W9-AXW-815

TO THE STUDENT: A study guide is available through your college bookstore under the title *Study Guide for Financial Accounting, Second Edition,* by Lawrence A. Klein. The *Study Guide* can help you with course material by acting as a tutorial, review, and study aid. If the *Study Guide* is not in stock, ask the bookstore manager to order a copy for you.

■ ABOUT THE AUTHORS*

Michael A. Diamond is the Dean of the School of Accounting, University of Southern California, and Director of the School's SEC and Financial Reporting Institute. He is a CPA and received his B.A. degree at the University of California, Berkeley, and his M.S. and Ph.D. degrees from the University of California, Los Angeles.

Dean Diamond's research interest relates to the use of accounting information, especially by managers in emerging companies. He is actively involved in international accounting research and has served in several capacities with the International Section of the American Accounting Association. His articles have appeared in the *Journal of Accountancy* and *Harvard Business Review*. Dean Diamond has conducted several research projects sponsored by national accounting firms and the Financial Executive Research Foundation.

Dean Diamond is active in the American Accounting Association, the American Institute of CPAs and the California Society of CPAs. He was recently named the recipient of the California Society of Certified Public Accountants 1989 Accounting Faculty Merit Award.

He has taught at California State University, Los Angeles, and has been a visiting professor at the University of California, Berkeley, the University of Southern California and the University of California, Los Angeles. Dean Diamond also has taught in executive education programs for a number of International accounting firms as well as Fortune 500 companies.

Eric G. Flamholtz is Professor of Accounting Information Systems and Human Resource Management at the Graduate School of Management, UCLA. He received his Ph.D. degree from the University of Michigan, where he served on the staff of the Institute for Social Research. His doctoral dissertation was co-winner of the McKinsey Foundation for Management Research Dissertation Award. He has served on the faculties at Columbia University and the University of Michigan, has been a Faculty Fellow at Price Waterhouse & Company, and has been an Assistant Project Director in the Accounting Research Division of the American Institute of CPAs. At UCLA, he has served as Director of the Accounting Information Systems Research Program. He is the author of more than fifty articles and chapters on a variety of accounting and management topics and has published a book entitled *Human Resource Accounting*. He has conducted research projects for the National Science Foundation, The National Association of Accountants, and the U.S. Office of Naval Research. He has also served as a member of the editorial board for *The Accounting Review* and *Accounting, Organizations and Society*. He has extensive experience as a consultant to firms ranging from entrepreneurships to members of Fortune's 500.

Diana Troik Flamholtz is the Executive Vice President of Management Systems Consulting Corporation and formerly an Associate Professor of Accounting in the College of Business, Loyola Marymount University, Los Angeles. She received her Ph.D. from the University of Michigan and did postdoctoral work in accounting at the Graduate School of Management, UCLA. Dr. Flamholtz has done writing and research in accounting history, with publications in *The Accounting Historians Journal* and *Accounting, Organizations and Society*. She has presented papers at the regional and national meetings of the American Accounting Association and The Institute of Management Science and serves on the editorial board of *The Accounting Historians Journal*. Dr. Flamholtz is co-author of a monograph published by Touche Ross & Company entitled "Organizational Control Systems—A Practical Tool for Emerging Companies" and has written and presented papers on accounting in The People's Republic of China. She has had a variety of consulting experiences, including cost behavior analysis, the development of contribution margin statements, and the conversion of accounting systems from manual to computerized systems.

* The authors have also written *Principles of Accounting*, PWS-KENT Publishing Company, copyright © 1986.

PREFACE

Financial Accounting is designed to be used in first-year accounting courses that cover one or two quarters or one semester. It presumes that the student has had no previous exposure to accounting. Because of the book's flexible organization, it can be used in introductory accounting courses at either the undergraduate or the graduate level.

As with the first edition of *Financial Accounting*, the second edition is based upon two premises. First, knowledge of accounting is important for all members of today's complex international economy, whether they are in industry, government, or professional accountancy. Therefore this book is written to meet the needs of the general student as well as of those who are prospective accounting majors. Second, accounting is an interesting subject, and we believe that the time spent in learning its concepts and practices should be enjoyable. For this reason, *Financial Accounting* is written in a highly readable, conversational style that will appeal to those students who often enter introductory accounting with a measure of trepidation.

In designing and writing this textbook, we were well aware that it must meet the needs of a wide range of students with varying interests and goals. Potential accounting majors must have a solid foundation in accounting concepts and practices if they are to complete their major requirements successfully. Other business majors, as well as nonbusiness majors, must be introduced to accounting concepts and practices in such a way that they can apply this knowledge to their various careers. To meet the needs of this diverse group, we have chosen the goal that all students should be able to read, understand, and reasonably interpret the financial statements contained in annual reports of major companies after completing their study of this text.

In addition to being an essential topic, we believe that accounting is fascinating. To complete successfully their first accounting courses, students spend many hours reading the text and preparing class materials. We have gone to considerable lengths to make this process interesting and enjoyable. The text includes extensive quotes from business journals such as *Forbes* and the *Wall Street Journal*, as well as many excerpts from actual financial statements and annual reports, to add realism and spark student interest. The financial statements of Toys "R" Us are used as an integrating force throughout the text. Whenever possible, we demonstrate the usefulness of specific accounting techniques so as to encourage further study.

■ CHANGES IN THE SECOND EDITION

The second edition of *Financial Accounting* has been revised to reflect current accounting changes and suggestions by various reviewers. However, like its predecessor, it has several features that aid student understanding: (1) balance between theory and practice; (2) emphasis on the use of accounting information in decision making; (3) contemporary theory and practice; (4) organizational flexibility; and (5) a complete and integrated learning package.

The second edition of *Financial Accounting* builds on the foundation of the first edition. Where appropriate, the text and end-of-chapter material have been updated to reflect current accounting standards. Thus, for example, the latest standards relating to deferred income taxes, consolidations, accounting for changing prices, and the statement of cash flows are explained at a level appropriate for an introductory book.

Several changes have been made to specific chapters. Chapter 7, "Management Control and Accounting for Cash," has been completely revised. The chapter now contains an overview of management control and fraudulent financial reporting, built around the report of the Treadway Commission. Accounting for cash is then discussed, as an example of how internal controls are built into an accounting system. The material relating to special journals, which was in Chapter 7 in the first edition, has now been placed in Appendix A.

Chapter 8, "Accounting for Short-term Monetary Assets," has been rewritten so that it includes only a short discussion of accounting for short-term investments but a more detailed discussion of accounting for receivables. This revised chapter is considerably shorter than the version in the first edition, which covered both cash and receivables in detail.

Chapter 13, "Corporate Organization and Capital Stock Transactions," has been reorganized. It now contains a discussion of treasury stock transactions that was previously in Chapter 14, "Stockholders' Equity—Retained Earnings and Dividends." The order of material in Chapter 14 has been rearranged. The discussion of corporate income statements has been moved from the first part of the chapter to the second part. Also, the material on earnings per share has been simplified.

Chapter 15, "Investment in Corporate Securities," has been revised to reflect the new FASB statement on consolidations. In addition, the coverage of the preparation of consolidated financial statements has been reduced to a level more appropriate to an introductory book.

The last three chapters have been reordered. Chapter 16, "The Statement of Cash Flows," has been completely rewritten to reflect the FASB's new statement on cash flows. Both the direct and the indirect methods are illustrated. Because of the FASB's preference for the direct method, however, this method is explained in more detail. We have moved the material on "Interpreting Financial Statement Data" from Chapter 18 to Chapter 17, and Chapter 18 now covers material related to special financial accounting problems. The title of the new Chapter 18 is "Accounting for Changing Prices and Problems Related to Multinational Corporations."

■ FEATURES

The second edition of *Financial Accounting*, like its predecessor, has several features that aid student learning and understanding: (1) balance between theory and practice; (2) emphasis on the use of accounting information in decision making; (3) contemporary theory and practice; (4) organizational flexibility; and (5) a complete and integrated learning package.

■ BALANCE BETWEEN THEORY AND PRACTICE

In writing this textbook, we carefully planned a blend of theory and practice that meets the needs of all its users. Financial statements and major accounting concepts are introduced in Chapter 1, before students are exposed to the mechanics of the accounting cycle. Details of the accounting cycle are explained patiently in Chapters 2 through 4. In Chapter 5, attention is turned back to the financial statements, and the actual financial statements of Toys "R" Us are first introduced to explain and illustrate key points. Throughout these chapters on the accounting cycle, the ongoing example of the Hartman Flower Company is used to illustrate relevant accounting concepts and procedures.

The remaining chapters are designed to reflect the proper balance between concepts and practice. For example, in Chapter 10, "Property, Plant, and Equipment; Natural Resources; and Intangible Assets," the concepts behind these topics are explained fully before the various depreciation methods are illustrated. In Chapter 16, "The Statement of Cash Flows," the uses and purposes of this statement are explained completely before the student is led carefully through an example illustrating its preparation. Other chapters are designed in a similar fashion.

■ EMPHASIS ON USING ACCOUNTING INFORMATION IN DECISION MAKING

In this text, we consistently approach accounting as an information system that provides useful financial data. This concept of accounting emphasizes its purpose in providing information for decisions rather than solely for its measurement procedures in recording, classifying, and summarizing financial information.

The emphasis on decision making is reflected in many of the features incorporated in the text. Ratios and other analytic tools are introduced at appropriate points in the specific chapter dealing with the related accounting concept. Chapter 17, "Interpreting Financial Statement Data," then draws all these ratios and tools together. However, this chapter does more than summarize ratio analysis; it shows students how they can use data from a variety of sources to analyze and interpret the financial statements of companies.

At the end of each chapter, in addition to a wide variety of other assignment material, we have added an "Understanding Financial Statements Problem" and a "Financial Decision Case." In these problems and cases, students are placed in the role of decision makers and are asked to analyze and interpret financial statements and quantitative data.

Management's role in the selection of accounting principles and in the preparation of the firm's financial statements is emphasized throughout the text. For example, the chapters that cover inventory methods, depreciation methods, leases, and purchase versus pooling all discuss the various effects that different methods can have on a firm's financial statements, which management must consider when choosing among these different approaches.

■ CONTEMPORARY THEORY AND PRACTICE

The second edition of *Financial Accounting* is contemporary in all respects. Where appropriate, current official pronouncements of authoritative accounting bodies are referenced. Because of its predominance in our economic system, the corporate form of business is the focus throughout. Problem material reflects our current economic environment, with emphasis on service and technology companies. Where appropriate, reference is made to current economic events such as mergers of major companies, the RJR Nabisco buyout, the purchase of Pillsbury by Grand Metropolitan, and the General Motors–Toyota joint venture.

The treatment of four particular topics—accounting for changing prices, international accounting, taxation, and computers—shows how up-to-date the text is. Chapter 18 contains clear, concise, and up-to-date coverage of two of the most perplexing problems facing the accounting profession—accounting for changing prices and international accounting. The coverage of inflation accounting in Chapter 18 reflects the changes made by FASB Statement No. 89. However, the effects of changing prices are not treated as an isolated subject; they are also discussed in other parts of the book, such as the chapter on inventories (Chapter 9) and the chapter on property, plant, and equipment (Chapter 10).

The second part of Chapter 18 discusses international accounting. The particular topics covered include accounting for foreign currency transactions, the translation of foreign currency statements, and international accounting standards. The coverage of these topics helps schools meet the current standards of the American Assembly of Collegiate Schools of Business regarding the coverage of international topics.

These topics are covered with the full understanding of both their complex nature and the fact that this is an introductory textbook. Thus students will gain an understanding of these international topics, as well as accounting for changing prices, without becoming overburdened by detail more appropriate to intermediate and advanced courses.

The effects of taxes on the firm's financial statements are discussed in the various chapters in which the relevant accounting principle is discussed. Thus the effects of income taxes are discussed in the chapter on inventories (Chapter 9) and in the chapter on property, plant, and equipment (Chapter 10). Chapter 11, on current liabilities, contains a discussion of interperiod income tax allocation at a level that is appropriate to an introductory textbook. Chapter 14 contains a discussion of intraperiod income tax allocation. This treatment reflects our view that income tax consideration plays an important role in management decisions and should be discussed when those decisions are covered, not in a separate chapter.

■ ORGANIZATIONAL FLEXIBILITY

Financial Accounting is written with the full understanding that accounting instructors have various teaching styles and different approaches to the subject. Also, even over a short period of time, the makeup of individual classes changes, and a text must have the flexibility to meet such changes.

The eighteen chapters in this book can be divided easily into three primary parts; two of them, covering the first fifteen chapters, contain the essential elements of an introductory course. The first part (Chapters 1 through 7) contains a complete explanation of the accounting cycle, as well as a chapter on accounting for merchandising firms (Chapter 6) and a chapter on management control (Chapter 7). These last two chapters can be omitted or covered in part without interrupting the flow of the text. However, as noted, Chapter 7 is quite contemporary in nature and contains a discussion of fraudulent financial reporting and ethics.

The next eight chapters make up the second part, a comprehensive discussion of the various financial accounting concepts and practices that both accounting and non-accounting majors should know. However, a considerable amount of flexibility is built into these chapters. For example, the end of Chapter 11, on current liabilities, contains a complete discussion of compound interest and present-value topics. If the instructor desires, this part of the chapter can be omitted.

The third part of this book contains chapters on (1) the statement of cash flows, (2) interpreting financial statements, and (3) accounting for changing prices and international accounting. Depending on the preference of the instructor and the amount of time available, some or all of the topics in the last three chapters can be covered. As previously noted, relevant discussions of ratio analysis and accounting for changing prices are contained in other chapters. The statement of cash flows is introduced in Chapter 1 and discussed again in Chapter 5. Therefore, if there is not enough time available to cover these last three chapters, the student will still have been introduced to some of the topics contained in them.

Finally, two appendixes cover more procedural matters. One contains a discussion of special journals; the second contains an overview of accounting for sole proprietorship and partnerships.

■ A COMPLETE AND INTEGRATED LEARNING PACKAGE

This text and the complete student's and instructor's support packages have been designed as an integrated unit.

■ PEDAGOGICAL FEATURES

We have gone to great lengths to design a pedagogically sound textbook. Each of the chapters contains a set of learning objectives at the beginning and a summary of these objectives at the end of the chapter. Each chapter concludes with the following end-of-chapter material: a list of Key Terms, Problem or Problems for Review, Questions, Exercises, Problems, Understanding Financial Statement Problems, and Financial Decision Cases. Beginning with Chapter 8, there are problems entitled Using the Computer.

■ LEARNING OBJECTIVES

Each chapter is preceded by a concise set of learning objectives. These objectives clearly indicate to the students what they should be able to accomplish after studying the chapter. Then each of these objectives is summarized in paragraph form at the end of the chapter.

■ KEY TERMS AND GLOSSARY

At the end of each chapter is a list of key terms discussed in that chapter. These terms are highlighted in **boldface** where they are introduced in the chapter. At the end of the book, in Appendix E, is a complete glossary of these key terms, arranged alphabetically for easy use.

■ PROBLEMS FOR YOUR REVIEW

At the end of each chapter is at least one review problem (in many cases two or three), emphasizing key points in the chapter. These problems are followed by detailed solutions, so that the students can compare their solutions with the correct one. Many review problems contain notes that anticipate student questions or problem areas.

■ END-OF-CHAPTER ASSIGNMENT MATERIALS

This text contains a varied set of end-of-chapter assignment materials. *Questions* relate to the major concepts and key terms introduced in the chapter. *Exercises* involve single concepts and provide the student with practice in applying those concepts. These Exercises, as well as the Questions, are arranged in the same order in which the material is introduced in the chapter.

Exercises are followed by *Problems*. These end-of-chapter Problems are more complex and usually cover several related topics. They are generally arranged in the order in which the topics are presented in the chapter. In the second edition, the end-of-chapter material has been expanded. Many of the exercises and problems have been revised, and new ones have been added. Each chapter now contains an exercise related to the Toys "R" Us financial statements.

As noted, each chapter also contains a problem called *Understanding Financial Statements; a Financial Decision Case*, and (beginning with Chapter 8) a problem entitled *Using the Computer.* Understanding Financial Statements problems are based on actual financial statements of major corporations. Students are asked to interpret these statements, relating subjects learned in the chapter to realistic situations. In the Financial Decision Cases, students are asked to analyze and interpret financial data and address business decisions based on this data. Using the Computer problems are straightforward exercises that are specially designed to be worked on any available spreadsheet. These problems introduce students to accounting calculations and problems that are readily adaptable to the power of spreadsheet programs.

■ THE STUDENT SUPPORT PACKAGE

The student support package contains a *Study Guide, Working Papers, Practice Set*, and a *Computerized Accounting Simulation*.

■ THE STUDY GUIDE

Prepared by Lawrence A. Klein of Bentley College, the Study Guide helps students develop the ability to apply concepts and techniques discussed in the main text. Each chapter corresponds to a text chapter, and contains an extensive chapter summary as well as fill-in the blank, multiple choice questions, and short answer problems that students can use to test their knowledge of text topics. The answers to all these questions and exercises, with complete explanations, are provided for the student.

■ WORKING PAPERS

Prepared by Raj Iyengar of University of Southern California, partially completed working papers are provided for each problem. They are designed to reduce the amount of nonproductive pencil work required of the student.

■ PRACTICE SET

Virginia Equipment Company. Prepared by Harry Dickinson of Virginia Commonwealth University, this puts students in the role of decision maker by allowing a choice of accounting methods for completing various transactions. It is to be used after coverage of inventory and cost of goods sold.

■ ON GUARD, INC.: A COMPUTERIZED ACCOUNTING INFORMATION SYSTEM

Prepared by Earl Weiss and Don Raun of California State University, Northridge, this unique microcomputer supplement provides a flexible set of eleven modules that are tied to the text. Students are required to analyze transactions, enter items into the microcomputer general ledger accounting system, and output financial statements. The modules are designed to enable instructors either to use the program throughout the entire course as an ongoing supplement or to assign a traditional accounting cycle practice set. In addition, students may use "WHAT-IF" questions to see the effect of various changes on the outputs of the accounting system.

■ THE INSTRUCTOR'S SUPPORT PACKAGE

The instructor's support package includes a *Solutions Manual,* an *Instructor's Manual,* a *Test Bank* (in book and microcomputer forms), *Transparencies*, and a *Check Figures*, and an *Annual Report*.

■ SOLUTIONS MANUAL

Prepared by Raj Iyengar, the Solutions Manual contains detailed solutions to all questions, exercises, problems, and other end-of-chapter materials. Complete solutions, including all intermediate calculations, are provided.

■ INSTRUCTOR'S MANUAL

Prepared by Raj Iyengar, the Instructor's Manual has been designed as a useful teaching aid and resource guide for the instructor. A flow chart diagram approach is taken to illustrate concepts, with examples for class use provided. A matrix of end-of-chapter material, organized by learning objective, is included for each text chapter. Included in the matrix are all questions, exercises, and problems, with their estimated level of difficulty and time required for completion.

An overview of the end-of-chapter material is followed by a chapter outline, also organized by learning goals. Additional examples of key computations and illustrations have been developed for selected chapters.

■ TEST BANK

Prepared by Mark S. Bettner of Bucknell University, the Test Bank contains over 1,200 test items. Included for each chapter and Appendices A and B are approximately 15 fill-in-the-blanks, 30 multiple-choice questions, and 16 exercises. Detailed solutions to all questions are included at the end, including explanations and computations where applicable.

■ COMPUTERIZED TEST BANK

The same test material appearing in the printed Test Bank is available on disk for use with the IBM PC or compatible.

■ TRANSPARENCIES

Acetate transparencies for problems are in oversized type for easy readability and are available from the publisher to adopters of the text.

■ CHECK FIGURES

For the instructor, a checklist of key figures for appropriate exercises and problems is available in quantity from the publisher.

■ ANNUAL REPORT

Copies of the current Toys 'R' Us Annual Report are available free to adopters from the publisher. The actual annual report reinforces illustrations used in the text.

■ ACKNOWLEDGMENTS

The second edition of this text would not have been completed successfully without the help of many of our colleagues and friends. Although it is impossible to list all who have made a contribution, we would like to acknowledge those who have provided so much help and insight.

Special mention goes to Raj Iyengar, who coordinated the supplement package and provided immeasurable help to us in many other ways. A special thanks also goes to Michael Vickerman and Donna Edgington, both of the University of Southern California, who provided much-needed help during the production phase of the book. We would also like to thank our colleagues at the University of Southern California and the University of California, Los Angeles, who provided professional and emotional support during this project.

Special mention goes to Mahmoud Nourayi, and to Mark Bettner of Texas Tech who, in addition to working on many of the supplements, provided a detailed critique of the entire manuscript. We would also like to thank Don Raun and Earl Weiss of California State University, Northridge, for the help in class testing the book and their efforts in preparing ON GUARD Inc., the computer supplement.

We have benefited from detailed and constructive reviews provided by many individuals, including:

Hobart W. Adams
University of Akron

Norman D. Berman
New York University

Phillip G. Buchanan
George Mason University

David M. Buehlmann
University of Nebraska at Omaha

Harold L. Cannon
State University of New York at Albany

Richard L. Cross
Bentley College

Anthony P. Curatola
Louisiana State University

Harry D. Dickinson
Virginia Commonwealth University

John A. Elliot
Cornell University

Patricia C. Elliot
University of New Mexico

Clarence E. Fries
University of Arkansas—Fayetteville

Martin L. Gosman
Boston University

Abo-El-Yazeed T. Habib
Mankato State University

Stanley H. Helm
University of Florida

David E. Hoffman
University of North Carolina

Merle W. Hopkins
University of Southern California

W. Elbert Jones
University of South Carolina

James M. Kreuger
University of Missouri—St. Louis

LaVern E. Kreuger
University of Missouri—Kansas City

Horace J. Landry
Syracuse University

Larry L. Lookabill
Western Washington University

Russell J. Peterson
University of Alabama

Don-Rice Richards
James Madison University

Joseph C. Rue
Syracuse University

George C. Sanderson
Moorhead State University

Barbara Schirappa
Trenton State College

Linda E. Sugarman
University of Akron

James R. Swearingen
Weber State College

Roy C. Weatherwax
University of Wisconsin—Whitewater

Our thanks to the Financial Accounting Standards Board for permission to reprint parts of various Statements and Concepts Statements. Copyright by Financial Accounting Standards Board, 401 Merritt 7, P.O. Box 5116, Norwalk, Connecticut, 06856-5116, USA. Reprinted with permission. Copies of the complete documents are available from the FASB.

Finally, this project would have never been completed without the assistance of the editorial and production staff of PWS–KENT. Those who contributed mightily to the production of this book include David Hoyt and Susan London with production and Rich Pellagrini, Deirdre Lynch, and Sue Purdy in editorial. A special note of thanks goes to Elaine and Jacob Diamond, who provided the emotional support required for the completion of this text.

Notwithstanding the assistance of all of these individuals, we are solely responsible for the final product. Any suggestions for improvement would be greatly appreciated.

M.A.D.
E.G.F.
D.T.F.

CONTENTS

CHAPTER 6

RECORDING SALES AND PURCHASES OF INVENTORY FOR A MERCHANDISING FIRM 214

CHAPTER 7

MANAGEMENT CONTROL AND ACCOUNTING FOR CASH 246

CHAPTER 10

PROPERTY, PLANT, AND EQUIPMENT; NATURAL RESOURCES; AND INTANGIBLE ASSETS   341

CHAPTER 11

CURRENT LIABILITIES, INCOME TAXES, AND CONCEPTS RELATED TO THE TIME VALUE OF MONEY 388

CHAPTER 12

ACCOUNTING FOR LONG-TERM LIABILITIES AND INVESTMENTS IN BONDS 429

CHAPTER 13

CORPORATE ORGANIZATION AND CAPITAL STOCK TRANSACTIONS 477

CHAPTER 14

STOCKHOLDERS' EQUITY—RETAINED EARNINGS AND DIVIDENDS 509

CHAPTER 15

INVESTMENT IN CORPORATE SECURITIES 547

ACCOUNTING: ITS NATURE AND FUNCTIONS

After studying this chapter, you should be able to:

1. Define accounting and discuss its functions.
2. Explain the relationship between accounting and different forms of business enterprises.
3. List the primary users of accounting information.
4. Discuss the work of accountants.
5. Explain which groups are involved in setting accounting standards.
6. Discuss the important accounting concepts on which financial statements are based.
7. Describe the primary financial statements, including:
   a. the balance sheet.
   b. the income statement.
   c. the retained earnings statement.
   d. the statement of cash flows.

ccounting was practiced in ancient societies such as Babylonia and Assyria. Then, as now, accounting not only helped individuals manage their businesses but also served a broader social function by facilitating the development of commerce. Today, accounting plays a central role in our day-to-day economic activities. Whether you decide to become a stockbroker, a production manager, or an advertising account executive, you will use accounting data. Even if you decide not to enter a business field, knowledge of accounting will help you manage your everyday affairs and help you understand the economic environment in which you live. For example, understanding international mergers and acquisitions, or the leveraged buyouts of Safeway Stores and RJR/Nabisco, requires a basic knowledge of accounting. Indeed, accounting is the language of business, and fluency in this language is needed in today's world. The purpose of this chapter is to introduce you to that language and to the nature and functions of accounting.

■ THE NATURE AND FUNCTIONS OF ACCOUNTING

The nature of accounting is, in part, a function of a specific country's economic, political, and social systems. It is a cultural phenomenon, much like language and law, and is used as a tool in understanding economic events. Because accounting has been created for economic purposes, it tends to evolve and adapt to changes in its environment. For example, modern accounting has its roots in the fourteenth century but has been able to adapt and cope with the relatively new phenomenon of multinational firms, such as IBM and ITT. Thus accounting, despite its use of numbers, is not a natural science, and unlike mathematics does not consist of a system of numbers that, once proven, does not change. Rather, accounting is dynamic and changes over time according to economic needs.

Accounting can be defined as a system of providing "quantitative information, primarily financial in nature, about economic entities that is intended to be useful in making economic decisions."[1] Its primary functions are to record, classify, and summarize in a significant manner and in monetary terms transactions that are of a financial character. This information is then used by groups such as the firm's managers and external parties to make a variety of decisions about an entity. The **accounting system** is the set of principles, methods, and procedures that is used to record, classify, and summarize the financial information to be distributed to users.

■ THE RECORD-KEEPING FUNCTION

All organizations that engage in economic activities need a method of keeping track of their transactions. **Transactions** are business events of a particular enterprise, measured in money and recorded in its financial records. Except in the smallest enterprises, failure to record sales or the purchase of goods or services systematically would lead to confusion. In order to be recorded in the accounting records, the transaction must be of a type that can be measured in money.

■ CLASSIFYING AND SUMMARIZING TRANSACTIONS

In order to summarize transactions meaningfully, they must first be classified into similar categories. That is, all of a firm's sales during a certain period are aggregated in order to determine its total sales. Likewise, all of the transactions affecting cash are

---

[1]American Institute of Certified Public Accountants, Accounting Principles Board, Statement No. 4, *Basic Concepts and Accounting Principles Underlying Financial Statements of Business Enterprises* (New York: AICPA, 1970), par. 9.

aggregated in order to determine the amount of cash on hand at any point in time, as well as to analyze how the cash was received and used.

Large firms enter into hundreds of thousands or even millions of transactions each year. For decision makers to use this data meaningfully, it must be summarized into accounting reports that are presented in useful formats. These reports are called *financial statements* and are the primary way in which financial information about an enterprise is communicated to users. **Financial statements** are concise reports that summarize specific transactions for a particular period of time. They show the financial position of the firm as well as the results of its operations.

■ ACCOUNTING AND DECISION MAKING

The definition and functions of accounting emphasize its purpose in providing information that is relevant in decision making. It is applicable to governmental and not-for-profit organizations such as museums, zoos, or churches as well as business enterprises. In this book, the primary concern will be with the role of accounting in business enterprises, especially corporations.

Exhibit 1–1 illustrates the relationships on which this book will focus. Central to the discussion is the corporation, the most important form of business organization in the United States. The primary users of corporate financial information are present and potential investors and creditors, the managers, governmental agencies such as the Internal Revenue Service, and the general public. Accountants in the firm prepare accounting information according to certain standards set by their profession. This helps ensure that the information will be useful to those in a decision-making capacity. This information is generally provided to these users in the form of financial statements. These relationships will be discussed next, focusing on:

1. The forms of business organizations.

2. The primary users of financial information.

3. Accountants, the providers of this information.

4. The setting of accounting standards.

5. Some of the concepts and conventions inherent in accounting information.

6. Financial statements, the primary means of communicating financial information to interested parties.

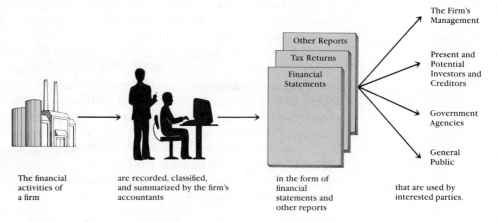

EXHIBIT 1–1

The Preparation and Dissemination of Accounting Information

The financial activities of a firm

are recorded, classified, and summarized by the firm's accountants

in the form of financial statements and other reports

that are used by interested parties.

Other Reports

Tax Returns

Financial Statements

The Firm's Management

Present and Potential Investors and Creditors

Government Agencies

General Public

■ ACCOUNTING AND THE FORMS OF BUSINESS ENTERPRISES

The three major types of business organizations are (1) the sole proprietorship, (2) the partnership, and (3) the corporation. Good accounting practices are necessary to each form of enterprise.

■ SOLE PROPRIETORSHIPS

A **sole proprietorship** is a business entity in which one person is the owner. The business may employ few or many people, but there is only one owner, who realizes either the profits or losses. A major advantage of a sole proprietorship is that it is easy to establish this form of organization with little cost and legal work. Although sole proprietorships often are relatively small businesses, some of today's great businesses began as individually owned enterprises. For example, companies such as the Ford Motor Company, Levi Strauss and Co., and McDonald's were originally founded and owned by one individual.

In accounting theory and practice, a business and its owner are different entities. A **business entity** is a distinct economic unit whose transactions are kept separate from those of its owners. As a result, the business has an existence independent of its owner's. The scope of accounting for the sole proprietorship is limited to the transactions of the business and does not include the owner's personal transactions. Despite this accounting treatment, under the law a sole proprietorship and its owner are not independent entities. This means that legally the sole proprietor is personally responsible for the debts and obligations of the business. The accounting distinction between the business and its owner points out that accounting is more concerned with the economic facts of an event than with its legal form.

■ PARTNERSHIPS

A **partnership** is a business entity that is owned by two or more individuals. Like a sole proprietorship, a partnership may employ few or many people. Some partnerships, such as the large international CPA firms, have hundreds or even thousands of partners. There are different types of partnership agreements. Individuals may be equal partners or have unequal interests in the partnership's profits and losses. There are silent partners, who contribute funds to the enterprise but do not engage actively in the management of the business, and active partners. In addition, corporations can become partners in joint ventures. For example, some of the large oil corporations such as ARCO have formed joint ventures in order to share the costs and risks of oil exploration in such areas as the North Sea or Alaska. The General Motors–Toyota venture to produce small cars in California is a partnership between two of the world's largest corporations.

Formation of a partnership does not require the formal approval of a state or other governmental agency. A partnership requires merely an oral or written agreement among the individuals or entities who are to be partners. The partnership agreement should provide for solutions to questions of admission and withdrawal, distributions of profits and losses, and settlements in the event of illness, incapacity, or death of a member.

From an accounting perspective, a partnership is an accounting entity distinct from its owners. Each individual partner has a predetermined interest in the enterprise's profits or losses; as with a sole proprietorship, the partners and the partnership are legally one entity.

■ CORPORATIONS

A **corporation** is a business entity that is viewed legally as separate and distinct from its owners, who are *stockholders*. In the United States, a business may be incorporated in any of the 50 states. To incorporate, an application must be filed with officials of the state in which incorporation is desired. If approved, the application becomes the Articles of Incorporation. The Articles of Incorporation include the corporate name, principal location of business, and the number of shares of stock that are authorized for sale. Ownership in a corporation is designated by stock certificates. Ownership of stock is ownership of a proportionate share of the corporation. State laws govern the sale or transfer of corporate stock from one stockholder to another.

In contrast with a sole proprietorship, a corporation is legally a separate entity. As a result, the owners of the corporation have **limited liability**, which means that they are not personally responsible, as individuals, for the debts incurred by the corporation, beyond the amount that they have invested in the corporation.

This limited liability feature of corporations enables them to obtain funds from many owners who want to invest. These owners may not wish to participate actively in the operations of the enterprise. Therefore, corporations, especially large ones, usually employ professional managers. The stockholders elect a board of directors, who may or may not be owners. The board, in turn, appoints the officers of the corporation (president, vice-president, treasurer, secretary, etc.) to manage the business.

Many large U.S. corporations are **publicly owned**, which means that the corporation's stock is bought and sold by the public often on exchanges such as the New York or American Stock Exchange. Through these exchanges, individuals can easily buy or sell shares of the stock of corporations. As a result, large publicly held corporations have hundreds of thousands or, in some cases, over a million shareholders. Not all corporations are publicly held; some are owned by families, a few shareholders, or a single individual, and the stock in these closely held corporations is not traded publicly. In some cases, government and not-for-profit organizations take the corporate form.

The role of accounting in corporations is important, especially because there is often a separation between ownership and management. Owners require financial reports to appraise the performance of management, as well as to decide whether to retain, sell, or add to their investment in the corporation.

■ THE PRIMARY USERS OF ACCOUNTING INFORMATION

The primary users of accounting information can be divided into two major categories: external and internal users. Major external users are present and potential investors and creditors, governmental agencies, and the general public. The firm's management represents the primary internal user of accounting information.

■ PRESENT AND POTENTIAL INVESTORS AND CREDITORS

Present and potential investors use financial statements as well as other information about an enterprise to make decisions about increasing, decreasing, or maintaining their investment in the entity. These same financial statements are used by creditors to evaluate whether the corporation can repay its debts or obligations. For example, a bank will analyze a company's financial statements to determine whether to make a new loan or to extend a current loan. In summary, one of the primary objectives of financial reporting has been stated as follows:

Financial reporting should provide information that is useful to present and potential investors and creditors and others in making rational investment, credit, and similar decisions. The information should be comprehensible to those who have a reasonable understanding of business and economic activities and are willing to study the information with reasonable diligence.[2]

■ GOVERNMENTAL AGENCIES

Governmental agencies are another major user of financial information about a firm. For example, the Internal Revenue Service uses some of the same information contained in financial statements to help determine the amount of taxes due to the government. Other federal agencies such as the Interstate Commerce Commission and the Securities and Exchange Commission use the firm's financial statements in their regulatory processes. State agencies, such as public utility commissions, also use financial statements and other accounting information in setting utility rates. In many circumstances, this information is based on the same accounting principles that govern the financial statements presented to investors and creditors. However, it does not necessarily have to be the same, and in some cases there are significant differences.

■ THE GENERAL PUBLIC

Many of us, whether investors, creditors, or just citizens, are interested in the activities of business entities. The affairs of large corporations affect individuals throughout the world. For example, IBM's decision regarding whether to manufacture computer components in the United States or abroad affects the employment and income of U.S. residents as well as residents of other countries. In order to evaluate the actions of IBM and other firms, the public often relies on the same financial information that is summarized in financial statements. Thus society uses a vast quantity of financial information in assessing its economic well-being.

■ CORPORATE MANAGEMENT

Corporate management is the internal user of financial information. The task of management is to plan and control operations in order to generate a profit. *Planning* involves deciding on the organization's objectives and on the means of accomplishing them. *Control* refers to the process of ensuring that the corporation's operations are successful in achieving these organizational objectives. **Management accounting** is the system and procedures related to providing information to management for planning and controlling the business. As a result, management accounting is primarily directed at providing information to internal users and can be tailored to meet individual managers' needs. The study of management accounting is the subject of a separate accounting course.

■ OTHER USERS

There also are other users of accounting information. For example, labor unions use financial statements to help them assess a company's ability to increase wage payments to employees. The financial information contained in a firm's financial statements is often a basis of the negotiations. In addition, in deciding whether to join a firm, potential employees may use financial information in evaluating the long-range prospects of the firm.

■ ACCOUNTANTS—THE PROVIDERS OF ACCOUNTING INFORMATION

Accountants are qualified through education and experience to perform accounting services. Professional accountants may work in public accounting, private accounting, or governmental accounting. In the course of an accountant's career, he or she may work in all three of these areas.

[2]Financial Accounting Standards Board, Concepts Statement No. 1, *Objectives of Financial Reporting by Business Enterprises* (Stamford, Conn.: November 1978), par. 34.

■ PUBLIC ACCOUNTING

Public accounting is the field of accounting that provides a variety of accounting services to clients for a fee. Professional accountants who work in public accounting firms are usually **certified public accountants (CPAs)** and work in firms called CPA firms. CPAs are licensed by individual states to practice accounting after having met a number of requirements. All states require that individuals pass the uniform CPA examination developed and administered by the **American Institute of Certified Public Accountants**, the professional organization of CPAs. In addition, states have varying requirements regarding education and experience for licensing a person as a CPA. In California, for example, besides passing the uniform examination, you must have a bachelor's degree and two years of qualified experience in order to become a CPA.

Certified public accounting firms range in size from one-person firms to large multinational firms. The large firms have offices in the principal cities in the United States and throughout the world. These large firms are organized as partnerships, and some have over 2,000 partners. Until recently there were eight multinational accounting firms, collectively known as the "Big Eight." However, during 1989, these large firms began to merge, leading to the possibility that only five will survive. As noted in Exhibit 1-2, a *Los Angeles Times* article, the remaining "Big Five" will have annual revenues ranging from $2.5 to $5.0 billion.[3]

| EXHIBIT 1—2 | The three pending or proposed mergers in the accounting industry would compress the list of firms known as the "Big Eight." |

FROM THE BIG EIGHT TO THE BIG FIVE

By BRUCE KEPPEL, *Times* Staff Writer

Two of the nation's largest accounting firms announced Thursday that they have agreed in principle to combine operations, and two even bigger concerns began formal merger talks.

If both deals succeed, the so-called Big Eight accounting firms would shrink to five multibillion-dollar giants in an effort to serve better their growing multinational clients in today's global economy.

"The pressure is for bigness as marketplaces internationalize," said Robert Crane, editor of *Accounting Today*. "The big, big companies are looking for their accounting firms to serve them on a worldwide basis."

Agreeing to merge were New York-based Deloitte Haskins & Sells and Touche Ross & Co. If partners of the two firms approve the merger, the new entity will be known as Deloitte & Touche, with 1989 revenue exceeding $4 billion and more than 65,000 employees worldwide, the companies said in a joint statement. In terms of 1988 revenue, Deloitte & Touche would rank fourth in the United States and fourth worldwide.

Meanwhile, an even bigger combination is afoot as the nation's No. 1 firm, Arthur Andersen & Co., and Price Waterhouse & Co. announced formal merger negotiations. Combined, they would create a global powerhouse with $5 billion in revenue. They would be nearly $1 billion larger than its closest rival, Ernst & Young, the result of the recently announced merger of two of the other Big Eight firms, Ernst & Whinney and Arthur Young.

Ernst & Young is expected to begin operations Oct. 1, pending approval by overseas partners.

The Big Eight		The Big Five	
Firm	World revenue (billions)	Firm	World revenue (billions)
KPMG Peat Marwick	$3.9	Andersen-Waterhouse	$5.0
Arthur Andersen	2.8	Ernst & Young	4.3
Coopers & Lybrand	2.5	KPMG Peat Marwick	3.9
Price Waterhouse	2.2	Deloitte Haskins Sells-Touche Ross	3.8
Ernst & Whinney	2.2	Coopers & Lybrand	2.6
Arthur Young	2.1		
Deloitte Haskins & Sells	1.9		
Touche Ross	1.8		

[3]*Los Angeles Times,* Friday, July 7, 1989, Section IV, p. 1. Copyright, 1989, *Los Angeles Times.* Reprinted by permission.

Auditing and Accounting Services

Auditing is one of the main functions of a CPA firm. An **audit** is an objective and independent third-party examination of an organization's financial statements. Publicly held corporations are required by federal securities laws to have their financial statements audited. Even if not required by law, many firms have their financial statements audited to satisfy banks and/or owners. The auditor evaluates the firm's accounting system, tests to see that economic transactions have been properly recorded, and gathers other evidence that the proper economic events have been appropriately recorded. After this examination, the auditor issues a report, called an **opinion**, on the findings regarding the financial statements. In this report, the auditor expresses a professional opinion as to the fairness of the financial statements. External users of financial statements can rely on this opinion, because the CPA must be independent of the firm it is auditing.

Many businesses, especially smaller ones, may not need or desire to have their financial statements audited. However, they often need some review of their records or help in preparing their financial statements. As a result, CPA firms also provide accounting services, called **reviews and compilations**.

Tax Preparation and Planning

Tax preparation and planning is another function of a public accountant. Because tax factors are important to most major financial decisions, CPAs are often asked for advice about the possible tax consequences of a particular decision. Also, CPAs are often asked to prepare income tax returns. Almost all CPA firms derive fees from tax practice.

Management Advisory Services

The accountant is more and more often being called upon to provide informal and formal business advice. In fact, one study noted that the accountant was named the primary business adviser to executives of smaller companies.[4] In order to serve their clients better, many firms have established management advisory service departments in addition to their audit and tax departments. Individuals who provide management services do not necessarily have to be CPAs or even accountants. They are often individuals with broad business education and backgrounds.

Today, management advisory services are among the fastest-growing practice areas in accounting firms. Before the mergers discussed in Exhibit 1-2, one-third of Arthur Andersen's business involved consulting. In fact, Arthur Andersen started a separate organization, called Andersen Consulting, to conduct this part of its business. In addition, many firms are expanding the traditional bounds of consulting services. For example, BDO/Seidman, a multinational accounting firm somewhat smaller than the "Big Five," recently established a separate organization for financial planning. This separate limited partnership will handle financial planning, asset monitoring, and life insurance analysis for clients.

■ PRIVATE ACCOUNTING

Private accounting is the practice of accounting in a single firm such as McDonald's or General Motors. Accountants who work for individual firms are employed in a variety of capacities. For example, the chief accounting officer for a private enterprise is typically known as the controller, and the head financial officer is often called the treasurer. Individuals working in accounting departments of businesses perform a variety

[4]Jerry Arnold et al., "Meeting the Needs of Private Companies: Executive Summary of Findings" (New York: Peat, Marwick, Mitchell & Co., 1983).

of tasks, such as determining the cost of items produced by the firm, budgeting, internal auditing, taxation, and financial reporting.

A number of certificate programs have been developed to provide professional recognition for individuals who work in private accounting. For example, the Institute of Management Accounting offers a program that allows accountants to earn a Certificate in Management Accounting (CMA). Although this is not a state license to practice as the CPA license is, it does show that the accountant has met certain experience and knowledge requirements.

■ GOVERNMENTAL ACCOUNTING

The management of governmental affairs requires the use of accounting for record-keeping, planning, and controlling operations. The practice of accounting as it relates to government organizations is called **governmental accounting**. Some governmental accountants work for regulatory agencies such as the Internal Revenue Service, the Federal Aviation Administration, and the Interstate Commerce Commission. Each of these agencies, as well as others, requires accountants to help them perform their functions. In addition, individual states, cities, counties, school districts, and other governmental bodies employ accountants for a variety of functions.

■ ACCOUNTING AS A CAREER

Accountants today are indeed information providers to a variety of clients. The profession has become a leader in the use of technological innovations. To a well-rounded student who has a strong background in liberal arts, oral and written communication skills, and strong analytical abilities, as well as an in-depth knowledge of accounting, the accounting profession offers a multitude of career paths. This is illustrated by Exhibit 1-3, an article from *Careers in Accounting*.[5]

EXHIBIT 1–3

ACCOUNTING CAREERS: THE CHALLENGES AND THE REWARDS

"Decision-maker" aptly describes the accounting professional of the 1980s.

The ability of companies to expand, invest and diversify has become the key to success in a complex global marketplace. For this, component information on budgets, expenditures and taxation issues has never been more necessary or more in demand.

Knowledge of state-of-the-art computer systems and the latest standards affecting financial reporting are just two examples of why opportunity and growth in both public accounting (CPA firms) and private accounting (business/industry) is projected to increase steadily into the mid-1990s.

Linked to this increasing demand for timely financial information is an equally strong push for accountants and financial professionals to assume greater responsibility for the numbers they generate.

The next few years will determine whether the accounting profession will continue with its present course of self-regulation or whether it will be subjected to greater accountability to government agencies. Either way, the profession's visibility stands to increase dramatically.

More responsibility will also raise salaries in the field. [*See table.*]

While attaining the position of partner at CPA firms will remain as lucrative and coveted as ever—only 2 percent of entrants to the larger firms eventually attain this status—qualified candidates will find a greater range of career paths in public accounting than ever before.

Aside from the traditional audit, tax and management consulting services, many CPA firms are now branching into related disciplines. Estate planning, employee compensation and pension consulting, litigation support and marketing analysis are just some of the additional services and specializations.

Many firms also offer clients support in the selection and implementation of software and mainframe computer systems for their in-

[5]"Accounting Careers: The Challenges and the Rewards," *Careers in Accounting*, September 1988, pp. 1–2. Reprinted with permission of *Careers in Accounting*, Lebhar-Friedman Inc.

EXHIBIT I–3   (continued)

ternal use. This growing specialization is one of the trends that has attracted the attention of the Federal Trade Commission, which is currently investigating the propriety of the profession's self-imposed ban on accepting commissions for the sale of computers, securities and real estate and for other services.

The American Institute of CPAs is currently faced with the delicate task of weaving the acceptance of commissions and other issues such as payment of contingency fees for merger and acquisition services into the professional code of ethics.

The need for more specially trained personnel is also being felt in private accounting.

Standards-setting bodies such as the Financial Accounting Standards Board and the Securities and Exchange Commission continue to refine the financial reporting process, forcing accountants in business and industry to constantly hone their technical skills.

Attention to maintaining a cost-effective and streamlined operating environment has placed renewed emphasis on cost accounting and financial planning. Changing policies in the area of tax reform have also placed a premium on business being able to attract and develop capable taxation specialists.

However, it is the technologically adept accountant who is most in demand. Candidates who can supervise and test the sophisticated internal control and information systems head the shopping lists of many U.S. corporations.

Many industries have begun to recognize and reward the increased workload taken on by financial personnel with compensation plans that used to be reserved for more product-oriented positions.

In small business, the accountant is also playing a more important role in planning and operations. The need for more technically trained applicants is being fueled by increased in-house use of personal computers (PCs) and breakthroughs in competitively-priced accounting software packages.

To maximize the opportunities presented by the accounting profession, career counselors offer some specific advice beyond the standard "work hard and you'll get ahead" variety.

Avoid overspecialization. Many firms in both public and private

accounting sometimes need to fill very specific niches when dealing with their day-to-day activities.

While these positions are often vital to an entity's ability to stay in business, and frequently are highly compensated, they are often limiting in terms of career potential. The result, personnel experts say, may be an income level within an organization that far exceeds the value of those skills on the open market.

According to many career counselors in the accounting field, individuals can avoid pricing themselves out of the job market and enhance their value to future employers by taking entry-level positions that offer as wide a range of experience as possible. As salary levels and responsibilities increase, the opportunity to explore different career paths within an organization dwindles.

Avoid complacency. Recruiters and personnel experts agree that there is a definite timetable leading to success in accounting even though this rigid schedule is slowly being abandoned in some sectors.

Those who remain satisfied with lower-level positions frequently find themselves working at dead-end jobs and being threatened by new employees on their way up.

At CPA firms, the optimal career path finds the college graduate spending about three years at the junior or staff level and another five years at a senior staff level before advancing to a manager's position.

The experts say this leap to a managerial position remains critical to long-term success in public accounting, since only those who show potential as partners are given supervisory positions.

A similar timetable exists in private accounting, according to personnel officers at larger companies. There, managers graduate to second-tier executive positions such as credit manager or lending officer before assuming senior-level jobs, such as controller and CFO.

Despite the decreasing numbers of college graduates entering the accounting profession in recent years, personnel experts agree that the race to advance will remain extremely competitive.

Their advice is that young accountants concentrate on improving their technical skills at entry level jobs and gradually build management capabilities, client relations and other "people" skills for the future.

1988 ACCOUNTING SALARIES
Average Entry-Level (less than one year experience) Salaries
in Thousands of Dollars for 15 Major Cities

	Bos.	N.Y.C.	Phil.	Atl.	Miami	D.C.	Chi.	Clev.	St. L.	Dal.	Hou.	K.C.	Den.	L.A.	S.F.
PUBLIC															
ACCOUNTANT	26.0	25.0	25.0	25.0	26.0	24.0	25.0	22.0	22.0	21.0	25.0	21.0	21.0	24.8	25.0
INDUSTRY															
Cost Accountant	22.0	23.0	22.0	21.0	21.5	20.0	24.0	22.0	20.0	19.0	19.0	21.0	20.0	22.0	22.0
EDP Auditor	24.2	25.0	23.0	22.0	26.0	22.2	25.0	22.0	22.0	24.0	23.0	24.0	22.0	24.0	24.0
General Accountant	20.3	23.0	20.0	20.0	21.1	20.8	22.0	17.7	19.0	21.0	20.0	20.0	18.0	22.8	22.0
Internal Auditor	24.2	24.0	18.0	20.0	23.0	22.5	24.0	22.3	20.0	21.0	21.0	22.0	19.0	24.0	23.0
Tax Accountant	24.5	26.0	20.0	22.0	25.1	23.8	24.0	23.0	20.0	23.0	22.0	22.0	21.0	24.8	22.0
Management Consulting	27.0	28.0	23.0	26.0	29.0	25.4	28.0	28.0	24.0	22.0	22.0	27.0	23.0	30.0	28.0

THE SETTING OF ACCOUNTING STANDARDS

The concepts and standards underlying accounting for financial reporting purposes are called **generally accepted accounting principles**, often referred to as GAAP. These principles represent the consensus at a particular time as to how accounting information should be recorded, what information should be disclosed, how it should be disclosed, and which financial statements should be prepared. Generally accepted accounting principles range from broad assumptions about the economic environment to specific methods of accounting for certain events. These principles help ensure the integrity and credibility of financial information. Thus generally accepted principles provide a common financial language to enable informed users to read and interpret financial statements.

The development of GAAP is a complex process involving a mixture of theory, governmental regulation, and conventions derived from actual practice. It is impossible to specify one source of GAAP or one book that codifies all of the accounting principles. However, the major groups involved in the standard-setting process include the American Institute of Certified Public Accountants (AICPA), the Financial Accounting Standards Board (FASB), the Securities and Exchange Commission (SEC), and the Americn Accounting Association (AAA).

THE AMERICAN INSTITUTE OF CERTIFIED PUBLIC ACCOUNTANTS

The AICPA was organized around the beginning of the century and is the major professional organization of CPAs. Over its more than 80-year history, the AICPA formed several committees to develop accounting standards. The two most important were the Committee on Accounting Procedures (CAP) and the Accounting Principles Board (APB).

The CAP was formed in the 1930s, and between that time and the 1950s it issued a number of Accounting Research Bulletins (ARBs) that recommended the use of certain accounting procedures and practices. By the 1950s, the AICPA became convinced that its efforts in the standard-setting process had to be expanded. In 1959, it set up the APB to develop accounting principles and methods. The APB formally issued 31 Opinions before it went out of existence in 1973. These Opinions carry the authority of the AICPA; the burden of justifying any departure from the board's Opinions has to be assumed by those adopting other practices.

Although the APB went out of existence in 1973, the AICPA continues to play an active role in the accounting standard-setting process. Several AICPA committees provide input to the FASB and set accounting guidelines for unique financial reporting problems facing specific industries. Auditing guidelines and standards continue to be set by the AICPA.

THE FINANCIAL ACCOUNTING STANDARDS BOARD

The APB was criticized because of its part-time nature and the board's perceived lack of independence from the accounting profession for which it was setting standards. In response to this criticism, the **Financial Accounting Standards Board** was created in 1973 as an organization independent of the AICPA. The primary purpose of the FASB is to develop accounting standards. The Opinions issued by the APB, however, are still in force today unless they have been superseded by Statements issued by the FASB.

The FASB consists of seven full-time members who are independent of other responsibilities. Among its members are CPAs and other individuals in private industry and academia. The FASB has a full-time accounting research and administrative staff and also appoints outside task forces to study various accounting issues. The FASB issues Statements of Financial Accounting Standards, relating to specific accounting issues, and Concepts Statements relating to broader issues. Through 1988, it issued 100 Statements and 6 Concepts Statements. The Statements issued by the FASB and the earlier Opinions issued by the APB are a major portion of generally accepted accounting principles, especially as they relate to specific methods of accounting for certain events.

THE SECURITIES AND EXCHANGE COMMISSION

The **Securities and Exchange Commission** was established by Congress during the Great Depression that followed the stock market crash of 1929. The securities laws of 1933 and 1934 that founded the SEC gave it the power to establish accounting principles governing the form and content of financial statements of companies issuing securities for sale to the public. Because most large U.S. corporations are publicly held, they are required to satisfy SEC accounting standards.

Because of its power to set accounting standards for publicly held corporations, the SEC's impact on the setting of accounting standards can be considerable. However, the SEC has explicitly recognized the FASB as the primary standard setter for all business entities. For many years, therefore, the SEC promulgated principles for publicly held companies that reflected the existing standards developed by the private sector of the accounting profession, the APB and the FASB. More recently, however, the SEC has moved in its own direction. For example, it issued several pronouncements that were at variance with those of the public accounting profession. In these cases, the accounting profession has usually had to conform its rules to those of the SEC. Although relatively rare, controversies such as these show that accounting rules are sometimes as much the result of political factors as of good accounting theory.

THE AMERICAN ACCOUNTING ASSOCIATION

The **American Accounting Association (AAA)** is a professional association of accountants, principally academics and practicing accountants, who are concerned with accounting education and research. Individually and collectively, members of the AAA contribute to the development of accounting concepts and standards through research studies. The AAA distributes these studies by issuing a series of research monographs and publishing an academic journal.

THE GOVERNMENTAL ACCOUNTING STANDARDS BOARD

In 1984, the Financial Accounting Foundation (the group that selects FASB members, funds their activities, and provides general oversight of the Board) created the **Governmental Accounting Standards Board (GASB)**. The purpose of the GASB is to establish and improve financial accounting standards for state and local governments. In most respects, the GASB is structured like the FASB. Although this book is primarily concerned with the standards issued by the FASB, GASB standards are important in the study of governmental accounting.

ACCOUNTING STANDARDS: A MULTIDIMENSIONAL PROCESS

In sum, generally accepted accounting principles include concepts, opinions, standards, and regulations from various sources. The SEC plays an important role in setting these principles, as do the private standard setters in the accounting profession. As noted, it is impossible to find these principles in a single book or in state or federal law. These principles represent a consensus at a particular point in time. Accounting principles are not set in this way in all countries, however. For example, in many European countries, such as France and Germany, the government is the primary standard setter, so accounting rules tend to be more uniform.

ACCOUNTING CONCEPTS AND CONVENTIONS INHERENT IN ACCOUNTING INFORMATION

The previous section discussed the groups that are involved in setting generally accepted accounting principles. This section provides an overview of basic concepts and conventions on which specific accounting standards and methods are based. Many of these basic concepts and conventions grew out of the APB's past work and the FASB's current work to develop a conceptual framework of accounting.

THE CONCEPTUAL FRAMEWORK OF ACCOUNTING

For many years, the accounting profession has been developing a theoretical framework for accounting. This project has become known as the **conceptual framework project**. Its purpose is to develop objectives and concepts that the FASB will use in deciding on the specific accounting standards for external financial reporting. According to the former research director of the FASB:

> A conceptual framework is the backbone of a standard-setting activity in the private enterprise system. Without a conceptual framework to guide its accounting policy, the FASB could not be distinguished from a government agency that would be forced to follow the policies and politics of the government in power, thereby setting accounting standards that would undoubtedly be inconsistent through time.[6]

In order to help accomplish this objective, the FASB issues Concepts Statements. Concepts Statement No. 2, *Qualitative Characteristics of Accounting Information*, is the basis for much of this overview.

This book will use the terms *concept* and *convention* to apply to general, more fundamental ideas on which financial reporting in the United States is based. The term *principle* will be used to refer to specific accounting methods. This use of the term *principle* is similar to what individuals mean when they speak of generally accepted accounting principles. Exhibit 1-4 summarizes 13 of the more important accounting concepts and conventions. It is divided into three categories: basic assumptions about the accounting environment, qualitative characteristics of accounting information, and the generally accepted accounting conventions that result from the above. The concepts outlined in the exhibit are developed in more detail and applied to specific accounting issues later in the text. At this point, it is important for you to understand that these concepts provide a general framework for the preparation and interpretation of financial statements.

EXHIBIT 1–4	Basic Assumptions about the Accounting Environment	
Accounting Concepts and Conventions	Business Entity	Business entities are separate economic units that control resources and obligations and must have separate and distinct records.
	Going Concern	There is an assumption that a particular business enterprise will continue in existence for a period of time long enough to carry out its objectives and commitments.
	Qualitative Characteristics of Accounting Information	
	Quantifiability	Money is the basic measuring unit. This means that in the United States, items included in the accounting system must be quantifiable in dollars.
	Relevance	Accounting information is relevant if it is capable of making a difference in a decision.
	Reliability	Accounting information is reliable if it measures without bias what it is supposed to. Verifiability is a prime ingredient of reliability.
		(continued)

[6] Michael O. Alexander, "After Eight Years, Is the End in Sight?" *FASB Viewpoints*, June 2, 1982, p. 2.

EXHIBIT 1–4

(continued)

Qualitative Characteristics of Accounting Information	
Comparability and Consistency	Accounting information is comparable if it enables users to identify similarities and differences between two sets of economic events. Consistency refers to using the same accounting principles in different periods.
Conservatism	Uncertainties in accounting are resolved by choosing from the alternatives the one that produces the lowest asset valuation or the least amount of income.
Materiality	Accounting information is material if the judgment of a reasonable user would have been changed or influenced by the omission or misstatement of the information.
Full Disclosure	All information useful to an informed decision maker should be disclosed.
Generally Accepted Conventions	
Historical Cost	Historical cost is the primary valuation method used in financial statements. Assets are recorded at their acquisition cost and are usually not adjusted for increases in value until a sale has occurred.
Time Period	Although a business enterprise is assumed to have an indefinite life, measurement of financial condition and operations must be made at relatively short intervals, such as quarterly or yearly.
Matching	Under the matching concept, expenses must be offset against the revenues earned in the period. Thus expenses of the period are matched against the revenues of the same period, and the result is net income or loss for the period.
Revenue Recognition	Revenue is usually recognized for accounting purposes when goods are delivered or services performed. In some cases, revenue is recognized before or after the delivery of goods or the performance of services.

FINANCIAL STATEMENTS AND THEIR ELEMENTS

Financial statements are one of the primary means by which economic information about a firm is communicated to interested users. The four main financial statements are the balance sheet, the income statement, the retained earnings statement, and the statement of cash flows. These statements summarize the many inputs into the accounting system and put them in a form that is useful to decision makers. Financial statements communicate information concerning the firm's position, its profitability, and significant changes in its resources and obligations.

For the information contained in financial statements to be useful, it must possess certain characteristics. These characteristics have been described in Exhibit 1-4. Perhaps the two most important are relevance and reliability. In this regard, accounting information is **relevant** if it is capable of making a difference in a decision. Relevant accounting information in financial statements will help external users predict the future course of the business by providing feedback on past decisions. **Reliability** means that the information is unbiased, accurate, and verifiable. These characteristics, as well as the others listed in the exhibit, are important to external users, who do not have access to a firm's accounting records.

THE BALANCE SHEET

A **balance sheet** presents the financial position of a firm at a particular point in time. Often called a statement of financial position, it shows the financial resources the firm owns or controls and the claims to those resources. One of its primary purposes is to help users assess the financial strength of a firm. A balance sheet is prepared at least yearly and, in many cases, more frequently.

The balance sheet for the Carson Corporation is presented in Exhibit 1-5. At the top of all financial statements is a heading that identifies the name of the entity, the title of the statement, and the period of time the statement covers or the date of the statement. The balance sheet is dated as of a certain date. The body of a corporate balance sheet contains three major categories or elements: assets, liabilities, and stockholders' equity. By convention, assets are listed first, followed by liabilities, and then stockholders' equity. This particular example is the **account form**, in which the assets are listed on the left and the liabilities and stockholders' equity on the right. In other cases, the balance sheet may be vertical, with the liabilities and stockholders' equity listed under the assets. This type of balance sheet is called the **report form**.

EXHIBIT 1-5

THE CARSON CORPORATION				
Balance Sheet				
January 1, 1990				
Assets		**Liabilities and Stockholders' Equity**		
Cash	$ 40,000	Liabilities		
Accounts receivable	75,000	Accounts payable		$ 96,000
Inventories	155,000	Notes payable		40,000
Supplies	30,000	Other payables		79,000
Land	130,000	Total liabilities		$215,000
Plant and equipment	115,000	Stockholders' equity		
		Capital stock	$270,000	
		Retained earnings	60,000	
		Total stockholders' equity		330,000
		Total liabilities and stockholders' equity		
Total assets	$545,000			$545,000

The **assets** represent the resources of the firm. The **liabilities** of the firm represent its obligations or the claims of its creditors. **Owners' equity** is a general term used to specify the owners' residual interest. Because the Carson Corporation is a corporation, its owners' equity is specified as **stockholders' equity**. Often the liabilities and owners' equity are collectively referred to as the **equities** of the firm.

The Accounting Equation

The total assets of the enterprise equal its liabilities and owners' equity. These relationships can be expressed through the basic **accounting equation**:

Assets = Liabilities + Owners' Equity

The balance sheet or statement of financial position is a detailed version of the accounting equation, listing the various assets, liabilities, and owners' equity at a particular point in time.

The two sides of the accounting equation must always be equal because they are two views of the same accounting entity. The left-hand side of the equation shows the economic resources controlled by a business, and the right-hand side shows the claims against these resources. Another way to view this equality is that the firm's assets must have sources, and the right-hand side of the equation shows from where those resources came. Using the data from the Carson Corporation in Exhibit 1-5, the accounting equation can be stated as follows:

Assets = Liabilities + Stockholders' Equity

$545,000 = $215,000 + $330,000

Because it is a corporation, the term *stockholders' equity* has been used, rather than *owners' equity*. In this case, the corporation has assets totaling $545,000. The creditors have claims against those assets of $215,000, and the stockholders' residual interest is $330,000.

Sometimes the accounting equation is also stated in the following form, which emphasizes that the owners' claims are secondary to those of the creditors:

Assets — Liabilities = Stockholders' Equity
$545,000 — $215,000 = $330,000

Assets

Assets are the firm's economic resources. They are formally defined by the FASB as "probable future economic benefits obtained or controlled by a particular entity as a result of past transactions or events."[7] This means that in order for an item to be considered an asset, it must (1) result from a past transaction, (2) have a historical cost, (3) provide future economic benefits, and (4) be owned or controlled by the enterprise. It is important to understand that from an accounting perspective, a firm need not legally own an item for it to be considered the firm's asset. All that is necessary is control. For example, in many states, if a firm purchases an automobile and finances that purchase through a bank loan, the bank will retain ownership of the automobile until the loan is paid off. However, the automobile is considered an asset of the firm because the firm has control over its use.

A business may have several different types of assets. Some assets have physical substance, including items such as cash, inventory, property, plant, and equipment. Other assets have no physical substance and represent legal claims and/or rights. They include such items as receivables and patents. Receivables are claims to future cash, and patents are the exclusive right granted by the federal government to make a product or to use a process. Assets are generally listed on the balance sheet in the order of their liquidity, which is the ease in which the item can be turned into cash. As a result, cash and items that can be turned into cash are listed first. The items such as supplies and equipment that are used in the operations of the business are listed next.

Liabilities

Liabilities are the economic obligations of the enterprise. They comprise primarily the money or services that the accounting entity owes to its creditors. The FASB formally defines liabilities as the "probable future sacrifices of economic benefits arising from present obligations of a particular entity to transfer assets or provide services to other entities in the future as a result of past transactions or events."[8] Liabilities are often sources of assets to a firm. For example, most businesses frequently buy goods on credit rather than paying cash, and this creates the liability called *accounts payable*. In addition, businesses often borrow money from banks and other lenders for various purposes, such as purchasing land, new machinery and equipment, or additional merchandise. These debts are *notes payable,* which are formal written promises to repay the lender at a certain time in the future. Notes payable may be short term (less than a year) or long term, and unlike accounts payable, they require the payment of interest to the lender. Other liabilities result from incurring expenses that are yet to be paid in cash, such as wages payable and interest payable. Liabilities are generally grouped on the balance sheet according to their due dates. That is, liabilities due within the coming year are listed before liabilities due after a year.

---

[7] Financial Accounting Standards Board, Concepts Statement No. 6, *Elements of Financial Statements* (Stamford, Conn.: FASB, December 1985), par. 25.

[8] Ibid., par. 35.

If a business fails to pay its creditors, the law may allow the creditors the right to force the business to sell some assets in order to satisfy their claims. Similarly, if a business is dissolved, its creditors legally must be paid first, and anything left goes to the owners. This is why the creditors have a primary claim on the assets of a business, and owners have a residual, or secondary, claim on its assets.

Owners' Equity

The owners' equity in a business enterprise is "the residual interest in the assets of an entity that remains after deducting its liabilities."[9] This definition emphasizes that creditors legally have first claim on the assets of a business, so the owners' equity is equal to assets minus liabilities. The term **net assets** is often used to refer to owners' equity, because it also equals assets minus liabilities. For example, the owners' equity of the Carson Corporation (its net assets) is $330,000 ($545,000 less $215,000).

Owners' equity is increased when the owners of the business invest assets in the firm. Owners' equity is also increased by the profitable operations of the firm, because the firm's profitable operations add to its net assets.

Owners' equity is decreased when the firm distributes cash or other assets to its owners. Essentially the firm is returning to its owners part of the investment that they made in the company or is distributing the assets earned through profitable operations. Owners' equity can also be decreased by unprofitable operations, because a net loss decreases the firm's net assets.

Stockholders' Equity

As noted, the owners' equity section of a balance sheet for a corporation is called *stockholders' equity*. The stockholders' equity section of the Carson Corporation is presented in Exhibit 1-6 and consists of two components: capital stock and retained earnings.

EXHIBIT 1−6

THE CARSON CORPORATION Stockholders' Equity	
Capital stock	$270,000
Retained earnings	60,000
Total stockholders' equity	$330,000

Capital Stock. When the owners of a corporation invest cash or other assets in the business, they receive shares of **capital stock** in exchange. Thus the amount of capital stock on the balance sheet represents the amount invested by the owners. In the case of the Carson Corporation, the owners have invested $270,000 in the business.

Individual units of capital stock are called *shares*, and one who invests in a corporation receives a stock certificate or certificates for the number of shares purchased. The more shares of stock owned, the greater the proportionate ownership interest in the corporation. Shares of stock in a publicly held corporation are easily transferable. The corporation itself is not affected by subsequent sale of shares.

To illustrate, assume that you invested $10,000 in a travel agency started by your friend. In exchange you received 1,000 shares of capital stock. Therefore you purchased each share from the corporation for $10. Other individuals also invested in the travel agency, and as a result 10,000 shares were originally issued. Thus you have a 10% interest in the business. A year later, you decide to sell half of your shares to your

[9]Ibid., par. 49.

brother at $14 a share. This is a transaction between you and your brother. The corporation is not affected, because the same total number of shares is in the hands of the owners. The only difference is that you now own 500 shares and your brother owns 500 shares. The corporation also is not affected by the fact that you were able to sell your shares for more than you paid for them. Again, this is a personal transaction between you and your brother. The corporation receives only what the original investors paid to the corporation for the shares.

Retained Earnings. The other component of stockholders' equity is retained earnings. **Retained earnings** represent the portion of stockholders' equity (resulting from the cumulative profitable operations) that have not been distributed to its owners. Thus, each year that the firm earns a profit, its retained earnings are increased by the profit amount. In effect, when a firm is profitable, its net assets increase, and this increase is assigned to the retained earnings component of stockholders' equity. If the firm suffers a loss in any year, retained earnings will be reduced by this loss. The Carson Corporation had retained earnings of $60,000 as of January 1, 1990. The term *retained* is used because the firm decided to keep $60,000 of its total lifetime earnings in the business instead of distributing them as a dividend in the form of cash or other assets to the owners. The total lifetime earnings of the Carson Corporation exceed the amount indicated as retained earnings; the $60,000 represents just the portion retained that has not yet been distributed to its shareholders.

Concepts and Conventions Related to the Balance Sheet

There are a number of important concepts and conventions related to the balance sheet. Included are the historical-cost convention, objectivity, and the going-concern assumption. The effect of inflation on the balance sheet must also be considered.

The Historical-cost Convention. Under the **historical-cost convention**, assets and liabilities are initially recorded in the accounting system at their original or historical cost and are not adjusted for subsequent changes in value. For accounting purposes, an asset's historical cost is the consideration given at the time of its acquisition. If cash is given as consideration at the time of purchase, the asset will be recorded at the amount of cash paid. If an asset other than cash is given in exchange, the asset received will be recorded at its equivalent cash price. Liabilities are also recorded in accordance with the historical-cost convention. When the liability is incurred, it is recorded at the current market value at the time resources were received.

In preparing subsequent balance sheets, the assets and liabilities usually continue to be shown at historical cost. For example, the Carson Corporation purchased land for possible future use as a building site, paying $130,000 for the property. When the land was acquired, it was recorded at its cost of $130,000. Currently the land might have a market value of $300,000. The current balance sheet, however, will continue to show the land at $130,000, its historical cost, until it is sold. The main reasons for this are the objectivity of that original cost and the going-concern assumption.

Objectivity. Historical cost is **objective** (not subject to different interpretations), thus meeting the characteristic of being reliable and verifiable. Owners, real estate brokers, or tax collectors might appraise the market value quite differently. The actual value of the land cannot be known until it is sold. Thus external users can best rely on the financial statements if assets and liabilities are recorded at the objective measure of historical cost.

The Going-concern Assumption. Another reason for using historical cost when recording and valuing assets and liabilities is the going-concern assumption. To illustrate, when a firm purchases assets such as plant and equipment, it does so with the intent of using these assets to produce income. Plant assets are used in the operations of the business and are not usually held for the purpose of resale. Furthermore, it is assumed that the firm will be in existence long enough to use these assets and derive their benefits. This is known as the **going-concern assumption**: Unless there is evidence to the contrary, it is assumed that a particular firm will continue to operate indefinitely. This does not mean that a firm will be profitable indefinitely, but only that it is expected to continue to operate. Thus the current liquidation value of these assets is not as important as it would be if the firm were about to sell its assets.

The Effect of Inflation. In recent years, the difference between the original cost and the current cost of many assets and liabilities has been magnified because of inflation. This is a problem especially for assets such as property, plant, and equipment that may have been acquired many years ago. Because of this, accountants have discussed the possibility of changing the way in which assets are measured in order to reflect more closely their current value. Those favoring such changes argue that accounting numbers would provide more useful information to decision makers, even though the information might not be as objective. In 1979, the FASB required firms with large amounts of assets to disclose the current costs of their inventories and property, plant, and equipment. Such information is not contained in the actual financial statements but is provided on a supplementary basis. However, in 1986 the FASB made the disclosure of this information voluntary, and most firms discontinued its disclosure.

■ THE INCOME STATEMENT

One of the primary objectives of any business enterprise is to earn a profit. The profit earned by an enterprise is a yardstick that managers, investors, and creditors use to evaluate the future prospects of the business. To many individuals, the **income statement** is the primary financial statement, because it provides information concerning the firm's profitability.

An income statement for the Carson Corporation is shown in Exhibit 1-7. The heading identifies the name of the enterprise, the title of the statement, and the period of time the statement covers. Because income is earned over a period of time, the heading must identify the period covered by the statement. In this statement, the period is one year, although income statements may be prepared more frequently.

EXHIBIT 1-7	

THE CARSON CORPORATION
Income Statement
For the Year Ended December 31, 1990

Revenues		
Sales	$620,000	
Rental revenue	10,000	
Total revenues		$630,000
Expenses		
Cost of goods sold	$370,000	
Salary expense	80,000	
Office rental expense	50,000	
Supplies expense	25,000	
Repairs and maintenance expense	10,000	
Utilities expense	7,000	
Interest expense	3,000	
Total expenses (other than taxes)		545,000
Income before taxes		85,000
Income taxes		40,000
Net income		$ 45,000

Below the heading is the body of the statement. The income statement for the Carson Corporation contains four major elements or categories: revenues, expenses, income before taxes, and net income. By convention, income taxes, which are an expense, are shown separately from the rest of the expenses. Under each category, specific items are listed. The detail contained under each caption depends on the intended users. For example, income statements prepared for management are likely to be more detailed than those prepared for external users.

Revenues

Revenues are the price of goods sold or services rendered by a firm to others in exchange for cash or other assets or to satisfy liabilities. In effect, revenues represent the inflows of resources resulting from the firm's operations and generally result from completed economic exchanges. When a firm sells its product or renders a service to another entity, it receives an asset. The asset received is usually cash, but if a sale is made or a service is rendered on credit, an account receivable is created. An account receivable is a promise to receive cash in the future. In effect, accountants do not differentiate between sales made or services rendered for cash or credit. They both represent revenues to the firm at the point of sale, regardless of when the cash is collected.

As a result of these completed transactions—the exchange of goods and/or services for cash or receivables—the firm recognizes revenue. The amount of revenue recognized is equal to the cash or the cash equivalent of the receivable and/or other resources received at the time the sale is made or the service is rendered. For retail firms such as Safeway Stores or manufacturing firms such as General Motors, sales are the major source of revenues. For service firms, such as law or accounting firms, fees earned are the major source of revenues. Other sources of revenues include interest, rentals, and investments.

Expenses

Expenses are the resources used up by the firm during a particular period of time in the process of earning revenues. In effect, expenses represent the efforts of the enterprise and also generally result from completed transactions. In order to earn revenues, a firm must expend some of its resources. In some situations, expenses require the immediate payment of cash or the use of another asset. In other cases, the payment of cash or the use of other resources is made after the expense is incurred by the firm. In this sense, *incur* refers to the time the firm receives the service or other benefit. The expense is recorded on the income statement for the period in which it was incurred, even though it may be paid in cash during a different period. For a retail or manufacturing firm, the major expense is the cost of the items sold to customers. Other expenses might include salaries, utilities, rent, interest, repairs and maintenance, and various taxes.

Net Income

Net income (or net loss) is the difference between revenues and expenses. If revenues exceed expenses, net income results. If, on the other hand, expenses exceed revenues, there will be a net loss. Revenues increase a firm's net assets or stockholders' equity (assets minus liabilities), and expenses use up its net assets. Therefore net income causes an increase in the firm's net assets during the period, whereas a net loss causes a decrease in the firm's net assets during the period. According to Exhibit 1-7, the Carson Corporation earned net income of $45,000 for the year. This means that because of profitable operations, the firm's net assets increased by $45,000 during the year. This $45,000 increase in net assets results in a corresponding increase in the retained earnings portion of the firm's stockholders' equity.

■ THE RETAINED EARNINGS STATEMENT

The **retained earnings statement** for the Carson Corporation is presented in Exhibit 1-8. The purpose of this statement is to detail the changes in the retained earnings account for a certain period. This statement is constructed by starting with the retained earnings balance at the beginning of the period, which is the amount listed for retained earnings on the balance sheet at that date. The net income from the income statement for that period is added to this beginning balance. If a net loss were incurred, it would decrease retained earnings. The amount of dividends that have been declared during the period will reduce the retained earnings. Dividends declared during the period are not expenses but are direct deductions in the earnings kept in the company. The result is the retained earnings at the end of the period. This balance at the end of period is the amount shown on the balance sheet of that date.

EXHIBIT 1–8

THE CARSON CORPORATION Retained Earnings Statement For the Year Ended December 31, 1990	
Retained earnings, January 1, 1990	$ 60,000
Add: Net income for the year	45,000
Subtotal	$105,000
Less: Dividends declared	(5,000)
Retained earnings, December 31, 1990	$100,000

In Exhibit 1-8, the beginning balance in retained earnings of $60,000 on January 1, 1990 is taken from the Carson Corporation's January 1, 1990 balance sheet. The net income of $45,000 comes from the income statement for the year ended December 31, 1990. Dividends are a direct deduction of retained earnings. The ending balance in retained earnings on the retained earnings statement for the year ended December 31, 1990 and on the balance sheet at December 31, 1990 is $100,000.

■ THE STATEMENT OF CASH FLOWS

The **statement of cash flows** for the Carson Corporation is presented in Exhibit 1-9.

EXHIBIT 1–9

THE CARSON CORPORATION Statement of Cash Flows For the Year Ended December 31, 1990		
Cash flows from operating activities		
Cash revenues	$570,000	
Less: cash expenses	555,000	
Net cash provided by operating activities		$15,000
Cash flows from investing activities		
Purchase of land	$ 45,000	
Purchase of plant and equipment	25,000	
Net cash used by investing activities		(70,000)
Cash flows from financing activities		
Issuance of note payable	$ 40,000	
Issuance of capital stock	30,000	
	70,000	
Less: Issuance of dividends	5,000	
Net cash provided from financing activities		65,000
Net increase in cash		10,000
Cash balance, January 1, 1990		40,000
Cash balance, December 31, 1990		$50,000

The purpose of this statement is to provide relevant information about the cash receipts and disbursements of an enterprise during a period. It helps statement users:

1. Assess the enterprise's ability to generate positive future net cash flows.
2. Assess the enterprise's ability to meet its obligations, its ability to pay dividends, and its needs for external financing.
3. Assess the reasons for differences between net income and associated cash receipts and payments.
4. Assess the effects on an enterprise's financial position of both its cash and noncash investing and financing transactions during the period.[10]

This information is important because many firms are entering into complex transactions such as repurchasing their own capital stock or converting some of their debt into capital stock. These transactions can be adequately disclosed only on the statement of cash flows.

A firm can obtain its cash from three primary sources: operating activities, investing activities, and financing activities. As indicated in Exhibit 1-9, the Carson Corporation's operating activities for the year provided a $15,000 source of cash. Cash inflow from operating activities is not equal to net income for the year. This is because net income includes revenues that have yet to be collected in cash (sales made on account in which the entire amount has not yet been collected) and expenses incurred in which the cash has not yet been paid. Thus cash flows from operating activities include only revenues and expenses received or paid in cash. In the Carson Corporation example, net income equals $45,000 (see the income statement, Exhibit 1-7), but cash inflow from operating activities equals $15,000.

Investing activities relate primarily to the receipt and payment of cash from the sale or purchase of property, plant, and equipment, other productive assets, and long-term investments. The Carson Corporation entered into two transactions that would be classified as investing activities. They are the $45,000 purchase of land and the $25,000 purchase of plant and equipment. In total, the total cash outflows from investing activities amounted to $70,000.

Financing activities have to do with obtaining resources from owners, paying dividends, and borrowing and repaying money to creditors on long-term debt. In Exhibit 1-9, the Carson Corporation had two sources of cash inflows from financing activities: the $40,000 received from issuing a note payable and the $30,000 received from issuing capital stock. The $5,000 of dividends paid represents a cash outflow from financing activities. The net result is a $65,000 increase in cash flows from financing activities.

At the end of the period, the firm's cash flows exceeded its uses by $10,000. When this is added to the beginning cash balance, the ending cash balance of $50,000 is obtained. This is the amount shown on the balance sheet of December 31, 1990.

■ THE RELATIONSHIP AMONG THE FINANCIAL STATEMENTS

The balance sheet, income statement, retained earnings statement, and statement of cash flows all are related to one another. This relationship is referred to as **articulation**, which means that the four financial statements all tie in with one another. The balance sheet at the beginning of the period describes the firm's financial position at that particular point in time. This financial position changes because the firm enters into various transactions. The firm's financial position is enhanced when a profit is earned and is weakened when a loss occurs. These transactions are summarized on

[10] Financial Accounting Standards Board, Statement No. 95, *Statement of Cash Flows* (Stamford, Conn.: 1987), par. 5.

EXHIBIT 1–10

The Relationship among Financial Statements

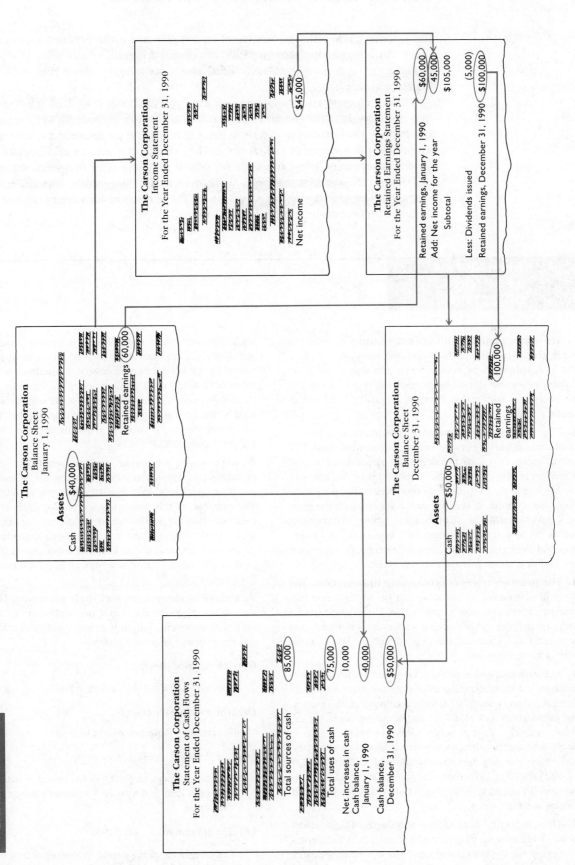

The Carson Corporation
Income Statement
For the Year Ended December 31, 1990

Net income $45,000

The Carson Corporation
Retained Earnings Statement
For the Year Ended December 31, 1990

Retained earnings, January 1, 1990 $60,000
Add: Net income for the year   45,000
   Subtotal $105,000
Less: Dividends issued   (5,000)
Retained earnings, December 31, 1990 $100,000

The Carson Corporation
Balance Sheet
January 1, 1990

Assets
Cash $40,000

Retained earnings   60,000

The Carson Corporation
Balance Sheet
December 31, 1990

Assets
Cash $50,000

Retained
earnings   100,000

The Carson Corporation
Statement of Cash Flows
For the Year Ended December 31, 1990

Total sources of cash   85,000

Total uses of cash   75,000
Net increases in cash   10,000
Cash balance, January 1, 1990   40,000
Cash balance,
   December 31, 1990 $50,000

the income statement. The net effect is also shown on the retained earnings statement. Thus the income statement and the retained earnings statement provide a link between two consecutive balance sheets and show how net assets have increased or decreased from operations.

A firm enters into a variety of investing and financing activities, many of which may not directly affect the firm's net income during the current period. These activities include the borrowing and repayment of loans, the purchase and sale of noncash assets, and the issuance of capital stock. They change the amount and composition of the firm's net assets. These transactions, as well as changes due to operations, are summarized on the statement of cash flows, which also links two consecutive balance sheets by detailing changes in a firm's cash. These relationships are presented for the Carson Corporation in Exhibit 1-10 on page 23.

SUMMARY OF LEARNING OBJECTIVES

1. The nature and function of accounting. Accounting is a system of recording, classifying, and summarizing financial information about economic entities that is useful in making economic decisions. Accounting is a tool created for economic use, and it changes according to the economic needs of society.

2. The relationship between accounting and different forms of business enterprise. Accounting is used by sole proprietorships, partnerships, and corporations. For all three forms of enterprise, the transactions of the business are kept separate from those of the owners. For a partnership, the accounting system must keep track of the partners' investments. For a corporation, whose stockholders are its owners, there is frequently a separation of ownership and management, and accounting reports inform the stockholders about management's performance.

3. The primary users of accounting information. The users of accounting information can be divided into two categories: external and internal users. The major external users are present and potential investors and creditors, governmental agencies, and the general public. The internal user of accounting information is the management.

4. Accountants—the providers of accounting information. Public accountants offer their services to the public for a fee and generally perform auditing and accounting, tax preparation and planning, and some management advisory services. Private accountants are employed by a single firm and perform such activities as cost accounting, budgetary planning and control, internal auditing, and financial reporting. Governmental accountants perform various accounting services for federal, state, and local governmental units and agencies.

5. The setting of accounting standards. The development of accounting concepts and standards is a complex process involving government and the accounting profession. The Securities and Exchange Commission has the legal authority from Congress to determine accounting standards but has basically accepted the standards determined by the accounting profession, sometimes modifying them or calling for different types of information. The Financial Accounting Standards Board is the organization created by the accounting profession to develop the concepts and standards that constitute generally accepted accounting principles (GAAP).

6. Accounting concepts and conventions. The accounting profession has been working for a number of years to develop a conceptual framework of accounting. The purpose of this project is to develop objectives and concepts that the FASB and others can use in developing specific accounting standards. The more important concepts and conventions that have been developed from this project and other related works have been summarized in Exhibit 1-4.

7. Financial statements and their elements. Financial statements represent the major product of the accounting information system. The four primary financial statements and their elements are as follows:

(a) The balance sheet:

Assets = Liabilities + Owners' equity

(b) The income statement:

Revenues − Expenses = Net Income

(c) The retained earnings statement:

Retained earnings, beginning of the period + net income (or − net loss) − dividends = retained earnings, end of the period

(d) The statement of cash flows:

Cash, beginning of the period + sources of cash − uses of cash = cash, end of the period

KEY TERMS

Account form of the balance sheet	Income statement
Accounting	Liabilities
Accounting equation	Limited liability
Accounting system	Management accounting
American Accounting Association (AAA)	Net assets
American Institute of Certified Public Accountants (AICPA)	Objectivity
	Opinion
Articulation	Owners' equity
Assets	Partnership
Audit	Private accounting
Balance sheet	Public accounting
Business entity	Publicly owned
Capital stock	Relevance
Certified public accountant (CPA)	Reliability
Conceptual framework project	Report form of the balance sheet
Corporation	Retained earnings
Equities	Retained earnings statement
Expenses	Revenues
Financial Accounting Standards Board (FASB)	Reviews and compilations
Financial statements	Securities and Exchange Commission (SEC)
Generally accepted accounting principles (GAAP)	Sole proprietorship
Going-concern assumption	Statement of cash flows
Governmental accounting	Stockholders' equity
Governmental Accounting Standards Board (GASB)	Transactions
Historical-cost convention	

PROBLEM FOR YOUR REVIEW

At the beginning of 1990, Patti Edwards decided to open a real estate firm called Real Property, Inc. During the first year of the firm's existence, the following transactions occurred.

Patti invested $100,000 of her personal funds in the business, in exchange for 1,000 shares of capital stock. In addition, some of Patti's friends decided to invest in her business. In exchange for $25,000, she issued them 250 shares of capital stock. In order to obtain additional funds for operating purposes, the firm obtained a $25,000 loan from a local bank. During the year, the real estate agency purchased, for $80,000 cash, a small building to use as an office. Finally, the firm purchased some office equipment for $8,000, $2,000 of which was paid in cash at the time and the remainder paid later in the year. Finally, various office supplies were purchased close to the end of the year. The supplies cost $2,500 and were purchased on account. No payments were made on this account during the current year.

The following revenue and expense transactions also occurred during the first year of operations:

1. Commissions earned during the year amounted to $300,000. By year-end, $230,000 of these commissions had been collected in cash.

2. Various operating expenses of $220,000 were incurred during the year. As of year-end, $190,000 of these expenses had been paid in cash.

3. Interest expense on the bank loan amounted to $2,500 and was unpaid at year-end.

4. Taxes of $15,500 were incurred and paid during the year.

REQUIRED: Using the information provided, prepare the following financial statements:

1. An income statement for the year ended December 31, 1990.

2. A balance sheet at December 31, 1990.

3. A statement of cash flows for the year ended December 31, 1990.

Use the financial statements in the text as an example. In the income statement, use the following expense categories: operating expenses, interest expense, and tax expense.

SOLUTION
(1)

REAL PROPERTIES, INC.
Income Statement
For the Year Ended December 31, 1990

Revenues		
Commissions earned		$300,000
Expenses		
Various operating expenses	$220,000	
Interest expense	2,500	
Total expenses before income taxes		$222,500
Income before taxes		77,500
Tax expense		15,500
Net income		$ 62,000

(2)

REAL PROPERTIES, INC.
Balance Sheet[a]
For the Year Ended December 31, 1990

Assets		Liabilities and Stockholders' Equity	
Cash	86,500	Liabilities	
Accounts receivable	70,000	Accounts payable	$ 32,500
Office supplies	2,500	Interest payable	2,500
Equipment	8,000	Bank loan payable	25,000
Building	80,000	Total liabilities	$ 60,000
		Stockholders' equity	
		Capital stock	125,000
		Retained earnings[b]	62,000
		Total stockholders' equity	187,000
		Total liabilities and	
Total assets	$247,000	stockholders' equity	$247,000

[a] The order of the accounts follows typical balance sheet order. Assets are shown first, with cash being the first asset, followed by items such as accounts receivable and supplies. The longer-term assets such as buildings and equipment are generally shown last.

[b] Because this is the firm's first year of operation, there is no beginning balance in retained earnings. In addition, no dividends were issued. As a result, the ending balance of retained earnings equals the net income for the year of $62,000.

(3)

REAL PROPERTIES, INC.
Statement of Cash Flows
For the Year Ended December 31, 1990

Cash flows from operating activities		
Cash commissions received	$230,000	
Less: Various expenses and taxes paid	205,500	
Net cash provided by operating activities		$ 24,500
Cash flows from operating activities		
Purchase of building	$ 80,000	
Purchase of office equipment	8,000	
Net cash used by investing activities		(88,000)
Cash flows from financing activities		
Issuance of bank loan payable	$ 25,000	
Issuance of capital stock	125,000	
Net cash provided from financing activities		150,000
Net increase in cash		86,500
Cash balance, January 1, 1990		0
Cash balance, December 31, 1990		$ 86,500

QUESTIONS

1. In broad terms, what is accounting?

2. What purposes does accounting serve in (a) a business enterprise and (b) society?

3. What are the similarities and differences among accounting, law, and mathematics? Explain.

4. In what ways do you think accounting would differ for business organizations and for the government?

5. In what ways do you think accounting differs for external and internal users?

6. Identify four outside groups that would be interested in a company's financial statements, and indicate their particular interest.

7. What are the characteristics of the corporate form of organization that would account for its popularity?

8. Is accounting more important in a corporation or in an individual proprietorship or partnership? Explain.

9. Describe in your own words the manner in which accounting standards are set in the United States. How do you think accounting standards would be set in a country with a centralized socialistic government?

10. Describe the role and function of each of the following groups:

(a) The Securities and Exchange Commission.

(b) The Financial Accounting Standards Board.

(c) The American Accounting Association.

(d) The Government Accounting Standards Board.

11. Financial statements are described as the major product of the accounting information system. Explain this statement, and briefly describe the four principal financial statements.

12. As the accountant for the Stanga Company, you have been asked to prepare the company's financial statements at the end of 1990. Prepare the headings for each of the four statements, and explain their differences.

13. List and define the three main elements of an income statement.

14. The main elements of a balance sheet are assets, liabilities, and owners' equity. Define and give at least two examples of each.

15. Describe the historical-cost convention, and explain its use in accounting.

16. Name two groups with claims on a firm's assets. Which has the primary claim? What are the reasons for this?

17. List two forms of the basic accounting equation. Why must it always be in balance?

18. If a transaction causes total liabilities to increase but does not affect owners' equity, what change is to be expected in total assets?

19. Assuming that you never took an accounting course and were asked to prepare a statement listing your assets and liabilities, would you do so at their historical cost or their current value? Why?

20. What are the disadvantages of using financial statements based on historical or original costs in a period of inflation?

21. Describe the going-concern assumption. What relevance does it have to the way accountants record assets?

22. A company purchased land ten years ago for $200,000. The land has just been appraised at $350,000. When do accountants recognize the fact that the land has increased in value?

23. What is the statement of cash flows, and what are its purposes?

24. The four main financial statements articulate with one another. Explain what this means.

25. What is the conceptual framework project, and what is its main purpose?

EXERCISES

E1. Users of Financial Statements. You are currently being interviewed for the position of manager of financial reporting for a large corporation. You have been asked to explain to the chief financial officer, your potential boss, why each of the following individuals or groups might be interested in the firm's financial statements:

(a) The current owners of the firm.

(b) The creditors of the firm.

(c) The management of the firm.

(d) The prospective stockholders of the firm.

(e) The Internal Revenue Service.

(f) The Securities and Exchange Commission.

(g) The firm's major labor union.

E2. Careers in Accounting. You have been asked to lecture on accounting careers to a group of prospective accounting students. Describe to them the types of work available in:

(a) CPA firms.

(b) Private industry.

(c) Government.

E3. Business Entities. Below are statements concerning sole proprietorships, partnerships, and corporations. Indicate whether each statement is true or false; if the statement is false, provide an explanation for your answer.

(a) If there are two or more owners of a business, it must be organized as a partnership.

(b) In a sole proprietorship, the owner and the business are legally one entity.

(c) The sole proprietorship and its owner represent the same accounting entity.

(d) Any two individuals, by oral agreement, can form a corporation.

(e) The owners of a corporation are not legally responsible for the individual debts incurred by the corporation.

(f) In a partnership, the partners and the partnership are legally one entity.

(g) All partners in a partnership must share the profits and losses equally.

(h) Ownership in a corporation is evidenced by a share of stock.

E4. The Accounting Equation. Answer each of the following independent questions:

(a) The New Company's assets equal $52,000, and its stockholders' equity totals $22,500. What is the amount of its liabilities?

(b) The liabilities of the Old Company are $25,200, and its owners' equity is $15,800. What is the amount of its assets?

(c) The Rose Corporation has total assets of $75,000 and total liabilities of $34,500. What is the amount of its owners' equity?

(d) The Barney Corporation started July with assets of $150,000 and liabilities of $90,000. During the month of July, stockholders' equity increased by $24,000 and liabilities decreased by $10,000. What is the amount of total assets at the end of July?

E5. **Recognition of Balance Sheet Items.** Classify the following items as assets, liabilities, or stockholders' equity. If you do not think that the item would be recognized as any of the above, so state and give your reasons.

(a) Cash   **(b)** Notes payable   **(c)** Office equipment

(d) Retained earnings   **(e)** Accounts payable   **(f)** Accounts receivable

(g) A firm's good management   **(h)** Office supplies   **(i)** Capital stock

(j) Notes receivable   **(k)** Land   **(l)** A trademark such as McDonald's golden arch

E6. **Balance Sheet Preparation.** The following data is available for Pam's Peanut Shop as of August 31, 1990.

Cash	$7,000	Accounts receivable	$ 2,500
Accounts payable	2,500	Supplies	4,500
Stockholders' equity	?	Notes payable	3,000
Office equipment	8,000	Land	15,000
		Taxes payable	2,000

REQUIRED: Prepare a balance sheet for the company as of August 31, 1990, in the format shown in Exhibit 1-5. Show figures for total assets, total liabilities, and stockholders' equity.

E7. **Balance Sheet Preparation.** The following data is available for Jose's Supply Store as of June 30, 1990:

(a) The purchase cost of all equipment owned by the store was $20,000. When making the purchase, a note for $18,000 was given to the supplier. An additional payment of $2,000 has subsequently been made on the note.

(b) Several years ago, the company purchased a plot of land for $100,000 cash, to be used for future store expansion. Although the land has yet to be used, the company still owns it. Recently it has been appraised at $140,000.

(c) Supplies on hand cost $15,000.

(d) Jose owed various suppliers $12,000.

(e) When the firm was organized, capital stock of $50,000 was issued.

(f) Various individuals owed the firm $2,500.

(g) Retained earnings amounted to $70,000.

(h) The firm had inventory for resale of $10,000.

(i) The firm had some cash in a checking account but was unable to determine the amount. All other items have been given to you.

REQUIRED: Prepare a balance sheet for Jose's Supply Store as of June 30, 1990, using the format of Exhibit 1-5.

E8. **Recognition of Revenue and Expense Transactions.** A summary of the Grant Corporation's transactions during November is reproduced below. State which of the events would be recorded on the income statement for November.

(a) The owners needed additional funds, and they borrowed $200,000 from the bank.

(b) The firm collected $20,000 on account from a sale made on account in October.

(c) Cash sales during November totaled $5,000.

(d) The firm received its November utility bill of $75.

(e) The firm paid $40 for October's utility bill.

(f) The firm made sales on account in November, totaling $7,500.

(g) A dividend of $500 was declared and paid in November.

E9. Recognizing Balance Sheet and Income Statement Items. Review the following items and state whether they are an asset, a liability, stockholders' equity, revenue, or expense account:

(a) Salary expense   (b) Supplies on hand   (c) Equipment

(d) Interest earned   (e) Capital stock   (f) Accounts payable

(g) Sales   (h) Retained earnings   (i) Cost of goods sold

(j) Wages payable   (k) Repairs and maintenance   (l) Patents

E10. Income Statement Preparation. Sam Houston, owner of Houston's Fun Ranch, wants to know the bottom line from his 1990 operations. Prepare an income statement using the following information:

(a) Salaries and wages expense was $56,000.

(b) House rental revenue came to $240,000.

(c) Insurance expense was $3,200.

(d) Interest earned on invested cash was $600.

(e) Rental revenue from horseback riding totaled $14,500.

(f) Horse feed and other expenses totaled $21,000.

(g) Advertising expense totaled $1,900.

(h) Income taxes totaled 20% of income before taxes.

(*Hint*: Income before taxes equals revenues minus all expenses other than taxes.)

E11. Income Statement Preparation. The University Book Store has just completed its busy fall season. Taking the following facts into consideration, construct an income statement for the month ending September 30:

(a) Sales, both cash and on account, totaled $965,000.

(b) Salary and wages equaled 12% of sales.

(c) All items were priced to sell at 1.25 times their cost.

(d) Insurance expense for the period was $1,100.

(e) Miscellaneous expenses equaled 1% of cost of goods sold.

(f) Advertising and promotion cost 5% of sales but was estimated to have attracted 45% of the current month's sales.

(g) Because the store is run by the university foundation, no taxes are levied.

E12. Income Statement Interpretation. As the accountant for the Software Circle Company, you have prepared the following income statement:

SOFTWARE CIRCLE COMPANY
Income Statement
For the Year Ended December 31, 1990

Revenues		
Cash sales	$160,000	
Sales on account	240,000	
Total revenues		$400,000
Expenses		
Cost of goods sold	$190,000	
Salary expense	60,000	
Advertising expense	50,000	
Rent expense	30,000	
Supplies used	10,000	
Total expenses		340,000
Income before taxes		60,000
Taxes		5,000
Net income		$ 55,000

REQUIRED: One of the directors of the company, an expert in marketing, knows little about accounting. She asks you the following questions, to which you should make a brief response:

  (a) If some of the sales made on account will not be collected until the next year, why are they included in this year's income statement?

  (b) The greatest part of the advertising was based on a promotion undertaken during the last quarter of the year. Although the advertisements ran before the end of the year, the payment to the advertising agency will not be made until early January. Why is the total amount listed on the current income statement?

  (c) At the end of the year, the firm purchased 100 new computers from AT&T. Why is this transaction not listed on the income statement?

  (d) The member of the board of directors knows the firm issued a $1,000 cash dividend, but she cannot find this amount listed on the income statement. Why?

E13. Analysis of Stockholders' Equity. When the Calbear Corporation was formed ten years ago, individuals invested $600,000 in the corporation. No additional subsequent investments have been made. Since then the company has been very profitable. At the end of the current year, December 1990, the firm's total assets had grown to $2,700,000. Liabilities were $1,150,000. During the past ten years, the firm has issued dividends equal to 25% of the current (December 1990) balance in the retained earnings account.

REQUIRED: **(a)** Prepare the stockholders' equity section of the balance sheet as of December 31, 1990.

  (b) How much in dividends has the firm issued since its inception?

  (c) Assuming that no dividends had been issued, what would the balance in stockholders' equity have been at the end of 1990?

E14. Preparation of the Retained Earnings Statement. At the beginning of the current year, January 1, 1991, the stockholders' equity section of the McKay Sporting Goods Corporation contained, the following items:

    Capital stock $250,000
    Retained earnings $435,000

During the year, the following events occurred:

- The company's net income amounted to $92,000.
- Dividends issued in cash amounted to $14,000.
- The firm issued additional capital stock for cash in the amount of $60,000.

REQUIRED: **(a)** Prepare the retained earnings statement for the year.

  (b) Prepare the stockholders' equity section of the balance sheet at the end of the year.

E15. Preparation of an Income Statement and Balance Sheet. Several years ago, Lisa Rios started an art supply store called Lisa's Art. The store has been very successful, and profits for last year reached a new high. Lisa asks you to help her prepare an income statement and balance sheet for the current year and gives you the following information:

Total sales	$800,000	Inventory	?
Cost of goods sold	?	Land	215,000
Salaries expense	60,000	Total assets	370,000
Rental expense	40,000	Accounts payable	30,000
Advertising expense	10,000	Salaries payable	10,000
Taxes	57,000	Capital stock	100,000
Net income	133,000	Retained earnings, January 1, 1991,	
Cash	25,000	beginning of period	97,000
Receivables	40,000		

REQUIRED: Assuming that all the items are listed, prepare (a) an income statement for the year ended December 31, 1991, and (b) a balance sheet at December 31, 1991.

E16. Preparing a Statement of Cash Flows. The Olympic Corporation began business at the beginning of 1990. As the accountant, you have been asked by management to prepare a statement of cash flows, for presentation to the board of directors. You obtained the following cash flow data for the year: revenues received in cash, $200,000; cash outflows for operating expenses, $140,000; purchased land and buildings for cash, $170,000; borrowings from a local bank, $50,000; issue of capital stock for cash, $100,000; and the issue of a cash dividend of $10,000.

REQUIRED: Using a format similar to Exhibit 1-9, prepare a statement of cash flows for the year ended December 31, 1990.

E17. Relationships among Financial Statements. The income statement for the Telsis Company is as follows:

THE TELSIS COMPANY
Income Statement
For the Year Ended December 31, 1990

Revenues		
Commissions earned	$700,000	
Rentals	80,000	
Total revenues		$780,000
Expenses		
Salaries expense	$300,000	
Advertising expense	150,000	
Building lease expense	60,000	
Supplies used	30,000	
Total expenses		540,000
Income before taxes		240,000
Taxes		30,000
Net income		$210,000

Additional information:

(a) Twenty percent of the commission revenues have not been collected in cash.

(b) All rental revenues were collected in cash.

(c) All salaries, except for $10,000, were paid in cash.

(d) The supplies that were used in the business were purchased and paid for in late 1989.

(e) All other expenses were paid for in cash during the current year.

REQUIRED: **(a)** Determine the amount of cash inflows or outflows from operations.

(b) Explain the difference between net income and cash inflow or outflow from operations.

PROBLEMS

P1-1 Recognition of Events. Amy Brooks opened a photographic studio on May 1, 1990. For each transaction that occurred in May, identify which would be recognized in preparing Amy's personal accounts and which would be recognized in accounting for her business entity, Brooks Studio. Some transactions may affect both entities, and some neither. In either case, be sure to so state and explain your reasoning.

(a) Amy received $7,000 in termination pay from her previous employer.

(b) Of this termination pay, $6,000 was deposited in the Brooks Studio's checking account in exchange for capital stock.

(c) Amy personally borrowed $25,000 from the local bank to open the studio. Her home was used as security for the loan.

(d) A three-year lease on a small building was signed. The building will be used for a studio. A $1,000 deposit was made by the firm at the time of signing.

(e) The $25,000 that Amy borrowed from the bank was invested in the business in exchange for additional capital stock.

(f) The studio bought $6,500 of photographic supplies on account.

(g) The printing of 10,000 brochures announcing the opening of the studio cost $1,000. None of the brochures has yet been distributed. Amy thinks she has enough brochures to last for one year.

(h) Amy hired an assistant at a monthly salary of $1,000. He will start work in June; no payments were made.

(i) Several of Amy's friends worked on the weekend, without pay, to help decorate the studio.

(j) Amy needed some money for her personal use and withdrew $1,000 of her investment from the corporation.

P1-2 Balance Sheet Preparation. The balance sheet items for Alfredo's Pizza Parlor at June 1, 1990 were as follows (in alphabetical order):

Accounts payable	$ 7,000	Loan receivable	$ 8,000
Capital stock	70,000	Note to bank	8,000
Cash	5,000	Restaurant furniture	60,000
Equipment	10,000	Retained earnings	?
Inventory of foods	12,000		

During June, the following transactions occurred:

(a) The company paid its suppliers $2,000 on account.

(b) Additional food inventory of $1,500 was purchased on account.

(c) The loan receivable was from a friend of the store's owner. A payment of one-half of the balance was made to the company.

(d) Additional equipment costing $600 was purchased for cash.

(e) A soft drink supplier wanted the pizza parlor to stock his brand of drink, so he agreed to sell the parlor 10 cartons of the soft drinks for a total of $100. The normal purchase price of the drinks is $150. The purchase was made on account.

REQUIRED:
(a) Prepare a balance sheet as of June 1, 1990.

(b) Prepare a balance sheet as of June 30, 1990.

(c) Have the balances in the stockholders' equity accounts changed? If so, by how much? Can you explain the change or lack of change in these accounts?

P1-3 Preparing an Income Statement and Statement of Retained Earnings. The following items were taken from the records of the Anasonic Corporation for the month ended October 31, 1990:

Sales revenue	$600,000
Salaries expense	80,000
Capital stock issued	120,000
Cost of goods sold	320,000
Service revenues	55,000
Rental expense	45,000
Repairs and maintenance expense	50,000
Retained earnings, October 1, 1990	220,000
Accounts payable	40,000
Taxes expense	30,000
Dividends declared and paid	10,000

REQUIRED:
(a) Prepare in good form an income statement and a retained earnings statement for the month ended October 31, 1990.

(b) During the month, the company made sales of $70,000 on credit, which have not yet been collected in cash. Why are these sales included in the October 1990 income statement?

(c) Is it accurate to say that when a firm earns net income during the period, its resources increase? Explain.

P1-4   The Entity Assumption and Preparation of a Balance Sheet. John Alexander owns a small retail store. He recently approached a bank for a loan to finance a planned expansion of the store. He was asked to submit the latest balance sheet for the store, which he prepared as follows:

ALEXANDER'S RETAIL OUTLET
December 31, 1990

Assets		Liabilities and Stockholders' Equity	
Cash	$ 2,500	Accounts payable	$ 5,000
Accounts receivable	8,000	Note payable on family car	2,500
Inventory	28,000	Mortgage on house	80,000
Equipment	10,000	Stockholders' equity	87,500
Personal residence	120,000		
Store supplies	1,500		
Family car	5,000		
Total	$175,000	Total	$175,000

In addition, John offered the following information:

(a) The inventory has an original cost of $25,000. It is listed on the balance sheet at what it would cost to purchase today.

(b) Of the cash listed on the balance sheet, $1,500 is in his personal account, and the remainder is in the store's account.

(c) The store has a delivery truck that it recently purchased for $10,000. It was financed through a bank loan, and the bank has legal title to the truck. To date, the store has paid $2,000 on the loan. John did not include the truck or the loan because it is not owned by either himself or the business.

REQUIRED: (a) Identify any errors in this balance sheet, and explain why they should be considered errors.

(b) Prepare a corrected balance sheet for the store.

P1-5   The Income Statement and Statement of Cash Flows. The Ocra Corporation began operations July 1, 1991. During the six months ended December 31, 1991, the following events took place:

(a) The owners invested $150,000 cash in exchange for capital stock.

(b) Total commissions earned amounted to $300,000, of which $60,000 had not yet been collected in cash by December 31.

(c) Total operating expenses amounted to $240,000, of which $35,000 had not yet been paid in cash at December 31.

(d) The firm borrowed $72,000 cash from a local bank.

(e) Various items of property, plant, and equipment were purchased for $125,000 cash.

(f) The firm declared and paid dividends in cash, amounting to $14,000.

(g) The firm invested $15,000 of excess cash in a long-term investment.

(h) During the six-month period, interest revenue earned on the investments amounted to $1,000, of which $800 was received in cash.

REQUIRED: (a) Prepare an income statement in condensed form and a statement of cash flows. (Taxes are ignored for simplicity.)

(b) What information does the statement of cash flows contain that cannot be learned from the income statement?

P1-6 Summary Problem. At the beginning of 1990, Jan Ochi decided to open an advertising agency called The Best Agency. During 1990, the following transactions occurred:

Jan and her family members invested $320,000 cash in the company in exchange for 3,000 shares of capital stock. In addition, the local bank lent the corporation $100,000. The company used the cash to purchase land for $60,000, a building for $100,000, and office furniture and fixtures for $80,000. In addition, the firm purchased another $50,000 of furniture and fixtures on account, all of which will be paid for next year.

The following summary revenue and expense transactions and other transactions took place during 1990:

(a) Commissions earned during the year amounted to $130,000. By the end of the year, $120,000 of these commissions had been collected in cash. The firm expects to collect the remaining cash early next year.

(b) Various operating expenses of $115,000 were incurred and paid in cash during the year.

(c) Interest expense of $1,000 on the bank loan was incurred but remained unpaid at December 31.

(d) The corporation declared and paid dividends of $5,000 during the year.

(e) Taxes of $2,000 were incurred and paid during the year.

REQUIRED: Using the above information, prepare the following financial statements:

(a) An income statement for the year ended December 31, 1990.

(b) A retained earnings statement for the year ended December 31, 1990.

(c) A balance sheet at December 31, 1990.

(d) A statement of cash flows for the year ended December 31, 1990.

■ UNDERSTANDING FINANCIAL STATEMENTS

P1-7 The following items, in random order, have been taken from a recent balance sheet of Hershey Foods Corporation (in thousands):

Property, plant, and equipment	$539,914
Accounts payable	110,582
Income taxes payable	85,165
Cash and short-term investments	17,820
Inventories	178,585
Capital stock	69,675
Prepaid assets	13,411
Notes payable (short-term)	19,579
Notes payable (long-term)	140,250
Investments and other assets	73,212
Retained earnings	462,820
Accounts receivable	65,129

REQUIRED: **(a)** Prepare a balance sheet for Hershey Foods at December 31.

(b) Describe what each item represents.

(c) Evaluate, as best as you can at this early point in your studies, the financial position of Hershey Foods Corporation.

■ FINANCIAL DECISION CASES

P1-8 Ben Racket is considering establishing a pro tennis team to compete in the new World Tennis League. He figures it will cost over $1 million to start up the team. A good part of this will go toward signing bonuses for players. Each of the five players will receive a $200,000 bonus for signing a three-year contract with the team.

Ben also feels that he will need substantial funds after the initial start-up, which will be used to obtain a stadium lease and for general operations. Although Ben will be the sole owner now, he might be willing to take in other investors, especially if he is unable to finance the team himself.

Ben is not very familiar with business practices or accounting and asks your advice on a number of items.

REQUIRED: **(a)** Ben has heard that he could organize his business as a sole proprietorship, partnership, or corporation. Advise him on his options and which you feel would be best.

(b) After making his initial $1.1 million investment in the business, Ben drew up the following balance sheet:

WEST PANASH ACES
Balance Sheet
April 1, 1990

Assets		Owners' Equity	
Cash	$ 100,000	Owners' equity	$1,100,000
Players' contracts	1,000,000		
Total assets	$1,100,000	Total owners' equity	$1,100,000

Ben never had accounting but looked in a dictionary and noted that it defined *asset* as any item owned by a person. As Ben had owned the players for three years, he listed their contracts as an asset. Do you agree with his interpretation of assets? Why or why not? How would you account for the players' contracts?

P1-9 One of your friends is the sole owner of a small company that makes banners. Although the firm has been relatively successful, it has grown little in the last few years. However, recently the company was contacted by an Olympic organizing committee to be the official banner supplier to the Olympics. As a result, the firm is planning to expand and needs funds for the expansion.

Your friend has always prepared his own financial statements. However, in negotiating a bank loan, the loan officer insisted that the statements be audited by a CPA. Because your friend was unfamiliar with the accounting profession, he asked you the following questions:

(a) What is a CPA, and what services are provided by CPA firms?

(b) The loan officer mentioned an audit. What is an audit, and why would the banker want my financial statements audited?

(c) The loan officer mentioned that my financial statements should be prepared in accordance with generally accepted accounting principles. What does she mean? Where can I go to find these generally accepted accounting principles? Who sets these principles?

REQUIRED: Write a brief memo responding to your friend's questions.

ACCOUNTING AS AN INFORMATION SYSTEM

After studying this chapter, you should be able to:

1. Explain why accounting is an information system.
2. Describe the characteristics of information admitted to the accounting system.
3. Explain the effects of transactions on the accounting equation.
4. Detail the components of the accounting system and steps in the accounting cycle.
5. Record balance sheet transactions in the journal and ledger.
6. Prepare a trial balance and describe its uses and limitations.

T his chapter begins the book's coverage of the accounting system, which is the set of methods and procedures used to record, classify, and summarize the financial information that is distributed to interested users. The first part of the chapter details which economic events are recorded in the accounting system. In the second part begins a discussion of the standard accounting procedures that are used to record, classify, and summarize the information handled in all accounting systems.

■ THE ACCOUNTING INFORMATION SYSTEM

Accounting is a system designed to provide financial information about economic entities. Any system, including accounting, may be viewed as comprising three parts: (1) inputs, (2) a transformation process, and (3) outputs. The inputs are the system's raw materials, and the transformation processes are the methods through which these raw materials are converted into outputs.

Exhibit 2-1 illustrates how the **accounting information system** transforms raw data into useful economic information. The inputs of the system are the economic events into which the firm enters. However, only those economic events that meet certain criteria become inputs of the system. The transformation process is the set of rules and conventions that accountants use to record, classify, and summarize the inputs. The outputs of the accounting system are the accounting reports provided for a variety of users. Most importantly, these outputs include financial statements for external users and management.

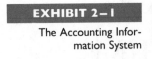

EXHIBIT 2–1

The Accounting Information System

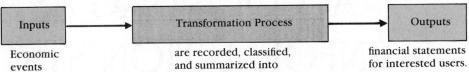

Inputs	Transformation Process	Outputs
Economic events	are recorded, classified, and summarized into	financial statements for interested users.

■ THE HARTMAN FLOWER COMPANY

To illustrate how accounting operates as an information system, assume that it is necessary to account for the activities of a retail flower business. Ken Hartman is presently a computer programmer with a yearly salary of $45,000 at a large corporation. He has always wanted to be in business for himself and, because his hobby is gardening, he has decided to open a flower shop. Hartman's plan is to grow flowers in the backyard of his home and to use his garage as a workshop and warehouse. Hartman plans to use the current and following months, April and May, to organize his business. He hopes to begin actually selling flowers in June.

Hartman's first step is to form a corporation, and on April 1 he invests $1,000 in his business in exchange for 100 shares of capital stock. Next, he purchases a license from the city for $120. He then buys seeds, fertilizer, and gardening tools ($200) from a local garden supply store, as well as containers ($30) and artificial soil ($150). Hartman also buys an old table ($75) at a used furniture store to keep in his garage as a display table.

At present, he accounts for his business using a checkbook. He makes all purchases by check and deposits all money received by his firm into a business checking account. So far, this has been reasonably satisfactory, but Hartman is not certain of how much he has spent on various individual items such as seeds and fertilizer. He could, of course, go through his checkbook and classify each check according to the different business items and then total the categories. However, he feels that there must be a better way of keeping track of his business activities.

When Hartman actually begins selling flowers in June, he will have to determine whether or not the shop is earning a profit. Furthermore, Hartman feels that if his business grows as he expects it to, he might need a loan from his local bank to help finance this growth. He knows that his banker is going to want to see some financial statements before a loan can be granted. Hartman is also concerned that he may have used a business check once or twice to pay a personal purchase of planting materials for family use.

Given this information, Hartman has to set up an accounting system for his business. How should he proceed? The first step is to decide what the inputs to his accounting system should be. Should he treat all data, economic and noneconomic, as inputs? If not all data, should he treat all economic data as inputs? As will become apparent, only specific economic data should be input into the system. A related question is: At what particular point in time should these inputs be recorded or recognized in Hartman's accounting records?

■ DATA INPUT INTO THE ACCOUNTING SYSTEM

For economic data to be an input of Hartman's accounting system, it must:

1. Be a transaction or event for the business entity, Hartman Flower Company.
2. Be quantifiable or measurable in monetary terms.
3. Be verifiable.

Business-entity Assumption

As noted in Chapter 1, an accounting system relates to a particular business entity. This is called the **business-entity assumption** of accounting—the concept that the business is independent and distinct from its owners, even though the owners clearly have a residual interest in the net assets of the business.

Because the accounting system is intended for a specified business entity, only the transactions and events concerning its economic activities should be included in the system. In the Hartman example, this means that only business transactions, not Hartman's personal transactions, can be admitted into the accounting system. For example, Hartman's purchase of planting materials for personal use is a transaction that should be excluded from the accounting system. If the accounting fails to distinguish between Hartman's business and personal expenditures, even though he is the owner of the business accounting reports for the business will be distorted.

Quantifiability

The accounting system admits as inputs only those transactions and events that can be represented in numerical (primarily monetary) terms. This characteristic is known as **quantifiability**. If it is not possible to express an event in numerical terms, the event is not treated as an input of the accounting system. For example, Hartman has spent considerable time and effort in developing a special type of rose. He feels that he has brought it to the point that he will soon be able to begin selling it to others. He wonders whether all his time and effort in development should be recorded in the accounting system. Unless there is some reasonable way to translate his time and effort into monetary terms, it cannot be an input of the system.

Verifiability

In addition to being quantifiable into monetary terms, an economic event should be verifiable before it is input in the accounting system. **Verifiability** means that the data pertaining to the transaction or event must be available and that if two or more qualified persons examined the same data, they would reach essentially the same conclusions about the data's accounting treatment. Verifiability adds to the usefulness and thus the reliability of the accounting information. For example, assume that Hartman could quantify in monetary terms the time and effort it took to develop the special rose mentioned earlier. It is doubtful that the resulting figure would be verifiable. It would be difficult for others to verify the time and effort spent on the development of the rose and to agree on a reasonable cost to assign to Hartman's efforts.

EXHIBIT 2–2

Analysis of Events and Transactions of the Hartman Flower Shop Admitted into the Accounting System		
Events and Transactions	**Inputs**	**Explanation**
1. Hartman's salary as a programmer	No	Not related to business entity
2. Land used to grow flowers	Maybe	If it can be quantified and verified
3. Hartman's investment in his business	Yes	Business receives funds
4. Development of special rose	Maybe	If it can be quantified and verified
5. City license	Yes	Related to business and quantifiable
6. Cost of seeds, fertilizer, and gardening tools	Yes	Related to business and quantifiable
7. Container	Yes	Related to business and quantifiable
8. Artificial soil	Yes	Related to business and quantifiable
9. Table	Yes	Related to business and quantifiable

Applying these input criteria to Hartman's business, the events and transactions pertaining to his operations may be analyzed. Exhibit 2-2 shows that there are three categories of events and transactions:

1. Those that clearly are admissible to the accounting system (Numbers 3, 5–9).

2. Those that are not admissible (Number 1).

3. Those that might be admissible if they can be quantified and verified (Numbers 2 and 4).

■ RECOGNIZING TRANSACTIONS

Once an event meets the necessary criteria to become an input of the system, one still must determine when to recognize the event in the accounting records. Accountants recognize transactions in the system only at specified points. For example, assume that the flower shop placed an order with the local wholesale nursery for a dozen flats of pansies. At that time, the flower shop sent the nursery a purchase order, which is a document indicating what it would like to order and the anticipated price. The pansies were delivered to the flower shop a week later, and two days after that the shop received the invoice, or bill. Two weeks later the invoice was paid in full. Finally, several weeks later, some of the pansies purchased were sold to a customer. In this example, there have been several distinct events:

1. An order was placed, and a purchase order was generated.

2. The flowers were delivered.

3. An invoice was received.

4. The invoice was paid in full.

5. Some flowers were sold.

Which of these events, all related to the purchase of the flowers, are recognized as transactions in the accounting system? Generally, accountants do not recognize mutual promises to perform. For example, in the first event, the wholesale nursery promised to deliver some flowers, and the flower shop promised to pay, but neither party had yet performed. Such mutual promises are not recorded as either assets or liabilities until one or both parties performs. Yet records and documents were generated; the flower shop sent the nursery a purchase order, which it used to keep track of what items were on order and when it could expect to receive them.

The transaction is first recorded in both the flower shop's and the nursery's accounting records when legal title to the flowers passes from the nursery to the shop.

Depending upon the terms of the agreement, this occurs either when the flowers leave the nursery or when they arrive at the shop. In any event, when title does pass, the flower shop records the purchase, and the nursery records the sale. Note that at this point the nursery has performed its part of the agreement by delivering the flowers, but the shop has only made a promise to pay in the future. This obligation is recorded in the flower shop's accounting records as a payable and in the nursery's records as a receivable.

The receipt of the invoice does not cause a transaction to be recorded in the flower shop's accounting records, because the purchase was recorded when the flowers were received. However, the invoice does enter the system and generates paperwork that will result in the payment of the invoice. The actual payment of the invoice is the second transaction that is recorded in the system. At that point, the shop is fulfilling its promise to pay. It is important to keep in mind that the purchase of the flowers first entered the accounting system at the time the shop received the flowers, two weeks and two days before it paid for them.

As Chapter 1 pointed out, business transactions enter the accounting system at their historical cost and are not changed if there are subsequent increases in value until another transaction has taken place. For example, assume that the dozen flats of pansies that the flower shop purchased cost $25. The shop records these flowers as an asset at their historical cost of $25. They remain at that amount, regardless of future price increases, until they are sold. If the pansies are sold for $40, it is at this point that the flower shop records the fact that it gave up an asset that cost $25 and received another asset (either cash or a promise to receive cash) that has a value of $40. Further, at this point the shop recognizes the $15 profit ($40 − $25) on the transaction.

■ EFFECTS OF TRANSACTIONS ON THE ACCOUNTING EQUATION

Chapter 1 introduced the accounting equation:

Assets = Liabilities + Stockholders' Equity

This equation, which is a condensation of the balance sheet, represents the assets, liabilities, and owners' equity of a business at a point in time. Let us return to the example of Ken Hartman's new flower business in order to see how the transactions that are admissible into the accounting system affect assets, liabilities, and stockholders' equity.

First, all transactions are recorded in accounts. An **account** is a record that summarizes all transactions that affect a particular category of asset, liability, or stockholders' equity. Specific accounts are set up by each company, depending on its specific needs and type of business. Accounts are added or deleted over time as the company grows and changes.

Second, for the accounting equation to remain in balance, each transaction must involve a change in at least two accounts. For example, if an asset is increased by $20, either another asset must be decreased by that amount, a liability must be increased by that amount, or stockholders' equity must be increased by that amount. Keep this fundamental relationship in mind as the transactions of the Hartman Flower Company are traced through the accounting system.

Hartman started his new business, Hartman Flower Company, by investing $1,000 of his cash on April 1. Hartman organized the business as a corporation, and the firm issued him 100 shares of its capital stock at a price of $10 per share. The effect of this transaction is to provide the business with cash. The source of that asset is Hartman's personal investment in the business. As a result, an asset, Cash, is increased, and a stockholders' equity account, Capital Stock, is increased.

	Assets	= Liabilities + Stockholders' Equity
	Cash =	Capital Stock
4/1	+1,000	+1,000

In order to conduct business the company purchased, on April 2, a license from the city for $120 cash. This transaction resulted in a decrease in Cash, but at the same time a new asset, the license, was acquired. The license is an asset because it provides the company future economic benefits:

	Assets		= Liabilities + Stockholders' Equity
	Cash +	License =	Capital Stock
4/1	1,000	=	1,000
4/2	−120	+120	
Bal.	880 +	120 =	1,000

On April 3, the company bought an old table for $75 cash, to be used for displaying flowers. In anticipation of future expansion, Hartman decided to classify this table as Store Furniture and Fixtures. This transaction decreases Cash in exchange for a new asset. Notice that each transaction affects at least two items and that after they are recorded, the accounting equation is still in balance.

	Assets			= Liabilities + Stockholders' Equity
	Cash +	License +	Store Furniture and Fixtures =	Capital Stock
4/2	880 +	120	=	1,000
4/3	−75		+75	
Bal.	805 +	120 +	75 =	1,000

The firm then purchased a variety of items from a garden supply store on April 4: tools for $100, seeds and fertilizer for $100, containers for $30, and potting soil for $150. Because he felt it would be wise to conserve the firm's cash, Hartman bought these items on credit. This transaction resulted in a liability, Accounts Payable, and a new asset, Garden Supplies. (Hartman decided to put all of these items into one account.)

	Assets				= Liabilities + Stockholders' Equity	
	Cash +	License +	Store Furniture and Fixtures +	Garden Supplies =	Accounts Payable +	Capital Stock
4/3	805 +	120 +	75		=	1,000
4/4				+380	+380	
Bal.	805 +	120 +	75	+380 =	380 +	1,000

After working with his materials for two weeks, Hartman decided that the table he had bought was not large enough for working on and displaying flowers. He therefore sold it for $75 to a friend, who asked to pay for it over six weeks. This transaction meant the loss of an asset, Store Furniture and Fixtures, and the creation of a new asset, Accounts Receivable. Revenues are not involved, as the sale of the table is not related to the main activities of the business. Furthermore, stockholders' equity is not involved, as the table was sold for exactly its cost. Thus this transaction is the exchange of one asset for another of the same cost.

| | Assets | | | | | = Liabilities + | Stockholders' Equity |
	Cash +	Accounts Receivable +	License +	Store Furniture and Fixtures +	Garden Supplies =	Accounts Payable +	Capital Stock
4/3	805 +		+ 120 +	75	+ 380 =	380 +	1,000
4/15		+75		−75			
Bal.	805 +	75 +	120 +	0	+ 380 =	380 +	1,000

On April 16, the company purchased two larger work tables, on credit, for $200. This transaction increased both assets and liabilities:

| | Assets | | | | | = Liabilities + | Stockholders' Equity |
	Cash +	Accounts Receivable +	License +	Store Furniture and Fixtures +	Garden Supplies =	Accounts Payable +	Capital Stock
4/15	805 +	75 +	120 +	0	+ 380 =	380 +	1,000
4/16				+200		+200	
Bal.	805 +	75 +	120 +	200	+ 380 =	580 +	1,000

At the end of the month, the flower company paid half of its bill to the garden supply store. This decreased both the asset, Cash, and the liability, Accounts Payable.

| | Assets | | | | | = Liabilities + | Stockholders' Equity |
	Cash +	Accounts Receivable +	License +	Store Furniture and Fixtures +	Garden Supplies =	Accounts Payable +	Capital Stock
4/16	805 +	75 +	120 +	200	+ 380 =	580 +	1,000
4/30	−190					−190	
Bal.	615 +	75 +	120 +	200	+ 380 =	390 +	1,000

On the same day, the company also received partial payment of $40 for the table it had sold. This transaction affected only assets, as Cash increased and Accounts Receivable decreased:

| | Assets | | | | | = Liabilities + | Stockholders' Equity |
	Cash +	Accounts Receivable +	License +	Store Furniture and Fixtures +	Garden Supplies =	Accounts Payable +	Capital Stock
4/30	615 +	75 +	120 +	200	+ 380 =	390 +	1,000
4/30	+40	−40					
Bal.	655 +	35 +	120 +	200	+ 380 =	390 +	1,000

Exhibit 2-3, on page 44, summarizes all of the transactions described so far.

Exhibit 2-4 is the balance sheet or statement of financial position that Hartman prepared for his corporation at the end of the first month. Note that when Hartman began his business, he invested $1,000, so at that time stockholders' equity (assets minus liabilities) was $1,000. As the balance sheet shows, at the end of April stockholders' equity is still $1,000 (assets of $1,390 less liabilities of $390). The firm's assets have increased to $1,390, from the $1,000 originally contributed by Hartman. In addition, instead of the assets being all in cash, the business now has a variety of assets. The additional $390 in assets was contributed by creditors. Thus, during April, the stockholders' equity of the firm has not changed from Hartman's original investment.

EXHIBIT 2–3

				HARTMAN FLOWER COMPANY						
				Summary of Transactions						
Assets								**= Liabilities + Stockholders' Equity**		
	Cash +	**Accounts** Receivable +	License +	**Store Furniture and Fixtures** +	**Garden** Supplies =	**Accounts** Payable +		**Capital Stock**		
4/1	+1,000					=		1,000		
4/2	−120		+120							
Bal.	880 +		120			=		1,000		
4/3	−75			+75						
Bal.	805 +		120 +	75		=		1,000		
4/4					+380	+380				
Bal.	805 +		120 +	75 +	380 =	380 +		1,000		
4/15		+75		−75						
Bal.	805 +	75 +	120 +	0 +	380 =	380 +		1,000		
4/16				+200		+200				
Bal.	805 +	75 +	120 +	200 +	380 =	580 +		1,000		
4/30	−190					−190				
Bal.	615 +	75 +	120 +	200 +	380 =	390 +		1,000		
4/30	+40	−40								
Bal.	655 +	35 +	120 +	200 +	380 =	390 +		1,000		

EXHIBIT 2–4

HARTMAN FLOWER COMPANY	
Balance Sheet	
April 30, 1990	
Assets	
Cash	$ 655
Accounts receivable	35
License	120
Table.	200
Garden supplies	380
Total assets	$1,390
Liabilities and Stockholders' Equity	
Liabilities	
Accounts payable	$ 390
Stockholders' equity	
Capital stock	$1,000
Total liabilities and stockholders' equity	$1,390

However, as previously noted, stockholders' equity is affected not only by what the owners invest, but by the profitability of the business as well. Because the corporation's first month of business activity was in preparation to start selling flowers, it has not yet generated revenues and expenses. Thus an income statement that would show whether or not the firm is profitable cannot be prepared. Chapter 3 will deal with transactions involving selling flowers, showing the effect of these sales on assets, liabilities, and stockholders' equity, as well as the preparation of an income statement.

It would be very difficult and costly for a business to prepare a balance sheet or accounting equation after each transaction, as has been done here. Therefore accountants have developed a means for storing and classifying transactions so that a balance sheet can be prepared easily and periodically. The next part of this chapter, as well as Chapters 3 and 4, will show how accounting systems store and classify information for this purpose. This is a part of the transformation process through which large amounts of input data are stored, classified, and summarized into accounting reports.

■ THE COMPONENTS OF THE ACCOUNTING SYSTEM

The major components of the accounting system are illustrated in Exhibit 2-5. Most transactions are written on business documents such as sales invoices, purchase invoices, cash-register tapes, and checks. These documents then serve as inputs into journals and ledgers, the two basic components of any accounting system, whether manual or computerized.

EXHIBIT 2–5

Components of the Accounting System

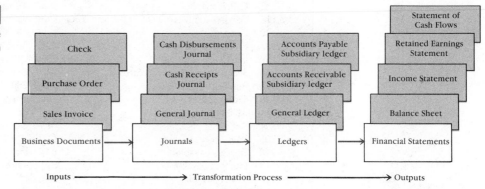

■ THE JOURNAL

The **journal** is the record or book in which each transaction is originally recorded. For this reason, it is often referred to as the *book of original entry*. The journal is in effect a chronological list of transactions into which the firm has entered. There are several types of journals, ranging from a general journal to specialized journals. General journals can be used to record all transactions, whereas specialized journals are used to record specific transactions, such as the receipt of cash or the disbursement of cash.

■ THE LEDGER

A **ledger** is a book or computer record of specific accounts. As noted, an account is a record that summarizes all transactions that affect a particular asset, liability, or stockholders' equity item. The **general ledger** is a book that contains all accounts on the financial statements and shows how transactions changed the balance in these accounts. **Subsidiary ledgers** contain backup or more detail of specific accounts. For example, the primary account, Accounts Receivable, is in the general ledger, whereas the individual accounts for each customer are contained in the Accounts Receivable subsidiary ledger. Transactions are first recorded in the journal, and at specified intervals these transactions are recorded in both the general and (when appropriate) subsidiary ledger accounts. The balances in the general ledger are then used to prepare financial statements.

The accounts used by a particular firm depend on its needs and the nature and size of the business. For example, a large, publicly owned corporation may have hundreds of accounts, whereas a small business may have a dozen or so accounts. Most firms maintain a **chart of accounts**, which is a list of all the accounts a firm uses. Accounts in the chart are sequentially numbered. The chart of accounts for the Hartman Flower Company is illustrated in Exhibit 2-6. Notice that there are more numbers than are currently being used, which gives management the flexibility to add new accounts as needed.

EXHIBIT 2–6	

HARTMAN FLOWER COMPANY
Chart of Accounts

100	ASSETS		400	REVENUES
	101 Cash in bank			401 Flower sales
	103 Marketable securities			405 Other revenues
	105 Notes receivable		500	COST OF GOODS SOLD
	106 Accounts receivable		600	EXPENSES—SELLING
	110 Inventory			601 Salaries expense
	115 Office supplies			605 Advertising expense
	116 Garden supplies		700	EXPENSES—GENERAL AND
	120 Licenses			ADMINISTRATIVE
	121 Prepaid insurance			701 Repairs and maintenance expense
	150 Land			703 Utility expense
	160 Store furniture and fixtures			705 License expense
	165 Buildings			707 Office supplies expense
	170 Other assets			709 Garden supplies expense
200	LIABILITIES			711 Insurance expense
	201 Accounts payable			715 Depreciation expense
	205 Bank loan payable		800	OTHER EXPENSES
	210 Salaries payable			801 Interest expense
	212 Interest payable			811 Taxes expense
	214 Taxes payable		1,000	INCOME SUMMARY
300	STOCKHOLDERS' EQUITY			
	301 Capital stock			
	311 Retained earnings			

■ ASSET ACCOUNTS

A firm is likely to have a number of asset accounts. The major ones include Cash, Marketable Securities, Receivables, Inventory, Prepaid Expenses, and Property, Plant, and Equipment.

Cash
The Cash accounts include such items as coins, currency, money orders, drafts, checks, and cash on hand. In effect, any medium of exchange that the bank will accept at its face value is considered cash. The number of specific Cash accounts that a firm has depends on the desires of management.

Marketable Securities
The Marketable Securities account is used to record purchases and sales of such items as investments in stocks and bonds of other companies.

Notes Receivable
Notes receivable are written promises from others to pay a specific amount of money at a specific time in the future. They may arise from cash loans or the sale of goods or

services. Notes receivable usually contain an interest element that must be paid by the borrower, in addition to the amount owed.

Accounts Receivable

Accounts receivable arise from sales on credit and represent future cash collections. When a sale on credit is made, Accounts Receivable is increased; when customers make payments on their accounts, it is decreased.

Inventory

All merchandising firms have an Inventory account, and items held for resale are recorded in this account. As the inventory is sold, this account is decreased, and an expense account, Cost of Goods Sold, is increased. A service firm such as a travel agency would not have an Inventory account, since it sells services rather than products.

Prepaid Expenses

Asset accounts such as Office Supplies, Garden Supplies, Prepaid Insurance, and Licenses all represent payment for goods or services that will be used in the future. As a group, these items are called Prepaid Expenses. At the time these goods or services are purchased, they are considered assets, but as they are used or consumed during operations, they become expenses. Thus, for each of these asset accounts, there is a related expense listed under General and Administrative Expenses in the chart of accounts. Although these assets usually expire daily, the asset account is decreased, and the related expense account is increased only at specified intervals, generally monthly.

Property, Plant, and Equipment

Land, Buildings, Equipment, and Furniture and Fixtures are often referred to as *operating,* or *fixed, assets*. These assets all provide long-term benefits to the firm. It is important to separate Land from other accounts because, except for Land, all these accounts are subject to wear and tear, obsolescence, or use that will eventually decrease their future benefits to the firm. As these assets lose their benefits, their cost must be allocated to that period. This process is called *depreciation* and is discussed in Chapters 4 and 10.

■ LIABILITY ACCOUNTS

Liability accounts represent the enterprise's obligations to make payments or to provide goods or services in the future. The principal liability accounts are Accounts Payable and Notes and Loans Payable.

Accounts Payable

Accounts payable arise from purchases of goods and services from vendors and suppliers for which the firm has not yet made payment. These payments are usually due within a short period, normally 30 days. When one company has an Account Payable, the company to which the cash or service is owed will have a corresponding Account Receivable.

Notes and Loans Payable

Notes and loans payable generally result from cash borrowings from banks and other creditors. These notes may be short-term, due within a period of a month or so, or long-term, due after one year or more. Like notes receivable, notes and loans payable usually have an interest element that must be repaid, in addition to the principal borrowed.

Other Liabilities

Finally, a firm is likely to have other short-term payable accounts arising at the time expenses are incurred, including Taxes Payable, Interest Payable, and Salaries Payable. These are the result of the firm's incurring an expense for which it has not made a cash payment.

STOCKHOLDERS' EQUITY

Because Hartman's flower company is organized as a corporation, the stockholders' equity accounts include Capital Stock and Retained Earnings. As noted, Capital Stock represents the owners' original and subsequent investments in the business. Normally owners invest cash, but other assets such as equipment can be contributed by the owners. When this occurs, the noncash assets are normally recorded at their value when invested in the business. Retained Earnings represents the assets that were generated through profitable operations and have been kept within the business (that is, have not been distributed as dividends). Revenues cause Retained Earnings to increase, and expenses and dividends cause Retained Earnings to decrease.

REVENUES AND EXPENSES

Although revenues and expenses, respectively, increase and decrease Retained Earnings, these transactions are not directly recorded in the Retained Earnings account. Rather, they are first recorded in separate revenue and expense accounts, then transferred at appropriate times to the Retained Earnings account. This enables management to gather relevant information and maintain control over the firm.

The exact title of the revenue and expense accounts depends on the nature, size, and complexity of the business, and the needs of management. The primary revenue account for the Hartman Flower Company is Flower Sales. A firm is likely to have a variety of different expense accounts. In some cases, such as the Hartman Flower Company, expense accounts are grouped under broad categories such as Selling, General and Administrative, and Other.

THE RECORDING PROCESS

In order to record economic transactions, accountants have developed a set of standardized procedures that are performed in sequence during every accounting period. Accounting periods can be monthly, quarterly, or yearly, depending on the needs of the business. This set of procedures is generally known as the **accounting cycle** and is outlined in Exhibit 2-7. The accounting system may be a manual, handkept set of records or a complex computerized system. Since the accounting remains the same, the discussion here will be based on a simple manual system, even though the concepts and procedures that you will learn are equally applicable to larger, more complex systems.

As Exhibit 2-7 illustrates, the first step in the accounting cycle is to record transactions in the journal. These entries are then periodically transferred to the ledger accounts. From a learning standpoint, however, it is more effective to start the discussion of the accounting cycle in reverse by explaining how transactions are entered in the ledger. This is because the rules for recording transactions in the accounting records are based on how they affect the ledger accounts. The discussion will then turn to how transactions are recorded in the journal. The remaining parts of the cycle will be covered in Chapters 3 and 4.

EXHIBIT 2–7	Steps in the Accounting Cycle

During the Period

- Record transactions in the journal.
- Periodically post entries to ledger accounts.

At End of Period

- Prepare the unadjusted trial balance.
- Prepare the worksheet—optional.
- Prepare adjusting entries.
- Post adjusting entries to the ledger accounts, balance the accounts, and prepare the adjusted trial balance.
- Prepare the financial statements.
- Prepare closing entries, post to the ledger accounts, and prepare a post-closing trial balance.

■ RECORDING TRANSACTIONS IN THE LEDGER

A ledger is a means of accumulating the effect of numerous transactions on specific accounts. In practice, a ledger contains a separate page for each account. Throughout this book, **T accounts** are used to represent individual ledger accounts. A sample T account looks like this:

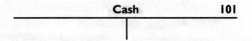

Depending on whether it is an asset, a liability, or a stockholders' equity account, one side is used to record increases, and the other side is used to record decreases. In all asset accounts, increases are recorded on the left side of the ledger account, and decreases are recorded on the right side of the account. Conversely, for all liability and stockholders' equity accounts, increases are recorded on the right side of the ledger account and decreases on the left side. These points are illustrated in the following T accounts.

Assets		Liabilities		Stockholders' Equity	
Increases	Decreases	Decreases	Increases	Decreases	Increases
+	−	−	+	−	+

Because of these conventions, each time an entry is made on the left side of an account, a corresponding entry or set of entries is made on the right side of another account. This is a direct reflection of the accounting equation. For example, an increase in an asset can come only from a decrease in another asset account or an increase in a liability or a stockholders' equity account. This means that when an entry is made on the left side of an asset account to record an increase in that account, there will be a corresponding entry on the right side of either another asset account to record a decrease, or an entry on the right side of a liability or a stockholders' equity account to record an increase in that account.

This is illustrated in the following two examples taken from the transactions of the Hartman Flower Company. On April 1, Hartman started his business by investing $1,000 cash. This transaction increases both an asset account, Cash, and a stockholders' equity account, Capital Stock. It results in an entry on the left side of the Cash account, which represents an increase of $1,000 in this account. There is a corresponding entry on the right side of the stockholders' equity account, Capital Stock, which represents an increase in that account. The T accounts reflect these transactions, and they are in balance:

Cash		Capital Stock	
4/1 1,000			4/1 1,000

A second example is the transaction on April 16 in which Hartman purchased (on account) two large work tables for $200. The increase in the asset account, Store Furniture and Fixtures, is recorded on the left side of the T account, and the increase in the liability account, Accounts Payable, is recorded on the right side of that account:

Store Furniture and Fixtures		Accounts Payable	
4/16 200			4/16 200

As is evident from these transactions, the system for recording transactions maintains the equality of the accounting equation: For every increase in asset accounts, there is a corresponding decrease in another asset account or an increase in an equity account. In addition, for every entry on the left side of an account, there is always a corresponding entry on the right side of another account.

Debits and Credits

Accountants have developed other conventions to help them easily and efficiently record transactions. Debits and credits are examples of these conventions. To **debit** an account means to make an entry on the left side of any ledger account. Therefore, a debit means that you are increasing an asset account or that you are decreasing an equity account. To credit an account means just the opposite. That is, a **credit** is an entry on the right side of a ledger account. It represents a decrease in an asset account and an increase in a liability or a stockholders' equity account. You should understand that *debit* and *credit* are just shorthand ways of saying that you are making an entry on the left (debit) side or right (credit) side of any ledger account. They have no other meanings and do not imply a favorable or unfavorable condition.

These accounting conventions are summarized in the following T accounts:

Assets		Liabilities		Stockholders' Equity	
Increase	Decrease	Decrease	Increase	Decrease	Increase
+	−	−	+	−	+
Debit	Credit	Debit	Credit	Debit	Credit

Referring back to the previous example, in order to record the $1,000 cash investment in Hartman's business, you would debit the asset account, Cash, and credit the stockholders' equity account, Capital Stock. To record the $200 purchase of tables on account, you would debit the asset account, Store Furniture and Fixtures, and credit the liability account, Accounts Payable.

Debits Must Equal Credits

The correct application of the debit and credit rules ensures that the accounting equation will always stay in balance. For example, if an asset account is increased (debited), there must be a corresponding decrease in another asset account (a credit) or an increase in an equity account (a credit). For this reason, this system of accounting is often referred to as **double-entry accounting**, because each transaction will have equal debit and credit effects on the accounting equation. However, the fact that debits must equal credits does not necessarily mean that a particular transaction was correctly recorded. For example, Cash could be credited by mistake when, in fact, Accounts Payable should have been credited. As long as a credit is recorded in either account, the accounting equation will remain in balance.

Balancing T Accounts

After all transactions for a specified period have been entered in the individual ledger accounts, the accounts are totaled and balanced. As an example, all of the cash transactions for the month of April for the Hartman Flower Company are shown in the following T account. As is indicated, each side of the account is totaled. These totals are referred to as *footings*; in this example, they are marked in color. The beginning balance plus debits, or increases, equals $1,040, and the credits or decreases equal $385. Subtracting the decreases on the right side, or credits, of $385 from the total of $1,040 on the left leaves a balance of $655. This is the ending balance on April 30 and will become the beginning balance for the period beginning May 1. In future examples, the footings will be eliminated, and only the new balance will be shown. It is customary that only the date and amount of a transaction be entered in the ledger account. The specific transaction is fully described in the journal.

	Cash				
4/1	Beginning balance	0	4/2	Purchase of license	120
4/1	Hartman's investment	1,000	4/2	Purchase of table	75
4/30	Receipt of payment		4/30	Payment on account	190
	on account	40			
		1,040			385
4/30	Ending balance	655			

As you would expect, all asset accounts normally have debit balances. Remember that debits represent increases in assets, and as a result there are very few situations in which it would be possible to have a credit balance in an asset account that would represent a negative asset. Liability and stockholders' equity accounts are totaled and balanced in the same way. Normally, these accounts have credit balances.

■ THE HARTMAN FLOWER COMPANY

As noted, on April 1, 1990, Hartman organized his new business, the Hartman Flower Company. April's transactions were discussed in the first part of this chapter. The balances on the April 30, 1990 balance sheet (Exhibit 2-4) are the opening balances in the ledger accounts on May 1. The month of May was used to continue organizing and preparing for the operations to begin on June 1.

During the month of May, the following transactions took place:

■ May 2: In addition to his original investment in April, Hartman and some of his friends purchased a total of 4,300 shares of capital stock at $10 per share.

■ May 7: The firm purchased land and a small building for $20,000. The land cost $5,000 and the building $15,000. The firm paid cash for both the land and building.

■ May 10: Numerous office supplies were purchased for cash. The total cost of these supplies was $1,000.

■ May 12: The company purchased a variety of additional furniture and fixtures for $10,000; $5,000 was paid in cash and the remaining $5,000 was borrowed from the bank.

■ May 18: In order to stock its shelves, the Hartman Flower Company made an initial purchase of assorted plants and flowers to be held for resale. The inventory of plants and flowers cost $5,000 and was purchased for cash.

■ May 22: The firm purchased a comprehensive insurance policy for $2,400 cash. The policy covers a two-year period from June 1, 1990 to May 31, 1992.

- May 25: The company made another purchase of flowers for resale. The total purchase amounted to $6,000 and was made on credit.
- May 28: The company made a $4,000 payment on accounts payable.
- May 29: Cash of $35 was received for the table sold in April.

Each of these transactions is analyzed from the standpoint of how they affect various accounts, and then they are entered in the appropriate ledger accounts. In thinking about how to record these transactions, you should go through a three-step process:

1. Determine the specific accounts that are affected by the transactions and whether they are asset, liability, or stockholders' equity accounts.

2. Decide which of these accounts are increased and/or decreased.

3. Finally, make the appropriate debit and credit entries in the specific ledger accounts.

■ ANALYSIS OF TRANSACTIONS

1. Transaction on May 2—Issuance of $43,000 of capital stock for cash.
   a. This transaction is an exchange of cash for capital stock. Thus the two accounts affected are Cash and Capital Stock.
   b. Cash, an asset account, is increased by $43,000 (4,300 shares times $10 per share), and Capital Stock, a stockholders' equity account, is increased by the same $43,000.
   c. The increase in cash is recorded on the left side of the Cash account as a debit. The increase in the stockholders' equity account, Capital Stock, is recorded on the right side of the account as a credit.

Cash				Capital Stock			
5/1	Bal.	655				5/1	Bal.	1,000
5/2		43,000				5/2		43,000

2. Transaction on May 7—Purchase of land and buildings for $20,000 cash.
   a. The three accounts affected by this transaction are Cash, Land, and Buildings.
   b. The two asset accounts, Buildings and Land, are increased $15,000 and $5,000, respectively. The asset account, Cash, is decreased by the total outlay of $20,000. Because more than two accounts are involved, this is referred to as a *compound transaction*.
   c. The increases in the Buildings and Land accounts are recorded on the left side of these accounts as debits. The decrease in the asset account, Cash, is recorded on the right side of the account as a credit.

Cash					Land			Buildings		
5/1	Bal.	655	5/7	20,000	5/7	5,000		5/7	15,000	
5/2		43,000								

3. Transaction on May 10—Purchase of office supplies for $1,000 cash.
   a. This transaction is an exchange of office supplies for cash.
   b. The asset account, Supplies, is increased, and the asset account, Cash, is decreased.
   c. The increase in the asset account, Supplies, is recorded on the left side as a debit. The decrease in the Cash account is recorded on the right side as a credit.

Cash					Office Supplies		
5/1	Bal.	655	5/7	20,000	5/10	1,000	
5/2		43,000	5/10	1,000			

4. Transaction on May 12—Purchase of $10,000 of store furniture and fixtures for $5,000 cash and a bank loan of $5,000.
   a. This is a compound transaction that involves two asset accounts, Store Furniture and Fixtures and Cash, and one liability account, Bank Loan Payable.

b. The asset account, Store Furniture and Fixtures, is increased and the asset account, Cash, is decreased. In addition, the liability account, Bank Loan Payable, is increased.

c. The increase in the asset account, Store Furniture and Fixtures, is recorded on the left side of the account as a debit. The decrease in the Cash account is recorded on the right side of the account as a credit. Finally, the increase in the liability account is recorded on the right side of that account as a credit.

Cash			
5/1	Bal.	655	5/7 20,000
5/2		43,000	5/10 1,000
			5/12 5,000

Store Furniture and Fixtures		
5/1	Bal.	200
5/12		10,000

Bank Loan Payable	
	5/12 5,000

5. Transaction on May 18—Purchase of inventory of plants and flowers for $5,000 cash.
  a. This transaction is an exchange of cash for inventory.
  b. The asset account, Inventory, is increased by $5,000, and the asset account, Cash, is decreased by $5,000.
  c. The increase in the Inventory account is recorded on the left side of the ledger account as a debit. The decrease in Cash is recorded on the right side of the account as a credit.

Cash			
5/1	Bal.	655	5/7 20,000
5/2		43,000	5/10 1,000
			5/12 5,000
			5/18 5,000

Inventory	
5/18 5,000	

6. Transaction on May 22—Purchase of a comprehensive insurance policy for $2,400 cash.
  a. The two accounts in this transaction are the asset account, Prepaid Insurance, and the asset account, Cash.
  b. The Prepaid Insurance account is increased, and the Cash account is decreased.
  c. The increase in the Prepaid Insurance account is recorded on the left side of the ledger account as a debit. The decrease in the Cash account is recorded on the right side of the ledger account as a credit.

Cash			
5/1	Bal.	655	5/7 20,000
5/2		43,000	5/10 1,000
			5/12 5,000
			5/18 5,000
			5/22 2,400

Prepaid Insurance	
5/22 2,400	

7. Transaction on May 25—Purchase of inventory of plants and flowers for $6,000 on account.
  a. This transaction involves an asset account, Inventory, and a liability account, Accounts Payable.
  b. The Inventory account is increased, and the Accounts Payable account is also increased.
  c. The increase in the asset account, Inventory, is recorded on the left side of the ledger account as a debit. The increase in the liability account, Accounts Payable, is recorded on the right side of the ledger account as a credit.

Inventory	
5/18 5,000	
5/25 6,000	

Accounts Payable		
	5/1 Bal.	390
	5/25	6,000

8. Transaction on May 28—$4,000 partial payment of accounts payable.
  a. This transaction involves the asset account, Cash, and the liability account, Accounts Payable.
  b. The asset account, Cash, is decreased, and the liability account, Accounts Payable, is decreased.

c. The decrease in the Cash account is recorded on the right side of the ledger account as a credit. The decrease in the Accounts Payable account is recorded on the left side of the account as a debit.

Cash					Accounts Payable				
5/1	Bal.	655	5/7	20,000			5/28	4,000	5/1	Bal.	390
5/2		43,000	5/10	1,000					5/25		6,000
			5/12	5,000							
			5/18	5,000							
			5/22	2,400							
			5/28	4,000							

9. Transaction on May 29—$35 received on accounts receivable.
   a. This transaction involves two asset accounts, Cash and Accounts Receivable.
   b. The Cash account is increased, and the Accounts Receivable account is decreased.
   c. The increase in the Cash account is recorded on the left side of the ledger account as a debit. The decrease in the Accounts Receivable account is recorded on the right side of the ledger account as a credit.

Cash					Accounts Receivable				
5/1	Bal.	655	5/7	20,000		5/1	Bal.	35	5/29	35
5/2		43,000	5/10	1,000						
5/29		35	5/12	5,000						
			5/18	5,000						
			5/22	2,400						
			5/28	4,000						

■ THE USE OF LEDGER ACCOUNTS IN PRACTICE

Throughout this book, T accounts are used to represent ledger accounts. In practice, however, more sophisticated account forms are used. Hartman's actual ledger account for Cash, illustrated in Exhibit 2-8, is an example of what an actual ledger account may look like.

A ledger account is designed for easy cross-reference to the journal where the original transaction is recorded. For example, the date column is used to record the

EXHIBIT 2–8

HARTMAN FLOWER COMPANY
Ledger Account for Cash

Cash   101

Date 19 90		Description	Ref	Debit	Credit	Balance	
						Debit	Credit
May	1		GJ–1	655 00		655 00	
	2		GJ–1	43000 00		43655 00	
	7		GJ–1		20000 00	23655 00	
	10		GJ–1		1000 00	22655 00	
	12		GJ–1		5000 00	17655 00	
	18		GJ–1		5000 00	12655 00	
	22		GJ–1		2400 00	10255 00	
	28		GJ–1		4000 00	6255 00	
	29		GJ–1	35 00			
		Balance				6290 00	

date on which the actual transaction took place. The same date will appear in the journal. The description column is generally not used unless it is necessary to make an unusual notation. Ref. is the abbreviation for reference. This column is used to indicate the page number of the journal where the complete journal entry can be found. The debit and credit columns are used to record the respective entries, and the balance column is used to keep a running balance.

In a ledger, the accounts are arranged in normal balance sheet order, so assets are listed first, followed by liabilities and stockholders' equity. As previously noted, each account is given a specific number for easy identification. The specific numbering system depends on the company's size and complexity.

■ RECORDING TRANSACTIONS IN THE JOURNAL

The use of journals and ledgers is interrelated. By first recording an entire transaction in the journal, all the specifics of the transaction are in one place and can be referred to at any future time. Remember that in a particular ledger account only part of the transaction is recorded.

The Use of the Journal

The transactions for the Hartman Flower Company for the month of May are recorded in the general journal (Exhibit 2-9). Although there are a variety of different journals,

EXHIBIT 2-9

HARTMAN FLOWER COMPANY General Journal				
Date	**Account Title**	**Ref.**	**Debit**	**Credit**
1990 May 2	Cash	101	43,000	
	Capital Stock	301		43,000
	To record sale of 4,300 shares of capital stock.			
7	Land	150	5,000	
	Buildings	165	15,000	
	Cash	101		20,000
	To record purchase of land and buildings.			
10	Office Supplies	115	1,000	
	Cash	101		1,000
	To record purchase of office supplies.			
12	Store Furniture and Fixtures	160	10,000	
	Cash	101		5,000
	Bank Loan Payable	205		5,000
	To record purchase of furniture and fixtures for cash and loan.			
18	Inventory	110	5,000	
	Cash	101		5,000
	To record purchase of inventory.			
22	Prepaid Insurance	121	2,400	
	Cash	101		2,400
	To record purchase of prepaid insurance.			
25	Inventory	110	6,000	
	Accounts Payable	201		6,000
	To record purchase of inventory on account.			
28	Accounts Payable	201	4,000	
	Cash	101		4,000
	To record payment of cash on account.			
29	Cash	101	35	
	Accounts Receivable	106		35
	To record receipt of cash on account.			

a standard two-column general journal will be used here. A number of points need to be made regarding how these transactions are journalized.

1. The date column is used to record the date on which the transaction took place. For the first entry of each month, it is customary to record both the month and day. For subsequent entries, only the specific day of the month is recorded.

2. The explanation or account title column is used to record the specific accounts. Accountants follow a number of conventions that simplify the use of the journal:
   a. Debits are always listed first, with the account title beginning at the extreme left margin of the explanation column.
   b. The credit portion of the entry is then recorded, indented slightly.
   c. If the transaction is a compound entry and thus involves more than two accounts, all the debits are recorded before the credits. The entry on May 7 is an example.
   d. The dollar amounts are put in the respective debit and credit columns on the same line as the account titles.
   e. Because a general journal is used for a number of different types of transactions, accountants generally write a short explanation under the entry. This makes it easier to understand the entry if it is referred to months or years later.

3. The Ref. (reference) column is used to cross-reference the journal to the ledger. The number of this ledger account to which the entry is posted is placed in this column at the time the entry is posted.

Posting to the Ledger

After transactions are entered into the journal, they are then summarized in the specific ledger accounts. This is referred to as **posting**. The size of the company and the number of entries usually determine how frequently entries are posted to the ledger. Posting can take place daily, semimonthly, monthly, or even yearly. If a computer is used to record transactions, the postings can be made instantaneously. Most of the examples and problem material in this book assume that entries are posted either monthly or yearly.

There are several things to remember about posting that will help you reduce errors. Each transaction should be posted in its entirety, one at a time. Using the entry on May 2 as an example, first post the debit to the Cash account and then the credit to the Capital Stock account before going on to the next transaction. If you have account numbers, as in this example, place the number of the account posted to in the reference column in the journal on the line of the account that you posted. If you are not using account numbers, place a check in this column. This will indicate to you that you have posted the entry. In addition, the page number of the journal where the entry is recorded should be placed in the reference column of the ledger account. If T accounts are used, only the date or number of the transaction should be placed beside the dollar amount.

For illustrative purposes, the journal entry on May 10 is posted to the appropriate accounts in Exhibit 2-10. After all of the accounts for the month have been posted, the T accounts for the Hartman Flower Company will appear as they are presented in Exhibit 2-11 on page 58.

■ THE TRIAL BALANCE

The **trial balance** is a list of the accounts in the general ledger with their respective debit or credit balances. It is the third step in the accounting cycle and is prepared after the transactions for the accounting period have been posted to the ledger ac-

EXHIBIT 2–10 Posting from the General Journal to Ledger Accounts

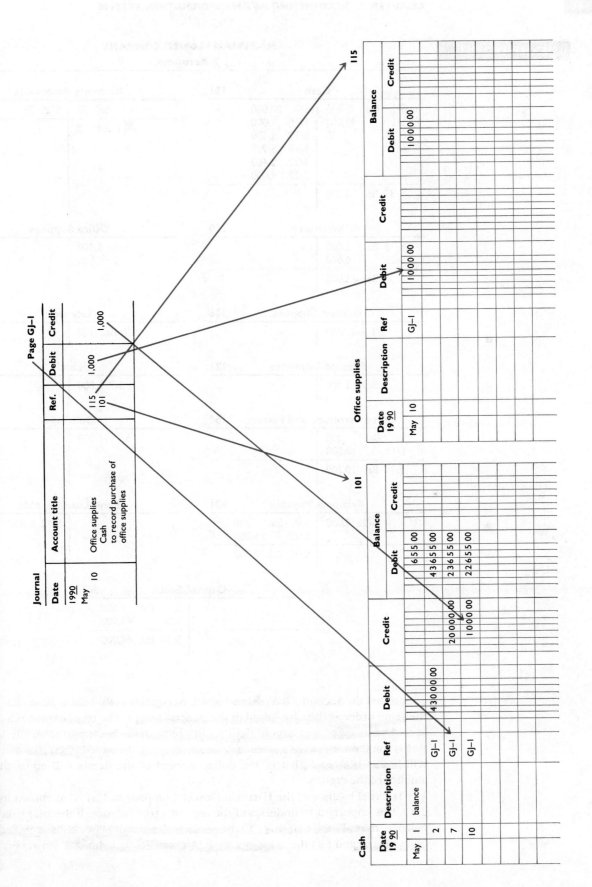

Journal

Date	Account title	Ref.	Debit	Credit
1990 May 10	Office supplies	115	1,000	
	Cash	101		1,000
	to record purchase of office supplies			

Page GJ–1

Office supplies   115

Date 19 90	Description	Ref	Debit	Credit	Balance Debit	Balance Credit
May 10		GJ–1	1 0 0 0 00		1 0 0 0 00	

Cash   101

Date 19 90	Description	Ref	Debit	Credit	Balance Debit	Balance Credit
May 1	balance				6 5 5 00	
2		GJ–1	4 3 0 0 0 00		4 3 6 5 5 00	
7		GJ–1		2 0 0 0 0 00	2 3 6 5 5 00	
10		GJ–1		1 0 0 0 00	2 2 6 5 5 00	

EXHIBIT 2–11

HARTMAN FLOWER COMPANY
T Accounts

Cash		101
5/1 Bal. 655	5/7 20,000	
5/2 43,000	5/10 1,000	
5/29 35	5/12 5,000	
	5/18 5,000	
	5/22 2,400	
	5/28 4,000	
5/31 Bal. 6,290		

Accounts Receivable		106
5/1 Bal. 35	5/29 35	
5/31 Bal. 0		

Inventory		110
5/18 Bal. 5,000		
5/25 6,000		
5/31 Bal. 11,000		

Office Supplies		115
5/10 1,000		

Garden Supplies		116
5/1 Bal. 380		

Licenses		120
5/1 Bal. 120		

Prepaid Insurance		121
5/22 2,400		

Land		150
5/7 5,000		

Store Furniture and Fixtures		160
5/1 Bal. 200		
5/12 10,000		
5/31 Bal. 10,200		

Buildings		165
5/7 15,000		

Accounts Payable		201
5/28 4,000	5/1 Bal. 390	
	5/25 6,000	
	5/31 Bal. 2,390	

Bank Loan Payable		205
	5/12 5,000	

Capital Stock		301
	5/1 Bal. 1,000	
	5/2 43,000	
	5/31 Bal. 44,000	

counts and the accounts have been footed. Accounts on the trial balance are listed in the same order as they are found in the general ledger. The trial balance is a check to see whether equal amounts of debits and credits have been posted to the ledger. If this is the case and all accounts have been correctly balanced, then the trial balance will be "in balance." That is, the dollar amount of the debits will equal the dollar amount of the credits.

The trial balance of the Hartman Flower Company at May 31 is shown in Exhibit 2-12. It is important to understand the uses of a trial balance. If the trial balance is in balance, this will tell you that (1) the same dollar amounts of debits and credits have been posted and (2) the accounts have been correctly balanced. However, the trial

EXHIBIT 2–12

HARTMAN FLOWER COMPANY Trial Balance May 31, 1990		
	Debits	Credits
Cash	$6,290	
Accounts receivable	0	
Inventory	11,000	
Office supplies	1,000	
Garden supplies	380	
Licenses	120	
Prepaid insurance	2,400	
Land	5,000	
Store furniture and fixtures	10,200	
Buildings	15,000	
Accounts payable		$ 2,390
Bank loan payable		5,000
Capital stock		44,000
Totals	$51,390	$51,390

balance will not tell you that each entry has been posted to the correct account. For example, assume that in the entry on May 10, you mistakenly posted the $1,000 debit to Office Supplies as a debit to Inventory. The Office Supplies account will be understated by $1,000, and the Inventory account will be overstated by the same $1,000. The errors would, in effect, cancel each other in the accounting equation, and no discrepancy would appear on the trial balance. It will be in balance, even though wrong.

■ ERRORS IN THE TRIAL BALANCE

There are a number of reasons why the total of the debits may not equal the total of the credits. Some of the more common errors that may occur in the trial balance are:

1. There simply may be an addition error in totaling the trial balance.

2. A debit may have been posted as a credit or vice versa. If this occurs, the difference between the totals will be twice the amount of the misposted entry. Therefore the way to locate errors of this type is to divide the difference between the totals of the debits and credits by two and see whether this amount is a debit that was posted as a credit or vice versa. If an account is listed incorrectly on the trial balance, an error of this type will also occur. For example, if the bank loan payable of $5,000 is listed under the debit column, the trial balance will be out of balance by $10,000.

3. Part of an entry may not have been posted. If this occurs, the difference in the total of the debit and credit columns will equal the part of the entry not posted.

4. You may have misposted a dollar amount. The most common errors of this type are transpositions or misplaced decimal points. An example of a transposition is posting $56 as $65. An example of a misplaced decimal point is posting $900 as $90. If there is any transposition or misplaced decimal point, the resulting difference between the total of the debit and credit columns will be evenly divisible by 9.

5. Other errors in the trial balance occur when ledger accounts are incorrectly balanced or if an incorrect balance is transferred to the trial balance from a ledger account.

The best way to avoid errors in the trial balance is to work slowly and carefully when you are journalizing and posting. However, errors will inevitably occur. When they do, first check to see whether you have correctly added the debit and credit columns of the trial balance. The next step is to analyze the difference in the totals of the debit and credit columns, using the techniques just described, to try to locate the error. If you still cannot locate the error, check to make sure the balance of each account in the trial balance is the same as the balance in the ledger account. If you are still unable to locate your error, stop your work for a while and do something else. Then, at a later time, resume your work, and you will probably find your error more quickly.

SUMMARY OF LEARNING OBJECTIVES

1. How accounting functions as an information system. Accounting is a system designed to provide certain information about economic entities. It is made up of three parts: (1) inputs, (2) a transformation process, and (3) outputs. Raw economic data is admitted into the accounting system where it is stored and classified during the transformation process in order to produce the outputs of the accounting system—financial reports for management and external users.

2. The characteristics of information admitted to the accounting system. For data to be input to the accounting system, it must:

(a) Be a transaction or event of the specified business entity.

(b) Be measurable in monetary terms.

(c) Be verifiable.

Economic events take place continually, and accountants must decide when to recognize and record them in the accounting system. Thus, for example, sales are not recorded until title passes from the seller to the buyer.

3. Effects of transactions on the accounting equation. All the economic events that qualify as inputs for the accounting system can affect one or more of the three parts of the accounting equation. The purchase of assets for cash, for example, affects only assets, whereas the purchase of assets on account affects both assets and liabilities. Similarly, transactions that result in the receipt of cash owed to the firm affect only asset accounts, but the payment of a liability affects assets and liabilities. All transactions affect at least two accounts—that is, two assets, assets and liabilities, assets and stockholders' equity, or liabilities and stockholders' equity.

4. The components of the accounting system. The journal and ledger are the two primary components of the accounting system. The journal is a listing of all transactions in the order in which they occurred. At specific intervals, these transactions are posted to the appropriate ac-

counts in the ledger. A ledger, whether maintained by computer or manually, is a book of all accounts the company has in its chart of accounts. The specific accounts used by a firm depend on the nature, size, and complexity of the business.

5. Recording accounting transactions in the journal and ledger. The following T accounts summarize the rules for recording changes in the balance sheet accounts:

Assets	
Increases	Decreases
+	−
Debits	Credits
Normal balance: debit	

Liabilities	
Decreases	Increases
−	+
Debits	Credits
	Normal balance: credit

Stockholders' Equity	
Decreases	Increases
−	+
Debits	Credits
	Normal balance: credit

6. The preparation and use of a trial balance. A trial balance is usually prepared after transactions have been posted from the journal to the ledger. It shows or is a list of the dollar balances of the general ledger accounts. If the trial balance is in balance, this will tell you that equal dollar amounts of debits and credits have been posted and that the accounts are correctly balanced. However, errors still may occur if incorrect accounts were debited or credited.

Account
Accounting cycle
Accounting information system
Business-entity assumption
Chart of accounts
Credit
Debit
Double-entry accounting
General ledger
Journal
Ledger
Posting
Quantifiability
Subsidiary ledger
T account
Trial balance
Verifiability

PROBLEM FOR YOUR REVIEW

On January 2, 1990, Bonnie Brinkley, an excellent cook, decides to open her own restaurant, BB's Fine Food. The following events occur during the month of January:

- January 2: Bonnie invests $100,000 cash in the business by issuing herself 1,000 shares of capital stock.

- January 10: The corporation purchases a small building, including land, for $60,000 cash. The land has a value of $10,000, and the building a value of $50,000.

- January 15: A variety of restaurant furniture and fixtures are bought for $10,000. Bonnie is able to finance the purchase through a one-year bank loan.

- January 21: Food and beverages totaling $5,000 are purchased on account. These items are recorded in an account called Food and Beverage Inventory.

- January 30: The corporation pays $3,500 on the account payable incurred on January 21.

REQUIRED:
1. Record the transactions in the general journal.
2. Post the transactions to the appropriate T accounts.
3. Prepare a trial balance at January 31.
4. Prepare a balance sheet at January 31.

SOLUTION

(1) JOURNAL ENTRIES

General Journal

Date		Account Title	Ref.	Debit	Credit
1990					
January					
2		Cash		100,000	
		Capital Stock			100,000
		To record issue of 1,000 shares of capital			
		stock to B. Brinkley for $100,000.			
10		Land		10,000	
		Building		50,000	
		Cash			60,000
		To record purchase of land and building for			
		$60,000.			
15		Furniture and Fixtures		10,000	
		Bank Loan Payable			10,000
		To record purchase of furniture and fixtures			
		through bank loan.			
21		Food and Beverage Inventory		5,000	
		Accounts Payable			5,000
		To record purchase of food and beverage on			
		account.			
30		Accounts Payable		3,500	
		Cash			3,500
		To record payment on account.			

(2) T ACCOUNTS

Cash			Food and Beverage Inventory	
1/2 100,000	1/10 60,000		1/21 5,000	
	1/30 3,500			
1/31 Bal. 36,500				

Furniture and Fixtures			Land	
1/15 10,000			1/10 10,000	

Building			Accounts Payable	
1/10 50,000			1/30 3,500	1/21 5,000
				1/31 Bal. 1,500

Bank Loan Payable			Capital Stock	
	1/15 10,000			1/2 100,000

(3) TRIAL BALANCE

BB'S FINE FOOD
Trial Balance
January 31, 1990

Account	Debit	Credit
Cash	$ 36,500	
Food and beverage inventory	5,000	
Furniture and fixtures	10,000	
Land	10,000	
Building	50,000	
Accounts payable		$ 1,500
Bank loan payable		10,000
Capital stock		100,000
	$111,500	$111,500

(4) BALANCE SHEET

BB'S FINE FOOD
Balance Sheet
January 31, 1990

Assets		Liabilities and Stockholders' Equity	
Cash	$ 36,500	Liabilities	
Food and beverage inventory	5,000	Accounts payable	$ 1,500
Furniture and fixtures	10,000	Bank loan payable	10,000
Land	10,000	Total liabilities	11,500
Building	50,000	Stockholders' equity	
		Capital stock	100,000
		Total liabilities and	
Total assets	$111,500	stockholders' equity	$111,500

QUESTIONS

1. What are the major parts of the accounting information system?

2. Explain what factors determine whether an event or transaction will be recognized as an input of the accounting system.

3. On January 20, the Gilbert Corporation enters into a contract to sell 100 dozen footballs to the University of California. The footballs are delivered on February 10 and February 15. The Gilbert Corporation receives full payment from the university on February 21. Which events are recognized in the accounting records of Gilbert and the University of California? Why?

4. Define the major components of an accounting system.

5. What is a chart of accounts? How might a chart of accounts for Carl's Market differ from that of Ohman and Rattan, attorneys?

6. Explain to your good friend, who has no knowledge of accounting, the purpose of a ledger and a journal and how they are related.

7. Complete the following chart by entering either increases or decreases on the appropriate line:

Account	Ledger Side	
	Left	Right
Assets		
Liabilities		
Stockholders' equity		

8. You overheard one of your friends telling another person that all credits must be good because every time she deposits money in the bank, she gets a credit memo. Is her reasoning correct? If not, explain the meaning of *credit* in accounting.

9. For any transaction, the total of debits must equal credits. Why?

10. Complete the following chart by entering either debit or credit on the appropriate line:

Account	Increase	Decrease
Accounts receivable		
Accounts payable		
Cash		
Inventory		
Wages payable		
Capital stock		

11. What is a compound journal entry?

12. Why is it necessary to post journal entries to ledger accounts? What determines how often postings are made?

13. How do T accounts differ from the running balance ledger accounts illustrated in the text?

14. Complete the following chart by indicating whether each account is an asset, liability, or stockholders' equity account and its normal balance (either debit or credit):

Account	Type of Account	Normal Balance
Accounts payable		
Buildings		
Cash		
Taxes payable		
Prepaid rent		
Land		
Capital stock		

15. Put the following six items into chronological order:
- **(a)** Enter transaction in journal.
- **(b)** Business event occurs.
- **(c)** Prepare trial balance.
- **(d)** Post entries to ledger.
- **(e)** Balance ledger accounts.
- **(f)** Prepare balance sheet.

16. One of your accounting classmates, after spending several hours doing her accounting homework, was able to balance the trial balance. Convinced her home-

work must be correct, she went to bed. Should she be as confident as she is?

17. The debit and credit columns of a trial balance are not equal. What could be some of the causes for this problem?

18. What is a balance sheet, and what does it tell us?

19. How are accounts listed on a typical balance sheet?

20. Explain the four transactions that appear in the following T accounts:

Cash	
[1] 100,000	40,000 [2]
	5,000 [3]
	10,000 [4]

Prepaid Insurance	
[3] 5,000	

Land	
[2] 60,000	

Bank Loan Payable	
[4] 10,000	20,000 [2]

Capital Stock	
	100,000 [1]

EXERCISES

E1. Recognition of Inputs. John Brown started his own legal practice on January 2 of the current year. Which of the following events and transactions would be recognized as an input of the accounting system for his business?

- **(a)** John invests $40,000 of his own money in exchange for capital stock of the law firm.
- **(b)** John receives $1,500 vacation pay from his previous law firm. He deposits the money in his own account.
- **(c)** John has a computer that he purchased with personal funds. He gives the computer to his new law firm.
- **(d)** The law firm purchases $2,500 of supplies to be paid in February. The supplies are received immediately.
- **(e)** The law firm purchases several items of office equipment for $15,000. These purchases are financed by a local bank. Because John's law firm is new, the bank insists that John personally guarantee the loan.

E2. The Accounting Equation. At the beginning of January of the current year, the Petini Corporation started out with total assets of $50,000. During January, the firm entered into a number of transactions. State whether each of the transactions increased total assets, decreased total assets, or had no effect on total assets. Also determine the amount of total assets at the end of January.

- **(a)** The firm purchased for cash office supplies at a total cost of $5,000.
- **(b)** The firm purchased for $10,000 a computer for office use. It paid $4,000 in cash and borrowed the rest from a local bank.
- **(c)** The firm was in need of additional cash and found an investor who invested $50,000 in exchange for capital stock.
- **(d)** A business license that allowed the firm to operate within the city for the rest of the year was purchased for $500 cash.

(e) A three-year insurance policy was purchased on account. The policy cost $3,600 and took effect immediately.

(f) One of the owners of the business withdrew $500 of the original investment she made.

E3. Analyzing Transactions. The Midway Corporation entered into a number of transactions during the month. State the effect that each transaction had on total assets, liabilities, and stockholders' equity. Use + for increase, − for decrease, and NE for no effect. If a transaction has the effect of both increasing and decreasing an item, use both a + and a − sign. Use the table below, which has been completed for the first transaction.

Transaction	Assets	Liabilities	Stockholders' Equity
a	−	−	NE

(a) Midway paid a liability.

(b) The firm purchased some stationery on account.

(c) The firm issued some capital stock in exchange for some land.

(d) The firm collected an account receivable.

(e) The firm distributed a cash dividend to its owners.

(f) Midway purchased a building by paying cash and issuing a note payable.

(g) Midway had an account payable to the Smith Co. The Smith Co. agreed to increase the payment period and take a note payable in exchange for the account payable.

(h) Midway paid in advance for a year's rent.

E4. Economic Transactions and the Entity Assumption. Indicate whether the following transactions of the Main Construction Corporation would increase, decrease, or have no effect on the company's total assets, liabilities, and stockholders' equity. Use + for increase, − for decrease, and NE for no effect. It may be that in some cases, none of the accounts is affected. Use the table below, which has been completed for the first transaction.

Transaction	Assets	Liabilities	Stockholders' Equity
a	+	+	NE

TRANSACTIONS: **(a)** The firm purchased land for $100,000, $20,000 of which was paid in cash and a note payable signed for the balance.

(b) The firm bought equipment for $40,000 on credit.

(c) The firm paid a $15,000 liability.

(d) The firm arranged for a $100,000 line of credit (the right to borrow funds as needed) from the bank. No funds have yet been borrowed.

(e) One of the investors wanted to make an additional investment in the company in the future and arranged a $20,000 personal bank loan.

(f) The firm borrowed $45,000 on its line of credit.

(g) The firm issued a $10,000 cash dividend to its stockholders.

(h) The individual in Item e invested the $20,000 in the company in exchange for additional capital stock.

E5. Analyzing Transactions. In this chapter, it was stated that in thinking about how to record transactions, you should go through this three-step process:

1. Determine the specific accounts that are affected.

2. Decide which of these accounts are increased or decreased.

3. Make the appropriate debit and credit entries in the T accounts.

Analyze each of the following transactions using the three steps shown above. Example (a) has been done for you.

(a) The Fazzi Corporation issued 1,000 shares of capital stock at a total price of $25,000.

(b) The firm purchased some equipment for $10,000 cash.

(c) Inventory of $5,000 is purchased on account.

(d) A month's rent of $1,000 is paid in advance.

(e) Some of the equipment that was purchased in Item b, at a cost of $2,000, was sold at its cost for cash.

(f) Accounts payable of $2,400 were paid.

EXAMPLE (a):   **1.** This transaction is an exchange of cash for capital stock.

2. Cash is increased by $25,000, and Capital Stock is increased by $25,000.

3. The T accounts.

Cash	Capital Stock
ᵃ25,000	25,000ᵃ

E6.   Recognition of Accounting Events. Crystal Kingdom, owner of Crystal Kingdom's Funland, has asked you to review the following transactions. For each event, state whether the transaction should be recorded on the books of the company, and state why.

(a) January 2: The firm places an order for three video games and two pinball machines at a cost of $1,300 each. The machines will be delivered next month.

(b) January 3: Three days later, Funland sends a deposit of $2,000 for the machines.

(c) February 1: The machines are delivered, and Funland receives an invoice for the balance.

(d) February 10: As she does each business day, one of Crystal's daughters, Rainbow, goes to the local bank and exchanges $200 cash for the same amount of quarters.

(e) February 12: The balance due on the machines is paid.

(f) February 22: The demand to play video games has far surpassed anyone's expectations. As a result, Funland has negotiated a line of credit to expand the business. The line of credit allows Funland to borrow up to $100,000 as the funds are needed. As of this date, the line of credit has not been used.

E7.   Making Entries in T Accounts. Enter the following transactions in the appropriate T accounts. Label each transaction with the date it occurred. Balance the T accounts.

(a) February 1: Lewis and Zorro started a CPA firm by issuing capital stock to themselves, for a total of $100,000.

(b) February 2: They rented an office and had to make a deposit of $4,000, which represented one month's rent. They will move in March.

(c) February 10: Supplies of $5,000 were purchased on account.

(d) February 15: A computer was purchased. The cost was $2,500, of which $500 was paid in cash and the remainder borrowed from the bank. Use the account Bank Loan Payable.

(e) February 22: The account payable that resulted from the purchase of supplies was paid.

E8.   Recognition of Accounts and Debits and Credits. For each of the following accounts, indicate whether the account is an asset, liability, or stockholders' equity account and whether the normal balance is a debit or credit. Arrange your answers by duplicating the following table:

Account	Type of Account	Normal Balance
(a) Cash		
(b) Inventory		
(c) Wages payable		
(d) Capital stock		
(e) Land		
(f) Equipment		
(g) Investment in ABC Corporation		
(h) Patent		
(i) Accounts receivable		
(j) Accounts payable		

E9. The Retained Earnings Account. Answer the following questions related to the Retained Earnings account:

(a) Should Retained Earnings be classified as an asset, a liability, or a stockholders' equity account?

(b) What is the normal balance in the Retained Earnings account?

(c) What activities cause Retained Earnings to increase and decrease?

E10. Journal Entries. J. J. Jay III has decided to open a car wash to offset his tuition for business school. Help J. J. get started by recording his first two months' transactions in his general journal. Make the appropriate explanation after each entry.

(a) His three cousins, J. P., Andy, and Mary, each bought 1,000 shares of stock in his corporation for $2 per share.

(b) J. J. purchased an abandoned car wash for $3,000 cash.

(c) He paid $200 for his local car wash license. It gave him the right to do business for the next two years.

(d) He also bought supplies for $760 on account.

(e) After being sued in small claims court, J. J. paid $900 to buy his first customer's car, because the windows were left down when it was washed. The car will be used in the business.

E11. Posting to the Ledger. Post the entries that you made in Exercise 10 to the appropriate T accounts. Balance the accounts.

E12. Analysis of the Accounting Equation. You have obtained the following data from the Heavy Corporation as of December 31, 1990. However, certain figures were smeared by the duplicating machine, and so you are to determine the missing figures.

HEAVY CORPORATION

Accounts payable	$15,630
Accounts receivable	?
Bank loan payable	6,000
Buildings	15,000
Cash	28,725
Inventory	14,800
Land	5,000
Licenses	225
Office supplies	1,280
Other assets	200
Prepaid insurance	2,400
Store furniture and fixtures	13,800
Total assets	91,630
Total liabilities	?
Total stockholders' equity	?

E13. Journal Entries and Posting. Computer Calisthenics Corporation began business on March 1 of the current year. During the month, the firm entered into the following transactions:

■ March 1: Issued capital stock to various investors for $125,000.

■ March 2: Arranged a $70,000 cash loan from the local bank. The cash was received immediately.

■ March 10: Purchased a small building on a downtown corner for $100,000 cash.

■ March 16: Purchased various types of exercise equipment for $25,000 on account.

■ March 20: Placed an order for $2,000 of various office supplies, including stationery. All supplies will be received next month. However, the stationery store required that the firm pay in advance. Full payment was made.

- March 25: Paid for equipment purchased on March 16.
- March 30: Purchased a three-year comprehensive insurance policy for $2,500.

REQUIRED: **(a)** Make the required journal entries.

(b) Create T accounts for each account, and post the journal entries to the ledger T accounts. Balance the ledger accounts.

E14. **Understanding and Explaining Journal Entries.**

(a) State the most reasonable explanation for each of the following entries:

		Dr.	Cr.
1.	Cash	5,000	
	Accounts Receivable		5,000
2.	Accounts Payable	3,000	
	Cash		3,000
3.	Inventory	10,000	
	Accounts Payable		10,000
4.	Accounts Payable	2,000	
	Notes Payable		2,000
5.	Stockholders' Equity	1,000	
	Cash		1,000

(b) The following entries are missing information. Complete them with the most reasonable account names.

		Dr.	Cr.
1.	_____	50,000	
	Capital Stock		50,000
2.	Loans Payable	1,000	
	_____		1,000
3.	_____	12,000	
	Accounts Receivable		12,000

E15. **Error Correction.** Some of the following journal entries are incorrect or are missing data. Make the complete correct journal entry for each item where appropriate. (*Note*: Dr. = debit, Cr. = credit.)

		Dr.	Cr.
a.	_____		
	Accounts Receivable		4,327
	To record payment received from customer on account.		
b.	Inventory	2,639	
	Cash		2,639
	To record inventory purchased for cash of $2,639.		
c.	Cash	50	
	Office Supplies		50
	To record purchase of office supplies for cash.		
d.	Land	15,000	
	Bank Loan Payable	10,000	
	Cash		5,000
	To record purchase of land costing $15,000. $5,000 paid in cash, the remainder borrowed from bank.		

E16. **Trial Balance and Effect of Errors.** Which of the following posting errors would cause the debit and credit columns of the trial balance not to balance? Briefly explain your reasoning.

(a) A receipt of cash from a payment on account was posted by debiting Cash for $2,500 and crediting Accounts Receivable for $25,000.

(b) A purchase of inventory on account was posted by debiting Inventory for $1,000 and crediting Cash for $1,000.

(c) When the following journal entry was posted, the debit to Accounts Payable was left out by mistake:

Accounts Payable	1,200	
Cash		1,200

(d) The purchase of supplies for cash was posted as a debit to Cash and a credit to Supplies for $500, respectively.

(e) When the following journal was posted, the debit to Cash was actually posted as a credit:

Cash	10,000	
Capital Stock		10,000

E17. Correcting Errors in the Trial Balance and Preparing a Balance Sheet. The accountant for LFN is having trouble balancing the trial balance and asks your help. You have obtained the following trial balance as well as the additional data:

LFN
Trial Balance
December 31, 1990

	Debit	Credit
Cash	$ 5,000	
Marketable securities	1,500	
Inventory	15,000	
Office supplies	2,000	
Prepaid rent	2,000	
Land	20,000	
Buildings	45,000	
Other assets		$ 5,000
Bank loans payable		10,000
Accounts payable		6,320
Mortgages payable		30,000
Capital stock		45,900
	$90,500	$97,220

Additional data:

(a) A purchase of marketable securities for $500 was not posted to the account.

(b) A cash payment on account of $570 was posted to Accounts Payable as a debit of $750. The credit was correctly posted.

(c) The Prepaid Rent ledger account was footed incorrectly and overstated by $200.

(d) When office supplies were purchased for $100, a credit was posted in that amount to the Office Supplies account, as well as the credit to the Cash account.

(e) Although the Capital Stock account was correctly footed in the ledger account at $49,500, it was listed in the trial balance as $45,900.

REQUIRED: **(a)** Prepare a corrected trial balance.　　**(b)** Prepare a balance sheet.

PROBLEMS

P2-1 **The Accounting Equation and Economic Transactions.** On December 31, 1989, the Last In, First Out Hamburger Store had the following account balances:

Cash + Loan Receivable + Supplies + Equipment =
$4,000 $3,500 $1,500 $7,000

Accounts Payable + Notes Payable + Stockholders' Equity
    $5,000 $2,000 $9,000

During January 1990, the following events occurred:

(a) Supplies were purchased for $3,500; $1,000 on credit and the rest for cash.

(b) The amount of $3,000 was collected on loans receivable.

(c) One of the owners of the business contributed a new word processor, at a value of $2,000 to the firm in exchange for capital stock.

(d) One of the old typewriters was sold for its original cost of $700, of which $300 was received in cash and the remainder on account. (Use the Loan Receivable account.)

(e) Accounts payable of $3,500 were paid.

(f) An installment payment of $500 was made on the note payable.

(g) The remainder due on the sale of the typewriter was collected.

REQUIRED: Prepare a table similar to Exhibit 2-3, showing the accounts and their balances at December 31 as column headings. Use a separate line on the table to show the effects of each transaction on the accounting equation. Total all columns after each transaction.

P2-2 **Understanding Transactions.** The balance sheet of Repair Store, Inc. at December 31, 1991 is shown below in equation form, followed by January transactions, whose effect on the accounting equation is also shown.

	Cash	+	Accounts Receivable +	Supplies +	Equipment =	Accounts Payable +	Capital Stock +	Retained Earnings
1.	$4,000 +4,000		$6,000 −4,000	$1,200	$10,000	$4,500	$10,000	$6,700
2.	8,000 −3,000		2,000	1,200	10,000 +3,000	4,500	10,000	6,700
3.	5,000		2,000	1,200 −500	13,000	4,500 −500	10,000	6,700
4.	5,000 −2,000		2,000	700	13,000	4,000 −2,000	10,000	6,700
5.	3,000 +1,500		2,000	700	13,000 −1,500	2,000	10,000	6,700
6.	4,500 +3,000		2,000	700	11,500	2,000	10,000 +3,000	6,700
	$7,500		$2,000	$ 700	$11,500	$2,000	$13,000	$6,700

REQUIRED: **(a)** Describe the nature of each of the numbered transactions that would produce the effect shown on the table.

(b) Determine the amount of net assets (assets minus liabilities or stockholders' equity) at the end of December and at the end of January after all the transactions have been recorded.

How much have they increased or decreased? Can you determine the reason for the change?

 P2-3 Recording Transactions. On January 2, 1990, Roy decided to start a business that performed children's acts at birthday parties. The business was called Children Are Fun. The following transactions occurred during the start-up month of January:

1. Roy invested $50,000 cash in the business, plus toys he had personally purchased recently at a cost of $20,000, in exchange for capital stock. (Put the toys in the Toy Supplies account.)

2. The company leased a small store at an annual rental of $15,000, all of which was paid in advance.

3. Various items of equipment including racks, tables, and an electronic clown were purchased for $10,000; $2,000 was paid in cash, and the remainder was put on account.

4. Additional toys costing $15,000 were purchased on account.

5. The business secured a $20,000 loan from a local bank.

6. $1,000 worth of the toys purchased in Transaction 4 arrived damaged. They were returned to the manufacturer, and the firm's account payable was decreased.

7. The remaining account payable from the purchase in Transaction 4 was paid by making an $8,000 cash payment and converting the remainder to a note payable.

8. A $5,000 installment was paid on the bank loan.

9. The firm decided to replace the electronic clown it had purchased with a small robot. (a) The clown, which cost $500, was sold for that amount of cash. (b) The new robot was purchased for $1,200 cash.

REQUIRED: Prepare a table similar to Exhibit 2-3, using the following accounts as column headings: Cash, Prepaid Rent, Toy Supplies, Store Equipment, Accounts Payable, Bank Loans Payable, and Capital Stock. Show the effect of each transaction on the accounting equation. You do not have to give totals after each transaction.

 P2-4 Analysis of Transactions. A number of transactions for Becky's Ice Parlor are described in the following chart.

REQUIRED: Complete the chart. Note that the increase/decrease columns are not necessarily intended to be in a debit/credit relationship.

	Asset		Liability		Owner's Equity	
Transaction	**Increase**	**Decrease**	**Increase**	**Decrease**	**Increase**	**Decrease**
a. Start business by investing $50,000 cash.						
b. Purchase freezer for $20,000— $15,000 in cash, and a bank loan for the remainder.						
c. Purchase various supplies costing $1,500 on account.						
d. A bank makes a $5,000 short-term loan to the firm.						
e. Payment of $1,000 made on Accounts Payable.						
f. An older freezer that cost $2,000 is sold at its cost for cash.						

P2-5 T-Account Analysis. The T accounts for Melissa's Maternity Mart follow, reflecting all the transactions for November. The firm was organized on November 1 of the current year.

Cash		Accounts Receivable		Inventory	
[1] 100,000	3,600 [3]	[7] 2,000	2,000 [10]	[11] 5,000	
[10] 2,000	10,000 [4]				
	240 [5]				
	400 [9]				

Prepaid Insurance		License		Office Supplies	
[3] 3,600		[5] 240		[6] 1,000	

Land		Buildings		Furniture and Fixtures	
[2] 20,000		[2] 40,000		[4] 10,000	2,000 [7]
				[8] 3,500	

Accounts Payable		Mortgage Payable		Capital Stock	
[9] 400	1,000 [6]		60,000 [2]		100,000 [1]
	5,000 [11]				3,500 [8]

REQUIRED: **(a)** For each of the numbered transactions (1 through 11), make the appropriate journal entry, including a complete explanation of the transaction.

(b) Determine the balances of the T accounts, and prepare a trial balance.

P2-6 Journal Entries, T Accounts, and Trial Balance. Will Miller decided to go into CPA practice for himself after three years of experience with another firm. The following events occurred in September, the month he organized his business:

- September 1: Will began his practice with $70,000. A local bank supplied a loan for half of the $70,000, and Will issued himself capital stock for the remaining half in exchange for cash.

- September 3: Will rented a small office for his practice. In accordance with the rental agreement, he prepaid the first six months at $2,100 per month.

- September 10: Various typewriters, calculators, and other office equipment were purchased for $7,500 on account from a local supplier. (Record all items in the Office Equipment account.)

- September 14: A two-year liability insurance policy with a cost of $4,000 was purchased for cash.

- September 18: One of the typewriters that cost $1,500 arrived damaged. Will returned it to his supplier and received a credit.

- September 24: Will purchased various pieces of office furniture at a cost of $4,000. All items were paid in cash.

- September 29: He paid the remainder of the balance on the purchase of office equipment.

- September 30: Will hired a part-time secretary, to begin work on October 1. Monthly wages will be $800.

REQUIRED: **(a)** Make the required journal entries.

(b) Set up the required T accounts and post the entries to these accounts.

(c) Prepare a trial balance at September 30.

P2-7 Journal Entries, T Accounts, and the Trial Balance. Laura Kline decided to open her own law practice after several successful years as a partner in a large local firm. The following events occurred in June, the month her practice was organized.

- June 1: Laura began her practice with $100,000 in exchange for capital stock, her brother lent her $40,000, and she invested the remaining $60,000 from her personal funds.

- June 3: The firm purchased a small building and the land on which it was situated for $120,000. A down payment of $24,000 was made, and a mortgage was taken out for the rest. Property records indicate that 40% of the total cost should be allocated to the land and 60% to the building.

- June 4: The firm purchased a small business computer for $10,000 cash.

- June 5: The firm purchased office furniture and fixtures for $15,000 on account.

- June 18: The firm purchased various office supplies for $2,400 cash.

- June 22: One of the pieces of furniture arrived broken. It had a cost of $1,200 and was returned to the seller. The firm's account was credited for $1,200.

- June 25: Just before opening her practice, Laura had purchased a new electronic typewriter for $2,200 with her own funds. She decided to use the typewriter in her business. She contributed the typewriter to the business in exchange for additional capital stock.

- June 27: The remaining balance due on the purchase of office furniture was made.

- June 30: Her first potential client came into her office. Laura agreed to begin working on his will in July for a total fee of $250.

REQUIRED: **(a)** Make the required journal entries.

(b) Set up the required T accounts and post the entries to these accounts.

(c) Prepare a trial balance at June 30.

P2-8 Journal Entries, Ledger Accounts, and Trial Balance. Sumi Kuramoto decided to open a children's book and record store called The Reading Store. The business was organized in January, and during that month the following transactions occurred:

- January 2: Sumi invested $40,000 of her own funds in the business and issued herself capital stock.

- January 3: Five of her good friends each invested $5,000 in the business and received capital stock in exchange.

- January 6: The business purchased land and a small building. The total cost was $75,000, of which two-thirds was applicable to the building and one-third to the land. A 20% down payment was made, and a bank loan was taken out for the remainder.

- January 11: The building appeared too small for the anticipated operations. The firm contracted with a local builder to add a new wing at a cost of $40,000. The work will begin next month, and the first cash payment is due on February 15.

- January 16: Sumi bought various books and records to be held for resale at a total cost of $10,000 on account.

- January 19: Various pieces of store equipment and furniture were purchased for $15,000 cash.

- January 23: The inventory purchased on January 16 was paid in full.

- January 24: Sumi decided that she could not use one of the pieces of furniture that cost $1,000. She sold it to one of her friends on account for that amount.

- January 29: Office supplies of $1,200 were bought on account.

- January 30: Her friend paid Sumi for one-half of the furniture purchased on January 24.

Sumi decided to use the following account titles and account numbers in the business:

Cash	110	Building	122
Accounts Receivable	112	Store Equipment and Furniture	124
Inventory	115	Bank Loan Payable	230
Office Supplies	118	Accounts Payable	232
Land	120	Capital Stock	340

REQUIRED: (a) Make the required journal entries for January.

(b) Post these entries to ledger accounts, using the running balance type shown in Exhibit 2-8.

(c) Prepare a trial balance at January 31.

P2-9   T Account Analysis. Frankie's Fish Hatchery has the following T accounts in its general ledger. (Note that BB indicates beginning balance.)

Cash		
BB 14,000	9/1 4,500	
9/15 5,426	9/12 3,500	
9/20 27,000	9/28 2,460	
	9/29 2,662	

Supplies		
BB 19,200		
9/15 3,750		
9/29 2,662		

Livestock		
BB 78,826		
9/10 6,240		

Accounts Payable		
9/1 4,500	BB 6,927	
9/28 2,460	9/5 3,750	
	9/10 6,240	

Other Assets		
BB 5,600		

Mortgage Payable		
9/12 3,500	BB 115,000	
	9/25 28,850	

Accounts Receivable		
BB 10,290	9/15 5,426	

Capital Stock		
	BB 290,616	
	9/20 27,000	

Equipment		
BB 52,650		
9/26 11,200		

Land		
BB 72,100		
9/25 13,250		

Note Payable		
	BB 32,700	
	9/26 11,200	

Building		
BB 192,577		
9/25 15,600		

Provide the following:

1. Ending balance of each account.

2. Beginning balance of assets.

3. Net change in the Cash account for September.

4. Net change in total assets for September.

5. Beginning balance of liabilities.

6. Ending balance of liabilities.

7. Amount of cash paid on mortgage.

8. Amount of net assets at the beginning of September.

9. Amount of net assets at the end of September.

10. Net change in owner's equity for September.

11. Explain the relationship between the change in net assets during September and the change in the Capital Stock account.

P2-10   Preparation of Balance Sheet from Incomplete Data. The accountant for Fortune Properties attempted to prepare the firm's balance sheet at December 31, 1990, but was unable to complete the job. You have obtained the following data:

FORTUNE PROPERTIES INCORPORATED
Balance Sheet
December 31, 1990

Assets		Liabilities and Stockholders' Equity	
Cash	$ 15,000	**Liabilities**	
Commissions receivable	?	Accounts payable	$ 16,000
Office supplies	?	Wages payable	6,420
Prepaid insurance	?	Property taxes payable	?
Office equipment	12,150	Bank note payable	?
Surveying equipment	46,220	Mortgage payable	?
Investment properties	944,600	Total liabilities	?
		Stockholders' equity	?
Total assets		Total liabilities and stockholders' equity	$1,030,129

ADDITIONAL DATA:

1. Insurance costs are $500 per month, and six months have been prepaid.

2. Property taxes owed equal 3% of the balance in the Investment Properties account.

3. The balance in the Mortgage Payable account represents 20% of the cost of the investment properties, and the Bank Note Payable represents 10% of the cost of the property.

4. All records pertaining to the Office Supplies account were lost. A count of the supplies at December 31, 1990 indicated that $4,500 remained on hand.

5. $500 of surveying equipment was incorrectly posted to the Office Equipment account.

REQUIRED: Prepare a corrected balance sheet at December 31, 1990.

P2-11 **Balance Sheet Analysis.** The balance sheet for Susan's Advertising Agency at December 31, 1990 is as follows:

SUSAN'S ADVERTISING AGENCY
Balance Sheet
December 31, 1990

Assets		Liabilities and Stockholders' Equity	
Cash	$ 8,000	Accounts payable	$12,000
Accounts receivable	10,000	Note payable	5,000
Note receivable	8,000	Mortgage payable	85,000
Supplies	10,000	Stockholders' equity	?
Office equipment	25,000		
Land	160,000		

In addition, you obtained the following information about the company:

1. The $40,000 worth of land shown in the land account was a personal purchase by Susan. She intends to develop it for resale. The remaining $120,000 in that account represents the latest market value for the land owned by the agency. It was purchased several years ago at a cost of $140,000.

2. The advertising agency recently moved. Included in the Supplies account is $2,000 worth of stationery with the old address. It all will have to be discarded.

3. The note receivable arose in 1988 because one of the agency's ex-employees was in need of emergency funds. However, after receiving the loan, the employee never showed up at work again and nobody knows his current whereabouts.

4. The agency is currently being sued by the City of Rolling Oceans for $5,600 because of the company's failure to pay back taxes. The company acknowledges the debt but has not recorded it.

REQUIRED: **(a)** Indicate what effect, if any, each of these items would have on the balance sheet. Justify your answer.

(b) Prepare a corrected balance sheet to reflect any of the changes that you think should be made.

■ UNDERSTANDING FINANCIAL STATEMENTS

P2-12 The following accounts have been taken from a recent annual report of Bristol Myers Company. The accounts have been purposely condensed to simplify the exercise. All amounts are shown in millions of dollars.

Accounts	Amount
Accounts payable	$ 191.5
Accounts receivable	559.1
Accrued payables	292.8
Capital stock	152.1
Cash	220.0
Goodwill	90.4
Inventories	559.1
Long-term debt	208.8
Marketable securities	391.6
Other assets	70.5
Other receivables	72.5
Prepaid expenses	139.5
Property, plant, and equipment	653.6
Retained earnings	1,562.3
Short-term borrowings	167.8
U.S. and foreign income taxes payable	181.0

REQUIRED: **(a)** What accounts do you think are included in Other Receivables? Why do you think that they are not included in Accounts Receivable?

(b) Goodwill is considered an asset. What do you think it represents, and why is it considered an asset?

(c) What items do you think are included under Accrued Payables?

(d) Prepare a balance sheet from the above data.

■ FINANCIAL DECISION CASES

P2-13 Ava Melbourne decided to open her own travel agency, called World Travel Unlimited. Because she had no accounting background, she made all of the initial payments and recorded all deposits in her personal checkbook. Her check and deposit register for July, the month Ava organized the business, is reproduced below.

Check Number	Date	Description of Transaction	Payment	Deposit	Balance
	May 31	Balance			$ 6,429
	June 1	Loan from bank to Ava		$20,000	
1023	June 2	World Travel Unlimited in exchange for capital stock	$15,000		
1024	June 3	Ralph's Market for groceries	45		
1025	June 4	American Travel Association for license	200		
1026	June 8	First Realty Company for deposit on office space for agency	1,000		
	June 15	Last paycheck from job		1,900	
1027	June 20	Purchase of supplies for travel agency	200		
1028	June 23	Purchase of typewriter for travel agency	800		
1029	June 30	Rent on apartment	750		10,334

In addition, Ava told you she had purchased a computer for $88,000 for use in the agency. The computer was purchased on account, and the agency agreed to make payment beginning next month.

REQUIRED: **(a)** Make the entries on the travel agency's books to record all transactions related to the travel agency.

(b) Prepare a balance sheet for World Travel Unlimited at the end of June.

(c) Explain to Ava why she should not continue to use her own checkbook to pay and deposit agency checks and deposits.

P2-14 One of your close friends has decided to open a business that offers accounting and tax courses to doctors and dentists. These courses are marketed to professional societies and meet the required continuing education requirement of these professions. During the first month of business, the following events occurred:

(a) Your friend Katie Longes invested $80,000, her entire savings, in the business in exchange for capital stock.

(b) The firm, which is called Great Tax Breaks, negotiated a line of credit with the bank in the amount of $50,000. A line of credit is a preapproved loan that can be used at the borrower's discretion. Currently, none of the line has been used.

(c) After several meetings with a number of professional societies, two of them agreed to use Katie's business. In three months, the firm will put on a tax seminar in Hawaii. In order to obtain the business, Katie agreed to waive any required deposits.

(d) The firm made a $5,000 down payment to the Coral Surf Hotel for the use of the facilities for the seminar.

(e) Katie contacted five of her associates who were professors at major universities, and they agreed to teach the classes for a fee of $1,000 a week. In order to show her good faith, she sent each of them $100.

(f) During the month, Katie worked very hard putting together the tax course. By the end of the month, she had outlined the highlights of individual taxation in over 100 typed pages. She estimates that the purchase price of similar materials would be over $1,000.

Katie was extremely pleased with the progress of her business in the first month of its existence. However, when her accountant prepared a balance sheet, presented below, she became very confused, feeling that the statement did not tell the true story of the business activities during the month.

GREAT TAX BREAKS
Balance Sheet
January 31, 1990

Assets		Equities	
Cash	$74,500		
Deposits	5,500	Stockholders' equity	$80,000
Total assets	$80,000	Total equity	$80,000

REQUIRED: Write a brief memo to Katie explaining how and why the accountant prepared the balance sheet. Be sure to explain which transactions were included and which were not and the reasons for their inclusion or lack of inclusion. Also, be sure to explain to Katie the relevant accounting concepts involved in this situation.

3

MEASURING
AND RECORDING
INCOME STATEMENT
TRANSACTIONS

After studying this chapter, you should be able to:

1. Discuss how accountants measure income and explain the roles of revenues and expenses, gains and losses, and net income in this measurement.
2. Explain the important concepts in determining net income.
3. Distinguish between the accrual and the cash bases of accounting.

4. Discuss the revenue-realization principle and identify the different points in the earnings cycle in which revenue can be recognized.
5. Record income statement transactions.
6. Describe the relationship among the balance sheet, income statement, and retained earnings statement.

T he ability of a business enterprise to earn a profit is essential to its continued operations. The profit earned by an enterprise is a yardstick that managers, investors, and creditors use to evaluate the future prospects of the business. Thus one of the most important parts of the accounting process is the recognition and recording of those economic transactions that affect the firm's income. These concepts are the main focus of this chapter.

THE MEASUREMENT OF INCOME

Net income is often measured by the increase in owners' equity that results from operations. However, economists define and measure this increase differently from the way accountants do for financial reporting purposes or the Internal Revenue Service does for tax return preparation. For financial reporting purposes, income is generally recognized when transactions have been completed. The accountant measures and records the transactions that occurred during the period and summarizes them on the income statement. The effect of these transactions, plus additional capital contributions, less withdrawals, is added to the historical cost of net assets at the beginning of the period in order to determine historical-cost net assets at the end of the period. This approach can be illustrated as in Exhibit 3-1. Accountants prefer this method because measurements of completed transactions are objective and verifiable. Thus the income statement that results from this process is a reliable financial statement that describes in detail the components of income: revenues and expenses, gains and losses, and net income.

EXHIBIT 3–1

| Historical-Cost Net Assets Beginning of the Period | ± | Income Statement Transactions during the Period | ± | Capital Contributions Withdrawals | = | Historical-Cost Net Assets End of the Period |

REVENUES AND EXPENSES

The definitions of revenues and expenses were introduced in Chapter 1. To review, revenues are the prices of goods sold or services rendered by a firm to others in exchange for cash or other assets. Conversely, expenses are the dollar amounts of the resources used up by the firm during a particular period of time in the process of earning revenues. Both revenues and expenses result from the firm's major operating activities, such as the sale of goods or services during the period.

In accounting, it is important to distinguish between receipts and revenues, as well as between expenditures and expenses. **Receipts** are inflows of cash or other assets. They do not always represent revenues. For example, a firm may receive cash from a bank loan or from a customer making a payment on account. The proceeds from a bank loan represent an increase in an asset, Cash, and an increase in a liability, Bank Loans Payable. Similarly, the collection of a receivable represents an exchange of one asset, Cash, for another asset, Accounts Receivable. In neither case is stockholders' equity affected. Receipts of cash or receivables that do represent revenues come primarily from products sold or services performed for customers.

Expenditures are outflows of cash or other assets or increases in liabilities. However, not all expenditures are expenses. For example, a firm may use its assets to purchase other assets such as buildings, inventories, or supplies. It might reduce its liabilities by paying off a bank loan. These transactions do not affect stockholders' equity.

Thus, if an expenditure was made in order to produce revenues in the current period and does not provide for future economic benefits, it is an expense that reduces retained earnings.

GAINS AND LOSSES

Gains are increases in equity (net assets) from activities other than revenues and investments by owners of the firm during a period. Conversely, **losses** are decreases in equity (net assets) from activities affecting the firm during the period, except for expenses and distributions to its owners. Gains and losses result from transactions that increase or decrease stockholders' equity (other than the investments by the owners or the distributions to the owners) but are not directly related to selling and producing its goods and services. An example of a transaction that might result in a gain or loss is the sale of an asset that was not intended for resale.

For example, assume that the Carson Corporation sold some marketable securities at an amount greater than their cost. The securities were originally purchased for $1,800 and were sold for $2,500 cash. The Carson Corporation records this transaction by increasing the asset, Cash, by $2,500, decreasing the asset, Marketable Securities, by $1,800, and recording a Gain on Sale of Marketable Securities for the difference of $700. This gain on sale represents an increase in retained earnings, because the firm received more assets than it gave up. This increase is assigned to Retained Earnings. You should note that only the net gain of $700 is recorded. That is, the firm does not show revenues of $2,500 and expenses of $1,800 in the way that it does when it is selling goods and services.

NET INCOME

Net income or loss is the difference between the total of revenues and gains and the total of expenses and losses. If revenues and gains exceed expenses and losses, net income results. If, on the other hand, expenses and losses exceed revenues and gains, a net loss results. Net income causes an increase in the firm's net assets during the period, whereas a net loss causes a decrease in the firm's net assets during the period.

DIVIDENDS

Corporations often pay dividends to stockholders. **Dividends** are a return to the stockholders of some of the assets that have increased because of the profits earned. Therefore dividends can generally be issued only if there is a positive balance in Retained Earnings. If a dividend were issued when there was a negative balance in Retained Earnings (called a *deficit*), the firm would be returning the corporation's original capital to the stockholders. These are called *liquidating dividends* and are issued only in very rare circumstances.

Although dividends can be issued in many forms, cash dividends are the most common. The important thing to remember is that dividends are not expenses but rather a distribution of assets resulting from the corporation's profits. Therefore they do not appear on the income statement, but instead are a direct deduction from Retained Earnings on the retained earnings statement.

IMPORTANT CONCEPTS IN DETERMINING INCOME

Accountants have developed a number of concepts and conventions to help determine net income. The most important include the time-period assumption, the matching convention, the accrual basis of accounting, and revenue and expense recognition.

■ THE TIME-PERIOD ASSUMPTION

Business enterprises are assumed to have an indefinite life unless there is evidence to the contrary (the going-concern assumption). However, users of financial statements, such as investors and creditors, do not wait until an enterprise ceases operating to measure the firm's performance. In order to make informed decisions, users need information, on a timely basis, about the enterprise's financial condition and performance. Thus the enterprise's life span is divided into time periods, which can be as short as a month or a quarter and are rarely longer than a year. This division of the enterprise's life span is called the **time-period assumption**.

At a minimum, firms prepare annual financial statements. If the year ends on December 31, it is considered a calendar year. However, some firms find it convenient to use a year that corresponds to their particular business cycle and so choose a year-end on the last day of another month, when inventory and activity may be lowest. For example, a magazine publisher may feel that its natural business period ends on January 31 and therefore choose that date as its year-end. A year that ends on the last day of a month other than December 31 is called a **fiscal year**. Publicly held corporations are required to issue quarterly financial statements, called **interim statements**. In addition, most firms prepare monthly financial statements for internal purposes.

■ THE MATCHING CONVENTION

The matching convention is the concept that accountants use to guide them in determining the net income for an accounting period. The **matching convention** simply states that the expenses incurred in one period to earn the revenues of that period should be offset against those revenues. Revenues are determined in accordance with revenue-recognition principles, and the expenses incurred in earning those revenues during the period are matched against them. This is a powerful convention in accounting and is the basis for many of the accounting concepts and procedures you will learn. In order to provide the best matching of expenses with revenues and the most useful income figure, the accrual basis of accounting has been developed. This is considered to be the generally accepted method of accounting and will be discussed next.

■ THE ACCRUAL VERSUS THE CASH BASIS OF ACCOUNTING

The accrual basis and the cash basis are the two basic methods of accounting. Each method uses a different set of rules for recognizing revenues and expenses. In the **accrual basis** of accounting, revenues, expenses, and other changes in assets, liabilities, and owners' equity are accounted for in the period in which the economic event takes place, not when the cash inflows and outflows take place. In the **cash basis** of accounting, revenues and expenses are not recognized until the cash is received or paid.

The Accrual Basis

As previously noted, the best matching of revenues and expenses takes place when the accrual basis of accounting is used. This means that the financial effects of transactions and economic events are recognized by the enterprise when they occur, rather than when the actual cash is received or paid by the enterprise. For example, sales are recognized as revenues when they are made, and services are recognized when they are performed and there is a right to receive payment, regardless of when the cash is actually collected. That is, a sale on account is recognized in the same manner as a cash sale is. The only difference is that Accounts Receivable rather than Cash is increased or debited at the time of sale. When the cash from the sale on account is collected, no revenue is recognized. The cash collection is just an exchange of one asset, Accounts Receivable, for another asset, Cash. The total amount of assets remains the same. The revenue and asset increases were recognized at the time the sale took place.

With the accrual basis of accounting, if cash, such as a deposit or a down payment, is received before the actual sale or the performance of a service, no revenue is recognized until performance. Instead, a liability to perform a future service or to deliver a product is recognized at the time the cash is received. This liability is usually referred to as an *unearned revenue*. When the service is finally performed or the sale is made, the revenue is then recognized, and the liability is decreased. The entries associated with this particular account will be discussed in Chapter 4.

Expenses are recognized in a similar manner. That is, expenses are considered to be incurred or used when the goods or services are consumed by the enterprise, not necessarily when the cash outflow takes place. For example, the Carson Corporation records as a June expense the salaries earned by its employees in that month, even though those salaries may not be paid until July. This is accomplished by recording Salaries Payable in June. When June's salaries are paid in July, no expense is recognized at that time. Both Salaries Payable and Cash are reduced at that time, but no expense is involved. The decrease in the firm's net assets and the corresponding expense were recorded in June.

In many cases, the cash is paid at the same time the expense is incurred. For example, plumbing repairs may be paid when the services are rendered. In this case, Repairs and Maintenance Expense would be recorded when the cash was paid. However, it is not the payment of cash that triggers the recognition of the expense. The expense is recognized because the plumbing services were received and an obligation to pay came into being. Finally, using the accrual basis of accounting, if cash is paid before incurring the expense, no expense is recognized at that time. For example, if a firm prepays its June rent in May, the prepayment is considered an asset in May and is not considered an expense until June, when the service has been received.

The Cash Basis

Under the cash basis of accounting, a revenue is recognized when the cash is received, and an expense is recognized when the cash is paid. The cash basis of accounting thus does not properly match revenues and expenses. This is because the recognition of revenue and expense is contingent upon the timing of cash receipts and disbursements; depending on this timing, the expenses of one period could be matched against the sales or services of another period. The cash basis of accounting is therefore not a generally accepted accounting principle for financial reporting purposes. However, many professionals, such as doctors and lawyers, who prepare financial statements solely for their own use, use the cash basis in order to simplify their record-keeping. In addition, most individuals use the cash basis of accounting for personal affairs and in determining their taxable income.

An Example of the Cash versus the Accrual Basis of Accounting

An example of the difference between the accrual and the cash bases of accounting is presented in Exhibit 3-2. This table shows how ten different transactions for the month of May affect accrual basis and cash basis income. As the exhibit shows, total accrual basis revenue is equal to cash sales made in May, plus all sales made on credit during this period. Total expenses during the period are equal to those incurred and paid in cash during May, plus expenses incurred on credit during the month. Cash basis net income is solely a function of when the cash is received and paid. In the remainder of this book, assume that the accrual basis of accounting is being used unless otherwise specified.

EXHIBIT 3–2

Comparison of Cash and Accrual Bases			
		Revenue/Expense Amounts Recognized in May	
Transactions in May		**Cash Basis**	**Accrual Basis**
1. Cash sales during May	$10,000	$10,000	$10,000
2. Credit sales during May	12,000		12,000
3. Cash collected from May's credit sales	4,000	4,000	
4. Cash collected from April's credit sales	5,000	5,000	
5. Cash deposit received in May for a sale in June	1,000	1,000	
Total revenues		$20,000	$22,000
6. Cash expenses incurred and paid in May	$ 8,000	8,000	8,000
7. Expenses incurred on account in May	7,000		7,000
8. Cash paid on May's expense incurred on account	4,000	4,000	
9. Cash paid in May on April's expenses incurred on account	3,000	3,000	
10. Insurance expense effective June 1 paid on May 17	2,000	2,000	
Total expenses		$17,000	$15,000
Net income		$ 3,000	$ 7,000

■ REVENUE AND EXPENSE RECOGNITION

In determining when revenue should be recognized, accountants follow what is often referred to as the **realization principle**. In short, this principle states that revenue is earned and therefore should be recognized when two events occur:

1. The earnings process is essentially complete.

2. There is objective evidence as to the exchange or sale price.

Depending on a firm's particular business and industry, these two events can take place at different points in the earnings cycle. Exhibit 3-3 depicts the different points at which these events may occur. However, the earnings process is continuous, and for most firms it is difficult to state at what exact point the earnings process is complete. At each point in the process, some earnings take place as the firm adds value to the products before their actual sale. Hartman's flower shop provides a good example of this problem. Assume that Hartman purchases some marigold seeds for $10. The seeds are then planted and eventually grow into plants that are sold for $25. At what point should Hartman recognize the $15 earned from the production and sale of the plants? Another way of looking at the issue is to ask, "When should the value of the plants be increased from their historical cost of $10 to their sales price of $25?"

EXHIBIT 3–3

Earnings Cycle

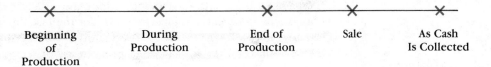

| Beginning of Production | During Production | End of Production | Sale | As Cash Is Collected |

Sale As the Point of Revenue Recognition

The application of the revenue-realization principle to most firms leads to the conclusion that the point of sale is the most realistic point at which to recognize revenue. Thus, in the above example, no revenue would be recognized until the marigold plants were sold. There are two reasons for this. First, at the point of sale an actual exchange takes place that provides objective evidence of the amount of revenue actually realized. That is, a transaction has been completed. Second, most accountants feel that the earnings process is not complete until an actual sale is made. The sale, therefore, represents the culmination of the earnings process, and so revenue should not be recognized before this point. For these reasons, the sale is considered to be the critical event in the earnings process.

For a service firm, revenues are normally considered earned when the services have been performed. Revenues from allowing others to use the firm's assets include interest, rents, and royalties. Revenues from these items are considered to be earned as time passes or as the assets are used. Finally, gains or losses from disposing of other assets are recognized as of the date of sale.

Alternative Recognition Points

Exhibit 3-3 points out that there are other times when revenue recognition can take place. These are based on industry characteristics that make it reasonable to recognize revenue at a time different from that of the actual sale. The percentage of completion, the completion of production, and the installment methods will be examined here.

Percentage of Completion. Large-scale construction projects can take several years to complete. The primary issue faced by accountants is whether to delay recognizing the revenue from the project until it is complete or to recognize a portion of the revenue in each of the years it takes to complete the project. In the completed-contract method, all of the profits earned from the contract are recognized in the year that the project is completed. An alternative method is the percentage-of-completion method. This method recognizes revenue during construction in proportion to the amount of work completed on the project; by its end, all revenue has been recognized. Because of the reliability principle, the percentage-of-completion method should be used only if reasonable estimates of construction progress and future costs can be made.

Completion of Production. In some situations, it is reasonable to recognize revenue at the point at which the production cycle is complete, but before sale. These situations occur when indistinguishable goods are sold in large, well-developed markets. Examples include certain agricultural products, such as wheat, and precious metals. Because the market can absorb all of the production of these products, a sale is ensured at harvest or mining, and an objective price can be obtained from the marketplace. Because the sale is ensured, the earnings process is complete at the end of production rather than at the point of sale.

Installment Basis. In a few situations, accountants will delay the recognition of revenue until the cash is collected from the sale. These installment sales are long-term payment plans, in which the buyer makes a relatively low down payment and the payments are spread over a number of years. In earlier years, many companies, such as land development firms, recognized all the revenue from their sales at the time of sale but collected only a small portion of the receivable before the buyer defaulted on the arrangement. As a result, accountants require the installment method of accounting to be used only in certain circumstances. Under the installment method, which is used only when there is a great deal of uncertainty regarding the collection of the receivable, revenues will be recognized only in proportion to the cash collected.

Expense Recognition

Expense recognition is the other essential ingredient of the matching convention. With the accrual basis of accounting, expenses are recognized when incurred and at that point are matched against revenues. This matching is accomplished by relating the expense to either (1) a particular product sold or a service rendered or (2) a particular time period in which the revenue is recognized.

Some expenses can be related directly to the product that the firm sells or the service it renders. Cost of goods sold is probably the most obvious example. Inventory costs are accumulated in the asset account, Inventory, and when the merchandise is sold, these costs are written off as expenses to Cost of Goods Sold in direct proportion to the units sold. Sales commissions are another example of an expense that is matched against revenues as the revenues are earned. This is because the amount of the commission is a direct function of the amount of the sale.

Most expenses of a business cannot be directly related to a product or service. These expenses are called **period expenses** and are matched against revenues in the period during which the expenses are incurred. Included in period expenses are what one normally thinks of as selling and general expenses. Examples include salaries other than direct commissions, insurance, and rent expense.

■ RECORDING INCOME STATEMENT TRANSACTIONS

This section will illustrate how to record income statement transactions. Following the pattern of Chapter 2, it will first cover the debit and credit rules and then the actual journal entries. Finally, transactions of the Hartman Flower Company will be analyzed.

■ DEBIT AND CREDIT RULES

The debit and credit rules for income statement transactions are based on the accounting equation and the definition of revenues and expenses. Remember that the accounting equation is

Assets = Liabilities + Stockholders' Equity

Stockholders' equity can be classified into two major components, Capital Stock and Retained Earnings. Therefore the accounting equation can be rewritten as

Assets = Liabilities + Capital Stock + Retained Earnings

One way to interpret this equation is to say that assets have several sources: the creditors (liabilities), the investors (capital stock), and the business itself through profitable operations (retained earnings). Thus retained earnings represent the increases in net assets contributed by the profitable operations of the business after all dividends have been deducted. Corporations must maintain separate accounts for Retained Earnings and Capital Stock because, in most states, dividends cannot exceed the cumulative earnings of the business.

These concepts can be summarized by successively expanding the accounting equation, as shown below. The essential point to remember is how income statement accounts fit into the overall accounting equation. These accounts are summarized through changes in retained earnings and corresponding changes in the net assets (assets minus liabilities) of the firm.

Assets =   Liabilities + Stockholders' Equity

Assets =   Liabilities + Capital Stock + Retained Earnings

Assets = Liabilities + Capital Stock + Retained Earnings, beginning of period + Net income − Dividends

Net Income =   Revenues + Gains − Expenses − Losses

Assets = Liabilities + Capital Stock + Retained Earnings, beginning of period + Revenues + Gains − Expenses − Losses − Dividends

Actually, it would be possible to record all income statement transactions directly in the Retained Earnings account. However, if this were done, it would be very difficult to determine separate revenue and expense accounts, such as Sales and Cost of Goods Sold. Therefore accountants use separate revenue and expense accounts during the period in order to capture this essential information. At the end of the period, the net effect of these accounts is transferred to Retained Earnings. Because separate revenue and expense accounts are used only during the period and are zeroed at the end of each period, they are often referred to as **temporary** or **nominal accounts**. In contrast, balance sheet accounts, including Retained Earnings, are often referred to as **real accounts**, because they maintain a running balance that extends beyond the accounting period.

The rules for revenue and expense accounts follow the same rules as those for the Retained Earnings account, which is part of stockholders' equity. These rules are illustrated below.

	Retained Earnings	
	Debit	Credit
	Decrease	Increase

Any Expense Account		**Any Revenue Account**	
Increase	Decrease	Decrease	Increase
+	−	−	+
Debit	Credit	Debit	Credit
Normal Balance:		Normal Balance:	
Debit		Credit	

These rules should be interpreted as follows:

1. Revenues represent increases in Retained Earnings. Increases in Retained Earnings are recorded on the right side of the ledger account as credits. Therefore increases in revenues are recorded on the right side of the ledger account as credits.

2. Expenses represent decreases in Retained Earnings. Decreases in Retained Earnings are recorded on the left side of the ledger account as debits. Therefore, because an increase in an expense represents a decrease in Retained Earnings, these increases are recorded on the left side of the expense ledger accounts as debits.

■ JOURNAL ENTRIES

Journal entry rules for income statement accounts parallel the rules for balance sheet transactions. Debits are recorded first at the left margin of the journal, and then credits are indented slightly. To illustrate how revenue and expense transactions are recorded, assume that a firm enters into the following eight transactions. After each transaction, the appropriate journal entry is made. For simplicity, the transaction number is entered into the date column, and the reference column is not used, since the transaction has not been posted.

1. **During the month, the firm made sales of $20,000, $5,000 on account and $15,000 for cash. The journal entry is:**

Date	Account Title	Ref.	Debit	Credit
1	Cash		15,000	
	Accounts Receivable		5,000	
	Sales			20,000
	To record sales for cash and on account.			

The increase in Sales is recorded as a credit because it represents an increase in Retained Earnings. The increases in Cash and Accounts Receivable are recorded as debits.

2. **The firm determines that the cost of inventory sold in Transaction 1 is $14,000. The journal entry is:**

Date	Account Title	Ref.	Debit	Credit
2	Cost of Goods Sold		14,000	
	Inventory			14,000
	To record cost of goods sold.			

The increase in the expense, Cost of Goods Sold, is a decrease in Retained Earnings and is therefore recorded as a debit. The decrease in the asset, Inventory, is a decrease in an asset account and is therefore recorded as a credit.

3. **The firm's employees earned salaries of $1,500 but will not be paid until next week. The journal entry is:**

Date	Account Title	Ref.	Debit	Credit
3	Salaries Expense		1,500	
	Salaries Payable			1,500
	To record salaries expense incurred but not yet paid.			

Again, the increase in the expense, Salaries, is a decrease in Retained Earnings and is thus recorded as a debit. The increase in the liability account, Salaries Payable, is recorded as a credit.

4. **The firm collected $1,000 of the sales made on account in Transaction 1. The journal entry is:**

Date	Account Title	Ref.	Debit	Credit
4	Cash		1,000	
	Accounts Receivable			1,000
	To record the collection of accounts receivable.			

This transaction does not involve the recognition of revenue. It is the collection of a receivable that was generated from the sale recorded in Transaction 1 and is an exchange of one asset, Cash, for another, Accounts Receivable. It is presented to point out once again that revenue and expense recognition is not necessarily tied to cash receipts and disbursements.

5. **Repairs and maintenance of $500 were incurred and immediately paid in cash. The journal entry is:**

Date	Account Title	Ref.	Debit	Credit
5	Repairs and Maintenance Expense		500	
	Cash			500
	To record payment of $500 in repairs and maintenance expense.			

This transaction illustrates the payment of an expense in cash rather than the incurrence of a liability. The increase in the Repairs and Maintenance Expense account decreases Retained Earnings and is thus recorded as a debit. The decrease in Cash is recorded as a credit.

6. **The firm paid the $1,500 of salaries owed that was generated from Transaction 3. The journal entry is:**

Date	Account Title	Ref.	Debit	Credit
6	Salaries Payable		1,500	
	Cash			1,500
	To record the payment			
	of salaries payable.			

This transaction does not involve the recognition of an expense. It is the payment of salaries payable that resulted from the recognition of salaries payable in Transaction 3. It is presented to point out once more that revenue and expense recognition is not necessarily tied to cash receipts and disbursements.

7. **The firm sold, for $1,000 cash, some marketable securities that it had purchased for $700 in a prior year. The journal entry is:**

Date	Account Title	Ref.	Debit	Credit
7	Cash		1,000	
	Marketable Securities			700
	Gain on Sale of Marketable Securities			300
	To record gain on sale of marketable			
	securities.			

This transaction shows how to record a gain or a loss. This transaction is recorded net, in the sense that a revenue of $1,000 and an expense of $700 are not shown. Only the net gain of $300 is shown in the account Gain on Sale of Marketable Securities.

8. **The firm declares and pays a $5,000 dividend. The journal entry is:**

Date	Account Title	Ref.	Debit	Credit
8	Retained Earnings		5,000	
	Cash			5,000
	To record the declaration and payment			
	of a $5,000 cash dividend.			

The declaration and payment of the cash dividend is recorded directly as a reduction of Retained Earnings and does not represent an expense to the firm. If the firm desired, the dividend could be debited to a Dividends Declared account. If this is done, the amount must eventually be transferred to Retained Earnings. In reality, dividends are often declared several weeks prior to their payment. If this is done, a liability, Dividends Payable, will be credited at the time of the declaration. When the dividend is paid, Cash is credited and Dividends Payable is debited. The debit is still to either the Retained Earnings or the Dividends Declared account.

■ TRANSACTIONS FOR THE HARTMAN FLOWER COMPANY

To illustrate further how to record income statement transactions, let us examine transactions for the Hartman Flower Company's first month of operations. Remember that the company was organized in April but did not record any sales until June. The trial balance as of May 31, 1990 is reproduced in Exhibit 3-4. June's transactions are recorded in the general journal, shown in Exhibit 3-5. After the journal entries have been posted to the appropriate accounts, the resulting T accounts are shown in Exhibit 3-6. Finally, the new trial balance as of June 30 is shown in Exhibit 3-7.

EXHIBIT 3–4

HARTMAN FLOWER COMPANY Trial Balance May 31, 1990		
	Debits	Credits
Cash	$6,290	
Accounts receivable	0	
Inventory	11,000	
Office supplies	1,000	
Garden supplies	380	
Licenses	120	
Prepaid insurance	2,400	
Land	5,000	
Store furniture and fixtures	10,200	
Buildings	15,000	
Accounts payable		$ 2,390
Bank loan payable		5,000
Capital stock		44,000
Totals	$51,390	$51,390

Transactions for the month of June

- June 2: The company placed an advertisement in a local newspaper. A bill of $100 was received from the newspaper company, payable within the month.

- June 15: Sales of plants and flowers for the first half of June totaled $8,000, of which $3,000 were for cash and $5,000 were on account.

- June 15: The cost of the flowers sold was $6,000.

- June 16: Salaries of $800 were paid in cash on June 16.

- June 20: The firm made another purchase of inventory of $13,100, on account.

- June 23: Accounts Receivable of $4,500 were collected.

- June 24: Repairs and Maintenance expense of $40 was paid in cash.

- June 26: The firm paid a utility bill of $200 for the month of June.

- June 29: Accounts Payable of $10,070 were paid.

- June 30: Sales for the second half of the month totaled $12,000, $7,000 for cash and $5,000 on credit.

- June 30: The cost of the inventory sold was $8,000.

EXHIBIT 3–5

HARTMAN FLOWER COMPANY General Journal				Page GJ-2
Date	Account Title	Ref.	Debit	Credit
1990 June 2	Advertising Expense	605	100	
	Accounts Payable	201		100
	To record advertisement placed in newspaper.			
15	Cash	101	3,000	
	Accounts Receivable	106	5,000	
	Sales	401		8,000
	To record sales for the first half of June.			

(continued)

EXHIBIT 3–5

(continued)

Date	Account Title	Ref.	Debit	Credit
1990 June				
15	Cost of Goods Sold	500	6,000	
	Inventory	110		6,000
	To record cost of flowers sold.			
16	Salaries Expense	601	800	
	Cash	101		800
	To record salaries for the first half of June.			
20	Inventory	110	13,100	
	Accounts Payable	201		13,100
	To record purchase of inventory on account.			
23	Cash	101	4,500	
	Accounts Receivable	106		4,500
	To record collection of cash on account.			
24	Repairs and Maintenance Expense	701	40	
	Cash	101		40
	To record repairs and maintenance expense paid in cash.			
26	Utility Expense	703	200	
	Cash	101		200
	To record payment of utility bill.			
29	Accounts Payable	201	10,070	
	Cash	101		10,070
	To record payment on account.			
30	Cash	101	7,000	
	Accounts Receivable	106	5,000	
	Sales	401		12,000
	To record sales for the last half of June.			
30	Cost of Goods Sold	500	8,000	
	Inventory	110		8,000
	To record cost of flowers sold.			

EXHIBIT 3–6

HARTMAN FLOWER COMPANY
T Accounts for June 1990

Cash			101
6/1 Bal. 6,290		6/16	800
6/15	3,000	6/24	40
6/23	4,500	6/26	200
6/30	7,000	6/29	10,070
6/30 Bal. 9,680			

Accounts Receivable			106
6/15	5,000	6/23 4,500	
6/30	5,000		
6/30 Bal. 5,500			

Inventory			110
6/1 Bal. 11,000		6/15 6,000	
6/20	13,100	6/30 8,000	
6/30 Bal. 10,100			

Office Supplies		115
6/1 Bal. 1,000		

Garden Supplies		116
6/1 Bal. 380		

License		120
6/1 Bal. 120		

Prepaid Insurance		121
6/1 Bal. 2,400		

Land		150
6/1 Bal. 5,000		

(continued)

EXHIBIT 3-6
(continued)

Store Furniture and Fixtures 160	
6/1 Bal. 10,200	

Buildings 165	
6/1 Bal. 15,000	

Accounts Payable 201

6/29 10,070	6/1 Bal.	2,390	
	6/2	100	
	6/20	13,100	
	6/30 Bal.	5,520	

Bank Loan Payable 205

	6/1 Bal. 5,000

Capital Stock 301

	6/1 Bal. 44,000

Sales 401

	6/15	8,000
	6/30	12,000
	6/30 Bal.	20,000

Cost of Goods Sold 500

6/15	6,000
6/30	8,000
6/30 Bal.	14,000

Salaries Expense 601

6/16 800	

Advertising Expense 605

6/2 100	

Repairs and Maintenance Expense 701

6/24 40	

Utility Expense 703

6/26 200	

EXHIBIT 3-7

HARTMAN FLOWER COMPANY		
Trial Balance		
June 30, 1990		
	Debits	**Credits**
Cash	$ 9,680	
Accounts receivable	5,500	
Inventory	10,100	
Office supplies	1,000	
Garden supplies	380	
License	120	
Prepaid insurance	2,400	
Land	5,000	
Store furniture and fixtures	10,200	
Buildings	15,000	
Accounts payable		$ 5,520
Bank loan payable		5,000
Capital stock		44,000
Sales		20,000
Cost of goods sold	14,000	
Salaries expense	800	
Advertising expense	100	
Repairs and maintenance expense	40	
Utility expense	200	
Totals	$74,520	$74,520

Three points need to be made about this example. The journal entries represent summary transactions for the month. In a real situation, journal entries would be made daily to record the transactions as they occur, but in this example, sales are recorded only twice a month rather than on a day-to-day basis. The trial balance as of June 30, 1990 (Exhibit 3-7) illustrates the manner in which the accounts should be listed. Note that the balance sheet accounts (assets, liabilities, and stockholders' equity) are listed first, followed by the income statement accounts (revenues and expense accounts). Finally, if the trial balance does not balance, you should follow the error identification suggestions made in the previous chapter.

■ FINANCIAL STATEMENTS

At this point in the accounting cycle, it is time to prepare a preliminary income statement, statement of retained earnings, and comparative balance sheet. These financial statements will help Hartman evaluate the progress of his business during its first full month of operation. However, these statements are only preliminary, because not all the steps in the accounting cycle have been completed. Hartman has recorded only **external transactions**. For example, a sale affects the firm and the buyer, an outside party, but there are a number of **internal transactions** or events that have not been recorded; these affect only the firm. For example, during the month of June, the Hartman Flower Company used some of the office supplies that it purchased in May. However, it is too time-consuming to make journal entries every time pencils or other supplies are taken from the supply closet. Therefore the amount of supplies used is determined at the end of the month, and an entry is made at that time to reflect this internal event. These transactions, called *adjustments*, will be discussed in the next chapter.

■ HARTMAN FLOWER COMPANY STATEMENTS

The financial statements for the Hartman Flower Company are shown in the next few exhibits. The income statement (Exhibit 3-8) covers a three-month period ending on June 30. Even though sales did not actually begin until June, the firm was in existence for that three-month period. The expenses are listed with the largest amount first. This is just one way to list them; they could also be listed alphabetically or by categories such as Selling and General and Administrative. Because of the preliminary nature

EXHIBIT 3-8

HARTMAN FLOWER COMPANY
Income Statement
For the Three Months Ended June 30, 1990

Revenues		
Sales		$20,000
Expenses		
Cost of goods sold	$14,000	
Salaries expense	800	
Utility expense	200	
Advertising expense	100	
Repairs and maintenance	40	
Total expenses		15,140
Net income		$ 4,860

of this chapter, income taxes have not been discussed. As the next chapter will show, income taxes are the subject of an adjustment.

The retained earnings statement (Exhibit 3-9) covers the same period as the income statement. Because the Hartman Flower Company was formed April 1, there is no balance in Retained Earnings at that date. The net income of $4,860 increases Retained Earnings. Since the company did not declare any dividends, the balance in Retained Earnings on June 30 is also $4,860. The retained earnings statement for the next month will show a beginning balance on July 1 of $4,860.

EXHIBIT 3–9

HARTMAN FLOWER COMPANY	
Retained Earnings Statement	
For the Three Months Ended June 30, 1990	
Retained earnings, April 1, 1990	$ 0
Add: Net income from April 1 to June 30	4,860
Retained earnings, June 30, 1990	$4,860

The June 30, 1990 and May 31, 1990 balance sheets for the Hartman Flower Company are presented in Exhibit 3-10. Because two periods are shown, this is referred to as a **comparative balance sheet**. Except for the Retained Earnings balance, the amounts for the June 30 balance sheet come from the June 30 trial balance (Exhibit 3-7). The balance in the Retained Earnings account is taken from the retained earnings statement (Exhibit 3-9). The data for the May 31 balance sheet is from the trial balance as of that date (Exhibit 3-4).

EXHIBIT 3–10

HARTMAN FLOWER COMPANY		
Comparative Balance Sheet		
Assets	June 30, 1990	May 31, 1990
Cash	$ 9,680	$ 6,290
Accounts receivable	5,500	0
Inventory	10,100	11,000
Office supplies	1,000	1,000
Garden supplies	380	380
License	120	120
Prepaid insurance	2,400	2,400
Land	5,000	5,000
Store furniture and fixtures	10,200	10,200
Buildings	15,000	15,000
Total assets	$59,380	$51,390
Liabilities and Stockholders' Equity		
Liabilities		
Accounts payable	$ 5,520	$ 2,390
Bank loan payable	5,000	5,000
Total liabilities	$10,520	$ 7,390
Stockholders' equity		
Capital stock	$44,000	$44,000
Retained earnings	4,860	0
Total stockholders' equity	$48,860	$44,000
Total liabilities and stockholders' equity	$59,380	$51,390

If you compare the stockholders' equity section of the two balance sheets in Exhibit 3-10, you will see that at June 30, Retained Earnings had a balance of $4,860, while at May 31, the balance was zero. The $4,860 represents an increase in the net assets due to the profitable operations of the business. This important point can also be seen by comparison of the net assets at June 30 and May 31, 1990:

Date	Net Assets	=	Assets	−	Liabilities
June 30	$48,860	=	$59,380	−	$10,520
May 31	44,000	=	51,390	−	7,390
	$ 4,860	=	$ 7,990	−	$ 3,130

You should note that retained earnings represents the increase in net assets, not just the increase in Cash. In this example, Cash alone increased $3,390 ($9,680 − $6,290) during the period. Other assets and liabilities also increased or decreased, causing a net increase of $4,860 in net assets.

At the beginning of this chapter, it was stated that accountants use the transaction approach to measure income. That is, the accountant measures the income and expense transactions that occurred during the period and then summarizes them on the income statement. The effect of these transactions, plus any additional capital contributions and less any withdrawals, is added to the historical-cost net assets at the beginning of the period in order to determine the historical-cost net assets at the end of the period. Using the diagram in Exhibit 3-1 and inserting the figures for the Hartman Flower Company results in Exhibit 3-11. This diagram shows how the balance sheet, income statement, and statement of retained earnings are related to one another. Two consecutive balance sheets are, in part, linked by the statement of retained earnings. The statement of retained earnings summarizes the factors that have caused Retained Earnings to change: net income or net loss and dividends. The income statement explains the change in Retained Earnings due to the profitable or unprofitable operations. The statement of cash flows, introduced in Chapter 1, further explains changes in the Cash account. The term *articulation* in accounting refers to this relationship among the financial statements.

EXHIBIT 3–11

Historical-Cost Net Assets 5/31/90 $44,000	+	Net Income for the Period $4,860	+	Capital Contributions $0 − Withdrawals $0	=	Historical-Cost Net Assets 6/30/90 $48,860

SUMMARY OF LEARNING OBJECTIVES

1. The measurement of income. There are various ways to define income. Accountants use a transaction approach to determine income; generally, only completed transactions affect income. Accountants believe that this provides the most objective measure of income. Revenues are inflows of net assets, and expenses are outflows of net assets caused by the primary operating activity of the enterprise. Gains and losses are related to other activities of the firm. Comprehensive net income or loss is the difference between the total revenues and gains and the total expenses and losses.

2. Important concepts in determining income. Accountants have developed several important concepts or conventions to help them determine income. The need for timely information requires that a firm's continuous economic activities be divided into monthly, quarterly, or yearly accounting periods. The matching convention requires that the expenses for a particular period be matched against the revenues of that period. This is best accomplished by using the accrual basis of accounting.

3. The accrual versus the cash basis of accounting. With the accrual basis of accounting, revenues are recognized when earned and expenses are recognized when incurred. With the cash basis of accounting, revenues are recognized when received and expenses are recognized when paid. The accrual basis of accounting is the generally accepted accounting method because it provides the best matching of revenues and expenses.

4. Revenue and expense recognition. With the accrual basis of accounting, revenue is recognized when it is earned. In most cases the point of sale has been chosen as the point of revenue recognition. This is because two events usually occur at the point of sale.

(a) There is objective evidence as to the exchange or sale price.

(b) The earnings process is essentially complete.

However, in limited situations, revenue may be recognized:

(a) During production, such as the percentage-of-completion method.

(b) At the end of production but prior to sale.

(c) As the cash is collected (the installment method).

Expenses are related to either a particular product sold or a service rendered, or a particular time period when revenue is recognized.

5. Recording income statement transactions. Increases in net assets from business activities are assigned to Retained Earnings and represent increases in that account. Conversely, decreases in net assets from business activities are also assigned to Retained Earnings but represent decreases. Thus the rules for revenue and expense accounts are the same as for Retained Earnings, which is a component of stockholders' equity. These rules are illustrated in the following T accounts:

Any Expense Account		Any Revenue Account	
Increase	Decrease	Decrease	Increase
+	−	−	+
Debit	Credit	Debit	Credit

6. The relationship among the financial statements. The balance sheet, income statement, and retained earnings statement are related to one another. Two consecutive balance sheets are linked by the retained earnings statement. The retained earnings statement summarizes the factors (net income or net loss and dividends) that have caused Retained Earnings to change. The income statement details the changes in Retained Earnings due to profitable or unprofitable operations. These relationships mean that the financial statements are articulated.

KEY TERMS

Accrual basis
Cash basis
Comparative balance sheet
Dividends
Expenditures
External transactions
Fiscal year
Gains
Interim statements
Internal transactions

Losses
Matching convention
Net income
Nominal (temporary) accounts
Period expenses
Real accounts
Realization principle
Receipts
Time-period assumption

**PROBLEM FOR
YOUR REVIEW**

You are the accountant for Rub-A-Dub-Dub, a large retail children's store, and have obtained the following information as of January 1, 1990.

<table>
<tr><td colspan="5" align="center">**RUB-A-DUB-DUB**
Balance Sheet
January 1, 1990</td></tr>
<tr><td>**Assets**</td><td></td><td colspan="3">**Liabilities and Stockholders' Equity**</td></tr>
<tr><td>Cash</td><td>$ 5,000</td><td>Liabilities</td><td></td><td></td></tr>
<tr><td>Accounts receivable</td><td>6,000</td><td>Accounts payable</td><td>$ 4,600</td><td></td></tr>
<tr><td>Inventory</td><td>12,000</td><td>Salaries payable</td><td>1,400</td><td></td></tr>
<tr><td>Office supplies</td><td>1,500</td><td>Bank loan payable</td><td>10,000</td><td></td></tr>
<tr><td>Land</td><td>25,000</td><td>Total liabilities</td><td></td><td>$ 16,000</td></tr>
<tr><td>Building</td><td>45,000</td><td>Stockholders' equity</td><td></td><td></td></tr>
<tr><td>Furniture and fixtures</td><td>15,000</td><td>Capital stock</td><td>$50,000</td><td></td></tr>
<tr><td></td><td></td><td>Retained earnings</td><td>43,500</td><td></td></tr>
<tr><td></td><td></td><td>Total stockholders' equity</td><td></td><td>$ 93,500</td></tr>
<tr><td></td><td></td><td>Total liabilities and stock-</td><td></td><td></td></tr>
<tr><td>Total assets</td><td>$109,500</td><td>holders' equity</td><td></td><td>$109,500</td></tr>
</table>

The following events occurred throughout 1990 and are numbered because they represent summary events for the year.

1. Inventory totaling $60,000 was purchased on account during the year.

2. The firm purchased a two-year comprehensive insurance policy for $3,600 cash. The policy takes effect on April 1, 1991.

3. Sales for the year amounted to $80,000, of which $50,000 was for cash and $30,000 was on account.

4. The cost of the inventory sold amounted to $52,000.

5. Salaries totaling $10,000 were paid during the year.

6. Salaries payable of $1,400 were paid.

7. Cash collections on account totaled $28,000.

8. Cash payments on account were $52,000.

9. Land that cost Rub-A-Dub-Dub $5,000 was sold for $5,200 cash.

10. The following expenses were paid in cash:

Advertising	$1,000
Utilities	750
Automobile expense	2,000
Repairs and maintenance	450

REQUIRED: **(1)** Make the journal entries to record these events.

            (2) Post the entries to ledger T accounts, and open new accounts where appropriate.

            (3) Prepare a trial balance.

SOLUTION
(1) JOURNAL ENTRIES

1.	Inventory	60,000	
	Accounts Payable		60,000
	To record purchase of inventory on account.		
2.	Prepaid Insurance	3,600	
	Cash		3,600
	To record purchase of two-year insurance policy.		
3.	Cash	50,000	
	Accounts Receivable	30,000	
	Sales		80,000
	To record sales on cash and credit.		
4.	Cost of Goods Sold	52,000	
	Inventory		52,000
	To record cost of goods sold.		
5.	Salaries Expense	10,000	
	Cash		10,000
	To record salaries for the period.		
6.	Salaries Payable	1,400	
	Cash		1,400
	To record payment of salaries.		
7.	Cash	28,000	
	Accounts Receivable		28,000
	To record cash collected on account.		
8.	Accounts Payable	52,000	
	Cash		52,000
	To record cash payments on account.		
9.	Cash	5,200	
	Gain on Sale of Land		200
	Land		5,000
	To record gain on sale of land.		
10.	Advertising Expense	1,000	
	Utilities Expense	750	
	Automobile Expense	2,000	
	Repairs and Maintenance Expense	450	
	Cash		4,200
	To record expenses for the period.		

(2) T ACCOUNTS

Cash

1/1	Bal.	5,000	(2)		3,600
(3)		50,000	(5)		10,000
(7)		28,000	(6)		1,400
(9)		5,200	(8)		52,000
			(10)		4,200
12/31	Bal.	17,000			

Accounts Receivable

1/1	Bal.	6,000	(7)	28,000
(3)		30,000		
12/31	Bal.	8,000		

Inventory

1/1	Bal.	12,000	(4)	52,000
(1)		60,000		
12/31	Bal.	20,000		

Office Supplies

1/1 1,500	

Prepaid Insurance

(2) 3,600	

Land

1/1	Bal.	25,000	(9)	5,000
12/31	Bal.	20,000		

Building	
1/1 Bal. 45,000	

Furniture and Fixtures	
1/1 Bal. 15,000	

Accounts Payable	
(8) 52,000	1/1 Bal. 4,600
	(1) 60,000
	12/31 Bal. 12,600

Salaries Payable	
(6) 1,400	1/1 Bal. 1,400

Bank Loan Payable	
	1/1 Bal. 10,000

Capital Stock	
	1/1 Bal. 50,000

Retained Earnings	
	1/1 Bal. 43,500

Sales	
	(3) 80,000

Cost of Goods Sold	
(4) 52,000	

Salaries Expense	
(5) 10,000	

Advertising Expense	
(10) 1,000	

Utilities Expense	
(10) 750	

Automobile Expense	
(10) 2,000	

Repairs and Maintenance Expense	
(10) 450	

Gain on Sale of Land	
	(9) 200

(3) TRIAL BALANCE

RUB-A-DUB-DUB
Trial Balance
December 31, 1990

Cash	$ 17,000	
Accounts receivable	8,000	
Inventory	20,000	
Office supplies	1,500	
Prepaid insurance	3,600	
Land	20,000	
Building	45,000	
Furniture and fixtures	15,000	
Accounts payable		$12,600
Salaries payable		0
Bank loan payable		10,000
Capital stock		50,000
Retained earnings		43,500
Sales		80,000
Cost of goods sold	52,000	
Salaries expense	10,000	
Advertising expense	1,000	
Utilities expense	750	
Automobile expense	2,000	
Repairs and maintenance expense	450	
Gain on sale of land		200
Totals	$196,300	$196,300

QUESTIONS

1. How does the accountant measure income? When is income generally realized?

2. What are the main components of an income statement?

3. Define revenues and expenses, and explain how they differ from gains and losses.

4. How do the time-period assumption and the matching concept relate to the measurement of income for the period?

5. Compare and contrast the accrual basis and the cash basis of accounting. Which method is favored by accountants, and why?

6. A friend of yours was told by his accountant that his business was profitable during the year. However, your friend is concerned because his cash decreased during the year. Explain to him how this can happen.

7. During the month, the Pfeifer Corporation sold 100 items for a total of $10,000, $8,000 of which was collected in the current month and $2,000 in the next month. The firm also collected $1,000 during the current month from last month's sales. How much revenue is recognized on the accrual basis? How much on the cash basis?

8. State the realization rule. Give an example, other than those in the text, of when a firm might recognize revenue at a time other than at a point of sale.

9. You have decided to enter the magazine business. All subscriptions are for two years, payable in advance. You will publish monthly. When should you recognize the revenue from the subscriptions?

10. Do you agree with the following statement? Why or why not? There is one point at which all firms should recognize revenue: the point of sale.

11. Why don't accountants directly enter revenue and expense transactions in the Retained Earnings account?

12. Why are revenue and expense accounts called *temporary* or *nominal* accounts?

13. Give three examples each of revenue and expense accounts. Describe the effect of a debit or a credit on each.

14. Why is an income statement reported for a specific period, whereas a balance sheet is reported at a specific time?

15. What happens to retained earnings if there is a loss during a certain period? Can dividends be distributed if there is a loss during the period?

16. If net income is a summary of revenues and gains minus expenses and losses, why can't you just take "cash in" minus "cash out" to determine net income?

17. What is meant by the statement that gains and losses are net concepts?

18. Why would a deposit or down payment received before a sale be considered a liability? Why would a prepaid expense be considered an asset?

19. What is the difference between a fiscal year and a calendar year?

20. Do you think it would be more difficult to maintain books on an accrual or a cash basis? Why?

EXERCISES

Note: Unless otherwise specified, assume that the accrual basis of accounting is used in all exercises and problems.

E1. Recognizing Accounts. Examine the following accounts and indicate whether they are asset, liability, stockholders' equity, revenue, or expense accounts. State whether a debit or a credit increases each account.

(a) Salary expense

(b) Prepaid insurance

(c) Buildings

(d) Interest earned

(e) Unearned rent

(f) Sales

(g) Retained earnings

(h) Cost of goods sold

(i) Taxes payable

(j) Commissions paid to salespeople

E2. Recognition of Revenue and Expense Transactions. A summary of the transactions into which the Usher Corporation entered during October and November is reproduced below. State which of the events affected the income statement during the month of October.

(a) The company needed additional funds, so the owners made an additional $50,000 investment.

(b) The firm collected $40,000 on account from credit sales made during September.

(c) Cash sales during October totaled $8,000.

(d) The firm paid its October salaries of $5,000 in early November.

(e) The firm paid $40 for some plumbing repairs made in August.

(f) October sales on account totaled $10,000.

(g) The firm repaid a bank loan. The original amount of the loan, made on October 1, was $5,000. At the end of October, the $5,000 was repaid, plus $50 in interest for the month.

(h) A customer placed an order for 50 dozen items at a sales price of $2,000. The order will be shipped in December. No deposit was received.

(i) A dividend of $1,000 was declared and paid in October.

(j) A dividend of $500 was paid in November.

(k) Another customer ordered a special item to be delivered in early January. The customer made a $1,000 deposit in October when the order was placed.

E3. Recording Journal Entries. The Golden Bear Company, a sporting goods store, entered into the following transactions during November:

- November 1: Purchased $30,000 of inventory on account.

- November 3: Placed an advertisement in the local paper for $200. Paid cash.

- November 16: Paid October's utility bill of $100. This bill was recorded as a payable at the end of October.

- November 29: Paid salaries of $8,000 for the month.

- November 30: Sales for the month amounted to $70,000, of which $45,000 was for cash.

- November 30: Cost of goods sold amounted to $50,000.

- November 30: November's utility bill of $85 was received. It will be paid in early December. Record in Accounts Payable.

REQUIRED: Prepare the necessary journal entries for the month of November.

E4. Income Statement Preparation. Sheri Ferraro is the owner of a small computer consulting service called The Professor. She has gathered the following data and asks you to help her prepare an income statement for the year ending on December 31, 1990.

(a) Salaries earned by various employees totaled $35,000. At year-end, only $28,000 of these had been paid in cash.

(b) Office rental expense for the year amounted to $20,000.

(c) Consulting fees earned during the year amounted to $110,000. Of this amount, the firm has not collected 10%.

(d) Sheri issued herself a $5,000 cash dividend.

(e) The firm sold some marketable securities for $13,000 that it had originally purchased for $20,000.

(f) Other operating expenses incurred during the year amounted to $22,000.

(g) The current tax rate is 30% of income before taxes.

REQUIRED: Prepare an income statement for the year ended December 31, 1990.

E5. Income Statement and Retained Earnings Preparation. The CBA Company runs a local news service. At the beginning of the current year, January 1, 1990, the balance in its Retained Earnings account was $25,000. During the year the following events occurred:

(a) Total subscription revenues earned amounted to $100,000.

(b) Interest revenue earned on investments totaled $2,000.

(c) Dividends declared during the year amounted to $5,000.

(d) Selling expenses incurred during the year were $54,000.

(e) General and administrative expenses incurred during the year amounted to $60,000.

(f) The owners made an additional $10,000 investment in exchange for additional capital stock.

(g) Interest expense incurred during the period amounted to $6,000.

REQUIRED: (a) Prepare an income statement for the year ended December 31, 1990.

(b) Prepare a statement of retained earnings for the year ended December 31, 1990.

E6. Income Statement Preparation. The Sandman Motor Inn has just completed its busy summer season. Taking the following facts into consideration, construct an income statement for the month ending September 30, 1990.

(a) Gross rentals were $965,312.

(b) Salary and wages equaled 30% of sales.

(c) Interest expense equaled 12% of sales.

(d) Insurance expense for the period was $1,100.

(e) Miscellaneous expenses equaled 1% of sales and wages.

(f) Advertising and promotion expenses totaled 5% of sales but were estimated to have attracted 45% of the current month's sales.

E7. Income Statement Concepts. Match the following statements from Gregory Simpson, president of Efficient Printing Services, Inc., to the relevant underlying accounting concept or concepts. There may be more than one answer for each question.

(a) Time-period assumption.

(b) Matching convention.

(c) Accrual versus cash basis of accounting.

1. "All I want to know is how you can tell me we had income of $32,000 and the bank says we're overdrawn."

2. "Well, I don't care, . . . how about not reporting income this year?"

3. "Shouldn't we wait and pay for the advertising after year-end so that our profits will look better for this period?"

4. "We're doing great! I finally collected on that $4,500 wedding invitations job we completed last year. This will improve current profits."

E8. Matching Concept. Sammy Sloppy, accountant for Good Times, Inc., has lately been ignoring the matching convention. Upon audit, you find the following trouble areas. Discuss the proper treatment of each. If Sammy did handle the issue properly, make a note of this.

(a) Good Times received $3,200 for unlimited passes to their amusement park. Although half of these passes were not valid until the following year, the entire amount was recorded currently as revenue.

(b) Two years ago, Good Times paid $2,790 for a three-year insurance policy. No insurance expense appeared on this year's income statement.

(c) At year-end, salaries earned but not yet paid equaled $850. These were not recorded until paid in the following year.

(d) Good Times bought equipment for $11,450 in the current year. Because no payments were made, neither the equipment nor the payable was recorded on the firm's books.

E9. Accrual versus Cash Basis. The Alpine Realty Corporation entered into the following transactions in July. Determine net income on the accrual and cash bases for the month of July.

1. Commissions earned and received in July	$7,100
2. Commissions earned in July but not yet received	2,125
3. Commissions received in advance on sale to close in August	500
4. Cash collected on commissions from May sales	1,000
5. Payment of June's utility and telephone bills	425

6. Payment of rent for six months, July through December   3,600

7. July's salaries paid in August   2,400

8. Received bill from plumber for services performed in
July, to be paid in August   50

E10.   Accounting Equation and Retained Earnings. The following data is available for three consecutive years of the Orazco Corporation:

	Year 1	Year 2	Year 3
Retained earnings, beginning balance	$95,000	$100,000	?
Net income	?	?	$24,000
Dividends	15,000	12,000	?
Retained earnings, ending	?	$96,000	$98,000

Complete the chart by filling in the missing amounts.

E11.   Journal Entries. Given the following facts for Instant Tan, Inc., record the proper summary journal entries for the year:

(a) Instant Tan sold 120 memberships for $395 each during the year. All memberships were sold for cash and are good only for the current year.

(b) Rent paid by Instant Tan totaled $850 per month, and all 12 months' rent was paid in cash.

(c) Members' guests are required to pay $10 for each visit. There were 450 guests for the first year. Forty percent of the guests' charges were placed on members' accounts, and the rest were paid in cash.

(d) Instant Tan's electric bills were $2,695 for the year, and all were paid in cash.

(e) During the year, Ultraviolet Repair Service was called 14 times, and their bills totaled $1,420, all of which was paid in cash.

E12.   Cash to Accrual. The income statement that follows is based on a cash basis of accounting instead of the accrual basis. Prepare an income statement on the accrual basis.

EXCAVATION INC.
Income Statement—Cash Basis
For the Year Ended December 31, 1990

Revenues		
Sales	$252,000	
Investment revenue	27,200	$279,200
Expenses		
Wages expense	$49,400	
Insurance expense	6,600	
Interest expense	12,950	
Utility expense	11,775	
Office expense	3,185	
Miscellaneous expense	1,210	85,120
Net income		$194,080

ADDITIONAL INFORMATION:

(a) At year-end, 10% of sales were not yet collected.

(b) In addition to investment revenue, Excavation owned land worth $45,000; this was $16,000 more than it was appraised for last year.

(c) One month's wages totaling $4,300 have not been paid yet.

(d) Three years of insurance was paid this year. One year's worth was considered used in the current year.

(e) Thirty-five percent of the office expense incurred during the year was unpaid at year-end.

E13. Error Correction. The Tanner Corporation made the following errors in preparing its financial statements for December 31, 1990:

1. Failed to record the purchase of supplies on account.

2. Failed to record a sale made on account.

3. Recorded a $500 cash sale as a $5,000 cash sale.

4. Failed to record the payment of a dividend during the year. The company's policy is to record dividends only when paid in cash.

5. Failed to record an expense for repairs incurred but not yet paid.

6. Recorded the purchase of inventory on account as a cash purchase. None of the inventory has been sold.

REQUIRED: Complete the following table using these abbreviations:

+ means the item is overstated

0 means the item is neither overstated nor understated

– means the item is understated

Effect on December 31, 1990	I	2	3	4	5	6
Total assets	——	——	——	——	——	——
Total liabilities	——	——	——	——	——	——
Total stockholders' equity	——	——	——	——	——	——
Net income	——	——	——	——	——	——

PROBLEMS

P3-1 Revenue Recognition. Following are a number of independent situations relating to revenue recognition principles:

1. The Aloha Company sells prepaid tours to Hawaii. All customers must pay two months in advance of their trip.

2. The Levian Corporation is the world's largest dam construction company. It recently received a $50 million contract to build a dam over the Los Angeles River. It will take five years to complete, but the company feels that it can make reasonable estimates of costs to complete as the dam is being built.

3. Bumby Aircraft Company recently received an order for 25 of its new generation of turbofan airliners. Each plane will take about 15 months to manufacture and will be delivered to the purchaser as manufactured. The firm received a $5 million down payment. The firm estimates that it has received enough orders from all airline companies to make a reasonable profit on the entire turbofan program.

4. ABC Appliance sells a variety of household appliances such as televisions and refrigerators to the general public. Most sales are made for cash, but some on account. The company has a no-questions-asked 30-day return policy.

REQUIRED: For each of the situations above, state when revenue should be recognized. Be sure to give your reasons.

P3-2 Journal Entries. The Jaminez Corporation summary transactions for April follow:

1. Paid a property tax bill of $2,800 that was recorded as a payable in March.
2. Paid its monthly rental of $2,400.
3. Sales during the month totaled $55,000; 30% of these were for cash, and the remainder were on credit.
4. The cost of the items sold equaled $49,000.
5. Purchased additional inventory on account for $10,200.
6. Cash collections from credit sales were:

   $14,000 from March's sales

   $21,000 from current month's sales

7. The following expenses were paid in cash:

Automobile	$2,000
Repairs	1,100
Utility	1,800

8. The firm made a $9,000 payment on the inventory purchased in Item 5.
9. The firm sold an extra parcel of land it owned. The land cost $42,000 and was sold for $38,000 cash.
10. Employee wages earned but not yet paid equaled $2,400.

REQUIRED: Make the journal entries with appropriate explanations to record each of the transactions.

P3-3 Journal Entries, Posting, and Trial Balance. Happy Helen's Hamburger Haven was organized in January. The following events occurred during that month:

- January 2: Helen organized the business by issuing herself capital stock for the following assets:

Cash	$50,000
Furniture and fixtures	24,000
Office equipment	15,000

- January 3: The company obtained additional financing by borrowing $18,000 from a local bank for one year. (Ignore interest.)
- January 5: Various items of inventory were purchased on account for $32,000.
- January 6: The company rented a storefront in which to conduct business. It signed a three-year lease and had to pay the first (January) and last months' rent of $2,000 per month.
- January 15: Sales for the first half of the month totaled $28,000, of which $14,000 was for cash and the remainder on account.
- January 15: The cost of the sales was $16,800.
- January 18: Additional inventory purchased for cash amounted to $18,000.
- January 20: Cash collections on account totaled $12,000.
- January 23: A $15,000 payment was made for the inventory purchased on January 5.
- January 30: Sales for the second half of January totaled $35,000, of which $25,000 was for cash and the remainder on account.
- January 30: The cost of the sales was $24,000.
- January 31: The following expenses were paid in cash:

Salaries	$10,000
Utilities	400
Taxes	2,000
Automobile	1,500

REQUIRED: **(a)** Make the appropriate journal entries to record the transactions.

(b) Set up the appropriate T accounts; post the entries to these accounts; and balance the accounts.

(c) Prepare a trial balance as of January 31.

P3-4 **Journal Entries, Posting, and the Trial Balance.** Mike and Associates, a management advisory service, was organized in April of the current year. The following events occurred during April:

■ April 1: Mike organized the business by contributing the following assets to the firm in exchange for capital stock:

Cash	$60,000
Furniture and fixtures	20,000
Office equipment	12,000

■ April 2: Mike realized that he would need additional financing, so he asked his best friend to lend the business $5,000 with no interest.

■ April 4: The firm purchased various office equipment for $32,000 on account.

■ April 7: The firm signed a lease on a vacant office. The lease runs for five years beginning on April 1 of the current year. The current month's rent of $1,400 plus a $4,000 deposit was paid.

■ April 15: Professional fees earned for the first half of April totaled $12,000, of which $6,000 was for cash. The remaining $6,000 was on credit.

■ April 17: Additional office equipment was purchased for $15,000 cash.

■ April 21: Cash collections from sales on account totaled $4,000.

■ April 23: A $28,000 payment was made for the office equipment purchased on April 4.

■ April 25: $800 worth of the equipment purchased on April 17 was damaged. Mike returned it and received a full cash refund.

■ April 30: Professional fees earned for the second half of April were $20,000, of which $12,000 was for cash, and the remainder on account.

■ April 30: The following expenses were paid in cash:

Salaries	$15,000
Utilities	2,000
Taxes	4,000

REQUIRED: **(a)** Make the appropriate journal entries to record the transactions.

(b) Set up the appropriate T accounts, post the entries to the accounts, and balance the accounts.

(c) Prepare a trial balance at April 30.

P3-5 **Journal Entries, Posting, Trial Balance, and Income Statements.** Elaine and Karen decided to open an ice-cream parlor, called Heavenly Ice. All the necessary preopening arrangements were made in January, and the doors opened for business on February 1.

The January 30, 1990 trial balance is as follows:

HEAVENLY ICE
Trial Balance
January 31, 1990

2/1/9ᶦ

	Debit	Credit
Cash	$10,000	
Inventory	42,000	
Prepaid insurance	2,000	
Store furniture	10,000	
Store equipment	25,000	
Accounts payable		$ 8,500
Bank note payable		15,500
Capital stock		65,000
Totals	$89,000	$89,000

In addition, the firm's chart of accounts is as follows:

Cash	10	Retained earnings	42
Investment in marketable securities	11	Dividends declared	49
		Sales	50
Accounts receivable	15	Interest revenue	51
Inventory	16	Gain on sales of	
Prepaid insurance	17	marketable securities	52
Interest receivable	19	Cost of goods sold	60
Store furniture	20	Advertising expense	70
Store equipment	22	Automobile expense	71
Accounts payable	30	Interest expense	72
Bank note payable	32	Repairs expense	73
Interest payable	33	Salaries expense	74
Capital stock	40	Rent expense	75

During the month of February the following events occurred:

- February 1: February's rent of $1,000 was paid in cash.
- February 2: Anticipating good business, Heavenly Ice purchased on account an additional $5,000 of inventory.
- February 4: The firm placed an advertisement in the local paper. It cost $400 and was paid in cash.
- February 15: Sales for the first half of the month totaled $35,000. All sales but $5,000 to a large corporate customer were for cash.
- February 15: The cost of the sales was $26,000.
- February 16: The firm had some excess cash and invested $5,000 in marketable securities.
- February 18: The inventory purchased on February 2 was paid in full.
- February 24: Cash ($4,200) was received from sales on account.
- February 25: Marketable securities with a cost of $2,000 were sold for $2,200 cash.
- February 28: Sales for the last half of the month were $27,000. All but $3,000 was for cash.
- Cost of goods sold for the last half of the month was $20,000.
- February 28: The following expenses were paid in cash:

Salaries	$9,000
Automobile	1,000
Repairs	1,500

- February 28: The firm received notification from its brokers that it had earned interest of $250 on its investment in marketable securities, to be received next month.

- February 28: The bank notified the firm that interest of $155 was incurred during February and was immediately payable. However, as of the end of February it had not been paid.

- February 28: Because business appeared to be good, dividends of $1,500 were paid in cash. Record these dividends in a Dividends Declared account.

REQUIRED: **(a)** Make the required entries to record these transactions in the general journal. Assume the journal starts with page 1 and reference it by using the abbreviation GJ-1.

(b) Post all entries to the running balance form of the ledger account. Use the account numbers from the chart of accounts.

(c) Balance the ledger accounts and prepare a trial balance.

(d) Prepare an income statement for the month ended February 28, 1990.

(e) Prepare a retained earnings statement for the month ended February 28, 1990.

P3-6 **Preparation of an Income Statement and a Balance Sheet.** You have obtained the following trial balance of the Tarkington Sports Store as of December 31, 1990:

TARKINGTON SPORTS STORE
Trial Balance
December 31, 1990

	Debit	Credit
Cash	$ 25,000	
Loans receivable	10,000	
Accounts receivable	30,000	
Inventory	60,000	
Office supplies	2,000	
Prepaid insurance	2,400	
Land held for future plant site	10,000	
Land	25,000	
Building	40,000	
Store equipment	15,000	
Patents	5,000	
Bank notes payable		$ 30,000
Accounts payable		4,800
Wages payable		3,200
Mortgages payable		50,000
Capital stock		50,000
Retained earnings		71,400
Sales		200,000
Interest revenue		500
Gain on sale of equipment		4,000
Cost of goods sold	160,000	
Advertising expense	2,000	
Automobile expense	500	
Entertainment expense	1,000	
Interest expense	700	
Repairs expense	300	
Taxes expense	5,000	
Wages expense	20,000	
Totals	$413,900	$413,900

Retained Earnings on the trial balance represents the beginning balance at January 1990 minus the cash dividends of $2,000 paid on April 1, 1990.

REQUIRED: (a) Prepare an income statement for the year ended December 31, 1990.

(b) Verify that the balance in the Retained Earnings account at January 1, 1990 is $73,400 and that the balance at December 31, 1990 is $86,400.

(c) Prepare the retained earnings statement for the year ended December 31, 1990.

(d) Prepare a balance sheet as of December 31, 1990.

P3-7 Preparing an Income Statement and Balance Sheet. You have obtained the following trial balance of the Crosby Engineering Design Company as of December 31, 1990:

CROSBY ENGINEERING DESIGN COMPANY
Trial Balance
December 31, 1990

Accounts	Debit	Credit
Cash	$ 40,000	
Notes receivable	10,000	
Accounts receivable	50,000	
Store supplies	2,000	
Prepaid rent	5,000	
Land and building	100,000	
Store equipment	70,000	
Office equipment	3,500	
Other assets	500	
Accounts payable		$ 35,000
Notes payable		10,000
Interest payable		3,000
B. Crosby, capital		101,000
Fees earned		380,000
Rental income		20,000
Advertising expense	15,000	
Delivery expense	1,200	
Interest expense	3,000	
Maintenance expense	1,800	
Office supplies used	500	
Promotion expense	2,500	
Wages expense	240,000	
Loss on sale of land	4,000	
Totals	$549,000	$549,000

The firm is organized as a sole proprietorship. The Capital account in the trial balance represents the beginning balance at January 1, 1990, minus cash withdrawals of $10,000 made by the owner on December 15, 1990, and directly debited to the Capital account.

REQUIRED: (a) Prepare an income statement for the year ended December 31, 1990.

(b) Verify that the balance in the Capital account at January 1, 1990 is $101,000 and that the balance at December 31, 1990 is $233,000.

(c) Prepare a balance sheet as of December 31, 1990.

P3-8 T-Account Analysis. The following data relate to several accounts. You are to supply the entry that would most likely account for the missing information. Assume that all items are independent.

(a) The beginning balance in the Accounts Receivable account is $65,000, and the ending balance is $56,000. All sales were made on account. Cash received on account totaled $56,000.

(b) The beginning balance in the Marketable Securities account is $70,000, and the ending balance is $88,000. During the year, the firm sold some securities for $105,000, on which they had a gain of $38,000.

(c) The beginning balance in the Interest Receivable account is $5,000, and the ending balance is $5,300. During the year, the firm received interest payments of $3,900.

(d) The beginning balance in the M. Burrell, Capital account is $57,000. During the year the firm earned net income of $12,000, and the ending balance in the Capital account is $53,400.

(e) The Accounts Payable account has a beginning balance of $56,000. All supplies purchases are made on account and the cash payments for the purchases totaled $83,000. The Accounts Payable account is only used to record supplies purchased on account. The ending balance in the account is $89,000.

(f) The beginning balance in the Notes Payable account is $100,000. During the year, the firm borrowed an additional $40,000, and at the end of the year the balance in the Notes Payable account is zero.

P3-9 **Cash versus Accrual Accounting.** The C G Ware Corporation was organized at the beginning of 1990 to provide management consulting services. The following represents the summary transactions for the year:

1. The firm was organized when five shareholders each contributed $13,000.

2. The firm rented some office space in a prestigious building. The rental was $2,000 per month for 12 months. In addition, the corporation had to make a $5,000 prepayment, which will be applied to the rent at the end of a four-year lease term.

3. The firm purchased various supplies on account for $6,000. At the end of the year, $1,500 of the supplies remained on hand.

4. Instead of purchasing office equipment and furniture, the Ware Corporation decided to lease it. The total required lease payments for the year were $16,200. However, December's payment was late and was not paid until January.

5. Total billings for professional services were $170,000. However, total cash collections for these services equaled $80,000.

6. Miscellaneous administrative expenses paid in cash were $4,500.

7. Payments on Accounts Payable from Item 3 were $6,000.

8. Salaries paid during the year were $88,000. However, $10,000 of those wages was a prepayment for services to be received next year. The prepayment was made in order to take advantage of the tax laws.

REQUIRED: **(a)** Prepare an income statement for the year on an accrual basis.

(b) Prepare an income statement for the year on a cash basis.

(c) Evaluate the performance of C G Ware Corporation. How much cash was on hand at the end of the year? Which method of accounting provides a better measure of performance? Why?

■ UNDERSTANDING FINANCIAL STATEMENTS

P3-10 The following is from a *Forbes* article on accounting practices in the airline industry:[1]

Perhaps the most peculiar aspect of airline accounting is how airlines figure out how much revenue to record and when. Says [Robert] Roth, [head of the AICPA committee that wrote the industry Audit Guide]: "Substantial portions of revenue are prepaid, because the airlines like you to purchase your ticket when

[1] Jane Carmichael, "The Wild Blue Yonder," *Forbes*, November 11, 1981, p. 94. Reprinted by permission of *Forbes* magazine. © Forbes, Inc., 1981.

you make your reservations. Then you may have several legs of your flight on different carriers. So the original carrier is selling space for other airlines. Large portions of the money coming in aren't even theirs."

Obviously, it wouldn't be fair for an airline to record revenue from your ticket before it has given you the service you paid for. So once a year, each airline opens an account called Air Traffic Liability or Unearned Transportation Revenue (you can look it up under the current liabilities in the balance sheet). When you pay for your ticket, that is where your money goes. Then, when you use the ticket, the airline moves those dollars from ATL into revenue.

Of course, with 300 million people flying every year and with up to 40 different types of fares on any given route, things get a lot more complicated. As one airline man puts it, "It's a real paper mill." You might think the airline would simply bundle together all the tickets it collects each day, add up the fares and make the proper adjustments to ATL and revenue. But only very small carriers that don't have many tickets to keep track of, and very large ones, like United and American, can afford to do so.

Instead, most airlines—Eastern, Delta and Braniff among them—use statistics to figure out how much money they have made—that is, how much they *think* they have made. Every day, they take a random sample of tickets and figure out an average revenue per passenger-mile. Then they assume all their tickets had that average revenue, and they multiply by total passenger-miles flown. This will get them within 1% or 2% of the real number. When the ATL account for the year is closed, months after the year is up, whatever remains is lumped into the current year's revenue. All the real dollars do get to the bottom line—it just takes time.

REQUIRED: (a) Discuss the different points at which an airline could recognize revenue. What do you think is the most appropriate point?

(b) Explain the procedure described in the article. Prepare sample journal entries.

P3-11 The following was taken from a recent Sears Roebuck annual report:

> **Notes to Summarized Dean Witter Financial Services Group Financial Statements. Dean Witter's principal business is securities brokerage.**
> *Securities-related transactions.* Securities-related transactions are recorded on the settlement date (the date the securities must be paid for). Commission revenues and related expenses for transactions are accrued on a trade date basis (the day the securities are bought or sold). Securities and commodities owned are valued at market and the unrealized gains and losses are included in income.

REQUIRED: (a) Comment on the policy of recording securities transactions on the settlement date and recording commission revenues and expenses on the trade date.

(b) Dean Witter values securities at market and recognizes unrealized gains and losses. This violates the historical-cost principle but is common in the industry. Explain what this means and why you think it is common in the industry.

P3-12 Princeville Development Corporation operates two business segments, resort operations and real estate development and sales, at the Princeville resort community located on the Hawaiian island of Kauai. In addition, the company, through a wholly owned subsidiary, has a significant ownership interest in a limited partnership that owns the Sheraton Princeville Hotel. Presented as follows is a consolidated statement of income.

PRINCEVILLE DEVELOPMENT CORPORATION
Consolidated Statement of Income

	Year Ended November 30, 1985
Revenues	
Resort operations	$4,969,291
Sales of real estate	2,918,487
Rental income (Note 6)	750,858
Interest and other income	1,136,012
	9,774,648

(continued)

PRINCEVILLE DEVELOPMENT CORPORATION
Consolidated Statement of Income

	Year Ended November 30, 1985
Costs and expenses	
Resort operating costs	4,067,618
Cost of real estate sales	344,284
Rental expense	250,761
Operating and selling expenses	2,104,885
Excise tax	334,805
Depreciation and amortization	193,798
	7,296,151
Operating income	$2,478,497

REQUIRED: **(a)** Using the data for the year ended November 30, 1985, calculate the percentage of each of the individual revenue items to total revenues. For example, resort operations of $4,969,291 are 50.8% of total revenues of $9,774,648, calculated as follows:

$$\frac{\$4,969,291}{\$9,774,648} \times 100 = 50.8\%$$

(b) Using the data for the year ended November 30, 1985 for resort operations, sales of real estate, and rental income, determine the percentage of the related expense to the revenue item. For example, resort operating costs of $4,067,618 are 81.9% of resort operation revenues of $4,969,291, calculated as follows:

$$\frac{\$4,067,618}{\$4,969,291} \times 100 = 81.9\%$$

Perform the same calculation for cost of real estate sales and sales of real estate, and rental expense and rental income.

(c) Based on the preceding information and your review of the partial income statement for the year ended November 30, 1985, which parts of the business contribute most to the overall revenues of the business? Which parts of the business appear to be the most profitable?

■ FINANCIAL DECISION CASES

P3-13 The president of A&D Associates, an advertising agency, is quite concerned about the current and future financial condition of her business. After reviewing the income statement for the year ended December 31, 1990 and the balance sheets at December 31, 1989 and 1990, she relates the following to you:

"I just don't understand our cash situation. As the years go on, we seem to have less and less cash. I started the business in early 1989 with $100,000 cash and also borrowed $60,000 from the bank. During 1989 and 1990, we were profitable. In fact, our net income in 1990 was 20% greater than it was in 1989. Yet our cash balance has decreased, and retained earnings have continued to increase."

She gives you the following financial statements and asks your advice:

A&D ASSOCIATES
Balance Sheets

	December 31	
Assets	**1990**	**1989**
Cash	$ 15,000	$ 55,000
Accounts receivable	92,000	60,000
Advertising supplies	38,000	30,000
Prepaids	15,000	10,000
Property and equipment	130,000	90,000
Total assets	$290,000	$245,000

Equities		
Accounts payable	$ 20,000	$ 35,000
Notes payable, due March 1991	60,000	60,000
Common stock	100,000	100,000
Retained earnings	110,000	50,000
Total equities	$290,000	$245,000

A&D ASSOCIATES
Income Statement
For the Year Ended December 31, 1990

Revenues		
Advertising fees		$250,000
Operating expenses		
Salaries	$100,000	
Advertising supplies used	40,000	
Commissions paid	25,000	
General office expenses	10,000	
Other	5,000	
Total expenses		180,000
Net income		$ 70,000

REQUIRED: Help explain the cash position of A&D Associates to the president by addressing the following questions:

(a) Reconcile the change in retained earnings with the net income for the period. What other event appears to have occurred?

(b) Explain to the president the relevance of her statement that the company's cash balance has decreased whereas its retained earnings have increased.

(c) Explain to her the possible reasons for the continued decrease in cash since the inception of the business.

(d) What future problems do you foresee for A&D Associates?

P3-14 For many years the yellow pages provided an important source of auxiliary income for AT&T. Under the divestiture order, the yellow pages became the property of the independent operating companies. Judge Greene's order was based on the presumption that the net profits of the yellow pages would help cover local operating cost deficits. Given the regulatory environment and local rate regulation, the determination of the net profits derived from the yellow pages is an important issue.

Revenue from the yellow pages is generated primarily through the sales of advertisements. Before the forthcoming issue can be put into production, a significant number of sales must be closed. In some cases, orders must be placed four to five months before the issue date. In some areas of the country, the customer is billed after the sale is made, and a substantial amount of the revenue is collected by the end of the production of the book or shortly thereafter. In other parts of the country, the customer is billed in monthly installments over the 12-month life of the issue.

During the production process, significant costs are incurred. In fact, other than distribution costs, almost all relevant costs are incurred prior to the delivery of the book.

REQUIRED:

(a) At what point or points in the yearly production and distribution cycle should the yellow pages recognize revenue? How should they account for their billings and cash receipts?

(b) How should the yellow pages account for the costs incurred in the production and distribution cycle?

(c) How should these costs be matched against the revenues for the period?

COMPLETING THE ACCOUNTING CYCLE

LEARNING OBJECTIVES

After studying this chapter, you should be able to:

1. Explain what adjusting entries are and why they are necessary.
2. Describe the major types of adjusting entries and be able to make these entries.
3. Make closing entries and complete the accounting cycle.
4. Prepare a worksheet and describe its use.
5. Make reversing entries (Special Supplement).

This chapter will complete the discussion of the accounting cycle. The second chapter analyzed balance sheet transactions, and the third chapter examined income statement transactions. This chapter will describe the final steps in the accounting cycle. These steps are preparing adjusting entries, financial statements, closing entries, and worksheets. Chapter 5 will discuss in more detail complex financial statements that are prepared and issued by publicly held corporations.

■ ADJUSTING ENTRIES

Adjusting entries are made at the end of the accounting period to update the accounts for internal transactions, such as the use of supplies or the recognition of salaries earned but not paid. Adjusting entries are necessary, since these transactions affect more than one accounting period. For example, supplies purchased in one year may not be used until the next year, or wages earned in one accounting period may not be paid until the next period. In order to make sure that the financial statements reflect all the events that occurred during a particular period and thus ensure the proper matching of revenues and expenses, adjusting entries to record internal transactions are made at the end of each accounting period.

Most of the examples in this chapter will illustrate adjusting entries that involve relatively small amounts, but in the accounting for actual business firms, adjusting entries usually involve only material amounts. For example, a mail order house is likely to use a significant amount of packaging materials. The amount of materials used during a particular period would be recorded by an adjusting entry at the end of each period. Failure to record as an expense the amount of packaging material used would seriously overstate net income and the net assets of the firm.

Two major events can cause economic transactions to affect more than one accounting period. In the first instance, an economic event occurs and is recorded in one period, but it is recognized over several subsequent periods. For example, a firm may pay for an asset that benefits many accounting periods. The purchase of a building in the current period is an illustration of this. In the second instance, an expenditure is incurred or an asset is received, but the firm has provided no economic benefits. For example, a firm may incur interest expense in the current period but may not pay that expense in cash until another period. Exhibit 4-1 lists the different categories of adjusting entries and specific examples of each.

EXHIBIT 4−1

Categories of Adjusting Entries	Specific Examples
Expenditures paid in one period that are used in subsequent periods	Supplies, prepaid insurance
Receipts received in one period that have earned in subsequent periods	Unearned revenue
Expenditures paid subsequent to use	Salaries payable
Receipts received subsequent to earning	Interest receivable

■ EXPENDITURES MADE IN ONE PERIOD THAT AFFECT SUBSEQUENT PERIODS

Enterprises make expenditures or incur liabilities for nonmonetary assets that affect several accounting periods. **Nonmonetary assets** are assets other than cash or legal claims to cash and usually benefit several periods. These assets include, among others, prepaid items, office supplies, inventories, buildings, and equipment. They are initially recorded at their historical cost, which represents the future benefits or services that an enterprise is to receive from these assets. As these services or benefits are consumed, the related cost must be matched against the revenues for the period. This allocation is accomplished by making adjusting entries at the end of the period.

Exhibit 4-2 illustrates this adjustment process. Note that expenditures made in the current period for assets not yet consumed are not recorded as expenses of the current period but are recorded as assets and are included in the current period's balance sheet. The portion of these assets that is consumed in a particular future period is recorded as an expense and is reported on the income statement for that period. The portion of these assets that remains unused at the end of a particular future period is included on that period's balance sheet.

EXHIBIT 4–2

Allocation Process for
Nonmonetary Assets

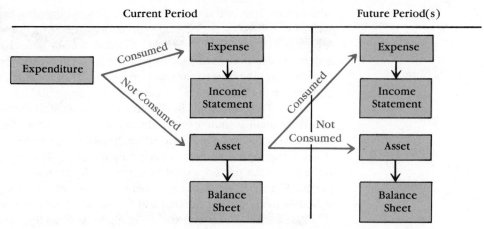

To demonstrate this allocation process, this section will discuss adjusting entries for supplies, prepaid assets, and equipment. You should remember, however, that although you are looking at different accounts, the process is the same; it is to allocate the cost that has been consumed or used (an expense) and the cost that has future economic benefits (an asset).

Supplies

Firms often purchase supplies at different times during the year. When these supplies are purchased, the original debit is usually made to an asset account, Office Supplies.[1] Firms generally do not record office supplies as they are used. Instead, at the end of the accounting period, the cost of the remaining supplies on hand is determined; once this amount is known, it is easy to calculate the cost of supplies used, by the method shown in Exhibit 4-3. An adjusting journal entry is necessary to record the amount of supplies used—in the case of Exhibit 4-3, $1,700.

EXHIBIT 4–3

Computation	Cost
Beginning balance of supplies	$ 900
+ Purchases of supplies during the year	1,500
= Supplies available for use	2,400
− Ending balance of supplies	700
= Supplies used during the period	$1,700

The journal entries to record the purchases of supplies on March 14 and on September 10, the adjusting entry at the end of the period, December 31, and the appropriate T accounts are shown in Exhibit 4-4. The figures in this example are based on the information just presented and the assumption that the firm makes adjusting en-

---

[1] It is possible to record the purchase of supplies by debiting Supplies Expense instead of the asset account, Supplies, for the amount of the purchase. In this case the journal entry would be:

| Supplies Expense | XXXX | |
| Cash | | XXXX |

However, the more common practice is to debit the asset account to record the purchase of nonmonetary assets such as supplies and prepaids. This is the method followed in the text and in the problem assignments.

tries only at the end of its calendar year. After the adjusting entry is posted, the balance in the Supplies account is $700, which represents the supplies on hand for future use. The balance of $1,700 in the Supplies Expense account represents the supplies used during the period.

EXHIBIT 4-4

	Purchase of Supplies		
March 14	Supplies	700	
	Cash		700
	To record purchase of supplies.		
September 10	Supplies	800	
	Cash		800
	To record purchase of supplies.		
December 31	Supplies Expense	1,700	
	Supplies		1,700
	To record $1,700 of supplies used during the year.		

Supplies				Supplies Expense		
1/1	Bal. 900	12/31	1,700	12/31	1,700	
3/14	700					
9/10	800					
12/31	Bal. 700					

Prepaid Assets

Prepaid assets are nonmonetary assets whose benefits affect more than one accounting period. They include items such as prepaid insurance and prepaid rent and essentially represent the right to receive future services. However, the rights to these future benefits or services rarely last more than two or three years. The matching convention requires allocation between the future economic benefits and the benefits used or consumed by the firm. The services to be received are a function of time, so the allocation process is related to the term of service.

The purchase of prepaid insurance is an example. Assume that the Smith Company, which has a yearly accounting period ending on December 31, purchases on April 1, 1990 a two-year comprehensive insurance policy for $2,400. When the insurance policy is purchased, the debit is to the asset account, Prepaid Insurance. The original journal entry, as well as the adjusting entry and the relevant T accounts, are illustrated in Exhibit 4-5. If it is assumed that the original entry for insurance was recorded in the asset account, Prepaid Insurance, it is necessary on December 31 to decrease the asset by the amount of insurance that has expired. In this case, the service represented by the asset expires equally each month, so the Prepaid Insurance account must be reduced by $900, or $100 per month. The balance of $1,500 in the Prepaid Insurance account represents the future benefits of the insurance policy, and the $900 balance in the Insurance Expense account represents the amount of expired benefits.

The adjusting entry for prepaid rent and other prepaid assets follows the same process. When you make adjusting entries for prepaid assets, you should follow these steps:

1. Estimate monthly benefits to be received from the asset, using this general formula:

$$\frac{\text{Cost of the asset}}{\text{Total number of months benefits are to be received}}$$

2. Expense the amount of the asset used, from the date the asset was acquired and the time in this accounting period. The adjusting entry decreases the asset account and records an expense for the amount of benefits used or expired.

EXHIBIT 4–5

		Prepaid Insurance Entries		
April 1	Prepaid Insurance		2,400	
	Cash			2,400
	To record purchase of 2-year insurance policy.			
Dec. 31	Insurance Expense		900	
	Prepaid Insurance			900
	To adjust prepaid insurance for 9 months.			

Amount of journal entry:

$$\frac{\text{Cost of insurance}}{\substack{\text{Number of months} \\ \text{benefits received}}} = \frac{\$2,400}{24 \text{ months}} = \$100 \text{ per month}$$

Adjusting entry = 9 months × \$100 = \$900

Prepaid Insurance			**Insurance Expense**	
4/1	2,400	12/31 900	12/31 900	
12/31 Bal.	1,500			

Depreciation Expense

Nonmonetary assets such as property, plant, and equipment are purchased by an enterprise because of the ability of these assets to generate future revenues for a very long time. In effect, these assets represent bundles of service potentials that the firm gradually uses up during future operations. This occurs because of wear and tear, obsolescence, and other factors. Other than land, which does not lose its future benefits, the matching convention requires that a portion of the cost of these assets be systematically allocated against the revenues generated by the use of these assets. **Depreciation** is the name given to this allocation process.

Although it is more difficult to imagine a building or piece of equipment giving up its benefits than it is to imagine supplies being physically used up or the term of an insurance policy expiring, the concept is the same. As the benefits from these assets are consumed, a portion of their cost should be written off to expense. In this sense, the term *write-off* means decreasing the asset account and increasing the expense account by the benefits that have been used or have expired.

To the accountant, depreciation is an allocation concept rather than a valuation concept. Although an asset's current market value may be increasing, accountants still allocate the historical cost as it gradually loses its ability to generate future operating revenues. Depreciation will be discussed in more detail in Chapter 10.

There are a number of acceptable methods to compute depreciation. For present purposes, assume that a firm uses the straight-line method. **Straight-line depreciation** assumes that depreciation is a constant function of time and results in an equal allocation of the asset's cost to each accounting period during its estimated service life.

In order to calculate depreciation expense, the asset's life and residual (or salvage) value must be estimated. Determining the life of a building or piece of equipment is much more difficult than determining the life or term of other nonmonetary assets. For example, an insurance policy has a fixed term, but there is clearly no fixed life for a building. Within broad guidelines established by the accounting profession, and past experience, management makes a best estimate of the useful life of buildings and other long-lived assets.

Residual (salvage) value is an estimate of what the asset will be worth at the end of its life. Again, management must make this estimate based on past experience and the asset's economic characteristics. When an asset has a residual value, this amount is not depreciated. Depreciation is limited to the asset's **depreciable base**, which is its acquisition cost less its estimated residual value. The following formula can be used to calculate straight-line depreciation:

$$\text{Depreciable base} = \frac{\text{acquisition cost} - \text{residual value}}{\text{Estimated useful life}}$$

Obviously, if the asset has an estimated residual value of zero, this component would be eliminated from the formula.

To illustrate these concepts, assume that on January 2, 1990, an enterprise purchases a new piece of equipment for $75,000 cash. The company has a yearly accounting period ending December 31 and makes adjusting entries only at that time. The firm estimates that the equipment has a service life of ten years and that at the end of the tenth year the equipment will have a residual value of $5,000. Exhibit 4-6 shows the journal entries to record the purchase of the equipment, the adjusting entry to record the annual depreciation expense of $7,000 made on each December 31 during the ten-year service life, and the relevant T accounts.

EXHIBIT 4–6

Journal Entries Related to Depreciation Expense

January 2, 1990	Equipment	75,000	
	Cash		75,000
	To record purchase of equipment for cash.		
December 31, 1990	Depreciation Expense	7,000	
and thereafter	Accumulated Depreciation—Equipment		7,000
through 1999	To record annual depreciation expense of $7,000.		

$$\text{Calculation of annual depreciation expense} = \frac{\text{Depreciable base}}{\text{Estimated useful life}}$$

$$\$7,000 = \frac{\$75,000 - 5,000}{10 \text{ years}}$$

Equipment		Accumulated Depreciation—Equipment	
1/2/90 75,000			12/31/90 7,000
			12/31/91 7,000
			12/31/92 7,000
			12/31/93 7,000
			12/31/94 7,000
			12/31/95 7,000
			12/31/96 7,000
			12/31/97 7,000
			12/31/98 7,000
			12/31/99 7,000
			70,000

Depreciation Expense	
12/31 each year 7,000	

It is important to note that the credit entry is made to an Accumulated Depreciation account rather than directly to the Equipment account. Accumulated Depreciation is considered a contra-asset account. A **contra account** partially or wholly offsets another account. Crediting this account rather than the Equipment account allows the accounting system to maintain both the original historical cost of the asset in one account (Equipment in this case) and to accumulate the depreciation to date in the Accumulated Depreciation account. Both of these accounts are shown on the asset side of the balance sheet. The Accumulated Depreciation account is deducted from the corresponding asset account. Going back to the original example, the proper balance sheet presentation as of December 31, 1990 is:

Property, plant, and equipment

Equipment (cost)	$75,000
Less: Accumulated depreciation	7,000
Net book value	$68,000

The difference between these two accounts, $68,000, at the end of the first year of the asset's life is often referred to as the asset's **net book value**.

Like other balance sheet accounts, the Accumulated Depreciation account has a cumulative balance. The balance in that account will be $14,000 at the end of 1991, and the net book value will be $61,000, determined as follows:

Property, plant, and equipment

Equipment (cost)	$75,000
Less: Accumulated depreciation	14,000
Net book value—12/31/91	$61,000

By the end of 1999, the Accumulated Depreciation account has a balance of $70,000, and the net book value equals $5,000, its estimated residual value. Later in this chapter, you will learn how the $7,000 yearly balance in the Depreciation Expense account is transferred to the Retained Earnings account at the end of the year.

Equipment was used for the depreciation example. The same concept applies to all operational assets except for land, which is not depreciable. Other examples are buildings, furniture and fixtures, automobiles, and machines. For each of these assets, different service lives and salvage values have to be estimated. In addition, a separate Accumulated Depreciation account is maintained for each major category. For example, an Accumulated Depreciation—Equipment account was used in Exhibit 4-6. For buildings, an Accumulated Depreciation—Buildings account would be used, and so forth.

■ RECEIPTS RECEIVED IN ONE PERIOD THAT AFFECT SUBSEQUENT PERIODS

The previous section examined expenditures made in one period that affect subsequent periods. This section will consider examples in which a firm acquires receipts representing revenues that are recognized in more than one accounting period. The portion of the revenues to be recognized in subsequent accounting periods is called *unearned revenues* and is a liability. Unearned revenues arise any time an enterprise receives cash or other assets prior to a sale or the performance of a service. At the time the firm receives the asset, a liability to deliver a product or perform a service exists. For example, a firm may rent part of a building it owns to others, on a yearly basis. The agreement calls for the tenant to pay a full year's rent of $18,000 in advance, on September 1, 1990. Assuming that the firm is on a calendar year, the revenue must be allocated between 1990 and 1991. The portion that is unearned at the end of 1990 must be reflected as a liability.

This allocation process is illustrated in Exhibit 4-7. In reviewing this diagram, note that receipts collected in the current period that are not yet earned are not re-corded as revenues of the current period, but are recorded as liabilities and are in-cluded on the balance sheet at the end of the current period. The portion of these liabilities that is earned in a particular future period is recorded as revenue and is reported on that period's income statement. The portion of these liabilities that re-mains unearned at the end of the future period is included on that balance sheet.

EXHIBIT 4–7

Allocation Process for
Unearned Revenues

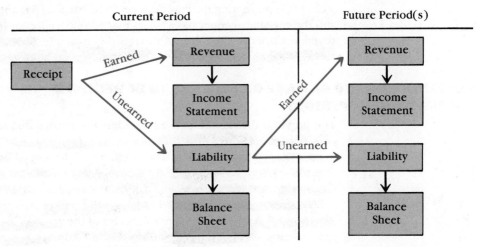

In a manner similar but opposite to that of prepaid assets, it is assumed that un-earned revenues are originally recorded as liabilities.[2] As the revenues are earned, the liability account is decreased, and the revenue account is increased. Using the data in the previous paragraph, the original entry, the adjusting entry, and the T accounts are illustrated in Exhibit 4-8. The entire $18,000 is originally recorded as a liability. Thus

EXHIBIT 4–8

	Recording Unearned Revenues		
September 1	Cash	18,000	
	Unearned Rent Revenue		
	To record receipt of 1 year's rent.		18,000
December 31	Unearned Rent Revenue	6,000	
	Rent Revenue		
	To adjust unearned rent for 4 months of earned revenue.		
			6,000
	Amount of journal entry:		

$$\frac{\text{Total receipt}}{\text{Number of months receipt applies}} = \frac{\$18,000}{12 \text{ months}} = \$1,500 \text{ per month}$$

Adjusting entry = 4 months × $1,500 = $6,000

Unearned Rent Revenue			**Rent Revenue**	
12/31 6,000	9/1 18,000			12/31 6,000
	12/31 Bal. 12,000			

[2]Again, it is possible to record this transaction by crediting a revenue account rather than the liability ac-count for the revenue received in advance. However, this would require a change in the way the adjusting entry is made. The more common method is to credit the unearned revenue account at the time the asset is received. This is the method used in the text and in the problem assignments.

the purpose of the adjusting entry at December 31 is to reduce the liability and to record revenues for the services performed, in this case the rent earned. Earned monthly revenues total $1,500 and are determined by dividing the total rental payment of $18,000 by 12 months. The $6,000 journal entry is necessary to reduce the liability and to increase the rental revenue earned from September 1 to December 31 (4 months).

Again, it is important to note the end result. The liability account has a balance of $12,000, representing the revenues yet to be earned (8 months at $1,500 per month), and the revenue account has a balance of $6,000, representing the 4 months of rental revenue earned by the firm. Although this example concerns rent, other unearned revenues, such as subscriptions and dues, are handled in the same manner.

■ EXPENDITURES TO BE MADE OR RECEIPTS TO BE RECEIVED IN SUBSEQUENT PERIODS

The previous discussion focused on adjusting entries that are necessary because receipts or expenditures of net assets were received prior to the proper timing of revenue and expense recognition. This section will discuss adjusting entries for accruals. **Accruals** recognize that certain expenses are incurred and revenues are earned over time but are recorded only periodically. As a result, adjustments must be made for revenues or expenses that continuously build up but are recorded only at the end of the accounting period. Payment or receipt of the asset or liability (usually cash) takes place during subsequent accounting periods. Adjusting entries are necessary for accruals because the accrual basis of accounting requires that revenue and expenses be recognized in the period earned or incurred, even if the receipt or payment of cash takes place in later periods. Common accruals include interest revenue, interest expense, and salaries expense. It is important to note that accruals are made only for revenues or expenses earned or incurred in one period in which the cash is received or paid in a subsequent period. If the cash is received or paid when the revenue or expense is recognized, an accrual is not made.

The difference between asset or liability allocation (discussed previously) and accruals is illustrated in Exhibit 4-9. As assets or liabilities are allocated over time to reflect benefits used or received, the prepaid or unearned portion decreases. Accruals, however, build up over the accounting period.

EXHIBIT 4–9	Asset or Liability Allocation	Revenue or Expense Accrual
Allocation versus Accrual		

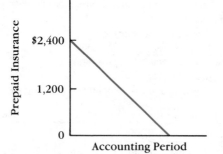

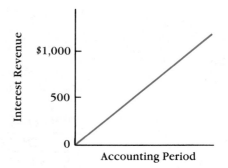

Accrued Revenues

Accrued revenues include items such as interest revenue, rental revenue, and investment revenue. Adjusting entries must be made for these items in order to recognize the revenue in the accounting period in which it is earned, even though the receipt of cash will take place in following periods. Revenues from these items are earned continuously, but in order to simplify the process, they are recorded only at the end of the accounting period by recognizing an accrued receivable and a corresponding revenue item.

A firm may have other accrued revenues that require adjusting entries. For example, a company may have earned a commission on the sale of a building in the current period for which it will not receive payment until the next period. In this case, an adjusting entry must be made at the end of the current period in order to accrue the commission earned but not yet received.

An Example of Accrued Interest. Interest is payment for the use of money. Most loans or notes are interest-bearing and have the following characteristics:

1. **Principal or face amount**—the amount lent or borrowed.
2. **Maturity date**—the date the loan must be repaid.
3. **Maturity value**—the total of the principal and interest at the maturity date.
4. **Interest rate**—the percentage rate of interest, which is usually stated in annual terms and must be prorated for periods shorter than a year.

In general, the correct amount of interest can be calculated by the following formula:

$i = p \times r \times t$ where

i = interest
p = principal of the loan
r = annual interest rate
t = applicable time period in fractions of a year

To illustrate the use of this formula, assume that the Ozark Company borrows $100,000 at 12% for nine months. In this example the principal of the loan is $100,000; the annual interest rate is 12%, and the maturity value is $109,000, calculated as follows:

Principal	$100,000
Interest for 9 months	
$100,000 \times .12 \times \frac{9}{12} =$	9,000
Maturity value	$109,000

To illustrate how interest accruals are calculated and recorded, assume that on June 1, 1990 the Smith Company lent $10,000 at 9% interest to one of its suppliers. The loan's maturity date is in nine months, February 28, 1991, at which time both the principal and the total interest are due. In this situation, 9% represents the interest for one year and must be prorated in order to determine the interest income for nine months. (In this example, as well as others, interest is based on 12 30-day months.)

Once the loan is made, the Smith Company immediately starts earning interest revenue. However, the revenue is not recorded until the end of the accounting period, in this case December 31. It would not be correct to wait until the due date of February 28 to recognize the interest revenue earned through December 31, 1990. This would violate the matching convention, because no revenue would be recognized in 1990 and too much would be recognized in 1991. Although it is possible to record the interest daily, this involves excess record-keeping, so an adjusting entry is made before financial statements are prepared at the end of the accounting period (a month, six months, or a year).

In this example, the $10,000, 9% note earns interest from June 1 to December 31, 1990 (seven months, each assumed to be 30 days), which amounts to $525 and is calculated as follows:

$$i = \$10,000 \times .09 \times \tfrac{7}{12}$$
$$= \$525$$

The total interest for the nine-month term of the loan is $675, or $10,000 \times .09 \times \tfrac{9}{12}$. Thus the interest revenue recognized in 1990 is $525 for seven months, and the interest earned for 1991 is $150 (total interest for nine months of $675 less $525 earned in 1990). These relationships are illustrated in the time line shown in Exhibit 4-10.

EXHIBIT 4–10

Total Interest Revenue
$675

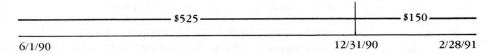

The appropriate journal entries on June 1, 1990, the date of the loan; December 31, 1990, the end of the accounting period; and February 28, 1991, the maturity date of the loan, are:

June 1, 1990	Loans Receivable	10,000	
	Cash		10,000
	To record issuance of loan.		
December 31, 1990	Interest Receivable	525	
	Interest Revenue		525
	To record 7 months' interest on $10,000, 9%, 9-month loan.		
February 28, 1991	Cash	10,675	
	Interest Receivable		525
	Interest Revenue		150
	Loans Receivable		10,000
	To record payment of principal and interest of loan.		

At the maturity date, Cash is debited for the entire value of the loan. Interest Receivable of $525 is credited for the interest recognized in the prior period. Interest Revenue is credited $150 for the interest earned during the current period. Finally, the principal of the loan of $10,000 is credited.

Accrued Expenses

Accrued expenses include such items as interest expense, salaries expense, tax expense, rental expense, and any other expense incurred in one accounting period that will be paid in subsequent periods. Adjusting entries must be made for these items in order to recognize the expense in the period in which it is incurred, even though the cash will not be paid until the following period. Like accrued revenues, the accrued expenses occur continuously, but in order to simplify the accounting process, they are recorded only at the end of the accounting period, by recognizing a payable and a corresponding expense item.

Accrued Interest Expense. The journal entry for accrued interest expense corresponds to the entry for accrued interest revenue, except that in this case a payable and an expense are recorded instead of a receivable and a revenue. For example, assume that on July 1, 1990, the Dogget Company borrows $10,000 from a local bank at 8%. Both principal and interest are payable in four quarterly installments, beginning October 1, 1990. The series of journal entries through January 2, 1991, including the December 31, 1990 adjusting journal entry, is shown in Exhibit 4-11.

EXHIBIT 4–11				
July 1, 1990	Cash		10,000	
	Note Payable			10,000
	To record $10,000, 8% loan from bank.			
October 1, 1990	Note Payable		2,500	
	Interest Expense		200	
	Cash			2,700
	To record first payment of interest and principal.			

$$i = p \times r \times t$$
$$= \$10,000 \times .08 \times \tfrac{3}{12}$$
$$= \$200$$

December 31, 1990	Interest Expense		150	
	Interest Payable			150
	To record accrued interest payable.			

$$i = p \times r \times t$$
$$= (\$10,000 - \$2,500) \times .08 \times \tfrac{3}{12}$$
$$= \$150$$

January 2, 1991	Note Payable		2,500	
	Interest Payable		150	
	Cash			2,650
	To record payment of second installment of principal and interest.			

This example is slightly more complex than the previous interest revenue example. In this case, the note and the interest are paid quarterly. The interest expense is based on the previous outstanding principal balance of the note. Therefore, on October 1, 1990, interest expense is $200, or 8% of $10,000 for three months. The interest expense for the next quarter is based on the new balance in the Note Payable account of $7,500. An adjustment must be made at December 31, 1990, to record the interest expense that was incurred between October 1, 1990 and December 31, 1990 but that will not be paid until January 2, 1991. Finally, the journal entry on January 2, 1991 reflects the second payment of principal and interest.

Accrued Salaries Expense. Salaries expense is another example of an accrued expense for which adjusting entries normally are made. An adjustment is necessary because the date that the salaries are paid does not necessarily correspond to the last date of the accounting period. Therefore accrued salaries payable must be recorded for salaries earned by employees but unpaid at the end of the accounting period.

For example, assume that a firm pays salaries on Friday for the work week ending on that day. For simplicity's sake, also assume that the firm began operations on Monday, January 1, 1990; the first payday of the year was Friday, January 5, 1990; and weekly salaries total $1,500. After the last full week of the year on December 28, 1990, the salaries T account appears as follows:

Salaries Expense

1/5	1,500
1/12	1,500
1/19	1,500
"	"
"	"
12/28	1,500
	78,000

Because the payday for the week beginning Monday, December 31, 1990 is not paid until Friday, January 4, 1991, it is necessary to make an adjusting entry to accrue salaries through December 31, 1990. This requires an entry to debit Salaries Expense and to credit Salaries Payable. In this case, the amount of accrued salaries at December 31, 1990 is for one day's salaries, or $300 ($1,500 ÷ 5 days = $300). The salaries for the next four days of the week, or $1,200, are an expense of the next year, 1991. The time line in Exhibit 4-12 shows the total amount of salaries expense for the week ended Friday, January 4, 1991, and how much expense should be allocated between the two years. Finally, the adjusting journal entry at December 31, 1990, the entry to record the payment of salaries on January 4, 1991, and the T accounts are shown in Exhibit 4-13.

EXHIBIT 4–12
Total Salaries $1,500

——— $300 ———	——————— $1,200 ———————
Monday December 31	Tuesday January 1	Friday January 4

EXHIBIT 4–13

December 31, 1990	Salaries Expense	300	
	Salaries Payable		300
	To record accrued salaries.		
January 4, 1991	Salaries Payable	300	
	Salaries Expense	1,200	
	Cash		1,500
	To record payment of salaries.		

Salaries Expense		Salaries Payable	
1/5 1,500			12/31 300
1/12 1,500			
1/19 1,500			
" "			
12/28 1,500			
12/31 300			
12/31 Bal. 78,300			

When the salaries are paid on January 4, Cash is credited for the full week's salaries. Salaries Payable is debited for the salaries owed at the end of the prior period, and Salaries Expense is debited for the current period's salaries.

■ OTHER ITEMS REQUIRING ADJUSTING ENTRIES

Other items requiring adjusting entries relate to specific items such as accounts receivable inventories and estimated liabilities such as warranties and guarantees whose accounts must be adjusted to their proper balances. These items will be covered in later chapters. In addition, bookkeeping errors are likely to occur, and these are usually corrected through adjusting entries at the end of the accounting period.

■ HARTMAN FLOWER COMPANY

Let us now examine the adjusting entries that are necessary before Hartman can complete the first (quarterly) accounting cycle for his new flower shop. The June 30, 1990 unadjusted trial balance for Hartman's flower shop is reproduced in Exhibit 4-14.[3] Assume that the firm's quarterly accounting period ends on June 30, 1990 and that adjusting entries must be made for the three-month period April 1 (the date the firm was organized) through June 30, 1990.

EXHIBIT 4-14

HARTMAN FLOWER COMPANY Unadjusted Trial Balance June 30, 1990		
	Debit	**Credit**
Cash	$ 9,680	
Accounts receivable	5,500	
Inventory	10,100	
Office supplies	1,000	
Garden supplies	380	
License	120	
Prepaid insurance	2,400	
Land	5,000	
Store furniture and fixtures	10,200	
Buildings	15,000	
Accounts payable		$ 5,520
Bank loan payable		5,000
Capital stock		44,000
Sales		20,000
Cost of goods sold	14,000	
Salaries expense	800	
Advertising expense	100	
Repairs and maintenance expense	40	
Utility expense	200	
Totals	$74,520	$74,520

Information containing the adjusting entries is presented below, and the actual adjusting entries are shown in Exhibit 4-15. The number of the adjusting entry is listed under the date column, and the number of the account is listed in the Ref. column in Exhibit 4-15.

1. The license purchased on April 2, 1990 has a life of one year. The appropriate expense must be recorded for April, May, and June.

2. A count of office supplies and garden supplies indicated that $300 and $200, respectively, remained on hand at the end of June.

3. Prepaid insurance must be written off. The policy was purchased on May 22, but it does not become effective until June 1. Therefore one month must be written off.

4. The furniture and fixtures have an estimated life of eight years with a $600 salvage value. The firm will take depreciation on both purchases from the beginning of May.

5. The small building has a life of 20 years with no salvage value. The firm will depreciate the building beginning in May.

6. The $5,000 bank loan to purchase furniture and fixtures has an annual interest rate of 9%. Both interest and principal are payable in one year. The loan was made on May 2. Assume an entire month's interest for May.

[3] Past chapters have referred to the unadjusted trial balance as just the *trial balance*. However, because it is produced from the general ledger balances prior to the adjustments, its proper name is the *unadjusted trial balance*.

7. Salaries expense for the second half of June totaled $1,200 and will be paid the first day of July.

8. Income taxes payable for the three months ending June 30 amounted to $900. This is based on a tax rate of 40% on income before taxes.

EXHIBIT 4–15

	HARTMAN FLOWER COMPANY Adjusting Journal Entries General Journal			
Date	**Account Titles**	**Ref.**	**Debit**	**Credit**
Adj 1	License Expense	705	30	
	License	120		30
	To write off three months of the license. Monthly write-off equals $10 or $120 ÷ 12 months or $30 for 3 months.			
2	Office Supplies Expense	707	700	
	Garden Supplies Expense	709	180	
	Office Supplies	115		700
	Garden Supplies	116		180
	To write off office supplies and garden supplies used during the period.			

	Balance/ unadjusted trial balance	Actual balance on hand	Required adjustment
Office Supplies	$1,000	$300	$700
Garden Supplies	380	200	180

3	Insurance Expense	711	100	
	Prepaid Insurance	121		100
	To write off one month of prepaid insurance. Monthly write-off = $100 or $2,400 ÷ 24 months.			
4	Depreciation Expense	715	200	
	Accumulated Depreciation—Store Furniture and Fixtures	260		200
	To record two months' depreciation expense.			

$$\frac{\$10,200 - \$600}{8\ years} = \$1,200\ per\ year\ or\ \$100\ per\ month\ or\ \$200\ for\ 2\ months$$

5	Depreciation Expense	715	125	
	Accumulated Depreciation—Buildings	265		125
	To record two months' depreciation expense.			

$$\frac{\$15,000}{20\ years} = \$750\ per\ year\ or\ \$62.50\ per\ month\ or\ \$125\ for\ 2\ months$$

6	Interest Expense	801	75	
	Interest Payable	212		75
	To record interest expense for two months.			
	$\$5,000 \times .09 \times \frac{2}{12} = \$75$			
7	Salaries Expense	601	1,200	
	Salaries Payable	210		1,200
	To record salaries payable for second half of June.			
8	Taxes Expense	811	900	
	Taxes Payable	214		900
	To record taxes payable.			

■ COMPLETION OF THE ACCOUNTING CYCLE

After the adjusting entries have been recorded in the general journal, five steps remain in the accounting cycle:

1. Post the adjusting entries to the ledger accounts.

2. Prepare an adjusted trial balance.

3. Prepare financial statements:
   a. The income statement.
   b. The retained earnings statement.
   c. The balance sheet.
   d. The statement of changes in financial position.
4. Make closing entries and post to the ledger accounts.
5. Prepare a post-closing trial balance.

■ POSTING ENTRIES TO THE GENERAL LEDGER

After the adjusting entries have been recorded in the general journal, they must be posted to the general ledger accounts. In fact, after any journal entries are recorded in the general journal, they should be posted to the ledger accounts. This will allow you to catch mathematical and posting errors at an earlier stage in the accounting cycle. The general ledger T accounts for the Hartman Flower Company after the adjusting entries have been posted are shown in Exhibit 4-16. The adjusting entries are posted to the T accounts with a reference A1 through A8.

EXHIBIT 4–16

HARTMAN FLOWER COMPANY
T Accounts
June 30, 1990, After Posting Adjusting Entries

Cash			101
6/1 Bal. 6,290	6/16	800	
6/15 3,000	6/24	40	
6/23 4,500	6/26	200	
6/30 7,000	6/29	10,070	
6/30 Bal. 9,680			

Accounts Receivable		106
6/15 Bal. 5,000	6/23 4,500	
6/30 5,000		
6/30 Bal. 5,500		

Inventory			110
6/1 Bal. 11,000	6/15 6,000		
6/20 13,100	6/30 8,000		
6/30 Bal. 10,100			

Office Supplies		115
6/1 Bal. 1,000	A2 700	
6/30 Bal. 300		

Garden Supplies		116
6/1 Bal. 380	A2 180	
6/30 Bal. 200		

License		120
6/1 Bal. 120	A1 30	
6/30 Bal. 90		

Prepaid Insurance		121
6/1 Bal. 2,400	A3 100	
6/30 Bal. 2,300		

Land		150
6/1 Bal. 5,000		

Store Furniture and Fixtures	160
6/1 Bal. 10,200	

Buildings		165
6/1 15,000		

Accumulated Depreciation— Furniture and Fixtures	260
	A4 200

Accumulated Depreciation— Building	265
	A5 125

(continued)

EXHIBIT 4–16

(continued)

Accounts Payable		201
6/29 10,070	6/1 Bal. 2,390	
	6/2 100	
	6/20 13,100	
	6/30 Bal. 5,520	

Bank Loan Payable	205
	6/1 Bal. 5,000

Salaries Payable	210
	A7 1,200

Interest Payable	212
	A6 75

Taxes Payable	214
	A8 900

Capital Stock	301
	6/1 44,000

Sales		401
	6/15 8,000	
	6/30 12,000	
	6/30 Bal. 20,000	

Cost of Goods Sold	500
6/15 6,000	
6/30 8,000	
6/30 Bal. 14,000	

Salaries Expense	601
6/16 800	
A7 1,200	
6/30 Bal. 2,000	

Advertising Expense	605
6/2 100	

Repairs/Maintenance Expense	701
6/24 40	

Utility Expense	703
6/26 200	

License Expense	705
A1 30	

Office Supplies Expense	707
A2 700	

Garden Supplies Expense	709
A2 180	

Insurance Expense	711
A3 100	

Depreciation Expense	715
A4 200	
A5 125	
6/30 Bal. 325	

Interest Expense	801
A6 75	

Taxes Expense	811
A8 900	

■ ADJUSTED TRIAL BALANCE

In order to check for posting errors, it is common to prepare an adjusted trial balance. An **adjusted trial balance** is just a listing of the general ledger T accounts and balances after the adjustments have been posted. The June 30, 1990 adjusted trial balance for the Hartman Flower Company is presented in Exhibit 4-17. In many situations, both the unadjusted and the adjusted trial balances are prepared as part of a worksheet. The preparation and purpose of a worksheet will be described later in this chapter.

EXHIBIT 4–17

HARTMAN FLOWER COMPANY		
Adjusted Trial Balance		
June 30, 1990		
	Debit	Credit
Cash	$ 9,680	
Accounts receivable	5,500	
Inventory	10,100	
Office supplies	300	
Garden supplies	200	
License	90	
Prepaid insurance	2,300	
Land	5,000	
Store furniture and fixtures	10,200	
Accumulated depreciation—Store furniture and fixtures		$ 200
Buildings	15,000	
Accumulated depreciation—Buildings		125
Accounts payable		5,520
Bank loan payable		5,000
Salaries payable		1,200
Interest payable		75
Taxes payable		900
Capital stock		44,000
Sales		20,000
Cost of goods sold	14,000	
Salaries expense	2,000	
Advertising expense	100	
Repairs and maintenance expense	40	
Utility expense	200	
License expense	30	
Office supplies expense	700	
Garden supplies expense	180	
Insurance expense	100	
Depreciation expense	325	
Interest expense	75	
Taxes expense	900	
Totals	$77,020	$77,020

■ FINANCIAL STATEMENT PREPARATION

All financial statements except for the statement of cash flows can be prepared from the adjusted trial balance. The income statement (Exhibit 4-18), statement of retained earnings (Exhibit 4-19), and the balance sheet (Exhibit 4-20) for the Hartman Flower Company are illustrated next.[4] The balance in the Retained Earnings account on the balance sheet is taken from the ending balance on the statement of retained earnings, because the retained earnings balance on the adjusted trial balance has yet to reflect any of the income statement transactions. Later in this chapter, it will become clear that the posting of closing entries to the general ledger makes the Retained Earnings account balance equal to the ending Retained Earnings balance presented on the June 30 balance sheet.

---

[4]Because the statement of cash flows cannot be prepared directly from the trial balance, it is not prepared for the Hartman Flower Company.

EXHIBIT 4–18

HARTMAN FLOWER COMPANY
Income Statement
For the Three Months Ended
June 30, 1990

Revenues		
Sales		$20,000
Expenses		
Cost of goods sold	$14,000	
Salaries	2,000	
Advertising	100	
Repairs and maintenance	40	
Utility	200	
License	30	
Office supplies	700	
Garden supplies	180	
Insurance	100	
Depreciation	325	
Interest	75	
Total expenses		17,750
Income before taxes		2,250
Income taxes		900
Net income		$1,350

EXHIBIT 4–19

HARTMAN FLOWER COMPANY
Retained Earnings Statement
For the Three Months Ended
June 30, 1990

Retained earnings, April 1, 1990	$ 0
Add: Income for the period	1,350
Total	1,350
Less: Dividends	0
Retained earnings, June 30, 1990	$1,350

EXHIBIT 4–20

HARTMAN FLOWER COMPANY
Balance Sheet
June 30, 1990

Assets			Liabilities and Stockholders' Equity		
Cash		$ 9,680	Liabilities		
Accounts receivable		5,500	Accounts payable	$ 5,520	
Inventory		10,100	Bank loan payable	5,000	
Office supplies		300	Salaries payable	1,200	
Garden supplies		200	Interest payable	75	
License		90	Taxes payable	900	
Prepaid insurance		2,300	Total liabilities		$12,695
Land		5,000	Stockholders' equity		
Store furniture and fixtures	$10,200		Capital stock	$44,000	
Less: Accumulated depreciation	200	10,000	Retained earnings	1,350	
Building	$15,000		Total stockholders' equity		45,350
Less: Accumulated depreciation	125	14,875			
			Total liabilities and stockholders' equity		
Total assets		$58,045	equity		$58,045

■ CLOSING ENTRIES

To accumulate information on the details of operations during a period, separate revenue and expense accounts are maintained. At the end of a period, this information is reported in the income statement. **Closing entries** are made at the end of the period and are used to accomplish two objectives:

1. To update retained earnings to reflect the results of operations.

2. To eliminate the balances in the revenue and expense accounts so that they may be used again in a subsequent period.

Closing Revenue Accounts

Revenue accounts such as Sales, Fees Earned, and Interest Revenue have credit balances. In order to close these accounts to a zero balance, they are debited for the amount of the ending balance. The credit part of the entry is to an Income Summary account. The **Income Summary account** is a temporary holding account used in the closing process. When a firm has several revenue accounts, only one compound closing entry that debits the individual revenue accounts and credits the Income Summary account is made.

In the following example, the Hartman Flower Company has only one revenue account, Sales, that is closed.

June 30, 1990	C-1	Sales		20,000	
		Income Summary			20,000
		To close sales account.			

After this entry is posted, the T accounts appear as follows:

Sales		401	Income Summary		1,000
	6/15	8,000		6/30 C-1	20,000
	6/30	12,000			
6/30 C-1 20,000	6/30 Bal.	20,000			

Closing Expense Accounts

Expense accounts generally have debit balances. In order to close these accounts to a zero balance, they are credited for the amount of their individual ending balances. The debit part of the entry is to the Income Summary account. One compound entry is used to close all the expense accounts.

The entry to close the expense accounts for the Hartman Flower Company is shown in Exhibit 4-21. After this entry is posted, the T accounts appear as shown in

EXHIBIT 4–21

6/30	C-2	Income Summary	18,650	
		Cost of Goods Sold		14,000
		Salaries Expense		2,000
		Advertising Expense		100
		Repairs and Maintenance Expense		40
		Utility Expense		200
		License Expense		30
		Office Supplies Expense		700
		Garden Supplies Expense		180
		Insurance Expense		100
		Depreciation Expense		325
		Interest Expense		75
		Taxes Expense		900
		To close expense accounts.		

EXHIBIT 4–22

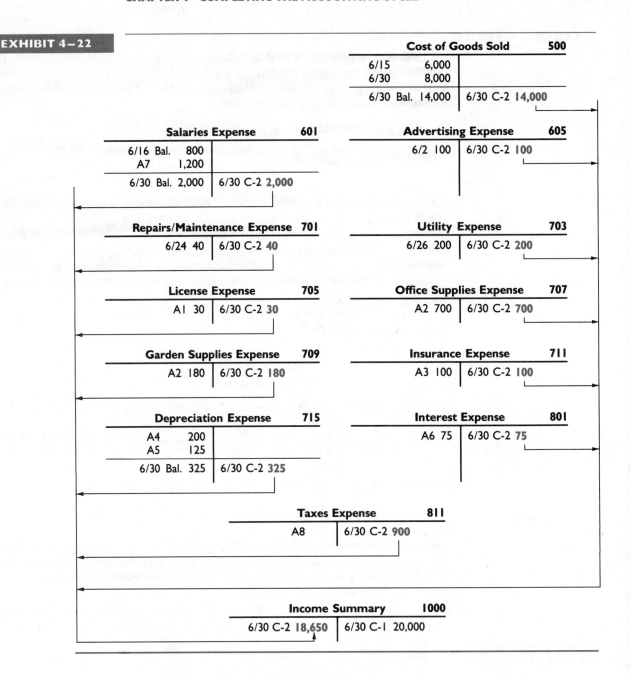

Cost of Goods Sold		500
6/15	6,000	
6/30	8,000	
6/30 Bal. 14,000	6/30 C-2 14,000	

Salaries Expense		601
6/16 Bal.	800	
A7	1,200	
6/30 Bal. 2,000	6/30 C-2 2,000	

Advertising Expense		605
6/2 100	6/30 C-2 100	

Repairs/Maintenance Expense	701
6/24 40	6/30 C-2 40

Utility Expense		703
6/26 200	6/30 C-2 200	

License Expense		705
A1 30	6/30 C-2 30	

Office Supplies Expense		707
A2 700	6/30 C-2 700	

Garden Supplies Expense		709
A2 180	6/30 C-2 180	

Insurance Expense		711
A3 100	6/30 C-2 100	

Depreciation Expense		715
A4	200	
A5	125	
6/30 Bal. 325	6/30 C-2 325	

Interest Expense		801
A6 75	6/30 C-2 75	

Taxes Expense		811
A8	6/30 C-2 900	

Income Summary		1000
6/30 C-2 18,650	6/30 C-1 20,000	

Exhibit 4-22. The arrows in Exhibit 4-22 indicate the flow of the closing entry that credits the various expense accounts and debits Income Summary.

Closing the Income Summary Account

The next step in the closing process is to close the Income Summary account into Retained Earnings. After the revenue and expense accounts have been closed into the Income Summary account, that account now shows all the effects of the income statement transactions. If the firm has made a profit, a debit will be required to close the Income Summary account. This is because more credits (revenues) have been transferred into this account than debits (expenses). The amount of the balancing debit will equal the net income for the period. Conversely, if the firm has suffered a net loss during the period, a credit will be required to close the Income Summary account.

This is because more debits (expenses) have been transferred into this account than credits (revenues). The amount of this balancing credit will equal the net loss for the period. The entry to close the Income Summary account for the Hartman Flower Company is as follows:

6/30	C-3	Income Summary	1,350	
		Retained Earnings		1,350
		To close income summary to retained earnings.		

After this entry has been posted to the appropriate T accounts, all income statement accounts have a zero balance, and the Income Summary and Retained Earnings accounts appear as follows:

Income Summary							Retained Earnings			
6/30	C-2	18,650	6/30	C-I	20,000		4/I	Bal.	0
6/30	C-3	1,350					6/30	C-3	1,350
		0					12/31	Bal.	1,350

Some firms shorten the closing process by not using an Income Summary account and instead making the closing entries directly to the Retained Earnings account. Either method is acceptable; the one chosen depends on the firm's accounting system.

Closing the Dividends Declared Account

If a firm records the issuance of dividends by directly debiting Retained Earnings, a closing entry for dividends is not required. However, if the declaration of dividends is recorded by debiting a Dividends Declared account, this account must also be closed to Retained Earnings. The Hartman Flower Company did not declare any dividends, so no closing entry is required. However, if $1,000 of dividends had been declared, the following closing entry would be required:

Retained Earnings	1,000	
Dividends Declared		1,000
To close dividends declared.		

The Closing Process—A Summary

To summarize, the closing process contains four steps:

1. Bring revenue accounts to zero by closing them to Income Summary. This is accomplished by debiting the revenue accounts and crediting Income Summary.

2. Bring expense accounts to zero by closing them to Income Summary. This is accomplished by crediting the expense accounts and debiting Income Summary.

3. Bring the Income Summary account to zero by closing it to Retained Earnings.

4. If a Dividends Declared account is used, close it to Retained Earnings.

■ POST-CLOSING TRIAL BALANCE

The **post-closing trial balance** is prepared from the ledger accounts after the closing entries have been posted and helps ensure that these entries have been correctly posted. The post-closing trial balance differs from the other trial balances in two ways. First, only balance sheet accounts are included, because all of the income statement accounts have been closed to zero balances. Second, as noted, the balance in the Retained Earnings accounts is the balance at the end of the accounting period. This is because the closing entries have recorded the effect of all of the income statement accounts into Retained Earnings. The beginning balances for the balance sheet accounts for the next period are taken from the post-closing trial balance. Hartman's post-closing trial balance is shown in Exhibit 4-23.

EXHIBIT 4–23

	Debit	Credit
HARTMAN FLOWER COMPANY		
Post-closing Trial Balance		
June 30, 1990		
Cash	$ 9,680	
Accounts receivable	5,500	
Inventory	10,100	
Office supplies	300	
Garden supplies	200	
License	90	
Prepaid insurance	2,300	
Land	5,000	
Store furniture and fixtures	10,200	
Accumulated depreciation—Store furniture and fixtures		$ 200
Building	15,000	
Accumulated depreciation—Building		125
Accounts payable		5,520
Bank loan payable		5,000
Salaries payable		1,200
Interest payable		75
Taxes payable		900
Capital stock		44,000
Retained earnings		1,350
Totals	$58,370	$58,370

THE WORKSHEET—A USEFUL TOOL

A **worksheet** is a common tool used by accountants to gather the information necessary to summarize several steps in the accounting cycle. It is prepared after the unadjusted trial balance is prepared. Adjusting entries, the adjusted trial balance, and data for the income statement and balance sheet all can be summarized on the worksheet.

There are several different types and forms of worksheets. The worksheet of the Hartman Flower Company shown in Exhibit 4-24 is only one of the common forms used. It is important to note that a worksheet does not eliminate the need for making adjusting entries or closing entries.

PREPARATION OF A WORKSHEET

A worksheet can be prepared after the accounts have been analyzed and the data necessary to prepare the adjusting entries has been generated. The steps in preparing a worksheet are (1) make the adjusting entries, (2) prepare an adjusted trial balance, and (3) prepare the income statement and the balance sheet.

The Unadjusted Trial Balance

Exhibit 4-24 shows a ten-column worksheet. However, at this point only the first six columns have been completed. There are two columns each for the unadjusted trial balance, the adjustments, the adjusted trial balance, the income statement, and the balance sheet. The first two columns represent the unadjusted trial balance, and if you compare these columns with the unadjusted trial balance (Exhibit 4-14), you will see that they are identical. You should note that accounts such as Interest Payable, Salaries Payable, and Depreciation Expense are inserted into the trial balance in their proper positions, although they have zero balances in the unadjusted trial balance. This

EXHIBIT 4–24

	1 Unadjusted Trial Balance Debit	2 Credit	3 Adjustments Debit	4 Credit	5 Adjusted Trial Balance Debit	6 Credit	7 Income Statement Debit	8 Credit	9 Balance Sheet Debit	10 Credit
HARTMAN FLOWER COMPANY Worksheet For the Three Months Ended June 30, 1990										
Cash	9,680				9,680					
Accounts receivable	5,500				5,500					
Inventory	10,100				10,100					
Office supplies	1,000			² 700	300					
Garden supplies	380			² 180	200					
License	120			¹ 30	90					
Prepaid insurance	2,400			³ 100	2,300					
Land	5,000				5,000					
Store furniture and fixtures	10,200				10,200					
Accumulated depreciation— Store furniture and fixtures				⁴ 200		200				
Buildings	15,000				15,000					
Accumulated depreciation— Building				⁵ 125		125				
Accounts payable		5,520				5,520				
Bank loans payable		5,000				5,000				
Salaries payable				⁷ 1,200		1,200				
Interest payable				⁶ 75		75				
Capital stock		44,000				44,000				
Retained earnings										
Sales		20,000				20,000				
Cost of goods sold	14,000				14,000					
Salaries expense	800		⁷ 1,200		2,000					
Advertising expense	100				100					
Repairs/maintenance expense	40				40					
Utility expense	200				200					
License expense			¹ 30		30					
Office supplies expense			² 700		700					
Garden supplies expense			² 180		180					
Insurance expense			³ 100		100					
Depreciation expense			⁵ 125 ⁴ 200		325					
Interest expense			⁶ 75		75					
Totals	74,520	74,520	2,610	2,610	76,120	76,120				
Income before taxes Totals										
Income before taxes										
Taxes expense										
Taxes payable										
Net income Totals										

makes subsequent work easier and guards against confusing balance sheet accounts with income statement accounts.

The Adjustments Columns

The adjustments columns numbered 3 and 4 in Exhibit 4-24 are used to enter the required adjusting entries. However, at this point the entry to record the taxes expense and taxes payable has not been made. This entry, usually the last adjusting entry, is made after the income statement columns have been used to determine income before taxes.

The first seven adjusting entries for the Hartman Flower Company shown in Exhibit 4-15 have now been entered in the adjustment columns of the worksheet. These entries should be numbered in order to make it easier to locate errors. The debit and credit columns are then totaled in order to ensure that an equal dollar amount of debits and credits was entered on the worksheet.

The Adjusted Trial Balance

The adjusted trial balance (columns 5 and 6) is the result of combining the adjusting entries with the corresponding account balances in the unadjusted trial balance. For example, the $1,000 unadjusted debit balance in the Office Supplies account is combined with the $700 credit adjustment to obtain the $300 debit balance in the adjusted trial balance. A comparison of the adjusted trial balance on the worksheet with the adjusted trial balance (Exhibit 4-17) indicates that they are identical except for the effect of the last adjusting entry to record taxes, which has not yet been recorded on the worksheet.

The Income Statement and Balance Sheet Columns

The completed worksheet showing all columns filled is shown in Exhibit 4-25. The last four columns—two for the income statement and two for the balance sheet—are used to prepare the financial statements. Balance sheet accounts have been transferred to the balance sheet columns, and income statement accounts have been transferred to the income statement columns. The income statement columns are totaled first. If there are more credits than debits, a debit entry will be needed to balance the two columns, which indicates that the firm has earned a profit before taxes for the period. If there are more debits than credits, this will indicate that a loss has been sustained for the period. In this example, a $2,250 debit is needed to balance the two income statement columns; it represents the amount of income before taxes. Remember that the income tax entry has not yet been made. At this point, the adjusting entry related to taxes is recorded in the adjustment columns of the worksheet:

8.	Taxes Expense	900	
	Taxes Payable		900
	To record income taxes payable.		

Because this entry is in fact an adjusting entry, it is entered in the adjustment columns. However, these columns have already been totaled, so it is not necessary to retotal them. The debit part of this entry, which represents the expense, is extended to the debit column in the income statement, and the credit part of this entry, which represents taxes payable, is extended to the credit column in the balance sheet. The final balancing figure of $1,350 represents net income.

Next the balance sheet columns are totaled, and the same $1,350 net income should be needed to balance these columns. However, in the balance sheet case a credit is required. The $1,350 debit to the income statement and the corresponding credit to the balance sheet are analogous to the closing entries debiting Income Summary and crediting Retained Earnings. The $1,350 increase in the net assets represents the $1,350 net income transferred to Retained Earnings and balances the balance sheet. Remember, the balance in the Retained Earnings account on the worksheet is the balance in the account at the beginning of the period minus the amount of any dividends declared if they have been debited directly to the Retained Earnings account. In this example, because this is the end of the first period, the beginning balance in Retained Earnings is zero, and the addition of $1,350 results in an ending balance of $1,350. Again, notice that this is the ending balance of Retained Earnings on the June 30 Retained Earnings statement and also on the balance sheet at June 30.

EXHIBIT 4–25

HARTMAN FLOWER COMPANY Worksheet For the Three Months Ended June 30, 1990										
	1 2 Unadjusted Trial Balance		3 4 Adjustments		5 6 Adjusted Trial Balance		7 8 Income Statement		9 10 Balance Sheet	
	Debit	Credit	Debit	Credit	Debit	Credit	Debit	Credit	Debit	Credit
Cash	9,680				9,680				9,680	
Accounts receivable	5,500				5,500				5,500	
Inventory	10,100				10,100				10,100	
Office supplies	1,000			² 700	300				300	
Garden supplies	380			² 180	200				200	
License	120			¹ 30	90				90	
Prepaid insurance	2,400			³ 100	2,300				2,300	
Land	5,000				5,000				5,000	
Store furniture and fixtures	10,200				10,200				10,200	
Accumulated depreciation— Store furniture and fixtures				⁴ 200		200				200
Buildings	15,000				15,000				15,000	
Accumulated depreciation— Building				⁵ 125		125				125
Accounts payable		5,520				5,520				5,520
Bank loans payable		5,000				5,000				5,000
Salaries payable				⁷ 1,200		1,200				1,200
Interest payable				⁶ 75		75				75
Capital stock		44,000				44,000				44,000
Retained earnings										
Sales		20,000				20,000		20,000		
Cost of goods sold	14,000				14,000		14,000			
Salaries expense	800		⁷ 1,200		2,000		2,000			
Advertising expense	100				100		100			
Repairs/maintenance expense	40				40		40			
Utility expense	200				200		200			
License expense			¹ 30		30		30			
Office supplies expense			² 700		700		700			
Garden supplies expense			² 180		180		180			
Insurance expense			³ 100		100		100			
Depreciation expense			⁵ 125 ⁴ 200		325		325			
Interest expense			⁶ 75		75		75			
Totals	74,520	74,520	2,610	2,610	76,120	76,120	17,750	20,000		
Income before taxes							2,250			
Totals							20,000	20,000		
Income before taxes								2,250		
Taxes expense			⁸ 900				900			
Taxes payable				⁸ 900						900
Net income							1,350			1,350
Totals							$ 2,250	$ 2,250	$58,370	$58,370

■ LIMITATIONS OF THE WORKSHEET

It is worth repeating that the worksheet does not replace steps in the accounting cycle; it is only a convenient tool to summarize the information necessary to prepare financial statements. Adjusting entries must be entered in the journal and then posted to the ledger accounts, and closing entries must be made. Furthermore, there are several forms of worksheets. The type and the manner in which a worksheet is used depend on the accounting system and the needs of management.

SUMMARY OF LEARNING OBJECTIVES

1. Why adjusting entries are necessary. Adjusting entries are made at the end of the accounting period in order to update various accounts to their proper balances. They result from the need to match economic events with accounting periods.

2. The major categories of adjusting entries and how to make these entries for different accounts. There are several different categories of adjusting entries commonly made by enterprises. These types of entries and the accounts usually involved are:

(a) Expenditures made in period that affect subsequent periods.

1. Typical accounts involved
   (i) Prepaid Assets
   (ii) Supplies
   (iii) Inventories
   (iv) Plant, Equipment, Furniture, and Fixtures

2. Form of the adjusting entry

Expense	XXX	
Nonmonetary Asset or Contra Account		XXX

(b) Receipts received in one period that affect subsequent periods.

1. Typical accounts involved
   (i) Unearned Rent
   (ii) Dues and Subscriptions Received in Advance

2. Form of the adjusting entry

Unearned Revenue	XXX	
Earned Revenue		XXX

(c) Expenditures made or receipts received in subsequent periods.

1. Typical accounts involved
   (i) Interest Receivable or Payable

   (ii) Salaries Payable
   (iii) Taxes Payable

2. Form of the adjusting entry
   (i) To record accrued receivable

Receivable	XXX	
Revenue		XXX

   (ii) To record accrued payables

Expense	XXX	
Payable		XXX

3. The accounting cycle. The accounting cycle includes the following steps:

During the period:

(a) Record business transactions in the journal.

(b) Post the journal entries to the ledger.

At the end of the period:

(a) Prepare the unadjusted trial balance.

(b) Prepare a worksheet—an optional step.

(c) Prepare adjusting entries.

(d) Post adjusting entries to the ledger.

(e) Prepare an adjusted trial balance.

(f) Prepare financial statements.

(g) Make closing entries and post to the ledger accounts.

(h) Prepare a post-closing trial balance.

4. The uses and preparation of a worksheet. A worksheet is a convenient tool to summarize the accounting information necessary to prepare financial statements. However, it does not eliminate the need to make adjusting entries, post them to the ledger, and prepare closing entries.

■ SPECIAL SUPPLEMENT: THE PREPARATION AND USES OF REVERSING ENTRIES

Reversing entries are optional entries that can be made to simplify the accounting process. They reverse adjusting entries and are made on the first day of the next accounting period. *Reversing entries are not used in connection with all adjusting entries, only with those involving routine future cash payments or receipts.*

To illustrate the use of reversing entries, let us return to the adjusting entry pertaining to salaries payable (Exhibit 4-13), in which Salaries Expense and Salaries Payable were used to record salaries earned but not yet paid at December 31, 1990. Exhibit 4-26 presents the adjusting entry, closing entry, the entry to record the subsequent payment of salaries on January 4, 1991, and the relevant T accounts. These entries and T accounts were made *without* a reversing entry.

EXHIBIT 4–26

	Adjusting Entry for Salaries without a Reversing Entry		
December 31, 1990	Salaries Expense	300	
	Salaries Payable		300
	To record accrued salaries.		
December 31, 1990	Income Summary	78,300	
	Salaries Expense		78,300
	To close salaries expense.		
January 4, 1991	Salaries Payable	300	
	Salaries Expense	1,200	
	Cash		1,500
	To record payment of salaries.		

Salaries Payable				**Salaries Expense**		
1/4/91	300	12/31/90 Adj. 300		1/5/90	1,500	
1/4/91 Bal.	0			1/12/90	1,500	
				1/19/90	1,500	
				"	"	
				"	"	
				"	"	
				12/28/90	1,500	
				12/31/90 Adj.	300	
					78,300	Closing 78,300
				12/31/90 Bal.	0	
				1/4/91	1,200	

Although these entries produce the desired result, they do cause extra problems for the accounting system, because all accounting systems, whether manual or computerized, are most efficient when routine transactions are recorded in the same way. This decreases the possibility of error or even fraud. In this particular example, each week's salaries expense is recorded by making the following entry:

Salaries Expense	1,500	
Cash		1,500
To record weekly salaries.		

However, because of the adjusting entry on December 31, 1990, the entry on January 4, 1991 is now different and does not take the same form as do all the other entries to record salaries expense during the year. The January 4, 1991 payment of $1,500 must be divided between Salaries Payable and Salaries Expense. This is not a routine entry, so it must be handled differently by the bookkeeper or computer. Whenever this happens, the possibility for error increases.

Reversing entries solve this problem. To illustrate, presented next is the same set of journal entries and T accounts, only this time using a reversing entry. The reversing entry on the first day of the next accounting period (in this case, January 1, 1991) is:

1/1/91	Salaries Payable	300	
	Salaries Expense		300
	To record accrued salaries.		

This entry accomplishes two things. First, the $300 balance in the Salaries Payable account is reduced to zero. Second, the payment of salaries on January 4, 1991 can be recorded in the same manner as all previous weekly entries to record the payment of salaries. You should note that immediately after the reversing entry is posted, the Salaries Expense account has a temporary credit balance of $300. However, when the $1,500 payment of salaries is recorded on January 4, 1991, the balance in the Salaries Expense account becomes $1,200, which represents the actual salaries expense for the first four days of 1991.

If you compare the series of entries without a reversing entry (Exhibit 4-26) with those with the reversing entry (Exhibit 4-27), you will see that on January 4, 1991, after all transactions have been posted, the balance in the Salaries Expense account is $1,200 and that the balance in the Salaries Payable account is zero, whether or not a reversing entry has been made. Thus, even though the results are the same, reversing entries allow the continued use of routine transactions.

Reversing entries can be made for any adjusting entry in which the expenditure or receipt of cash is made in subsequent periods. Thus accrued expenses such as sala-

EXHIBIT 4–27

Adjusting Entry for Salaries with a Reversing Entry

December 31, 1990	Salaries Expense	300	
	Salaries Payable		300
	To record accrued salaries.		
December 31, 1990	Income Summary	78,300	
	Salaries Expense		78,300
	To close salaries expense.		
January 1, 1991	Salaries Payable	300	
	Salaries Expense		300
	To reverse 12/31/90 adjusting entry.		
January 4, 1991	Salaries Expense	1,500	
	Cash		1,500
	To record payment of salaries for week ended 1/2/91.		

Salaries Payable		
1/1/91 300	12/31/90 Adj. 300	
Reversing		
1/1/91 Bal. 0		

Salaries Expense	
1/5/90 1,500	
1/12/90 1,500	
1/19/90 1,500	
" "	
" "	
" "	
12/28/90 1,500	
12/31/90 300	
12/31/90 Bal. 78,300	Closing 78,300
1/4/91 1,500	1/1/91 300
	Reversing
1/4/91 Bal. 1,200	

ries, interest, taxes, and accrued revenues such as interest and commissions all are candidates for reversing entries. However, they are not required, and their use depends on the design of the accounting system. Accrued salaries that are paid routinely are the most common example of adjusting entries that are reversed. *The examples in this book and the homework assignments assume that reversing entries are not used.*

KEY TERMS

Accruals
Accrued expenses
Accrued revenues
Adjusted trial balance
Adjusting entries
Closing entries
Contra account
Depreciable base

Depreciation
Income Summary account
Interest rate
Maturity date
Maturity value
Net book value
Nonmonetary assets

Post-closing trial balance
Principal
Residual (salvage) value
Reversing entries
Straight-line depreciation
Unadjusted trial balance
Worksheet

PROBLEM FOR YOUR REVIEW

This problem is a continuation of the review problem in Chapter 3. As the accountant for Rub-a-Dub-Dub children's store, you have been able to prepare an unadjusted trial balance as shown below. In addition, you have determined the data listed at the top of page 144.

RUB-A-DUB-DUB
Unadjusted Trial Balance
December 31, 1990

Cash	$ 17,000	
Accounts receivable	8,000	
Inventory	20,000	
Office supplies	1,500	
Prepaid insurance	3,600	
Land	20,000	
Building	45,000	
Furniture and fixtures	15,000	
Accounts payable		$ 12,600
Salaries payable		0
Bank loan payable		10,000
Capital stock		50,000
Retained earnings		43,500
Sales		80,000
Cost of goods sold	52,000	
Salaries expense	10,000	
Advertising expense	1,000	
Utilities expense	750	
Automobile expense	2,000	
Repairs and maintenance expense	450	
Gain on sale of land		200
Totals	$196,300	$196,300

1. At the end of the year, office supplies on hand totaled $400.

2. The prepaid insurance policy was purchased during the year for $3,600. It became effective on April 1, 1990 and has a two-year term.

3. The building and furniture and fixtures were purchased at the beginning of the year. The building has a 30-year life and no salvage value. The furniture and fixtures have a six-year life and a salvage value of $3,000.

4. Salaries earned but unpaid at year-end were $1,500.

5. The bank loan has been outstanding all year. The interest rate is 12%. Both interest and principal are due next year.

6. A December 1990 utility bill for $50 did not arrive until early January (see note below).

REQUIRED: **1.** Prepare the necessary adjusting entries.

2. Post these entries to the ledger T accounts.

3. Prepare an adjusted trial balance.

4. Prepare an income statement, a statement of retained earnings, and a balance sheet.

5. Prepare closing entries.

6. Prepare a post-closing trial balance.

Note: Although the firm's year-end is December 31, this does not mean that all the steps in the accounting process will take place by that date. Usually it takes a firm at least one month to complete many of the steps and prepare financial statements. During this month, the firm has the opportunity to record transactions such as Item 6 that relate to December but for which the paperwork will not be received until January. In many cases, such transactions are recorded as adjusting entries.

SOLUTION
(1) ADJUSTING
ENTRIES

Adj 1.	Office Supplies Expense	1,100	
	Office Supplies		1,100
	To record office supplies used during period.		
2.	Insurance Expense	1,350	
	Prepaid Insurance		1,350
	To record insurance used during period.		
	$3,600 \div 24$ months $= \$150$		
	$\$150 \times$ 9 months $= \$1,350$		
3.	Depreciation Expense	3,500	
	Accumulated Depreciation—Building		1,500
	Furniture and Fixtures		2,000
	To record depreciation expense for period.		
	Building $\dfrac{\$45,000}{30 \text{ years}} = \$1,500$ per year		
	Furniture and Fixtures $\dfrac{\$15,000-\$3,000}{6 \text{ years}} = \$2,000$ per year		
4.	Salaries Expense	1,500	
	Salaries Payable		1,500
	To record salaries payable.		
5.	Interest Expense	1,200	
	Interest Payable		1,200
	To record interest payable.		
	$\$10,000 \times .12 = \$1,200$		
6.	Utilities Expense	50	
	Accounts Payable		50
	To record December utility bill received in January.		

(2) T ACCOUNTS

Cash			
1/1 Bal.	5,000	(2)	3,600
(3)	50,000	(5)	10,000
(7)	28,000	(6)	1,400
(9)	5,200	(8)	52,000
		(10)	4,200
12/31 Bal.	17,000		

Accounts Receivable			
1/1 Bal.	6,000	(7) 28,000	
(3)	30,000		
12/31 Bal.	8,000		

Inventory			
1/1 Bal.	12,000	(4) 52,000	
(1)	60,000		
12/31 Bal.	20,000		

Office Supplies		
1/1 Bal. 1,500	Adj. 1 1,100	
12/31 Bal. 400		

Prepaid Insurance		
(2) 3,600	Adj. 2 1,350	
12/31 Bal. 2,250		

Land		
1/1 Bal. 25,000	(9) 5,000	
12/31 Bal. 20,000		

Building	
1/1 Bal. 45,000	

Furniture and Fixtures	
1/1 Bal. 15,000	

Accumulated Depreciation—Buildings	
	Adj. 3 1,500

Accumulated Depreciation—Furniture and Fixtures	
	Adj. 3 2,000

Accounts Payable			
(8) 52,000	1/1 Bal.	4,600	
	(1)	60,000	
	12/31	12,600	
	Adj. 6	50	
	12/31 Bal.	12,650	

Salaries Payable		
(8) 1,400	1/1 Bal. 1,400	
	Adj. 4 1,500	

Bank Loan Payable	
	1/1 Bal. 10,000

Interest Payable	
	Adj. 5 1,200

Capital Stock	
	1/1 Bal. 50,000

Retained Earnings	
	1/1 43,500

Sales	
	(3) 80,000

Cost of Goods Sold	
(4) 52,000	

Salaries Expense		
(5)	10,000	
Adj. 4	1,500	
12/31 Bal.	11,500	

Advertising Expense	
(11) 1,000	

Utilities Expense		
(10)	750	
Adj. 6	50	
12/31 Bal.	800	

(continued)

Automobile Expense			Repairs and Maintenance Expense	
(10) 2,000			(10) 450	

Gain on Sale of Land			Office Supplies Expense	
	(9) 200		Adj. 1 1,100	

Insurance Expense			Depreciation Expense	
Adj. 2 1,350			Adj. 3 3,500	

Interest Expense	
Adj. 5 1,200	

(3) ADJUSTED TRIAL BALANCE

RUB-A-DUB-DUB
Adjusted Trial Balance
December 31, 1990

Accounts	Debit	Credit
Cash	$ 17,000	
Accounts receivable	8,000	
Inventory	20,000	
Office supplies	400	
Prepaid insurance	2,250	
Land	20,000	
Buildings	45,000	
Accumulated depreciation—Buildings		$ 1,500
Furniture and fixtures	15,000	
Accumulated depreciation—Furniture and fixtures		2,000
Accounts payable		12,650
Salaries payable		1,500
Interest payable		1,200
Bank loan payable		10,000
Capital stock		50,000
Retained earnings		43,500
Sales		80,000
Cost of goods sold	52,000	
Salaries expense	11,500	
Advertising expense	1,000	
Utilities expense	800	
Automobile expense	2,000	
Depreciation expense	3,500	
Repairs and maintenance expense	450	
Insurance expense	1,350	
Office supplies expense	1,100	
Interest expense	1,200	
Gain on sale of land		200
Totals	$202,550	$202,550

(4) INCOME STATEMENT, STATEMENT OF RETAINED EARNINGS, AND BALANCE SHEET

RUB-A-DUB-DUB
Income Statement
For the Year Ended December 31, 1990

Revenue		
Sales	$80,000	
Gain on sale of land	200	$80,200
Expenses		
Cost of goods sold	$52,000	
Salaries	11,500	
Advertising	1,000	
Utilities	800	
Automobile	2,000	
Depreciation	3,500	
Repairs and maintenance	450	
Insurance	1,350	
Supplies used	1,100	
Interest	1,200	74,900
Net income		$ 5,300

At this point, the exact order of the expenses on the income statement is not important. Some firms list them alphabetically or in the order of their magnitude. For simplicity, taxes are ignored.

RUB-A-DUB-DUB
Retained Earnings Statement
For the Year Ended December 31, 1990

Retained earnings—1/1/90	$43,500
Plus: Net income	5,300
Less: Dividends	0
Retained earnings—12/31/90	$48,800

RUB-A-DUB-DUB
Balance Sheet
December 31, 1990

Assets			Liabilities and Stockholders' Equity	
Cash		$ 17,000	Liabilities	
Accounts receivable		8,000	Accounts payable	$12,650
Inventory		20,000	Salaries payable	1,500
Office supplies		400	Interest payable	1,200
Prepaid insurance		2,250	Bank loan payable	10,000
Land		20,000	Total liabilities	$25,350
Buildings	$45,000		Stockholders' equity	
Less: Accumulated depreciation	1,500	43,500	Capital stock	$ 50,000
Furniture and fixtures	$15,000		Retained earnings	48,800
Less: Accumulated depreciation	2,000	13,000	Total stockholders' equity	$ 98,800
			Total liabilities and	
Total assets		$124,150	stockholders' equity	$124,150

(5) CLOSING ENTRIES

1. Sales	80,000	
Gain on Sale of Land	200	
Income Summary		80,200
To close revenue accounts.		
2. Income Summary	74,900	
Cost of Goods Sold		52,000
Salaries Expense		11,500
Advertising Expense		1,000
Utilities Expense		800
Automobile Expense		2,000
Depreciation Expense		3,500
Repairs and Maintenance Expense		450
Insurance Expense		1,350
Supplies Expense		1,100
Interest Expense		1,200
To close expense accounts.		
3. Income Summary	5,300	
Retained Earnings		5,300
To close Income Summary to Retained Earnings.		

(6) POST-CLOSING TRIAL BALANCE

RUB-A-DUB-DUB
Post-closing Trial Balance
December 31, 1990

Accounts	Debit	Credit
Cash	$ 17,000	
Accounts receivable	8,000	
Inventory	20,000	
Office supplies	400	
Prepaid insurance	2,250	
Land	20,000	
Buildings	45,000	
Accumulated depreciation—Buildings		$ 1,500
Furniture and fixtures	15,000	
Accumulated depreciation—Furniture and fixtures		2,000
Accounts payable		12,650
Salaries payable		1,500
Interest payable		1,200
Bank loan payable		10,000
Capital stock		50,000
Retained earnings		48,800
Totals	$127,650	$127,650

QUESTIONS

1. What is the relationship between the need to prepare financial statements on a timely basis and the matching convention?

2. Give three examples of an expenditure that is made in the current period but affects both the current and subsequent periods. What is the accounting problem related to these expenditures?

3. Why is it necessary to make adjusting entries? Can you think of a situation in which adjusting entries would not be required?

4. Prepaid insurance amounted to $1,500 at the beginning of the year and $700 at the end of the year. The income statement for the year showed insurance expense of $2,000. How much insurance was purchased during the year?

5. During the current year, the accountant for the Hamlet Company debited all purchases of office supplies to Supplies Expense. At year-end, the firm still had a large amount of supplies remaining in the storeroom. Which accounts are over- or understated?

6. Explain to your friend how a building that has an increasing market value must be depreciated for financial-reporting purposes.

7. Several years ago, a piece of equipment was purchased. It cost $120,000 and had no salvage value. Yearly depreciation on the straight-line method was $6,000, and at the end of 1990 the accumulated depreciation account had a credit balance of $36,000. When was the equipment purchased? What is the life of the equipment?

8. Give two examples of receipts received in one period that affect current and subsequent periods.

9. At the beginning of the year, the balance in a firm's Unearned Subscription Revenue account was $1,200, and at the end of the year, it was $450. During the year, the firm received an additional $2,000 in subscription receipts. Supply the missing entry.

10. Describe to an individual who is unfamiliar with accounting the difference between adjusting entries that involve write-offs and those that involve accruals.

11. Jones owns a 12% note receivable that was acquired on January 2, 1990. On July 30, 1990, the Interest Receivable account showed a balance of $1,400, and there have been no receipts of interest or principal. What is the principal of the note?

12. What is the purpose of closing entries? When are they made? Describe the logic of debiting revenue accounts in the closing process.

13. Describe the difference between an adjusted trial balance and a post-closing trial balance.

14. Retained earnings on January 1, 1990 were $58,000 and were $78,000 on December 31, 1990. During that time, the firm issued $30,000 of cash dividends, debited to Retained Earnings. Make the required closing entry that has not been made.

15. What is the purpose of a worksheet? When is it prepared?

16. The income statement columns on a worksheet are prepared before the balance sheet columns are. Why?

17. During the preparation of a worksheet, the debit column of the income statement columns exceeded the credit column by $5,000. Did the firm earn a profit or incur a loss? Explain your reasoning.

18. Why is the adjusting entry for income taxes handled differently from the other adjusting entries on the worksheet?

19. A friend of yours stated that she never has to prepare adjusting or closing entries because she prepares a worksheet at the end of each accounting period. Is this a correct technique? Why or why not?

20. What steps, if any, in the accounting cycle can a worksheet replace?

21. (*Refers to material in the Special Supplement.*) A friend of yours who was taking an accounting course said that his accounting instructor stated that reversing entries are more trouble than they are worth. Do you agree? Why or why not?

22. (*Refers to material in the Special Supplement.*) Which of the following types of adjusting entries are candidates for a reversing entry? Why?

  (a) Recording depreciation expense.

  (b) Recording unearned rent that has been earned during the period.

  (c) Accrual of payroll.

  (d) Accrual of interest receivable.

  (e) Recording supplies used during the period.

EXERCISES

E1. **The Accounting Cycle.** Following is a list of steps in the accounting cycle. Arrange them in the proper sequence by placing the appropriate number to the left of the step. The first step should be numbered 1, and so on.

_____ Preparing financial statements.	_____ Preparing a post-closing trial balance.
_____ Posting journal entries to the ledger.	_____ Preparing closing entries.
_____ Recording transactions in the journal.	_____ Preparing adjusting entries.
_____ Preparing an unadjusted trial balance.	_____ Posting adjusting entries and preparing an adjusted trial balance.

E2. Making Adjusting Entries. Make the necessary entries for each of the following two independent situations:

(a) On April 1, the O'Neil Company received $5,400 for a three-year subscription to its political newsletter. The firm closes its books once a year, on December 31. Make the entry to record the receipt of the subscription and the adjusting entry at December 31. The firm uses an account called Unearned Subscription Revenue.

(b) The McDonald Company pays its salaries every Friday for the five-day work week. Salaries of $60,000 are earned equally throughout the week. December 31 of the current year is a Wednesday.

    1. Make the adjusting entry at December 31.

    2. Make the entry to pay the week's salaries on Friday, January 2, of the next year. (Ignore reversing entries and assume that all employees are paid for New Year's Day.)

E3. Making Adjusting Entries. The Deloitte Company closes its books on December 31 and makes adjusting entries once a year at that time. For each of the following items, make the appropriate adjusting journal entry, if any:

(a) At the beginning of the year, the firm had $800 of supplies on hand. During the year, another $2,400 worth was purchased on account and recorded in the asset account, Supplies. At the end of the year, the firm determined that $550 of supplies remained on hand.

(b) On October 1 of the current year, the firm lent the Rosevsky Co. $10,000 at 12% interest. Principal and interest are due in one year.

(c) Three full years ago, the firm purchased a building and land for $500,000. Two-fifths of the cost was allocated to the land and three-fifths to the building. The building has a life of 20 years with no salvage value.

(d) On July 1 of the current year, the firm borrowed $8,000 at 10% interest. As of December 31 of the same year, the Interest Expense account showed a balance of $400.

(e) On March 1 of the current year, the firm rented to another firm some excess space in one of its buildings. The Deloitte Company received a year's rent, $15,000, at that time.

E4. Adjusting Entries for Interest. On October 1, 1990, the Cooper Company lent $100,000 to Lybrand Company at 14% interest. Both interest and principal are due on September 30, 1991. Both firms have a December 31 year-end and close their books annually at that time. Make the required entries for both firms at October 1, 1990; December 31, 1990; and September 30, 1991.

E5. Making and Analyzing Adjusting Entries. The Brokow Company opened a news service on January 2 of the current year. The firm's year-end is December 31, and it makes adjusting entries once a year at that time. For each of the following items, make the initial entry, where appropriate, to record the transaction and, if necessary, the adjusting entry at December 31:

(a) On March 31 the Brokow Company rented a new office. Before it could move, it had to prepay a year's rent of $18,000 cash.

(b) On January 31, the firm borrowed $100,000 from a local bank at 12%. The principal and interest on the loan are due in one year but no interest payments have yet been made.

(c) On March 15, the firm purchased $500 of supplies for cash. On September 14, it made another cash purchase of $900. During the current year, the firm's accountant determined that $1,100 of supplies had been used.

(d) The firm charges its customers in advance for subscribing to its news service. During the year, the firm received $120,000 cash from its customers. The firm's accountant determined that 15% of that had not yet been earned.

(e) Before closing its books, the Brokow Company found a bill for $1,200 from a local newspaper for an advertisement that was placed in a November paper.

(f) Wages accrued but unpaid at December 31 totaled $1,400.

E6. Determining the Ending Balance in Certain Accounts. The Dunesberry Company is preparing its September 30, 1991 financial statements. State at what amounts the following assets should be shown:

(a) On January 2, 1990, the firm bought a three-year comprehensive insurance policy for $5,400.

(b) A piece of equipment was purchased on June 30, 1989 for $125,000. It has an eight-year life with an estimated salvage value of $5,000. Depreciation is taken from July 1, 1989. Give the proper balance in the Accumulated Depreciation account.

(c) On January 2, 1988, the firm bought some land for $150,000, which is currently being used as a parking lot. It expects to sell the land by the end of 1991 and feels it will get approximately $256,000 at that time. It recently received a cash offer for $187,000.

(d) The firm purchases several types of supplies. During the year, the firm purchased 4,250 boxes of staples at a total cost of $14,875. On September 30, 1991, the firm had 2,250 boxes of staples left.

(e) On July 1, 1990, the firm lent $50,000 to one of its best customers at 14% interest for two years. Interest is due yearly, the principal at the end of two years. What amount of interest receivable should be shown on the September 30, 1991 balance sheet?

E7. Closing Entries. Some of the accounts of the Grant Company at the end of the current year are listed in alphabetical order. All accounts have normal balances, and all adjusting entries have been made.

Accounts	Amount
Accounts payable	$ 26,000
Accounts receivable	35,000
Accumulated depreciation—	
Furniture and fixtures	12,000
Capital stock	100,000
Cash	12,000
Cost of goods sold	250,000
Depreciation expense	24,000
Furniture and fixtures	100,000
General and administrative expenses	80,000
Interest receivable	3,000
Interest revenue	5,000
Inventory	80,000
Land	120,000
Loss on sale of furniture	6,000
Retained earnings	124,000
Sales	450,000
Selling expenses	106,000

REQUIRED: **(a)** Prepare the necessary closing entries at the end of the year.

(b) Assuming that dividends of $1,000 were declared and paid during the year, what was the balance in the Retained Earnings account at
1. the beginning of the year?
2. the end of the year?

E8. Closing Entries. The accountant for the Fonda Corporation made the following closing entries at the end of the firm's year. After reviewing these entries,

(a) Discuss the errors, if any.

(b) Make the correct closing entries.

1. Interest Revenue	4,200	
Accounts Payable	900	
Capital Stock	5,000	
Sales	25,000	
Income Summary		35,100
To close accounts with credit balances.		

2. Income Summary	32,700	
Cost of Goods Sold		22,000
Accounts Receivable		2,000
Operating Expenses		4,200
Loss on Sale of Land		1,000
Other Assets		3,500

To close accounts with debit balances.

3. Income Summary	2,400	
Retained Earnings		2,400

To close Income Summary to Retained Earnings.

E9. Analysis of the Accounting Equation. For each of the following five independent situations, determine the net income or loss for the period:

a.	Net assets at the beginning of the year	$ 37,000
	Net assets at the end of the year	44,000
	Dividends declared	0
	Capital stock issued	0
b.	Net assets at the beginning of the year	$ 35,000
	Net assets at the end of the year	44,000
	Dividends declared	2,000
	Capital stock issued	0
c.	Net assets at the beginning of the year	$ 29,000
	Net assets at the end of the year	46,000
	Dividends declared	400
	Capital stock issued	5,000
d.	Net assets at the beginning of the year	$ 74,000
	Net assets at the end of the year	125,000
	Dividends declared	10,000
	Capital stock issued	15,000
e.	Net assets at the beginning of the year	$100,000
	Net assets at the end of the year	140,000
	Dividends declared	5,000
	Capital stock issued	50,000

E10. The Accounting Equation. Answer each of the following two questions:

(a) You have obtained the following information for the Cal Company: Total assets at January 1, 1991 were $150,000 and at December 31, 1991 were $200,000. Total liabilities at January 1, 1991 were $85,000 and at December 31, 1991 were $100,000. During the year the firm's total sales were $500,000. Cost of goods sold was $420,000. Capital stock of $10,000 was issued during the year, and dividends of $2,000 were declared. Determine:

1. The net income for 1991.
2. The total of all other expenses excluding cost of goods sold for 1991.

(b) You have determined the following data for the independent situations in the table. Calculate the missing figures:

	Year-end Amounts			Retained Earnings, Beginning	Net Income (Loss)	Dividends Declared	Retained Earnings, Ending
	Total Assets	Total Liabilities	Capital Stock				
a.	$ 80,000	?	$15,000	$22,000	$15,000	$7,000	?
b.	?	$65,000	20,000	?	20,000	5,000	$30,000
c.	120,000	70,000	?	30,000	?	4,000	20,000

E11. Accrual to Cash Basis of Accounting. You have determined the following balance sheet data for the Oregon Company:

	1/1/91	12/31/91
Accounts receivable	$150,000	$210,000
Supplies	8,000	9,200
Salaries payable	17,000	15,000
Unearned rent revenue	8,200	7,000

The income statement data for the year showed the following data:

Sales—all credit	$570,000
Supplies used	10,000
Salaries expense	42,000
Rent revenue	23,000

You are to calculate the following information:

(a) Cash received on account.

(b) Cash paid for supplies—all supplies purchased for cash.

(c) Salaries paid in cash.

(d) Cash collected for rent.

E12. Cash to Accrual Basis of Accounting. You have determined the following balance sheet data for the Washington Corporation:

	1/1/91	12/31/91
Interest receivable	$2,500	$2,800
Prepaid insurance	1,400	900
Interest payable	900	1,100
Dividends payable	2,000	1,500

During the year, the company made the following cash payments or received cash related to the items listed above:

Cash received on interest receivable	$4,000
Cash paid for additional insurance covering several periods	6,700
Interest paid	3,000
Dividends paid	9,000

You are to calculate the following information:

(a) Interest earned during the year.

(b) Insurance expense for the year.

(c) Interest expense for the period.

(d) Dividends declared during the year.

E13. Preparing Adjusting Entries from Worksheet Data. The partial worksheet for the Tuggle Company is reproduced on page 154. From this data, determine the seven adjusting entries that were made, and explain each adjusting entry.

Accounts	Unadjusted Trial Balance		Adjusted Trial Balance	
	Debit	Credit	Debit	Credit
Cash	$ 10,000		$ 10,000	
Accounts receivable	14,000		14,000	
Inventory	30,000		30,000	
Supplies	1,200		400	
Prepaid insurance	4,100		2,200	
Land	15,000		15,000	
Building	75,000		75,000	
Accumulated depreciation—Building		$ 12,000		$ 13,000
Accounts payable		9,600		10,000
Interest payable		0		1,400
Salaries payable		0		3,800
Unearned rent revenue		1,800		100
Capital stock		40,000		40,000
Retained earnings		61,600		61,600
Sales		100,000		100,000
Rent revenue				1,700
Gain on sale of land		2,500		2,500
Cost of goods sold	62,000		62,000	
Advertising expense	4,200		4,200	
Automobile expense	1,800		2,200	
Employee salaries	10,200		14,000	
Depreciation	0		1,000	
Supplies used	0		800	
Insurance expense	0		1,900	
Interest expense	0		1,400	
Totals	$227,500	$227,500	$234,100	$234,100

E14. Post-closing Trial Balance. Using the data in Exercise 13, prepare the closing entries and a post-closing trial balance.

E15. Computations and Analysis. In doing these computations, be sure to show your calculations.

(a) On January 1, 1991, the Broccoli Company received a 12%, $15,000 note receivable. If accrued interest on December 31, 1991 equals $450, through what date was the interest paid?

(b) On August 1, 1991, the Carrot Company received a $12,000 note. At December 31, 1991, the firm had not yet received any interest payments. If the Interest Receivable had a balance of $750, what would the interest rate be?

(c) The Tomato Company purchased a large machine on January 2, 1987. It is being depreciated at a straight-line rate of $9,000 per year. At the end of its useful life, it will have a salvage value of $3,000. As of December 31, 1990, the machine has a remaining life of four years. What was the machine's purchase price?

(d) The Onion Organization owns a small building that is being depreciated at the rate of $7,500 per year. The building has a remaining life of 24 years from December 31, 1991. Assuming that the building originally cost $235,000 and has no salvage value, determine when it was purchased.

E16. Reversing Entries. (*Refers to material in the Special Supplement.*) As she was closing the firm's books on December 31, 1991, the Rodriguez Company's accountant obtained the following information concerning two adjusting entries:

1. The company pays its payroll every Friday for that week's five days of work. December 31, 1991 is a Tuesday, and the entire week's wages of $18,000 will be paid on Friday, January 3, 1992. Wages are earned equally throughout the week, including January 1.

2. On February 1, 1991, the firm borrowed $15,000 from a local bank at 14% interest. The entire principal and interest are due on January 31, 1992.

REQUIRED: **(a)** Make the adjusting entries on December 31, 1991, and the entries on January 3 and January 31, 1992, assuming that no reversing entries are made.

(b) Make the same set of entries, assuming that reversing entries are made on January 1, 1992.

(c) Compare and contrast the results in (a) and (b). Which do you prefer and why?

PROBLEMS

P4-1 **Adjusting Entries.** The accountant for the Selsun Company obtained the following information while preparing adjusting entries for the year ended December 31, 1990:

(a) During the year the company made the following purchases of supplies:

February 12	$1,700
April 17	1,900
November 11	2,300

At the end of the year, it was determined that $1,450 of supplies remained on hand.

(b) The Selsun Company publishes a monthly beauty newsletter. All customers are required to subscribe to 12 issues, or one per month for the entire year. Subscriptions are renewed annually, but the subscribers list is staggered so that one-fourth of the subscribers renew at the beginning of each quarter. The following subscriptions were received during the year and credited to unearned subscription revenue:

Date	Yearly Subscription
January 1	$1,800
April 1	2,700
July 1	4,500
October 1	3,600

(c) On April 1, 1990, the firm borrowed $12,000 at 12% from the South City National Bank. Principal and interest on the unpaid balance are due quarterly on:

July 1, 1990	January 1, 1991
October 1, 1990	April 1, 1991

(d) As of January 1, 1990, the balance in the firm's Prepaid Rent account was $9,000 and represented four months of prepaid rent. The lease was renewed in 1990 at an increase of 10% of last year's full rent. The full year's rent was prepaid as of the beginning of the new lease term on May 1, 1990.

(e) Land, buildings, and equipment all were purchased at the beginning of 1987. All assets were given a zero salvage value. As of January 1, 1991, you obtained the following account balances:

Accounts	Balance
Land	$80,000
Accumulated depreciation—Building	21,000
Accumulated depreciation—Equipment	36,000

REQUIRED: Make the necessary adjusting entries at December 31, 1990.

P4-2 **Adjusting Entries.** The accountant for the Lloyd Corporation obtained the following data as she was preparing the firm's adjusting entries for the firm's fiscal year ending June 30, 1990:

1. On July 1, 1989, the balance in the firm's Prepaid Insurance account was $2,200, representing four months of prepaid insurance. When the policy expired, the firm purchased for cash a new three-year policy for $24,300.

2. On July 1, 1989, the balance in the firm's Supplies account was $2,400. On November 1989, $8,700 of supplies were purchased on account. As of June 30, 1990, all of the original supplies had been used, and two-thirds of the supplies purchased in November had been used.

3. The Lloyd Corporation lent its main customer some needed cash. Analysis of the loans indicates the following:

Date of Loan	Principal	Interest Rate	Interest Paid Through
9/1/88	$10,000	9%	9/1/89
11/1/89	10,000	9	4/30/90
3/1/90	25,000	12	5/31/90

All loan due dates are after June 30, 1990. Interest on the 9/1/88 loan is paid annually.

4. The firm's rental agreement on its office and stores calls for a monthly rental of $1,200 per month plus 1% of the firm's gross revenues. The monthly portion of $1,200 is payable at the beginning of each month. The 1% portion is payable once a year, on July 15, based on the prior year's gross revenues. Gross revenues for the year ended June 30, 1990 were $675,000.

REQUIRED: **(a)** Make the journal entries where appropriate to record the initial transactions between July 1, 1989 and June 30, 1990.

(b) Make the necessary adjusting entries at June 30, 1990.

P4-3 **Completion of the Accounting Cycle from the Unadjusted Trial Balance.** The bookkeeper of Financial Management Consultants gave you the unadjusted trial balance at December 31, 1990 (below) and the additional information on page 157.

FINANCIAL MANAGEMENT CONSULTANTS
Unadjusted Trial Balance
December 31, 1990

Accounts	Debit	Credit
Cash	$ 8,000	
Investment in marketable securities	10,000	
Accounts receivable	16,500	
Interest receivable	0	
Supplies	2,800	
Prepaid rent	1,400	
Land	25,000	
Buildings	120,000	
Accumulated depreciation—Buildings		$ 8,000
Accounts payable		9,400
Bank notes payable		20,000
Salaries payable		0
Interest payable		0
Capital stock		25,000
Retained earnings		35,600
Fees earned		200,000
Salaries expense	90,000	
Rent expense	20,000	
Legal and accounting expense	1,800	
Utility expense	1,000	
Delivery expense	1,500	
Totals	$298,000	$298,000

ADDITIONAL INFORMATION:

1. The firm was notified by its brokers that it had earned interest revenue of $850 from its various marketable securities.

2. Supplies on hand at the end of the year amounted to $300.

3. Prepaid Rent of $1,200 was used during the year.

4. The building was purchased on January 2, 1988 and has no salvage value.

5. The interest rate on the note is 8%. No interest has been paid on the note since July 1, 1990.

6. Salaries payable at year-end amounted to $2,000.

7. The December 31, 1990 telephone bill of $250 arrived in January 1991 and was not included in the utilities expense of $1,000 listed in the unadjusted trial balance. Use the Accounts Payable account.

REQUIRED:

(a) Set up T accounts with the December 31, 1990 balances from the unadjusted trial balance.

(b) Make the adjusting entries in the general journal. Set up new accounts where appropriate.

(c) Post the adjusting entries to the ledger accounts.

(d) Prepare an adjusted trial balance.

(e) Prepare an income statement, retained earnings statement, and balance sheet.

(f) Make the closing entries.

(g) Post the closing entries to the ledger accounts.

(h) Prepare a post-closing trial balance.

P4-4 Completing the Accounting Cycle from the Unadjusted Trial Balance. The unadjusted trial balance for the Lynch Accounting Firm for the fiscal year ended October 31, 1990 is presented below:

LYNCH ACCOUNTING FIRM
Unadjusted Trial Balance
October 31, 1990

Accounts	Debit	Credit
Cash	$ 19,700	
Accounts receivable	23,000	
Notes receivable	5,000	
Interest receivable	0	
Office supplies	7,200	
Prepaid rent	12,000	
Prepaid insurance	8,400	
Land	30,000	
Building	70,000	
Accumulated depreciation—Building		$ 17,500
Accounts payable		15,000
Property taxes payable		0
Salaries payable		0
Capital stock		50,000
Retained earnings		41,160
Fees earned		104,000
Interest revenue		0
Insurance expense	0	
Advertising expense	700	
Salaries expense	8,490	
Utilities expense	550	
Rent expense	42,000	
Miscellaneous expense	620	
Totals	$227,660	$227,660

ADDITIONAL INFORMATION:

1. The note receivable is a one-year note. The interest rate is 10%, and both the interest and principal are due on February 1, 1991.

2. Supplies on hand at the end of the year cost $2,500.

3. Nine hundred dollars of the prepaid rent was used during the year.

4. The prepaid insurance is for a two-year period beginning April 1, 1990.

5. The building has a useful life of ten years with no salvage value.

6. Property taxes are based on the fair market value of the property owned by the firm, at a rate of 15% of its fair market value on July 1, 1990. At that date, the property had an estimated fair market value of $170,000. Property taxes for the year ended October 31, 1990 are payable on November 10, 1990 but are assessed as of October 31, 1990.

7. Salaries earned but not yet paid at the end of the year amounted to $3,400.

REQUIRED: **(a)** Set up ledger accounts with the October 31, 1990 balances from the unadjusted trial balance.

     (b) Make the adjusting entries in the general journal. Set up new accounts if needed.

     (c) Post the adjusting entries to the T accounts.

     (d) Prepare an adjusted trial balance.

     (e) Prepare an income statement for the year ended October 31, 1990 and a balance sheet at October 31, 1990.

     (f) Make the closing entries.

     (g) Post the closing entries to the T accounts.

     (h) Prepare the post-closing trial balance.

 P4-5 **Accrual and Cash Basis of Accounting.** The comparative December 31, 1990 and 1989 balance sheets and the income statement for the year ended December 31, 1990 for the Kennedy Corporation are presented below and on page 159.

KENNEDY CORPORATION
Comparative Balance Sheets
December 31, 1990

Assets	1990	1989
Cash	$ 14,320	$ 6,200
Accounts receivable	10,500	3,400
Notes receivable	22,000	10,000
Inventory	32,000	25,000
Prepaid rent	3,400	2,500
Supplies	2,100	4,200
Land	65,000	65,000
Buildings, net of accumulated depreciation	165,600	172,800
Other assets	10,000	10,000
Total assets	$324,920	$299,100

Liabilities and Stockholders' Equity		
Liabilities		
Accounts payable	$ 8,200	$ 10,000
Notes payable	20,000	25,000
Salaries payable	4,700	5,200
Interest payable	820	1,200
Other payables	4,000	0
Total liabilities	$ 37,720	$ 41,400
Stockholders' equity		
Capital stock	$100,000	$100,000
Retained earnings	187,200	157,700
Total stockholders' equity	$287,200	$257,700
Total liabilities and stockholders' equity	$324,920	$299,100

KENNEDY CORPORATION
Income Statement
For the Year Ended December 31, 1990

Revenues		
Sales	$600,000	
Interest revenue	1,500	
Total revenues		$601,500
Expenses		
Cost of goods sold	$400,000	
Salaries expense	60,000	
Rent expense	25,000	
Depreciation	7,200	
Supplies expense	4,250	
Interest expense	3,500	
Total expenses		499,950
Income before taxes		101,550
Income taxes		40,000
Net income		$61,550

REQUIRED: **(a)** Prepare the necessary closing entries.

(b) Prepare a statement of retained earnings for the year ended December 31, 1990.

(c) Answer each of the following questions:

1. How much cash was collected from customers on account during 1990? Assume that all fees earned were originally recorded in Accounts Receivable.

2. If no notes receivable were repaid, by how much did the firm increase its Notes Receivable?

3. How much cash was paid out for rent during 1990?

4. Assuming that all purchases of supplies were paid in cash, how much cash was paid out for supplies during 1990?

5. How much cash was paid out for salaries during the year?

6. How much cash was paid out for interest during the year?

P4-6 Computations and Analysis. Make the necessary computations for each of the following independent situations. In all cases, assume that the year-end is December 31, 1990 and that the firm has made all required adjusting entries for the year.

(a) The Mynard Co. acquired an $18,000, 10% note on August 1, 1990. On December 31, 1990, the Interest Receivable account had a balance of $150. How much cash interest did the Mynard Co. collect on this note during 1990, and through what date had interest been received?

(b) The Arthur Corporation borrowed $14,250 on September 30, 1990. The note is due in six months, and the total interest paid when the note is due will be $855. What is the interest rate on the note?

(c) On January 1, 1986, the Jackson Corporation bought a machine for $80,000. It has a 12-year useful life. On December 31, 1990, after the adjusting entry to record depreciation, the book value of the machine is $50,000. What is its estimated salvage value?

(d) On January 1, 1987, the Hawkins Company purchased a new machine for $89,000 with a $4,000 salvage value. The machine has an estimated useful life of ten years. What is its book value on December 31, 1990, after the adjusting entry to record depreciation is made?

(e) The Waco Company purchased a building for $1,400,000. The building has a $200,000 salvage value and an estimated useful life of 30 years. On December 31, 1990, after the entry to record depreciation expense, the building's current book value is $1,300,000. When was the building purchased?

P4-7 Computations and Analysis. For each of the following independent situations, make the necessary computations. For each case, assume that the year-end is December 31, 1990 and that that is the only time that adjusting entries are made.

(a) Bobby Jones's Barber Shop borrowed $25,000 from a local bank on July 1, 1990. The note had an interest rate of 15%. On December 31, 1990, the Interest Payable account had a balance of $1,875. How much cash interest did the barber shop pay on this note during 1990? What was the total interest expense for 1990 for this note?

(b) The Young Company borrowed $17,500 from City National Bank at 9%. The total interest expense for the year 1990 will be $525. How many months has the loan been outstanding during 1990?

(c) On January 2, 1990, the Hannah Company purchased equipment at a cost of $130,000. The equipment had an estimated salvage value of $8,000. Assuming that after the December 31, 1990 adjusting entry for depreciation the book value of the equipment was $117,800, what is the estimated useful life of the equipment?

(d) On January 1, 1989, the Speedy Delivery Company purchased a new truck with an estimated useful life of five years and a salvage value of $2,000. Depreciation expense for 1990 was $2,800. What was the purchase price of the truck?

(e) On July 1, 1986, the Mathy Company purchased a building for $492,000. The building has an estimated useful life of 40 years. Six months' depreciation was taken in the year of purchase, and the book value of the building on December 31, 1990, after the depreciation adjusting entry, is $437,550. What is the salvage value of the building?

P4-8   Worksheet Preparation. The December 31, 1990 unadjusted trial balance for the International Toy Company follows:

INTERNATIONAL TOY COMPANY
Unadjusted Trial Balance
December 31, 1990

Assets	Debit	Credit
Cash	$ 10,400	
Accounts receivable	14,000	
Notes receivable	15,000	
Inventory	28,000	
Supplies	3,200	
Prepaid insurance	4,200	
Land	30,500	
Building	60,000	
Accumulated depreciation—Building		$ 6,000
Equipment	18,000	
Accumulated depreciation—Equipment		9,000
Other assets	4,000	
Accounts payable		24,000
Salaries payable		0
Capital stock		60,000
Retained earnings		41,950
Sales		540,000
Interest revenue		1,350
Cost of goods sold	370,000	
Salaries expense	60,000	
Rent expense	45,000	
Delivery expense	12,000	
Repairs and maintenance expense	6,200	
Loss on sale of land	1,800	
Totals	$682,300	$682,300

ADDITIONAL INFORMATION: **1.** The note receivable has an interest rate of 12% and has been outstanding since October 1, 1990.

2. Supplies on hand at the end of year were $670.

3. Prepaid insurance of $3,800 expired during the year.

4. The building has a life of 25 years and no salvage value. The equipment has a useful life of six years and no salvage value.

5. Salaries accrued but unpaid were $4,000 at year-end.

6. The tax rate is 30% of income before taxes.

REQUIRED: **(a)** Prepare a ten-column worksheet similar to Exhibit 4-25.

(b) Make the necessary closing entries in the general journal.

(c) Prepare an income statement for the year ended December 31, 1990, and a balance sheet at December 31, 1990.

 P4-9 **Worksheet Preparation.** The unadjusted trial balance for Architects and Assoc. at year-end September 30, 1990 is presented below.

ARCHITECTS AND ASSOC.
Unadjusted Trial Balance
September 30, 1990

Accounts	Debit	Credit
Cash	$ 34,500	
Marketable securities	25,000	
Accounts receivable	23,800	
Supplies	7,900	
Land	34,000	
Building	175,000	
Accumulated depreciation—Building		$15,000
Equipment	63,700	
Accumulated depreciation—Equipment		23,250
Other assets	81,500	
Accounts payable		17,500
Note payable		30,000
Unearned rent revenue		43,000
Salaries payable		0
Capital stock		100,000
Retained earnings		245,050
Fees earned		93,400
Rental income		6,700
Salaries expense	85,000	
Advertising expense	30,000	
Delivery expense	7,000	
Repairs and maintenance	3,900	
Utilities expense	2,600	
Totals	$573,900	$573,900

ADDITIONAL INFORMATION:

1. Supplies used during the year amounted to $2,500.

2. The building has a useful life of 35 years and no salvage value. The equipment has an estimated useful life of eight years and a salvage value of $1,700.

3. The note payable has an interest rate of 13% and has been outstanding for seven months during the year.

4. $21,000 of the unearned rent revenue was earned during the year.

5. Earned but unpaid salaries amounted to $6,200 at year-end.

REQUIRED: **(a)** Prepare a ten-column worksheet similar to Exhibit 4-25.

(b) Prepare an income statement for the year ended September 30, 1990 and a balance sheet at September 30, 1990.

(c) Make the necessary adjusting and closing entries in the general ledger.

P4-10 **Error Analysis.** The accountant for the Watergate Corporation had very little experience in preparing financial statements. After examining the worksheet, the controller determined that a number of errors had been made. These errors are listed below. For each error, indicate the effect on income before taxes, total assets, and total liabilities for Year 1 and Year 2. In completing the following table use these codes:

+ = Overstated

− = Understated

0 = No effect

Assume that Year 1 is the first year of the firm's existence and that each error is independent of the others. The first one is completed for you as an example.

| | Income before Taxes | | End of Year | | | |
| | | | Assets | | Liabilities | |
Errors	Year 1	Year 2	Year 1	Year 2	Year 1	Year 2
1. A two-year insurance policy purchased at the beginning of Year 1 was completely expensed in Year 1.	−	+	−	0	0	0
2. Interest incurred by the firm in Year 1 was not recorded until paid in Year 2.						
3. Depreciation expense on asset purchased in Year 1 was not recorded in Year 1. Twice the amount was recorded in Year 2.						
4. Unearned revenue received in Year 1 was recorded as revenue in Year 1. Services were provided in Year 2.						
5. Dividends declared in Year 1 were not recorded until paid in Year 2.						

P4-11 **Summary Review Problem.** The Fenton-Brenner Company was organized on January 2, 1990. During the year the following summary events occurred:

1. Ten thousand shares of capital stock were issued in exchange for $100,000.

2. A $50,000 bank loan was obtained on February 1 at 12%. The principal and interest are due in one year.

3. On April 1, the firm purchased for $3,600 cash a comprehensive two-year insurance policy.

4. Inventory costing $180,000 was purchased on account.

5. The firm signed a lease on April 30 to rent office space. Because the firm is new, the lessor required a full year's rent of $24,000, to be paid immediately.

6. Sales during the first half of the year were $260,000, of which $180,000 was on account and the remainder was for cash.

7. Cost of goods sold amounted to $165,000.

8. Payments on inventory purchases in Item 4 were $150,000.

9. Collections on accounts were $130,000.

10. Additional inventory purchases on account were $250,000.

11. Supplies totaling $4,300 were purchased for cash.

12. Various pieces of store furniture and fixtures were purchased for $100,000. A 20% down payment was made, and the remainder was obtained through a 12% mortgage payable issued on May 1.

13. Sales for the second half of the year were $320,000, of which $200,000 was on account and $120,000 was for cash.

14. Cost of goods sold was $195,000.

15. Cash collections on account amounted to $200,000.

16. Payments on account for inventory purchases amounted to $235,000.

17. The following expenses were paid in cash:

Salaries	$80,000
Legal and accounting	52,400
Advertising	25,000
Delivery	5,000
Repairs	4,200
Utilities	2,400

18. The firm declared and paid dividends of $4,000.

ADDITIONAL INFORMATION:

(a) Interest on the bank loan and the mortgage payable must be accrued.

(b) The necessary amount of prepaid insurance must be written off.

(c) Prepaid rent must be written off.

(d) Supplies totaling $3,500 were used during the year.

(e) The store furniture and fixtures have a ten-year life with a $5,000 salvage value. Take a full year's depreciation on the store furniture and fixtures.

(f) Salaries of $1,400 must be accrued at year-end.

(g) A December utility bill of $200 was received in January. This amount has not been included in the utility expense listed on the unadjusted trial balance. Use the Accounts Payable account to record the transaction.

(h) The tax rate is 30% of income before taxes.

The firm's chart of accounts is as follows:

Cash	101	Retained earnings	311
Accounts receivable	102	Sales	400
Inventory	103	Cost of goods sold	501
Supplies	105	Salaries expense	502
Prepaid insurance	106	Legal and accounting expense	503
Prepaid rent	107	Advertising expense	504
Store furniture and fixtures	110	Delivery expense	506
Accumulated depreciation—		Repairs expense	507
Store furniture and fixtures	111	Utility expense	508
Accounts payable	201	Depreciation expense	509
Bank loan payable	202	Insurance expense	510
Taxes payable	203	Rent expense	511
Mortgage payable	205	Supplies expense	512
Specialist fees payable	209	Interest expense	513
Salaries payable	210	Taxes expense	520
Interest payable	212	Income summary	1000
Capital stock	310		

REQUIRED:

(a) Make the summary journal entries for the year, and post them to the running balance ledger accounts. As a posting reference, use the number of the account and page 1 of the general journal.

(b) Prepare an unadjusted trial balance.

(c) Prepare a ten-column worksheet.

(d) Prepare an income statement, statement of retained earnings, and a balance sheet.

(e) Prepare closing entries and post them to the ledger accounts.

(f) Prepare a post-closing trial balance.

P4-12 Summary Review Problem. On January 2, 1990, John Naperski started his own CPA firm. During the year the following summary events occurred:

1. Naperski invested $170,000 cash, in exchange for capital stock, in order to start his practice.

2. Two years' rent of $19,200 was paid in advance on January 3, 1990.

3. Office supplies of $8,200 were purchased for cash.

4. Office furniture and fixtures were purchased for $25,000 cash.

5. Office equipment of $5,000 was purchased on account.

6. Marketable securities for short-term investment were purchased for $95,000 cash.

7. Fees earned during the first half of the year were $42,000, of which $22,000 was on account and the remainder was for cash.

8. A $5,000 advance for services yet to be performed was received.

9. Utilities expense for the first half of the year amounted to $750 and was paid in cash.

10. Salaries of $19,200 were paid in cash during the first half of the year.

11. On July 1, the firm purchased a comprehensive three-year insurance policy for $6,000 cash.

12. Supplies costing $3,400 were purchased on account.

13. The firm accepted a $15,000 note receivable from a client for services rendered on August 1, 1990. The note has an interest rate of 10% and is due in a year.

14. On November 1, the firm paid $3,000 cash in advance for a three-year subscription to a professional journal.

15. The firm paid the full amount due for office equipment purchased in Item 5.

16. The firm returned $1,500 of the supplies purchased in Item 12 because they were defective. Its account was credited, and the remaining balance was paid in full.

17. Supplies costing $2,500 were purchased on account.

18. Fees earned during the second half of the year amounted to $63,000, of which 85% was on account and the remainder was received in cash.

19. One-half of the marketable securities were sold for $49,000 cash.

20. The following expenses were paid in cash during the second half of the year:

    Salaries $13,900
    Utilities   950
    Legal   1,500

21. Cash collections on account were $34,000.

22. Land was purchased for $25,000 cash.

23. Naperski withdrew $12,000 cash as a dividend for his personal use.

ADDITIONAL INFORMATION:

(a) Interest on the note receivable must be accrued.

(b) The necessary amount of prepaid insurance must be written off.

(c) The necessary amount of prepaid subscriptions must be written off.

(d) Prepaid rent must be written off.

(e) Supplies on hand at December 31, 1990 amounted to $3,700.

(f) The office furniture and fixtures have a seven-year life and a $4,000 salvage value.

(g) The office equipment has a five-year life and no salvage value.

(h) Salaries of $1,300 were earned but unpaid at year-end.

(i) Fees of $2,000 were earned at year-end, for which the receivable and the revenue have not yet been recorded.

The firm's chart of accounts is as follows:

Cash	101	Accounts payable	201
Marketable securities	102	Unearned accounting fees	202
Accounts receivable	103	Salaries payable	203
Note receivable	104	Capital stock	300
Interest receivable	105	Retained earnings	310
Supplies	106	Accounting fees earned	400
Prepaid rent	107	Supplies expense	500
Prepaid insurance	108	Salaries expense	501
Prepaid subscriptions	109	Legal expense	502
Land	110	Utilities expense	503
Office furniture and fixtures	120	Subscription expense	504
Accumulated depreciation—		Insurance expense	505
Office furniture and fixtures	130	Rent expense	506
Office equipment	140	Depreciation expense	507
Accumulated depreciation—		Gain on sale of marketable securities	600
Office equipment	150	Interest revenue	610
		Income summary	1000

REQUIRED: Depending on your instructor's directions, either use T accounts or a three-column running balance ledger account in completing the following work. If required by your instructor, Item c can be prepared on a worksheet.

(a) Make the summary journal entries for the year, and post them to the ledger accounts. As a posting reference, use the number of the account and page 1 of the general journal.

(b) Prepare an unadjusted trial balance.

(c) In order to complete the accounting cycle:
1. Prepare the adjusting entries and post them to the ledger accounts.
2. Prepare an adjusted trial balance.

(d) Prepare an income statement, a statement of owner's equity, and a balance sheet.

(e) Prepare closing entries and post them to the ledger accounts.

(f) Prepare a post-closing trial balance.

■ UNDERSTANDING FINANCIAL STATEMENTS

P4-13 The consolidated financial statement of income (in thousands) for Browning-Ferris Industries, Inc. and subsidiaries is as follows:

	Year Ended September 30,		
	1988	**1987**	**1986**
Revenues	$2,067,405	$1,656,616	$1,328,393
Cost of operations	1,307,037	1,036,784	836,413
Gross profit	760,368	619,832	491,980
Selling, general, and administrative expense	375,383	296,056	243,077
Income from operations	384,985	323,776	248,903
Interest expense	37,417	22,361	12,359
Interest income	(12,534)	(5,773)	(4,257)
Income before income taxes	360,102	307,188	240,801
Income taxes	133,238	135,163	103,948
Net income	$ 226,864	$ 172,025	$ 136,853

In addition, you have gathered the following balance sheet data (in thousands):

	September 30,	
	1988	1987
Cash	$ 8,135	$ 5,522
Retained earnings	749,170	590,011

REQUIRED: **(a)** Make the summary closing entries that Browning-Ferris would have made.

(b) What amount of dividends did the company declare during 1988?

(c) What are the relationships, if any, between the increase in retained earnings and the increase in cash during 1988?

■ FINANCIAL DECISION CASE

P4-14   Bill Gilroy is considering buying an apartment house. The building will cost $500,000, and Bill will make a 20% down payment and will finance the remainder through a 10%, 30-year mortgage. Monthly payments including principal and interest will be $3,510. Bill put together the following projected income statement for the first year. He expects this statement to reflect the operations of the apartment house for the next two years, except that interest expense will decrease very slightly.

Revenues		
Rents		$55,000
Expenses		
Interest	$33,000	
Depreciation	16,667	
Repairs and maintenance	6,000	
Insurance	2,400	
Net loss		58,067
		($ 3,067)

Bill is concerned that he will be unable to generate enough cash flow from the building to pay the necessary cash outflows. He gives you the following additional information and asks you to prepare a statement of cash flows for the first year:

1. All rents will be paid in cash at the beginning of each month. No prepayments or deposits are required.

2. The building has a 30-year life and no salvage value.

3. The insurance expense of $2,400 represents one-half the cost of the two-year comprehensive insurance policy he purchased.

4. Finally, in preparing your statement, do not consider the 20% down payment as part of the cash outflows.

   In addition to your statement, write a brief memo to Bill explaining the differences in the two statements.

FINANCIAL STATEMENTS— THE OUTPUTS OF THE SYSTEM

After studying this chapter, you should be able to:

1. Discuss the need for and purpose behind the establishment of objectives of financial reporting.
2. Discuss the qualitative characteristics of financial information.
3. Prepare a classified balance sheet.
4. Explain the uses and limitations of a classified balance sheet.
5. Prepare both forms of a classified income statement—the single-step and the multistep income statement.
6. Explain the uses and limitations of classified income statements.
7. Explain the uses and limitations of the retained earnings statement and the statement of changes in stockholders' equity.
8. Explain the uses and limitations of the statement of cash flows.
9. Discuss the uses of other financial data in the annual report.

F inancial statements are the principal product of the accounting information system. The four required financial statements are the balance sheet, the income statement, the retained earnings statement, and the statement of cash flows. These statements communicate to external users information concerning the enterprise's financial position, liquidity, and profitability and significant changes in its resources and obligations. These financial statements were introduced in Chapter 1; the goals of this chapter are to explain the objectives and concepts behind their construction. In addition, a set of actual financial statements from Toys "R" Us will demonstrate these concepts.

OBJECTIVES OF FINANCIAL REPORTING

As part of its conceptual framework project, the Financial Accounting Standards Board (FASB) has spent considerable time and energy in developing **objectives of financial reporting**. The purpose of these objectives and related concepts is to help users better understand the content and limitations of financial statements. In Concepts Statement 1, the FASB identified three main objectives of financial reporting:

1. Financial reporting should provide information that is useful to present and potential investors and creditors and other users in making rational investment, credit, and similar decisions. The information should be comprehensible to those who have a reasonable understanding of business and economic activities and are willing to study the information with reasonable diligence.

2. Financial reporting should provide information to help present and potential investors and creditors and other users in assessing the amounts, timing, and uncertainty of prospective cash receipts from dividends or interest and the proceeds from the sale, redemption, or maturity of securities or loans. Since investors' and creditors' cash flows are related to enterprise cash flows, financial reporting should provide information to help investors, creditors, and others assess the amounts, timing, and uncertainty of prospective net cash inflows to the related enterprise.

3. Financial reporting should provide information about the economic resources of an enterprise, the claims to those resources (obligations of the enterprise to transfer resources to other entities and owners' equity), and the effects of transactions, events, and circumstances that change resources and claims to those resources.[1]

The FASB considers present and potential investors and creditors to be the primary users of financial statements, and it notes that these users need information concerning the possibility of receiving cash flows from investments or loans. This data can best be provided by giving investors and creditors information about the enterprise's resources, claims to those resources, and changes in them. However, the FASB is quite clear in noting that business and economic activities are complex and that financial statement users must be willing to study the information carefully.

QUALITATIVE CHARACTERISTICS OF FINANCIAL INFORMATION

According to the FASB, to be useful in decision making, accounting information must possess certain qualitative characteristics, including quantifiability, relevance, and reliability. Quantifiability was discussed in Chapter 2. Relevance and reliability as well as other qualitative characteristics will be covered in this chapter.

RELEVANCE AND RELIABILITY

According to the FASB, relevance and reliability are the two primary qualities that make accounting information useful. "Relevant accounting information is capable of making a difference in a decision by helping users to form predictions about the out-

---

[1]Financial Accounting Standards Board, Concepts Statement No. 1, *Objectives of Financial Reporting by Business Enterprises* (Stamford, Conn.: FASB, November 1978), pars. 34, 37, and 40.

come of past, present, and future events or to confirm or correct prior expectations." [2] That is, information is relevant if it has predictive and/or feedback value to users. This means the information helps users predict the future or evaluate past decisions. Further, timeliness is an important ingredient of relevance. If information is not given to users when it is capable of influencing their decision, it loses its relevance.

Information is reliable to the extent it measures what it should. From an accounting perspective, information is reliable if users can depend on it to represent the economic conditions or events that it purports to represent. For example, if receivables are shown on the balance sheeet at $500,000, this figure will be reliable only if the real collectibility of these receivables closely approximates $500,000. We use the word *approximate* because informed users of accounting information know that estimates and approximations rather than exact measures must often be made.

Verifiability is an important ingredient of reliability. Verifiability is similar to objectivity and means that several individuals or measurers would reach similar conclusions. For example, the $500,000 balance in Accounts Receivable is verifiable if several individuals could agree that the net realizable value of the receivables is in fact $500,000. Verifiability is important because external users do not have access to a firm's accounting records and must rely on published financial statements as well as other public data in making their decisions. Verifiable and objective information increases users' confidence in accounting information.

In their attempt to provide useful information, accountants are often forced to make a trade-off between relevance and reliability. In many cases, the more relevant the information is, the less reliable it becomes. The controversy surrounding the use of certain current-cost data is an example of a debate that involves this trade-off. Many individuals feel that current-cost data is more relevant than historical-cost data to users in decision making. For example, if you were to measure your net worth and owned a plot of land, its current cost might be more relevant to you than its historical cost would be. However, current-cost data is less reliable. You may have several individuals appraise the land and receive a different appraisal value from each of them. There might be no measurement consensus. Accountants are often confronted with this trade-off; as with other issues in accounting, there is no single solution—the accountant's judgment is required.

■ COMPARABILITY AND CONSISTENCY

Comparability and **consistency** are important factors in evaluating the usefulness of accounting information. Accounting information is comparable if it allows users to identify similarities and differences between two sets of economic events. When accounting information is comparable, it can be used to evaluate the financial position and performance of one firm over time or in comparison with other firms. However, comparability does not imply that accounting procedures or methods should be the same for all firms. This would disguise real differences that exist in the economic circumstance reported.

Consistency is related to comparability and is also an important quality of accounting information. Consistency means that a firm uses the same accounting procedures and policies from one period to the next. It presumes that once an accounting principle has been adopted, it will not be changed in accounting for similar events. For example, once a firm selects a certain depreciation method, it should not change

[2] Financial Accounting Standards Board, Concepts Statement No. 2, *Qualitative Characteristics of Accounting Information* (Stamford, Conn.: FASB, May 1980), Summary.

the method in one period and then switch back to the original method in the following period. However, as the FASB notes, such consistency should not inhibit necessary changes in accounting principles and practices. If such a change is made, the full disclosure principle requires that the effect of this change on net income be fully noted.

CONSERVATISM

Although conservatism may qualify more as a convention than as a qualitative characteristic of accounting information, it has been a pervasive factor in U.S. accounting for over 50 years. Generally, **conservatism** means prudence in financial reporting because of the uncertainty surrounding business and economic activities. According to Statement 4 of the Accounting Principles Board,

> Frequently, assets and liabilities are measured in a context of significant uncertainties. Historically, managers, investors, and accountants have generally preferred that possible errors in measurement be in the direction of understatement rather than overstatement of net income and net assets. This has led to the convention of conservatism. . . .[3]

This convention developed in the early stages of financial reporting, when bankers and lenders were the main users of financial reports, especially balance sheets. To the banker, the further the assets were understated, the greater the margin of safety the assets provided as security for loans. The tendency to recognize losses as soon as they become evident, while not recognizing gains until they become assured, is an example of conservative accounting that gives bankers such security.

In Concepts Statement 2, the FASB clearly stated: "Conservatism in financial reporting should no longer connote deliberate, consistent understatement of net assets and profits."[4] The board correctly noted that understatement in one period leads to overstatement in another period. To demonstrate how this works, assume that an enterprise started operating on January 2, 1987 and ceased operating three years later, on December 31, 1989. At the end of the three-year period, it can be determined with certainty that the firm earned net income of $300,000. However, during the life of the firm, its income in each one of these years cannot be known with certainty. Accountants must therefore make estimates and allocations in order to match income and expense in each year. If income in Years 1 and 2 is deliberately understated by a total of $50,000, income in Year 3 must be overstated by $50,000 if total income over the three-year period is to equal $300,000.

Nonetheless, conservatism is still a reasonable reaction to the uncertainties inherent in business and economic events. For example, if two estimates of the amounts to be collected on an account receivable are equally likely, the less optimistic estimate should be used. However, if the two estimates are not equally likely and the more optimistic one is more likely, it would be an incorrect application of conservatism to use the less optimistic one.

MATERIALITY

In an accounting context, **materiality** refers to the relative importance or significance of an item to an informed decision maker. An item or event is material if it is probable that the judgment of a reasonable person, relying on that information, would have been changed or influenced by its omission or misstatement. If a particular item or transaction is not considered material, it does not make any difference whether it is

---

[3]American Institute of Certified Public Accountants, Accounting Principles Board, Statement No. 4, *Basic Concepts and Accounting Principles Underlying Financial Statements of Business Enterprises* (New York: AICPA, 1970), par. 171.

[4]FASB Concepts Statement 2, par. 93.

accounted for in the theoretically correct manner. For example, if a firm purchases a wastepaper basket for $2.50, this item theoretically should be considered an asset and be depreciated over its lifetime. However, because of the immaterial nature of the account, a firm would most likely consider the entire $2.50 an expense of the current period. Clearly, this decision would not affect the decisions of informed users of financial statements.

Many decisions regarding materiality are less clear-cut than the above example and call for the careful application of the accountant's judgment. The application of materiality often depends on the size of the particular item in relation to the overall size of the firm. Obviously, what is material to Smith's Shoe Store is not material to General Motors. Because of the difficulty in applying the materiality concept, a rule of thumb is often used. For example, an accountant may decide that an item is material if it equals or exceeds 5% of net income or 10% of total assets. Although such yardsticks are helpful, they do not replace the accountant's judgment.

■ QUALITATIVE CHARACTERISTICS AND GENERAL-PURPOSE FINANCIAL STATEMENTS

Collectively, the purpose of the qualitative characteristics is to ensure that the financial information is useful to the variety of groups who are likely to use it for decision-making purposes. Among these groups are stockholders, creditors, labor unions, regulatory agencies, attorneys, educators, and internal management. Each of these groups uses financial statements for overlapping but somewhat different purposes. Because it is costly to prepare special-purpose financial statements for each user group, general-purpose financial statements are prepared, aimed primarily at present and potential investors and creditors and also serving the needs of a wide range of users.

For financial statements to meet these needs, they must be presented in a manner that allows investors and creditors to evaluate the financial strength and profitability of business enterprises. Therefore financial statements are often divided into categories that allow for meaningful interfirm and interperiod comparison. These statements are called **classified financial statements** and will be discussed in reference to the Hartman Flower Company and Toys "R" Us.

■ CLASSIFIED BALANCE SHEETS

The purpose of the balance sheet is to present the financial position of a company at a specific date. This statement aids financial statement users in assessing the company's financial strength and liquidity and is used to answer the following types of questions:

1. What is the company's overall financial strength?

2. How liquid is the company?

3. Will the company be able to meet its short-term obligations?

4. What proportion of the company's assets has been contributed by creditors and investors, respectively?

5. How does the company's financial position compare with that of others in that industry?

The classified balance sheet for the Hartman Flower Company at June 30, 1990 is presented in Exhibit 5-1, and the consolidated balance sheets for Toys "R" Us is presented in Exhibit 5-2. The particular subcategories listed under the major categories of assets, liabilities, and stockholders' equity are the decisions of management. Although the classification scheme generally revolves around specific firm and industry characteristics, there is a great deal of uniformity in the statements of U.S. companies. Thus the statements presented in this chapter are typical of those found in major U.S.

EXHIBIT 5–1

HARTMAN FLOWER COMPANY				
Balance Sheet				
June 30, 1990				

Assets			Liabilities and Stockholders' Equity		
Current assets			Current liabilities		
Cash		$ 9,680	Accounts payable		$ 5,520
Accounts receivable		5,500	Bank loan payable		1,000[a]
Inventory		10,100	Salaries payable		1,200
Office supplies		300	Interest payable		75
Garden supplies		200	Taxes payable		900
License		90	Total current liabilities		8,695
Prepaid insurance		2,300	Long-term debt		
Total current assets		$28,170	Bank loan payable		4,000[a]
Property, plant, and equipment			Total liabilities		$12,695
Land		$ 5,000	Stockholders' equity		
Store furniture and fixtures	$10,200		Capital stock		$44,000
Less: Accumulated depreciation	200	10,000	Retained earnings		1,350
Buildings	$15,000		Total stockholders' equity		$45,350
Less: Accumulated depreciation	125	14,875			
Total property, plant, and equipment		$29,875	Total liabilities and stockholders'		
Total assets		$58,045	equity		$58,045

[a] The $5,000 bank loan is divided between current liabilities and long-term debt.

corporations. In considering a French or Dutch company, however, the classifications used and the order of the particular elements within the balance sheet would be considerably different, because generally accepted accounting principles are the result of the economic and political systems within particular countries, so there are many variations.

When examining the Toys "R" Us balance sheets (Exhibit 5-2), notice that Toys "R" Us's year-end is on a different date for the two years. Toys "R" Us has chosen as a year-end what is referred to as a *52–53 week fiscal year*, which allows a firm to choose a year-end on the same day of the week each year. Toys "R" Us is on a 52–53 week fiscal year that ends on the Saturday nearest to the end of January. This means that sometimes its year ends in the last week of January and other times in the first week of February. Thus Toys "R" Us's year always ends on a Saturday, which is the end of its natural business week. This type of fiscal year is very common for retailing firms. January is the month following the end of their busiest time of the year, the holiday season. At this time, their inventories are at a low point and their business is slowest. This simplifies its accounting and closing process. Because of this choice of fiscal year, the accounting period for Toys "R" Us has 52 weeks in some years and 53 weeks in others.

The Toys "R" Us balance sheet, as well as its other financial statements, are **consolidated statements**. Toys "R" Us owns a number of other companies, called *subsidiaries*, and because of the entity concept, the balance sheet of Toys "R" Us and its subsidiaries are consolidated into one statement. This enables the users of the statement to assess the financial position of Toys "R" Us based on all of the assets under its control.

EXHIBIT 5–2

TOYS "R" US, INC. AND SUBSIDIARIES

Consolidated Balance Sheets

(In thousands)   *Fiscal Year Ended*

	January 31 1988	February 1 1987
ASSETS		
Current Assets:		
Cash and short-term investments	$ 45,996	$ 84,379
Accounts and other receivables, less allowance for doubtful accounts of $1,386 and $1,133	62,144	37,502
Merchandise inventories (Note 1)	772,833	528,939
Prepaid expenses	5,050	3,566
Total Current Assets	886,023	654,386
Property and Equipment (Notes 1, 2 and 3):		
Real estate, net of accumulated depreciation of $31,238 and $22,400	762,082	600,747
Other, net of accumulated depreciation and amortization of $116,980 and $86,207	351,037	240,218
Leased Property Under Capital Leases, net of accumulated depreciation of $16,840 and $15,797 (Note 4)	11,397	12,440
Other Assets	16,520	15,175
	$ 2,027,059	$1,522,966
LIABILITIES AND STOCKHOLDERS' EQUITY		
Current Liabilities:		
Short-term notes payable to banks	$ 17,657	$ —
Accounts payable	403,105	305,705
Accrued expenses, taxes and other liabilities	167,280	118,260
Federal income taxes (Note 6)	71,003	73,059
Current portion:		
Long-term debt (Note 3)	876	973
Obligations under capital leases (Note 4)	1,071	968
Total Current Liabilities	660,992	498,965
Deferred Income Taxes (Note 6)	53,356	40,321
Long-Term Debt (Note 3)	159,788	63,966
Obligations Under Capital Leases (Note 4)	17,602	18,673
Commitments (Note 4)		
Stockholders' Equity (Note 5):		
Common stock par value $.10 per share:		
Authorized 200,000,000 shares		
Issued 130,530,467 and 127,110,608	13,053	12,711
Additional paid-in capital	252,493	239,721
Retained earnings	854,421	650,499
Foreign currency translation adjustments	23,586	8,449
Treasury shares, at cost	(5,929)	(5,571)
Receivable from exercise of stock options	(2,303)	(4,768)
	1,135,321	901,041
	$2,027,059	$1,522,966

See notes to consolidated financial statements.

Published balance sheets of publicly held companies are comparative and present data for at least two years. Toys "R" Us presents two years of comparative data. The financial statements for the Hartman Flower Company are not comparative, because this is the first year of operation.

■ ASSETS

Most balance sheets contain up to five categories in the assets section: (1) current assets; (2) long-term investments; (3) property, plant, and equipment; (4) intangible assets; and (5) other assets. Not all of these categories will be found on all balance sheets, and particular firms often use slightly different classifications and labels.

Current Assets

The Accounting Principles Board defined **current assets** as:

> . . . cash and other assets that are reasonably expected to be realized in cash or sold or consumed during the normal operating cycle of a business or within one year if the operating cycle is shorter than one year.[5]

The **operating cycle** of a business is the time it takes a firm to go from cash back to cash. That is, an enterprise uses its cash or incurs payables to purchase or manufacture merchandise for resale. The inventory is then sold, and the enterprise receives cash or a receivable. The operating cycle is completed when the receivables from credit sales are collected and the payables are paid.

Most firms have an operating cycle of less than one year. However, because some firms have operating cycles that extend for several years, assets that are used up or turned into cash during that cycle are considered current. Examples of such companies are construction companies, tobacco growers, distillers, and cattle breeders. Some firms have several operating cycles of different lengths. For example, a bank might have a short operating cycle for checking accounts and a long operating cycle for notes and mortgages. As a result, the current/noncurrent categories often are not used on bank balance sheets.

Current assets include cash, short-term investments, accounts receivable, inventories, supplies, and various prepaid items. Only in rare situations is cash not included as a current asset. An example is when a firm maintains cash in a foreign country and currency regulations prohibit the transfer of cash to the United States. Investments can be classified as current or noncurrent. In some cases, management will invest idle cash in the capital stock of other companies. If such investments are on a temporary basis and if the securities are readily marketable, they are classified as a current asset. If the investment does not meet these criteria, it is classified as a noncurrent asset in the long-term investment section of the balance sheet.

Trade accounts receivable and other loans or notes receivable due within one year or the operating cycle are classified as current. Because some accounts receivable will not be collected, a contra account called Allowance for Doubtful Accounts is established. The balance in this account represents management's estimate of the uncollectible accounts. On the balance sheet, the total in this account is deducted from the total in Accounts Receivable. As a result, the net amount in Accounts Receivable represents the total estimated to be collected, or the net realizable value of the receivables. The techniques used to estimate and record the Allowance for Doubtful Accounts will be described in Chapter 8.

[5] APB Statement 4, par. 198.

Inventories, supplies, and prepaid expenses are current assets because they will be sold or used up during the following year or operating cycle. In some situations, prepaid expenses may benefit several years or operating cycles. However, because these amounts are usually not material, the entire amount is usually shown as a current asset. If they are material, the noncurrent portion of these long-term prepaids will be listed in the Other Assets section of the balance sheet and are often called *deferred charges*.

When you examine the balance sheets shown in Exhibits 5-1 and 5-2, you see that current assets are listed in order of their liquidity. That is, cash is shown first and then those items that are most easily converted into cash (monetary assets). Nonmonetary current assets are shown last.

Investments

Long-term investments include cash not available for current use and holdings in securities (stocks and bonds) not classified as current. Property, plant, and equipment not used in production but held for resale or future use are often listed in this category. Other assets listed under investments include special cash accounts called *sinking funds*, which are established to purchase property, plant, and equipment or to repay bonds and other long-term debts.

Property, Plant, and Equipment

Assets classified under property, plant, and equipment represent the firm's productive capacity. These assets are used in the purchasing, production, selling, and delivery of the firm's goods and services. Other than land, which does not give up its future benefits, assets listed under this category are depreciated. As discussed in Chapter 4, plant, equipment, and other productive assets are shown net of accumulated depreciation. Although the specific order in which the assets are listed in this category varies, land is usually shown first. Other titles for this section of the balance sheet include Operating Assets, Long-lived Assets, Tangible Assets, and Fixed Assets.

The property, plant, and equipment sections of the Hartman Flower Company and Toys "R" Us are typical of those found in the balance sheets of many U.S. companies. Toys "R" Us also includes in this category Leased Property Under Capital Leases. These are stores that Toys "R" Us has leased under long-term agreements. Generally accepted accounting principles require that these leases be treated as if the stores had been purchased outright. Chapter 12 will show how accounting for leases results in an asset account, Property Under Capital Leases, to be included in the balance sheet of Toys "R" Us.

Intangible Assets

Intangible assets are assets that have no physical or tangible characteristics, as do buildings or equipment. They are agreements, contracts, or rights that provide the firm future economic benefits, because they give it the right to use a certain production process, trade name, or similar item. Typical assets included in this category are patents, trademarks, copyrights, franchises, and goodwill. **Goodwill** refers to anticipated future benefits that will accrue to the firm because of its ability to earn a rate of return exceeding the normal return expected for firms using similar resources. If the purchaser pays more than the fair market value for the net assets acquired, the difference is considered goodwill. Goodwill cannot be recorded unless a firm is purchased by another. Only in this way can the amount of goodwill be verified. Because all intangible assets eventually lose their economic benefits, their costs are written off over the shorter of their useful or economic life. This process is called *amortization* and will be explored further in Chapter 10. The Hartman Flower Company does not have any intangible assets. The intangible assets of Toys "R" Us are included as other items under the Property and Equipment heading.

Other Assets

Other assets is a catchall category that many firms use to list assets that do not fit well elsewhere. Examples are long-term receivables, if not listed under the investment category, and long-term prepayments.

■ LIABILITIES

Liabilities represent the economic obligations of the firm. For balance sheet purposes, they are usually classified in two categories, current liabilities and long-term liabilities or debt.

Current Liabilities

Current liabilities are those that will either be paid or require the use of current assets within one year or one operating cycle, if the operating cycle exceeds one year. Typical current liabilities are short-term notes and loans payable, accounts payable, taxes payable, wages, other accrued expenses, and unearned income or advances from customers. Some liabilities, such as mortgages, are payable in equal monthly installments over a specified number of years. The portion of these liabilities that is payable within 12 months from the balance sheet date is called **current portion of long-term debt** and is classified as a current liability. The remaining portion is classified as a noncurrent liability. In Exhibit 5-2, for example, two such items, current obligations under capital leases and the current portion of long-term debt, are shown in the current liability section.

Long-term Liabilities

Liabilities that do not meet the criteria to be considered current are classified as noncurrent or long-term. Included in this category are bonds payable, mortgages payable, leases, and long-term bank loans payable. Remember that the portion of these liabilities that is due within the next 12 months is classified as current.

Toys "R" Us lists two additional categories in the liability section of its balance sheet: deferred income taxes and commitments. **Deferred income taxes** are those that Toys "R" Us has incurred in the current year but that are not payable until a future period. Deferred income taxes are complex; the topic is discussed briefly in Chapter 11.

Commitments are listed on the balance sheet with no dollar amount shown. These represent executory contracts that will cause a future outflow of cash but that do not meet the recognition criteria to be recorded as liabilities. The category is shown on the balance sheet and referenced to a footnote. This is to call the reader's attention to the item. For Toys "R" Us, commitments for future payments on non-cancelable leases are not recorded as actual liabilities.

■ STOCKHOLDERS' EQUITY

Because both the Hartman Flower Company and Toys "R" Us are organized as corporations, the term *stockholders' equity* is used to describe this section of their balance sheets. Included in this category are the following accounts: common stock (or the more general term, capital stock), additional paid-in capital, certain direct adjustments to stockholders' equity such as foreign currency adjustments, and retained earnings. The total of the common stock and the additional paid-in capital represents the stockholders' permanent investment in the corporation.

For the Hartman Flower Company, the total capital stock account equals $44,000 and represents the corporation's permanent capital. This capital was contributed by Hartman and his friends. For Toys "R" Us, the total permanent investment by stockholders at January 31, 1988 equals $265,546,000 ($13,053,000 in common stock and $252,493,000 in additional paid-in capital). The fact that this investment is divided between the Common Stock account and the Additional Paid-in Capital account is not significant, but the reasons for this arbitrary division will be explained in Chapter 13.

By just looking at the Toys "R" Us balance sheet, it is impossible to say how many current stockholders there are. It is clear only that Toys "R" Us is authorized to issue 200,000,000 shares of common stock and had 130,530,467 shares outstanding on January 31, 1988. How they are divided among individual stockholders is impossible to determine from this information.

Under current accounting standards, some items are treated as direct deductions to stockholders' equity. These include treasury stock and cumulative foreign currency translation adjustments, which will be mentioned in appropriate chapters in the text.

As noted in Chapter 3, retained earnings represent the accumulated earnings of the business less any dividends issued. Because the Hartman Flower Company has just begun operations, its Retained Earnings account has a balance of only $1,350. Toys "R" Us's balance in its Retained Earnings account is $854,421,000. The changes that affect this account during the year are described in the retained earnings statement.

■ THE USES AND LIMITATIONS OF CLASSIFIED BALANCE SHEETS

This discussion began with a list of questions that present and potential investors and creditors can answer from the balance sheet. These questions usually center on measuring a company's overall financial strength. This can be accomplished through financial statement analysis, using ratios to highlight important relationships. Some significant ratios and other analytic data will be considered next. Chapter 17 contains a more complete discussion of financial statement analysis and interpretation.

■ MEASURING LIQUIDITY

As noted, financial statement users are interested in a firm's liquidity. That is, they would like to know whether a firm has enough current assets to pay its current liabilities and/or to respond to changes in the business environment. Two measures, working capital and the current ratio, are commonly used to make this assessment.

Working Capital

Working capital, or net working capital, is defined as current assets minus current liabilities. Thus working capital represents the amount of current assets that the firm has available to respond to its business needs after repaying all of its current liabilities. Firms need enough working capital to continue operating on a day-to-day basis. Even profitable firms that are unable to maintain a significant amount of working capital can face financial difficulties. Consequently, a firm's creditors often require it to maintain a certain level of working capital. The following footnote taken from the recent financial statements of Genesco, a large publicly held corporation, illustrates such a restriction:

> Genesco's revolving credit agreement requires the Company, among other things, to maintain working capital of at least $90,000,000; a current ratio of not less than 1.5:1.

Working capital is calculated for both the Hartman Flower Company and Toys "R" Us in Exhibit 5-3. As these calculations show, working capital for the Hartman Flower Company is $19,475 and for Toys "R" Us $225,031,000. Several questions come to mind. How much working capital is sufficient? Which is in better financial position, Hartman or Toys "R" Us? The answer to the first question depends on the company's particular needs and the characteristics of the industry within which the firm operates. One way to answer this question is to compare the amount of working capital of

EXHIBIT 5–3

Determination of
Working Capital and the
Current Ratio

Working Capital	Current Ratio
Current Assets less Current Liabilities	$\dfrac{\text{Current Assets}}{\text{Current Liabilities}}$

HARTMAN FLOWER COMPANY

$$\$28,170 - \$8,695 = \$19,475 \qquad \frac{\$28,170}{\$\,8,695} = 3.24$$

TOYS "R" US

$$\$886,023,000 - \$660,992,000 = \$225,031,000 \qquad \frac{(\$886,023,000)}{(\$660,992,000)} = 1.34$$

a particular firm with that of other firms of similar size in the industry or with an industry average. In addition, working capital over several years should be compared and analyzed.

Answering the second question is more difficult. Interfirm comparisons are tentative, because the firm's absolute size affects the amount of its working capital. Because Toys "R" Us is thousands of times larger than the Hartman Flower Company, one would expect Toys "R" Us to have more working capital. But whether Toys "R" Us is in better financial shape than Hartman cannot be answered by just comparing the dollar amount of the working capital of the two companies.

The Current Ratio

One solution to this problem is to calculate a ratio called the *current ratio*. The **current ratio** is determined by dividing the total current assets by the total current liabilities. It allows meaningful comparisons among firms of different sizes, because all dollar amounts are standardized by the ratio. The current ratio for the Hartman Flower Company is 3.24, and for Toys "R" Us it is 1.34. These calculations are given with the working capital calculations in Exhibit 5-3.

From this data, the Hartman Flower Company appears to be more liquid than Toys "R" Us. However, other items must be considered. For example, firms in some industries traditionally have higher current ratios than do firms in other industries. Thus a firm's specific ratio should be compared with its industry average. For example, the average current ratio for firms in the retail toy and hobby industry is 1.5. Thus the Toys "R" Us current ratio appears to be slightly below the average. In any event, most financial analysts would probably agree that a ratio of 2.0 to 1 or 3.0 to 1 is sufficiently high for most firms.

The particular makeup of the current assets is also important. Approximately 54% of Hartman's current assets (cash and accounts receivable) can quickly be turned into cash. Conversely, for Toys "R" Us this figure is only about 12%. This is due to the large amount of inventory that Toys "R" Us must maintain.

■ LONG-TERM MEASURES OF FINANCIAL STRENGTH

Investors and creditors are also interested in a firm's long-term strength and financial viability. The amount of debt in relation to total equity or total assets is an indication of this strength. Two ratios, debt to equity and debt to total assets, are often calculated to help individuals assess a firm's long-term strength.

Debt-to-equity Ratio

The **debt-to-equity ratio** is calculated by the following formula:

$$\frac{\text{Total liabilities}}{\text{Total stockholders' equity}}$$

This ratio measures the relative risk assumed by creditors and owners. The higher this ratio, the more difficult it will be for a firm to raise additional capital by increasing long-term debt. The debt-to-equity ratios for the Hartman Flower Company and for Toys "R" Us are calculated in Exhibit 5-4. For the Hartman Flower Company, the ratio is 28%, and for Toys "R" Us it is 78.5%. Toys "R" Us has a much greater percentage of debt to stockholders' equity than Hartman does, which reflects the fact that Toys "R" Us is a strong, mature company that is able to command a large amount of external financing from creditors. This figure is below the industry average of about 170%. Hartman is a young company with much of its financing coming from its stockholders.

EXHIBIT 5–4

Determination of the Debt-to-equity Ratio and the Debt-to-total-assets Ratio

Debt-to-equity Ratio	**Debt-to-total-assets Ratio**
$\dfrac{\text{Total Liabilities}}{\text{Total Stockholders' Equity}}$	$\dfrac{\text{Total Liabilities}}{\text{Total Assets}}$

HARTMAN FLOWER COMPANY

$$\frac{\$12,695}{\$45,350} = 28\% \qquad \frac{\$12,695}{\$58,045} = 21.9\%$$

TOYS "R" US

$$\frac{\$891,738,000}{\$1,135,321,000} = 78.5\% \qquad \frac{\$891,738,000}{\$2,027,059,000} = 44\%$$

Debt-to-total-assets Ratio

The **debt-to-total-assets ratio** is determined by applying the following formula:

$$\frac{\text{Total liabilities}}{\text{Total assets}}$$

This ratio indicates the amount of assets provided by the creditors versus the amount provided by the stockholders. As you may recall, assets must be provided by either creditors or stockholders and profitable operations. This ratio indicates the relative percentage of assets contributed by each group. A higher ratio indicates that creditors have provided a larger share of the firm's assets. When there is a higher ratio of debt to total assets, a prospective banker or other creditor may be unwilling to extend additional credit.

The debt-to-total-assets ratios for the Hartman Flower Company and for Toys "R" Us are also shown in Exhibit 5-4. As this calculation indicates, for Hartman, the ratio is 21.9%, and for Toys "R" Us it is 44%. Again, this reflects the difference in the ability of each company to command external financing.

■ LIMITATIONS OF THE BALANCE SHEET

This chapter has pointed out some of the ways that a balance sheet helps financial statement users evaluate financial position and strength. However, a number of problems inherent in the accounting model limit the usefulness of balance sheets. These problems include the way in which accountants define assets, the use of historical cost, the need for arbitrary cost allocations, and the use of different methods of accounting.

Definition of Assets

In Chapter 1, assets were defined as economic resources, controlled by an enterprise, that have future benefits. For transactions to be admitted into the accounting system, they must be quantifiable in monetary terms and have benefits that are measurable and verifiable. A number of items that one might consider assets, such as good management and research and development efforts, do not meet these criteria and are not considered assets. Accordingly, not all of the real economic assets that a firm owns or controls are listed on the balance sheet.

Historical Costs

Net assets on a firm's balance sheet are recorded at their historical cost or net book value (historical cost less accumulated depreciation). Remember that accountants do not record increases in value or market value until an external transaction occurs. Except in the case of a newly formed company, the balance sheet generally does not indicate the current or market value of the company's net assets. Therefore investors or creditors cannot use the balance sheet to determine the current cost or value of the company's net assets.

Arbitrary Allocation

Investors and creditors need information about an enterprise on a periodic and timely basis. The matching principle ensures that the cost of assets that benefit several periods are allocated to those periods. This requires a number of allocations, such as depreciation, that are inherently estimates. To the extent to which these required estimates are arbitrary management decisions, the balance sheet is less useful to investors and creditors.

Use of Different Accounting Methods

Another limitation of the balance sheet, as well as of other financial statements, is that alternative generally accepted accounting principles are available under current standards. For example, as will become clear in later chapters, firms can use different depreciation methods. Management can choose among alternatives and often does. This makes it difficult to compare and contrast the financial positions of various firms.

■ CLASSIFIED INCOME STATEMENTS

The purpose of the income statement is to provide financial statement users with information concerning the profitability of an enterprise for a particular period of time. This statement lists all of the revenues, expenses, gains, and losses that the enterprise earned or incurred during the accounting period. The difference between the total of revenues plus gains and the total of expenses plus losses is either net income or net loss. The income statement has become very important because, as Concepts Statement 1 notes, "the primary focus of financial reporting is information about . . . earnings and its components."[6]

By analyzing the income statement, the investor or creditor can answer such questions as:

1. Did the company earn a profit this year, and if so, how does it compare with its profits from other years?

2. What is the company's gross margin on sales, and is it large enough to cover other operating expenses?

3. What are the various components of revenues and expenses, and how do they compare with those of prior years?

4. Did the firm generate enough revenues from operations to pay the current interest charges?

5. How profitable is the firm compared with others in its industry?

As with the balance sheet, management has some discretion over the exact format of the income statement, but there are two typical formats used by most businesses in

---

[6]FASB Concepts Statement 1, par. 43.

the United States: the single-step and the multistep forms. Both of these income statements for the Hartman Flower Company are presented in Exhibit 5-5 (single-step) and 5-6 (multistep). Note that in both formats net income is the same. The consolidated income statements of Toys "R" Us for the years ended January 31, 1988, February 1, 1987, and February 2, 1986, are shown in Exhibit 5-7. Keep in mind that the income statements are typical of most U.S. firms but that a foreign firm may issue an income statement showing a different format.

EXHIBIT 5–5

HARTMAN FLOWER COMPANY		
Income Statement—Single-Step		
For the Three Months Ended June 30, 1990		
Revenues		
Sales		$20,000
Expenses		
Cost of goods sold	$14,000	
Selling	2,100	
General and administrative	1,575	
Interest	75	
		17,750
Income before taxes		2,250
Taxes		900
Net income		$ 1,350

EXHIBIT 5–6

HARTMAN FLOWER COMPANY		
Income Statement—Multistep		
For the Three Months Ended June 30, 1990		
Sales		$20,000
Cost of goods sold[a]		14,000
Gross margin on sales		6,000
Operating expenses		
Selling		
Advertising	$2,000	
Salaries	100	
Total selling expenses		$2,100
General and administrative		
Office supplies	$ 700	
Depreciation	325	
Utility	200	
Garden supplies	180	
Insurance	100	
Repairs and maintenance	40	
License	30	
Total general and administrative expenses	1,575	
Total operating expenses		3,675
Income from operations		2,325
Other expenses		
Interest		75
Income before taxes		2,250
Taxes		900
Net income		$ 1,350

[a]Some multistep income statements also present the components of cost of goods sold. These components will be discussed in detail in the next chapter.

EXHIBIT 5–7

TOYS "R" US, INC. AND SUBSIDIARIES

Statements of Consolidated Earnings

(In thousands except per share information)   *Fiscal Year Ended*

	January 31 1988	February 1 1987	February 2 1986
Net sales	$3,136,568	$2,444,903	$1,976,134
Costs and expenses:			
Cost of sales	2,157,017	1,668,209	1,322,942
Selling, advertising, general and administrative	584,120	458,528	408,438
Depreciation and amortization	43,716	33,288	26,074
Interest expense	13,849	7,890	6,999
Interest income	(8,056)	(7,229)	(8,093)
	2,790,646	2,160,686	1,756,360
Earnings before taxes on income	345,922	284,217	219,774
Taxes on income (Note 6)	142,000	132,000	100,000
Net earnings	$ 203,922	$ 152,217	$ 119,774
Net earnings per share (Note 8)	$1.56	$1.17	$.93

■ THE SINGLE-STEP STATEMENT

Usually, the **single-step income statement** has only five major categories: revenues, expenses, income before taxes, taxes, and net income. Individual expense accounts, other than interest and taxes, are combined into functional categories: selling and general and administrative. Selling expenses include the costs that directly relate to the firm's efforts to sell and dispose of its goods and services. Typical expenses included in this category are salespersons' salaries and commissions and advertising, promotion, and delivery expense. In Exhibit 5-5, the Hartman Flower Company's selling expenses include salaries and advertising. General and administrative expenses is a catchall category that includes general office expenses, salaries of personnel other than the sales force, and other general expenses. Because some expenses, such as depreciation and insurance expense, affect both selling and general and administrative expenses, they are often split so that a portion is allocated to each category. Most published income statements are a type of single-step statement; although these statements are simple to prepare, there is a significant condensation of information.

■ THE MULTISTEP STATEMENT

The **multistep income statement** has several steps or categories. The major steps are gross margin or gross profit on sales, operating expenses, income from operations, other income and expenses, income before taxes, and net income.

Gross Margin on Sales

Gross margin on sales is simply sales less cost of goods sold. The gross margin figure is significant to evaluate a company's ability to earn enough profit on its sales to cover its operating expenses. In addition, analysts and other financial statement users calculate a ratio called the *gross margin ratio*, which provides information about the percentage relationship between sales, cost of goods sold, and gross margin. This ratio will be examined in more detail later in this chapter.

Operating Expenses

Operating expenses are generally divided into two categories, selling and general and administrative. A complete multistep income statement (for example, Exhibit 5-6) lists all the individual expenses under the selling and general and administrative categories. Many published financial statements condense this data and report only the total expenses in each category.

Income from Operations

Income from operations (or operating income) is the next category on the income statement. It is the difference between the gross margin on sales and the total of the operating expenses. If the firm's total operating expenses exceed its gross margin on sales, the category will be labeled *loss from operations*.

Other Income and Expenses

A firm often earns revenues from sources other than sales and incurs expenses other than from operations. On a multistep income statement, these items are listed under a category called *other revenues and expenses*. Other revenue items include rent revenue, investment revenue from dividends and interest, and gains from sales of property, plant, and equipment. Other expenses include losses from sales of plant and equipment and interest expense. Accountants consider interest to be a financing charge and not an operating expense.

Income before Taxes and Net Income

Income before taxes is determined by adding or subtracting other revenues and expenses from income from operations. From that total figure, the income tax expense for the period is deducted, and net income is determined. Again, because of the significance of income taxes, they are shown separately as the last item before net income.

Other Data

Income statements of publicly held corporations include earnings-per-share data and may include such categories as discontinued operations, extraordinary items, and the effects of changes in accounting methods. These last three are unusual items that, under generally accepted accounting principles, must be shown separately. On the Toys "R" Us income statement, the only one of these items shown is net income per share, which is another name for **earnings per share**. Although this can be complicated to calculate for a company as complex as Toys "R" Us, it is basically determined by dividing net income by the average number of common shares outstanding during the year. Earnings per share is used by many financial analysts to compare earnings among firms; it will be examined in Chapter 14. Because the Hartman Flower Company is owned by a few individuals, and its stock is not publicly traded, accounting standards do not require the disclosure of earnings per share.

■ THE USES AND LIMITATIONS OF CLASSIFIED INCOME STATEMENTS

The preceding main section began with a list of questions investors and creditors could use the income statement to answer. These questions center on measuring and evaluating a firm's profitability.

■ MEASURING PROFITABILITY

One way to measure and evaluate a firm's profitability is to compute percentages that compare particular income statement items, such as gross margin and net income, to sales. Two such percentages are the **gross margin percentage** and the **profit margin percentage.** These ratios for both the Hartman Flower Company and Toys "R" Us are calculated in Exhibit 5-8.

EXHIBIT 5–8

Determination of Gross
Margin Percentage and
Profit Margin Percentage

Gross Margin Percentage	Profit Margin Percentage
Gross Margin on Sales **Sales**	**Net Income** **Sales**

HARTMAN FLOWER COMPANY

$$\frac{\$\,6,000}{\$20,000} = 30\% \qquad\qquad \frac{\$\,1,350}{\$20,000} = 6.75\%$$

TOYS "R" US

Sales	$3,136,568,000
Cost of goods sold	$2,157,017,000
Gross margin on sales	$ 979,551,000

$$\frac{\$\,979,551,000}{\$3,136,568,000} = 31.2\% \qquad \frac{\$\,203,922,000}{\$3,136,568,000} = 6.5\%$$

Gross Margin Percentage

The gross margin percentage is determined by dividing gross margin by sales. This ratio provides information concerning the percentage of sales to cost of goods sold and gross margin on sales. For the Hartman Flower Company, the gross margin percentage is 30%, and for Toys "R" Us it is 31.2%. Conversely, for Hartman the cost of goods sold percentage equals 30% and for Toys "R" Us 69%. As with all ratios, individual percentages should be evaluated in terms of industry norms. For example, the average gross margin percentage for retail toy and hobby stores is 38.4%.

Profit Margin Percentage

The profit margin percentage relates net income to total sales. It is calculated by dividing net income by sales. For Hartman this percentage is 6.75%, and for Toys "R" Us it is 6.5%. (See previous calculations.) This means that for every dollar of sales, both Hartman and Toys "R" Us net about six cents in profits. Retail firms such as Toys "R" Us tend to be high-volume, low profit-margin businesses.

■ RETURN ON INVESTMENT

A number of ratios can be used by investors and creditors to determine how effectively management is operating a business and the return that is accruing to the various equity holders. Two such common ratios are return on assets and return on stockholders' equity. These ratios are computed in Exhibit 5-9 at the top of page 185 for both Hartman and Toys "R" Us.

Return on Assets

In its simplest form, the ratio **return on assets** is determined by dividing net income by average total assets.[7] In ratios that use an income statement figure in the numerator and a balance sheet figure in the denominator, the denominator should be an average.

---

[7]There are more complex ways to calculate this ratio, which are explored in Chapter 17. However, the method used in this chapter conveys the essential meaning of the ratio. Hartman's statements are for a three-month period, whereas those of Toys "R" Us are for the entire year, so direct comparisons should not be made.

EXHIBIT 5–9

Determination of Return on Assets and Return on Stockholders' Equity

Return on Assets	Return on Stockholders' Equity
$$\frac{\text{Net Income}}{\text{Average Total Assets}}$$	$$\frac{\text{Net Income}}{\text{Average Stockholders' Equity}}$$

HARTMAN FLOWER COMPANY

$$\frac{\$ 1,350}{\$58,045^a} = 2.3\%$$ $$\frac{\$ 1,350}{\$45,350^a} = 3.0\%$$

TOYS "R" US

$$\frac{\$203,922,000}{\dfrac{(\$2,027,059,000 + \$1,522,966,000)}{2}} = 11.5\%$$ $$\frac{\$203,922,000}{\dfrac{(\$1,135,321,000 + \$901,041,000)}{2}} = 20.0\%$$

[a] Balance at end of year is used, as Hartman has been in existence only three months.

This is because revenue and expense items are for a period of time, and it is most appropriate to relate these items to average assets for that period. The return-on-asset ratio is important because it measures how efficiently a firm is using the assets at its command. A high ratio is evidence that management is using the firm's assets or resources efficiently to produce profits. For Hartman, this ratio is 2.3%, and for Toys "R" Us it is 11.5%.

Return on Stockholders' Equity

The **return on stockholders' equity** measures the return that the stockholders are receiving on their investment. It is calculated by dividing net income by average stockholders' equity. This ratio is also calculated in Exhibit 5-9; it is 3.0% for Hartman and 20.0% for Toys "R" Us. Again, evaluation of these ratios depends on industry norms and firm trends. The average in the retail toy industry for large firms is about 23%.

■ LIMITATIONS OF THE INCOME STATEMENT

Clearly, the income statement is extremely useful for evaluating and measuring a firm's profitability. However, as with all financial statements, there are limitations to its usefulness. Because the income statement is linked to the balance sheet, some of the criticisms regarding the balance sheet also apply to the income statement. These include the use of historical costs, the problems associated with cost allocation, and the use of different accounting methods.

■ THE RETAINED EARNINGS STATEMENT OR STATEMENT OF CHANGES IN STOCKHOLDERS' EQUITY

As previously noted, the retained earnings statement discloses the items that caused a change in retained earnings. This fairly simple statement shows the effect of net in-

EXHIBIT 5–10

HARTMAN FLOWER COMPANY Retained Earnings Statement For the Three Months Ended June 30, 1990	
Retained earnings, April 1, 1990	$ 0
Add: Net income for the period	1,350
Total	$1,350
Less: Dividends	$ 0
Retained earnings, June 30, 1990	$1,350

EXHIBIT 5–11

TOYS "R" US, INC. AND SUBSIDIARIES

Statements of Consolidated Stockholders' Equity

(In thousands except shares information)	Common stock Issued Shares	Amount	Common stock In treasury Shares	Amount	Additional paid-in capital	Retained earnings	Foreign currency translation adjustments	Receivable from exercise of stock options	Total
Balance, February 3, 1985	83,153,924	$ 8,315	(1,690,368)	$(4,352)	$200,323	$382,821	$ (383)	$(7,611)	$ 579,113
Net earnings for the year						119,774	–	–	119,774
Exercise of stock options and other	899,992	90	(1,903)	(71)	5,713	–	–	(554)	5,178
Tax benefit from exercise of stock options	–	–	–	–	10,894	–	–	–	10,894
Foreign currency translation gain	–	–	–	–	–	–	2,435	–	2,435
Balance, February 2, 1986	84,053,916	8,405	(1,692,271)	(4,423)	216,930	502,595	2,052	(8,165)	717,394
Three-for-two stock split effected in the form of a 50% stock dividend payable June 27, 1986	42,338,594	4,234	(864,629)	–	–	(4,313)	–	–	(79)
Net earnings for the year	–	–	–	–	–	152,217	–	–	152,217
Exercise of stock options	718,098	72	(33,817)	(1,148)	4,107	–	–	(92)	2,939
Tax benefit from exercise of stock options	–	–	–	–	18,684	–	–	–	18,684
Repayment of stock option loans	–	–	–	–	–	–	–	3,489	3,489
Foreign currency translation gain	–	–	–	–	–	–	6,397	–	6,397
Balance, February 1, 1987	127,110,608	12,711	(2,590,717)	(5,571)	239,721	650,499	8,449	(4,768)	901,041
Net earnings for the year	–	–	–	–	–	203,922	–	–	203,922
Exercise of stock options	3,419,859	342	(9,265)	(358)	7,739	–	–	(1,313)	6,410
Tax benefit from exercise of stock options	–	–	–	–	5,033	–	–	–	5,033
Repayment of stock option loans	–	–	–	–	–	–	–	3,778	3,778
Foreign currency translation gain	–	–	–	–	–	–	15,137	–	15,137
Balance, January 31, 1988	130,530,467	$13,053	(2,599,982)	$(5,929)	$252,493	$854,421	$23,586	$(2,303)	$1,135,321

come or loss and dividends on retained earnings. Such a statement for the Hartman Flower Company is shown in Exhibit 5-10 on page 185.

The statement as shown is adequate for smaller companies that do not have significant changes in other stockholder equity accounts. Large, publicly held firms are likely to enter into various transactions, such as issuing additional common stock or converting bonds into common stock, that affect a variety of stockholders' equity accounts. These firms prepare a more extensive statement, called a **statement of changes in stockholders' equity**. This statement, which is reproduced in Exhibit 5-11 on page 186 for Toys "R" Us, details the changes in all the stockholders' equity accounts.

■ THE STATEMENT OF CASH FLOWS

The statement of cash flows is the fourth required financial statement. The purpose of this statement is to provide relevant information about the cash receipts and disbursements of an enterprise during a period. It is useful in answering the following questions:

1. What are the sources of the firm's cash?

2. What proportion of the firm's cash is generated internally or from operations?

3. What other financing and/or investing activities took place during the year?

4. Why was the firm profitable, although there was only a slight increase in cash?

The statements of cash flows for the Hartman Flower Company and Toys "R" Us are shown in Exhibits 5-12 and 5-13, respectively. Chapter 16 explains the actual preparation of this statement; the purpose here is to introduce you to its usefulness.

The statement of cash flows for the Hartman Flower Company indicates that operating activities resulted in a use of cash of $9,245, even though net income for the period amounted to $1,350. This is not an uncommon situation in a new business; the collection of receivables is slow, but payables must be met quickly. Furthermore, cash is needed to build up inventories for future sales. Thus Hartman had to rely on the sale of capital stock to provide initial cash needs for operating activities as well as the purchase of land, buildings, and store equipment.

The statement of cash flows for Toys "R" Us shows that operating activities resulted in a positive cash flow of $135,017,000. Cash was used to purchase various

EXHIBIT 5-12

HARTMAN FLOWER COMPANY
Statement of Cash Flows
For the Three Months Ended June 30, 1990

Cash flows from operation activities		
Cash revenues	$14,575	
Less: Cash expenses	23,820	
Net cash used by operating activities		$ (9,245)
Cash flows from investing activities		
Purchase of land	$ 5,000	
Purchases of building	15,000	
Purchase of store furniture & fixtures	5,075	
Net cash used by investing activities		(25,075)
Cash flows from financing activities		
Issue of capital stock		44,000
Net increase in cash		9,680
Cash balance at April 1, 1990		0
Cash balance, June 30, 1990		$ 9,680

EXHIBIT 5–13

TOYS "R" US, INC. AND SUBSIDIARIES

Statements of Consolidated Cash Flows

(In thousands)   *Fiscal Year Ended*

	January 31 1988	February 1 1987	February 2 1986
CASH FLOWS FROM OPERATING ACTIVITIES			
Net income	$203,922	$152,217	$119,774
Adjustments to reconcile net income to net cash provided by operating activities:			
Depreciation and amortization	43,716	33,288	26,074
Deferred taxes	13,035	14,184	9,669
Change in operating assets and liabilities:			
Accounts and other receivables	(24,642)	(11,531)	(2,564)
Merchandise inventories	(243,894)	(115,446)	(15,580)
Prepaid expenses	(1,484)	(320)	(1,215)
Accounts payable, accrued expenses and taxes	144,364	102,382	(153)
Total adjustments	(68,905)	22,557	16,231
Net cash provided by operating activities	135,017	174,774	136,005
CASH FLOWS FROM INVESTING ACTIVITIES			
Capital expenditures-net	(314,827)	(259,388)	(221,794)
Other net	13,792	10,952	11,053
Net cash used in investing activities	(301,035)	(248,436)	(210,741)
CASH FLOWS FROM FINANCING ACTIVITIES			
Short-term borrowings-net	17,663	(1,136)	(19,118)
Long-term borrowings	96,611	—	2,493
Long-term debt repayments	(1,860)	(2,027)	(3,819)
Exercise of stock options	15,221	25,033	16,072
Net cash provided by financing activities	127,635	21,870	(4,372)
CASH AND SHORT-TERM INVESTMENTS			
Decrease during year	(38,383)	(51,792)	(79,108)
Beginning of year	84,379	136,171	215,279
End of year	$ 45,996	$ 84,379	$136,171

SUPPLEMENTAL DISCLOSURES OF CASH FLOW INFORMATION

The Company considers all highly liquid investments purchased as part of its daily cash management activities to be short-term investments.

During the years ended January 31, 1988, February 1, 1987 and February 2, 1986, the Company made income tax payments of $119,722,000, $79,934,000 and $70,205,000 and interest payments (net of amounts capitalized) of $9,610,000, $8,044,000 and $6,857,000 respectively.

See notes to consolidated financial statements.

capital items such as stores and equipment. Cash was raised through various financing activities, mainly long-term borrowings. During the year, cash and short-term investments, which are considered part of the company's daily cash management activities, decreased $38,383,000.

■ OTHER ELEMENTS OF AN ANNUAL REPORT OF A PUBLICLY HELD COMPANY

The financial statements themselves are only one aspect of the financial information that an enterprise makes available to users. This is especially true of publicly held companies, which are required to disclose various other items. This section will cover the footnotes to the financial statements, which are an integral part of the financial statements of all firms, the auditors' report, and other aspects of an annual report.

■ FOOTNOTES TO THE FINANCIAL STATEMENTS

It is impossible to include in the body of the financial statements all important information. Yet the **full-disclosure principle** requires that a firm's financial statements provide users with all relevant information about the various transactions of the firm. As a result, financial statements must have **footnotes**, which are narrative explanations of the important aspects of various items. Toys "R" Us has footnotes that range from an explanation of its significant accounting policies (footnote 1) to quarterly information (footnote 9). Toys "R" Us's complete financial statements, including all footnotes, are reproduced in Appendix D. As an example, footnote 7, concerning the company's profit-sharing plan, is shown in Exhibit 5-14.

EXHIBIT 5–14
Toys "R" Us

> **7. PROFIT-SHARING PLAN**
>
> The Company has a profit-sharing plan with a 401(k) salary deferral feature for eligible employees, which may be terminated at its discretion. Provisions of $9,523,000, $6,573,000, and $6,422,000 have been charged to operations in the years ended January 31, 1988, February 1, 1987 and February 2, 1986, respectively.

■ THE AUDITORS' REPORT

The management of all public companies, as well as a number of private companies, are required to use certified public accountants (CPAs) to audit their financial statements. Public companies are required by U.S. securities laws to engage CPAs to conduct an audit. Owner-managers of private companies may want an audit for several reasons, including the desire to assure themselves that their financial statements conform with generally accepted accounting principles. Bankers and other creditors also may require an audit. In all cases, the purpose of the audit is to assure users that the financial statements prepared by the firm's management are in conformity with generally accepted accounting principles.

The **auditors' report** for Toys "R" Us is reproduced in Exhibit 5-15. It is a traditional, two-paragraph report that indicates that the financial statements of Toys "R" Us present fairly the financial position of the company and its results of operations. Recently, this traditional report has been replaced by a different form, which spells out more clearly the responsibilities of management and the auditors and has a middle paragraph that indicates what an audit includes. This change was made by the accounting profession in order to make clear the function and purposes of an audit. An example of the new report form for the Walgreen Co. is shown in Exhibit 5-16. Future auditors'

EXHIBIT 5–15

Traditional Auditors'
Report

TOYS "R" US, INC. AND SUBSIDIARIES

▌Auditors' Report

Board of Directors and Stockholders
Toys "R" Us, Inc.
Rochelle Park, New Jersey

We have examined the consolidated balance sheets of Toys "R" Us, Inc. and subsidiaries at January 31, 1988 and February 1, 1987 and the related consolidated statements of earnings, stockholders' equity and cash flows for each of the three years in the period ended January 31, 1988. Our examinations were made in accordance with generally accepted auditing standards and, accordingly, included such tests of the accounting records and such other auditing procedures as we considered necessary in the circumstances.

In our opinion, the consolidated statements referred to above present fairly the financial position of Toys "R" Us, Inc. and subsidiaries at January 31, 1988 and February 1, 1987, and the results of their operations and cash flows for each of the three years in the period ended January 31, 1988 in conformity with generally accepted accounting principles applied on a consistent basis.

Touche Ross & Co.

March 16, 1988
New York, New York

Certified Public Accountants

EXHIBIT 5–16   New Auditors' Report

REPORT OF INDEPENDENT PUBLIC ACCOUNTANTS

To the Board of Directors and Shareholders of Walgreen Co.:

We have audited the accompanying balance sheets of Walgreen Co. (an Illinois corporation) and Subsidiaries as of August 31, 1988 and 1987, and the related statements of earnings, retained earnings and cash flows for each of the three years in the period ended August 31, 1988. These financial statements are the responsibility of the Company's management. Our responsibility is to express an opinion on these financial statements based on our audits.

We conducted our audits in accordance with generally accepted auditing standards. Those standards require that we plan and perform the audit to obtain reasonable assurance about whether the financial statements are free of material misstatement. An audit includes examining, on a test basis, evidence supporting the amounts and disclosures in the financial statements. An audit also includes assessing the account-

ing principles used and significant estimates made by management, as well as evaluating the overall financial statement presentation. We believe that our audits provide a reasonable basis for our opinion.

In our opinion, the financial statements referred to above present fairly, in all material respects, the financial position of Walgreen Co. and Subsidiaries as of August 31, 1988 and 1987, and the results of its operations and its cash flows for each of the three years in the period ended August 31, 1988, in conformity with generally accepted accounting principles.

Arthur Andersen + Co.

Chicago, Illinois,
October 18, 1988.

reports for Toys "R" Us will look like Exhibit 5-16. As the new audit report clearly indicates, financial statements are the responsibility of management. Management also explicitly notes this in a statement in the annual report, placed immediately before the auditors' report. Such a statement for Toys "R" Us is shown in Exhibit 5-17.

EXHIBIT 5–17

Toys "R" Us

Report of Management

Responsibility for the integrity and objectivity of the financial information presented in this Annual Report rests with Toys "R" Us management. The accompanying financial statements have been prepared from accounting records which management believes fairly and accurately reflect the operations and financial position of the Company. Management has established a system of internal controls to provide reasonable assurance that assets are maintained and accounted for in accordance with its policies and that transactions are recorded accurately on the Company's books and records.

The Company's comprehensive internal audit program provides for constant evaluation of the adequacy of and adherence to management's established policies and procedures. The Company has distributed to key employees its policies for conducting business affairs in a lawful and ethical manner.

The financial statements of the Company have been examined by Touche Ross & Co., independent certified public accountants. Their accompanying report is based on an examination conducted in accordance with generally accepted auditing standards, including a review of internal accounting controls and financial reporting matters.

Charles Lazarus
Chairman of the Board

Michael Goldstein
Executive Vice President-
Finance and Administration

■ OTHER ASPECTS OF THE ANNUAL REPORT

All public companies issue annual reports to their stockholders and other interested users. These reports contain the firm's audited financial statements, including footnotes, management's discussion and analysis of operations, the president's letter, summaries of significant financial statistics, and other data. How to use this data to analyze and interpret financial statements is covered in Chapter 18. Also, Appendix D includes relevant portions of the Toys "R" Us annual report, including all financial statements and footnotes. In addition, for your comparison, the appendix includes the financial statements of the Heineken Company, a multinational Dutch firm.

SUMMARY OF LEARNING OBJECTIVES

1. The objective of general-purpose financial statements. Financial statements are the major outputs of the accounting information system and are aimed at the general-purpose user. One objective of financial statements is to provide relevant and useful information to present and potential investors and creditors that increases their ability to assess future cash flows. This is best accomplished by providing information about an enterprise's economic resources and obligations and changes in them.

2. The qualitative characteristics of financial information. According to the FASB, to provide information that is useful in decision making, accounting information must possess certain qualitative characteristics, including quantifiability, relevance, and reliability. Information is relevant if it has predictive and/or feedback value to users. Reliability is an indication of whether the information measures what it should.

3. The construction of classified balance sheets. Given accounting norms and conventions, the actual format of the balance sheet is at the discretion of a firm's management. However, most balance sheets of U.S. firms include at least some of these major categories: Current Assets; Long-term Investment; Property, Plant, and Equipment; Intangible Assets; Other Assets; Current Liabilities; Long-term Liabilities; and Stockholders' Equity.

4. The uses and limitations of classified balance sheets. Investors and creditors can use a balance sheet to analyze a firm's financial position, liquidity, and strength. This can be accomplished by considering such items and ratios as working capital, the current ratio, the debt-to-equity ratio, and the total-debt-to-assets ratio. However, there are limitations to the usefulness of the balance sheet because of the way in which assets are defined, the use of historical costs, the use of different accounting methods, and the need for cost allocation.

5. The construction of classified income statements. As with balance sheets, the usefulness of income statements can be increased by classifying items that appear on the statement. The degree of detail depends on whether a firm prepares a single-step or a multistep income statement. Both types of statements are typical of those prepared in U.S. firms.

6. The uses and limitations of classified income statements. Classified income statements are useful to investors and creditors in evaluating a firm's profitability and the returns that accrue to each equity group. Percentages and ratios such as the gross margin percentage, the profit margin percentage, the return on total assets, and the return on stockholders' equity are useful in this evaluation. However, as with the balance sheet, there are limitations to the usefulness of the income statement. These include the use of historical costs, cost allocations, and the existence of alternative generally accepted accounting principles.

7. The retained earnings statement and the statement of changes in stockholders' equity. The retained earnings statement details the factors that caused changes in the retained earnings account. The statement of changes in stockholders' equity details the changes in all of the stockholders' equity accounts. In recent years, large firms have begun to prepare the statement of changes in stockholders' equity rather than the retained earnings statement. This is because firms are entering into more complex transactions that can best be disclosed in this statement.

8. The statement of cash flows. In order to gain a full understanding of a company, an investor or creditor must look beyond the balance sheet, the income statement, and the statement of changes in stockholders' equity. The statement of cash flows is useful in gaining an understanding of how a firm obtains and uses its cash.

9. Other financial data in the annual report. The full-disclosure principle requires that all of the relevant information pertaining to a firm's economic activities be disclosed. Such items as footnotes, summaries of financial statistics, and the auditors' report are found in published annual reports and provide essential information to users.

KEY TERMS

Auditors' report
Classified financial statements
Commitments
Comparability
Conservatism
Consistency
Consolidated statements
Current assets
Current liabilities
Current portion of long-term debt
Current ratio
Debt-to-equity ratio
Debt-to-total-assets ratio
Deferred income taxes
Earnings per share
Financial statement footnotes

Full-disclosure principle
Goodwill
Gross margin on sales
Gross margin percentage
Intangible assets
Long-term investments
Materiality
Multistep income statement
Objectives of financial reporting
Operating cycle
Profit margin percentage
Return on assets
Return on stockholders' equity
Single-step income statement
Statement of changes in stockholders' equity
Working capital

PROBLEMS FOR YOUR REVIEW

A. Classified Balance Sheet. The post-closing trial balance of the Artesian Company is shown below (in alphabetical order):

ARTESIAN COMPANY
Post-closing Trial Balance
December 31, 1990

Accounts payable	$10,000	Land	$40,000
Accounts receivable	12,500	Marketable securities, held for temporary investments	4,500
Accumulated depreciation— Plant and equipment	20,000		
Bonds payable	50,000	Mortgage payable less current portion	20,000
Bond sinking fund	15,000	Patent	5,000
Cash	8,000	Prepaid insurance	2,000
Common stock	30,000	Plant and equipment	100,000
Current maturities of long-term debt	12,000	Retained earnings	?
Inventories	18,000	Salaries payable	5,000
Investments, long term	5,000	Taxes payable	3,000

REQUIRED: Prepare in good form a classified balance sheet at December 31, 1990 for the Artesian Company.

SOLUTION

ARTESIAN COMPANY
Balance Sheet
December 31, 1990

Assets			Liabilities and Stockholders' Equity	
Current assets			**Current liabilities**	
Cash		$ 8,000	Current maturities of long-term debt	$ 12,000
Marketable securities		4,500	Accounts payable	10,000
Accounts receivable		12,500	Salaries payable	5,000
Inventories		18,000	Taxes payable	3,000
Prepaid insurance		2,000		
Total current assets		45,000	Total current liabilities	30,000
Investments			**Long-term liabilities**	
Long-term investments		5,000	Bonds payable	50,000
Bond sinking fund		15,000	Mortgage payable	20,000
Total long-term investments		20,000	Total long-term liabilities	70,000
Property, plant, and equipment			Total liabilities	$100,000
Land		40,000	**Stockholders' equity**	
Plant and equipment	$100,000		Common stock	30,000
Less: Accumulated depreciation	20,000	80,000	Retained earnings	60,000
Total property, plant, and equipment		120,000	Total stockholders' equity	90,000
Intangible assets				
Patents, net of amortization		5,000		
Total assets		$190,000	Total liabilities and stockholders' equity	$190,000

Points to consider:

1. The marketable securities are considered a current asset because they are marketable and held temporarily.

2. Intangible assets such as patents are usually shown net of amortization, whereas for plant and equipment both the historical costs and the accumulated depreciation are disclosed.

3. Current maturities of long-term debt must be classified as a current liability.

4. The order within the current liabilities section is not particularly significant.

5. In this example, retained earnings must be calculated. It is the amount needed to make the equities equal the assets, or $190,000 − $130,000 = $60,000.

B. Classified Income Statement. The revenue expense and related accounts of the Artesian Company are listed below in alphabetical order.

REQUIRED:

1. Prepare in good form a multistep income statement.

2. Prepare in good form a single-step income statement.

3. Prepare in good form a statement of retained earnings. (The amount of dividends must be determined.)

ARTESIAN COMPANY

Revenues and Expense and

All Related Accounts

Year Ended December 31, 1990

Advertising expense*	$ 3,500
Beginning retained earnings	39,500
Commission*	4,500
Cost of goods sold	167,000
Depreciation and amortization	10,000
Dividends paid	?
Insurance expense	3,000
Interest expense	2,000
Repairs and maintenance	1,000
Sales	250,500
Salespersons' salaries*	12,000
Income tax rate	40%

*Indicates selling expenses

SOLUTION

(1)

ARTESIAN COMPANY

Multistep Income Statement

For the Year Ended December 31, 1990

Sales			$250,500
Cost of goods sold			167,000
Gross margin			$ 83,500
Selling expenses			
Salespersons' salaries	$12,000		
Commissions	4,500		
Advertising	3,500		
Total selling expenses		$20,000	
General and administrative expenses			
Depreciation and amortization	$10,000		
Insurance expense	3,000		
Repairs and maintenance	1,000		
Total general and administrative expenses		14,000	
Total operating expense			34,000
Income from operations			49,500
Other expenses			
Interest			2,000
Income before taxes			47,500
Taxes—40%			19,000
Net income			$ 28,500

(2)

ARTESIAN COMPANY
Single-step Income Statement
For the Year Ended December 31, 1990

Revenues		
Sales		$250,500
Expenses		
Cost of goods sold	$167,000	
Selling	20,000	
General and administrative	14,000	
Interest	2,000	
		203,000
Income before taxes		47,500
Income taxes—40%		19,000
Net income		$ 28,500

---

(3)

ARTESIAN COMPANY
Statement of Retained Earnings
For the Year Ended
December 31, 1990

Retained earnings, 1/1/90	$39,500
Added: Net income	28,500
	68,000
Less: Dividends[a]	(8,000)
Retained earnings 12/31/90	$60,000

---

[a]The dividends figure must be calculated. Because beginning and ending retained earnings are given and net income is determined above, dividends can be calculated as follows:

$39,500	Retained earnings, 1/1/90
28,500	(See income statements)
68,000	
−60,000	Retained earnings, 12/31/90
$ 8,000	Dividends

C. Analysis. Using the data in parts A and B, calculate the following ratios for the Artesian Company:

(a) Working capital.   (e) Gross margin percentage.

(b) Current ratio.   (f) Profit margin percentage.

(c) Debt to equity ratio.   (g) Return on assets.

(d) Total debt to total assets.   (h) Return on stockholders' equity.

SOLUTION

a. Working Capital = Current Assets − Current Liabilities
$15,000   = $45,000   − $30,000

b. Current Ratio = $\dfrac{\text{Current Assets}}{\text{Current Liabilities}}$ $\qquad \dfrac{\$45,000}{\$30,000} = 1.5$

c. Debt-to-equity Ratio = $\dfrac{\text{Total Liabilities}}{\text{Total Stockholders' Equity}}$ $\qquad \dfrac{\$100,000}{\$ 90,000} = 1.11$

d. Total Debt to Total Assets = $\dfrac{\text{Total Liabilities}}{\text{Total Assets}}$ $\qquad \dfrac{\$100,000}{\$190,000} = .526$

$$\text{e.}\quad \text{Gross Margin Percentage} = \frac{\text{Gross Margin}}{\text{Sales}} \qquad \frac{\$\,83,500}{\$250,500} = .333$$

$$\text{f.}\quad \text{Profit Margin Percentage} = \frac{\text{Net Income}}{\text{Sales}} \qquad \frac{\$\,28,500}{\$250,500} = .114$$

$$\text{g.}\quad \text{Return on Assets} = \frac{\text{Net Income}}{\text{Average Total Assets}} \qquad \frac{\$\,28,500}{\$190,000^{a}} = .15$$

$$\text{h.}\quad \text{Return on Stockholders' Equity} = \frac{\text{Net Income}}{\text{Average Total Stockholders' Equity}} \qquad \frac{\$28,500}{\$90,000^{a}} = .317$$

^aOnly year-end balance available.

QUESTIONS

1. Because of the special selection and training of the upper management of the Roberto Company, the board of directors believes that management should be considered as an asset. What advice would you give them concerning recording management as an asset? What accounting concept supports your conclusions?

2. Define *reliability*. How does the concept of verifiability affect reliability?

3. What do accountants mean by conservatism? Why do you think that this characteristic of financial information has been part of accounting for so long? Are there situations in which it is possible to be too conservative? When?

4. Because of a change in general economic conditions, a firm decides to switch from one acceptable accounting method to another. What principle is being violated, and what principle would require that the change be noted in the financial statements?

5. The Winwrich Co., a large conglomerate, has a policy of expensing in the current period all asset purchases under $1,000. Do you agree with this policy? What accounting characteristic is involved?

6. Below are some of the common groups that are likely to use financial statements. List at least two uses each group would make of financial statements.
    (a) Labor unions
    (b) Stockbrokers
    (c) Regulatory agencies such as the Securities and Exchange Commission or the Federal Trade Commission
    (d) Internal management

7. If different groups use financial statements for different purposes, why are general-purpose financial statements prepared?

8. Why did the FASB develop objectives of financial statements? Describe the three primary purposes of financial statements.

9. Describe classified financial statements, and explain why they are prepared.

10. What are the primary purposes and uses of a balance sheet? How does it enable a user to analyze a company?

11. What are the important limitations of a balance sheet, and what are their causes?

12. Describe the differences among a calendar year, a fiscal year, and a 52–53 week year.

13. Define and give examples of:
    (a) Current assets
    (b) Long-term investments
    (c) Property, plant, and equipment
    (d) Intangible assets
    (e) Current liabilities
    (f) Long-term liabilities
    (g) Stockholders' equity

14. What is the operating cycle of a business? Describe the operating cycles of the following businesses:
    (a) Distillery
    (b) Savings and loan company
    (c) Gas station
    (d) Construction company
    (e) Book publisher

15. Assume a firm made the following two investments:
    (a) One thousand shares of General Motors stock
    (b) One hundred fifty thousand shares (a 15% ownership interest) in DLX Motors

    How would each of the above investments likely be classified on a balance sheet? Why?

16. Describe the two common measures used to assess a firm's liquidity.

17. What does the debt-to-equity ratio measure?

18. Why would the amount of assets provided by credi-

tors versus the amount provided by owners be important?

19. What are the purposes of the income statement, and what information does it provide to users?

20. What are the limitations of the income statement, and what are some of their causes?

21. What are the differences between a single-step and a multistep income statement? In what circumstances should each type of statement be prepared?

22. What measures can an investor use to assess a firm's profitability?

23. What measures can an investor use to determine how effectively management is operating a business?

24. In recent years, many large firms have decided to prepare statements of changes in stockholders' equity rather than retained earnings statements. What is the reason for this change?

25. What is the purpose of the statement of cash flows? What information does it provide?

26. What is the full-disclosure principle, and what is its relationship to financial statement footnotes?

27. What are the footnotes to the financial statements? Describe several types of information contained in the footnotes.

28. In addition to financial statements, what other parts of a firm's annual report are useful to investors?

29. What are the purposes of an audit of financial statements conducted by CPAs? What information is contained in the auditors' report? What is management's responsibility in relation to the data contained in the financial statements?

30. Describe the differences between the traditional and the new auditors' reports.

EXERCISES

E1. **Review of Financial Accounting Concepts.** For each of the following independent situations, describe the accounting assumptions, characteristics, or conventions that have been violated. There may be more than one answer for each situation. The concepts involved have been discussed in this as well as earlier chapters.

(a) Hilary Wong is the sole proprietor of Wong Jewelry Imports. During March, the following items were recorded as expenses on the firm's books:

Rent on office	$500
Employees' wages	700
Supplies for personal use	100
Advertising	250
Pleasure travel	800

(b) The Wright Corporation began business in 1988. The company produces a magazine for nature enthusiasts. Two-year subscriptions are offered. Since its inception, the firm has adopted the policy of recognizing revenues when the cash is received. Expenses are recognized as incurred.

(c) The Weiss Corporation spent $200,000 in employee training during the current year. This amount was listed in the intangible asset section of the balance sheet, with the caption "Investment in Employees."

(d) Over the last few years, the president of the Federal Company has purchased a number of paintings to decorate her office. Recently one of the artists died, and his paintings have increased in value by over 200%. The president has therefore instructed the accounting department to increase the recorded cost of the paintings to reflect this change.

E2. **Accounting Conventions and Principles.** For each of the following independent situations, state the accounting convention, characteristic, or assumption that is involved. There may be more than one answer for each question. The concepts involved have been discussed in this as well as earlier chapters.

(a) Earth Airlines has suffered huge losses in recent years and may not be able to continue to operate. The firm's public accountants feel that this information should be disclosed in their opinion.

(b) The following footnote was taken from an annual report of General Motors:

There are various claims and pending actions against the Corporation and its subsidiaries with respect to commercial matters, including warranties and product liability, governmental regulations including environmental and safety matters, civil rights, patent matters, taxes and other matters arising out of the conduct of the business. Certain of these actions purport to be class actions, seeking damages in very large amounts. The amounts of liability on these claims and actions at December 31, 1982 were not determinable but, in the opinion of the management, the ultimate liability resulting will not materially affect the consolidated financial position or results of operations of the Corporation and its consolidated subsidiaries.

(c) The Crazy Accounting Supply Co. is not a publicly held company but is owned by ten investors. The company's president, who is also one of the owners, has decided not to prepare financial statements this year because the company suffered huge losses.

(d) A fancy staple machine costing $125 was debited to the office equipment account and will be depreciated over ten years.

E3. Classification of Balance Sheet Accounts. Below are the classifications commonly found on classified balance sheets. In the space next to each of the numbered items, write the letter that best indicates to which classification it belongs.

(a) Current assets   **(f)** Current liabilities

(b) Long-term investments   **(g)** Long-term liabilities

(c) Property, plant, and equipment   **(h)** Stockholders' equity

(d) Intangible assets   **(i)** Not a balance sheet item

(e) Other assets

_____ **1.** Trucks used in business   _____ **11.** Accounts receivable

_____ **2.** Copyright owned by firm   _____ **12.** Retained earnings

_____ **3.** Accounts payable   _____ **13.** Accumulated depreciation—Truck

_____ **4.** Prepaid insurance   _____ **14.** Current maturities of long-term debt

_____ **5.** Supplies on hand   _____ **15.** Inventory

_____ **6.** Supplies used   _____ **16.** Rent expense

_____ **7.** Unearned rent   _____ **17.** Common stock

_____ **8.** Bonds payable   _____ **18.** Marketable securities

_____ **9.** Land held for future use   _____ **19.** Note receivable, due in five years

_____ **10.** Land   _____ **20.** Additional paid-in capital

E4. Preparation of a Classified Balance Sheet. Using the following data, prepare a classified balance sheet for the Nigel Corporation as of December 31, 1990:

Accounts payable	$ 15,600	Inventory	$20,000
Accounts receivable	20,500	Long-term investments	5,000
Accumulated depreciation—		Interest payable	3,500
Building	20,000	Land	50,000
Accumulated depreciation—		Long-term note payable	30,000
Equipment	2,500	Marketable securities	2,500
Building	100,000	Retained earnings	77,000
Cash	16,000	Short-term note payable	10,400
Cash in sinking fund	5,000		
Common stock	100,000		
Equipment	40,000		

E5. Preparation of a Classified Balance Sheet. The following items were taken from the record of the Hart Corporation at the end of 1990:

Cash	$ 22,000	Patent	$ 15,000
Investment in short-term		Long-term note receivable	6,000
government securities	25,000	Accounts payable	60,000
Accounts receivable	50,000	Current maturities of long-term	
Inventory	85,000	debt	50,000
Long-term investment	10,000	Long-term debt	100,000
Land	100,000	Common stock, $10 par value,	
Building	200,000	20,000 shares outstanding	200,000
Accumulated depreciation—		Additional paid-in capital	35,000
Building	25,000	Retained earnings	?
Equipment	60,000		
Accumulated depreciation—			
Equipment	10,000		

REQUIRED: Prepare a classified balance sheet for the Hart Corporation as of December 31, 1990.

E6. Balance Sheet Analysis. The balance sheet for the Mendez Corporation is as follows:

THE MENDEZ CORPORATION
Balance Sheet
December 31, 1990

Assets		Liabilities and Stockholders' Equity	
Current assets		Current liabilities	
Cash	$ 7,000	Accounts payable	$10,000
Accounts receivable	14,000	Salaries payable	5,000
Total current assets	$21,000	Total current liabilities	15,000
Long-term investments	$24,000	Long-term liabilities	
Property, plant, and		Note payable—due 1/92	15,000
equipment, net	$40,000	Total liabilities	30,000
		Stockholders' equity	
		Common stock	50,000
		Retained earnings	5,000
			$55,000
		Total liabilities and	
Total assets	$85,000	stockholders' equity	$85,000

REQUIRED: **(a)** Calculate the following:

    1. Net working capital

    2. Current ratio

    3. Debt-to-equity ratio

    4. Total-debt-to-total-assets ratio

  (b) If you were considering making a $20,000, two-year loan to the firm, how would you assess its financial strength and stability? Would you make the loan?

E7. Classification of Income Statement Accounts. Below are classifications commonly found on a multistep income statement. In the space next to each of the numbered items, write the letter that best indicates to which classification it belongs.

  (a) Revenues   **(d)** General and administrative expenses

  (b) Cost of goods sold   **(e)** Other revenue and expense

  (c) Selling expenses   **(f)** Not an income statement item

_____	**1.** Sales	_____	**8.** Sales commissions paid
_____	**2.** Taxes	_____	**9.** Rent received in advance
_____	**3.** Supplies on hand	_____	**10.** President's salary
_____	**4.** Gain on sale of land	_____	**11.** Office rent
_____	**5.** Dividends declared	_____	**12.** Delivery expense
_____	**6.** Interest payable	_____	**13.** Interest expense
_____	**7.** Depreciation expense— Administrative office equipment	_____	**14.** Advertising expense
		_____	**15.** Prepaid insurance

E8. Preparation of a Single-step Income Statement. Given the following information, prepare a single-step income statement for the Pauline Perfume Shop for the year ended December 31, 1990.

Rent expense	$10,000
Taxes expense	2,250
Sales	60,000
Selling expense	6,000
Cost of goods sold	35,000
General and administrative expense	2,500

E9. Preparation of a Multistep Income Statement. You have obtained the following information for the Ponce Pickle Factory. Prepare a multistep income statement for the year ended December 31, 1990. Assume a tax rate of 30% of income before taxes.

Sales	$150,000
Depreciation expense*	8,000
Insurance expense*	2,500
Salaries expense*	22,000
Delivery expense	1,500
Cost of goods sold	60,000
Interest expense	3,000
Rental income	1,000

*Split 60% general and administrative expense and 40% selling expense.

E10. Income Statement and Balance Sheet Analysis. Answer each of the following two independent questions:

(a) The Ching Toy Company had net income for the year ended December 31, 1990 of $25,000. Its total beginning assets were $1,000,000, and its total ending assets were $1,500,000. Its total stockholders' equity at January 1, 1990 was $500,000, and on December 31, 1990 it was $700,000. Calculate the return on total assets and the return on owners' equity.

(b) On January 1, 1990, McGinn's Book Store had current assets of $672,000 and current liabilities of $531,000. At the end of the year, its current assets increased to $783,750 and its current liabilities to $670,325. Determine the increase or decrease in working capital that occurred during the year. Did the current ratio change? If so, by how much?

E11. Financial Statement Analysis. You have obtained the following data for the Marigold Company for the year ended December 31, 1990. (Some income statement items are missing.)

Cost of goods sold	$410,000
General and administrative expenses	55,000
Interest expense	5,000
Net income	66,000
Sales	650,000
Tax rate	20%

Answer each of the following questions:

(a) What is the gross margin on sales?

(b) What is the amount of income from operations?

(c) What is the amount of selling expenses?

(d) What is the gross margin percentage?

(e) If the return on total assets is 2.5%, what were the average total assets during 1990?

(f) If the return on stockholders' equity is 5%, what was the amount of average stockholders' equity during 1990?

(g) What is the profit margin percentage?

E12. **Balance Sheet Analysis.** Answer each of the following two independent questions:

(a) State whether each of the following transactions would increase, decrease, or have no effect on (1) net working capital and (2) current ratio of a business. Assume that the firm is in a positive working capital position.

1. Cash is received on account.

2. Prepaid insurance is written off to expense in an adjusting entry.

3. Supplies are purchased on account.

4. An automobile is purchased. The firm makes a down payment and finances the remainder through a four-year bank loan, due in monthly installments.

5. A cash payment is made on an open account payable.

(b) State whether each of the following transactions would increase, decrease, or have no effect on a debt-to-equity ratio that is now 32%.

1. Cash is received on account.

2. The liability, unearned rent, is written off to income in an adjusting entry.

3. The firm borrows $100,000 from a bank. The principal and interest on the loan are due in 18 months.

4. Excess land is sold; the firm recorded a $100,000 loss on the sale.

E13. **Income Statement Analysis.** The Furillo Company makes both cash and credit sales. You have obtained the following data from the company's records:

Credit sales for November	$210,000
Cash received in November:	
From October credit sales	86,000
From November credit sales	43,000
From November cash sales	70,000
Gross margin	30%
Profit margin	16%
Income tax rate	30%
Selling expenses are one-third of general and administrative expenses	

REQUIRED: Prepare a single-step income statement for the month ended November 30, 1990.

E14. **Analyzing Financial Statements.** The Searfoss Corporation is a medium-sized company in a fast-growing industry. The company anticipates revenues and earnings growth of more than 20% for each of the next three years. It may need additional financing to accomplish this growth. Throughout much of the current year, the firm's current assets totaled $500,000 and its current liabilities $400,000. During November and December of the current year and January of the next year, the firm entered into the following transactions:

1. The firm entered into an aggressive campaign to collect its outstanding receivables by allowing customers a 2% discount for all receivables paid within twenty days of the notice of the campaign.

2. The firm allowed its merchandise inventories to decrease by not making any inventory purchases during December. The firm replenished its merchandise inventories in January and February.

3. Using the cash received from its receivable collection campaign, the firm paid many of its outstanding accounts payable. The president of the firm even ordered its accountant to pay some bills that were not due until January.

4. The firm had been contemplating for some time the purchase for cash of a new computer system costing $100,000. The purchase was made during the first week of January.

REQUIRED: Discuss the significance of each of the above on the firm's financial position. What do you think it is trying to accomplish by the moves listed?

E15. **Toys "R" Us Financial Statements.** Using the data from the Toys "R" Us financial statements for *the year ended February 1, 1987* (Exhibits 5-2, 5-7, 5-11, and 5-13), calculate the following items:

(a) Working capital

(b) Current ratio

(c) Debt-to-equity ratio

(d) Debt-to-total-assets ratio

(e) Gross margin percentage

(f) Profit margin percentage

(g) Return on assets (use 1987 balance sheet data only)

(h) Return on stockholders' equity (use 1987 balance sheet data only)

How do these ratios compare with those for 1988?

PROBLEMS

P5-1 **Review of Financial Accounting Concepts.** For each of the following independent situations, state which accounting concept, if any, has been violated. If more than one concept has been violated, so state. If you feel the item has been appropriately handled, so state. Be sure to explain your answers.

(a) Recently, Cardulucci's Fine Restaurant hired one of the country's outstanding chefs. Based on the anticipated increased earnings, the firm debited goodwill and credited stockholders' equity for $100,000.

(b) For years the Watts Equipment Corporation has been using straight-line depreciation on its plant and equipment. During the year, the plant suffered a two-month strike, and the president decided not to depreciate the plant and equipment during that time.

(c) The Ecological High Tech Company began operations early in 1990. However, because of high start-up costs, the firm suffered a large loss during 1990. However, the company's prospects appear to be very good in 1991 and beyond. In order not to discourage the firm's stockholders, the president of Ecological High Tech decided not to issue financial statements until 1991 or until the firm can show a profit.

(d) Natural Foods, Inc. is a large producer of natural foods. During the last half of 1990, the firm undertook a large advertising campaign in an attempt to increase its market share. Because the firm believes that the expenditures for advertising will benefit several years, it has decided to consider the costs an asset and to write them off over five years.

(e) The Colossas Oil Co. has always had difficulty taking a physical inventory because its inventory is spread across the entire world. As a result, the chief financial officer decided to estimate this year's inventory by increasing the amount of last year's by 10% for estimated price increases.

P5-2 Accounting Concepts. For each of the following independent situations, state which accounting concept, if any, is violated. If more than one concept is violated, say so. If you feel the item has been appropriately handled, say so. Be sure to explain your answer.

(a) Industrial Technology, Inc. has just completed a new project. Based on the anticipated increased earnings on the new product, Industrial Technology debited an asset account for all expenses for this project.

(b) Due to the economic situation, Tommy's Restaurant chain suffered a great loss in 1990. As a result, current liabilities exceed current assets by $20 million. In anticipation of future losses, Tommy's has already sold or closed many restaurants. Tommy's prepares financial statement using historical costs.

(c) Doggy and Kathy Corporation has just changed the manner in which it calculates depreciation. In order to show a better result for this year, the firm did not mention this change in its financial statements.

(d) At the year-end, the president of Jack and Sons Company found that the inventory on hand has increased in value over 50%. He decided to give this information to the firm's creditors by writing up inventory to fair market value.

(e) Graham and Sons Company has experienced an extremely profitable year. In order to smooth out earnings, the president decided to expense all merchandise when purchased during the year rather than when it was sold.

P5-3 Preparation of a Classified Balance Sheet. The post-closing account balances of the Vera Video Games Company are presented below (in alphabetical order). All accounts have normal balances.

VERA VIDEO GAMES COMPANY Post-closing Account Balances December 31, 1990	
Accounts payable	$10,000
Accounts receivable	30,000
Accumulated depreciation—Plant and equipment	25,000
Bonds payable	25,000
Cash	17,000
Common stock	50,000
Copyright	10,000
Current maturities of long-term debt	14,000
Inventories	60,000
Investments, long-term	5,000
Marketable securities, held for temporary investment	10,000
Mortgage payable, less current portion	20,000
Plant and equipment	70,000
Prepaid insurance	5,000
Retained earnings	41,000
Salaries payable	5,000
Supplies on hand	1,000
Taxes payable	8,000
Unearned commissions	10,000

REQUIRED: Prepare in good form a classified balance sheet at December 31, 1990.

P5-4 Preparation of a Classified Income Statement. The revenue, expense, and related accounts of the Weiss Company for the year ended June 30, 1990 are listed.

Advertising expense*	$ 2,500	Interest expense	$ 500
Beginning retained earnings	42,750	Repairs and maintenance expense	2,500
Cost of goods sold	25,000	Sales	75,000
Delivery expense*	6,850	Salaries expense*	5,000
Depreciation expense	10,000	Supplies expense	750
Insurance expense	1,000	Tax rate	30%

*Indicates selling expenses. Other expenses besides interest are general and administrative.
Included in the salaries of $5,000 are $1,000 of dividends paid to the owner, E. Weiss.

REQUIRED: **(a)** Prepare in good form a single-step income statement.

(b) Prepare in good form a multistep income statement.

(c) Prepare in good form a retained earnings statement.

P5-5   Ratio Analysis. The following financial data is taken from the records of the Compeq Company:

THE COMPEQ COMPANY
Comparative Balance Sheet
December 31

Assets	1990	1989
Cash	$ 30,000	$ 21,000
Accounts receivable	4,000	7,000
Inventory	240,000	215,000
Property, plant, and equipment, net	40,000	40,000
Total assets	$314,000	$283,000

Liabilities and Stockholders' Equity

	1990	1989
Current liabilities	$ 45,000	$ 33,000
Noncurrent liabilities	109,000	100,000
Stockholders' equity	160,000	150,000
Total liabilities and stockholders' equity	$314,000	$283,000

THE COMPEQ COMPANY
Comparative Income Statement
For the Year Ended December 31

	1990	1989
Sales	$500,000	$430,000
Cost of goods sold	220,000	180,000
Gross margin on sales	280,000	250,000
Operating expenses	190,000	165,000
Net income	$ 90,000	$ 85,000

REQUIRED: **(a)** Compute the following ratios for 1989 and 1990:

1. Working capital.

2. Current ratio.

3. Debt to equity.

4. Debt to total assets.

5. Gross margin percentage.

6. Profit margin percentage.

7. Return on total assets (1988 total assets, $251,000).

8. Return on owner's equity (1988 stockholders' equity, $140,000).

(b) Have the firm's performance and financial position improved from 1989 to 1990? Explain.

P5-6 Preparation of Financial Statements and Analysis. The following accounts have been taken from the December 31, 1990 adjusted trial balance of the Porter Press Corporation. They are not listed in any particular order, and all accounts have normal balances.

Notes receivable—Due in		Accrued salaries and other	
6 months	$ 5,000	payables	$ 8,000
Accumulated depreciation—		Interest payable	5,000
Building	14,000	Depreciation expense	18,000
Common stock	10,000	Machinery and equipment	20,000
Sales	600,000	Patents, net	6,000
Salaries expense	45,000	Additional paid in capital	2,000
Cash	25,000	Retained earnings	13,000
Accounts payable	38,000	Repairs and maintenance expense	6,000
Long-term debt	39,000	Inventory	30,000
Land	12,000	Interest expense	20,000
Building	50,000	Cost of goods sold	450,000
Taxes expense	10,000	Accumulated depreciation—	
Rent expense	12,000	Machinery and equipment	7,000
Gain on sale of land	5,000	Supplies expense	9,000
Accounts receivable	6,000	Long-term investments	15,000
Prepaid assets	2,000		

REQUIRED: (a) Assume that all expenses other than interest are split into one-third selling and two-thirds general and administrative. Prepare in good form the following statements:

 1. A multistep income statement.

 2. A single-step income statement.

 3. A balance sheet.

(b) In what circumstances do you feel that a multistep income statement is more useful than a single-step?

(c) Based on the above data, calculate:

 1. Working capital.

 2. The current ratio.

 3. Debt-to-equity ratio.

 4. Total-debt-to-total-assets ratio.

 5. Gross margin percentage.

 6. Profit margin percentage.

 7. Return on total assets (use end-of-year figures only in denominator).

 8. Return on stockholders' equity (use end-of-year figures only in denominator).

P5-7 Balance Sheet Analysis. Below is a partial list of the accounts for the Diamond Company. Referring to these figures, where appropriate, answer the questions on page 206.

Accounts payable	$28,000	Investment, long-term	$ 20,000
Accounts receivable	45,000	Long-term debt	30,000
Interest payable	12,000	Notes receivable, due in	
Cash	30,000	12 months	5,000
Current portion of long-term		Retained earnings	45,000
debt	30,000	Sales	400,000
Inventories	60,000		

REQUIRED: **(a)** What is the amount of working capital?

(b) What is the current ratio?

(c) For this question only, assume that the company has a current ratio of 3:1. If the company purchased $5,000 of inventory on account, what effect (that is, increase, decrease, or no effect) would this transaction have on:

  1. working capital?

  2. current ratio?

(d) Again for this question, assume that the company has a current ratio of 3:1. If the company purchased some equipment for $10,000 cash, what effect would this transaction have on:

  1. working capital?

  2. current ratio?

(e) Assume the same current ratio as in Item d and the same purchase, but now assume that the equipment purchased was on account with the payable due in two years. For simplicity, assume that there is no interest on the note. What effect would this transaction have on:

  1. working capital?

  2. current ratio?

P5-8 **Effect of Errors.** The accountant for the Micropress Company made the following errors in preparing its 1989 calendar year financial statements:

  1. Failed to record a purchase of inventory on account. As of the end of the year, the inventory was not sold.

  2. Recorded the payment of several payables based on the fact that checks were written for these payables prior to the end of the year. However, the checks were not mailed until early in the next year.

  3. Failed to record accrued rent receivable.

  4. Failed to record depreciation expense for the year.

  5. Recorded the cash purchase of supplies as a purchase on account. That is, an increase in a payable rather than a decrease in cash was recorded.

REQUIRED: Complete the table below by using the following codes:

  + = item overstated
  − = item understated
  0 = item neither understated nor overstated

	Item Number				
Effect on 12/31/89	1	2	3	4	5
Total assets					
Total liabilities					
Total stockholders' equity					
Working capital					
Current ratio					
Debt to total assets					
Profit margin percentage					
Return on assets					

P5-9 **Analysis of Financial Statements.** The financial statements for the R.J.P. Company are presented on the next page. (All accounts are listed.)

R.J.P. COMPANY
Balance Sheet
December 31, 1990

Assets		Liabilities and Stockholders' Equity	
Cash	$25,000	Accounts payable	$ d
Accounts receivable	a	Total liabilities	e
Total current assets	45,000	Stockholders' equity	f
Property, plant, and equipment	b	Total liabilities and	
Total assets	$ c	stockholders' equity	$ g

R.J.P. COMPANY
Income Statement
For the Year Ended December 31, 1990

Revenues		
Sales		$ h
Expenses		
Cost of goods sold	$35,000	
Selling	20,000	
General and administrative	6,000	
Interest	900	
City taxes	1,100	
Total expenses		i
Net income		$ j

In addition, you have gathered the following data:

Net working capital = $7,500
Current ratio = 1.2:1
Debt to equity ratio = 1.25
Gross margin percentage = 50%
Profit margin percentage = 10%

REQUIRED: Complete the financial statements of R.J.P. Company by determining the amount of Items a through j. It is not necessary to determine the missing figures in order.

■ UNDERSTANDING FINANCIAL STATEMENTS

P5-10 The financial statements on pages 208 and 209 were taken from the annual report of Albertson's, Inc., a large market chain in the West.

REQUIRED: Answer each of the following questions about the financial statements:

(a) What type of income statement is presented?

(b) Why do you think that cash and marketable securities are shown together as one item on the balance sheet?

(c) Explain the difference between accounts payable and other current liabilities.

(d) Compute the following data for 1989 and 1988:

1. Net working capital
2. Current ratio
3. Debt-to-equity ratio
4. Total-debt-to-total-assets ratio

5. Gross margin percentage
6. Profit margin percentage
7. Return on total assets

(e) Would you say that the firm's financial performance and position had improved from 1988 to 1989? Explain.

ALBERTSON'S, INC.
Consolidated Balance Sheets
(in thousands)

Assets	February 2, 1989	January 28, 1988	January 29, 1987
Current assets			
Cash and marketable securities	$ 81,641	$ 201,381	$ 245,762
Accounts and notes receivable	43,399	43,830	40,492
Inventories	432,322	361,579	316,473
Prepaid expenses	8,813	9,190	7,553
Deferred income tax benefits	20,027	18,981	15,004
Refundable income taxes	5,748		
Total current assets	591,950	634,961	625,284
Other assets	39,329	36,793	25,853
Land, buildings, and equipment			
Land	182,239	136,073	105,570
Buildings	422,418	307,399	240,549
Fixtures and equipment	602,645	489,432	427,945
Leasehold improvements	122,455	98,338	84,204
Assets under capital leases	148,137	144,150	139,658
	1,477,894	1,175,392	997,926
Less accumulated depreciation and amortization	518,187	449,932	388,785
	959,707	725,460	609,141
Deferred income tax benefits		4,861	4,378
	$1,590,986	$1,402,075	$1,264,656

Liabilities and Stockholders' Equity

	February 2, 1989	January 28, 1988	January 29, 1987
Current liabilities			
Accounts payable	$ 375,786	$ 328,307	$ 278,781
Salaries and related liabilities	64,458	54,613	52,000
Taxes other than income taxes	23,570	20,775	15,307
Income taxes		14,085	13,504
Other current liabilities	13,492	11,976	10,785
Current maturities of long-term debt	5,655	5,554	5,461
Current obligations under capital leases	5,429	4,693	4,201
Total current liabilities	488,390	440,003	380,039
Long-term debt	64,041	69,696	75,003
Obligations under capital leases	113,046	113,455	112,220
Deferred credits and other long-term liabilities			
Deferred investment tax credits	8,464	11,149	14,381
Deferred compensation	16,864	15,147	14,051
Deferred income taxes	4,208		
Deferred rents payable	49,862	46,558	40,081
Other long-term liabilities	45,615	40,859	34,502
	125,013	113,713	103,015
Stockholders' equity			
Common stock	66,929	66,361	33,408
Capital in excess of par value	36,317	26,800	82,266
Retained earnings	697,250	572,047	478,705
	800,496	665,208	594,379
	$1,590,986	$1,402,075	$1,264,656

ALBERTSON'S, INC.
Consolidated Earnings
In Thousands (except share and per share data)

	53 Weeks February 2, 1989	52 Weeks January 28, 1988	52 Weeks January 29, 1987
Sales	$6,773,061	$5,869,423	$5,379,643
Cost of sales	5,260,459	4,554,297	4,168,578
Gross profit	1,512,602	1,315,126	1,211,065
Operating and administrative expenses	1,251,995	1,098,306	1,022,420
Operating profit	260,607	216,820	188,645
Interest expense, net	(11,979)	(10,267)	(9,961)
Other income, net	8,366	5,301	6,097
Earnings before income taxes	256,994	211,854	184,781
Income taxes	94,449	86,469	84,629
Net earnings	$ 162,545	$ 125,385	$ 100,152
Earnings per share	$2.44	$1.88	$1.50
Average number of shares outstanding	66,606,351	66,870,408	66,666,846

P5-11 The statements that follow were taken from the annual report of the Pacific Gas and Electric Company (a large West Coast utility).

REQUIRED: **(a)** In what significant ways do these statements differ from those of Toys "R" Us? What do you think the reasons are for the differences in format?

(b) What is the Construction Work in Progress account, and why is it an asset?

(c) What do you think the Reinvested Earnings account is?

(d) Compute the following data for 1987:

  1. Net working capital.

  2. Current ratio.

  3. Return on total assets.

PACIFIC GAS AND ELECTRIC COMPANY
Statement of Consolidated Income
Years Ended December 31
In Thousands (except per share amounts)

	1987	1986*	1985*
Operating revenues			
Electric	$5,133,028	$5,567,438	$5,819,983
Gas	2,052,673	2,249,223	2,610,998
Total operating revenues	7,185,701	7,816,661	8,430,981
Operating expenses			
Cost of electric energy	1,383,497	1,252,414	2,072,548
Cost of gas	859,882	1,074,392	1,749,207
Transmission	175,534	148,788	148,479
Distribution	189,782	188,499	173,081
Customer accounts and services	283,965	339,583	357,189
Administrative and general	708,200	635,792	591,926
Other	263,585	333,038	302,326
Maintenance	341,118	352,230	312,531

(continued)

	1987	1986*	1985*
Depreciation	875,208	693,675	535,654
Income taxes	603,012	927,647	652,669
Property and other taxes	240,217	216,978	166,012
Total operating expenses	5,924,000	6,163,036	7,061,622
Operating income	1,261,701	1,653,625	1,369,359
Other income and (income deductions)			
Allowance for equity funds used during construction	2,564	69,164	247,367
Interest income	99,011	120,431	132,985
Disallowed project costs	(8,689)	—	(58,882)
Other—Net	19,001	(37,760)	11,763
Total other income and (income deductions)	111,887	151,835	333,233
Income before interest expense	1,373,588	1,805,460	1,702,592
Interest expense			
Interest on long-term debt	698,233	707,975	709,258
Other interest charges	77,845	58,802	55,588
Allowance for borrowed funds used during construction	316	(42,540)	(93,059)
Net interest expense	776,394	724,237	671,787
Income before change in recording unbilled revenues	597,194	1,081,223	1,030,805
Cumulative effect as of January 1, 1987 of accruing unbilled revenues, net of income taxes of $77,045	91,323	—	—
Net income	688,517	1,081,223	1,030,805
Preferred dividend requirement	110,782	156,190	164,230
Earnings available for common stock	$ 577,735	$ 925,033	$ 866,575
Weighted average common shares outstanding	377,723	355,937	326,838
Earnings per common share before change in recording unbilled revenues	$1.29	$2.60	$2.65
Cumulative effect as of January 1, 1987 of accruing unbilled revenues	.24	—	—
Earnings per common share	$1.53	$2.60	$2.65
Dividends declared per common share	$1.92	$1.90	$1.81

*Changed to conform to 1987 presentation.

PACIFIC GAS AND ELECTRIC COMPANY
Consolidated Balance Sheet
(In Thousands)

	December 31,	
Assets	**1987**	**1986***
Plant in service (at original cost)		
Electric	$17,760,570	$16,659,173
Gas	3,594,959	3,335,255
Total plant in service	21,355,529	19,994,428
Accumulated depreciation	(6,208,992)	(5,466,767)
Net plant in service	15,146,537	14,527,661
Construction work in progress	923,746	1,178,254
Nuclear fuel and other capital leases	381,376	434,303
Gas exploration costs	96,107	235,791
Advances to gas producers	334,767	367,426
Funds held by trustee	217,226	243,161
Investments	86,840	123,062
Customer conservation loans receivable (net of current portion $24,142 in 1987; $33,697 in 1986)	40,045	60,935
Total	17,226,644	17,170,593

(continued)

	December 31,	
Assets	**1987**	**1986***
Current assets		
Cash	8,632	5,618
Short-term investments (at cost which approximates market)	136,925	112,586
Accounts receivable		
Customers (including unbilled amounts of $311,604 in 1987)	962,922	556,648
Other	471,258	460,673
Allowance for uncollectible accounts	(8,340)	(8,951)
Regulatory balancing accounts receivable	633,897	361,380
Inventories (Note 1)		
Fuel oil	100,590	223,472
Gas stored underground	224,196	263,507
Materials and supplies	168,246	165,223
Prepayments	34,925	31,754
Total current assets	2,733,251	2,171,910
Deferred charges		
Diablo Canyon balancing accounts (net of deferred revenue and interest of $804,667 as of December 31, 1987)	871,144	871,144
Project costs pending regulatory action	16,970	16,970
Unamortized project costs	123,097	116,084
Workers' compensation and disability claims recoverable	91,900	93,500
Unamortized debt expense	47,218	37,459
Unamortized loss net of gain on reacquired debt	305,461	303,049
Other—Net	317,967	221,544
Total deferred charges	1,773,757	1,659,750
Total assets	$21,733,652	$21,002,253

Capitalization and Liabilities

Capitalization		
Common stock	$ 1,941,543	$ 1,840,636
Additional paid-in capital	2,611,654	2,319,344
Reinvested earnings	2,699,108	2,855,748
Common stock equity	7,252,305	7,015,728
Preferred stock without mandatory redemption provision	1,010,195	1,207,865
Preferred stock with mandatory redemption provision	195,000	225,285
Long-term debt	7,998,265	7,255,956
Total capitalization	16,455,765	15,704,834
Noncurrent liabilities		
Capital lease obligations	318,524	351,680
Customer advances for construction	159,907	125,212
Workers' compensation and disability claims	91,900	93,500
Customer conservation loans payable	59,300	80,300
Other	113,481	34,352
Total noncurrent liabilities	743,112	685,044
Current liabilities		
Short-term borrowings	554,024	1,101,213
Accounts payable		
Trade creditors	482,938	459,255
Other	244,180	217,104
Accrued taxes	101,627	49,834
		(continued)

Capitalization and Liabilities	December 31,	
	1987	1986*
Current liabilities		
Deferred income taxes—Current portion	275,245	153,168
Long-term debt—Current portion	71,620	84,314
Capital lease obligations—Current portion	77,874	89,892
Interest payable	75,228	76,345
Dividends payable	186,001	176,602
Amounts due customers	77,983	59,295
Other	81,928	76,962
Total current liabilities	2,228,648	2,543,984
Deferred credits		
Deferred investment tax credits	553,481	519,351
Deferred income taxes	1,499,155	1,517,194
Other	253,491	31,846
Total deferred credits	2,306,127	2,068,391
Contingencies		
Total capitalization and liabilities	$21,733,652	$21,002,253

*Changed to conform to 1987 presentation.

■ FINANCIAL DECISION CASE

P5-12   Rebecca Webb is head of the loan department at Wilshire National Bank. She has been approached by two firms in the retail toy business. Each firm is requesting a nine-month term loan in order to purchase inventory for the holiday season. She must make her recommendation to the loan committee and has gathered the following data in order to make her analysis.

The Fun Toy Company was organized in early 1986. The first year of operations was fairly successful, as the firm earned net income of $45,000. Total sales for the year were $600,000, and total assets at year-end, December 31, 1989, were $350,000. A condensed balance sheet at September 30, 1990 follows. The firm is requesting a $100,000 loan.

Assets	
Cash	$ 60,000
Accounts receivable	65,000
Inventory	125,000
Prepaids	5,000
Furniture and fixtures, net	155,000
Total assets	$410,000

Liabilities and Stockholders' Equity	
Accounts payable	$ 70,000
Note payable, due 10/5/91	100,000
Stockholders' equity	240,000
Total liabilities and stockholders' equity	$410,000

The Toy Store, the other firm, has been in business for many years. The firm's net income is $100,000 on total sales of $2,000,000. Total assets at year-end, December 31, 1989, were $1,250,000. A condensed balance sheet at September 30, 1990 follows. The firm is seeking a $200,000 loan.

Assets	
Cash	$ 60,000
Accounts receivable	100,000
Inventory	400,000
Supplies	10,000
Prepaids	5,000
Property, plant, and equipment	825,000
Total assets	$1,400,000

Liabilities and Stockholders' Equity	
Accounts payable	$ 350,000
Current bank loan payable	150,000
Long-term debt	400,000
Stockholders' equity	500,000
Total liabilities and stockholders' equity	$1,400,000

REQUIRED: **(a)** Calculate the ratios that you think will help Rebecca Webb in her analysis.

(b) Based on the above and your further analyses, what should Rebecca Webb recommend to the loan committee regarding each firm's request? Explain your reasoning.

6

RECORDING SALES AND PURCHASES OF INVENTORY FOR A MERCHANDISING FIRM

LEARNING OBJECTIVES

After studying this chapter, you should be able to:

1. Explain how merchandising firms account for sales transactions, including trade and quantity discounts, sales discounts, credit card sales, and sales returns and allowances.

2. Distinguish between the perpetual and the periodic inventory systems, and the accounting entries related to these systems.

3. Account for purchases of merchandise for resale, including trade and quantity discounts, purchase discounts, purchase returns and allowances, and freight-in.

4. Discuss the taking of a physical inventory.

5. Prepare a worksheet for a merchandising firm using the periodic inventory system, and construct the sales and cost of goods sold section of a multistep income statement.

T he main activities of many business enterprises are the purchase or manufacture of inventory for resale and the subsequent sale of those goods and related services. This chapter will describe the accounting for the sales and purchases of inventory for a merchandising firm. A **merchandising firm** purchases finished products for resale. Examples of such firms include retail department and food stores, pharmacies, and computer stores.

ACCOUNTING FOR SALES

The essential activity of the merchandising concern is the sale of its product or products. It is at this point that the firm's earnings process is complete, objective evidence as to the sales price is available, and revenue is recognized under generally accepted accounting principles. It does not make any difference whether the sale is for cash or is on account. In either case, an exchange has taken place, and revenue is earned through the generation of cash and/or a receivable. The journal entry to record a sale of $1,000, of which $400 is for cash and $600 is on account, is:

Cash	400	
Accounts Receivable	600	
Sales		1,000
To record cash and credit sales.		

The source of the data for this entry is the cash register or electronic point-of-sale device. In a manual system, hand postings are made to both the general ledger Accounts Receivable and the subsidiary Accounts Receivable ledger. A subsidiary ledger contains detailed information about a control account in the general ledger—in this case, an account for each individual customer. If management desires, sales can be broken down further by department. An electronic point-of-sale device may be able to make these postings instantaneously as well as to update quantities of inventory on hand.

A number of issues are related to accounting for sales, including trade and quantity discounts, sales discounts, credit card sales, and sales returns and allowances.

TRADE AND QUANTITY DISCOUNTS

Merchandising firms often allow reductions from list or catalogue prices. **Trade discounts** are discounts offered to a certain class of buyers. For example, a furniture store may allow certain trade discounts to professional decorators but charge the general public the full retail price. **Quantity discounts** are reductions from the list price based on quantity purchases. For example, the price of pens may be $21 per dozen, but large discounts may be offered on the following bulk purchases:

Quantity Purchased	% Discount
Below 50 dozen	0%
50 to 99 dozen	5%
100 to 199 dozen	10%
Above 200 dozen	15%

Both trade and quantity discounts are price adjustments on the sales price, and generally accepted accounting principles require that transactions be recorded at the agreed-upon price, net of these discounts. Thus there is no accounting recognition of these discounts. To illustrate, assume that an individual purchased 60 dozen pens on account for $21 per dozen. The total sales price is $1,197(60 × $21 = $1,260 × 95% = $1,197), and the transaction is recorded in the following manner:

Accounts Receivable	1,197	
Sales		1,197
To record cash sales.		

Although financial reporting rules do not require explicit recognition of trade or quantity discounts, management may want to keep records of these discounts to monitor their quantity and effectiveness. This can be important in certain retail areas, such as automobile dealerships, in which discounts from the list price are common and salespeople are paid on a commission. Indiscriminate use of discounts may be in the salesperson's short-run best interest but not in the long-run best interest of the firm. By establishing a separate discount account (offset against the Sales account when external financial statements are prepared), this potential problem can be controlled.

■ SALES DISCOUNTS

A **sales discount** is a cash reduction offered to customers to encourage prompt payment. In effect, the seller is willing to accept less cash than the agreed-upon sales price if the customer will pay within a specified period of time. The seller benefits because prompt payment decreases the probability of bad debts and also the need for short-term financing. In a cash-tight economy, the prompt conversion of receivables into cash is essential to maintain liquidity.

The type and amount of the sales discount depend on the credit terms set by the seller. Exhibit 6-1 lists and explains the more common types of sales discounts and credit terms. Sales discounts such as those listed are mainly offered to wholesale customers and are infrequently available to retail customers.

EXHIBIT 6–1

Common Credit Terms

Type of Credit Term	Explanation
2/10, n/30	A 2% discount is allowed if payment is made within 10 days of the invoice date. The full price is due within 30 days of the invoice date.
1/10, n/30	A 1% discount is allowed if payment is made within 10 days of the invoice date. The full price is due within 30 days of the invoice date.
5 EOM	The full invoice price is due within five days after the end of the month of the sale.
n/30	The entire invoice price is due within 30 days of the invoice date.

The purchaser generally should take a sales discount when it is offered. The following example points out the potential benefits to the purchaser. Assume that a customer made a $1,000 purchase on account and that the terms of the sale are 2/10, n/30. In this situation the customer has two choices: pay $980 on Day 10 or $1,000 on Day 30. Because there is no additional benefit to paying before Day 10, or if the discount is not taken before Day 30, we can assume that there are only two choices: pay on Day 10 or on Day 30. By not taking the discount, the customer has the use of the additional $20 for 20 days. This represents an annual interest rate of 36.7% for the use of the money.

These relationships are diagrammed in Exhibit 6-2. Obviously, the lower the allowable discount, the lower the effective annual interest rate. If the terms were 1/10, n/30, the annual rate would be 18.2%. However, because most firms can borrow

EXHIBIT 6–2

Day	$1,000 Invoice	$980 Due	$20	$1,000
	1	10		30
	Invoice date	Last day to take discount		Full invoice amount due

Number of 20-day periods in one year:

$$\frac{360}{20} = 18 \text{ periods}$$

Annual interest rate:

$$\frac{\$20 \times 18 \text{ periods}}{\$980} = \frac{360}{\$980} = 36.7\%$$

funds at less than 36.7% or, in many cases, at less than 18.2%, they would benefit by taking the discount even if they had to borrow funds from other creditors to do so. Because of the high cost to the seller and the relatively high interest rates in recent years, some firms have stopped using cash discounts and instead levy an interest charge of 1% to $1\frac{1}{2}$% per month on accounts that are outstanding over 30 days. This service or finance charge, if and when accrued, should be credited to interest income.

Unlike trade or quantity discounts, explicit accounting recognition is given to sales discounts. There are two popular methods used to record sales discounts, the gross method and the net method. The journal entries for both of these alternatives, based on a $100 sale on account with stated terms of 2/10, n/30, are shown in Exhibit 6-3.

EXHIBIT 6–3

Journal Entries to Record Sales Discounts
$100 Sale—Stated Terms 2/10, n/30

Transaction	Gross Method			Net Method		
1. Sale of $100 of merchandise on account	Accounts Receivable Sales	100	100	Accounts Receivable Sales	98	98
2a. Customer pays within discount period	Cash Sales Discounts Accounts Receivable	98 2	100	Cash Accounts Receivable	98	98
2b. Customer *does not* pay within discount period	Cash Accounts Receivable	100	100	Cash Sales Discounts Not Taken Accounts Receivable	100	2 98

The Gross Method

The **gross method of recording sales discounts** records the sale and receivable at the gross amount before any discount. If the customer takes the discount, the account entitled Sales Discounts must be debited. In the example above, a $2 debit is made to that account, Cash is debited for $98, and Accounts Receivable is credited for $100. Remember, Accounts Receivable was originally debited for the full invoice price of $100 and so must be credited for $100 in order to clear the customer's account. Sales Discounts is a contra sales account, which means that it is a deduction from gross sales to arrive at net sale on the income statement. If the customer fails to take the discount, the entry to record the eventual payment is straightforward. Cash is debited for $100, and Accounts Receivable is credited for $100, the full invoice price paid.

The gross method is commonly used, because most manual and/or electronic systems are designed to record invoices at the billed price. Nonetheless, there are problems with this method. It is based on the assumption that the customer will not take the discount, though it is generally to the purchaser's advantage to do so. To the extent that customers eventually take the discount, both accounts receivable and sales are overstated at the time the sale is recorded. Furthermore, the gross method highlights the discounts taken, whereas management may be more interested in identifying those customers who fail to take the discount. Because it generally benefits the purchaser to take the discount, the failure to do so may indicate potential credit problems with that customer. That is, those customers not paying within the discount period may be experiencing cash flow problems. Because of the shortcomings of the gross method, some firms use the net method of recording sales.

The Net Method

As the journal entries above illustrate, the net method records the receivable and sale net of the allowable discount. The **net method of recording sales discounts** is based on the assumption that the customer will indeed take the discount. As noted before, this is a reasonable assumption. The receivable is stated at the expected cash receipts at the time of the sale. Likewise, the sale is recorded at the lowest cash price that the seller is willing to take. If payment is made within the discount period, Cash and Accounts Receivable are respectively debited and credited at the amount that the receivable was originally recorded. In the example, this amount is $98.

If the customer does not make the payment in the discount period, the full invoice price must be paid. The difference between this full invoice price and the net amount at which the receivable was recorded is credited to an account called Sales Discounts Not Taken. This is a revenue account and is generally shown under the caption Other Revenues and Expenses in the income statement.

The net method is theoretically preferable because accounts receivable are recorded at their net realizable value (expected cash collection) at the time of the sale. In addition, the account Sales Discounts Not Taken highlights those customers who fail to take the discount. As noted, this is important information for management control.

■ CREDIT CARD SALES

Credit card sales are a common part of American business. All sizes and types of merchandisers are likely to accept one or more of the following credit cards: VISA, MasterCard, American Express, Diners' Club, and Carte Blanche. Even large retail chains such as J. C. Penney accept national credit cards in addition to their own charge cards. Credit cards are accepted by retailers because they stimulate business; cash is often received sooner than are payments on accounts carried by the business; and it can be cheaper to accept a national credit card than to carry individual accounts. The accounting for credit cards depends on whether a bank card or a nonbank card is accepted.

Bank Cards

Bank cards such as VISA or MasterCard are issued by banks. In order to receive reimbursement on bank card sales, the retailer simply deposits the signed drafts directly in the bank with the rest of the day's receipts. These drafts are immediately credited to the retailer's account and are treated like cash.

All of the national banks or credit card companies charge for their services. This charge is based on a number of factors, such as the volume of the retailer's gross charge sales. For example, to process the sale, most credit card companies charge in the vicinity of 2 to 5% of the gross sales price. This charge is deducted from the total cash receipts credited to the retailer's account when the charge slips are deposited at the bank, or as a service charge at the end of the month. To illustrate, assume that Lisa's Athletic Store recorded bank credit card sales of $500 for the day. The credit card company charges 4%, which is immediately deducted by the bank when the charge slips are deposited with the day's cash receipts. Based on this data, Lisa's Athletic Store makes the following entry:

Cash	480	
Credit Card Fees	20	
Sales		500
To record credit card sales of $500 and a 4%, or $20, fee.		

Nonbank Cards

Reimbursement on nonbank credit cards such as American Express and Diners' Club are usually handled differently. Instead of being deposited directly into the bank, the drafts are periodically mailed to the credit card company, which then forwards the payment, less the service charge, to the retailer.

To illustrate, assume that Lisa's Athletic Store recorded nonbank credit card sales of $300 for the day. At the end of the day the store makes the following entry:

Accounts Receivable, credit card company	300	
Sales		300
To record credit card sales for the day.		

By the end of the week, Lisa has made total nonbank credit card sales of $2,000 and mails the drafts to the credit card company. The credit card company remits the payment, less a 4% service charge, and the store makes the following entry:

Cash	1,920	
Credit Card Fees	80	
Accounts Receivable, credit card company		2,000
To record receipt of payment from credit card company less $80 fee.		

Most companies consider credit card fees to be a selling expense. This is based on the assumption that these fees replace the expenses that the firm would incur in carrying its own receivables. However, some individuals argue that credit card fees should be shown as a reduction to gross sales in determining net sales. Because many companies are beginning to offer discounts to customers who pay with cash rather than with credit cards, the latter treatment appears to be more appropriate. In any event, the effect is to reduce net income by the amount of the credit card fee.

■ SALES RETURNS AND ALLOWANCES

Like credit cards, sales returns and allowances are a fact of everyday life for the retailer or merchandiser. **Sales returns** occur when a customer returns an item for a cash refund or a credit on account. It is called a credit because, from the retailer's point of view, it reduces accounts receivable or cash. **Sales allowances** are a reduction in the actual sales price, and the customer keeps the merchandise. A retailer might accept this subsequent allowance because the particular item did not perform to expectations or had other defects. In most situations, one account, Sales Returns and Allowances, is used to record these types of transactions. Although it would be possible to debit these returns and allowances directly to the Sales account, this would not provide as much control as does the use of a Sales Returns and Allowances account, whereby a firm can monitor the dollar amount of returns and allowances.

To demonstrate the use of a Sales Returns and Allowances account, assume that the Lloyd Corporation purchased on account $10,000 of goods from the Austin Company. The Lloyd Corporation determined that these goods were defective and returned them for a credit. The Austin Company made the following entry to record this return:

Sales Returns and Allowances	10,000	
Accounts Receivable		10,000
To record return of defective merchandise.		

If the sale had been made for cash and a cash refund granted, the credit would be made to the Cash account rather than to Accounts Receivable.

The method just described assumes that sales returns and allowances are recorded in the period in which the item is returned or the allowance granted, regardless of whether the sale took place in that or the preceding period. Because of the matching requirement, sales returns and allowances should be recorded in the period of the sale. This requires making an estimate of sales returns and allowances when financial statements are prepared. However, for most companies, sales returns and allowances are not material, and over time there is usually little variation in the amounts, so such an estimate is not employed. If a firm (such as a mail-order house) does have material sales returns and allowances, the matching rule requires that such an estimate be made.

■ INCOME STATEMENT PRESENTATION

The manner in which sales are presented on the income statement depends on the form of the income statement and varies across firms. In a full multistep statement, all accounts affecting sales are presented. For example, the sales section of such an income statement might look like Exhibit 6-4. Most published income statements are not as detailed as Exhibit 6-4, because sales returns and allowances and sales discounts generally are not large when compared with total sales. Thus only one figure, net sales, is disclosed on the income statement. In those cases in which sales returns are an important item, such as the mail-order firm discussed previously, this account should be disclosed as a deduction from total sales.

EXHIBIT 6—4

JIGS' DO-IT-YOURSELF STORE		
Income Statement		
For the Year Ended December 31, 1990		
Sales		$1,500,000
Less		
Sales returns and allowances	$10,000	
Sales discounts	12,000	22,000
Net sales		$1,478,000

■ ACCOUNTING FOR INVENTORY PURCHASES

The purchase of inventory for resale represents the other major activity of a merchandising firm. **Inventories** are items held for resale to customers in the normal course of business or items that are to be consumed in producing or manufacturing goods or rendering services. For merchandising and manufacturing companies, inventories are often the single largest current asset. For example, at January 31, 1988, the inventories of Toys "R" Us totaled over $772 million and represented 87% of the current assets and over 38% of its total assets.

Accounting information for inventory purchases must be designed to allow management to maintain the proper level of inventories and to ensure that ending inventories and cost of goods sold are properly recorded and costed. This section will cover the nature of inventories, the recording of inventory purchases, and the related issues of purchase discounts, and purchase returns and allowances. Chapter 9 will deal with how a firm determines the cost of its ending inventory and the cost of those items sold during the period.

Two different accounting information systems have been developed to deal with accounting for inventories: the perpetual and the periodic inventory systems. Up to this point in the book, it has been assumed that a perpetual system is being used. Both the perpetual and the periodic systems will now be described.

■ PERPETUAL INVENTORY SYSTEM

A **perpetual inventory system** keeps a running balance of both inventory on hand and the cost of goods sold. These balances can be kept in units or in units and dollars. Management is therefore always aware of inventory levels and is able to make timely purchases to maintain desired inventory levels. The use of perpetual inventory systems has been enhanced in recent years through the use of electronic point-of-sale devices and computers. However, even with such sophisticated equipment, perpetual records may be kept only in units; the costs of ending inventories and goods sold are determined by the periodic system. For example, optical scanners in markets keep track of inventory quantities, but at the end of the accounting period, a physical inventory is taken to compute the cost of goods sold during the period and the appropriate cost of the ending inventory.

Accounting for Perpetual Inventories

The accounting for perpetual and later for periodic inventories is shown in the following example. Assume that a firm started the year with a beginning inventory of pens that cost $10,000. During the quarter, the following summary of transactions occurred:

Date	Amount of Sale	Cost of Inventory Sold*	Cost of Inventory Purchased
1. 1/20	$12,000	$ 8,000	
2. 1/28			$25,000
3. 2/10	30,000	24,000	
4. 3/28			$10,000

*On a periodic system, this data would not be computed; it is given here for illustrative purposes.

These illustrations will assume that all sales are for cash and purchases made on account. The appropriate journal entries for both the perpetual and the periodic systems are presented in Exhibit 6-5.

| EXHIBIT 6–5 | Comparative Journal Entries for Merchandise Purchaser | | | | |

Transaction	Journal Entries—Perpetual System		Journal Entries—Periodic System		
1/20 sale for $12,000 with a cost of $8,000	Cash	12,000		Cash	12,000	
	Sales		12,000	Sales		12,000
	Cost of Goods Sold	8,000		No entry to record cost		
	Merchandise Inventory		8,000	of goods sold.		
1/28 purchase for $25,000	Merchandise Inventory	25,000		Purchases	25,000	
	Accounts Payable		25,000	Accounts Payable		25,000
2/10 sale for $30,000 with a cost of $24,000	Cash	30,000		Cash	30,000	
	Sales		30,000	Sales		30,000
	Cost of Goods Sold	24,000		No entry to record cost		
	Merchandise Inventory		24,000	of goods sold.		
3/28 purchase for $10,000	Merchandise Inventory	10,000		Purchases	10,000	
	Accounts Payable		10,000	Accounts Payable		10,000

Under the perpetual system, when inventory is purchased, the Merchandise Inventory account is debited. (In previous chapters, this account was just entitled Inventory.) As the inventory is sold, the Merchandise Inventory account is credited, and Cost of Goods Sold is debited for the cost of the inventory sold. One of the features of the perpetual system is to provide the firm with information concerning its inventory levels. The system's design reflects this goal. As the series of journal entries in Exhibit 6-5 shows, the balance in the Merchandise Inventory account at a particular time should reflect the actual cost of the goods on hand at that time. In the example, the ending balance in the Merchandise Inventory account is $13,000, which should represent the actual cost of inventory on hand.

Merchandise Inventory					Cost of Goods Sold			
1/1	Bal.	10,000	8,000	1/20		1/20	8,000	
1/28		25,000	24,000	2/10		2/20	24,000	
3/28		10,000						
3/30	Bal.	13,000				3/30	Bal.	32,000

The word *should* was used because the balance in the merchandise inventory account will not always equal the cost of the items remaining in the inventory. This is due to clerical errors, spoilage, theft, and similar problems. An actual physical inventory count should be made at specified intervals—usually once a year. The balance in the Merchandise Inventory account is then adjusted to the actual ending inventory as determined by the physical count.

A typical perpetual inventory record is presented in Exhibit 6-6. The data shown in the record pertain to the journal entries shown in Exhibit 6-5. In this perpetual record, both units and costs are maintained. Furthermore, in order to simplify the illustration, all items are assumed to have had the same cost, $2. As noted, some perpetual records maintain only a record of units.

Although the perpetual inventory system provides management with a great deal of information, it is costly and time-consuming to maintain unless the firm has completely computerized its inventory control system. Many firms, therefore, use a periodic inventory system.

EXHIBIT 6–6

Inventory Record **Quarter Ended March 31, 19XX**												
Item	Pens								Minimum Stock	1,000	
Code No.	P-24								Maximum Stock	17,000	
										Average Reorder Time	2 weeks

		Items Purchased			**Items Sold**			**Balance Remaining**		
Date	**Description**	**Units Received**	**Unit Cost**	**Total Cost**	**Units Sold**	**Unit Cost**	**Total Cost**	**Units**	**Unit Cost**	**Total Cost**
January 1	Beginning balance							5,000	$2.00	$10,000
January 20	Sales				4,000	$2.00	$ 8,000	1,000	2.00	2,000
January 28	Purchases	12,500	$2.00	$25,000				13,500	2.00	27,000
February 10	Sales				12,000	2.00	24,000	1,500	2.00	3,000
March 28	Purchases	5,000	2.00	10,000				6,500	2.00	13,000
	Recap for Quarter Purchases Sales Balance	17,500	$2.00	$35,000	16,000	$2.00	$32,000	6,500	$2.00	$13,000

■ PERIODIC INVENTORY SYSTEMS

Periodic inventory systems do not keep continuous track of ending inventories and cost of goods sold. Instead, these items are determined only periodically: at the end of each quarter, each year, or other accounting period. Although this system may be easier to use for record-keeping purposes, it results in a significant loss of information for managerial decision-making purposes. However, the sheer volume of transactions in some merchandising businesses makes it impossible to use anything but a periodic system for purposes of inventory costing.

Accounting under the Periodic System

The journal entries necessary to record inventories under the periodic system are also shown in Exhibit 6-5. When the periodic system is used, no entry is made to record the cost of the inventory sold for a particular sale. Furthermore, as the journal entries show, inventory purchases are not debited to the Merchandise Inventory account. Rather, they are accumulated in a separate account called Purchases. As a result, there are no entries during the period to the asset account, Merchandise Inventory. Therefore, before any adjusting entries, the balance in the Merchandise Inventory account will reflect the amount of inventory at the beginning of the year, as indicated in the following T accounts.

Purchases			**Merchandise Inventory**	
1/28	25,000		1/1 Bal.	10,000
3/28	10,000			
3/30 Bal.	35,000			

Determining Cost of Goods Sold and Ending Inventory

Before financial statements can be prepared under the periodic system, the cost of goods sold during the period as well as the ending inventory must be calculated. This is done by taking a physical inventory, or counting the end-of-period inventory, to determine the quantity and the cost of the ending inventory and then applying this formula (the data is from the current example):

	Beginning	$10,000	
Plus	+ Inventory Purchases	35,000	
Equals	= Goods Available for Sale	45,000	
Less	− Ending Inventory	13,000	
Equals	= Cost of Goods Sold	$32,000	

In effect, the total of the beginning inventory and purchases during the period represents the total of all goods that the firm had available for sale. If the ending inventory is subtracted from this total, the remaining balance represents the cost of the items sold.

Determining the cost of the ending inventory and the resulting cost of goods sold is extremely important to determining the periodic income and financial position. Chapter 9 examines the alternative accounting methods that have been developed to do this. At this point, it is assumed that these amounts have been determined, and the journal entries to record these figures are illustrated here.

Adjusting and Closing Entries under the Periodic System

Once the ending inventory and cost of goods sold have been determined, the accounts must be adjusted to reflect the ending inventory balance and the cost of goods sold. There are several ways to do this; the authors recommend that the following adjusting and closing entries be made:[1]

Adjusting and Closing Entries at End of Accounting Period		
Adjusting Entry:		
Merchandise Inventory (ending)	13,000	
Cost of Goods Sold	32,000	
Purchases		35,000
Merchandise Inventory (beginning)		10,000
To adjust inventory to ending balance and create Cost of Goods Sold account.		
Closing Entry:		
Income Summary	32,000	
Cost of Goods Sold		32,000
To close Cost of Goods Sold account.		

The adjusting entry is based on the formula to calculate cost of goods sold. That is, the two credits, Purchases and Merchandise Inventory (beginning), are added together and represent goods available for sale. The debit, Merchandise Inventory (ending), is subtracted from that total to determine the balancing debit to Cost of Goods Sold. For convenience, Merchandise Inventory is labeled *beginning* and *ending*; how-

---

[1] An alternative method to record the ending inventory and to determine cost of goods sold is by means of the following closing entry:

Merchandise Inventory (ending)	13,000	
Income Summary	32,000	
Purchases		35,000
Merchandise Inventory (beginning)		10,000

Although this method requires one less entry, cost of goods sold is not specifically determined. However, this account is necessary in order to prepare the income statement.

ever, there is only one ledger account, Merchandise Inventory. Note that the result of this adjusting entry is to adjust the Merchandise Inventory account to its proper ending balance, to zero out the Purchases account, and to create a Cost of Goods Sold account. The entry to close Cost of Goods Sold to Income Summary or Retained Earnings is like all entries to close expense accounts.

After the adjusting and closing entries have been posted, the T accounts appear as follows:

Merchandise Inventory			
1/1 Bal.	10,000	Adj. Entry	10,000
Adj. Entry	13,000		
3/30 Bal.	13,000		

Purchases			
1/23	25,000	Adj. Entry	35,000
3/28	10,000		
	0		

Cost of Goods Sold			
Adj. Entry	32,000	Cl. Entry	32,000
	0		

Income Summary		
Cl. Entry	32,000	

■ ISSUES INVOLVED IN RECORDING PURCHASES

There are several other issues in recording merchandise purchases. It is important that inventory purchases be recorded at the time title passes from the seller to the buyer and that inventory purchases be recorded in accordance with the historical-cost principle. In this regard, historical cost includes the cash-equivalent price of the item plus all costs paid for freight and handling in order to deliver the merchandise to a location for its use or sale. Specific items that affect the historical cost of inventory purchases include purchase discounts, purchase returns and allowances, and freight charges. Accounting for each of these items will be explained next. Because the periodic inventory system is the most commonly used, it will be the basis for the discussion.

Accounting for **purchase discounts** is similar to accounting for sales discounts. The two methods, gross and net, are illustrated next, in the journal entries shown in Exhibit 6-7. The example is based on a $100 purchase with terms of 2/10, n/30.

EXHIBIT 6–7

JOURNAL ENTRIES TO RECORD PURCHASE DISCOUNTS
$100 Purchase—Stated Terms 2/10, n/30

Transaction	Gross Method			Net Method		
1. Purchase of $100 of merchandise on account	Purchases[a]	100		Purchases	98	
	Accounts Payable		100	Accounts Payable		98
2a. Firm pays within discount period	Accounts Payable	100		Accounts Payable	98	
	Purchase Discounts		2	Cash		98
	Cash		98			
2b. Firm *does not* pay within discount period	Accounts Payable	100		Accounts Payable	98	
	Cash		100	Purchase Discount Lost	2	
				Cash		100

[a]This illustration assumes the use of the periodic inventory system. If a perpetual system is used, the debit is to the Merchandise Inventory account in all places where the Purchases account is debited. All other aspects of the entry are the same.

The Gross Method of Recording Purchase Discounts

The **gross method of recording purchase discounts** records the purchase and the payable at the gross amount before any discount. If the firm takes the discount, an account titled Purchase Discounts will be credited for the amount of the discount. This account is eventually closed into Cost of Goods Sold at the time an adjusting entry is made to compute the cost of goods sold. The result is to reduce cost of goods sold by the amount of the discounts taken.

If the business fails to take the discount, the entry to record the payment will be straightforward. Accounts Payable is debited, and Cash is credited for $100, the full invoice price. Like the gross method of recording sales discounts, the gross method of recording purchase discounts is very common. However, it also suffers from the same criticisms made against recording sales at the gross amount when discounts are offered.

The Net Method of Recording Purchase Discounts

As Exhibit 6-7 indicates, the **net method of recording purchase discounts** records the purchase and the accounts payable net of the allowable discount. If the payment is made within the discount period, Accounts Payable should be debited, and Cash should be credited for the amount at which the payable was originally recorded. If the firm does not pay within the discount period, the full invoice price is paid. The difference between the amount at which Accounts Payable is debited and Cash is credited is debited to an account titled Purchase Discounts Lost. This account is treated as a financial cost or interest expense. The argument for treating discounts lost as interest expense is based on the fact that the firm consciously chose not to pay within the allowable discount period, thus causing an additional cost. This additional cost represents a cost for the use of money and therefore is considered interest.

As in the case of sales discounts, the net method is preferable. Accounts payable are recorded at their expected cash payment at the time of purchase. Furthermore, the use of the Purchase Discounts Lost account highlights the total cost of not paying within the discount period. As noted previously, this can be a significant cost, and it is generally in the firm's best interest to pay within the discount period.

Purchase Returns and Allowances

The accounting treatment for **purchase returns and allowances** is similar to that for sales returns and allowances, except that it involves the accounts Purchases Returns and Allowances and Accounts Payable. To illustrate, assume that the Russell Company purchased, for future resale, ten television sets at a total cost of $2,800. The periodic inventory system is used, and the payable is recorded at the gross or invoice price. If one television costing $280 is found defective and is returned, the Russell Company will make the following entry:

Accounts Payable	280	
Purchase Returns and Allowances		280
Return of defective merchandise.		

The Purchase Returns and Allowances account is offset against total purchases in computing cost of goods sold. The ultimate effect is to reduce cost of goods sold. Although the Purchases account could be directly credited for any returns and allowances, the use of the Purchases Returns and Allowances account gives management more control over these items.

Freight

The cost of freight for goods purchased for resale is referred to as *freight-in*, or transportation-in. In some circumstances the seller pays the freight, and in other circumstances the purchaser does. Freight charges paid by the purchaser are debited to an account called Freight-in and are an addition to the cost of merchandise purchased and ultimately to cost of goods sold. This is in accordance with the historical-cost principle and ensures that the purchases carry their full cost. Freight charges paid by the seller are referred to as *freight-out*. They are considered a selling expense and as such are not included in the computation of cost of goods sold.

Deciding who pays the freight is a negotiable item in determining the terms of sale and is based on legal concepts concerning the legal passage of title. If the terms of the sale are **FOB (Free on Board) destination**, legal title to the goods does not pass until they reach the buyer's receiving point, and so the seller pays the freight. Conversely, when the goods are shipped **FOB shipping point**, title to the goods passes when they leave the seller's warehouse, so the buyer pays the freight charges. The following table summarizes these points:

Terms	Who Pays Freight Charges	When Title to Goods Passes
FOB shipping	Purchaser	At shipment
FOB destination	Seller	Upon delivery

As the previous discussion pointed out, freight-in ultimately becomes an addition to cost of goods sold. Other expenses that could be considered additional inventory costs and ultimately part of cost of goods sold include such items as the expenses of the merchandise-receiving department, warehousing, insurance cost, and other costs of carrying inventory. Clearly, these costs are incurred because of the inventory and logically could be allocated to the cost of inventory and the cost of goods sold. However, because of the difficulty of allocating these items, accountants consider them to be period expenses and include them in either selling or general and administrative expenses. Only items such as freight-in, which are directly related to the inventory, are included in the cost of the inventory.

■ TAKING A PHYSICAL INVENTORY

Taking a physical inventory is an important part of maintaining control over merchandising operations. When a perpetual inventory system is used, the physical inventory verifies that the firm does in fact have the inventory that its records show it does. When a periodic inventory system is used, a physical inventory is needed to determine cost of goods sold. The two steps in taking a physical inventory are the inventory count and the determination of the inventory's cost. This section will consider the issues pertaining to the item count; the issues pertaining to the cost of the ending inventory will be studied in Chapter 9.

In taking a physical inventory, special care must be taken to ensure that all items of inventory to which the firm has legal title are counted. In addition, care must be taken to ensure that items that have been sold are not counted in the seller's year-end inventory. In this regard, items that require special analysis are goods in transit, goods on consignment, and goods in public warehouses.

Goods in Transit

Goods in transit are goods that have been purchased but have not yet been received by the purchaser. These goods can be easily overlooked when counting the ending inventory because they are not physically located at either the seller's or the purchaser's warehouse. In accounting for goods in transit, the main question is whether a sale has taken place, resulting in the passage of title to the buyer. If this is the case, the seller records a sale and a receivable or cash and does not include the item in the ending inventory. The purchaser records the payable or the payment of cash and the purchase and includes the item in the ending inventory. Conversely, if title has not passed, no sale or purchase has taken place, so the inventory is included in the seller's ending inventory.

As noted, from a legal standpoint, title passes when goods reach the FOB point. Therefore, when goods are shipped FOB shipping point, title passes from the seller to the buyer at the shipping point. Because title has passed, the seller recognizes the sale, the buyer recognizes the purchase, and the inventory is included in the buyer's ending inventory. If goods are shipped FOB destination, title does not pass until the goods reach the buyer's receiving point. In this situation, goods in transit belong to the seller, and neither a sale nor a purchase is recorded until the goods reach the buyer.

Goods on Consignment

Goods on consignment are goods held by a firm for resale, but title remains with the manufacturer of the product. In effect, the merchandiser has agreed to display the goods but, for a variety of reasons, is not willing to purchase them. When and if the retail firm sells the consigned goods, it receives a commission. However, until the sale takes place, the title to the goods remains with the manufacturer, although they are on the premises of a different firm. The manufacturer of the items is willing to accept such an agreement in order to get new or unusual goods into the hands of retailers for possible sale. Retailers agree to this arrangement because they do not have to accept the risks of ownership and will still receive a commission if the goods are sold.

Goods in Public Warehouses

Merchandising firms often store goods in public warehouses. If the firm has title to the goods in the warehouses, they must be included in the ending inventory. Failure to count these items will understate the ending inventory, net assets, and profits for the period.

WORKSHEET TECHNIQUES FOR A PERIODIC INVENTORY SYSTEM

Chapter 4 discussed worksheet techniques when a perpetual inventory system is used. This section will explain the worksheet techniques when a periodic inventory system is used. A worksheet for Jacob's Pet Supplies Company for the year ended December 31, 1990 is presented in Exhibit 6-8. All of the new accounts discussed in this chapter are highlighted.

THE UNADJUSTED TRIAL BALANCE

The amounts listed in the unadjusted trial balance columns of Exhibit 6-8 come from the unadjusted general ledger accounts. The important points to note are that the $24,000 balance in the Inventory account represents the amount of the beginning inventory and that additional inventory purchases of $98,000 are accumulated in the Purchases account. There also is an account titled Cost of Goods Sold in the unadjusted trial balance, but at this point it has a zero balance.

ADJUSTING ENTRIES AND THE ADJUSTED TRIAL BALANCE

The accountant for Jacob's Pet Supplies analyzed the accounts and made the following adjusting journal entries for the year ended December 31, 1990. The accountant determined the data on page 230 related to cost of goods sold.

EXHIBIT 6–8

JACOB'S PET SUPPLIES
Worksheet
For the Year Ended December 31, 1990

	1	2	3	4	5	6	7	8	9	10
	Unadjusted Trial Balance		Adjustments		Adjusted Trial Balance		Income Statement		Balance Sheet	
Account	Debit	Credit	Debit	Credit	Debit	Credit	Debit	Credit	Debit	Credit
Cash	4,000				4,000				4,000	
Accounts receivable	12,000				12,000				12,000	
Merchandise inventory	24,000		¹ 37,000	¹ 24,000	37,000				37,000	
Supplies	1,200			² 400	800				800	
Prepaid insurance	2,600			³ 1,300	1,300				1,300	
Long-term investments	8,000				8,000				8,000	
Land	15,000				15,000				15,000	
Store equipment	30,000				30,000				30,000	
Accumulated depreciation— Store equipment		2,000		⁶ 1,000		3,000				3,000
Accounts payable		3,000				3,000				3,000
Salaries payable				⁴ 1,200		1,200				1,200
Current maturities of long- term debt		2,500				2,500				2,500
Interest payable				⁵ 2,250		2,250				2,250
Mortgages payable		20,000				20,000				20,000
Common stock		25,000				25,000				25,000
Retained earnings		35,300				35,300				35,300
Sales		125,000				125,000		125,000		
Sales returns and allowances	1,500				1,500		1,500			
Sales discounts	3,500				3,500		3,500			
Purchases	98,000			¹ 98,000						
Purchase returns and allowances		2,000	¹ 2,000							
Purchase discounts		4,000	¹ 4,000							
Freight-in	1,000			¹ 1,000						
Cost of goods sold			¹ 80,000		80,000		80,000			
Sales salaries expense	7,000		⁴ 700		7,700		7,700			
Office salaries expense	7,600		⁴ 500		8,100		8,100			
Advertising expense	2,100				2,100		2,100			
Freight-out	1,300				1,300		1,300			
Supplies expense			² 400		400		400			
Insurance expense			³ 1,300		1,300		1,300			
Depreciation expense			⁶ 1,000		1,000		1,000			
Interest expense			⁵ 2,250		2,250		2,250			
Totals	218,800	218,800	129,150	129,150	217,250	217,250	109,150	125,000		
Income before taxes							15,850			
Totals							125,000	125,000		
Income before taxes								15,850		
Income taxes expense			⁷ 6,340				6,340			
Income taxes payable				⁷ 6,340						6,340
Net income							9,510			9,510
							15,850	15,850	108,100	108,100

Cost of Goods Sold:		
Beginning Inventory		$ 24,000
Purchases	$98,000	
Less: Purchase Returns and Allowances	(2,000)	
Purchase Discounts	(4,000)	
Net Purchases		92,000
Add: Freight-in		1,000
Goods Available for Sale		117,000
Less: Ending Inventory		37,000
Cost of Goods Sold		$ 80,000

Therefore the following adjusting entry is made to record cost of goods sold. In addition, adjusting entries 2 through 6 are made to record other adjustments.

1. Merchandise Inventory (ending)	$37,000	
Purchase Returns and Allowances	2,000	
Purchase Discounts	4,000	
Cost of Goods Sold	80,000	
Purchases		$98,000
Freight-in		1,000
Merchandise Inventory (beginning)		24,000
To record cost of goods sold and adjust ending inventory to its actual balance.		
2. Supplies Expense	400	
Supplies		400
To write off supplies used.		
3. Insurance Expense	1,300	
Prepaid Insurance		1,300
To write off prepaid expenses.		
4. Office Salary Expense	500	
Sales Salary Expense	700	
Salaries Payable		1,200
To record salaries payable.		
5. Interest Expense	2,250	
Interest Payable		2,250
To record interest payable.		
6. Depreciation Expense	1,000	
Accumulated Depreciation—Store Equipment		1,000
To record depreciation expense.		

After these adjusting journal entries are recorded in the proper worksheet columns, an adjusted trial balance can be prepared. This adjusted trial balance is in columns 5 and 6 of Exhibit 6-8.

■ THE INCOME STATEMENT AND BALANCE SHEET COLUMNS

After the adjusted trial balance is prepared, the figures can be spread to the appropriate income statement and balance sheet columns. In the income statement columns of Exhibit 6-8, the debits total $109,150, and the credits total $125,000. The difference of $15,850 represents income before taxes. The adjustments do not yet include a tax accrual; this accrual must be made before the worksheet can be completed.

The current tax rate is 40%, so this adjusting journal entry must be made:

Income Taxes Expense	6,340	
Income Taxes Payable		6,340
To record income taxes expense.		
$6,340 = $15,850 × .40		

Because this entry is in fact an adjusting entry, it is entered in the adjustment column. However, these columns are already totaled, and so it is not necessary to retotal them. The debit part of this entry, which represents the expense, is extended to the debit column in the income statement, and the credit part of this entry, which represents taxes payable, is extended to the credit column in the balance sheet. The final balancing figure of $9,510 represents net income.

■ PREPARATION OF FINANCIAL STATEMENT AND CLOSING ENTRIES

Financial statements can be prepared directly from the worksheet. A multistep income statement for Jacob's Pet Supplies is shown in Exhibit 6-9, in which the sales and

EXHIBIT 6–9

JACOB'S PET SUPPLIES Income Statement For the Year Ended December 31, 1990			
Revenues			
Gross sales			$125,000
Less: Sales returns and allowances		$ 1,500	
Sales discounts		3,500	5,000
Net sales			120,000
Cost of goods sold			
Beginning inventory		24,000	
Purchases	$98,000		
Less: Purchase returns and allowances	(2,000)		
Purchase discounts	(4,000)		
Net purchases		92,000	
Add: Freight-in		1,000	
Goods available for sale		117,000	
Less: Ending inventory		37,000	
Cost of goods sold			80,000
Gross margin on sales			40,000
Operating expenses			
Selling expenses			
Sales salaries	7,700		
Advertising	2,100		
Freight-out	1,300		
Depreciation*	400		
Total selling expenses		11,500	
General and administrative expenses			
Office salaries	8,100		
Insurance	1,300		
Depreciation*	600		
Supplies	400		
Total general and administrative expenses		10,400	
Total operating expenses			21,900
Income from operations			18,100
Other expenses			
Interest			2,250
Income before taxes			15,850
Taxes			6,340
Net income			$ 9,510

*Allocated 40% to selling expenses and 60% to general and administrative expenses.

cost of goods sold section have been expanded to show how all of the accounts covered in this chapter are placed on the income statement. The balance sheet for Jacob's Pet Supplies is shown in Exhibit 6-10.

EXHIBIT 6–10

JACOB'S PET SUPPLIES
Balance Sheet
December 31, 1990

Assets			Liabilities and Stockholders' Equity		
Current assets			Current liabilities		
Cash		$ 4,000	Accounts payable		$ 3,000
Accounts receivable		12,000	Salaries payable		1,200
Inventory		37,000	Taxes payable		6,340
Supplies		800	Interest payable		2,250
Insurance expense		1,300	Current maturities		
Total current assets		55,100	Long-term debt		2,500
Long-term investments		8,000	Total current liabilities		15,290
Property, plant, and			Long-term liabilities		
equipment			Mortgage payable		20,000
Land		15,000	Total liabilities		35,290
Store equipment	$30,000		Stockholders' equity:		
Accumulated			Common stock	$25,000	
depreciation	3,000	27,000	Retained earnings	44,810	69,810
Total property, plant,			Total liabilities and		
and equipment		42,000	stockholders' equity		$105,100
Total assets		$105,100			

The last step in the cycle is to prepare the closing entries. These entries for Jacob's Pet Supplies are shown next:

Sales	125,000	
Income Summary		120,000
Sales Returns and Allowances		1,500
Sales Discounts		3,500
To close revenue accounts to Income Summary		
Income Summary	110,490	
Cost of Goods Sold		80,000
Sales Salaries		7,700
Office Salaries		8,100
Freight-out		1,300
Advertising Expense		2,100
Depreciation Expense		1,000
Insurance Expense		1,300
Supplies Expense		400
Interest Expense		2,250
Taxes		6,340
To close expense accounts to Income Summary.		
Income Summary	9,510	
Retained Earnings		9,510
To close Income Summary to Retained Earnings.		

**SUMMARY OF
LEARNING
OBJECTIVES**

1. How merchandising firms account for sales transactions, including trade and quantity discounts, sales discounts, credit card sales, and sales returns and allowances. Merchandising firms may offer their customers trade and quantity discounts and/or sales discounts. Trade and quantity discounts are adjustments to arrive at an agreed-upon price, and no accounting recognition is given. That is, the sale is recorded net of any of these discounts. Sales discounts may be recorded gross or net, although the net method is preferable. Separate accounts are maintained for credit card fees, and they are usually considered selling expenses. Sales returns and allowances are deducted from sales in order to determine net sales.

2. The difference between the perpetual and the periodic inventory systems, and the accounting entries related to each system. Both the perpetual and periodic inventory systems are acceptable. The perpetual system records and provides management a continuous record of inventories on hand and cost of goods sold. The record-keeping involved is complex and, without electronic point-of-sale devices or other computer systems, can be costly to maintain. The periodic system records only the cost of purchases. The entries for each system are as in the table:

3. How merchandising firms account for purchases, including trade and quantity discounts, purchase discounts, purchase returns and allowances, and freight. The accounting for purchases parallels the accounting for sales. Accounting recognition is not given to trade or quantity discounts. The net and gross methods can be used to record purchase discounts. Although the gross method is the more common, the net method is preferable. Because freight-in is directly related to merchandise purchases, it ultimately becomes part of cost of goods sold and inventory. Other costs, such as warehouse expenses, which are only indirectly related to inventory purchases, are considered period expenses.

4. Issues involved in taking a physical inventory. In taking a physical inventory, special care must be taken to ensure that all items of inventory to which the firm has legal title are counted. Thus goods in transit to which the firm has title, goods on consignment, and goods in public warehouses must be included in the ending inventory. Finally, care must be taken to ensure that items that have been sold are not counted in the seller's year-end inventory.

Transaction	Perpetual			Periodic		
1. To record sales	Accounts Receivable	XX		Accounts Receivable	XX	
	Sales		XX	Sales		XX
2. To record cost of goods sold at time of sale	Cost of Goods Sold	XX		No Entry		
	Inventory		XX			
3. To record inventory purchases	Inventory	XX		Purchases	XX	
	Accounts Payable		XX	Accounts Payable		XX

If the periodic system is used, an adjusting entry must be made at the end of the accounting period in order to determine cost of goods sold and the ending balance in the Merchandise Inventory account. The form of this entry, based on the formula to compute cost of goods sold, is:

Merchandise Inventory (ending)	XXX	
Cost of Goods Sold	XXX	
Purchases		XXX
Merchandise Inventory (beginning)		XXX

5. Worksheet Techniques for a Merchandising Firm. The construction of a worksheet for a merchandising firm is similar to the worksheet outlined in Chapter 4. The difference is the addition of new accounts related to sales and purchases. A multistep income statement would show all these accounts, whereas a single-step income statement would show only net sales and cost of goods sold.

KEY TERMS

FOB destination

FOB shipping point

Goods in transit

Goods on consignment

Gross method of recording sales discounts	Purchase discounts
Gross method of recording purchase discounts	Purchase returns and allowances
Inventories	Quantity discounts
Merchandising firm	Sales allowances
Net method of recording sales discounts	Sales discounts
Net method of recording purchase discounts	Sales returns
Periodic inventory system	Trade discounts
Perpetual inventory system	

PROBLEM FOR YOUR REVIEW

During the month of October, Tiny Tots, Inc. (the seller) entered into the following transactions with Little Kids (the purchaser):

- October 2: Tiny Tots, Inc. sold merchandise to Little Kids on account. The sale totaled $10,000 and was made under the following terms: 2/10, n/30.
- October 8: Little Kids returned $1,000 of the merchandise because it was defective.
- October 9: Tiny Tots, Inc. made an additional sale of $5,000 on account to Little Kids. The terms of the sale were 2/10, n/30.
- October 10: Tiny Tots, Inc. received the required payment for the October 2 sale.
- October 25: Tiny Tots, Inc. received full payment on the October 9 purchase from Little Kids.

REQUIRED: Make all the required entries on the books of both Tiny Tots, Inc. and Little Kids, assuming that:

(a) Each company uses the gross method of recording sales and purchases.

(b) Each company uses the net method of recording sales and purchases.

Assume each firm uses the periodic inventory system.

SOLUTION

(a) GROSS METHOD:

	Tiny Tots, Inc. (Seller)			Little Kids (Buyer)		
October 2	$10,000 sale on account, terms 2/10, n/30					
	Accounts Receivable	10,000		Purchases	10,000	
	Sales		10,000	Accounts Payable		10,000
October 8	Return of $1,000 of defective merchandise					
	Sales Returns and Allowances	1,000		Accounts Payable	1,000	
	Accounts Receivable		1,000	Purchase Returns		
				and Allowances		1,000
October 9	$5,000 sale on account, terms 2/10, n/30					
	Accounts Receivable	5,000		Purchases	5,000	
	Sales		5,000	Accounts Payable		5,000
October 10	Receipt of payment on October 2 sale					
	Cash	8,820*		Accounts Payable	9,000	
	Sales Discounts	180		Purchase Discounts		180
	Accounts Receivable		9,000	Cash		8,820*
October 25	Receipt of payment on October 9 sales					
	Cash	5,000		Accounts Payable	5,000	
	Accounts Receivable		5,000	Cash		5,000

*$8,820 = .98 × $9,000

(b) NET METHOD:

	Tiny Tots, Inc. (Seller)			Little Kids (Buyer)		
October 2	$10,000 sale on account, terms 2/10, n/30					
	Accounts Receivable	9,800*		Purchases	9,800*	
	Sales		9,800	Accounts Payable		9,800
October 8	Return of $1,000 of defective merchandise					
	Sales Returns and Allowances	980†		Accounts Payable	980†	
	Accounts Receivable		980	Purchase Returns		
				and Allowances		980
October 9	$5,000 sale on account, terms 2/10, n/30					
	Accounts Receivable	4,900‡		Purchases	4,900‡	
	Sales		4,900	Accounts Payable		4,900
October 10	Receipt of payment on October 2 sale					
	Cash	8,820		Accounts Payable	8,820	
	Accounts Receivable		8,820	Cash		8,820
October 25	Receipt of payment on October 9 sale					
	Cash	5,000		Accounts Payable	4,900	
	Accounts Receivable		4,900	Purchase Discounts Lost	100	
	Sales Discounts Not Taken		100	Cash		5,000

*$9,800 = .98 × $10,000
†$980 = .98 × $1,000
‡$4,900 = .98 × $5,000

QUESTIONS

1. What are the characteristics of a merchandising firm? How do they differ from those of a manufacturing firm?

2. Define: (a) trade discounts, (b) sales discounts, and (c) quantity discounts.

3. Why would a firm offer a sales discount to its buyers?

4. What is meant by (a) 3/10, n/30, (b) 7 EOM, and (c) n/30?

5. Describe the difference between the gross method and the net method of recording sales discounts. What are the basic assumptions of each method?

6. What are the theoretical problems with the gross method of recording sales or purchase discounts?

7. Briefly discuss the difference between the perpetual inventory system and the periodic inventory system. Under what circumstances is each system used?

8. When goods are shipped FOB destination, who must pay the cost of freight? Who must pay if the goods are shipped FOB shipping point?

9. Would a hardware store be likely to use a perpetual or periodic inventory system?

10. What costs, in addition to the initial purchase price, should be included in the inventory cost and the cost of goods sold?

11. Using the periodic system, how is the cost of goods sold determined?

12. What problems can occur with goods in transit when determining the ending inventory?

13. What is meant by goods on consignment?

14. Edward's Radio Shop sells a particular radio for $50. However, if a customer buys ten radios, the total cost will be $450. How would such a sale be recorded? Why?

15. How are bank credit card fees accounted for?

16. What are sales returns and allowances, and how are they accounted for?

17. What is the effect of purchase returns and allowances in computing the cost of goods sold?

18. In examining an unadjusted trial balance, how can you tell whether a firm has used the periodic or the perpetual inventory system?

19. In what ways, if any, would the cost of goods sold section of an income statement differ when a firm uses the gross method of recording sales discounts rather than the net method?

EXERCISES

E1. **Accounting for Trade and Quantity Discounts.** Perry's Paint Store offers both trade and quantity discounts. Quantity discounts are given as follows:

Quantity Purchased	% Discount
1–9 cans	0
10–19 cans	3
More than 20 cans	5

Professional painters also receive an additional 5% discount on the list price per gallon before any quantity discounts. Finally, cash buyers receive an additional 3% off the total price. The retail price of each can of paint is $10.

REQUIRED: Make the entry to record the sale for each of the following two situations:

1. Joe Kelly, a professional painter, purchases 30 cans of paint. The purchase is made on account.

2. Al Companies, a do-it-yourself painter, purchases 15 cans. He pays cash.

E2. **Recording Sales Discounts.** The following transactions were selected from the records of McKelvey Retailers:

- January 2: Sold merchandise to the Vox Corporation for $6,000 cash.
- January 12: Sold merchandise on account to the Chief Company for $4,000. Terms 3/10, n/30.
- January 15: Sold merchandise on account to the Foothill Company for $8,000. Terms 2/10, n/30.
- January 21: Received payment from Foothill Company net of the discount.
- January 30: Received payment from the Chief Company.

REQUIRED: Prepare the necessary entries to record these sales, assuming that McKelvey Retailers uses (a) the gross method and then (b) the net method of recording sales discounts.

E3. **Recording Sales Discounts and Sales Returns.** The PGM Corporation sells plumbing supplies to various plumbing stores. During March, the following transactions occurred. The gross method of recording sales discounts was used.

- March 2: Supplies with a price of $6,000 sold on account to LM Plumbing. Terms 2/10, n/30.
- March 4: Sale of merchandise for $1,500 cash.
- March 6: LM returned $1,000 of supplies and received a credit.
- March 10: LM paid the amount owed to PGM.
- March 15: Sale of $9,000 of merchandise to Ramsey Corporation. Terms 2/10, n/30.
- March 17: Sale of $3,500 of merchandise to Ron Corporation. Because this is a new customer, terms are 5 EOM.
- March 20: Payment received from Ramsey Corporation.
- March 31: Payment received from Ron Corporation.

REQUIRED: Record the above transactions on the books of the PGM Corporation.

E4. **Credit Card Sales.** During March, the King Corporation had bank credit card sales of $7,500. The fees are 3% and are deducted when the charge slips are deposited.

Also during March, the firm made nonbank credit card sales of $4,000. The service charge on these sales is 5%. The drafts are mailed to the credit card firm, and the firm receives payment net of the service charge on April 10.

REQUIRED: Make the entries to record all of these transactions.

E5. The Periodic versus the Perpetual System of Accounting. The Honey Company began business during the current year. The following summary of events occurred during its first month of operation:

- January 2: Merchandise costing $6,000 was purchased for cash.

- January 10: Merchandise costing $9,000 was purchased on account. Terms n/30.

- January 15: Sales for the first half of January totaled $14,000. Of this amount, $9,000 was for cash and the remaining on account. The cost of goods sold was $11,000.

- January 20: Merchandise costing $16,000 was purchased on account. Terms n/30.

- January 31: Sales for the last half of January were $20,000. Of this amount, $15,000 was for cash and the remaining on account. The cost of goods sold was $14,000.

REQUIRED: Prepare the necessary entries to record these transactions, assuming that the firm uses (a) the periodic system and then (b) the perpetual system. (Ignore adjusting and closing entries.)

E6. Determining Cost of Goods Sold. Given the following information, determine the missing amounts:

	Case 1	Case 2	Case 3
Sales	$25,000	$18,050	$?
Beginning inventory	8,000	8,000	10,000
Purchases	15,000	?	23,000
Purchase returns and allowances	1,500	2,000	?
Goods available for sale	?	17,000	28,500
Ending inventory	4,000	?	2,150
Cost of goods sold	?	11,500	?
Gross margin on sales	?	?	7,500

E7. Accounting for Purchase Discounts. Sue's Fabric Shop entered into the following transactions during May:

- May 2: Purchased $6,000 of fabric on account. Terms 1/10, n/30.

- May 10: Purchased $8,000 of fabric on account. Terms 2/10, n/30.

- May 10: Returned $500 of goods purchased on May 2 because they were defective. The company's account was credited.

- May 11: Made the required payment on the May 2 purchase.

- May 20: Received $200 freight bill on the May 10 purchase, payable at the end of the month.

- May 30: Made the required payment on the May 10 purchase. Also paid the related freight bill received on May 20.

The company uses the periodic inventory system.

REQUIRED: Make the necessary entries, assuming that the company used (a) the gross method and then (b) the net method of recording purchase discounts.

E8. Accounting for Purchases and Transportation. On December 28, 1990, the Golden Company entered into the following transactions:

(a) Merchandise costing $17,000 was purchased from Manchester Corporation, terms 1/10, n/30, FOB destination. Transportation costs were $1,200. The goods arrived on January 3, 1991. All required payments were made on January 4, 1991.

(b) Merchandise costing $15,000 was purchased from the London Industries, 5 EOM FOB shipping point. Transportation costs were $500. The goods arrived on January 4, 1991. All required payments were made on January 5, 1991.

REQUIRED: Assuming that the Golden Company uses the periodic inventory system and records purchases using the net method, prepare the necessary journal entries for these transactions. Now assume that any transportation charges payable by the Golden Company are not subject to a discount. Which goods should be included in the December 31, 1990 ending inventory?

E9. Analysis. Given the following information, compute the beginning inventory:

Purchases returns and allowances	$ 7,280
Transportation-in	2,375
Purchases	134,890
Cost of goods sold	112,710
Ending inventory	38,575
Sales returns	6,250
Freight-out	1,246

E10. Determining the Cost of the Ending Inventory. The Gould Antique Shop asks your help in determining the cost of its ending inventory at December 31. It has counted all the items in its store and determined their cost to be $102,475. In addition, the shop gives you the following information:

(a) Goods costing $24,000 were held by others on consignment.

(b) Goods costing $56,000 were in transit from England. They were shipped FOB shipping point.

(c) The Gould Antique Shop held items costing $62,000 on consignment for others. These items were included in the ending inventory count.

(d) Goods costing $10,000 were in transit from Spain. They were shipped FOB destination.

What is the cost of their ending inventory?

E11. Periodic System—Adjusting and Closing Entries. The following accounts were taken from the trial balance of the Jose Corporation on December 31:

Sales	$500,000
Beginning inventory	40,000
Transportation-in	4,000
Ending inventory	42,000
Sales discounts	5,000
Purchases	331,000
Purchase returns and allowances	2,400
Sales returns and allowances	15,000
Purchase discounts	7,400

REQUIRED: **(a)** Prepare an income statement in good form through gross margin on sales.

(b) Prepare the necessary adjusting and closing entries.

E12. Perpetual Inventory—Recording Transactions. The Conners Company is a small distributor of radiators for specialty automobiles. The firm carries only three different models and uses the perpetual inventory system. At the beginning of March, the firm had 100 radiators, Model 467, that it purchased for $27 per radiator. During March, the following cash purchases and sales took place in regard to this model:

- March 8: Purchased 40 radiators at $40 each.

- March 15: Sold 80 radiators for $60 each. (Assume that the radiators are sold in the order that they are purchased. Thus all radiators in the beginning inventory are sold before those purchased on March 8, and so forth.)

- March 20: Purchased 50 radiators at $35 each.

- March 22: Returned two of the radiators purchased on March 20 as they were defective.
- March 30: Sold 30 radiators for $60 each.

REQUIRED: **(a)** Make the necessary journal entries to reflect the purchases and sales during March.

(b) Prepare an inventory record similar to the one in the text for radiator Model 467.

E13. Receivables and Inventory Analysis. The adjusted trial balance of the Hoyle Company indicated an Accounts Receivable balance of $8,000. However, as the accountant you are concerned about the validity of this figure, given the volume of sales and your knowledge of the business. You decided to investigate and obtained the following data in your analysis.

	Beginning Balance	Ending Balance
Accounts receivable	$15,000	$ 8,000*
Accounts payable	8,000	10,000
Merchandise inventory	40,000	36,000

*Represents reported balance.

OTHER DATA: **1.** All sales and all merchandise purchases are on account.

2. The gross margin percentage is 20%.

3. Payments on account during the year were $200,000.

4. Collections on account during the year were $220,000.

REQUIRED: Determine the errors, if any, in the reported accounts receivable balance.

E14. Toys "R" Us Financial Statements. Using the data from the Toys "R" Us financial statements in Appendix D, determine:

(a) Gross margin on sales for 1988 and 1987.

(b) Net purchases of inventory for 1988.

PROBLEMS

P6-1 Recording Purchase and Sales Transactions. The Barbara Company uses the periodic inventory system. Assume that the company uses the gross method of recording discounts. The following transactions relating to sales and purchases occurred during the month of October:

- October 3: Purchased merchandise on account, $8,000, from Tiger Company. Terms 2/10, n/30.
- October 4: Sold merchandise to Sue Corporation for $1,400 cash.
- October 6: Sold merchandise to Elvia Company on account, $3,800, 5 EOM, FOB shipping point.
- October 8: Made required payment to Tiger Company on October 3 purchase.
- October 10: Purchased merchandise for $4,200 from the Kelly Company. Terms 2/10, n/30.
- October 15: Sold merchandise to Kaufman Corporation on account, $3,000, 1/10, n/30.
- October 17: Permitted Kaufman Corporation to return for credit $700 of merchandise purchased on October 15.
- October 24: Received required cash due from Kaufman Corporation for October 15 sale.
- October 25: Made required payment to the Kelly Company on October 10 purchase.

REQUIRED: Prepare the necessary journal entries for the above transactions.

P6-2   Recording Purchases and Sales Transactions. The Davidson Company uses the periodic inventory system and the gross method of recording sales and purchase discounts. The following transactions relating to sales and purchases occurred during March:

- March 3: Purchased merchandise on account for $8,000 from the Washington Company. Terms 2/10, n/30.
- March 4: Sold merchandise to the Jefferson Company on account for $1,500. Terms 1/10, n/30.
- March 5: Sold merchandise to Adam Company on account for $3,500. Terms 7 EOM, FOB shipping point.
- March 8: Made the required payment to Washington Company for the March 3 purchase.
- March 12: Purchased merchandise on account for $6,000 from the Lincoln Company. Terms 2/10, n/30.
- March 13: Received payment from the Jefferson Company, net of the discount.
- March 16: Sold merchandise to Grant Company on account for $4,000. Terms 1/10, n/30.
- March 21: Received required payment from Adam Company for March 5 sale.
- March 31: Made payment to the Lincoln Company for the March 12 purchase.

REQUIRED: Prepare the necessary journal entries for the above transactions.

P6-3   Recording Purchase Transactions. Amy's Antique Shoppe made the following purchase transactions during the month of February. The firm uses the periodic inventory system and the net method to record purchase discounts.

- February 2: Five tables were purchased on account from London Furniture Company, terms 2/10, n/30. The selling price of each table is $500. Amy's Antique Shoppe was given a 5% trade discount.
- February 6: A $400 desk was delivered on consignment from the Old England Guild.
- February 7: Ten rocking chairs were purchased on account from American Corporation, terms 2/10, n/30, FOB shipping point. The chairs cost $175 each. Freight charges payable to Smith Freight were $210, n/30.
- February 8: 100 mirrors were purchased from Smithe Glass Company for $1,000 cash.
- February 10: 25 of the mirrors purchased from Smithe Glass Company were received damaged and were returned for a cash refund.
- February 15: Three dressers costing $1,300 each were purchased from the Old England Guild on account, terms n/30, FOB shipping point. Freight charges were $75, which was paid in cash.
- February 16: A check for the full payment due was written to the American Corporation.
- February 17: The Smith Freight Company was paid for the freight charges of February 7.
- February 25: A check for the full payment due was written to the Old England Guild for the February 15 purchase.
- February 28: A check for the full payment due was written to the London Furniture Company.

REQUIRED: Record the necessary journal entries for Amy's Antique Shoppe.

P6-4   Gross and Net Methods of Recording Discounts. The Stardust Company, which uses the periodic inventory system, entered into the following transactions during April:

- April 2: Purchased inventory items from the Lite Company for $2,400. Terms 2/10, n/30.
- April 6: Sold merchandise on account to the Mercury Company for $15,000. Terms 1/10, n/30.
- April 9: Paid freight charges of $75 in cash on items purchased on April 2.
- April 10: Made the required payment to the Lite Company on the April 2 purchase.
- April 13: $1,000 worth of the merchandise sold on April 6 was returned because of defects. Accounts Receivable was credited.

■ April 15: Received required payment from the Mercury Company.

■ April 20: Purchased $9,000 of merchandise from the Mars Company. Terms 2/10, n/30.

■ April 23: Sold various items of merchandise to Jupiter, Inc., for $7,000. Terms 1/10, n/30.

■ April 29: Made the required payment to the Mars Company.

REQUIRED: **(a)** Make the necessary journal entries, assuming that the firm uses the gross method of recording purchase and sales discounts.

(b) Prepare the cost of goods sold section of the income statement, assuming that the beginning inventory is $6,800 and the ending inventory is $4,700.

(c) Make the necessary journal entries, now assuming that the firm uses the net method of recording purchase and sales discounts.

(d) Prepare the cost of goods sold section of the income statement using the data from Item b but assuming that the net method is used.

(e) Compare and contrast the two income statements prepared in Items b and d.

P6-5 **Income Statement of a Merchandising Company.** The following information was taken from the records of the Newton Company at year-end:

	Year 1	Year 2
Gross sales	$235,000	$238,430
Sales returns and allowances	5,000	?
Net sales	?	?
Beginning inventory	36,050	?
Purchases	101,530	?
Purchase returns and allowances	3,250	4,535
Ending inventory	?	7,254
Cost of goods sold	?	?
Gross margin on sales (45%)	?	?
Operating expenses	33,570	27,280
Pretax income	?	?
Income tax expense (30%)	?	?
Net income	?	53,694

REQUIRED: Supply the missing information. Show all computations, rounding them to the nearest dollar.

P6-6 **Computing Income Statement Amounts.** Complete the following table by filling in the missing dollar amounts for the income statement of the Blue Monday Corporation. Each case is independent, and all amounts are in dollars.

BLUE MONDAY CORPORATION
Income Statement

Case	Sales Revenue	Beginning Inventory	Purchases	Goods Available for Sale	Ending Inventory	Cost of Goods Sold	Gross Margin on Sales	Operating Expenses	Pretax Income (Loss)
1	2,100	250	1,600	?	420	?	?	300	?
2	2,400	350	?	?	300	1,900	?	240	?
3	2,400	300	1,800	?	?	?	?	250	100
4	3,000	?	2,500	?	200	?	250	?	(100)
5	1,800	?	1,100	?	400	?	?	300	110

P6-7 **Income Statement Preparation.** The accounting records of the Rainbow Company are maintained on a fiscal year ended August 31. All necessary adjusting entries, other than those relating to inventory and taxes, have been made. The trial balance is presented on the next page.

REQUIRED: **(a)** Does the Rainbow Company use the perpetual or the periodic inventory system? How do you know?

  (b) Prepare any remaining adjusting entries.

  (c) Prepare a multistep income statement for the Rainbow Company for the year ended August 31, 1990.

  (d) Prepare the required closing entries.

RAINBOW COMPANY
Adjusted Trial Balance
August 31, 1990

	Debit	Credit
Cash	$ 38,150	
Accounts receivable	55,004	
Inventory (September 1, 1989)	45,325	
Supplies	2,925	
Land	75,000	
Furniture and fixtures	135,000	
Equipment	40,000	
Accumulated depreciation—Furniture and fixtures		$ 75,750
Accumulated depreciation—Equipment		10,000
Accounts payable		47,890
Note payable		70,000
Long-term debt		65,750
Capital stock		100,000
Retained earnings		29,265
Sales		263,140
Sales returns and allowances	23,260	
Purchases	133,160	
Purchase returns and allowances		3,785
Transportation-in	3,320	
Office, salaries, and wages*	25,876	
Depreciation expense*	33,000	
Supplies expense*	15,530	
Rent*	15,780	
Sales commissions	24,250	
Totals	$665,580	$665,580

The ending inventory was determined to be $65,725. Tax rate is 30%.
*Split 50-50 between selling and general and administrative expense.

P6-8 Worksheet Preparation. The unadjusted trial balance of Tommy's Toy Store on September 30, 1990 is presented on the next page. The following additional information was determined on September 30, 1990:

1. Ending inventory was $125,000.

2. Depreciation on both the building and equipment is 10% a year.

3. Supplies on September 30, 1990 were worth $700.

4. Prepaid insurance was $1,000.

5. Interest has accrued for 12 months, not yet paid.

TOMMY'S TOY STORE
Unadjusted Trial Balance
September 30, 1990

	Debit	Credit
Cash	$ 5,000	
Accounts receivable	14,300	
Inventory	105,000	
Supplies	2,000	
Prepaid insurance	3,000	
Long-term investment	5,000	
Land	50,000	
Building	220,000	
Accumulated depreciation—Building		$ 40,000
Store equipment	90,000	
Accumulated depreciation—Equipment		17,500
Accounts payable		14,000
Mortgage payable (10%)		180,000
Capital stock		100,000
Retained earnings		25,000
Sales		250,000
Sales returns and allowance	8,000	
Sales discounts	4,500	
Purchases	115,500	
Purchase returns and allowance		7,800
Purchase discounts		2,000
Freight-in	2,000	
Selling expenses	8,000	
General expenses	4,000	
Totals	$636,300	$636,300

REQUIRED: **(a)** Prepare a ten-column worksheet for the year ended September 30, 1990.

(b) Prepare a classified income statement. Split all expenses two-thirds to selling expenses and one-third to general and administrative expenses, except for interest expense. Ignore income tax.

(c) Prepare a classified balance sheet.

(d) Make the closing entries.

P6-9 Cost of Goods Sold Analysis. Following is a list of some of the accounts for Alexander & Co. for the year ended December 31, 1990:

Sales	$2,987,450
Purchases	1,848,270
Freight-in	25,000
Purchase returns and allowances	28,475
Purchase discounts	36,525
Sales discounts	54,320
Ending inventory	900,470
Sales returns and allowances	384,500
Beginning inventory	?
Gross margin on sales	264,630

REQUIRED: **(a)** Compute the amount of beginning inventory.

(b) Prepare in good form a partial income statement using the accounts presented above.

■ UNDERSTANDING FINANCIAL STATEMENTS

P6-10   The following data was taken from a recent annual report of Carter Hawley Hale Stores, Inc., a diversified North American retailer operating department stores, high-fashion specialty stores, and specialized merchandising operations:

CARTER HAWLEY HALE
(In Thousands)

Sales	$4,089,794
Inventories, beginning	776,831
Inventories, ending	755,971
Cost of goods sold	2,898,213

REQUIRED: **(a)** Determine the amount of gross margin on sales for the year and the amount of net purchases that the firm made during the year.

(b) Do you think that Carter Hawley Hale uses the perpetual or the periodic system in accounting for inventories in its department stores? Explain your reasoning.

(c) Do you think that the firm allows its customers to take a sales discount? Why or why not?

(d) Carter Hawley Hale's fiscal year ends on the Saturday closest to January 31. What type of year-end is this, and why do you think management picked this particular year-end?

P6-11   The following information was taken from recent annual reports of IBM and Lucky Stores, Inc. (volume-oriented retail stores, primarily food):

	IBM (in millions)	Lucky Stores (in millions)
Gross income		
Sales	$23,274	$7,972
Rentals	9,230	0
Services	7,676	0
Cost of goods sold	16,395	6,131
Net income	5,485	92
Accounts receivable	5,735	44
Total current assets	17,270	890
Total assets (average)	37,243	1,609

REQUIRED: **(a)** Calculate the following ratios:

1. Gross margin percentage.

2. Profit margin percentage.

3. Ratio of accounts receivable to total current assets.

4. Return on total assets.

(b) Based on your knowledge of both companies and the industries in which they operate, explain the difference in the ratios you calculated.

■ FINANCIAL DECISION CASE

P6-12   David Schwartz recently decided to open a new-car dealership. The dealership will sell expensive imported cars and offer both engine and body repairs. David plans to organize the business into two divisions: One will sell the cars, and the other will provide the repair services. David has asked your advice concerning two matters:

1. David is in the process of setting up inventory systems for both divisions. The inventory of the car division will be made up of no more than 40 to 50 new cars at any one time. The repair division inventory will be made up of more than 3,000 different parts, in varying quantities, which must be inventoried and controlled. David is concerned about maintaining adequate quantities of fast-moving parts, about 30% of the parts in inventory.

2. David will offer repair services on credit. He is trying to decide whether to carry his own receivable accounts or to use bank cards such as VISA or MasterCard. He estimates that his annual repair service revenues will be $300,000 per year. If he uses bank cards, he figures that about 80% of the revenues will be charged on the cards. The bank card companies will charge David a 5% fee. Because of some fraud, all but .5% of total charges, less the fee, will be remitted to David. If David decides to carry his own accounts, he estimates that 70% of the revenues will be charged on account. If he carries his own accounts, he will have to hire a part-time bookkeeper at $8,000 per year. Finally, he estimates that about 3% of the charges will never be paid.

REQUIRED: Write David a memo outlining (1) his options concerning inventory systems (periodic versus perpetual) and (2) a quantitative and qualitative analysis of whether he should carry his own accounts or use a bank card. Assume that he will not do both.

MANAGEMENT CONTROL
AND
ACCOUNTING FOR CASH

LEARNING OBJECTIVES

After studying this chapter, you should be able to:

1. State the need for management controls and internal controls.

2. Discuss the financial reporting system for a public company and its role in preventing fraudulent financial reporting.

3. State the principles of internal control and explain the attributes of a strong internal control system.

4. Determine what items are considered cash.

5. Discuss bank checking transactions and prepare a bank reconciliation.

6. Establish and account for a petty cash fund.

T hroughout this book, various components of financial reporting are discussed, including the preparation and dissemination of financial statements. This chapter will concentrate on the extremely important issues of management controls and internal controls, the problems that result when these controls are absent or not functioning, and the application of these controls in one specific instance: accounting for cash.

■ THE NEED FOR MANAGEMENT CONTROLS AND INTERNAL CONTROLS

Through the application of management controls and internal controls, management carries out its important responsibility of ensuring that the financial statements it prepares are free of material misstatements, whether intentional or unintentional. Unfortunately, there have been a number of recent instances of intentional misstatement in financial statements. Companies such as E.S.M. Government Securities, ZZZZ Best, Penn Square Bank, and Drysdale Government Securities have become involved in cases of alleged fraudulent financial reporting. Because of these alleged frauds, millions of dollars have been lost by the companies themselves, their stockholders, their employees, and others.

These cases, although relatively rare, have brought public and congressional attention to the financial reporting process. In the public mind, there has arisen an "expectations gap": the "difference between what the public and financial statement users believe accountants and auditors are responsible for and what accountants and auditors themselves believe they're responsible for."[1] The public and financial statement users believe that auditors should:

a. Assume more responsibility for the detection and reporting of fraud and illegal acts.

b. Improve audit effectiveness—that is, improve detection of material misstatements.

c. Communicate to users of financial statements more useful information about the nature and results of the audit process—including early warnings about the possibility of business failure.

d. Communicate more clearly with audit committees and others interested in or responsible for reliable financial reporting.[2]

In the minds of many, including influential congressmen, the accounting profession has not lived up to these expectations. Congress has responded in various hearings investigating the role of the auditor in fraud detection, oversight procedures by the SEC, and other matters related to the audit process and fraudulent financial reporting. The private sector, through various groups such as the AICPA and AAA, responded by sponsoring and funding the National Commission on Fraudulent Financial Reporting, known as the Treadway Commission (after its chairman, James C. Treadway, Jr.). As the result of this commission's findings and pressure from others, the AICPA revised some of its auditing standards and issued new ones, referred to as the "expectation gap standards," which have expanded the role of the auditor in evaluating internal control and detecting fraud.

■ THE FINANCIAL REPORTING SYSTEM FOR PUBLIC COMPANIES

The financial reporting system for a public company is outlined in Exhibit 7-1. The three major components shown are public companies, independent public accountants, and oversight bodies such as the SEC. Clearly, "the company and its management are the key players in the financial reporting system; they bear the primary responsibility for the preparation and content of the financial statements."[3] The CPA, through its audit opinion, reports on the fairness of the financial statements, and the several oversight bodies affect financial reporting through standard setting and monitoring of compliance.

[1] Dan M. Guy and Jerry D. Sullivan, "The Expectation Gap Auditing Standards," *Journal of Accountancy*, (April, 1988), p. 36.

[2] Ibid. Reprinted by permission of the *Journal of Accountancy.*

[3] Report of The National Commission on Fraudulent Financial Reporting (October 1987), p. 17.

EXHIBIT 7–1

Financial Reporting System[4]

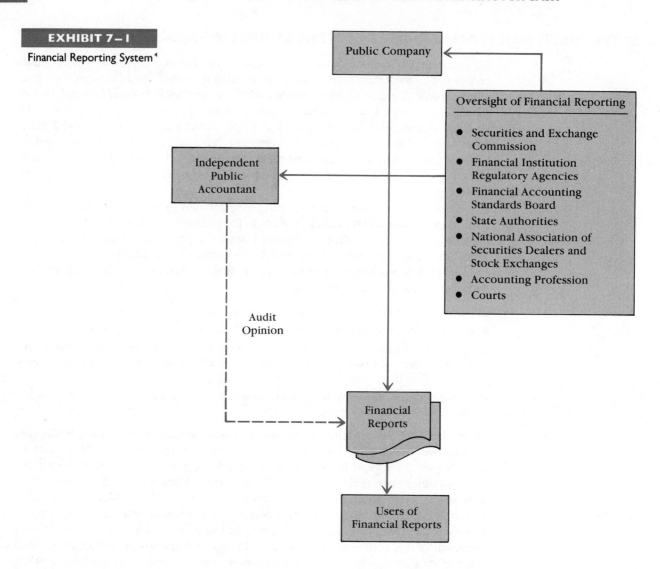

PREVENTING FRAUDULENT FINANCIAL REPORTING

The Treadway Commission defines **fraudulent financial reporting** as:

> . . . intentional or reckless conduct, whether act or omission, that results in materially misleading financial statements. Fraudulent financial reporting can involve many factors and take many forms. It may entail gross and deliberate distortions of corporate records, such as inventory count tags, or falsified transactions, such as fictitious sales or orders. It may entail the misapplication of accounting principles. Company employees at any level may be involved, from top to middle management to lower-level personnel.[5]

One of the most well-known examples of alleged fraudulent financial reporting is the ZZZZ Best Company. In this case, the president of the firm was found guilty of recording major sales that never took place. He also went to great lengths to create false records and bogus transactions in order to enhance the value of the firm's stock.

---

[4] Ibid., p. 18. Reprinted by permission of the AICPA.

[5] Report of the National Commission on Fraudulent Financial Reporting (October 1987), p. 2.

The Treadway Commission felt that companies and their management play a key role in reducing the potential for fraudulent financial reporting. Management is responsible for establishing the appropriate tone, the overall control environment in which financial reporting occurs. On a more detailed level, management should "maximize the effectiveness of the functions within the company that are critical to the integrity of financial reporting, the accounting function, the internal audit function, and the audit committee of the Board of Directors."[6] Thus management must have an internal control function in place—a crucial element in preventing fraudulent financial reporting as well as unintentional misstatements.

ELEMENTS OF AN INTERNAL CONTROL STRUCTURE

"An entity's **internal control structure** consists of the policies and procedures established to provide reasonable assurance that specific entity objectives will be achieved."[7] According to the AICPA, an entity's control structure consists of three elements: the control environment, the accounting system, and control procedures.

THE CONTROL ENVIRONMENT

The **control environment** results from the effects of several factors in establishing, enhancing, or mitigating the effectiveness of specific policies and procedures. Some of the factors noted in the AICPA's latest statement on internal control are:

- Management's philosophy and operating cycle
- The entity's organizational structure
- The functioning of the board of directors and its committees, particularly the audit committee
- Methods of assigning authority and responsibility
- Management's control methods for monitoring and following up on performance, including internal auditing
- Personnel policies and practices
- Various external influences that affect an entity's operations and practices, such as examinations by bank regulatory agencies[8]

Exhibit 7-2 illustrates the control environment of a public company, as described by the Treadway Commission. Clearly, such a control environment is essential for maintaining strong and effective internal controls. If it is perceived that management is lax with regard to the control environment, fraudulent financial reporting is more likely to occur.

THE ACCOUNTING SYSTEM

The **accounting system** consists of the methods and records established by management to identify, assemble, analyze, classify, record, and report an entity's transactions and to maintain accountability for the firm's assets and liabilities. According to the AICPA, an effective accounting system attempts to establish methods and records that will accomplish the functions listed at the top of the next page.

---

[6] Ibid.

[7] "Consideration of the Internal Control Structure in a Financial Statement Audit," *Statement on Auditing Standards 55*, AICPA (April 1988) par. 6. Emphasis supplied.

[8] Ibid., par. 9.

- Identify and record all valid transactions.

- Describe on a timely basis the transactions in sufficient detail to permit proper classification of transactions for financial reporting.

- Measure the value of transactions in a manner that permits recording their proper mandatory value in the financial statements.

- Determine the time period in which transactions occurred, to permit recording of transactions in the proper accounting period.

- Present properly the transactions and related disclosures in the financial statements.[10]

EXHIBIT 7–2

The Public Company[9]

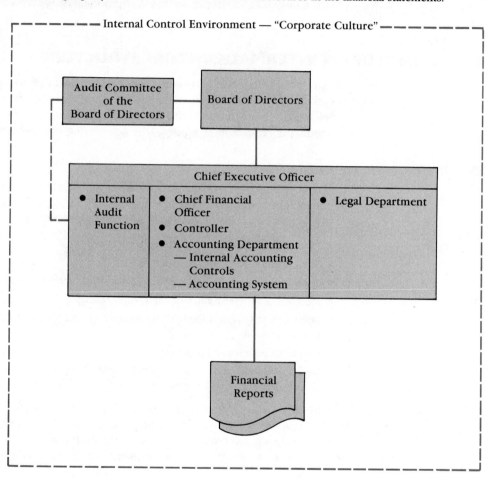

— Internal Control Environment — "Corporate Culture" —

Audit Committee of the Board of Directors

Board of Directors

Chief Executive Officer

- Internal Audit Function

- Chief Financial Officer
- Controller
- Accounting Department
  — Internal Accounting Controls
  — Accounting System

- Legal Department

Financial Reports

■ CONTROL PROCEDURES

Control procedures are those established by management to provide reasonable assurance that the firm's objective will be met. Again according to the AICPA, control procedures pertain to:

- Proper authorization of transactions and activities.

- Segregation of duties that reduce the opportunities to allow any person to be in a position to both perpetrate and conceal errors or irregularities in the normal course of his duties—dif-

[9]Source: Report of The National Commission on Fraudulent Financial Reporting (October 1987), p. 19. Reprinted by permission of the AICPA.

[10]"Consideration of the Internal Control Structure in a Financial Statement Audit," *Statement on Auditing Standards 55*, AICPA (April 1988), par. 10.

ferent people should be in charge of authorizing transactions and maintaining the custody of assets.

- Design and use of adequate documents and records to help ensure the proper recording of transactions and events, such as monitoring the use of prenumbered shipping documents.
- Adequate safeguards over access to and use of assets and records, such as secured facilities and authorization for access to computer programs and data files.
- Independent checks on performance and proper valuation of recorded amounts, such as clerical checks, reconciliations, comparison of assets with recorded accountability, computer-programmed controls, management review of reports that summarize the detail of account balances (for example, an aged trial balance of accounts receivable), and user review of computer-generated reports.[11]

Control procedure should be designed to meet a firm's specific needs. Nevertheless, any well-designed internal controls must center on a properly designed accounting system and include sound personnel and personnel practices, as well as separation of duties.

■ LIMITATIONS TO INTERNAL CONTROL SYSTEMS

No system of internal control can be completely foolproof. This is especially true if top management is trying to override the system. The costs of completely foolproofing the system, even if possible, would probably outweigh the benefits derived. However, a properly designed and executed system can eliminate many potential problems and offer management a reasonable assurance that its policies are being carried out and that the firm's assets are being safeguarded.

■ FRAUDULENT FINANCIAL REPORTING, THE ACCOUNTING PROFESSION, AND ETHICS: A SUMMARY

The combination of business failures, increases in the incidence of fraudulent financial reporting, and ethical questions has increased scrutiny of the accounting profession. As this book is being written, the Government Accounting Office has charged the accounting profession with poor-quality audits of many savings and loan institutions that have gone bankrupt. The revelation that a CPA participated with management in the fraudulent financial reporting of an entity has caused many to question the ethical standards of the accounting profession. Lack of confidence in the profession can have far-reaching consequences for our economic system. This was clearly spelled out by Joe Conner, formerly head of Price Waterhouse, when he stated:

> Confidence in business and confidence in the accounting profession are inseparable. The profession's primary role is to help sustain confidence in our business and economic system by ensuring the integrity of financial information. When the public's faith in our effectiveness in carrying out that role wanes, so does faith in the system itself.[12]

The leadership of the accounting profession is responding to these challenges. A new code of ethics was adopted in early 1988, and the "expectation gap" auditing standards were adopted. The profession has been quick to call for increased teaching of ethics in business schools. In addition, state organizations such as the California Society of Certified Public Accountants have initiated programs to increase the ethical

---

[11] Ibid., par. 11.
[12] Ralph Walters, "Operation Highroad: A Plan to Restore Confidence and Balance," *Ethics in the Accounting Profession* (May 1986), p. 69. Reprinted by permission of the University of Southern California.

and technical standards of their members. These initiatives should lead to a closing of the "expectations gap."

■ ACCOUNTING FOR CASH

The application of internal controls relates to all aspects of a firm's accounting system. However, the accounting issues related to cash are particularly affected by internal controls. In this section, these internal controls are discussed in detail.

In the broadest sense, **cash** is any medium of exchange that a bank will accept for deposit, including coins, paper money, money orders, checks, certified and cashier's checks, and money on deposit in a bank. However, IOUs, postdated checks (the date on the checks is beyond the present date), and postage stamps are not considered cash, and a bank would not accept them for deposit. Cash in savings accounts, certificates of deposit, commercial paper, and money market accounts are cash equivalents because they can quickly be converted into cash. Equivalents that can be immediately converted into cash are usually included in the cash category on the balance sheet if they are available for unrestricted use. Most savings accounts and money market accounts fall into this category. However, if there are restrictions on withdrawals, such as those on certain certificates of deposit and Treasury certificates, the item should not be included in the cash category. It should be shown as a short-term investment. For practical purposes, though, many firms combine cash and all cash equivalents into one category.

Cash and cash equivalents are current assets and are the first item shown on the balance sheet. Although a firm may have separate ledger accounts for each of its individual bank accounts, savings accounts, and so forth, all are combined into one classification for balance sheet presentation. However, in a number of situations, cash may be excluded from the current asset section of the balance sheet. They all relate to cases in which there are restrictions on the use of the cash that make it unavailable for current use. For example, a firm may set aside cash in a special fund to repay bonds or for the future purchase of a building. The funds are often called *sinking funds* and are shown in the long-term investment section of the balance sheet. Another situation is cash on deposit in banks in foreign countries which cannot be returned to the United States. In this case, the cash is not shown as a current asset. Finally, there are times when the company overdraws its bank account and has a cash overdraft. Cash overdrafts are not shown as a negative item in the current asset section but as a liability in the current liability section of the balance sheet.

■ MANAGEMENT CONTROL OVER CASH

The management and control of cash are essential management functions. The responsibility of management is to develop, implement, and maintain a cash management and control system that:

1. Prevents losses, theft, and the misappropriation of cash.
2. Provides accurate records of all cash receipts, disbursements, and other cash transactions.
3. Offers accurate and timely information about cash balances to enable management to control the amount of cash on hand at any time.

The first and second objectives pertain to the internal control of cash transactions; these are the items discussed in this chapter. In recent years, the third objective has become more and more important. In a credit- and cash-tight economy, management must make maximum use of its cash resources. This means that the control system must provide information that can be used to prepare cash budgets and projections. These budgets can then be used to ensure that only minimal amounts of cash are held in non-interest-bearing accounts or to enable a firm to establish lines of credit with banks to provide for cash shortfalls. The preparation of cash budgets and other problems related to use of cash are topics explored in managerial accounting courses.

■ INTERNAL CONTROL OVER CASH

Most business transactions involve cash receipts and disbursements, and many employees play a role in the collection and payment of cash. Furthermore, cash is a firm's most liquid asset, and thus it is the most difficult to control. As Exhibit 7-3[13] points out, these two features make it imperative that a firm devise a strong internal control system to prevent losses from theft, fraud, and misappropriation.

EXHIBIT 7–3

HOW TO PREVENT AN EMPLOYE FROM RIPPING OFF THE FIRM

By SANFORD L. JACOBS
Staff Reporter of THE WALL STREET JOURNAL

Could someone be ripping off your business? What about the bookkeeper, that godsend who relieves you of the accounting stuff that bores you stiff? How about the old-timer who is so darn good at filling orders you let him run the shipping department with an iron fist? Not them, you say, they're trusted employes. Well, consider how a few "trusted" employes cheated small companies recently.

A bookkeeper diverted $750,000 of bill payments to her bank account in three years. Another bookkeeper made off with $80,000 in less than a year by drawing checks to herself and forging the owner's signature on them. A fellow in charge of paying bills paid himself $250,000 of company money. An employe of 28 years, who was a crackerjack at filling and shipping orders, shipped thousands of dollars of merchandise to himself.

Small companies can be easy prey. Their accounting systems usually lack tight controls because of the extra expense involved. A few employes normally do a number of critical jobs, weakening the first line of defense against employe dishonesty: segregating duties.

The bookkeeper who makes bank deposits, opens the mail and draws checks—even for someone else's signature—can divert receipts or forge checks and doctor the books to hide the loss.

Some simple precautions can make larceny difficult. "Segregation of duties is the biggest single deterrent," says Thomas Frey, of Arthur Andersen & Co., accountants. For example, the person who makes accounts-receivable entries shouldn't be the one who receives checks, because that person could divert the checks and cover up by juggling the records. One juggling method is to credit customer accounts for fictitious returns of goods or price adjustments.

Another employe should open the mail, list, endorse and total incoming checks, and, perhaps, make up a bank deposit. If that person diverts checks, receivables won't be adjusted to hide the fraud, and eventually customers will squawk about being billed or dunned for sums they already have paid. Complaints about statement balances from customers can signal something wrong: bookkeeping may be sloppy, someone may be embezzling—or both.

Sloppy record-keeping invites cheating, for employes know when money or merchandise can disappear without immediate detection. "Eventually you may know there is a shortage," says Al Roberts of the accounting firm of Arthur Young & Co., "but the records are such that you can't track the shortage."

Good controls mean nothing moves in or out of inventory without documents, such as purchase orders, receiving tickets, bills of lading, invoices, sales orders and shipping tickets. Different people should process forms to act as a check on one another. Then fraud could be covered up only by collusion of two or more employes. Prenumbered forms provide some protection if access is limited and someone checks to assure that the correct numerical order is being kept.

The design of an internal control system over cash depends on the firm's specific size, complexity, and nature. For example, separation of duties is an important cornerstone of any control system. Yet, the smaller the organization and/or the accounting staff, the more difficult it will be to separate duties properly. Thus the controls described next are meant to be general in nature and cannot be applied to all firms.

If possible, the control system over cash should include the following features:

1. The duties of those handling cash and keeping records of cash transactions should be segregated. For example, the individual who prepares the bank reconciliation should not handle cash receipts and/or disbursements.

2. Only a limited number of clearly designated and bonded employees should have access to cash.

[13] Reprinted by permission from *The Wall Street Journal* (May 10, 1982). © Dow Jones & Company, Inc., 1982. All Rights Reserved Worldwide.

3. All procedures relating to cash receipts and disbursements should be clearly stated in the accounting manual. Compliance checks should be made regularly, and surprise audits should be made randomly.

4. All cash receipts should be deposited intact daily in the bank account. Only a small amount of cash should be maintained on hand in a petty cash fund. All but minor cash payments should be made by check.

5. All cash expenditures should be approved and the amounts verified by an employee not involved in the disbursement process.

These controls, along with the other parts of a strong internal control system, will help ensure that unauthorized cash disbursements are not made and that all cash receipts are properly deposited to the company's bank account.

■ BANK CHECKING ACCOUNT TRANSACTIONS

To ensure strong internal control over cash, most firms have a policy that requires all disbursements except minor petty transactions to be made by check. This requires the maintenance of a checking account and the implementation of controls over that account.

Elements of a Checking Account

All business firms maintain at least one checking account. When a business opens a checking account, its bank will require certain information such as proof of a business name and a business license. If the business is a corporation, certain other data may also be required, such as a resolution by the board of directors authorizing certain individuals to sign checks. A signature card that lists those authorized to sign checks, as well as their signatures, must be completed. This is used by the bank to verify the signatures on checks presented for payment. Large firms often have an automatic check imprinter that signs all checks.

Once a checking account is opened, the firm receives personalized deposit slips and checks. It is imperative that these personalized documents be used because they contain magnetic numbers that identify both the company and the bank. These are important elements of the internal control over cash and play a part in the electronic funds transfer system currently being put in place in the United States.

The Bank Statement

Every month the bank prepares a **bank statement** and mails it to the depositor. The statement should be addressed to a designated individual in the depositor's organization and should be opened only by that person. The statement lists the beginning balance in the account, all deposits received, checks paid, other debits (charges) and credits (receipts), and the ending balance of the account.

In recent years, bank statements have become more complex as banks have begun to handle a variety of different types of transactions and as their data-processing capabilities have increased. The bank statement for A&D Associates for the month of November is shown in Exhibit 7-4. It contains four sections, which have been numbered for easy reference. The first section summarizes all the transactions during the month. As indicated, the beginning balance on November 1 is $2,156.43. During the month, total credits (only deposits in this case) of $27,883.87 increased the balance, and total debits (checks paid of $28,099.26 plus the $108.00 NSF returned check) of $28,207.26 were paid, which decreased the balance. Interest of $18.50 earned on the average balance in the checking account was added to the balance, and service charges of $15.00 were deducted, resulting in an ending balance of $1,836.54.

The second section lists all the checks that the bank paid during the period. Each check is listed in order of check number. The checks can be listed this way because the check number is magnetically listed on the check, and this magnetic number is

EXHIBIT 7–4

A&D ASSOCIATES
5151 State University Dr.
Los Angeles, CA 90032
Bank Statement

Checking Account Number

11768-05130

From: 11/1/90
Through: 11/30/90

	Beginning Balance	+ Total Credits	− Total Debits	+ Interest	− Service Charge	= Ending Balance
(1)	2,156.43	27,883.87	28,207.26	18.50	15.00	1,836.54

Check Activity

	Check	Date	Amount	Check	Date	Amount
(2)	221	11/4	683.24	235	11/22	147.75
	222	11/4	500.00	236	11/30	386.25
	223	11/7	1,246.32	237	11/29	152.40
	224	11/9	1,056.22	238	11/21	2,456.20
	226	11/12	247.32	239	11/29	425.00
	227	11/7	1,022.28	240	11/30	2,167.67
	228	11/12	746.46	241	11/25	843.13
	229	11/21	1,000.01	243	11/22	52.30
	230	11/15	4,331.00	245	11/24	1,105.00
	231	11/17	2,456.56	246	11/27	785.15
	232	11/19	1,132.24	250	11/30	42.40
	233	11/30	1,010.00	251	11/30	542.36
	234	11/27	3,562.00			

Deposits

	Date	Amount	Date	Amount
(3)	11/1	1,050.25	11/16	725.00
	11/4	4,200.01	11/23	1,022.43
	11/7	653.24	11/25	7,101.83
	11/8	1,524.87	11/26	500.24
	11/11	2,220.00	11/27	603.36
	11/12	2,600.24	11/28	1,050.23
	11/15	532.15	11/30	4,100.02

Other Transactions

	Date	Amount	Explanation
(4)	11/5	−5.00	Check Printing Fee
	11/21	−10.00	NSF Check Return Charge
	11/28	−108.00	NSF Check
	11/30	+18.50	Interest

used in preparing the bank statement. The date on which the check cleared the bank is also listed on the statement.

The third section lists all the deposits made by A&D Associates and received by the bank. In this case, A&D does not make deposits daily. (This has been done in order to simplify the illustration.) These deposits are listed on the statement by date.

The last section of this statement lists other transactions. These usually consist of service charges such as check-printing fees and monthly maintenance charges. In this illustration, there are two service charges: $5.00 for printing checks and $10.00 for processing a deposit that was returned because of nonsufficient funds (NSF). That is, the deposit of 11/23 included a check for $108.00 that, when presented for payment at the payer's bank, was returned because the party that wrote the check had insufficient funds. The $108.00 debit is included with the total debits of $28,207.26 in the first section of the statement.

Other miscellaneous credits are also included in the third section of the statement. An example is the bank's collection of a note for a customer which the bank deposited directly in the customer's account. Other examples are interest on checking account balances and proceeds from bank loans. In this illustration, A&D earned $18.50 interest.

The Bank Reconciliation

A **bank reconciliation** is an essential part of any internal control system for cash. If the cash balance per the bank statement can be reconciled with the cash balance per the firm's general ledger, this will ensure the accuracy of the cash receipts and disbursement journals. This is because the bank statement is prepared by the bank independently of the firm's accounting system. Whenever a third party's records can be used to verify internal records, the firm has good evidence of the accuracy of its records. However, in order to maintain this independence, the bank reconciliation must be prepared by an independent individual within the firm who neither handles cash nor maintains the accounting records for cash.

At the end of the month or any period, the balance on the bank statement will not equal the balance shown in the cash account in the general ledger. This is because the bank and the depositor are likely to record certain transactions at different times. The depositor will record certain events before they are recorded by the bank. Examples are deposits in transit and outstanding checks. Deposits in transit result: When a deposit is made by the depositor, it is added to the general ledger cash account, but the bank does not credit the depositor's account until the following day. Deposits in transit can be determined by comparing the deposits listed in the cash receipts journal with those on the bank statement. Deposits in transit will most likely be the deposits close to or at the end of the month. Outstanding checks occur when the check is written by the depositor and is immediately deducted from the Cash account. However, there is a lag of a few days before the bank pays the check and deducts the amount from the depositor's account. Outstanding checks can be determined by comparing the checks listed in the cash payments journal with those paid by the bank, as shown on the bank statement. Conversely, the bank may record certain transactions before they are recorded by the depositor. There are several such items, but the most common are service charges, charges for NSF checks, and interest earned. These items are evidenced by debit and credit memos issued by the bank. Debit memos must be deducted from the depositor's general ledger, and credit memos must be added to the general ledger cash balance.

Finally, both the bank and the depositor may make errors. If the bank makes an error, such as charging the depositor's account for a check drawn on a different depositor, the balance shown on the bank statement will be too small. If the error is in the depositor's records, the cash balance must be corrected also.

An Example of a Bank Reconciliation

Several methods are used to prepare bank reconciliations. For example, the balance per the bank statement may be reconciled to the general ledger cash balance, or the general ledger cash balance may be reconciled to the bank's balance. However, the best method is to reconcile both the balance per the bank and the balance per the books or general ledger to the actual cash balance. This is accomplished by focusing on those items that are recorded at different times by the bank and the depositor.

The November 30 bank statement for A&D Associates, shown in Exhibit 7-4, will be used to illustrate the preparation of a bank reconciliation. As this statement indicates, the balance per the bank at November 30 is $1,836.54. In addition, it is determined that the general ledger cash balance is $2,414.47, as indicated in the following Cash T account:

	Cash	
11/1 Bal. 2,023.44		
Cash receipts 28,482.81	Cash disbursements 28,091.78	
11/30 Bal. 2,414.47		

The bank reconciliation for A&D Associates (shown in Exhibit 7-5) is prepared by the following procedures. The balance, taken from Exhibit 7-4, is $1,836.54. The deposits in transit of $1,524.31 and $124.88 are determined by comparing the deposits on the cash receipts journal with the deposits listed on the bank statement.

EXHIBIT 7–5

A&D ASSOCIATES Bank Reconciliation November 30, 1990		
Balance per bank, November 30		$1,836.54
Add: Deposits in transit		
11/29	$1,524.31	
11/30	124.88	1,649.19
Less: Outstanding checks		
225	100.00	
242	158.10	
244	91.78	
247	100.25	
248	31.41	
249	22.12	
252	601.29	
253	88.81	(1,193.76)
Adjusted balance		$2,291.97
Balance per books, November 30		2,414.47
Add: Interest revenue		18.50
Less: Service charges	$ 15.00	
NSF check	108.00	
Error check no. 236	18.00	(141.00)
Adjusted balance		$2,291.97

Must equal

The outstanding checks listed on the bank reconciliation were determined by comparing all the checks listed in the cash payments journal with the checks paid by the bank. As a result, eight checks totaling $1,193.76 were determined to be outstanding. When the deposits in transit are added to the bank balance and the outstanding checks are subtracted, the adjusted cash balance of $2,291.97 is determined. There were no bank errors that need adjustment.

The balance in the cash general ledger account is $2,414.47, as shown in the T account. Interest revenue of $18.50 credited by the bank has not been recorded in the cash receipts journal and must be added to the balance per the books. The service charges of $15.00 and the NSF check for $108.00 must be subtracted. Finally, check number 236 was written for $386.25 and cleared the bank for that amount. However, by mistake it was recorded as $368.25 in the cash disbursements journal. Automobile expense was also originally debited for the incorrect amount. Thus the cash disbursements are understated by $18.00 ($386.25 − $368.25), and this amount must be deducted on the bank reconciliation. When these adjustments are made, the adjusted balance equals $2,291.97, and the bank account is reconciled.

The last step in the bank reconciliation process is to make adjusting entries for all the items required to adjust A&D Associates' general ledger cash account to the adjusted balance as determined on the bank reconciliation (that is, the items on the bottom half of the bank reconciliation). These entries are:

Nov. 30	Cash	18.50	
	Interest Revenue		18.50
	To record interest revenue earned on bank account.		
	Service Charge	15.00	
	Accounts Receivable	108.00	
	Automobile Expense	18.00	
	Cash		141.00
	To record adjustment from bank reconciliation, NSF checks from Grant Co. recorded as a receivable and automobile expense debited for error in recording check no. 236.		

After these adjusting entries are posted, the Cash account will appear as follows:

Cash

11/1	Bal.	2,023.44			
	Cash receipts	28,482.81	Cash disbursements		28,091.78
	Adj.	18.50		Adj.	141.00
	11/30 Bal.	2,291.97			

If these entries are not made, the general ledger will never be adjusted to the correct balance determined by the bank reconciliation.

■ PETTY CASH

Although it would be preferable if all disbursements were made by check and all receipts were deposited intact, most firms usually maintain a small amount of cash on hand for miscellaneous expenditures such as postage, delivery expense, and minor office supplies such as coffee. The greatest degree of internal control can be maintained when a petty cash fund is established under the control of one individual. A **petty cash fund** is used to make small disbursements of cash.

Creating a Petty Cash Fund
In order to create a petty cash fund, a check is written to the petty cashier for an amount such as $75 or $100. The size of the fund depends on the firm's needs but should be large enough to last at least three to four weeks. The check is cashed and the money put under the control of a designated custodian. This ensures that one individual will be held responsible for the cash in the fund. The entry to record the establishment of a $100 petty cash fund is:

Petty Cash	100	
Cash		100
To establish petty cash fund.		

Making Disbursements from the Fund
The custodian of the petty cash fund approves and makes all disbursements from the fund and must prepare a petty cash voucher for each expenditure. This **voucher** indi-

cates the purpose of the expenditure and the date and is signed by the person receiving the cash. The voucher is attached to the receipt, which has been stamped "paid" to ensure that it is not used again. Because a petty cash voucher is prepared for all disbursements, the total of the vouchers and the remaining cash should always equal the amount of the fund (in this case $100) unless an error has been made.

Replenishing the Fund

During the month, the custodian will make various disbursements from the petty cash fund, and at some time the fund will have to be replenished. For example, assume that during April disbursements totaling $84.32 were made from the $100 petty cash fund previously established. Analysis of the petty cash vouchers indicates that the $84.32 of disbursements were for the following expenses: postage, $24.10; delivery expense, $16.31; supplies, $15.39; and taxi fares, $28.52. Actual cash remaining on hand is $15.48, which indicates a shortage of $.20 ($100 − $84.32 = $15.68 should be on hand; only $15.48 is on hand, so there is a $.20 shortage). The shortage is recorded in a Cash Over and Short account.

In order to replenish the petty cash fund to its $100 balance, a check is drawn for $84.52, cashed, and returned to the fund. The following entry is made:

Postage Expense	24.10	
Delivery Expense	16.31	
Supplies Expense	15.39	
Taxi Expense	28.52	
Cash Over and Short	.20	
Cash		84.52
To record replenishment of petty cash fund.		

Notice that the appropriate expense accounts are debited and that Cash is credited. No entry is made to the Petty Cash account. No entry is made to Petty Cash unless the firm wants to increase or decrease the fund above or below $100. For example, if the firm decided to increase the petty cash from $100 to $150, it would make the following entry:

Petty Cash	50	
Cash		50
To increase petty cash fund to $150.		

The petty cash fund is replenished as needed. However, it should always be replenished at the end of the accounting period to ensure proper matching. Finally, surprise petty cash counts should be made by management to maintain good internal control over the fund.

SUMMARY OF LEARNING OBJECTIVES

1. The need for management controls and internal controls. One of the most important functions of management is to ensure that the financial statements it prepares are free of material misstatements. In recent years, public attention has focused on cases of fraudulent financial reporting, which have led to an "expectations gap."

2. The financial reporting system for a public company and its role in preventing fraudulent financial

reporting. The components of a financial reporting system for a public company are independent public accountants and oversight bodies such as the SEC. In this reporting system, the management of a public company plays the essential role in reducing the potential for fraudulent financial reporting.

3. The principles of internal control and the attributes of a strong internal control system. A firm's internal control structure consists of three elements: the control environment, the accounting system, and the control procedures. Accounting systems should be designed to meet the needs of individual firms. These systems should process information efficiently, accurately, and on a timely basis. The system must also be designed to meet the firm's internal control needs, including duplication of records and the separation of duties.

4. What is included in cash on the balance sheet. Cash is any medium of exchange that a bank will accept for deposit. Thus cash includes coins, paper money, money orders, checks, certified and cashier's checks, and money on deposit in a bank. IOUs and postdated checks are not included in cash. If it is available for current use, cash is considered a current asset.

5. Bank checking transactions, including the purpose and preparation of the bank reconciliation. All cash disbursements should be made by check. A bank reconciliation should be prepared monthly by a responsible individual who neither handles cash transactions nor has access to the cash-related accounting records. A bank reconciliation is prepared by reconciling the bank's and the ledger's cash balance to the same adjusted amount. A bank reconciliation takes the following general form:

Balance per bank	$7,500
Add: Deposits in transit	2,000
Less: Outstanding checks	(3,500)
Plus or minus bank errors	0
Adjusted balance	$6,000
Balance per books	$5,875
Add: Interest	75
Collection on notes	260
Less: Service charge	(10)
NSF checks	(200)
Other charges	0
Plus or minus firm errors	0
Adjusted balance	$6,000

Adjusting journal entries must be made for any item required to reconcile the general ledger balance to the adjusted balance.

6. Accounting for the establishment and maintenance of a petty cash fund. All cash disbursements not made by check should be made from a petty cash fund. The fund should be under the control of a single custodian. The following entries pertain to petty cash funds:

To establish the fund		
Petty Cash	100	
Cash		100
To replenish the fund		
Delivery Expense	20	
Freight-in	15	
Postage	30	
Office Supplies	22	
Cash		87

KEY TERMS

Accounting system

Bank reconciliation

Bank statement

Cash

Control environment

Control procedures

Fraudulent financial reporting

Internal control structure

Petty cash fund

Voucher

PROBLEM FOR YOUR REVIEW

Bank Reconciliations. As the accountant for the Hall Corporation, you are to prepare its March 31 bank reconciliation. You have obtained the following additional data:

1. The ending balance on the March 31 bank statement is $8,975.

2. During your examination of the bank statement, you noticed that the bank charged your account for $170 for a check that should not have been charged to the Hall Corporation's account. Furthermore, you find that the bank credited your account for a note it collected on your behalf. The credit was for $1,090. The principal of the note is $1,000, and the interest for the month is $100. The bank charged a fee for making the collection. This note has not yet been recorded in the firm's accounts.

3. The balance in the Cash general ledger account is $7,258. You determined that the deposits on 3/30 and 3/31 for $1,567 and $432, respectively, have not yet been credited to your account by the bank.

4. Analysis of the cash payments journal indicated that the following checks have not yet been paid by the bank:

No.	Amount
842	$ 170
863	243
867	190
868	586
869	320
870	1,450

While verifying checks, you discovered that check no. 832, written to Smith Janitorial Service, was recorded in the cash disbursements journal as $57. The actual amount of the check was $75, and that is the amount paid by the bank.

5. A debit memo for $20 for monthly maintenance fees and a debit memo for $125 for an NSF check from A. Spielberg were included in the returned checks. These items have not yet been recorded on Hall Corporation's books.

REQUIRED: 1. Prepare a bank reconciliation at March 31.

2. Make the required adjusting journal entry.

SOLUTION
(1) BANK
RECONCILIATION

HALL CORPORATION
Bank Reconciliation
March 31

Balance per bank statement			$8,975
Add: Deposit in transit 3/30		$1,567	
3/31		432	1,999
Bank error check charged against wrong account			170
Less: Outstanding checks	No.	Amount	
	842	$ 170	
	863	243	
	867	190	
	868	586	
	869	320	
	870	1,450	(2,959)
Adjusted balance			$8,185
Balance per general ledger			$7,258
Add: Note collection and interest less collection charge			1,090
Less: Maintenance fee		$ 20	
NSF check		125	
Error on check no. 832 ($75–$57)		18	(163)
Adjusted balance			$8,185

(2) JOURNAL ENTRIES

Cash	1,090	
Service Charge	10	
Note Receivable		1,000
Interest Revenue		100
To record collection of notes.		
Service Charge	20	
Accounts Receivable	125	
Repairs and Maintenance	18	
Cash		163

To record service charge, NSF check by Spielberg, and error in check no. 832.

QUESTIONS

1. Describe the need for management controls and internal controls.

2. What is the expectations gap? Why did it arise?

3. An entity's control system has three elements; the control environment, the accounting system, and control procedures. Describe and give examples of each of these elements.

4. The ABCD Company is a medium-sized business with several individuals in the accounting department. Under current job assignments, the employee who makes entries in the cash receipts journal is also the individual who makes the daily bank deposit. Does this represent good internal control? Why or why not?

5. One of your fellow students was overheard saying that if all people were honest there would be no need for internal control systems. Do you agree? Why or why not?

6. Which of the following item(s) would not be included in the current asset section under cash when preparing a December 31, 1990 balance sheet?

    (a) Certified checks.

    (b) Cash on hand.

    (c) A check dated January 2, 1991.

    (d) Cash held in a building fund.

    (e) Petty cash.

7. Is it possible to have too much cash? Explain your answer.

8. Why do you think it is important that those authorized to handle cash do not do the record-keeping for cash?

9. Why would a firm establish a petty cash fund? Why should the fund be replenished at the end of each accounting period, regardless of the cash remaining in the fund at that time?

10. List and explain three items that may be required to adjust the bank balance to a corrected bank balance when performing a bank reconciliation.

11. Why is it necessary to adjust the cash general ledger balance after preparing a bank reconciliation?

12. What items may cause the differences between the total debits charged against a depositor's account and the depositor's total cash disbursements for the month?

13. What items may cause the differences between the total credits on a depositor's bank account and the total cash receipts in the depositor's cash receipts journal?

14. During the month, the Irmhoff Co. was charged a $5 service charge fee. Assuming the firm's accountant did not record this charge on the books, how would it be handled on a bank reconciliation? If the firm's accountant had entered $5 in the cash disbursements journal prior to the reconciliation, how would this item be handled on the bank reconciliation?

EXERCISES

E1. **Internal Control.** The Allowance Company recently redesigned its accounting department to increase its efficiency. Several employees were terminated, and several jobs were combined. As a result of the reorganization, two employees now have the following jobs:

- Employee A: Makes entries in the purchases journal and the cash payments journal.
- Employee B: Makes entries in the sales journal and the cash receipts journal. Employee B also has access to the general journal.

Furthermore, the head of the accounting department will allow all employees to receive overtime pay instead of taking their regularly scheduled vacations.

REQUIRED: What internal control problems, if any, might result from the reorganization?

E2. Internal Control. The Discount Warehouse is a discount apparel store in southern California. The company has a small accounting department made up of three individuals, who must perform the following functions:

(a) Record purchases from suppliers in the purchases journal.

(b) Record sales on account in the sales journal and cash sales in the cash receipts journal.

(c) Make cash payments to suppliers and record these payments in the cash payments journal.

(d) Record customers' payments on accounts in the cash receipts journal and make the daily deposits.

(e) Make entries in the general journal for purchase returns and allowances and sales returns and allowances.

REQUIRED: List the tasks for which each employee should be responsible. Use good internal control techniques. If necessary, each employee may have more than one task.

E3. Bank Reconciliation. From the following data, prepare the bank reconciliation for the E. O. Smith Corporation as of April 30, 1990: (a) balance per bank statement April 30, $1,150.25; (b) balance per books April 30, $1,048.34; (c) outstanding checks, $342.85; (d) interest income earned on average cash balance, $12.40; (e) deposit in transit, $246.34; and (f) check-printing charge, $7.00. In addition, prepare any necessary journal entries.

E4. Bank Reconciliation—Determine Missing Data. In preparing the bank reconciliation for the Hopie Company, you obtained the following information: (a) balance per bank, $10,465; (b) balance per books, $10,072; (c) outstanding checks, $1,058; (d) notes collected by bank for firm, $125; and (e) service charge, $6. What is the amount of the deposit in transit?

E5. Bank Reconciliation—Determine Missing Data. The Kenney Company conducts all of its cash transactions by check. Thus all receipts and payments are received or made by check. You obtained the following information:

Bank Reconciliation
September 30

Balance per bank	$10,025
Add: Deposits in transit	2,150
Less: Outstanding checks	(1,825)
Balance per books	$10,350

Data from October Bank and Book Records

	Per Bank	Per Books
October deposits	$10,650	$11,985
October checks	9,940	9,175

REQUIRED: Given the above information, figure as of October 31:

(a) Deposits in transit.

(b) Outstanding checks.

E6. Petty Cash Transactions. The Harvey Company maintains a petty cash fund of $100. At the end of March, the fund contained the following:

Cash and currency		$ 17.57
Expense vouchers		
Postage		20.00
Delivery expense		34.30
Office supplies		15.65
Parking		12.48
Total		$100.00

Prepare the necessary journal entry at March 31 to replenish the fund.

E7. Petty Cash Transactions. The Corona Company currently maintains a petty cash fund of $200.00. At December 31, the fund contained the following items:

Cash and currency		$ 9.10
Expense vouchers		
Delivery expense		22.30
Office supplies		105.00
Postage		20.00
Travel expense (taxi)		15.00
Parking		18.50
Donation to Cancer Fund		10.00
Total		$199.90

Recent experience indicates that $200 is not enough for the fund, so the firm decides to increase the fund to $300. Make the necessary journal entry or entries to replenish and to increase the fund.

E8. Toys "R" Us Financial Statements. Refer to the financial information and financial statements of Toys "R" Us in Appendix D.

(a) Does management make any statements concerning its responsibility for the financial statements? If so, where?

(b) Describe the relative responsibilities of Toys "R" Us management and Touche Ross & Co., the company's auditor.

PROBLEMS

P7-1 Internal Control. William Stolen works in the accounting department of Computech, a retail minicomputer store. He is in charge of the purchasing function, as well as accounts payable. Many of the computers purchased by Computech are delivered by the manufacturer directly to Computech's clients without first being delivered to the Computech store.

Stolen decided to divert the firm's computers to his own use in the hope of opening his own store. In order to do this, Stolen did the following: He first prepared fake purchase orders under Computech's name for computers and peripheral equipment. He had the suppliers deliver the merchandise to a little store he rented called Specialty Computer Sales. When the order arrived at Specialty, Stolen entered them in the purchases journal as:

Purchase	XXX	
Accounts Payable		XXX

When the invoices were due, Stolen prepared the checks and sent them to the treasurer for signature. Based on a purchase order and vendor's invoice, the checks were signed and mailed to the vendor.

REQUIRED: **(a)** Discuss the weaknesses in internal control, if any, in the system just described.

(b) What suggestions would you make?

P7-2 Internal Control. The Lovable Egg Museum operates a small museum in Minneapolis. Members of the Lovable Egg Society are allowed to enter the museum free of charge. Nonmembers pay a $2 entrance fee, which is collected by two clerks who are stationed at the museum entrance.

At the end of each day, one of the clerks takes the proceeds to the museum treasurer. The treasurer then counts the cash in the presence of the clerk and puts the cash in the safe. On Friday of each week, the clerk takes the cash to the bank and receives a signed deposit slip from the bank clerk, which serves as the basis for the weekly entry to the cash receipts journal.

REQUIRED: **(a)** Identify the weaknesses in the internal control system.

(b) What recommendations would you make?

P7-3 Bank Reconciliation. Using the following information, prepare a bank reconciliation for the month ended December 31 for Southern California, Inc. In addition, make any required journal entries.

1. The bank statement showed an ending balance of $6,719.79 at December 31. The general ledger Cash account showed an ending balance of $6,385.96 at December 31.

2. Your examination showed that included with the bank statement was a credit memo indicating that the bank collected $1,100 in accounts receivable for you. The bank charged a $5 fee.

3. A credit memo showed $33.74 interest earned on average balance.

4. A debit memo showed a $3 monthly service charge.

5. A deposit of $1,374.29 representing December 31 cash receipts was not posted in the bank statement.

6. Your review of the bank statement and cash disbursements journal indicated that the following checks written in December were not returned: no. 1034 for $125.27; no. 1036 for $83.78; no. 1037 for $378.54; no. 1040 for $21.79.

7. Check no. 1030, issued for monthly rent and properly paid by the bank for $596, was recorded in the book for $569.

P7-4 Bank Reconciliation. As the accountant for Central Communication Co., you are preparing the bank reconciliation as of September 30, 1990. You have obtained the following data:

1. The bank statement showed an ending balance as of 9/30/90 of $3,785. The general ledger Cash account showed a balance of $5,303 as of that date.

2. Deposits of $769 and $338 representing cash receipts of 9/28 and 9/30 were not posted by the bank.

3. The following items were returned with the bank statement:

(a) A credit memo in the amount of $17 for interest earned in September.

(b) A debit memo for $176 for a NSF check written by GEE Company.

(c) A debit memo for $1,300 for an automatic repayment of a bank loan. The interest portion is $1,245.

(d) A debit memo for $5 for monthly service charge.

4. The following checks were written by Central Communication Co. but not yet paid by the bank: no. 3479 for $126; no. 3480 for $374; no. 3483 for $29; no. 3485 for $273; no. 3487 for $137; no. 3488 for $114.

REQUIRED: **(a)** Prepare a bank reconciliation at September 30, 1990.

(b) Make any required journal entries.

P7-5 Bank Reconciliation—Missing Data. Standard Company makes all cash receipts and disbursements by check. You have obtained the following information for November and December 1990:

STANDARD COMPANY
Bank Reconciliation
November 30, 1990

Balance per bank	$14,785
Add: Deposit in transit	1,756
Less: Outstanding checks	(3,574)
Adjusted balance	$12,967
Balance per book	$12,972
Less: Service charge	(5)
Adjusted balance	$12,967

TRANSACTIONS DURING DECEMBER:

	Per Bank Statement	Per Book
Balance, December 31	$17,595	$18,388
December deposits per book		24,599
December deposits per bank, includes a collection on accounts receivable of $1,771 less collection fee of $15	23,574	
December checks	20,759	19,178
Service charge	5	

REQUIRED: **(a)** Determine the following as of December 31:

    1. Deposits in transit.

    2. Outstanding checks.

(b) Prepare a bank reconciliation at December 31.

(c) Make the required adjusting entries, if any. Assume there is no interest income involved in accounts receivable collected.

P7-6 **Petty Cash Transactions.** The Boggs Farm Equipment Corporation decided in November to establish a $200 petty cash fund. The following transactions affected the fund during November and December:

- November 1: A check for $200 is drawn to establish the fund.

- November 30: Examination of the fund indicates that $72.40 in cash is on hand. The following expense vouchers are also on hand:

Donations	$12.00
Office supplies	47.56
Parking	24.32
Delivery expense	30.42
Repairs	15.60

A check is drawn to replenish the fund.

- December 31: Examination of the fund indicates that $12.36 is on hand. The following expense vouchers are also on hand:

Travel	$48.00
Freight-out	17.00
Postage	23.46
Store supplies	96.18

The firm decides to increase the fund to $350. A check is drawn to replenish and increase the fund.

REQUIRED: Make all necessary entries to record these transactions.

UNDERSTANDING FINANCIAL STATEMENTS

P7-7 The following statement was taken from a recent annual report of Safeway Stores:

MANAGEMENT'S RESPONSIBILITY FOR FINANCIAL STATEMENTS

The consolidated financial statements of Safeway Stores, Incorporated and its subsidiaries have been prepared in accordance with generally accepted accounting principles applied on a consistent basis and include amounts that are based on Management's best estimates and judgments. Management is responsible for the integrity and objectivity of the data in these statements. Financial information elsewhere in this Annual Report is consistent with that in the financial statements.

To fulfill its responsibilities, Management has developed and maintained a strong system of internal accounting controls. There are inherent limitations in any control system in that the cost of maintaining a control should not exceed the benefits to be derived. However, Management believes the controls in use are sufficient to provide reasonable assurance that assets are safeguarded from loss or unauthorized use and that the financial records are reliable for preparing the financial statements. The controls are supported by careful selection and training of qualified personnel, by the appropriate division of responsibilities, by communication of written policies and procedures throughout the Company, and by an extensive program of internal audits.

Peat, Marwick, Mitchell & Co., independent certified public accountants, whose report follows the consolidated financial statements, are engaged to provide an independent opinion regarding the fair presentation in the financial statements of the Company's financial condition and operating results. They obtain an understanding of the Company's systems and procedures and perform tests of transactions and other procedures sufficient to provide them reasonable assurance that the financial statements are neither misleading nor contain material errors.

The Board of Directors, through its Audit Committee composed of outside Directors, is responsible for assuring that Management fulfills its responsibilities in the preparation of the financial statements. The Board, on the recommendation of the Audit Committee and in accordance with stockholder approval, selects and engages the independent public accountants. The Audit Committee meets with the independent accountants to review the scope of the annual audit and any recommendations they have for improvements in the Company's internal accounting controls. To assure independence, the independent accountants have free access to the Audit Committee and may confer with them without Management representatives present.

REQUIRED: **(a)** Do you agree with the statement that "there are inherent limitations in any control system in that the cost of maintaining a control should not exceed the benefits to be derived." Provide specific examples in which the cost of maintaining such a system in a market may outweigh the benefits derived.

(b) Safeway's management lists a number of items that support the controls. Do these items meet the attributes a good internal control system should have?

(c) In what ways do you think the Audit Committee influences the system of internal control at Safeway?

FINANCIAL DECISION CASE

P7-8 The Metro Gold Store is owned by two partners, Ed Roebuck and Sharon Sears. Their primary business is the purchase and resale of gold bars and gold coins. Each day a large number of cash receipts and disbursements are made. All transactions are conducted by check. The company has grown in recent years, and the firm has been able to obtain a $200,000 line of credit from the bank.

Controlling the daily cash balance is an important aspect of their business. Ed is primarily in charge of this aspect. At the end of each day, he calls the bank and finds out what the current balance is in their account. He then adds the amount of the day's deposits, and this gives him the amount of cash available to use. He then writes checks for that amount, and in some cases in excess of that amount. He feels comfortable writing checks in excess of the amount available, because he knows that it will take a few days before those checks are paid.

As the firm's business has expanded, the available cash balance has continued to decrease, and they have been forced to use most of their line of credit. They are both happy in the increase in sales as the price of gold has increased, but they are concerned with their cash position.

REQUIRED: **(a)** Comment on the procedures that Ed uses to control the firm's cash. Explain to him why he may not be getting an accurate cash figure.

(b) What circumstances could cause their cash problems as their sales continue to rise?

(c) Describe several procedures the firm could institute to gain better control over the daily cash balance.

ACCOUNTING FOR SHORT-TERM MONETARY ASSETS

LEARNING OBJECTIVES

After studying this chapter, you should be able to:

1. Differentiate between short-term and long-term investments.
2. Account for short-term investments and understand the lower-of-cost-or-market rule for equity investments.
3. Explain the nature of accounts receivable.
4. Explain the nature of uncollectible accounts and apply the accounting procedures related to the allowance method of accounting for uncollectible accounts, including the percentage-of-sales and the aging methods.
5. Evaluate management controls over receivables.
6. Explain the nature of notes receivable and the elements of a promissory note.
7. Describe how a firm uses receivables to generate cash.
8. Explain the presentation of receivables on a balance sheet.

T he purpose of this chapter is to discuss the accounting concepts and procedures related to short-term monetary assets other than cash. **Monetary assets** are considered to be cash and those items that represent claims to specific amounts of cash. These assets are liquid, can be quickly converted into cash when needed, and include cash, short-term investments, and accounts and notes receivable. In contrast, **nonmonetary assets** are generally used in the productive cycle of the business and include such assets as inventories, long-term investments, and property, plant, and equipment. Cash was discussed in Chapter 7; short-term investments and receivables are discussed in this chapter.

SHORT-TERM INVESTMENTS

One of the purposes of a cash management control system is to ensure that the firm maintains adequate cash balances to meet its working capital needs. However, a firm does not want to let excess cash lie idle, without earning interest. Thus it is likely to invest cash that is in excess of its working capital needs in marketable securities such as stocks, government securities, and corporate bonds. These are called **short-term investments**, because management generally does not intend to hold them longer than one year. If the investments are not marketable, or if management intends to hold them for an indefinite period, they should be excluded from the current assets section and included under the caption "long-term investments."

ACCOUNTING FOR SHORT-TERM INVESTMENTS

When short-term investments are acquired, they are recorded at cost, which includes all commissions, fees, taxes, and other items that must be incurred to acquire the investment. When dividends or interest are received, Investment Revenue is credited.

To illustrate, assume that the Able Corporation purchases 1,000 shares of Beta Stores, at $28 per share, including all commissions. Able Corporation would make the following entry to record this investment:

Short-term Investments	28,000	
Cash		28,000
To record purchase of 1,000 shares of Beta Stores, at $28 per share.		

Subsequently, Beta Stores declares a quarterly dividend of 75 cents per share. Able records the receipt of this $750 dividend as follows:

Cash	750	
Investment Revenue (or Dividend Revenue)		750
To record receipt of 75¢ per share dividend (1,000 × 75¢ = $750).		

When some or all of the shares of stock are sold, Able will record a gain or loss equal to the difference between the sales price and the recorded cost of the securities. To illustrate, assume that Able sells 500 shares of Beta for $30 per share, net of commission. The firm makes the following entry to record this transaction:

Cash	15,000	
Gain on Sale of Short-term Investments		1,000
Short-term Investments		14,000
To record $1,000 gain on sale of 500 shares of Beta stock at $30 per share.		

In this case, a $1,000 gain (or $2 per share) is recorded. If a loss had occurred, the account Loss on Sale of Short-term Investments would be debited for the amount of the loss.

VALUATION OF SHORT-TERM INVESTMENTS

Under current accounting practices, short-term marketable equity investments (i.e., stocks as opposed to bonds, which are debt investments) must be valued at the lower of their cost or market value at each balance sheet date.[1] This means that if the market value of the securities on the balance sheet date is below their cost, they must be written down to that amount. The amount of the write-down is shown on the income statement as an unrealized loss. The amount is unrealized because the securities have not been sold. Conversely, if the market value is above the cost of the securities, they are left at the lower (cost) amount. The lower-of-cost-or-market standards in FASB Statement 12 do not have to be applied to debt securities such as bonds or government securities. However, a firm may, if it wishes, value these securities at the lower of cost or market.

APPLICATION OF THE LOWER-OF-COST-OR-MARKET RULE

To illustrate the application of the lower-of-cost-or-market rule, assume that on December 31 Able still holds the remaining 500 shares of the Beta stock. At that date, the current market value of Beta Stores is $27 per share. Because the total market value of the shares—$13,500 ($27 × 500 shares)—is less than their remaining cost—$14,000 ($28 × 500 shares)—the shares must be shown at market. After this write-down, the Short-term Investments account appears on the balance sheet as follows.

Current Assets	
Cash	10,000
Short-term Investments	
(at market, which is below cost)	13,500

The loss of $500 ($14,000 − $13,500) is shown on the income statement as an unrealized loss.

Actually, the accounting procedures related to valuing equity securities at the lower of cost or market can be more complicated than just illustrated. Because these procedures parallel those used for long-term investments, they are discussed in greater detail in Chapter 15.

ACCOUNTING FOR RECEIVABLES

Accounts receivable arise from credit sales, and the accounting issues related to the recognition of credit sales and accounts receivable were discussed in Chapter 6. This section will focus on accounting for subsequent cash collections and uncollectible accounts. **Uncollectible accounts** are receivables that the firm is unable to collect in full from the customer.

CREDIT SALES

A major portion of wholesale and retail sales in the United States are on credit. As a result, some firms have a substantial portion of their current assets in the form of accounts receivable. For example, at the end of 1987, Sears, Roebuck and Company's accounts receivable totaled over $26 billion, and IBM's totaled over $12 billion. The ability of these firms, as well as others, to collect these amounts affects their cash liquidity and financing needs. This is an essential aspect of overall cash management.

The ability of a firm to collect its credit sales depends on (1) the initial decision regarding to whom credit is extended, (2) the particular credit policies of the firm, such as the use of sales discounts or interest charges on uncollected accounts, and (3)

[1] Financial Accounting Standards Board, Statement No. 12, *Accounting for Certain Marketable Securities* (Stamford, Conn.: FASB, 1975).

general economic conditions. A firm obviously has more control over the first two factors than over the third.

In large firms, the credit department has the responsibility of granting credit as well as subsequently collecting accounts. In smaller firms, this responsibility often lies with the owner-manager. In deciding whether originally to grant credit or to extend credit limits, the firm must obtain information about customers, such as their financial condition and past credit history. This information can be obtained through credit applications and the services of credit-rating bureaus.

■ CREDIT POLICIES

A firm could adopt a very conservative credit policy and extend credit only to customers with excellent credit ratings. Although this type of policy virtually eliminates bad debts or uncollectible accounts, the firm can lose sales and profits by not extending credit to individuals or firms with less-than-perfect credit histories which might fully pay their accounts. In theory, a firm should extend credit to all customers if the ultimate cash collected would (through either partial or full payment on account) exceed the total of the cost of goods sold, plus other incremental selling and general and administrative expenses. If a firm follows such a credit policy, it would still incur some bad debts or uncollectible accounts. However, as long as these uncollectible accounts do not exceed the incremental profits from sales to customers in this credit class, the firm will be better off.

For large firms, the cost of administering a credit department and the associated bad debts can be substantial. In an attempt to reduce the cost of their products, some firms have decided to eliminate retail credit sales. For example, Arco decided in 1982 to eliminate its retail gas credit cards in the hope of saving $73 million. Recently, ARCO has replaced these credit cards with bank debit cards, which automatically charge the customer's bank account for the amount of any purchase.

■ UNCOLLECTIBLE ACCOUNTS

The primary accounting issue regarding accounting for uncollectible accounts is matching the bad debts with the sales of the period that gave rise to the bad debts. That is, the bad-debt expense should be recognized in the period in which the sale took place and the receivable was generated, not in the period in which management determined that the customer was unable or unwilling to pay. The accounting problem arises because it may be the following year before management discovers that a sale made in the current year will not be collectible. Waiting to record the bad-debt expense in the year following the sale would violate the matching convention.

In order to provide the best matching, the allowance method is used. Under the **allowance method**, the uncollectible accounts expense for the period is matched against the sales for that period. This requires estimating the uncollectible accounts expense in the period of the sale. An estimate is required because it is impossible to know with certainty which outstanding accounts at the end of the year will become uncollectible during the next year. This estimate is usually recorded through an adjusting journal entry at year-end. Although estimates are uncertain, accountants feel that the benefits of applying the matching convention outweigh the uncertainties associated with estimates.

Using the Allowance Method to Record Uncollectible Accounts Expense

To demonstrate the application of the allowance method, the necessary journal entries will be discussed first, and then the different methods used to make the required estimates will be examined.

In order to understand the required journal entries used with the allowance method, assume that during 1990, Delta Company's first year in business, sales totaled $1 million. All sales were made on credit, and cash collections on account totaled $750,000. After analyzing the ending balance of $250,000 in Accounts Receivable, management estimated that $12,500 of these accounts would ultimately become uncollectible.

Journal Entries to Record Original Estimate. The summary journal entries required to record the sales, cash collections, and the $12,500 in uncollectible accounts are:

Summary entries for the year:

Accounts Receivable	1,000,000	
Sales		1,000,000
To record sales during the year.		
Cash	750,000	
Accounts Receivable		750,000
To record cash collected on account during the year.		

December 31, 1990—Adjusting entry:

Uncollectible Accounts Expense	12,500	
Allowance for Uncollectible Accounts		12,500
To record estimated uncollectible accounts.		

The first two entries are to record sales on account and the subsequent collection of cash. However, the adjusting entry on December 31, 1990, to record the estimated uncollectible accounts, needs to be explained.

The debit part of the adjusting entry is made to the Uncollectible Accounts Expense account. Another title for this account is Bad Debt Expense. This account is generally shown as a selling expense on the income statement and is closed to Income Summary. However, some firms show this item as a deduction from gross sales in arriving at net sales. The credit part of the entry is to an account called Allowance for Uncollectible Accounts, a contra asset. This account, rather than Accounts Receivable, is credited because the firm is only making an estimate of uncollectible accounts and does not know which particular account will ultimately prove uncollectible. If a firm knows that a particular account is, in fact, uncollectible, it should already have been written off.

The **Allowance for Uncollectible Accounts** account is a contra-asset account with a credit balance. Other titles for this account include Allowance for Doubtful Accounts and Allowance for Bad Debts. In preparing a balance sheet, the Allowance account is netted against Accounts Receivable. This amount represents management's estimate of the net realizable value of the receivables. Exhibit 8-1 shows the current assets section of the Delta Company's balance sheet at December 31, 1990 after the adjusting entry has been made. Because this is the first year of the firm's operations, the balance in the Allowance account equals the amount of the journal entry. However, in future years this may not be the case.

To extend this illustration, assume that the following events occur in 1991:

1. On April 14, Corona Company, one of Delta's customers, informs Delta that it is entering bankruptcy proceedings. Because Delta's management feels that it is unlikely that it will be able to collect anything from the $6,000 balance in Corona's account, it decides to write off the entire balance.

2. On November 29, Delta receives $400 from the bankruptcy court as the final settlement of Corona's account.

EXHIBIT 8–1

DELTA COMPANY Partial Balance Sheet December 31, 1990		
Current assets		
Cash		$ 15,000
Temporary investments		5,000
Accounts receivable	$250,000	
Less: Allowance for uncollectible accounts	12,500	237,500
Inventory		180,000
Prepaids		2,500
Total current assets		$440,000

Journal Entries to Record Actual Write-Off. Based on these data, Delta makes the following entry on April 14, 1991, to write off the $6,000 account:

Apr. 14, 1991	Allowance for Uncollectible Accounts	6,000	
	Accounts Receivable—Corona		6,000
	To write off balance in Corona Company's		
	account receivable.		

As this entry shows, the debit part of the entry is to the Allowance account. The entry is not to the Uncollectible Accounts Expense account because it is assumed that the $6,000 is included in the $12,500 debit to expense as part of the December 31, 1990 adjusting entry. The credit part is to Accounts Receivable—Corona. This part of the entry must be posted to both the general ledger accounts receivable and to Corona's account in the accounts receivable subsidiary ledger.

After the $6,000 entry to write off the specific account, the net amount of accounts receivable (Accounts Receivable less Allowance for Uncollectible Accounts) remains the same, as illustrated in Exhibit 8-2. The entry on April 14, 1991 decreases the Allowance account and the Accounts Receivable account by the same amount, $6,000, to write off the account, but has no effect on the net. Once a particular account is determined to be bad, the balance that pertains to that account is taken out of both the Allowance account and the Accounts Receivable account, and there is no effect on net receivables. The decrease in the net occurred when the estimate was recorded at December 31, 1990.

EXHIBIT 8–2

	Balances	
Account	**Before Write-off of Accounts**	**After Write-off of Accounts**
Accounts receivable	$250,000	$244,000
Less: Allowance for uncollectible accounts	12,500	6,500
Net accounts receivable	$237,500	$237,500

Journal Entries to Record Subsequent Collection of Accounts Previously Written Off. In some cases, a customer whose account has been written off will subsequently pay part or all of the account. For example, in the Corona case, Delta's management decided it was prudent to write off the entire balance when Corona entered bankruptcy proceedings, because in Delta's opinion the outcome of such proceedings is uncertain. In November 1991, when Delta received $400 as its full settlement, it had to make the following two entries:

Nov. 29, 1991	Accounts Receivable—Corona	400	
	Allowance for Uncollectible Accounts		400
	To reinstate $400 of Corona's account receivable.		
	Cash	400	
	Accounts Receivable—Corona		400
	To record receipt of $400 cash.		

The first entry reinstates Corona's account receivable in the amount collected, $400. This entry is a reversal of the entry to write off the receivable and reinstates the account receivable. The second entry is the normal cash receipts entry to record a collection from a customer. These two entries should not be combined. First, there may be a lag between the notification of the intention to pay and the actual receipt of the cash. Second, the two entries create a complete record in Corona's subsidiary accounts receivable account of the actual bad debt. A combined entry would not accomplish this. Finally, an entry that debits Cash and credits an Allowance account cannot arise from normal external transactions. For internal control purposes, therefore, unusual entries or combinations of entries should be avoided.

The previous entries demonstrate the entries made to write off an account declared uncollectible and reinstate an account that had previously been written off. During the year, similar entries are made to record other accounts declared uncollectible. At the end of 1991, the Delta Company would again make an estimate of its uncollectible accounts at December 31, 1991 and make the necessary adjusting entry to Uncollectible Accounts Expense and the Allowance for Uncollectible Accounts. How this estimate is made will be considered next.

How to Estimate Uncollectible Accounts Expense

It has been shown that the allowance method is based on the accountant's ability to estimate future uncollectible accounts that result from current year's sales. The percentage-of-net-sales method and the aging method are the two methods that are used to make this estimate.

Percentage-of-net-sales Method. The **percentage-of-net-sales method** determines the amount of uncollectible accounts expense by analyzing the relationship between net credit sales and uncollectible accounts expense of prior years. This method is often referred to as the *income statement approach* because the accountant attempts to measure the expense account Uncollectible Accounts as accurately as possible. The balance in the Allowance for Uncollectible Accounts is the result of the entry to record the estimated uncollectible accounts expense for the period.

To demonstrate the percentage-of-net-sales method, assume that at the end of 1990 you have gathered the data shown in Exhibit 8-3, prior to any adjusting entries, for the Porter Company. This assumes that all accounts determined to be uncollect-

EXHIBIT 8–3

Account	Balance 12/31/90 (Before Adjustments)
Credit sales	$1,020,000
Sales returns and allowances (relating to credit sales)	15,000
Sales discounts (relating to credit sales)	5,000
Accounts receivable	200,000
Allowance for doubtful accounts—Credit balance	2,000

ible during the period have already been written off against Accounts Receivable and the Allowance account. The management of the Porter Company has analyzed the relationship of the losses from uncollectible accounts and net credit sales for the last five years and determined that uncollectible accounts expense will be approximately 2% of credit sales:

Year	Credit Net Sales	Losses Resulting from Uncollectible Accounts
1985	$ 650,000	$12,000
1986	680,000	15,000
1987	780,000	14,820
1988	850,000	17,850
1989	940,000	18,330
	$3,900,000	$78,000

Average percentage
$78,000 ÷ $3,900,000 = 2%

Based on this data, the debit to the Uncollectible Accounts Expense is 2% of net credit sales of $1 million ($1,020,000 − $15,000 − $5,000), or $20,000. The correct adjusting entry at December 31, 1990, to record this estimate is:

Uncollectible Accounts Expense	20,000	
Allowance for Uncollectible Accounts		20,000
To record uncollectible accounts expense based on 2% of net sales.		

After this entry is posted, the relevant T accounts appear as follows:

Allowance for Uncollectible Accounts		Uncollectible Accounts Expense	
	12/31/90 Bal. 2,000	12/31/90 Adj. 20,000	
	12/31/90 Adj. 20,000		
	12/31/90 Adj. Bal. 22,000		

The balance in the Uncollectible Accounts Expense account represents 2% of net credit sales. The balance in this account will always be a function of a predetermined percentage of credit sales if the percentage-of-net-sales method is used. The balance in the Allowance for Uncollectible Accounts account is $22,000—$2,000 from prior years' sales that have not been written off as uncollectible and $20,000 from 1990 sales. At the end of any particular year, the credit balance in this account will fluctuate, and only by coincidence will it equal the balance in Uncollectible Accounts Expense.

To continue with this illustration, assume that during 1991 the following events related to accounts receivable took place:

1. The accounts receivable balance at December 31, 1991, prior to any receivable write-offs or adjusting entries, is $230,000.

2. Management determined that $20,600 of accounts actually became uncollectible during the year and had to be written off.

3. Net credit sales for the year (after deducting sales returns and allowances and discounts) totaled $1,350,000, and 2% of these are estimated to be uncollectible.

The entries to record the write-off of the actual uncollectible accounts and the adjusting entry at the end of 1991 to record the estimated uncollectible accounts are as follows:

Summary entry for the year:

Allowance for Uncollectible Accounts	20,600	
Accounts Receivable		20,600
To record accounts written off during the year.		

December 31, 1991—Adjusting entry

Uncollectible Accounts Expense	27,000	
Allowance for Uncollectible Accounts		27,000
To record estimated uncollectible accounts expense for the year.		

$$.02 \times \$1,350,000 = \$27,000$$

After these entries are posted, the relevant T accounts are as follows:

Allowance for Uncollectible Accounts		**Uncollectible Accounts Expense**	
During year 20,600	12/31/90 Bal. 22,000 12/31/91 Adj. 27,000	12/31/91 Adj. 27,000	
	12/31/91 Adj. Bal. 28,400		

The balance in the Allowance account is now $28,400, which represents $1,400 ($22,000 − $20,600) for the prior years' sales and $27,000 for 1990 sales. At December 31, 1991, the accounts receivable would be shown as follows in the current assets section of the balance sheet:

Accounts receivable	$209,400
Less: Allowance for uncollectible accounts	28,400
	$181,000

The Aging Method. The **aging method** is based on determining the desired balance in the account Allowance for Uncollectible Accounts. The accountant attempts to estimate what percentage of outstanding receivables at year-end will ultimately not be collected; this amount becomes the desired ending balance in the Allowance for Uncollectible Accounts, and an entry to this account is made to adjust the previous balance to the new, desired balance. The offsetting part of this entry is to the account Uncollectible Accounts Expense. The aging method is often referred to as the *balance sheet approach* because the accountant attempts to measure, as accurately as possible, the net realizable value of Accounts Receivable, at the balance sheet date.

The method to estimate the desired balance in the Allowance account is called an aging of accounts receivable. This is done by analyzing the individual customer balance by age categories based on the length of time they have been outstanding. Categories such as current, 31–60 days, 61–90 days, and over 90 days are often used. On the assumption that the longer an account is outstanding, the less likely its collection is, an increasing percentage is applied to each of these categories. The total of these figures represents the desired balance in the account Allowance for Uncollectible Accounts.

To demonstrate the application of the aging method, we will use the data for the Porter Company from Exhibit 8-3. At the end of 1990, the balance in Accounts Receivable was $200,000, and an aging schedule is presented in Exhibit 8-4. For simplicity, it is assumed that the entire $200,000 balance in Accounts Receivable is owed by only five customers.

EXHIBIT 8–4

PORTER COMPANY
Aging of Accounts Receivable
December 31, 1990

Customer	Total	Current	31–60 Days	61–90 Days	Over 90 Days
			Age of Receivables		
A. B. Dick	$ 30,000	$ 10,000	$15,000	$ 5,000	
T. V. Marsh	65,000	45,000	15,000	5,000	
J. Ong	45,000	30,000	5,000	5,000	$5,000
L. Tse	10,000	9,000			1,000
M. S. Worth	50,000	40,000	5,000	5,000	
	$200,000	$134,000	$40,000	$20,000	$6,000
Percentage estimated to be uncollectible		×	5% ×	10% ×	30% ×	50%
Desired balance in Allowance account	$19,700 =	$ 6,700 +	$ 4,000 +	$ 6,000 +	$3,000
Current credit balance	2,000				
Required entry	$ 17,700				

Based on the data in Exhibit 8-4, the Porter Company makes the following adjusting entry at December 31, 1990, to record the uncollectible accounts expense:

Uncollectible Accounts Expense	17,700	
Allowance for Uncollectible Accounts		17,700

To record uncollectible accounts expense based on the aging method.

After this entry is posted, the relevant T accounts appear as follows:

Allowance for Uncollectible Accounts		Uncollectible Accounts Expense	
	12/31/90 Bal. 2,000	12/31/90 Adj. 17,700	
	12/31/90 Adj. 17,700		
	12/31/90 Adj. Bal. 19,700		

A number of points need to be made about this example. First, the amount of the journal entry is the amount needed to bring the Allowance account to the desired balance of $19,700. Because the Allowance account had a $2,000 credit balance prior to adjustment, the required entry is for $17,700, or the difference between $19,700 and $2,000. In some situations, the Allowance account may have a debit balance before the adjustment. This may occur if during the year more accounts were written off than had been estimated for in the prior year. In this situation, the debit balance should be added to the desired credit balance in the Allowance account to determine the correct amount of the entry. For example, if the Porter Company's Allowance account had a $300 debit balance before the entry to record the uncollectible accounts expense was made, the Allowance account would require a credit entry of $20,000 in order to establish the necessary ending balance of $19,700.

The second issue is how the accountant determines what percentages to apply to each age category. Generally, the percentages are based on past experience adjusted for current economic and credit conditions; they should be evaluated on a regular basis and adjusted when necessary.

Finally, in some cases the aging of the accounts receivable will indicate that a particular account has no possibility of collection. If this occurs, this account should be written off by debiting the Allowance account and crediting Accounts Receivable before determining the desired ending balance in the Allowance account. In effect, this particular customer account is eliminated from the aging process, as it is already considered uncollectible.

To continue with this illustration, again assume that the following events occurred during 1991. (These are the same items used in the previous illustration relating to the percentage-of-sales method.) That is,

1. The accounts receivable balance prior to any receivable write-offs or adjusting entries is $230,000.

2. Management determined that $20,600 of accounts actually became uncollectible during the year and had to be written off.

3. In addition, accounts receivable at December 31, 1991 total $209,400.

The aging schedule of accounts receivable on Dec. 31, 1991 is shown in Exhibit 8-5.

EXHIBIT 8-5

PORTER COMPANY
Aging of Accounts Receivable
December 31, 1991

Customer	Total	Current	Age of Receivables		
			31–60 Days	61–90 Days	Over 90 Days
A. B. Dick	$ 40,000	$ 13,000	$21,000	$ 6,000	
T. V. Marsh	60,400	42,000	15,400	3,000	
J. Ong	52,000	38,000	4,000	7,000	$3,000
L. Tse	12,900	8,000	1,000	2,000	1,900
M. S. Worth	44,100	36,000	5,100	3,000	
	$209,400	$137,000	$46,500	$21,000	$4,900
Percentage estimated to be uncollectible		× 5% ×	10% ×	30% ×	50%
Desired balance in Allowance account	$20,250 =	$ 6,850 +	$ 4,650 +	$ 6,300 +	$2,450
Current debit balance	900 debit (see T account below)				
Required entry	$ 21,150				

T Account Prior to 12/31/91 Adjusting Entry
Allowance for Uncollectible Accounts

Write-off during year	20,600	12/31/90 Bal.	19,700
Bal. before adj. 12/31/91	900		

As the schedule illustrates, the accounts receivable balance at December 31, 1991 is $209,400. This is the amount after the $20,600 write-off for uncollectible accounts during 1991 has been posted. The $209,400 is split among the firm's five customers. The computation shows that the amount of required entry is $21,150, because the balance in the Allowance account prior to the adjusting entry is a debit of $900. Remember, the $20,600 write-off has also been posted as a debit to this account and causes this account to have a temporary debit balance. The journal entries to record these events are:

Summary entry for the year:

Allowance for Uncollectible Accounts	20,600	
Accounts Receivable		20,600
To record write-off of accounts receivable.		

December 31, 1991—Adjusting entry

Uncollectible Accounts Expense	21,150	
Allowance for Uncollectible Accounts		21,150
To record estimate of uncollectible accounts expense per aging schedule.		

After these entries are posted, the relevant T accounts are as follows:

Allowance for Uncollectible Accounts		Uncollectible Accounts Expense	
During year 20,600	12/31/90 Bal. 19,700	12/31/91 Adj. 21,150	
	12/31/91 Adj. 21,150		
	12/31/91 Adj. Bal. 20,250		

Comparison of the Methods. Both the percentage-of-net-sales and the aging methods are generally accepted accounting methods, in that they both attempt to match revenues and expenses. The percentage-of-net-sales method is aimed at determining the amount of uncollectible accounts expense, and the aging method is aimed at determining the net realizable balance of accounts receivable for the balance sheet. These methods thus will probably show different balances in both the expense and contra-asset accounts. This is illustrated below, using the data from the 1990 Porter Company example.

	Balance—12/31/90	
Method	**Allowance for Uncollectible**	**Uncollectible Accounts Expense**
Percentge of net sales	$22,000	$20,000
Aging	19,700	17,700

These differences point out that management can choose among methods of applying generally accepted accounting principles and that these choices affect the firm's financial statements. Once a method of estimating bad debts is chosen, it should be consistently followed to enhance the comparability of the financial statements.

Both the aging and the percentage-of-net-sales methods are found in practice. The percentage-of-net-sales method is easier to apply, but the aging method forces management to analyze the status of accounts receivable and credit policies annually. Some firms use the percentage-of-net-sales method to prepare monthly and quarterly statements, and the aging method to make the final adjustment at year-end.

Difference between Estimates and Actual Experience

Regardless of which method is used, the actual accounts written off seldom equal the estimates made in the prior year. However, this presents no problem. If fewer accounts are written off than previously estimated, the Allowance account will have a credit balance prior to the adjustment. The adjustment will then increase this balance to reflect management's new estimate of the uncollectible accounts. If more accounts are written off than previously estimated, the Allowance account will have a temporary debit balance prior to the year-end adjustment. This debit balance will be eliminated when the new adjusting entry is made.

Estimates are inherent in accounting, because the accountant attempts to match revenues and expenses. Most individuals feel that the benefits of this proper matching outweigh the disadvantages of using estimates. Furthermore, for stable companies, the amount of receivables and uncollectible accounts tends to be steady from year to year. This point can be illustrated by looking at the data in Exhibit 8-6.

EXHIBIT 8-6

J. C. PENNEY Key Credit Information (In millions)			
	1986	1985	1984
Customer receivables			
Regular plan	$3,110	$3,122	$2,792
Major purchase plan	1,181	1,111	984
Total customer receivables	$4,291	$4,233	$3,776
Number of accounts with balances	18.3	17.6	16.5
Finance charge revenue	$ 703	$ 671	$ 587
Net bad debts written off	$ 153	$ 101	$ 71
Percent of customer charges	2.0	1.4	1.1
Provision for doubtful accounts	$ 160	$ 109	$ 65
Accounts 90 days or more past due as a percent of customer receivables	2.5	2.1	1.8

The Company's policy is to write off accounts when the scheduled minimum payment has not been received for six consecutive months, or if any portion of the balance is more than 12 months past due, or if it is otherwise determined that the customer is unable to pay. Collection efforts continue subsequent to write-off, and recoveries are applied as a reduction of bad debt losses.

As this section has shown, reasonable errors in estimates are adjusted in current and future years; the accountant does not retroactively change a prior year's statement. However, if estimates are materially and consistently incorrect, management should reevaluate the method used to make the estimate.

■ MANAGEMENT CONTROL AND ANALYSIS OF RECEIVABLES

Management control and analysis of receivables are important parts of the overall cash management system. A previous chapter covered various aspects of internal control over cash transactions. An additional point regarding the proper authorization of receivables to be written off as uncollectible must be emphasized. Only the controller or an individual who does not have day-to-day operational control over receivables or cash should authorize a write-off or a sales return. Written authorization should be attached to the customer's subsidiary ledger or file. This separation of duties and these control procedures will ensure that an employee is not able to steal a cash payment on account and conceal the theft by recording the transaction in a customer's account as a bad debt or a sales return.

Other control procedures include monitoring the age and size of the Accounts Receivable balance. Being able to convert receivables into cash quickly is important in maintaining the firm's liquidity. A regular aging of accounts receivable and a review of credit policies can help ensure that the collections of receivables do not lag.

To help management monitor receivables, the **receivable turnover** and the **average collection period** (in days) are often calculated. The receivable turnover is computed by dividing credit sales by the average accounts receivable for the period. For example, a firm with annual credit sales of $2.5 million and average accounts receivable of $500,000 has a receivable turnover of 5 times, calculated as follows:

$$\frac{\text{Receivable}}{\text{turnover}} = \frac{\text{Credit sales}}{\text{Average accounts receivable}}$$

$$5 \text{ times} = \frac{\$2,500,000}{\$500,000}$$

This turnover figure can easily be converted into the average number of days that the receivables are outstanding, by dividing 365 days by the turnover. In this case, receivables are outstanding an average of 73 days (365 days ÷ 5). Within the constraints of the firm's credit policies, management is interested in reducing the turnover period and thus quickly turning receivables into cash. If sales are made on a 2/10, n/30 basis, the turnover should be close to 12 times in a year, and the average age of receivables should be less than 30 days. The company in the preceding illustration (5 times and 73 days) has a severe collection problem.

■ NOTES RECEIVABLE

A **note receivable** is a written, unconditional promise by an individual or business to pay a definite amount at a definite date or on demand. The individual or business that signs the note is referred to as the **maker** of the note, and the person to whom the

EXHIBIT 8–7

PROMISSORY NOTE RECEIVABLE

$ .... 5,000 .... April 5 ..... **1990**

For Value Received .... J. Hart ....

....

promises to pay to .... C. Brecker .... *or order, the sum*

of .... Five Thousand .... *Dollars*

.... at San Francisco, CA ....

....

in ..... lawful money of the United States, ninety days .... *from this date,*

with interest annually at the rate of .... 12% .... *per annum,*

during said term, and for such further time as said principal sum, or any part thereof shall remain unpaid; provided however, that if any default shall be made in the payment of any installment of principal or interest and such default continues for .... thirty ..... *days, the whole principal sum then remaining unpaid, together with interest shall, at the option of the holder hereof, become due and payable on demand.*

Signed in the presence of

D. Dinelly   *J. Hart*

---

payment is to be made is called the **payee**. Exhibit 8-7 shows a common form of a note receivable, in which J. Hart is the maker and C. Brecker is the payee. In this illustration, C. Brecker records the note as an asset, and J. Hart records the note as a payable. The journal entries to record the note by each individual on April 5, 1990, the date of the note, are as follows:

C. Brecker

Note Receivable	5,000	
Cash		5,000

To record $5,000 note receivable at 12% interest.

J. Hart

Cash	5,000	
Note Payable		5,000

To record $5,000 note payable at 12% interest.

Although this chapter is primarily concerned with accounting for notes receivable, the concepts here apply equally well to notes payable (see Chapter 11).

There are several types of notes receivable that arise from economic transactions. For example, trade notes receivable result from written obligations by a firm's customers. In some industries, it is common for a seller to insist on a note rather than an open account for certain types of sales, such as the sale of equipment or other personal or real property, in which payment terms are normally longer than is customary for an open account. In other cases, a particular customer's credit rating may cause the seller to insist on a written note rather than relying on an open account. Further, if a particular customer is delinquent in paying an account, the seller may insist that the customer sign a note for the balance. Other notes receivable result from cash loans to employees, stockholders, customers, or others. For purposes of this discussion, all notes will be referred to as **promissory notes**.

■ ELEMENTS OF PROMISSORY NOTES

There are several elements to promissory notes that are important to a full understanding of accounting for notes. These are principal, maturity date, duration, interest rate, and maturity value.

The Principal

The principal of the note is the amount that is lent or borrowed. It does not include interest. The principal of the note shown in Exhibit 8-7 is $5,000. Together, the principal and interest portions represent the maturity value. The principal is often referred to as the *face amount* or *face value*.

Maturity Date

The maturity date is the date that the note becomes due and payable. This date either is stated on the note or can be determined from the facts on the note. For example, a note may have a stated maturity date, such as December 31, or be due in a specific number of days or months, such as three months after the note's date. The note shown in Exhibit 8-7 is due 90 days from its date (April 5), or on July 4. This July 4 maturity date is computed as follows:

Days remaining in April (30 − 5)	25
Days in May	31
Days in June	30
Days in July (number of days required to make 90 days)	4
	90 days

Duration

The **duration of the note** is the length of time that the note is outstanding. This period of time is important in determining the interest charges on the note. In order to determine the duration of the note, both the date of the note and its maturity date must be known. For example, a note dated July 15 with a maturity date of September 15 has a duration of 62 days.

Days remaining in July (July 31 − July 15; date of origin not included)	16
Days in August	31
Days in September (date of payment included)	15
	62 days

In this example, interest is based on the note's being outstanding for 62 days.

Interest Rate

Interest is the revenue or expense from lending or borrowing money. To the lender or payee, interest is revenue, and to the maker or borrower, it is an expense. The total interest related to a particular note is based on the note's principal, rate of interest, and duration. It can be calculated by using the following formula:

$$i = P \times R \times T$$
Interest = Principal × Interest rate × Time

Interest rates are stated in annual terms unless specified otherwise. For example, the total interest related to a $10,000, 12% note that is due in one year is $1,200, or

$1,200 = $10,000 × .12 × 1 (or $\frac{12}{12}$)

If this same note had a term of only five months, the interest would be $500, calculated as follows:

$500 = $10,000 × .12 × $\frac{5}{12}$

In some cases, the term of the note is expressed in days, and the exact number of days should be used in the interest computation. For simplicity, assume a 360-day year. For example, the interest related to a $10,000, 12% note with a 90-day term is $300, computed as follows:

$300 = $10,000 × .12 × $\frac{90}{360}$

■ ACCOUNTING FOR NOTES RECEIVABLE

When a note is received from a customer, the account Notes Receivable is debited. The credit can be to Cash, Sales, or Accounts Receivable, depending on the transaction that gave rise to the note. In any event, the Notes Receivable account is debited at the face, or principal, of the note. No interest revenue is recorded at the date of the issue, since no interest has yet been earned. Interest is recorded at the maturity date or at the end of the accounting period, by an adjusting entry.

Receipt of the Note

To show the initial recording of a note receivable, assume that on July 1 the Fenton Company accepts a $2,000, 12%, four-month note receivable from the Zoe Company in settlement of an open account receivable. The following entry is made to record this transaction:

July 1	Notes Receivable—Zoe	2,000	
	Accounts Receivable—Zoe		2,000
	To record 12%, 4-month note.		

In some situations the receipt of the note results from a previous sale of merchandise on account. For example, assume that a $5,000 sale was made to a customer on account. The customer was unable to pay the account when due, and the seller agreed to accept a note in payment. In this case, the following two entries are made:

Accounts Receivable	5,000	
Sales		5,000
To record $5,000 sale.		
Notes Receivable	5,000	
Accounts Receivable		5,000
To record receipt of note in exchange for open account receivable.		

Payment of the Note

When the payment on the note is received, Cash is debited, Notes Receivable is credited, and Interest Revenue is credited. For example, assume that the $2,000 note from the Zoe Company recorded on July 1 is paid in full on October 31. The entry is:

October 31	Cash	2,080	
	Notes Receivable—Zoe		2,000
	Interest Revenue		80
	To record full payment of note and interest of $80.		

$$\$80 = \$2,000 \times .12 \times \tfrac{4}{12}$$

In some cases, the note is received in one accounting period and collected in another. In these situations, interest must be accrued at year-end. For example, assume that the Bullock Company received a three-month, 18% note for $5,000 on November 1, 1990, in exchange for cash. The firm's year-end is December 31, and the note matured on January 31, 1991. The entries, that the Bullock Company made on November 1, 1990, December 31, 1990, and January 31, 1991 are:

November 1, 1990	Notes Receivable	5,000	
	Cash		5,000
	To record receipt of $5,000, 18%, 3-month note.		
December 31, 1990	Interest Receivable	150	
	Interest Revenue		150
	To record interest revenue for November and December 1990.		
	$150 = \$5,000 \times .18 \times \tfrac{2}{12}$		
January 31, 1991	Cash	5,225	
	Interest Receivable		150
	Notes Receivable		5,000
	Interest Revenue		75
	To record full collection of loan as follows:		
	Total Interest = $5,000 \times .18 \times \tfrac{3}{12}$ = $225		
	Interest Accrued to 12/31/90 150		
	Interest Revenue for 1/91 $ 75		

Defaulted Notes Receivable

When the borrower, or maker of the note, fails to make the required payment at maturity, the note is considered to be **defaulted**. At that point, the note becomes worthless and should be transferred to Accounts Receivable. Accounts Receivable is debited for the maturity value (the principal and the unpaid interest). For example, if the Zoe Company defaults on its $2,000, 12% note, the Fenton Company will make the following entry on October 31:

Accounts Receivable—Zoe	2,080	
Notes Receivable—Zoe		2,000
Interest Revenue		80

To record default by the Zoe Company on $2,000, 12%, 4-
month loan, including interest of $80 = ($2,000 $\times$ .12 $\times$ $\frac{4}{12}$).

Although it may seem strange to record interest revenue on a defaulted note receivable, the Zoe Company is still obligated to pay both the interest and the principal. The account receivable is a valid claim, even though the note receivable is worthless. Furthermore, by transferring the note to Accounts Receivable, the balance in the Note Receivable account in the general ledger contains only the notes that have not yet matured. The Fenton Company should also indicate the default in the subsidiary accounts receivable ledger. Subsequently, if the account receivable proves uncollectible, it must be written off against the Allowance account.

■ USING RECEIVABLES TO GENERATE CASH

Both accounts and notes receivable can be used to generate immediate cash. Accounts receivable can be assigned, pledged, or factored. Essentially, in all these situations the company that owns the receivable either sells it to a bank or other lender or borrows against it to obtain immediate cash. The ability to raise cash in this manner is especially important to small- and medium-sized businesses, which are often strapped for cash. Accounting for the assigning, pledging, or factoring of accounts receivable are topics covered in an intermediate accounting text.

Discounting Notes Receivable

Notes receivable can also be used to obtain immediate cash. This is done by selling or discounting the note to a bank or other lender prior to its maturity date. The term **discount** is used because the bank deducts the interest it charges from the note's maturity value and thus discounts the note. The note is usually discounted *with recourse*. This means that the company discounting the note, called the *endorser*, guarantees the eventual full payment of its maturity value. If the maker fails to make the required payments, the bank will present the note to the endorser and demand full payment.

By discounting a note with recourse, the endorser has a contingent liability. A **contingent liability** is a possible liability that may or may not occur, depending on some future event. In many cases, such liabilities are not included in the balance sheet with other liabilities. Rather, they are usually referred to in the footnotes to the financial statements. If the maker pays the bank, the contingent liability will end; if the maker defaults, the contingent liability will become a real liability. However, before being accepted, most discounted notes are reviewed for creditworthiness by both the bank and the endorser, so this type of contingent liability rarely turns into a real liability. (Contingent liabilities are discussed in more detail in Chapter 11.)

Accounting for a Discounted Note

When the note is discounted, the endorser obtains an amount of cash less than the maturity value. This amount of cash is called the *proceeds* of the note; it is computed by applying the interest rate charged by the bank (the discount rate) to the note's maturity value for only the time between the date of the discount and the maturity date.

For example, assume that on April 1 the Schwartz Company receives a $10,000, 12%, 90-day note from Ruth, Inc. The maturity date is June 30. Because of the need for immediate cash, the Schwartz Company discounts the note at the Second National Bank, with recourse, on April 16. (At this point, the note has 75 days until maturity.) The bank charges an interest rate, often called the *discount rate*, of 16%. The Schwartz Company will receive proceeds of $9,957, computed as follows:

Principal of note	$10,000
Add: Interest on note from	
date of issue to maturity date	
$10,000 \times .12 \times \frac{90}{360} =$	300
Maturity value	$10,300
Less: Bank discount charge—16%	
$10,300 \times .16 \times \frac{75}{360} =$	343*
Proceeds	$ 9,957

*Rounded off—actual amount equals $343.33.

The journal entry to record this transaction is:

Cash	9,957	
Interest Expense	43	
Note Receivable		10,000

To record discounting of note receivable at a 16% rate.

In this case, the firm incurs net interest expense of $43, the difference between the principal of $10,000 and the proceeds of $9,957, or the difference between the interest expense of $343 and the total interest of $300. In other situations, the proceeds may exceed the principal, and the endorser records interest revenue in the amount of the difference. Whether interest expense or interest revenue results depends on the interest rate, the discount rate, and the time remaining when the note is discounted.

After the note is discounted, the Second National Bank will notify Ruth, Inc. that it is now the holder of the note and that Ruth must pay the bank the maturity value of $10,300 when the note matures. When Ruth makes the payment, the bank will notify the Schwartz Company that the note has been fully paid.

If Ruth fails to make the required payment, the bank will notify Schwartz and demand payment. The Schwartz Company must pay the bank and make the following entry:

Accounts Receivable—Ruth	10,300	
Cash		10,300

To record account receivable from Ruth, Inc. due to default on note.

If a note is defaulted, a bank will often charge a protest fee that must be paid by the endorser. If this occurs, the protest fee is added to the accounts receivable and the cash payment.

■ CLASSIFICATION OF RECEIVABLES

This portion of the chapter has examined several types of receivables. Trade accounts receivable that arise from ordinary sales are usually collected within 30 days and are thus classified as current assets. Other receivables that arise from loans to outsiders, employees, or stockholders should be shown separately from trade receivables. If the receivable is due within a year or the operating cycle, it should be classified as current. If the receivable arises from a loan to a stockholder or employee and there is no definite due date, it should be considered noncurrent and included in either the long-term investment or other asset section of the balance sheet.

When receivables are discounted with recourse, the issue arises as to whether the transfer should be treated as a sale or as collateral for a loan. The FASB has rules (beyond the scope of this book) related to this issue. In any event, any contingent liability arising from discounted notes should be disclosed in notes to the financial statements.

SUMMARY OF LEARNING OBJECTIVES

1. The difference between short-term and long-term investments. Short-term investments are investments in such marketable securities as stocks, government securities, and bonds. These are considered short-term because management generally does not intend to hold them longer than one year. If the investment is not marketable or if management intends to hold them for an indefinite period, they should be considered long-term.

2. Accounting for short-term investments. When short-term investments are acquired they are recorded at cost, which includes all commissions, fees, and other items. Subsequently, equity securities are recorded at the lower of cost or market at each balance sheet date. Any write-downs to market are recorded on the income statement as unrealized losses.

3. Accounts receivable. Accounts receivable result from credit sales, and for many retailing firms they represent a substantial portion of current assets. The function of the credit department is to establish and enforce credit policies. Credit policies should protect the firm against excessive bad debts but should not be so restrictive as to eliminate customers who, although they do not have a perfect credit rating, are likely to pay.

4. Accounting for uncollectible accounts. Uncollectible accounts are a fact of life in business. The allowance method attempts to match the uncollectible accounts against the sale in the period the sale takes place. This is accomplished by estimating uncollectible accounts in the period of the sale.

Both the percentage-of-net-sales and the aging methods are acceptable to estimate uncollectible accounts. The percentage-of-net-sales method is often called the *income statement approach* because it attempts to estimate the amount of uncollectible accounts expense, whereas the aging method is often called the *balance sheet method* because it attempts to estimate the net realizable value of the accounts receivable.

5. Management and control and analysis of receivables. To help management monitor receivables, two statistics—the receivable turnover and the average collection period in days—are often calculated. The receivable turnover is computed by dividing credit sales by the average accounts receivable for the period. This turnover figure is converted into the average number of days that the receivables are outstanding by dividing 365 days by the turnover.

6. Notes receivable. Notes receivable are unconditional promises in writing to pay a definite amount at a definite time. Notes arise from a variety of transactions. A major accounting issue is the computation of interest.

7. Using receivables to generate cash. Both accounts and notes receivable can be used to generate immediate cash. Accounts receivable can be pledged, assigned, or factored. Notes receivable can be discounted at banks or with other secured lenders.

8. Presentation of receivables. Different types of receivables should be classified separately. Trade accounts receivable are not mixed with loans to employees, stockholders, or others. Interest receivable is also shown separately from the face value of the note.

KEY TERMS

Aging method
Allowance for uncollectible accounts
Allowance method
Average collection period
Contingent liability
Default

Discount
Duration of the note
Maker
Monetary assets
Nonmonetary assets
Note receivable

Payee
Percentage-of-net-sales method
Promissory note

Receivable turnover
Short-term investments
Uncollectible accounts

**PROBLEMS FOR
YOUR REVIEW**

A. **Uncollectible Accounts.** During your review of the financial statements of the SBC Company, you have gathered the following data relating to receivables as of December 31, 1991 (prior to any adjusting entries):

Net sales, all on credit	$5,000,000
Accounts receivable balance	800,000
Allowance for uncollectible account—Debit balance	5,000

REQUIRED: **1.** Assuming the firm estimates that $1\frac{1}{2}\%$ of all credit sales will become uncollectible,

(a) Make the required adjusting entry at 12/31/91.

(b) What are the balances in the (1) Uncollectible Accounts Expense account and (2) Allowance for Uncollectible Accounts account after the 12/31/91 adjusting entry?

2. Assume that an aging of accounts receivable at 12/31/91 reveals the following:

Age	Total	Estimated Percentage Uncollectible	
Current	$450,000	5%	22 500
30–60 days	150,000	10	15 000
61–90 days	75,000	15	11 250
91–120 days	100,000	20	20 000
Over 120 days	25,000	50	12 500
Total	$800,000		81 250

(a) Make the required adjusting entry at 12/31/91.

(b) What are the balances in the (1) Uncollectible Accounts Expense account and (2) Allowance for Uncollectible Accounts account after the 12/31/91 adjusting entry?

**SOLUTION
(1) PERCENTAGE-OF-
NET-SALES METHOD:**

(a) Estimate of uncollectible accounts expense

$5,000,000 \times .015 = \$75,000$

Adjusting entry, 12/31/91

Uncollectible Accounts Expense	75,000	
Allowance for Uncollectible Accounts		75,000

(b) Balance in accounts

Uncollectible Accounts Expense	
Adj. 75,000	
12/31/91 Bal. 75,000	

Allowance for Uncollectible Accounts	
	12/31/91 5,000
	Adj. 75,000
	12/31/91 Bal. 70,000

(2) AGING METHOD: **(a)** Estimate of uncollectible accounts expense

Age	Total	Estimated Percentage Uncollectible	Total
Current	$450,000	5%	$22,500
31–60 days	150,000	10	15,000
61–90 days	75,000	15	11,250
91–120 days	100,000	20	20,000
Over 120 days	25,000	50	12,500
	Required balance		$81,250
	Unadjusted balance—debit		5,000
	Amount of adjusting entry		$86,250

Adjusting entry—12/31/91
Uncollectible Accounts Expense   86,250
    Allowance for Uncollectible Accounts   86,250

(b) Balance in accounts

Uncollectible Accounts Expense	
Adj. 86,250	

Allowance for Uncollectible Accounts	
	12/31/91 5,000
	Adj. 86,250
	12/31/91 Bal. 81,250

B. **Discounting.** The Weiss Corporation discounted a $2,000, 12%, 60-day note receivable of the Cobb Company, dated April 1, 1991. The note was discounted on April 21, 1991, at a discount rate of 14%.

1. What are the proceeds of the note to Weiss?

2. Make the journal entry that Weiss should make to record the discount.

SOLUTION
(1) MATURITY VALUE:

Face value	$2,000.00
Interest	
$2,000 × .12 × $\frac{60}{360}$	40.00
Maturity value	$2,040.00
Discount	
$2,040 × .14 × $\frac{40}{360}$*	31.73
Proceeds	$2,008.27

*The remaining term of the loan is 40 days.

(2) JOURNAL ENTRY:

Cash	2,008.27	
Interest Revenue		8.27
Note Receivable		2,000.00
To record discount of note receivable.		

QUESTIONS

1. What are monetary assets? Give three examples.

2. What factors determine whether an investment is classified as short-term or long-term?

3. The Smith Company purchased 100 shares of IBM at $135 per share. In addition, the company paid a brokerage commission of $100 and a state transfer tax of $50. What is the recorded historical cost of the investment?

4. On April 1, 1990, the Zahary Company purchased 2,000 shares of Murphy's Milk Company at a total cost of $8,500. On December 31, 1990, the Zahary Company's year-end, the stock had a market value of $7,900. At what amount would these securities be shown on the December 31, 1990 balance sheet?

5. What factors affect a firm's ability to collect its credit sales?

6. The controller for Switch and Save Stores is proud of herself because she has eliminated all bad debts by giving credit to only a small number of customers. Do you think this is a good policy? Why or why not?

7. Briefly describe the allowance method of accounting for uncollectible receivables. Include a discussion of the two methods of estimating uncollectible accounts expense.

8. The Allowance for Uncollectible Accounts is a contra-asset account. Explain what this means to your friend, who has no knowledge of accounting.

9. What is the accounting procedure that a firm should use to reinstate a receivable that has previously been written off as uncollectible?

10. In estimating the amount of future uncollectible accounts, a business may use the balance sheet approach or the income statement approach. Briefly describe these two approaches.

11. In what situation would there be a debit balance in the account Allowance for Uncollectible Accounts?

12. Prior to the year-end adjustment, the Grant Co. had a debit balance in its Allowance for Uncollectible Accounts of $1,500. If the firm uses the aging method and estimates $10,000 of the accounts to be uncollectible, what should be the amount of the entry? If the firm uses the percentage-of-sales method and determines that uncollectible accounts expense should be $11,000, what should be the amount of the entry?

13. Define the following terms regarding notes receivable:

   (a) Payee.   **(d)** Maturity value.

   (b) Maker.   **(e)** Duration of note.

   (c) Face value.   **(f)** Interest rate.

14. List four examples in which a promissory note might be issued.

15. How can accounts and notes receivable be used to generate cash?

EXERCISES

E1. Accounting for Short-term Investments. The Kline Company has been very profitable over the last few years and has accumulated a large amount of cash. Management decided to invest some of the excess cash in short-term investments. On June 1, the company purchased 1,000 shares of Liqco Company at $50 per share and 500 shares of International Equity at $120 per share. On July 1, the firm received cash dividends of $2.00 per share from Liqco and $2.50 per share from International Equity. On November 1, the Kline Company sold all the shares of International Equity for $100 per share. At year-end, the market value of the Liqco Company shares was $60 per share.

REQUIRED: **(a)** Make the required entries to record the above events.

           (b) Show how the short-term investments should be shown on the year-end balance sheet.

E2. Uncollectible Accounts Journal Entries. During your examination of the Paton Co., you discovered the following series of journal entries:

1990	a. Uncollectible Accounts Expense	2,500	
	Allowance for Uncollectible Accounts		2,500
	b. Allowance for Uncollectible Accounts	250	
	Accounts Receivable		250
1991	c. Accounts Receivable	100	
	Allowance for Uncollectible Accounts		100
	d. Cash	100	
	Accounts Receivable		100

Describe the events that caused these entries. What effect did each of these transactions have on net income, gross accounts receivable, allowance for uncollectible accounts, and net accounts receivable?

E3. **Recording Sales and Uncollectible Accounts.** During 1990, Baker's Department Store had total sales of $950,000, of which 65% were on credit. During the year, $621,500 was collected on credit sales. Management uses the allowance method and estimates that $20,750 of accounts receivable will be uncollectible.

Prepare the journal entries to record:

(a) Sales during the year.

(b) Cash collected on account.

(c) The establishment of the account Allowance for Uncollectible Accounts.

E4. **Recording Sales and Uncollectible Accounts.** On March 15, 1991, the Hernandez Company purchased on account from the Stepanskie Manufacturing Company merchandise costing $32,000. On December 31, 1991, the accounts receivable of the Stepanskie Manufacturing Company showed a balance of $750,000, including $32,000 owed to it by the Hernandez Company. Stepanskie's management estimates that 4% of the accounts receivable will be uncollectible. At December 31, 1991, there is no balance in either the Uncollectible Accounts Expense account or in the Allowance for Uncollectible Accounts account.

On February 4, 1992, the Hernandez Company enters into bankruptcy proceedings. The Stepanskie Manufacturing Company feels that only 10% of Hernandez's outstanding receivable balance will ever be collected.

On November 12, 1992, Stepanskie receives $4,000 from Hernandez in payment of the receivable. No other funds will be received on this account.

Prepare the necessary journal entries on Stepanskie's books:

(a) March 15, 1991.   **(c)** February 4, 1992.

(b) December 31, 1991.   **(d)** November 12, 1992.

E5. **Accounting for Uncollectible Accounts.** The following data were taken from the unadjusted trial balance of the Yokotake Company:

	Debit	Credit
Accounts receivable	$250,000	
Allowance for uncollectible accounts		$ 2,200
Total sales—40% for cash		660,000

Actual uncollectible accounts written off during the year amounted to $2,500.

REQUIRED: If the firm uses the allowance method to record uncollectible accounts, compute uncollectible accounts expense under each of the following assumptions:

(a) Two percent of total sales.

(b) Three percent of credit sales.

(c) The Allowance for Uncollectible Accounts account is increased to 5% of the ending receivable balance.

E6. Uncollectible Accounts—Percentage-of-sales Method. The following information has been taken from the records of the Lord Company prior to any adjusting entries on December 31, 1990:

Account	Balance—12/31/90
Credit sales	$3,750,000
Sales returns and allowances	23,000
Sales discounts	8,000
Accounts receivable	410,000
Allowance for uncollectible accounts, credit balance	3,500

All accounts have normal balances. Management uses the percentages of net credit sales to estimate uncollectible accounts. Actual credit sales and uncollectibles for the five previous years have been:

Year	Net Credit Sales	Uncollectible Accounts
1985	$ 450,000	$11,250
1986	532,000	17,500
1987	950,000	25,050
1988	1,300,000	42,060
1989	2,200,000	39,940

Using the above information, prepare the adjusting entry to record the uncollectible accounts expense for 1990. What is the balance in the Allowance for Uncollectible Accounts account after the adjusting entry?

E7. Uncollectible Accounts—Aging Method. On December 31, 1990, the balance in the Accounts Receivable account of the McClain Company is $217,820. The company sells highly specialized products to a small number of customers. The following aging schedule was prepared by the company's bookkeeper:

Customer	Totals	Current	Age of Accounts Receivable 31–60 Days	61–90 Days	Over 90 Days
M. A. Pagano	$ 30,500	$ 500	$12,000	$18,000	$ 0
G. M. Wright	52,700	3,100	24,000	15,000	10,600
J. E. Francis	65,950	0	33,450	0	32,500
S. A. Chent	68,670	60,000	0	8,670	0
Totals	$217,820	$63,600	$69,450	$41,670	$43,100

Based on past experience, management makes the following estimate of uncollectible accounts:

Age	%
Current	5
31–60 days	12
61–90 days	30
Over 90 days	60

Prior to any adjustment, the Allowance for Uncollectible Accounts account has a debit balance of $2,000.

Prepare the necessary journal entry to record the uncollectible accounts expense at December 31, 1990.

E8. Receivables Management. K & J Electronics had total credit sales of $1,940,000 during 1990. The beginning balance in the Accounts Receivable account was $340,000, and the ending balance in the account was $630,000.

Figure the receivable turnover rates and the average number of days that the receivables were outstanding. Explain what these figures mean. What advice can you give to management to improve these figures?

E9. Notes Receivable. On March 12, 1991, the Griffith Company received a 90-day note receivable for $40,000, with a stated interest rate of 12%. Determine the following amounts or items:

(a) The principal of the note.

(b) The interest revenue computed on a 360-day year.

(c) The maturity value of the note.

(d) The date the note is due.

E10. Notes Receivable. On October 1, 1991, the Jackson Co. sold a piece of fine furniture to the LuLu Company for $2,000. One month later, Jackson took a three-month, 15% note in exchange for the full account receivable. Jackson's accounting period ends on December 31. LuLu makes the appropriate payment when the note becomes due on February 1, 1992.

Make all the necessary entries to record these events on Jackson's books.

E11. Notes Receivable. On July 15, 1990, Ken Mynard received a $28,000, 16% note from the Williams Company, with a maturity date of September 20, 1990. Using a 360-day year, determine the interest amount associated with the note.

E12. Notes Receivable. On April 15, 1990, Milli received $3,600 from Judi, representing full payment on a note receivable plus interest. If Milli charged Judi a rate of 15.8% and if 1% of Judi's total payment represents interest, on what date did Milli receive the note from Judi? Use a 360-day year.

E13. Defaulted Notes Receivable. The Stover Company was the payee on a $3,000, 14%, 60-day promissory note, due on May 4, 1991, from the sale of merchandise. The maker of the note was the Rau Company, a steady customer. The Rau Company began to experience financial difficulties and on May 5 defaulted on the note. The Stover Company still feels that there is some possibility it will ultimately be able to collect the funds.

Prepare the necessary journal entries to record the receipt and subsequent default on the note. How would your answer differ, if at all, if the Stover Company felt that it would never be able to collect on the note?

E14. Discounted Notes Receivable. On November 1, 1991, Rainbow Oil Company received a $66,000, 14%, 90-day note from Spenser, Inc. On December 1, 1991, Rainbow discounted the note at the First City Bank, with recourse. The bank's discount rate at that time was 18%.

Figure the amount of cash Rainbow Oil Company will receive from discounting the note, and prepare the necessary journal entry.

E15. Toys "R" Us Financial Statements. The current asset section of Toys "R" Us balance sheet is reproduced below.

TOYS "R" US, INC. AND SUBSIDIARIES

(In thousands)		Fiscal Year Ended
	January 31 1988	February 1 1987
ASSETS		
Current Assets:		
Cash and short-term investments	$ 45,996	$ 84,379
Accounts and other receivables, less allowance for doubtful accounts of		
$1,386 and $1,133	62,144	37,502
Merchandise inventories (Note 1)	772,833	528,939
Prepaid expenses.	5,050	3,566
Total Current Assets	886,023	654,386

Net sales for the year, all on account, totaled $3,136,568,000.

REQUIRED: Based on this information, answer the following questions:

1. How much cash did the company collect from its accounts and other receivables during the year ended January 31, 1988?

2. The company determined that $2,200,000 of receivables previously allowed for were uncollectible and decided to write them off. Determine the amount of uncollectible accounts expense for the year ended January 31, 1988.

P8-1 Accounting for Short-term Investments. The Gar Oil Company entered into the following transactions related to short-term investments.

- February 12: Purchased 1,500 shares of Crunchy Nut at $40 per share.
- May 30: Purchased 2,000 shares of Diversified Inc. at $80 per share.
- September 20: Received cash dividends of $3 per share on Crunchy Nut stock.
- December 1: Sold all of its shares of Diversified at $90 per share.
- December 30: Received special $1 per share dividend on Crunchy Nut stock.
- December 31: The market value of Crunchy Nut's stock is $45 per share.

REQUIRED: (a) Make the necessary journal entries to record the above transactions.

(b) Show how the securities would be shown on the December 31 balance sheet.

P8-2 Uncollectible Accounts Expense. The Europe Company has been experiencing a high rate of bad debts in the last few years. On December 31, 1990, before the company made any year-end adjustments, the balance in Europe's Accounts Receivable account was $800,000, and the Allowance for Uncollectible Accounts had a debit balance of $4,000. The Allowance for Uncollectible Accounts account will be adjusted using the aging method and applying the following schedule:

Days Account Is Outstanding	Amount	Probability of Default
Current	$450,000	.05
Between 30 and 60 days	240,000	.10
Between 61 and 90 days	80,000	.20
Between 91 and 120 days	20,000	.30
Over 121 days	10,000	1.00

REQUIRED: (a) Make the journal entry or entries to record the required adjustment.

(b) What is the appropriate balance for the Allowance for Uncollectible Accounts on December 31, 1990?

(c) Show how Accounts Receivable would be presented on the balance sheet prepared on December 31, 1990.

(d) What is the dollar effect of the year-end uncollectible accounts expense adjustment on income for 1990?

P8-3 Uncollectible Accounts Expense. The YU Company operates in an industry that has been experiencing a high rate of bad debts. On December 31, 1990, before the company made any year-end adjustments, the balance in the YU Company's Accounts Receivable account was $5 million, and the Allowance for Uncollectible Accounts account had a normal balance of

$250,000. The Allowance for Uncollectible Accounts account will be adjusted using the aging method and applying the schedule shown below:

Days Account Outstanding	Amount	Probability of Collection
Less than 15 days	$3,000,000	.98
Between 16 and 30 days	1,000,000	.90
Between 31 and 45 days	500,000	.80
Between 46 and 60 days	300,000	.70
Between 61 and 75 days	100,000	.60
Over 75 days	100,000	.00

REQUIRED: **(a)** What is the appropriate balance for the Allowance for Uncollectible Accounts account at December 31, 1990?

(b) Make the journal entry or entries to record the required adjustment.

(c) Show how Accounts Receivable would be presented on the balance sheet prepared at December 31, 1990.

(d) What is the dollar effect of the year-end uncollectible accounts expense adjustment on the income for 1990?

P8-4 Uncollectible Accounts Expense. The following items were taken from the financial statements of Hard-Rock Wholesale Grocery Company at year-end before adjustments, except as noted.

1. Accounts receivable balance, beginning of the year	$ 560,000
2. Allowance for uncollectible accounts—Debit balance	2,400
3. Sales—All on credit	1,700,000
4. Sales returns and allowances	2,500
5. Cash received from customers on account, net of sales discounts of $4,500	1,737,500

The company uses the gross method to record accounts receivable.

REQUIRED: **(a)** Make the necessary journal entries to record the summary events in Items 3 through 5.

(b) Assuming that the firm decides to estimate its uncollectible accounts expense as 2% of net sales before discounts, make the appropriate adjusting entry.

(c) Independent of your answer to (b), now assume that the firm decides to use the aging method to estimate the balance in the Allowance for Uncollectible Accounts account. After aging the accounts, the firm decides that the Allowance for Uncollectible Accounts account should have a balance of $34,800. Make the appropriate entry.

(c) Prepare partial balance sheets showing Accounts Receivable and Allowance for Uncollectible Accounts for each of the methods used to estimate uncollectible accounts described in (b) and (c). Compare and contrast the two.

P8-5 Accounting for Notes Receivable. During the current year, the Green, Patrick, and Kiley Company entered into the following transactions pertaining to notes receivable:

■ March 1: One of the firm's customers, the O'Leary Company, which purchased a large amount of inventory on open account, was unable to pay the bill. As a result, Green, Patrick, and Kiley took a $10,000, 12%, 180-day note in exchange.

■ April 5: In order to obtain immediate cash, the firm discounted the note with recourse at the Third Bank of Berkeley, at 14%. Assume the note has 145 days remaining until its maturity.

■ May 1: Green, Patrick, and Kiley lent $25,000 to one of its best customers. The terms of the note call for interest of 10%. Principal and interest are due in one year.

■ July 15: The firm sold some merchandise to the Blarney Company. Since the Blarney Company is a poor credit risk, Green, Patrick, and Kiley insisted on a note. The principal of the note is $9,000, is due in 90 days, and has an interest rate of 15%.

- July 31: The note from Blarney was discounted at the bank at a discount rate of 16%. Assume the note has 75 days remaining until its maturity.

- September 1: Green, Patrick, and Kiley received notice from the Third Bank of Berkeley that the note discounted on April 5 was paid in full.

- September 10: A note was due from Bad Way Company. However, Bad Way informed Green, Patrick, and Kiley it could not pay the note at this time. The note had a face value of $15,000 with accrued interest of $2,925 as of September 1.

- October 20: The firm received notice from the bank that the Blarney Company had defaulted on its note. Green, Patrick, and Kiley made the required payment plus a $10 protest fee.

- November 1: The firm lent another customer $5,000 cash. The note was due in 90 days and had an interest rate of 14%.

REQUIRED: **(a)** Make all the entries to record these transactions.

(b) Make any required adjusting entries at December 31. (For purposes of adjusting entries, assume a 360-day year.)

P8-6 Accounting for Notes Receivable. The Dream Company needed a considerable amount of cash to undertake production expansion next year. The firm decided to take the following actions relative to its accounts and notes receivable:

1. An open account amounting to $50,000 from the Ray Company was 60 days overdue. The Dream Company insisted that the Ray Company sign a 90-day, 15% note. The note was signed on November 1, 1990.

2. The treasurer decided to discount the existing notes. The relevant data for each of these notes follow:

Company	Principal of Note	Length of Note	Date of Note	Interest Rate	Discount Date	Discount Rate
Ray Co.	$50,000	90 days	Nov. 1	15%	Dec. 1	15%
Almost Inc.	90,000	60 days	Dec. 1	12	Dec. 16	15
West Inc.	40,000	120 days	Dec. 1	12	Dec. 16	15

Ray and Almost paid their notes to the bank when they were due. However, West defaulted on its note. The bank charged the Dream Company a protest fee of $20.

REQUIRED: Make the necessary entries to record the above events.

P8-7 Analysis of Uncollectible Accounts. You have obtained the following data relative to the accounts receivable balance at 6/30/90 of The Sandman, Inc.

1. Sales for the year ended 6/30/90		$2,450,000
2. Accounts Receivable		389,500
3. The T accounts for Uncollectible Accounts Expense and		

Allowance for Uncollectible accounts are presented below:

Uncollectible Accounts Expense

6/20/90	Sales returned for credit	5,000	Various times during the year	Accounts written off	25,000
6/30/90	3% of total credit sales	55,125			

Allowance for Uncollectible Accounts

Various times during the year	Accounts written off	25,000	7/1/89	Beg. Bal.	42,875
			6/20/90	Sales returned for credit[a]	5,000
			6/30/90	3% of total credit sales	55,125

Due to past experience, you feel that The Sandman, Inc. should now use the aging method. Your analysis of the accounts receivable indicates the following:

Age	Net Balance	% Considered Uncollectible
Current	$147,000[a]	2%
31–60 days	117,600	6
61–90 days	70,560[b]	15
91–120 days	31,040[b]	30
Over 120 days	23,300[b]	70
Total	$389,500	

[a] Sale that was returned for credit was made on June 15, 1990 and returned on June 20, 1990.
[b] 50% of the accounts written off during the year were over 120 days, 30% were in the 91–120 day category, and 20% were in the 61–90 day category.

REQUIRED:

(a) Make the summary journal entry to record sales for the year.

(b) Make the required analysis and journal entries and then adjust the accounts to the aging method.

P8-8 Notes Receivable—Determining Missing Values. Answer each of the following questions.

(a) Mark DeFond discounted a $12,000, 18%, 120-day note with his local bank when the note had 90 days remaining until maturity. As a result of this transaction, Mark recognized interest expense of $75. Determine the discount rate used by Mark's banker.

(b) Brent Inman, Inc. discounted a $10,000, 15%, 90-day note with its local bank, at a discount rate of 20%. As a result of this transaction, Brent recognized no interest expense or interest income. Calculate the days remaining until maturity on Brent's note at the time it was discounted.

■ USING THE COMPUTER

P8-9 The controller of the Computer Graphics Company has asked you to prepare an aging of accounts receivable on a common computer spreadsheet program. She provides you with the following data concerning outstanding accounts receivable as of December 31:

Customer	Sales Date	Amount
Atwater Co.	October 5	$4,000
	December 8	6,000
Beckwith Corp.	November 20	2,000
	December 15	6,000
Lotuse Inc.	October 16	1,000
	November 22	500
	December 2	3,000
Perset Ltd.	August 17	5,000
Visiadd Co.	September 13	5,000
	October 22	2,500
	November 12	1,000

The controller estimates that the following schedule should be used in estimating the necessary amount for the journal entry to record uncollectible accounts as of December 31:

Days Account Outstanding	Probability of Default
Current	.02
Between 31 and 60 days	.05
Between 61 and 90 days	.10
Between 91 and 120 days	.25
Over 120 days	.50

Finally, prior to any adjustment, the balance in the Allowance for Uncollectible Accounts account was a credit balance of $1,000.

REQUIRED: **(a)** Using a spreadsheet program available at your school, prepare an aging of accounts receivable that determines the amount of the required adjusting entry at December 31. Use a format similar to that in the text.

(b) The controller now tells you that she feels the economy may not be as good as she originally thought. She would like you to repeat the analysis using the following estimates of uncollectible accounts:

Days Account Outstanding	Probability of Default
Current	.05
Between 31 and 60 days	.10
Between 61 and 90 days	.25
Between 91 and 120 days	.50
Over 120 days	1.00

■ UNDERSTANDING FINANCIAL STATEMENTS

P8-10 The following note is taken from the 1987 annual report of Citicorp.

4. Changes in the Allowance for Possible Credit Losses (in millions of dollars)			
	1987	1986	1985
Balance at beginning of year	$1,698	$1,235	$ 917
Deductions			
Consumer credit losses	1,271	1,172	719
Consumer credit recoveries	(247)	(214)	(134)
Net consumer credit losses	$1,024	$ 958	$ 585
Commercial credit losses	$ 617	$ 489	$ 442
Commercial credit recoveries	(144)	(76)	(65)
Net commercial credit losses	$ 473	$ 413	$ 377
Additions			
Provision for possible credit losses	$4,410	$1,825	$1,243
Other (principally from allowance balances of acquired companies and translation of overseas allowance balances)	7	9	37
Balance at end of year	$4,618	$1,698	$1,235

REQUIRED: **(a)** Determine the amount of receivables written off as uncollectible during 1987.

(b) Determine the increase in the Allowance account during 1987.

(c) Make the entries Citicorp would have made to record the accounts written off during 1987 and the provision for possible credit losses made at the end of 1987.

■ FINANCIAL DECISION CASE

P8-11   The Muppett Computer Store sells computers and software to individuals and to businesses. Because of the high price of the goods it sells, Muppett has always had a very stringent credit policy and will sell on credit only to customers with a AAA credit rating. However, the president of the company has begun to notice that many of the firm's competitors have begun to advertise that they welcome credit sales. As a result, the president is concerned that the firm's profits are suffering by its insistence on such a tough credit policy. She gives you the following data and asks your advice as to whether the firm's credit policies should be relaxed.

Current sales are running about $10 million a year, of which only 10% are currently made on credit. The firm's gross margin on sales is 30% or, correspondingly, cost of goods sold equals 70% of sales. Current uncollectible accounts amount to only 1% of credit sales. The firm has analyzed its potential customers and feels that there are three additional classes of credit customers to which it could extend credit. If it does, the firm expects to increase sales and to incur the following amount of uncollectibles and additional selling expenses for each of the three classes:

Class Rating	Additional Sales	Percent Uncollectible	Additional Expenses
A	$100,000	5	$10,000
B	60,000	10	11,000
C	90,000	20	13,000

REQUIRED: **(a)** Advise the president as to whether the firm's credit policies should be revised and, if so, to what extent. Include a discussion of what effect there will be on profits if sales are made to the additional customers.

       (b) What else should the president take into consideration before making a final decision on extending credit to these potential customers?

ACCOUNTING
FOR INVENTORIES

LEARNING OBJECTIVES

After studying this chapter, you should be able to:

1. Explain the relationship between inventories and income determination.
2. Determine the cost of ending inventories.
3. Apply the four methods of attaching costs to the ending inventory, using the periodic and perpetual systems.
4. Explain the factors that management considers in selecting among generally accepted accounting principles.
5. Apply the lower-of-cost-or-market rule as it relates to inventories.
6. Use inventory data in decision making.
7. Use the gross margin and retail inventory methods to estimate ending inventories (Special Supplement).

This chapter will focus on how accountants determine both the cost of ending inventories and the cost of the goods sold during the period. The problems here are typical of those found with all nonmonetary assets. In addition, inventories will be used as an example to examine how management chooses among alternative accounting methods. Finally, the Special Supplement will deal with other issues related to inventories, including procedures such as the gross margin and the retail methods.

301

■ INVENTORIES AND INCOME DETERMINATION

Inventories are nonmonetary assets. As noted in Chapter 4, one of the major accounting issues regarding nonmonetary assets is determining the cost of the current benefits used or consumed (the expense of the period) and the cost of the future benefits (the cost of the asset at the end of the period). This process helps ensure that the costs of these assets are matched against the revenues they produce. For inventories, this requires allocating the cost of all goods available for sale between the items sold and the items remaining in ending inventory. The AICPA has stated:

> A major objective of accounting for inventories is the proper determination of income through the process of matching appropriate costs against revenues.[1]

Exhibit 9-1 illustrates this allocation process. As the exhibit indicates, the cost of inventories at the end of the period is determined and subtracted from the cost of goods available for sale to derive the cost of goods sold. The accounting methods and procedures that accountants use to make this allocation are the main focus of this chapter.

EXHIBIT 9–1

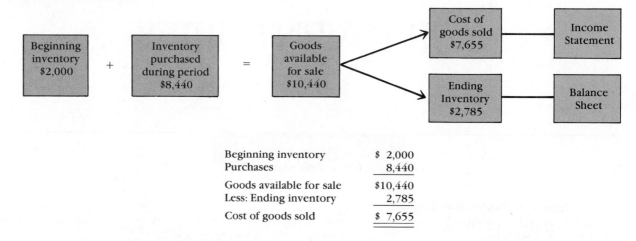

Beginning inventory	$ 2,000
Purchases	8,440
Goods available for sale	$10,440
Less: Ending inventory	2,785
Cost of goods sold	$ 7,655

■ MEASURING ENDING INVENTORIES AND INCOME

The allocation of the cost of the goods available for sale between the ending inventories and the goods sold affects both the balance sheet and the income statement. Ending inventories are usually a significant current asset, and an improper allocation of costs to the ending inventory can cause a serious error in current assets, total assets, working capital, and the current ratio. The cost of goods sold is often the largest expense item on the income statement. For some firms, this figure can reach 75% to 80% of total sales. A measurement error in cost of goods sold affects the gross margin amount, the gross margin percentage, and the net income. Furthermore, a measurement error in determining the ending inventory has a two-period effect, because the ending inventory for one period becomes the beginning inventory for the next period.

The effects of inventory on the determination of income can be demonstrated by analyzing the effect of an inventory measurement error. The first column in Exhibit 9-2 presents the data used to illustrate these effects. The data in Column 1 shows the current amount of ending inventory as well as all other items. As the statements show, the gross margins for Years 1 and 2 are $25,000 and $20,000, respectively. The total gross margin for the two-year period is $45,000.

---

[1] American Institute of Certified Public Accountants, Committee on Accounting Procedure, Accounting Research Bulletin No. 43, *Restatement and Revision of Accounting Research Bulletins* (New York: AICPA, 1961), Chapter 4, Statement 2.

EXHIBIT 9–2	Effect of Inventory Errors

Column 1 Correct Ending Inventory in Year 1			Column 2 (Case A) Ending Inventory in Year 1 Overstated by $5,000			Column 3 (Case B) Ending Inventory in Year 1 Understated by $5,000		
Year 1			**Year 1**			**Year 1**		
Sales		$110,000	Sales		$110,000	Sales		$110,000
Cost of goods sold			Cost of goods sold			Cost of goods sold		
Beginning			Beginning			Beginning		
inventory	$ 10,000		inventory	$ 10,000		inventory	$ 10,000	
Purchases	90,000		Purchases	90,000		Purchases	90,000	
Goods available			Goods available			Goods available		
for sale	100,000		for sale	100,000		for sale	100,000	
Less			Less			Less		
Ending inventory	15,000		Ending inventory	20,000		Ending inventory	10,000	
Cost of goods sold		85,000	Cost of goods sold		80,000	Cost of goods sold		90,000
Gross margin		$ 25,000	Gross margin		$ 30,000	Gross margin		$ 20,000
Year 2			**Year 2**			**Year 2**		
Sales		$135,000	Sales		$135,000	Sales		$135,000
Cost of goods sold			Cost of goods sold			Cost of goods sold		
Beginning			Beginning			Beginning		
inventory	$ 15,000		inventory	$ 20,000		inventory	$ 10,000	
Purchases	120,000		Purchases	120,000		Purchases	120,000	
Goods available			Goods available			Goods available		
for sale	135,000		for sale	140,000		for sale	130,000	
Less			Less			Less		
Ending inventory	20,000		Ending inventory	20,000		Ending inventory	20,000	
Cost of goods sold		115,000	Cost of goods sold		120,000	Cost of goods sold		110,000
Gross margin		$ 20,000	Gross margin		$ 15,000	Gross margin		$ 25,000
Total for 2 years		$ 45,000	Total for 2 Years		$ 45,000	Total for 2 Years		$ 45,000

Ending Inventory Overstated

Case A in Column 2 shows the effect of a $5,000 overstatement of ending inventory in Year 1. Let us assume that this error is the result of miscounting the items in the ending inventory. Keep in mind that this is the only error in the example; all other items are correct. The effect of this error in Year 1 is to understate the cost of goods sold by $5,000, from $85,000 to $80,000. Thus there is a corresponding overstatement of the gross margin from $25,000 to $30,000. Generally, everything else being equal, the higher the overstatement of ending inventory is, the higher the overstatement of the gross margin.

In Year 2, the ending inventory from Year 1 becomes the beginning inventory. As a result, the beginning inventory in Year 2 is overstated by $5,000, from $15,000 to $20,000. Therefore goods available for sale and cost of goods sold are overstated by $5,000, and gross margin is understated by $5,000. Again, everything else being equal, the higher the overstatement of the beginning inventory is, the more understated the gross margin will be.

Comparing Columns 1 and 2, you can see that over a two-year period, the gross margin in both cases is $45,000. In effect, the one overstatement of $5,000 in the ending inventory of Year 1 and the beginning inventory of Year 2 cancel each other out, so that Year 2's ending inventory and retained earnings are correctly stated. However, there are important differences within each period. In Year 1, ending inventory and gross margin are overstated, and in Year 2, beginning inventory is overstated and gross margin is understated. Thus, although inventory errors can be self-correcting, there are serious allocation errors between the accounting periods that affect gross margin and income trends.

Ending Inventory Understated

Case B in Column 3 illustrates the effect of a $5,000 understatement of the ending inventory in Year 1. Again, keep in mind that this is the only error; all other items are correct. The effect of this error in Year 1 is to overstate cost of goods sold by $5,000, from $85,000 to $90,000, and to understate the gross margin by the same $5,000. Generally, all else being equal, understating the ending inventory will cause the gross margin to be understated.

In Year 2, the ending inventory from Year 1 becomes the beginning inventory. As a result, the cost of goods sold is understated by $5,000, from $115,000 to $110,000, and there is a corresponding $5,000 overstatement in the gross margin, from $20,000 to $25,000. Again, everything else being equal, an understatement in the beginning inventory will cause an overstatement in the gross margin.

Comparing Columns 1, 2, and 3, you can see that over a two-year period, the total gross margin in all three columns is $45,000. This emphasizes that a single inventory error is self-canceling over a consecutive two-year period, but that serious allocation errors occur each year. The data and the relationships in this illustration are summarized in Exhibit 9-3.

EXHIBIT 9–3

Effect of Inventory
Measurement Errors

Year 1	Cost of Goods Sold			Gross Margin		
Ending Inventory	Year 1	Year 2	Total	Year 1	Year 2	Total
Correct	$85,000	$115,000	$200,000	$25,000	$20,000	$45,000
Overstated $5,000	80,000	120,000	200,000	30,000	15,000	45,000
Understated $5,000	90,000	110,000	200,000	20,000	25,000	45,000

Relationships between Inventories and Gross Margins

1. Overstating the ending inventory overstates the gross margin.

2. Understating the ending inventory understates the gross margin.

3. Overstating the beginning inventory understates the gross margin.

4. Understating the beginning inventory overstates the gross margin.

■ DETERMINING THE COST OF ENDING INVENTORIES

In order to calculate the total cost of ending inventories, it is necessary first to determine the actual quantity of items on hand at the end of the period and then to attach a cost to these items. This is usually done by taking a physical inventory, most often at year-end. A physical inventory is required at least once a year, regardless of whether a firm uses the perpetual or the periodic inventory system. After the quantity of items is is determined, a particular cost flow pattern is assumed, and costs are attached to each item in the inventory. The total of the costs times the quantity equals the cost of the ending inventory.

Ending Inventory Quantities

Determining the actual quantity of items in the ending inventory usually requires a physical count. This count can take more than a day and often requires the firm to halt operations. For example, imagine the effort to count the ending inventory of a large department store. For this reason, some firms, especially those in the retail sales business, use estimation procedures, some of which will be discussed later in this chapter.

When the ending inventory is counted, the firm must ensure that all the items to which it has legal title are counted, including goods stored in public warehouses and goods in transit. Goods in transit include both sales on an FOB destination basis and purchases on an FOB shipping basis. Goods sold but still on hand should not be included.

Costs Included in the Ending Inventory

Under generally accepted accounting principles, the presumption is that inventories should be recorded at cost. The AICPA defines cost "as the price paid or consideration given to acquire an asset. As applied to inventories, cost means . . . the sum of the applicable expenditures and charges directly or indirectly incurred in bringing an article to its existing condition and location."[2] For the retailer, this means that acquisition costs include the purchase price less any cash discounts, plus other freight charges, insurance in transit, and sales taxes that are incurred to get the product ready for sale. However, costs such as freight charges and insurance are usually small, and the cost of trying to allocate them to individual items outweighs the benefit. Thus most firms will use the net invoice price when attaching a cost to an individual item in the ending inventory. These other costs then become part of cost of goods sold. As noted in Chapter 6, such indirect costs as selling and warehouse expenses are not included in the cost of inventory, because of the difficulty in reasonably allocating them to particular items. They are therefore treated as period expenses and reduce the current period's income.

After determining the quantity of the ending inventory and deciding what to include in the acquisition cost, a decision still must be made as to what cost to attach to the particular items on hand. In other words, the problem is how the accountant determines the acquisition cost or price paid for each item on hand when the items have been purchased at different times at different costs.

■ METHODS OF ATTACHING COSTS TO THE ENDING INVENTORY

At first glance, it would seem easy to determine the acquisition cost of each item that is sold or that is in ending inventory. However, imagine a firm that sells identical products, such as molded plastic chairs, that have been purchased at different prices and at different times through the year. Or imagine a large department store that sells a variety of products in different sizes and styles, again purchased at different prices. Even with a well-developed electronic record-keeping system, it is difficult, if not impossible, to determine the exact or actual acquisition price of each item remaining at the end of the year.

If all items are purchased at the same price, there will be no problem in determining the cost of either the ending inventory or the items sold. However, prices do not remain stable, so accountants have developed alternative methods to attach costs to inventory items. These methods use a cost flow assumption, rather than the actual physical flow. That is, an assumption is made that costs flow in four different patterns, regardless of how the goods physically move into and out of the firm. These cost flow assumptions are (1) first-in, first-out (FIFO), (2) last-in, first-out (LIFO), (3) average cost, and (4) in some limited situations, specific identification.

First-in, first out assumes that the costs attached to the first goods sold are the costs of the first goods purchased. In effect, the items are assumed to be sold in the order that they were purchased, and thus the cost of the ending inventory is from the most recent purchases. **Last-in, first-out** makes the opposite assumption about

[2] Ibid., Statement 3.

the flow of costs. Thus the costs attached to the last purchases made are assumed to be the cost of the first items sold. In effect, items are assumed to be sold in the opposite order from that in which they were purchased, and thus the cost of the ending inventory is that of the earliest purchases. **Average cost** attaches a weighted average cost to both the cost of goods sold and the ending inventory, determined by dividing the total cost of goods available for sale by the number of units available for sale. Finally, the **specific-identification method** determines the actual acquisition cost of each item in the ending inventory. Management is free to choose any one of these cost flow patterns, regardless of the physical flow of goods.

■ APPLYING DIFFERENT COST FLOW ASSUMPTIONS—PERIODIC SYSTEM

The data for the Cerf Company shown in Exhibit 9-4 will be used to demonstrate the computations required to apply the three cost flow assumptions and the specific identification method, using a periodic system. Three points should be made about this example. First, it is simplistic in that only six purchases are made during the year. However, the procedures in this example hold for more complex purchasing patterns. Second, the example uses a periodic inventory system, which for cost flow purposes does not require keeping track of the dates upon which sales are made. In a perpetual system (discussed later in this chapter), the dates of the sales are important. Third, each of these methods is an acceptable alternative under generally accepted accounting principles.

EXHIBIT 9–4

CERF COMPANY Data for Cost Flow Illustration Year Ended December 31, 1990			
	Unit	Acquisition Cost	Total Cost
Beginning inventory	500	$4.00	$ 2,000
Purchases during year			
January 24	200	4.10	820
March 18	400	4.20	1,680
May 5	300	4.50	1,350
July 31	350	4.50	1,575
September 27	400	4.60	1,840
November 29	250	4.70	1,175
Goods available for sale	2,400		$10,440
Less: Items in ending inventory	600		
Items sold	1,800		
Total dollar value of sales	$10,800		

First-in, First-out (FIFO)

Under the FIFO method, the costs attached to the first goods sold are assumed to be the costs of the first goods purchased, and the cost of the ending inventories consists of the costs of the latest goods purchased. FIFO refers to a means of determining the cost of goods sold during the period. However, when applying the FIFO method, the cost of the ending inventory is determined and the cost of the goods sold is derived from it.

Using the data in Exhibit 9-4, the cost of the ending inventory under FIFO is $2,785, and the cost of goods sold is $7,655. These figures are determined as shown in Exhibit 9-5. As Exhibit 9-5 indicates, the 600 units in the ending inventory consist of

EXHIBIT 9–5

Cost of goods available for sale			$10,440
Cost of Ending Inventory—FIFO			
Date Purchased	**Units**	**Acquisition Cost**	**Total Cost**
November 29	250	$4.70	$1,175
September 27	350	$4.60	1,610
Total	600		2,785
Cost of goods sold			$7,655

(1) the 250 units purchased on November 29 and (2) 350 of the 400 units purchased on September 27. The 50 items remaining from the September 27 purchase, as well as the units from prior purchases and the beginning inventory, are assumed to have been sold. However, we could calculate the cost of goods sold directly, as shown in Exhibit 9-6. This approach is rarely used, because firms sell many more goods than they have on hand at the end of the year, and so it is easier to count and cost what is on hand.

EXHIBIT 9–6

Date Purchased	Units	Acquisition Cost	Total Cost of Goods Sold
Beginning inventory	500	$4.00	$2,000
January 24	200	4.10	820
March 18	400	4.20	1,680
May 5	300	4.50	1,350
July 31	350	4.50	1,575
September 27	50	4.60	230
	1,800		$7,655

In 1991, the 1990 ending inventory of $2,785 becomes the beginning inventory. Although this inventory consists of two distinct layers of 250 and 350 units, respectively, each purchased at different prices, it is usually not necessary to maintain these layers. The inventory can be brought forward as 600 units at a cost of $2,785. The reason that these two layers can be merged is that under the FIFO method, these goods will be assumed to be the first ones sold in the next year. When they become part of the goods sold, the cost becomes part of a large pool in which the identity of the layers is not important.

Although most goods physically move on a FIFO basis, this is not a necessary criterion. For example, think of a large barrel of nails in a hardware store. As additional nails are added to the barrel, they are placed on top of the older nails, and when the nails are sold, the top nails are sold first. In this situation, the nails move in a last-in, first-out pattern. Nonetheless, the management of the hardware store is free to choose the FIFO method of pricing its inventories.

Last-in, First-out (LIFO)

Under the LIFO method of costing inventories, the cost attached to the last goods purchased is assumed to be the cost of the first goods sold. Therefore the cost of the ending inventory is from the earliest purchases.

Using data from Exhibit 9-4, the cost of the ending inventory under LIFO is $2,410, and the cost of goods sold is $8,030. These figures are determined as shown in Exhibit 9-7. As the exhibit indicates, the 600 units in the ending inventory are as-

EXHIBIT 9–7

Cost of goods available for sale			$10,440
Cost of Ending Inventory—LIFO			
Date Purchased	**Units**	**Acquisition Cost**	**Total Cost**
Beginning inventory	500	$4.00	$2,000
January 24	100	4.10	410
Total	600		2,410
Cost of goods sold			$8,030

sumed to be (1) 500 units from the beginning inventory and (2) 100 units from the January 24 purchase. As in the previous example, the cost of the goods sold could be calculated as $8,030 instead of deriving it by subtracting the ending inventory of $2,410 from the goods available for sale of $10,440.

When the LIFO method is used, it is important to maintain separate layers of costs of ending inventory. Therefore, in the illustration, the beginning inventory for the following period is carried forward in two layers comprising 500 units at $4.00 and 100 units at $4.10. If next year's ending inventory falls below 600 units, the 100 units represented by the January 24 purchase would be included in cost of goods sold before the 500 units represented by the beginning inventory. That is, inventory is decreased in the order that it was originally added, and because the January 24 layer was added last, under the LIFO method it is considered to be sold first.

Average Cost

Under the average-cost method, a weighted average cost per unit is calculated by dividing the total cost of the goods available for sale for the year by the total number of units available for sale during the year. For the Cerf Company, this calculation is:

$$\frac{\text{Cost of goods available for sale}}{\text{Units available for sale}} = \frac{\$10,440}{2,400} = \$4.35 \text{ average cost per unit}$$

This $4.35 cost per unit is applied to both the ending inventory and the goods available for sale as follows:

$$
\begin{aligned}
\text{Ending inventory} &= 600 \text{ units} \times \$4.35 &&= \$\ 2,610 \\
\text{Cost of goods sold} &= 1,800 \text{ units} \times \$4.35 &&= \underline{\ \ 7,830} \\
&&&\underline{\$10,440}
\end{aligned}
$$

In 1991, the beginning inventory consists of 600 units at an average cost of $2,610.

Specific Identification

In some situations, it is practical to determine the specific acquisition cost of the items remaining in the ending inventory. For example, an automobile dealer has records of the exact cost of every car sold and every car remaining in inventory, by using auto serial numbers. Other examples of such firms are furniture companies, antique stores, and coin and stamp dealers. Depending on the product, costs, and benefits, other firms might want to maintain such records.

To illustrate this method, assume that the Cerf Company is able to determine that the 600 items in the ending inventory are from the specific purchases listed in Exhibit 9-8 and thus computes the cost of the ending inventory to be $2,640 and the cost of goods sold to be $7,800.

EXHIBIT 9-8

Cost of goods available for sale			$10,440
Cost of Ending Inventory—Specific Identification			
Date Purchased	**Units**	**Acquisition Cost**	**Total Cost**
March 18	250	$4.20	$1,050
July 31	200	4.50	900
September 27	150	4.60	690
Total	600		2,640
Cost of goods sold			$7,800

In addition to the practical problems of keeping track of the costs of the specific items in the inventory, there are theoretical problems involved in using the specific-identification method. For example, assume that a firm produces only one product and that all its products are identical (fungible). Wheat and other commodities are examples of fungible goods. Buyers of such products are indifferent as to which specific item or lot they buy, so the firm's management is free to sell the specific lot(s) it desires. That is, the buyer of 10 ounces of gold does not care which lot the gold comes from, as long as all the gold is of the same quality. Thus the firm's management can sell the gold from any lot it chooses.

Management is able to manipulate income by selling lots with certain acquisition costs. To demonstrate this point, assume that the management of the Cerf Company wants to maximize its income for the current year. In this situation, the firm sells those goods with the lowest acquisition costs (that is, the items purchased at $4.00 and $4.10). Next year, if management decides to minimize its income, it will sell those products with the highest acquisition prices. Therefore it has more ability to manipulate the firm's income.

■ APPLYING DIFFERENT COST FLOW ASSUMPTIONS—PERPETUAL SYSTEM

Point-of-sale devices and computers have made the use of the perpetual system more popular. This section takes the data from the Cerf Company and applies the FIFO, LIFO, and average-cost methods under a perpetual inventory assumption. With the perpetual system, the date of the sale is important, so this information is included in the basic data shown in Exhibit 9-9.

EXHIBIT 9-9

CERF COMPANY DATA			
Date	**Purchase**	**Sales**	**Balance**
Beginning inventory	500 @ $4.00		500 units
January 24	200 @ $4.10		700 units
March 1		400 units	300 units
March 18	400 @ $4.20		700 units
May 5	300 @ $4.50		1,000 units
May 29		650 units	350 units
July 31	350 @ $4.50		700 units
September 27	400 @ $4.60		1,100 units
October 9		750 units	350 units
November 29	250 @ $4.70		600 units

To review, the main difference between the periodic and the perpetual systems is the timing of the recognition of the cost of goods sold. Under the perpetual system, an entry to recognize cost of goods sold is made at the point of sale. Application of the various cost flow methods will be different under the perpetual system. To illustrate the application of the perpetual system, refer to the January 24 purchase of inventory on account and the March 1 sale on account. Assume that each unit is sold for $6. Under the perpetual system, the entries to record this inventory purchase and sale (assuming FIFO) are:

January 24	Inventory (200 × $4.10)	820	
	Accounts Payable		820
	To record inventory purchase on account.		
March 1	Accounts Receivable (400 × $6)	2,400	
	Sales		2,400
	To record sales on account.		
March 1	Cost of Goods Sold (400 × $4)	1,600	
	Inventory		1,600
	To record cost of goods sold.		

FIFO Perpetual

When the FIFO perpetual system is used, the inventory balance must be determined after each purchase or sale. The earliest layers are assumed to have been sold first. To illustrate the application of FIFO perpetual, refer to the perpetual inventory record for the data from the Cerf Company in Exhibit 9-10. After the purchase on January 24, the total inventory of $2,820 now contains two layers: 500 units at $4.00 (the beginning inventory) and 200 units at $4.10 (the January 24 purchase). When the cost of goods sold for the March 1 sale is recorded, 400 units from the beginning inventory are assumed to have been sold (using FIFO). Thus cost of goods sold is recorded at $1,600. The remaining inventory of $1,220 now contains the two layers:

100 units (beginning inventory) @ $4.00 = $ 400
200 units (January 24 purchase) @   4.10 =   820
                                      $1,220

EXHIBIT 9–10

FIFO Perpetual												
	Purchase			**Sales**			**Balance**					
Date	**Units**	**Acqui-sition Cost**	**Total**	**Units**	**Acqui-sition Cost**	**Total**		**Units**	**Acqui-sition Cost**		**Total**	
Beginning inventory								500	@ $4.00	=	$2,000	
January 24	200	@ $4.10 =	$ 820					500	@ $4.00	=	$2,000	
								200	@ $4.10	=	820	
								700			$2,820	
March 1				400	@ $4.00 =	$1,600		100	@ $4.00	=	$ 400	
								200	@ $4.10	=	820	
								300			$1,220	
											(continued)	

EXHIBIT 9–10   continued

Date	Purchase Units	Purchase Acqui-sition Cost	Purchase Total	Sales Units	Sales Acqui-sition Cost	Sales Total	Balance Units	Balance Acqui-sition Cost	Balance Total
March 18	400 @	$4.20 =	$1,680				100 @ 200 @ 400 @ ___700	$4.00 = $4.10 = $4.20 =	$ 400 820 1,680 _____ $2,900
May 5	300 @	$4.50 =	$1,350				100 @ 200 @ 400 @ 300 @ ___1,000	$4.00 = $4.10 = $4.20 = $4.50 =	$ 400 820 1,680 1,350 _____ $4,250
May 29				100 @ 200 @ 350 @ ___650	$4.00 = $4.10 = $4.20 =	$ 400 820 1,470	50 @ 300 @ ___350	$4.20 = $4.50 =	$ 210 1,350 _____ $1,560
July 31	350 @	$4.50 =	$1,575				50 @ 300 @ 350 @ ___700	$4.20 = $4.50 = $4.50 =	$ 210 1,350 1,575 _____ $3,135
September 27	400 @	$4.60 =	$1,840				50 @ 300 @ 350 @ 400 @ ___1,100	$4.20 = $4.50 = $4.50 = $4.60 =	$ 210 1,350 1,575 1,840 _____ $4,975
October 9				50 @ 300 @ 350 @ 50 @ ___750	$4.20 = $4.50 = $4.50 = $4.60 =	$ 210 1,350 1,575 230	350 @	$4.60 =	$1,610
November 29	250 @	$4.70 =	$1,175				350 @ 250 @	$4.60 = $4.70 =	$1,610 1,175
Total			$8,440			$7,655	600		$2,785

FIFO perpetual results in the same inventory cost as does FIFO periodic, because the first goods acquired are assumed to have been sold first. This order remains the same throughout the period; therefore, whether the cost of goods sold is recorded when the sales are made or at the end of the period, the result will be the same.

LIFO Perpetual

Unlike FIFO, LIFO perpetual results in a different ending inventory than LIFO periodic, because LIFO perpetual matches each sale with the immediately preceding LIFO layers, whereas LIFO periodic matches sales after all purchases for the period have been made. The inventory record for the Cerf Company on a LIFO perpetual basis is presented in Exhibit 9-11.

EXHIBIT 9–11

	LIFO Perpetual									
	Purchase			Sales			Balance			
Date	Units	Acqui-sition Cost	Total	Units	Acqui-sition Cost	Total	Units	Acqui-sition Cost	Total	
Beginning inventory							500 @ $4.00 =		$2,000	
January 24	200 @ $4.10 =		$ 820				500 @ $4.00 =		$2,000	
							200 @ $4.10 =		820	
							700		$2,820	
March 1				200 @ $4.10 =		$ 820	300 @ $4.00 =		$1,200	
				200 @ $4.00 =		800				
				400						
March 18	400 @ $4.20 =		$1,680				300 @ $4.00 =		$1,200	
							400 @ $4.20 =		1,680	
							700		$2,880	
May 5	300 @ $4.50 =		$1,350				300 @ $4.00 =		$1,200	
							400 @ $4.20 =		1,680	
							300 @ $4.50 =		1,350	
							1,000		$4,230	
May 29				300 @ $4.50 =		$1,350	300 @ $4.00 =		$1,200	
				350 @ $4.20 =		1,470	50 @ $4.20 =		210	
				650			350		$1,410	
July 31	350 @ $4.50 =		$1,575				300 @ $4.00 =		$1,200	
							50 @ $4.20 =		210	
							350 @ $4.50 =		1,575	
							700		$2,985	
September 27	400 @ $4.60 =		$1,840				300 @ $4.00 =		$1,200	
							50 @ $4.20 =		210	
							350 @ $4.50 =		1,575	
							400 @ $4.60 =		1,840	
							1,100		$4,825	
October 9				400 @ $4.60 =		$1,840	300 @ $4.00 =		$1,200	
				350 @ $4.50 =		1,575	50 @ $4.20 =		210	
				750			350		$1,410	
November 29	250 @ $4.70 =		$1,175				300 @ $4.00 =		$1,200	
							50 @ $4.20 =		210	
							250 @ $4.70 =		1,175	
Total			$8,440			$7,855	600		$2,585	

After the January 24 purchase, there are now two layers: 500 units at $4.00 and 200 units at $4.10. Under LIFO perpetual, the March 1 sale first wipes out 200 units from the January 24 layer, the last layer added. The remaining 200 units sold are assumed to come from the beginning inventory, thus reducing that layer to 300 units at $4. At this point, the total inventory is $1,200. After the next purchase on March 18, an additional layer of 400 units at $4.20 is added. On May 5, another layer of 300 units at $4.50 is added. Because this is the last layer added, the 650 units sold on May 29 are first assumed to have come out of the May 5 layer and then from the March 18 layer. At the end of the year, the cost of the ending inventory under LIFO perpetual is $2,585, compared with $2,410 under LIFO periodic. Cost of goods sold under LIFO perpetual equals $7,855.

Average-cost Perpetual

Average-cost perpetual is often referred to as a *moving-average* method. Under this method, a new average must be computed after each purchase. The perpetual record using the weighted moving-average method is shown in Exhibit 9-12. To illustrate how the weighted average is calculated, refer to the January 24 purchase. After this purchase, a new moving average of $4.03 per unit is computed as follows:

$$
\begin{array}{llll}
500 \text{ units} & @ & \$4.00 & = \$2,000 \\
\underline{200} \text{ units} & @ & 4.10 & = \underline{\ \ \ 820} \\
700 \text{ units} & & & = \$2,820
\end{array}
$$

$$
\text{Average cost per unit} = \frac{\$2,820}{700} = \$4.03 \text{ (rounded)}
$$

On the perpetual record, all per-unit costs are rounded off to two decimal points, and the total inventory costs are rounded off to whole dollars.

When the March 1 sale is recorded, Cost of Goods Sold is debited for 400 units at $4.03 per unit, or $1,612. This leaves 300 units in the ending inventory at an average

EXHIBIT 9–12

	Average-cost Perpetual									
	Purchase			**Sales**			**Balance**			
Date	Units	Acqui-sition Cost	Total	Units	Acqui-sition Cost	Total	Units	Acqui-sition Cost		Total
Beginning inventory							500	@ $4.00	=	$2,000
January 24	200 @ $4.10		= $ 820				700	@ $4.03*	=	$2,821
March 1				400 @ $4.03		= $1,612	300	@ $4.03	=	$1,209
March 18	400 @ $4.20		= $1,680				700	@ $4.13	=	$2,889
May 5	300 @ $4.50		= $1,350				1,000	@ $4.24	=	$4,240
May 29				650 @ $4.24		= $2,756	350	@ $4.24	=	$1,484
July 31	350 @ $4.50		= $1,575				700	@ $4.37	=	$3,059
September 27	400 @ $4.60		= $1,840				1,100	@ $4.45	=	$4,895
October 9				750 @ $4.45		= $3,338	350	@ $4.45	=	$1,558
November 29	250 @ $4.70		= $1,175				600	@ $4.55	=	$2,733
Total			$8,440			$7,706				

*All average-cost figures rounded off to two decimal places.

cost per unit of $4.03, or a total of $1,209. After the next purchase of 400 units at $4.20 on March 18, a new moving average must be calculated, as follows:

$$
\begin{array}{ll}
300 \text{ units @ } \$4.03 = & \$1,209 \\
\underline{400} \text{ units @ } \ \ 4.20 = & \underline{\ \ 1,680} \\
\underline{\underline{700}} \text{ units} \qquad \ \ \ = & \underline{\underline{\$2,889}}
\end{array}
$$

$$
\text{Average cost per unit} = \frac{\$2,889}{700} = \$4.13
$$

Under the moving-average method, the ending inventory is $2,733, versus $2,610 under the average-cost periodic. Cost of goods sold equals $7,706 under the perpetual system.

■ COMPARING THE METHODS

Exhibit 9-13 is a comparison of the effect of the FIFO, average cost, and LIFO cost flow assumptions on ending inventory, cost of goods sold, and gross margin for the Cerf Company for both the periodic and the perpetual systems.[3] The highest gross margin and ending inventory and lowest cost of goods sold result when FIFO is used; the lowest gross margin and ending inventory and highest cost of goods sold result when LIFO is used. Average cost falls between these two extremes. This is because the acquisition price of the inventory consistently rose during the year, from $4.10 to $4.70. This example was deliberately constructed to reflect rising prices, which are more common than falling prices in today's economy. However, in some sectors of the economy, such as electronics, prices have been falling. In this case, the income statement and balance sheet effects of LIFO and FIFO would be the opposite of the rising-price situation. That is, LIFO would produce the highest gross margin and the highest ending inventory cost.

EXHIBIT 9-13

CERF COMPANY **Comparison of Three Cost Flow Assumptions**						
	Periodic			**Perpetual**		
	FIFO	**Average-cost**	**LIFO**	**FIFO**	**Average-cost**	**LIFO**
Sales	$10,800	$10,800	$10,800	$10,800	$10,800	$10,800
Cost of goods sold	7,655	7,830	8,030	7,655	7,706	7,855
Gross margin	$ 3,145	$ 2,970	$ 2,770	$ 3,145	$ 3,094	$ 2,945
Ending inventory	$ 2,785	$ 2,610	$ 2,410	$ 2,785	$ 2,733	$ 2,585

Rising Prices and FIFO

In a period of rising prices, FIFO produces the highest gross margin and the highest ending inventory. The high gross margin is produced because the earliest and thus the lowest costs are allocated to cost of goods sold. Thus cost of goods sold is the lowest of the three inventory costing methods, and gross margin is correspondingly the highest of the three methods. Ending inventory reflects the highest cost under FIFO be-

[3]Specific identification has not been included in this comparison because of its limited use.

cause the latest and highest costs are allocated to ending inventory. These results are logical, given the relationship between ending inventories and gross margin.

Many accountants approve of using FIFO because ending inventories are recorded at costs that approximate their current acquisition or replacement cost. Thus inventories are realistically valued on the firm's balance sheet. On the other hand, accountants criticize FIFO because it matches the earliest cost against current sales and results in the highest gross margin. Some accountants argue that these profits are overstated because, in order to stay in business, a going concern must replace its inventory at current acquisition prices or replacement costs. These overstated profits are often referred to as **inventory profits**.

To illustrate the concept of inventory profits, assume that a firm enters into the following transactions:

- January 2: Purchases one unit of inventory at $60.
- December 15: Purchases a second unit of inventory at $85.
- December 31: Sells one unit at $100. Current replacement cost of inventory, $85.

On a FIFO basis, the firm reports a gross margin of $40 ($100 − $60). However, if it is to stay in business, the firm will not have $40 available to cover operating expenses. This is because it must replace the inventory at a cost of at least $85. Thus, in reality, the firm has only $15 ($100 − $85) available to cover its operating expenses. The $25 difference between the $85 replacement cost and the $60 historical cost is the inventory profit and is considered a holding gain that is caused by the increase in the acquisition price of the inventory between the time that the firm purchased the item and when it was sold. This holding gain is not available to cover operating costs because it must be used to repurchase inventory at higher prices.

Rising Prices and LIFO

In a period of rising prices, LIFO results in the lowest gross margin and the lowest ending inventory. The low gross margin results when the latest and highest costs are allocated to cost of goods sold. Thus cost of goods sold is the highest of the three inventory costing methods, and gross margin is the lowest. Also, under LIFO, the ending inventory is recorded at the lowest cost of the three methods, because the earliest and lowest prices are allocated to it. In fact, if a company had switched to LIFO 20 years ago, the original LIFO layers, if unsold, would be costed at 20-year-old prices.

LIFO has the opposite effect from FIFO on the balance sheet and income statement. Consequently, LIFO is criticized because the inventory cost on the balance sheet is often unrealistically low. Therefore working capital, the current ratio, and current assets tend to be understated. This possible effect can be significant, as illustrated by the following excerpt from a recent annual report of Albertsons, a Western United States grocery chain.

INVENTORIES

Approximately 95% of the Company's inventories are valued using the last-in, first-out (LIFO) method. If the first-in, first-out (FIFO) method had been used, inventories would have been $114,485,000, $97,081,000 and $88,086,000 higher at the end of 1988, 1987 and 1986. Net earnings would have been higher by $10,986,000 ($.16 per share) in 1988, $5,280,000 ($.07 per share) in 1987 and $4,449,000 ($.07 per share) in 1986. The replacement cost of inventories valued at LIFO approximates FIFO cost.

Physical counts of all inventories were made by the Company at year end. Retail store inventories comprise approximately 71% of total inventories at February 2, 1989.

Many accountants argue, however, that LIFO provides a more realistic income figure because it eliminates a substantial portion of inventory profit. If you refer to the transactions on page 315, you will see that on a LIFO basis the firm's gross margin is $15, because the December 15 purchase is matched against the $100 sale. In this case, the acquisition price of the inventory did not change between the last purchase on December 15 and its sale on December 31, so all the inventory profits are eliminated. In reality, LIFO will not eliminate all inventory profits but will substantially reduce them.

In summary, in a period of rising prices, FIFO and LIFO have opposite effects on the balance sheet and income statement. LIFO usually provides a realistic income statement at the expense of the balance sheet. Conversely, FIFO provides a realistic balance sheet at the expense of the income statement. In a period of falling prices, the opposite is true. In either case, average cost will fall between FIFO and LIFO.

■ HOW CURRENT COST CAN ALLEVIATE THE PROBLEM

The current-cost method can alleviate the need for a cost flow assumption and can thus help solve the problem of choosing between a realistic income statement and a realistic balance sheet. In general, current cost is the cost of currently acquiring an item. Cost of goods sold is recorded at the current cost of the item at the time of its resale. Thus the gross margin figure, which is the difference between sales and the current cost of goods sold, represents income available to the firm to cover operating expenses after maintaining its ability to purchase new inventory. On the balance sheet, ending inventory is recorded at the current cost at the statement date. The difference between the current cost of the ending inventory and its historical cost is considered an unrealized holding gain. Thus the figures on the income statement and balance sheet represent realistic amounts.

Current-cost accounting is not a generally accepted accounting principle for primary financial statements. Many accountants feel that the information is difficult to obtain and does not meet the reliability criterion. However, because of the perceived relevance of these data to present and potential investors and creditors, the FASB encourages certain companies to disclose selected current-cost data on a supplemental basis. In regard to inventories, FASB Statement No. 33, as amended by Statement No. 89, suggests that firms disclose income from continuing operations on a current-cost basis and the current-cost amounts of inventory and property, plant, and equipment at the end of the year. Current-cost accounting is examined in detail in Chapter 18.

■ CHOOSING AMONG GENERALLY ACCEPTED ACCOUNTING PRINCIPLES

The choice a firm's management has in selecting among alternative inventory cost flow assumptions is representative of the choice management has in general in selecting among acceptable accounting principles. For example, there are several acceptable depreciation methods, different methods of estimating uncollectible accounts, and two ways of accounting for construction contracts. The choice involves not only financial reporting considerations but also tax considerations, and in many instances management can choose one method for tax purposes and another for financial reporting purposes.

Even after selecting an accounting method, management can still change methods in future years, even though the comparability characteristic of accounting information requires that accounting methods and principles be applied consistently across accounting periods. The Accounting Principles Board noted this concept when discussing accounting changes:

> In the preparation of financial statements there is a presumption that an accounting principle once adopted should not be changed in accounting for events and transactions of a similar type. Consistent use

of accounting principles from one accounting period to another enhances the utility of financial statements to users by facilitating analysis and understanding of comparative accounting data.[4]

When a change in accounting principles is made, the auditor's report must be modified to indicate the nature of the change and the fact that the financial statements are not consistent with those of preceding years. For tax purposes, most accounting changes require the approval of the IRS commissioner and also cannot be made at will.

■ MOTIVATION FOR SELECTING CERTAIN ACCOUNTING METHODS

The motivation of management is often straightforward when selecting accounting methods or principles for tax purposes: to postpone or reduce current tax payments. By doing so, the cash flows to the firm are increased and stockholders' wealth is increased. The selection of accounting principles for external financial reporting is considerably more complex. Not all managements have the same motivation. Considerations such as increasing the bottom line, enhancing management's own compensation, and providing reliable financial reports all play a part. The management of a public company may also have different pressures and motivations from those of the owner-manager of a private company.

The motivations in selecting accounting principles for tax purposes may conflict with those in selecting accounting principles for financial reporting purposes, because in many cases, management wishes to reduce taxable income while at the same time increasing reported accounting income. In many cases, however, this is not a problem: Management can select one principle for tax purposes and another for financial reporting purposes. Yet, when deciding whether to use FIFO or LIFO, this is not the case.

■ SELECTING FIFO OR LIFO

The Internal Revenue Code contains a provision called the LIFO conformity rule, which requires a company to use LIFO for financial reporting purposes if LIFO is used for tax purposes. This is one of the few situations in which the choice of accounting principles for tax and financial reporting purposes cannot be made independently. This conformity rule applies only to LIFO. That is, a firm can use FIFO for external financial report purposes and average cost for tax purposes. This rule was inserted in the Code by Congress in order to keep businesses from reporting low earnings to the government while at the same time reporting high earnings to stockholders and other financial statement users.

This conformity rule has important implications, given the tax effects of LIFO. To demonstrate these effects, assume the following facts for the Golden Bear Company at year-end 1990:

Sales	$1,500,000
Cost of goods sold—FIFO	800,000
Cost of goods sold—LIFO	1,100,000
All other operating expenses	100,000
Tax rate	25%

The summary income statements based on both FIFO and LIFO are shown in Exhibit 9-14. If the firm uses the LIFO method, its income before taxes will be reduced by $300,000, the difference between the FIFO and the LIFO inventories. Thus taxes using the LIFO method are only $75,000, versus $150,000 using the FIFO method.

[4]American Institute of Certified Public Accountants, Accounting Principles Board, Opinion No. 20, *Accounting Changes* (New York: AICPA, 1971), par. 15.

EXHIBIT 9-14

GOLDEN BEAR COMPANY Summary Income Statement Year-end 1990		
	FIFO	**LIFO**
Sales	$1,500,000	$1,500,000
Cost of goods sold	800,000	1,100,000
Gross margin on sales	700,000	400,000
Operating expenses	100,000	100,000
Income before taxes	600,000	300,000
Taxes—25%	150,000	75,000
Net income	$ 450,000	$ 225,000

This represents a cash savings of $75,000, or 25% of the $300,000 difference between FIFO and LIFO inventories.

Given the conformity rule and the tax effects of LIFO, what inventory cost method should management select? In a period of rising prices, because LIFO reduces the current period's taxable income and taxes and thus increases cash flows to the firm, many accountants argue that LIFO should be selected, even at the expense of lower reported earnings. The argument is made that increased cash flows enhance stockholders' wealth, even though reported earnings are lower. Furthermore, many financial analysts have begun to evaluate a firm's **quality of earnings**. For example, in a period of rising prices, if a firm chooses FIFO and other accounting principles that tend to increase reported earnings, analysts may consider the quality of such earnings not to be as high as earnings determined by more conservative accounting principles. Indeed, accounting research has generally indicated that the stock market is not fooled by reported earnings and recognizes the value of the increased cash flows available to LIFO firms versus those available to FIFO firms.

This discussion is not meant to imply that all firms should use LIFO or should switch to LIFO. As will be seen later, there are practical and economic reasons that do not make LIFO advantageous for all firms. However, the number of firms using LIFO has grown in recent years, and in fact, the 1986 AICPA survey shown in Exhibit 9-15 indicates that 66% of the 600 firms sampled used LIFO.[5]

EXHIBIT 9-15

AICPA Inventory Cost								
	1986		**1985**		**1984**		**1983**	
Method	**Number**	**%**	**Number**	**%**	**Number**	**%**	**Number**	**%**
LIFO	393	66	402	67	400	67	408	68
FIFO	383	64	381	64	377	63	366	61
Average cost	223	37	223	37	223	37	235	39
Other	53	9	48	8	54	9	52	9
Totals*	1,052		1,054		1,054		1,061	

*Totals and percentages are more than 600 and 100%, respectively, because many firms use more than one method of inventory costing. For example, a firm with three different classes of inventory may elect to use a different cost flow method for each class. (Percentages based on total sample of 600.)

Although an increasing number of firms use LIFO, some have changed from LIFO to FIFO. Chrysler Corporation's 1970 change from LIFO to FIFO is an example. Esti-

[5] AICPA, *Accounting Trends and Techniques,* 41st ed. (New York: AICPA, 1987), p. 126. Reprinted with permission of the AICPA.

mates indicate that this change cost Chrysler $75 million in future taxes. Why did Chrysler make a change that might increase its taxes by $75 million? The effect of this change was to decrease the current year's losses and to increase the current ratio and retained earnings. To a management concerned with short-term goals of decreasing losses and meeting loan agreements related to maintaining a current ratio and debt-to-equity ratio, such a change may seem worthwhile, even at the expense of short- and long-run cash flows.

■ ISSUES RELATED TO LIFO

A number of issues and problems related to LIFO can decrease its advantages. Some of the more important ones are the effects of falling prices, LIFO liquidation, purchasing behavior, and inventory turnover.

Falling Prices

When prices decrease, LIFO shows higher earnings, and higher taxes result. This is because the latest and, in this case, the lowest prices are allocated to cost of goods sold. In some industries, prices are volatile and thus unpredictable. For example, in 1974 a number of sugar companies changed to LIFO as sugar prices rose at a rapid pace. By switching to LIFO, these companies reduced their taxable income and their resulting tax payments. However, in 1975, sugar prices declined. The result of this decline was an increase in earnings and tax payments over what they would have been on a FIFO basis.

LIFO Liquidation

The potential of **LIFO liquidation** is a major concern to LIFO users. As noted, at least a portion of the inventories costed under LIFO is priced at the firm's early purchase prices, which might go back to the date when LIFO was adopted. LIFO liquidation occurs when a firm sells in any year more units than it purchases. Thus LIFO layers that have been built up in the past are liquidated—that is, included in the current period's cost of goods sold. In effect, a firm is apt to sell units that may have 1950 or 1960 costs attached to them. The result is a lower cost of goods sold, higher gross margin, and higher taxes. Although firms can often plan for LIFO liquidation, events sometimes happen that are beyond management's control. For example, a supplier's strike or an unanticipated demand can cause unplanned LIFO liquidation. The effect of a LIFO liquidation is illustrated by the following excerpt of a footnote taken from a recent financial statement of Burlington Northern, Inc.:

> Inventories valued using the LIFO method comprised approximately 65% of consolidated inventories at September 27, 1986 and 76% at September 28, 1985.
>
> The 1986 decrease in excess of average cost over LIFO was due to the liquidation of LIFO inventory quantities carried at lower costs prevailing in prior years, principally due to the sale of the company's Domestics division, and lower cotton prices. The effect of the liquidation of LIFO inventory quantities was to increase fiscal 1986 net earnings by approximately $8,875,000 or 32 cents per share of which $6,003,000 or 21 cents per share was related to the sale of the company's Domestics division.

Purchasing Behavior

The use of LIFO, especially in connection with the periodic inventory method, offers management a certain degree of flexibility to manipulate profits. From management's perspective, this certainly is not a problem, but critics of LIFO point to this ability as a disadvantage of LIFO. In any event, by timing purchases at year-end, management is able to determine what costs will be allocated to cost of goods. Remember that under LIFO, the latest purchase will be included in cost of goods sold. Thus, by making a purchase at year-end, the cost of that purchase will be included in cost of goods sold. A purchase at the beginning of the next year, however, could end up in next year's ending inventory as a new LIFO layer if the units purchased during this year exceed the units sold.

Inventory Turnover

Inventory turnover, or the rate at which a company sells its inventory, can affect the differential between FIFO and LIFO. When a company has a high turnover rate, the advantage of LIFO over FIFO is not as great, because with a high turnover rate, a FIFO-based cost of goods will approximate a LIFO-based or current-cost cost of goods sold. Thus inventory profits usually found in connection with FIFO are substantially decreased.

In summary, the selection of accounting principles for both financial reporting and tax purposes is an important management decision. In the LIFO-versus-FIFO case, it is even more important because of the LIFO conformity rule, whereby management is forced to consider the utility of increased cash flows versus the effect LIFO will have on the balance sheet and income statement.

■ INVENTORY VALUATION—LOWER OF COST OR MARKET

The preceding paragraphs explained how to determine the cost of ending inventory. As noted, under generally accepted accounting principles, the presumption is that inventories will be recorded at cost. If, however, the utility of the goods in inventory is not as great as their cost, the goods must be written down to the **lower of cost or market**. Although this is a violation of the historical-cost principle, accountants feel that losses should be recorded as soon as they become evident. Thus, in this case, the concept of conservatism takes precedence over the historical-cost convention. Approximately 90% of the 600 companies surveyed by the AICPA in 1986 reported their inventory at the lower of cost or market.[6]

■ THE THEORY OF LOWER OF COST OR MARKET

In applying the lower-of-cost-or-market rule, cost is determined by one of the cost methods; market, in this case, generally means replacement cost, or the cost to purchase a similar item. The use of lower of cost or market is based on the theory that if replacement cost decreases during the current period, present sales price will ultimately decrease. Because accountants feel that all losses should be recognized when they occur, this loss should be recognized in the period that it occurs—that is, when the price declines—not in a later period, when the item is eventually sold.

To illustrate the theory behind the lower-of-cost-or-market rule, assume the following facts:

1. During Year 1, the Shanken Company purchases one item of inventory for $80. The normal selling price is $100, which represents a gross margin percentage of 20%.

2. The item is held during the entire year. However, replacement cost falls 10%, from $80 to $72. No other transactions take place during the year.

3. During Year 2, the item is sold for $90.

The analysis in Exhibit 9-16 shows the effect on reported earnings over a two-year period, both with and without the application of the lower-of-cost-or-market rule. This example assumes that when the replacement cost dropped 10%, or $8 from $80

---

[6]American Institute of Certified Public Accountants, *Accounting Trends and Techniques*, 41st ed. (New York: AICPA, 1987), p. 127.

EXHIBIT 9–16

SHANKEN COMPANY
Illustration of Lower of Cost or Market

Case 1: With the Application of Lower of Cost or Market

Year 1		Year 2		Total
Sales	$0	Sales	$90	$90
Loss on write-down of inventory	8[a]	Cost of goods sold	72	80
Gross margin	($8)	Gross margin	$18	$10

Case 2: Without the Application of Lower of Cost or Market

Year 1		Year 2		Total
Sales	$0	Sales	$90	$90
Loss on write-down of inventory	0	Cost of goods sold	80	80
Gross margin	$0	Gross margin	$10	$10

[a] This inventory write-down would be accomplished by the following journal entry:

Loss on Decline in Market		
Value of Inventory	8	
Inventory		8

to $72, there was a corresponding decrease of 10%, or $10 from $100 to $90, in the item's selling price.

Case 1 shows the effect of applying the lower-of-cost-or-market rule. In Year 1, there is a reported loss of $8 due to the decline in the replacement cost. In Year 2, when the actual sale takes place, there is an $18 gross margin on sales. This $18 gross margin represents a 20% gross margin percentage, the normal gross margin percentage that the Shanken Company earns. The result of applying the lower of cost or market is to force the company to take a loss in Year 1, the year of the price decline, but it allows the company to earn its normal gross margin percentage in future years. Over the two-year period, the combined income is $10.

Case 2 shows the effect of not applying the lower-of-cost-or-market rule. There is no income or loss in Year 1; the entire effect is felt in Year 2, when the sale takes place. In Year 2, the gross margin falls to $10, and the gross margin percentage falls to 11%. Over a two-year period, combined income is $10, the same as it is in Case 1. Thus the application of lower of cost or market changes the allocation of income within the two-year period but does not change the combined income.

This illustration is based on the assumption that a decrease in the replacement cost of the item will result in a corresponding decrease in the sales price. In reality, however, that one-for-one relationship does not always hold. For example, assume that although the replacement cost of the inventory item held by the Shanken Company drops 10%, there is little or no change in the sales price. To apply lower of cost or market in this situation would understate income in Year 1 and overstate income in Year 2; thus it would be an improper application of conservatism. Lower of cost or market must be applied with caution.

■ THE APPLICATION OF LOWER OF COST OR MARKET

The application of lower of cost or market is a two-step process. In the first step, **market**, defined as replacement cost, is determined. This can usually be done by examining vendors' invoices at the end of the year. In the second step, market or replacement cost is compared with cost, and if necessary, the inventory is reduced to the lower of cost or market (LCM). Under generally accepted accounting principles, this comparison can be made on (1) an item-by-item basis, (2) a group-of-items basis, or (3) the inventory as a whole.

The LCM comparison on all three bases is shown in Exhibit 9-17. When the item-by-item basis is used, individual comparisons of cost to market for each item must be made. This results in an LCM value of $24,000. Under the group basis, the inventory is divided into a luxury group and a standard group, and the comparison is then made by the total of each group. For example, in the luxury group the cost of $22,500 is compared with the market of $22,000, so the LCM of the group is determined to be $22,000. The same comparison is then made for the standard group, and its LCM is $2,750. This results in a total LCM value of $24,750. On a whole basis, the cost and the market of the entire inventory are compared, resulting in an LCM value of $24,800.

EXHIBIT 9–17

		Per Unit		Total		LCM		
	Quantity	Cost	Market	Cost	Market	Item-by-item	Group	Total Inventory
Lower of Cost of Market (LCM)								
Luxury group								
Item A	100	$50	$40	$ 5,000	$ 4,000	$ 4,000		
Item B	250	70	72	17,500	18,000	17,500		
Total luxury group				$22,500	$22,000		$22,000	
Standard group								
Item C	50	$25	$20	$ 1,250	$ 1,000	1,000		
Item D	100	15	18	1,500	1,800	1,500		
Total standard group				$ 2,750	$ 2,800		2,750	
Total inventory				$25,250	$24,800			$24,800
Inventory value—item by item						$24,000		
Inventory value—group basis							$24,750	
Inventory value—total								$24,800

Comparing all three methods, it is clear that the item-by-item method is the most conservative; that is, it results in the lowest inventory value. This is because increases in the value of one item cannot offset decreases in other items, as is the case under the group and whole inventory methods.

■ LOWER OF COST OR MARKET AND INCOME TAXES

The Internal Revenue Code contains rules pertaining to the use of lower of cost or market for federal tax purposes. Two of these provisions differentiate the use of lower of cost or market for tax purposes from financial reporting purposes. First, for tax purposes, only FIFO (not LIFO) can be used in conjunction with lower of cost or market. For generally accepted accounting purposes, however, LIFO combined with lower of cost or market is a valid method. Second, for tax purposes, lower of cost or market can be applied only on an item-by-item basis. The group or total inventory method cannot be used.

■ USING INVENTORY DATA FOR DECISION MAKING

Because inventories have a substantial effect on both the balance sheet and the income statement, they offer important data to investors and managers in evaluating a firm's financial performance and position. Two ratios are often used in this evaluation—the gross margin percentage and the inventory turnover. As noted, the gross margin percentage is gross margin on sales divided by sales and has several uses, including estimating inventories (which is discussed in the Special Supplement).

Inventory turnover indicates how quickly a firm is able to sell its inventory. In effect, the quicker the inventory turns over, the less cash the firm has tied up in inventory and the less need there is for inventory financing. Furthermore, the quicker the turnover is, the less obsolescence or spoilage. However, too quick a turnover may indicate that certain items are not available to meet consumer demand, and sales may be lost as a result. The optimal inventory turnover therefore depends on the firm's characteristics and policies.

The inventory turnover is computed by dividing cost of goods sold by average inventory. Generally, the average inventory is determined by taking the average of the beginning and ending inventories. For example, if a firm had cost of goods sold of $1.2 million and average inventories of $100,000, the inventory would turn over 12 times during the year, calculated as follows:

$$\frac{\text{Cost of goods sold}}{\text{Average inventory}} = \frac{\$1,200,000}{\$100,000} = 12 \text{ times}$$

If the inventory turnover is divided into 365 days, the result will be the average number of days that the inventory is on hand. In this case the average time is about 30 days, or one month.

When evaluating inventory data and ratios, remember that they are sensitive to the cost flow assumption adopted. For example, inventory turnover under LIFO is apt to be higher than under FIFO. This is because under LIFO, cost of goods sold (the numerator) is higher, and average inventories (the denominator) is lower. The result is higher turnover. Thus accounting data must be used carefully when evaluating a firm or comparing several firms.

SUMMARY OF LEARNING OBJECTIVES

1. The relationship between inventories and income determination. Inventories are nonmonetary assets; the major accounting issue is allocating the cost of goods available for sale between the ending inventory and the cost of goods sold. The process of matching these costs against revenues helps ensure the proper determination of income. The measurement of ending inventories affects two accounting periods, because the ending inventory for the first year becomes the beginning inventory of the second year. Although a single measurement error is self-canceling, there is an improper allocation of income between the two accounting periods.

2. How the cost of ending inventories is determined. The cost of ending inventory is determined by multiply-

ing the quantity on hand by the acquisition cost of the items. The quantity on hand is determined by taking a physical inventory. Cost is the price paid to bring the item to its existing condition, ready for sale. When items are purchased at different prices, the accountant must still use a cost flow assumption to attach acquisition costs to the ending inventory.

3. The four methods of attaching costs to the ending inventory. There are four generally accepted accounting methods of determining cost of inventory quantities: (1) FIFO, (2) LIFO, (3) average cost, and (4) specific identification. FIFO assumes that the costs attached to the first goods sold are the costs of the first goods purchased. The cost of the ending inventory is that of the most recent purchase. LIFO makes the opposite assumption; the costs of the latest purchase are assumed to be the cost of the first item sold. Thus the cost of the ending inventory is that of the earliest purchases. Average cost attaches a weighted average cost, determined by dividing the total cost of the goods available for sale by the number of units available for sale, to both the cost of goods sold and the ending inventory. Specific identification determines the actual acquisition cost of each item in the ending inventory. Because of practical problems, this method is not often used. In a period of changing prices, the selection of a particular cost flow assumption may have a dramatic effect on a firm's balance sheet and income statement. These cost flow assumptions can be applied using either the periodic or the perpetual system.

4. The factors management considers in selecting among generally acceptable accounting principles. Management has a choice in selecting among generally accepted accounting principles for both financial reporting and tax purposes. The LIFO conformity rule, however, requires management to use LIFO for financial reporting purposes if it is adopted for tax purposes. As a result, management is often confronted with choosing between increased

cash flows caused by lower tax payments with LIFO and higher reported profits with FIFO.

5. The lower-of-cost-or-market rule. Generally accepted accounting principles assume that inventories should be valued at cost, unless the replacement cost of the items falls below cost. In applying the lower-of-cost-or-market rule, market, which is generally considered replacement cost, is compared with cost; if necessary, the inventory is written down to the lower of the two. This comparison can be made on an item-by-item basis, a group basis, or a whole inventory basis. The lower-of-cost-or-market rule is an excellent example of the conservatism convention in accounting.

6. Using inventory data for decision making. Because inventories and cost of goods sold are substantial components of the balance sheet and the income statement, they provide important data for evaluating a firm's financial position and profitability. In this respect, two common ratios used are the gross margin percentage and the inventory turnover. However, because these ratios are very sensitive to the cost flow assumption adopted, they must be used with caution.

■ SPECIAL SUPPLEMENT: ESTIMATING ENDING INVENTORIES

This Special Supplement illustrates two methods that are commonly used to estimate the cost of ending inventories when it is impractical to determine their actual cost: the gross margin method and the retail inventory method. For example, a firm's inventory may have been destroyed by fire or flood, and the cost of the inventory lost must be estimated. The gross margin method can be used in such circumstances. For a retail store, taking inventory at cost is very difficult for interim statements. The inventory may be valued at retail and then converted to cost. This is referred to as the *retail inventory method.*

■ THE GROSS MARGIN METHOD

The **gross margin method** may be used when a firm wishes to estimate its ending inventory without actually taking a count. For example, firms that wish to determine their ending inventories on a monthly basis certainly cannot take a physical inventory every month. Some firms have inventories in so many locations that a complete physical count would be impossible. When there are losses from disasters, fires, or floods, it may be impossible to take an ending inventory. In these cases, the gross margin method can be used to estimate ending inventories.

The gross margin method is based on the fact that most firms have a gross margin percentage that remains stable. The firm's past gross margin percentage therefore can be used to estimate ending inventories. To illustrate, assume that the Wong Company began the month of January with an inventory of $20,000 and made net purchases of $170,000 during January. Net sales for the month totaled $200,000, and the firm's gross margin percentage has remained at 20%. A 20% gross margin implies that cost of goods sold is 80% of sales.

This data is inserted into the formula to calculate cost of goods sold. Goods available for sale of $190,000 can be determined from existing records by adding the amount of beginning inventory to the purchases during the period. The cost of goods sold is estimated to be equal to 80% of sales, or $160,000. The ending inventory of

$30,000 is the difference between the cost of goods available for sale of $190,000 and the estimated cost of goods sold of $160,000.

Sales		$200,000
Cost of Goods Sold		
Beginning Inventory	$ 20,000	
Net Purchases	170,000	
Goods Available for Sale	190,000	
Less: Ending Inventory	?	
Cost of Goods Sold (80% of sales)		160,000
Gross Margin (20% of sales)		$ 40,000

■ THE RETAIL INVENTORY METHOD

Retail firms such as department stores and grocery stores use the **retail method** to determine their ending inventories. In essence, the inventory is taken at retail prices and then converted to cost. Because the inventories that are displayed on the shelves are priced at retail, the entire inventory for a store, such as a large market, can be taken at retail in just a few hours. Two or three individuals read the quantity of the items and their retail prices into tape recorders. The tapes are then transcribed and extended, and the result is the total inventory at retail prices. This inventory is then converted to cost by using a cost-to-retail percentage. This process is considerably less time-consuming than trying to determine the cost of each item using a cost flow assumption.

The heart of the retail method is determining a cost-to-retail percentage. This percentage is often calculated by dividing goods available for sale at cost by goods available for sale at retail. This means that a firm using the retail method must keep records of inventories and purchases at both cost and retail. This is not as difficult as it seems, because most retailers know the retail prices they set on the goods they purchase.

The retail method can be used to estimate ending inventories even if a physical inventory is not taken. This is done by first determining goods available for sale at retail and then subtracting sales that are at retail. The result is an estimated ending inventory at retail. The ending inventory at cost is then determined by applying the cost-to-retail percentage to the ending inventory at retail. This procedure is illustrated for the Martinez Grocery Store in Exhibit 9-18. In this case, the cost-to-retail percentage is 80%, or goods available for sale at cost of $190,000 divided by goods available for sale at retail of $237,500. The ending inventory at retail of $37,500 is multiplied by this ratio to determine the ending inventory at cost of $30,000.

EXHIBIT 9–18

MARTINEZ GROCERY STORE Retail Inventory Method		
	Cost	**Retail**
Beginning inventory	$ 20,000	$ 26,000
Net purchases	168,000	211,500
Freight-in	2,000	—
Goods available for sale	$190,000	$237,500
Ratio of cost to retail $\frac{\$190,000}{\$237,500} = 80\%$		
Less: Net sales during period		200,000
Ending inventory, at retail		37,500
Ratio of cost to retail		.80
Ending inventory at cost		$ 30,000

Although this example is a simplified version of the retail method, it does indicate the theory behind its application. In practice, different cost percentages can be used to cost inventories at FIFO, LIFO, and average cost. This and other complications are considered in intermediate accounting textbooks.

KEY TERMS

Average cost	Inventory turnover	Market
First-in, first-out (FIFO)	Last-in, first-out (LIFO)	Quality of earnings
Gross margin method	LIFO liquidation	Retail method
Inventory profits	Lower of cost or market	Specific-identification method

PROBLEMS FOR YOUR REVIEW

A. Cost Flow Assumption. The following data relates to the beginning inventory and purchases of the Valenzuela Company:

	Purchases		Sale	Balance
Date	Units	Cost	Units	Units
Beginning inventory	200	$ 9.75		200
January 3	50	10.00		250
January 10	100	10.50		350
January 15			175	175
January 20	225	10.80		400
January 31			150	250

REQUIRED: Assuming that the Valenzuela Co. uses a periodic inventory system, calculate the ending inventory and cost of goods sold as of January 31, based on the following methods:

1. FIFO.

2. LIFO.

3. Average cost.

SOLUTIONS Total goods available for sale are calculated as follows:

	Units	Acquisition Cost	Total Cost
Beginning balance	200	$ 9.75	$1,950
Purchases			
January 3	50	10.00	500
January 10	100	10.50	1,050
January 20	225	10.80	2,430
	575		$5,930
Sales	325		
Ending inventory	250		

(1) FIFO:

Goods available for sale	$5,930.00

Ending inventory—FIFO

225 × $10.80 = $2,430.00
25 × $10.50 =   262.50

Ending inventory	2,692.50
Cost of goods sold	$3,237.50

(2) LIFO:

Goods available for sale	$5,930.00

Ending inventory—LIFO

200 × $ 9.75 = $1,950.00
50 × $10.00 =   500.00

Ending inventory	2,450.00
Cost of goods sold	$3,480.00

(3) AVERAGE COST:

$$\frac{\text{Goods available for sale}}{\text{Units available for sale}} = \frac{\$5,930.00}{575} = \$10.31 * \text{Unit}$$

Ending inventory	250 @ $10.31 =	$2,577.50
Cost of goods sold	325 @ $10.31 =	3,352.50[†]
Goods available for sale		$5,930.00

*Rounded off.

†Rounded off so that ending inventory and cost of goods sold equal goods available for sale.

B. Lower of Cost or Market. The Duffy Company uses the lower-of-cost-or-market convention in valuing its inventory. The company has divided its products into two groups, with two types within each group. The following schedule presents the relevant data as of December 31.

	Group 1		Group 2	
	Type A	Type B	Type C	Type D
Number of units	50	100	100	200
Selling price per unit	$30	$40	$35	$20
Replacement cost per unit—12/31	20	28	26	16
Cost per unit	19	29	27	15

REQUIRED: Determine at what amount the ending inventory should be shown, assuming that the firm applies the lower-of-cost-or-market rule on

1. An item-by-item basis.

2. A group basis.

3. A total inventory basis.

SOLUTION

Group 1

Type A	Cost = 50 × $19 = $ 950	Market = 50 × $20 = $1,000
Type B	Cost = 100 × $29 = $2,900	Market = 100 × $28 = $2,800
Total Group 1	$3,850	$3,800

Group 2

Type C	Cost = 100 × $27 = $2,700	Market = 100 × $26 = $2,600
Type D	Cost = 200 × $15 = $3,000	Market = 200 × $16 = $3,200
Total Group 2	$5,700	$5,800
Total inventory	$9,550	$9,600

1. Item-by-item = $\underline{\underline{\$9,350}}$ = $950 + $2,800 + $2,600 + $3,000

2. Group basis = $\underline{\underline{\$9,500}}$ = $3,800 + $5,700

3. Total inventory = $\underline{\underline{\$9,550}}$

QUESTIONS

1. What is the main accounting issue regarding inventories, and why is it so important?

2. Assume that the ending inventory in Year 1 is overstated by $1,000 and that all other items in the cost of goods sold computation are correct. What is the impact on:

(a) the beginning inventory in Year 2?

(b) gross margins for Years 1 and 2?

(c) retained earnings balance at the end of Year 2?

3. One of your fellow students stated, "Determining the quantity of items in the ending inventory is easy—you just count the number of items in the storeroom." Do you agree? Why or why not?

4. What costs should be included in the ending inventory? In practice, how are these costs handled?

5. Explain to a friend who knows nothing about accounting why it is necessary to make cost flow assumptions that often differ from the actual physical flow of the goods.

6. Explain the four cost flow assumptions that are considered generally accepted accounting principles.

7. Safeway Stores uses the LIFO method of determining the cost of its inventories. Another large grocery chain uses the FIFO method. In a period of rising prices, how does this affect each firm's (a) total assets and (b) net income?

8. Why do some accountants feel that the specific-identification method is not appropriate in many circumstances?

9. Briefly describe the difference in applying the following inventory costing methods when a perpetual system rather than a periodic system is used:

(a) FIFO.   **(b)** LIFO.   **(c)** Average cost.

10. The Quick Chip Company is in an industry in which material prices have been declining. If the firm wants to report the highest gross margin and ending inventory and lowest cost of goods sold, what inventory cost method should it use?

11. For a number of years, the Jackson Co. has been using the FIFO method of costing its inventories. During the last few years, the prices of its inventory have been steadily rising. The controller is concerned that the firm's reported gross margin may not reflect its economic ability to repurchase future inventories for resale. Do you agree or disagree with the controller? Why?

12. Descript the concept of inventory profits.

13. The Financial Accounting Standards Board requires large companies to disclose the current cost of their inventories. Why do you think the Board adopted this policy? If inventories are reported on a current-cost basis, how do you think the inventory account and cost of goods sold would be affected?

14. How do the regulations contained in the Internal Revenue Code affect management's choice of inventory methods for financial reporting purposes?

15. What are some of the factors that management considers when selecting an inventory costing method?

16. If you were the president of a newly formed high-tech firm, what inventory method would you choose? Why?

17. What is the accounting concept behind the lower-of-cost-or-market rule? Should lower of cost or market be applied in all circumstances?

18. The Regal Company began business at the beginning of the current year. The firm has decided to use the FIFO method of inventory costing. If LIFO inventory costing had been used, the cost of the ending inventory would have been higher. Can you determine the direction that the cost of the purchases moved in during the year? If so, in what direction did they move?

19. (This applies to material covered in the Special Supplement.) What is the gross margin method of estimating inventories? When is its use most appropriate?

20. (This applies to material covered in the Special Supplement.) What is the retail method of estimating inventories? When is its use most appropriate?

21. (This applies to material covered in the Special Supplement.) In applying the retail method, how does the accountant convert the retail price of the inventory to its cost?

E1. Inventory Errors. During 1989, the Edward Corporation had sales of $800,000 and made inventory purchases of $570,000. Inventories on January 1, 1989 amounted to $325,000, and inventories at December 31, 1989 were $285,000.

REQUIRED: **(a)** Compute cost of goods sold and the gross margin for 1989.

(b) Now assume that an error was made in determining the ending inventory in 1987, and as a result the inventory was overstated by $40,000. What is the effect of this error on the gross margin for 1988 and 1989? What is the effect on the balance in the Retained Earnings account at the end of 1989?

E2. Inventory Errors. Shown below are condensed income statements for the TG Company for two consecutive years.

	Year 1	Year 2
Sales	$800,000	$850,000
Cost of goods sold	560,000	612,000
Gross margin on sales	240,000	238,000
Operating expenses	140,000	125,000
Net income	$100,000	$113,000

At the beginning of the third year, the new controller of the TG Company found that there had been two inventory errors in Year 1. She determined that the beginning inventory had been overstated by $4,000 and that the ending inventory had been understated by $6,000. At the end of Year 2, the Retained Earnings account had a balance of $290,000.

REQUIRED: **(a)** Determine the correct amount of net income for both Years 1 and 2.

(b) Compute the correct balance in the Retained Earnings account at the end of Year 2.

E3. Comparison of Inventory Costing Methods. The Robinson Football Equipment Company gives you the following data regarding one of its inventory items, football helmets:

Date	Quantity	Cost per Unit
Beginning	40 units	$130
2/28 purchase	100	125
6/24 purchase	85	122
10/4 purchase	110	120

The ending inventory consisted of 50 units.

REQUIRED: **(a)** Determine the cost of the

1. goods available for sale,

2. ending inventory, and

3. goods sold,

under the FIFO, LIFO, and average-cost inventory methods.

* Where appropriate, work all exercises and problems based on the periodic inventory system unless otherwise noted.

(b) Explain the relationship between the cost of goods sold figure under each of the methods. That is, which is higher and lower and what are the reasons for this relationship?

E4. Determining the Cost of Ending Inventories. The Brenner Brin Company uses the periodic inventory system. During March, the following sales and purchases of inventories were made:

	Number of Units	Cost per Unit	Total Cost
March 1 inventory	100	$13.20	$1,350
March 3 sale	75		
March 15 purchase	250	15.00	3,750
March 20 sale	125		
March 29 purchase	150	16.00	2,400
March 30 sale	110		

Determine the ending inventory and cost of goods sold for the Brenner Brin Company under the following cost flow assumptions:

(a) First-in, first-out.   **(b)** Last-in, first-out.   **(c)** Average cost.

E5. Determining the Cost of Ending Inventories. The following data were taken from the records of the Imdieke Co. regarding the purchases of its main inventory item, instant gold:

April 1:	Beginning inventory	400 units @ $10.00 per unit
April 4:	Purchase	900 units @ $10.20 per unit
April 10:	Purchase	700 units @ $10.25 per unit
April 18:	Purchase	900 units @ $10.25 per unit
April 30:	Purchase	600 units @ $10.40 per unit

At the end of the month, there were 1,200 units remaining in the ending inventory.

Determine the cost of the ending inventory and the cost of goods sold under each of the following cost flow assumptions, assuming the periodic inventory system is used:

(a) First-in, first-out.   **(b)** Last-in, first-out.   **(c)** Average cost.

E6. Specific-identification Method. Smith's Specialty Desk Company uses the specific-identification method of inventory costing. You obtained the following records for the year:

Quantity Purchased	Purchase Price per Unit	Units on Hand at End of the Year
10	$120.00	2
15	130.00	4
12	124.50	4
20	122.00	0
15	128.00	6

REQUIRED: **(a)** Determine the cost of the ending inventory using the specific-identification method.

(b) Assume that all the desks are substantially identical and that their selling price is $200 each. Determine the gross margin from the sales. How would your answer differ if the entire inventory of 15 units was from the items purchased at $122 per unit? What does this suggest about some of the conceptual problems with the specific-identification method?

E7. Determining the Cost of Ending Inventories—Perpetual System. The Payton Company uses the perpetual inventory system. During March, the following sales and purchases of inventories were made:

	Number of Units	Cost per Unit
March 1 inventory	200	$8.00
March 8 sale	150	
March 11 purchase	220	8.10
March 20 sale	240	
March 25 purchase	150	8.15
March 31 sale	140	

All sales are made at $14 per unit. Prepare a condensed income statement through gross margin on sales, assuming the firm uses (a) the FIFO method and (b) the LIFO method.

E8. Use the data from Exercise 4, but now assume that the firm uses the perpetual inventory system. Determine the ending inventory and the cost of goods sold for the Brenner Brin Company under the following cost flow assumptions:

(a) First-in, first-out.   **(b)** Last-in, first-out.   **(c)** Average cost.

E9. Inventory Costing Methods—Two-period Analysis. The Marshall Company began business on January 1, 1989. During 1989 and 1990, the firm made the following purchases:

1989:
January 2	75 units @ $2.00
February 5	50 units @ $2.10
April 14	125 units @ $2.20
July 14	100 units @ $2.20
September 28	80 units @ $2.25
November 29	70 units @ $2.30

1990:
January 14	100 units @ $2.35
March 25	600 units @ $2.40
August 19	400 units @ $2.38
December 4	60 units @ $2.36

During 1989 and 1990, the firm sold 360 units and 1,200 units, respectively.

REQUIRED: Determine the amount of cost of goods sold and the ending inventories for 1989 and 1990 under both the FIFO and the LIFO methods. Assume that the periodic inventory system is used.

E10. Effects of Different Inventory Cost Methods. The president of Pete's Pickles is confused about the effects of different inventory cost methods on income. The firm has been in business since the beginning of 1987, and the president gives you the following inventory data for 1987 through 1989:

Date	LIFO Cost	FIFO Cost	Average Cost
12/31/87	$6,000	$6,500	$6,300
12/31/88	5,200	5,400	5,325
12/31/89	5,800	5,600	5,540

REQUIRED: **(a)** Which inventory method will show the highest net income in each of the years?

(b) Which inventory method will show the lowest net income in each of the years?

E11. Inventory Turnover. The following information was taken from the records of the Mc-Ginnis Company:

Beginning inventory—1/1/90	$ 56,000
Net purchases	210,000
Ending inventory—12/31/90	28,000

Determine the inventory turnover and the average number of days that the inventory is on hand.

E12. LIFO Liquidation. The president of the Red Baron Corporation is concerned about the company's potential tax situation for the current year. The company has been on the LIFO method of inventory cost for many years. The president gives you the following data, which reflects inventory sales and purchases through December 15 of the current year:

Beginning inventory	1,000 units @ $5.00 per unit
Sales during the year	50,800 units @ $50.00 per unit
Purchases during the year	50,000 units @ $35.00 per unit
Current replacement cost per unit	$40.00 per unit

The company has the opportunity to purchase an additional 2,000 units at the current replacement cost prior to year-end.

Assuming that the tax rate is 40%, advise the president whether another purchase should be made before year-end. (*Hint*: Calculate cost of goods sold with and without an additional purchase. Assume that all expenses other than taxes remain the same.)

E13. Inventory Methods and Taxes. You have obtained the following information for the Rodriguez Company:

Sales	$950,000
Operating expenses	235,500
Interest expense	26,000
Tax rate	30%

This is the first year of the company's operations. Its accounting records are currently based on the FIFO method. Under FIFO, cost of goods sold is $555,000, and the ending inventory is $50,000. However, in order to lower its taxes, the company's controller is considering using either LIFO or the average-cost method. The controller has determined that ending inventories would be $30,000 under LIFO and $42,000 under the average-cost method.

REQUIRED: **(a)** Determine cost of goods sold under LIFO and under average cost.

(b) Compute income before taxes, tax expense, and net income under the three inventory methods.

(c) Compare and contrast the effects of the three methods. What constraints does management face in choosing inventory methods?

E14. Inventory Methods and Ratio Analysis. The Alto Teck Company has always used the FIFO method of computing inventory cost. As of December 31, 1990, you have been given the following data by the company's president:

Average inventories during 1990	$ 6,000,000
Cost of ending inventory at year-end 1990	6,500,000
Cost of goods sold for the year ended 1990	36,000,000
Current assets at year-end 1990	10,000,000
Current liabilities at year-end 1990	6,000,000
Net income for the year ended 1990	8,000,000

The president is giving serious thought to converting to the LIFO cost flow assumption. She has determined that if LIFO had been used during 1990, ending inventories would have decreased by $1,000,000 and average inventories by $500,000.

REQUIRED: **(a)** The president is concerned that switching to LIFO will have a negative effect on several ratios. Calculate the following amounts and ratios using both the FIFO and LIFO data:

1. Working capital.   **3.** Profit margin ratio.

2. The current ratio.   **4.** Inventory turnover.

EXERCISES

(b) Which ratios are affected and why?

(c) If you were a banker evaluating this company for a loan, what would you think of the possible change?

E15. Lower of Cost or Market. The following information pertains to the ending inventory of the Great Dane Corporation:

Item	Cost per Unit	Replacement Cost per Unit
A	$50	$65
B	80	75
C	75	67
D	25	19
E	45	46

The firm values its inventory using lower of cost or market on an item-by-item basis.

REQUIRED: **(a)** At what value should the ending inventory be shown on the balance sheet?

(b) Can you think of a situation when it would not be appropriate to use lower of cost or market?

E16. Toys "R" Us Financial Statements. Refer to the Toys "R" Us financial statements in Appendix D. Based on that information, answer the following questions.

(a) What method does the company use to determine the cost of its ending inventories?

(b) Calculate the amount of net working capital and the current ratio for the years ended 1988 and 1987.

(c) Determine the gross margin ratio and inventory turnover for the years ended 1988 and 1987.

(d) Were there any significant changes in the above ratios from 1987 to 1988?

(e) If the company used FIFO, would there be any change in the above ratios?

E17. The Gross Margin Method. (This applies to material covered in the Special Supplement.) On August 15 of the current year, the entire inventory of Youngblood's Bookstore was destroyed in a freak tornado in San Diego. In order to file a claim with the insurance company, the owner of the store compiled the following information regarding the purchases and sales of inventory for the month of August just prior to the tornado:

Beginning inventory	$15,000
Purchases	45,000
Sales	50,000

During the last few years, the gross margin percentage has been averaging 25%.

Compute the amount of inventory destroyed in the tornado. Also compute the cost of goods sold from August 1 to August 15.

E18. Retail Inventory Method. (This applies to material covered in the Special Supplement.) Sunset Drug Store uses the retail inventory method to estimate its ending inventory. You have been able to determine the following information for the year ended December 31, 1990:

	Cost	Retail
Beginning inventory	$12,000	$20,000
Net purchases	30,000	40,000
Net sales		42,000

Determine the cost of the ending inventory and the cost of goods sold during the year.

PROBLEMS

P9-1   Inventory Errors. You have just been hired as the accountant for Youngsters, Inc., the makers of Murfs. During your review of the records, you found that the following errors were made in calculating the year-end inventory amounts:

	Overstated	Understated
12/31/85	0	
12/31/86	$9,000	
12/31/87	9,500	
12/31/88		$6,500
12/31/89		4,500
12/31/90	2,200	
12/31/91	0	

REQUIRED: **(a)**   For each year, determine the dollar error on (1) total assets and (2) net income.

(b)   At the end of 1991, by how much is retained earnings misstated, and in which direction?

P9-2   Inventory Errors. The Taktech Company uses the periodic inventory system. The accountant for the company prepared the following condensed income statements for the years ended June 30, 1989 and 1990:

	1989	1990
Net sales	$700,000	$950,000
Cost of goods sold		
Beginning inventory	80,000	110,000
Purchases, net	580,000	770,000
Goods available for sale	660,000	880,000
Less: Ending inventory	110,000	150,000
Cost of goods sold	550,000	730,000
Gross margin on sales	150,000	220,000
Operating expenses	70,000	100,000
Net income	$ 80,000	$120,000

During 1991, the accountant found that several errors were made in determining the amount of ending inventories:
1989:

1. On June 30, the company had several personal computers that were not included in Taktech's ending inventory, held on consignment by some retailers. These computers had a cost of $6,500.

2. A sale was made in late June; the customer did not take delivery of the equipment until sometime in July. As a result, ending inventory was overstated by $3,500, and sales were understated by $4,700.

1990:

3. A purchase was made on June 25, 1990; the merchandise did not arrive until July. The purchase had been recorded properly in the purchases journal, but the item was not included in the ending inventory. The merchandise had a cost of $11,000.

4. Some equipment that was held on consignment for others was included in Taktech's ending inventory. As a result, ending inventory was overstated by $2,200.

REQUIRED: **(a)** Prepare a correct set of income statements for the years ended June 30, 1989 and 1990.

(b) Assume that the firm had net assets of $300,000 and $340,000, respectively, prior to any corrections for the preceding items. Determine the correct amount of net assets after you have made the necessary corrections.

P9-3 **Inventory Determination.** The Hawk Steamer Company uses the periodic inventory system and prepares financial statements every December 31. You have gathered the following data regarding the main item in the inventory:

	Number of Units	Unit Cost	Total Cost
1989			
Beginning inventory	0		
Purchases: January	600	$2.00	$1,200.00
April	400	2.10	840.00
July	400	2.25	900.00
Total for year	1,400		
Less items sold	800		
Ending inventory	600		
1990			
Beginning inventory	600		
Purchases: February	400	3.00	1,200.00
June	800	3.10	2,480.00
November	200	3.20	640.00
Total for year	2,000		
Less items sold	1,600		
Ending inventory	400		

REQUIRED: Determine the cost of the ending inventory and the cost of goods sold for each year, assuming the firm uses the following inventory methods:

(a) FIFO. **(b)** LIFO. **(c)** Average cost.

P9-4 **Inventory Determination.** Ekbog Inc. stocks and sells a single product. During 1989 and 1990, the firm made the following inventory purchases:

	1989		
	Quantity	Price	Total
Beginning inventory	200	$ 5.00	$1,000
Purchases: 2/20	300	9.00	2,700
5/20	200	9.50	1,900
8/15	300	9.25	2,775
11/15	400	9.20	3,680
Ending inventory	450	?	?
	1990		
Beginning inventory	450	?	?
Purchases: 3/15	600	$ 9.50	$5,700
6/15	200	10.00	2,000
9/15	200	10.50	2,100
12/15	300	10.20	3,060
Ending inventory	400	?	?

REQUIRED: Determine the cost of the ending inventory and cost of goods sold for 1989 and 1990 under each of the following methods. (Assume that the periodic inventory system is used.)

(a) FIFO.   **(b)** LIFO.   **(c)** Average cost.

P9-5   Inventory Determination. Eddite, Inc. is a one-product merchant. During 1990 and 1991, the firm had the following purchases:

	1990		
	Quantity	**Price**	**Total**
Beginning inventory	1,000	$3.98	$ 3,980
Purchases: 1/15	1,500	5.00	7,500
4/15	2,300	5.30	12,190
7/15	2,700	5.50	14,850
10/15	1,500	5.40	8,100
Ending inventory	1,200	?	?
	1991		
Beginning inventory	1,200	?	?
Purchases: 2/1	1,700	$5.35	$ 9,095
5/1	2,100	5.45	11,445
8/1	2,500	5.50	13,750
11/1	2,000	5.60	11,200
Ending inventory	1,500	?	?

REQUIRED: Determine the cost of the ending inventory and the cost of goods sold for 1990 and 1991 under each of the following methods. (Assume that the periodic inventory system is used.)

(a) FIFO.   **(b)** LIFO.   **(c)** Average cost.

P9-6   Perpetual Inventory Method. The Z-Image Company sells X-ray machines. The firm uses the perpetual inventory system to keep track of its major product, Unit 145. The record of inventory purchases and sales during the current year is as follows:

Beginning inventory		10 units @ $400 per unit
Purchases and sales		
February 1:	Purchase	30 units @ $450 per unit
March 15:	Sale	35 units
May 2:	Purchase	20 units @ $460 per unit
June 4:	Purchase	25 units @ $470 per unit
August 8:	Sale	20 units
September 1:	Sale	15 units
November 12:	Purchase	60 units @ $480 per unit
December 1:	Purchase	10 units @ $485 per unit
December 31:	Sale	55 units

REQUIRED: Determine cost of goods sold and ending inventory, assuming the firm uses the following inventory methods:

(a) FIFO.   **(b)** LIFO.   **(c)** Weighted moving average.

Where necessary, round off unit costs and total inventory costs to two decimal points.

P9-7   Perpetual Inventory System. The Copy-It Company sells duplicating machines. The firm uses the perpetual inventory system to keep track of its major product, the Image Maker. The record of inventory purchases and sales during the current year is as follows:

Beginning inventory	20 units @ $1,000 per unit		
Purchases and sales			
February 10:	Purchase	50 units @	980 per unit
March 25:	Sale	45 units	
April 29:	Purchase	25 units @	975 per unit
June 12:	Purchase	25 units @	970 per unit
July 30:	Sale	35 units	
September 15:	Sale	25 units	
November 12:	Purchase	100 units @	965 per unit
December 9:	Purchase	40 units @	960 per unit
December 24:	Sale	130 units	

REQUIRED: Determine cost of goods sold and ending inventory, assuming the firm uses the following inventory methods:

(a) FIFO. **(b)** LIFO. **(c)** Moving average.

Where necessary, round off unit costs and total inventory costs to two decimal points.

P9-8 Perpetual Inventory System. Using the data from Problem 9-4, determine the cost of the ending inventory and cost of goods sold for 1989 and 1990 under each of the following methods:

(a) FIFO. **(b)** LIFO. **(c)** Average cost.

Assume that sales during the period occurred as follows:

1989		1990	
January 10:	50 units	February 2:	200 units
April 14:	200 units	March 20:	350 units
July 6:	250 units	June 24:	250 units
September 29:	300 units	November 1:	100 units
October 30:	150 units	December 16:	450 units

P9-9 Inventory Methods and Income Taxes. The chief financial officer of the Raider Company gave you the following data for the year ended December 31, 1990:

Sales	$1,000,000
Inventory, January 1, 1990	100,000
Inventory, December 31, 1990	150,000
Inventory turnover	5 times
Other operating expenses	70,000
Average tax rate	30%

The company currently uses the FIFO method of costing its inventory but is considering changing to the LIFO method. The chief financial officer has estimated the cost of goods sold on a LIFO basis would be 130% of FIFO cost of goods sold. The chief financial officer has asked you to prepare an analysis comparing the effects of FIFO and LIFO.

REQUIRED: **(a)** Prepare comparative income statements for the year ended December 31, 1990. Use the following form:

	FIFO	LIFO
Sales		
Cost of goods sold		
Gross margin on sales		
Operating expenses		
Income before taxes		
Taxes		
Net income		

(b) Explain the reasons for the differences in the two statements.

(c) From your analysis, can you determine whether prices paid for the inventory have fallen or risen during the year? Explain your reasoning.

P9-10   Lower of Cost or Market. The Rimbau Company sells home and office telephones. It has divided its product into a basic and a luxury group and has two different telephones in each group. The firm uses the lower-of-cost-or-market rule in determining the value of its ending inventory. Data pertaining to the December 31 inventory is presented below.

	Luxury Group		Basic Group	
	Type 1	Type 2	Type 3	Type 4
Number of units	60	150	120	250
Selling price per unit	$60	$80	$75	$40
Replacement cost	40	56	52	32
Purchase cost	38	58	54	30

REQUIRED: Determine the value of the December 31 ending inventory, applying the lower-of-cost-or-market rule under each of the following independent assumptions:

(a) applied individually to each item.

(b) applied to each group of products.

(c) applied to the inventory as a whole.

P9-11   Gross Margin Method. (This problem applies to material in the Special Supplement.) The Winrich Company has been taking a physical inventory every quarter in order to prepare its quarterly financial statements. Because this process is very time-consuming, the president of the company is wondering whether there is a more efficient way to determine the cost of inventories for its quarterly reports.

You have been provided with the following information and asked to figure a better way to determine quarterly inventories:

THE WINRICH COMPANY

Partial Income Statement

For the Year Ended December 31, 1990

Net sales		$655,000
Cost of goods sold		
Beginning inventory	$ 80,000	
Purchases, net	575,000	
Goods available for sale	655,000	
Less: Ending inventory	223,000	432,000
Gross margin on sales		$223,000

You have obtained the following additional data:

(a) In early 1991, it was determined that a sale for $5,000 recorded in late 1990 was actually an item provided to a good customer on consignment. The cost of the item, $3,000, was not included in the ending inventory. The item was subsequently returned unsold in early 1991.

(b) Gross margin percentages for the previous years were 1986, 32%; 1987, 35%; 1988, 33%; and 1989, 36%.

(c) Data for the first quarter of 1991 were: sales, $280,000; net purchases, $130,000.

REQUIRED: **(a)** Explain to the president how the ending inventory for the first quarter of 1991 can be estimated.

(b) Estimate the ending inventory at the end of the first quarter of 1991.

(c) Explain other uses for the gross margin method.

P9-12 Retail Inventory Method. (This problem relates to material covered in the Special Supplement.) The Diamond Computer Store uses the retail method to determine its cost of goods sold and ending inventory. You have gathered the following information for the month of July:

	Cost	Retail
Beginning inventory	$100,000	$135,000
Purchases	450,000	600,000
Purchase returns	5,100	6,800
Freight-in	1,250	
Sales		586,200
Sales returns		7,000

REQUIRED: Determine the cost of the ending inventory and cost of goods sold for July.

■ USING THE COMPUTER

P9-13 The EDP manager of the Clean Washing Machine Company is considering computerizing the firm's inventory valuation system and asks your help. The firm wholesales two types of washers, the Super Wash model and the Clean Wash model. Data regarding the cost, market, and units on hand for each model are as follows:

	Super Wash		Clean Wash	
	Model A	Model B	Model C	Model D
Units on hand	200	300	100	80
Cost per unit	$300	$325	$225	$250
Replacement cost per unit				
Optimistic	340	320	220	255
Conservative	315	308	215	251

REQUIRED: Using an electronic spreadsheet available at your university, prepare a lower-of-cost-or-market analysis using the format shown in Exhibit 9-17. Prepare a separate analysis using first the optimistic replacement cost and then the conservative value.

■ UNDERSTANDING FINANCIAL STATEMENTS

P9-14 After analyzing one of the recent annual reports of Safeway Stores, you obtained the following information (all figures in thousands):

Purchases	$13,193,000
Cost of sales	12,966,000
Beginning inventory, FIFO	1,268,000
Ending inventory, FIFO	1,495,000

In discussing and analyzing operations, management noted that the current cost of the ending inventory was $1,501,000 and that cost of goods sold on a replacement-cost basis was $13,020,000.

REQUIRED: **(a)** Determine the amount of inventory profits included in Safeway's reported net income of $115,000,000.

(b) How do you think your analysis would differ when Safeway reported its inventories on the LIFO basis?

■ FINANCIAL DECISION CASE

P9-15 In mid-December, the Diamond Gold Company is reviewing its financial and tax position prior to year-end. The price of gold has been falling, and the company is considering making an additional purchase of 5,000 ounces of gold prior to year-end. The following data reflects inventory purchases and sales through mid-December:

	Ounces of Gold	Cost per Ounce	Total Cost
Beginning inventory	6,000	$200	$1,200,000
Purchases during year			
First	10,000	400	4,000,000
Second	8,000	380	3,040,000
Third	12,000	350	4,200,000

During the year, the company sold 34,000 ounces of gold and does not expect to make any additional sales prior to year-end. The company has been offered 5,000 ounces of gold at $340 per ounce. Although this price appears attractive, the company feels that the price of gold will continue to decline and finally stabilize at $300 per ounce at the beginning of the next year. The company uses the LIFO method of inventory cost and has an average tax rate of 30%.

REQUIRED: **(a)** Determine cost of goods sold, assuming that (1) the purchase is not made and (2) the purchase is made.

(b) Assume that the 34,000 ounces of gold were sold at $450 per ounce and that all expenses other than taxes amounted to $1 million. Determine net income, assuming that (1) the purchase is not made and (2) the purchase is made.

(c) Determine the difference in cash flows to the firm if the purchase is made in December at $340 per ounce or in January at $300 per ounce.

(d) What course of action would you suggest that the firm take?

PROPERTY, PLANT, AND EQUIPMENT; NATURAL RESOURCES; AND INTANGIBLE ASSETS

LEARNING OBJECTIVES

After studying this chapter, you should be able to:

1. Explain the accounting concepts and problems related to noncurrent, nonmonetary assets.
2. Discuss the importance of differentiating between capital and revenue expenditures.
3. Measure the acquisition cost of property, plant, and equipment and record their acquisition.
4. Explain the accounting concept of depreciation.
5. Compute depreciation expense under four different methods.
6. Identify depreciation problems relating to a par-

tial year, revision of depreciation rates, and depreciation and inflation.
7. Account for subsequent expenditures related to plant and equipment.
8. Account for disposal of assets.
9. Explain accounting concepts related to natural resources and depletion.
10. Describe the accounting concepts related to intangible assets and their amortization.

T his chapter will consider the accounting concepts and procedures related to noncurrent, nonmonetary assets other than long-term investments. Specifically, the material will concentrate on accounting for property, plant, and equipment, the related concept of depreciation, and the dispositions of these assets. This chapter will also examine the accounting concepts related to natural resources and intangible assets and the related concepts of depletion and amortization.

■ NONCURRENT, NONMONETARY ASSETS

Noncurrent, nonmonetary assets, often called *operational* assets, are often categorized as either tangible or intangible. **Tangible assets** include property, plant, and equipment and other similar productive assets. These assets have physical substance and capabilities. Natural resources are also considered tangible assets. **Natural resources** are physical substances that, when taken from the ground, produce revenues for a firm. Included in this category are oil, natural gas, coal, iron ore, uranium, and timber.

    Intangible assets have no physical substance; rather, they give the enterprise the right of ownership or use. Included in this category are patents, copyrights, leaseholds, trademarks, and franchises.

    All noncurrent, nonmonetary assets have the following common characteristics:

1. They represent future economic services acquired for use in the business and are usually not held for resale.

2. The future services will benefit a firm for several accounting periods.

3. The cost of consumed services is systematically allocated to the periods in which revenues are earned (except for land).

■ FUTURE SERVICES NOT HELD FOR RESALE

Property, plant, and equipment, as well as other noncurrent, nonmonetary assets, are acquired by an enterprise because of their ability to generate future revenues. In effect, these assets are viewed as future service potentials that are consumed in the merchandising or production cycle. For example, accountants are not concerned with the physical properties of a lathe but rather with its ability to produce a product that will provide future benefits.

    Assets not used in the merchandising or production process, including assets that are held for resale, are not included in this category. For example, a warehouse that is no longer being used or land held for speculation is not classified under the category of property, plant, and equipment. Rather, these assets are included in the long-term investment category on the balance sheet. Similarly, land a real estate firm holds for resale is shown in the inventory section of the balance sheet.

■ LONG-TERM NATURE OF THE ASSETS

The economic or service life of a noncurrent, nonmonetary asset is the period of time that a firm expects to receive benefits from the asset, which depends on economic and legal factors. A building generally has an economic life of at least 20 to 30 years; a delivery truck may have a life of 100,000 miles. Intangible assets have a legal life as well as an economic life. For example, a patent has a legal life of 17 years, but its economic life may be shorter than 17 years. Generally, any asset that has a life longer than one year is included in the noncurrent section of the balance sheet.[1]

■ ALLOCATION OF BENEFITS TO ACCOUNTING PERIODS

The matching convention requires that the cost of expired benefits be matched with the revenues they produce. Accountants do this for all nonmonetary assets (other than land), whether classified as current or noncurrent. For example, when prepaid assets such as insurance are written off as their benefits expire or are consumed, the asset is reduced and an expense is recorded. Further, as noted in Chapter 9, various cost flow assumptions are used to allocate the cost of goods available for sale to ending inventory and cost of goods sold. This chapter will consider how the cost of noncurrent, nonmonetary assets, other than site land, is systematically allocated to accounting periods. Land is not depreciable, since its benefits are considered to last indefinitely.

Listed below are the major categories of noncurrent, nonmonetary assets and the expenses associated with the cost allocation process:

Asset Category	Expense
Tangible assets	
Land	None
Plant, buildings, equipment, and other similar assets	Depreciation
Natural resources (e.g., oil and gas)	Depletion
Intangible assets	Amortization

■ MAJOR ACCOUNTING ISSUES ASSOCIATED WITH NONCURRENT, NONMONETARY ASSETS

The major accounting issues related to noncurrent, nonmonetary assets include:

1. Distinguishing between capital and revenue expenditures.

2. Measuring and recording acquisition cost.

3. Measuring the costs of using the assets, including depreciation, depletion, and amortization expense and subsequent expenditures.

4. Accounting for the disposal of such assets.

The following sections of this chapter are concerned with these issues as they relate to property, plant, and equipment, natural resources, and intangible assets.

■ CAPITAL VERSUS REVENUE EXPENDITURE

Throughout this book, the term *expenditure* has been used to refer to a payment of an asset or the incurrence of a liability in exchange for another asset or for a service rendered. That is, the expenditure is made in cash or on credit and results in the firm's receiving another asset, such as a delivery truck, or in using a service, such as the repair of a delivery truck. When the expenditure produces another asset, it is called a **capital expenditure**. Thus the term *capitalize*, when used in this sense, means to consider an expenditure as an asset. When the expenditure results in a service whose benefits are consumed in the current period, it is called a **revenue expenditure**.

[1] Long-term prepaid expenses represent an exception to this. In Chapter 5, it was noted that prepaid expenses that benefit several years are still classified as current, because these items are not material and thus the financial statements are not distorted.

EXHIBIT 10–1

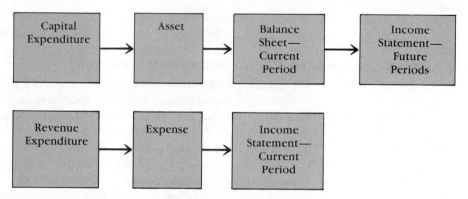

Revenue expenditures are current expenses such as ordinary repairs, maintenance, fuel, and other items required to keep the asset in normal working condition. Exhibit 10-1 illustrates the difference between capital and revenue expenditures. This distinction is important in determining periodic net income, because capital expenditures affect several future accounting periods, whereas revenue expenditures affect only the current period. If an error is made and a capital expenditure, such as the purchase of equipment, is recorded as a revenue expenditure, the net income of both the current period and future periods will be misstated. The current period's income will be understated because the entire expenditure was expensed when only a portion of it, the current year's depreciation, should have been. Future periods' income will be overstated because no depreciation expense is recorded in those years. Over the useful life of the asset the error is self-correcting, but the interim income is misstated.

How do firms decide what is a capital and what is a revenue expenditure? Clearly, the purchase of a delivery truck is a capital expenditure, whereas an engine tune-up is a revenue expenditure, but what about the purchase of a wastepaper basket or a major engine overhaul that practically constitutes a new engine? In order to have consistent accounting policies that can be followed from year to year, firms develop guidelines or formal policies to handle these items. Materiality plays a large part in the design of such policies. Most firms put some minimum dollar limit for capital expenditures. The minimum can range from one hundred dollars for small companies to several thousand dollars for large companies.

This problem is further complicated by the fact that the same item can sometimes be considered a capital expenditure and at other times a revenue expenditure. For example, the labor cost to install a new machine is considered a capital expenditure and part of the acquisition cost of the machine, because the expenditure is necessary to get the machine ready for use. On the other hand, the same labor cost subsequent to installation is a revenue expenditure, because it is a normal and recurring repair. Thus both the purpose and the nature of the expenditure must be considered when deciding whether an item is a capital or a revenue expenditure.

■ MEASURING AND RECORDING THE ACQUISITION COST OF PROPERTY, PLANT, AND EQUIPMENT

According to the FASB, "the historical cost of acquiring an asset includes the costs necessarily incurred to bring it to the condition and location necessary for its intended use."[2] In terms of property, plant, and equipment, this means that all the rea-

[2]Financial Accounting Standards Board, Statement No. 34, *Capitalization of Interest Cost* (Stamford, Conn.: FASB, October 1979), par. 6.

sonable and necessary costs required to get the asset in place and ready for use are included in the acquisition cost. For example, the acquisition cost of equipment includes any transportation charges, insurance in transit, installation, testing costs, and normal repairs before putting the asset into service. All of these costs are necessary to bring the equipment to a location and condition to make it ready for its intended use. However, the acquisition cost does not include unexpected costs, such as the cost of repairing damage incurred in transportation, purchase discounts lost, or, in most cases, interest costs. These costs, as well as normal repairs and maintenance expenses incurred in subsequent periods, are considered period expenses when incurred.

Each type of asset within the property, plant, and equipment category has special conventions regarding which items should be included in the acquisition cost. For example, when land is purchased, various incidental costs that must be included in acquisition cost include real estate commissions; title fees; legal fees; draining, grading, and clearing costs; and delinquent property taxes. However, in many cases, judgment must be used to determine which items should be capitalized.

■ CASH ACQUISITIONS

When property, plant, and equipment are purchased for cash, the acquisition price is easy to determine. It is the cash price paid plus all other costs necessary to get the asset ready to use. To illustrate, assume the Miller Company purchases a lathe from the Arnold Company. The price of the lathe is $15,000, and the terms of sale are 2/10, n/30. Sales tax is 6%, freight charges are $850, and installation costs are $150. The total acquisition cost of the equipment is $16,600, computed as follows:

Purchase price		$15,000
Less: Discount of 2%		(300)
Net price		14,700
Add: Sales tax (6% of $15,000)	$900	
Freight charges	850	
Installation charges	150	1,900
Total acquisition cost		$16,600

If the discount is not taken, the $300 should not be included in the cost of the equipment but instead should be considered interest expense.

■ OTHER METHODS OF ACQUIRING PROPERTY, PLANT, AND EQUIPMENT

An enterprise can acquire property, plant, and equipment in a variety of ways other than by a direct cash purchase. These include basket purchases, noncash exchanges such as in exchange for the firm's own capital stock, donation, and self-construction. The determination of cost for these types of acquisitions is more difficult than a straightforward cash exchange and thus warrants special attention.

Basket or Group Purchases

Whether or not the purchase is for cash, property, plant, and equipment are often purchased together in one lump sum. For example, when an existing building is purchased, the land on which that building is situated is usually purchased. The agreed-upon purchase price represents the total cost of both the building and the land, and in many cases the total purchase price is more or less than the fair market values of the building and the land individually. As a result, the total purchase price must be allocated between the individual assets. This is especially important because the building is subject to depreciation, whereas the land is not. The allocation is often based on appraisals or real estate tax records.

To illustrate, assume that the H. Jones Company purchases an existing office building and site land. The total purchase price is $1 million. An independent appraiser determines that the building and land have fair market values of $900,000 and $300,000, respectively. The $1 million purchase price is allocated as follows:

	Appraised Value	Relative Percentage of Total Appraised Value[a]	Purchase Price		Allocation of Cost
Building	$ 900,000	75% ×	$1,000,000	=	$ 750,000
Land	300,000	25 ×	1,000,000	=	250,000
Total	$1,200,000	100			$1,000,000

[a]$900,000 ÷ $1,200,000 = 75%.
$300,000 ÷ $1,200,000 = 25%.

As this example illustrates, acquisition cost is the basis for recording assets, even though their individual appraised values may be higher.

Noncash Exchanges

In some situations, property, plant, or equipment is purchased through noncash transactions. For example, a firm may purchase land and, in exchange, issue the firm's stock to the seller. In such transactions, the application of the cost method requires that the acquisition price of the asset be equal to any cash given plus the fair market value of any noncash consideration. However, if it is difficult or impossible to determine with reasonable accuracy the fair market value of the noncash consideration, the market value of the particular asset that is purchased should be used.

To illustrate, assume that the Orange Company, a large public company, purchases site land in downtown Los Angeles on which to build its corporate office. In exchange for the land, the Orange Company issues 10,000 shares of its capital stock to the seller. At the time of the transaction, Orange Company's stock is selling on a national exchange for $78 per share. To record this transaction, the Orange Company makes the following entry:

Land	780,000	
Capital Stock		780,000
To record purchase of land in exchange for capital stock.		

If the stock of the Orange Company is not traded on an exchange and it is otherwise difficult to determine its fair market value, then the land should be recorded at its fair market value.

Acquisition through Donation

There are circumstances in which an enterprise may acquire its property, plant, or equipment through donation. For example, in order to entice General Motors or any other large corporation to locate within its boundaries, a city may give the company the site land on which to build its plant. In these rare situations, if the historical-cost convention were strictly followed, accountants would assign a zero cost to the land. Because this would be clearly misleading, accountants record the asset at its fair market value at the time it is received. The credit portion of the entry is to a stockholders' equity account, Donated Capital.

To illustrate, assume that the WLH Corporation acquires at no cost 100 acres of land from the city of Lost Acres. At the time of the donation, the land is appraised at a fair market value of $100,000. To record this transaction, the WLH Corporation makes the following entry:

Land	100,000	
Donated Capital		100,000
To record donated land		
at fair market value.		

Self-constructed Assets

In some circumstances, a building or a piece of equipment is constructed by the enterprise itself. The assets are called *self-constructed assets*, and their acquisition costs include materials and labor used directly in the construction process as well as a portion of overhead. Overhead costs include supervisory labor, utilities, and depreciation on the factory building.

Capitalization of Interest. Interest is the time cost of money and is therefore generally considered an expense in the period incurred. Thus, when property, plant, or equipment is purchased through the issuance of a note, the interest related to that note is expensed when incurred. However, in 1979 the FASB issued Statement 34, which requires that in limited circumstances interest be capitalized and thus be included in the acquisition cost of certain noncurrent, nonmonetary assets.[3] In particular, Statement 34 requires that when an enterprise constructs its own assets, or has another entity construct an asset for it, and there is an extended period to get it ready for use, interest incurred in the construction period should be capitalized as part of the acquisition or construction cost of the asset. The complex rules relating to capitalized interest are discussed more fully in intermediate accounting texts.

THE ACCOUNTING CONCEPT OF DEPRECIATION

Depreciation is probably the most misunderstood and yet one of the most important of all the accounting concepts that you will study. Perhaps the best way to understand the nature of depreciation is to explore what depreciation is and what it is not.

THE NATURE OF DEPRECIATION

Noncurrent, nonmonetary assets are purchased because they represent future benefits. All of these assets, with the exception of site land, eventually give up these benefits as the firm uses them to produce revenues. Depreciation, as noted in Chapter 4, is the process of allocating the cost of plant and equipment to the period in which the enterprise receives the benefit from these assets. **Depletion** refers to the allocation of the cost of natural resources, and **amortization** refers to intangible assets. The concept of depreciation will be analyzed next, but the theoretical concepts are the same, and the analysis applies equally well to depletion and amortization.

Depreciation Is an Allocation Process

From an accounting perspective, depreciation is an allocation process. That is, the cost of the asset is allocated to the periods in which the enterprise receives benefits from the assets. Theoretically, when an enterprise buys an asset such as delivery equipment, it can account for it in three different ways:

[3] Ibid.

1. Write off to expense the entire cost of the asset at the time of purchase—that is, consider it a revenue expenditure.

2. Record the expenditure as an asset at the time of purchase and make no further adjustment until the asset is sold, abandoned, or otherwise disposed of, at which time the entire cost of the asset is written off to expense.

3. Record the expenditure as an asset at the time of purchase and systematically allocate the cost to the periods in which the asset benefits the firm (depreciation).

Clearly, the third option provides the best matching of revenue and expense; it is the only one considered to be a generally accepted accounting principle. Although estimates such as useful lives and salvage value must be made, accountants believe that the benefits of the depreciation process outweigh the subjectivity of these estimates.

Depreciation Is Not a Valuation Concept

Unfortunately, many individuals think that depreciation represents a decrease in the value of an asset.[4] Accounting records do not attempt to show the current value of an asset, and depreciation is not used to value plant or equipment. For example, because of market conditions, the value of a building may substantially increase over a specific period of time. However, accountants would continue to depreciate the building because they know that eventually the building will give up its benefits to the firm, and the matching concept requires that as these benefits expire, they should be offset against the revenues they help produce. Also, the assumption is made that productive assets will not be sold but will be consumed in the operations of the business (the going-concern assumption). Thus, depreciation is used to allocate the cost of an asset over its estimated useful life, regardless of current market value.

Depreciation Is Not a Direct Source of Cash

Another common misconception regarding depreciation is that it is a source of cash. Depreciation is a noncash expense in that it does not require a cash payment at the time the expense is recorded. This is no different from the write-off of prepaid insurance or rent. The cash outlay takes place when the payment for the related asset is made. As a result, depreciation does not result in a direct cash outflow or inflow, nor does the balance in the Accumulated Depreciation account represent cash. The balance in this account represents only the total of the expired costs of the particular asset and is recorded as a debit to Depreciation Expense and a credit to the Accumulated Depreciation account. Neither Cash nor any other current asset or current liability account is involved. Unless a company purposely sets aside cash by taking it out of its regular cash account and putting it into a special fund, there is no guarantee that the firm will have the funds to replace its plant and equipment.

There is one way, however, in which depreciation is an indirect source of cash to a firm. Depreciation is a noncash expense that reduces taxable income. The lower the firm's income is, the lower the cash outflows due to tax payments will be. Thus the higher the depreciation expense for tax purposes, the more cash the firm will be able to retain through lower tax payments. Only in this way does depreciation affect cash flow. As will be seen later in this chapter, using depreciation for tax purposes is closely tied to reducing taxable income.

■ WHAT CAUSES DEPRECIATION?

There are two factors that cause a tangible asset to give up its economic benefits: deterioration and obsolescence.

---

[4] From an economic viewpoint, this may be the case. However, from an accounting perspective, depreciation is strictly an allocation concept.

Physical Deterioration

Tangible assets deteriorate because of use, the passage of time, and exposure to the elements such as weather and other climatic factors. Clearly, a good maintenance policy can keep a firm's tangible assets in good repair and performing according to expectations. However, even the best-maintained asset will eventually wear out and need to be replaced. Thus depreciation is recorded for all tangible assets other than land, no matter how well maintained. In addition, depreciation is recorded for those items included in the Plant and Equipment account, even if they are temporarily not in use. This is because as time passes, physical deterioration takes place to a certain extent, regardless of use.

Obsolescence

Obsolescence is the process of becoming outdated, outmoded, or inadequate. Certain high-tech equipment, such as computers and other electronic devices, are subject to rapid obsolescence. Although these assets continue to perform, new technology makes them outdated in a relatively short period of time. Some assets, although technologically sound, become obsolete because they are no longer able to produce at the increased levels required as a result of expanded growth and sales.

Physical deterioration and obsolescence are factors that cause depreciation. However, it is not necessary to distinguish between them in determining depreciation. They are primarily related to determining the economic useful life of assets, and no attempt is made to separate these joint factors in that determination.

■ RECORDING PERIODIC DEPRECIATION

In Chapter 4, the process of recording periodic depreciation was introduced. Before describing the various methods of computing depreciation, let's review the recording process. When a tangible asset is purchased, an asset account is debited. The credit part of the entry depends on how the asset is acquired. Periodic depreciation expense is recorded by debiting Depreciation Expense and crediting the contra-asset account, Accumulated Depreciation.

To illustrate, assume that a firm purchases a delivery truck for $8,500 cash on January 2 of the current year. Yearly depreciation is determined to be $1,700. The necessary journal entries to record these events and the correct balance sheet presentation at December 31 are shown in Exhibit 10-2. Two points should be emphasized when studying this example. The $6,800 figure, referred to as the asset's *net book value* or *carrying value*, is calculated by subtracting the balance in the asset's Accumulated Depreciation account from its historical cost. In addition, separate accumulated depreciation ledger accounts are maintained for each asset or group of asset ac-

EXHIBIT 10–2

Jan. 2	Delivery Truck	8,500	
	Cash		8,500
	To record purchase of delivery truck.		
Dec. 31	Depreciation Expense	1,700	
	Accumulated Depreciation—Delivery Truck		1,700
	To record depreciation for the year.		

Partial Balance Sheet
December 31

Delivery truck	$8,500
Less: Accumulated depreciation	1,700
	$6,800

counts, such as Buildings, Delivery Equipment, and Office Equipment. However, for balance sheet presentation, large companies often combine all of these balances into one Accumulated Depreciation account.

■ METHODS OF COMPUTING PERIODIC DEPRECIATION

As is the case with determining the cost of ending inventory, there are acceptable alternative methods of computing periodic depreciation. The primary guideline is that the method be rational and systematic. The four most common depreciation methods are straight-line, units-of-production, and two accelerated methods, declining-balance and sum-of-the-years-digits. Management is free to choose any of these methods and can depreciate one class of assets using one method and another class of assets using a different method. As will become clear later, another form of depreciation is usually calculated for tax purposes.

■ FACTORS IN COMPUTING DEPRECIATION

Regardless of which depreciation method is used, certain factors must be considered: (1) the asset's acquisition cost, (2) its residual or salvage value, (3) its depreciable cost, and (4) its estimated useful or economic life.

Acquisition Cost

The previous portions of this chapter explained how the acquisition cost of tangible assets is determined. The proper determination of this figure is important, because it serves as a foundation for many other figures on which periodic depreciation is based.

Residual or Salvage Value

The residual or salvage value is management's best estimate of what an asset will be worth at the time of its disposal—that is, the amount that the firm expects to receive or recover from the asset, less any cost to dispose of it. In many cases, a firm will assume that the cost to dispose of the asset is about equal to what it will recover and thus gives the asset a zero residual value. The residual value is obviously an estimate and is often based on management's past experience. Assets are not depreciated below their salvage value.

Depreciable Cost

Depreciable cost is determined by subtracting an asset's estimated residual value from its acquisition cost. The starting point for most depreciation methods is the asset's depreciable cost. Often this amount is referred to as the asset's *depreciable base*.

Estimated Useful or Economic Life

The asset's estimated useful or economic life is a measure of the service potential that the current user may expect from the asset. Thus when a used asset is purchased, it is assigned a life based on its use to the new owner, regardless of the life assigned to it by the former owner. It can be in years, percentage rates, or units produced, such as expected miles. For example, a delivery truck may have a five-year life. A five-year life represents a 20% per-year depreciation rate ($1 \div 5 = 20\%$). In the case of a delivery truck, it may be appropriate to express its estimated life in terms of expected miles, such as 150,000 miles. All of these methods of expressing useful or economic lives are used for various assets.

Of the factors that affect the depreciation computation, the estimated useful life of an asset is perhaps the most difficult to estimate. Information such as past experience, the asset's physical condition, the firm's maintenance policy, and the state of technology all are used to help estimate an asset's life.

■ METHODS OF COMPUTING DEPRECIATION

To demonstrate the previous concepts, as well as the various depreciation methods, the following data will be used:

Equipment purchase date	January 2, 1990
Cost	$40,000
Residual value	$ 4,000
Depreciable cost	$36,000
Useful life	5 years

Straight-line Depreciation

Straight-line depreciation is the simplest of the various depreciation methods. Under this method, yearly depreciation is calculated by dividing an asset's depreciable cost by its estimated useful life. For example, using the above data, yearly straight-line depreciation is $7,200, calculated as follows:

$$\frac{\text{Cost} - \text{Salvage value}}{\text{Useful life}} = \frac{\$40,000 - \$4,000}{5} = \$7,200$$

When the straight-line method is used, the depreciable cost of the asset is spread evenly over its life, in this case at a uniform rate of 20% ($1 \div 5 = 20\%$). Therefore depreciation expense is the same each year, and by the end of the fifth year, the asset's book value has been reduced to its estimated residual value of $4,000. Even if the equipment is still being used past the fifth year, it is left at its book value of $4,000. These points are summarized in the following schedule:

Year	Acquisition Cost	Yearly Depreciation	Accumulated Depreciation	Book Value
1990	$40,000	$7,200	$ 7,200	$32,800
1991	40,000	7,200	14,400	25,600
1992	40,000	7,200	21,600	18,400
1993	40,000	7,200	28,800	11,200
1994	40,000	7,200	36,000	4,000

This example assumed that an entire year's depreciation is taken in the year of acquisition. However, a firm purchases assets at different times during the year, and a full year's depreciation need not be taken on a midyear purchase. Furthermore, depreciation is often calculated monthly or quarterly for the preparation of interim statements. To illustrate the calculation of partial-year depreciation, assume that in the previous example the asset was purchased on April 1 rather than on January 2. In this case, only nine months of depreciation expense, or $5,400 ($7,200 $\times \frac{9}{12}$, is recorded on December 31.

Straight-line depreciation is widely used because of its simplicity and the fact that it allocates an equal amount of expense to each period of the asset's life. From a conceptual perspective, straight-line depreciation is most appropriate for assets that give up their benefits on a fairly uniform basis, but management can choose straight-line depreciation regardless of the pattern in which the asset gives up its benefits.

Units-of-production Method

The cost of some assets can be more easily allocated according to their estimated production or output, rather than their life. The **units-of-production method** assumes that the primary depreciation factor is use rather than the passage of time and so is appropriate for assets such as delivery trucks and equipment, when there are substantial variations in use. To illustrate, assume that the equipment described above is estimated to produce 120,000 units over its useful life. In this case, depreciation per unit is $0.30, determined as follows:

$$\frac{\text{Cost} - \text{Salvage value}}{\text{Estimated production in units}} = \frac{\$40,000 - \$4,000}{120,000 \text{ units}} = \$0.30 \text{ per unit}$$

This cost per unit is then applied to the units produced during the year. For example, the following schedule shows yearly depreciation over the equipment's life:

Year	Acquisition Cost	Units Produced	Yearly Depreciation	Accumulated Depreciation	Book Value
1990	$40,000	22,000	$6,600	$ 6,600	$33,400
1991	40,000	24,000	7,200	13,800	26,200
1992	40,000	18,000	5,400	19,200	20,800
1993	40,000	26,000	7,800	27,000	13,000
1994	40,000	30,000	9,000	36,000	4,000
		120,000			

It has been assumed that the 120,000 units produced by the equipment are spread over five years. However, when the units-of-production method is used, the life in years is of no consequence.

The units-of-production method requires that the production base, or output measure, be appropriate to the particular asset. For example, miles driven or flown might be most appropriate for a delivery truck or airplane, whereas units produced is most appropriate for a lathe or other equipment. The units-of-production method meets the criterion of being rational and systematic and provides a good matching of expenses and revenues for those assets for which use is an important factor in depreciation. However, for static assets such as buildings, the units-of-production method is inappropriate.

ACCELERATED-DEPRECIATION METHODS

Accelerated-depreciation methods allocate a greater portion of an asset's cost to the early years of its useful life and consequently less to later years. These methods are based on the assumption that some assets produce greater benefits or revenues in their earlier years, and thus a greater portion of their cost should be allocated to those years. The two most common accelerated methods are declining-balance and sum-of-the-years-digits.

Declining-balance Method

Under the **declining-balance method**, yearly depreciation is calculated by applying a fixed percentage rate to an asset's remaining book value at the beginning of each year. Because twice the straight-line rate is generally used, this method is often referred to as *double-declining-balance depreciation*.

In the equipment example, the equipment has a five-year life. This results in an annual straight-line percentage rate of 20% ($1 \div 5 = 20\%$). The double-declining-balance rate is 40% ($2 \times 20\%$). This rate is applied to the asset's remaining book value at the beginning of each year. When applying the double-declining-balance method, the asset's residual value initially is not subtracted from the asset's acquisition cost to arrive at a depreciable cost, as it is when applying the straight-line method, the units-of-production method, and (as will be seen later) the sum-of-the-years-digits method. Residual value is considered only in the last year of the asset's life, when that year's depreciation is limited to the amount that will reduce the asset's book value to its residual value. These points are illustrated in the following schedule, which computes yearly depreciation for the equipment:

Year	Cost	Yearly Depreciation Computation		Expense	Accumulated Depreciation	Book Value
1990	$40,000	$40,000 × .40	=	$16,000	$16,000	$24,000
1991	40,000	24,000 × .40	=	9,600	25,600	14,400
1992	40,000	14,400 × .40	=	5,760	31,360	8,640
1993	40,000	8,640 × .40	=	3,456	34,816	5,184
1994	40,000	*		1,184	36,000	4,000

*Depreciation expense in 1994 is the amount required to reduce the equipment's book value to its residual value of $4,000 ($5,184 − $4,000 = $1,184).

Partial-year depreciation can also be calculated by using the declining-balance method. For example, if the equipment in the previous illustration is purchased on October 1 rather than on January 2, depreciation for the period between October 1 and December 31 is $4,000 ($16,000 × $\frac{3}{12}$). In the second year, depreciation is calculated in the regular manner by multiplying the remaining book value of $36,000 ($40,000 − $4,000) by 40%.

The previous example assumed a depreciation rate equal to twice the straight-line rate. However, many firms use a rate equal to one and one-half the straight-line rate; this is called *150% declining-balance depreciation*. It is calculated in the same manner as is double-declining-balance depreciation, except that the rate is 150% of the straight-line rate.

Sum-of-the-years-digits

The **sum-of-the-years-digits** method is another variation of accelerated depreciation. Under this method, the asset's depreciable base is multiplied by a declining rate. Note that the asset's residual value is subtracted from its acquisition cost to determine its depreciable base. This rate is a fraction, in which the numerator is the number of years remaining in the asset's life at the beginning of the year and the denominator is the sum of the digits of the asset's useful life. To demonstrate how this fraction is computed, assume that an asset has a five-year life. In the first year, the rate is a fraction that has a numerator of 5, the number of years remaining at the beginning of the year. The denominator is 15, or $1 + 2 + 3 + 4 + 5$.[5] In the second year, the fraction is $\frac{4}{15}$, and so forth. The depreciation schedule using the sum-of-the-years-digits method for the equipment appears on page 354.

---

[5] The denominator of the fraction can easily be computed from the following formula:

$$N \frac{(N + 1)}{(2)}$$

where N equals the asset's life. In the above illustration, the denominator is calculated as follows:

$$5 \frac{(5 + 1)}{(2)} = 5(3) = 15$$

If the asset's life is 10 years, the denominator is 55, calculated as follows:

$$10 \frac{(10 + 1)}{(2)} = 10(5.5) = 55$$

Year	Cost	Depreciation Calculation			Accumulated Depreciation	Book Value
		Depreciable Cost ×	Fraction =	Expense		
1990	$40,000	$36,000	× $\frac{5}{15}$ =	$12,000	$12,000	$28,000
1991	40,000	36,000	× $\frac{4}{15}$ =	9,600	21,600	18,400
1992	40,000	36,000	× $\frac{3}{15}$ =	7,200	28,800	11,200
1993	40,000	36,000	× $\frac{2}{15}$ =	4,800	33,600	6,400
1994	40,000	36,000	× $\frac{1}{15}$ =	2,400	36,000	4,000

As with the double-declining-balance method, the sum-of-the-years-digits method allocates more depreciation in early years and less in later years. However, unlike the double-declining-balance method, the sum-of-the-years-digits method is calculated by applying a declining rate to a constant base, the asset's depreciable cost.

Partial-year depreciation can also be calculated under the sum-of-the-years-digits method. For example, now assume that the equipment is purchased on October 1 of the current year. In this case, the equipment is in use for only three months during the year, and the sum-of-the-years-digits depreciation is $3,000, calculated as follows:

$$\$3,000 = \tfrac{3}{12} \times \$12,000, \text{ or } \tfrac{3}{12} \times (\$36,000 \times \tfrac{5}{15})$$

In the second year, the depreciation expense of $11,400 must be calculated in two steps, as follows:

$$\tfrac{9}{12} \times (\$36,000 \times \tfrac{5}{15}) = \quad \$\,9,000$$
$$\tfrac{3}{12} \times (\$36,000 \times \tfrac{4}{15}) = \quad \underline{\;2,400\;}$$
$$\$11,400$$

Depreciation expense for the remaining three years is calculated in a similar manner.

Both declining-balance and sum-of-the-years-digits are examples of accelerated depreciation. From a conceptual perspective, these methods are most appropriate for assets that give up a greater portion of their benefits in their early years. Therefore most of the cost of these assets should be allocated to these same early years. High-tech products are examples of assets in which the decline of benefits is likely to follow such a pattern. Accelerated depreciation is also appropriate for assets that have a greater amount of repair expense in later years. This results in a reasonably constant expense related to the asset because depreciation expense declines as repair expense increases.

Regardless of these conceptual arguments, the management of a firm can choose either accelerated-depreciation method for any depreciable asset. The only guideline is that the depreciation method be systematic and rational; as noted, all of the depreciation methods discussed so far meet this requirement. Furthermore, management can choose straight-line depreciation for financial reporting purposes and accelerated depreciation for tax purposes. This allows a firm to report higher income for financial statement purposes and lower income for tax return purposes.

■ COMPARISON OF VARIOUS DEPRECIATION METHODS

Exhibit 10-3 compares the four depreciation methods graphically, and Exhibit 10-4 compares them in tabular fashion. One of the most important points to note is that in all cases, total depreciation expense over all five years is $36,000. As a consequence, the balance in the Accumulated Depreciation account at the end of the fifth year is also $36,000 in all four cases. This shows that it is a matter of various ways to allocate the same depreciable cost of $36,000, and that each method results in a different expense pattern within the five-year period. These differences are significant and can

EXHIBIT 10–3

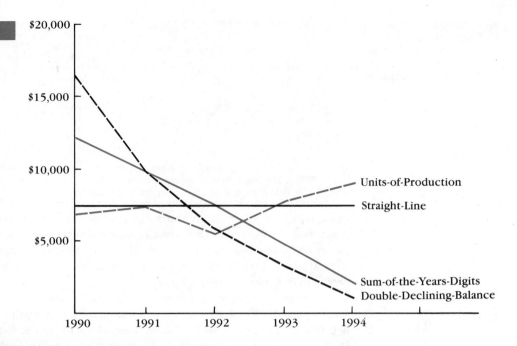

EXHIBIT 10–4 Comparison of Four Depreciation Methods

	Depreciation Expense				Accumulated Depreciation			
Year	Straight-line	Units-of-production	Double-declining-balance	Sum-of-the-years-digits	Straight-line	Units-of-production	Double-declining-balance	Sum-of-the-years-digits
1990	$ 7,200	$ 6,600	$16,000	$12,000	$ 7,200	$ 6,600	$16,000	$12,000
1991	7,200	7,200	9,600	9,600	14,400	13,800	25,600	21,600
1992	7,200	5,400	5,760	7,200	21,600	19,200	31,360	28,800
1993	7,200	7,800	3,456	4,800	28,800	27,000	34,816	33,600
1994	7,200	9,000	1,184	2,400	36,000	36,000	36,000	36,000
Total	$36,000	$36,000	$36,000	$36,000				

have a great effect on earnings for each year. For example, in the first year, double-declining depreciation is $16,000, and depreciation under the units-of-production method is only $6,600. These differences tend to lessen in the middle years of the asset's life and again increase in the last years of the asset's life. However, in the last years, the differences reverse. That is, straight-line and units-of-production depreciation is greater than depreciation under either of the accelerated methods. Of course, the pattern under the units-of-production method could vary in different situations.

Selecting a Depreciation Method for Financial Reporting Purposes

Because all four of the depreciation methods are generally accepted accounting methods, management has the option of selecting any of them for financial reporting purposes. In fact, it is possible to use one method to depreciate equipment and another method to depreciate buildings. All of these methods are used in practice. However, a survey of 600 companies (Exhibit 10-5) shows that the straight-line method is the most popular. Theoretically, the best depreciation method is the one that allocates the cost of the individual asset to the years of its useful life in the same pattern as do the benefits or revenues that the asset produces. Because different assets have different revenue patterns, all of the methods are appropriate in specific circumstances. However, the theoretical soundness of a depreciation method is not an absolute re-

EXHIBIT 10–5

Depreciation Methods
Used by 600 Major
Companies[a]

	Number of Companies[b]			
	1986	**1985**	**1984**	**1983**
Straight-line	561	563	567	564
Declining-balance	49	53	54	57
Sum-of-the-years-digits	14	16	15	17
Accelerated method—Not specified	77	73	76	74
Units-of-production	48	54	60	65
Other	12	12	13	12

[a]Source: AICPA, *Accounting Trends and Techniques,* 41st ed. (New York: AICPA, 1987), p. 296. Reprinted with permission of the AICPA.
[b]Adds up to more than 600, as some companies use more than one method.

quirement for its use. In choosing a particular method for financial reporting purposes, management is usually more concerned with practical motives, such as simplicity and financial statement effects. To a large extent, this explains the popularity of straight-line depreciation. It is easy to compute and results in a constant expense spread over the asset's useful life.

Because the choice of depreciation methods can have a significant effect on a firm's financial statements, current accounting rules require that a firm disclose how it depreciates its assets. This disclosure is usually made in the footnote to the financial statements that summarizes the firm's accounting policies. Such a footnote from the Toys "R" Us financial statements reads in part as shown in Exhibit 10-6.

EXHIBIT 10–6

Toys "R" Us

C. Property and Equipment
Property and equipment are recorded at cost. Depreciation and amortization are provided using the straight-line method over the estimated useful lives of the assets, or where applicable, the terms of the respective leases, whichever is shorter.

2. PROPERTY AND EQUIPMENT

(In thousands)	Useful Life (In years)	January 31 1988	February 1 1987
Land		$275,012	$234,780
Buildings	20 · 50	473,397	361,732
Furniture and equipment	5 · 15	320,491	222,356
Leaseholds and leasehold improvements	12½ · 50	147,526	104,069
Construction in progress		44,911	26,635
		1,261,337	949,572
Less accumulated depreciation and amortization		148,218	108,607
		$1,113,119	$840,965

■ CHOOSING A DEPRECIATION METHOD FOR TAX PURPOSES

Since 1981, Congress has made several significant changes in the depreciation rules for tax purposes. The changes were made in the name of tax reform and tax simplification, but they have served to confuse the tax rules related to depreciation. If assets have been placed in service at various times during the 1980s, they will be depreciated under different tax rules.

Under the tax laws put into place by the Tax Reform Act of 1986, depreciable business property other than real estate is assigned to one of six classes. These classes, called *recovery periods*, prescribe the length of time various assets can be written off or depreciated. Current recovery periods range from three to twenty years. Primary types of assets included in each are:

- The *three-year class* includes small tools.

- In the *five-year class* are light trucks, automobiles, computer equipment, typewriters, calculators, and copiers. Also included: assets used in research and development, oil and gas drilling, construction, and the manufacture of certain products, such as chemicals and electronic components.

- Assets in the *seven-year class* include office furniture and fixtures and most other machinery and equipment.

- There are also *ten-*, *fifteen-*, and *twenty-year classes*, but only a small number of assets—including land improvements, such as drainage pipes—fall into these categories.[6]

Assets in the three-, five-, and seven-year classes can be depreciated using the double-declining-balance method. Assets in the other classes must be depreciated using the 150% declining-balance method. The tax rules for depreciation also involve a rule called the *half-year convention*: For tax purposes, property is depreciated for half the taxable year in which it is placed in service, regardless of when use actually begins. Finally, the salvage or residual value of the asset can be ignored for tax purposes.

To illustrate, assume that a piece of equipment costing $100,000 is purchased and placed into service in 1990. For tax purposes, the asset is placed in the five-year class. Straight-line depreciation is used for financial reporting purposes for all depreciable assets. (The half-year convention is used.) For tax purposes, double-declining-balance depreciation is allowed. However, the tax laws allow a switch to straight-line when it begins to yield a higher depreciation than double-declining-balance. This occurs in the fourth year; at that point, a switch is made to straight-line. Depreciation expense for the asset's life for both tax and financial reporting purposes is calculated in Exhibit 10-7.

EXHIBIT 10–7

Comparison of Depreciation for Tax and Financial Reporting Purposes

Year	Computation	Depreciation Expense
Tax—Double-declining-balance Depreciation, $100,000 Asset Cost, 5-year Life		
1990	$100,000 $\times$ .40 $\times$ $\frac{1}{2}$	$ 20,000
1991	($100,000 − $20,000) $\times$ .40	32,000
1992	($100,000 − $20,000 − $32,000) $\times$ .40	19,200
1993	Convert to straight-line depreciation ($100,000 − $20,000 − $32,000 − $19,200) / $2\frac{1}{2}$ years remaining life	11,520
1994	Straight-line depreciation	11,520
1995	Straight-line depreciation—$\frac{1}{2}$ year	5,760
	Total depreciation	$100,000
Financial Reporting—Straight-line Depreciation, $100,000 Asset Cost, 5-year Life		
1990	$100,000 / 5 years $\times$ $\frac{1}{2}$	$10,000
1991	$100,000 / 5 years	20,000
1992	$100,000 / 5 years	20,000
1993	$100,000 / 5 years	20,000
1994	$100,000 / 5 years	20,000
1995	$100,000 / 5 years $\times$ $\frac{1}{2}$	10,000
	Total depreciation	$100,000

[6] *The Price Waterhouse Personal Tax Adviser* (New York: Simon & Schuster, 1990). Reprinted with permission of Price Waterhouse and Simon & Schuster.

As indicated in Exhibit 10-7, the depreciation for tax purposes provides substantial tax benefits in the asset's first years. Under the tax method, total depreciation expense for the first three years equals $71,200, as compared to $50,000 for financial reporting purposes. Higher depreciation expense for tax purposes means lower net taxable income and thus lower tax payments. In later years, these benefits reverse—depreciation for financial reporting purposes exceeds that for tax purposes. However, the fact that tax payments are deferred until later years benefits the firm, since it is able to earn interest on the money saved in the early years. This issue is discussed further in Chapter 11, pages 398–403.

■ OTHER PROBLEMS RELATED TO DEPRECIATION

In order to explain depreciation concepts, the examples and illustrations so far have been purposely simplified. Actual businesses confront a number of practical problems related to depreciation, including depreciation for partial years, revision of depreciation patterns, and the effects of inflation on depreciation.

Depreciation for a Partial Year

Productive assets are purchased and disposed of at various times during the year. When this occurs, firms often calculate annual depreciation expense for the number of nearest full months since the purchase and up to the full month closest to its disposal. In explaining how depreciation is calculated under the four depreciation methods, it was shown how partial-year depreciation could be computed. Unless other methods were indicated, partial-year depreciation should be computed based on the nearest full month since the purchase or up to the full month closest to the time of disposal. However, because depreciation is inherently an estimate, many firms do not feel that it is necessary to calculate partial-year depreciation so precisely. Two common conventions are often used. Under one convention, depreciation expense is calculated for the entire year if the asset is purchased in the first half of the year. If the asset is purchased in the last half of the year, no depreciation is taken. Under another convention, six months of depreciation is taken in the year of purchase and six months in the year of retirement or disposal, regardless of the date when the asset is actually purchased or disposed of. This six-month convention is built into the IRS tax recovery tables for assets other than real estate.

Revision of Depreciation Patterns

Factors such as economic lives and residual values are estimates made at the time the asset is purchased. Later events may require that these original estimates be revised. For example, improved maintenance techniques may increase the life of an airplane an additional five years beyond the estimate made at the time it was purchased. Failure to revise these estimates for the new information will cause a mismatching of revenue and expense.

A change in estimate is not an error correction. As noted, new events or new information may require a revision of the original estimates. Because of this, changes in depreciation estimates, such as a revision in useful life, are handled by spreading the remaining undepreciated base (undepreciated cost or book value less estimated residual value) of the asset over the years of the new remaining useful life. That is, there is no correction of prior years' statements; only current year's and future years' depreciation are affected. This treatment is required by the accounting profession in APB Opinion No. 20.

To illustrate, assume that on January 2, 1987, the Pen and Ink Company purchases a piece of equipment for $12,000 with a $2,000 residual value. The firm estimates that the equipment will have a useful life of ten years and elects to use straight-line depreciation. At the beginning of the asset's fourth year of life, January 2, 1990, management decides the asset still has a remaining life of ten years instead of seven years. Further, it is estimated that the asset's residual value will be $1,000 at the end of its new remaining useful life. The first step in determining the revised depreciation pattern is to calculate the asset's undepreciated cost, or book value, at the beginning of the fourth year, January 2, 1990. From that value, $9,000 in this case, the new estimated residual value of $1,000 is subtracted. The resulting amount is the remaining depreciable base, which is then spread over the remaining new life. This is done as follows:

Asset's historical cost:	$12,000
Asset's depreciable cost: $12,000 − $2,000 = $10,000	
Yearly depreciation: $10,000 ÷ 10 years = $1,000	
Accumulated depreciation as of 1/2/87: $1,000 × 3 =	(3,000)
Book value at January 2, 1990	$ 9,000
Remaining depreciable base ($9,000 − $1,000 residual value)	$ 8,000
Remaining life based on new estimate	10 years
Yearly depreciation for 1990 and afterwards ($8,000 over 10 years)	$ 800

A change in the estimated lives of the depreciable assets of a firm can have a significant effect the firm's earnings in current and future periods. For example, in 1987 General Motors increased the lives of its tools, dies, and other equipment used to manufacture automobiles. This change is estimated to reduce GM's pretax expenses by $1.5 billion a year. The significance of this change is illustrated in the excerpt from a *Forbes* article[7] reproduced in Exhibit 10-8.

EXHIBIT 10−8

READING THE NUMBERS

Most auto manufacturers write off tools—such as the dies and equipment used to manufacture car bodies—over the life of the body type. GM, long leaning toward conservative bookkeeping, has expensed these tools about twice as fast as Ford and three times as fast as Chrysler. But this is about to change. By slowing down the amortization of these tools, GM will add between $2 and $4 per share to its earnings.

GM now writes off machinery in 10 years, compared with Ford's 12 years and Chrysler's 11 years. GM takes 28 years to write off buildings, compared with 30 years at Ford and 26 at Chrysler.

"Right now," says Drexel Burnham auto analyst David Healy,

"they [GM] are roughly as conservative as Ford, a good deal more so than Chrysler. If GM went through with this change, they would be less conservative than Ford but still more so than Chrysler."

"When we get done we will still be more conservative than the majority of the industry," claims Chairman Roger Smith. "All GM is trying to do is get to the middle of accounting practices."

But by changing its bookkeeping system, GM's timing may be off. Smart investors will interpret the less rigorous bookkeeping as a sign of the company's weakness—an admission that GM has not dealt with its fundamental problems.

A change in depreciation method is another event that will revise the future depreciation pattern. Under current accounting rules, a change in method, such as a change from sum-of-the-years-digits to straight-line depreciation, requires a catch-up adjustment that affects the current period's income. The accounting procedures for this type of depreciation revision will be outlined in Chapter 14.

Arbitrary Allocation

In Chapter 5, it was mentioned that financial statements are based on many estimates as costs are allocated to accounting periods. Depreciation expense, no matter how

[7]Reprinted by permission of *Forbes* magazine, August 24, 1987 (p. 32). © Forbes Inc., 1987.

calculated, is an example of an allocation that is based on estimates. Even though some of the methods, such as double-declining-balance and sum-of-the-years-digits, appear quite scientific, they are based on estimated lives and salvage values. In analyzing financial statements with ratios and other techniques, it is important to keep in mind that these estimates do limit the usefulness of the financial information. However, without making such estimates it would be impossible to prepare periodic financial statements.

Inflation and Depreciation

Historical cost is the primary method of recording assets; periodic depreciation is based on the historical cost of such assets. Many individuals feel that when price levels rise in the economy, historical-cost depreciation overstates profits and does not provide a reasonable picture of a firm's financial position.

To illustrate, assume that a firm purchases a piece of equipment for $2 million in 1980. Over the asset's ten-year life, straight-line depreciation is used. In 1990, the firm purchases a similar asset as a replacement. However, the cost of the new machine is $4 million. In this situation, many accountants feel that the $2 million of depreciation is not adequate and that depreciation expense should have totaled $4 million. This represents the expenditure that the firm must ultimately make to maintain its productive capacity and should therefore be charged to expense over the life of the original asset. That is, depreciation expense is based on the asset's replacement cost rather than on its historical cost. This means that depreciation expense increases as the asset's replacement cost increases.

Because of the difficulty in obtaining objective data on replacement costs, it is not the primary method used in recording assets; rather, the historical cost of the assets is maintained in the records. However, because of the conceptual importance of replacement cost data, the FASB urges public companies to make supplemental disclosure of certain current cost data. With respect to productive assets, large firms are urged to disclose the current cost of their property, plant, and equipment and the related depreciation expense based on current costs. Accounting for inflation will be discussed in Chapter 18.

■ ACCOUNTING FOR SUBSEQUENT EXPENDITURES

Subsequent expenditures made on property, plant, and equipment can be in the form of either capital or revenue expenditures. As noted, the distinction between the two is often hazy and depends on the accounting policies developed by management. However, the distinction is important because it affects the determination of current and future periods' income.

■ REVENUE EXPENDITURES

Revenue expenditures are expenditures whose benefits are used up or consumed in the current period. In terms of plant and equipment, revenue expenditures are usually called *repairs and maintenance*. Technically, a repair or maintenance is an expenditure that maintains the asset's expected level of service or output and neither extends its useful life nor decreases the quantity or quality of its output. These expenditures are expensed in the current period by debiting the expense account Repairs and Maintenance or a similar account.

■ CAPITAL EXPENDITURES SUBSEQUENT TO PURCHASE

Capital expenditures are those that benefit several accounting periods. In terms of plant and equipment, capital expenditures made in periods subsequent to putting an asset in service are considered additions, betterments, or extraordinary repairs. **Additions** are enlargements, such as the addition of a new wing to an existing plant. **Betterments** are improvements to existing assets, such as the installation of a computer-controlled temperature-monitoring system in a department store. **Extraordinary repairs** are a major reconditioning or overhaul of existing assets, such as a major overhaul or the installation of a new engine. Regardless of how these expenditures are described, they either extend the asset's useful life or increase the quantity or quality of its output. Accounting for these expenditures is often accomplished by debiting the asset's Accumulated Depreciation account or, in the case of an addition, debiting the asset account itself. In either case, Cash or an appropriate liability account is credited. The asset's book value is increased by the amount of the capital expenditure, and subsequent depreciation expense is revised.

■ DISPOSAL OF PROPERTY, PLANT, OR EQUIPMENT

Disposal of plant assets can occur through retirement of discarded assets, sales, involuntary conversions, or trade-ins. No matter how the disposal is accomplished, the accounting procedures are quite similar. Depreciation must be recorded up to the date of disposal and, where appropriate, a gain or loss must be recorded on the disposal. These concepts are explained by demonstrating the accounting for the sale and trade-in of plant assets.

■ SALE OF PLANT ASSETS

In some cases, plant assets are sold, rather than retired for no value. An asset can be sold during its useful life when it has a positive book value or at the end of its life when it is fully depreciated. In either situation, a gain or loss will usually result. A gain occurs if the cash or other assets received (referred to as *consideration*) are greater than the book value at the time of sale. Conversely, a loss occurs if the consideration received is less than the book value at the time of sale.

To illustrate, assume that a delivery truck with a historical cost of $35,000 and accumulated depreciation to date of $30,000 (book value of $5,000) is sold for cash; in Case 1 for $7,000 and in Case 2 for $4,000. The journal entries are shown in Exhibit 10-9. As the journal entries show, both the cost of the asset and the amount of related accumulated depreciation are removed from the books. Furthermore, these examples assumed that depreciation has been recorded up to the date of the disposal of the delivery truck. However, in most cases, assets are sold or otherwise disposed of at various dates throughout the year. If depreciation is normally recorded at a date (quarter or year-end) other than the sale date, an entry is required to record the de-

EXHIBIT 10-9

Case 1: Sale Price $7,000			Case 2: Sale Price $4,000		
Cash	7,000		Cash	4,000	
Accumulated Depreciation	30,000		Accumulated Depreciation	30,000	
Delivery Truck		35,000	Loss on Disposal of Asset	1,000	
Gain on Disposal of Asset		2,000	Delivery Truck		35,000
To record $2,000 gain on disposal of asset:			To record a $1,000 loss on disposal of asset:		
Cash Received	$7,000		Cash Received	$4,000	
Book Value of Delivery Truck	5,000		Book Value of Delivery Truck	5,000	
Gain	$2,000		Loss	($1,000)	

preciation expense from the date of the previous depreciation entry to the date of the sale.

■ TRADE-IN OF PLANT ASSETS

Depreciable assets, such as automobiles, computers, and copy machines, are often traded in for similar new assets. In most cases, the trade-in allowance on the asset might be considerably different from its book value. If the trade-in allowance is higher than the book value, a gain will be realized on the trade-in. Conversely, if the trade-in allowance is less than the book value, a loss will be realized. However, care must be exercised when using a trade-in allowance to measure a gain or loss. Dealers such as automobile companies often set an unrealistically high list price in order to offer an inflated trade-in allowance. This is done in order to make the transaction appear more attractive to the buyer.

The accounting procedures that govern trade-ins are quite complex, but for present purposes they can be stated as follows:

1. Realized gains on the trade-in of assets for similar assets are not usually recognized as accounting gains. The cost basis of the new asset is the book value of the old, plus the additional cash or other consideration paid.

2. Realized losses on the trade-in of similar assets are always recognized.[8]

Both of these situations will be described next.

Gain Realized But Not Recognized

To illustrate the accounting procedures when a gain on a trade-in is realized, assume that the Jackson Company trades in a delivery truck for a new one. At the time of the trade-in, the old delivery truck has a historical cost of $40,000 and accumulated depreciation to date of $30,000 (book value equals $10,000). The new truck has a list price of $65,000, and the dealer gives the Jackson Company a trade-in allowance of $14,000 for the old truck, which is assumed to be equal to its fair market value at that time. Thus a cash payment of $51,000 ($65,000 − $14,000) is made for the difference. Since the asset was traded in for a similar one, the realized gain of $4,000 (trade-in allowance of $14,000 less book value of $10,000) is not recognized in the accounting records, and the cost basis of the new truck is $61,000, computed as follows:

Book Value of Old Truck	$10,000
Cash Paid	51,000
Cost Basis of New Truck	$61,000

The entry to record this trade-in is:

Delivery Truck, New	61,000	
Accumulated Depreciation	30,000	
Delivery Truck, Old		40,000
Cash		51,000
To record trade-in of old delivery truck		
and purchase of new delivery truck.		

At first, it may seem strange that a realized gain is not recognized in the accounting records. The APB felt that revenue should not be recognized merely because one productive asset is exchanged or substituted for a similar one. According to the APB, revenue flows from the production and sale of the goods and services are made possible by the new asset, not from the exchange of one asset for another.[9] In effect, the

---

[8]American Institute of Certified Public Accountants, Accounting Principles Board, Opinion No. 29, *Accounting for Nonmonetary Transactions* (New York: AICPA, 1973), par. 22.

[9]Ibid., par. 16.

realized gain of $4,000 is just postponed. It is ultimately realized through lower depreciation charges in future years, which are based on a cost of $61,000 rather than at its list price of $65,000. Furthermore, because the new asset has a lower book value than if the realized gain of $4,000 had been recognized, a larger gain or a smaller loss will be recognized if and when it is finally disposed of other than by another trade-in.

Loss Realized and Recognized

Because of the conservatism concept in accounting, any realized loss on a trade-in must be recognized in the accounting records. For example, assume the same facts in the previous example, but now the dealer offers a trade-in allowance of only $8,000, which is now assumed to be equal to the asset's fair market value. As a result, a loss of $2,000 ($10,000 book value less $8,000 trade-in allowance) is both realized and recognized. Because the trade-in allowance is only $8,000, a cash payment of $57,000 must also be made by the Jackson Company. Finally, the new asset cannot be recorded at a value higher than the fair market value of $65,000. Failure to record the loss would inflate the cost of the new asset above its present fair value. The appropriate entry is:

Delivery Truck, New	65,000	
Accumulated Depreciation	30,000	
Loss on Disposal	2,000	
Delivery Truck, Old		40,000
Cash		57,000
To record $2,000 loss on trade-in		
and purchase of new delivery truck.		

■ NATURAL RESOURCES

Natural resources are physical substances that, when extracted from the ground, are converted into inventory, and when sold, produce revenues for the firm. Natural resources include oil, natural gas, coal, iron, uranium, and timber. These assets are often referred to as *wasting assets*, because once they are removed from the ground or physically consumed, they cannot be replaced.

Natural resources give up their benefits as the resources are removed. This process is called *depletion*. It is computed in the same manner as units-of-production depreciation. That is, in order to determine the cost per unit of output, the capitalized cost, less residual or salvage value, of the natural resources is divided by the estimated output. This per-unit cost is then charged to depletion expense as the resources are removed.

To show how depletion is calculated, assume that the JDD Company pays $18 million for land on which to drill oil. Other capitalized costs relating to exploration and development are $14 million, so the total cost is $32 million. The company estimates that there will be a $2 million residual value at the end of the project, so the total depletable cost is $30 million. Geologists estimate that the oil field will produce 15 million barrels of oil over the project's life. The depletion charge is $2 per barrel, calculated as follows:

$$\frac{\text{Accumulated cost} - \text{Residual value}}{\text{Estimated barrels of oil to be produced}}$$

$$\frac{\$32,000,000 - \$2,000,000}{15,000,000 \text{ barrels}} = \$2.00 \text{ per barrel}$$

Assuming that 4.5 million barrels were produced in the current year, the depletion charge is $9 million ($4,500,000 × $2.00), and the required journal entry is:

Depletion Expense   9,000,000
  Oil Field   9,000,000
To record depletion expense of $9,000,000 based
on production of 4,500,000 barrels of oil during
the period.

By convention, the credit is made directly to the asset account rather than a contra-asset account. The depletion expense ultimately becomes part of the cost of the oil inventory that eventually will be sold. This allocation can be accomplished by making the following journal entry:

Inventory of Oil   9,000,000
  Depletion Expense   9,000,000
To transfer depletion expense
to inventory of oil.

Other production costs such as transportation and direct labor must be included as part of the inventoriable cost of the oil. To continue the same example, assume that during the year these costs amounted to $7.5 million. They would be recorded as follows:

Inventory of Oil   7,500,000
  Cash, Accounts Payable, etc.   7,500,000
To record production costs of $7,500,000.

After these entries, and assuming that no sales have yet taken place, the relevant section of JDD's balance sheet would be as follows:

JDD CORPORATION		
Partial Balance Sheet		
Current assets		
Inventory of oil	$16,500,000	
Natural resources		
Oil fields, net	23,000,000	

The inventory of oil is recorded in the current asset section, and the book value of the oil fields is shown in the noncurrent section under natural resources. Finally, when the barrels of oil are sold, the sale and cost of sale are recorded in the usual manner.

■ ESTABLISHING A DEPLETION BASIS— SUCCESSFUL EFFORTS VERSUS FULL COST

In recent years, there has been considerable controversy related to determining the proper cost for an oil well. Once the firm obtains exploration rights, it will incur certain exploration costs. These exploration costs can be immense for companies such as ARCO and Exxon, and the way they are accounted for can have a significant effect on an oil company's financial statements.

Most large oil companies use what is called the **successful-efforts method** of accounting. Under this method, only the exploration costs of successful finds are capitalized into the Natural Resource asset account. Exploration cost of unsuccessful activities are immediately written off to expense in the current period. Because of the immediate expensing of the costs associated with dry wells, many accountants consider the successful-efforts method to be the more conservative method.

Some firms follow what is referred to as the **full-cost method**. Under this method, all exploration costs are capitalized into the cost of the natural resource asset account. Thus the cost of producing oil wells includes the exploration cost of those wells in addition to the costs of the dry wells. Depletion is then based on this full cost.

Because exploration costs of unsuccessful wells are capitalized instead of written off in the current period, the full-cost method tends to improve earnings in early years. Each method will produce considerably different periodic income figures, but both are acceptable under current accounting practices.

In 1977, the FASB issued Statement 19, which required all firms to use the successful-efforts method. This Statement generated considerable controversy, and strong opposition arose from smaller oil companies, many of which were using the full-cost method. These smaller oil companies felt that if they were forced to switch to successful-efforts, their earning performance would decline and their ability to raise capital for further exploration would be hurt. Because of this controversy and the intervention of the Securities and Exchange Commission, the FASB suspended that Statement and, as noted, both methods are currently acceptable.

■ INTANGIBLE ASSETS

Intangible assets are noncurrent assets that have no physical properties. They generate revenues because of the right of ownership or use. However, there is generally a higher degree of uncertainty concerning the benefits generated from intangible assets than concerning tangible assets. In addition, intangible assets are differentiated from nonphysical assets, such as accounts receivable or prepayments, because intangible assets are long-term in nature and contribute to the production or operating cycle of a business.

Intangible assets are generally divided into two categories: those that are specifically identifiable and those that are not. **Specifically identifiable intangible assets** are those intangibles whose costs can be easily identified as part of the cost of the asset and whose benefits generally have a determinable life. Examples include patents, trademarks, franchises, and leaseholds. Conversely, intangibles that are not specifically identifiable represent some right or benefit that has an indeterminate life and whose cost is inherent in a continuing business. The primary example of such an intangible is goodwill. Exhibit 10-10 contains a list of the most common intangible assets.

EXHIBIT 10–10 Common Intangible Assets	

Type of Intangible Asset	Description
Specifically Identifiable Patent	An exclusive right to use, manufacture, process, or sell a product granted by the U.S. Patent Office. Patents have a legal life of 17 years, but their economic life may be shorter.
Copyright	The exclusive right of the creator or heirs to reproduce and/or sell an artistic or published work. Granted by the U.S. government for a period of 50 years after the death of the creator.
Leaseholds	A contractual agreement between a lessor (owner of the property) and a lessee (user of the property) that gives the lessee the right to use the lessor's property for a specific period of time in exchange for cash payments.
Leasehold Improvements	Improvements that are made by the lessee that at the end of the lease term revert to the ownership of the lessor.
Trademark and Trade Name	A symbol or name that allows the holder to use it to identify or name a specific product or service. A legal registration system allows for an indefinite number of 20-year renewals.
Organization Cost	Costs incurred in the creation of a corporation, including legal fees, registration fees, and fees to underwriters. <div align="right">(continued)</div>

EXHIBIT 10–10

(continued)

Type of Intangible Asset	Description
Franchise	An exclusive right to use a formula, design, technique, or territory.
Not Specifically Identifiable Goodwill	Present value of expected excess earnings of a business above average industry earnings. Recorded only when a business is purchased at a price above the market value of the individual net assets of the business.

■ ACCOUNTING PROBLEMS RELATED TO INTANGIBLE ASSETS

The accounting treatment of intangible assets parallels the accounting treatment of tangible noncurrent assets. Thus it is necessary to (1) measure and capitalize their acquisition cost; (2) amortize their cost over the shorter of their legal life, if any, or their economic life (in no case can the amortization period exceed 40 years); and (3) account for any gain or loss at their disposition.

Determining Acquisition Cost

Intangible assets are originally recorded at cost. As with tangible assets, cost includes all the expenditures necessary to get the intangible asset ready for its intended use. Included in the acquisition cost are the purchase price and any legal fees. If an intangible asset such as a trademark or goodwill is acquired without a cost, it is not shown on the balance sheet. Subsequent valuation of intangibles is at net book value (that is, at cost less accumulated amortization to date).

Operating Expenses and Intangible Assets. Because intangible assets are characterized by a lack of physical qualities, it is difficult to determine the value of their future benefits and the life of those benefits. As a consequence, it is difficult to separate expenditures that are essentially operating expenses from those that give rise to intangible assets. For example, advertising and promotion campaigns and training programs provide future benefits to the firm. If this were not the case, firms would not spend the millions of dollars on these programs that they do. However, it is extremely difficult to measure the amount and life of the benefits generated by such programs. Therefore expenditures for these and similar items are written off as an expense in the period incurred. When recurring expenditures are made for these items in approximately equal amounts, the effect on periodic income is not much different than if they were capitalized and then amortized over their estimated life.

Research and Development Costs. Research and development costs are expenditures incurred in discovering, planning, designing, and implementing a new product or process. Accounting for these costs has presented the accounting profession with significant problems. Clearly, they provide the firm with some future benefits. The billions of dollars spent by firms such as IBM result in new successful products but also in products that never reach the marketplace or are unsuccessful in the marketplace. Thus it is difficult to measure the ultimate benefits that accrue from research and development expenditures that are made in 1991 but that may not result in a product until 1998. Furthermore, in today's highly competitive world economy, it is almost impossible to measure how long any of the benefits produced by research and development expenditures will last. The failure of IBM's PC Jr. is a good example of this. Because of these problems and the diversity of accounting practices that existed, the FASB now requires that all research and development costs be expensed in the period incurred.[10]

---

[10] Financial Accounting Standards Board, Statement No. 2, *Accounting for Research and Development Costs* (Stamford, Conn.: FASB, October 1974), par. 12.

Amortization of Intangible Assets

For accounting purposes, intangible assets do not have an indefinite life, so their cost must be systematically written off to expense over their useful life.[11] This is generally done by debiting the Amortization Expense account and crediting the Intangible Asset account directly. By convention, an Accumulated Amortization account is not used, although there is no reason why it could not be.

Estimating the useful life of intangible assets is quite difficult. Some assets, such as patents, have legal lives, whereas others, such as trademarks, have indefinite lives. If a legal life exists, the intangible asset should be amortized over its useful economic life or legal life, whichever is shorter. The APB ruled that if an intangible asset has a legal life of over 40 years or has an indeterminate economic life, the period of amortization should not exceed 40 years.[12] In practice, straight-line amortization is used, although any systematic, rational method can be used.[13]

Gains and Losses on Disposition

When intangible assets are sold or otherwise disposed of, a gain or a loss equal to the difference between the amount received for the asset (if any) and its book value is recorded. If there has been a substantial or permanent decline in the value of an intangible asset still on hand, the unamortized cost should be reduced or written off as an expense of the current period.

■ ACCOUNTING FOR SPECIFIC INTANGIBLE ASSETS

Exhibit 10-10 listed some of the more common intangible assets. The following section will outline the accounting for the more significant intangible assets.

Patents

A **patent** is an exclusive right to use, manufacture, process, or sell a product; it is granted by the U.S. Patent Office. Patents can either be purchased from the inventor or holder or generated internally. When a patent is purchased from the inventor, its capitalized cost includes its acquisition cost and other incidental costs, such as legal fees. The legal costs of successfully defending a patent are also capitalized as part of its cost.

If a patent results from successful research and development efforts, its cost is only the legal or other fees necessary to patent the invention, product, or process. This is because all the research and development costs expended to develop the patent, including those in the year the patent is obtained, must be written off to expense in the period the expenditure occurs.

A patent has a legal life of 17 years. In many cases, however, its useful economic life is less than 17 years. As a result, patents should be amortized over their remaining legal life or economic life, whichever is shorter. For example, assume that a patent is purchased from its inventor for $240,000. At that time, the patent has a remaining legal life of ten years but has an estimated economic life of eight years. In this case, the patent should be amortized on a straight-line basis over eight years, with the journal entry made each year as shown on page 368.

---

[11] In previous years, some accountants argued that some intangibles had an indefinite life. This view was rejected by both the AICPA and the FASB.

[12] American Institute of Certified Public Accountants, Accounting Principles Board, Opinion No. 17, *Intangible Assets* (New York: AICPA, 1970), par. 29.

[13] Under the current Internal Revenue Code regulations, goodwill or other intangible assets that the IRS considers to resemble goodwill cannot be amortized for tax purposes. Therefore amortization of those intangibles does not reduce taxable income.

| Amortization Expense | 30,000 | |
| Patent | | 30,000 |

To amortize the patent at $30,000
per year ($240,000 over 8 years).

Copyrights

A **copyright** is the exclusive right of the creator or heirs to reproduce and/or sell an artistic or published work. The copyright is granted by the U.S. government for the life of the creator plus 50 years. The cost to the creator of obtaining a copyright from the government is the modest sum of $10, which is usually charged to an expense account when incurred. However, when a copyright is purchased by someone other than the creator, its cost may be substantial and should be capitalized. The capitalized cost should then be amortized over its remaining economic life, which is usually substantially shorter than its original legal life.

Leaseholds and Leasehold Improvements

A **lease** is a contractual agreement between the lessor (the owner of the property) and the lessee (the user of the property), giving the lessee the right to use the lessor's property for a specific period of time in exchange for stipulated cash payments. The rights contained in this agreement are usually called *leaseholds*.

Leases are classified into two types: operating leases and capital leases. **Capital leases**, which are complex financing arrangements, will be briefly discussed in Chapter 12. **Operating leases** usually require regular monthly payments by the lessee, but the lessor retains control and ownership of the property. The property or equipment always reverts to the lessor at the end of the lease term. Renting office space on a monthly or yearly basis is an example of an operating lease. Leases of this type do not result in a leasehold. The lessee records the lease by debiting Rent or Lease Expense and crediting Cash. The leased property remains on the books of the lessor.

Some operating lease payments require the prepayment of the final month's rent. When this occurs, this payment is classified as a prepaid expense and remains on the books until the lease is terminated. Leases may also require a lump-sum rental payment that represents additional rent over the life of the lease. This is usually a significant amount in relation to the monthly payment and should be written off over the life of the lease.

Leasehold improvements are improvements made by the lessee to leased property. They consist of such items as air conditioning, partitioning, and elevators. These improvements are permanent in nature and become the property of the lessor when the leased property reverts to the lessor at the termination of the operating lease. These expenditures should be recorded in an asset account called Leasehold Improvements and amortized over the shorter of their useful life or the remaining term of the lease.

Franchises

A **franchise** is a right to use a formula, design, or technique or the right to conduct business in a certain territory. Franchises can be granted by either a business enterprise or a governmental unit. Many businesses, such as fast-food restaurants and convenience markets, are operated as franchises. For example, the parent company of 7-Eleven Markets sells franchises to individual owner-operators. Cities and municipalities also often grant franchises, such as a taxi franchise that allows a company to operate in a specified territory for a designated period of time.

If the cost of a franchise is substantial, it should be capitalized and amortized over its useful life, not to exceed 40 years. If the cost is insignificant, the expenditure can be treated as an expense and immediately written off.

Goodwill

Goodwill has a specific meaning in accounting. It represents the value today of the excess earnings of a particular enterprise. Excess earnings represent earnings above what is normal in that industry. That is, the firm is able to earn a rate of return on its recorded net assets above the industry average rate of return. Such excess earnings are the result of a number of factors, including superior management, well-trained employees, good location, monopoly, and manufacturing efficiencies. Unlike the other intangible assets, goodwill is not specifically identifiable and is not separable from the firm. Thus goodwill can be recorded only when purchased. The existence of internally generated goodwill is verified only when a firm is purchased by another party; at that time, the goodwill (if any) is paid for and recorded.

To illustrate the concept of goodwill, assume that a group of investors purchases an electronic components manufacturing business. At the time of the purchase, the fair market value of the firm's net assets totals $1 million, consisting of the following:

Inventory	$ 400,000
Property, plant, and equipment, net	900,000
Other assets	200,000
Total assets acquired	$1,500,000
Total liabilities assumed	500,000
Net assets acquired	$1,000,000

The agreed-upon purchase price is $1,250,000; this implies goodwill of $250,000—the purchase price of $1,250,000 less the identifiable net assets acquired of $1 million. The entry to record the purchase is as follows:

Inventory	400,000	
Property, Plant, and Equipment	900,000	
Other Assets	200,000	
Goodwill	250,000	
Liabilities		500,000
Cash		1,250,000

As this journal entry shows, the purchase price is first allocated to the identifiable net assets based on their fair market value. Any remaining portion is considered goodwill and is recorded by a debit to the Goodwill account. Subsequently, goodwill is amortized over a period not exceeding 40 years.

SUMMARY OF LEARNING OBJECTIVES

1. The accounting concepts and issues related to noncurrent, nonmonetary assets. Noncurrent, nonmonetary assets include both tangible and intangible assets. Tangible assets include property, plant, and equipment and natural resources. Intangible assets have no physical substance and include such assets as patents, franchises, and goodwill. All noncurrent, nonmonetary assets

(a) Are future economic services.

(b) Affect several accounting periods.

(c) Are systematically allocated over the periods in which the benefits are received (except for land).

2. Differentiating between capital and revenue expenditures. When a firm makes an expenditure that results in the acquisition of an asset, it is called a *capital expenditure*. When the expenditure results in a service whose benefits are consumed in the current period, it is called a *revenue expenditure*. The distinction between capital and revenue expenditures is important when determining periodic net income, because capital expenditures affect several periods, whereas revenue expenditures affect only the current period's income.

3. Measuring the acquisition cost of property, plant, and equipment. The historical cost of plant assets includes all the costs necessary to get the assets to their location and in condition to be used. Included are such costs as transportation charges, insurance in transit, installation, and testing costs. When the purchase is made for cash, the acquisition cost is the net cash price. When a noncash acquisition is made, the acquisition cost is equal to the cash given plus the fair market value of the noncash consideration given. If it is difficult or impossible to obtain the fair market value of the noncash consideration given, the transaction should be recorded at the fair market value of the asset received.

4. The accounting concept of depreciation. Depreciation is the process of allocating the cost of plant and equipment to the period in which the enterprise receives the benefits from the assets. Depreciation is not a valuation concept, nor is it a direct source of cash. Rather, it is caused by such factors as physical deterioration and obsolescence.

5. Methods of computing periodic depreciation. There are several alternative methods of computing depreciation, all of which meet the criteria of being systematic and rational. The four most common methods are straight-line and units-of-production and two accelerated methods, declining-balance and sum-of-the-years-digits. Management is free to choose any of these methods for financial reporting purposes. For tax purposes, depreciation is calculated under the IRS recovery tables.

6. Other problems related to accounting for depreciation. There are several other problems related to accounting for depreciation: depreciation for partial years, revision of depreciation rates, and the effects of inflation.

7. Accounting for subsequent expenditures. Expenditures made on plant and equipment consist of either revenue expenditures or capital expenditures. Revenue expenditures are generally for repairs and maintenance that maintain the asset's expected level of service. They neither extend the asset's useful life nor increase the quantity or quality of its output. Capital expenditures after acquisition benefit several accounting periods; they may be additions, betterments, or extraordinary repairs.

8. Disposal of plant assets. Disposal of plant assets occurs through retirements, sales, or trade-ins. In most cases, a firm will realize a gain or loss on disposal. The gain or loss is measured by the difference between the book value of the disposed asset and the consideration (if any) received for it. However, when the plant asset is traded in for a similar one, a gain is not recognized, though a loss is always recognized. The following table summarizes these concepts:

Method of Disposal	Is the Gain/Loss to Be Recognized for Accounting Purposes?
Sale of asset at realized gain	Yes
Sale of asset at realized loss	Yes
Trade-in of asset for similar asset at realized gain	No
Trade-in of asset for similar asset at realized loss	Yes

9. Accounting for natural resources. Natural resources are physical substances that are extracted from the ground; they are often called *wasting assets*. Their cost must be allocated on a prorated basis over the units produced. This process is called *depletion*. The depletable base of natural resources includes the acquisition cost of the site land, exploration costs, and development costs.

10. Intangible assets. Intangible assets have no physical properties. They generate revenue for the firm because they give it the right of ownership or use. Intangible assets include patents, trademarks, franchises, leaseholds, and goodwill. (See Exhibit 10-10.) Intangible assets have a definite life and must be amortized over the shorter of their legal life or economic life. In no case, however, can the amortization period exceed 40 years.

KEY TERMS

Accelerated depreciation

Additions

Amortization

Betterments

Capital expenditure

Capital lease

Copyright

Declining-balance method

Depletion

Depreciable cost

Extraordinary repairs

Franchise

Full-cost method

Intangible assets

Lease

Leasehold improvements

Natural resources

Obsolescence

Operating lease

Patent

Research and development costs

Revenue expenditure

Specifically identifiable intangible assets

Straight-line depreciation

Successful-efforts method

Sum-of-the-years-digits method

Tangible assets

Units-of-production method

PROBLEMS FOR YOUR REVIEW

A. Acquisition Cost of Assets. During 1990, the C. Price Company purchased the following assets:

■ January 15: Purchase of land and building in which to conduct business. The entire cost was $5,000,000, cash. The assets were appraised at the following individual values:

| Land | $1,500,000 |
| Buildings | 4,500,000 |

■ April 14: Store equipment with a list price of $10,000 was purchased on account. The terms were 2/10, n/30. Other costs incurred for cash were:

Shipping	$500
Insurance in transit	50
Installation	100
Repair for damage in transit	200

REQUIRED: Make all the required journal entries. It is not necessary to make the December 31, 1990 depreciation entries for the plant's assets still on hand.

SOLUTION

January 15	Land	1,250,000	
	Buildings	3,750,000	
	Cash		5,000,000

To record purchase of land and
buildings, allocated as follows:

Account	Fair Market Value	%	Total Purchase Price	Allocation of Total Purchase Price
Land	$1,500,000	25% × $5,000,000 =	$1,250,000
Building	4,500,000	75% × $5,000,000 =	3,750,000
	$6,000,000		$5,000,000

April 14	Store Equipment	10,450*	
	Repair	200	
	Accounts Payable		9,800
	Cash		850

To record purchase of store
equipment on account.
*$10,450 = ($10,000 × .98) + $500 + $50 + $100

B. Commute Air, a small commuter airline, purchased an airplane for $6 million. The president of the company is trying to decide how to depreciate the plane. She asks you to calculate the annual depreciation for each of the next three years under each of the following methods:

1. straight-line.

3. double-declining-balance.

2. units-of-production.

4. sum-of-the-years-digits.

In each case, the asset has a ten-year life, or a 110 million-mile life. Miles flown are:

Year	Miles Flown
1	8,800,000
2	10,000,000
3	15,000,000

The plane has an estimated residual value of $500,000.

SOLUTION

	Year 1	Year 2	Year 3
Straight-line[a]	$ 550,000	$550,000	$550,000
Units-of-production[b]	440,000	500,000	750,000
Double-declining-balance[c]	1,200,000	960,000	768,000
Sum-of-the-years-digits[d]	1,000,000	900,000	800,000

a. $\dfrac{\$6,000,000 - \$500,000}{10 \text{ years}} = \$550,000$ per year

b. $\dfrac{\$6,000,000 - \$500,000}{110,00,000 \text{ miles}} = \$.05$ per mile

c. Year 1 $\$6,000,000 \times .20* =$ $1,200,000

   Year 2 $(\$6,000,000 - \$1,200,000) \times .20 =$ 960,000

   Year 3 $(\$4,800,000 - \$960,000) \times .20 =$ 768,000

d. Year 1 $(\$6,000,000 - \$500,000) \times \frac{10†}{55} =$ $1,000,000

   Year 2 $(\$6,000,000 - \$500,000) \times \frac{9}{55} =$ 900,000

   Year 3 $(\$6,000,000 - \$500,000) \times \frac{8}{55} =$ 800,000

*Straight-line rate = 10%; twice the straight-line rate = 20%. Salvage value is not considered until the last year.

$†N \dfrac{(N+1)}{2} = 10 \dfrac{(11)}{2} = 55$

C.   The property, plant, and equipment section of the Ken and Bob Company's December 31, 1990 balance sheet contained the following items:

Property, plant, and equipment		
Land		$1,000,000
Radio studio	$5,000,000	
Less accumulated depreciation	250,000	4,750,000
Radio and broadcasting		
Equipment	$ 600,000	
Less accumulated depreciation	120,000	480,000
Total property, plant, and equipment		$6,230,000

In addition, you gathered the following information:

1. All assets were acquired on January 2, 1988.

2. The firm depreciates all assets on a straight-line basis with no residual value and with the following lives:

  (a) Radio studio   40 years

  (b) Radio and broadcasting equipment   10 years

3. The following transactions occurred during 1990:

- April 1: A new additional broadcasting studio was finished. The studio had a cost of $1 million and the new equipment a cost of $50,000. All items were paid for in cash.
- July 15: Repairs of $5,000 were made for cash on certain pieces of radio equipment.
- September 30: Radio equipment with a cost of $100,000 and accumulated depreciation of $20,000 (as of 12/31/89) was sold for $82,000 cash.
- December 30: Radio equipment with a cost of $50,000 and accumulated depreciation of $10,000 (as of 12/31/89) was traded in for new equipment. The firm received a trade-in allowance of $32,000. The list price of the new equipment is $85,000.

REQUIRED: Make all the required journal entries. It is not necessary to make the December 31, 1990 depreciation entries for the plant assets still on hand.

SOLUTION

April 1	Radio Studio	1,000,000	
	Radio and Broadcasting Equipment	50,000	
	Cash		1,050,000
	To record addition to radio studio and purchase of new equipment.		
July 15	Repair and Maintenance Expense	5,000	
	Cash		5,000
	To record $5,000 repair on radio equipment.		
Sept. 30	Depreciation Expense	7,500	
	Accumulated Depreciation—Radio and Broadcasting Equipment		7,500
	To record depreciation for 9 months on radio and broadcasting equipment to be sold.		
	$100,000 × .10 × $\frac{9}{12}$ = $7,500		
	Cash	82,000	
	Accumulated Depreciation—Radio and Broadcasting Equipment	27,500	
	Gain on Sale of Radio and Broadcasting Equipment		9,500
	Radio and Broadcasting Equipment		100,000
	To record gain on sale of equipment of $9,500, computed as follows:		

Historical Cost		$100,000
Accumulated Depreciation		
to 12/31/89	$20,000	
from 1/2/90 to 9/30/90	7,500	27,500
Book Value on 9/30/90		72,500
Cash Received		82,000
Gain		$ 9,500

Dec. 30	Depreciation Expense	5,000	
	Accumulated Depreciation—Radio and Broadcasting Equipment		5,000
	To record depreciation for the year 1990 on equipment trade-in.		
	$50,000 × .10 = $5,000		
	New Radio and Broadcasting Equipment	85,000	
	Accumulated Depreciation—Radio and Broadcasting Equipment	15,000	
	Loss on Trade-in	3,000	
	Old Radio and Broadcasting Equipment		50,000
	Cash		53,000
	To record trade-in of radio equipment, computed as follows:		

Historical Cost		$50,000
Accumulated Depreciation		
to 12/31/89	$10,000	
from 1/2/89 to 12/31/90	5,000	15,000
Book Value at 12/31/90		35,000
Trade-in Allowance		32,000
Loss		($ 3,000)

Because this trade-in resulted in a loss, it must be recognized. If a gain had occurred, it would not be recognized.

QUESTIONS

1. What are the similarities and differences between tangible and intangible assets? Give three examples of each.

2. Why must the cost of noncurrent, nonmonetary assets be allocated to future accounting periods? What are some of the problems with this allocation process?

3. Explain the meaning of *capital expenditure*. How does it differ from a revenue expenditure? From an accounting perspective, describe the consequences of recording a capital expenditure as a revenue expenditure.

4. Smith Corporation purchased a computer for $500,000. Freight charges amounted to $750 and were paid by Smith. Smith also incurred costs of $1,500 to have the old computer taken out and $2,500 to have the new one installed. Subsequently, the old computer was sold for $20,000. At what amount should Smith record the new computer?

5. If interest of $80,000 is capitalized as part of the acquisition cost of self-constructed assets, what effect does this have on current and future periods' income?

6. Explain the accountant's concept of depreciation. Why do accountants insist on depreciating a building whose fair market value is increasing?

7. Your best friend, who knows very little about accounting, made the following statement after purchasing a new car: "I just bought this car for $8,500, and as soon as I drove it off the lot it depreciated by one-third." How would you respond?

8. What is meant by each of the following terms, and how are they estimated?

(a) residual or salvage value.

(b) economic or useful life.

(c) depreciable cost.

9. How is depreciation determined for tax purposes? How does it compare with depreciation methods used for financial reporting purposes? Why do you think the Internal Revenue Code is different from generally accepted accounting principles?

10. In examining the annual reports of the Flemming and Jose companies, you notice that the Flemming Company uses straight-line depreciation and the Jose Company uses double-declining balance. Both firms are in the same industry, are about the same size, and pur-chase similar assets. Isn't one firm's depreciation policy incorrect? Why or why not?

11. Why would a company change its original estimate of an asset's useful life? How is this change accounted for?

12. The Southern Iowa Utility Company is in the process of building a nuclear power plant. The cost of the plant is $25 million. Under the current Iowa laws, the plant must be dismantled after 50 years. Southern Iowa estimates that it will cost $10 million to dismantle the plant. How should this $10 million be handled from an accounting perspective? What is the depreciable cost of the nuclear plant?

13. Many individuals argue that in a period of inflation, historical-cost depreciation overstates earnings. What do they mean, and how can this problem be overcome?

14. Define the following terms:

(a) additions.

(b) betterments.

(c) extraordinary repairs.

(d) revenue expenditures.

15. Briefly describe the accounting procedures for the sale or retirement of plant assets. How is the gain or loss on the sale or retirement of plant assets determined?

16. Briefly describe the accounting procedures when a trade-in allowance is given on the purchase of a new asset that is similar to the old asset.

17. Why is a gain not recognized when an asset is traded in for a similar one? What is the ultimate effect of not recognizing the gain on the firm's financial statements over the life of the new asset?

18. Why are natural resources often referred to as *wasting assets*? What costs are commonly included in the acquisition of natural resources?

19. What is depletion, and how is it calculated?

20. What is the difference between full-cost and successful-efforts accounting?

21. The Found-It Gas Company recognized $1.50 depletion for each metric ton of gas taken from the well head. During the year, the firm produced 1 million metric tons of gas, of which 750,000 tons were delivered to customers. The remaining was stored for future delivery. How much depletion expense should Found-It recognize in the current year?

22. Briefly define and describe intangible assets. How do these assets offer future benefits to a firm?

23. What are research and development costs? Under current accounting principles, how are these costs accounted for? Do you agree with this treatment? Why or why not?

24. Why must intangible assets be amortized? What factors should you consider in determining the useful life of an intangible asset?

25. The Alfredo Invention Company recently acquired two patents. The first patent was purchased from the Klein-Smith Corporation for $2.5 million. The second patent was developed internally. The previous year's research and development costs were $1.5 million. During the current year, additional R&D costs amounted to $750,000. Also during the year, legal fees of $250,000 were incurred to obtain the patent. How should each of these patents be recorded on Alfredo's books?

26. One of your good friends owns a fashionable restaurant. In recent years, the restaurant has been extremely profitable. As a result, your friend has decided to recognize goodwill by debiting Goodwill and crediting Paid-in Capital. Is this in accordance with generally accepted accounting principles? Why or why not?

27. The Jackson Corporation recently purchased Way Out Video Games for $1 million. The appraisers for Jackson estimated that the fair market value of Way Out's net tangible assets was $850,000. How much goodwill, if any, should Jackson recognize on this transaction? How should the goodwill, if any, be subsequently accounted for?

EXERCISES

E1. **Revenue versus Capital Expenditures.** Identify each of the following items as a revenue or capital expenditure. If you cannot make a clear distinction, state why not.

(a) Immediately after the purchase of a new warehouse and before its use, it was painted at a cost of $50,000.

(b) Immediately after the purchase of a used delivery truck, new tires were purchased at a cost of $200.

(c) Purchased a wastepaper basket for the office at a cost of $7.

(d) Installed air conditioning in an office building that had been owned for several years. The cost of the air conditioning was $24,000.

(e) Purchased land for possible future use as a site for a new building. Paid a guard $200 per week to protect the site.

(f) Acme Freight Corporation decided to overhaul one of its trucks instead of purchasing a new one. Total overhaul cost is $3,500, including a new drive train.

E2. **Determining Acquisition Cost.** For each of the following independent situations, determine the appropriate acquisition cost:

(a) Coral, Inc. purchased a tract of land for $420,050 as a potential building site. In order to acquire the land, the firm paid a $25,000 commission to a real estate agent. Additional costs of $18,000 were incurred to clear the land.

(b) On August 15, the Nigerian Export Company purchased a tract of land for $775,000. Additional expenses incurred by the company were a $45,000 commission paid to a real estate agent, $75,000 clearing fees, and $90,000 in delinquent property taxes. This property was adjacent to the Nigerian Export Company's present warehouse, and two months later the company incurred expenses of $60,000 for paving and $4,500 for fencing in order to turn the land into a parking lot.

(c) New office equipment was purchased by the Davenport Corporation. The equipment had a list price of $95,000. Terms of purchase were 2/10, n/30. State taxes were 6%. Davenport incurred the following additional costs in connection with the purchase:

Transportion	$360
Installation	480
Removal of old equipment	200
Testing of new equipment	500
Repair of damage incurred in transit	240

Determine the acquisition cost of the new equipment assuming that (1) payment was made within the discount period and (2) payment was not made within the discount period.

E3. Lump-sum Purchase. On November 15, the Hutch Company acquired four pieces of machinery for a lump sum of $743,000. The company then paid $4,000 to have the machines installed. Hutch Company also paid $2,500 to determine the appraised value of the machinery. These appraised values were:

Machine 1	$ 200,000
Machine 2	300,000
Machine 3	400,000
Machine 4	100,000
Total	$1,000,000

Determine the acquisition cost of each machine.

E4. Exchange of Assets for Stock. On October 15, Annabel, Inc., a private company, purchased a used machine from the Street Company. The machine had a book value of $57,000 on Street's books and a fair market value of $82,000. In return for the machine, Annabel, Inc. gave the Street Company $3,000 and 1,000 shares of its capital stock. Because Annabel, Inc. is a private company, it is almost impossible to determine the fair market value of the stock.

Prepare the journal entry to record this transaction on the books of Annabel, Inc. Would your answer be different if Annabel, Inc. were a public company and its stock were trading at $75 per share? Why?

E5. Depreciation Concepts. You overheard the following conversation about depreciation among five of your friends:

- Sumi—As generally used in accounting, depreciation applies to all items of property, plant, and equipment.

- Helene—No, depreciation does not apply to land and is used to value operational assets.

- Jay—You are both wrong. Depreciation records only the decline in value of nonmonetary assets other than land. Accountants do not record increases in value.

- Michelle—No, depreciation is essentially an allocation concept used to match revenues and expenses. And it does not apply to land.

- Ernesto—You all are wrong. Depreciation has nothing to do with cost or value. It is used solely to generate cash for the firm.

Evaluate each of their comments.

E6. Calculating Depreciation. The Brett Aviation Corporation at the beginning of the current year purchased a 12-passenger commuter plane for $3.5 million. The plane has an estimated salvage value of $750,000.

REQUIRED: **(a)** If the airplane has a useful life of eight years and the firm uses straight-line depreciation, calculate the annual depreciation for the first four years of the asset's life.

(b) Now assume that the firm believes that the plane will fly 2 million miles and that it has decided to use the units-of-production method of calculating depreciation. Calculate the depreciation for each of the first four years, assuming the plane flew the following miles:

Year 1	300,000
Year 2	250,000
Year 3	275,000
Year 4	240,000

E7. Calculating Depreciation. Equipment with a useful life of five years was purchased by Hondo, Inc. on January 2, 1990 for $38,000. Salvage value is estimated to be $2,000. Compute annual depreciation expense relating to this equipment for the next five years, using the following methods:

(a) straight-line.

(b) double-declining-balance.

(c) sum-of-the-years-digits.

E8. Analysis of Depreciation Calculations. Answer each of the following independent questions:

(a) At the beginning of 1988, the Lombardi Company purchased a heavy-duty power generator for $240,000. The firm estimates that the generator will have a $30,000 salvage value at the end of its useful life. The firm uses sum-of-the-years depreciation, which was as follows for years 1989 and 1990:

Year	Annual Depreciation
1989	$56,000
1990	42,000

What would be depreciation for 1990, assuming that the straight-line basis was always used?

(b) Jigs' Self-service Storage bought a warehouse for $23 million. It estimates that this building will have a useful life of 35 years and a salvage value of $2 million. On the firm's December 31, 1990 financial statements, the warehouse's book value was $20.6 million. Assuming that the firm uses straight-line depreciation, when was the warehouse purchased?

(c) On January 2, 1990, Smile Cosmetics bought a machine that liquifies certain chemicals. The firm estimates that the machine will have a useful life of 12 years and a salvage value of $1,800. On December 31, 1995, the machine will have a book value of $22,300 based on straight-line depreciation. If the firm had used double-declining-balance depreciation rather than straight-line, what would be the depreciation expense for the years ended December 31, 1990 and December 31, 1991?

E9. Partial Year's Depreciation. On March 1, 1989, Radar Enterprises purchased a machine for $410,000. The machine has a useful life of eight years and a salvage value of $20,000. The policy of Radar Enterprises is to calculate depreciation expense from the beginning of the month the asset was purchased.

Calculate depreciation expense for 1989 and 1990, assuming that the firm uses (a) sum-of-the-years-digits depreciation and (b) double-declining-balance depreciation.

E10. Comparing Depreciation for Accounting and Tax Purposes. In April of the current year, the West Valley Company purchased for $70,000 a new light truck to use for delivery purposes. For financial reporting purposes, the asset was given a five-year life with a $500 residual value and will be depreciated using the straight-line method. The firm's policy is to take six months' depreciation in the year of purchase. For tax purposes, the truck falls into the five-year life class. At the beginning of the fourth year, the firm will switch to straight-line for tax purposes.

REQUIRED: (a) Prepare a five-year schedule comparing annual depreciation expense for financial reporting purposes and for tax purposes.

(b) Assume that the firm's income before taxes and depreciation for both financial reporting purposes and tax purposes over the five years of the asset's life are as follows: Year 1, $200,000; Year 2, $220,000; Year 3, $260,000; Year 4, $290,000; and Year 5, $310,000. In addition, the firm's tax rate is 30%. For each, determine the firm's net income for financial reporting purposes and the firm's taxable income.

(c) Explain the benefit the firm received, if any, from using depreciation for tax purposes.

E11. Revision of Depreciation Estimates. At the beginning of 1989, the Porter-Fitch Corporation purchased a piece of heavy equipment for $600,000. The firm estimates that the asset will have a $60,000 residual value at the end of its 15-year life. The firm uses straight-line depreciation. At the beginning of 1992, the firm decides the machine has a remaining life of only ten years. Calculate depreciation for 1992, given the new estimate of the asset's economic life.

E12. Revenue versus Capital Expenditures. The following expenditures were made by the R&G Corporation. For each item, indicate whether the expenditure is a capital expenditure, a revenue expenditure, or neither. If you cannot make a clear-cut decision, so state and explain why.

(a) Paid $500 for a small machine.

(b) Paid $600 for ordinary repairs to a large machine.

(c) Paid premiums of $760 for insurance for the firm's officers.

(d) Paid $1,500 for a patent.

(e) Paid $10 for an electric pencil sharpener.

(f) Paid $1,750 to overhaul a large delivery truck.

(g) Removed a wall during installation of a new computer, $500.

E13. Extraordinary Repairs. Hollis Answering Service began operations on January 2, 1987. At that time, the firm purchased switchboard equipment for $23,000 cash. The equipment had an estimated useful life of ten years and a salvage value of $2,000. The company uses straight-line depreciation. During 1990, ordinary repairs totaling $500 were made and paid in cash. At the beginning of 1991, an employee spilled coffee on the equipment. As a result, a major overhaul of the equipment was made. The equipment was upgraded at the same time. The total cost was $8,000, which was paid in cash. These expenditures will increase the total useful life of the equipment from 10 years to 15.

REQUIRED: **(a)** Prepare the required entries to record the $500 expenditure in 1990 and the depreciation expense in 1990.

(b) Prepare the required entries to record the $8,000 expenditures in 1991 and the depreciation expense in 1991.

E14. Retirement of Plant Assets. On March 31, 1990, Flip Pockets, Co. retired a machine used in manufacturing designer jeans. The machine was acquired on May 1, 1987. Straight-line depreciation was used. The asset had an estimated salvage value of $200 and a five-year life. On December 31, 1989, the balance in the Accumulated Depreciation account was $3,200. The machine was scrapped without Flip Pockets' receiving any consideration.

REQUIRED: **(a)** Make the entry to record the depreciation expense for the period January through March 1990. Depreciation is calculated from the date of acquisition. (*Hint*: You must first determine the acquisition cost of the machine.)

(b) Make the entry to record the retirement of the asset on March 31, 1990.

E15. Sale of Plant Assets. On September 30, 1990, Schneider's Maintenance Service sold one of its vans. The acquisition cost of the van was $9,500. It had an estimated useful life of five years and a salvage value of $500. Straight-line depreciation was used. The balance in the Accumulated Depreciation account at December 31, 1989 was $4,950.

REQUIRED: **(a)** Calculate the gain or loss on the sale assuming that the asset is sold for either (1) $4,200 or (2) $2,300. In both cases the sale is for cash.

(b) Make the necessary journal entries to record the transaction for each of the cases in Requirement (a).

(c) Now assume that the van was scrapped without any consideration. Make the journal entry to record the retirement.

E16. Asset Sale. On December 31, 1990, the records of the Benson Company showed the following information with regard to one of the company's delivery trucks.

Delivery truck	$8,500
Accumulated depreciation—12/31/90	4,875

Depreciation is based on a four-year useful life, a $2,000 salvage value, and straight-line depreciation. On February 1, 1991, the truck is sold for $4,000 cash.

REQUIRED: **(a)** How old was the truck on January 1, 1991? Show your computations.

(b) Prepare the necessary journal entries to record the sale of the truck.

(c) Prepare the necessary journal entries to record the sale, now assuming a cash sale price of $2,000.

E17. Asset Trade-in. On July 1, 1990, Drake Co. traded a machine used in the production of bottle caps for a newer model. Drake received a trade-in allowance of $10,000 on the new machine, which had a list price of $65,000. The old machine was purchased seven years and three months ago at a price of $42,000. It had an estimated useful life of ten years and a salvage value of $3,000. Straight-line depreciation was used.

REQUIRED: **(a)** How much cash did Drake have to pay for the new machine?

(b) Make the necessary journal entry to record the acquisition of the new machine.

E18. Asset Disposition. The Yangtse Company acquired an asset that had a cost of $130,000. The asset is being depreciated over five years using the sum-of-the-years-digits method of depreciation. The asset has an estimated salvage value of $10,000. Make the journal entry to record the disposition of the asset under each of the following independent assumptions:

(a) At the end of the third year, the asset was sold for $38,000 cash.

(b) At the end of the second year, the asset was traded in for a similar one. The new asset had a list price of $150,000. The firm received a trade-in allowance of $60,000. Assume that the trade-in allowance represents the fair market value of the old asset.

(c) At the end of the sixth year, the asset was retired and given to a scrap dealer in exchange for $1,000.

(d) At the end of the third year, the asset was traded in for a similar one with a list price of $80,000. The firm paid $62,000 cash. The trade-in allowance represented the fair market value of the old asset.

E19. Depletion. During 1990, Fortune Company purchased a mine for $16.8 million. In addition, the firm capitalized exploration and development costs of $6,450,000. The firm estimates that the property will have a salvage value of $8 million when the mine is finally closed. A geological survey indicates that 25 million units of the mineral can be extracted over the life of the mine. If 1.2 million units are extracted in 1990 and 2 million are extracted in 1991, determine the depletion expense for each year.

E20. Intangible Assets. Imagination, Inc. has the following intangible assets on December 31, 1990, which is the end of the firm's year:

(a) A patent was purchased on January 2, 1990 for cash of $5,896. This patent had been registered with the U.S. Patent Office on January 2, 1984 and is to be amortized over its remaining legal life.

(b) On January 2, 1989, the company purchased a copyright for cash of $12,600. The remaining legal life is 20 years; however, management estimates that the copyright would have no value at the end of 15 years.

(c) On July 1, 1990, the company received a patent on a product developed by the firm. Expenses of $26,500 were incurred in the development of the product. Legal fees and costs associated with obtaining the patent amounted to $5,100. The company will amortize the patent over its legal life beginning on July 1, 1990.

(d) On January 2, 1990, Imagination, Inc. hired a public relations firm to develop a trademark. The fees to the firm amounted to $25,000. Legal fees associated with the trademark amounted to $5,000. Assume a 20-year life.

Determine the amortization expense for 1990 and the book value of each of the intangible assets that should be shown on the December 31, 1990 balance sheet.

E21. Determining Goodwill. The Mann Corporation is negotiating the purchase of the Horace Company. After auditing the Horace Company's books, the accountant for the Mann Corporation gathered the following information:

Accounts	Book Value	Fair Market Value
Current assets	$100,000	$150,000
Property, plant, and equipment	500,000	600,000
Other assets	40,000	5,000
Current liabilities	80,000	80,000
Long-term debt	200,000	240,000
Stockholders' equity	360,000	435,000

After considerable negotiation, the Mann Corporation agreed to purchase the Horace Company for $500,000 cash. As part of the agreement, the Mann Corporation will acquire all of the Horace Company's assets as well as assume all of its liabilities.

REQUIRED: **(a)** Determine the amount of goodwill that the Mann Corporation should record as a result of this purchase.

(b) Make the necessary journal entries on the books of the Mann Corporation to record the acquisition of the Horace Company.

E22. Toys "R" Us Financial Statements. Using the information contained in the annual report of Toys "R" Us, found in Appendix D, answer the following questions:

(a) How much interest did the firm capitalize during the years ended January 1, 1988 and February 1, 1987?

(b) What effect do you think that the capitalization of interest had on net income during 1988?

(c) During the year, the firm made net additions to property and equipment. Using the information in the balance sheet and the income statement, determine the amount of the net additions.

PROBLEMS

P10-1 Acquisition of Nonmonetary Assets. The following transactions were made during 1989 by Dawson Enterprises, a manufacturer of novelty tee-shirts:

(a) A tract of land was acquired for $250,000. In addition, commissions of $25,000 were paid to real estate agents, and a special assessment for late taxes of $5,000 was also incurred. The taxes and fees were paid in cash. A 15% down payment was made, and a 20-year mortgage was used to finance the project.

(b) A small building and tract of land were purchased for a lump sum of $635,000 cash. The property was appraised for tax purposes near the end of 1988 as follows: building $230,000 and land $270,000. The building has an estimated useful life of 20 years and a salvage value of $25,000. The company will be using double-declining-balance depreciation and will take a full year's depreciation in the year of purchase.

(c) A machine is acquired in exchange for 40,000 shares of Dawson Enterprises capital stock. The stock had a closing market value of $17 per share on a national stock exchange on the date the machine was acquired. The machine has an estimated useful life of five years and no salvage value. The company decided to use straight-line depreciation, and a full year's depreciation was taken in 1989.

(d) The city of Hidden Hills donates a parcel of land to Dawson Enterprises on the condition that the firm build a new factory. Hidden Hills acquired the land several years ago at a cost of $150,000. At the time the land was donated to the firm, it had a current market value of $220,000.

REQUIRED: **(a)** Prepare the necessary journal entries to record the above acquisitions.

(b) Make the required adjusting entries for depreciation expense for 1989. Make a separate entry for each depreciable asset.

P10-2 **Calculating Depreciation.** Washington, Inc. purchased an automated conveyer belt on April 1, 1988 at a cost of $175,000. The machine had an estimated useful life of ten years and a $10,000 salvage value. Washington, Inc. estimates that the machine will be able to handle 3.3 million units before it must be scrapped. Actual output in the first three years was: Year 1, 900,000 units; Year 2, 750,000 units; and Year 3, 600,000 units.

REQUIRED: Determine the annual depreciation expense and book value of the conveyer belt under each of the following methods at the end of the first three years of the asset's life. Assume that the firm takes a full year's depreciation in the year of purchase.

1. Straight-line.

2. Units-of-production.

3. Sum-of-the-years-digits.

4. Double-declining-balance.

P10-3 **Calculating Depreciation.** Jefferson Co. owns several radio stations and recently acquired some new broadcasting equipment for $550,000. The equipment has a useful life of eight years and a salvage value of $50,000. Jefferson estimates that the equipment will work 5 million hours over its useful life. Actual hours used during the first two years were: Year 1, 800,000 hours; Year 2, 600,000 hours.

REQUIRED: Determine the annual depreciation expense and book value of the equipment under each of the following methods at the end of the first two years of the asset's life. Assume that the firm takes a full year's depreciation in the year of purchase.

(a) Straight-line.

(b) Units-of-production.

(c) Sum-of-the-years-digits.

(d) Double-declining-balance.

P10-4 **Depreciation Calculations and Adjusting Entries.** Cooper and Sons Ltd. is an automobile parts importer. You have obtained the following data relative to the firm's depreciable assets:

	Building	Furniture	Equipment	Trucks
Date acquired	7/1/84	1/2/87	7/6/89	10/3/89
Cost	$250,000	$16,500	$8,000	$16,000
Salvage value	$10,000	$0	$800	$1,000
Useful life	30 years	10 years	8 years	5 years
Method of depreciation	Straight-line	Sum-of-the-years-digits	Double-declining	Sum-of-the-years-digits

The policy of Cooper and Sons is to calculate depreciation expense from the beginning of the month the asset is purchased.

REQUIRED: **(a)** For each asset group, determine the balance in the Accumulated Depreciation account as of January 1, 1990.

(b) Make the adjusting entries to record depreciation expense for the year ended December 31, 1990. Make a separate entry for each asset group.

P10-5 **Revision of Depreciation Rates.** Rick Monday's Sports Manufacturing Co. owns a special machine that makes baseballs. The machine was purchased at the beginning of 1989 for a price of $200,000. The machine is being depreciated on the straight-line basis. It has an estimated life of 15 years and a salvage value of $20,000. At the beginning of 1991, new information was presented that made the firm change the estimated life to 20 years instead of 15. Salvage value was also reduced from $20,000 to $5,000.

REQUIRED: **(a)** Compute the amount of depreciation expense that should be recorded in 1990 and the book value of the machine on December 31, 1990.

(b) Compute the amount of depreciation expense for 1991. Show all computations and round to the nearest dollar, if necessary.

P10-6 **Selecting Depreciation Methods.** You are the controller of the J. C. Ray Company. The firm has just purchased a specialized piece of equipment for $300,000. The equipment has a salvage value of $12,000 and an estimated useful life of eight years. In order to choose the most beneficial depreciation method, you have been asked to determine the following data:

(a) At what point in the equipment's life does sum-of-the-years-digits depreciation exceed double-declining-balance depreciation?

(b) At what point in the equipment's life does straight-line exceed both sum-of-the-years-digits and double-declining-balance depreciation?

(c) If the equipment falls into the five-year class under tax depreciation, what would annual depreciation be for the next five years? (Assume that the firm switches to straight-line at the beginning of the fourth year.)

(d) Assuming the firm desires to smooth earnings for financial reporting purposes and to increase cash flows by decreasing tax payments, which method or methods should the firm choose?

P10-7 **Analyzing Depreciation Calculations.** Answer each of the following independent questions:

(a) On July 1, 1986, Kickson Co. acquired equipment with an estimated useful life of eight years and a residual value of $5,000. On December 31, 1988, the Accumulated Depreciation account for this equipment amounted to $37,500, including the depreciation expense for 1988. If the firm only took six months' depreciation in 1986, determine the acquisition cost of the equipment. The firm uses straight-line depreciation.

(b) On January 2, 1987, Pinky Co. purchased a building with an estimated useful life of 20 years and a residual value of $20,000. Depreciation expense for the year ended December 31, 1989 was $16,200. The firm uses double-declining-balance depreciation. Determine the acquisition cost of the building.

(c) On January 2, 1988, the Bingo Company acquired a machine with a cost of $300,000. The firm estimated that the machine would have an estimated life of seven years. The policy of Bingo is to use straight-line depreciation. On December 31, 1990, the book value of the machine was $180,000. Determine the residual value of the machine.

P10-8 **Analyzing Depreciation Calculations.** Answer each of the following independent questions:

(a) On January 2, 1987, Pagano, Inc. purchased a specialized drilling machine with an estimated useful life of ten years and a salvage value of $2,500. For the year ended December 31, 1989, depreciation expense for this machine totaled $24,000. Determine the acquisition cost of the machine, assuming the firm uses straight-line depreciation.

(b) On January 2, 1989, the Eddows Corporation purchased a machine with an estimated useful life of five years and a salvage value of $2,000. Depreciation expense for 1987 was $18,000. The company uses the double-declining-balance method of depreciation for financial reporting. Determine the acquisition cost of the machine on January 2, 1989.

(c) On January 2, 1988, Heller Manufacturing Products bought a lathe that cost $140,000. The firm estimates that the lathe will have a useful life of six years. The company uses straight-line depreciation. At December 31, 1989, the lathe had a book value of $95,000. What was the asset's estimated salvage value?

P10-9 **Purchase and Depreciation of Equipment.** During your examination of the records of the Current Deterrent Company, you obtained the following information concerning the purchase of a new piece of equipment called an Exoinic:

Acquisition date	4/1/89
Purchase price	$260,000
Terms	2/10, n/30
Installation costs	$ 7,500
Freight costs	$ 500
Repairs required for damage while in transit	$ 200
Normal repairs and maintenance, 12/1/85	$ 1,000
Estimated useful life	10 years
Salvage value	$ 0
Depreciation method	straight-line

REQUIRED: **(a)** Determine the acquisition cost of the equipment.

(b) Assuming that depreciation is calculated from the month of purchase, determine the depreciation expense for 1989 and 1990.

(c) Now assume that on January 2, 1991, the firm performs a complete rebuilding of the machine for $40,000. Because of this the firm believes that the asset's life will be extended an additional ten years from the beginning of 1991. Determine the correct amount of depreciation expense for 1991.

P10-10 Plant Asset Transactions. During 1989, the Travis Company entered into the following transactions related to various items of property, plant, and equipment:

■ January 2: A delivery truck owned by the firm was overhauled at a cost of $4,000, which was paid in cash. The truck had been purchased on January 2, 1987 at a price of $13,000. At that time, the firm estimated that the truck would have a salvage value of $1,000 and a five-year life with no salvage value. After the overhaul, Travis estimated that the life of the truck should be extended two more years from the date of the overhaul.

■ February 1: Sold a used machine that had a book value of $2,500 on the date of the sale. The machine had a historical cost of $72,000, and the firm received $2,300 cash.

■ March 31: A fully depreciated machine purchased several years ago was scrapped for no consideration. The machine had an original cost of $15,000, a useful life of six years, and a salvage value of $1,500.

■ July 1: Travis sold one of its computers for $8,000. The computer, which was purchased on January 2, 1988 for $25,000, had a useful life of five years and a $4,000 salvage value. The firm uses sum-of-the-years-digits depreciation on this asset. No depreciation has been taken since December 31, 1988. Of the $8,000 selling price, the firm received 20% down and a 12%, 1-year note for the remainder.

REQUIRED: **(a)** Make the journal entries to record the above transactions.

(b) Make any necessary adjusting entries for depreciation and interest. Assume that the firm closes its books once a year, on December 31. The firm calculates depreciation from the beginning of the month in which the asset is purchased.

P10-11 Disposal of Plant Assets. The Corona Company purchased a metal crusher for $140,000 on January 2, 1987. The asset has a five-year useful life and a salvage value of $5,000. The firm uses sum-of-the-years-digits depreciation.

REQUIRED: Make the entry to record the disposition of the asset under each of the following independent situations. Assume that depreciation has been recorded to the date of sale. (You do not have to make the depreciation entry unless so instructed.)

(a) The asset is retired without consideration at the end of its useful life.

(b) The asset is sold for cash at the end of its useful life for $5,500.

(c) The asset is sold for cash on March 31, 1990, for (1) $60,000 and (2) $20,000. Depreciation for the period January 1, 1990 to March 31, 1990 must be recorded.

(d) The asset is traded in for a similar one on January 2, 1991. A trade-in allowance of (1) $35,000 and (2) $5,000 is received. In both Cases 1 and 2, assume that the trade-in allowance represents the fair market value of the asset given up at that time. The list price of the new machine is $100,000.

P10-12 Purchase and Disposal of Equipment. On January 2, 1987, the Lewis Corporation purchased a piece of equipment for $80,000. The asset is depreciated on the double-declining-balance method with a life of ten years and a $5,000 salvage value. On January 2, 1989, the asset was traded for a similar one. The new equipment had a list price of $100,000, but after the trade-in allowance, which approximated the fair market value of the old asset at that time, Lewis paid only $40,000 in cash. The Lewis Corporation decided the new asset should have a life of five years and a salvage value of $10,000. The double-declining-balance method was again used. Depreciation expense for 1989 on the new machine amounted to $40,000.

REQUIRED: **(a)** From your analysis of the above facts, did Lewis properly record the trade-in of the old equipment? Why or why not? Assume that the depreciation calculation on the new asset is mathematically correct.

(b) Make one entry to correct the books at January 2, 1989 and another to correct the depreciation expense for 1989.

P10-13 Purchase and Disposal of Equipment. On January 2, 1986, the Perkins Corporation purchased for cash a piece of high-tech equipment. The equipment, which cost $200,000, had a five-year life and a $20,000 salvage value. Straight-line depreciation is used. Installation costs were $10,000. At the beginning of 1988, the firm decided to upgrade the equipment and spent $50,000 in the process. The asset's Accumulated Depreciation account was debited for this amount. As a result, the asset is now considered to have a life of six years from the beginning of 1988. In addition, the salvage value was increased by $5,000. However, at the end of 1989, a new machine came on the market that made the old equipment obsolete. As a result, Perkins traded its old piece of equipment for a new one. The trade-in was made on December 31, 1989, but prior to any adjusting entries. The list price of the new equipment was $180,000, and Perkins received a $40,000 trade-in allowance on the old equipment. The trade-in allowance was equal to the asset's fair market value at that time.

REQUIRED: **(a)** Record the purchase of the equipment on January 2, 1986.

(b) Record depreciation expense for 1986 and 1987.

(c) Record the relevant entries for 1988, including the depreciation expense.

(d) Record all the relevant entries for 1989, including the depreciation expense.

P10-14 Patents. Think, Inc. manufactures state-of-the-art electronic products. Its products are manufactured under two patents.

The first patent, no. 106-235, was developed by the firm. During 1989 and 1990, the firm incurred research and development costs of $600,000 and $200,000, respectively. In addition, in 1990, the firm incurred $100,000 of legal and other related costs to have its work patented. Management estimates that the patent will have a ten-year economic life, although the legal life is 17 years.

The second patent, no. 203-589, was purchased at the beginning of 1988 from its inventor for $120,000. The firm decided to amortize it over 15 years. During 1989, the firm was sued for patent infringement in connection with this patent. Think, Inc. was successful in defending the suit. Legal costs were $56,000. As a result of this suit, management decided that beginning in 1990, the remaining useful life of the patent should be reduced to ten years.

REQUIRED: **(a)** Make all the entries for 1989 and 1990 relative to each patent. Make a separate set of entries for each patent. Assume that the firm's year-end is December 31 and that adjusting entries are made yearly at this time.

(b) At what amount should each patent be shown on the firm's December 31, 1990 balance sheet?

P10-15 Determination of Goodwill. Brenner Electronics is considering the purchase of one of its competitors, Kress Technology. Kress Technology has been very profitable and has been averaging an annual net income of $88,500 since its inception six years ago.

Under the terms of the proposed purchase agreement, Brenner will pay a price equal to the fair market value of Kress's identifiable net assets plus goodwill as of December 31, 1989. Goodwill is to be determined by multiplying excess earnings by 5. Excess earnings are the amount by which Kress's average annual earnings exceed the industry norm of 10% of identifiable net assets at their fair market value. Brenner will make the purchase by issuing Kress enough shares of its capital stock at the current market value of $80 per share to cover the agreed-upon purchase price.

The balance sheet of Kress Technology at December 31, 1989, is as follows:

KRESS TECHNOLOGY
Balance Sheet
December 31, 1989

Assets

Current assets		$100,000
Property, plant, and equipment		
Land	$200,000	
Buildings, net	320,000	
Plant and equipment, net	100,000	620,000
Other assets		10,000
Total assets		$730,000

Liabilities and Stockholders' Equity

Current liabilities	$ 75,000
Long-term liabilities	140,000
Total liabilities	$215,000
Stockholders' equity	
Capital stock	$200,000
Retained earnings	315,000
Total stockholders' equity	$515,000
Total liabilities and stockholders' equity	$730,000

The following additional information is available:

(a) The fair market value of the current assets approximates their book value.

(b) The fair market value of the property, plant, and equipment is as follows:

Account	Amount
Land	$300,000
Buildings, net	360,000
Plant and equipment, net	140,000

(c) The other assets consist of an advance to Kress's principal stockholder. The debt is being forgiven when the purchase is made, so that shareholder has no intention of repaying it.

(d) Kress has a patent that has been developed internally. As a result, all costs related to this patent have been expensed. The management of Brenner feels that the fair market value of this patent is $50,000.

(e) The fair market values of all liabilities approximate their book values.

REQUIRED: **(a)** Determine the amount of excess earnings.

(b) Determine the amount of goodwill in the transaction.

(c) Determine the total purchase price Brenner will pay to Kress. How many shares will Brenner have to issue to Kress to effect the purchase?

(d) Make the entry on Brenner's books to record both the purchase of the assets and the assumption of the liabilities of Kress. Assume that the property, plant, and equipment are recorded at fair market value.

■ USING THE COMPUTER

P10-16   At the beginning of the current year, the Prindle Company purchased three depreciable assets. Information pertaining to these assets follows:

	Asset A	Asset B	Asset C
Cost	$10,000	$25,000	$55,000
Depreciation data for financial reporting purposes			
Method	SL	DDB	SYD
Residual value	0	0	0
Life	5 yrs	10 yrs	10 yrs
Depreciation for tax purposes			
Class life—double-declining-balance (no switch to straight-line)	3 yrs	5 yrs	5 yrs

OTHER DATA: **(a)**   For financial reporting purposes, a full year's depreciation is taken in the year of purchase.

(b)   The firm's average tax rate is 40%.

The controller asks you to develop an electronic spreadsheet program that calculates for each asset the annual depreciation expense for both financial reporting purposes and tax purposes. She would also like to know the annual difference in tax payments from using tax depreciation versus what the payments would have been if the method for financial reporting was also used for tax purposes. She suggests that you develop a table like the following:

	Yearly Depreciation								
	Financial Reporting				**Tax Purposes**				**Tax Payment Difference**
Year	Asset A	Asset B	Asset C	Total	Asset A	Asset B	Asset C	Total	
1									
2									
3									
.									
.									
10									
Totals									

■ UNDERSTANDING FINANCIAL STATEMENTS

P10-17   In its 1986 annual report, the Campbell Soup Company reported supplemental information on the effects of changing prices. Management reported the following information:

	As Reported in the Primary Statements	Adjusted for Changes in Specific Prices (Current Costs)
Depreciation expense	$ 120,761,000	$ 247,206,000
Cost of plant assets, net	1,168,129,000	1,472,550,000
Net income	223,225,000	
Dividends declared	84,367,000	

REQUIRED: Based on the above information, answer the following questions:

(a)   If there are no other changes other than depreciation expense between historical-cost net income as reported in the primary financial statements, what would have been the reported profit of Campbell Soup Corporation on a current cost basis?

(b) Calculate the following ratios based on reported net income and net income as adjusted in Requirement (a) for current costs and reported total assets and assets adjusted for the increase in the current cost of plant and equipment:

1. Profit margin ratio

2. Dividend payout calculated as follows:

$$\frac{\text{Dividends declared}}{\text{Net income}}$$

3. Rate of return on total assets—use only year-end figures for total assets.

(c) Based on your answers to Requirement (b), comment on the effects of changing prices on the operating results and financial condition of Campbell Soup.

■ FINANCIAL DECISION CASE

P10-18   The Oldham Corporation is in the paper products industry. This industry is very capital-intensive, and it has been using the standard industry policy to calculate depreciation on the straight-line basis. The company is contemplating the purchase of a large milling machine that will cost $3 million. The machine will probably have a useful life of ten years, at which time the machine's salvage value will be negligible. However, the machine is most productive in its first five years. After that, increasing repairs and maintenance requirements will increase the machine's downtime and decrease its efficiency. Prior experience indicates that repairs and maintenance expense will be $40,000 in the first year and will increase at a rate of 10% per year.

REQUIRED: The president is contemplating the use of different depreciation methods and asks you, his financial adviser, the following questions:

(a) I have read in a business magazine that for this type of asset an accelerated depreciation method such as double-declining-balance is conceptually the most appropriate method. Why is that so? If you disagree, please let me know why.

(b) Most firms in the industry use straight-line depreciation. Prepare a comparative schedule for me showing the annual expense related to this machine if (1) straight-line or (2) double-declining-balance depreciation is used. Include both depreciation and repairs and maintenance expense in your schedule. (Round off to whole dollars where appropriate.)

(c) I am concerned that if I use double-declining-balance depreciation, the earnings of the company, especially in the early years, will not look good in comparison with those firms using straight-line depreciation. Because I am interested in selling the company in the near future, how will a potential buyer view our earnings, in comparison with those of other companies in the industry?

(d) Our present machine is fully depreciated, and although not as productive as the new one would be, it is still working. I understand there would be some tax benefits to buying the new machine. Explain to me how depreciation is calculated for tax purposes and what the potential tax benefits are. (Assume the equipment falls into a five-year-life class.)

CURRENT LIABILITIES, INCOME TAXES, AND CONCEPTS RELATED TO THE TIME VALUE OF MONEY

LEARNING OBJECTIVES

After studying this chapter, you should be able to:

1. Define liabilities and state the criteria used to recognize and classify them.
2. Explain the accounting concepts and procedures for different types of current liabilities, including:
   a. liabilities that are definitely determinable.
   b. liabilities that represent collections for third parties or are conditioned on operations.
   c. contingent liabilities.
3. Account for corporate income taxes and understand the need for interperiod income tax allocation.
4. Explain the concepts related to the time value of money and solve various time-value-of-money problems.

L iabilities represent the economic obligations of the enterprise. In recent years, as many firms have struggled to maintain an adequate level of liquidity, issues involving the determination, measurement, and recognition of liabilities have become increasingly important. This chapter will discuss the accounting concepts and procedures related to current liabilities. In addition, corporate income taxes and how to account for them will be introduced. Finally, concepts concerning the time value of money will be examined. This topic is particularly important because it is related to the valuation of liabilities.

■ DEFINITION AND RECOGNITION OF LIABILITIES

The FASB defines liabilities as "probable future sacrifices of economic benefits arising from present obligations of a particular entity to transfer assets or provide services to other entities in the future as a result of past transactions or events."[1] To recognize a liability, a firm need not know the actual recipient of the assets that are to be transferred or for whom the services are to be performed. For example, when General Motors guarantees or warrants an automobile, a liability must be recorded, even though at the time of sale GM does not know which particular customer's automobile may require repair.

For a liability to exist, an event or transaction must already have occurred. In effect, only present (not future) obligations are liabilities. For example, the exchange of promises of future performance between two firms or individuals does not result in the recognition of a liability or the related asset. The signing of a labor contract between a firm and an individual does not cause the firm to recognize a liability; rather, it is recognized when the employees perform services for which they have not yet been compensated. In the automobile warranty case, the liability occurs at the time of sale, because at that time the firm obligates itself to make certain repairs. Thus the event has occurred, and a present obligation is incurred.

Liabilities can be either monetary or nonmonetary. **Monetary liabilities** are obligations that are payable in a fixed sum. Examples of monetary liabilities are accounts, notes payable, and accruals such as wages and interest payable. **Nonmonetary liabilities** are obligations to provide fixed amounts of goods and services. They include items such as revenues received in advance of a sale or the performance of a service.

■ CLASSIFICATION OF LIABILITIES ON THE BALANCE SHEET

In preparing a balance sheet, liabilities are classified as either current or long-term. **Current liabilities** require the use of existing resources that are classified as current assets or require the creation of new current liabilities. Current liabilities include such accounts as Accounts Payable, Short-term Notes Payable, Current Maturities of Long-term Debt (the principal portion of a long-term liability due within the next 12 months), Taxes Payable, and other Accrued Payables. **Long-term liabilities**, discussed in the next chapter, are those liabilities that will not be satisfied within one year or the operating cycle (if longer than one year). Included in this category are Mortgages Payable, Bonds Payable, and Lease Obligations. However, the current portion, if any, of these long-term liabilities is classified as current liabilities.

[1] Financial Accounting Standards Board, Concepts Statement No. 6, *Elements of Financial Statements* (Stamford, Conn.: FASB, December 1985), par. 35.

■ MEASUREMENT AND VALUATION OF CURRENT LIABILITIES

Like assets, liabilities are originally measured and recorded according to the cost principle. That is, when incurred, the liability is measured and recorded at the current market value of the asset or service received. Because current liabilities are payable within a relatively short period of time, they are recorded at their face value, which is the amount of cash needed to discharge the principal of the liability. No recognition is given to the fact that the present value of these future cash outlays is less. **Present value** is related to the idea of the time value of money. Essentially, it means that cash received or paid in the future is worth less than the same amount of cash received or paid today. This is because cash on hand today can be invested and thus can grow to a greater future amount. Thus the value of the liability at the time incurred is actually less than the cash required to be paid in the future.

In connection with current liabilities, the difference between value today and future cash outlay is not material, because of the short time span between the time the liability is incurred and when it is paid. Current liabilities are therefore shown at the amount of the future principal payment. However, present-value concepts are applied to long-term liabilities, liabilities with no stated interest, and liabilities with a stated interest rate materially different from the market rate for similar transactions. These cases will be explored in the next chapter.

■ TYPES OF CURRENT LIABILITIES

Liabilities are often divided into three categories: (1) those that are definitely determinable in amount, (2) collections for third parties and those liabilities conditioned on operations, and (3) contingent liabilities.

■ LIABILITIES THAT ARE DEFINITELY DETERMINABLE

Definitely determinable current liabilities are those liabilities that are known and are definite in amount. Included in this category are accounts such as Accounts Payable, Trade Notes Payable, Current Maturities of Long-term Debt, Interest Payable, and Dividends Payable. The major accounting problems associated with these liabilities are determining their existence and ensuring that they are recorded in the proper accounting period. For example, if the cost of an item is included in the ending inventory but a corresponding payable and/or purchase is not recorded, there will be an understatement of both cost of goods sold and total liabilities.

Accounts Payable

Accounts payable, or **trade accounts payable**, are monies owed to the enterprise's suppliers or vendors for the purchase of goods and services. Most purchases take place on credit; under the accrual basis of accounting, the liability must be recorded at the time title passes for the assets purchased or when the services are received. Proper internal control procedures require using subsidiary accounts payable ledgers or a voucher register.

Notes Payable

As with notes receivable, **notes payable** can result from different types of transactions, but the most likely sources are from purchases of goods and services through trade notes payable or from bank loans through notes payable. Notes payable to banks will be discussed here; the concepts related to these notes can easily be applied to other forms of notes payable.

Notes Issued to Banks

Short-term bank loans are a major source of funding for all types and sizes of businesses. There are two different types of notes that can be issued to banks. One type is an interest-bearing note, which is drawn to include the principal or face amount and a separate interest element (see Exhibit 11-1). The other is a zero-interest-bearing note, which does not explicitly state an interest rate on the face of the note. It is drawn in such a way that the face amount includes the interest charge (see Exhibit 11-2).

EXHIBIT 11-1

Note with Interest Element Stated Separately

PROMISSORY NOTE

$ .... 5,000 .... October 1 ..... **1990**

For Value Received .... S. F. Giant

promise(s) to pay to .... L. A. Dodger .... *or order, the sum*

of .... Five Thousand .... *Dollars*

.... at Los Angeles, CA

in .... lawful money of the United States in 120 days .... *from this date,*

with interest annually at the rate of .... 12% .... *per annum,*

during said term, and for such further time as said principal sum, or any part thereof shall

remain unpaid; provided however, that if any default shall be made in the payment of any

installment of principal or interest and such default continues for . thirty . . *days, the whole*

principal sum then remaining unpaid, together with interest shall, at the option of the holder

hereof, become due and payable on demand.

Signed in the presence of

Susan Lardon   *S. F. Giant*

EXHIBIT 11-2

Note with Interest Element Included

PROMISSORY NOTE

$ .... 5,200 .... October 1 ..... **1990**

For Value Received .... S. F. Giant

promise(s) to pay to .... L. A. Dodger .... *or order, the sum*

of .... Five Thousand Two Hundred .... *Dollars*

.... at Los Angeles, CA

in .... lawful money of the United States in four months .... *from this date,*

with interest annually at the rate of .... included .... *per annum,*

during said term, and for such further time as said principal sum, or any part thereof shall

remain unpaid; provided however, that if any default shall be made in the payment of any

installment of principal or interest and such default continues for . thirty . . *days, the whole*

principal sum then remaining unpaid, together with interest shall, at the option of the holder

hereof, become due and payable on demand.

Signed in the presence of

H. Lantz   *S. F. Giant*

The note in Exhibit 11-1 is drawn in the principal amount of $5,000. The interest element of 12% is stated separately. The note in Exhibit 11-2 is drawn for $5,200, and the interest element is not stated separately. There is interest, however, since the borrower is required to pay back at maturity an amount greater than that received at the date the note is issued. When the note is issued, the borrower, S. F. Giant, receives in cash the discounted value of the note, which is equal to the face value of the note at maturity less the interest or discount rate charged by the lender, L. A. Dodger. Thus S. F. Giant receives only $5,000 instead of $5,200, the face value of the note. The actual interest rate or discount rate is slightly less than 12%.[2]

Issuance of the Note

The journal entries to record this note under each of the two cases are as follows. (Case 1 corresponds to Exhibit 11-1, and Case 2 is for Exhibit 11-2.)

Case 1: Interest Stated Separately			Case 2: Interest Not Stated Separately		
October 1, 1990			October 1, 1990		
Cash	5,000		Cash	5,000	
Notes Payable		5,000	Discount on Notes Payable	200	
To record $5,000, 12%, 120-day note payable.			Notes Payable		5,200
			To record $5,200, 120-day discounted note payable.		

The entry in Case 1 is straightforward. Cash is debited, and Notes Payable is credited for $5,000. In Case 2, Notes Payable is credited for $5,200, the maturity value of the note, but S. F. Giant receives only $5,000 cash. The $200 difference is debited to the account Discount on Notes Payable. This is a contra-liability account and is offset against the Notes Payable account on the balance sheet. Interest expense is not debited, because interest is a function of time. The discount simply represents the total potential interest expense to be incurred if the note remains unpaid for the full 120 days. Over the life of the note, the discount is written off as interest expense is recognized. The partial balance sheets for both cases as of the date of the note are as follows:

Case 1: Partial Balance Sheet		Case 2: Partial Balance Sheet	
Current liabilities		Current liabilities	
Notes payable	$5,000	Notes payable	$5,200
		Less: Discount on notes payable	200
			$5,000

Interest Accrual

Because the interest on the notes is not payable until maturity, an interest accrual must be made at year-end. This accrual is for three months, as adjusting entries are assumed to be made only at year-end, December 31. The entry in each case is:

---

[2]The actual rate charge is 11.824%. This rate equates maturity value of $5,200 and the cash proceeds of $5,000 over the four-month period. The general procedure for making this calculation is explained in the present-value section of the chapter.

Case 1: December 31, 1990			Case 2: December 31, 1990		
Interest Expense	150		Interest Expense	150	
Interest Payable		150	Discount on Notes Payable		150
To record 90 days of accrued interest.			To amortize discount on straight-line basis for 90 days.		
$150 = \$5,000 \times .12 \times \frac{90}{360}$			$150 = \$200 \times \frac{3}{4}$		

The adjusting journal entry in Case 1 is similar to the entries to accrue interest made in Chapter 4. Interest Expense is debited, and Interest Payable is credited for three months of accrued interest. The entry in Case 2 needs additional explanation. At the origin of the note, the account Discount on Notes Payable represents interest charges related to future accounting periods. At the end of the note's term, all of these interest charges have been recognized, so the balance in this discount account becomes zero. To accomplish this process, the Discount on Notes Payable account is written off over the life of the note. This write-off is referred to as *amortization of the discount*.

In the journal entry in Case 2, the discount is amortized on a straight-line basis.[3] That is, an equal amount of the discount ($200 \div 4 = \$50$) is charged each month to interest expense. The entry is for $150 because the amortization entry is for a three-month period. After the entry on December 31, the discount account has a balance of only $50. This increases the net liability to $5,150, which represents the $5,000 proceeds from the note plus $150 of interest incurred since the inception of the loan. Partial balance sheets at December 31, 1990 for Cases 1 and 2 appear as follows:

Case 1: Partial Balance Sheet		Case 2: Partial Balance Sheet	
Current liabilities		Current liabilities	
Notes payable	$5,000	Notes payable	$5,200
Interest payable	150	Less: Discount on notes payable	50
			$5,150

As these partial balance sheets show, the total liability related to notes and interest is $5,150 in both cases.

Payment at Maturity of the Note

When the note matures on January 31, 1991, S. F. Giant must pay the entire principal and, in the first case, the accrued interest. In both cases, the final month's interest expense, $50, is recognized. The journal entries for both cases are as follows:

Case 1: January 31, 1991			Case 2: January 31, 1991		
˙Notes Payable	5,000		Notes Payable	5,200	
Interest Payable	150		Interest Expense	50	
Interest Expense	50		Discount on Notes Payable		50
Cash		5,200	Cash		5,200
To record payments of $5,000 principal and $150 of interest payable and to record interest expense for 30 days of $50.			To record payment of $5,200 note and to amortize discount of $50 on note payable for 30 days.		

[3]Under the straight-line basis, interest expense is the same each period. This is similar to straight-line depreciation. Chapter 12 will show that in some cases a method called the *effective-interest method* is preferable.

In summary, the two cases represent different ways in which notes can be written. In the first case, the firm receives the total face value of $5,000 and ultimately repays principal and interest of $5,200. In the second case, the firm receives the same $5,000, but the note is written for $5,200. The interest is deducted from the note at the time of its origin. Eventually, however, the firm must repay the full $5,200.

Current Portion of Long-term Debt

Current maturities of long-term debt are those portions of long-term liabilities that are payable within one year of the balance sheet date and thus are classified as current. For example, the principal portion of the next 12 payments due on a 30-year mortgage following the balance sheet date is classified as current. The remaining portion is considered long-term.

Dividends Payable

Corporations often issue cash dividends to common and/or preferred shareholders. A corporation is under no legal obligation to issue dividends, but once they are declared by the board of directors, the dividends become a liability of the corporation. Because the liability is usually paid within a month or so after it is declared, it is classified as a current liability.

Other Definitely Determinable Liabilities

Other definitely determinable liabilities include accrued liabilities such as interest and wages payable and unearned revenues. Recognition of accrued liabilities requires periodic adjusting entries. Failure to recognize accrued liabilities overstates income and understates liabilities.

A firm may receive cash in advance of performing some service or providing some goods. Because the firm has an obligation to perform the service or provide the goods, this advance payment is a liability. These advance payments are called *unearned revenues*; they include such items as subscriptions or dues received in advance, prepaid rent, and deposits. These nonmonetary liabilities are generally classified as current, because the goods or services are usually delivered or performed within one year or the operating cycle (if longer than one year). If this is not the case, they should be classified as noncurrent liabilities.

■ LIABILITIES THAT REPRESENT COLLECTIONS FOR THIRD PARTIES OR ARE CONDITIONED ON OPERATIONS

Firms are often required to make collections for third parties such as unions and governmental agencies. For example, taxes are levied on the consumer and/or the firm, and the firm is required to collect the tax on behalf of the taxing agency. Included in this category are sales and excise taxes, social security taxes, withholding taxes, and union dues. Other liabilities such as federal and state corporate income taxes are conditioned or based on the results of the enterprise's operations.

Sales Taxes

Most states and some counties and cities impose sales or excise taxes. These taxes are usually imposed on the consumer, but the retailer usually collect must them and remit them to the taxing authority. When collected by the retailer, the tax is a liability and is not included in total sales. For example, assume that the Lottery Corporation makes a $500 sale on account that is subject to a 6% sales tax. The entry to record this sale is:

Accounts Receivable	530	
Sales		500
Sales Taxes Payable		30

To record $500 sales on account plus 6% sales tax.
$30 = $500 × .06

When the sales tax is remitted to the taxing agency, usually on a monthly or quarterly basis, the Sales Taxes Payable account is debited, and Cash is credited.

Payroll Tax Liabilities

As employees earn wages, certain federal and state taxes are incurred by the employee and the employer. Included are federal and state withholding taxes, social security taxes, and unemployment taxes. The employer must account for these taxes and file appropriate tax returns on a quarterly or yearly basis. This section will provide an overview of accounting for payroll taxes.

FICA (Federal Insurance Contributions Act) taxes are usually referred to as social security taxes. These taxes are a combination of Old Age Survivors and Disability Insurance (OASDI) and Medicare Insurance. FICA taxes are levied on both the employer and the employee. These taxes are a certain percentage of the employee's wages. In 1989, the tax rate was 7.51% of the first $48,000 on both the employer and employee, based on the first $45,000 of each individual salary. This rate is subject to change in future years.

Besides their share of social security taxes, employers must also pay federal and state unemployment taxes. Federal unemployment taxes (FUTA) are currently 6.0% of the employee's first $7,000 of wages. However, employers can receive a maximum credit of 5.4% against these federal taxes for state unemployment taxes incurred, thereby lowering their federal unemployment taxes to 0.6%. The actual amounts and limits of state unemployment taxes vary from state to state. The tax in most states differs from firm to firm, depending on the unemployment claims made by the former employees of the specific firm.

The federal government and many states have adopted pay-as-you-go requirements for the collection of individual income taxes. This requires the employer to withhold income taxes from employees' paychecks and to remit these taxes to the appropriate federal and state governments.

To demonstrate these points, assume that the monthly payroll of the Walters Company is $60,000. Assume that the entire payroll is subject to FICA taxes of 7.5% for both the employee and the employer, but only $40,000 of the wages is subject to state unemployment taxes of 2.7% and federal unemployment taxes of 0.8%. Finally, federal income taxes of $9,800, state income taxes of $3,500, and union dues of $600 are withheld. The entries to record the payroll and payroll taxes are as follows:

Wages Expense	60,000	
Federal Withholding Income Taxes Payable		9,800
State Withholding Income Taxes Payable		3,500
Union Dues Withheld		600
FICA Taxes Payable		4,500
Cash		41,600

To record wages for the month.
FICA taxes = $4,500, or $60,000 × .075

Payroll Taxes Expense	5,900	
FICA Taxes Payable		4,500
State Unemployment Taxes Payable		1,080
Federal Unemployment Taxes Payable		320

To record employer's share of payroll taxes.
FICA = $4,500, or $60,000 × .075
SUT   = $1,080, or $40,000 × .027
FUTA = $ 320, or $40,000 × .008

The timing of the actual payment of these taxes to the appropriate government agency depends on the size of the firm's payroll. Payments can be required on a weekly or a monthly basis. Generally, the payroll tax returns are filed on a quarterly basis. The entry to record the payables just shown is as follows:

FICA Taxes Payable	9,000	
Federal Withholding Income Taxes Payable	9,800	
State Withholding Income Taxes Payable	3,500	
Union Dues Withheld	600	
State Unemployment Taxes Payable	1,080	
Federal Unemployment Taxes Payable	320	
Cash		24,300
To record payment of various payroll taxes and union dues withheld.		

Compensated Absences

Although compensated absences do not represent collections for third parties, they are closely related to payroll taxes and thus will be covered here. As employees work, they accrue certain fringe benefits that allow them time off with full or partial pay. These **compensated absences** include such benefits as vacation and sick pay.

Under current accounting practices, a firm should accrue the liability for these benefits as they are earned. For example, many employees receive a two-week paid vacation every year. As the employee works throughout the year, he or she earns a portion of that vacation, so an estimated liability should be accrued for that amount. To illustrate, assume that during the current quarter, a firm estimates that its employees have earned 20 vacation days at an average salary of $200 per day. Thus the firm should accrue a $4,000 ($200 × 20 days) liability as follows:

Vacation Pay Expense	4,000	
Accrued Vacation Pay		4,000
To record an estimated liability of $4,000 for vacation pay.		

As the employees take their vacation and are paid, the liability account Accrued Vacation Pay is debited and Cash is credited.

Corporate Federal Income Taxes

Corporations are taxed by the federal as well as many state governments. These taxes are based on the results of the firm's operations as defined by the Internal Revenue Code. However, during the year, corporations are required to make quarterly payments based on their estimated tax for the entire year.

CONTINGENT LIABILITIES

Contingent liabilities are potential future liabilities whose existence is contingent upon some future event. In effect, a contingent liability is the result of an existing condition or situation whose final resolution depends on some future event. Generally, the amount of these liabilities must be estimated; the actual amount cannot be determined until the event that confirms the liability occurs. Furthermore, in many cases the actual person to whom payment will be made is not known until the future event occurs.

Examples of contingent liabilities include product warranties and guarantees, pending or threatened litigation, and the guarantee of others' indebtedness. In all these situations, a past event has occurred that may give rise to a liability depending on some future event. For example, when General Motors sells a car, it gives the purchaser a 64,000-mile or six-year guarantee against defects. Thus the event—the sale of a car—has taken place. However, the actual amount of the liability and the person to whom it will be paid depend on some future action—the customer's presenting the automobile for repair.

Contingent Liabilities That Are Accrued

Under generally accepted accounting principles, contingent liabilities are recorded as actual liabilities only if the potential liability is probable and its amount can be reasonably estimated.[4] An automobile guarantee or other product warranties are examples of contingent liabilities that are usually recorded on a company's books. Past experience indicates that a certain percentage of products will be defective, and past experience can also be used to make a reasonable estimate of the amount of the future expenditure required by the warranty. The matching convention requires the expense to be recorded in the period of the sale, not when the repair is made. As of December 31, 1986, General Motors had a $3.9 billion liability recorded for warranty claims and other allowances.

To illustrate, assume that the Micro Printing Company manufactures and sells high-speed laser printers for personal computers. The retail price per unit is $1,200, and each printer is guaranteed for three years; that is, the firm will repair the unit free of charge during this period. During the 1989 calendar year, the firm sold 2,000 printers. Past experience indicates that Micro Printing will incur an average of $40 in repair expense for each of the printers sold. Finally, during 1989, the company actually incurred $35,000 of warranty expenditures related to these printers. The following summary journal entries were made by Micro Printing Company in 1989 to reflect these events:

Cash or Accounts Receivable	2,400,000	
Sales		2,400,000
To record sales for the year.		
$2,400,000 = 2,000 units × $1,200		
Product Guarantee Expense	80,000	
Estimated Liability for Product Guarantees		80,000
To record estimated liability for product guarantees.		
$80,000 = 2,000 units × $40		
Estimated Liability for Product Guarantees	35,000	
Cash, Supplies, Accrued Wages, etc.		35,000
To record actual expenditures incurred for product guarantees during the year.		

For each accounting period, the entries are repeated. As the firm makes sales, an estimated liability is accrued. And as the guarantee expenditures are made by the firm, the liability is debited, and the appropriate accounts are credited.

Contingent Liabilities That Are Not Accrued

Contingent liabilities that are not probable and/or whose amount cannot be reasonably estimated are not accrued on the company's books. Instead, they are usually disclosed in the footnotes to the financial statements. These types of contingencies usually include pending litigation and guarantees of indebtedness that exist when a company guarantees the collectibility of a receivable that it has discounted at the bank. The following example, taken from a recent annual report of General Motors, shows how such contingent liabilities are disclosed.

> There are serious potential liabilities under government regulations pertaining primarily to environmental, fuel economy and safety matters. There are also various claims and pending actions against the Corporation and its subsidiaries with respect to commercial matters, including warranties and product liability, civil rights, antitrust, patent matters, taxes and other matters arising out of the conduct of the business. Certain of these actions purport to be class actions, seeking damages in very large amounts. The ultimate

---

[4]Financial Accounting Standards Board, Statement No. 5, *Accounting for Contingencies* (Stamford, Conn.: FASB, March 1975).

liability under these government regulations and the amounts of liability on these claims and actions at December 31, 1986 were not determinable but, in the opinion of the management, the ultimate liability resulting should not have a material adverse effect on the Corporation's consolidated financial position.

■ BALANCE SHEET PRESENTATION OF CURRENT LIABILITIES

The particular order in which current liabilities are presented on the balance sheet is a management decision. The current liability section of Colgate-Palmolive Company's balance sheet, shown in Exhibit 11-3, is typical of those found in the balance sheets of many U.S. companies. That is, notes and loans are usually listed first, then accounts payable, and finally accrued liabilities and taxes.

EXHIBIT 11–3

COLGATE-PALMOLIVE COMPANY Partial Balance Sheet (in thousands)		
Liabilities	1988	1987
Current Liabilities		
Notes and loans payable	$ 84,253	$ 192,126
Current portion of long-term debt	21,205	25,024
Accounts payable	489,920	496,521
Accrued income taxes	114,230	68,055
Other accruals	362,247	495,241
Total current liabilities	$1,071,855	$1,276,967

■ ACCOUNTING FOR CORPORATE INCOME TAXES

This book has pointed out various differences between generally accepted accounting principles (GAAP) and the provisions of the Internal Revenue Code (IRC). These differences result from the differing objectives of GAAP and the IRC. The objectives of GAAP are aimed at providing investors and other users of financial statements with reliable and relevant financial information. The objectives of the tax law contained in the IRC include social equity, ease of administration, political considerations, and ensuring that individuals and corporations are taxed when they have the ability to pay. Furthermore, there are many cases when the management of a firm will use one accounting method, such as straight-line depreciation, for accounting purposes and another method, such as declining-balance depreciation, for tax purposes. A prudent management will select those accounting methods allowed by the IRC that will minimize the firm's taxable income and thus reduce its cash outflow for taxes. On the other hand, the same management may select a different set of accounting principles for financial reporting purposes.

■ SOURCES OF DIFFERENCES BETWEEN ACCOUNTING INCOME AND TAXABLE INCOME

Differences between accounting income and taxable income can be classified into permanent and temporary differences. **Permanent differences** enter into the determination of accounting income but never into the determination of taxable income. They are, in effect, statutory differences between GAAP and the IRC. An example of a permanent difference is interest on state and local bonds. Although interest on these items represents revenue from an accounting perspective, it is not included in taxable income in either the year received or the year earned. Congress did this in order to make it easier for states and local governments to raise revenues by making the interest on their obligations nontaxable. Because these differences are indeed permanent, they are not of concern.

Temporary differences are the other reason that accounting income in any year may be different from taxable income. Temporary differences result from the fact that some transactions affect taxable income in a different period from when they affect pretax accounting income. Over the life of a particular transaction, the amount of income or expense for accounting and tax purposes is the same, but it is different within the various periods.

An example of a temporary difference is the use of straight-line depreciation based on the asset's economic life for financial reporting purposes and the use of accelerated depreciation for tax purposes. Generally, in the first few years of the asset's life, accelerated depreciation exceeds straight-line depreciation, and pretax accounting income is reduced less than taxable income as the result of depreciation expense. In later years, however, the temporary difference reverses. Straight-line depreciation now exceeds accelerated depreciation, causing a greater reduction in accounting income than in taxable income as the result of differences in depreciation expense.

To illustrate, return to the example outlined in Exhibit 10-7 in Chapter 10. Recall that equipment costing $100,000 is purchased and placed into service in 1990. For tax purposes, the asset is placed in the five-year class. Straight-line depreciation is used for financial reporting purposes for all depreciable assets. Remember that for tax purposes, double-declining-balance depreciation is allowed. In both cases, only half a year's depreciation is taken in the first year, and salvage value is ignored. However, the tax laws allow a switch to straight-line when it begins to yield a higher depreciation than double-declining-balance. This occurs in the fourth year, and at that point a switch is made to straight-line. Depreciation expense for the asset's life for both tax and financial reporting purposes is calculated in Exhibit 11-4. Note that over the asset's life, total depreciation expense equals $100,000; it is just allocated differently among the years under each method. Exhibit 11-5 compares the annual and total depreciation under each method.

EXHIBIT 11–4

Comparison of Depreciation for Tax and Financial Reporting Purposes

Tax—Double-declining-balance Depreciation, 5-year Life		
Year	**Computation**	**Depreciation Expense**
1990	$100,000 × .40 × $\frac{1}{2}$	$ 20,000
1991	($100,000 − $20,000) × .40	32,000
1992	($100,000 − $20,000 − $32,000) × .40	19,200
1993	Convert to straight-line depreciation ($100,000 − $20,000 − $32,000 − $19,200) / $2\frac{1}{2}$ years remaining life	11,520
1994	Straight-line depreciation	11,520
1995	Straight-line depreciation—$\frac{1}{2}$ year	5,760
	Total depreciation	$100,000

Financial Reporting—Straight-line Depreciation, 5-year Life		
Year	**Computation**	**Depreciation Expense**
1990	$100,000 / 5 years × $\frac{1}{2}$	$ 10,000
1991	$100,000 / 5 years	20,000
1992	$100,000 / 5 years	20,000
1993	$100,000 / 5 years	20,000
1994	$100,000 / 5 years	20,000
1995	$100,000 / 5 years × $\frac{1}{2}$	10,000
	Total depreciation	$100,000

EXHIBIT 11–5

Depreciation Method	Years						Total
	1990	1991	1992	1993	1994	1995	
Tax	20,000	32,000	19,200	11,520	11,520	5,760	100,000
Financial reporting	$10,000	$20,000	$20,000	$20,000	$20,000	$10,000	$100,000
Difference	$10,000	$12,000	($ 800)	($ 8,480)	($ 8,480)	($ 4,240)	$ 0

There are several other temporary differences between taxable income and accounting income. Some of the more important ones are summarized in Exhibit 11-6. You should remember two points. Temporary differences affect two or more periods: the period in which the difference originates and the later periods when it turns around or reverses. However, over the life of a single transaction, the amount of accounting and taxable income or expense related to that transaction will be the same. It is just a question of when temporary differences affect accounting and taxable income.

EXHIBIT 11–6

Summary of Selected Temporary Differences

Transaction	Accounting Method	Tax Method
Rent received in advance	Recognized when earned	Recognized when cash received
Installment sales	Recognized at point of sale	Installment basis; income recognized as cash collected
Construction contracts	Percentage-of-completion	Completed contract
Inventories	FIFO	Average cost
Depreciation	Straight-line	Accelerated

■ THE NEED FOR INTERPERIOD INCOME TAX ALLOCATION

The temporary differences just discussed illustrate that certain transactions affect accounting and taxable income in different periods. In order to deal with this problem, accountants follow a procedure called *interperiod income tax allocation*, in which the tax effects of temporary differences are reflected in the balance sheet as assets and liabilities. These tax effects reconcile the differences between pretax accounting income and taxable income. Thus the total tax liability for a period is the tax liability based on taxable income plus or minus the tax effect of the temporary difference.

To illustrate the application of interperiod income tax allocation, assume that the Price Corporation uses the same accounting principles for financial reporting purposes as it does for tax purposes, except for depreciation methods. For financial reporting purposes, the firm uses straight-line depreciation; for tax purposes, double-declining-balance. At the beginning of 1990, the firm purchases equipment as described in Exhibit 11-4. The annual depreciation for both accounting and tax purposes is also described in Exhibit 11-4. The calculations necessary to compute the tax liability are shown in Exhibit 11-7.

As Exhibit 11-7 shows, the firm's total tax liability is composed of two parts: the taxes payable based on taxable income and the tax effect of the temporary difference. In the first two years, the tax effect of the temporary difference (excess depreciation) is added to the tax liability based on taxable income to arrive at the total liability. In 1990, for example, the firm's total tax expense is $16,000. The liability for financial reporting purposes is also $16,000 and comprises the $12,000 currently payable and the $4,000 deferred until future years. The tax effect of the excess depreciation in 1990 ($10,000 × .40) is the reconciling item between the tax liability based on accounting income and taxable income.

EXHIBIT 11–7

PRICE CORPORATION Determination of Tax Liability						
	Year[a]					
	1990	1991	1992	1993	1994	1995
1. Taxable income before depreciation and taxes	$50,000	$51,000	$54,000	$56,000	$62,000	$70,000
2. Tax depreciation	20,000	32,000	19,200	11,520	11,520	5,760
3. Taxable income	30,000	19,000	34,800	44,480	50,480	64,240
4. Taxes payable—40%	$12,000	$ 7,600	$13,920	$17,792	$20,192	$25,696
5. Temporary difference (see Exhibit 11–5)	$10,000	$12,000	($800)	($8,480)	($8,480)	($4,240)
6. Tax rate[b]	.40	.40	.40	.40	.40	.40
7. Tax effect of temporary difference	$ 4,000	$ 4,800	($320)	($3,392)	($3,392)	($1,696)
8. Total tax liability (row 4 + row 7)	$16,000	$12,400	$13,600	$14,400	$16,800	$24,000

[a] The exhibit must include six years, since the firm takes only one-half of a year's depreciation in the first year.

[b] Although the actual corporate tax rate is now below 40%, this figure is used for ease of calculation.

The journal entries to record taxes expense for the first two years of the asset's life are as follows:

	1990		1991	
Income Tax Expense	16,000		12,400	
Income Tax Payable		12,000		7,600
Deferred Income Tax		4,000		4,800

In the remaining years of the asset's life, Income Taxes Payable exceeds Income Tax Expense, because the depreciation expense for financial reporting purposes associated with the equipment exceeds the depreciation expense for tax purposes. Thus the Deferred Income Tax account is debited in these years. These entries are as follows:

	1992	1993	1994	1995	
Income Tax Expense	13,600	14,400	16,800	24,000	
Deferred Income Tax	320	3,392	3,392	1,696	
Income Taxes Payable	13,920	17,792	20,192	25,696	

This case deals with a single asset purchase in which salvage values are ignored, the asset is held its entire life, and the tax rate is a constant 40%. Therefore the temporary difference completely reverses, and by the end of the asset's life, the Deferred Income Tax account has a zero balance. This is shown in the following Deferred Income Tax T account:

Deferred Income Tax			
12/31/92	320	12/31/90	4,000
12/31/93	3,392	12/31/91	4,800
12/31/94	3,392		
12/31/95	1,696		
Bal. 12/31/95	0		

When the Deferred Income Tax account has a credit balance, it is shown as a liability on the balance sheet. The FASB believes that the Deferred Income Tax account, when calculated according to its latest pronouncement, meets its definition of a liability: a probable future sacrifice of economic benefits arising from present obligations of an enterprise to transfer assets or provide services in the future. Likewise, when the Deferred Income Tax account has a debit balance, it is shown as an asset on the balance sheet, assuming it will result in predictable future tax savings.

A related question is whether the Deferred Income Tax account should be shown as a current or noncurrent asset or liability. The FASB feels that the current/noncurrent classification depends on whether or not the temporary difference is related to an identifiable asset or liability. Basically, if the temporary difference is related to a current asset such as inventory, the resulting deferred tax account should be classified as current. On the other hand, if the temporary difference is related to a noncurrent asset such as equipment, the resulting deferred tax account should be classified as noncurrent. However, temporary differences that relate to items that will result in net taxable or deductible amounts during the next year should be classified as current.

■ THE CONTROVERSY SURROUNDING ACCOUNTING FOR INCOME TAXES

Accounting for income taxes has always generated much controversy in the accounting profession. In December 1987, the FASB issued Statement No. 96, *Accounting for Income Taxes*, which replaced the long-standing Accounting Principles Board Opinion related to taxes. This statement added significant complexities to accounting for taxes and has not met with much enthusiasm from preparers of financial statements.

Much of the past controversy surrounding accounting for income taxes centered around the increasing size of the deferred tax liability account. Research studies have shown that prior to the issuance of Statement No. 96, deferred tax liabilities increased over the years; for many firms, they represent a large item in the liability section of the balance sheet. The primary reasons for this are the current use of accelerated depreciation methods for tax purposes. A company that has a relatively stable or growing investment in depreciable assets and that uses straight-line depreciation in determining pretax accounting income but uses accelerated depreciation in determining taxable income will be likely to have an increasing credit balance in its Deferred Income Tax account. This is because the continued investment in higher-priced assets indefinitely postpones the total reversal of the temporary difference, even though differences due to individual assets completely reverse. That is, as the effect of accelerated depreciation reverses on assets purchased in earlier years, it is offset by the effect of higher-priced assets purchased in the current year.

This raises the issue of how to treat the deferred tax account in analyzing financial statements. If, in fact, there is substantial evidence that the balance in the deferred tax liability account will not be reduced by future tax payments, should this account be classified as a liability? Many analysts feel that in such cases this account should be considered part of stockholder's equity or at least not be considered a liability in computing debt-to-equity ratios. The way in which this account is treated can have a substantial impact on the meaning of the resulting ratios.

For example, at the end of 1986 and 1985, ARCO had $3.562 billion and $2.405 billion, respectively, in its Deferred Income Tax account. These amounts represented 22% and 16% of total liabilities, respectively, and 68% and 44% of stockholders' equity, respectively. The deferred tax account grew by 48% from 1985 to 1986—the difference between the annual tax provision and what ARCO actually paid various governments in taxes. If the $3.562 billion in deferred taxes at the end of 1986 is considered a liability, the debt-to-equity ratio for ARCO is 311%. If that same amount in deferred taxes is considered part of stockholders' equity, the debt-to-equity ratio drops to 145%.

Statement No. 96 changed the manner in which the deferred tax account is calculated. This, in conjunction with the lowering of maximum corporate tax rates from 46% to 34%, will probably cause a reduction in the Deferred Income Tax account, with a corresponding increase in income. For example, Grumman adopted FASB Statement No. 96 in 1987. As a result of this adoption, a loss of $.20 per share was turned into income of $.94 per share.[5]

Although some companies like the effect FASB Statement No. 96 will have on income, they are quite concerned about the complexity of the statement and the estimates needed to determine the amount of deferred taxes. As a result of these complexities, the FASB issued Statement No. 100, which pushed back the effective date of the new standard to December 16, 1989. As this book went to press, it appeared that the effective date would be pushed back until at least September 1990. Thus the full effect of this statement on financial reports will not be seen until then.

■ INTEREST AND THE TIME VALUE OF MONEY

Perhaps you have heard the advertisements that claim that if you invest $2,000 a year in an Individual Retirement Account (IRA) beginning at age 30, you will accumulate over $500,000 by the time you retire at age 65. As the advertisements claim, you will receive substantially more than the $70,000 ($2,000 × 35 years) you invested, because of the interest that you will earn on your investment. This points out the importance of interest and how quickly it accumulates over a period of time. The focus of this section is on the time value of money and how this concept is used in personal and business financial decisions.

All investment decisions involve giving up a certain amount of money today in the hope of receiving a greater amount at some future time. In order to determine whether you have made a wise investment, you must consider the time value of money. For example, assume that you are given the following investment opportunity: A real estate developer offers to sell you a vacant lot today for $100,000 and guarantees to repurchase it ten years later for a minimum of $250,000. Does that sound like a good investment? Although it is tempting to say yes, because you would be making a profit of $150,000, you must also consider the time value of money. The $250,000 you will receive in ten years is not really comparable to the $100,000 you have to give up today. Money that you will receive in the future will not be as valuable as money you receive today, due to the fact that money received today can be invested and, as a result, will increase in amount. In the example, if you did not make the investment but instead put the $100,000 in a savings account that earned 12% interest per year, you would accumulate over $310,000 at the end of ten years.

The best way to analyze investment opportunities such as this is to determine the rate of return they offer. In this example, if you invested $100,000 today and received $250,000 in ten years, you would earn a rate of return of about 9.6%. You can compare this rate of return with those of other investments of similar risk and logically decide which one presents the best opportunity. In order to make this and similar analyses, you must understand five concepts:

1. simple versus compound interest.

2. the future value of a single amount.

3. the present value of a single amount.

4. the future value of an annuity.

5. the present value of an annuity.

[5] Arthur Young, *Financial Reporting & Accounting, 1988 Update* (Arthur Young, November 1988), p. 16.

■ SIMPLE VERSUS COMPOUND INTEREST

Interest is payment for the use of money for a specified period of time. Interest can be calculated on either a simple or a compound basis. The distinction between the two is important because it affects the amount of interest earned or incurred.

Simple Interest

Simple interest means that the interest payment is computed on only the amount of the principal for one or more periods. That is, if the original principal of the note is not changed, the interest payment will remain the same for each period. Most of the examples in this book so far have assumed simple interest. For example, if you invested $10,000 at 12% interest for three years, your yearly interest income would be $1,200 (($10,000 × .12). The total interest earned over the three years would be $3,600, and you would eventually receive $13,600 ($10,000 + $3,600).

Compound Interest

Compound interest means that interest is computed on the principal of the note plus any interest that has accrued to date. That is, when compound interest is applied, the accrued interest of that period is added to the principal to determine the amount on which future interest is to be computed. Thus, by compounding, interest is earned or incurred not only on the principal but also on the interest left on deposit.

To demonstrate the concept of compound interest, assume that the interest in the previous example now will be compounded annually rather than on a simple basis. As Exhibit 11-8 shows, in this case, your total interest income will be $4,049.28 rather than the $3,600 in the case of simple interest. During Year 1, interest income is $1,200, or 12% of $10,000. Because the interest is compounded, it is added to the principal to determine the accumulated amount of $11,200 at the end of the year. Interest in Year 2 is thus $1,344.00, or 12% of $11,200, and the accumulated amount at the end of Year 2 is now $12,544.00. The interest and the accumulated amount at the end of Year 3 are calculated in the same manner.

EXHIBIT 11–8			
Year	Principal Amount at Beginning of Year	Annual Interest Income, 12%	Accumulated at End of Year
1	$10,000.00	$1,200.00	$11,200.00
2	11,200.00	1,344.00	12,544.00
3	12,544.00	1,505.28	14,049.28

Interest Compounded More Often Than Annually

Interest can be compounded as often as the lender desires. The more often interest is compounded, the more quickly it will increase. For example, many savings and loans institutions compound interest daily. This means that interest is calculated on the beginning balance of your account each day. This interest is then added to the accumulated amount to determine the base for the next day's interest calculation. Clearly, this is more advantageous than if interest is compounded yearly.

When calculating interest that is compounded more than annually, it is quite easy to make the necessary adjustments. If interest is compounded more often than annually, there is more than one interest period each year. For example, if interest is compounded quarterly, there are four interest periods in each year. In the example of a three-year investment, there would be 12 interest periods if interest were compounded quarterly. However, the interest rate that is stated in annual terms must be reduced accordingly. Thus, instead of using an interest rate of 12% in the example, the interest rate would be 3% each quarter. As a general rule, the annual interest rate is divided by the number of compounding periods to determine the proper interest rate each period.

If interest is compounded quarterly in the previous $10,000, 12% example, it will equal $4,257.60, and the total amount of the investment will grow to $14,257.60. This is shown in Exhibit 11-9. In this straightforward example, the total interest increases by $208.32, from $4,049.28 to $4,257.60, when interest is compounded quarterly instead of annually.

EXHIBIT 11-9

Period	Principal Amount at Beginning of Period	Amount of Interest Each Period at 3%	Accumulated Amount at End of Period
1	$10,000.00	$300.00	$10,300.00
2	10,300.00	309.00	10,609.00
3	10,609.00	318.27	10,927.27
4	10,927.27	327.82	11,255.09
5	11,255.09	337.65	11,592.74
6	11,592.74	347.78	11,940.52
7	11,940.52	358.22	12,298.74
8	12,298.74	368.96	12,667.70
9	12,667.70	380.03	13,047.73
10	13,047.73	391.43	13,439.16
11	13,439.16	403.17	13,842.33
12	13,842.33	415.27	14,257.60

■ FUTURE VALUE OF A SINGLE AMOUNT

The previous example was an attempt to determine what the future amount of $10,000 invested at 12% for three years would be, given a certain compounding pattern. This is an example of determining the **future value of a single amount**. *Future value* means the amount to which the investment will grow at a future date if interest is compounded. The single amount means that a lump sum was invested at the beginning of Year 1 and was left intact for all three years. Thus there were no additional investments or withdrawals. These future-value or compound interest calculations are important in many personal and business financial decisions. For example, an individual may be interested in determining how much an investment of $50,000 will amount to in five years if interest is compounded semiannually versus quarterly, or what rate of return must be earned on a $10,000 investment if $18,000 is needed in seven years. All of these situations relate to determining the future value of a single amount.

One way to solve problems of this type is to construct tables similar to Exhibit 11-9. However, this method is time-consuming and not very flexible. Mathematical formulas can also be used. For example, the tables used in Exhibits 11-8 and 11-9 and in Appendix C to determine the accumulated amount of a single deposit at different compounded rates are based on the following formula:

Accumulated amount $= p(1 + i)^n$ where
p = Principal amount
i = Interest rate
n = Number of compounding periods

That is, in the example of the $10,000 compounded annually for three years at 12%, the $14,049.28 can be determined by the following calculation:

$14,049.28 = $10,000(1 + .12)^3$

One of the simplest methods is to use tables that give the future value of $1 at different interest rates and for different periods. Essentially, these tables interpret the mathematical formula just presented for various interest rates and compounding periods for a principal amount of $1. Once the amount for $1 is known, it is easy to determine the amount for any principal amount by multiplying the future amount for $1 by the required principal amount. Many hand calculators also have function keys that can be used to solve these types of problems.

To illustrate, Exhibit 11-10, an excerpt from the compound interest and present-value tables in Appendix C at the end of the book, shows the future value of $1 for ten interest periods for interest rates ranging from 2% to 15%. Suppose that you want to determine the future value of $10,000 at the end of three years if interest is compounded annually at 12% (the example previously used). In order to solve this, look down the 12% column in the table until you come to the third interest period. The factor from the table is 1.40493, which means that $1 invested today at 12% will accumulate to $1.405 at the end of three years. Because you are interested in $10,000 rather than $1, just multiply the factor of 1.40493 by $10,000 to determine the future value of the $10,000 principal amount. The amount is $14,049.30, which, except for a slight rounding error, is the same as was determined from Exhibit 11-8.

EXHIBIT 11–10   Future Value of a Single Amount

(n) Periods	2%	4%	6%	8%	10%	12%	15%	(n) Periods
1	1.02000	1.04000	1.06000	1.08000	1.10000	1.12000	1.15000	1
2	1.04040	1.08160	1.12360	1.16640	1.21000	1.25440	1.32250	2
3	1.06121	1.12486	1.19102	1.25971	1.33100	1.40493	1.52088	3
4	1.08243	1.16986	1.26248	1.36049	1.46410	1.57352	1.74901	4
5	1.10408	1.21665	1.33823	1.46933	1.61051	1.76234	2.01136	5
6	1.12616	1.26532	1.41852	1.58687	1.77156	1.97382	2.31306	6
7	1.14869	1.31593	1.50363	1.71382	1.94872	2.21068	2.66002	7
8	1.17166	1.36857	1.59385	1.85093	2.14359	2.47596	3.05902	8
9	1.19509	1.42331	1.68948	1.99900	2.35795	2.77308	3.51788	9
10	1.21899	1.48024	1.79085	2.15892	2.59374	3.10585	4.04556	10

The use of the future-value table can be generalized by using the following formula:

Accumulated amount = Factor (from the table) × Principal

$14,049.30 = 1.40493 × $10,000

This formula can be used to solve a variety of related problems. For example, as noted above, you may be interested in determining what rate of interest must be earned on a $10,000 investment if you want to accumulate $18,000 at the end of seven years. Or you may want to know the number of years an amount must be invested in order to grow to a certain amount. In all these cases, you have two of the three items in the formula, and you can solve for the third.

Interest Compounded More Often Than Annually

As previously stated, interest usually is compounded more often than annually. In such situations, simply adjust the number of interest periods and the interest rate. If you want to know what $10,000 will accumulate to at the end of three years if interest is compounded quarterly at an annual rate of 12%, just look down the 3% column until you reach 12 periods (see Table 1 in Appendix C). The factor is 1.42576, and (employing the general formula) the accumulated amount is $14,257.60, determined as follows:

$$\text{Accumulated amount} = \text{Factor} \times \text{Principal}$$
$$\$14,257.60 = 1.42576 \times \$10,000$$

Determining the Number of Periods or the Interest Rate

There are many situations in which the unknown variable is the number of interest periods that the dollars must remain invested or the rate of return (interest rate) that must be earned. For example, assume that you invest $5,000 today in a savings and loan association that will pay interest at 10% compounded annually. You need to accumulate $8,857.80 for a certain project. How many years does the investment have to remain in the savings and loan association? Using the general formula, the answer is six years, determined as follows:

$$\text{Accumulated amount} = \text{Factor} \times \text{Principal}$$

$$\text{Factor} = \frac{\text{Accumulated amount}}{\text{Principal}}$$

$$1.77156 = \frac{\$8,857.80}{\$5,000.00}$$

Looking down the 10% column in Table 1 of Appendix C, the factor of 1.77156 appears at the sixth-period row. Because the interest is compounded annually, the sixth period is interpreted as six years. This example was constructed so that the factor equals a round number of periods. If it does not, interpolation is necessary. The examples, exercises, and problems in this book will not require interpolation.

You can use the same method to determine the required interest rate. For example, assume that you invest $10,000 for eight years. What rate of return or interest rate compounded annually must you earn if you want to accumulate $30,590.23? Using the general formula, the answer is 15%, determined as follows:

$$\text{Accumulated amount} = \text{Factor} \times \text{Principal}$$

$$\text{Factor} = \frac{\text{Accumulated amount}}{\text{Principal}}$$

$$3.05902 = \frac{\$30,590.23}{\$10,000.00}$$

Looking across the eighth-period row, you find the factor of 3.05902 at the 15% column.

■ PRESENT VALUE OF A SINGLE AMOUNT

In many business and personal situations, you are interested in determining the value today of receiving a set single amount at some time in the future. For example, assume that you want to know the value today of receiving $15,000 at the end of five years if a rate of return of 12% is earned. Another way of asking this question is, what is the amount that would have to be invested today at 12% (compounded annually) if you wanted to receive $15,000 at the end of five years? These are **present-value-of-a-single-amount** problems, because you are interested in knowing the present value, or the value today, of receiving a set sum in the future.

Intuitively, it is clear that the present value will be less than the future value. For example, if you had the choice of receiving $12,000 today or in two years, you would take the $12,000 today. This is because you can invest the $12,000 so that it will accumulate to more than $12,000 at the end of two years. Another way of looking at this is to say that because of the time value of money, you would take an amount less than $12,000 if you could receive it today, instead of $12,000 in two years. The amount you would be willing to accept depends on the interest rate or the rate of return you receive.

In present-value situations, the interest rate is often called the *discount rate*. This is because a future value is being discounted back to the present. Some individuals refer to present-value problems as *discounted* present-value problems.

One way to solve present-value problems is to use the general formula previously developed for future-value problems. For example, returning to the previous example, assume that at the end of five years, you wish to have $15,000. If you can earn 12% compounded annually, how much do you have to invest today? Using the general formula for Table 1 in Appendix C, the answer is $8,511.40, determined as follows:

$$\text{Accumulated amount} = \text{Factor} \times \text{Principal}$$

$$\text{Principal} = \frac{\text{Accumulated amount}}{\text{Factor}}$$

$$\$8,511.40 = \frac{\$15,000}{1.76234}$$

This is equivalent to saying that at a 12% interest rate, compounded annually, it does not matter whether you receive $8,511.40 today or $15,000 at the end of five years. Thus, if someone offered you an investment at a cost of $8,000 that would return $15,000 at the end of five years, you would take it if the minimum rate of return were 12%. This is because at 12% the $15,000 is actually worth $8,511.45 today, but you would need to make an outlay of only $8,000.

Using Present-value Tables

Rather than using future-value tables and making the necessary adjustments to the general formula, you can use present-value tables. As is the case with future-value tables, present-value tables are based on the mathematical formula used to determine present values. Because of the relationship between future and present values, the present-value table is the inverse of the future-value table. Exhibit 11-11 presents an excerpt from the present-value tables (Table 2) found in Appendix C. The table works the same as the future-value table does, except that the general formula is

$$\text{Present value} = \text{Factor} \times \text{Accumulated amount}$$

EXHIBIT 11-11

Present Value of a
Single Amount

(n) Periods	2%	4%	6%	8%	10%	12%	15%	(n) Periods
1	.98039	.96154	.94340	.92593	.90909	.89286	.86957	1
2	.96117	.92456	.89000	.85734	.82645	.79719	.75614	2
3	.94232	.88900	.83962	.79383	.75132	.71178	.65752	3
4	.92385	.85480	.79209	.73503	.68301	.63552	.57175	4
5	.90573	.82193	.74726	.68058	.62092	.56743	.49718	5
6	.88797	.79031	.70496	.63017	.56447	.50663	.43233	6
7	.87056	.75992	.66506	.58349	.51316	.45235	.37594	7
8	.85349	.73069	.62741	.54027	.46651	.40388	.32690	8
9	.83676	.70259	.59190	.50025	.42410	.36061	.28426	9
10	.82035	.67556	.55839	.46319	.38554	.32197	.24719	10

For example, if you want to use the table to determine the present value of $15,000 to be received at the end of five years, compounded annually at 12%, simply look down the 12% column and multiply that factor by $15,000. Thus the answer is $8,511.45, determined as follows:

$$\text{Present value} = \text{Factor} \times \text{Accumulated amount}$$

$$\$8,511.45 = .56743 \times \$15,000$$

Other Present-value Situations

As in the future-value case, you can use the general formula to solve other variations, as long as you know two of the three variables. For example, assume that you want to know what interest rate compounded semiannually you must earn if you want to accumulate $10,000 at the end of three years, with an investment of $7,049.60 today. The answer is 6% semiannually or 12% annually, determined as follows:

$$\text{Present value} = \text{Factor} \times \text{Accumulated amount}$$

$$\text{Factor} = \frac{\text{Present value}}{\text{Accumulated amount}}$$

$$.70496 = \frac{\$\,7{,}049.60}{\$10{,}000.00}$$

Looking across the sixth-period row, we come to .70496 at the 6% column. Because interest is compounded semiannually, the annual rate is 12%.

Distinguishing between Future Value and Present Value

In beginning to work with time-value-of-money problems, you should be careful to distinguish between present-value and future-value problems. One way to do this is to use time lines to analyze the situation. For example, the time line relating to the example in which you determined the future value of $10,000 compounded at 12% for three years is as follows:

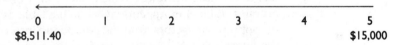

0	1	2	3
$10,000			$14,049.28

But the time line relating to the present value of $15,000 discounted back at 12% for five years is:

0	1	2	3	4	5
$8,511.40					$15,000

■ THE FUTURE VALUE OF AN ANNUITY

An **annuity** is a series of equal payments made at specified intervals. Interest is compounded on each of these payments. Annuities are often called *rents* because they are like the payment of monthly rentals. Annuity payments can be made at the beginning or the end of the specified intervals. If they are made at the beginning of the period, the annuity is called an *annuity due*, and if the payment is made at the end of the period, it is called an *ordinary annuity*. The examples in this book use ordinary annuities, so we will always assume that the payment takes place at the end of the period.

Annuities are commonly encountered in business and accounting situations. For example, a lease payment or a mortgage represents an annuity. Life insurance contracts involving a series of equal payments at equal times are another example of an annuity. In some cases, it is appropriate to calculate the future value of the annuity; in other cases, it is appropriate to calculate the present value of the annuity.

Determining the Future Value of an Annuity

The **future value of an annuity** is the sum of all the periodic payments plus the interest that has accumulated on them. To demonstrate how to calculate the future value of an annuity, assume that you deposit $1 at the end of each of the next four years in a savings account that pays 10% interest, compounded annually. Exhibit 11-12 shows how these $1 payments will accumulate to $4.6410 at the end of the

EXHIBIT 11–12

End of Year in Which
Investment Is Made

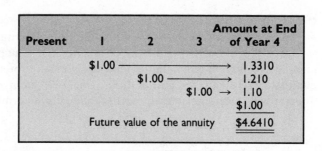

fourth period, or year in this case. The future value of each dollar is determined by compounding interest at 10% for the appropriate number of periods. For example, the $1 deposited at the end of the first period earns interest for three periods. It earns interest for only three periods because it was deposited at the end of the first period and earns interest until the end of the fourth. Using the factors from Table 1 in Appendix C, the future value of this first $1.00 single payment is $1.3310, determined as follows:

Future value = Factor × Principal
    $1.3310 = 1.3310 × $1.00

The second payment earns interest for two periods and accumulates to $1.2100, and the third payment earns interest for only one period and accumulates to $1.10. The final payment, made at the end of the fourth year, does not earn any interest, because the future value of the annuity is being determined at the end of the fourth period. The total of all payments compounded for the appropriate number of interest periods equals $4.6410—the future value of this ordinary annuity.

Fortunately, you do not have to construct a table like this one in order to determine the future value of an annuity. You can use tables that present the factors necessary to calculate the future value of an annuity of $1, given different periods and interest rates. Table 3 in Appendix C is such a table. It is constructed by simply summing the appropriate factors from the compound interest table. For example, the factor for the future value of a $1.00 annuity at the end of four years at 10% compounded annually is $4.6410, which is the amount determined when the calculation was performed independently by summing the individual factors.

Problems Involving the Future Value of an Annuity

By using the general formula below, you can solve a variety of problems involving the future value of an annuity:

Future value of an annuity = Factor × Annuity payment

As long as you know two of the three variables, you can solve for the third. Thus you can solve for the future value of the annuity, the annuity payment, the interest rate, or the number of periods.

Determining Future Value. Assume that you deposited in a savings and loan association $4,000 per year at the end of each of the next eight years. How much will you accumulate if you earn 10% compounded annually? The future value of this annuity is $45,743.56, determined as follows:

Future value of an annuity = Factor × Annuity payment
    $45,743.56 = 11.43589 × $4,000

Determining the Annuity Payment. Assume that at the end of 15 years, you need to accumulate $100,000 to send your daughter to college. If you can earn 12% at your local savings and loan association, how much must you deposit at the end of each of the next 15 years in order to accumulate the $100,000 at the end of the fifteenth year? The annual payment is $2,682.42, as determined in the following:

$$\text{Future value of an annuity} = \text{Factor} \times \text{Annuity payment}$$

$$\text{Annuity payment} = \frac{\text{Future value of an annuity}}{\text{Factor}}$$

$$\$2{,}682.42 = \frac{\$100{,}000}{37.27972}$$

Determining the Interest Rate. In some cases, you may want to determine the interest rate that must be earned on an annuity in order to accumulate a predetermined amount. For example, assume that you invest $500 per quarter for ten years and want to accumulate $30,200.99 at the end of the tenth year. What interest rate is required? You need to earn 2% quarterly, or 8% annually, determined as follows:

$$\text{Future value of an annuity} = \text{Factor} \times \text{Annuity payment}$$

$$\text{Factor} = \frac{\text{Future value of an annuity}}{\text{Annuity payment}}$$

$$60.40198 = \frac{\$30{,}200.99}{\$500}$$

Because the annuity payments are made quarterly, you must look across the fortieth-period (10 years $\times$ 4) row until you find the factor. In this case it is at the 2% column. Thus the interest rate is 2% quarterly, or 8% annually.

In some situations, the interest rate is known, but the number of periods is missing. These problems can be solved by using the same technique you used to determine the interest rate. When the factor is determined, you must be sure to look down the appropriate interest column to find the factor on the annuity table.

■ PRESENT VALUE OF AN ANNUITY

The value today of a series of equal payments or receipts to be made or received on specified future dates is called the **present value of an annuity**. As in the case of the future value of an annuity, the receipts or payments are made in the future. Present value is the value today, and future value relates to accumulated future value. Furthermore, the present value of a series of payments or receipts will be less than the total of the same payment or receipts, because cash received in the future is not as valuable as cash received today. On the other hand, the future value of an annuity will be greater than the sum of the individual payments or receipts, because interest is accumulated on the payments. It is important to distinguish between the future value and the present value of an annuity. Again, time lines are helpful in this respect.

Mortgages and certain notes payable in equal installments are examples of present-value-of-annuity problems. For example, assume that a bank lends you $60,000 today, to be repaid in equal monthly installments over 30 years. The bank is interested in knowing what series of monthly pyaments, when discounted back at the agreed-upon interest rate, is equal to the present value today of the amount of the loan, or $60,000.

Determining the Present Value of an Annuity

Assume that you want to determine the value today of receiving $1 at the end of each of the next four years. The appropriate interest or discount rate is 12%. To solve this, construct a table that determines the present values of each of the receipts, as shown in Exhibit 11-13. The exhibit shows that the present value of receiving the four $1.00 payments is $3.03735 when discounted at 12%. Each of the individual dollars was discounted by using the factors in the present-value of a single amount table in Exhibit

EXHIBIT 11–13

End of Year in Which
$1.00 Is to Be Received

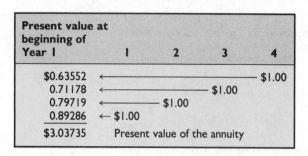

Present value at beginning of Year 1	1	2	3	4
$0.63552				⟵ $1.00
0.71178			⟵ $1.00	
0.79719		⟵ $1.00		
0.89286	⟵ $1.00			
$3.03735	Present value of the annuity			

11-11. For example, the present value of the dollar received at the end of Year 4, when discounted back four years, is $0.63552. It must be discounted back four years because the present, or today, is the beginning of Year 1. The dollar received at the end of Year 3 must be discounted back three periods; the dollar received at the end of Year 2 must be discounted back two periods; and so forth.

As with the calculation of the future value of an annuity, you can use prepared tables. Table 4 in Appendix C is such a table. It is constructed by summing the individual present values of $1 at set interest rates and periods. Thus the factor for the present value of four $1.00 to be received at the end of each of the next four years, when discounted back at 12%, is 3.03735, the value that was determined independently.

Problems Involving the Present Value of an Annuity

Problems involving the present value of an annuity can be solved by using the following general formula:

Present value of an annuity = Factor × Amount of the annuity

As long as you know two of the three variables, you can solve for the third. Thus, you can determine the present value of the annuity, the interest rate, the number of periods, or the amount of the annuity.

Determining the Present Value. To demonstrate how to calculate the present value of an annuity, assume that you were offered an investment that paid $2,000 a year at the end of each of the next ten years. How much would you pay for it if you wanted to earn a rate of return of 8%? This is a present-value problem, because you would pay the value today of this stream of payments discounted back at 8%. This amount is $13,420.16, determined as follows:

Present value of an annuity = Factor × Amount of the annuity
$13,420.16 = 6.71008 × $2,000

Another way to interpret this problem is to say that it makes no difference whether you keep $13,420.16 today or receive $2,000 a year for ten years, if you want to earn 8%.

Determining the Annuity Payment. A common variation of present-value problems requires computing the annuity payment. In many cases, these are loan or mortgage problems. For example, assume that you purchase a house for $100,000 and make a 20% down payment. You will borrow the rest of the money from the bank at 10% interest. To make the problem easier, assume that you will make 30 yearly payments at the end of each of the next 30 years. (Most mortgages require monthly payments.) How much will your yearly payments be?

In this case, you are going to borrow $80,000 ($100,000 × 80%). The yearly payment would be $8,486.34, determined as follows:

$$\text{Present value of an annuity} = \text{Factor} \times \text{Amount of the annuity}$$

$$\text{Amount of the annuity} = \frac{\text{Present value of an annuity}}{\text{Factor}}$$

$$\$8,486.34 = \frac{\$80,000}{9.42691}$$

Determining the Number of Payments. Assume that the Black Lighting Co. purchased a new printing press for $100,000. The quarterly payments are $4,326.24 and the interest rate is 12% annually, or 3% per quarter. How many payments will be required to pay off the loan? In this case, 40 payments are required, determined as follows:

$$\text{Present value of an annuity} = \text{Factor} \times \text{Amount of the annuity}$$

$$\text{Factor} = \frac{\text{Present value of an annuity}}{\text{Amount of the annuity}}$$

$$23.11477 = \frac{\$100,000}{\$4,326.24}$$

Looking down the 3% column in Table 4 in Appendix C, you find the factor 23.11477 at the fortieth-period row. Thus 40 quarterly payments are needed to pay off the loan.

Combination Problems. Many accounting applications related to the time value of money involve both single amounts and annuities. For example, say that you are considering purchasing an apartment house. After much analysis, you determine that you will receive net yearly cash flows of $10,000 from rental revenue, less rental expenses from the apartment. To make the analysis easier, assume that the cash flows are generated at the end of each year. These cash flows will continue for 20 years, at which time you estimate that you can sell the apartment building for $250,000. How much should you pay for the building, assuming that you want to earn a rate of return of 10%?

This problem involves an annuity—the yearly net cash flows of $10,000—and a single amount—the $250,000 to be received once at the end of the twentieth year. As a rational person, the maximum that you would be willing to pay is the value today of these two cash flows discounted at 10%. That value is $122,296, as determined below:

Present value of the annuity of $10,000 a year for 20 years $10,000 × 8.51356 (Table 4)	$ 85,136
Present value of the single amount of $250,000 to be received at the end of year 20 $250,000 × .14864 (Table 2)	37,160
Total purchase price	$122,296

■ ACCOUNTING APPLICATIONS OF THE TIME VALUE OF MONEY

The concepts related to the time value of money, especially present value, have many applications in financial and managerial accounting. For example, from a theoretical perspective, assets and liabilities should be valued at the present value of the future cash inflows expected from the asset or of the cash outflows from the liability. Accountants rarely use this valuation method to value assets, because of the difficulty of estimating future cash flows and discount rates. However, present value is often used to value long-term liabilities at their valuation date, because the cash flows for liabilities such as mortgages and bonds are known with certainty. For example, a bond has a stated interest rate and a set principal amount. As the next chapter will show, bonds are recorded at the present value of these cash outflows, based on the yield interest rate at the time of their issuance.

SUMMARY OF LEARNING OBJECTIVES

1. Definition and recognition of liabilities. Liabilities are probable future sacrifices of economic benefits arising from present obligations to transfer assets or provide services. Liabilities, like assets, are classified as either current or noncurrent. Current liabilities are valued on the balance sheet at their face value.

2. Types of current liabilities. Current liabilities can be classified into three categories:

Category	Example
Definitely determinable	Accounts and notes payable and accrued liabilities
Collection for third parties and liabilities conditioned on operations	Sales taxes payable, payroll taxes, and corporate income taxes
Contingent liabilities	Warranties, guarantees, and litigations

3. Accounting for corporate income taxes. Because of differing objectives, there are significant differences between taxable income as defined by the IRC and pretax accounting income as defined by GAAP. Management often takes advantage of these differences to report taxable income that is lower than pretax accounting income. The differences are either permanent or temporary. Temporary differences make interperiod income tax allocation necessary. The total tax for the period is the tax liability based on taxable income plus or minus the tax effect of the temporary differences.

4. Concepts related to the time value of money. Money paid or received in the future is not as valuable as is money paid or received today, because money received today can be invested and thus will increase in value. Many investment decisions require using time-value-of-money concepts:

(a) Simple versus compound interest.

(b) The future value of a single amount.

(c) The present value of a single amount.

(d) The future value of an annuity.

(e) The present value of an annuity.

The following table summarizes time-value-of-money concepts:

Concept	Typical Situation
Future value of a single amount	How much will $5,000 grow to at the end of five years if deposited today and earning 12% compounded annually?
Present value of a single amount	What is the value today of receiving $10,000 at the end of ten years, discounted at 10%, compounded quarterly?
Future value of an annuity	How much will $2,000 a year, deposited in a bank at the end of each of the next ten years at 8%, compounded yearly, accumulate to at the end of ten years?
Present value of an annuity	What is the value today of receiving $6,000 at the end of each of the next seven years, discounted at 10% per year?

KEY TERMS

Accounts payable
Annuity
Compensated absences

Compound interest
Current liabilities
Current maturities of long-term debt

FICA (Federal Insurance Contributions Act) taxes	Permanent differences
Future value of an annuity	Present value
Future value of a single amount	Present value of an annuity
Long-term liabilities	Present value of a single amount
Monetary liabilities	Simple interest
Nonmonetary liabilities	Temporary differences
Notes payable	Trade accounts payable

PROBLEMS FOR YOUR REVIEW

A. On November 1, 1989, the British Corporation signed a $10,000 note to the French Co. The note has an interest rate of 12% and is due in six months, on April 30, 1990. The British Corporation has a December 31 year-end. Make the appropriate journal entries on the books of the British Corporation, the borrower, on November 1, 1989, on December 31, 1989, and on April 30, 1990, assuming that:

1. The note contains a separate interest element so that British receives proceeds of $10,000.

2. The note is discounted so that it is written for $10,600, but the British Corporation receives only an amount less the discount of $600. (The interest is not stated separately.)

SOLUTION

Case 1: Separate Interest Element			Case 2: No Separate Interest Element		
November 1, 1989					
Cash	10,000		Cash	10,000	
Notes Payable		10,000	Discount on Notes Payable	600	
			Notes Payable		10,600
To record issuance of $10,000, 12%, 6-month note.			To record issuance of $10,600, 6-month discounted note payable.		
December 31, 1989					
Interest Expense	200		Interest Expense	200	
Interest Payable		200	Discount on Notes Payable		200
To record accrued interest from 11/1 to 12/31. $200 = \$10,000 \times .12 \times \frac{2}{12}$			To amortize discount on notes payable for 2 months on a straight-line basis. $200 = (\$600 \div 6 \text{ months}) \times 2$		
April 30, 1990					
Notes Payable	10,000		Notes Payable	10,600	
Interest Payable	200		Interest Expense	400	
Interest Expense	400		Discount on Notes Payable		400
Cash		10,600	Cash		10,600
To record payment of loan and interest expense.			To record payment of loan and discount amortization.		

B. Solve each of the following time-value-of-money problems:

1. Determine the future value of:

(a) a single payment of $15,000 at 8%, compounded semiannually, for ten years.

(b) ten annual payments of $2,000 at 12%.

2. Determine the present value of:

(a) six semiannual payments of $1,000 at 10%, compounded semiannually.

(b) a single payment of $12,000 discounted at 12% annually, received at the end of five years.

3. You have decided that you would like to take a trip around the world at the end of ten years. You expect that the trip will cost $150,000. If you can earn 10% annually, how much would you have to invest at the end of each of the next ten years to accumulate the $150,000?

SOLUTION   **1(a).** Future value of single amount—$15,000, 8% compounded semiannually for ten years (4% × 20 periods)

Principal × Factor = Accumulated amount

$15,000 × 2.19112 = $32,866.80

1(b). Future value of an ordinary annuity—ten payments, 12% interest

Annuity payment × Factor = Future value of annuity

$2,000 × 17.54874 = 35,097.48

2(a). Present value of six semiannual payments discounted at 5% semiannually

Annuity payment × Factor = Present value of annuity

$1,000 × 5.07569 = 5,075.69

2(b). Present value of single payment of $12,000 discounted at 12% for five years

Future value × Factor = Present value

$12,000 × .56743 = $6,809.16

3. Determine annual payment required to accumulate $150,000 at the end of ten years at 10% interest (future value of an annuity)

$$\text{Annuity payment} = \frac{\text{Future value of annuity}}{\text{Factor}}$$

$$\$9,411.81 = \frac{\$150,000}{15.93743}$$

QUESTIONS

1. In your own words, define *liabilities*.

2. Distinguish current liabilities from noncurrent liabilities. Why is the classification of liabilities important to an enterprise?

3. What is meant by present value? Discuss the application of present-value concepts to the valuation of current liabilities.

4. The Santa Cruz Co. entered into an agreement with the Los Padres Co. to purchase 100,000 tons of iron ore. The first delivery is to be made in one month. No cash or other consideration has changed hands. Should the Santa Cruz Co. recognize a liability? Why or why not?

5. What are the characteristics of liabilities that are classi-fied as definitely determinable in nature? Give three examples of liabilities in this category. What are the important accounting problems related to this liability?

6. What is a discount on notes payable, and how does it arise?

7. Describe the difference between a note that explicitly states an interest rate and one in which the interest element is not explicitly stated.

8. Define and give two examples of monetary and non-monetary liabilities.

9. List the most common payroll taxes incurred by employees and those incurred by employers.

10. What is a compensated absence? Give three examples.

11. What are contingent liabilities? How do they differ, if at all, from other types of liabilities?

12. Give an example of a contingent liability that is accrued and one that is just disclosed in the financial statements. Explain what criteria are used in deciding whether to accrue a liability.

13. In December 1988, there was an accident at the No-Nuke Nuclear Power Plant. As a result, personal injury suits totaling $10 million have been filed against the company owning the plant. Although it appears that the company will lose several of the lawsuits, there is no way to make a reasonable determination of the final amount of the loss. In preparing its December 31, 1988 financial statements, how do you think these facts should be accounted for? Would your answer be different if the accident had taken place in early January 1989, but before the firm's December 31, 1988 financial statements were prepared?

14. In your opinion, what is the primary objective of determining pretax accounting income according to GAAP? How does this objective differ from the objectives of determining taxable income as defined by the IRC?

15. What are temporary differences, and how do they relate to accounting for income taxes?

16. There are several instances when the management of a firm can use one accounting method in determining pretax accounting income and a different method in computing taxable income. Give four examples.

17. The books of the Bowmant Co. for the year ended December 31, 1988 showed pretax income of $200,000. In computing taxable income for federal tax purposes, Bowmant deducted $10,000 of depreciation in excess of depreciation recorded on the books. Assuming the current tax rate is 40%, make the entry to record the tax expense and the taxes payable.

18. Explain the difference between simple and compound interest. If all else were equal, would you rather earn simple or compound interest?

19. Describe the differences among the following:

(a) The future value of a single amount.

(b) The future value of an annuity.

(c) The present value of a single amount.

(d) The present value of an annuity.

20. You are considering purchasing a car that will be financed through a bank loan. The bank loan will be for $7,000 at 12% for four years. Payments are to be made monthly. You are attempting to determine the monthly payments. Describe how you would solve this problem. It is not necessary to make the actual calculations.

21. Assume that you are determining the future value of an annuity. If the interest you can earn falls from 15% to 10%, what will happen to the future value of the annuity?

22. Your firm is considering establishing a fund that will be used in ten years to retire a large amount of long-term debt. You need to accumulate $5 million. You are contemplating making annual payments in a fund that will earn 7%, and you want to know how much you must contribute to the fund. Describe how you would solve this problem. It is not necessary to make the actual calculations.

23. Assume that you are trying to determine the present value of an annuity. If the discount rate increases from 10% to 12%, what effect will this have on the present value of the annuity?

24. Below are several situations. Which of them, if any, do not involve time-value-of-money concepts? Explain your answer.

(a) Determining the monthly mortgage payment on a loan.

(b) Determining whether you should make an investment today that will provide you with $1,000 a year for the next ten years.

(c) Deciding whether you should pay cash or take out a five-year loan when purchasing a new car.

(d) Deciding whether to purchase a new machine that will increase cash flows by $5,000 a year for five years.

EXERCISES

E1. Types of Liabilities. Following are descriptions of liabilities commonly found on balance sheets:

(a) An amount of money owed on a note.

(b) An amount of money owed to the government, based upon the corporation's income.

(c) An amount of money withheld from an employee's paycheck, used to fund retirement benefits.

(d) Services owed to client because of fees received previously.

(e) An amount of money owed to creditors for the acquisition of merchandise held for resale.

(f) An amount of money owed to others for the use of money.

(g) An amount of money owed to the state based on the gross sales of the firm.

(h) An amount of money received from subscribers for magazines to be delivered next year.

REQUIRED: For each item, state the account title normally used on the balance sheet. In addition, state whether each item is considered a monetary or nonmonetary liability.

E2. Recording Notes Payable. On January 31, 1989, the Lynch Co. purchased equipment from the Andersen Corporation for $425,000. A one-year, 12% note was signed. Assuming Lynch has a December 31 year-end, make all the appropriate entries related to this note.

E3. Notes Payable. The Maxwell Corporation signed on March 1, 1989 a $250,000, one-year, 16% discounted note payable to the Olympic National Bank. What cash proceeds did the Maxwell Corporation receive? Make the necessary journal entries related to this note, assuming that the firm has a December 31 year-end. In addition, show how the note payable would be disclosed on a December 31, 1989 balance sheet.

E4. Notes Payable. The Reds Corporation borrowed $10,000 at 12% from Wilshire West National Bank. The loan was made on September 1 and is due in one year. Assume that the firm closes its books once a year on December 31.

Make the entries to record (1) the note, (2) the adjustment at year-end, and (3) the payment of the note, assuming that the note:

(a) is drawn in the principal amount of $10,000 and interest is stated separately.

(b) is drawn in the face amount of $11,200, is discounted, and does not contain a separate interest element.

E5. Sales Taxes. M&T Shoes had $35,000 of sales during the first quarter of 1989. The sales tax for the state in which the store operates is 6%. All sales are on account. Prepare the necessary entries to record the sales and subsequent payment of the sales taxes on May 1, 1989.

E6. Payroll and Payroll Taxes. The payroll expense for the Ziggy Corporation for the week ending August 15, 1989 is $7,500. The entire payroll is subject to FICA taxes of 7.5%, but only 75% is subject to state unemployment taxes of 2.7% and federal unemployment taxes of 0.8%. Federal income taxes of $1,300, state income taxes of $600, and $250 payable to the pension funds were withheld.

Prepare the necessary journal entries to record the payroll and the payroll taxes.

E7. Compensated Absences. The Holmes Company's policy regarding paid vacations is as follows: Each employee is allowed 15 days paid vacation after working for the company one full year. After reviewing payroll records, the controller estimates that 60% of the individuals employed during November will qualify for vacation pay. Total payroll for November is $100,000, and vacation pay is accrued monthly.

Compute the amount of estimated vacation pay liability for November and make the entry to record the liability.

E8. Accounting for Warranties. The Ring Corporation manufactures and sells executive telephones. The telephones sell for $100 and are warranted for two years. Any defects during this period will be fixed by the company without charge. During the year, the firm sold 50,000 telephones. Past experience indicates that 10% of the telephones will need some type of repair during the warranty periods. In the past, the firm has incurred expenditures of $7 on each telephone in need of repair. At the beginning of the year, the Estimated Liability for Warranties account had a credit balance of $4,000. Actual expenditures for warranties amounted to $36,000 during the year.

Prepare the journal entries to record the transactions regarding the warranties. What is the balance in the Estimated Liability for Warranties account at the end of the year, and where should it be disclosed on the balance sheet?

E9. Accounting for Income Taxes. The MacKnee Corporation's accounting income before depreciation and taxes for 1988, 1989, and 1990 was $300,000, $350,000, and $370,000, respectively. The depreciation expense pertains to an asset purchased at the beginning of 1987 for $200,000. For financial accounting purposes, the firm uses straight-line depreciation, with a five-year life and no salvage value. The firm took one-half year's depreciation in 1987. For tax purposes, the asset has a five-year class life, and double-declining-balance depreciation is used. At the beginning of the fourth year of the asset's life (1990), a switch to straight-line is made. This is the only difference between accounting income and taxable income.

Prepare the journal entries to record the tax liability and tax expense for 1988 through 1990. Assume a tax rate of 40% in all three years. What is the balance in the Deferred Tax account at the end of 1990, and how should it be disclosed on the balance sheet?

E10. Accounting for Income Taxes. The Barter Corporation reported the following taxable income and pretax accounting income for 1987 through 1989:

	1987	1988	1989
Taxable income	$360,000	$400,000	$580,000
Pretax accounting income	440,000	410,000	480,000

Assume that the tax rate is 40% in all years and that the differences between taxable income and pretax accounting income are due to temporary differences in the recognition of an installment receivable.

Prepare the required journal entries for 1987 through 1989 to record the company's tax expense and tax liability. What is the balance in the Deferred Income Tax account at the end of 1989? Assume that the balance in that account at the beginning of 1987 was zero.

E11. Accounting for Income Taxes and Financial Statement Analysis. You have gathered the following data for the Technical Phone Company:

	Year Ended	
	1990	1989
Deferred taxes (credit balance)	$ 50,000	$ 35,000
Total liabilities	200,000	180,000
Stockholders' equity	100,000	80,000

REQUIRED:
1. Compute the debt-to-equity ratio and the debt-to-total-assets ratio, based on the following assumptions:

   (a) Deferred taxes are considered a liability and have already been included in the total liability figure presented above.

   (b) Deferred taxes are considered part of stockholders' equity.

   (c) Deferred taxes are ignored in the computation of the ratios.

2. Comment on the significance of the above. Assume that the industry averages for the ratios are:

   Debt to equity = 1.5 to 1
   Debt to total assets = .55 to 1

E12. Toys "R" Us Financial Statements. Refer to the Toys "R" Us financial statements in Appendix D. From the data on the financial statements and footnotes, determine the following:

   (a) The amount of income tax expense for year-end 1988 and 1987.

   (b) The amount of income taxes payable to the government based on taxable income for year-end 1988 and 1987.

   (c) Comment on the changes in the Deferred Income Tax account.

The exercises on pages 420 and 421 refer to the time value of money. Their descriptions are intentionally not included, because a major part of understanding time-value-of-money concepts is determining the type of problem you are dealing with.

E13. Determine the future value of $10,000 deposited in a savings and loan association for five years at 12% interest under each of the following compounding assumptions:

(a) Annual compounding.

(b) Semiannual compounding.

(c) Quarterly compounding.

E14. Assume that you invested $10,000 today at 10% interest, compounded annually. Several years later, you had accumulated $25,937. For how many years did your investment compound?

E15. At the end of ten years, you will receive $25,000. If the interest rate is 10%, what is the present value of this amount, assuming that the interest is compounded:

(a) annually?

(b) semiannually?

(c) quarterly?

E16. If you have a $2,000 investment that will accumulate to $3,077.25 at the end of five years, what rate of interest did you earn, compounded annually?

E17. You are approached with the following investment opportunity: If you invest $7,000 today, you will receive a guaranteed payment of $13,000 at the end of six years. If you desire a 15% rate of return for this type of investment, would you make the investment? Why or why not?

E18. Mr. Fumble is considering the following two investment alternatives:

(a) $10,000 in a savings account earning interest at 10%, compounded semiannually for four years.

(b) $10,000 in a thrift account earning 11% simple interest for four years.

Which one should he make?

E19. If $500 is invested at the end of each of the next four years at 8% interest, compounded annually, what will it accumulate to at the end of the seventh year?

E20. At the end of ten years, you are planning to take a cruise around the world on the QE2 that will cost $81,215. You are planning to save for this cruise by making yearly deposits in a savings and loan association. If you can earn 15% interest compounded annually and the payments are made at year-end, how much must the yearly deposits be?

E21. At the end of ten years, you wish to accumulate $226,204 by making $3,000 quarterly deposits in your interest-earning money market account. What interest rate do you have to earn on a quarterly basis? All payments are made at quarter-end.

E22. What is the present value of receiving $10,000 at the end of each of the next 12 years at an interest rate of 8%, compounded annually?

E23. Charlie Kaplan is considering making a $95,076 investment that will provide a guaranteed return of $12,500 at the end of each of the next 15 years. What interest rate, compounded annually, will Charlie earn on this investment?

E24. Lisa West is considering whether to borrow $6,000. Under the proposed terms of the loan, she will have to repay the loan in 36 equal monthly payments, including interest at 2% per month on the unpaid principal. What will the amount of Lisa's monthly payments be?

E25. You are deciding whether to undertake the following investment: You must make an initial payment of $2,500 and then an additional $100 per quarter at the end of each of the next 40 quarters. If the investment earns 10%, compounded quarterly, how much will it be worth at the end of ten years?

E26. The Walbanger Corporation is planning a major plant expansion in eight years. However, it wants to start accumulating the funds today in a special interest-earning account. The firm estimates that it will need $2.5 million to finance the expansion. The company decides to invest 20% of the funds today and the rest on a quarterly basis for the next eight years. If the firm can earn 8%, compounded quarterly, what will be the amount of its quarterly deposits into the special fund? All payments are made at quarter-end.

E27. You have been offered the following investment opportunity: You will receive $100,000 at the end of 15 years. In addition, you will receive semiannual payments of 4% of the $100,000 until the $100,000 is paid. If you want to earn 10%, compounded semiannually, what is the maximum that you would pay for this investment?

E28. A local used car dealer is advertising interest-free 48-month loans. However, after shopping around for comparable cars, you notice that his prices are higher than those of other dealers. Why do you think this is so?

E29. In order to enjoy her retirement, Becky Webb is contemplating the purchase of a small travel agency. She would like you to help her determine the amount she should pay, based solely on the cash flows that will be generated by the agency. Becky expects to operate the agency for ten years and sell it at the end of that time for $200,000. During the ten years she expects to run the agency, she estimates that it will generate the following net cash inflows:

Years 1–7: $50,000 per year
Years 8–10: $40,000 per year

If all the yearly cash flows are received at the end of each year and Becky wants to earn a 10% rate of return, compounded annually, what is the maximum she should pay for the agency?

PROBLEMS

P11-1 Accounting for Notes Payable. The Deferral Corporation's fiscal year ends on June 30. During the year ended June 30, 1989 and the next two months of the next fiscal year, the firm entered into the following transactions regarding various notes payable. All adjusting entries are made once a year on June 30. Assume a 360-day year.

- December 31, 1988: Signed an agreement with Filmore National Bank establishing a $500,000 line of credit at 12% interest. Immediately borrowed $200,000.

- March 1, 1989: Signed a six-month, 15% term loan. The face value of the note was $107,500, but the firm received net proceeds of only $100,000 because the note was discounted.

- April 1, 1989: Repaid $100,000 of the line of credit, plus all accrued interest to date.

- April 30, 1989: The firm was granted a 90-day extension on an open trade account payable in exchange for signing an $8,000 note at 10%. The interest element was stated separately.

- May 15, 1989: Was notified by the bank that its $20,000, 10%, one-year loan was discounted by the payee. The note that is due on June 30, 1989 should now be paid to Adams-Madison National Bank.

- June 1, 1989: Borrowed an additional $300,000 under the terms of the revolving line of credit.

- June 30, 1989: Made the required payment to the Adams-Madison National Bank. No interest has been accrued on the note.

- June 30, 1989: Made all adjusting entries.

- July 31, 1989: Repaid the April 30 loan.

- August 31, 1989: Repaid the March 1 loan.

REQUIRED: Make all the journal entries to reflect the above transactions. Assume that the firm does not make reversing entries.

P11-2 Accounting for Notes Payable. The Smith Company's fiscal year ends on March 31. During the year ended March 31, 1990, the firm entered into the following transactions relating to notes payable. Adjusting entries are made once a year on March 31. Assume a 360-day year.

- April 15, 1989: Signed an agreement with Hollywood National Bank establishing a $100,000 line of credit at 10% interest. Immediately borrowed $10,000.

- May 10, 1989: Signed a nine-month, 12%, $109,000 term loan. The note was discounted and the firm received $100,000.

- June 15, 1989: Repaid $5,000 of the line of credit plus all interest accrued to date.

- July 1, 1989: The firm was granted a one-year extension on an open trade account payable in exchange for signing a $60,000, one-year note at 12%.

- August 1, 1989: The firm was notified by Santa Ana National Bank that its $50,000, 12%, one-year-term loan payable was discounted by Grannett Company, the payee. The note (which is due on November 1, 1989) should now be paid to Santa Ana.

- September 15, 1989: Borrowed an additional $50,000 under the terms of its revolving line of credit.

- November 1, 1989: Made the required payment on the note now owed to Santa Ana National Bank. Interest has been accrued to March 31, 1989.

- February 10, 1990: Paid the May 10, 1989 loan.

- March 1, 1990: Borrowed $100,000 on a 10% loan from First Savings and Loan. The note is due and payable on September 1, 1990.

- March 31, 1990. Made all adjusting entries.

REQUIRED: Make all the journal entries to reflect the above transactions. Assume that the firm does not make reversing entries.

P11-3   Analysis of Notes Payable and Receivable. The accountant for the Papaya Company prepared the partial balance sheet at October 31, 1990. However, the accountant failed to make the required monthly adjusting entries. Company policies require that these entries be made monthly.

During your analysis, you have obtained the following additional information:

1. The $200,000 accounts payable general ledger balance includes an account with a debit balance of $3,975, which resulted when the Papaya Company returned some defective goods. Papaya has asked the vendor to refund its money.

2. The interest payable relates to a $60,000 note that was signed six months ago.

3. When the firm records its sales, applicable sales taxes are included in the sales account. At the end of each month, an adjusting entry is made to reverse out the amount of the sales taxes and to set up a payable account. During October, sales were $212,000 including sales taxes of 6%.

REQUIRED: **(a)** Make the necessary adjusting entries at October 31, 1990.

(b) Prepare a revised partial balance sheet as of October 31, 1990.

PAPAYA COMPANY
Partial Balance Sheet
October 31, 1990

Current assets		
Accounts receivable	$243,875	
Less allowance for uncollectible accounts	1,250	
		$242,625
Note receivable		32,700
Current liabilities		
Accounts payable		$200,000
Interest payable		2,500
Notes payable		60,000

P11-4   Accounting for Current Liabilities. Tracy's Tennis Stores entered into the following transactions during the current calendar year:

1. Inventory purchases of $50,000 were made on account. (Assume periodic system.)

2. On April 1, a light truck was purchased for $10,000. A 25% down payment was made and a 10% note was signed for the balance. Principal and interest are due in one year.

3. The inventory purchased in Item 1 was paid in full.

4. On July 31, the firm signed a $78,400 note at a local bank. It received proceeds of $70,000 at that time. The note is due in one year.

5. Sales for the year amounted to $180,000. All sales are for cash. State sales taxes are 6%.

6. During the holiday season, the firm issues gift certificates. Gift certificates totaling $5,000 were sold for cash. By the end of the calendar year, only 30% of the certificates had been redeemed. Sales of certificates are credited to the Sales Revenue account.

7. Wages of $30,000 were paid during the year. Federal and state income taxes withheld amounted to $4,400, and union dues of $200 were also withheld. The FICA rate is 7% for both the employee and employer, and all wages but $5,000 are subject to these taxes. State unemployment taxes of 2.7% are levied on $10,000 of wages.

8. Sales, union dues, and payroll taxes were paid in full prior to year-end.

REQUIRED: **(a)** Make the necessary journal entries to record these events.

(b) Make the necessary adjusting entries, other than depreciation.

P11-5 **Accounting for Current Liabilities.** Super O Discount Stores entered into the following transactions during the current fiscal year:

(1) On March 1, the store purchased a delivery truck for $20,000. A 20% down payment was made, and the firm signed a 12%, one-year note for the balance. Both principal and interest are due at the maturity date.

(2) The firm purchased inventory for $60,000 on account (use the periodic method).

(3) The store purchased some additional office equipment for $10,000, subject to credit terms of 2/10, n/30. (Use the gross method of recording discount.)

(4) $1,000 of the inventory purchased in (2) above arrived damaged and was returned to the manufacturer. Super O's account was credited.

(5) The office equipment purchased in (3) above was paid for within the discount period.

(6) Sales for the year amounted to $130,000, of which 40% were on account and the remainder were for cash. State and local sales taxes amounted to 5%.

(7) The department store rents part of its space to Tasty Croissants. The agreement calls for Tasty to pay a year's rent in advance. Tasty began business on October 1 and made the $4,800 required payment to Super O on that date.

(8) Super O's payroll for the year amounted to $30,000, all of which was paid in cash. Applicable payroll taxes and related items were as follows: federal and state income taxes withheld, $2,400 and $800, respectively; FICA taxes, 7.5% for both employee and employer on entire payroll; state unemployment taxes of 2.7% on $20,000 of the payroll; and federal unemployment taxes of 0.8% on $20,000 of the payroll.

(9) Sales and payroll taxes were fully paid before year-end.

REQUIRED: **(a)** Make the necessary journal entries to record the above transactions.

(b) Make any necessary adjusting entries at February 28 other than depreciation.

P11-6 **Product Warranty.** The Wolfer Company manufactures and sells high-quality stereo equipment. It has a special line of speakers that sell for $1,000 apiece. The parts on the speaker are guaranteed for three years. During the first year, all labor for repairs is performed free of charge. During the next two years of the guarantee, there is a set labor charge of $40 per repair. During 1989, the firm sold 500 of these speakers. Past experience indicates that 20% of these units will need repair within the guarantee period and that average replacement parts will cost $80 and labor costs will be $50. During the year, the firm incurred $5,000 in labor costs and $6,000 in replacement costs. Also during the year, the firm collected $2,800 in revenue from labor performed on guarantee work. At the end of 1989, before any adjustments were made, the account Estimated Liability for Guarantee Work had a credit balance of $500.

REQUIRED: **(a)** Would it be possible for the account Estimated Liability for Guarantee Work to have a debit balance prior to the adjusting entry at the end of the year? If so, how would this occur? What was the actual balance in this account at the beginning of 1989?

(b) Prepare the summary journal entries to record the above events related to guarantees. Assume that all sales are made on credit.

(c) Determine the balance in the Estimated Liability for Guarantee Work account at the end of 1989 after all adjusting entries have been made.

P11-7 Payroll Taxes and Compensated Absences. The Bubble Laundry Company had four employees on its payroll for the fourth quarter of 1990. The unemployment compensation at the state level is 2.7%; the federal unemployment rate is 0.8%. The maximum unemployment wage is $7,000 for both federal and state unemployment taxes. Current FICA taxes are 7.5% of the first $45,000 of the current year's wages. Each employee is entitled to two weeks' compensated vacation pay yearly. The pay is based on the average salary for the year assuming a 50-week year. Each quarter, the firm accrues 25% of that amount as an estimated liability.

During your review of Bubble Laundry's records, you have obtained the following information:

Name	Earnings to 9/30/90	Earnings 4th Quarter 1990
J. Korman	$ 35,920	$11,490
O. Jones	24,280	6,890
T. Glasson	16,230	2,780
R. Sato	40,500	15,000
Totals	$116,930	$36,160

REQUIRED: **(a)** For each employee, determine the correct amount of payroll taxes for the fourth quarter.

(b) Assume that the federal income tax withheld and state income tax withheld equaled $3,800 and $1,300, respectively, for the quarter. Make the journal entries to record the payroll and related expenses for the fourth quarter.

(c) Determine the amount of vacation pay each employee is entitled to. Make the journal entry to record the estimated liability for the fourth quarter.

P11-8 Accounting for Income Taxes. Below are the condensed income statements for the Morango Corporation for the last six years:

	1986	1987	1988	1989	1990	1991
Revenues	$300,000	$320,000	$360,000	$450,000	$475,000	$490,000
Expenses	210,000	240,000	290,000	370,000	375,000	385,000
Pretax accounting income	$ 90,000	$ 80,000	$ 70,000	$ 80,000	$100,000	$ 95,000

At the beginning of 1986, the firm purchased a new piece of equipment that cost $100,000. For financial accounting purposes, the firm uses straight-line depreciation based on a four-year life with no salvage value. A half-year's depreciation was taken in the first year. Depreciation is included in expenses in the condensed income statements. For tax purposes, the firm uses double-declining-balance depreciation, and the asset falls into the five-year class life. The tax rate is a flat 40%. At the beginning of the fourth year of the asset's life, the switch is made to straight-line for tax purposes.

REQUIRED: **(a)** For each year, determine the amount of taxable income and the actual tax liability.

(b) For each year and the total over six years, determine net income, assuming that interperiod income tax allocation is *not* used.

(c) For each year and the total over six years, determine net income, assuming that interperiod income tax allocation *is* used. Compare your results with those obtained in item (b). Comment on the differences.

(d) Prepare the journal entries to record the income taxes payable and income tax expense, assuming that interperiod income tax allocation is used. What is the balance in the Deferred Income Tax account at the end of 1991? Comment on the figure you determined.

P11-9 Accounting for Income Taxes. You have obtained the following tax information from the records of the Marshall Co.:

	1984	1985	1986	1987	1988	1989
Taxable income	$110,000	$140,000	$125,000	$150,000	$160,000	$175,000

At the beginning of 1984, the firm purchased a new piece of equipment for $120,000. For tax purposes, the firm uses double-declining-balance depreciation, and the asset falls into the five-year class life. However, for financial statement purposes, the firm uses straight-line depreciation based on a five-year life with no salvage value. A half-year's depreciation was taken in 1984. The tax rate is a flat 40%. At the beginning of the fourth year of the asset's life, the switch is made to straight-line for tax purposes.

REQUIRED: (a) For each year, determine the amount of pretax accounting income and income tax expense.

(b) For each year and the total over six years, determine net income assuming that interperiod income tax allocation is used.

(c) Prepare the journal entries to record the income taxes payable and income tax expense, assuming that interperiod income tax allocation is used. What is the balance in the Deferred Tax account at the end of 1989? Comment on the figure that you determined.

P11-10 Time-value-of-money Concepts. Paul Kupcheck's dog died recently. Paul, who loved his dog very much, had the foresight to take out an insurance policy on the dog's life. After the dog died, the insurance company gave Paul the following options:

(a) taking $100,000 immediately.

(b) taking $30,000 immediately and then receiving annual payments of $11,067, to be made at the end of each of the next ten years.

(c) taking $20,000 immediately and then receiving quarterly payments of $5,196, to be made at the end of each quarter for the next five years.

(d) taking $30,000 immediately, $30,000 at the end of Year 3, $30,000 at the end of Year 6, and another $30,000 at the end of Year 9.

REQUIRED: Assuming an interest rate of 10% per annum, which option should Paul take, and why?

P11-11 Time-value-of-money Concepts. Bill Smith, an instructor of accounting, opens a tax-deferred retirement account with the university. He plans to deposit $5,000 a year in that account, which will pay interest of 10%, compounded annually. He will make his first deposit at the end of the year and make 19 additional deposits at the end of each of the following 19 years. (A total of 20 deposits will be made.)

REQUIRED: (a) How much cash will Bill Smith have accumulated in the account when he retires at the end of 20 years?

(b) How much of the amount calculated above will be interest? Principal?

(c) Bill plans to withdraw the funds in ten equal installments immediately after the end of the 20th year or at the beginning of the 21st year. Assuming an interest rate of 10%, how much will he be able to withdraw each year?

■ USING THE COMPUTER

P11-12 The law firm of Simmer, Smith, and Sental employs six administrative employees in addition to its professional staff. The administrative staff is paid on an hourly basis and receives time-and-one-half for overtime. Employees are paid every Friday for the week's work. All employees are subject to FICA taxes of 7.5% of their first $45,000 of wages. The firm is subject to FICA taxes of 7% on the same basis. State unemployment taxes are 2.7%, and federal unemployment taxes are 0.8% on the first $7,000 of each employee's wages. In addition, the firm withholds 5% of each employees's wages for health insurance and $5 for parking.

The data relating to the December 22, 1990, payroll is as follows:

Name	Hours Worked Regular	Overtime	Hourly Pay Rate	Earnings to Date prior to Current Period	Federal and State Income Tax Withheld
T. Johnson	40	5	$ 8.50	$24,000	$180
J. Collins	40	7	8.00	23,500	140
J. C. Ray	40	3	7.25	21,000	100
E. Weiss	40	0	20.00	46,000	278
M. Tofukagi	35	0	18.00	45,000	190
R. Williams	40	2	15.00	37,000	210

REQUIRED: Using an electronic spreadsheet, prepare a payroll register similar to the following:

Payroll Register
Payroll Period: December 22–29, 1990

Employee	Earnings Regular	Overtime	Total	Deductions FICA—7.5%	Withholdings	Total	Amount Paid

UNDERSTANDING FINANCIAL STATEMENTS

P11-13   The following information was taken from the 1987 annual report of USAir:

(5) Income Taxes

The Company files a consolidated Federal income tax return with its wholly-owned domestic subsidiaries.

The components of the provisions for income taxes are as follows:

	1987	1986	1985
			(in thousands)
Current provision			
Federal	$ 31,410	$ 737	$(11,533)
State and other	7,988	1,202	1,470
Total current provision	39,398	1,939	(10,063)
Deferred provision			
Federal	57,842	64,343	63,840
State	3,840	5,268	5,123
Total deferred provision	61,682	69,611	68,963
Provision for income taxes	$101,080	$71,550	$58,900

The credit for the current portion of the 1985 Federal provision is due to the carryback of investment tax credits which resulted in a refund of taxes paid in a prior year.

Investment tax credits on qualifying progress payments on aircraft are recognized for financial reporting purposes to the extent the Company, or one of its subsidiaries, plans to purchase rather than lease aircraft or the Company expects to retain investment tax credits on leased aircraft.

Deferred income taxes result from differences in the recognition of revenue and expenses and investment tax credits for tax and financial reporting purposes. The major items resulting in these differences and the related tax effects are as follows:

	1987	1986	1985
			(in thousands)
Equipment depreciation and amortization	$77,634	$64,380	$69,003
Gain on sale and leaseback transactions	(33,436)	—	—
Employee benefit plans	2,305	5,307	(8,025)
Tax benefits purchased	6,314	6,461	6,633
Investment tax credits	17,170	(5,719)	1,550
Other	(8,305)	(818)	(198)
Total deferred provision	$61,682	$69,611	$68,963

A reconciliation of taxes computed at the statutory Federal tax rate on earnings before income taxes and equity in net income of Piedmont to the provisions for income taxes is as follows:

	1987	1986	1985
			(in thousands)
Tax computed at statutory rate	$102,546	$78,155	$80,951
Investment tax credits	(15,667)	(9,726)	(26,142)
State income taxes, net of Federal tax benefit	7,097	3,494	3,560
Other	7,104	(373)	531
Provision for income taxes	$101,080	$71,550	$58,900
Effective tax rate	39.4%	42.1%	33.5%

At December 31, 1987, the Company had investment tax credits available to reduce future Federal income taxes payable of approximately $18 million, substantially all of which expire in 2002. All available investment tax credits have been utilized for financial reporting purposes.

Federal income tax returns for 1979 through 1985 are currently being reviewed by the Internal Revenue Service. Various adjustments, mainly dealing with the timing of tax deductions, are under consideration. No adjustments have been proposed for which adequate provision has not been made.

In late December 1987 the Financial Accounting Standards Board issued Statement of Financial Accounting Standards No. 96, "Accounting for Income Taxes." Application of Statement No. 96, which must be adopted by January 1, 1989, will require the Company to change from the deferred method to a liability method in accounting for income taxes. While the Company does not presently expect Statement No. 96 to have a significant impact on the current provision for income taxes, recording the cumulative effect on prior years of the change in accounting will have a significant effect on deferred income taxes and net income after the cumulative effect of the change. For USAir it is presently estimated the cumulative effect of the adoption of Statement No. 96 would be a reduction in deferred taxes and increase in net income of approximately $70 to $80 million.

REQUIRED:
(a) What is the amount of the total tax expense for 1987?
(b) How much did the deferred tax liability increase during 1987?
(c) What is the main reason for the substantial amount of deferred taxes over the last three years?
(d) What effect does the company estimate the adoption of Statement No. 96 will have?

■ FINANCIAL DECISION CASE

P11-14   The Packwood Corporation is an emerging company that began business in 1985. In the first couple of years of the company's existence, the firm invested about $1 million a year in plant and equipment. However, recently the firm has increased this investment and expects to continue to do so. In fact, the president estimates that in the next 10 to 15 years, investment in new plant and equipment will outstrip retirements of plant and equipment by three to one.

The president has given you the following accounting and tax data since the company's inception:

	1985	1986	1987	1988
Tax expense	$200,000	$240,000	$280,000	$310,000
Tax liability	110,000	100,000	130,000	172,000

The president explains that the major difference between the tax expense and the tax liability comes from using accelerated depreciation for tax purposes. He estimates that by the end of the 1980s, the balance in the Deferred Tax Liability account will grow to over $3 million. After that time, he expects it to decrease slowly as the rapid investment in new plant and equipment decreases.

In preparing the 1988 financial statements, the president objects to recording the deferred taxes of $138,000. He feels that the tax expense should be recorded at the amount of the tax liability. After all, he argues, this is the amount that is due and payable. He questions whether the deferred taxes will ever be payable at their full amount. Furthermore, he contends that if the deferred taxes are recorded, they should be recorded at their present value. His analysis indicates that the $518,000 balance in the Deferred Tax Liability account at the end of 1988 will not be payable until 1993 at the earliest. He has prepared the following schedule indicating his best guess as to when these deferred taxes might be payable:

	End of				
	1993	1994	1995	1996	**Total**
Amount payable	$100,000	$120,000	$98,000	$200,000	$518,000

Although he is not an expert on time-value-of-money concepts, his intuition tells him that the value of that liability at December 31, 1988 was substantially less than $518,000, based on the company's 12% cost of capital.

REQUIRED: **(a)**   Reproduce the journal entries that were made from 1985 to 1988 to record the income tax expense and income tax payable for each year.

(b)   Assuming that the president is correct and that $138,000 of 1988 deferred taxes will be paid at the end of 1996, make the appropriate journal entry to record taxes for the year.

(c)   Write a memo to the president responding to his comments. Calculate for him the present value of the deferred taxes as of the end of 1988, given the company's cost of capital. Be sure to explain to him the accounting profession's point of view, as well as your own.

ACCOUNTING FOR LONG-TERM LIABILITIES AND INVESTMENTS IN BONDS

LEARNING OBJECTIVES

After studying this chapter, you should be able to:

1. Explain the nature and features of bonds payable.
2. Account for bonds issued at par value.
3. Account for bonds issued at either a discount or a premium.
4. Amortize a discount or premium on both the straight-line and the effective-interest methods.
5. Discuss the other issues related to bonds payable, including bonds issued between interest dates, year-end accruals, and bond issue costs.
6. Account for the retirement of bonds.
7. Account for bonds purchased by an investor.
8. Account for other forms of long-term debt, including notes payable, mortgages, and leases.

Long-term liabilities are the obligations of an enterprise that are not due within the next 12 months or the operating cycle (if longer than a year). Included in the long-term liability section of a typical balance sheet are accounts such as Bonds Payable, Mortgages Payable, Long-term Notes Payable, and Leases. Because bonds are a common form of long-term debt, they will be used to explain the key accounting procedures for long-term liabilities. Because of their similarities with long-term liabilities, investments in bonds are also covered in this chapter.

BONDS

A **bond** is a written agreement between a borrower and a lender in which the borrower agrees to repay a stated sum on a future date and to make periodic interest payments at specified dates. Bonds can be issued by local, state, or federal governments, but this section will concentrate on bonds issued by corporations to public investors.

FEATURES OF BONDS

If you purchase a bond, you will receive a bond certificate. This certificate spells out the terms of agreement between the issuer and the investor. These terms include the denomination or principle of the bond, maturity date, the stated rate of interest, the interest payment terms, and any other agreements made between the borrower and lender.

Denomination of the Bond

Individual bonds usually have a **denomination** of $1,000, although in recent years $5,000 and $10,000 bonds have become common. In this chapter and the homework assignments, it will be assumed that all bonds are in $1,000 denominations unless stated otherwise. The denomination, or principal, of a bond is often referred to as *face value*, *maturity value*, or *par value*; it is always on this amount that the required interest payment is calculated.

A total bond issue usually contains several hundreds or thousands of individual bonds. For example, a $10 million bond issue might be made up of 10,000 individual $1,000 bonds. Investors can purchase as many of these individual bonds as they wish. After bonds are issued by a large publicly held company, they trade on the New York Bond Exchange. This enables present and potential investors to sell and purchase bonds after their initial issue, just as they do with shares of stock.

Maturity Date

The date that the principal of the bond is to be repaid is called the *maturity date*. Bonds usually mature in from 5 years to more than 30 years from their date of issue. Bonds whose entire principal is due in one payment are called **term bonds**, and bonds that are payable on various dates are called **serial bonds**.

Stated Interest Rate and Interest Payment Dates

Most bonds have a **stated interest rate,** which is part of the bond agreement. This rate is often referred to as the **nominal interest rate** and is specified on the bond at the time it is issued. This rate does not change over the life of the bond. The stated rate of interest is fixed by the firm's management in conjunction with its financial advisers. They attempt to set the rate as close as they can to the **market interest rate** that exists at the time the bond is issued. The market rate is the interest rate that the money market establishes through hundreds of individual transactions; it depends on such factors as prevailing interest rates in the economy and the perceived risk of the company.

Most bonds pay interest semiannually, or every six months. However, the stated interest rate is an annual rate based on the face value of the bond. For example, a $1,000, 12% bond that pays interest on January 2 and July 1 will pay interest of $60 ($1,000 \times .12 \times \frac{6}{12}$) on each of these dates until it matures. In effect, the bond in this example pays 6% interest every six months.

Other Agreements

Bondholders are unable to vote for corporate management or otherwise participate in corporate affairs in the way that shareholders do. Therefore bondholders often insist on written convenants as part of the bond agreement. These agreements are often referred to as **bond indentures**. They can take a variety of forms, but they usually include restrictions as to dividends, working capital, and the issuance of additional long-term debt. The purpose of these agreements is to ensure that the borrower will maintain a strong enough financial position to meet the interest and principal payments.

■ TYPES OF BONDS

There are several different types of bonds, including term, serial, coupon, registered, secured, unsecured, convertible, and callable bonds.

Term versus Serial Bonds

Term bonds are bonds whose entire principal amount is due at a single date. Most corporate bonds are term bonds. In contrast, serial bonds have principal payments that are required at specific intervals. Serial bonds are often issued by state or local municipalities. To illustrate, assume that the city of San Francisco issues $5 million of serial bonds whose terms require that $500,000 of the bonds are to be repaid every five years beginning five years after the date of issue. Thus, for the first five years, $5 million of bonds will be outstanding; for the second five years, $4.5 million will be outstanding, and so forth. From both the investors' and the issuer's point of view, serial bonds help ensure that the issuer will be able to repay the entire principal.

Coupon versus Registered Bonds

Some bonds are bearer or **coupon bonds**. This means that the bonds are not registered in the name of individual holders but are negotiable by whoever holds them. In order to receive their interest payments, the current holders simply clip off a coupon and redeem it at an authorized bank. Because coupon bonds do not offer much safety to the holder, most currently issued bonds are registered. This means that the bonds are registered in the name of the holder and that all interest payments are made by the issuing company directly to the current bondholder.

Secured versus Unsecured Bonds

Unsecured bonds, called *debentures*, are issued without any security to back them. Investors purchase them based on the creditworthiness of the company. Some bonds are secured by the borrower's collateral or specified assets. These secured bonds are often referred to as *mortgage bonds*.

Convertible Bonds

Convertible bonds are convertible at some future specified date into the firm's common stock; thus they enable the bondholder eventually to obtain an equity interest in the firm. This conversion feature allows the firm to issue the bond at a lower interest rate. Convertible bonds are usually *callable*, which means that the borrower, or issuer, is able to call the bonds prior to their maturity. Thus the bondholder is forced either to convert the bonds or to have them called prior to their maturity.

■ BOND PRICES

Traditionally, bond prices are quoted in terms of 100. A price of 100 means that the bond is quoted at 100% of its face value, or $1,000. This is often referred to as the bond's *selling at par*. If a bond is quoted at 104, this means that its price is $1,040, or $1,000 × 104%. Any time the bond's price is above 100, the bond is selling *at a premium*. Conversely, if the bond is quoted at $97\frac{1}{2}$%, its price is $975, or $1,000 × 97.5%. Any time the bond's price is below 100, the bond is selling *at a discount*.

Bond Quotations on the Bond Exchange

Exhibit 12-1 presents a portion of the bond page from the *Wall Street Journal*. The list for AT&T, underlined in the exhibit, is reproduced below.

Bond		Cur Yld	Vol	Close	Net Chg
AT&T	$7\frac{1}{8}$03	8.8	26	$80\frac{7}{8}$	$-1\frac{3}{8}$

As can be seen from the exhibit, there are several issues of AT&T bonds. The issue underlined has a stated interest rate of $7\frac{1}{8}$ and is due in 2003. Its current yield is 8.8%, which means that if the bonds were purchased at their closing price of $80\frac{7}{8}$, the investor would earn an 8.8% rate of return to maturity. To illustrate, the bond pays interest of 7.125% on the stated value of $1,000, or $71.25 per bond. If the bond sells for $80.875, or $808.75, the return is 8.8% ($71.25 ÷ $808.75). During the day, 26 bonds were traded, and the closing price was $80\frac{7}{8}$. The closing price represented a decrease of $1\frac{3}{8}$ from the previous day's closing price.

How Bond Prices Are Determined

Bond prices at the issue date and during subsequent trading are the result of the interaction among the stated interest rate, the prevailing market rate, and the length of time to maturity. When a bond is issued, the company will receive the full face amount of the bond only if the stated rate of interest equals the market rate at the time of issue. That is, when $100,000, 12%, ten-year bonds are issued, the company will receive $100,000 only if the prevailing market rate is 12% for bonds of that duration and perceived risk. If the prevailing market rate is above 12%—say, 14%—the bond will be issued at a discount, and the firm will receive less than $100,000. Conversely, if the market rate of interest for such bonds is below 12%—say, 10%—the bonds will be issued at a premium, and the firm will receive more than $100,000 at the time of issue. The amount of the discount or the premium is the difference between the face value of the bond and the amount for which the bond was actually issued. You should keep in mind that the issuing company is obligated to repay the full face amount of the bond, regardless of whether the bond is issued at a discount or at a premium. Furthermore, all interest payments are based on this face value.

To demonstrate further this relationship between interest rates and bond prices, assume that you are considering investing in a $1,000, five-year, 10% bond that pays 6% interest semiannually. Therefore you will receive $60 every six months ($1,000 × 6%). Because this stated interest rate will not change, you will receive this $60 every six months for five years, regardless of what happens to future interest rates.

EXHIBIT 12–1 [1]

Corporation Bonds Volume, $38,300,000				
Bonds	**Cur Yld**	**Vol**	**Close**	**Net Chg**
AVX $8\frac{1}{4}$12	cv	5	106	$+ 1\frac{1}{2}$
AbbtL 9.2s99	9.3	15	99	$- \frac{3}{8}$
AbbtL 11s93	10.8	15	102	$- \frac{3}{8}$
Advst 9s08	cv	45	89	$+ 1\frac{7}{8}$
AetnLf $8\frac{1}{8}$07	9.3	40	$87\frac{1}{4}$	$+ \frac{1}{4}$
AlaP $8\frac{7}{8}$s03	9.6	5	92	$- \frac{1}{8}$
AlaP $9\frac{3}{4}$s04	9.8	20	99	...
AlaP $10\frac{7}{8}$05	10.6	7	$102\frac{3}{8}$	$+ \frac{3}{8}$
AlaP $10\frac{1}{2}$05	10.4	20	$101\frac{1}{4}$	$- \frac{1}{8}$
AlaP $9\frac{1}{4}$07	9.7	2	$95\frac{3}{4}$	$+ \frac{1}{4}$
AlaP $9\frac{1}{2}$08	9.9	45	$95\frac{3}{4}$	$- \frac{3}{4}$
AlaP $9\frac{5}{8}$08	9.9	50	$96\frac{3}{4}$	$- \frac{5}{8}$
AlaP $12\frac{5}{8}$10	12.0	3	$105\frac{1}{8}$	$+ \frac{1}{8}$
AlskH $12\frac{7}{8}$93	12.4	4	104	...
viAlgl $10\frac{3}{4}$99f	...	2	$90\frac{1}{4}$	...
viAlgl 10.4s02f	...	53	$64\frac{1}{4}$	$- \frac{3}{4}$
viAlgl 9s89f	...	15	$89\frac{7}{8}$	$- 1$
AlldC zr92	...	13	$70\frac{7}{8}$	...
AlldC zr98	...	2	$41\frac{1}{2}$	$- \frac{5}{8}$
AlldC zr2000	...	33	$33\frac{3}{4}$	
AlldC zr01	...	30	$31\frac{1}{8}$	$+ \frac{7}{8}$
AlldC zr09	...	155	$14\frac{1}{2}$	$+ \frac{1}{4}$
AMAX $14\frac{1}{4}$90	13.6	32	$104\frac{1}{2}$	$- \frac{1}{2}$
AAirl $4\frac{1}{4}$92	5.1	50	$83\frac{1}{2}$	$- \frac{1}{2}$
AAir dc$6\frac{1}{4}$96	7.0	20	89	$- 1$
ACyan $8\frac{3}{8}$06	9.5	10	$88\frac{1}{8}$	$- 1\frac{1}{8}$
AExC $14\frac{3}{4}$92	14.4	20	$102\frac{1}{4}$	$+ \frac{1}{8}$
AHoist $5\frac{1}{2}$93	cv	3	$88\frac{1}{2}$	$- 5\frac{1}{2}$
AmMed $9\frac{1}{2}$01	cv	7	98	$- \frac{1}{8}$
AmMed $8\frac{1}{4}$08	cv	25	75	...
ATT $3\frac{7}{8}$s90	4.1	25	$94\frac{1}{4}$	$- \frac{1}{8}$
ATT $3\frac{7}{8}$90r	4.1	8	94	...
ATT $5\frac{5}{8}$95	6.9	5	$81\frac{7}{8}$	$+ \frac{1}{8}$
ATT 6s00	7.9	106	$75\frac{3}{4}$	$- \frac{1}{4}$
ATT $5\frac{1}{8}$01	7.3	63	$69\frac{3}{4}$	$+ \frac{1}{4}$
ATT $8\frac{3}{4}$00	9.4	310	93	$- 1\frac{1}{4}$
ATT 7s01	8.5	43	82	$- \frac{3}{8}$
ATT $7\frac{1}{8}$03	8.8	26	$80\frac{7}{8}$	$- 1\frac{3}{8}$
ATT 8.80s05	9.4	49	$93\frac{3}{4}$	$- \frac{1}{8}$
ATT $8\frac{5}{8}$s07	9.5	62	$91\frac{1}{4}$	$- \frac{5}{8}$
ATT $8\frac{5}{8}$26	9.7	30	$89\frac{1}{8}$	$- \frac{7}{8}$
Ames 10s95	10.2	6	$98\frac{1}{2}$	$- \frac{1}{2}$
Amoco 6s91	6.5	10	$92\frac{3}{4}$	$- \frac{1}{8}$
Amoco 9.2s04	9.4	50	$97\frac{1}{2}$	...
Amoco $8\frac{3}{8}$05	9.3	126	$90\frac{3}{8}$	$- \frac{3}{4}$
Amoco $7\frac{7}{8}$07	9.1	79	$86\frac{1}{8}$	$- 1\frac{7}{8}$
Amoco $8\frac{5}{8}$16	9.5	25	$90\frac{5}{8}$	$- 1$
AmocoCda $7\frac{3}{8}$13	7.4	229	99	$- \frac{1}{2}$
Ancp $13\frac{7}{8}$02f	cv	11	101	$+ \frac{1}{2}$
Andarko $5\frac{3}{4}$12	cv	12	96	$- 2$
Apch $7\frac{1}{2}$12	cv	30	$82\frac{1}{4}$	...
ArizP $10\frac{5}{8}$00	10.6	34	$100\frac{1}{2}$	$- \frac{5}{8}$

[1] Source: *Wall Street Journal,* February 10, 1989, p. C-15. Reprinted by permission of the *Wall Street Journal.* © Dow Jones & Company, Inc., 1989. All Rights Reserved Worldwide.

However, assume that you have an alternative $1,000, five-year investment that represents the same risk as the bond investment. The alternative investment pays 14%, or 7% every six months. Clearly, the second alternative is more valuable, because it pays a semiannual interest of $70, versus $60 for the first investment. If you wanted to purchase the first investment, one way to equalize the difference between the two investments would be to pay less than $1,000 for the first investment. By paying less than $1,000 and still receiving $60 every six months, your rate of return would increase. In effect, as a rational economic person, you would pay for the first investment only an amount that would provide a return of 14%. Such an amount would be less than $1,000.

This is exactly what happens with bonds. Bonds having a stated rate less than the prevailing market rate for investments of similar risk will attract investors only if they are issued at a discount. In effect, the price of the bonds will be bid down until they yield a rate of return equal to the prevailing market rate of return for investments of similar risk. Conversely, if the stated rate is higher than the market rate, the demand for these bonds will cause their price to be bid up, and they will be issued at a premium. The actual rate at which the bond is issued is referred to as the **yield rate** or **effective rate**.

To illustrate this concept, an example will show how the price of a bond can actually be computed. Assume that $100,000, 12%, five-year bonds are issued to yield 14%. Given this data—the prevailing market interest rate, the stated or coupon interest rate, and the maturity date—bond prices can be calculated using present-value techniques. When bonds are issued, the borrower agrees to make two different types of payments: an annuity made up of the future cash interest payments and a single future amount constituting the bond's maturity value. Rational investors would not pay any more than the present value of these two future cash flows, discounted at the market rate of interest or desired yield. The issue price of $92,976 is calculated in Exhibit 12-2. As this exhibit indicates, the issue price is composed of the present value of the maturity payment of $100,000 discounted at 7% for ten periods, and the present value of semiannual cash interest payments of $6,000 ($100,000 × .06) also discounted at 7%. Ten periods are used because the five-year bonds pay interest semiannually. The discount rate is the semiannual yield, or an effective rate of 7%. You should remember that the $6,000 annuity, which is the cash interest payment, is calculated on the actual semiannual coupon rate of 6%.

EXHIBIT 12–2 Determination of Bond Price ($100,000, five-year, 12% bonds issued to yield 14%)	
Present value of $100,000 to be received at end of ten periods at 7% semiannually	
$100,000 × .50835	$ 50,835
Present value at 7% of semiannual interest payments of $6,000 ($100,000 × .06) to be received at the end of each of the next ten interest dates	
$6,000 × 7.02358	42,141
Total issue price	$ 92,976
Amount of discount	
Face value of bonds	$100,000
Total issue price	92,976
Amount of discount	$ 7,024

If the bonds were issued at par (that is, to yield 12%), the issue price would be $100,000, as calculated in Exhibit 12-3. Borrowers and investors need not make these calculations. Various bond tables are available that determine the correct prices at

EXHIBIT 12–3

Determination
of Bond Price
($100,000, five-year, 12%
bonds issued to yield 12%)

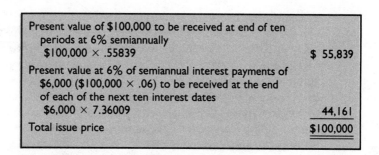

Present value of $100,000 to be received at end of ten periods at 6% semiannually $100,000 × .55839	$ 55,839
Present value at 6% of semiannual interest payments of $6,000 ($100,000 × .06) to be received at the end of each of the next ten interest dates $6,000 × 7.36009	44,161
Total issue price	$100,000

different yield rates and maturity dates. Calculating prices for bonds issued at a premium is discussed later in this chapter.

The same relationships hold after the bonds are issued and are trading in the marketplace. Remember that the stated rate is specified on the bond and does not change over its life. However, market rates of interest constantly change as economic conditions change. Taken as a whole, when there is a general rise in interest rates, the bond market declines, and when interest rates decline, bond prices tend to rise. Exhibit 12-4 shows these relationships graphically.[2] Because of the historical-cost convention, however, subsequent price changes in the bonds are not reflected in the accounting records.

EXHIBIT 12–4

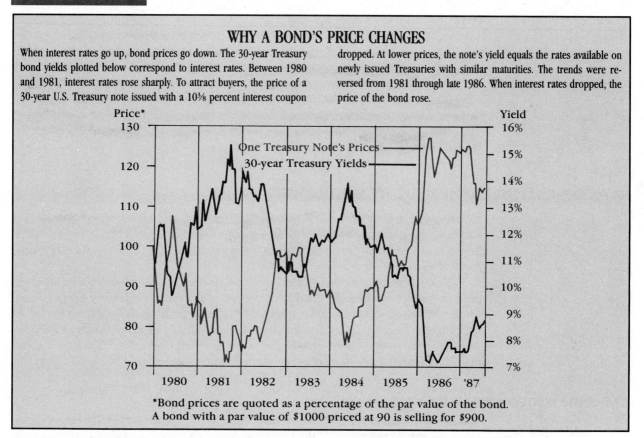

WHY A BOND'S PRICE CHANGES

When interest rates go up, bond prices go down. The 30-year Treasury bond yields plotted below correspond to interest rates. Between 1980 and 1981, interest rates rose sharply. To attract buyers, the price of a 30-year U.S. Treasury note issued with a 10⅜ percent interest coupon dropped. At lower prices, the note's yield equals the rates available on newly issued Treasuries with similar maturities. The trends were reversed from 1981 through late 1986. When interest rates dropped, the price of the bond rose.

*Bond prices are quoted as a percentage of the par value of the bond. A bond with a par value of $1000 priced at 90 is selling for $900.

[2]Source: *Consumer Reports*, September 1987, p. 571. Reprinted with permission of Consumer's Union and Shearson Lehman Hutton.

Determining Interest Rates

Obviously, interest rates play an important role in determining bond prices. As previously noted, the stated interest rate is set by management and in some cases by the underwriters. Underwriters help the issuing company market the bond. They often agree to purchase the entire bond issue at a certain price and then assume the risks involved in selling the bonds to institutions and/or private investors. Management and the underwriters attempt to set the stated or face interest rate as close as possible to the prevailing market rate. The stated rate must be decided on far enough in advance of the actual issue date to allow regulatory bodies such as the Securities and Exchange Commission to approve the issue and then to allow the firm to have the bond certificate printed. There is a consequent lag time between the time the decision must be made concerning the stated interest rate and the time the bonds are actually issued. A number of economic and financial events during the interim period may cause the prevailing market rate to change. Thus there is likely to be a difference between the two rates, so bonds are often issued at a discount or a premium.

The determination of market interest rates is as difficult to understand as the rates are to predict. They are effected by the federal government's economic policies, the Federal Reserve Board, investors' expectations about inflation, the risk of the particular investment, and various other factors. In recent years, these rates have been very volatile, reaching new highs and lows. For example, the cost of borrowing through traditional debt instruments, such as bonds, rose sharply in the early 1980s, and the number of new bond issues at that time dropped correspondingly.

Determining the Risk of a Bond

As noted, there are different market rates of interest for bonds of different risk. All else being equal, investors will demand a higher interest rate on investments that are perceived to be of greater risk than other investments are. One way in which a bond's risk can be measured is through bond ratings. Financial advisory services such as Standard and Poor's and Moody's rate the bonds of major corporations, states, and cities. The higher the rating, the less risky the bond will be in the opinion of the rating service. Thus firms with high ratings can issue bonds with a lower stated interest rate than firms with lower ratings.

■ ACCOUNTING FOR BONDS BY BORROWERS

Accounting for the issuance of bonds by the issuer and accounting for the purchase of bonds by the investor closely parallel each other. The accounting procedures will first be discussed in detail from the issuer's, or borrower's, point of view, then from the investor's point of view.

The decision to issue bonds represents a major financial commitment by an enterprise. Approval must be obtained by its board of directors, regulatory agencies, and often stockholders. The bond issue can be made through underwriters or issued directly to the public and to private institutions without the aid of underwriters. Regardless of the method used to issue the bonds or whether the bonds are issued at par, discounted, or at a premium, the accounting issues are similar.

■ BONDS ISSUED AT PAR OR FACE VALUE

Bonds will be issued at par or face value if the stated interest rate equals the prevailing rate for similar investments at the issue date. Because bonds can be issued on an interest date or between interest dates, both cases will be discussed.

Bonds Issued on an Interest Date

If bonds are issued at par or face value on an interest date, the entry is straightforward. Cash is debited for proceeds received, and Bonds Payable is credited for the face value of the bond issue. For example, assume that on January 2, 1989, the Valenzuela Corporation issues $100,000, five-year term bonds with a stated interest rate of 12%. The bonds pay interest every January 2 and July 1. The bonds were issued to yield 12%, which is another way of saying that they were issued at par, and thus the company received the full $100,000. The entry to record this bond issue is as follows:

Jan. 2, 1989	Cash	100,000	
	Bonds Payable		100,000
	To record the issuance of $100,000, 5-year, 12% bonds at face value.		

The Valenzuela Corporation is required to make semiannual interest payments of $6,000, or $100,000 × 6%. The entry on July 1, 1989 is:

July 1, 1989	Interest Expense	6,000	
	Cash		6,000
	To record payment of semiannual interest of $6,000.		

The next interest payment is due on January 2, 1990. The corporation's year-end is December 31, and the firm must make an adjusting entry to record interest expense for the six-month period, July 1 to December 31. This adjusting entry and the entry to record the subsequent payment are:

Dec. 31, 1989	Interest Expense	6,000	
	Interest Payable		6,000
	To record interest accrual for 6 months on $100,000, 12%, 5-year bonds.		
Jan. 2, 1990	Interest Payable	6,000	
	Cash		6,000
	To record payment of 6 months' accrued interest.		

In this case, the interest accrual is for the entire six-month period, because the last interest payment was on July 1. If the year-end were other than December 31, the interest accrual would be for less than six months.

Bonds Issued at Par between Interest Dates

Bonds are often issued between interest dates. When this occurs, the investors pay the issuing corporation for the interest that has accrued since the last interest date. This is because the investors receive the entire six months' interest on the next interest payment date, regardless of how long they have held the bonds. This procedure has definite record-keeping advantages for the issuer, whether or not the bonds are registered. If the bonds are registered, the corporation does not have to maintain records of when each particular bond was purchased or to compute individual partial interest payments. Interest on unregistered or coupon bonds is paid by authorized banks upon presentation of the coupon. Banks, however, will not honor a partial coupon. These problems are alleviated by the fact that the accrued interest is collected from the investors when the bonds are sold, thus allowing the corporation to pay investors the full six months' interest.

For example, now assume that the Valenzuela Corporation issues $100,000, five-year, 12% bonds on March 1, 1989. The bonds, dated January 2, 1989, pay interest semiannually, on January 2 and July 1. In this situation, the investor must pay the Valenzuela Corporation for two months of accrued interest (from January 2 to February 28), or $2,000 ($100,000 × .06 × $\frac{2}{6}$ = $2,000). The entry to record this transaction is:

Mar. 1, 1989	Cash	102,000	
	Interest Payable		2,000
	Bonds Payable		100,000
	To record issuance of $100,000, 5-year, 12%		
	bonds on March 1 plus accrued interest of $2,000.		

Several points should be emphasized about this entry. Bonds Payable is always credited for the face value of the issue, so the accrued interest element must be accounted for separately. This is done by crediting Interest Payable for the two months of accrued interest, or $2,000. Interest Payable is credited because these funds are owed on the next interest date. Cash is debited for the entire proceeds.

When the next interest payment is made on July 1, the following entry is recorded:

July 1, 1989	Interest Expense	4,000	
	Interest Payable	2,000	
	Cash		6,000
	To record interest payment for 6 months' interest		
	on 7/1/89.		

In this entry, Cash is credited for $6,000, Interest Payable is debited for $2,000, and Interest Expense is debited for $4,000. The result is that there is a zero balance in the Interest Payable account and a $4,000 balance in the Interest Expense account. This $4,000 balance represents the actual interest expense that the Valenzuela Corporation incurred from March 1, 1989 to July 1, 1989 ($100,000 × .06 × $\frac{4}{6}$). These relationships are illustrated in the diagram below and in the relevant T accounts.

$2,000	+	$4,000	=	$6,000
Accrued interest		Interest expense		Total paid
1/2/89		3/1/89		7/1/89
Start of interest period		Date bonds issued		First interest payment date

Interest Payable				Interest Expense		
	7/1 2,000	3/1 2,000		7/1 4,000		
		0		4,000		

■ BONDS ISSUED AT OTHER THAN FACE VALUE

As previously noted, bonds are often issued above or below their face value. If the prevailing market interest rate is above the stated rate, the bonds will be issued at a discount. Conversely, if the prevailing interest rate is below the stated rate, the bonds will be issued at a premium.

Recording Bonds Issued at a Discount

To illustrate the issuance of bonds at a discount, assume that on January 2, 1989, the Valenzuela Corporation issues $100,000, five-year, 12% term bonds. Interest of 6% is payable semiannually on January 2 and July 1. The bonds were issued when the prevailing market interest rate for such investments was 14%. Thus the bonds were issued at a discount to yield 14%. This rate is also called the *effective interest rate*.

Based on this effective rate, the bonds would be issued at a price of 92.976, or $92,976. The calculation of this issue price was illustrated in Exhibit 12-2.

The journal entry to record the Valenzuela bonds shown is:

Jan. 2, 1989	Cash	92,976	
	Discount on Bonds Payable	7,024	
	Bonds Payable		100,000
	To record issuance of $100,000, 5-year, 12% bonds for $92,976.		

As this entry illustrates, Cash is debited for the proceeds received, and Bonds Payable is credited for the face value of the bonds. The difference of $7,024 is debited to an account called Discount on Bonds Payable.

The Discount on Bonds Payable account is a contra-liability account, in that it is deducted from the Bonds Payable account on the balance sheet in order to arrive at the bonds' net carrying value. To illustrate, a balance sheet prepared on January 2, 1989, immediately after the bonds were issued, would include the long-term liability section shown in Exhibit 12-5.

EXHIBIT 12-5

VALENZUELA CORPORATION
Partial Balance Sheet
January 2, 1989

Long-term liabilities	
Bonds payable, 12% due 1/2/94	$100,000
Less: Discount on bonds payable	7,024
	$ 92,976

The Nature of the Discount Account

It is important to understand the nature of the Discount on Bonds Payable account. In effect, the discount should be thought of as additional interest expense that should be amortized over the life of the bond. Remember that the bond was issued at a discount because the stated rate was below the market rate. The bondholders are receiving only $6,000 every six months, whereas comparable investments yielding 14% are paying $7,000 every six months ($100,000 × .07). The discount of $7,024 represents the present value of that $1,000 difference that the bondholders are not receiving over each of the next ten interest periods (five years' interest paid semiannually). Essentially, the company incurs that additional interest of $7,024 at the time of issuance by receiving only $92,976 rather than $100,000. Because of the matching concept, this cost of $7,024 cannot be expensed when the bonds are issued but must be written off over the life of the bond.

As a result of issuing the bonds at a discount, the total interest expense incurred by the Valenzuela Corporation over the five-year life of the bond is $67,024, calculated as follows:

Interest expense paid in cash to bondholders	
Face value of bonds	$100,000
Semiannual stated interest rate	.06
Semiannual interest	$ 6,000
Number of interest periods	× 10
Total cash interest	$ 60,000
Discount on issuance	7,024
Total interest expense incurred	$ 67,024

Another way to view this is to look at the difference between the cash that the company will eventually repay the bondholders versus what it received at the time of issuance. This calculation is:

Total cash repaid to bondholders		
Principal	$100,000	
Cash interest—see above	60,000	
	160,000	
Total cash received at issuance	92,976	
Total interest expense incurred	$ 67,024	

Amortizing the Discount

The discount of $7,024 must be written off or amortized over the life of the bond. There are two methods used to do this: the straight-line method and the effective-interest method. The effective-interest method is conceptually preferable, and accounting pronouncements require its use unless there is no material difference from the periodic amortization computed by the straight-line method. However, the straight-line method is easy to compute and understand, so it is examined first in order to aid in your understanding of the concepts. The effective-interest method will be discussed later in the chapter.

The Straight-line Method. The straight-line method simply allocates the discount evenly over the remaining life of the bond. Thus there is a constant interest charge each period. An entry is usually made on every interest date, and if necessary, an adjusting journal entry is made at the end of each period to record the discount amortization.

To demonstrate the application of the straight-line method, let's return to the Valenzuela Corporation example. In this case, the discount of $7,024 will be amortized over ten interest periods at a rate of $702 per interest period ($7,024 ÷ 10). The total interest expense for each period is $6,702, consisting of the $6,000 cash interest and the $702 amortized discount. Another way to calculate the $6,702 is to divide the total interest cost, $67,024, into the ten interest periods of the bond's life. The journal entry at July 1, 1989 and each interest payment date thereafter is:

July 1, 1989	Interest Expense	6,702	
	Discount on Bonds Payable		702
	Cash		6,000
	To record cash interest payment and		
	amortization of discount on the straight-line		
	method.		

As the bonds approach maturity, their carrying value increases, and the result of this and subsequent entries is to reflect this increase in the carrying value of the bonds. This is because the discount account, which is offset against bonds payable in arriving at the bonds' carrying value, is decreased each time a credit entry is made to that account. To illustrate, the relevant T accounts and a partial balance sheet as of July 1, 1989 are presented in Exhibit 12-6. In each interest period, the bond's carrying value will be increased by $702. Thus, by the time the bond matures, the balance in the Discount on Bonds Payable account will be zero, and the bond's carrying value will be $100,000. Exhibit 12-7 presents an amortization schedule for this bond on the straight-line method. Thus, when the company repays the principal, it makes the following entry:

Jan. 2, 1994   Bonds Payable   100,000

                      Cash   100,000

                      To record the repayment of $100,000,

                      12-year bonds.

EXHIBIT 12–6

Bonds Payable		Interest Expense	
1/2/89 100,000		7/1/89 6,702	

Discount on Bonds Payable	
1/2/89 7,024	7/1/89 702
7/1/89 Bal. 6,322	

VALENZUELA CORPORATION
Partial Balance Sheet
July 1, 1989

Long-term liabilities
    Bonds payable $100,000
    Less: Discount on bonds payable   6,322
                                 $ 93,678

EXHIBIT 12–7

Discount Amortization—
Straight-line

Date	Cash Interest	Discount Amortization	Total Interest Expense	Carrying Value of Bonds
	(1)	(2)	(3)	(4)
1/2/89				$ 92,976
7/1/89	$6,000	$702	$6,702	93,678
1/2/90	6,000	702	6,702	94,380
7/1/90	6,000	702	6,702	95,082
1/2/91	6,000	702	6,702	95,784
7/1/91	6,000	702	6,702	96,486
1/2/92	6,000	702	6,702	97,188
7/1/92	6,000	702	6,702	97,890
1/2/93	6,000	702	6,702	98,592
7/1/93	6,000	702	6,702	99,294
1/2/94	6,000	706	6,706	100,000

(1) $6,000 = $100,000 × .06

(2) $ 702 = $\dfrac{\$7,024}{10 \text{ periods}}$ = $702.40 rounded to $702

(3) $6,702 = $6,000 + $702

(4) Carrying value at beginning of period plus discount amortization for period ($93,678 = $92,976 + $702). Last year's interest expense rounded to make carrying value $100,000.

Bonds Issued at a Premium

To show how to account for bonds issued at a premium, let us now assume that on January 2, 1989, the Valenzuela Corporation issues $100,000, five-year, 12% term bonds. Interest is payable semiannually on January 2 and July 1. In this case, however, the bonds are issued when the prevailing market interest rate for such investments is 10%. The bonds therefore are issued at a premium to yield 10% and are sold at a price of 107.7212, or $107,722. Exhibit 12-8 shows how the issue price of $107,722 is determined. The calculations are similar to those of the discount example in Exhibit 12-2, except that the cash flows are discounted at a semiannual yield rate of 5%. The entry to record this bond issue is:

Jan. 2, 1989   Cash   107,722
                   Premium on Bonds Payable   7,722
                   Bonds Payable   100,000
                   To record issuance of $100,000, 5-year,
                   12% bonds at 107,722.

This entry is similar for recording bonds issued at a discount, except that a premium account is involved. Cash is debited for the entire proceeds, and Bonds Payable is credited for the bonds' face amount. The difference in this case is a credit to the Premium on Bonds Payable account of $7,722.

EXHIBIT 12-8

Determination
of Bond Price
($100,000, five-year, 12%
bonds issued to yield 10%)

Present value of $100,000 to be received at the end of ten periods at 5% semiannually $100,000 × .61391	$ 61,391
Present value of 5% of semiannual interest payments of $6,000 ($100,000 × .06) to be received at the end of each of the next ten interest dates $6,000 × 7.72173	46,331
Total issue price	$107,722
Amount of premium	
Total issue price	$107,722
Face value of bonds	100,000
Amount of premium	$ 7,722

The Premium on Bonds Payable is called an **adjunct account** because it is added to the Bonds Payable account in determining the bonds' carrying value. To illustrate, the Valenzuela balance sheet prepared on January 2, 1989, immediately after the bonds were issued, would include the long-term liability section shown in Exhibit 12-9.

EXHIBIT 12-9

VALENZUELA CORPORATION
Partial Balance Sheet
January 2, 1989

Long-term liabilities	
Bonds payable, 12% due 1/2/94	$100,000
Plus: Premium on bonds payable	7,722
	$107,722

The Nature of the Premium Account

In effect, the premium should be thought of as a reduction in interest expense that should be amortized over the life of the bond. The bonds were issued at a premium because the stated interest rate was higher than the prevailing market rate. The bondholders are receiving $6,000 ($100,000 × .06) every six months when comparable investments were yielding only 10% and paying $5,000 ($100,000 × .05) every six months. The premium of $7,722 represents the present value of that extra $1,000 difference that the bondholders will receive in each of the next ten interest periods. Because the bond is an attractive investment, its price is bid up to $107,722, and the premium of $7,722 is considered a reduction of interest expense. Although the borrower receives all of the funds at the time of the issue, the matching convention requires that the premium be recognized over the life of the bond.

After issuing the bonds at premium, the total interest expense incurred by the Valenzuela Corporation over the five-year life of the bonds is $52,278, calculated as follows:

Interest expense paid in
cash to bondholders

Face value of bonds	$100,000
Semiannual interest rate	.06
Semiannual interest	6,000
Number of interest periods	× 10
Total cash interest	$ 60,000
Premium upon issuance	(7,722)
Total interest expense	$ 52,278

Again, another way to view this is to consider what the company will ultimately repay the bondholders versus what it received at the time of issuance. This calculation is:

Total cash repaid to bondholders	
Principal	$100,000
Cash interest	60,000
	160,000
Total cash received at issuance	107,722
Total interest expense incurred	$ 52,278

Amortizing the Premium

The premium of $7,722 is amortized by using either the straight-line method or the effective-interest method. Again, the straight-line method will be discussed first, then the effective-interest method will be discussed for both the discount and premium examples.

The Straight-line Method. Under the straight-line method, the premium of $7,722 is amortized over ten interest periods at a rate of $772 ($7,722 ÷ 10) per period. Thus the total interest expense for each period is $5,228, consisting of the $6,000 cash interest less the premium amortization of $772. Another way to calculate the $5,228 is to divide the total interest cost of $52,278, as just calculated, into the ten interest periods of the bond's life. Exhibit 12-10 presents an amortization schedule for

EXHIBIT 12–10

Premium Amortization—
Straight-line

Date	Cash Interest Payment	Premium Amortization	Total Interest Expense	Carrying Value of Bond
	(1)	(2)	(3)	(4)
1/2/89				$107,722
7/1/89	$6,000	$772	$5,228	106,950
1/2/90	6,000	772	5,228	106,178
7/1/90	6,000	772	5,228	105,406
1/2/91	6,000	772	5,228	104,634
7/1/91	6,000	772	5,228	103,862
1/2/92	6,000	772	5,228	103,090
7/1/92	6,000	772	5,228	102,318
1/2/93	6,000	772	5,228	101,546
7/1/93	6,000	772	5,228	100,774
1/2/94	6,000	774	5,230	100,000

(1) $6,000 = $100,000 × .06

(2) $ 772 = $\dfrac{\$7,722}{10 \text{ interest periods}}$ = $772.20 rounded to $772

(3) $5,228 = $6,000 − $772

(4) Carrying value = carrying value at beginning of period, less premium amortized during period ($106,950 = $107,722 − $772). 1/2/91 rounded up to equal $100,000.

this bond issue, on a straight-line basis. The journal entry at July 1, 1989 and each interest payment date thereafter is:

July 1, 1989	Interest Expense	5,228	
	Premium on Bonds Payable	772	
	Cash		6,000
	To record cash interest payment and amortization		
	of the premium on the straight-line method.		

The effect of this and subsequent entries is to decrease the carrying value of the bonds as the premium account is reduced each period. By the time the bonds reach maturity, their carrying value will have been reduced to their face value of $100,000. The relevant T accounts and partial balance sheet as of July 1, 1989 are presented in Exhibit 12-11.

EXHIBIT 12–11

Premium on Bond Payable

7/1/89	772	1/2/89	7,722
		7/1/89 Bal.	6,950

Bonds Payable

	1/2/89	100,000

Interest Expense

7/1/89	5,228

VALENZUELA CORPORATION
Partial Balance Sheet
July 1, 1989

Long-term liabilities	
Bonds payable	$100,000
Premium on bonds payable	6,950
	$106,950

The Effective-interest Method

Although the straight-line method is simple to use, it does not produce the accurate amortization of the discount or premium. It makes the unrealistic assumption that the interest cost for each period is the same, even though the carrying value of the liability is changing. For example, under the straight-line method, interest expense is the same each period, so as the carrying value of the bond increases or decreases, the actual interest rate correspondingly decreases or increases. For example, the Valenzuela bonds issued at a discount (see Exhibit 12-7) had a carrying value of $92,976 at the date of their issue. The interest expense based on straight-line amortization for the period between January 2, 1989 and July 1, 1989 is $6,702. This results in an interest rate of 7.2%, or $6,702 ÷ $92,976. In the next period, the interest expense for the period remains at $6,702, but as shown in Exhibit 12-7, the bond's carrying value has increased to $93,678. The interest rate is now 7.15% or $6,702 ÷ $93,678. Over the life of the bond, this interest rate continues to decrease until January 2, 1991, when it reaches 6.7%, or $6,702 ÷ $99,294.

With a premium example, the same conceptual problem occurs, except that the percentage rate continuously increases as the carrying value of the bond decreases from $107,722 to $100,000, since the semiannual interest expense remains constant at $5,228.

Because of the conceptual problem with the straight-line method, the Accounting Principles Board (APB) requires that the effective-interest method be used unless there are no material differences between the two.[3] Under the **effective-interest method**, a constant interest rate, equal to the market rate at the time of issue, is used to calculate periodic interest expense. Thus the interest rate is constant over the term of the bond, but the amount of interest expense changes as the carrying value of the bond changes. Furthermore, when the effective-interest method is used, the carrying value of the bonds will always equal the present value of the future cash outflow at an amortization date. The effective-interest method will be illustrated for both the discount and the premium cases.

Discount Amortization—Effective-interest Method. As illustrated, the $100,000, five-year, 12% bonds issued to yield 14% were sold at a price of $92,976, or at a discount of $7,024. Exhibit 12-12 shows how this discount is amortized using the effective-interest method over the life of the bond. The effective periodic bond interest expense is calculated by multiplying the bond's carrying value at the beginning of the period by the semiannual yield rate determined at the time the bond was issued. In this case, the interest expense of $6,508 in Column 2 at July 1, 1989 is equal to $92,976 multiplied by 7%. The difference between the required cash interest payment of $6,000 in Column 3 ($100,000 × 6%) and the effective-interest expense of $6,508 is the required discount amortization of $508 in Column 4. Finally, the unamortized discount of $6,516 at July 1, 1989 in Column 5 is equal to the original discount of $7,024, less the amortized discount of $508. The carrying value of the bond in Column 6 is thus increased by $508, from $92,976 to $93,484. Alternatively, the

EXHIBIT 12–12 Discount Amortization Table—Effective-interest Method

Date	Carrying Value at Beginning of the Period (1)	Debit — Effective Bond Interest Expense, 7% of Carrying Value from Col. 1 (2)	Credit — Cash Interest Paid, 6% of $100,000 (3)	Credit — Discount Amortization Col. 2 − Col. 3 (4)	Unamortized Discount Balance at End of the Period— Previous Balance Less Col. 4 (5)	Carrying Value of Bond at End of the Period Col. 1 + Col. 4 (6)
1/2/89					$7,024	$ 92,726
7/1/89	$92,976	$ 6,508[a]	$ 6,000	$ 508	6,516	93,484
1/2/90	93,484	6,544	6,000	544	5,972	94,028
7/1/90	94,028	6,582	6,000	582	5,390	94,610
1/2/91	94,610	6,623	6,000	623	4,767	95,233
7/1/91	95,233	6,666	6,000	666	4,101	95,899
1/2/92	95,899	6,713	6,000	713	3,388	96,612
7/1/92	96,612	6,763	6,000	763	2,625	97,375
1/2/93	97,375	6,816	6,000	816	1,809	98,191
7/1/93	98,191	6,873	6,000	873	936	99,064
1/2/94	99,064	6,936[b]	6,000	936	—	100,000
		$67,024	$60,000	$7,024		

[a] Rounded to whole dollars.
[b] Rounded to balance.

[3] "Interest on Receivables and Payables," *Accounting Principles Board Opinion No. 21* (New York: AICPA, 1971), par. 15.

bond's carrying value on July 1, 1989 is equal to $100,000 less the unamortized discount of $6,516.

The information for the journal entry to record the semiannual interest expense can be drawn directly from the amortization schedule. The entry on July 1, 1989 is:

July 1, 1989	Interest Expense	6,508	
	Discount on Bonds Payable		508
	Cash		6,000
	To record semiannual interest expense based on the effective-interest method.		

Exhibit 12-13 compares the two different methods of discount amortization for the first three interest periods and for the total over all ten periods. Under the straight-line method, the interest expense for each period is $6,702, and the total over all ten periods is $67,024. Under the effective-interest method, the semiannual interest expense is $6,508 in the first period and increases thereafter as the carrying value of the bond increases. With the effective-interest method, as with the straight-line method, the total interest expense is $67,024. The important point is that there is no difference in the total interest expense but only in the allocation within the five-year period of time.

EXHIBIT 12–13

	Interest Expense	
	Straight-line	Effective-interest
Date		
July 1, 1989	$ 6,702	$ 6,508
January 2, 1990	6,702	6,544
July 1, 1990	6,702	6,582
.	.	.
.	.	.
.	.	.
January 2, 1994	6,702	6,936
Total for all 10 interest periods	$67,024	$67,024

Premium Amortization—Effective-interest Method. Exhibit 12-8 showed that the $100,000, five-year, 12% bonds issued to yield 10% were issued at a price of $107,722, or at a premium of $7,722. The schedule in Exhibit 12-14 shows how the premium is amortized under the effective-interest method. This schedule is set up in the same manner as the discount amortization schedule in Exhibit 12-12, except that the premium amortization reduces the cash interest expense every period. For each period, the interest in Column 2 is the semiannual yield rate at the time of issue, 5%, multiplied by the carrying value of the bonds at the beginning of the period. The difference between this amount and the cash interest in Column 3 is the premium amortization in Column 4. The carrying value of the bond at the end of the period in Column 6 is reduced by the premium amortization for the period.

The journal entry to record the semiannual interest expense can be drawn directly from this schedule. The entry on July 1, 1989 is:

July 1, 1989	Interest Expense	5,386	
	Premium on Bonds Payable	614	
	Cash		6,000
	To record semiannual interest expense based on the effective-interest method.		

As with the discount example, the total interest expense over the life of the bond under the straight-line and the effective-interest methods is the same. However, it is

| EXHIBIT 12–14 | Premium Amortization Table—Effective-interest Method |

Date	Carrying Value at Beginning of the Period (1)	Debit Effective Bond Interest Expense, 5% of Carrying Value from Col. 1 (2)	Credit Cash Interest Paid, 6% of $100,000 (3)	Debit Premium Amortization Col. 3 – Col. 2 (4)	Unamortized Premium Balance at End of the Period— Previous Balance Less Col. 4 (5)	Carrying Value of Bond at End of the Period Col. 1 – Col. 4 (6)
1/2/89					$7,722	$107,722
7/1/89	$107,722	$ 5,386ᵃ	$ 6,000	$ 614	7,108	107,108
1/2/90	107,108	5,355	6,000	645	6,463	106,463
7/1/90	106,463	5,323	6,000	677	5,786	105,786
1/2/91	105,786	5,289	6,000	711	5,075	105,075
7/1/91	105,075	5,254	6,000	746	4,329	104,329
1/2/92	104,329	5,216	6,000	784	3,545	103,545
7/1/92	103,545	5,177	6,000	823	2,722	102,722
1/2/93	102,722	5,136	6,000	864	1,858	101,858
7/1/93	101,858	5,093	6,000	907	951	100,951
1/2/94	100,951	5,049ᵇ	6,000	951	—	100,000
		$52,278	$60,000	$7,722		

ᵃ Rounded to whole dollars.
ᵇ Rounded to balance.

allocated differently among periods. In both the discount and the premium examples, the difference between the straight-line and the effective-interest amortization methods is not significant, but for large bond issues, the difference between these two methods can become significant. If this is the case, generally accepted accounting principles require that the effective-interest amortization be used.

■ OTHER ISSUES RELATED TO BONDS PAYABLE

Besides the basic concepts and procedures related to the issuance and subsequent accounting for bonds payable, you should be familiar with other issues concerning bonds.

Bonds Issued at a Premium or Discount between Interest Dates

Bonds are likely to be sold between interest dates at either a discount or a premium. When this occurs, the discount or premium and the accrued interest must be accounted for separately. To demonstrate, assume that the Valenzuela Corporation issues $100,000, 12%, five-year term bonds on March 11, 1989. The bonds are dated January 2, 1989. They are issued at a discount to yield 14% and pay interest semiannually on January 2 and July 1. The price of the bonds net of the discount is 93.0939, and the accrued interest is $2,000 ($100,000 × .06 × $\frac{2}{6}$ = $2,000). The entry to record this issue is:

Mar. 1, 1989	Cash	95,094	
	Discount on Bonds Payable	6,906	
	Interest Payable		2,000
	Bonds Payable		100,000
	To record the issue of $100,000, 12%, 5-year bonds for March 1, 1989, to yield 14%. The discount equals $6,906 ($100,000 – $93,094).		

In this example, the cash proceeds that the firm receives of $95,094 consist of the proceeds from the bond of $93,094 plus the accrued interest of $2,000. The discount of $6,906 is the difference between the face value of $100,000 and the issue price net of the interest of $93,094. The bonds payable are recorded at their face value of $100,000.

When the first interest payment is made, the entry in Exhibit 12-15 is made (assuming straight-line amortization). Note that the discount is amortized over only 58 months, or four years and ten months, not five years, because the bonds had a remaining life of only 58 months when they were issued on March 1, 1989. Subsequent interest payments and discount amortization should be made in the usual way.

EXHIBIT 12–15	July 1, 1989 Interest Expense	4,476	
	Interest Payable	2,000	
	Discount on Bonds Payable		476
	Cash		6,000

To record semiannual interest payment and amortize discount on a straight-line basis.

Discount Amortization

$$\frac{\$6,906}{58 \text{ months}} = \$119*/\text{month} \times 4 \text{ months} = \underline{\$476}$$

Interest Expense: $\$100,000 \times .06 \times \frac{4}{6} = \$4,000$

$$\$4,000 + \$476 = \underline{\$4,476}$$

*Rounded to whole dollars.

Year-end Accruals of Interest Expense

It is likely that the issuing firm's year-end will not coincide with an interest payment date. A previous example showed the proper accounting procedures to handle this situation when bonds are issued at par; it is a simple extension to handle premiums or discounts in this new situation. To demonstrate, the data from the Valenzuela Corporation from the previous example will be used, except that the company's year-end will be September 30. An adjusting entry must be made on this date to record an interest accrual of three months since the last interest payment date on July 1, 1989. This entry, assuming straight-line amortization, is:

Sept. 30, 1989 Interest Expense	3,357	
Discount on Bonds Payable		357
Interest Payable		3,000

To record interest expense on bonds payable from 7/1/89 to 9/30/89.

Interest payable: $\$100,000 \times .06 \times \frac{3}{6} = \$3,000$

Discount Amortization

$$\frac{\$6,906}{58 \text{ months}} = \$119/\text{month} \times 3 \text{ months} = 357$$

Total Interest Expense $\underline{\$3,357}$

As this entry shows, the cash interest must be accrued and the discount must be amortized for three months.

On January 2, 1990, when the interest is paid, the entry at the top of page 449 is made:

Jan. 2, 1990	Interest Expense	3,357	
	Interest Payable	3,000	
	Discount on Bonds Payable		357
	Cash		6,000
	To record interest payment and 3 months' discount amortization.		

Discount Amortization:	$119 \times 3 =$	$ 357
Cash Interest Expense: $100,000 $\times$ .06 $\times \frac{3}{6} =$		3,000
Total Interest Expense		$3,357

In this entry, the Interest Payable account is debited, and Interest Expense is recorded for the three-month period from October 1, 1989 to January 2, 1990. The Discount on Bonds Payable is also amortized for the same three-month period.

Bond Issue Costs

When a corporation issues bonds, various expenses are incurred, such as printing and engraving and legal and accounting costs. Furthermore, many bonds are marketed through investment bankers, who receive a commission for underwriting the bond issue. These costs result in the issuer's receiving less cash proceeds than a corporation otherwise would. Current accounting principles require that these costs be accumulated in a noncurrent asset account called Bond Issue Costs and be amortized over the life of the bond on a straight-line basis.

■ ACCOUNTING FOR THE RETIREMENT OF BONDS

Bonds can be retired in different ways, including repayment at maturity, early extinguishment of the debt before maturity, and conversion into capital stock.

Retirement of Bonds at Maturity and Bond Sinking Funds

When bonds are repaid at maturity, the journal entry is straightforward: Bonds Payable is debited and Cash is credited. There are no problems with discounts or premiums, since they have been amortized to zero at the time of the last interest payment.

In order to ensure the repayment of the principal, some bond agreements require that the issuing corporation create and maintain a sinking fund. A **sinking fund** is a collection of cash (or perhaps other assets such as marketable securities) that is set aside to be used only for a specified purpose. This fund is generally under the control of a trustee or agent who is independent of the enterprise that established the fund. The issuing corporation makes periodic payments to its sinking fund. These monies are then invested by the trustee and eventually used to pay the interest and to repay the principal of the bond. The amount of periodic payments to the fund is based on the expected return that the trustee can earn on the assets in the fund.

The sinking fund is shown under the investment section on the balance sheet of the issuing corporation. The accounting procedure regarding interest expense recognition and other aspects of bonds is not affected by the existence of a bond sinking fund.

Early Extinguishment of Debt

Early extinguishment of debt occurs whenever a firm's long-term debt is retired before maturity. Management can accomplish this extinguishment by repurchasing the bonds on the market. Other bonds are callable and give the issuing corporation the right to buy back the bonds before maturity at a specified price. This price is usually set above the par or face value of the bond because the bondholder will be foregoing future interest income. The amount above par is often referred to as a *call premium*.

The early extinguishment of long-term debt is a financing decision of management. It depends on such factors as cash flows and past, existing, and anticipated interest rates. For example, it may be advantageous for a firm to repurchase bonds if market interest rates have risen since the original bond issue date. To demonstrate, assume that the Tracy Hospital Company issued $50,000, 6%, 20-year bonds at face at the beginning of 1980. Because the bonds were issued at face or par, it can be assumed that the market interest rates were equivalent to the stated rates for this type of bond. By the beginning of 1988, interest rates rose to 10%, so the market value of the bonds decreased to $36,201. Therefore the Tracy Hospital Company can repurchase for that amount all the bonds on the open market to liquidate a $50,000 debt for only $36,201, as well as save interest payments for 13 years. This situation occurred often in the late 1970s and early 1980s when market interest rates rose, and many firms did retire their debt early.

When a firm extinguishes its debt prior to maturity, there will be a gain or loss: the difference between the reacquisition price and the carrying value of the bonds. In the example of the Tracy Hospital bonds, the firm would record a gain of $13,799, or $50,000 less the reacquisition price of $36,201. Prior to recording the gain or loss, the carrying value must be adjusted for any amortization to the date the bonds are retired. If the carrying value exceeds the reacquisition price, there is a gain; conversely, if the reacquisition price exceeds the carrying value, there is a loss. Under current accounting practices, this gain or loss is considered extraordinary and must be shown as a separate item on the income statement.[4]

It is important to recognize that an accounting gain on the early extinguishment of debt may not represent a real economic gain. In fact, the result may be higher cash outflows for interest expense. For example, if the Tracy Hospital Company liquidates its $50,000 debt for only $36,201, it records an extraordinary gain of $13,799. However, if the company then issues new bonds at higher interest rates to meet current financing needs, it will incur higher cash outflows for interest expense than if the old bonds were still outstanding. If additional financing is not needed, the firm is probably better off retiring the debt and saving future interest payments.

To illustrate the accounting for the early extinguishment of debt, assume that the $100,000, 12%, five-year term bonds that were issued at a discount of $7,024 by the Valenzuela Corporation were called on July 1, 1991. The bonds were reacquired at a price of 104. The firm uses the straight-line method of amortization. The entries to record (1) the payment of interest and the amortization of the discount and (2) the retirement of the bonds are as follows. (See Exhibit 12-7 for the necessary data.)

July 1, 1991	Interest Expense	6,702	
	Discount on Bonds Payable		702
	Cash		6,000
	To record semiannual		
	interest payment and		
	discount amortization.		

---

[4]"Reporting Gains and Losses from Extinguishment of Debt," *Statement of Financial Accounting Standards No. 4* (Stamford, Conn.: FASB, 1975). For an item to be considered extraordinary, it must meet certain criteria. If it meets these criteria, the item is disclosed separately on the income statement. Extraordinary items are discussed in detail in Chapter 14.

July 1, 1991	Bonds Payable	100,000	
	Extraordinary Loss on Early		
	Extinguishment of Debt	7,514	
	Discount on Bonds Payable		3,514
	Cash		104,000
	To record early retirement of bonds at 104.		

Reacquisition price ($100,000 × 1.04)	$104,000
Less: Carrying value—See Exhibit 12-7	96,486
Loss on Reacquisition	$ 7,514

The first entry records the interest payment and the discount amortization from January 2, 1991 to July 1, 1991. The second entry records the actual extinguishment of the debt. There is a loss in this case because the reacquisition price exceeds the carrying value of the bonds.

Conversion of Bonds into Capital Stock

As noted previously, many corporations issue convertible bonds because of the advantages that accrue to the bondholders and to the issuing corporation. When convertible bonds are issued, no recognition is given to the conversion feature. That is, the entire issue is treated as debt. For example, assume that the Farr Corporation issues $500,000, ten-year, 10% bonds. These bonds are convertible into 50 shares of capital stock and are issued at a price of 95. The entry to record the bond issue on January 2, 1989 is:

Jan. 2, 1989	Cash	475,000	
	Discount on Bonds Payable	25,000	
	Bonds Payable		500,000
	To record issuance of $500,000 convertible bonds.		

When the bonds are converted into capital stock, the capital stock is recorded at the carrying value of the bonds, and no gain or loss is recognized on the conversion. For example, assume that all the bonds of the Farr Corporation are converted into 25,000 shares on July 1, 1993, when the unamortized discount is $13,750 and the carrying value of the bonds is $486,250. The firm issues 25,000 shares because 500 ($500,000 ÷ $1,000) bonds were converted and the conversion agreement calls for each bond to be converted into 50 shares of stock. The entry to record this conversion is:

July 1, 1993	Bonds Payable	500,000	
	Discount on Bonds Payable		13,750
	Capital Stock		486,250
	To record issuance of 25,000 shares of capital stock in exchange for outstanding bonds.		

Bonds Payable is debited for the face value of the converted bonds. The unamortized discount of $13,750 is written off. The 25,000 shares of capital stock are recorded at the bonds' carrying value at the date of conversion.

ACCOUNTING FOR BONDS BY THE INVESTOR

Accounting for bonds by the investor is similar to that by the issuer, except that the investor records an asset, Investment in Bonds, rather than a liability, Bonds Payable. The Investment in Bonds account can be classified as either a current asset or a long-term investment, depending on the marketability of the bonds and management's plans for converting into cash. Thus bonds can be purchased in order to invest idle cash on a short-term basis, to make a long-term investment in another company, or to accumulate funds for future expansion plans. The accounting procedures followed by investors in long-term bonds will be outlined in the next section.

ACCOUNTING FOR THE ACQUISITION OF BONDS

The acquisition cost of bonds includes their purchase price, brokerage commission, and any other costs related to the purchase. Bonds may be purchased at their face value, at a discount or premium, and at or between interest dates. In practice, the debit to the Investment in Bonds account is cost, including all acquisition costs but excluding the accrued interest element. A separate account is not maintained for the premium or discount. This practice varies from the accounting procedures used by the issuer and the recommendation found in official pronouncements.[5] However, the investor seldom purchases an entire bond issue, and the amount of the discount or premium is not material. The remaining portion of the chapter will not use a separate discount or premium account in accounting for investments.

If bonds are purchased between interest dates, the investor must pay the issuer or the previous bondholder for any interest accrued since the last interest date, since the purchaser will collect the full six months' interest on the next interest date. To illustrate these procedures, assume that the Cinzano Corporation purchased 12 $1,000, 10%, five-year bonds on March 1, 1989. The bonds are dated January 1, 1989. The total face value of the bonds was $12,000. The bonds pay interest semiannually on January 2 and July 1 and were purchased at a price of 98. The entry to record this investment is as follows:

Mar. 1, 1989	Investment in Bonds	11,760	
	Interest Receivable	200	
	Cash		11,960
	To record purchase of $12,000 bonds		
	at 98 plus accrued interest of $200.		

Cash payment required
  Acquisition cost
    $12,000 × .98   = $11,760
  Interest receivable
    $12,000 × .05 × $\frac{2}{6}$ =   200
                                  $11,960

The Investment in Bonds account is recorded at $11,760, net of the discount of $240 ($12,000 − $11,760). The $11,760 also represents the carrying value of the bonds at their purchase date. Interest Receivable is debited for the two months' interest that has accrued since the last payment date on January 2. The receivable is debited because the investor will receive all six months' interest on July 1, 1989.

---

[5]"Interest on Receivables and Payables," *Accounting Principles Board Opinion No. 21* (New York: AICPA, 1971).

■ AMORTIZING THE DISCOUNT OR PREMIUM

The straight-line method or the effective-interest method can be used to amortize the bond discount or premium. As noted, if there are material differences between the two methods, the effective-interest method should be used. However, for ease of illustration, the straight-line method will be used in this part of the chapter. Regardless of which method is used, a discount is amortized by debiting the Investment in Bonds account, and a premium is a credit to the Investment in Bonds account. This procedure ensures that after the discount or premium is fully amortized, the investment account will reflect the bond's maturity value.

To demonstrate these concepts, let's continue with the Cinzano Corporation example. The first interest payment is on July 1, 1989, and the following entry would be made to record the receipt of the cash interest and the amortization of the discount:

July 1, 1989	Cash	600	
	Investment in Bonds	17	
	Interest Receivable		200
	Interest Revenue		417
	To record semiannual interest payment		
	and discount amortization.		

In this entry, Cash is debited for $600, which is the full six months' interest payment ($12,000 × .05). The Investment in Bonds account is debited for four months of discount amortization. The total discount is $240 and is amortized over the remaining 58 months of the bond's life at the time of issue. This equals $4.14 ($240 ÷ 58 months = $4.14) per month, and four months' amortization from March 1, 1986 to July 1, 1989 is $16.56 ($4.14 × 4). This is rounded off to $17 in the journal entry. Interest revenue is credited for $417. This $417 consists of four months' cash interest plus $17 of the amortized discount. Note that from the investor's perspective, the discount increases interest revenue, and from the issuer's point of view, it increases interest expense.

Thereafter, the Cinzano Corporation would make the following set of journal entries each year until the bonds mature or until they are sold. The corporation has a December 31 year-end.

Dec. 31	Interest Receivable	600	
	Investment in Bonds	25	
	Interest Revenue		625
	To record accrual of 6 months' interest		
	plus the amortization of 6 months' interest.		
	($4.14 × 6 = $24.84, rounded off to $25)		
Jan. 1	Cash	600	
	Interest Receivable		600
	To record receipt of accrued interest receivable.		
July 1	Cash	600	
	Investment in Bonds	25	
	Interest Revenue		625
	To record receipt of 6 months' interest and		
	amortization of discount.		

These examples illustrate the accounting procedures for discounts. Premiums are handled in a similar manner, except that the premium decreases interest revenue and is recorded by crediting the Investment in Bonds account.

■ SALE OF BONDS PRIOR TO MATURITY

Investors often sell bonds prior to their maturity. The sale is recorded by debiting Cash for the net proceeds received (sale price less commission and fees). The Investment in Bonds account is credited for the net carrying value of the bonds, and a gain or loss is recorded for the difference between the cash proceeds and the carrying value of the bonds. If the bonds are sold between interest dates, the seller also receives the interest that has accrued since the last interest date.

To illustrate, assume that the Cinzano Corporation decides to sell its bonds on October 1, 1991 for $11,500 plus accrued interest. As of the last interest date, July 1, 1991, the balance in the Investment in Bonds account is $11,877, as shown in the following T account:

Investment in Bonds

3/1/89	11,760
7/1/89	17
12/31/89	25
7/1/90	25
12/31/90	25
7/1/91	25
Bal.	11,877

The first step is to record the discount amortization for the three months from July 1 to October 1, 1991. This amounts to $12 ($4.14 × 3 = $12.42, rounded to $12) and is recorded as follows:

Oct. 1, 1991	Investment in Bonds	12	
	Interest Revenue		12
	To record discount amortization for 3 months.		

After this entry, the Investment in Bonds account has a balance of $11,889 ($11,877 + $12). Because the firm sold the bonds for $11,500, it suffered a $389 loss, recorded as follows:

Oct. 1, 1991	Cash	11,800	
	Loss on Sale	389	
	Investment in Bonds		11,889
	Interest Revenue		300
	To record sale of bonds and interest income		
	for 3 months.		

The cash proceeds of $11,800 represent the sale price of $11,500 plus three months' accrued interest of $300 ($12,000 × 5% × $\frac{3}{6}$) that the buyer is paying the Cinzano Corporation. There is a corresponding credit of $300 to the Interest Revenue account. This represents the cash portion of the interest revenue, and the $12 from the previous October 1, 1991 entry represents the amortized discount portion. Thus over the three-month period from July 1 to October 1, interest revenue of $312 is earned by the Cinzano Corporation. Again, the loss is the difference between the carrying value of the bond and the sale price of $11,500, excluding interest.

■ OTHER FORMS OF LONG-TERM DEBT

This chapter has been concerned primarily with accounting problems related to bonds, but there are other types of long-term debts, including notes payable, mortgages payable, and leases.

■ NOTES PAYABLE

A firm may issue a long-term note payable for a variety of reasons. For example, notes may be issued to purchase equipment or other assets or to borrow money from the bank for working capital purposes. Generally, there are no particular problems with accounting for these notes. The asset received is debited, and the note is credited. As interest accrues, it is periodically recorded and eventually paid.

A problem does arise, however, when an obligation has no stated interest or the interest rate is substantially below the current rate for similar notes. This situation may occur when a seller, in order to make a particular transaction appear more favorable, increases the list or cash price of an item but offers the buyer interest-free repayment terms. The APB noted that "the use of an interest rate that varies from the prevailing interest rate warrants evaluation of whether the face amount and the stated interest rate of a note or obligation provide reliable evidence of properly recording the exchange and subsequent related interest."[6] The APB required that in these situations the note, the sales price, and the cost of property, goods, or services exchanged for the note be recorded at the cash-equivalent price of the property, goods, or services, or the market value of the note if it is easier to determine. If neither of these amounts can be determined, the note should be recorded at its present value, using an appropriate interest rate for that type of note.

To demonstrate, assume that on January 2, 1989, the Ng Corporation agrees to purchase a custom piece of equipment. The agreement calls for the Ng Corporation to make three equal payments of $6,245 at the end of the next three years, for a total payment of $18,735. No interest is provided for in the agreement. If the item had been purchased outright for cash, its price would have been $15,000. In reality, there is an implied interest rate in this trasaction, because the Ng Corporation will be paying a total of $18,735 over the next three years for what it could have purchased immediately for $15,000. Present-value techniques illustrated in the previous chapter can be used to determine that this implied interest rate is 12%.

It would be inappropriate to record this transaction by debiting the Equipment account and crediting Notes Payable for $18,735, the total amount of the cash outflows. This would overstate the acquisition cost of the equipment and subsequent depreciation charges and understate subsequent interest expense. The equipment and note should be recorded at their cash equivalent price of $15,000. The correct journal entry is:

Jan. 2, 1989	Equipment	15,000	
	Discount on Note Payable	3,735	
	Note Payable		18,735
	To record purchase of equipment and issuance of note requiring 3 payments of $6,245 with implied interest rate of 12%.		

The discount is amortized over each of the next three years to Interest Expense. Exhibit 12-16 shows how this is done. Each payment of $6,245 is divided between interest and principal. The interest portion is 12% of the note's carrying value at the beginning of each year. For example, the interest in 1989 is $1,800, or $15,000 × .12, and the interest in 1990 is $1,267, or $10,555 × .12. The principal portion is just the total payment less the amount allocated to interest. Each year, the unamortized discount is reduced by the interest expense for the year. This treatment ensures that the interest element is accounted for separately from the cost of the asset.

---

[6] Ibid., par. 1.

EXHIBIT 12–16

Interest Amortization
Table

Year	Total Payment	12% Interest	Principal	Unamortized Discount	Carrying Value
1/2/89				$3,735	$15,000
12/31/89	$6,245	$1,800	$4,445	1,935[a]	10,555[b]
12/31/90	6,245	1,267	4,978	668	5,577
12/31/91	6,245	668	5,577	0	0
		$3,735			

[a]$1,935 = $3,735 − $1,800.
[b]$10,555 = $15,000 − $4,445.

The journal entry to record the payment for the first year is:

Dec. 31, 1989	Interest Expense	1,800	
	Note Payable	6,245	
	Discount on Note Payable		1,800
	Cash		6,245
	To record first payment of $6,245 and		
	discount amortization of $1,800.		

The result of this entry is to record interest expense of $1,800 and to reduce the carrying value of the note to $10,555, as shown in the following T accounts:

Note Payable				Discount on Note Payable				Interest Expense		
12/31/89	6,245	1/2/89	18,735	12/31/89	1,800	1/2/89	3,735	12/31/89	1,800	
		Bal.	12,490			Bal.	1,935			

Carrying value of note on 12/31/89:

Note Payable	$12,490
Less: Discount	1,935
	$10,555

The entries in the following years would be made in the same manner. The important points to remember are that the depreciation expense is now based on an acquisition cost of $15,000, the cash-equivalent price, and that the interest expense of $3,735 is recorded over the three-year duration of the note.

■ MORTGAGES PAYABLE

A **mortgage** is a promissory note secured by an asset whose title is pledged to the lender. Mortgages are generally payable in equal installments consisting of interest and principal. To demonstrate the accounting procedures, assume that on January 2, 1989, the Grant Corporation purchases a small building for $1 million and makes a down payment of $200,000. The mortgage is payable over 30 years at a rate of $8,229 monthly. The annual interest rate is 12%, and the first payment is due on February 1, 1989. The entry to record the purchase of the building is:

Jan. 2, 1989	Building	1,000,000	
	Mortgage Payable		800,000
	Cash		200,000
	To record purchase of building and issuance of		
	12%, 30-year mortgage.		

Subsequent entries are based on dividing the monthly payment of $8,229 between principal and interest. A mortgage amortization table can be used for this purpose, and such a table for the first 5 months of 1989 is shown in Exhibit 12-17. Each month, the total payment of $8,229 is divided into interest and principal. The interest is based on 1% (12% ÷ 12 months) of the note's carrying value at the beginning of the month. On February 1, the interest is $8,000 (or $800,000 × 1%), and the principal portion of the payment is thus $229 (or $8,229 − $8,000). In March, the interest is $7,998, or 1% of $799,771, and this pattern continues monthly. The journal entry for February 1989 is:

Feb. 1989	Interest Expense	8,000	
	Note Payable	229	
	Cash		8,229
	To record February mortgage payment of $8,229.		

EXHIBIT 12–17

Mortgage Amortization Table

Date	Total Payment	1% Monthly Interest	Principal	Carrying Value of Mortgage
January 1				$800,000
February 1	$8,229	$8,000	$229	799,771
March 1	8,229	7,998	231	799,540
April 1	8,229	7,995	234	799,306
May 1	8,229	7,993	236	799,070
June 1	8,229	7,991	238	798,832

Because most mortgages are payable in monthly installments, the principal payments for the next 12 months following the balance sheet date must be shown in the current liability section as a current maturity of long-term debt. The remaining portion is, of course, classified as a long-term liability.

LEASES

A **lease** is a contractual agreement between the **lessor** (owner of the property) and the **lessee** (the user of the property), giving the lessee the right to use the lessor's property for a specific period of time in exchange for stipulated cash payments. As an alternative to full ownership, leases have become very popular in recent years, because the lessee does not have to assume full financial and operating risk for the leased property. All types of companies lease various kinds of property. For example, airlines currently lease a large percentage of their planes, and railroads lease much of their train equipment. Leasing is also very popular in the retail, hotel, and computer industries. In fact, leasing is one of the largest sources of corporate financing.

The accounting treatment of leases has long been a controversial subject. The basic controversy centers on the classification and accounting treatment for capital leases that are essentially equivalent to installment purchases.

Types of Leases

From the lessee's point of view, there are two types of leases: *operating leases* and *capital leases*. The distinction between them is important because a different accounting treatment is required for each; there are substantial effects on the balance sheet and income statement according to whether a lease is classified as a capital or an operating lease.

According to FASB Statement No. 13, "Accounting for Leases," a lease should be classified as a capital lease if the lease meets one or more of the following criteria:

1. The lease transfers ownership of the property to the lessee at the end of the lease term.

2. The lease contains a bargain purchase option (the asset can be purchased by the lessee at a price significantly lower than its then fair market value).

3. The lease term is 75 percent or more of the leased property's estimated economic life.

4. The present value of the minimum lease payments is 90 percent or more of the fair market value of the property to the lessor at the inception of the lease.[7]

Thus capital leases are accounted for essentially as purchases of equipment or other property. A lease rather than a bank loan is used to finance the purchase. Accounting for such leases requires that the asset and the liability be recorded on the lessee's books just as if a purchase had taken place.

A lease that does not meet any of the criteria just listed is considered an operating lease. With this type of lease, the lessor retains control and ownership of the property, which reverts back to the lessor at the end of the lease term. Accounting for an operating lease requires only that the lessee record an expense for the periodic lease payments as they are made. Keep in mind that these two types of leases are not alternatives for the same transaction. If the terms of the lease agreement meet any of the previously enumerated four criteria, the lease must be accounted for as a capital lease.

Accounting for Leases

To demonstrate the proper accounting for leases, assume that on January 2, 1989, the Scully Corporation enters into a lease with the Porter Company in which the Scully Corporation agrees to lease a piece of equipment for five equal annual payments of $13,870. Each payment is made at year-end.[8] This data will be used to compare and contrast the accounting treatment for operating and capital leases. Note that this is for illustrative purposes only—in reality, the lease must be considered either a capital lease or an operating lease.

Accounting for Operating Leases

Assuming this agreement is an operating lease, the Scully Corporation does not make any entry on January 2, 1989, when the lease agreement is signed. At this point, the lease is considered just an agreement or contract that neither party has yet carried out. The Scully Corporation makes the following entry on December 31 of each of the next five years:

Equipment Lease Expense	13,870	
Cash		13,870
To record annual lease payment.		

The entire lease payment is shown as an expense. The equipment is still on the books of the lessor and is depreciated by the lessor. Over the five-year lease term, the Scully Corporation incurs total lease expenses of $69,350, or $13,870 × 5.

Accounting for Capital Leases

Under a capital lease, the Scully Corporation actually records the equipment as an asset and the required lease payments as a liability. The asset and liability are recorded at the present value of the required lease payments by using an appropriate interest rate (assume 12% for this lease). Subsequently, the Scully Corporation makes the yearly payments, which are divided between principal and interest, and also depreciates the equipment. In a corresponding manner, the lessor takes the leased equipment off his or her books and records a receivable at the present value of the lease payments.

The present value of the lease payments of $13,870, based on an interest rate of 12%, is $50,000.[9] Based on this data, the Scully Corporation makes the entry shown at the top of page 459 on January 2, 1989, the inception of the lease:

---

[7]"Accounting for Leases," *Statement of Financial Accounting Standards No. 13* (Stamford, Conn.: FASB, 1976), par. 7. Reprinted by permission.

[8]Most lease payments are made monthly. However, annual payments are assumed here for ease of illustration.

[9]This is determined by discounting the annuity of $13,870 for five years at 12%. The factor from Table 4 in Appendix C is 3.60490; thus the present value is $50,000 or $13,879 × 3.60490.

```
Jan. 2, 1989   Leased Equipment under Capital Lease           50,000
                   Obligation under Capital Lease                          50,000
               To record capital lease with payment of $13,870
               at 12%.
```

The account Leased Equipment under Capital Lease is a noncurrent asset, generally shown under the property, plant, and equipment section. The account Obligation under Capital Lease is a liability, of which part is classified as current and part as long-term. At the end of each year, the Scully Corporation makes a $13,870 annual payment. Exhibit 12-18 shows how these payments are divided between interest and principal. The interest each year is based on 12% of the balance of the lease obligation at the beginning of the year. In 1989, for example, interest is $6,000 (or 12% of $50,000), and in 1990, it is $5,056 (or 12% of $42,130). The difference between the annual lease payment and the interest portion is the principal portion. The entry to record the first payment is:

```
Dec. 31, 1990   Interest Expense                              6,000
                Obligation under Capital Lease                7,870
                    Cash                                                    13,870
                To record first lease payment of $13,870.
```

EXHIBIT 12-18

Lease Payment Schedule

Date	Annual Lease Payment	12% Interest	Principal Portion	Balance of Lease Obligation
1/2/89				$50,000
12/31/89	$13,870	$ 6,000	$ 7,870	42,130
12/31/90	13,870	5,056	8,814	33,316
12/31/91	13,870	3,998	9,872	23,444
12/31/92	13,870	2,813	11,057	12,387
12/31/93	13,870	1,483	12,387[a]	0
	$69,350	$19,350		

[a] Rounded to reduce lease obligation to zero.

The Scully Corporation needs to make one additional entry each year to record depreciation expense on the leased equipment. The leased equipment is depreciated over its life of five years using straight-line depreciation and no salvage value. Thus the Scully Corporation makes the following adjusting entry at the end of each year:

```
Dec. 31   Depreciation Expense                                 10,000
              Accumulated Depreciation—Leased Equipment                   10,000
          To record annual depreciation expense of $10,000.
```

$$\frac{\$50,000}{5 \text{ years}} = \$10,000$$

Operating versus Capital Leases

Exhibit 12-19 shows the difference between accounting for this lease as an operating lease and as a capital lease. Over the entire five-year period, the total expense in both cases is $69,350, which represents the total cash outflows. However, each method results in a different expense pattern within the five-year period of time. In the first three years, the capital lease method results in a higher annual expense than does the operating lease method. This means that annual net income is lower in these years. This pattern then reverses in the last two years of the lease term.

EXHIBIT 12–19

	Operating Lease Equipment Lease Expense (1)	Capital Lease Interest (2)	Depreciation (3)	Total (Cols. 2 + 3) (4)	Difference between Operating and Capital Lease Expense (Cols. 4 − 1) (5)
1989	$13,870	$ 6,000	$10,000	$16,000	$2,130
1990	13,870	5,056	10,000	15,056	1,186
1991	13,870	3,998	10,000	13,998	128
1992	13,870	2,813	10,000	12,813	(1,057)
1993	13,870	1,483	10,000	11,483	(2,387)
	$69,350	$19,350	$50,000	$69,350	0

These relationships lie at the heart of the controversy over the accounting for leases. Prior to the issuance of Statement 13, companies had a good deal of latitude in deciding whether a lease should be classified as an operating or a capital lease. Most companies felt that it was in their best interest to classify as many leases as possible as operating leases, and some obvious purchases that were being financed through leases were considered operating leases when they should have been considered capital leases.

If a lease is considered to be an operating lease, no liability is recorded on the balance sheet for the required lease payments. This means that the lessee's working capital position or current ratio is not affected by the lease agreement. Remember that if a liability were recorded on a balance sheet, the next year's payment would have to be considered a current liability, whereas the entire balance in the account Leased Equipment under Capital Lease is considered a noncurrent asset. The fact that the lessee was in substance making an installment purchase but did not have to record the asset or liability on the balance sheet is referred to as **off-balance-sheet financing**. Off-balance-sheet financing also has a tendency to decrease a firm's debit-to-equity ratio and to increase its return on investment. Furthermore, the annual expense associated with an operating lease is less in the first few years of the lease term than that with a capital lease. Because of these facts and the fear that creditors might react adversely if leases were capitalized on the balance sheet, some managers had a definite bias to classify leases as operating leases.

The criteria set forth in Statement 13 corrected a number of obvious situations in which agreements that were in substance capital leases were being accounted for as operating leases. The four criteria in this Statement ensure that leases that are in fact installment purchases are recorded as capital leases. Thus the appropriate asset and liability, interest expense, and depreciation are recorded. In addition, current accounting rules require substantial footnote disclosure concerning lease terms and agreements.

SUMMARY OF LEARNING OBJECTIVES

1. The nature and features of bonds payable. A bond is a written agreement between a borrower and a lender, in which the borrower agrees to repay a stated sum on a future date and to make periodic interest payments. Most bonds are in $1,000 denominations and pay interest semi-annually. There are various types of bonds, including term, serial, secured, convertible, and callable bonds.

The issue price of bonds and subsequent trading prices

depend on the relationship between the stated rate of interest and the prevailing market rates. For investments of similar risk, these two rates are often different. If the prevailing interest rate is above the stated interest, the bond will be issued or subsequently traded at a discount. Conversely, if the prevailing rate of interest is below the stated rate, the bond will be issued or traded at a premium.

2. **Accounting for bonds issued at par.** Bonds will be issued at par or face value if the stated interest rate equals the prevailing market rate. In this situation, the journal entry to record the issuance of the bonds is straightforward and takes the following form:

Cash	XXXX	
Bonds Payable		XXXX

If the bond is issued between interest dates, the accrued interest element is accounted for separately by crediting Interest Payable.

3. **Bonds issued at other than face value.** Bonds are often issued at other than face or par value. Any discount or premium should be accounted for separately and should be thought of as an additional interest expense or a reduction of interest expense to be amortized over the life of the bond. The journal entries to record bond issues in these cases take the following form:

record the interest accrual and the appropriate amortization. Finally, any bond issue costs incurred by the issuing firm are generally accumulated in a deferred charge account and amortized on a straight-line basis over the bond's life.

6. **Accounting for the retirement of bonds.** When bonds mature, they are repaid by the firm. The journal entry is a debit to Bonds Payable and a credit to Cash. The premium or discount account should have already been amortized to zero. If a bond is retired prior to its maturity, a gain or loss will usually result. This gain or loss is the difference between the reacquisition price and the carrying value of the bonds and is considered to be extraordinary.

Some bonds are convertible into capital stock. At the time these bonds are issued, the proceeds represent a liability. At the time of conversion, the carrying value of the converted bonds is transferred to owners' equity.

7. **Accounting for bonds by the investor.** Accounting for bonds by the investor generally parallels accounting for bonds by the issuer. However, by convention, a separate account is not maintained for the discount or premium account. The discount account increases the investor's periodic interest revenue, and the premium reduces the investor's periodic interest revenue.

8. **Other forms of long-term debt.** Other common

Discount			Premium		
Cash	XXX		Cash	XXX	
Discount on Bonds Payable	XXX		Premium on Bonds Payable		XXX
Bonds Payable		XXX	Bonds Payable		XXX

4. **The straight-line and effective-interest methods.** The straight-line and effective-interest methods are used to amortize the discount or premium. Unless there is little difference between the two, the effective-interest method should be used. The following table summarizes each:

types of long-term debt include bank loans and notes payable, mortgages payable, and leases. The concepts that apply to bonds payable apply to other forms of long-term debt, except for leases.

Accounting for leases centers on whether the lease is

Method	Calculation/Interpretation
Straight-line	Amortization is determined by dividing discount or premium by the remaining life of bonds. Result is equal amount of interest expense each period.
Effective-interest	Amortization is determined by multiplying semiannual yield or effective interest rate by bonds' carrying value at beginning of period. Thus interest expense is a constant rate, although amount changes with carrying value.

5. **Other issues related to bonds payable.** If bonds with a discount or premium are issued between interest dates, the interest must be accounted for separately. This is done by crediting Interest Payable for the interest accrued since the last interest date. If the issuing company's year-end is not an interest date, an adjusting entry must be made to

classified as an operating lease or a capital lease. If a lease meets the criteria established by the FASB, it is a capital lease, and if not, it is an operating lease. Lease payments related to operating leases are expensed when paid. Capital leases are recorded at their present value on the lessee's books as both an asset and a liability.

KEY TERMS

Adjunct account	Lessor
Bond	Market interest rate
Bond indentures	Mortgage
Convertible bonds	Nominal interest rate
Coupon bonds	Off-balance-sheet financing
Denomination	Serial bonds
Early extinguishment of debt	Sinking fund
Effective-interest method	Stated interest rate
Effective interest rate	Term bonds
Lease	Unsecured bonds
Lessee	Yield rate

PROBLEM FOR YOUR REVIEW

On January 2, 1988, the Garvey Corporation issued $200,000, 14%, ten-year term bonds. The bonds were issued at a premium to yield 12%. The issue price was 111.4699, and the bonds pay interest every January 2 and July 1.

REQUIRED: **1.** Make the entry to record the issue of the bonds on January 2, 1988.

2. Make the entry to record the first interest payment on July 1 and premium amortization, assuming that:

  (a) straight-line amortization is used.

  (b) effective-interest amortization is used.

3. If the Garvey Corporation has an August 31 year-end, make the appropriate entries at August 31, 1988, assuming that:

  (a) straight-line amortization is used.

  (b) effective-interest amortization is used.

4. The Garvey Corporation repurchased all bonds on January 2, 1991, at a price of 107. Assume that all interest payments and premium amortization for January 2, 1991 have been made and that the firm uses the straight-line method of amortization.

5. (Optional if present-value techniques are used.) Using present-value techniques, prove that the carrying value of the bonds on July 1, 1988, after the premium is amortized using the effective-interest method, is equal to the present value of the future cash outflows on that date.

SOLUTION
(1) JANUARY 2, 1988

Cash	222,940	
Premium on Bonds Payable		22,940
Bonds Payable		200,000

To record issuance of $200,000 bonds at a price of 111.4699.

	$200,000
	× 1.114699
Issue Price	$222,940
Face Value	− 200,000
Premium	$ 22,940

(2) JULY 1, 1988 **(a) STRAIGHT-LINE METHOD**	Interest Expense	12,853
	Premium on Bonds Payable	1,147
	Cash	14,000

To record interest payment and premium amortization on a straight-line basis, calculated as follows:

Cash Interest $200,000
                × .07
                $ 14,000

Premium Amortization

$$\frac{\$22,940}{20 \text{ interest periods}} = \$1,147 \text{ per period}$$

(b) EFFECTIVE-INTEREST METHOD	Interest Expense	13,376
	Premium on Bonds Payable	624
	Cash	14,000

To record interest payment and premium amortization on effective-interest basis, calculated as follows:

Carrying Value 1/2/88	$222,940
Yield Rate	.06
Effective Interest	$ 13,376
Cash Interest	14,000
Premium Amortization	(624)
Carrying Value 1/2/88	222,940
Carrying Value 7/1/88	$222,316

(3) 8/31/88—YEAR-END ACCRUALS (2 MONTHS FROM 7/1 to 8/31/88) **(a) STRAIGHT-LINE METHOD**	Interest Expense	4,285
	Premium on Bonds Payable	382
	Interest Payable	4,667

To record 2 months' interest accrual and premium amortization, calculated as follows:

Interest Payable = $200,000 × .07 × $\frac{2}{6}$ = $4,667
  Premium Amortization = $1,147 × $\frac{2}{6}$ = (382)
Interest Expense $4,285

(b) EFFECTIVE-INTEREST METHOD	Interest Expense	4,446
	Premium on Bonds Payable	221
	Interest Payable	4,667

To record 2 month's interest accrual and premium amortization, calculated as follows:

Carrying Value 7/1/88	$222,316	(see Item 2 above)
Yield Rate	.06	
	13,339*	
Two-months' Adjustment	× $\frac{2}{6}$	
Interest Expense	$ 4,446	
Interest Payable	4,667	
Premium on Bonds Payable	$ 221	

*Rounded to whole dollars.

**(4) 1/2/91
REPURCHASE
OF BONDS**

Bonds Payable	200,000	
Premium Bonds Payable	16,058	
Extraordinary Gain		2,058
Cash		214,000

To record repurchase of bonds at 107. Gain, which is extraordinary, is calculated as follows:

Carrying Value of Bonds on 1/2/91

Face Value	$200,000	
Unamortized Premium		
(see T account, below)	16,058	
	216,058	
Repurchase Price	214,000	
Gain	$ 2,058	

Premium on Bonds Payable

7/1/88	1,147	1/2/88	22,940
1/2/89	1,147		
7/1/89	1,147		
1/2/90	1,147		
7/1/90	1,147		
1/2/91	1,147		
	6,882		
		1/2/91	16,058

Note: This T account ignores year-end accruals and records just the January 2 entries.

(5) As of July 1, 1988, there are 19 interest periods remaining. The cash flows, discounted at 6% for 19 periods, equal $222,316, the carrying value of the bonds on that date. The calculations are:

Present value of $200,000 to be received at the end of 19 periods at 6% semiannually ($200,000 × .33051)	$ 66,103
Present value of $14,000 semiannual interest payments ($200,000 × .07) to be received at end of each of the next 19 periods ($14,000 × 11.1581)	156,213
Total	$222,316

QUESTIONS

1. What is a term bond? Describe the common features of bonds.

2. Define the following terms regarding bonds:
   (a) Face value.
   (b) Maturity value.
   (c) Maturity date.
   (d) Stated interest rate.
   (e) Market interest rate.

3. Describe the following types of bonds:
   (a) Serial bonds.
   (b) Term bonds.
   (c) Bearer bonds.
   (d) Coupon bonds.
   (e) Debentures.
   (f) Convertible bonds.

4. What are written convenants, and why are they included in certain bond agreements?

5. Several months ago, you purchased a $1,000, 8% bond of the Marlow Corporation at a price of 102. You recently looked in the paper and noticed that the latest price was 98.
   (a) How much did you pay for the bond?
   (b) How much interest will you receive every six months?
   (c) If you sold the bond today, how much would you receive? (Assume all interest has been paid.)

6. What factors are considered in setting the stated rate of interest on a bond? How does this stated rate affect the bond's issue price?

7. One of your fellow students does not understand how a bond with a stated rate of interest of 10% set by management can be issued at a discount. Explain how this can happen.

8. Explain the relationship among the stated interest rate, the market interest rate, and the price at which the bond is issued.

9. Several years ago the Newburyport Corporation issued bonds with a stated interest rate of 12%, which approximated the market rate at the time. However, in recent years, interest rates in the economy have fallen to about 8%. What effect will this have on the current price of the bond? Why?

10. What is the proper method of presenting bonds payable and any related premium or discount on the balance sheet?

11. Recently, the Diome Corporation issued 100 $1,000, 8% bonds at 98. Were the bonds issued at a premium or a discount, and what is the amount of that premium or discount? How much cash did the firm receive from the issue? (Assume the bonds were issued on an interest date.)

12. The Jiffy Computer Corporation recently issued $100,000 of 10% bonds at 103. Interest is paid semiannually. The bonds were issued on an interest date.

(a) Were the bonds issued at a premium or a discount?

(b) How much cash did the company receive from the issue?

(c) What was the amount of interest expense in the first six-month period, assuming the firm uses the straight-line method of amortization and the bond will mature in ten years?

13. Describe the straight-line amortization method and the effective-interest amortization method. Which method is considered preferable?

14. What are bond issue costs, and how are they handled under current accounting practices?

15. What is a bond sinking fund, and what is its purpose?

16. In some situations, notes are issued with no interest rate or with an interest rate that is unreasonably low. Under current accounting practices, how should these notes be handled?

17. Define leases and describe the different types.

18. Many individuals consider capital leases to be essentially purchases. Why? In answering the question, also include the characteristics of capital leases.

19. Why would a business wish to classify a lease as an operating lease rather than as a capital lease?

20. The Always Late Delivery Company recently leased one of its trucks. Under the terms of the lease, the company had to make monthly payments of $500 for the next five years. At the end of the lease term, Always Late can purchase the truck for $100. What type of lease is this, and why?

EXERCISES *

E1. **The Issuance of Bonds.** The Rugless Corporation issued $1 million of bonds on an interest date at a price of 105.

(a) Determine the total cash the company received from the bond issue.

(b) Did the bonds sell at par, at a discount, or at a premium?

(c) Make the journal entry to record the issue of the bonds.

E2. **Recording the Issuance of Bonds.** On January 2, 1989, the Alpha Beta Corporation issued $100,000 of ten-year term bonds with a stated rate of interest of 14%. The bonds pay interest semiannually on January 2 and July 1. At the time of the issue, the current market interest rate was also 14%. Prepare the necessary journal entries to record:

(a) The issue of the bond on January 2, 1989.

(b) The interest payment on July 1, 1989.

(c) The necessary adjusting entry on December 31, 1989—the firm's year-end.

(d) The interest payment on January 2, 1990.

*Note: Unless otherwise indicated, assume that all premiums and discounts are amortized at each interest date and at each adjustment date.

E3. **Bonds Issued between Interest Dates.** The Homestead Corporation issued $100,000 of 20-year, 9% term bonds on March 1, 1989. The bonds were issued at par and pay interest semiannually every January 2 and July 1. Prepare the necessary journal entries to record:

(a) The issuance of the bonds on March 1, 1989.

(b) The interest payment on July 1, 1989.

(c) The adjusting entry on December 31, 1989—the firm's year-end.

E4. **Issue of Bonds Not at Face Value.** On January 2, 1989, Vacation Cruises sold ten-year term bonds with a face value of $250,000. The bonds had a stated interest rate of 13%, payable semiannually on January 2 and July 1. The bonds were sold to yield 15%, and were therefore issued at a price of $224,513.

(a) Prepare the journal entry to record the issuance of the bonds.

(b) Show how the bonds would be disclosed on the balance sheet immediately after their issue.

(c) Make the entry to record the interest payment on July 1, 1989. Assume that straight-line amortization is used.

(d) Show how the bonds would be disclosed on the balance sheet immediately after the interest payment on July 1, 1989.

E5. **Issue of Bonds Not at Face Value.** El Cholos Restaurants, a franchiser of Mexican restaurants, issued $100,000 of ten-year, 12% bonds on January 2, 1989. Interest is payable on January 2 and July 1. These bonds were issued to yield 10% and were sold at a price of $112,462.

(a) Prepare the journal entry to record the issuance of the bonds.

(b) Show how the bonds would be disclosed on the balance sheet immediately after their issue.

(c) Assuming the firm uses the straight-line amortization method, make the required journal entry to record the interest payment on July 1, 1989.

(d) Show how the bonds would be disclosed on the balance sheet on July 1, 1989, after the payment of the interest.

E6. **Effective Interest Method of Amortization.** Using the data from (a) Exercise 4 and (b) Exercise 5, prepare the journal entries to record the payment of interest on July 1, 1989 and the interest accrual on December 31, 1989, assuming the firms use the effective-interest method of amortization.

E7. **Bonds Issued between Interest Dates above Face Value.** On March 1, 1989, the Downing Manufacturing Corporation issued $200,000 of 12%, ten-year term bonds dated January 2, 1989. The bonds were issued to yield 14% and pay interest semiannually on January 2 and July 1. The bonds were issued at a price of 89.44389 net of the discount. The firm uses the straight-line method of amortization. Prepare the entries to record:

(a) the issuance of the bonds on March 1, 1989.

(b) the interest payment on July 1, 1989.

(c) the interest accrual on December 31, 1989—the firm's year-end.

E8. **Early Extinguishment of Bonds.** On January 2, 1986, South Central Airlines issued $500,000 of 20-year, 12% bonds at 102. The bonds pay interest every January 2 and July 1. On July 1, 1989, immediately after the interest payment, the bonds were called at a price of 105. The firm uses the straight-line method of amortization. Prepare the journal entries at:

(a) January 2, 1986—the date of issue.

(b) July 1, 1989—to record the interest payment and premium amortization.

(c) July 1, 1989—to record the extinguishment of the bonds.

E9. **Conversion of Bonds.** On April 1, 1987, the Orwell Company issued $100,000 of 8%, five-year convertible bonds at 98. The bonds pay interest every April 1 and October 1. Each bond is convertible into five shares of capital stock. On April 1, 1990, immediately after the required interest payment, all the bonds were converted into capital stock. Make the required entries to record:

(a) the issuance of the bonds.

(b) the interest payment on April 1, 1990 (using straight-line amortization).

(c) the conversion of the bonds into capital stock.

E10. Investment in Bonds. On March 1, 1989, the Vargo Specialty Manufacturing Company purchased $15,000 of 12%, five-year bonds. The bonds were dated January 1, 1989. They pay interest semiannually on January 2 and July 1. The company purchased the bonds for $16,160. Straight-line amortization is used. Prepare the journal entries to:

(a) record the initial investment on March 1.

(b) record the receipt of the first interest collection on July 1.

(c) Assume that the company sold the bonds at 104 on April 1, 1990. Make the entry to record the sale.

E11. Non-interest-bearing Notes. The Fargo Corporation purchased a new piece of equipment from the Soong Company on July 1, 1988. The Soong Company accepted a non-interest-bearing note that is payable in four equal installments of $14,415, beginning on July 1, 1989. The cash-equivalent price of the equipment is $42,000, which means that there is an implicit interest rate of 14%.

REQUIRED: **(a)** Prepare the journal entry to record the purchase of the equipment on July 1, 1988.

(b) What is the amount of interest expense that should be recognized from this transaction during 1988?

(c) Assuming that the equipment is to be depreciated on the straight-line basis over five years, prepare the journal entry to record the depreciation for 1988. Assume that the firm takes a full year's depreciation in the year of purchase and that there is no salvage value.

(d) Why would it be incorrect to record the equipment at the sum of the total of the four payments of $14,415 each? What effect will there be on matching income and expense if the equipment is recorded in this manner?

E12. Accounting for Leases. On January 2, 1989, the Rainbow Company entered into a ten-year lease with the IQ Computer Co. to lease one of their new computers. The Rainbow Company agreed to make ten equal annual payments of $10,619, beginning on December 31, 1989.

(a) Assuming that the lease is properly recorded as an operating lease, prepare the necessary journal entry to record the first yearly payment.

(b) Again, assuming that the lease is properly recorded as an operating lease, how much expense will the firm record on its books relative to this lease over its ten-year life?

(c) Now assume that the lease is properly recorded as a capital lease with a present value of $60,000 based on a 12% interest rate. Make the entry to record the lease on January 2, 1989 and the first payment on December 31, 1989.

(d) Again, assuming that the lease is properly recorded as a capital lease, how much expense will the firm record relative to the lease over its ten-year life? Assume that the computer is depreciated on a straight-line basis over a ten-year useful life with no salvage value.

(e) Compare and contrast the effects on the firm's financial statements over the ten-year period if the lease is recorded as a capital lease rather than as an operating lease.

E13. Accounting for Capital Leases. On January 2, 1989, the Buchanon Company leased a small building from Sun Dance Properties, Inc. The Buchanon Company agreed to make annual lease payments of $12,369 on December 31, 1989 and for the following nine years (a total of ten payments). Assume that the lease has a present value of $76,000 based on a 10% interest rate. The Buchanon Company estimates that the building will have an eight-year life and will use straight-line depreciation with no salvage value.

REQUIRED: **(a)** Prepare the necessary journal entries to record the lease for the Buchanon Company on January 2, 1989 and the first payment on December 31, 1989. Include the entry for the recognition of the depreciation expense related to the lease.

(b) How would the building and the related lease liability be shown on the December 31, 1989 balance sheet of the Buchanon Company?

E14. Analysis Relating to Bond Amortization. On January 2, 1988, the Old Time Brewer Co. issued $100,000 of 12%, 20-year bonds at a price of 86.667 that resulted in a 14% yield. The bonds pay interest semiannually on January 2 and July 1.

REQUIRED: **(a)** How much cash did the firm receive from the issue of the bonds?

(b) Assuming the firm uses the straight-line method of amortizing any discount or premium:

1. How much cash did the firm expend for interest from January 2, 1988 to January 2, 1989?
2. How much interest expense did the firm incur from January 2, 1988 to January 2, 1989?
3. How much interest expense did the firm incur because of the bond over its 20-year life?

(c) Assuming that the firm uses the effective-interest method of amortizing any discount or premium:

1. How much cash did the firm expend for interest from January 2, 1988 to January 2, 1989?
2. How much interest expense did the firm incur from January 2, 1988 to January 2, 1989?
3. How much interest expense did the firm incur because of the bond over its 20-year life?

E15. Determining the Price of a Bond. (Requires present-value calculations.) On January 2, 1989, the Whodunit Corporation issued $200,000 of ten-year, 8% bonds to yield 10%. The bonds pay interest semiannually on January 2 and July 1.

REQUIRED: **(a)** Make the entry to record the issuance of the bonds on January 2, 1989.

(b) Assuming that the firm uses the straight-line method of amortization, make the required entry at July 1, 1989.

(c) Assuming that the firm uses the effective-interest method of amortization, make the required entry at July 1, 1989.

E16. Determining the Price of a Bond. (Requires present-value calculations.) The Bendot Corporation issued $300,000 of five-year, 12% bonds on July 1, 1988, to yield 10%. Interest is payable semiannually on July 1 and January 2.

REQUIRED: **(a)** Make the entry to record the issuance of these bonds on July 1, 1988.

(b) Assuming the firm uses the straight-line amortization method, make the required entries at January 2, 1989. The firm's year-end is June 30.

(c) Assuming the firm uses the effective-interest method of amortization, make the required entries at January 2, 1989.

E17. Determining Bond Prices. (Requires present-value calculations.) The Brocolli Alfalfa Corporation has decided to issue $500,000 of 9%, ten-year bonds payable. The firm's policy has been to use the straight-line method of amortization. The bonds were issued on January 2, 1990 and pay interest on January 2 and July 1.

REQUIRED: **(a)** How much cash would the firm receive if the bonds were issued:

1. at par?
2. to yield 10%?
3. to yield 8%?

(b) Show how the bonds would be listed on the firm's December 31, 1990 balance sheet under each of the above issue prices.

E18. Determining the Discount. (Requires present-value calculations.) The Brett Corporation issued $100,000 of ten-year, 9% term bonds to yield 12% on January 2 of the current year. Interest is payable semiannually on July 1 and January 2. Using present-value techniques, directly determine the amount of the discount.

E19. Accounting for Notes Payable. (Requires present-value calculations.)

(a) The following example was provided on page 455: On January 2, 1989, the Ng Corporation agrees to purchase a custom piece of equipment. The agreement calls for the Ng Corporation to make three equal payments of $6,245 at the end of the next three years. No interest is provided for in the agreement. The cash purchase price is $15,000.

REQUIRED: Prove that the implied interest rate is 12%.

(b) The following example was provided on page 456: On January 2, 1989, the Grant Corporation purchases a small building for $1 million and makes a down payment of $200,000. The mortgage is payable monthly over 30 years, at an annual interest rate of 12%. You have determined the following interest factors for 1% and 360 periods:

Future value of single amount	35.9496
Present value of a single amount	0.0278
Future value of an annuity	3494.9641
Present value of an annuity	97.2183

REQUIRED: Prove that the monthly mortgage payment is $8,229.

E20. Accounting for Mortgages. On January 1, 1991, the Caster Corp. purchased a building for $500,000. The firm made a 20% down payment and took out a 10% mortgage payable over 30 years at a rate of $3,510.29 monthly. The first payment is due February 1, 1991.

REQUIRED: **(a)** Make the entry to record the purchase of the equipment.

(b) Make the entries to record the first two mortgage payments on February 1 and March 1.

E21. Accounting for Notes Payable. The DeFond Group purchased a mainframe computer on January 1, 1990. The purchase agreement calls for the DeFond Group to make five equal payments of $13,189.87 at the end of each of the next five years. If the item had been purchased outright for cash, it would have cost $50,000. Although no interest is specified in the agreement, a fair interest rate would be 10%.

REQUIRED: **(a)** Make the entry to record the purchase of the equipment on January 1, 1990.

(b) Make the entry to record the first two note payments on December 31, 1990 and December 31, 1991.

E22. Toys "R" Us Financial Statements. Refer to the financial statements of Toys "R" Us in Appendix D to answer the following questions:

(a) What types of leases has Toys "R" Us entered into?

(b) What is the total amount of the liability, if any, recorded for lease obligations for year-end 1988?

(c) What is the total rental expense recorded for leases for year-end 1988?

(d) Assuming that no leases are canceled or other lease agreements entered into, what is the estimate of lease rentals for year-end 1989?

PROBLEMS

P12–1 Accounting for Bonds. The Hemsted Corporation is considering issuing bonds and has asked your advice concerning several matters. The firm plans to issue $500,000 of 20-year 10% bonds. Bond interest payments are on April 1 and October 1. The firm has a December 31 year-end.

REQUIRED: **(a)** If the bonds are issued on April 1 at a price of 91.977 to yield 11%, how much cash will the firm receive? Explain to the president of the corporation the difference in interest expense the firm will incur during the first year if the effective-interest method of amortization rather than the straight-line method is used. How will the firm's cash flow be affected in the first year?

(b) If the bonds are issued on April 1 at a price of 109.201 to yield 9%, how much cash will the firm receive? Explain to the president of the corporation the difference in interest expense the firm will incur during the first year if the effective-interest method rather than the straight-line method of amortization is used. How will the firm's cash flow be affected in the first year?

(c) If the bonds are issued on June 1 at par, how much cash will the firm receive? Determine for the president the amount of interest expense the firm will incur relative to the bonds for the period between June 1 and April 1 of the following year. Ignore the 12/31 year-end.

P12–2   Bond Transactions—Straight-line Amortization. At the beginning of 1989, the long-term debt section of the China Export Corporation's balance sheet appeared as follows:

10% bonds payable	$200,000
Premium on bonds payable	3,600
	$203,600

The bonds were issued on January 2, 1988 and will mature in ten years from that date. The firm uses the straight-line method of amortization for bond issues. Interest on these bonds is payable semiannually on January 2 and July 1. During 1989 and 1990, the following transactions regarding bonds took place.

- January 2, 1989: The interest payment on the 10% bonds was made. Assume that the company has a December 31 year-end and that all proper accruals were made at that time.
- March 1, 1989: The firm issued $100,000 of 8%, ten-year bonds dated February 1 at 97. The bonds pay interest semiannually on February 1 and August 1 of every year.
- July 1, 1989: The interest payment on the 10% bonds was made, and the premium was amortized.
- August 1, 1989: The interest payment on the 8% bonds was made, and the discount was amortized.
- December 31, 1989: The firm's year-end, and all interest accruals must be made.
- January 2, 1990: The interest payment on the 10% bonds was made.
- February 1, 1990: The interest payment on the 8% bonds was made, and the discount was amortized.
- July 1, 1990: Immediately after the interest payment was made on the 10% bonds, they were called at a price of 104.
- August 1, 1990: The interest payment on the 8% bonds was made, and the discount was amortized.
- December 31, 1990: Year-end interest accruals were made.

REQUIRED: (a) Make the necessary journal entries for 1989 and 1990.

(b) Prepare the long-term debt section of the firm's balance sheet at December 31, 1989 and 1990.

(c) Make the entry to record the last interest payment on the 8% bonds and their repayment at maturity.

P12–3   Bond Transactions—Straight-line Amortization. At the beginning of 1990, the long-term debt section of Julia International, Inc. appeared as follows:

8% bonds payable	$300,000
Less: Discount on bonds payable	4,800
	$295,200

The bonds were issued on January 2, 1988 and mature in ten years from that date. The firm uses the straight-line method of amortization for all bond issues. Interest on these bonds is payable semiannually on January 2 and July 1. During 1990 and 1991, the following transactions relative to bonds took place:

- January 2, 1990: The interest payment on the 8% bonds was made.
- April 1: The firm issued $500,000 of 10%, ten-year bonds at 104. The bonds pay interest semiannually on April 1 and October 1.
- July 1: The interest payment on the 8% bonds was made, and the discount was amortized.

- October 1: The interest payment on the 10% bonds was made, and the premium was amortized.
- December 31: The firm's year-end and all interest accruals are made.
- January 2, 1991: The interest payment on the 8% bonds was made.
- April 1: The interest payment on the 10% bonds was made, and the premium was amortized.
- July 1: Immediately after the interest payment was made on the 8% bonds, they were called at a price of 99.
- October 1: The interest payment on the 10% bonds was made and the premium was amortized.
- December 31: The firm's year-end and all interest accruals are made.

REQUIRED: **(a)** Make the necessary journal entries for 1990 and 1991 to record these events.

(b) Prepare the long-term debt section of the firm's balance sheet at December 31, 1990 and 1991.

(c) Make the entry to record the last interest payment on the 10% bonds and their repayment at maturity.

P12–4 **Bond Transactions—Effective-interest Amortization.** The AB-Smith Corporation is about to undertake a major business expansion. On July 1, 1989, the firm issued $100,000 of 10% bonds to yield 11%. As a result, the issue price was $94,025. The bonds mature on July 1, 1999 and pay interest semiannually on July 1 and January 2. The firm uses the effective-interest method of amortization. The long-term debt section of the firm's December 31, 1989 balance sheet appeared as follows:

Long-term debt	
10% bonds payable	$100,000
Less: Unamortized discount	5,804
	$ 94,196

During 1990 and 1991, the following events occurred regarding bonds:

- January 2: The firm's year-end is December 31. The interest accrual made on that date for the 10% bonds was paid.
- July 1: The semiannual interest payment on the 10% bonds was made, and the discount was amortized.
- September 1: The firm issued $500,000 of 10% bonds at 106.5040 to yield 9%. The bonds mature in ten years and pay interest every September 1 and March 1.
- December 31: Year-end interest accruals and amortizations were made.
- January 2, 1991: The interest payment on the $100,000 bonds was made.
- March 1: The interest payment on the $500,000 bonds was made, and the proper amount of premium was amortized.
- July 1: The interest payment on the $100,000 bonds was made, and the proper amount of discount was amortized. Immediately thereafter, all of these bonds were called at a price of 101.
- September 1: The interest payment on the $500,000 was made, and the proper amount of premium was amortized.
- December 31: The proper interest accruals and amortizations were made at year-end.

REQUIRED: **(a)** Prepare the journal entries to record the above transactions.

(b) Prepare the long-term debt section of the firm's balance sheet at December 31, 1990 and 1991.

P12–5 **Bond Transactions—Effective-interest Amortization.** Bill Smith and Associates needs additional financing in order to begin a new product line. The board of directors authorizes the company to issue $400,000 of 10% bonds on September 1, 1990. The bonds mature on September 1, 2000 and pay interest semiannually on September 1 and March 1. Because of market conditions, the bonds were issued to yield 12%. The firm uses the effective-interest method of amortization for all bond issues. The long-term debt section of the firm's balance sheet at December 31, 1990 appears as follows:

10% bonds payable	$400,000
Less: Discount on bonds payable	45,050
	$354,950

During 1991 and 1992, the following events relative to the bonds occurred:

■ March 1, 1991: The interest payment on the $400,000 10% bonds was made, and the discount was amortized.

■ July 1: The firm issued $200,000 of 10% bonds at 113.59 to yield 8%. The bonds mature in ten years and pay interest on January 2 and July 1.

■ September 1: The interest payment on the $400,000 10% bonds was made, and the discount was amortized.

■ December 31: The firm's year-end and interest accruals and amortizations were made.

■ January 2, 1992: The interest payment on the $200,000 10% bonds was made.

■ March 1: The interest payment on the $400,000 10% bonds was made, and the discount was amortized.

■ July 1: The interest payment on the $200,000 10% bonds was made, and the premium was amortized.

■ September 1: The interest payment on the $400,000 10% bonds was made, and the discount was amortized. Immediately thereafter, all the bonds were called at a price of 95.

■ December 31: The firm's year-end and interest accruals and amortizations were made.

REQUIRED: **(a)** Prepare the journal entries to record the above bond transactions during 1991 and 1992.

(b) Prepare the long-term debt section of the firm's balance sheet at December 31, 1991 and 1992.

P12–6 Interest Amortization Tables. On January 2, 1990, the Peacock Corporation issued $500,000 of five-year bonds. The bonds have a stated rate of interest of 10% and were issued at 107.986 to yield 8%. Interest is payable *annually* on January 2 of each year.

REQUIRED: Prepare an amortization table for the bonds similar to Exhibits 12-10 and 12-14, assuming that (a) the straight-line method of premium amortization is used and (b) the effective-interest method of premium amortization is used. You should use the following headings for your table:

(a) Date.

(b) Carrying value of the bonds at the beginning of the period.

(c) Cash interest paid.

(d) Interest expense.

(e) Premium amortization.

(f) Unamortized premium at the end of the period.

(g) Carrying value of the bonds at the end of the period.

P12–7 Bond Analysis. The accountant for J.C. Lee Enterprises prepared an amortization table for a $500,000, ten-year bond issue. The interest payments are made on March 1 and September 1.

Date	Interest Expense	Interest Paid	Amorti-zation	Unamortized Amount	Carrying Value of Bonds
3/1/89				$57,352	$442,648
9/1/89	$26,559	$25,000	$1,559	55,793	444,207
3/1/90	26,652	25,000	1,652	54,141	445,859

REQUIRED: **(a)** Were the bonds issued at a premium, at a discount, or at par?

(b) What is the stated rate of interest on the bonds?

(c) What interest rate were the bonds issued to yield?

(d) Is the firm using the straight-line or the effective-interest method of amortization? Explain the reasoning behind your answer.

(e) Continue the table through 9/1/91.

P12–8 **Investment in Bonds.** On May 1, 1989, the Price-Fischer Corporation issued $100,000 of five-year, 10% bonds dated January 2, 1989 at a price of 98. All of these bonds were purchased by Helen Chen. The bonds pay interest every July 1 and January 2.

REQUIRED: **(a)** Assuming that both Price-Fischer and Chen use the straight-line method of interest amortization, make the entries for these bonds for both Price-Fischer and Chen through January 2, 1990. Assume that both parties have a December 31 year-end.

(b) On July 1, 1990, after the interest payment, Price-Fischer calls one-half of the bonds at a price of 102. Make the entries to record this event on the books of both Price-Fischer and Chen.

P12–9 **Mortgage and Note Payable Transactions.** During 1989, the West Corporation entered into the following transactions:

- January 2: The corporation agrees to purchase a specially made piece of equipment from the Gernon Co. Under the terms of the agreement, West agrees to make five annual payments of $16,645, beginning on December 31, 1989. No interest is stated in the agreement. However, you have determined that the cash purchase price of the equipment is $60,000, which means that there is an implicit interest rate of 12%.

- April 1: The corporation borrows $100,000 from the local bank. The loan is payable in full in five years. Interest of 10% is payable annually on April 1.

- December 31: The firm purchased a building for $600,000. A $100,000 down payment was made, and a 30-year mortgage was taken out for the remaining $500,000. Under the terms of the mortgage, payments of $71,408 are to be made annually for 30 years, beginning on December 31, 1990. The mortgage has a stated interest rate of 14%.

REQUIRED: **(a)** Make the journal entries for these notes and mortgages for 1989 and 1990. Assume that the firm has a December 31 year-end.

(b) Assuming that these are the firm's only long-term liabilities and that the only recorded short-term payables other than interest are accounts payable of $20,000, prepare the liability section of the firm's December 31, 1989 balance sheet.

P12–10 **Leases.** On January 2, 1988, the Wakefield Corporation leased a building to the Migglin Corporation. The lease agreement is for 20 years, cannot be canceled, and has the following terms:

(a) Annual rental payments are $100,000 and are due on December 31 of each year.

(b) The building has an estimated useful life of 25 years with no salvage value. If appropriate, straight-line depreciation will be used.

(c) Assuming that 10% is an appropriate interest rate, the present value of the required lease payments is $851,400. The building has an estimated fair market value of $900,000.

REQUIRED: **(a)** Is this lease an operating or a capital lease? Explain your reasoning.

(b) Assuming the lease is a capital lease, make the necessary journal entries on the books of the Migglin Corporation for 1988 and 1989.

(c) Assuming the lease is an operating lease, make the necessary journal entries on the books of the Migglin Corporation for 1988 and 1989.

(d) Prepare a table similar to Exhibit 12-19 to compare expense patterns of the capital lease versus the operating lease for the first five years of the lease.

(e) If you were part of Migglin's management, would you prefer to account for the lease as a capital lease or an operating lease? Why? What choice do you have?

P12–11 Determining Bond Prices. (Requires present-value calculations.) The Zentos Corporation issued $400,000 of five-year, 9% bonds to yield 10%. The bonds were issued on April 1, 1989 and pay interest every April 1 and October 1.

REQUIRED: (a) Compute the issue price, and determine the amount of any discount or premium.

(b) Make the journal entry to record the issuance of the bonds.

(c) Prepare an amortization table for the term of the bonds using the effective-interest method of amortization. Use a form similar to Exhibit 12-12 or 12-14.

(d) Using present-value techniques, independently determine the carrying value of the bonds on April 1, 1990, as shown in the amortization table.

(e) Assume that the firm retired the bonds on April 1, 1991 at a price of 102. Make the entry to record the interest payment and the amortization on that date, and then the entry to record the retirement of the bonds.

P12–12 Determining Bond Prices. (Requires present-value calculations.) The Bradfield Corporation issued $1 million of five-year, 14% bonds to yield 12%. The bonds were issued on January 2, 1990 and pay interest every January 2 and July 1.

REQUIRED: (a) Compute the issue price, and determine the amount of any discount or premium.

(b) Make the journal entry to record the issuance of the bonds.

(c) Prepare an amortization table for the term of the bonds, using the effective-interest method of amortization. Use a form similar to Exhibit 12-12 or 12-14.

(d) Using present-value techniques, independently determine the carrying value of the bonds on July 1, 1991, as shown in the amortization table.

(e) Assume that the firm retired the bonds on July 1, 1992 at a price of 104. Make the entry to record the interest payment and the amortization on that date, and then make the entry to record the retirement of the bonds.

P12–13 Notes and Leases. (Requires present-value calculations.) The Grosse Corporation entered into the following transactions during 1988:

■ January 2, 1988: The firm signed an agreement with the Peritt Company to purchase a specially designed graphic printer. Under the terms of the agreement, Grosse agreed to make five annual payments of $24,000, beginning on December 31, 1988. The agreement did not mention any interest, and because the printer is specially made, there is no cash-equivalent price. Grosse was recently able to negotiate a loan with the local bank for 12%.

■ December 31, 1988: The firm signed a lease on a building that will be used to house its corporate offices. The terms of lease call for 30 annual payments of $40,000 to be made at the end of each year, beginning on December 31, 1989. The lessor determined the annual lease payments in order to guarantee a return of 12%. The lease should be recorded as a capital lease.

REQUIRED: Make the appropriate entries for each of these transactions for 1988 and 1989. Assume that the firm has a December 31 year-end. (Ignore depreciation and amortization.)

■ USING THE COMPUTER

P12–14 The Carey Corporation borrowed $250,000 at 15%. The note is to be repaid in 60 equal monthly installments, beginning at the end of the first month. Using an electronic spreadsheet, prepare a loan amortization table similar to Exhibit 12-17. Use the spreadsheet feature to determine the monthly payment. Use the following format:

	Loan Amortization Table			
	Data Entry Area			
	Principal: $250,000			
	Interest: 15%			
	Term: 60 months			
Month	**Total Payment**	**Interest Portion**	**Principal Portion**	**Carrying Value of Mortgage**

Now repeat the amortization schedule, assuming that the interest is only 12%.

P12–15 The Star Gazer Corporation issued $700,000 of ten-year, 14% term bonds to yield 12%. Interest is payable semiannually on January 2, the issue date, and July 1. Using an electronic spreadsheet, prepare a premium amortization table similar to Exhibit 12-14. Use the same column headings.

■ UNDERSTANDING FINANCIAL STATEMENTS

P12–16 A note taken from the 1988 financial statement of Bell Atlantic follows. Based on this note, answer these questions:

1. For 1988, how much of the total long-term debt will be shown as current? As long-term?

2. The net unamortized discount and premium is $133.7 million. Is this net a discount or a premium?

3. Explain the difference between the debentures and mortgage and installment notes.

BELL ATLANTIC
Long-term Debt
(dollars in millions)
December 31, 1988

			1988	1987
Communications and related services	**Interest Rates**	**Maturities**		
Telephone subsidiaries' debentures	$2\frac{3}{4}\%-7\frac{1}{2}\%$	1989–2013	$1,702.0	$1,757.0
	$7\frac{3}{4}\%-8\frac{7}{8}\%$	2006–2026	1,630.0	1,630.0
	$9\%-11\frac{3}{8}\%$	1992–2026	1,855.0	1,870.0
			5,187.0	5,257.0
Unamortized discount and premium, net			(133.7)	(144.7)
Capital lease obligations—average rate 10.6% and 10.5%			122.6	124.6
Other			57.4	35.8
Total			5,233.3	5,272.7
Financial and real estate services	**Interest Rates**	**Maturities**		
Notes payable	$5\frac{4}{5}\%-10\frac{9}{10}\%$	1989–1997	1,523.0	1,248.2
Mortgage and installment notes	$7\frac{3}{4}\%-17\%$	1989–2011	211.6	320.3
Non-recourse notes	$8\%-18\frac{1}{4}\%$	1989–2003	73.2	56.6
Subordinated notes	—	—	—	26.8
Capital lease obligations—average rate 10.0% and 9.8%			46.4	78.9
			1,854.2	1,730.8
Less: Maturing within one year			530.3	262.0
Total			$6,557.2	$6,741.5

■ FINANCIAL DECISION CASE

P12–17 (Requires present-value calculations.) On January 2, 1978, the Lafler Corporation issued $600,000 of 20-year, 8% bonds to yield 10%. The bonds pay interest semiannually on January 2 and July 1. By January 2, 1988, interest rates in the economy had risen, and current market rates for investments of risk similar to that of the Lafler Corporation were 12%. As a result, the current aggregate market value of the bonds on January 2, 1988 ($500,000) was below their carrying value. The president of the firm is considering repurchasing all these bonds in the open market at that price. However, to do that the firm will have to issue new 30-year bonds with a stated rate of interest of 12%. Bonds with a face value of $500,000 would be issued at par. The president asks your advice on the feasibility of this proposed repurchase.

REQUIRED: **(a)** Determine the carrying value of the bonds on January 2, 1988. Assume that the firm uses the straight-line method of amortization.

(b) Make the journal entry to issue the new bonds and retire the old bonds. Make two separate journal entries.

(c) Is there a gain or a loss from the repurchase?

(d) Present to the president the economic factors that you think should be considered in this proposed repurchase.

CORPORATE ORGANIZATION AND CAPITAL STOCK TRANSACTIONS

LEARNING OBJECTIVES

After studying this chapter, you should be able to:

1. List the major characteristics of a corporation.
2. Explain how corporations are formed and organized.
3. List the characteristics of capital stock: common and preferred.
4. Discuss the components of stockholders' equity.
5. Make the journal entries for the issuance of capital stock.
6. Record treasury stock transactions and the retirement of capital stock.
7. Use stock information in making decisions.

Perhaps more than any other symbol, the corporation characterizes U.S. business. Although sole proprietorships and partnerships outnumber corporations, the corporation is the dominant form of organization in the United States. Most major businesses, other than service-oriented businesses such as large accounting and law firms, are organized as corporations. The purpose of this chapter is to introduce you to corporate organizations, their formation, and related capital stock transactions. The next chapter will discuss other issues related to corporations, such as retained earnings, dividend transactions, and corporate income statements.

CHARACTERISTICS OF A CORPORATION

A corporation is a separate legal entity, created by the state, owned by one or more persons, and having rights, privileges, and obligations that are distinct from those of its owners. A corporation may sue or be sued and may be taxed, just as an individual may. However, it does not go out of existence with the death of the owners or a change in ownership.

ADVANTAGES OF CORPORATIONS

A corporation has certain characteristics that give it advantages over business organizations in other forms. These advantages include limited liability for the shareholders, transferability of ownership, ease of capital formation, and professional management.

Limited Liability of the Shareholders

A corporation is responsible for its own obligations. Its creditors can look only to the assets of the corporation to satisfy their claims. The owners' total liability is generally limited to the amount they invested in the corporation. Thus, if you invested $5,000 in a corporation, your liability would be limited to that investment regardless of the debts the corporation might eventually incur. However, in many smaller corporations owned by families or a few individuals, the shareholders often are required to guarantee corporate loans from banks and other creditors.

Transferability of Ownership

Ownership in a corporation is evidenced by a share of stock. These shares are generally transferable without any restrictions. Large stock exchanges such as the New York and the American stock exchanges, as well as regional exchanges, exist to facilitate the exchange of stock between individuals. Once the stock of a corporation is issued, the corporation is not affected by subsequent stock transactions among individual shareholders, other than the fact that its list of shareholders will change.

Ease of Capital Formation

Limited liability and transferability of ownership make it relatively easier for a corporation to raise capital than for sole proprietorships and partnerships. Many individuals can invest small amounts of capital that, in total, will meet the capital needs of a major corporation. It is attractive to individuals to invest in corporations, because they know the amount of their total risk and are usually able to liquidate their investment when they desire.

Professional Management

In a large publicly held corporation, the owners generally have no direct management control. They give this control to the president and other senior officers of the corporation. This separation between ownership and control allows corporations to attract top-level professional management. In most sole proprietorships and partnerships, the owner is also the manager. An owner who has considerable engineering skills may not have the necessary management skills to operate a business successfully.

DISADVANTAGES OF CORPORATIONS

Some of the same corporate characteristics that provide advantages to incorporating may also result in some disadvantages. These disadvantages are especially relevant to smaller businesses.

Double Taxation

Double taxation is one of the major disadvantages of a corporation. The earnings of a corporation are subject to taxes up to 34%. When corporate earnings are distributed to stockholders in the form of dividends, these dividends are not deductible by the corporation but are taxable to the recipient. In effect, corporate earnings are taxed twice, once at the corporate level and again when distributed to the individual shareholder.

Government Regulation

Corporations are chartered by a state and thus must comply with various state and federal regulations. Several reports and documents must be filed with state and federal agencies. For smaller companies, the cost of complying with these regulations may outweigh the other benefits of the corporate form of business organization. Although government regulation applies to all forms of business enterprise, it is generally not as great for sole proprietorships and partnerships.

Limited Liability

For smaller companies, the limited liability feature of a corporation may be a disadvantage in raising capital. Because of this feature, creditors have claims against only the assets of a corporation. If a corporation defaults, the creditors have no recourse against the owners. As a result, loans from bankers and other creditors are often limited to the amount of security offered by the corporation. In other cases, the shareholders may have to sign an agreement pledging their personal assets as security.

In other situations, the owners of a small corporation may raise capital with the help of venture capitalists. A *venture capitalist* is an individual or group of individuals who provide capital to growing and emerging firms. In return for their capital, these individuals usually demand an equity position in the firm. Thus the original owners may have to give up their control of the corporation as the price of obtaining capital.

■ THE FORMATION AND ORGANIZATION OF A CORPORATION

The procedures to form a corporation and subsequently to conduct business are a function of state law; as you might expect, all states have somewhat different laws. For example, it has historically been easier to incorporate in some states (such as Delaware) than in other states (such as California). To a large extent, this has been because of the regulatory environment in California. The following discussion is thus based on the general procedures found in most states.

■ FORMING A CORPORATION

The first step in forming a corporation is for at least three individuals, generally the corporate president, vice-president, and secretary-treasurer, to file an application with the appropriate state official, often the secretary of state. Among the items included in the application are the articles of incorporation, which list:

1. the name and place of business of the corporation.
2. the main purpose of the business.
3. the names of the principal officers of the corporation.
4. the names of the original stockholders.
5. the type of stock to be issued; the number of authorized shares; their par value, if any; and their dividend and voting rights.

Once the articles of incorporation have been approved by the appropriate state official, they are referred to as the *corporate charter*.

ORGANIZATION COSTS

During the organization process, a corporation incurs certain costs, including filing and incorporation fees to the state, attorney's fees, promotion fees, printing and engraving fees, and similar items. These costs all are necessary to get the corporation started. Because they are considered to have future benefit, they are capitalized and are referred to as **organization costs**. They are usually listed in the Other Assets section of the balance sheet.

Although these costs benefit the corporation over its entire life (considered to be indefinite under the going-concern assumption), they are normally written off over a five-year period of time. This is because the income tax laws allow these costs to be written off over a minimum of five years. Accountants do not necessarily follow tax laws in setting accounting principles, but they do so in this case, because organization costs are usually not material.

ORGANIZING THE CORPORATION

Immediately after the corporation's charter is issued, the shareholders must organize the firm to conduct future business. A board of directors must be elected; it, in turn, appoints the new officers of the corporation. Corporate bylaws are drafted to establish rules of order for the operation of the new corporation. Exhibit 13-1, which presents a typical corporate organization chart, shows the relationship among the stockholders, the board of directors, and senior corporate management.

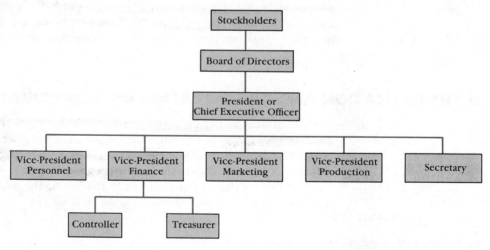

EXHIBIT 13–1

Typical Corporate Organization Chart

Stockholders

The stockholders are the owners of the corporation, and this ownership is evidenced by stock certificates. A sample stock certificate from The Thomson Corporation is reproduced in Exhibit 13-2. A stock certificate is a legal document that shows the number, type, and par value (if any) of the shares issued by the corporation. Stock certificates are serially numbered and may include other data required by state laws.

In large corporations, the shareholders do not participate in the day-to-day operation of the business. They elect the board of directors and vote on important issues at the annual stockholders' meeting. The **board of directors** is charged with establishing broad corporate policies and appointing senior corporate management. However, stockholders do have certain rights, which include:

EXHIBIT 13–2

A Share of Common Stock
in The Thomson
Corporation

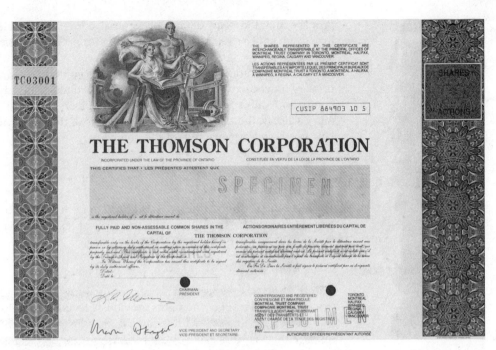

1. The right to attend all stockholders' meetings, to vote for the board of directors, and to vote on major corporate policies and decisions such as proposed mergers and consolidations. The number of votes is based on the number of shares owned. Stockholders who do not attend the meetings are able to vote through a proxy. A **proxy** gives another individual or individuals, usually the current management, the right to vote the shares in the manner they deem best.

2. The right to receive a proportionate share of all dividends declared by the board of directors.

3. The right to a proportionate share of remaining corporate assets upon the liquidation of the corporation. Remember that the stockholders' interest is a residual one and that they are only entitled to the remaining assets after all the claims of the creditors and other equity holders have been satisfied.

4. The preemptive right, which gives the existing stockholders the right to purchase shares from a new stock issue in proportion to the shares already owned. This right ensures that the ownership of the current stockholders is not diluted by the issuance of additional shares. To illustrate, assume that Mark Wilson owns 5% of the outstanding shares of the Ironside Corporation. If the corporation decides to issue 100,000 new shares, Mark Wilson will have the right to purchase 5,000 (100,000 × .05) additional shares. Of course, Wilson does not have to purchase these shares. Stockholders often waive this right in order to facilitate mergers that require the issuance of additional shares.

5. The right to dispose of or transfer their shares if and when they desire. In some situations, this right of free transferability is limited. Such limitations, if and when they exist, are clearly noted on the stock certificate.

The Board of Directors and Senior Management

The board of directors and the chairperson of the board are elected by the stockholders. The board usually consists of senior management and outside members. Outside members are individuals who are not otherwise employed by the company and thus are independent of senior management. In recent years, it has become commonplace for a majority of the board to be made up of such outside members. The board's primary function is to determine general corporate policies and to appoint senior management. The board is also charged with protecting the interest of stockholders and creditors.

The corporation's senior management is appointed by the board. Obviously, the primary function of senior management is to conduct the day-to-day operations of the company. Exhibit 13-1 shows some of the officers typically found in general management. Clearly, the designations and functions of these individuals depend on the specific needs and organization of the company.

TYPES OF CAPITAL STOCK

Throughout this book, the term *capital stock* has been used to refer to the stock issued by a corporation. In reality, there are at least two major types of capital stock: common stock and preferred stock.

COMMON STOCK

Common stock is capital stock that must be issued by all corporations. Common stockholders have all of the rights previously listed. Generally, because common stock is the only type of stock with voting rights, common stockholders control the corporation. However, they have only a residual interest in its net assets. This means that in the event of a corporate liquidation, common shareholders will not receive any assets until the claims of the creditors and the preferred stockholders are satisfied.

Some states allow different classes of common stock. For example, a corporation may issue Class A and Class B common stock. Depending on state laws and the corporate charter, Class A stock may be voting, whereas Class B is not. However, it is relatively rare for large, publicly held corporations to issue two classes of common stock.

PREFERRED STOCK

In addition to common stock, a corporation may issue a type of stock called *preferred stock*. Preferred stock does not necessarily mean better; the term *preferred* means that this type of stock has certain preferences over common stock. **Preferred stock** generally has the following preferences and characteristics:

1. Preference as to dividends.

2. Preference over common stockholders upon liquidation.

3. No voting rights.

4. Cumulative and callable.

Preferred Dividends

Preferred stock has a preference in regard to dividends, which means that the preferred stockholders must receive all of the dividends to which they are entitled before any dividends can be declared and paid to the common stockholders. Unlike common stock, preferred stock usually has the amount of its dividends stated on the stock certificate. This is done in one of two ways. The actual dollar amount of the dividend may be stated on the stock certificate. For example, one issue of preferred stock for USX is stated at $3.50 per share. This means that if a dividend is declared by the board of directors, each stockholder will receive a dividend of $3.50 per share. In the second case, the dividend is stated as a percentage of par value. *Par value* is a stated amount printed on the stock certificate. For example, Koppers, another publicly held corporation, has issued $100 par value, 4% preferred stock. This means that if and when dividends are declared, the preferred stockholder will receive an annual per-share dividend of $4, or 4% × $100. Because the amount of preferred dividends is stated, many individuals consider the stock more stable and less risky than common stock.

Cumulative versus Noncumulative Dividends

As previously noted, a corporation does not have to issue a dividend. Only when the board of directors declares a dividend does it become an actual liability of the corporation. Many issues of preferred stock are cumulative. This means that preferred stockholders do not lose their claim to undeclared dividends. The right to receive these undeclared dividends accumulates over time and must be fully paid before common stockholders can receive any dividends. This is an attractive feature, so most preferred issues are cumulative. Conversely, if the stock is noncumulative, any dividends not declared in the current year will lapse, and preferred stockholders will lose their claim to such dividends.

To demonstrate, assume that the Place Publishing Corporation issued 10,000 shares of $3 cumulative preferred stock. At the beginning of 1988, all stated preferred dividends for prior years had been declared and paid. During 1988, profits were down, so Place decided to declare only $20,000 of preferred dividends. As a result, there was a shortfall of $10,000, calculated as follows:

Required dividend, $3.00 × 10,000	$30,000
Dividends declared	20,000
Dividends in arrears	$10,000

This shortfall is called **dividends in arrears**. Although this $10,000 is not a liability of the Place Publishing Corporation, if dividends are declared the next year (1989), the dividends in arrears of $10,000 plus the 1989 preferred dividends of $30,000 must be paid before common stockholders will receive anything.

To continue the illustration, assume that in 1989, Place decided to declare total dividends of $75,000 to preferred and common stockholders. In this case, preferred stockholders would receive $40,000, and common stockholders would receive the residual of $35,000, calculated as follows:

Total dividend		$75,000
Preferred dividends		
Dividends in arrears	$10,000	
1989 current year's dividend	30,000	
Total to preferred stockholders		40,000
Total to common stockholders		$35,000

As previously noted, dividends in arrears are not liabilities of the corporation. However, full disclosure requires that any dividends in arrears be disclosed in the footnotes to the financial statements. For example, the following note was taken from an annual report of Western Airlines:

> The company has omitted payment of the quarterly dividends on the Series A (cumulative) Preferred Stock beginning the first quarter of 1982. The total amount of the dividends in arrears at January 1, 1984 was $4,785,000. Various loan agreements currently prohibit payment of dividends on preferred stock. Because more than six quarterly dividends have been omitted, holders of preferred stock have the right (unless all dividend arrearages have been cured) to elect two additional members to the Company's Board of Directors at the next annual meeting of the shareholders.

Participating versus Nonparticipating

In some situations, preferred stock has a participating feature. This means that in addition to the stated dividend, preferred stockholders can also participate with common shareholders in additional dividends. This participation feature can range from limited to full. When full participation exists, the common shareholders receive dividends at the same rate as preferred, and any excess dividends are split on a proportionate basis between common and preferred shareholders.

Most preferred stock, however, is not participating; the preferred stockholder receives only the stated dividend rate, regardless of how profitable the company is. This is one of the major disadvantages of preferred stock. After the stated preferred dividend rate is paid, all of the benefits of above-average profitable years may accrue to the common stockholders through higher dividends. In effect, the stockholder who has purchased cumulative nonparticipating preferred stock trades off a possible higher return for less risk.

Preference on Liquidation

Normally, preferred stock has preference in the event of corporate liquidation. This means that after the creditors are satisfied, preferred shareholders must be fully satisfied before common stockholders can receive any assets. Furthermore, dividends in arrears are included in this liquidation preference. Most preferred stock has an actual stated liquidation value per share that the shareholder will receive if liquidation occurs. Current accounting practices require that this liquidation value be disclosed in the stockholders' equity section of the balance sheet.

Other Features of Preferred Stock

In some situations, a corporation may issue **convertible preferred stock**. This enables preferred stockholders to convert their preferred stock for common stock at a stated rate and time. This conversion feature allows preferred stockholders to enjoy the stability of preferred dividends, and, if it becomes advantageous, they can convert to common stock and benefit from increases in the price of the common shares. The issuing corporation also benefits from the conversion feature, because it can issue preferred stock with a lower stated dividend rate than it otherwise could have.

Preferred stock can be redeemable or callable. Under certain conditions, **redeemable preferred stock** can be returned, for a stated price, to the issuing corporation by the owner of the stock. Some preferred stock has mandatory redemption requirements, by which the corporation can force redemption at a certain price and time.

Callable preferred stock gives the issuing corporation, at its option, the right to retire the stock at a specified price. The specified price (call price) is usually above the stated par value of the stock, and the difference between the call price and the par value is called the **call premium**. To illustrate, $100 par value preferred stock with a call price of $108 has a call premium of $8. When the issuing corporation calls the stock, the total price paid is the call price plus any dividends in arrears.

There are several reasons why a corporation may wish to issue callable, or redeemable, preferred stock. If the stock is also convertible, the call provision will allow the corporation to force conversion by threatening to call the stock. In addition, if interest and investment rates change in the economy, the call provision will give the corporation flexibility by allowing it to retire preferred stock with a high dividend rate and replace it with new stock at a lower rate. Finally, if the corporation has considerable amounts of excess cash, it may wish to retire its preferred stock and thus avoid paying dividends in the future.

■ THE COMPONENTS OF STOCKHOLDERS' EQUITY

Stockholders' equity represents the stockholders' residual interest in the corporation's assets. Although terminology and form differ among firms, the shareholders' equity section of the Borden, Inc. consolidated balance sheet, presented in Exhibit

13-3, is typical of those found in most U.S. corporate balance sheets. Although not specifically designated as such in most published balance sheets, stockholders' equity consists of the following components: (1) contributed capital, including preferred and common stock and additional paid-in capital; (2) retained earnings; (3) treasury stock; and, in some situations, (4) certain debit items. You should keep in mind that the total of these categories represents owners' claims; they are subdivided only for legal and accounting purposes.

EXHIBIT 13-3

BORDEN, INC. Shareholders' Equity (in thousands)		
	December 31,	
	1988	1987
Capital stock		
Preferred stock—no par value		
Authorized 10,000,000 shares		
Issued series B convertible—10,354		
shares and 13,022 shares, respectively		
(involuntary liquidating value of $299 or		
$28.88 per share at December 31, 1988)	43	54
Common stock—$1.25 par value		
Authorized 240,000,000 shares		
Issued 100,991,687 shares	$ 126,240	$ 126,240
Paid-in capital	295,771	288,205
Accumulated translation adjustment	(49,844)	(40,308)
Retained earnings	1,980,241	1,778,713
Total	2,352,451	2,152,904
Less common stock in treasury (at cost)—		
27,082,089 shares and 27,338,882 shares,		
respectively	(503,836)	(494,055)
Total	$1,848,615	$1,658,849

CONTRIBUTED CAPITAL

Contributed capital is the total capital contributed by all the stockholders as well as others. This capital comes from the original issue of common and preferred stock, subsequent issues of stock, and other sources such as donations to the corporation. Contributed capital has two components: the **legal (stated) capital** of the corporation and the **additional paid-in capital**. The total contributed capital of Borden, Inc. at December 31, 1988 is $422.054 million, consisting of legal capital of $126.283 million (preferred stock of $43,000 and common stock of $126.240 million) and additional paid-in capital of $295.771 million.

Legal Capital or Stated Capital

The definition of legal or stated capital depends on the laws of the state in which the corporation is chartered. Generally, it pertains to the number of shares of common and (if any) preferred stock, and their par values, stated values, or issue price if no par stock is issued. Thus, the legal capital of Borden, Inc. is $126.283 million, consisting of the $43,000 issue price of the preferred stock and the $126.240 million par value of the common stock. The definition and determination of legal capital have important legal implications. Many courts have ruled that if a corporation's legal capital is reduced through dividend payments or actions other than unprofitable operations, its creditors have a claim against the current stockholders to the extent of that reduction. As note, the amount of legal capital is closely tied to the concept of par value, which will be explored next.

Par Value

Par value is an accounting term that often is misunderstood. The **par value** of common or preferred stock is an amount designated in the articles of incorporation or by the board of directors and is printed on the stock certificate. It does not represent the amount that the board feels the stock will sell for when issued or in the future. In fact, it does not represent value at all.

Par value is a concept developed around 1900 in order to protect the creditors and investors of corporations. It was meant to provide an amount of assets that could not be distributed to shareholders if there were other creditors' and investors' claims that would be impaired by this distribution. However, the concept of par value has lost much of its significance today. The board of directors has the right to set the par value of the stock at any amount it desires. Because it is unlawful in most states to issue stock below its par value, the board usually sets a relatively low par value, such as $1, $5, or $10. For example, the par value of Borden, Inc. common stock is $1.25 per share. From an accounting perspective, the main significance of par value is that it is often a basis on which the amount of the preferred stock dividends is derived.

No Par Stock

Many states now allow corporations to issue no par stock. True **no par stock** has no stated value placed on it by the board of directors. In some situations, the board of directors will place a stated value on the no par stock. No par stock with a stated value is treated in the same way that par value stock is.

Shares Authorized and Issued

Under current accounting practices, the par value or stated value of a firm's capital stock and the number of shares authorized, issued, and outstanding must be disclosed in its financial statements. The number of shares authorized is stated in the articles of incorporation and is simply the number of shares that the corporation is allowed to issue. For example, Borden, Inc. is authorized to issue 10 million and 240 million shares of preferred and common stock, respectively. The number of shares authorized in Borden's articles of incorporation is clearly large enough to meet its present and future needs.

The shares issued represent the number of shares the corporation has actually issued to date. Borden has issued and outstanding 10,354 and 13,022 shares of no par value preferred at December 31, 1988 and December 31, 1987, respectively. Borden has issued 100,991,687, $1.25 par value common shares at December 31, 1988 and December 31, 1987. Because of the common shares held in treasury, not all of the issued shares were still outstanding. Stock that is authorized but unissued (or issued and no longer outstanding) has no rights associated with it.

Additional Paid-in Capital

Because par value or stated value is arbitrary and often a low figure, the concept of contributed capital is more meaningful. **Contributed capital** is equal to the legal capital plus any additional capital contributed to the stockholders or others. One of the primary sources of additional paid-in capital is the issue of stock in excess of the par or stated value. For example, if you want to know how much a corporation received from the issuance of other than true no par common stock, you must combine both the balance in the Common Stock account and the additional paid-in capital account, Paid-in Capital from the Issue of Common Stock in Excess of Par. Other sources of additional paid-in capital include donated capital and the resale of treasury stock

(stock repurchased by the corporation) above its cost. Borden's additional paid-in capital equals $295.771 million, and as noted, the total contributed capital equals $422.054 million, consisting of preferred stock, common stock, and additional paid-in capital.

Donated capital is another source of additional paid-in capital. Several transactions can give rise to donated capital, including donated assets, stock returned to the corporation by stockholders, and forgiveness of corporate debt by a stockholder. The most common situation involving donated assets occurs when a city or municipality offers to a corporation, at no cost, land on which to locate its plant. Cities do this in the hope of improving local employment and increasing tax revenues. As shown in Chapter 10, such donated assets are recorded at their fair market value, by debiting the appropriate asset account and crediting the paid-in capital account, Donated Capital.

■ RETAINED EARNINGS

The second category in the stockholders' equity section is retained earnings. Retained earnings result from a business's profitable operations and represent part of the owners' residual claim. Dividends reduce retained earnings. Transactions that affect this account will be discussed in the next chapter.

■ TREASURY STOCK

The stockholders' equity section of Borden, Inc. (Exhibit 13-3) includes a listing for treasury stock. **Treasury stock** represents the cost of Borden's own stock that the company itself repurchased. Treasury stock will be considered later in this chapter.

■ DEBIT ITEMS IN STOCKHOLDERS' EQUITY

Under current accounting standards, there are a number of items other than treasury stock that are treated as direct deductions to stockholders' equity. These include unrealized losses on long-term investments and cumulative foreign currency translation adjustments. Cumulative foreign currency adjustments, which are briefly examined in Chapter 18, amount to $49.844 million for Borden, Inc.

■ ACCOUNTING FOR THE ISSUANCE OF STOCK

When a corporation is formed, it must issue common stock. In addition, it may issue preferred stock. Subsequently, if the corporation needs additional capital, it may decide to issue common stock, preferred stock, or bonds. Large public corporations often issue stock through **underwriters**—brokerage firms such as Merrill Lynch or groups of firms that purchase the entire stock issue for a stated price. The underwriters assume the risks in marketing the stock to their clients. Some firms sell their stock directly to the public. Smaller firms that are going to issue only limited amounts of stock often do so through private solicitations and private placements. The decision as to how to market a stock issue is an important management decision but does not affect the way in which the stock is recorded in the firm's books and records.

■ STOCK ISSUED FOR CASH

Large public corporations usually issue stock in exchange for cash. To illustrate the accounting entries, assume that on January 2, 1990, The Jackson Corporation decides to issue 5,000 of the 20,000 authorized shares of common stock and receives $25 per share. The following three independent cases will be considered:

1. The stock has a par value of $10 per share.
2. The stock is no par with no stated value.
3. The stock is no par but has a stated value of $5 per share.

Although common stock is used in these examples, the same concepts apply to preferred stock.

Exhibit 13-4 presents the appropriate journal entries for all three cases as well as the stockholders' equity section of the balance sheet immediately after the stock issue. In the first case, as in all of the cases, Cash is debited for the total proceeds received, $125,000 (5,000 × $25 = $125,000). When common stock has a par value, the Common Stock account is credited for the par value of the total stock issued, or $50,000 (5,000 × $10 = $50,000), and the paid-in capital account Paid-in Capital from Issue of Common Stock in Excess of Par is credited for the difference of $75,000 (5,000 × [$25 − $10] = $75,000). The partial balance sheet pictured under Case 1 in Exhibit 13-4 shows that the corporation's contributed capital is divided into the legal capital of $50,000 (the par value of the stock) and the additional paid-in capital of $75,000. Total stockholders' equity, which does not include retained earnings (because the corporation has just been organized), equals $125,000.

EXHIBIT 13–4	Issue of 5,000 Shares of Stock at $25 per Share

Case 1 $10 Par Value Stock	Case 2 No Par, No Stated Value	Case 3 No Par, $5 Stated Value

January 2, 1989
Cash   125,000
  Common Stock   50,000
  Paid-in Capital from Issue of
  Common Stock in Excess of
  Par   75,000
To record issue of 5,000 shares of $10 par value stock at $25 per share.
	Cash 125,000
	  Common Stock 125,000
	
	To record issue of 5,000 shares of no par stock at $25 per share.
		Cash 125,000
		  Common Stock 25,000
		  Paid-in Capital from Issue of
		  Common Stock in Excess of
		  Stated Value 100,000
		To record issue of 5,000 shares of no par, $5 stated value stock at $25 per share.

THE JACKSON CORPORATION **Partial Balance Sheet** **January 2, 1990**	**THE JACKSON CORPORATION** **Partial Balance Sheet** **January 2, 1990**	**THE JACKSON CORPORATION** **Partial Balance Sheet** **January 2, 1990**

Contributed capital
  Common stock, $10 par
    value, 20,000 shares
    authorized, 5,000 shares
    issued and outstanding $ 50,000
Additional paid-in capital   75,000
  Total stockholders' equity $125,000
	Contributed capital
	  Common stock, no par
	    value, 20,000 shares
	    authorized, 5,000 shares
	    issued and outstanding $125,000
	
	  Total stockholders' equity $125,000
		Contributed capital
		  Common stock, no par with $5
		    stated value, 20,000 shares
		    authorized, 5,000 shares
		    issued and outstanding $ 25,000
		Additional paid-in capital 100,000
		  Total stockholders' equity $125,000

In Case 2, the stock is no par and has no stated value. Again, Cash is debited for the entire proceeds of $125,000. However, in this case, Common Stock is also credited for the entire proceeds of $125,000. There is no entry to an additional paid-in capital account. Since different stock issues are apt to be sold at different prices, there is no uniform price per share recorded in the capital stock, as it is for par value stock. In this case, the corporation's legal capital is $125,000; the total stockholders' equity is still $125,000.

In Case 3, the stock is no par but has a stated value of $5 per share. As before, Cash is debited for $125,000, but now Common Stock is credited for only $25,000 (5,000 × $5 = $25,000), or the stated value of the entire issue. The account Paid-in Capital from Issue of Common Stock in Excess of Stated Value is credited for the difference of $100,000 (5,000 × [$25 − $5] = $100,000). Assuming that the stock's stated value remains the same, there will be a uniform amount per share recorded in the Capital Stock account. Most states consider that the corporation's legal capital is the stock's total stated value—in this case $25,000. Total stockholders' equity, as with the other two cases, is $125,000.

There are a number of points to keep in mind when reviewing these examples. In all cases, total stockholders' equity remains the same. The difference is just in the manner in which contributed capital is divided between legal capital and other paid-in capital. Although the distinction between legal capital and contributed capital may have important legal ramifications, especially on liquidation, it has little accounting significance.

■ STOCK ISSUED FOR NONCASH ASSETS

There are some circumstances in which stock is issued for noncash assets or for services. For example, in payment for their services, attorneys and other promoters may accept stock in a corporation instead of cash. In other circumstances, a corporation may receive land, buildings, or other assets in exchange for its stock. In either case, the transaction should be recorded in accordance with the cost principle. This means that the assets or services acquired should be recorded at the fair market value of the stock issued at the date of the transaction—that is, the consideration given. In those transactions for which it is not feasible to determine the fair market value of the stock that has been issued, the fair market value of the assets or services received should be used.

To illustrate, assume that Rebecca Webb, the attorney for the Secco Corporation, agrees to take 1,000 shares of the corporation's $5 par value stock in exchange for the services she performed in organizing the corporation. Her normal fee for such work is $7,500. Because the corporation is owned by only a few individuals and is not traded on an exchange, its market value cannot be determined, so the value of the services performed will be used to value the transaction. The entry to record this transaction is:

Organization Costs	7,500	
Common Stock		5,000
Paid-in Capital from Issue of Common Stock in Excess of Par		2,500
To record issue of 1,000 shares of $5 par value stock in exchange for attorney's fees of $7,500.		

The intangible asset account Organization Costs is debited for the fair market value of the attorney's service; Common Stock is credited for the par value of the stock; and Additional Paid-in Capital is credited for the difference.

If stock is exchanged for noncash assets such as land or buildings, the entry would be similar. For example, now assume that the Secco Corporation issues 5,000 shares of its $100 par value preferred stock in exchange for land and a building. At the time of the transaction, the preferred stock has a fair market value of $120 per share, and so the total transaction is valued at $600,000 (5,000 × $120 = $600,000). The land and the building are valued at $200,000 and $400,000, respectively. The entry to record this transaction is:

Land	200,000	
Building	400,000	
Preferred stock		500,000
Paid-in Capital from Issue of Preferred Stock in Excess of Par		100,000
To record issue of 5,000 shares of $100 par value preferred stock in exchange for land and building. Market value of preferred stock is $120 per share.		

If it is impossible to determine the fair market value of the stock, the fair market value of the land and building should be used to value the transaction. If this figure cannot be determined, then the board of directors would have to set a value for the transaction.

CONVERSION OF PREFERRED STOCK TO COMMON

As previously noted, some issues of preferred stock are convertible into common shares after some specified date. When this occurs, the convertible preferred stock is originally recorded in the normal way. That is, the Preferred Stock account is credited for the par value of the shares, and Paid-in Capital is credited for the difference, if any, between the issue price and the par value. When the stock is converted, it is done so at its book value. No gain or loss is recorded.

To illustrate, assume that the BAFS Corporation issues 5,000 shares of $100 par value convertible stock at $130. Each preferred share is convertible into five shares of $1 par value common. Subsequently, 1,000 shares of preferred are converted into 5,000 shares of common. The journal entries to reflect these transactions are:

Cash	650,000	
Preferred Stock		500,000
Paid-in Capital from Issue of Preferred Stock in Excess of Par		150,000
To record issue of 5,000 shares of $100 convertible preferred stock at $130 per share.		
Preferred Stock	100,000	
Paid-in Capital from Issue of Preferred Stock in Excess of Par	30,000	
Common Stock		5,000
Paid-in Capital from Issue of Common Stock in Excess of Par		125,000
To record conversion of 1,000 shares of preferred stock into 5,000 shares of $1 par value common.		

Notice that when the preferred stock is converted, the Preferred Stock account is debited for the total par value of the converted stock. The Paid-in Capital account is also debited for the amount per share credited to that account when the stock is originally issued. In this case, that amount is $30,000, or $30 × 1,000 shares. Common Stock is credited at par, and Paid-in Capital is credited for the difference. Although total stockholders' equity remains the same, its components have changed.

TREASURY STOCK AND RETIREMENT OF CAPITAL STOCK

To this point, the issuance of capital stock has been the subject of discussion. Next are the accounting concepts and procedures when a corporation either repurchases or retires its capital stock.

TREASURY STOCK

Treasury stock is the corporation's own capital stock, either common or preferred, that has been issued and subsequently reacquired by the firm but not canceled. Such stock, held in the corporate treasury, loses its right to vote, receive dividends, or receive assets upon liquidation.

There are a number of valid business reasons why a firm may reacquire its own capital stock. For example, a firm may need to acquire additional shares (1) for employee stock option or bonus plans, (2) for mergers and acquisitions, (3) in order to support the price of its stock, (4) because the firm may believe the stock is a good investment, or (5) to stop a hostile takeover.

EXHIBIT 13-5

STANDARD BRANDS PAINTS TO BUY BACK 53% OF SHARES

By Keith Bradsher, TIMES STAFF WRITER

Standard Brands Paint, a leading do-it-yourself home decorating chain under takeover pressure, announced Tuesday that it intended to buy back more than half of its stock.

The Torrance-based company said it would borrow $190 million and stop paying its quarterly dividend to pay for the repurchase. In all, the company said it expects to buy 6 million shares—53% of its outstanding common stock—at a price of between $25 and $28 a share.

The company also said it will issue stock rights that may only be exercised in the event of a takeover struggle.

The moves will make Standard Brands much less vulnerable to a hostile takeover and may boost earnings per share next year, said

Ward P. Lindenmayer, a consumer stock analyst for Sutro & Co., a San Francisco-based brokerage.

But by increasing interest expenses, the moves may also hurt the company's ability to expand and compete in the already hotly contested home improvement industry, he said.

"They can do it and have it contribute to earnings . . . [but] I'm not so sure two or three years out this will be as beneficial as next year," he said.

Standard Brands, which had 1986 sales of $326.6 million, made its announcement after the close of trading Tuesday. The company's stock closed on the New York Stock Exchange at $21.50, up 25 cents.

In November 1987, for example, Standard Brands Paints announced its intention to repurchase 53% of its stock to stop a hostile takeover bid. Exhibit 13-5, an article from the *Los Angeles Times*, describes this repurchase.[1]

In October 1987, the stock market crashed; the New York Stock Exchange's Dow Jones Average fell more than 500 points in one day. Many firms, in an effort to prop up their share prices and show stockholders and others that management had confidence in the firm, undertook major stock repurchases. The following part of a press release issued by Ames Department Stores, Inc. is illustrative of the actions of many large corporations at that time.

> *October 29, 1987*: Ames Department Stores, Inc. (NYSE:ADD) today announced that the Board of Directors has authorized the repurchase of up to 10% of its outstanding shares.
>
> Peter B. Hollis, Chief Executive Officer, stated that Ames will repurchase up to 3,800,000 shares from time to time in the open market and through privately negotiated transactions, subject to general market and other conditions. The buy-back program will be financed out of Ames' general corporate funds and borrowings under its revolving credit agreement. Mr. Hollis added that the stock repurchase program reflects the Company's confidence in its long-term prospects.
>
> Ames operates 337 discount department stores and 142 variety stores.[2]

Accounting for Treasury Stock

Treasury stock is not considered an asset; it is a reduction in stockholders' equity. Nor can a firm record a profit on the subsequent sale of treasury stock. Any difference between the reacquisition price and the selling price is either an increase in paid-in capital if the shares sold at a gain, or a decrease in paid-in capital and/or retained earnings if the shares sold at a loss. Finally, no treasury stock held by the corporation has any dividend or voting rights.

Recording the Purchase of Treasury Stock. To show how the purchase of treasury stock is recorded, assume that the stockholders' equity section of the Linefsky Corporation at September 30, 1989 is as shown in Exhibit 13-6. On October 1, the corporation repurchased 1,000 shares of its common stock at $24 per share. This transaction is recorded by debiting the stockholders' equity account Treasury Stock and crediting Cash for the cost of the purchase, as shown at the top of page 492.

[1]*Los Angeles Times*, November 11, 1987, p. 10–12. Copyright, 1987, *Los Angeles Times*. Reprinted by permission.

[2]Source: Financial Press Release, Ames Department Stores, Inc., October 29, 1987.

Oct. 1, 1989	Treasury Stock	24,000	
	Cash		24,000
	To record purchase of 1,000 shares of treasury stock at $24 per share.		

EXHIBIT 13-6

LINEFSKY CORPORATION	
Stockholders' Equity	
September 30, 1989	
Common stock, $5 par value, 100,000 shares authorized,	
10,000 shares issued and outstanding	$ 50,000
Additional paid-in capital from issue of common stock above par	150,000
Retained earnings	700,000
Total stockholders' equity	$900,000

Immediately after this purchase, the stockholders' equity section of the Linefsky Corporation appeared as shown in Exhibit 13-7. As this partial balance sheet shows, treasury stock is not shown as an asset but as a negative item in stockholders' equity. The effect of the transaction is to reduce both assets and stockholders' equity by $24,000.

EXHIBIT 13-7

LINEFSKY CORPORATION	
Stockholders' Equity	
October 1, 1989	
Common stock, $5 par value, 100,000 shares authorized,	
10,000 shares issued, of which 9,000 are outstanding	$ 50,000
Additional paid-in capital from sale of common stock above par	150,000
Retained earnings	700,000
Less 1,000 shares of treasury stock at cost	(24,000)
Total stockholders' equity	$876,000

The corporation can sell its treasury stock any time that it desires. The subsequent resale can be either above or below its repurchase price. However, in no case is net income for the current period affected.

Recording Resale above Cost. When treasury stock is resold above its cost, Cash is debited for the entire proceeds. Treasury Stock is credited for the total cost of the shares sold, and the account Additional Paid-in Capital from the Sale of Treasury Stock above Cost is credited for the difference. The Additional Paid-in Capital account is credited for the economic gain, because current accounting and tax rules do not allow a corporation to record a profit and thus to increase retained earnings by dealing in its own stock.

To demonstrate, now assume that on November 29, 1989, 500 shares of the treasury stock purchased at $24 per share were sold at $30 per share. To record this sale, the Linefsky Corporation made the following entry:

Nov. 29, 1989	Cash	15,000	
	Treasury Stock		12,000
	Paid-in Capital from Sale of Treasury Stock		
	above Cost		3,000
	To record sale of treasury stock. Cost of treasury stock, $12,000 = 500 × $24.		

Recording Resale below Cost. If treasury stock is resold below cost, there will be an economic loss. This loss does not affect the current period's income but reduces the credit balance in the Paid-in Capital account that resulted from other treasury stock transactions. If there are no previous treasury stock transactions, or the balance in this Paid-in Capital account is not large enough to cover the loss, or there is no other Paid-in Capital account from the same class of stock, Retained Earnings is debited.

To illustrate, now assume that the remaining 500 shares of treasury stock were resold on December 24 at $15 per share. The following journal entry is made to record this sale:

Dec. 24, 1989	Cash	7,500	
	Paid-in Capital from Sale of Treasury Stock above Cost	3,000	
	Paid-in Capital from Sale of Common Stock above Par	1,500	
	Treasury Stock		12,000
	To record sale of 500 shares of treasury stock at $15 per share.		

In this case, Paid-in Capital from Sale of Treasury Stock above Cost is debited for only $3,000, the balance in this account that resulted from the previous resale. The remaining $1,500 difference of the $4,500 economic loss is charged to Paid-in Capital from Sale of Common Stock above Par. If there had not been a credit balance in this paid-in capital account, the difference would have been debited to Retained Earnings.

■ RETIREMENT OF CAPITAL STOCK

Occasionally, a corporation may repurchase its stock with the intent to retire it rather than to hold it in the treasury. Essentially, a corporation retires its stock for some of the same reasons that it purchases treasury stock. Like treasury stock transactions, income or loss for the current period is not affected, nor can retained earnings be increased when capital stock is retired.

Accounting for stock retirements depends on the original issue price and the price that must be paid to retire it. For example, assume that the Kishi Corporation issued 10,000 shares of $10 par value common stock at $25 per share and made the following entry to record this issue:

Cash	250,000	
Common Stock		100,000
Paid-in Capital from Issue of Common Stock in Excess of Par		150,000

Several years later, the firm repurchased and retired 1,000 shares of its stock at a price of (1) $25 per share, (2) $20 per share, and (3) $30 per share. The journal entries to record each of these three independent cases are:

Case 1—Repurchase price, $25 per share

Common Stock	10,000	
Paid-in Capital from Issue of Common Stock in Excess of Par	15,000	
Cash		25,000
To record retirement of 1,000 shares of $10 par value stock originally issued at $25 per share and retired at $25 per share.		

Case 2—Repurchase price, $20 per share

Common Stock	10,000	
Paid-in Capital from Issue of Common Stock in Excess of Par	15,000	
Paid-in Capital from Retirement of Common Stock		5,000
Cash		20,000

To record retirement of 1,000 shares of $10 par value stock
originally issued at $25 per share and retired at $20
per share.

Case 3—Repurchase price, $30 per share

Common Stock	10,000	
Paid-in Capital from Issue of Common Stock in Excess of Par	15,000	
Retained Earnings	5,000	
Cash		30,000

To record retirement of 1,000 shares of $10 par value common
stock originally issued at $25 per share and retired at $30
per share.

In each case, both the Common Stock account and the Paid-in Capital from Issue of Common Stock in Excess of Par account are debited for the amounts per share for which they were originally credited. In the first case, when the retirement price is equal to the original issue price, the only remaining entry is a credit to Cash. In the second case, when the stock is retired at a price below its original issue price, Paid-in Capital from the Retirement of Common Stock is credited. In the third case, when the stock is retired at a price above its original issue price, Retained Earnings is debited for the difference.

■ USE OF STOCK INFORMATION

After the stock of a major corporation is issued, it trades on a national exchange such as the New York or the American stock exchange or possibly on a regional exchange. To help them evaluate a corporation, present and potential investors and creditors look at the market price of the stock as well as other indicators.

■ MARKET VALUE

The market value per share refers to the price at which a particular stock is currently trading. Clearly, this market price is most objective when there is a large market for the stock on a national exchange. In effect, the price is set by many individuals all acting independently as they buy and sell shares of stock. Such factors as general economic conditions, interest rates, the perceived risk of the company, expectations concerning future profits, and present and expected dividends all contribute to the stock's current market price.

The Stock Page

The current market price of stocks traded on a major exchange are listed in major newspapers. A recent stock-page listing for IBM is reproduced as follows:

52-week										
High	Low	Stock	Dividend	Yield	P-E Ratio	Sales 100's	High	Low	Last	Change
$175\frac{7}{8}$	102	IBM	4.40	3.7	16	24284	$117\frac{7}{8}$	$114\frac{3}{4}$	$117\frac{3}{4}$	$+2\frac{1}{8}$

The 52-week high and low columns show the highest and lowest price of the stock during the previous 52 weeks, plus the current week. In this situation, IBM's high for the previous year was $175.875, and its low was $102. The dividend column shows the latest annual dividend, which, in IBM's case, is $4.40.

The yield column indicates the rate of return that a stockholder would receive if the stock were purchased at its latest price. In the IBM example, an annual dividend of $4.40 on an investment of $117.75 (last price) represents a yield of 3.7%, calculated as follows:

$$\text{Yield} = \frac{\text{Annual dividend}}{\text{Current market price}}$$

$$3.7\% = \frac{\$4.40}{\$117.75} \times 100$$

The **price-earnings ratio** (P-E) is a ratio used by many investors and analysts to compare stocks. The P-E ratio is calculated by means of the following formula:

$$\frac{\text{Current market price}}{\text{Earnings per share}}$$

Earnings per share (EPS), which is discussed in detail in the next chapter, shows the amount of current earnings available to common shareholders on a per-share basis. It is calculated by dividing the earnings available to common stockholders (net income less preferred dividends) by the average number of shares outstanding. The P-E ratio uses this data to help investors compare firms having different market prices and earnings. For IBM, the P-E ratio of 16 is calculated as follows:

$$16 = \frac{\$117.75}{7.36}$$

This means that IBM was selling at a multiple of 16, or 16 times its EPS. This can be used to compare alternative investments. For example, Digital Equipment, a somewhat comparable company, had a P-E ratio of 8.9.

The last five columns are relatively straightforward. The sales column, which is in 100s, indicates the total sales for the day. During the day we are considering, 2,428,400 shares of IBM stock changed hands. The high and low columns show the highest and lowest price at which the stock traded during the day. The next column indicates the price of the last trade of the day, and the change column shows the net change from the prior day's last trade.

■ BOOK VALUE PER SHARE

Book value per share of common stock indicates the net assets represented by one share of common stock. Thus book value is the equity that the owner of one share of common stock has in the net assets (assets − liabilities) or stockholders' equity of the corporation. It is the amount that each share would receive if the firm were liquidated and the firm received the amount shown on the balance sheet for the various assets less the liabilities. It is important to remember, however, that the term *value* in this sense does not mean market value or current value. Because the firm's net assets are recorded at historical cost less the write-offs to date, value is in terms of these historical costs, not in terms of market value or liquidation value. Thus there is no particular reason that book value and market value per share should be related.

Book Value When Only Common Stock Is Issued

When a firm has only common stock outstanding, the book value per share is equal to

$$\frac{\text{Total stockholders' equity}}{\text{Number of common shares outstanding}}$$

To illustrate, the 1988 stockholders' equity section of C. R. Bard, Inc., a multinational developer, manufacturer, and marketer of health-care products, is reproduced in Exhibit 13-8. The book value per share of $5.83 is calculated as follows:

$$\$5.83 = \frac{\$328,600,000}{56,346,609 \text{ shares}}$$

In comparison, the price of Bard's stock ranged between $16.875 and $24.625 during 1988.

EXHIBIT 13–8

C. R. BARD, INC. Stockholders' Equity Year-end 1988	
Shareholders' investment	
Preferred stock, $1 par value, authorized 5,000,000 shares; none issued	
Common stock, $.25 par value, authorized 150,000,000 shares; issued and outstanding 56,346,609 shares in 1988; issued 61,361,984 shares and outstanding 57,605,194 shares in 1987	$ 14,100
Capital in excess of par value	4,500
Retained earnings	310,000
Total shareholders' investment	$328,600

Book Value When Both Common and Preferred Stock Are Outstanding

Book value refers to the common stockholders' interest in the firm's net assets. Thus, when preferred stock is outstanding, total stockholders' equity must be reduced by the preferred stockholders' claims, in order to arrive at the common stockholders' equity. This is usually done by subtracting the liquidation or redemption value of the preferred stock and any dividends in arrears from the total stockholders' equity. To demonstrate, the balance sheet of Borden, Inc. will once again be used. The stockholders' equity section of Borden's balance sheet is reproduced in Exhibit 13-3. Total stockholders' equity is $1,848,615,000. The liquidation value of the preferred stock, $299,000, must be subtracted to determine the common stockholders' equity. The firm had 73,909,598 shares issued and outstanding (100,991,687 issued less 27,082,089 held in treasury), so the book value per share is $25.01, calculated as follows:

$$\$25.01 = \frac{\$1,848,615,000}{73,909,598 \text{ shares}}$$

At year-end, Borden's common stock was selling at $59.25—more than twice its book value.

In these examples, the common stocks of both companies were trading above their respective book values. However, this is not always the case. Market conditions, investor expectations, and other factors can cause a firm's stock to trade below its book value.

SUMMARY OF LEARNING OBJECTIVES

1. The main characteristics of corporations. Corporations are separate legal entities with a continuous life. Corporations are characterized by the following features:

(a) Limited liability.

(b) Transferability of ownership.

(c) Ease of capital formation.

(d) Centralization of management.

(e) Continuity of existence.

2. The formation and organization of a corporation. Corporations are chartered by individual states and must comply with state and federal regulations. Control of a corporation lies ultimately with the common stockholders, but they give this power to the board of directors. The board is responsible for setting broad corporate policies and appointing senior management.

3. Types of capital stock. Common and preferred stock are the two major types of capital stock. All corporations must issue common stock, and common shareholders have the following rights:

(a) The right to vote.

(b) The right to a proportionate share of dividends when declared.

(c) The right to a proportionate share of assets upon liquidation.

(d) The preemptive right.

Preferred stockholders have certain preferences over common shareholders with respect to dividends and assets upon liquidation.

4. Components of stockholders' equity. Stockholders' equity consists of contributed capital; retained earnings; treasury stock, if any; and, possibly, special debit items. Contributed capital is often divided into legal capital and additional paid-in capital. Legal capital is based on the par or stated value of the issued and outstanding shares. If true no par stock is issued, the legal capital will be the entire issue price of the stock. Sources of additional paid-in capital include the issue of capital stock in excess of par, sale of treasury stock above par, and donated capital.

5. The accounting concepts and procedures regarding the issuance of capital stock. If par value or no par stock with a stated value is issued, the Capital Stock account should be credited for the par or stated value. Additional Paid-in Capital from the Sale of Capital Stock in Excess of Par or Stated Value is credited for the difference between the issue price and the par or stated value. If true no par stock is issued, the capital stock should be credited for the entire amount.

6. Accounting for treasury stock transactions and the retirement of capital stock. A firm may repurchase its own stock for a number of reasons. This stock is called *treasury stock*. These transactions neither result in an asset nor affect the current period's income. Any economic gain on the subsequent resale of treasury stock is credited to Additional Paid-in Capital, and any economic loss is debited to Additional Paid-in Capital and/or Retained Earnings. Occasionally, a firm will repurchase and then retire its capital stock. When this occurs, the Capital Stock and Additional Paid-in Capital accounts, if any, are debited for the original amounts per share for which they were credited. If the stock is retired at a price below its original purchase price, Additional Paid-in Capital is credited. Conversely, if the stock is retired at a price above its original issue price, Retained Earnings is debited.

7. Uses of stock information. Present and potential investors use stock information in their evaluation of a particular company. Included are such data as the stock's current market price, its P-E ratio, and EPS. Book value per share is also used, but it does not provide data on market or liquidation values.

KEY TERMS

Additional paid-in capital
Board of directors
Book value
Callable preferred stock
Call premium

Common stock
Contributed capital
Convertible preferred stock
Dividends in arrears
Legal (stated) capital

No par stock
Organization costs
Par value
Preferred stock
Price-earnings ratio

Proxy
Redeemable preferred stock
Treasury stock
Underwriters

PROBLEMS FOR YOUR REVIEW

A. The Square Pizza Corporation was organized in 1989 to manufacture and distribute square pizzas. The corporation was authorized to issue 5 million shares of $5 per value common stock and 1 million shares of $100, 6% par value convertible preferred stock. The following transactions took place during 1989:

- January 25: Issued 100,000 shares of common stock at $20 per share.
- April 10: Issued 1,000 shares of common stock to the firm's attorneys in connection with the organization of the corporation. The fair market value of the attorney's fees was $25,000.
- July 1: Issued 10,000 shares of preferred stock at par.
- November 20: Converted 5,000 shares of preferred stock into common shares at the rate of two common shares for each preferred. At the time of conversion, the common stock was selling at a price of $30 per share.

REQUIRED: **(a)** Make the journal entries to record these events.

(b) Assuming that net income for the year amounted to $500,000 and no dividends were declared, prepare the stockholder's equity section of the balance sheet at December 31, 1989.

SOLUTION

Jan. 25, 1989	Cash	2,000,000	
	Common Stock (100,000 × $5)		500,000
	Paid-in Capital from Issue of Common Stock in Excess of Par		1,500,000
	To record issue of 100,000 shares of $5 par value common stock at $20 per share.		

April 10, 1989	Organization Costs	25,000	
	Common Stock (1,000 × $5)		5,000
	Paid-in Capital from Issue of Common Stock in Excess of Par		20,000
	To record issue of 1,000 shares of common stock in connection with organization costs.		

July 1, 1989	Cash	1,000,000	
	Preferred Stock		1,000,000
	To record issue of 10,000 shares of preferred stock at par.		

Nov. 20, 1989	Preferred Stock	500,000	
	Common Stock*		50,000
	Paid-in Capital from Issue of Common Stock in Excess of Par		450,000
	To record conversion of 5,000 shares of preferred stock into 10,000 shares of common stock.		

*Note: The conversion to common is made at the book value of the preferred. The market value of the preferred stock is not relevant.

THE SQUARE PIZZA CORPORATION
Partial Balance Sheet
December 31, 1989

Preferred stock, 6%, $100 par value, 1,000,000 shares authorized and 5,000 shares issued and outstanding	$ 500,000
Common stock, $5 par value, 5,000,000 shares authorized and 111,000 shares issued	555,000
Paid-in capital from issue of common stock in excess of par	1,970,000
Retained earnings	500,000
Total stockholders' equity	$3,525,000

B. Synder Football Equipment Corporation has 100,000 shares of $5 par value common stock outstanding. All stock was originally issued at $12 per share. During the current year, the company entered into the following transactions related to its common stock:

- March 12: The company repurchased 10,000 shares of its common stock at a price of $22 per share.
- May 19: The company resold 6,000 of these shares at $26 per share.
- July 1: The company resold the remaining 4,000 shares held in treasury at $17 per share.
- November 29: The firm retired 1,000 shares at a price of $15 per share.

REQUIRED: Make the journal entries to record these events.

SOLUTION

March 12	Treasury Stock	220,000	
	Cash (10,000 × $22)		220,000
	To record purchase of 10,000 shares of stock at $22 per share.		
May 19	Cash (6,000 × $26)	156,000	
	Paid-in Capital from Sale of Treasury Stock above Cost (6,000 × $4)		24,000
	Treasury Stock (6,000 × $22)		132,000
	To record sale of 6,000 shares of treasury at $26 per share.		
July 1	Cash (4,000 × $17)	68,000	
	Paid-in Capital from Sale of Treasury Stock above Cost (4,000 × $5)	20,000	
	Treasury Stock (4,000 × $22)		88,000
	To record sale of 4,000 shares of treasury stock at $17 per share.		
Nov. 29	Common Stock (1,000 × $5)	5,000	
	Paid-in Capital from Issue of Common Stock in Excess of Par (1,000 × $7)	7,000	
	Retained Earnings ($1,000 × $3)	3,000	
	Cash (1,000 × $15)		15,000
	To record the retirement of 1,000 shares of stock at $15 per share.		

QUESTIONS

1. List and discuss the major characteristics of a corporation.

2. Why have corporations become the dominant form of business organization in the United States?

3. A famous business school professor recently stated that all businesses should be organized as corporations in order to take advantage of their special tax and legal treatment. Do you agree with this statement? Why or why not?

4. Describe the purposes or functions of each of the following:

  (a) Articles of incorporation.

  (b) Board of directors.

  (c) Senior management.

5. Shareholders have certain rights. Describe and discuss these rights and how they differ between common and preferred shareholders.

6. You overheard a fellow student say that he had recently invested in the preferred stock of a major corporation because his stockbroker told him that preferred stock is a better investment because it is less risky. Do you agree? Why or why not?

7. You recently purchased 100 shares of cumulative preferred stock, which has a stated dividend of $2 per share. Because the current year's operations were barely profitable, the firm did not declare any dividends. How much in dividends will you be entitled to in the next year?

8. Describe the major components of stockholders' equity.

9. One of your friends invests only in stock that has a par value above $10, because she feels that this will guarantee that the price of the stock will not fall below this amount. Do you agree with her investment strategy? Why or why not?

10. Recently a number of states have allowed corporations to issue stock that does not have a par value. What factors have led to this policy?

11. Which of the following statements, if any, regarding par value is correct? Explain your answer.

  (a) All stock must be issued at its par value.

  (b) When stock has a par value, the total issue price is credited to the Capital Stock account.

  (c) Par value differs from stated value because the par value is set by the board of directors and the stated value is set by the stock market.

  (d) When stock has a par value, the Capital Stock account is credited for the par value, and the Paid-in Capital account is credited for the excess of the issue price over the par value.

12. In some circumstances, a corporation issues stock in exchange for services or other assets such as land and buildings. In these situations, what factors must the accountant consider in assigning a dollar value to the exchange?

13. The purchase of treasury stock is recorded by a debit to the Treasury Stock account and a credit to Cash. Treasury stock is shown as an asset on the balance sheet. Comment on these statements.

14. Why does a firm purchase its own stock? Once the purchase is made and the stock is resold, how is the economic gain or loss on the transaction, if any, recorded?

15. When a corporation retires its common stock at a price below its issue price, what accounts are affected?

16. Describe the yield on common stock and the P-E ratio and how they are used by investors.

17. Explain how the book value per share of common stock is calculated (a) when a corporation has only common shares outstanding and (b) when it has both common and preferred shares outstanding.

18. Discuss the meaning and usefulness of book value per share of common stock. Does it provide a good measure of the stock's current or market value?

19. Would you purchase stock in a company just because the price of the stock was below its book value? Why or why not?

EXERCISES

E1. Identification of Accounts. State whether each of the following items should be classified as an asset, liability, stockholders' equity, revenue, or expense.

  (a) Organization costs.

  (b) Paid-in capital from issue of common stock in excess of par.

(c) Common stock.

(d) Cumulative foreign currency adjustments.

(e) Preferred stock.

(f) Donated capital.

(g) Dividends declared.

(h) Interest paid on bonds.

(i) Dividends received on investments.

E2. Dividends on Preferred and Common Stock. The El Tota Corporation has the following shares of stock outstanding:

Common stock, no par	50,000 shares
Preferred stock, cumulative, stated dividend $2	10,000 shares

The company had been very profitable until 1987, when its business and profits fell. In 1987, for the first time in its history, the company was unable to pay all of its required dividends. The board of directors made the following funds available for dividends during 1987, 1988, and 1989:

1987	$12,000
1988	25,000
1989	30,000

Determine the amount of dividends that the preferred and common shareholders will receive each year.

E3. Issuance of Stock. The Software Corporation is authorized to issue 50,000 shares of common stock. During the current year, it decides to issue 10,000 shares. Make the required entry to record the issuance of the common stock under each of the following independent situations:

(a) The shares have a $5 par value and were sold for $20 per share.

(b) The shares are no par but have a stated value of $10. The total issue price was $300,000.

(c) The shares are no par and have no stated value. They were issued at $25 per share.

(d) The shares are no par and have no stated value. They were issued to an attorney in exchange for services rendered in connection with organizing the corporation. The attorney normally charges $40,000 for these services. There is no reasonable way to determine the fair market value of the stock.

E4. Preparation of the Stockholders' Equity Section. The Baker Corporation was formed in early 1988. At that time, the corporation was authorized to issue 100,000 shares of $5 par value common stock and 50,000 shares of 6%, $100 par value cumulative preferred stock. At the time the corporation was formed, 20,000 shares of common stock were issued at $25 per share. Net income during 1988 amounted to $10,000.

At the beginning of 1989, the firm issued 5,000 shares of the preferred stock at par. Net income during 1989 amounted to $50,000. In addition to the preferred dividends, the firm declared common dividends of $5,000. Prepare the stockholders' equity section of the balance sheet as of December 31, 1989, the end of the firm's year.

E5. Determining Missing Value. The stockholders' equity section on the December 31, 1989 balance sheet of Advanced Technologies appeared as follows:

Preferred stock, 5%, $100 par value, cumulative, 50,000 shares, authorized	
___?___ issued	$2,000,000
Common stock, $5 par value, 100,000 shares authorized, 25,000 issued	?
Paid-in capital from sale of common stock in excess of par	750,000
Retained earnings	650,000

Answer each of the following questions:

(a) How many preferred shares were issued?

(b) What was the total issue price of the preferred shares?

(c) What amount should be recorded in the Common Stock account?

(d) What was the total issue price per share of the common shares?

(e) What is the amount of required preferred dividends?

(f) What is the amount of required common dividends?

(g) What is the amount of total stockholders' equity?

E6. **Determining Missing Values.** The stockholders' equity section on the December 31, 1990 balance sheet of Microexpress appeared as follows:

Preferred stock, 8%, $50 par value, 200,000 shares authorized, 70,000 shares issued	$?
Common stock, $2 stated value, 500,000 shares authorized, ? issued and ? outstanding	200,000
Paid-in capital from issue of common stock in excess of par	600,000
Retained earnings	1,000,000
Less: Common stock held in treasury at cost, 10,000 shares	(30,000)
Total stockholders' equity	$?

Answer each of the following questions:

(a) What is the total issue price of the preferred stock?

(b) How many shares of common stock were issued?

(c) How many shares of common stock are outstanding?

(d) What was the total issue price of the common stock?

(e) What is the total legal capital of the corporation?

(f) What is the total contributed capital of the corporation?

(g) What is the total stockholders' equity?

(h) For how much per share was the treasury stock purchased?

(i) What is the amount of the required preferred dividends?

E7. **Stock Issued for Noncash Consideration.** On July 1, 1991, the West Corporation exchanged 1,500 shares of its $5 par value common stock for site land. A few months ago, the land was appraised by an independent appraiser for $100,000.

REQUIRED: Make the required journal entry to record this transaction, given the two following independent assumptions:

(a) West Corporation's stock is currently trading on the New York Stock Exchange at $65 a share.

(b) West Corporation is a privately held corporation whose stock is owned by five family members. They estimate the stock has a fair market value of $70 per share.

E8. **Conversion of Preferred Stock to Common.** The capital structure of the Santa Anita Corporation is as follows:

Preferred stock: 5%, $100 par value convertible preferred stock, 10,000 shares authorized, issued, and outstanding	$1,000,000
Common stock: $1 par value common stock, 100,000 shares authorized, issued, and outstanding	100,000
Paid-in capital from sale of common stock in excess of par	500,000

Each preferred share is convertible into five shares of common stock. During the current year, 5,000 shares of the preferred shares were converted into common shares.

REQUIRED: **(a)** Make the required journal entry to record the conversion.

(b) Now make the entry, assuming that (1) the common stock is no par and has no stated value and (2) the common stock is no par and the stock has a $10 stated value.

E9. **Treasury Stock Transactions.** Make the appropriate journal entries to record the following treasury stock transactions:

■ January 5: The Truly Modern Corporation repurchases 500 shares of its $5 par value common stock at its current price of $30 per share.

■ April 15: The company resells 200 shares of the treasury stock at $40 per share.

- November 29: The firm resells 200 additional treasury shares at $24 per share.
- December 15: The firm sells the remaining 100 shares still held in the treasury at $18 per share.

E10. **Retirement of Common Stock.** Several years ago, EGBOK, Inc. issued 100,000 shares of $5 par value common stock at $14 per share. During the current year, the firm repurchased and retired 10,000 shares.

REQUIRED: **(a)** Make the journal entry to record the original issue of the 100,000 shares.

(b) Make the entry to record the repurchase and retirement, assuming the shares were purchased for (1) $14 per share, (2) $25 per share, and (3) $12 per share.

E11. **Book Value per Share.** You have gathered the following data from the 1989 annual report of the STN Corporation:

Total common stockholders' equity	$2,380,000
Net income from 1989	$1,120,000
Number of common shares outstanding	560,000
Dividends declared during 1989	$1.25 per share
Market price at end of 1989	$10.00 per share
EPS for 1989	$2.00

Determine each of the following at the end of 1989:

(a) Dividend yield.

(b) P-E ratio.

(c) Book value per share.

E12. **Book Value per Share—Preferred Stock Outstanding.** Stockholders' equity of the Logus Corporation as of December 31, 1989 is as follows:

Preferred stock, 5%, $100 par value, 20,000 shares authorized and issued (total liquidation value $2,100,000)	$2,000,000
Common stock, no par value, 50,000 shares authorized and issued	1,000,000
Donated capital	500,000
Retained earnings	4,500,000
Total stockholders' equity	$8,000,000

Determine book value per common share, given the following two independent assumptions:

(a) All preferred dividends are fully paid.

(b) The preferred shares are cumulative, and the board of directors has decided to forgo all dividends this year.

E13. **Toys "R" Us Financial Statements.** Using the information contained in the Toys "R" Us financial statements in Appendix D, answer the following questions:

(a) What is the total legal capital of the corporation?

(b) What is the total contributed capital of the corporation?

(c) Determine the book value per share at January 31, 1988.

(d) Earnings per share for the year ended January 31, 1988 were $1.56, and the common stock closed on that day at a price of $40.375. Determine the P-E ratio.

PROBLEMS

P13–1 **Preparation of Stockholders' Equity Section.** At the beginning of the current year, 1989, the Softlite Corporation was formed. The firm issued 50,000 of the 100,000 shares that were authorized of $5 par value common stock for $30 per share. In addition, the firm issued all

1,000 authorized shares of 6%, $100 par value preferred. During the year the firm's net income amounted to $60,000. All dividends on the preferred shares were declared; no dividends on the common were declared. Finally, at the end of the year, the city of Westbridge donated a plot of land to the firm. The land was originally purchased by the city for $100,000 and had a fair market value of $60,000 at the time it was donated to Softlite.

REQUIRED: Prepare in good form the stockholders' equity section of Softlite's balance sheet at the end of 1989.

P13—2 Issuance of Stock. In early 1989, Gerald Weinstein and several associates formed the Pico National Bank. The corporation was authorized to issue 500,000 shares of $100, 6% par value preferred stock and 1 million shares of $10 par value common stock. The following transactions occurred during 1989:

- March 1: Sold 100,000 shares of common stock to a group of investors at $40 per share.
- March 9: Issued 4,375 shares of the preferred stock to an individual in exchange for a building. The building was appraised at $525,000. It was impossible to determine the fair market value of the stock.
- April 1: Issued 1,000 shares of common stock to the bank's attorney in exchange for services rendered in forming the corporation. The stock was currently selling at $50 a share. All parties agreed that this represented the value of the attorney's services.
- December 1: Issued an additional 625 shares of preferred stock at $130 per share.
- December 15: The bank had a very profitable year, so the board of directors decided to declare the stated dividend to the preferred shareholders as well as a $1 per share dividend to the common shareholders.
- December 31: The dividends were paid in cash.

REQUIRED: (a) Make the journal entries to record these transactions.

(b) Assuming that net income for the year amounted to $2 million, prepare the stockholders' equity section of the balance sheet at the end of December.

P13—3 Stock Transactions. Jackson Corporation was authorized to issue 800,000 shares of $100, 8% par value preferred stock and 1.5 million shares of no par $10 stated value common stock. The following transactions occurred during 1990:

- January 2: 20,000 shares of common stock were sold to a group of investors at $20 per share.
- January 15: 5,000 shares of preferred stock were issued to an individual in exchange for a plot of land to be held for future development. The land was appraised at $750,000. The preferred stock was not actively traded.
- March 31: 1,500 shares of common stock were issued to an attorney in exchange for services rendered in forming the corporation. The stock was currently trading at $30 a share. All parties agreed that this represented the value of the attorney's services.
- October 20: An additional 5,000 shares of common stock were issued at $45 per share.
- October 31: 1,000 shares of common stock were repurchased at $32 per share. The shares are to be held in treasury.
- November 15: An additional 1,000 shares of preferred stock were issued at $125 a share.
- November 30: The firm resold 400 shares of the stock held in treasury at a price of $36 per share.
- December 31: Preferred dividends were declared and paid in cash.

REQUIRED: (a) Make the journal entries to record these transactions.

(b) Assuming that net income for the year amounted to $100,000, prepare the stockholders' equity section of the balance sheet at the end of December.

P13—4 Preparation of the Stockholders' Equity Section. Adventure, Inc. was formed in early 1988. The following events occurred from 1988 through 1990:

1988

(a) Issued 500,000 shares of 1,000,000 authorized of no par, no stated value common stock at $20 per share.

(b) Issued 10,000 shares of 20,000 authorized of $100, 5% cumulative preferred stock at $105 per share.

(c) The net loss for the year was $200,000. No dividends were declared.

1989

(d) An additional 10,000 shares of common stock were issued at $15 per share.

(e) Issued 5,000 shares of 10,000 authorized of $100, 8% preferred stock at par.

(f) The net income for the year was $10,000. No dividends were declared.

1990

(g) A plot of land was donated to the corporation by the city. The land was appraised at $100,000.

(h) The firm repurchased 10,000 shares of its common stock at a price of $22 per share. The shares will be held in treasury.

(i) Net income for the year amounted to $800,000. A $.10 per share dividend was paid on common stock. In addition, all required preferred dividends were declared and paid.

REQUIRED: Prepare in good form the stockholders' equity section of the balance sheet as of December 31, 1990.

P13–5 Formation of a Corporation. Dennis Murphy is a successful computer programmer and has decided to begin a business that develops and markets computer learning games for young children. The corporation, called Learn with Computers, was authorized to issue the following stock:

- 100,000 shares of 10% convertible $100 par value preferred stock.

- 500,000 shares of $2 par value common stock.

The following events occurred during the first quarter of 1989:

- January 2: Murphy issued 5,000 shares of common stock to himself in exchange for computers and various software with fair market values as follows:

Computers	$25,000
Software	15,000

- January 30: Twenty of Murphy's friends each purchased 2,000 shares of common stock at $10 per share.

- February 1: The attorney submitted a bill for $5,000 in connection with services performed in organizing the corporation. The attorney agreed to take half of the payment in cash and 250 shares of common stock. The stock in Learn with Computers is not traded on an exchange, and so it is difficult to determine its fair market value.

- February 15: A venture capitalist purchased 10,000 shares of the convertible preferred stock at $100 per share.

- March 1: The venture capitalist converted 5,000 shares of preferred stock into 20,000 shares of common stock.

- March 31: The firm repurchased for retirement 2,000 shares of common at a price of $12 per share. The shares were from the lot issued on January 30.

REQUIRED: **(a)** Make the necessary journal entries to record these transactions.

(b) Prepare in good form the stockholders' equity section of the firm's balance sheet. Net income for the first quarter amounted to $100,000, and no dividends were issued.

(c) Why does a firm such as Learn with Computers issue convertible preferred stock, and why would the venture capitalist purchase it?

P13–6 Determining Missing Figures. Recently, California Valley Federal Savings and Loan converted from a depositor-owned savings and loan association to a publicly held one. The stockholders' equity section of its 1989 balance sheet appears as follows (after conversion and with certain details omitted):

> Stockholders' equity
>
> | | |
> |---|---:|
> | 5% preferred stock, $100 par value, authorized 100,000 shares (liquidation value $110 per share) | $1,000,000 |
> | Common stock, no par value, stated value $5, authorized 1,000,000, issued 500,000 | ? |
> | Paid-in capital from sale of common stock in excess of stated value | 4,000,000 |
> | Retained earnings | 8,000,000 |

REQUIRED: Based on the above information, answer the following questions:

(a) How many shares of preferred stock are outstanding?

(b) At what price was the preferred stock issued?

(c) What is the total of stockholders' equity?

(d) What was the average issue price of the common stock?

(e) What is the total contributed capital of the savings and loan association?

(f) What is the total legal capital of the savings and loan association?

(g) What is the book value per share of common stock?

(h) What is the total dividend requirement on the preferred stock?

(i) What is the total dividend requirement on the common stock?

P13–7 Common and Preferred Dividends. The KABC Corporation began operations in January 1986. During the first five years of operations, it reported the following net loss or income:

1986	$ 300,000	loss
1987	260,000	loss
1988	240,000	loss
1989	1,500,000	income
1990	1,120,000	income

At December 31, 1990, KABC's capital accounts were as follows:

Common stock, par value $10 per share; authorized, issued, and outstanding 100,000 shares	$1,000,000
4% nonparticipating, noncumulative preferred stock, par value $100 per share; authorized, issued, and outstanding 2,000 shares	200,000
8% nonparticipating, cumulative preferred stock, par value $100 per share; authorized, issued, and outstanding 20,000 shares	2,000,000

KABC has never paid a cash dividend or any other type of dividend. KABC is incorporated in California, and under California law, dividends can be paid only if there is a positive balance in retained earnings. There has been no change in the capital structure since the firm's inception.

REQUIRED: **(a)** Determine the maximum amount of dividends that can be paid each year and how it would be distributed between common and preferred shareholders.

(b) What does the participating feature of preferred stock mean? Without recalculating your figures, explain how your answer to (a) would be different if the 8% preferred stock were fully participating.

■ USING THE COMPUTER

P13–8 The European Corporation has 100,000 shares of preferred stock and 300,000 shares of common stock outstanding. The preferred stock has a stated dividend rate of $2 per share and is cumulative and nonparticipating. As of the beginning of the year, there were no preferred dividends in arrears. Using an electronic spreadsheet, determine the amount of dividends distributed to preferred and common shareholders under each of the three independent cases shown at the top of page 507.

	Total Dividends Distributed	
	Current Year	Next Year
Case 1	$ 50,000	$100,000
2	150,000	300,000
3	300,000	400,000

	Case 1	Case 2	Case 3
Current year			
Preferred dividends			
Common dividends			
Total dividends			
Next year			
Preferred dividends			
Common dividends			
Total dividends			

■ UNDERSTANDING FINANCIAL STATEMENTS

P13–9 The following stockholders' equity section was taken from the 1988 and 1987 comparative balance sheets of Lockheed Corporation.

Dollar Figures in Millions	1988	1987
Common stock, $1 par value, 100,000,000 shares authorized; 66,341,786 shares issued (66,005,083 in 1987)	66	66
Additional capital	484	473
Retained earnings (November 29, 1981)	2,205	1,674
Less treasury shares at cost	(279)	(126)
Total	$6,643	$6,460

ADDITIONAL INFORMATION:

	1988	1987
Cash dividends per share of common stock	$ 1.55	$ 1.30
EPS	10.30	6.41
Year-end market price	42.75	36.75

REQUIRED:
(a) Calculate the dividend yield on the common stock at the end of 1988 and 1987.

(b) Determine the P-E ratio at the end of both years.

(c) Determine the book value per share of common stock for both years.

(d) Describe the relationship, if any, between book value and the market price of the stock.

(e) If the average number of common shares outstanding for 1988 was 60,200,000, what was the net income for 1988?

■ FINANCIAL DECISION CASE

P13–10 The Myers Corporation is a successful company owned solely by the members of the Myers family. The company manufactures and distributes animal care products. It has recently developed a new antiflea pill that will protect animals from fleas for up to one year. The formula is patented, and it appears that if the company can finance its manufacturing and distribution, the product will dominate that part of the animal care market.

The firm has been existence for several years. There are currently 1,000 shares of $1 par value common stock outstanding, all of which are held by family members. The stockholders' equity section of the June 30, 1990 balance sheet is as follows:

Common stock, $1 par value, 1,000 shares authorized and issued	$ 1,000
Additional paid-in capital from issue of common stock in excess of par	499,000
Retained earnings	3,450,000
Total stockholders' equity	$3,950,000

Although the company has been profitable, it needs additional cash in order to finance the production and distribution of the new product. Maintaining adequate cash has always been a problem for the firm. L.D. Myers, the current president of the company, tells you that the company is considering three alternatives to raising additional capital:

1. Borrowing $3 million in a five-year term loan from the bank at a 12% interest rate. Interest is due annually; the principal at the end of five years.

2. Issuing 30,000 shares of 8%, $100 par value cumulative convertible preferred stock to a venture capitalist. Each share could be converted into five shares of common stock, beginning in five years.

3. Going public by issuing 50,000 shares of common stock at an estimated price of $6 per share. At their discretion, family members could purchase some of this stock at the $6 price.

Myers tells you that the family has two considerations. The first has to do with forced cash payments due to interest and/or dividends. He reminds you that maintaining adequate cash has always been a problem for the firm. He informs you that interest is deductible for tax purposes but dividend payments are not. The firm is currently in a 34% tax bracket. The second consideration has to do with family control. The company has always been family-owned, and Myers is concerned that the family may have to relinquish that control.

REQUIRED: Write a memo to Myers outlining the advantages and disadvantages of each proposal. Be sure to consider the issues the family has raised.

STOCKHOLDERS' EQUITY— RETAINED EARNINGS AND DIVIDENDS

LEARNING OBJECTIVES

After studying this chapter, you should be able to:

1. Prepare the entries to record corporate dividends.
2. Differentiate between stock splits and stock dividends and be able to record them.
3. Prepare a corporate income statement.
4. Calculate earnings per share and understand its uses.

5. Make prior period adjustments and appropriate retained earnings.
6. List the purposes of the statement of stockholders' equity.

This chapter continues the discussion of the stockholders' equity section of a corporate balance sheet, concentrating on those transactions that affect retained earnings, including corporate net income and dividends. In addition, you will be introduced to the concepts behind earnings per share.

The supplemental statement of retained earnings for AMPCO-Pittsburgh Corporation is shown in Exhibit 14-1. As this statement shows, net earnings and dividends are the two primary events that affect retained earnings. Obviously, net earnings increase

EXHIBIT 14–1

AMPCO-PITTSBURGH CORPORATION Consolidated Statements of Retained Earnings For the Years Ended December 31			
	1987	1986	1985
Retained earnings at beginning of year	$37,232,787	$86,391,909	$85,821,625
Net income (loss)	5,351,405	(46,294,304)	3,434,323
	42,584,192	40,097,605	89,255,948
Less cash dividends declared, $.30 per share	2,870,876	2,864,818	2,864,039
Retained earnings at end of year	$39,713,316	$37,232,787	$86,391,909

retained earnings, and a net loss and dividends decrease retained earnings. Retained earnings can also be affected by prior period adjustments as well as treasury stock transactions discussed in the previous chapter. Our discussion will first start with dividends.

DIVIDENDS

Corporate income is the principal means by which retained earnings are increased. Other than losses, dividends are the principal cause of retained earnings decreases. Dividends, which represent a distribution of assets to shareholders, can be in the form of cash, other assets, or, in some cases, the corporation's own stock.

CASH DIVIDENDS

Most investors purchase either common or preferred stock with the expectation of receiving cash dividends. The amount and regularity of cash dividends are two of the factors that affect the market price of a firm's stock. Many corporations therefore attempt to establish a regular quarterly dividend pattern that is maintained or slowly increased over a number of years. In profitable years, the corporation may issue a special year-end dividend in addition to the regular dividends. Such stable dividend policies increase the attractiveness of the firm's stock. The following, taken from a recent General Electric Company annual report, shows how one corporation implements this policy:

> Dividends declared totaled $1.314 billion in 1988, or $1.46 per share. At the same time, the Company retained sufficient earnings to support enhanced productive capability and to provide adequate financial resources for internal and external growth opportunities. The fourth-quarter increase of 17% in dividends declared marked the 13th consecutive year of dividend growth.

As this quotation indicates, management gives considerable thought to the amount and timing of dividends. In addition to the desire to maintain a stable dividend policy, other factors also affect the amount of cash dividends declared in any one year—for example, the amount of retained earnings or the firm's cash position and business needs.

From a theoretical and practical point of view, there must be a positive balance in retained earnings in order to issue a dividend. If there is a deficit (negative balance) in retained earnings, any dividend would represent a return of invested capital and is called a *liquidating dividend*. A corporation can still issue a normal dividend (a dividend other than a liquidating one) even if it incurred a loss in any one particular year, as long as there is a positive balance in retained earnings.

Because there must be a positive balance in retained earnings before a normal dividend can be issued, the phrase "paying dividends out of retained earnings" developed. However, this is a misnomer. Dividends are not paid out of retained earnings; they are a distribution of assets and are paid in cash or, in some circumstances, in other assets or even stock. Retained earnings are the increase in the firm's net assets due to profitable operations and represent the owners' claim against net assets, not just cash.

The maximum amount of dividends that can be issued in any one year is the total amount of retained earnings. However, this is rarely, if ever, done. Again, in order to pay a cash dividend, a firm must have the necessary cash available, and the amount of cash on hand is not directly related to retained earnings. Furthermore, as is evident from the statement in the GE annual report, a firm has other uses for its cash. Most mature and stable firms restrict their cash dividends to about 40% of their net earnings. Returning to the example of AMPCO-Pittsburgh Corporation, the company declared a consistent amount of dividends even in 1986, a loss year. In other years, dividends were more than 50% of net income.

Declaring Dividends

All dividends must be declared by the board of directors before they become a liability of the corporation. There are three dates that are significant to the declaration and payment of dividends: the declaration date, the date of record, and the payment date.

The **declaration date** is the date on which the board of directors declares the dividend. At that time, the dividend becomes a liability of the corporation and is recorded on its books. The declaration date is usually several weeks prior to the payment date. A typical dividend announcement may be:

> The Board of Directors on December 1 declared a $1.20 per share dividend payable on January 4 to common shareholders of record on December 21.

Only the stockholders as of the **date of record** are eligible for the dividend. Because of the time involved in compiling the list of stockholders at any one date, the date of record usually is two to three weeks after the declaration date, but before the actual payment date.

The **payment date** is the date that the dividend is actually paid. It usually occurs about a month after the declaration date.

Journal Entries to Record Cash Dividends

To demonstrate the journal entries required when a cash dividend is declared and paid, return to the above example, in which the board of directors declared on December 1 a $1.20 per-share dividend payable on January 4 to the common shareholders of record on December 21. Because there are 100,000 common shares outstanding, the total cash dividends will be $120,000.

Dec. 1	Declaration Date		
	Retained Earnings	120,000	
	Dividends Payable		120,000
	To record declaration of $1.20 per-share dividend on 100,000 shares of outstanding common stock. Dividend is payable on January 4 to shareholders of record on December 21.		
Dec. 21	Date of Record		
	No Entry		
Jan. 4	Payment Date		
	Dividends Payable	120,000	
	Cash		120,000
	To record payment of $1.20 per-share dividend declared on December 1.		

When recording the declaration of a dividend, some firms debit an account titled Dividends Declared, rather than debiting Retained Earnings. There is nothing wrong with this procedure, except that a closing entry must be made to close the Dividends Declared account into Retained Earnings. As a result of this entry, the ultimate effect is to reduce retained earnings by the amount of the dividend.

■ NONCASH DIVIDENDS

Occasionally, a firm will issue a dividend in which the payment is in an asset other than cash. Noncash dividends, which are called *property dividends*, are more likely to occur in private corporations than in publicly held ones. Under current accounting pronouncements, the property is revalued to its current market value, and a gain or loss is recognized on the disposition of the asset.[1]

To illustrate, assume that the Ironside Corporation declared a property dividend on December 1, to be distributed on January 4. Marketable securities held by the firm that have a cost of $750,000 and a fair market value (FMV) of $1 million are to be distributed to the shareholders. The journal entries to reflect these transactions are:

Dec. 1	Date of Declaration		
	Investment in Marketable Securities	250,000	
	Gain on Revaluation of Marketable Securities		250,000
	To record revaluation of marketable securities.		

$$\begin{array}{ll} \text{FMV} = & \$1,000,000 \\ \text{Cost} & \underline{750,000} \\ & \underline{\underline{\$\ 250,000}} \end{array}$$

	Retained Earnings	1,000,000	
	Property Dividends Payable		1,000,000
	To record declaration of property dividend payable on January 4.		
Jan. 4	Distribution of Property Dividend		
	Property Dividends Payable	1,000,000	
	Investment in Marketable Securities		1,000,000
	To record distribution of property dividend.		

■ STOCK DIVIDENDS AND STOCK SPLITS

Stock dividends and stock splits both result in the distribution of additional shares to existing stockholders. Because of their similarities, they will be discussed in turn.

■ STOCK DIVIDENDS

Many corporations issue stock dividends instead of, or in addition to, cash dividends. A **stock dividend** is a distribution to current shareholders on a proportional basis of the corporation's own stock. That is, the current holders of stock receive additional shares of stock in proportion to their current holdings. For example, if you own 10,000 shares of common stock in a corporation and it issues a 15% stock dividend, you will receive an additional 1,500 shares ($15\% \times 10,000 = 1,500$). Most stock dividends are given to common stockholders.

When investors receive a stock dividend, the cost per share of their original shares is reduced accordingly. For example, assume that an individual owns 1,000

[1] American Institute of Certified Public Accountants, Accounting Principles Board, Opinion No. 29, *Accounting for Nonmonetary Transactions* (New York: AICPA, 1973), par. 18.

shares of South Gulf Oil Company. These shares were purchased at $60 per share, for a total cost of $60,000. Subsequently, South Gulf issues a 20% stock dividend, so the investor will receive an additional 200 shares (1,000 × .20). Therefore the cost per share to the investor is reduced to $50 per share ($60,000 ÷ 1,200 shares), from the original $60 per share. Thus no income is recognized on the stock dividends when they are received. The reduced cost per share will increase the gain or decrease the loss on subsequent sales of the stock.

Why Stock Dividends Are Issued

A corporation may issue a stock dividend rather than a cash dividend for a number of reasons. Clearly, a stock dividend conserves cash and thus allows the firm to use its cash for growth and expansion. Corporations experiencing growth are generally more likely to issue a stock dividend than are stable, mature firms. In addition, stock dividends transfer a part of retained earnings to permanent capital. This is referred to as **capitalizing retained earnings**; it makes that part of retained earnings transferred to permanent capital unavailable for future cash dividends.

Recording Stock Dividends

When a stock dividend is declared and issued, the corporation debits Retained Earnings for the total fair market value of the stock dividend. Assuming that the stock is immediately issued, the Common Stock account is credited for its par value, if any. Additional Paid-in Capital from the Issue of Common Stock in Excess of Par is credited for the difference between the market value and par value. If the stock has neither a par nor a stated value, Common Stock is credited for the entire market value.[2]

After all these entries have been made, total stockholders' equity remains the same, because there has not been a distribution of cash or other assets. The only difference is in the components of stockholders' equity. Retained earnings is decreased, and contributed capital is increased. As noted, this is often referred to as capitalizing retained earningss, because a portion of retained earnings becomes part of the firm's permanent invested capital. In effect, after the stock dividend, each individual shareholder owns the same proportionate share of the corporation as he or she did before.

EXHIBIT 14-2

KOREAN EXPORT CORPORATION Stockholders' Equity November 30, 1990—Before Stock Dividend	
Common stock, $5 par value, 1,000,000 shares authorized, 60,000 shares issued and outstanding	$ 300,000
Paid-in capital from issue of common stock in excess of par	800,000
Retained earnings	1,900,000
Total stockholders' equity	$3,000,000

To demonstrate the journal entries to record stock dividends, assume that the stockholders' equity of the Korean Export Corporation immediately before the issue of a 10% stock dividend appears as shown in Exhibit 14-2. On November 30, 1990, the corporation issues a 10% stock dividend distributed immediately. At the time of the declaration, the stock is selling at $40 per share. As a result of the 10% dividend, a

[2]In this example, it is assumed that the dividend was declared and issued at the same time. In reality, a period of time may elapse before the declared stock dividend is actually issued to the stockholders. Although this changes the required journal entries slightly, it does not change the effect of the dividend when either declared or issued.

total of 6,000 shares ($10\% \times 60,000 = 6,000$) is issued. Based on this data, the following journal entry is made:

Nov. 30, 1990	Retained Earnings	240,000	
	Common Stock		30,000
	Paid-in Capital from Issue of Common		
	Stock in Excess of Par		210,000
	To record declaration of 10% stock dividend;		
	6,000 shares distributed. FMV of stock at time		
	of declaration is $40 per share.		

The stockholders' equity section of the Korean Export Corporation's balance sheet at November 30, immediately after the issuance of the stock dividend, appears as shown in Exhibit 14-3.

EXHIBIT 14–3

KOREAN EXPORT CORPORATION
Stockholders' Equity
November 30, 1990—After Stock Dividend

Common stock, $5 par value, 1,000,000 shares authorized, 66,000 shares issued and outstanding	$ 330,000
Paid-in capital from issue of common stock in excess of par	1,010,000
Retained earnings	1,660,000
Total stockholders' equity	$3,000,000

The most important thing to note in comparing the stockholders' equity section in both balance sheets is that the total is $3 million in both cases. The only difference is the total of the various accounts within stockholders' equity.

Large versus Small Stock Dividends

Up to this point, the discussion has involved small stock dividends, which range up to 20% or 25%. Occasionally, a corporation will issue a large stock dividend. The accounting profession defines a large stock dividend as one in excess of 20% to 25%. Some stock dividends are as large as 100%, and these have the effect of proportionately reducing the market price of the corporation's stock. Large stock dividends are recorded by debiting Retained Earnings and crediting Common Stock for the total par value of the stock issued by the stock dividend. The market value of the stock is ignored.

■ STOCK SPLITS

A **stock split** happens when a corporation increases the number of its common shares and proportionally decreases their par or stated value. The end result is a doubling, tripling, or quadrupling of the number of outstanding shares and a corresponding decrease in the market price per share of the stock. This price decrease is the main reason that a corporation decides to split its stock. When the market price per share is too high, the stock loses its attractiveness to many investors, because it is most economical to purchase stock in round lots of 100. A stock price that is too high makes round-lot purchases impossible for some potential investors. For example, if a firm's stock is currently selling for $240, and the firm splits its stock 4 for 1, the price per share will fall to around $60. Thus it takes only $6,000 rather than $24,000 to purchase 100 shares.

To demonstrate the accounting for stock splits, assume that the Moreno Corporation's stockholders' equity accounts are as shown in Exhibit 14-4. The corporation's stock is currently selling at $90 per share. The firm decides to issue a 3-for-1 stock

EXHIBIT 14–4

MORENO CORPORATION Stockholders' Equity— Before Stock Split	
Common stock, $15 par value, 1,000,000 shares authorized, 50,000 shares issued and outstanding	$ 750,000
Additional paid-in capital	1,450,000
Retained earnings	1,800,000
Total stockholders' equity	$4,000,000

split. As a result, the corporation reduces the par value of its stock from $15 to $5 and increases the number of shares issued and outstanding from 50,000 to 150,000. Although no journal entry is required, some firms will make a memorandum entry noting the stock split. Immediately after the stock split, the Moreno Corporation's stockholders' equity accounts are as shown in Exhibit 14-5. As you can see by comparing the corporation's stockholders' equity accounts before and after the stock split, there is no change in either total stockholders' equity or the individual components. Only the par value and the number of issued and outstanding shares are different.

EXHIBIT 14–5

MORENO CORPORATION Stockholders' Equity— After Stock Split	
Common stock, $5 par value, 3,000,000 shares authorized, 150,000 shares issued and outstanding	$ 750,000
Additional paid-in capital	1,450,000
Retained earnings	1,800,000
Total stockholders' equity	$4,000,000

From the investor's viewpoint, each stockholder receives two additional shares for each share owned. In effect, the old shares are canceled, and shares with the new par value are issued. Because the price of the firm's stock is likely to fall to about $30, the total market value of each stockholder's investment immediately after the split will be about the same as it was before the split.

Stock splits and large stock dividends are quite similar. They both serve to reduce the market price per share and increase the number of shares issued and outstanding. In each circumstance, total stockholders' equity remains the same, because there has been neither an increase nor a decrease in the entity's net assets. For example, a 2-for-1 stock split is similar to a 100% stock dividend. In both cases, the number of shares issued and outstanding doubles, and the market price per share will fall accordingly. However, if this event is a stock dividend, there will be no change in the stock's par or stated value, but there will be a decrease in the Retained Earnings account and an increase in the Common Stock account. If this event is a stock split, there is no change in either Retained Earnings or Common Stock, just a decrease in par value and an increase in the number of issued and outstanding shares.

■ CORPORATE INCOME STATEMENTS

A corporation or even a large private enterprise usually derives income and incurs expenses from many sources. Since the mid-1960s, the accounting profession has felt that net income should be a comprehensive figure. That is, comprehensive net income "includes all changes in equity during a period except those resulting from investments by owners and distributions to owners [dividends]."[3]

The notion of comprehensive income, however, does present a problem for users of the income statement. One of the primary purposes of this statement is to help users predict future income patterns. Yet when a firm derives income from various types of transactions, it is difficult to separate recurring from nonrecurring transactions, so the predictive ability of the income statement may be decreased. As the FASB noted:

> Characteristics of various sources of comprehensive income may differ significantly from one another, indicating a need for information about various components of comprehensive income.[4]

Exhibit 14-6, an article from *Forbes* magazine, illustrates the need for many users to be able to distinguish among various sources of comprehensive income.[5]

EXHIBIT 14—6

UNREAL ACCOUNTING

Suppose your metal-bending company owns an old desk. It's on the books for $100. One day you discover the old desk belonged to Ben Franklin; Sotheby's auctions it off for $50,000.

Comes now the end of the year and you're calculating your company's operating earnings from bending metal. Question: Should you include the $49,900 profit from selling that old desk in "operating earnings"?

Don't laugh. In their reported operating earnings, lots of big companies include gains (and losses) from once-only events. As a result, says David Hawkins, professor of accounting at Harvard Business School, "investors cannot just take the bottom-line numbers before or after extraordinary items and assume that they understand what is going on." Doing so, Hawkins warns, "can be dangerous to your wealth."

Consider Time Inc. For 1986, the august publisher reported income, before taxes, of $626 million. Aftertax net came to $376 million, $5.95 per share, up 89% from 1985. With earnings momentum like that, maybe Time was worth the $100-plus a share it was selling for before Bloody Monday ripped it to $81. (It recovered to $88 two days later.)

But did Time's ongoing, operating businesses really earn $376 million? Is the figure a good basis from which to project 1987's earnings and buy its stock? Not necessarily.

Look at the $376 million reported profit, and you'll see it includes the equivalent of Ben Franklin's desk. To wit: In 1986, when the stock market was hot, Time sold 20% of a cable television subsidiary, American Television Communications Corp., to the public for a pretax gain of $318 million. Time booked this one-time gain as operating earnings—even though the only way it might realize a comparable gain next year would be to sell off yet another 20%.

Time also threw a $33 million profit on another investment, and $113 million in one-time expenses from relocating offices and reducing staff, into pretax earnings. Eliminate these once-only gains from selling off investments, and Time's aftertax operating earnings from ongoing businesses was around $129 million last year, down over 35% from 1985.

What's going on here? We called John Shank, professor of accounting at Dartmouth's Tuck School. Don't blame Time Inc., said Shank. Blame the accountants. Their rules make companies include such unusual items as stock sale profits and office relocation expenses in income, even though they are unrelated to current, or future, operations.

Sometimes the accounting rules understate a company's earnings from its ongoing businesses. Take Eastman Kodak. In 1985 Kodak decided to get out of the instant photography business, and close some plants. Total writeoff: $563 million. Where should Kodak show this amount? Its accountants made the company deduct it from operating earnings. As a result, Kodak reported earnings on its continuing photographic, copier and chemical businesses of $332 million, whereas in reality those businesses earned $597 million aftertax.

Then, in 1986, Kodak wrote off more assets and sacked people, at a cost of $654 million. Again, this one-time item was deducted from operating earnings, with the result that Kodak reported earnings from ongoing operations of $374 million. But this time the charge made sense: The 1986 writeoff was, after all, associated with Kodak's ongoing businesses. The 1985 writeoff was on a business, instant photography, on which Kodak had irrevocably pulled the plug.

Why do the accountants insist that companies report, as income from operations, gains or losses that will never recur? In essence, because they have come to the conclusion over the years that anything

(continued)

---

[3] Financial Accounting Standards Board, Concepts Statement No. 6, *Elements of Financial Statements* (Stamford, Conn.: FASB, December 1985), par. 76.

[4] Ibid., par. 61.

[5] Subrata N. Chakravarty, "Unreal Accounting," *Forbes*, November 16, 1987, pp. 74, 78. Reprinted by permission of *Forbes* magazine. © Forbes Inc., 1987.

EXHIBIT 14–6 continued

that produces income or expense in a given year must be dragged through the income statement in that year. If a metal-bending company earns $49,900 on an antique desk in 1986, that profit has to show up in 1986's net. Where else, argue the accountants, could it show up?

The accountants have been arguing this so-called dirty surplus problem for years. Back in the go-go accounting of the 1960s, companies had enormous latitude in reporting nonrecurring income and losses. The income they would usually report as income; the losses they would deduct from their retained earnings account, so as to manage earnings better. They could thus avoid acknowledging errors long enough until they could smoothly wipe them off the books. "So there was something called dirty surplus," recalls Dartmouth's John Shank, "which betrayed the bias of those who didn't like it."

The accounting rule writers quickly moved to solve that problem by encouraging companies to report nonrecurring income and loss on their income statements, but labeling them "Extraordinary Items." A new problem was born. "The practice [of reporting extraordinary items] created nothing but confusion because companies would take the good stuff into earnings and call the bad stuff extraordinary," explains Harvard's David Hawkins. The result was a new rule—Accounting Principles Board Opinion 30, issued 1973—which significantly tightened the definition of extraordinary items, defining them as events that were unrelated to the company's business and unlikely to recur. Under Opinion 30, any special event that did not qualify as an "extraordinary event" should be reported as an "unusual item."

Opinion 30 worked all right as long as there weren't too many unusual items. But then came the 1980s and widespread corporate restructuring—office closing, asset sales and all sorts of "unusual" items, some of which are related to operations and some of which are not.

So here the matter stands: By accounting rules, income from nonrecurring events—like selling the old desk, or selling off part of a cable TV system—must be included as part of net income. So must items relating to errors and omissions of past years, even if their effect is to seriously distort current earnings with a one-time adjustment. If investors and other users of financial statements aren't clever enough to read all the explanatory footnotes to see how the company's ongoing businesses are doing—well, too bad for the investors.

The problem becomes more acute when you remember that Value Line, Standard & Poor's and other statistical services generally pick up only a single number—net income—to report a company's profitability.

This single, often meaningless number than gets reflected in return on equity, growth rate calculations, averages and the like.

"There are items that cause earnings to appear to be more volatile than they actually are on a continuing basis," says Hawkins. "But whether they make companies look better or worse, they are, in every case, a poor indicator of the companies' future earnings prospects." More relevant accounting, anyone?

In order to meet this need, generally accepted accounting principles require that the major components of income be segregated on the income statement. These major components are:

1. Income from continuing operations.
2. Discontinued operations.
3. Extraordinary items.
4. Cumulative effect of changes in accounting methods or principles.
5. Earnings per share for each of the above items.

An income statement that includes all of these components is shown in Exhibit 14-7. In reviewing this income statement, keep in mind that it is unlikely that an enterprise would have income from all of these sources in any one year; they all are presented for illustrative purposes only. Furthermore, if all these categories do in fact exist, they must be listed in the manner and order shown in Exhibit 14-7.[6]

■ INCOME FROM CONTINUING OPERATIONS

Income from continuing operations includes all of the recurring and usual transactions that the firm enters into as it produces its goods and services. Thus such items

[6] In December 1984, the FASB issued Concepts Statement No. 5, *Recognition and Measurement in Financial Statements of Business Enterprises* (Stamford, Conn.). In that Statement, the FASB suggested reformulating the income statement. The major change would be differentiating earnings from comprehensive net income. Cumulative effects of changes in accounting methods would not be included in earnings, but they would be included in net income. These changes are only suggestions, and the Board expects only gradual change.

EXHIBIT 14–7

THE EXACTO COMPUTER CORPORATION
Comparative Income Statement
For the Years Ended December 31 (in millions)

	1990	1989
Net sales	$6,000	$5,700
Cost of goods sold	3,900	3,648
Gross margin	2,100	2,052
Selling and general and administrative expenses	1,260	1,230
Operating income	840	822
Other income		
Gain on sale of building	15	0
Interest income	5	2
	860	824
Other expenses		
Interest expense	10	6
Income from continuing operations, before taxes	850	818
Provision for income taxes	340	327
Income from continuing operations	510	491
Discontinued operations		
Loss from operations of discontinued segment, net of tax savings of $18 in 1990 and $14 in 1989	(27)	(16)
Gain on disposal of business segment, net of applicable taxes of $27	33	0
Income before extraordinary items and cumulative effect of accounting change	516	475
Extraordinary item—Gain on expropriation of subsidiary, net of applicable taxes of $45	0	55
Cumulative effect of change in accounting method for depreciation, net of taxes of $23	27	0
Net income	$ 543	$ 530
Earnings per share		
Income from continuing operations	$ 2.04	$ 1.96
Discontinued operations	.02	(.06)
Income before extraordinary items and cumulative effect of accounting change	2.06	1.90
Extraordinary gains	0	.22
Cumulative effect of accounting change	.11	0
Net income	$ 2.17	$ 2.12

as sales, cost of goods sold, operating expenses, and other income and expense items all are included in income from continuing operations. For 1990 and 1989, income from continuing operations for the Exacto Computer Corporation is $510 million and $491 million, respectively. The significance of these amounts is that as decision makers use the income statement to make predictions about the future, these items indicate how profitable the corporation has been and how profitable it might be on a recurring and continuing basis.

Two important points need to be made about this example. First, either a single-step or a multistep format (shown in Chapter 5) can be used. Regardless of which form is used, income from continuing operations must be the same. Second, the total income tax expense is divided among the four components of the income statement. This is called **intraperiod income tax allocation**. It means that the total income tax expense for the period is related to the proper component that caused the income. Conversely, **interperiod income tax allocation**, discussed in Chapter 11, refers to the allocation of income taxes among different accounting periods. Intraperiod income tax allocation is necessary in order to maintain an appropriate relationship between income tax expense and income from continuing operations, discontinued operations, extraordinary items, and cumulative effects of accounting changes.

To illustrate, the total income tax expense for 1990 for Exacto is $372 million, computed as in Exhibit 14-8. Instead of showing just one figure for taxes, $372 million, this amount is allocated to the various components of net income. Thus the reader of the income statement knows how each item affected the firm's total tax expense and what the income tax expense can be expected to be in the future on a recurring basis.

EXHIBIT 14–8

THE EXACTO COMPUTER CORPORATION Income Tax Expense for 1990 (in millions)		
	Before-tax Amount	Tax (Tax Savings)
Income from continuing operations before taxes	$850	$340
Discontinued operations		
Loss from operations	(45)	(18)
Gain on sale	60	27
Cumulative effect of accounting change	50	23
	$915	$372
Net income ($915 − $372) = $543		

At first glance, it may seem strange that a loss is reduced on a tax savings. For example, as noted in Exhibit 14-7, the firm suffered a loss on discontinued operations of $45 million in 1990. Because a loss reduces income, income tax is less by a portion of the loss. Thus, in this example, total taxes are reduced by $18 million because of this loss, and this tax savings is netted against the before-tax loss of $45 million to arrive at the net loss of $27 million. By convention, discontinued operations, extraordinary items, and cumulative effects of accounting changes are shown net of their tax effects, whereas income from continuing operations is shown both before and after taxes.

■ DISCONTINUED OPERATIONS

The Accounting Principles Board, in Opinion 30, stated that results from discontinued operations and the gain or loss from the disposal of the discontinued segment should be shown separately from income from continued operations. These figures should be disclosed immediately below income from continuing operations.

According to professional pronouncements, a **segment** of a business is a "component of an entity whose activities represent a separate major line of business or class of customer."[7] A segment may be a subsidiary, a division, or a department, as long as its activities can be clearly distinguished from other assets both physically and operationally for financial reporting purposes. A few years ago, for example, CBS discontinued its CBS Cable division, which produced certain cable programming. This represents a discontinued operation. However, if CBS sold one of its corporate-owned

[7]American Institute of Certified Public Accountants, Accounting Principles Board, Opinion No. 30, *Reporting the Results of Operations* (New York: AICPA, 1973), par. 13.

television stations, this would not be considered a discontinued operation, because CBS still owns several other stations and has several hundred affiliates.

The discontinued operations segment of the income statement of the Exacto Computer Corporation that is illustrated in Exhibit 14-7 is reproduced in Exhibit 14-9. As this partial income statement shows, the two types of events listed under the discontinued operations segment are income or loss from operations and the gain or loss on the actual disposal of the segment. As noted before, each item is shown net of its tax effect. Income or loss from operations represents the net of the revenues and the expenses related to that particular segment. In the case of Exacto, there is a loss of $27 million, net of taxes, in 1990.

EXHIBIT 14–9

THE EXACTO COMPUTER CORPORATION Partial Income Statement For the Years Ended December 31 (in millions)		
	1990	**1989**
Income from continuing operations	$510	$491
Discontinued operations		
Loss from operations of discontinued segment, net of tax savings of $18 in 1990 and $14 in 1989	(27)	(16)
Gain on disposal of business segment, net of applicable taxes of $27	33	0
Income before extraordinary items and cumulative effect of accounting change	$516	$475

The treatment for 1989 in the comparative 1990 and 1989 income statement is important to understand. In this example, the segment was disposed of in 1990, so if one looked at the comparative income statement covering 1988 and 1989, the entire discontinued operations segment would not exist. All income and expenses from this particular segment were included with the regular income and expenses categories found in income from continuing operations. However, when the comparative statement covering 1989 and 1990 was prepared in 1990, the 1989 statement was changed. The relevant revenues and expenses were pulled out of their regular categories, netted, and shown after their tax effects, at a loss of $16 million. This was done in order to make the 1990 and 1989 statements comparative.

The second item under the discontinued segment category is a gain or loss on the actual disposal. In the example, the Exacto Computer Corporation incurred a $33 million gain, net of taxes. There is no comparable gain shown in 1989 because the disposal did not occur until 1990.

■ EXTRAORDINARY ITEMS

Extraordinary items are gains and losses that result from transactions that are both unusual in nature and infrequent in occurrence. Because these transactions are unusual and infrequent, they need to be separated from continuing operations so that investors can better use the income statement to predict future income.

Criteria for Determining Extraordinary Items
The criteria for determining whether an item is extraordinary have caused much controversy. Prior to the issuance of Opinion 30 in 1973, the management of a firm had considerable discretion in determining whether an item was extraordinary. Thus several items were considered extraordinary when, under current accounting principles, they would be included in income from continuing operations. For example, there was considerable controversy over Penn Central's decision in 1969 to consider the sale of certain real estate as an ordinary gain rather than an extraordinary gain. Many

observers felt that this classification was made in order to conceal operating losses during the year.[8] In order to limit the number and type of extraordinary items, current accounting pronouncements restrict them to those transactions that are both unusual and infrequent.

An unusual event or transaction is one that is highly abnormal or is clearly only incidentally related to the enterprise's ordinary and typical activities, taking into account the environment in which the entity operates. For an event to be infrequent in occurrence, it should be of a type that would not reasonably be expected to recur in the foreseeable future, again taking into account the environment in which the entity operates.

Although an event or transaction must meet both of these criteria to be extraordinary, considerable judgment is still needed to apply them. For example, in order to determine a business's ordinary and typical activities, the specific characteristics of the entity, such as its scope of operations and line of business, should be considered. The entity's environment includes such factors as the characteristics of the industry in which the entity operates, its geographical location, and the extent of governmental regulation. Thus an item may be unusual and/or infrequent for one enterprise but not for another, because of the differences in their environments.

To demonstrate the judgment required in this area, assume that a Florida citrus grower's crop of oranges is destroyed by frost. Is this an extraordinary item? No, frost damage in Florida is normally experienced every three to four years; given the environment in which the entity operates, the infrequency-of-occurrence criterion has not been met.[9] However, if it were a California grower, would the answer be different? Most likely yes, because damage from frost is unusual and infrequent in California, so any loss would be extraordinary.

Examples of Extraordinary Items

Because of the judgment involved in determining extraordinary items, both the APB and FASB have stated that certain items or transactions definitely are and are not extraordinary items. The more important ones are listed in Exhibit 14-10. Some of the

EXHIBIT 14–10	**Considered Extraordinary**	**Not Considered Extraordinary**
Illustration of Extraordinary Items*	1. Destruction by an earthquake of one of the oil refineries owned by a large, multinational oil company.	1. Write-downs or write-offs of receivables, equipment, or similar items.
	2. Destruction of a large portion of a tobacco manufacturer's crops by a hailstorm in an area in which severe damage from hailstorms is rare.	2. Gains and losses from a disposal of a segment.
	3. Expropriation of assets by a foreign government.	3. Gains and losses from the sale or abandonment of property, plant, or equipment.
	4. Gains or losses due to a prohibition under a newly created law.	4. Effects of strikes against the firm and/or competitors and major suppliers.
	5. Gains and losses on early extinguishment of debt.†	5. Changes in accounting estimates and methods.

*Sources:

1. APB Opinion No. 30, *Reporting the Results of Operations* (New York: AICPA, 1973).

2. Accounting Interpretations of APB Opinion No. 30, *Reporting the Results of Operations* (New York: AICPA, 1973).

†FASB Statement 4 requires these gains and losses, if material, to be treated as extraordinary, regardless of the criteria set forth by Opinion 30.

[8] Abraham Briloff, *Unaccountable Accounting* (New York: Harper & Row, 1972), p. 194.

[9] American Institute of Certified Public Accountants, Accounting Principles Board, Accounting Interpretations of APB Opinion 30, *Reporting the Results of Operations* (New York: AICPA, 1973).

items that are not considered extraordinary in the exhibit are classified that way because they are unusual or infrequent but not both. In these cases, the item should be recorded as a separate component of income from continuing operations. However, these accounting pronouncements have not entirely quieted the arguments surrounding the proper classification of certain nonoperating items.

The income statement in Exhibit 14-7 shows how both extraordinary items and transactions that do not meet both criteria are disclosed. The extraordinary item in this example is a gain from an expropriation of a subsidiary. The gain occurred because the firm received compensation in excess of the book value of its subsidiary. The 1989 gain of $55 million is shown net of tax. Thus the actual gain of $100 million is reduced by the related taxes of $45 million. It is disclosed on the income statement immediately after discontinued operations, if any. If there were no discontinued operations, extraordinary items would follow income from operations. The gain on the sale of the building, which does not meet both criteria, is shown before taxes in the continuing operations section of the income statement.

TYPES OF ACCOUNTING CHANGES

Over a period of time, a firm is likely to make two different types of accounting changes: a change in accounting methods and a change in accounting estimates. A **change in accounting method** results when a firm changes from one generally accepted accounting principle or method to another generally accepted one. A **change in accounting estimate** occurs when a firm changes a particular estimate, such as an asset's depreciable life, as a result of new information that was not available when the original estimate was made.

Change in Method or Principle

As previously noted, management can sometimes choose among acceptable accounting methods. For example, there are different methods of determining bad debts, cost of goods sold, and depreciation expense. Once a particular method is chosen, accountants feel that it should be consistently used unless a change to a different method is preferable, or a particular accounting standard is changed that mandates the switch. When there is a change in accounting method, current accounting rules generally require that the cumulative effect of the change be included in income of the current period.[10] The cumulative effect is the amount required to adjust the asset or liability to what it would have been had the new accounting method always been used. This amount, which is either a gain or a loss, is shown on the income statement, net of taxes, immediately before net income.

To illustrate, assume that on January 2, 1988, a firm purchased a piece of equipment at a cost of $100,000. The equipment has a useful life of ten years with no residual value. In 1988 and 1989, the firm used double-declining-balance depreciation, but at the beginning of 1990, the third year of the asset's life, the firm switched to straight-line. The difference of $16,000 between what the depreciation was for the first two years on double-declining-balance and what it would have been had the straight-line method been used is a cumulative effect of an accounting change, as calculated in Exhibit 14-11.

The cumulative effect of $16,000 can be calculated either by comparing the difference in the total depreciation expense for the two years or by comparing the as-

---

[10] American Institute of Certified Public Accountants, Accounting Principles Board, Opinion No. 20, *Accounting Changes* (New York: AICPA, 1971). There are several exceptions to this general rule. For example, when a firm changes from FIFO to LIFO, a cumulative effect *is not calculated*, because the layering process of LIFO makes it impossible to calculate the cumulative effect. Concepts Statement 5 recommends that cumulative-effect-of-accounting changes be included in comprehensive income but not earnings.

EXHIBIT 14–11

Calculation of Cumulative Effect of Change in Depreciation

Difference in Depreciation			
	Double-declining-balance	Straight-line	Difference
Year 1, 1988	$20,000[a]	$10,000[c]	$10,000
Year 2, 1989	16,000[b]	10,000	6,000
	$36,000	$20,000	$16,000

Difference in Book Value			
	Double-declining-balance	Straight-line	Cumulative Effect of Accounting Change
Historical cost	$100,000	$100,000	$ 0
Accumulated depreciation	36,000[d]	20,000[d]	16,000
Book value	$ 64,000	$ 80,000	$16,000

[a]$100,000 × .20 = $20,000
[b]($100,000 − $20,000) × .20 = $16,000
[c]$100,000 × .10 = $10,000
[d]From previous schedule.

set's net book value under each of the depreciation methods. For example, at the beginning of Year 3, 1990, the asset had a book value of $64,000 under the double-declining-balance method. If straight-line depreciation had been used for the two previous years, the asset would have had a book value of $80,000. Thus a cumulative gain of $16,000 is needed to increase the book value of the asset from $64,000 to $80,000. The gain, net of any tax effect, is shown on the 1990 income statement. Depreciation expense for 1990 is calculated on the straight-line method and is $10,000. If it were necessary to decrease the book value of the asset, a loss would be recorded.

In the example in Exhibit 14-7, there is a gain resulting from the cumulative effect of a change in depreciation method. The total gain is $50 million but is shown at $27 million, or net of the tax effect of $23 million. Full disclosure requires that the effect of this change be reported in the footnotes to the financial statements as well as in the auditor's report.

Change in Accounting Estimate

In order to make the allocations required under the matching convention, accountants must make estimates. Examples of some of these estimates are service lives, uncollectible receivables, residual value, and warranty costs. Because an estimate is inherently uncertain, new information may require a change in the original estimate. This is quite common in accounting and does not require a cumulative catch-up. A change in estimate affects only the current period in which the change is made and future periods.

To demonstrate, assume that an enterprise purchases equipment at a cost of $40,000 on January 2, 1988. The asset, with no residual value, is depreciated over an estimated life of ten years using the straight-line method. At the beginning of 1990, Year 3 of the asset's life, the firm decides to decrease the service life of the equipment from ten years to eight. Thus, with a new total life of eight years, there are only six years remaining at the beginning of 1990 (eight years less the two years that expired in 1988 and 1989). This change in estimate is handled by now spreading the book value of $32,000 at January 2, 1990 over the remaining six years. This depreciation expense in 1990 and for each of the next five years is $5,333, calculated as follows:

Yearly depreciation from 1/2/88 to 12/31/89: $\dfrac{\$40,000}{10 \text{ yrs.}} = \underline{\$4,000}$ per year

Book value 1/2/90:	Historical cost	$40,000
	Accumulated depreciation,	
	1/2/88 to 12/31/89	8,000
		$32,000

Depreciation expense, 1990 and thereafter: $\dfrac{\$32,000}{6 \text{ yrs.}} = \underline{\$5,333}$

Thus depreciation expense in 1990 is $5,333, and there is no cumulative effect of a change in accounting method on the income statement.

EARNINGS PER SHARE

Earnings per share (EPS) is one of the most popular—if not *the* most popular—financial statistic reported in financial publications. The relationship between EPS and the stock's market price is called the *price-earnings ratio* (P-E ratio) and is presented for most stocks listed on the stock page of newspapers. Thus an understanding of how EPS is calculated and its uses and limitations is necessary in order to be an informed user of financial information.

CALCULATING EPS—THE BASICS

The complex rules regarding the calculation of EPS are spelled out primarily in APB Opinion 15.[11] The purpose here is to present an overview of the calculation. In the simplest sense, EPS is calculated by dividing net income available to common shareholders by the weighted average number of outstanding common shares.

$$\text{EPS} = \frac{\text{Net income available to common shareholders}}{\text{Weighted average number of common shares outstanding}}$$

EPS is meaningful only in regard to common stockholders. This is because preferred shareholders have claims only to the stipulated dividend.

Net Income Available to Common Shareholders

Net income available to common shareholders is equal to net income less preferred stock dividends declared.[12] If there is no preferred stock, the numerator of the formula will be simply net income. To illustrate, assume that the Mori Corporation earned net income of $1,562,500 for the year ended December 31, 1990. The firm declared the following dividends during 1990:

| Common dividends | $125,000 |
| Preferred dividends | 62,500 |

In this case, net income available to common shareholders is $1,500,000, or $1,562,500 − $62,500. The common dividends declared are ignored, because all

---

[11] American Institute of Certified Public Accountants, Accounting Principles Board, Opinion No. 15, *Earnings per Share* (New York: AICPA, 1969).

[12] If the preferred stock is cumulative, the dividends relating to the stock must be deducted from net income whether or not they are declared, because preferred shareholders do not lose their claim to undeclared dividends on cumulative stock.

the earnings after preferred dividends are theoretically available to common shareholders, whether or not returned in the form of dividends.

Weighted Average Number of Common Shares Outstanding

If a corporation has not issued any additional common stock, the denominator of the EPS formula will be simply the number of common shares outstanding at the end of the year. In many cases, however, firms issue additional shares of common stock at various times during the year. In these cases, it is incorrect to take the total number of shares outstanding at the end of the year, because the firm did not have use of the cash or other assets generated from the additional stock issue for the entire year. Therefore a weighted average number of shares must be calculated, based on the number of months that the shares were outstanding.

To demonstrate, assume that the Mori Corporation has 1 million shares of common stock outstanding on January 1, 1990. During the year, the firm issued the following additional common stock:

Beginning		1,000,000
April 1, 1990	250,000	
September 30, 1990	150,000	400,000
Ending		1,400,000

The weighted average number of common shares outstanding is 1,225,000, calculated as follows:

Number of Shares		Fraction of Year Outstanding		Weighted Average Number of Shares
1,000,000	×	$\frac{3}{12}$	=	250,000
1,250,000	×	$\frac{6}{12}$	=	625,000
1,400,000	×	$\frac{3}{12}$	=	350,000
		$\frac{12}{12}$		
Weighted average number of common shares outstanding				1,225,000

In effect, the number of shares outstanding for any part of the year is multiplied by the fraction of the year they were outstanding. In a full year, 12 12ths must be accounted for.

Based on this data, EPS for the Mori Corporation is $1.22 (rounded), determined by the following calculation:

$$\frac{\$1,500,000}{1,225,000} = \$1.22$$

EPS of $1.22 is more realistic than a figure determined by using 1.4 million shares, the number of common shares outstanding at year-end. Using 1.4 million shares would decrease EPS and would be based on the assumption that the firm had use for the entire year of the cash from the additional stock issued on April 1 and September 30.

■ CALCULATING EPS FOR MORE COMPLEX CAPITAL STRUCTURES

Many large corporations have **complex capital structures**, which contain certain types of bonds, preferred stock, or other securities that are convertible into common shares. These types of convertible securities are often dilutive, because if they were converted into common stock, increasing the number of common shares outstanding, EPS could be reduced. Accounting rules require that when a firm has a complex capital structure, two separate EPS figures must be calculated: primary and fully diluted EPS.

Primary EPS

Primary earnings per share is calculated by dividing net income available to common shareholders by the weighted average number of shares outstanding plus those dilutive securities that meet the definition of a common stock equivalent. A **common stock equivalent** is a dilutive security that, because of the terms or circumstances at the time of its issue, is essentially equivalent to common stock. That is, a common stock equivalent is not common stock *per se*, but it does allow the holder to become a common stock holder at some future date. Therefore the market value of the common stock equivalent tends to vary in relation to the common stock to which it is related. Common stock equivalents include stock options and, under certain circumstances specified by the accounting profession, convertible preferred stock and bonds.[13] Because common stock equivalents so closely resemble common stock, they are treated as common stock in the EPS calculation. Thus the formula to calculate primary EPS is:

$$\text{Primary EPS} = \frac{\text{Net income available to common shareholders}}{\text{Weighted average number of common shares}\atop\text{outstanding plus common stock equivalents}}$$

Fully Diluted EPS

Fully diluted EPS is calculated by dividing net income available to common shareholders by the weighted average number of common shares outstanding plus all dilutive securities, whether or not they are considered common stock equivalents. The purpose of presenting fully diluted EPS is to show the worst possible case, which assumes that all the dilutive securities were converted. Thus present and potential investors can see what their earnings per share would be, assuming maximum dilution. The formula to calculate fully diluted EPS is:

$$\text{Fully diluted EPS} = \frac{\text{Net income available to common shareholders}}{\text{Weighted average number of common shares}\atop\text{outstanding and common stock equivalents and}\atop\text{all other dilutive securities}}$$

Although the numerator in both cases represents net income available to common shareholders, the actual dollar amounts are likely to be different. This distinction and the actual calculation of primary and fully diluted earnings per share are covered in more advanced books.

EPS and Stock Splits and Dividends

Stock dividends and stock splits affect the number of common shares issued and outstanding, which in turn affects the EPS calculation. The current year's EPS is calculated by using the number of common shares after any stock dividends and stock splits. This means that when comparative statements are issued, or five- and ten-year summaries are presented, the number of common shares on which EPS is determined in these statements must be retroactively adjusted for these dividends or splits. This ensures

---

[13] The accounting profession has definite rules governing which dilutive securities are common stock equivalents. These rules are far beyond the scope of this book; they can be found in APB Opinion 15 and FASB Statements 55 and 85.

that the EPS figures will be comparable. These points regarding stock splits and EPS are illustrated in the following footnote taken from an annual report of Albertson's, Inc.:

> On August 31, 1987 the Board of Directors approved a two-for-one stock split, effected in the form of a stock dividend, payable October 5, 1987 to stockholders of record on September 18, 1987. Accordingly, January 28, 1988 balances reflect the split with an increase in common stock and a reduction in capital in excess of par value of $33,620,000. Stock option and per share data have also been retroactively adjusted to reflect the split.

■ PRESENTING EPS ON CORPORATE INCOME STATEMENTS

All publicly held corporations are required to present EPS data on their income statements.[14] Primary EPS must be disclosed, and if fully diluted EPS is at least 3% less than primary EPS, fully diluted EPS also must be disclosed. EPS data also should be presented for major categories on the income statement, such as income from continuing operations and discontinued operations. Exhibit 14-7 shows the EPS presentation for the Exacto Computer Corporation, and Exhibit 14-12 presents the income statement for Carter Hawley Hale Stores, Inc., a large retailer, including the relevant EPS disclosures.

■ USES AND LIMITATIONS OF EPS DATA

EPS is a popular financial statistic that provides useful comparisons among companies. It also provides a basis for other ratios such as the price-earnings ratio. However, one must be extremely careful in using this data. As noted, the rules for calculating EPS are complex, and it is often impossible for even a sophisticated user to calculate EPS from just looking at published financial data. Furthermore, if you are relying on published EPS data, you still must be careful. For example, are the published P-E ratios based on primary or fully diluted EPS? Is EPS from continuing operations used, or is the figure based on other income statement categories? Generally, the P-E ratio is based on primary EPS calculated on income from continuing operations. These are only a few examples of the issues that must be considered in using EPS data.

■ PRIOR PERIOD ADJUSTMENTS AND APPROPRIATIONS OF RETAINED EARNINGS

To this point, the discussion has focused on the two major events that affect retained earnings: net income or loss and dividends. There are three other events that can affect retained earnings: prior period adjustments, appropriations, and treasury stock transactions. Treasury stock transactions were discussed in Chapter 13. Prior period adjustments and appropriations are discussed next.

■ PRIOR PERIOD ADJUSTMENTS

Under the all-inclusive concept of income, with a few exceptions, all items of profit and loss recognized during the period are included in net income for the period. These exceptions relate mainly to **prior period adjustments**, and they are accounted for by an adjustment to the beginning balance of retained earnings. However, there has been considerable controversy about what causes an event to qualify as a prior period adjustment. Only two events are considered prior period adjustments:

---

[14] Financial Accounting Standards Board, Statement 21, *Suspension of the Reporting of Earnings per Share and Segment Information by Nonpublic Enterprises* (Stamford, Conn.: FASB, April 1978). Before the issuance of this Statement, all corporations had to disclose EPS data, which was of limited use to nonpublic entities.

1. Correction of an error in the financial statements of a prior period.

2. Adjustments that result from realization of income tax benefits of pre-acquisition operating loss carryforwards of purchased subsidiaries.[15]

Because the realization of tax benefits is a specialized topic, this section will examine only prior period adjustments that relate to error corrections.

EXHIBIT 14–12

CARTER HAWLEY HALE STORES, INC. Consolidated Statement of Earnings (In thousands, except per share data)	1986 52 Weeks	1985 52 Weeks	1984 53 Weeks
Sales	$4,089,794	$3,977,913	$3,724,294
Costs and expenses			
Cost of goods sold, including occupancy and buying costs	2,898,213	2,850,599	2,702,055
Selling, general, and administrative expenses	932,361	923,504	862,272
Interest expense and discount, net	119,005	131,235	117,237
	3,949,579	3,905,338	3,681,564
Earnings from continuing operations before nonoperating items and income taxes	140,215	72,575	42,730
Nonoperating items			
Loss on sale of John Wanamaker	(2,200)		
Loss on sale of Holt Renfrew		(2,450)	
Costs relating to restructuring program	(25,000)		
Costs relating to unsolicited tender offer			(7,100)
	(27,200)	(2,450)	(7,100)
Earnings from continuing operations before income taxes	113,015	70,125	35,630
Income taxes	65,400	22,100	8,500
Earnings from continuing operations	47,615	48,025	27,130
Discontinued operations, net of income taxes of $28,800			62,540
Net earnings before extraordinary item and cumulative effect of change in accounting	47,615	48,025	89,670
Extraordinary item—costs relating to early retirement of long-term debt, net of income tax benefit of $28,804	(29,253)		
Cumulative effect of change in accounting, net of income tax benefit of $15,505	(14,148)		
Net earnings	$ 4,214	$ 48,025	$ 89,670
Primary earnings per common share			
Continuing operations	$ .87	$ .92	$
Discontinued operations			2.75
Extraordinary item	(1.44)		
Cumulative effect of change in accounting	(.70)		
	$ (1.27)	$ .92	$ 2.75
Fully diluted earnings per common share*			
Continuing operations	$	$	$ .83
Discontinued operations			1.89
	$ *	$ *	$ 2.72

*Fully diluted earnings per common share are not shown, as the effect of the calculation is anti-dilutive.

[15] Financial Accounting Standards Board, Statement No. 16, *Prior Period Adjustments* (Stamford, Conn.: FASB, June 1977), par. 11.

Occasionally, a firm will discover a material error in a prior year's financial statements. Material errors are very rare, especially when a firm's financial statements are audited by a CPA firm. However, when they do occur and are discovered, the manner in which the error is corrected depends on whether the firm publishes single-year or comparative financial statements and on the year in which the error was made.

When single-year statements are published, the error is corrected by adjusting the beginning balance of retained earnings on the retained earnings statement. To demonstrate accounting for prior period adjustments in a single-year statement, assume that during the audit of its 1990 statements, the Mondrian Corporation discovered that depreciation in 1989 had been understated by $100,000, ignoring taxes. Because this is a material error, a prior period adjustment is required. The following journal entry is made at year's-end to correct this error:

Dec. 31, 1990	Retained Earnings	100,000	
	Accumulated Depreciation—Building		100,000
	To record error in 1989 through a prior period adjustment.		

The 1990 statement of retained earnings would appear as shown in Exhibit 14-13. In addition, the prior period adjustment is explained in the footnotes to the financial statement.

EXHIBIT 14–13

MONDRIAN CORPORATION Statement of Retained Earnings For the Year Ended December 31, 1990		
Retained earnings, January 1, 1990	$5,000,000	
Less: Prior period adjustment for error correction, net of tax	(100,000)	
Retained earnings, January 1, 1990, restated		4,900,000
Net income for 1990		650,000
Less: Dividends		(150,000)
Retained earnings, December 31, 1990		$5,400,000

When comparative financial statements are presented, the procedure is different. If the error is in an earlier financial statement that is being presented for comparative purposes, that statement should be revised to correct the error. As a result, net income will be corrected, and after that corrected net income figure is reflected on the retained earnings statement, no further adjustment is required. If the error is in a year for which the financial statements are not being presented, the correction is made through a prior period adjustment to the earliest retained earnings balance presented.

■ APPROPRIATION OF RETAINED EARNINGS

An **appropriation of retained earnings** occurs when the board of directors transfers a portion of the Retained Earnings account into a separate Appropriated Retained Earnings account. The sole purpose of such a transfer is to indicate to stockholders and others that the balance in the Appropriated Retained Earnings account is not available for dividends. Thus, by appropriating retained earnings, the firm limits the amount of dividends it can declare.

The board may appropriate retained earnings in order to limit dividends voluntarily in the hope of conserving cash for projects such as the purchase of new buildings. In other cases, creditors may force the board to appropriate retained earnings and thus limit dividends. The creditors do so in the hope that the firm will not use its cash to pay dividends rather than make timely interest and principal payments.

In order to appropriate retained earnings, the firm debits Retained Earnings and credits Appropriated Retained Earnings. For example, if the Clayborn Corporation decides to appropriate retained earnings of $1 million for future plant expansion, out of a total of $7,435,000 in retained earnings, it will make the following entry:

Retained Earnings	1,000,000	
Appropriated Retained Earnings—Plant Expansion		1,000,000
To appropriate $1,000,000 of retained earnings for future plant expansion.		

Immediately after this entry, the stockholders' equity section of the Clayborn Corporation appears as shown in Exhibit 14-14. If the appropriation is no longer needed or required, the Retained Earnings account will be credited, and Appropriated Retained Earnings will be debited.

EXHIBIT 14–14

CLAYBORN CORPORATION	
Stockholders' Equity	
Common stock, no par, 1,000,000 shares issued, 500,000 shares issued and outstanding	$2,465,000
Unappropriated retained earnings	6,435,000
Appropriated retained earnings, future plant expansion	1,000,000
Total stockholders' equity	$9,900,000

These entries point out the problem with the appropriation of retained earnings and some of the confusion surrounding it. If you review the entry to appropriate retained earnings, you will see that no cash is involved. Thus retained earnings can be appropriated each year, but there is no guarantee that the cash will be there for its intended use. Although the amount of dividends is limited by appropriating retained earnings, cash can still be used for other purposes. The only way to ensure the availability of cash is to create a special cash fund and to set aside a certain amount each year. To the extent that users believe that appropriated retained earnings ensure that cash in that amount is available, it is a misleading concept.

Because of these issues, corporations seldom appropriate retained earnings. Instead, voluntary or required dividend restrictions are disclosed in the footnotes to the financial statements. For example, the following footnote was in a financial statement of Shaw Industries, Inc.:

The 8.63% term notes payable are due in semi-annual payments of $5,000,000. These note agreements contain, among other provisions (1) restrictions as to creation or assumption of liens, payments of cash dividends and acquisitions of the Company's stock, (2) limitation as to new indebtedness and lease obligations, and (3) financial requirements as to minimum working capital ($115,000,000) and current ratio (225%). At June 27, 1987, working capital was $141,679,000 and the current ratio was 253%. Retained earnings of $94,611,000 are restricted with respect to the payment of cash dividends and the acquisition of the Company's stock.

■ STATEMENT OF STOCKHOLDERS' EQUITY

In today's corporate environment, many corporations enter into complex transactions that directly affect stockholders' equity. A simple statement of retained earnings does not adequately disclose all of the information needed by financial statement users. Many corporations therefore substitute a broader statement, called a *statement of stockholders' equity*, which presents the changes that affected all of the stock-holders' equity accounts. If this statement is not presented as a fourth financial state-ment, information regarding changes in stockholders' equity accounts can be found in the footnotes to the financial statements. Exhibit 14-15 is an example of a statement of stockholders' equity.

EXHIBIT 14–15

BORDEN, INC.
Consolidated Statements of Shareholders' Equity
Three Years Ended December 31, 1988
(In thousands)

| | Capital Stock Issued | | | Accumulated | | |
	Preferred Series B	Common	Paid-in Capital	Translation Adjustment	Retained Earnings	Treasury Stock
Balance, December 31, 1985	$71	$126,240	$263,537	$(94,018)	$1,461,125	$(349,160)
Net income					223,312	
Cash dividends						
Common stock					(81,327)	
Preferred series B					(20)	
Translation adjustment for the period				14,581		
Stock reacquired for acquisitions and treasury						(144,784)
Preferred series B stock converted	(13)		(148)			161
Stock issued for exercised options			4,880			4,721
Stock issued for acquisitions						9,585
Balance, December 31, 1986	58	126,240	268,269	(79,437)	1,603,090	(479,477)
Net income					267,056	
Cash dividends						
Common stock					(91,416)	
Preferred series B					(17)	
Translation adjustment for the period				39,129		
Stock reacquired for acquisitions and treasury						(25,222)
Preferred series B stock converted	(4)		(62)			66
Stock issued for exercised options			3,933			2,619
Stock issued for acquisitions			16,065			7,959
Balance, December 31, 1987	54	126,240	288,205	(40,308)	1,778,713	(494,055)
Net income					311,882	
Cash dividends						
Common stock					(110,339)	
Preferred series B					(15)	
Translation adjustment for the period				(9,536)		
Stock reacquired for acquisitions and treasury						(47,930)
Preferred series B stock converted	(11)		(150)			161
Stock issued for exercised options and award plans			7,716			7,724
Stock issued for acquisitions						30,264
Balance, December 31, 1988	$43	$126,240	$295,771	$(49,844)	$1,980,241	$(503,836)

SUMMARY OF LEARNING OBJECTIVES

1. Corporate dividends. The amount and type of dividend to issue is a strategic decision made by a corporation's board of directors. Firms attempt to establish a stable dividend policy. Most firms issue cash dividends, but they can also declare stock and property dividends.

2. Stock splits and their relationship to stock dividends. Stock splits are used by firms to decrease the price of their stock in order to make round-lot purchases more attractive to investors. Neither stock dividends nor stock splits change the firm's total net assets or total stockholders' equity. Stock dividends do, however, change the balances in retained earnings and common stock and possibly additional paid-in capital.

3. Preparation of the corporate income statement. Large businesses generally earn income and incur expenses from a variety of sources. Because users of financial statements want to use the income statement to make predictions about future income flows, the various income sources must be segregated. There may be up to four separate categories on the income statement: (1) income from continuing operations, (2) discontinued operations, (3) extraordinary items, and (4) cumulative effect of a change in accounting principles. Intraperiod income allocation requires that the income tax expense that relates to each of the categories be allocated to it.

4. Calculation, use, and limitations of EPS. Earnings per share is one of the most widely used of the financial statistics. In simple situations, EPS is calculated by the following formula:

$$\frac{\text{Net income available to common shareholders}}{\text{Weighted average number of common shares outstanding}}$$

Firms that have complex capital structures generally must make a dual presentation of EPS that discloses both primary and fully diluted EPS. The primary EPS calculation includes only common stock equivalents, whereas the fully diluted EPS calculation includes all dilutive securities.

5. Prior period adjustments and appropriation of retained earnings. In recent years, the accounting profession has limited the items that qualify as prior period adjustments. Under current pronouncements, only error corrections and certain tax benefits qualify. Prior period adjustments are generally handled by adjusting the beginning balance of retained earnings on the retained earnings statement.

The appropriation of retained earnings is either voluntary or required in order to restrict dividend payments. However, the balance in the appropriated earnings account does not imply that an equal amount of cash is available. Instead of appropriating retained earnings, most firms just disclose dividends and/or other restrictions in the footnotes to the financial statements.

6. Purpose of the statement of stockholders' equity. Because of the importance and complexity of transactions that affect stockholders' equity, many firms replace the retained earnings statement with a more comprehensive statement called a *statement of stockholders' equity*, which summarizes all of the items that have changed the stockholders' equity accounts.

KEY TERMS

Appropriation of retained earnings
Capitalizing retained earnings
Change in accounting estimate
Change in accounting method
Common stock equivalent
Complex capital structure
Date of record
Declaration date
Dividend payment date
Earnings per share (EPS)

Extraordinary items
Fully diluted EPS
Income from continuing operations
Interperiod income tax allocation
Intraperiod income tax allocation
Primary earnings per share
Prior period adjustments
Segment
Stock dividend
Stock split

As the treasurer of the Gernow Airline Corporation, you have been asked to prepare the firm's 1989 income statement and retained earnings statement. Your assistant has provided you with the following data:

1. Income before taxes, $5 million.

2. Included in the above figure are the following items:

(a) One of the firm's planes crashed. No one was hurt, and the crash resulted in a $500,000 gain from the insurance proceeds.

(b) One of the planes was struck by lightning at an airport in southern California. Lightning very rarely occurs in this area, and the firm suffered a $400,000 loss.

(c) The corporation had been incurring substantial losses in its catering business. It therefore sold that part of the business and now operates only the airline. Losses from operation totaled $600,000 for 1989, and there was a gain of $100,000 on disposal of the segment.

(d) All amounts are before taxes, which is currently 40% on all transactions.

3. Retained earnings at the beginning of 1989 equaled $18 million. The firm had 100,000 shares of $5 par value common stock outstanding and issued the following dividends:

(a) April 15, 1989—10% stock dividend. At the time of the stock dividend, the price per share was $20.

(b) December 15, 1989—$1.00 per-share cash dividend declared.

REQUIRED: (a) Prepare an income statement for 1989; begin with income from continuing operations before taxes. Ignore earnings per share.

(b) Prepare a statement of retained earnings for 1989.

SOLUTION
(a)

GERNOW AIRLINE CORPORATION
Partial Income Statement
For the Year Ended December 31, 1989

Income from continuing operations, before taxes		$5,900,000
Provision for taxes		2,360,000
Income from continuing operations		3,540,000
Discontinued operations		
Loss from operations, net of tax savings of $240,000	($360,000)	
Gain on disposal of segment, net of taxes of $40,000	60,000	(300,000)
Income before extraordinary items		3,240,000
Extraordinary items—Loss on destruction of airplane, net of tax savings of $160,000		(240,000)
Net income		$3,000,000

Notes:

A.	Income from continuing operations =	
	Income before taxes (as given)	$5,000,000
	Plus: Loss on operations of discontinued segment	600,000
	Loss on destruction of airplane	400,000
	Less: Gain on disposal of segment	(100,000)
		$5,900,000

Proof:

Income before taxes	$5,000,000
Less total taxes (40% × 5,000,000)	2,000,000
Net income	$3,000,000

B. Catering business is treated as a discontinued operation.

C. Plane crash does not meet criteria of extraordinary—not unusual or infrequent in airline business.

D. Plane destroyed by lightning is extraordinary because unusual and infrequent, given the environment.

(b)

GERNOW AIRLINE CORPORATION
Statement of Retained Earnings
For the Year Ended December 31, 1989

Retained earnings, beginning balance		$18,000,000
Add: Net income for the year		3,000,000
Less: Stock dividends[a]	$200,000	
Cash dividend[b]	110,000	(310,000)
Retained earnings, ending balance		$20,690,000

---

[a] 100,000 × 10% =   10,000 shares
                   × $20 per share
                      $200,000

[b] 100,000 × 110% =   110,000 shares
                    × $1 per share dividend
                       $110,000

QUESTIONS

1. What is the statement of retained earnings, and what items are likely to affect the balance in the Retained Earnings account?

2. What significance does each of the following dates have to the declaration and payment of cash dividends?

 (a) Declaration date.   **(b)** Date of record.
 (c) Payment date.

3. What is a stock dividend? What are the benefits of stock dividends, if any, to the issuing corporation and the existing stockholders?

4. After a stock dividend is issued, what changes occur in total stockholders' equity and within the individual components of stockholders' equity?

5. You overheard a friend of yours saying that stock dividends and stock splits are essentially the same. Do you agree or disagree? Why or why not?

6. Describe the major components of a corporate income statement. Are they all likely to be found on a single-year income statement? Why is it necessary to distinguish among these components?

7. What items are included in the category *loss from continuing operations*, and what is the significance of this figure?

8. One of your fellow students stated that income tax expense was income tax expense, and he did not understand the need to go to all the trouble to apply intraperiod income tax allocation. How would you respond?

9. On the income statement of the Jigs Corporation, you noticed the following item:

Extraordinary item—Loss on early extinguishment of debt, net of tax savings of $25,000	$50,000

Explain the concept of a tax savings. What is the amount of the loss before the tax savings?

10. What constitutes a segment for purposes of disclosing a discontinued operation? Explain how the operations and the gain or loss on the disposition of a discontinued operation must be disclosed on the income statement.

11. What are the criteria for determining whether an item should be classified as extraordinary? Why do you think that the environment in which the entity operates must be considered?

12. Recently, an airplane of a large airline slid off the runway. Although no one was seriously injured, the plane was completely destroyed. The airline received insurance proceeds in excess of the book value of the airplane. How should this item be classified on the income statement? Why?

13. Recently, the IAC Corporation changed the way it calculates its bad debts expense, from the percentage-of-sales method to the aging method. What type of accounting change is this, and how should it be disclosed on the income statement? How would your answer differ if the firm had remained on the percentage-of-sales method but changed the percentage from 2% of net credit sales to 3% of net credit sales?

14. Two years ago, the Peters Corporation purchased a new machine for $100,000. The machine had a ten-year useful life and no salvage value. At the beginning of the third year, the firm changed from the double-declining-balance method of depreciation to the straight-line method. Determine the amount of depreciation for the third year, and show how this change should be disclosed on the income statement for the third year. Assume a tax rate of 40%.

15. Earnings per share is one of the most looked at of all the financial statistics. Describe earnings per share. Why do you think so many financial statement users attach so much importance to it?

16. What are the basic components that go into the earnings-per-share calculation? How are they affected by additional issues of common stock during the year?

17. What is the essential difference between primary and fully diluted earnings per share? Under what circumstances is it necessary to disclose both, and what is the purpose of this dual disclosure?

18. What is a complex capital structure, and what is its importance in the calculation of earnings per share?

19. Describe common stock equivalents. How do they affect the calculation of primary and fully diluted earnings per share?

20. A famous stock market adviser suggests that all of his clients make their stock purchase and sales decisions solely on whether a stock's EPS is increasing or decreasing. Do you think that is good advice? Why or why not?

21. What items are currently considered prior period adjustments, and how are they accounted for?

22. What does the appropriation of retained earnings accomplish?

EXERCISES

E1. Cash Dividends. Informatics has 100,000 shares of $5 par value common stock outstanding and 50,000 shares of 5%, $100 par value preferred stock outstanding. During December, the board of directors made the following dividend declarations:

On December 1, the board of directors declared that the preferred dividend would be paid on January 4 to preferred shareholders of record on December 25.

On December 10, the board of directors declared a $2 per-share dividend payable on January 4 to common shareholders of record on December 25.

REQUIRED: **(a)** Make all the necessary entries related to the declaration and payment of the preferred dividends.

(b) Make all the necessary entries related to the declaration and payment of the common dividends.

E2. Property Dividends. The Klinger Company is a closely held family corporation. On December 10, 1989, the board of directors decided to declare a property dividend. The dividend was to consist of a plot of land held by the corporation. The land was purchased several years ago at a cost of $140,000. Recently, the land was appraised at $250,000. On January 2, 1990, title to the land was transferred to the Klinger Family Trust.

REQUIRED: Make the entries to record the property dividend.

E3. Stock Dividends. The Mister Mo Mart has 150,000 shares of $5 par value common stock outstanding. Although the company has been profitable, it has decided to issue stock dividends instead of cash dividends in order to conserve cash for future expansion. On December 10, when the common stock was selling at $25 per share, the board of directors declared a 5% stock dividend to be distributed immediately.

REQUIRED: **(a)** Make the entries to record the stock dividend.

(b) Assume that you own 100 shares of Mister Mo stock that you purchased at $12 per share. How would the stock dividend affect your investment, and how would you account for it?

(c) Independent of (a) and (b), now assume that Mister Mo declared a 30% stock dividend instead of the 5% dividend. Make the necessary entry to record the stock dividend.

E4. **Stock Dividends and Stock Splits.** On December 31, 1990, the stockholders' equity section of the Price-Moran Corporation appeared as follows:

PRICE-MORAN CORPORATION
Partial Balance Sheet
December 31, 1990

Stockholders' equity	
Common stock, $10 par value, 500,000 shares authorized, 200,000 shares issued and outstanding	$2,000,000
Paid-in capital from issue of common stock in excess of par	1,000,000
Retained earnings	5,000,000
Total stockholders' equity	$8,000,000

REQUIRED: **(a)** Assume that on January 2, 1991, the board of directors declared and issued a 10% stock dividend. At that time, the stock was selling at $25 per share. Prepare the stockholders' equity section of the balance sheet after the declaration.

(b) Now assume that instead of issuing a stock dividend, the board of directors declared a 2-for-1 stock split on January 2. Prepare the stockholders' equity section of the balance sheet after the stock split.

E5. **Corporate Income Statements.** The controller of Moreno Technical Systems gave you the following information for the year ended December 31, 1990:

Sales	$4,000,000
Cost of goods sold	2,800,000
Selling expenses	500,000
General and administrative expenses	200,000
Income from discontinued operations	100,000
Loss on disposal of discontinued operations	40,000
Extraordinary loss from earthquake damage	70,000
Tax rate on all items	30%

Prepare in good form the income statement for the year ended December 31, 1990.

E6. **Extraordinary Items.** During a very eventful year, the following happened to the Bacuall Corporation:

(a) The first hurricane in 100 years occurred in the area where the corporation's headquarters was located, and its headquarters building was completely destroyed.

(b) The company recorded a loss on the abandonment of some equipment formerly used in the business.

(c) Uncollectible accounts of $20,000 were written off during the year.

(d) One of the company's major employee unions went on strike, and the firm was shut down for several weeks. Management estimates that profits of $500,000 were lost.

REQUIRED: Which of the above items should be classified as extraordinary, and why?

E7. Change in Accounting Methods. Air North is a small commuter airline. At the beginning of the current year, 1990, it made the following accounting changes:

   (a) The firm decided to change the method of depreciation on one of its newer airplanes. The plane was purchased at the beginning of 1987 at a price of $3 million. The plane has a useful life of ten years and no salvage value. The firm had been using double-declining-balance depreciation but has now decided to change to straight-line.

   (b) The firm decided to change the remaining life of one of its older aircraft. The plane was purchased at the beginning of 1986 at a cost of $1.5 million. At that time, the firm estimated that the aircraft would have a useful life of 20 years and no salvage value. However, at the beginning of 1990, the firm estimated that the aircraft would have a remaining useful life of only ten years but would now have a salvage value of $10,000. Straight-line depreciation has always been used on this particular aircraft.

REQUIRED: Assuming these are the only depreciable items, determine the amount of depreciation expense for 1990 and the cumulative effect of the change in accounting principle. Ignore taxes.

E8. Earnings per Share. At the beginning of the current year, the Batitta Corporation had 120,000 shares of common stock outstanding. During the year, the following stock transactions occurred:

   ■ March 1: 60,000 additional common shares were issued.

   ■ July 1: 30,000 additional common shares were issued.

   ■ November 1: 30,000 common shares were repurchased and held in the treasury for the rest of the year.

   ■ December 1: The firm issued 10,000 shares of nonconvertible preferred stock. This was the first issue of preferred stock.

   Net income during the year amounted to $650,000. The firm issued preferred dividends of $20,000 and common dividends of $40,000.

REQUIRED: Determine the weighted average number of common shares outstanding and the earnings per share for the year.

E9. Earnings per Share. At the beginning of the current year, 1989, the Totita Corporation had 450,000 common shares outstanding. On April 1, 1989, the company issued an additional 200,000 common shares of stock for cash. All 650,000 shares were outstanding on December 31, 1989.

   At the beginning of 1989, Totita issued 5,000 shares of 8%, $100 par value preferred stock at par. Net income during the year amounted to $1.5 million.

REQUIRED: Calculate earnings per share for 1989.

E10. Prior Period Adjustments. At the beginning of 1990, Newtonian Incorporated's retained earnings balance was $500,000. During the year, the firm's net income amounted to $100,000, and dividends of $30,000 were paid. During the preparation of the 1990 financial statements, it was discovered that a piece of equipment that had been purchased at the beginning of 1989 at a cost of $50,000 had been entirely expensed in that year. Management feels the equipment has a five-year life and should be depreciated on the straight-line basis with no salvage value.

REQUIRED: **(a)** Assuming that the current year's books have not been closed and that reported income of $100,000 does not reflect the depreciation on the equipment, make the necessary entries to correct the error. Ignore taxes.

   (b) If single-year statements are published, prepare the retained earnings statement for 1990, based on the corrections made in (a).

   (c) If comparative 1990 and 1989 statements were prepared, explain how you would handle the error correction. Do not actually prepare new statements.

E11. Appropriation of Retained Earnings. The Oops Chemical Corporation has been producing an insect spray for a number of years. Recently, it has discovered that this spray is very dangerous, and the company has been sued over the illness of a number of individuals. The board of directors, on December 31, 1990, decided to appropriate retained earnings in the amount of $50 million to cover future lawsuits. Just before the appropriation, the firm had 100,000 shares of no par, no stated value common stock outstanding that had been issued at an average price of $15 per share. In addition, total retained earnings at that time amounted to $120 million. Several years later, when all the lawsuits had been settled (the ultimate cost to the company was $47 million), the appropriation was removed by the board.

REQUIRED:

(a) Make the entry to record the appropriation.

(b) Prepare the stockholders' equity section of the balance sheet immediately after the appropriation.

(c) Make the journal entry to record the removal of the appropriation.

(d) Did the appropriation ensure that the firm had the cash to pay the lawsuits? What other method besides appropriation of retained earnings is available to handle situations such as these?

E12. Toys "R" Us Financial Statements. Based on the Toys "R" Us financial statements in Appendix D, answer the following questions:

(a) During 1986, Toys "R" Us had a 3-for-2 stock split, effected in the form of a 50% dividend.

1. How many shares of stock were issued?

2. What was the amount of the debit to Retained Earnings and the credit to Common Stock? Speculate on why these amounts are not equal.

(b) In computing earnings per share, does Toys "R" Us have any common stock equivalents? If so, what are they? How did they affect the EPS computation?

PROBLEMS

P14–1 Stockholders' Equity Transactions. The stockholders' equity section of Federated Markets' balance sheet at December 31, 1990 is as follows:

Common stock, $10 stated value stock, authorized 1,000,000 shares, issued 60,000 shares	$ 600,000
Paid-in capital in excess of stated value	400,000
Paid-in capital from sale of treasury stock in excess of cost	25,000
Retained earnings	700,000
Total stockholders' equity	$1,725,000

The following events occurred during 1991:

- January 2: Sold 10,000 shares of unissued common stock for $20 per share.

- January 20: Declared a cash dividend of $.20 per share, payable on February 20 to shareholders of record on February 10.

- February 5: Exchanged 5,000 shares of authorized but unissued common stock for 600 acres of land. The stock had a fair market value of $25 per share.

- February 20: Dividend declared on January 20 paid.

- March 1: A 2-for-1 stock split was declared: per share market value $40.

- July 1: Federated Markets purchased 1,000 shares of its own stock at the current market price of $35 per share.

- July 18: A 10% stock dividend was declared and issued. Market value is currently $30 per share.

- August 20: Sold 600 shares of treasury stock at $30 per share.

- August 30: Declared a cash dividend of $0.10 per share, payable on September 10.

REQUIRED: **(a)** Make the appropriate journal entries to record these transactions. It may be useful to use T accounts as you proceed.

(b) Prepare the stockholders' equity section of the balance sheet at December 31, 1991. Assume that net income during the year amounted to $200,000.

P14-2 Stockholders' Equity Transactions. The stockholders' equity section of the Crikos Company's balance sheet as of December 31, 1990 is as follows:

Common stock, par value $10 per share; authorized 1,000,000 shares, issued and outstanding 200,000 shares	$2,000,000
8% convertible preferred stock, par value $100 per share; 10,000 shares authorized, issued, and outstanding. Each share is convertible into five shares of common stock	1,000,000
Paid-in capital in excess of par, common stock	2,000,000
Paid-in capital in excess of par, preferred stock	2,000,000
Retained earnings	800,000
Total stockholders' equity	$7,800,000

The following events occurred during 1991:

- January 2: 20,000 shares of common stock were issued and sold for $45 per share.

- January 31: A cash dividend on preferred stock was declared. In addition, a cash dividend of $.10 per share on common stock was declared.

- February 15: Both preferred and common dividends were paid.

- June 1: The Crikos Company purchased 3,000 shares of its own stock at the current price of $50 per share.

- August 1: A 5% common stock dividend was declared and issued. Market value is currently $40 per share.

- September 1: Issued 10,000 shares of common stock in exchange for a building. At the time, the stock had a fair market value of $45 per share.

- October 1: A 2-for-1 stock split was declared. The market value of the stock is currently $50 per share.

REQUIRED: **(a)** Make the appropriate journal entries to record these transactions. It may be useful to use T accounts as you proceed.

(b) Prepare the stockholders' equity section of the balance sheet at December 31, 1991. Assume that net income during the year amounted to $500,000.

P14-3 Stock Splits and Stock Dividends. Jerry Dunphy purchased 1,000 shares of common stock of the Little Corporation for a price of $20,000 several years ago. At the end of 1990, the stockholders' equity section of the balance sheet is as follows:

LITTLE CORPORATION Partial Balance Sheet December 31, 1990	
Stockholders' equity	
Common stock, $10 par value, 100,000 shares authorized, 80,000 shares outstanding	$ 800,000
Paid-in capital from issue of common stock in excess of par	450,000
Retained earnings	700,000
Total stockholders' equity	$1,950,000

REQUIRED: For each of the following situations, make the appropriate journal entries or answer the required questions:

(a) On June 30, 1991, the firm decided on a 2-for-1 stock split. At the time, the stock was trading at $30 per share.

   1. What entry should the firm make to record the stock split?

   2. What effect do you think that the split will have on Jerry's investment?

   3. If Jerry decided to sell some shares at $12 per share, how much gain or loss would he record per share?

(b) On September 30, 1991, the firm declared a cash dividend of $.50 per share payable October 31.

   1. Make the entry required on the books of the Little Corporation.

   2. After the cash dividend is declared, what is the balance of the Retained Earnings account, and what is the total stockholders' equity?

(c) On December 31, 1991, the firm declared and distributed a 5% stock dividend. At the time of declaration, the stock was trading at $20 per share.

   1. Make the required entry on the books of the Little Corporation.

   2. What effect does this dividend have on stockholders' equity and its various components?

   3. Assuming Jerry Dunphy has never sold any shares of stock, what is his new basis per share after all of the above transactions?

P14–4 Stockholders' Equity—Comprehensive Problem. The stockholders' equity section of Davison's, Inc. follows:

DAVISON'S, INC.

Partial Balance Sheet

December 31, 1990

Stockholders' equity
Common stock, $20 par value, authorized 500,000 shares, issued and outstanding 100,000 shares	$2,000,000
Paid-in capital from issue of common stock in excess of par	1,500,000
Retained earnings	2,000,000
Total stockholders' equity	$5,500,000

During the month of January 1991, the following events occurred:

- January 12: A 2-for-1 stock split was declared by the board of directors. At the time of split, the market price was $100 per share.

- January 20: A 5% stock dividend was declared and issued by the board of directors. At the time of the declaration, the market price of the stock was $45 per share.

- January 22: The corporation repurchased 4,000 shares of its common stock at a price of $40 per share.

- January 28: A cash dividend of $.40 per share was declared by the board of directors, payable February 28.

- January 30: A 25% stock dividend was declared and issued. At the time of declaration, the market price of the stock was $42 per share.

- January 31: The net income for the month amounted to $100,000.

REQUIRED: Answer each of the following questions:

   (a) After the stock split on January 12, what was the amount of total stockholders' equity?

   (b) After the stock split on January 12, what was the balance in the Common Stock account?

   (c) After the stock dividend on January 20, what was the balance in the Retained Earnings account?

(d) After the stock dividend on January 20, what was the amount of the firm's total net assets?

(e) After the treasury stock purchase, by how much did the firm's assets increase or decrease, if at all?

(f) Make the journal entry for stock dividend on January 30.

(g) What was the total balance in retained earnings after all transactions for January were completed?

P14–5 **Stockholders' Equity—Comprehensive Problem.** The stockholders' equity section on the December 31, 1989 balance sheet of the Sandy Bean Corporation appeared as follows (certain details omitted):

SANDY BEAN CORPORATION
Partial Balance Sheet
December 31, 1989

Preferred stock, 5%, $40 par value authorized 100,000 shares; ? issued	$2,400,000
Common stock, $5 par value, authorized 100,000 shares; ? issued	
of which 1,000 are held in treasury	250,000
Paid-in capital in excess of par, common	750,000
Paid-in capital from sale of treasury stock	10,000
Donated capital	20,000
Retained earnings	560,000
Cost of treasury stock, common	22,000

REQUIRED: Answer each of the following questions:

(a) How many shares of preferred stock were issued?

(b) Was the preferred stock issued at par, above par, or below par?

(c) How many shares of common stock were issued?

(d) How many shares of common stock are outstanding?

(e) What was the average issue price of the common stock?

(f) Have the treasury stock transactions increased or decreased the firm's net assets, and by what amount?

(g) How much did the treasury stock cost per share?

(h) What is the total amount of dividends, both preferred and common, that the board of directors could legally declare? How would they be divided between preferred and common shareholders?

(i) What is the amount of the corporation's total contributed capital?

(j) What is the amount of total stockholders' equity?

P14–6 **Statement of Changes in Stockholders' Equity.** The stockholders' equity section on the June 30, 1989 balance sheet of the Learning Circuit is as follows:

Preferred stock, 6%, $100 par value convertible preferred stock,	
100,000 shares authorized, 10,000 shares issued and outstanding	$ 1,000,000
Common stock, $1 par value, 5,000,000 shares authorized, 120,000	
shares issued, of which 10,000 are held in the treasury	120,000
Paid-in capital from issue of common stock in excess of par	5,280,000
Paid-in capital from sale of treasury stock in excess of cost	5,000
Retained earnings	6,000,500
Treasury stock, at cost	(245,000)
Total stockholders' equity	$12,160,500

For the year ended June 30, 1990, the following events regarding stockholders' equity are listed in chronological order:

(a) Converted 8,000 shares of the convertible preferred stock into common. Each share is convertible into two shares of common.

(b) A 10% stock dividend was declared and issued. At that time, the common stock was selling at $40 per share.

(c) Sold 5,000 shares of treasury stock at $50 per share.

(d) Declared and paid $75,000 of dividends.

(e) Net income for the year amounted to $1 million.

REQUIRED: Prepare a statement of changes in stockholders' equity similar in form to Exhibit 14-15.

P14—7 Income Statement Construction. During the current year, 1990, the Fullerton Manufacturing Company sold its carpet manufacturing division because of consistently poor performance. In addition, you obtained the following information about the events that affected the firm during 1990:

	Continuing Operations	Discontinued Operations
Sales	$4,500,000	$1,800,000
Expenses		
Cost of goods sold	3,000,000	1,500,000
Operating expenses	500,000	500,000
Loss on disposal of discontinued operations		(300,000)
Gain on expropriation of assets by foreign country	300,000	
Gain on sale of building	100,000	
Cumulative effect (gain) of change from average cost to FIFO	50,000	

All of the above items are shown prior to any tax effect. Assume that a tax rate of 30% applies to all items. In addition, assume that the firm had 200,000 shares of common stock outstanding for the entire year.

REQUIRED: Prepare an income statement in good form for the year ended December 31, 1990. Include earnings per share.

P14—8 Income Statement Preparation. Shelly Grant is the accountant for Air Churchill, a successful commuter airline. Because Shelly is just beginning to learn accounting, she asks for your help in preparing the firm's income statement. She has prepared the following condensed statement of income and retained earnings for the year ended December 31, 1990.

AIR CHURCHILL
Condensed Statement of Income and Retained Earnings
For the Year Ended December 31, 1990

Revenues		
Ticket revenue	$1,000,000	
Gain on sale of used airplane	50,000	
Gain on sale of hotels	150,000	$1,200,000
Expenses		
Selling, general, and administrative	$ 600,000	
Depreciation	300,000	
Interest	100,000	1,000,000
Income before extraordinary item		200,000
Extraordinary item		300,000
Income before taxes		500,000
Taxes—30%		150,000
Net income		350,000
Retained earnings, January 1		700,000
Retained earnings, December 31		$1,050,000

In addition, you have obtained the following information:

(a) The firm changed the estimated lives of its airplanes at the beginning of 1990. The effect was to decrease this year's depreciation expense by $50,000. The decrease is reflected in the depreciation expense shown on the income statement. If the company had always used the new figure for estimated lives, the effect on all prior years' income would have been an increase of $100,000.

(b) Included in selling and general and administrative expense is a $25,000 cash dividend issued by the company in July 1990.

(c) The extraordinary gain is the result of a plane crash in which no one was injured or killed, though the plane was completely destroyed. The insurance proceeds exceeded the book value of the plane by $300,000.

(d) On January 2, 1988, the company acquired some maintenance machinery at a cost of $150,000. The company adopted the double-declining-balance method of depreciation for this machinery and had been recording depreciation over an estimated useful life of ten years with no salvage value. At the beginning of 1990, a decision was made to adopt the straight-line method of depreciation for this machinery. Depreciation was recorded on the straight-line method for 1990.

(e) Air Churchill sold one of its older airplanes. Because this is a relatively new company, it is the first sale of this kind. The pretax gain as indicated on the income statement is $50,000.

(f) At the end of 1990, Air Churchill decided to sell its small chain of hotels. In the past, this segment of the company had been unprofitable. The sale of the hotel chain resulted in a pretax gain of $150,000. The company determined that its loss from operations on hotels during 1990 amounted to $20,000. This amount was included in selling and general and administrative expenses. The company intends to restrict all of its future operations to the airline business.

REQUIRED: Prepare a revised income statement and retained earnings statement. Assume a tax rate of 30% on all items. Ignore earnings per share.

P14–9 **Income Statement Preparation.** You are the accountant for Camus Manufacturing Company. The condensed statement of income and retained earnings for the year ended December 31, 1990 has been provided for you.

CAMUS MANUFACTURING COMPANY
Condensed Statement of Income and Retained Earnings
For the Year Ended December 31, 1990

Revenues		
Sales	$5,000,000	
Gain on sale of used equipment	150,000	$5,150,000
Expenses		
Cost of goods sold	2,700,000	
Selling, general, and administrative	$1,200,000	
Depreciation	300,000	
Interest	300,000	4,500,000
Income before extraordinary item		650,000
Extraordinary item		(100,000)
Income before taxes		550,000
Taxes—40%		220,000
Net income		330,000
Retained earnings, 1/1/90		150,000
Retained earnings, 12/31/90		$ 480,000

In addition, the following information is available to you:

(a) The firm changed the estimated lives of its equipment at the beginning of 1990. The effect was to decrease this year's depreciation by $20,000. The decrease is reflected in the depreciation expense shown on the income statement. If the company had always used the new lives, the effect on all prior years' income would have been $120,000.

(b) Included in selling, general, and administrative expense is a $400,000 cash dividend issued by the company in December of 1989.

(c) The extraordinary item is the result of a lawsuit that was brought to court by a group of consumers due to product defects.

(d) On January 2, 1988, the company acquired a piece of machinery at a cost of $110,000. The company adopted the sum-of-years-digits method of depreciation to depreciate this machinery over a useful life of ten years with no salvage value. At the beginning of 1990, a decision was made to adopt the straight-line method of depreciation for this machinery. Depreciation was recorded on the straight-line method for 1990.

REQUIRED: Prepare a revised income statement and retained earnings statement AMR. Assume a tax rate of 40% on all items. Ignore earnings per share.

■ USING THE COMPUTER

P14–10   The stockholders' equity section on the December 31, 1989 balance sheet of News Company, Incorporated, is as follows:

Preferred stock, 5%, $100 par value, 500,000 shares authorized, 100,000 shares issued and outstanding	$10,000,000
Common stock, $5 par value, 1,000,000 shares authorized, 200,000 shares issued, of which 10,000 are held in treasury	1,000,000
Paid-in capital from issue of common stock in excess of par	12,000,000
Retained earnings	14,000,000
Treasury stock, at cost	(200,000)
Total stockholders' equity	$36,800,000

During 1990 and 1991, the following events occurred:

1990

- Issued 1,000 shares of preferred stock at $100 per share.
- Net income for the year amounted to $4 million.
- Dividends declared during the year amounted to $1 million.

1991

- Issued 10,000 shares of common stock at $25 per share.
- Sold 5,000 shares of treasury stock at $30 per share.
- Net income for the year amounted to $5 million.
- Dividends declared during the year amounted to $2 million.

REQUIRED: Using an electronic spreadsheet, prepare a statement of changes in stockholders' equity, using the format at the top of page 545.

■ UNDERSTANDING FINANCIAL STATEMENTS

P14–11   The following data was taken from the 1988 annual report of AMR (the parent company of American Airlines):

Earnings per share	
Primary	$7.92
Fully diluted	$7.66

NEWS COMPANY, INCORPORATED
Statement of Changes in Stockholders' Equity
For the Years Ended December 31, 1990 and 1991

	Preferred Stock	Common Stock	Paid-in Capital Sale of Common	Sale of Treasury Stock	Retained Earnings	Treasury Stock	Total
January 1, 1990	$10,000,000	$1,000,000	$12,000,000	$0	$14,000,000	($200,000)	$36,800,000
Transactions during 1990							
.							
.							
.							
Transactions during 1991							
.							
.							
.							
Totals							

REQUIRED:

(a) Why did the company report both primary and fully diluted EPS? What type of securities do you think would cause primary EPS to differ from fully diluted EPS?

(b) According to the footnotes to the financial statements, EPS is computed on the basis of the weighted average number of shares outstanding. The company reported that for 1988, the weighted average number of shares used to compute primary EPS was 59,103,000. Determine the amount of net income for the year.

(c) The following footnote was taken from the same annual report:

In 1986, AMR sold three of its wholly-owned subsidiaries, Flabship and American Airlines Training Corporation at gains and AMR Energy Corporation at a loss, and wrote off certain assets of AMR Energy Corporation not included in that sale. These transactions resulted in a pretax gain of $60.3 million.

How would this item be shown on the company's income statement? That is, how should it be classified? Explain your answer.

■ FINANCIAL DECISION CASE

P14–12 Michael Day is president of Day's Donuts, a chain of successful doughnut shops. Until recently, Day owned all of the company's stock. However, last year the company issued a significant amount of stock to the public, and the stock is now trading on a major exchange. At the end of the current year, the stockholders' equity section of the firm's balance sheet appeared as follows:

Common stock, $10 par value, 100,000 shares issued and outstanding	$1,000,000
Paid-in capital from issue of common shares in excess of par	1,000,000
Retained earnings	2,000,000
Total stockholders' equity	$4,000,000

In addition, total assets amounted to $7 million. Michael Day tells you that the stock of Day's Donuts has recently been selling at around $100 a share. He is somewhat mystified by the high price of the stock in comparison with its book value. He is considering several courses of action to reduce the price of the stock, to make it more attractive to potential stockholders:

1. A 20% stock dividend.

2. A 100% stock dividend.

3. A 2-for-1 stock split.

REQUIRED: **(a)** What is the relationship between the book value per share and the market price per share?

(b) Write a memo to Michael Day outlining how each of the above alternatives would affect stockholders' equity and book value per share and describing the likely effect on the stock's market price. Calculate the new totals for stockholders' equity and book value per share under each alternative.

INVESTMENT IN CORPORATE SECURITIES

After studying this chapter, you should be able to:

1. Discuss the nature and role of publicly held corporations and security exchanges.
2. Measure and record investments in current marketable securities, including:
   a. equity securities.
   b. debt securities.
3. Measure and report long-term investments.
4. Account for investments when there is no significant influence or control.
5. Account for ownership interests between 20% and 50%.
6. Account for ownership interests above 50%, including:
   a. the preparation of consolidated financial statements.
   b. the difference between the purchase and the pooling-of-interests methods of accounting for acquisitions.

T he securities of business firms are purchased by many groups and individuals, including corporations, mutual funds, bank trust departments, and individual investors. Individuals or other entities may invest in the securities of other firms for several reasons. The investment may be made in order to invest idle cash in the hope of realizing a gain or in order to have significant influence or control over another corporation. In recent years, many companies have taken over others, through either friendly merger or hostile takeover. General Electric's purchase of RCA is a good example of a friendly takeover; Texaco's purchase of Getty Oil is an example of what can happen during a hostile takeover attempt.

Equity and debt securities are the two major types of securities purchased by investors. **Equity securities** are preferred and common stock, and **debt securities** are bonds. Accounting for investments in long-term bonds was discussed in Chapter 12. This chapter will focus on accounting for both short- and long-term investments in equity securities.

Most investors purchase the securities of publicly held corporations. A **publicly held corporation** is one whose stock is owned by outside investors and whose stock and/or bonds are listed on national and regional exchanges. National exchanges include the New York Stock Exchange, the American Stock Exchange, and the national over-the-counter market. The stocks of the largest publicly held corporations are listed on the New York Stock Exchange, and the stocks of smaller corporations are listed on the American Stock Exchange or regional exchanges such as the Pacific Stock Exchange. The stocks of some corporations are not listed on an organized exchange, but rather on the over-the-counter market. The over-the-counter market is maintained by numerous brokerage firms buying and selling securities for their customers. Corporations whose stock is traded on this market are generally smaller corporations or ones that have recently issued stock for the first time (often referred to as *going public*).

Publicly held corporations must comply with regulations of both the Securities and Exchange Commission (SEC) and the exchange on which its stock is listed. For example, these companies must file an annual report, called a 10-K, with the SEC. In effect, this report is an expanded version of the financial data contained in the annual report to shareholders. The 10-K form must contain the corporation's financial statements, which have been audited by a certified public accounting firm. These same corporations must also file condensed quarterly reports called 10-Qs. Stock exchanges also have certain filing requirements. For example, the listing agreement between the New York Stock Exchange and member companies provides for the timely disclosure of earnings statements, dividend notices, and other financial information that might reasonably be expected to have a material effect on the market for a firm's securities.

■ ACCOUNTING FOR CURRENT MARKETABLE SECURITIES

Investment in securities refers to investments in equity and debt securities of corporations as well as the debt securities of federal and local governments and agencies. If these investments are made in publicly held corporations or governmental agencies, they are usually readily marketable and thus can easily be turned into cash. Conversely, if the investment is in a nonpublicly held or closely held corporation, it may not be liquid. Depending on their marketability and management's intention, investments are classified as either current assets or long-term investments. This section of the chapter will examine accounting for marketable securities that are considered current. This is an expansion of the brief discussion of marketable securities found in Chapter 8. Later, accounting for marketable securities, and other investments that are classified as long-term, will be discussed.

In order for an investment in securities to be considered a current asset, it must meet two criteria:

1. It must be readily marketable. In order to be readily marketable, there must be an established market for the security.

2. It must be management's intention to convert the securities into cash within the normal operating cycle of the business or one year, whichever is longer.

If either or both of these criteria are not met, the investment cannot be considered a current asset and is classified as long-term.

Marketable securities are usually purchased in order to invest idle cash. Management needs to maintain a certain level of cash in order to meet its current obligations and working capital requirements. Excess cash is often invested in securities to provide a return. The ability to turn these investments into cash quickly is important, as management constantly monitors its immediate cash needs.

Marketable securities include both equity and debt securities. When more than one security of either or both types is purchased, the investor is considered to be holding a portfolio, which is made up of several different securities and which allows the investor to decrease risk through diversification. Because the accounting treatment differs slightly for equity and debt securities, both of them will be discussed.

■ ACCOUNTING FOR CURRENT EQUITY SECURITIES

When equity securities are purchased, they are recorded at cost in an account titled Investment in Marketable Securities. Under the historical-cost convention, cost includes all brokerage commissions, other costs, and taxes incurred at acquisition. To illustrate, assume that during the first year of business, 1989, the EFP Corporation made the following purchases of current marketable equity securities:

Security	Number of Shares	Price per Share*	Total Cost
Kahn, Inc.—Common	100	$ 75	$ 7,500
Webb Construction—Preferred	100	200	20,000
Stern-Price Piano—Common	50	60	3,000
Total Cost			$30,500

*Includes all brokerage commissions.

In order to record this purchase, the EFP Corporation made this summary entry:

Investment in Current Marketable Securities	30,500	
Cash		30,500
To record purchase of marketable securities.		

All the securities are recorded in one general ledger account, Investment in Marketable Securities. Subsidiary ledger accounts are also maintained for each security. In most cases, the subsidiary ledger account consists of a separate card for each security, showing the acquisition date, the total cost, the number of shares or bonds owned, the dividends or the interest received, and the gain or the loss on disposition.

Accounting for Subsequent Events

Investors purchase the stock of another company in the hope of realizing a return on their investment. Their return is in the form of dividends received while the stock is held and/or a gain or loss when the securities are sold.

An investor usually records the dividends as income when the dividend checks are received, rather than when they are declared by the issuing company. Although this is not in accordance with strict accrual accounting, the financial statements are usually not materially misstated, and it does simplify the accounting records. To demonstrate, assume that the EFP Corporation still owns 100 shares of Kahn, Inc. On December 1, Kahn, Inc. declares a $.75 per-share dividend payable on December 20. On December 20, EFP makes the following entry:

Dec. 1   Cash   75
              Dividend Revenue   75
              To record dividend received of $75.
              ($.75 × 100 shares)

Besides expecting to receive dividends, investors expect to sell their stock at a future date at a price above their original purchase price. The market price of equity securities reacts to general economic conditions as well as to specific events that affect the firm. Thus the market price of the investor's stock may rise or fall during a particular accounting period. The investor may choose to sell the stock and realize a gain or loss on the transaction or to hold the stock and incur an unrealized gain or loss. (The gain or loss is unrealized because the stocks have not been sold.) One of the issues confronting the accounting profession is how to account for unrealized gains or losses on marketable equity securities.

The Lower-of-cost-or-market Rule

In 1975, the FASB issued Statement 12, which requires that after acquisition, investments in marketable equity securities be valued at the lower of cost or market and that the necessary adjustments be made on each balance sheet date. Essentially, this statement requires that firms divide their marketable equity securities into a current portfolio and a noncurrent portfolio and that each portfolio be shown on the balance sheet at the lower of its aggregate cost or market value. Thus, if the total market value of the securities in a portfolio is below its cost, an unrealized loss must be recognized. An Allowance account, similar to the Allowance for Doubtful Accounts, is used to reduce the securities to market. This reduction is made whether the price decline is temporary or permanent; but if the market price of the stock rises above its cost, the stock cannot be written up above its original cost.

EXHIBIT 15–1

CURRENT MARKETABLE EQUITY SECURITY PORTFOLIO December 31, 1989			
Security	Total Cost	Total Market Value	Unrealized Gain or (Loss)
Kahn, Inc.—Common	$ 7,500	$ 6,000	$(1,500)
Webb Construction—Preferred	20,000	21,400	1,400
Stern-Price Piano—Common	3,000	2,100	(900)
Total	$30,500	$29,500	$(1,000)
Present balance in allowance account			0
Required adjustment			$ 1,000

To illustrate the application of the lower-of-cost-or-market rule (LCM rule) as applied to current marketable equity securities, let us continue with the EFP example. Because EFP prepares its balance sheet once a year on December 31, it must apply the LCM rule at that date. At December 31, 1989, the end of the firm's first year in business, the cost and market value of the portfolio are as shown in Exhibit 15-1. The total market value of the portfolio, $29,500, is $1,000 below its cost of $30,500. Notice that the valuation is based on the total portfolio, not just on the two stocks that decreased in value. Thus the $1,400 increase in the Webb Construction stock offsets the combined $2,400 decreases in the prices of the other two stocks. However, the individual unrealized gains and losses are calculated, because Statement 12 requires footnote disclosure of the aggregate unrealized gains and losses. The following adjusting entry is made for the purpose of recording the unrealized loss at December 31, 1989:

Dec. 31, 1989	Unrealized Loss on Marketable Securities	1,000	
	Allowance to Reduce Marketable Securities		
	to Market		1,000
	To record the unrealized loss on marketable securities.		

It is important to understand the nature of the two accounts involved in the adjusting journal entry. The Allowance account works just as the Allowance for Doubtful Accounts does when the aging method is used. That is, the amount of the adjusting entry is that amount necessary to bring the Allowance account to a predetermined balance. That balance is the difference between the cost and the market value of the portfolio at the balance sheet date. In this case, because this is the first year of the firm's operations, the balance in the Allowance account before adjustment is zero; the required balance is $1,000, so the adjusting entry is made for that amount.

The Unrealized Loss account is an income statement account and is included in the other income and expense category. However, because the loss is unrealized, it should be shown as a separate item in order to distinguish it from actual realized gains or losses on the sale of securities.

Balance Sheet Presentation

The account Allowance to Reduce Marketable Securities to Market is a contra-asset account and is offset against the Marketable Securities account. The partial December 31, 1989 balance sheet for EFP is shown in Exhibit 15-2. As noted, the Unrealized Loss account appears on the income statement under the other income and expense category.

EXHIBIT 15-2

EFP CORPORATION Partial Balance Sheet December 31, 1989		
Current assets		
Cash		$124,000
Marketable securities	$30,500	
Less: Allowance to reduce marketable securities to market	(1,000)	29,500
Accounts receivable	89,000	
Less: Allowance for uncollectible accounts	(4,000)	85,000

To continue the example, assume that two events occurred in 1990 involving current marketable securities: (1) On April 14, 1990, EFP sold 50 shares of Kahn, Inc. at $65 per share, and (2) an adjustment was made at December 31, 1990 to value the portfolio at the lower of cost or market. The entry to record the sale of 50 shares of Kahn, Inc. is:

April 14, 1990	Cash	3,250	
	Realized Loss on Sale of Marketable Securities	500	
	Investment in Marketable Securities		3,750
	To record sale of 50 shares of Kahn, Inc. at $65 per share.		

Notice that a loss of $500 is recorded. This loss is the difference between the recorded cost of the securities at $3,750 ($75 per share × 50 shares) and the sale price of $3,250 ($65 per share × 50 shares). The Allowance account is not involved, because this account is not directly associated with any specific security in the portfolio. Remember that the Allowance account reduces the entire cost of the portfolio to market but has no effect on the individual securities in the portfolio.

The cost and market of the portfolio at December 31, 1990 are shown in Exhibit 15-3. Again, the fact that the makeup of the portfolio has changed over the year is not important. The amount of the required adjusting entry is based on only the total cost and market value of the portfolio.

EXHIBIT 15–3

Current Marketable Equity Security Portfolio December 31, 1990			
Security	Total Cost	Total Market	Unrealized Gain or (Loss)
Kahn, Inc.—Common	$ 3,750	$ 3,600	$ (150)
Webb Construction—Preferred	20,000	21,000	1,000
Stern-Price Piano—Common	3,000	1,800	(1,200)
Totals	$26,750	$26,400	$ (350)
Balance in allowance account, 1/1/90			1,000
Required entry to reduce allowance account to balance based on market value on 12/31/90			$ 650

At the end of 1990, the total market value of the securities is only $350 below their cost. Because the Allowance account currently has a balance of $1,000, it must be reduced by $650 to reflect the new balance of $350. The following adjusting entry is made to accomplish this:

Dec. 31, 1990	Allowance to Reduce Marketable Securities to Market	650	
	Reduction in Unrealized Loss on Marketable Securities		650
	To reduce Allowance account to required balance of $350.		

The Allowance account is debited, and an income statement account, Reduction in Unrealized Loss, is credited. This account can be considered an unrealized gain, though it is not so labeled here. In effect, the firm is simply reducing a loss recorded in the prior year. This account is shown as an income item in the other income and expense category of the income statement. After this entry is posted, the Allowance account appears as follows:

Allowance to Reduce Marketable Securities to Market

12/31/89 Adj. 650	12/31/89 1,000	
	12/31/90 Bal. 350	

The correct balance sheet is shown in Exhibit 15-4, and the income statement presentation is shown in Exhibit 15-5. As before, the Allowance account is offset against the Investment account. Both the realized loss and the unrealized gain are shown separately on the income statement.

EXHIBIT 15—4

EFP CORPORATION Partial Balance Sheet December 31, 1990		
Current assets		
Cash		$150,000
Marketable securities	$ 26,750	
Less: Allowance to reduce marketable securities to market	350	26,400
Accounts receivable	120,000	
Less: Allowance for uncollectible accounts	8,000	112,000

EXHIBIT 15—5

EFP CORPORATION Partial Income Statement For the Year Ended December 31, 1990		
Income from continuing operations		$240,000
Other income (expense)		
Rental income	$24,000	
Reduction of unrealized loss on marketable securities held	650	
Loss on sale of marketable securities	(500)	24,150

Securities Cannot Be Recorded above Cost

According to Statement 12, marketable securities cannot be valued above cost. Thus the Allowance account will have either a zero or a credit balance. To demonstrate, assume that the entire portfolio is held throughout 1991 and that at the end of 1991, the market value of the portfolio has increased to $30,000. In this case, market exceeds the cost of $26,750, so the balance in the Allowance account should be zero. Because the balance before any adjustment is $350, the following adjusting entry should be made at December 31, 1991:

Dec. 31, 1991	Allowance to Reduce Marketable Securities to Market	350	
	Reduction in Unrealized Loss on Marketable Securities		350
	To reduce allowance account to a zero balance.		

In effect, this entry writes the securities back up to their cost, but no accounting recognition is given to the fact that the market value now exceeds the cost by $3,250 ($30,000 − $26,750).

In summary, Statement 12 should be applied to marketable equity securities. If the total price of the current portfolio is below cost, an Allowance account should be established for the entire portfolio, regardless of the composition of the securities in the portfolio. Any changes in the Allowance account should be included in net income in the period in which they occur. According to Statement 12, no accounting recognition is given to an increase in market value above cost. Finally, under the full-disclosure principle, both the cost and the market value of the securities should be disclosed in the financial statements or in the footnotes.

Evaluation of Lower of Cost or Market

Many accountants feel that the accounting profession was correct in moving away from the strict use of cost in valuing marketable securities. However, many of these same individuals feel that lower of cost or market is too conservative and that marketable equity securities should be valued at market, regardless of whether market is below or above cost. This is because market values are objectively determined in the capital market; gains and losses occur when the value of the security changes, not when the investment is sold; and the market price can be realized at any time management desires. The main argument given by those against the use of market is that fluctuations in earnings that have not or may not become realized would have to be recorded in the accounting records. Furthermore, market fluctuations are outside the control of management.

■ ACCOUNTING FOR CURRENT DEBT SECURITIES

The accounting treatment for current investments in debt securities is slightly different from that for current equity securities. First, at acquisition, accounting recognition must be given to any interest that has accrued since the last interest date. This interest is recorded in an Interest Receivable account. This is not the case with dividends on stock. Dividends do not accrue, and no accounting recognition is given to dividends until declared by the board of directors of the issuing company. Second, the lower-of-cost-or-market rule of Statement 12, as it applies to temporary price declines, does not have to be applied to investments in debt securities.

To illustrate the accounting issues related to investments in current debt securities, assume that on May 1, 1990, the Doggett Corporation purchases 20 $1,000, 12% bonds that pay interest every January 2 and July 1. The bonds are purchased at a price of 102 plus $100 in brokerage commissions. The total cash outlay is $21,300, which is calculated by adding the cost of the bonds of $20,500 ($20,000 \times 1.02 = $20,400 + 100 brokerage commission $= $20,500$) to the accrued interest of $800 ($20,000 \times .12 \times \frac{4}{12} = 800). The following entry is made on May 1, 1990 to record this purchase:

May 1, 1990	Investment in Marketable Securities	20,500	
	Interest Receivable	800	
	Cash		21,300
	To record purchase of twenty $1,000 bonds at 102 plus brokerage commissions and accrued interest.		

On July 1, 1990, the Doggett Corporation will receive interest of $1,200, and the following entry is made to record the interest:

July 1, 1990	Cash	1,200	
	Interest Receivable		800
	Interest Revenue		400
	To record receipt of six months' interest		

The Interest Receivable account is reduced to zero, and two months' interest revenue representing May and June is recorded ($20,000 \times .12 \times \frac{2}{12} = 400).

Recording a Gain or Loss

Chapter 12 considered the need to amortize the premium or discount on long-term bond investments. The premium or discount is amortized on long-term investments because it is assumed that they will be held to maturity. In effect, the market price of the bond will move toward the maturity or face value as the bond nears maturity. Thus it makes sense to amortize the discount or premium over the life of the bond, by using the effective-interest method.

Short-term bond investments, however, are usually not held to maturity. The investment account is therefore carried at cost, and any difference between the cost of the bonds and their current selling price represents a gain or loss in the period of sale. Since these investments are held for a relatively short period of time, amortizing a discount or premium would not provide a more meaningful measurement basis than would leaving the investment at cost.

To show how a gain or loss on a sale of a short-term bond investment is measured and recorded, assume that on December 1, 1990, ten of the $1,000, 12% bonds purchased on May 1, 1990 were sold at a price of 104, less brokerage commissions of $50. The total price received for the bonds was $10,350, or $10,000 × 1.04 − $50. A gain of $100, or $10,350 minus $10,250 (one-half of the acquisition cost of $20,500), is recognized. Finally, because the bonds were sold between interest dates, the seller will receive the interest accrued since July 1. This amounts to $500, or $10,000 × .12 × $\frac{5}{12}$. Therefore the total cash received is $10,850, or $10,350 plus $500. The following entry is made to record the sale:

Dec. 1, 1990	Cash	10,850	
	Interest Revenue		500
	Gain on Sale of Bonds		100
	Investment in Marketable Securities		10,250
	To record gain on sale of 10 $1,000, 12% bonds.		

LCM Not Required

In addition to the fact that no recognition is given to discount or premiums on short-term debt investments, the lower-of-cost-or-market (LCM) rule in Statement 12 need not be applied. Thus no accounting recognition need be given to a temporary decline in the market value of a bond below its recorded cost. The term *need be* is used because Statement 12 does not prohibit a firm from valuing the debt securities at lower of cost or market; it just requires this treatment for equity securities. Nonetheless, in order to simplify their accounting process, many firms treat current debt and equity investments in the same way and thus apply the LCM rule to all short-term investments.

■ FINANCIAL STATEMENT PRESENTATION OF CURRENT MARKETABLE SECURITIES

Marketable securities are shown in a variety of ways on the balance sheets of major corporations. For example, some companies include these temporary investments with cash. Other companies show their investment in marketable securities as a separate item immediately following cash. These two approaches are illustrated by two excerpts from annual reports, shown in Exhibit 15-6.

EXHIBIT 15−6

BR COMMUNICATIONS		
	Year-end	
	1985	1984
Current assets		
Cash including short-term investments of $3,100,000 and $3,400,000	$3,507,985	$4,384,965
SAFEWAY STORES, INC.		
	Year-end	
	1985	1984
Current assets		
Cash	$ 54,593,000	$49,179,000
Marketable securities	170,921,000	25,263,000

There are two interesting points about these disclosures. First, note in each case the relative proportion of cash and investments. These firms are practicing good cash management by not maintaining large amounts of cash relative to their temporary investments. Second, in both reports no separate disclosure is made of any Allowance account. This is so because there is no material difference between the cost and the market value of the securities. This treatment is very common in published financial statements.

■ LONG-TERM INVESTMENTS

Investments that do not meet the criteria to be considered as current assets are shown in the long-term investment section of the balance sheet. Either these securities are not readily marketable, or management's intention is to hold them for a long period of time or for purposes of control. Accounting for long-term debt investments was explained in Chapter 12. This portion of the chapter will consider accounting for long-term equity investments.

Exhibit 15-7 summarizes the accounting treatment for long-term equity investments. The correct accounting treatment depends on the degree of the investor's control over the investee (the firm whose stock has been purchased). The accounting pronouncements differentiate among three levels of control: no significant influence or control, significant influence but not control, and controlling interest.[1]

<table>
<tr><td>**EXHIBIT 15–7**
Accounting on Long-term Equity Investments</td><td colspan="3">

Amount of Influence or Control	Percentage of Common Stock Owned	Accounting
1. No significant influence or control	Less than 20%	Cost method and lower-of-cost-or-market valuation
2. Significant influence but not control	20% to 50%	Equity method—no LCM valuation
3. Controlling interest	More than 50%	Consolidated financial statements

</td></tr>
</table>

No significant influence or control exists when the investor is unable to have an important impact on either the financing or operating policies of the investee. The accounting pronouncements presume that ownership of less than 20% of the voting stock or any amount of the investee's nonvoting stock will not result in any significant influence or control. This presumption can be overcome, however, if economic circumstances dictate.

Significant influence but not control exists when an investor can influence, but cannot control, the operating and financing policies of the investee. In many situations, this influence is evidenced by the investor's having a seat on the board of directors of the investee company, other participation in the policy-making process, material intercompany transactions, the interchange of management personnel, and technological interdependencies. The accounting pronouncements presume that sig-

---

[1] Four related pronouncements govern accounting for long-term investments: American Institute of Certified Public Accountants, Accounting Principles Board, Opinions No. 16, *Business Combinations* (New York: AICPA, 1970), and No. 18, *The Equity Method of Accounting for Investments in Common Stock* (New York: AICPA, 1971); Financial Accounting Standards Board, Statement No. 12, *Accounting for Certain Marketable Securities* (Stamford, Conn.: FASB, December 1975); and Financial Accounting Standards Board, Statement No. 94, *Consolidation of All Majority-Owned Subsidiaries* (Stamford, Conn.: FASB, October 1987).

nificant influence but not control exists when the investor holds at least 20% but not more than 50% of another company. In this situation, an investor can influence the investee's operating policies but cannot control them, because the investor does not have majority control.

Finally, a controlling interest exists when an investor is able to determine both the financial and the operating policies of the other company. Control is presumed when the investor owns more than 50% of the stock of another company.

■ NO SIGNIFICANT INFLUENCE OR CONTROL

When the ownership interest is less than 20%, the investor is presumed not to have significant influence or control over the operations of the investee company. Under current practices, the cost method of accounting is used to account for these types of investments.[2] Thus, at acquisition, the investment is recorded at cost and is subsequently valued at lower of cost or market. Income from the investment is recognized when dividends are received by the investor. With the exception of a few variations in applying the LCM rule, measuring and recording long-term investments of ownership interests of less than 20% are the same as for short-term marketable equity securities.

Accounting at Acquisition

Like short-term equity securities, acquisition cost includes whatever expenditures are necessary to acquire the securities. Thus brokerage fees, commissions, and taxes all are included in the initial acquisition cost. For example, assume that on July 1, 1989 the Popper Company purchased 100 shares of Bailey, Inc. at $40 per share and 100 shares of Essence, Inc. at $60 per share. The Popper Company made the following entry at July 1, 1989:

July 1, 1989	Long-term Investments in Securities	10,000	
	Cash		10,000
	To record purchase of long-term investments.		

Accounting for Subsequent Events

Under the cost method of accounting for investments, dividends are recorded as income when they are received. Furthermore, at each balance sheet date the securities must be valued at the lower of cost or market.

To illustrate, assume that on December 1, 1989, the Popper Company received cash dividends of $2 per share on the 100 shares of Essence. The entry to record the receipt of the dividends is:

Dec. 1, 1989	Cash	200	
	Dividend Revenue		200
	To record dividends of $2 per share of		
	Essence stock.		

On the balance sheet date, the securities must be valued at lower of cost or market. Assume that on December 31 the Bailey, Inc. stock was selling at $34 per share, and the Essence, Inc. stock at $62 per share. The cost and market value of the long-term portfolio are as shown in Exhibit 15-8. Because the aggregate market value of $9,600 is $400 below its $10,000 cost and the Allowance account currently has a zero balance (assuming first purchase of securities), this account must be credited for

[2]Opinion 18.

EXHIBIT 15–8

POPPER COMPANY Long-term Equity Security Portfolio December 31, 1989			
Security	**Total Cost**	**Total Market Value**	**Unrealized Gain or (Loss)**
Bailey, Inc.	$ 4,000	$3,400	$(600)
Essence, Inc.	6,000	6,200	200
Total	$10,000	$9,600	$(400)
Present balance in the Allowance account			0
Required adjustment			$ 400

this amount. Accordingly, the Popper Company would make the following entry on December 31:

Dec. 31, 1989	Unrealized Loss on Long-term Investment	400	
	Allowance to Reduce Long-term Equity		
	Investments to Market		400
	To record decrease in market value of		
	securities.		

The Allowance account is a contra-asset account that is offset against the Investment account on the balance sheet. This is the same treatment as for short-term investments.

The Unrealized Loss account, however, is not an income statement account, as it is when short-term investments are involved. For long-term investments, the Unrealized Loss account is a debit item in stockholders' equity (a contra-equity account) and is shown immediately after retained earnings. Thus both accounts in the adjusting entry are balance sheet accounts. This treatment is based on the view that long-term investments will not be sold in the near future, so unrealized losses will not immediately affect income.

In most other respects, the application of LCM requirements is the same as for short-term equity investments.[3] That is, if the securities subsequently increase in value so that market exceeds cost, the contra-equity account can be eliminated. Since the investments cannot be valued at higher than cost, the Unrealized Loss on Long-term Investment account cannot have a credit balance.

Exhibit 15-9 shows the stockholders' equity section for the GAF Corporation, together with the relevant note. This illustrates how unrealized losses on long-term marketable securities are disclosed.

■ OWNERSHIP INTEREST BETWEEN 20 AND 50 PERCENT

Significant influence but not control is presumed to exist when an investor holds an interest in the investee of at least 20% but not more than 50%. In this situation, the investor can influence the investee's operating and financial policies but cannot completely control them. For example, the investor may control one or two seats on the investee's board of directors, gained through the exercise of a large block of stock, but the investor is unable to control the investee completely.

[3] There are other variations in applying LCM to long-term investments. For example, if the decline is considered permanent, realized loss is recorded. This, as well as other complexities, are topics for intermediate accounting textbooks.

EXHIBIT 15–9

GAF CORPORATION
Partial Consolidated Income Statement
For the Years Ended December 31
(in thousands)

	1987	1986
Shareholders' equity		
Preferred stock, $1 par value per share: authorized 6,000,000 shares	$ —	$ —
Common stock, $1 par value per share: authorized 100,000,000 shares; issued shares: 1987 and 1986—36,008,117	36,008	36,008
Additional paid-in capital	46,565	44,736
Retained earnings	753,438	519,207
Accumulated translation adjustment	18,134	3,928
Net unrealized loss on marketable equity securities	(22,038)	—
Treasury stock, at cost	(323,790)	(2,381)
Shareholders' equity	508,317	601,498

Notes to Consolidated Financial Statements

Note 2 (in part): Short-term Investments and Marketable Securities

As of December 31, 1987, the Company held positions in several publicly-owned companies. These investments, classified as marketable securities, had an aggregate cost of $332.4 million at December 31, 1987, while the aggregate market value was $299 million. The unrealized loss in market value of the equity securities is reflected on an after tax basis as a reduction of shareholders' equity since management does not deem such unrealized losses to be permanent.

When this relationship exists between the investor and the investee, dividends paid to the investor by the investee are no longer a proper measure of income received. This is because the investor is able to influence the investee's dividend policy. Thus an investor may pressure an investee to pay dividends in an amount that has little to do with the investee's profitability. For example, this may occur if the investee is forced to issue a large dividend that otherwise would not be issued. In this situation, the cost method of accounting is not appropriate, and the equity method should be used.

The Equity Method of Accounting

The primary differences between the equity and cost methods of accounting are the way in which income from the investment is recognized and the fact that LCM is not applied when the equity method is used. Under the **equity method** of accounting, the investment is first recorded at its acquisition cost. Subsequently, the Investment account is adjusted to reflect the proportionate increase or decrease in the investee's stockholders' equity that results from the investee's net income or loss for the period. That is, as the investee earns net income, its stockholders' equity increases, and so the investor recognizes its proportionate share of the increase as investment income. If the investee suffers a loss, the investor will recognize a proportionate share of the loss.

Under the equity method of accounting, dividends declared are not considered income but rather reduce the Investment account. A cash dividend reduces the net asset or stockholders' equity of the investee, so the investor records a proportionate decrease in its Investment account. In effect, dividends received represent a conversion of the investment into cash. Thus, under the equity method, investors recognize revenue as the investee earns it rather than at the time dividends are declared.

Illustration of the Equity Method

Accounting for the equity method is illustrated by the following example. Assume that at the beginning of the year, the Jackson Corporation purchased for $300,000 a 30% interest in Wildcat Ventures. At the time of purchase, Wildcat Ventures' net assets totaled $1 million, so the $300,000 purchase exactly equaled a 30% interest in Wildcat's net assets.[4] During the year, Wildcat Ventures reported net income of $70,000 and declared cash dividends of $25,000. Jackson Corporation would make the following entries to reflect these events:

At time of acquisition		
Investment in Wildcat Ventures	300,000	
Cash		300,000
To record 30% interest in Wildcat Ventures.		
At Jackson's year-end		
Investment in Wildcat Ventures	21,000	
Investment Income		21,000
To record increase in investment from 30% share of net income earned by Wildcat, $70,000 × 30% = $21,000.		
Cash	7,500	
Investment in Wildcat Ventures		7,500
To record decrease in investment due to receipt of dividends, $25,000 × 30% = $7,500.		

Note that after these events, Wildcat Ventures' net assets or stockholders' equity is $1,045,000, or the book value of $1 million at acquisition plus the net income of $70,000 less the dividends of $25,000. The balance in the investment account is now $313,500, or the original investment of $300,000 plus Jackson's share of the net income, $21,000 less its share of the dividend, $7,500. Thus the balance in the investment account equals 30% of the net assets of Wildcat Ventures ($1,045,000 × 30% = $313,500). The equity method ensures that the balance in the investment in the investee account equals the investor's proportionate share of the net assets purchased. These points are illustrated in the following T accounts:

Wildcat's Books
Stockholders' Equity,
Wildcat Ventures

			1,000,000	
Dividends	25,000		70,000	Net income
			1,045,000	

Jackson's Books
Investment in
Wildcat Ventures

		300,000	7,500	Dividends
Net income		21,000		
		313,500		

---

[4] In reality, the purchase price rarely equals the book value of the investee's net assets. This assumption has been made in order to simplify the illustration. Although beyond the scope of an introductory book, adjustments can be made if the purchase price is more or less than the book value.

To summarize, the equity method of accounting for long-term investments ensures that the investor reflects in its statements, during the period it was earned, the income or loss of the company in which it invested. The lower-of-cost-or-market method is not applied, so no adjustments are made for declines (if any) in the investment's market value.

■ OWNERSHIP INTEREST ABOVE 50 PERCENT

Often, a corporation owns more than 50% of the stock of another corporation. The corporation that owns the majority of stock is called the **parent company**, and the corporation that is wholly or partially owned is called a **subsidiary**. One parent often owns several subsidiaries. The degree of ownership interest in these subsidiaries may vary between 50 and 100 percent.

Once a corporation owns more than 50% of the stock of another company, the parent corporation can elect the board of directors of the subsidiary and can control its operating and financial policies. In effect, the parent and subsidiary or subsidiaries represent one economic unit, and the entity assumption requires that it be reported as such.

The parent company and the subsidiary or subsidiaries are separate legal entities, so they each maintain separate records and prepare separate financial statements for internal purposes and, under some circumstances, for external purposes. On the parent's books, the investment in the subsidiary is accounted for by the equity method of accounting. Since the parent and subsidiary represent one economic unit, the parent company prepares consolidated financial statements to be distributed to external users. These consolidated balance sheets and income statements show the financial position and operating results of the entire economic unit.

Consolidated Financial Statements

Consolidated financial statements should not be confused with combined financial statements. Although the assets, liabilities, revenues, and expenses of all the entities are combined to provide a single set of financial statements, certain eliminations and adjustments are made. These eliminations are necessary to ensure that only arm's-length transactions between independent parties are reflected in the consolidated statements. For example, a parent and subsidiary may make intercompany sales and/or loans and borrowings. Viewed independently, the transactions represent sales and expenses or assets and liabilities on the books of the respective entities. When consolidated statements are prepared, these intercompany transactions must be eliminated. This ensures that only arm's-length transactions between independent parties are reflected in the consolidated statements; transactions between related parties are not counted.

When to Use Consolidated Financial Statements

If one company owns more than 50% of the voting stock of another company, consolidated financial statements must be prepared unless control of the subsidiary is temporary or does not rest with the majority owner.[5] Prior to 1987, many firms did not consolidate their financing subsidiaries. For example, General Motors did not consolidate GMAC, its huge financing subsidiary. (GMAC is the subsidiary that provides auto loans for customers of General Motors.) It was shown on the balance sheet as a one-line item, Investments in Unconsolidated Subsidiaries, accounted for by the equity

---

[5] Financial Accounting Standards Board, Statement No. 94, *Consolidation of All Majority-Owned Subsidiaries* (Stamford, Conn.: FASB, October 1987).

method of accounting. In effect, only one number representing General Motor's equity in GMAC appeared on the balance sheet. However, that one number represented the net of billions of dollars of assets and liabilities of GMAC.

The FASB, as well as users of financial statements, were concerned that allowing companies not to consolidate majority-owned financing subsidiaries made it difficult to determine the true financial picture of the consolidated company. Huge liabilities of these subsidiaries were not fully disclosed. This phenomenon, called *off-balance-sheet financing*, was and continues to be a major problem in financial reporting. In late 1987, the FASB decided to act; it issued Statement No. 94, which requires the consolidation of all majority-owned subsidiaries besides the two minor exceptions previously noted. The FASB stated:

> The Board believes that the objectives of financial reporting are better met if significant amounts of assets, liabilities, revenues, and expenses are not omitted from balance sheets. That omission is an important factor in what is often criticized as "off balance sheet financing." By requiring consolidation of all subsidiaries, Statement 94 is a major step in resolving the problem of off balance sheet financing.[6]

Methods of Accounting for Consolidations

There are various ways in which a parent may acquire a controlling interest in a subsidiary. For example, the investor may acquire it by paying cash, by issuing stock for stock, or through a combination of stock and cash. How the investment is made and other circumstances surrounding the investment or business combination determine the correct accounting method of consolidation. Either the **purchase method** or the **pooling-of-interests method** must be used. Each will produce significantly different consolidated statements. These methods are not interchangeable, and the circumstances of the acquisition determine which method should be used. First, the purchase method will be explained. It is appropriate when the investment is made for cash, through the issue of stock or bonds, or a combination of these. Later in the chapter, the pooling-of-interests method will be discussed. It is appropriate only when stock of the parent company is exchanged for substantially all of the stock of its subsidiary.

■ PREPARING CONSOLIDATED FINANCIAL STATEMENTS

Accounting procedures for consolidation are quite complex; they occupy many chapters in advanced accounting texts. The purpose here is to introduce you to the basics so that you will be able to interpret and understand consolidated financial statements. First to be considered is consolidation of a 100% owned subsidiary acquired at book value. A more complex situation will be treated later.

Consolidation of a 100% Owned Subsidiary at Date of Acquisition

To illustrate the preparation of consolidated financial statements, assume that on January 2, 1990, Scientific Instruments purchased 100% of the common stock of Technical Tools, Inc. The purchase price was $100,000, which represented the book value of Technical Tool's net assets at that time. Before the purchase, Scientific Instruments had made a $25,000, non-interest-bearing loan to Technical Tools. The individual balance sheets of the two companies immediately after the purchase are shown in Exhibit 15-10.

---

[6] Financial Accounting Standards Board, Status Report No. 190 (Stamford, Conn.: FASB, October 30, 1987), p. 1.

EXHIBIT 15–10

	SCIENTIFIC INSTRUMENTS AND TECHNICAL TOOLS Balance Sheets January 2, 1990	
Accounts	Scientific Instruments	Technical Tools
Cash	$ 20,000	$ 18,000
Notes receivable from Technical Tools	25,000	—
Accounts receivable, net	60,000	22,000
Investment in Technical Tools	100,000	—
Other assets	165,000	140,000
Total assets	$370,000	$180,000
Notes payable to Scientific Instruments	—	25,000
Accounts payable	10,000	5,000
Other liabilities	60,000	50,000
Common stock	175,000	55,000
Retained earnings	125,000	45,000
Total liabilities and stockholders' equity	$370,000	$180,000

The worksheet to prepare consolidated financial statements immediately after acquisition is shown in Exhibit 15-11. Remember that each firm maintains separate books and records. Thus a worksheet is needed to prepare a consolidated balance sheet. However, the elimination entries on the worksheet are not made in the individual accounting records of the parent or subsidiary; they are made for consolidation purposes only.

EXHIBIT 15–11

			Consolidated Balance Sheet Worksheet January 2, 1990—Acquisition Date		
			Intercompany Eliminations		
Accounts	Scientific Instruments	Technical Tools	Debit	Credit	Consolidated Balance Sheet
Cash	$ 20,000	$ 18,000			$ 38,000
Notes receivable from Technical Tools	25,000	—		$ 25,000[b]	
Accounts receivable, net	60,000	22,000			82,000
Investment in Technical Tools	100,000	—		100,000[a]	
Other assets	165,000	140,000			305,000
Total assets	$370,000	$180,000			$425,000
Notes payable to Scientific Instruments	—	25,000	$ 25,000[b]		—
Accounts payable	10,000	5,000			15,000
Other liabilities	60,000	50,000			110,000
Common stock	175,000	55,000	55,000[a]		175,000
Retained earnings	125,000	45,000	45,000[a]		125,000
Total liabilities and stockholders' equity	$370,000	$180,000	$125,000	$125,000	$425,000

[a] To eliminate investment in Technical Tools against stockholders' equity of Technical Tools.
[b] To eliminate intercompany debt.

As noted, certain elimination entries must be made before a consolidated balance sheet is prepared. Typical intercompany eliminations pertain to intercompany stock ownership, intercompany debt, and intercompany revenue and expenses. Since this example involves constructing a consolidated balance sheet, only the first two elimination entries will be shown. Eliminations of revenue and expense accounts are more complex matters, discussed in advanced textbooks.

Elimination of Intercompany Stock Ownership. The first entry eliminates the Investment in Technical Tools account. This entry is necessary in order to keep from double-counting the amount of the investment. Before the consolidation, the $100,000 investment in Technical Tools was shown in the Investment account. However, the purpose of the consolidated balance sheet is to combine the individual accounts of the parent and subsidiary. Thus the $100,000 Investment account must be eliminated so that the individual assets and liabilities of Technical Tools that net to $100,000 can be added to the respective accounts of Scientific Instruments to form the consolidated balance sheet.

The elimination of the Investment account is made against the stockholders' equity accounts of Technical Tools. Essentially, there are no external stockholders of Technical Tools. All the stock is owned internally by the consolidated entity. Ownership of a company's own stock does not give rise to either an asset or stockholders' equity. Thus the purpose of the entry is to eliminate the Investment account on Scientific Instruments' books against the stockholders' equity accounts of Technical Tools.

Elimination of Intercompany Debt. Before Scientific Instruments purchased Technical Tools, it lent the firm $25,000. Scientific Instruments thus recorded a note receivable, and Technical Tools recorded a note payable. From a consolidated entity point of view, this transaction results only in the transfer of cash from one part of the entity to another and does not give rise to a receivable or a payable. Thus, in preparing a consolidated balance sheet, an entry must be made to eliminate the notes receivable and payable.

Preparation of a Consolidated Balance Sheet. After the two elimination entries are posted to the worksheet, the remaining assets and liabilities and stockholders' equity accounts are combined to prepare the consolidated balance sheet columns in the worksheet shown in Exhibit 15-11. The actual consolidated balance sheet is presented in Exhibit 15-12.

EXHIBIT 15–12

SCIENTIFIC INSTRUMENTS, INC.
Consolidated Balance Sheet
January 2, 1990

Assets		Liabilities and Stockholders' Equity		
Cash	$ 38,000	Liabilities		
Accounts receivable	82,000	Accounts payable		$ 15,000
Other assets	305,000	Other liabilities		110,000
		Stockholders' equity		
		Common stock	$175,000	
		Retained earnings	125,000	300,000
		Total liabilities and		
Total assets	$425,000	stockholders' equity		$425,000

Purchase above or below Book Value

In order to simplify the discussion, it has been assumed that the purchase price has been equal to the book value of the net assets acquired. Usually this will not be the case. The price that an investor is willing to pay for a business depends on several factors, such as general economic conditions, market prices, estimates of future anticipated earnings, and the relative bargaining position of the buyer and seller. The book value of a subsidiary's net assets therefore bears little relation to what a buyer may be willing to pay for them. For example, a parent will pay more for a business if it feels that the potential subsidiary's assets are undervalued, that there is a potential for future excess earnings, or perhaps that the subsidiary owns a valuable patent needed by the parent. On the other hand, the parent may pay less than the book value for a potential subsidiary's net assets if these assets are overvalued, the firm is in a declining industry, or it has suffered losses in the past.

The Accounting Principles Board has developed a number of guidelines to be used when the purchase method is used and when the purchase price differs from the book value of the net assets acquired.[7] Briefly, the purchase method follows the principles normally found under historical-cost accounting in regard to the purchase of assets. Thus when the purchase price exceeds the book value of the net assets acquired, the purchase price is first allocated to the identifiable assets acquired and liabilities assumed, based on their respective fair market values. The excess cost of the acquired company over the amounts assigned to the identifiable assets, less liabilities assumed, should be recorded as goodwill. In effect, the acquired net assets of the acquired company are recorded at their fair market value, and any excess cost is considered goodwill. This is based on the assumption that the reason the parent is willing to pay more for a subsidiary than the fair market value of its identifiable net assets is the existence of goodwill.

In some circumstances, the parent will purchase the subsidiary at a price below the book value of the subsidiary's net assets. This implies that some assets are recorded at amounts above their current values. In this situation, the assets of the company are written down to their fair market value. Negative goodwill is rarely recorded.

Purchase above Fair Market Value. To demonstrate the preparation of a consolidated balance sheet when the parent pays more than the book value of the subsidiary's net assets, assume that on December 31, 1990, the Peter Corporation purchased 100% of the Mary Company for $140,000. The book value of Mary Company's net assets on the date of acquisition (see Exhibit 15-13) is $130,000 (common stock plus

EXHIBIT 15–13

MARY COMPANY Balance Sheet December 21, 1990			
Assets		**Equities**	
Cash	$ 10,000	Current liabilities	$ 20,000
Accounts receivable, net	15,000	Long-term debt	15,000
Inventory	40,000	Common stock	50,000
Property, plant, and		Paid-in capital	25,000
equipment, net	100,000	Retained earnings	55,000
		Total liabilities and	
Total assets	$165,000	stockholders' equity	$165,000

[7]Opinion 16.

paid-in capital plus retained earnings). The Peter Corporation paid $10,000 in excess of the book value of Mary's net assets. The Peter Corporation evaluated the fair market value of the Mary Company's net assets and decided to increase the property, plant, and equipment by $7,500. The remaining $2,500 is allocated to goodwill.

The consolidated worksheet is shown in Exhibit 15-14. The following entry is made to write off the investment account against the stockholders' equity accounts of the Mary Company, to increase the property, plant, and equipment account to fair market value, and to record goodwill:

Property, Plant, and Equipment	7,500	
Goodwill	2,500	
Common Stock	50,000	
Paid-in Capital	25,000	
Retained Earnings	55,000	
Investment in Mary Company		140,000

Goodwill must be amortized over a maximum of 40 years, whereas the plant and equipment will be depreciated over their useful lives. The allocation between goodwill and other assets will affect future periods' income. The other entry is made to eliminate intercompany receivables and payables.

EXHIBIT 15–14

Consolidated Balance Sheet Worksheet December 31, 1990					
Accounts	**Peter Corporation**	**Mary Company**	**Eliminations**		**Consolidated Balance Sheet**
			Debit	**Credit**	
Cash	$ 24,000	$ 10,000			$ 34,000
Accounts receivable	36,000	15,000		$ 6,000[b]	45,000
Inventory	80,000	40,000			120,000
Investment in Mary Company	140,000	0		140,000[a]	0
Property, plant, and equipment, net	200,000	100,000	$ 7,500[a]		307,500
Goodwill	0	0	2,500[a]		2,500
Total assets	$480,000	$165,000			$509,000
Current liabilities	60,000	20,000	6,000[b]		74,000
Long-term debt	100,000	15,000			115,000
Common stock	100,000	50,000	50,000[a]		100,000
Paid-in capital	50,000	25,000	25,000[a]		50,000
Retained earnings	170,000	55,000	55,000[a]		170,000
Total liabilities and stockholders' equity	$480,000	$165,000	$146,000	$146,000	$509,000

[a] To eliminate investment account and to increase property, plant, and equipment to fair market value and to record goodwill.
[b] To eliminate intercompany debt of $6,000.

Purchase below Book Value of Net Assets. Occasionally, a parent will purchase a subsidiary at a price below the book value of the subsidiary's identifiable net assets. As previously noted, this may occur if the book value of the subsidiary's net assets is greater than their current fair market value and/or the acquired firm has suffered heavy losses in the immediate past. In this case, the book value of the subsidiary's assets must be written down by the amount of the excess of the book value of the acquired identifiable net assets over the purchase price. Rarely, if ever, is this excess used to record negative goodwill.

Consolidated Income Statement

To this point, the illustration has involved only the preparation of consolidated balance sheets at the date of acquisition. Consolidated income statements and statements of retained earnings are also prepared. Essentially, a consolidated income statement is prepared by combining the revenues and expenses of the parent and subsidiary companies after eliminating intercompany revenues and expense transactions such as sales, cost of goods sold, and interest revenue and expense. Because of their complex nature, the preparation of consolidated income statements is not illustrated here.

■ THE POOLING-OF-INTERESTS METHOD VERSUS THE PURCHASE METHOD

In all of the examples to this point, it has been assumed that the purchase method of accounting has been used. The purchase method must be used when the acquisition is made for cash and/or if the parent company issues debt or equity securities to the previous shareholders of the subsidiary. This method assumes that the company's shareholders have sold out their interest to the parent company. Therefore accounting principles applied to any purchase of assets are followed, and the acquired assets are recorded at their fair market value. Any goodwill resulting from the excess of the purchase price over the fair market value of the identifiable net assets is amortized over a maximum of 40 years.

In some situations, the acquisition is structured in a different manner. Substantially all of the subsidiary's stock may be acquired in exchange for the parent's common stock. If this occurs and if certain other restrictive requirements are met, the acquisition must be considered a pooling of interests rather than a purchase. Essentially, a pooling of interests assumes that the subsidiary's stockholders are now stockholders of the parent company and that a mutual pooling of interests rather than an outright purchase has taken place.

If in fact a pooling of interests has taken place, then there has not been a sale of the subsidiary's net assets. The subsidiary's net assets are therefore not revalued to their fair market value, as they are when the purchase method is used. Thus, when a consolidated balance sheet is prepared under the pooling-of-interests method, the book value of the parent's assets and liabilities is combined with the corresponding book value of the subsidiary's assets and liabilities. As a result, no goodwill is recognized, and there is no subsequent goodwill amortization.

There is another difference between the purchase and the pooling-of-interests methods of consolidating financial statements. Under the purchase method, only the subsidiary's earnings after the acquisition date are combined with the parent's earnings. Thus, if a purchase took place on October 1, only the subsidiary's earnings from that date to the year-end would be consolidated with the parent's earnings for the entire year.

However, under the pooling-of-interests method, in the year of acquisition, the subsidiary's earnings for the entire year would be combined with the parent's earnings, regardless of the date of the acquisition. Thus, even if an acquisition took place on October 1, the subsidiary's earnings for the entire year would be consolidated with the parent's earnings when preparing a consolidated income statement for the year ending December 31. This is based on the idea that the two companies have merely combined their resources and operations.

These factors explain the popularity of the pooling method of accounting with the managements of many companies. If the pooling-of-interests method is used when the purchase price exceeds the value of the acquired assets, the consolidated net assets will be recorded at lower amounts than if the purchase method is used. Furthermore, in the year of acquisition, earnings can be consolidated for the entire year. Ratios such as return on investment and earnings per share will be better when the pooling-of-interests method is used than if the purchase method is used. Exhibit 15-15 summarizes the major differences between these two methods of accounting for acquisitions.

EXHIBIT 15–15

	Method of Consolidation	Recording of Net Assets	Subsidiary's Earnings
Purchase Method	Acquisition of more than 50% of subsidiary's voting stock for cash and/or other assets, debt or securities.	Subsidiary's assets are revalued to fair market value. Excess of cost over fair market value, if any, is considered goodwill. Goodwill amortized over a maximum of 40 years.	In year of acquisition, earnings of subsidiary are combined with those of the parent from date of acquisition.
Pooling-of-interests Method	Acquisition of substantially all (90% or more) of the subsidiary's voting stock for voting stock of parent.	Subsidiary's net assets are shown on consolidated balance sheet at book value. As a result, no goodwill recognized. Retained earnings of subsidiary are carried over.	In year of acquisition, earnings of subsidiary are combined with those of the parent for the entire year.

Because of the dramatic effect that the pooling-of-interests method can have on consolidated statements, as well as its abuse during the 1960s, the Accounting Principles Board set certain conditions that must be met if the pooling-of-interests method is to be used. There are 12 requirements, the essence of which is that the transaction must be structured as an exchange of the parent's stock for substantially all of the subsidiary's stock. If all 12 requirements are not met, the purchase method must be used. In effect, the purchase and pooling-of-interests methods are not alternatives for the same acquisition, and the correct accounting treatment depends on the nature of the transaction.

To demonstrate the pooling-of-interests method, return to the Peter Corporation's acquisition of 100% of the Mary Company for a total price of $140,000. (See Exhibit 15-14.) Now assume that instead of making the acquisition for cash, the Peter Corporation issues 10,000 shares of its $10 par value common stock, which currently has a fair market value of $14, for all of the shares of the Mary Company. Under the pooling-of-interests method, the investment in Mary Company is recorded at the book value of the net assets acquired—$130,000—not at the fair market value of the stock exchanged—$140,000—as it would be if the purchase method were used. The journal entry to record this acquisition under the pooling-of-interests method is:

Investment in Mary Company	130,000	
Common Stock, $10 Par		100,000
Paid-in Capital from Issue of Common Stock in Excess of Par		30,000
To record investment in Mary Company under the pooling-of-interests method.		

The worksheet to consolidate these companies under the pooling-of-interests method is shown in Exhibit 15-16. The investment elimination entry is as follows:

Common Stock	50,000	
Paid-in Capital	80,000	
Investment in Mary Company		130,000
To eliminate investment account against capital accounts.		

EXHIBIT 15—16

Consolidated Balance Sheet Worksheet—Pooling of Interests December 31, 1990—Acquisition Date					
Accounts	Peter Corporation	Mary Company	Eliminations		Consolidated Balance Sheet
			Debit	Credit	
Cash	$164,000	$ 10,000			$174,000
Accounts receivable	36,000	15,000		$ 6,000[b]	45,000
Inventory	80,000	40,000			120,000
Investment in Mary Company	130,000	0		130,000[a]	0
Property, plant, and equipment, net	200,000	100,000			300,000
Total assets	$610,000	$165,000			$639,000
Current liabilities	60,000	20,000	$ 6,000[b]		74,000
Long-term debt	100,000	15,000			115,000
Common stock	200,000	50,000	50,000[a]		200,000
Paid-in capital	80,000	25,000	80,000[a]		25,000
Retained earnings	170,000	55,000			225,000
Total liabilities and stockholders' equity	$610,000	$165,000	$136,000	$136,000	$639,000

[a] To eliminate investment account.

[b] To eliminate intercompany debt.

In this entry, the investment account is first eliminated against Mary Company's common stock and then against the paid-in capital account. However, under the theory of a pooling of interests, the Mary Company's retained earnings are carried over in total. It is assumed that the two companies have always been one. Finally, because all the net assets of the Mary Company are carried over at their net book value, no revaluation of assets is made, nor is goodwill recorded. The consolidated balance sheet under the pooling-of-interests method, compared with the purchase method, is shown in Exhibit 15-17.

EXHIBIT 15—17

PETER CORPORATION Consolidated Balance Sheets December 31, 1990		
Assets	Purchase	Pooling of Interests
Cash	$ 34,000	$174,000
Accounts receivable	45,000	45,000
Inventory	120,000	120,000
Property, plant, and equipment, net	307,500	300,000
Goodwill	$ 2,500	
Total	$509,000	$639,000
Liabilities and Stockholders' Equity		
Current liabilities	$ 74,000	$ 74,000
Long-term debt	115,000	115,000
Common stock	100,000	200,000
Paid-in capital	50,000	25,000
Retained earnings	170,000	225,000
Total	$509,000	$639,000

Under the purchase method, the Investment in Mary Company account is recorded at $140,000, the fair value of the shares exchanged. The $10,000 paid in excess of the book value of the net assets required is allocated $7,500 to the property, plant, and equipment and $2,500 to goodwill. After the elimination entry, the stockholders' equity of the subsidiary is completely eliminated, and consolidated retained earnings is equal to the parent's retained earnings of $170,000.

SUMMARY OF LEARNING OBJECTIVES

1. The nature of publicly held corporations and security exchanges. Publicly held corporations are those whose securities are owned by outside investors and whose stocks and/or bonds are listed on a national or regional stock exchange. These exchanges include the New York Stock Exchange, the American Stock Exchange, and the over-the-counter market. Publicly held corporations are required to file certain reports with the Securities and Exchange Commission and various exchanges.

2. The accounting issues regarding accounting for current marketable securities. Investments in securities are listed as current assets if they are readily marketable and management's intention is to turn them into cash within the operating cycle of the business. Investments in current marketable securities include both equity and debt securities.

(a) Current equity securities are originally recorded at their acquisition costs and at each balance sheet date valued at lower of cost or market (LCM). A valuation account is established to reduce the securities to market when market falls below cost. The unrealized loss is shown as a separate item in the current period's income statement. Prior years' losses can be recaptured, but the securities are never valued above cost.

(b) Debt securities are recorded at cost. However, the interest that has accrued since the last interest date must be accounted for separately. Because of materiality, there is no subsequent amortization of any discounts or premiums. Furthermore, debt securities do not have to be valued at lower of cost or market, though many firms do so for simplicity's sake.

3. Long-term investments and the differences in control exercised by the investor. Long-term investments are those investments that do not meet the criteria to be classified as current. The accounting for long-term investments is based on the degree of control exercised by the investor over the investee. This degree of control is based on whether the investor owns less than 20% of the investee's stock, between 20% and 50% of its stock, or more than 50% of its stock.

4. Accounting for investments when there is no significant influence or control. No significant influence or control is presumed to exist when the investor owns less than 20% of the investee's stock. In this circumstance, the investment is originally recorded at cost and is subsequently valued at lower of cost or market. When applying the LCM rule, unrealized losses are shown as a debit item in stockholders' equity. Dividends are recorded as income when received.

5. Accounting for ownership interest between 20 and 50%. Significant influence but not control is presumed to exist when an investor owns between 20 and 50% of an investee's stock. Because the investor can influence the operating policies of the investee, the cost method of accounting is not appropriate; rather, the equity method is used. Under the equity method, the investor records as income the proportionate share of the investee's income. Dividends declared serve to decrease the investment account. Thus the investment account is carried at an amount equal to the investor's proportionate share of the purchased net assets of the investee.

6. Accounting for ownership interest above 50%. Complete control exists when the investor owns more than 50% of the investee's stock. In these situations, consolidated financial statements should be prepared. The preparation of these statements requires using certain elimination entries. These entries eliminate the investment account against the subsidiary's stockholders' equity as well as all intercompany transactions.

(a) Acquisitions must be accounted for by using either the purchase or the pooling-of-interests method. These methods are not alternatives for the same acquisition; rather, the use of a particular one depends on how the acquisition is structured.

(b) When the purchase method is used, all assets and liabilities are revalued to their fair market values, and any remaining excess cost is considered goodwill. When the pooling-of-interests method is used, all of the assets and liabilities of the subsidiary are combined with the parent's assets and liabilities at their net book value. Furthermore, under a pooling-of-interests, in the year of acquisition the subsidiary's earnings for the entire year are combined with the parent's earnings.

KEY TERMS

Consolidated financial statements

Debt securities

Equity method

Equity securities

Parent company

Pooling-of-interests method

Publicly held corporation

Purchase method

Subsidiary

PROBLEMS FOR YOUR REVIEW

A. At the beginning of the current year, West Coast Silicon held the following portfolio of current marketable equity securities:

Security	Number of shares	Total Cost	Market Value
Allied, Inc.	50	$ 4,000	$ 4,600
Gora Company	100	2,500	2,300
Leaky Oil and Gas	200	6,000	5,400
		$12,500	$12,300

During the current year, West Coast Silicon entered into the following transactions:

(a) Sold 100 shares of Leaky Oil and Gas for $2,800 net of commissions.

(b) Purchased 100 shares of EG&P for $40 per share, including commissions.

(c) Current market values at the end of the year are:

Stock	Total Market Value
Allied, Inc.	$ 4,400
Gora Company	2,200
Leaky Oil and Gas	2,000
EG&P	4,100
	$12,700

REQUIRED:
1. Prepare all the necessary journal entries for the year.
2. How would the marketable securities be shown on the balance sheet?
3. Assume that all securities were held throughout the next year and that at the end of the year their market values totaled $14,000. Make the required entry at year-end.

SOLUTION
1.

1. Cash	2,800	
Loss on Sale of Marketable Securities	200	
Investment in Marketable Securities		3,000
To record loss on sale of securities.		
2. Investment in Marketable Securities	4,000	
Cash		4,000
To record purchase of 100 shares of EG&P at $40 per share.		

3. Unrealized Loss on Marketable Securities   600

      Allowance to Reduce Marketable Securities to Market   600

    To record unrealized loss.

Current Market Value	$12,700	
Cost ($4,000 + $2,500 + $3,000 + $4,000)	13,500	
Required balance in Allowance account	800	
Current balance in Allowance account		
($12,500 − $12,300)	200	
Amount of adjusting entry	$ 600	

2.   Investment in marketable securities $13,500

      Less: Allowance to reduce marketable securities to market   (800)

      $12,700

3.   Allowance to Reduce Marketable Securities to Market   800

      Reduction in Unrealized Loss on Marketable Securities   800

    To reduce allowance account to zero as market exceeds cost.

B. Several years ago, the Anger Company purchased a 25% interest in the Zebra Corp. The purchase price was $50,000, which represented a 25% interest in the book value of Zebra's net assets at that time. At the beginning of the current year, the book value of Zebra's net assets was $350,000. During the current year, Zebra reported the following:

Net Income	$75,000
Dividends Paid	40,000

REQUIRED: **1.**   Make the appropriate entries on Anger's books to reflect these events during the current year.

            2.   What is the balance in the Investment in Zebra account at end of the year?

SOLUTION   Investment in Zebra   18,750

     1.   Investment Revenue   18,750

      To record investment revenue.

      Cash   10,000

        Investment in Zebra   10,000

      To record receipt of dividend.

2.   Balance in Investment account

Net book value at beginning of year	$350,000	
Anger's interest	.25	
Current year's transaction	$ 87,500	
Income	18,750	
Dividend received	(10,000)	
Net book value at end of year.	$ 96,250	

QUESTIONS

1. What is a publicly held corporation? How does one acquire stock in such a corporation?

2. Investment in securities can be classified as either a current asset or a long-term investment. What criteria are used in making this distinction?

3. Marketable securities include debt securities and equity securities. What is the distinction between these types of securities? Why would an investor hold a portfolio that includes both debt and equity securities?

4. In order to invest idle cash, the Orleans Corporation purchased 100 shares of General Motors stock at $65 per share, plus brokerage commissions of $100 and state taxes of $50. At what amount should this investment be recorded on the balance sheet? Where should it be classified on the balance sheet?

5. At the beginning of the current year, the Juarez Co. purchased 1,000 shares of California Federal Savings stock at $20 per share, including brokerage commissions. During the year, the firm received dividends of $1.50 per share. At the time Juarez was preparing its year-end balance sheet, California Federal Savings stock was selling at $18 per share. Assuming that this is the only stock Juarez owns, how much income or loss should the firm record regarding this stock?

6. Lower-of-cost-or-market is applied to various situations in accounting. Compare and contrast the application of lower-of-cost-or-market to marketable securities with its application to inventories.

7. Malibu Publishing Co. owns several stocks classified as current marketable securities. At the end of 1990, the firm had a credit balance of $2,500 in the account Allowance to Reduce Marketable Securities to Market. By the end of 1991, the market value of the firm's stock investments had risen and now exceeds its cost by $1,000. Make the appropriate entry at the end of 1991 to record this fact.

8. Some accountants argue that marketable securities should be valued at market, regardless of whether market is above or below cost. What is the basis for their argument? Do you agree or disagree? Why?

9. To what types of investments does FASB Statement 12 apply?

10. Briefly describe the difference in accounting for current equity securities and for current debt securities.

11. Describe the accounting treatment for long-term equity investments of less than 20%. How is the lower-of-cost-or-market rule applied to these investments?

12. When the market value of a portfolio of either current marketable securities or long-term investments is less than its cost, an account titled Allowance to Reduce Marketable Securities to Market is credited. How does this account differ if the portfolio consists of long-term investments rather than current investments?

13. Briefly describe the equity method of accounting, why it is used, and when it is used.

14. Explain to a fellow accounting student why dividends received are not considered revenue when the equity method of accounting for long-term investments is applied.

15. At the beginning of 1989, the Metro Co. owned 30% of the Freeway Corporation. At that time, the balance in the investment in the Freeway account was $200,000. During the year, Freeway issued cash dividends totaling $100,000 and earned net income of $400,000. What should be the balance in the investment in the Freeway account after these events are considered?

16. Under what circumstances should consolidated statements be prepared? How do these consolidated statements differ from just combining the financial statements of two companies?

17. List and describe at least three different elimination entries. Why must these entries be made?

18. At the beginning of the current year, Symphony, Inc. purchased a 100% interest in Software Centers, Inc. for $400,000. At the time of the purchase, Software's stockholders' equity accounts were as follows: common stock, no par $350,000; retained earnings $150,000. Make the entry on a consolidated worksheet to eliminate Symphony's investment in Software Centers, Inc.

19. Often when one company purchases another, the purchase is made at a price above the net book value of the assets acquired. Describe the accounting procedures to handle this when the purchase method of accounting is used.

20. Compare and contrast the purchase method of accounting for acquisitions with the pooling-of-interests method. If you were the manager of a company that was about to acquire another company, what factors would you consider in deciding which method to use?

EXERCISES

E1. Accounting for Current Marketable Equity Securities. On February 2, 1990, the Chaise Lounge Co. purchased 100 shares of Pops Brewery at $45 per share, plus brokerage commissions of $1 per share. During 1990 and 1991, the following events occurred regarding this investment:

- December 15, 1990: Pops Brewery declares and pays a $1.50 per-share dividend.
- December 31, 1990: The market price of Pops Brewery's stock is $40 per share at year-end.

- December 1, 1991: Pops Brewery declares and pays a dividend of $1 per share.
- December 31, 1991: The market price of Pops Brewery's stock is $42 per share at year-end.

REQUIRED: Assuming that this is the only investment that Chaise Lounge made during 1990 and 1991, record the entries to reflect these events. How would the investment in marketable securities be disclosed on the December 31, 1991 balance sheet?

E2. Accounting for Current Marketable Equity Securities. The following items were taken from the December 31, 1990 balance sheet of the Simmonds Company:

SIMMONDS COMPANY
Partial Balance Sheet
December 31, 1990

Current assets	
Cash	$ 50,000
Accounts receivable, less allowance for uncollectible accounts of $6,000	120,000
Investment in Akro Corporation, less allowance to reduce marketable	
equity securities to market of $1,000	15,000

The investment in Akro Corporation consisted of 1,000 shares of Akro common stock purchased on November 29, 1990.

REQUIRED:
(a) What was the purchase price per share of the Akro Corporation common stock?

(b) What was the market price per share of the Akro Corporation common stock on December 31, 1990?

(c) On April 1, 1991, the Simmonds Company sold 500 shares of Akro at $18 per share. Make the necessary journal entry to record this sale.

(d) Simmonds held the remaining 500 shares of Akro throughout the remaining year. At December 31, 1991, Akro was selling at $15.75 per share. Make the necessary entry, if any, to value the securities at lower of cost or market at December 31, 1991.

E3. Application of the Lower-of-Cost-or-Market Rule. During 1990, the Ambrosia Corp. made several purchases of current marketable equity securities. No securities were owned prior to 1990. None of these purchases represented an interest of 20% or more. The cost and market value of these securities are as follows:

		Market Value— December 31,		
Securities	Total Cost	1990	1991	1992
BPOE Inc.	$ 1,500	$ 1,200	$ 1,100	$ 1,600
Laird, Inc.	5,600	5,700	5,600	5,500
Showboat Co.	4,900	4,400	4,300	4,600
Total	$12,000	$11,300	$11,000	$11,700

REQUIRED:
(a) Make the adjusting entries at December 31 of each year to reflect these changes in market values.

(b) How should the account Investment in Marketable Equity Securities be disclosed on the December 31, 1992 balance sheet?

E4. Accounting for Debt Securities. On September 1, 1990, the Thesaurus Co. purchased ten $1,000, 12% bonds of Webster Corporation. The bonds were purchased at 97 plus $100 of brokerage commissions and accrued interest. The bonds pay interest every January 2 and July 1. Because the Thesaurus Co. intends to hold these bonds as a short-term investment, it does not plan to amortize any discount or premium. On February 1, 1991, the firm sold all the bonds at 102 less $125 brokerage commissions plus accrued interest.

REQUIRED: **(a)** Make the required journal entries on September 1, 1990, December 31, 1990 (the firm's year-end), January 2, 1991, and February 1, 1991 to record these bond transactions.

(b) If the price of the bonds had declined below their cost at December 31, 1990, would the Thesaurus Co. have to make an entry to reflect this fact?

E5. **Accounting for Current and Long-term Equity Investments.** At the end of 1989, the CIJI Corporation owned two equity investments that it classified as current marketable securities. The relevant cost and market data at December 31, 1989 is as follows:

Security	Cost	Market
Lockness, Inc.	$6,700	$6,200
Scottish Co.	5,400	5,500

During 1990, CIJI Corporation sold all of its holdings in Lockness, for $6,500 after commissions. In addition, the firm purchased 500 shares of English Inc. on November 1, 1990 at a price of $27 per share including commissions. CIJI considers this to be a long-term investment.

At December 31, 1990, Scottish Co. had a market value of $6,000, and English Inc. had a market value of $13,200.

REQUIRED: **(a)** Prepare the journal entries to record the transactions that took place during 1990.

(b) How much income or loss would CIJI report during 1990 regarding these stock transactions? How would this income or loss be classified?

(c) Determine the December 31, 1990 balances in the balance sheet accounts regarding these stock investments.

E6. **Cost and Equity Method of Accounting for Long-term Investments.** At the beginning of 1990, the El Paso Corp. purchased two long-term investments. The first purchase was a 30% interest (30,000 shares) in the common stock of Houston Inc. for $1.5 million. The second purchase was a 15% interest (15,000 shares) in the common stock of Lubbock Inc. for $495,000. The following data is available regarding these companies:

Company	Reported Income	Dividends Declared and Paid	Market Price per Share, 12/31/90
Houston	$ 500,000	$100,000	$45
Lubbock	$1,000,000	$300,000	$35

REQUIRED: **(a)** Which of these investments should be accounted for on the cost or equity method? Why?

(b) As a result of these two investments, what should be the income reported by El Paso for the year ended December 31, 1990?

(c) As a result of these two investments, what should be the balance in the Investments account for El Paso at December 31, 1990?

E7. **Equity Method of Accounting.** At the beginning of the current year, the Bond Company purchased for $300,000 as a long-term investment common stock representing a 30% interest in the Spy Corporation. This represented a 30% interest in the book value of Spy Corporation's net assets. During the year, Spy declared and issued dividends totaling $80,000. Spy reported net income of $200,000 during the current year.

REQUIRED: **(a)** Make the required journal entries on the Bond Company's books to record these events.

(b) What is the balance in the Investment in Spy Corporation account at the end of the current year?

E8.   Accounting for Long-term Investments. For several years, Southworth Corporation has held a 40% interest in the Corona Co. At the time of purchase, Corona's net assets were $1 million and Southworth paid $400,000 for its interest. At the end of 1989, Southworth reported a balance of $1.6 million in its Investment in Corona account.

During 1990, Corona reported a loss of $100,000. Because management considered this loss to be temporary, Corona declared dividends of $20,000.

REQUIRED: **(a)** Does Southworth use the cost or the equity method of accounting for its investment in Corona? Explain your answer.

(b) Make the appropriate journal entries to record the events that occurred during 1990.

(c) As a result of these transactions, what is the December 31, 1990 balance in the Investment in Corona account?

E9.   Elimination Entries—Date of Acquisition. During the year, First Air purchased 100% of the common stock of Royal Hotels for $600,000 in cash. At the time of the purchase, the book value of Royal Hotels' net assets was $600,000, consisting of common stock of $200,000 and retained earnings of $400,000. Also at the time of acquisition, First Air had an accounts receivable on its books in the amount of $10,000 from Royal Hotels. Royal Hotels had a corresponding accounts payable.

Prepare the elimination entries that would be made on the worksheet required for the preparation of a consolidated balance sheet.

E10.   Elimination Entries. During June 1990, Oniix Inc. purchased 100% of the common stock of Praim for $650,000 cash and a note of $112,000. At the time of the purchase, Praim's stockholders' equity accounts were common stock of $450,000 and retained earnings of $190,000. Included in Oniix's accounts payable at the time of acquisition was a $5,000 liability to Praim. A corresponding receivable was on Praim's books. Any excess of cost and book value should be assigned to goodwill.

REQUIRED: **(a)** Prepare the journal entry to record Oniix's purchase of Praim.

(b) Prepare the elimination entry that would appear on a worksheet necessary to prepare a consolidated balance sheet at the date of acquisition.

E11.   Accounting for Consolidations and Goodwill. On April 1, 1990, the Pual Co. purchased 100% of the common stock of Santos Inc. for $175,000 cash. Immediately after the purchase, the balance sheet of each company appeared as follows:

Assets	Pual Co.	Santos Inc.
Cash and receivables	$ 50,000	$ 20,000
Inventory	80,000	35,000
Investment in Santos	175,000	—
Property, plant, and equipment, net	240,000	200,000
Total assets	$545,000	$255,000

Equities		
Accounts payable	$ 60,000	$ 15,000
Long-term debt	80,000	85,000
Common stock, no par	200,000	60,000
Retained earnings	205,000	95,000
Total equities	$545,000	$255,000

After evaluating the assets of Santos, Pual decided that the fair market value of the inventory was $40,000 and that the fair market value of the property, plant, and equipment was $210,000. The remaining cost of the acquisition over the assets acquired should be considered goodwill.

REQUIRED: **(a)** Prepare the entry to record the acquisition of Santos by Pual.

(b) Prepare the elimination entry that would be made on the worksheet required to prepare a consolidated balance sheet at the date of acquisition.

(c) After consolidation, what will be the amount of the total assets of the consolidated entity?

(d) After consolidation, what will be the amount of the total stockholders' equity of the consolidated entity?

E12. Consolidation Worksheet. On November 1, 1990, the Rosenberg Rose Co. purchased 100% of the stock of the Seedy Seed Co. for $180,000 cash. Immediately after the purchase, the condensed balance sheets of the two companies were as follows:

	Rosenberg Rose	Seedy Seed
Receivable from Seedy	$ 10,000	$ 0
Other assets	800,000	250,000
Investment in Seedy	180,000	0
Total assets	$990,000	$250,000
Payable to Rosenberg	$ 0	$ 10,000
Other liabilities	300,000	100,000
Capital stock, no par	400,000	100,000
Retained earnings	290,000	40,000
Total equities	$990,000	$250,000

After a detailed analysis, Rosenberg has decided that the fair market value of Seedy's assets approximates their book value, and so any excess of the cost of the investment over the book value of the acquired net assets should be considered goodwill.

REQUIRED: Prepare a worksheet consolidating the two companies as of the date of acquisition.

E13. Purchase versus Pooling. On March 1, 1991, Northstar Tech purchased 100% of Tahoe Limited by exchanging 10,000 shares of its $5 par value common stock for all of Tahoe's common stock. Tahoe's common stock is no par and has a balance of $100,000. At the acquisition date, Northstar's common stock was selling at $21 per share. At the time of the purchase, the book value and fair market value of Tahoe's net assets appeared as follows:

	Book Value	Fair Market Value
Monetary assets	$ 50,000	$ 50,000
Inventory	75,000	85,000
Property, plant, and equipment, net	150,000	175,000
Total assets	$275,000	$310,000
Total liabilities	$100,000	$100,000

Tahoe's net income during the year amounted to $150,000, earned as follows:

January 2, 1991 to February 28, 1991	$ 40,000
March 1, 1991 to December 31, 1991	110,000

REQUIRED: (a) Assuming that the purchase method of accounting is used, make the required entries and answer the following questions:

1. Make the entry to record the acquisition.

2. Make the elimination entry that would be made on the date of acquisition.

3. At what dollar amount would Tahoe's net assets be consolidated with Northstar's assets?

4. How much income would Northstar report on its consolidated income statement from Tahoe's operations?

(b) Make the required entries and answer the preceding questions, assuming that the pooling-of-interests method of accounting is used.

E14. Toys "R" Us Financial Statements. Based on the Toys "R" Us financial statements (Appendix D), answer the following questions:

(a) How does Toys "R" Us disclose its short-term investments?

(b) Does Toys "R" Us consolidate all its subsidiaries? How did you arrive at your conclusion?

PROBLEMS

P15—1   Accounting for Current Marketable Securities. At the beginning of 1990, the Rose Corporation held the following current marketable equity securities:

Security	Number of Shares	Total Cost	Total Market
MG, Inc.	1,000	$35,000	$30,000
Drof Co.	500	10,000	12,000

During 1990, the following transactions took place:

- March 1: Purchased 200 shares of Joellen Inc. at $45 per share including commissions.
- March 31: Received dividends of $1.50 per share on MG, Inc. stock.
- May 2: Sold all of the shares in Drof Co. for $22 per share.
- September 1: Sold 500 shares of MG, Inc. for $29 per share.
- September 30: Received cash dividends of $1.50 per share on MG, Inc. stock.
- December 1: Purchased ten $1,000, 12% bonds of United Inc. at 98 plus accrued interest for five full months. The company does not intend to amortize any discounts or premiums.
- December 31: Received the semiannual interest payment on the United Inc. bonds.
- December 31: You have obtained the following market values as of December 31, 1990:

Joellen Inc.	$46 per share
MG, Inc.	34 per share
United Inc. bonds	97 per unit

The company applies the lower-of-cost-or-market rule to debt as well as equity securities.

REQUIRED: **(a)** Prepare the journal entries to record the above transactions regarding the marketable securities.

(b) Show how the marketable securities would be disclosed on the December 31, 1990 balance sheet.

P15—2   Accounting for Current Marketable Securities. At the beginning of 1990, the Modem Corporation held the following current marketable equity securities:

Security	Number of Shares	Total Cost	Total Market
Tele Inc.	2,000	$80,000	$74,000
Byte Co.	800	16,000	29,000

During 1990, the following transactions took place:

- February 1: Purchased 300 shares of Alexis Inc. at $60 per share including commissions.
- March 31: Received dividends of $1 per share of Tele Inc. stock.
- April 14: Sold 400 of the shares in Byte Co. for $22 per share.
- August 14: Sold 1,000 shares of Tele Inc. for $39 per share.
- September 30: Received cash dividends of $1 per share on Tele Inc. stock.
- November 1: Purchased 20 $1,000, 10% bonds of Americo, Inc. at 102 plus accrued interest for four full months. The company does not intend to amortize any discounts or premiums.
- December 31: The company receives the semiannual interest payment on the Americo, Inc. bonds.
- December 31: You have obtained the following market values as of December 31, 1990:

Alexis Inc.	$ 61 per share
Tele Inc.	38 per share
Byte Co.	23 per share
Americo bonds	100 per unit

The company applies the lower-of-cost-or-market rule to debt as well as equity securities.

REQUIRED: **(a)** Prepare the journal entries to record the above transactions related to the marketable securities.

(b) Show how the marketable securities would be disclosed on the December 31, 1990 balance sheet.

(c) Describe how the income statement accounts relative to these transactions would be shown on the income statement.

P15–3 Valuation of Marketable Equity Securities. Included in the information contained in the footnotes to the financial statements of Grenada Corporation at December 31, 1991 is the following information related to current marketable equity securities:

	1991	1990
Marketable securities, at cost	$160,000	$75,000
Gross unrealized gains	14,300	5,100
Gross unrealized losses	(17,200)	(2,300)
Marketable securities, at market	$157,100	$77,800

During 1991, the firm sold securities with a cost of $30,000 for $38,500.

REQUIRED: Based on this information, answer the following questions:

(a) At what amount should the marketable equity securities be shown on the balance sheet for 1991 and 1990?

(b) What should be the balance (if any) for 1991 and 1990 in the account titled Allowance to Reduce Marketable Equity Securities to Market, and where is this account disclosed?

(c) What are the amounts of the unrealized gains and/or losses, if any, for 1991 and 1990 that should be disclosed, and where should these amounts be disclosed?

(d) What is the amount of realized gain or loss for 1991 that should be disclosed, and where should this amount be disclosed?

(e) What is the cost of the securities purchased by the Grenada Corporation during 1991?

P15–4 Investment in Long-term Securities. During 1990 and 1991, the Crafty Tool Corporation entered into the transactions shown at the top of page 580 related to long-term investments. All investments represent less than a 20% interest in the related companies. Prior to 1990, Crafty Tool had no long-term investments.

1990:

- January 29: Purchased 200 shares of Fast Industries for $60 per share.
- March 24: Purchased 300 shares of Celeste at $45 per share.
- September 30: Received a $2 per-share cash dividend on Fast Industries' stock.
- October 13: Purchased 2,000 shares of Cool Pen for $20 per share.
- December 30: Received a 20% stock dividend on Celeste stock.
- December 31: The market value per share of stocks was:

Fast Industries	$63
Celeste	35
Cool Pen	19

1991:

- February 12: Purchased an additional 100 shares of Fast Industries at $65 per share.
- May 29: Sold 200 shares in Celeste for $34 per share.
- September 30: Received a $2 per-share dividend on Fast Industries stock.
- December 31: The market value of the stocks held at December 31, 1991 was as follows:

Fast Industries	$66.00 per share
Celeste	32.00 per share
Cool Pen	19.25 per share

REQUIRED: **(a)** Make the appropriate journal entries for 1990 and 1991.

(b) Prepare the long-term investment section of the balance sheet at December 31, 1990 and 1991.

P15–5 Investment in Long-term Securities. During 1990 and 1991, the Hubbard Scientific Corporation entered into the following transactions regarding long-term investments. All investments represent less than a 20% interest in the related companies. Prior to 1990, Hubbard Scientific had no long-term investments.

1990

- January 15: Purchased 500 shares of Saco Industries for $25 per share.
- April 14: Purchased 100 shares of Listo Lecon for $80 per share.
- September 30: Received a $1 per-share cash dividend on Saco Industries stock.
- November 29: Purchased 1,000 shares of Inca Ink for $30 per share.
- December 15: Received a 10% stock dividend on Listo Lecon stock.
- December 31: The market value per share of stocks was:

Saco Industries	$22
Listo Lecon	84
Inca Ink	28

1991

- February 1: Purchased an additional 500 shares of Saco Industries at $26 per share.
- April 28: Sold all the shares in Listo Lecon for $81 per share.
- October 1: Received $1 per-share dividend on Saco Industries stock.
- December 31: The market value of the stocks held at December 31, 1991 was as follows:

Saco Industries	$22 per share
Inca Ink	32 per share

REQUIRED: **(a)** Make the appropriate journal entries for 1990 and 1991.

(b) Prepare the long-term investment section of the balance sheet at December 31, 1990 and 1991.

P15-6 Equity Method of Accounting. At the beginning of 1990, Eastbound Inc. purchased a 40% interest (representing 40,000 shares) in Earth Co. for $1,008,000 cash. Earth had a good year during 1990 and reported net income of $250,000. In addition, on June 30, 1990, the firm declared and issued a 5% stock dividend. On December 30, 1990, the firm also declared and paid a $1 per-share dividend. At year-end, the price per share of Earth's stock was $22 per share.

During 1991, business increased significantly, and Earth reported a net income of $400,000 for the year. The firm declared and paid dividends of $1.50 per share. Because of the firm's strong performance, the price per share of its stock at year-end increased to $30.

REQUIRED: **(a)** Make the journal entries to record these transactions during 1990 and 1991.

(b) How much income would Eastbound report from this investment during 1990 and 1991?

(c) Prepare the long-term investment section of Eastbound's balance sheet at December 31, 1990 and 1991.

(d) If this investment was accounted for under the cost method of accounting for long-term investment, how much income would Eastbound report from this investment during 1990 and 1991?

P15-7 Cost versus Equity Method of Accounting. During 1990, the Strawberry Company made the following two investments:

■ January 2: Strawberry purchased for cash and notes 30% of the 1 million shares of common stock of the Adam Computer Co. The purchase was made for $2 million cash and notes of $1 million. Adam Computer Co.'s net income for the year ended December 31, 1990 was $500,000. In addition, Adam Computer paid total dividends of $1.50 per share. At December 31, 1990, the market price of Adam Computer's stock was $31.50 per share.

■ April 1: Strawberry purchased 50,000 shares of Chow Inc. for $600,000 cash. This purchase represented a 10% interest in Chow. Chow's net loss during 1990 was $100,000, and Chow paid dividends of $.10 the last day of each quarter during 1990. At December 31, 1990, the market price of Chow's stock was $5 per share. However, Strawberry considers this to be a temporary price decline.

These are the only two long-term investments made by the Strawberry Company.

REQUIRED: **(a)** Make the journal entries to record these investments.

(b) At the end of 1990, what is the balance in the investment account of the Strawberry Company?

(c) What should be the income reported by the Strawberry Company related to these two investments during 1990?

P15-8 Consolidation Worksheet and Balance Sheet. On June 1, 1990, the Upbeat Corporation purchased a 100% interest in the Deadbeat Co. for $250,000 cash. At the date of acquisition, the condensed balance sheets of each company are as follows:

Assets	Upbeat Corporation	Deadbeat Company
Cash	$ 60,000	$ 15,000
Accounts receivable	107,000	24,000
Inventory	300,000	126,000
Investment in Deadbeat	250,000	0
Property, plant, and equipment, net	525,000	180,000
Total assets	$1,242,000	$345,000

Equities		
Current liabilities	$ 220,000	$ 95,000
Long-term debt	150,000	0
Common stock, no par	600,000	100,000
Retained earnings	272,000	150,000
Total equities	$1,242,000	$345,000

Included in the accounts receivable and current liabilities is intercompany debt amounting to $8,000.

REQUIRED: **(a)** Prepare a worksheet to consolidate Upbeat and Deadbeat.

(b) Prepare a consolidated balance sheet at the date of acquisition.

P15–9 **Consolidated Worksheet and Balance Sheet.** On April 1, 1990, the Canfield Corporation purchased a 100% interest in the Skinner Company for $187,500 cash. At the date of acquisition, the condensed balance sheets of each company were as follows:

Assets	Canfield Corporation	Skinner Company
Cash	$ 12,500	$ 12,000
Accounts receivable	72,000	18,000
Inventory	165,000	112,500
Investment in Skinner	187,500	0
Property, plant, and equipment, net	400,000	130,000
Total assets	$837,000	$272,500
Equities		
Current liabilities	$140,000	$ 85,000
Long-term debt	100,000	0
Common stock, no par	400,000	100,000
Retained earnings	197,000	87,500
Total equities	$837,000	$272,500

Included in the accounts receivable and current liabilities is intercompany debt amounting to $5,000.

REQUIRED: **(a)** Prepare a worksheet to consolidate Canfield and Skinner.

(b) Prepare a consolidated balance sheet at the date of acquisition.

P15–10 **Consolidated Worksheet and Balance Sheet.** On September 1, 1990, the Button Corporation purchased a 100% interest in the Zipper Co. for $400,000 cash. The condensed balance sheets of each company at the date of acquisition are as follows:

Assets	Button Corporation	Zipper Company
Cash	$ 62,000	$ 75,000
Accounts receivable	85,000	45,000
Inventory	178,000	85,000
Investment in Zipper	400,000	0
Property, plant, and equipment, net	360,000	200,000
Total assets	$1,085,000	$405,000
Equities		
Current liabilities	$ 105,000	$ 50,000
Long-term debt	180,000	55,000
Common stock, $2 par value	400,000	100,000
Paid-in capital	80,000	25,000
Retained earnings	320,000	175,000
Total equities	$1,085,000	$405,000

Button decided to allocate the 70% excess of the purchase price over the book value of the net assets acquired to increase the inventory of Zipper to its fair market value. The remaining amount of the excess is considered goodwill. Included in the accounts receivable and current liabilities is $4,000 of intercompany debt.

REQUIRED: **(a)** Prepare a worksheet to consolidate the two companies at the date of acquisition.

(b) Prepare a consolidated balance sheet at the date of acquisition.

P15–11 Purchase versus Pooling of Interests. The Minneapolis Company intends to merge with the St. Paul Corporation by exchanging 10,000 shares of its common stock for 100% of the shares of the St. Paul Corporation. At the time of the merger, the Minneapolis Company's common stock was selling for $18 per share. Presented below are the condensed balance sheets of the two firms immediately prior to the acquisition.

Assets	Minneapolis Company	St. Paul Corporation
Current assets	$100,000	$ 45,000
Property, plant, and equipment, net	250,000	150,000
Total assets	$350,000	$195,000

Equities		
Current liabilities	$ 40,000	$ 30,000
Long-term debt	140,000	45,000
Common stock, $1 par value	75,000	50,000
Paid-in capital	40,000	25,000
Retained earnings	55,000	45,000
Total equities	$350,000	$195,000

REQUIRED: **(a)** Prepare journal entries to record the acquisition of St. Paul by Minneapolis, assuming that (1) the pooling-of-interests method is used and (2) the purchase method is used.

(b) Prepare a worksheet as of the date of acquisition, assuming that (1) the pooling-of-interests method is used and (2) the purchase method is used. (Apply the excess cost over the book value of net assets acquired to goodwill.)

(c) Prepare a consolidated balance sheet at the date of acquisition for the two different methods. Compare and contrast the two balance sheets.

■ USING THE COMPUTER

P15–12 The Horn Corporation acquired 100% of the Gren Company on July 1, 1990 for $700,000 cash. At the date of acquisition, the condensed balance sheets of the two companies were as follows:

Assets	Horn Corporation	Gren Company
Cash	$ 165,000	$175,000
Accounts receivable	185,000	145,000
Inventory	278,000	185,000
Investment in Gren Company	550,000	0
Property, plant, and equipment, net	460,000	400,000
Total assets	$1,638,000	$905,000

Equities		
Current liabilities	$ 205,000	$150,000
Long-term debt	280,000	155,000
Common stock, $2 par value	500,000	300,000
Paid-in capital	180,000	125,000
Retained earnings	473,000	175,000
Total equities	$1,638,000	$905,000

The excess purchase price over the book value of the net assets acquired is allocated as 60% to the property, plant, and equipment on Gren's books and the remainder to goodwill.

REQUIRED: Using an electronic spreadsheet, prepare a worksheet to consolidate the two entities at the date of acquisition.

■ UNDERSTANDING FINANCIAL STATEMENTS

P15–13   The following footnote appeared in the financial statements of the Pennzoil Company:

	1987	1986
Current assets (in thousands)		
Cash	$ 22,186	$ 21,371
Temporary cash investments	164,103	126,287
Marketable equity securities	159,127	242,482

Notes to Consolidated Financial Statements

1 (in part): Summary of Significant Accounting Policies—Marketable Equity Securities

At December 31, 1987, the current and noncurrent portfolios of marketable equity securities are each carried at the lower of aggregate cost or market value (as detailed below). Current marketable equity securities are comprised of a managed portfolio of common and preferred stocks.

	December 31, 1987		
	Cost	Market	Gross and Net Unrealized (Loss)
Current	$183,863,000	$159,127,000	$(24,736,000)
Noncurrent	$ 29,644,000	$ 22,921,000	$ (6,723,000)

At December 31, 1986, the current and noncurrent marketable equity securities portfolios totaled $242,482,000 and $31,441,000, respectively, and were carried at cost which approximated market. At December 31, 1985, a valuation allowance for unrealized losses on noncurrent marketable equity securities of $4,679,000 was charged to shareholders' equity.

The following sales of marketable equity securities occurred during the periods indicated below. The cost of the securities sold was based on the average cost of all the shares of each security held at the time of sale. There was no resulting material effect from the sale of marketable equity securities in 1986.

	Net Realized Gain (Loss)
1987	$(21,813,000)
1985	$ 13,546,000

REQUIRED: **(a)** For the years ended 1987 and 1986, are the marketable equity securities carried at cost or market?

(b) During 1987, the company had a net realized loss on the sale of the marketable equity securities. On what financial statement is the loss shown?

(c) During 1987, the company had gross and net unrealized losses on marketable current equity securities of $24,736,000. On what financial statement is this loss shown?

(d) Assume that the company did not purchase any additional marketable current equity securities during 1987, and that all securities sold during 1987 were current. For how much were the securities sold?

■ FINANCIAL DECISION CASE

P15–14   The Space Parts Company has been in business for several years. However, in the last couple of years growth in the industry has slowed down and the company is facing its first net loss. In order to increase its future prospects, the company is considering purchasing 100% of a competing company called High Tech Parts.

The president of Space Parts asks your advice concerning the contemplated purchase of High Tech Parts. He tells you that it is now December 1, and it appears that Space Parts will have a loss of $300,000 for the year ended December 31, 1990. On the other hand, High Tech has had a successful year, with estimated profits through November of $500,000. Profits for December are estimated to be another $75,000. Further, the president of Space Parts feels that the net assets of High Tech are substantially undervalued. The purchase price will be substantially above the net book value of High Tech's net assets and probably above the fair value of the net assets.

The president of Space Parts had heard about purchase and pooling-of-interests accounting, but he is confused about the difference between them. He asks your advice on the following points:

(a) In structuring the contemplated purchase of High Tech, do I have a choice between using purchase accounting and pooling-of-interests accounting?

(b) I am considering either purchasing High Tech entirely with cash or exchanging common stock of Space Parts for all the common stock of High Tech. What effect does this have, if any, on whether I can use the purchase or the pooling method of accounting? Compare for other possible effects of using the two different methods on Space Parts' financial statements.

(c) Prepare a schedule for me that compares the effect on Space Parts' current period's income of using the pooling-of-interests method versus the purchase method.

REQUIRED: Answer the president's questions.

16

THE STATEMENT
OF CASH FLOWS

LEARNING OBJECTIVES

After studying this chapter, you should be able to:

1. Describe a statement of cash flows and give its purpose.
2. Differentiate among investing, financing, and operating activities.
3. Determine cash flows from operating activities using both the direct and the indirect methods.
4. Prepare a statement of cash flows using a worksheet.

■ THE PURPOSES OF THE STATEMENT OF CASH FLOWS

The **statement of cash flows** is a required financial statement, along with the balance sheet, income statement, and retained earnings statement or statement of changes in stockholders' equity. Until recently, firms could prepare a related statement—the statement of changes in financial position, which was often used to describe changes in working capital rather than cash. Since many users of financial statements questioned the relevance of changes in working capital in assessing liquidity, the FASB decided that future statements should focus on flows of cash rather than flows of working capital. Thus the statement of cash flows is now the required statement.

The two primary purposes of the cash flow statement are to provide information about the firm's cash receipts and cash payments and information about the investing and financing activities of the firm. This statement is useful to present and potential investors and creditors because it helps them assess:

1. The firm's ability to generate future cash flows.
2. The firm's ability to meet its obligations and pay dividends and its needs for outside financing.
3. The reasons for the differences between income and cash receipts and payments.
4. Both the cash and noncash aspects of the firm's investing and financing activities.

Exhibit 16-1 shows a simplified cash flow statement. (An actual statement would show more detail under the category operating activities.) ETR Sound Systems was able to obtain cash from its operations, from various financing activities such as the issuance of common stock and bonds, and from investing activities such as the sale of equipment. On the other hand, ETR used cash to settle its long-term debt, pay dividends, and purchase a building. Looking at this statement as a whole, it appears that ETR is financing its expansion through the issuance of long-term debt and common stock. As these outside resources become less available in the future, ETR must begin to generate additional cash from operations.

EXHIBIT 16–1

ETR SOUND SYSTEMS		
Statement of Cash Flows		
For the Year Ended December 31, 1991		
Cash flows from operating activities		$ 16,500
Cash flows from investing activities		
Proceeds from sale of equipment	$ 20,000	
Purchase of building	(100,000)	
Net cash used by investing activities		(80,000)
Cash flows from financing activities		
Proceeds from issuing common stock	$ 50,000	
Proceeds from issuing bonds	80,000	
Payments to settle long-term debt	(40,000)	
Dividends paid	(6,000)	
Net cash provided by financing activities		84,000
Net increase in cash		$ 20,500

WHAT IS MEANT BY CASH FLOWS

The FASB feels that the cash flow statement should explain changes in both cash and cash equivalents. **Cash equivalents** are short-term, highly liquid investments such as Treasury bills, commercial paper, and money market funds. These investments are readily convertible to known amounts of cash and are so near their maturity that there is little risk of change in values due to fluctuating interest rates. The purchase and sale of these investments are part of a firm's cash management activities and are included in the overall definition of cash. Thus changes in cash flows mean changes in both cash and cash equivalents.

CAUSES OF CHANGES IN CASH FLOWS

The three major activities of a firm that cause changes in its cash flows are investing, financing, and operations. When a statement of cash flows is prepared, the FASB feels that these activities should be clearly distinguished from one another.

Investing Activities
Investing activities include cash inflows and outflows from (1) lending money and collecting on those loans, and (2) acquiring and selling securities and productive assets such as property, plant, and equipment. Cash inflows from investing activities

thus include collections on loans made to others, receipts from the sale of invest-ments in the debt or equity securities of other firms that are not cash equivalents, and the receipts from the sale of property, plant, and equipment. Cash outflows from in-vesting activities include loans made to others, investments in the debt or equity se-curities of other firms, and cash payments to acquire property, plant, and equipment.

Financing Activities

Major **financing activities** include obtaining resources from owners and providing them a return on their investment and obtaining resources from creditors and repay-ing those borrowings. Common examples of cash inflows from financing activities in-clude the issuance of notes, bonds, mortgages, and other short- or long-term borrow-ings, and the issuance of common and preferred stock. Common examples of cash outflows from financing activities include repayment of these borrowings, the pay-ment of cash dividends, and the purchase of treasury stock.

Operating Activities

Operating activities include all transactions not considered either investing or finan-cing. Therefore they consist primarily of delivering or producing goods for sale and providing services. Cash flows from operating activities are really the cash effect of the transactions that enter into the determination of net income. Thus cash inflows from operating activities primarily include cash receipts from the sale of goods or ser-vices. Cash inflows from operating activities also include the cash receipts from re-turns on loans and equity securities, such as interest and dividends received. Cash outflows from operating activities include cash payments to suppliers for the pur-chase of inventory, to employees for salaries, to governments for taxes, and to other suppliers for various expenses. Cash outflows from operating activities also include cash payments to lenders and other creditors for interest.

The FASB had a difficult time determining how to classify interest and dividends paid or received. The Board finally declared that dividends paid to equity investors result from financing activity, and dividends received and interest paid and received result from an operating activity. This distinction is based on the notion that dividends are a distribution of income, whereas interest is a determinant of net income. Exhibit 16-2 summarizes these various cash inflows and outflows by type of activity.

EXHIBIT 16–2

Classification of Activities[1]

Operating
  Payments
    To suppliers for inventory
    To employees for services
    To governments for taxes
    To other suppliers for other expenses
    To creditors for interest
  Receipts
    From sale of goods or services
    From dividends received
    From interest received
Investing
  Payments
    To purchase property, plant, and equipment—includes capitalized interest
    To acquire a business
    To purchase debt or equity securities (other than cash equivalents) of
      other entities
    To make loans to another entity
    To purchase loans from another entity

(continued)

[1] Adapted from Ernst & Whinney, *Financial Reporting Developments,* "Statement of Cash Flows, Under-standing and Implementing FASB Statement No. 95," January 1988. Reprinted by permission of Ernst & Young.

EXHIBIT 16–2

(continued)

> Receipts
>> From sale of property, plant, and equipment
>> From sale of a business unit
>> From sale of debt or equity securities (other than cash equivalents)
>> From collection of principal on loans to another entity
>> From sale of loans made by the entity
> Financing
>> Payments
>>> To shareholders as dividends
>>> To repay amounts borrowed—includes amounts related to short-term debt, long-term debt, and capitalized lease obligations
>> Receipts
>>> From the sale of equity securities
>>> From the issuance or sale of bonds, mortgages, notes, and other short- or long-term borrowings

■ INVESTING AND FINANCING ACTIVITIES NOT INVOLVING CASH FLOWS

Most investing and financing activities involve cash inflows and outflows. For example, a building is purchased with cash, or common stock is issued for cash. Occasionally, however, a firm enters into a **noncash activity**—an exchange of an asset or equity not involving cash. For instance, a firm may issue common stock in exchange for land or convert bonds into common stock. Because these transactions do not affect cash flows, they could be ignored in the preparation of the statement of cash flows. However, to do so would ignore important financing and investing activities. Therefore the FASB requires that information about these noncash investing and financing activities be summarized in a separate schedule or disclosed in narrative form. These transactions should be clearly identified as not involving cash receipts or payments.

■ PREPARING A STATEMENT OF CASH FLOWS

A statement of cash flows can be prepared by identifying only those transactions that resulted in a cash receipt or payment, plus noncash investing and financing activities. This would be rather tedious, because it would be necessary to review all the transactions the firm entered into during the period. Instead, the information contained in the balance sheet, the income statement, and the statement of changes in stockholders' equity can be utilized to prepare the statement of cash flows. Thus this statement is usually the last one prepared. A worksheet is often used to facilitate its preparation. The three steps involved in preparing the worksheet and ultimately the statement are determining cash flows from (1) operating activities, (2) investing activities, and (3) financing activities.

■ DETERMINING CASH FLOWS FROM OPERATING ACTIVITIES

The first step in preparing a cash flow statement is to determine cash flows from operating activities. There are two alternative methods of presenting operating activities: the direct method and the indirect method. The **direct method** involves reporting the major types of operating receipts and cash payments, such as receipts from the sales of goods and services and payments to suppliers for inventory. Cash flows from operating activities are the difference between the total of the operating receipts and the total of the operating payments. The **indirect method** involves presenting a reconciliation between net income and cash flows from operation. Essentially, the accrual-based income statement is reconciled to a cash-based statement.

The FASB decided to allow both methods of presenting cash flows from operating activities, although the Board prefers the direct method. Regardless of which method is used, interest and income taxes paid must be disclosed. The sections that follow discuss both methods, with the emphasis on the direct method.

■ THE DIRECT METHOD

As previously stated, the direct method involves reporting the major types of operating receipts and payments. The partial cash flow statement presented in Exhibit 16-3 shows the categories of cash receipts and payments that the FASB suggests be disclosed. In this particular example, there is no interest received or paid. If there were, they would be shown under operating activities. Furthermore, no dividends have been received.

EXHIBIT 16-3		

EAST-WEST CORPORATION		
Partial Statement of Cash Flows		
For the Year Ended December 31, 1991		
Cash flows from operating activities		
Cash received from customers		$488,500
Cash paid to suppliers and employees	$450,000	
Taxes paid	6,000	
Cash disbursed for operating activities		456,000
Net cash flows from operating activities		$ 32,500

A literal application of the direct method would require firms to keep their records on a cash rather than an accrual basis. The FASB expects firms to derive the necessary information by analyzing changes in appropriate balance sheet and income statement accounts. The best way to understand the required procedures is to work through the example that follows.

Exhibit 16-4 presents the December 31, 1990 and 1991 balance sheets for the East-West Corporation, and Exhibit 16-5 is the income statement for the year ended December 31, 1991. Since the statements are prepared according to generally accepted accounting principles, they are based on the accrual method. In order to simplify the example, the following assumptions are made:

1. All sales are on account.

2. All inventory purchases are made on account. The Accounts Payable account is used solely for this purpose.

3. All operating expenses except for prepaids used are first recorded in the Accrued Liabilities account.

4. Additions to prepaids are made in cash.

5. Income taxes are recorded in the Income Taxes Payable account.

6. There have been no sales or additions to Property, Plant, and Equipment.

7. No interest has been paid or received. No dividends have been received.

In order to determine cash flows from operating activities, adjustments must be made to sales, cost of goods sold, and the various other operating expenses. This is best accomplished by analyzing the related balance sheet accounts.

EXHIBIT 16–4

EAST-WEST CORPORATION Balance Sheets December 31					
Assets	**1991**	**1990**	**Equities**	**1991**	**1990**
Cash	$ 42,500	$ 10,000	Accounts payable	$ 30,000	$ 35,000
Accounts receivable	36,500	22,000	Accrued liabilities	20,000	17,000
Inventory	60,000	40,000	Taxes payable	2,000	3,000
Prepaids	3,000	5,000	Stockholders' equity	152,000	92,000
Property, plant, and equipment	62,000	70,000			
Total assets	$204,000	$147,000	Total equities	$204,000	$147,000

EXHIBIT 16–5

EAST-WEST CORPORATION Income Statement For the Year Ended December 31, 1991		
Revenues		
Sales		$503,000
Expenses		
Cost of goods sold	$340,000	
Depreciation	8,000	
Prepaids used	10,000	
Other operating expenses	80,000	
Taxes	5,000	
Total expenses		443,000
Net income		$ 60,000

Cash Inflows from Operations

Cash received from customers (or cash-basis sales) is the primary source of cash flows from operations. It represents cash collected from customers on account as well as cash sales during the period. In this example, there were no cash sales; all sales were made on credit. The relationship between accrual-basis and cash-basis sales can be illustrated by examining the following Accounts Receivable T account from the East-West Corporation.

Accounts Receivable

1/1/91 Bal. 22,000 Accrual Sales 503,000	? Cash Collections
12/31/91 Bal. 36,500	

The beginning and ending balances in the Accounts Receivable account are known, from the data in the balance sheet. Accrual-basis sales cause increases in the Accounts Receivable account. Cash collections cause decreases or credits to the Accounts Receivable account. If the firm were on the cash basis, these cash collections would represent the revenues for the period. From these data, it can be determined that cash-basis sales, the missing figure, totaled $488,500 ($22,000 + $503,000 − $36,500).

From an analytical view, it is clear that the beginning balance of the Accounts Receivable account ($22,000) plus the accrual sales of $503,000 represent the maximum cash collections ($525,000) the firm could receive during the year. The fact that the ending balance in the Accounts Receivable account is $36,500 indicates that this is the amount of credit sales that remains uncollected at year-end. Thus cash collections in this case are only $488,500. If the Accounts Receivable balance increases during the year, cash-basis sales will be less than accrual-basis by the amount of the increase. Similar reasoning indicates that if the Accounts Receivable balance decreases during the year, cash-basis sales will exceed accrual-basis sales by that amount. To see this, rework the previous example, only this time assume that the December 31, 1991 Accounts Receivable balance is only $15,000. You will see that in this situation, cash-basis sales are $510,000.

In general, the relationship between accrual-basis and cash-basis income arising from receivables is illustrated as follows:

Accrual-basis revenue	+ Decrease in receivables	=	Cash-basis
(Sales, interest)	− Increase in receivables		revenue

Thus, in the accounts receivable example, cash-basis income (or cash received from customers) is $488,500, determined as follows:

Accrual-basis sales	$503,000
Less: Increase in accounts receivable during the period	14,500
Cash received from customers	$488,500

Cash Outflows from Operations

The two major categories of cash outflows are cash paid to suppliers and employees and cash disbursed for taxes.

Cash Paid to Suppliers and Employees. Cash paid to suppliers and employees includes cash payments to suppliers for inventory purchases, to employees for wages, and to others for all other operating expenses. Taxes are shown as a separate item in determining cash flows from operations, and they are not included with cash paid to suppliers and employees.

Cash Paid to Suppliers. Accrual-based cost of goods sold is represented by inventory decreases during the year. However, for a cash flow statement, cost of goods is simply the cash paid for inventory during the year. If all inventory purchases are made on account through Accounts Payable, what must be determined is the decrease or debit to the Accounts Payable account. This represents the amount paid in cash for inventories during the period. Thus the relationship between accrual- and cash-based cost of goods sold involves both the Inventory and Accounts Payable accounts.

The first step is to analyze the Inventory account. From the balance sheet, the amount of the beginning and ending inventory is known, and the income statement shows the amount of cost of goods sold. Using these data, it can be determined that the amount of inventory purchased during the year was $360,000, as follows:

Cost of goods sold	$340,000
Ending inventory	60,000
Cost of goods available for sale	400,000
Less: Beginning inventory	(40,000)
Inventory purchases	$360,000

Since it was assumed that all inventory purchases are made on credit, the inventory purchases of $360,000 also represent an increase in Accounts Payable. Therefore the cash purchases for inventory are determined to be $365,000, as follows:

Beginning balance in Accounts Payable	$ 35,000
Inventory purchases	360,000
Maximum that could be paid	395,000
Less: Ending balance in Accounts Payable	(30,000)
Cash payments for purchases of inventories	$365,000

In effect, when the Inventory account increases, this indicates that the company purchased more goods during the year than it sold. In this case, the Inventory account increased $20,000, so inventory purchases were $20,000 greater than the cost of goods sold. The decrease of $5,000 in the Accounts Payable account indicates that $5,000 more goods were paid for during the year than were purchased. Thus actual cash payments during the year were $365,000. The $365,000 cash-basis expense is $25,000 more than cost of goods sold on the accrual basis, as a result of the combination of the $20,000 Inventory increase and the $5,000 Accounts Payable decrease. These relationships are illustrated as follows:

Accrual cost of goods sold	+ Increases in inventory − Decreases in inventory	=	Net purchases during the year
Net purchases during the year	+ Decreases in accounts payable − Increases in accounts payable	=	Cash payments for purchases of inventories during the period

Cash Paid for Operating Expenses. Having determined cash paid to suppliers for inventory purchases, it is now necessary to determine cash paid to employees and others for various operating expenses. In the example, two accounts are involved—Prepaids and Accrued Liabilities.

Let's look at the Prepaids account. Using the data in Exhibit 16-4, the Prepaids T account appears as follows:

Prepaids

1/1/91 Bal. 5,000		
Additions to Prepaids account ? in cash	10,000 Prepaids used	
12/31/91 Bal. 3,000		

In this case, it is clear that $10,000 worth of prepaids were used or expired during the year. This is represented by the $10,000 credit to the Prepaids account. Prepaid expenses on the cash basis represent additions to the Prepaids account; in this case, they amount to $8,000 ($3,000 + $10,000 − $5,000). Remember that it has been assumed that all additions to the Prepaids account are made in cash; on the cash basis, all prepaids are expensed as incurred. Therefore prepaid expenses on an accrual basis are $2,000 less than cash-based prepaid expense. In effect, the $2,000 decrease in the balance of the Prepaids account means that $2,000 more of prepaids expired than were purchased during the year, so accrual-based expenses are $2,000 more than cash-based expenses. In general, a decrease in the balance of any prepaid account means that accrual-basis expense will exceed cash-basis expense by that amount, and an increase in the balance of any prepaid account means that cash-basis expense will exceed accrual-basis expense by that amount.

The relationship between accrual-basis and cash-basis expenses arising from the expiration of various prepayments is as follows:

Accrual-basis expenses (Insurance, supplies)	+ Increase in related prepayments − Decrease in related prepayments	=	Cash-basis expenses

Thus, in the example, cash outflows for various prepayments included in operating expenses are $8,000, determined as follows:

Prepaid expense	$10,000
Less: Decrease in the Prepaids account during the period	2,000
Cash outflows for prepaids	$ 8,000

Cash outflows for all other operating expenses, including salaries and wages and payments to suppliers other than those providing inventory, can be determined by analyzing the Accrued Liabilities account. Recall that all other operating expenses in the example were originally recorded in the Accrued Liabilities account. Based on the data in Exhibit 16-4, the Accrued Liabilities T account appears as follows:

Accrued Liabilities

	1/1/91	
Accrued expenses	Bal.	17,000
paid in cash	Accrued	
	expenses	80,000
	12/31/91	
	Bal.	20,000

The Accrued Liabilities account is analyzed in the same way as the Accounts Payable account. In the example, cash outflows for other operating expenses of $77,000 are determined as follows:

Other operating expenses	$80,000
Less: Increase in the Accrued Liabilities account during the period	3,000
Cash outflows for other operating expenses	$77,000

Combining the cash outflows for the three items just discussed gives the total of cash paid to suppliers and employees. This amount is $450,000, determined as follows:

Cash payments for purchases of merchandise	$365,000
Cash payments for prepaids	8,000
Cash payments for other operating expenses	77,000
Total cash paid to suppliers and employees	$450,000

It was not necessary to make any adjustment for depreciation expense. In the example, depreciation was disclosed as a separate item on the income statement and was not included with the operating expenses. If it were included in operating expenses, it would have to be subtracted from the total of the operating expenses to determine cash paid to suppliers and employees. Remember that depreciation expense is a noncash expense in that it does not affect cash flows at the time it is recorded.

Cash Paid for Taxes. The final category that is disclosed in determining cash flows from operations is cash paid for taxes. The amount of cash paid for taxes can be determined by analyzing the Taxes Payable account in the same manner as the Accounts Payable and the Accrued Liabilities accounts. That is, the general relationship is:

Accrual-basis	+ Decrease in taxes payable	=	Cash outflow
tax expense	− Increase in taxes payable		for taxes

In the example, cash paid for taxes is $6,000, determined as follows:

Taxes expense	$5,000
Plus: Decrease in the taxes payable liability during period	1,000
Cash paid for taxes	$6,000

Cash Flows from Operating Activities—A Summary

All the information derived above can now be summarized to determine cash flows from operating activities using the direct method. The cash flows statement for the East-West Corporation (Exhibit 16-6) shows this disclosure. In this example, there were no other changes in the balance sheet accounts, so the $32,500 cash inflow from operating activities actually equals the cash inflow for the period.

EXHIBIT 16–6

EAST-WEST CORPORATION		
Partial Statement of Cash Flows—Direct Method		
For the Year Ended December 31, 1991		
Cash flows from operating activities		
Cash received from customers		$488,500
Cash paid to suppliers and employees	$450,000	
Taxes paid	6,000	
Cash disbursed for operating activities		456,000
Net cash flows from operating activities		$ 32,500

■ THE INDIRECT METHOD

The indirect method involves a reconciliation between net income and cash flows, or a change from accrual-basis to cash-basis income. This reconciliation involves both current and noncurrent balance sheet accounts, as well as income statement accounts.

The analysis required for current balance sheet accounts was explained when the direct method was presented. Exhibit 16-7 summarizes the relationships just discussed. Notice that when the balance in an asset account decreases during the year, cash-basis income is higher than accrual-basis income. When the balance in these same asset accounts increases, cash-basis income is lower than accrual-basis income.

EXHIBIT 16–7   Current Balance Sheet Accounts Reconciling Net Income to Cash Flows from Operations

Account	Balance during Year	Effect on Income or Expense Account	Cash-basis Net Income in Relation to Accrual-Basis
Accounts receivable	Decrease	Cash-basis sales exceed accrual-basis sales.	Higher
Other receivables (e.g., interest)	Decrease	Cash-basis income exceeds accrual-basis income.	Higher
Other nonmonetary assets (e.g., supplies, prepaids)	Decrease	Accrual-basis expense exceeds cash-basis expense.	Higher
Payables, including interest	Increase	Accrual-basis expense exceeds cash-basis expense.	Higher
Accounts receivable	Increase	Accrual-basis sales exceed cash-basis sales.	Lower
Other receivables (e.g., interest)	Increase	Accrual-basis income exceeds cash-basis income.	Lower
Other nonmonetary assets (e.g., supplies, prepaids)	Increase	Cash-basis expense exceeds accrual-basis expense.	Lower
Payables, including interest	Decrease	Cash-basis expense exceeds accrual-basis expense.	Lower

The opposite occurs when liability accounts are involved. Then increases in these liability accounts cause cash-basis income to exceed accrual-basis income and vice versa.

Exhibit 16-8 shows how the data developed in the previous discussion can now be used to reconcile East-West Corporation's net income to cash flows from operating activities. Notice that the amount of net cash flows from operating activities is the same as before. The only difference is in the format of the disclosures. However, as required by the FASB, taxes paid are disclosed separately. If any interest had been paid, it would also be included in the disclosures. Finally, Exhibit 16-9 shows how the net increase of $35,000 in receivables, inventories, prepaids, and payables is determined. The depreciation adjustment is explained in the next section.

EXHIBIT 16–8

EAST-WEST CORPORATION Partial Cash Flows Statement—Indirect Method For the Year Ended December 31, 1991	
Net cash flows from operating activities	
Net income	$60,000
Noncash expenses and revenues included in income	
Depreciation	8,000
Net increase in receivables, inventories, prepaids, and payables	(35,500)
Net cash flows from operating activities	$32,500

EXHIBIT 16–9

| | December 31, | | Increase |
Account	1990	1991	(Decrease)
Accounts receivable	$22,000	$36,500	$14,500
Inventory	40,000	60,000	20,000
Prepaids	5,000	3,000	(2,000)
Accounts payable	35,000	30,000	5,000
Accrued liabilities	17,000	20,000	(3,000)
Taxes payable	3,000	2,000	1,000
Net increase			$35,500

Other Adjustments Required to Determine Cash Flows from Operating Activities

In the East-West example, adjustments had to be made only for the balance sheet current accounts and depreciation. In order to prepare the statement of cash flows, other adjustments must often be made to net income to determine cash flows from operating activities. That is, adjustments to accrual-based net income must be made for items affecting noncurrent accounts such as depreciation, amortization, and bond discounts and premiums that affected net income but did not affect cash flows.

Expenses That Do Not Reduce Cash

There are a number of expenses that reduce net income but do not reduce cash. Included are such items as depreciation, amortization of intangible assets, and amortization of discounts on bonds payable. The accounts related to these expenses are noncurrent assets or liabilities and ultimately retained earnings; cash is not involved. The following two journal entries illustrate these points:

Transaction	Journal Entry	Debit	Credit	Effect on Net Income	Cash
1. Depreciation	Depreciation Expense	10,000			
	Accumulated Depreciation		10,000	(10,000)	0
2. Amortization of bond discount	Interest Expense	2,500			
	Discount on Bonds Payable		2,500	(2,500)	0

Thus, to determine cash flows from operating activities, net income must be *increased* for all these expenses that reduced net income but did not reduce cash.

One additional point must be emphasized. Items that are added back to net income to determine cash from operations are not sources of cash. They are added back because they were deducted in calculating net income, which is used as the starting figure to determine cash flows from operating activities. Because depreciation is a very common example of this, many people consider depreciation as a source of cash. This is an incorrect interpretation; depreciation is just one of the expenses that have no effect on cash.

Income Items That Do Not Increase Cash

Occasionally, a firm will earn revenue or have an expense reduced by an item that does not increase cash. Perhaps the most common example is the amortization of a premium on a bond. The following entry decreases interest expense and thus increases income without affecting cash:

Premium on Bonds Payable	500	
Interest Expense		500

To determine cash flows from operations, these items must be subtracted from net income.

Nonoperating Gains and Losses

Cash flows from operating activities include only items generated from the operating activities of the firm. Gains and losses from nonoperating or financial changes, such as the sale or disposal of noncurrent assets or the early extinguishment of debt, are not included in income from operations. Rather, the proceeds from these transactions are included, in total, in the investing and/or the financing activities section of the statement of cash flows.

Assume that a firm sold a parcel of land for $120,000. The land had a historical cost of $100,000, so the $20,000 gain was included in the net income for the period. In preparing the statement of cash flows, the entire $120,000 is included in the section called "cash flows from investing activities." As a result, the $20,000 gain must be deducted from net income in determining cash flows from operations. If this were not done, the $20,000 would be double-counted, because the full $120,000 is included in the investing activities section.

Similarly, nonoperating losses must be added back to net income in determining cash flows from operations. Again, assume that a firm sold land for $100,000 cash, but now assume that the land had a historical cost of $120,000. The $100,000 cash is included in the same investing activities section of the statement. The $20,000 must then be added back to net income. This assures that the $20,000 loss is not double-counted and that cash flows from operating activities include only transactions resulting from the regular operating activities of the firm.

Exhibit 16-10 illustrates the typical items that must be added back to or subtracted from net income in determining cash flows from operating activities when the indirect method is used.

EXHIBIT 16—10

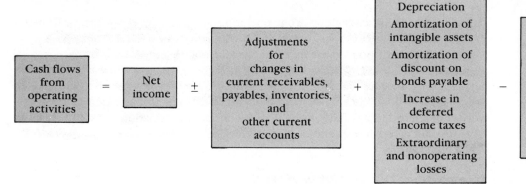

■ INVESTING AND FINANCING ACTIVITIES

After cash flows from operating activities are calculated, the next step in the preparation of a statement of cash flows is to determine cash flows from investing and financing activities. This is accomplished by analyzing the changes in the other balance sheet accounts not affecting cash flows from operations. These include most noncurrent assets, short- and long-term debt, and stockholders' equity accounts. This analysis, as well as the determination of cash flow from operating activities, is usually done by utilizing a worksheet. This approach is discussed next.

■ USING A WORKSHEET TO PREPARE A STATEMENT OF CASH FLOWS

The essence of the worksheet approach is to explain all changes in cash by detailing the changes in the other balance sheet accounts. The following steps are used in this approach:

1. Set up the worksheet.

2. Determine the change in cash and cash equivalents for the period.

3. Analyze changes in balance sheet accounts other than cash using the balance sheet, the income statement, and, if necessary, the statement of changes in stockholders' equity. Determine whether these transactions affected operating, investing, or financing activities. Use these data to complete the worksheet.

4. Prepare the statement of cash flows.

Exhibit 16-11 presents a comparative balance sheet for BMI Computers, and Exhibit 16-12 is the income statement. These statements, as well as the following supplemental data, will be used to complete the worksheet. The direct method is used to determine cash flows from operations.

EXHIBIT 16–11

BMI COMPUTERS
Comparative Balance Sheet
December 31

Assets	1991	1990	Liabilities and Stockholders' Equity	1991	1990
Current assets			Current liabilities		
Cash	$ 33,000	$ 20,000	Current maturities of notes payable	$ 90,000	$ 80,000
Accounts receivable, net	85,000	60,000	Accounts payable	52,000	60,000
Inventory	150,000	140,000	Dividends payable	15,000	20,000
Prepaids	4,000	5,000	Other accrued liabilities	5,000	9,000
Total current assets	$ 272,000	$225,000	Interest payable	2,000	1,000
			Total current liabilities	$ 164,000	$170,000
Property, plant, and equipment			Long-term liabilities		
Land	$ 300,000	$200,000	Notes payable, long-term	170,000	260,000
Building	500,000	400,000	Bonds payable	200,000	100,000
Less: Accumulated depreciation	(40,000)	(30,000)	Total liabilities	$ 534,000	$530,000
Equipment	135,000	120,000			
Less: Accumulated depreciation	(21,000)	(24,000)	Stockholders' equity		
			Common stock, $10 par	$ 100,000	$ 80,000
Total property, plant, and equipment	$ 874,000	$666,000	Paid-in capital in excess of par	200,000	120,000
			Retained earnings	320,000	170,000
Other assets			Total stockholders' equity	$ 620,000	$370,000
Goodwill, net	$ 8,000	$ 9,000			
Total assets	$1,154,000	$900,000	Total liabilities and stockholders' equity	$1,154,000	$900,000

EXHIBIT 16–12

BMI COMPUTERS
Income Statement
For the Year Ended December 31, 1991

Revenues		
Sales	$2,500,000	
Gain on sale of equipment	10,000	
Total revenues		$2,510,000
Expenses		
Cost of goods sold	$1,625,000	
Selling	240,000	
General and administrative	300,000	
Interest	52,000	
Taxes	93,000	
Total expenses		2,310,000
Net income		$ 200,000

Supplemental Information

1. Net income for the year is $200,000. (See Exhibit 16-12.)

2. Depreciation and amortization expense included in selling and general and administrative expenses are:

   (a) Depreciation—building = $10,000.

   (b) Depreciation—equipment = $12,000.

   (c) Amortization—goodwill = $1,000.

3. (a) Equipment with a historical cost of $55,000 and accumulated depreciation to date of $15,000 was sold.

   (b) Additional equipment was purchased for cash during the year.

4. The firm issued $100,000 of bonds at par in exchange for land.

5. A building was purchased for $100,000 cash.

6. Long-term notes payable of $90,000 due in 1992 were reclassified to current liabilities. The $80,000 December 31, 1990 balance in the current maturities of notes payable was paid in 1991.

7. The dividends payable at December 31, 1990 were paid. During 1991, the firm declared dividends totaling $50,000, of which $35,000 was also paid during 1991.

8. 2,000 shares of $10 par value common stock were issued at $50 per share.

■ SETTING UP THE WORKSHEET

An illustrative worksheet for BMI Computers is presented in Exhibit 16-13. This worksheet has two major parts. The first has a line for cash and a list of the other individual balance sheet accounts; the second is a skeleton statement of cash flows using the direct method to disclose cash flows from operations.

EXHIBIT 16–13

BMI COMPUTERS
Statement of Cash Flows—Worksheet
For the Year Ended December 31, 1991

A	B	C	D	E
	Account Balances 12/31/90	Analysis of Interim Transactions for 1991		Account Balances 12/31/91
Description		Debit	Credit	
Debits				
Cash	$ 20,000	✔ $ 13,000		$ 33,000
Accounts receivable	60,000	2a. 25,000		85,000
Inventory	140,000	2b. 10,000		150,000
Prepaids	5,000		2e. $ 1,000	4,000
Land	200,000	4b. 100,000		300,000
Building	400,000	5. 100,000		500,000
Equipment	120,000	3b. 70,000	3a. 55,000	135,000
Goodwill	9,000		2f. 1,000	8,000
Total debits	$ 954,000			$1,215,000
Credits				
Current maturities—Notes payable	80,000	6a. 80,000	6b. 90,000	90,000
Accounts payable	60,000	2c. 8,000		52,000
Dividends payable	20,000	7b. 55,000	7a. 50,000	15,000
Other accrued liabilities	9,000	2d. 4,000		5,000
Interest payable	1,000		2g. 1,000	2,000
Accumulated depreciation—Buildings	30,000		2f. 10,000	40,000
Accumulated depreciation—Equipment	24,000	3a. 15,000	2f. 12,000	21,000
Notes payable—Long-term	260,000	6b. 90,000		170,000
Bonds payable	100,000		4a. 100,000	200,000
Common stock—$10 par	80,000		8. 20,000	100,000
Paid-in capital in excess of par	120,000		8. 80,000	200,000
Retained earnings	170,000	7a. 50,000	1. 200,000	320,000
Total credits	$ 954,000	$ 620,000	$ 620,000	$1,215,000
				(continued)

EXHIBIT 16–13 (continued)

	Increases		Decreases	
Operating activities				
Cash received from customers	1. $2,500,000			
Less: Accounts receivable increase			2a. $	25,000
Cash paid to suppliers and employees			1.	2,165,000
Add: Inventory increase			2b.	10,000
Accounts payable decrease			2c.	8,000
Other accrued liabilities decrease			2d.	4,000
Less: Prepaids decrease	2e.	1,000		
Depreciation	2f.	12,000		
	2f.	10,000		
Amortization	2f.	1,000		
Cash paid for taxes			1.	93,000
Cash paid for interest			1.	52,000
Less: Interest payable decrease	2g.	1,000		
Investing activities				
Gain on sale of equipment	1.	10,000	3a.	10,000
Sale of equipment	3a.	50,000		
Purchase of equipment			3b.	70,000
Purchase of land			4b.	100,000
Purchase of building			5.	100,000
Financing activities				
Issuance of bonds	4a.	100,000		
Repayment of current notes			6a.	80,000
Payment of dividends			7b.	55,000
Issue of common stock	8.	100,000		
Increase in cash			✔	13,000
	$2,785,000		$2,785,000	

The first part of the worksheet can be set up by using the comparative balance sheet (Exhibit 16-11). All the individual accounts should be placed in the first column of the worksheet (A). The account balances at the end of the prior year, 1990 in this case, should be placed in the next column (B). At this point, Columns C and D, which are used to analyze the interim transactions during the year, are not filled in. The relevant account balances at the end of the current year, 1991 in this case, are then inserted in Column E.

The second part of the worksheet contains a skeleton statement of cash flows. The major headings are cash flows from operating activities, from investing activities, from financing activities, and increase (decrease) in cash. In setting up this skeletal statement, make sure that you leave yourself enough room to insert all the necessary transactions.

■ DETERMINING CHANGES IN CASH DURING THE PERIOD

Comparison of the beginning and ending balances in the Cash account indicates that the balance increased $13,000 during the period. This change is put in Column C on the first part of the worksheet on the cash line. It is a debit, because cash increased during the period. The $13,000 is also inserted in Column D on the line called "increase in cash" in the second part of the worksheet. This $13,000 should make the skeletal statement balance. A check mark is used for reference.

■ ANALYZING THE CHANGES IN OTHER BALANCE SHEET ACCOUNTS

The next step in completing the worksheet is to analyze the changes in the balance sheet accounts other than cash. Essentially, this means trying to recreate the summary journal entries that caused these accounts to change. These journal entries are then inserted on the worksheet. The first part of the entry goes on the top part of the worksheet and details the changes in these accounts. The second part of the entry classifies the changes as operating, investing, or financing and is placed on the bottom portion of the worksheet, with the appropriate description in Column A.

Cash Flows from Operating Activities

Determining cash flows from operating activities is the most logical place to begin. As previously noted, this essentially involves converting the accrual-basis net income of $200,000 to cash flows from operations. This is accomplished by making a journal entry that places the accrual-basis income statement on the worksheet. This entry is labeled as 1 and is as follows:

Increase in Cash Flows from Operations—Sales	2,500,000	
Increase in Cash Flows from Investing Activities—Gain on		
Sale of Equipment	10,000	
Decrease in Cash Flows from Operations—Suppliers		
and Employees		2,165,000
Decrease in Cash Flows from Operations—Taxes		93,000
Decrease in Cash Flows from Operations Interest		52,000
Retained Earnings		200,000

The debits in this entry are the $2,500,000 in accrual-basis sales and the $10,000 gain on the sale of the equipment. This gain is not an operating activity as far as this statement is concerned; rather, it is classified as an investing activity. The credits are the accrual-basis expenses. The $2,165,000 decrease in cash flows from operations is made up of cost of goods sold of $1,625,000, selling expenses of $240,000, and general and administrative expenses of $300,000. The other credits represent decreases in cash flows due to taxes and interest, net income of $200,000.

Changes in Current Assets and Liabilities Affecting Operations

Entries labeled 2a through 2g on the worksheet (shown in full below) relate to the changes in the current assets and liabilities affecting operations. For example, entry 2a debits Accounts Receivable and credits Cash Flows from Operating Activities. On the top portion of the worksheet, $25,000 is inserted as a debit to Accounts Receivable in Column C. The offsetting part of the entry is made in the decrease column (D) to Cash Flows from Operating Activities in the bottom portion of the worksheet. The logic behind this worksheet entry is as follows: Accounts Receivable increased during the period, which means that $25,000 less cash was collected during the period than was considered in the determination of accrual-based net income. Therefore accrual-based net income must be decreased by $25,000 to determine cash flows from operating activities. The same reasoning applies to entries 2b through 2e.

2a. Accounts Receivable	25,000	
Decrease in Cash Flows from Operations		25,000
2b. Inventories	10,000	
Decrease in Cash Flows from Operations		10,000
2c. Accounts Payable	8,000	
Decrease in Cash Flows from Operations		8,000
2d. Other Accrued Liabilities	3,000	
Decrease in Cash Flows from Operations		3,000
2e. Increase in Cash Flows from Operations	1,000	
Prepaids		1,000
2f. Increase in Cash Flows from Operations	23,000	
Accumulated Depreciation—Building		12,000
Accumulated Depreciation—Equipment		10,000
Amortization Expense		1,000

2g. Increase in Cash Flows from Operations   1,000
      Interest Payable   1,000

Depreciation and Amortization

Journal entry 2f relates to depreciation and amortization. Item no. 2 in the supplemental information list indicates the amount of depreciation and amortization expense included in the operating income of BMI Computers. Because these items all reduce net income but do not affect cash flows, they must be added to net income to determine cash flows from operating activities.

These items help explain the changes in the Accumulated Depreciation accounts and the Goodwill account. After these items are inserted on the worksheet, the appropriate T accounts would appear as follows:

Accumulated Depreciation—Building			**Accumulated Depreciation—Equipment**	
	Bal. 30,000			Bal. 24,000
	(2) 10,000			(2) 12,000
	Bal. 40,000			Bal. 21,000
	✔			

Goodwill		
Bal. 9,000	(2) 1,000	
Bal. 8,000		
✔		

The accounts with the check mark beneath them indicate that after these items are inserted on the worksheet, all entries affecting the account are explained. The Accumulated Depreciation—Equipment account does not yet balance, indicating that there is a reduction in that account that has not been explained.

The Equipment Account

The third entry relates to the gain on the sale of equipment. Item no. 3 in the supplemental information list indicates that the net book value of the equipment sold equaled $40,000. The income statement (Exhibit 16-12) shows that the firm recorded a gain of $10,000 on the sale of equipment. As the following formula indicates, there is now enough information to calculate the receipts from the sale. This figure is important because it represents an increase in cash flows from investing activities.

Receipts from sale	$?
− Net book value	40,000
= Gain or (loss)	$10,000

Receipts from the sale equal $50,000 ($40,000 + $10,000). Note that as long as two items of information in the formula are available, the third can be calculated.

Enough information has now been gathered to make worksheet entry no. 3a.

3a. Increase in Cash Flows from Investing Activities   50,000
      Accumulated Depreciation—Equipment   15,000
          Decrease in Cash Flows from Investing Activities
            due to Gain on Sale of Equipment   10,000
          Equipment   55,000

The gain of $10,000 must be entered in the decreases column and labeled Gain on Sale of Equipment in the bottom portion of the worksheet. Although this $10,000 does not really represent a decrease in cash, it is subtracted from net income to reach cash flows from investing activities. The entire $50,000 proceeds are then entered on the worksheet in the increase column and called Proceeds from the Sale of Equipment.

The sold equipment's historical cost and its related accumulated depreciation are now inserted into the proper accounts on the worksheet. The historical cost of $55,000 relating to the sold equipment is credited because the Equipment account is reduced. Similarly, the accumulated depreciation of $15,000 relating to the sold equipment is debited because the Accumulated Depreciation account is also reduced. After these entries are made, these accounts appear as follows:

Equipment				Accumulated Depreciation—Equipment			
Bal.	120,000					Bal.	24,000
		(3a)	55,000	(3a)	15,000	(2)	12,000
Bal.	135,000					Bal.	21,000
							✔

Again, the check mark indicates that all the transactions affecting the Accumulated Depreciation account have been accounted for. However, the Equipment account still does not balance. A $70,000 debit is still needed ($135,000 − $120,000 + $55,000). Logic and the supplemental information list tell us that the cause of this debit is a purchase of additional equipment.

The journal entry to reflect this purchase for worksheet purposes is as follows:

3b. Equipment	70,000	
Decrease in Cash Flows from Investing Activities		70,000

After the $70,000 purchase of equipment is recorded in the worksheet, all items that affected the Equipment account have been analyzed. The following T account illustrates this:

Equipment			
Bal.	120,000	(3a) 55,000	
(3b)	70,000		
Bal.	135,000		
	✔		

Issuance of Bonds in Exchange for Land

Supplemental item no. 4 indicates that BMI issued additional bonds at par in exchange for a plot of land. This is an example of a noncash investing and financing transaction that must be disclosed on a separate statement. For purposes of the worksheet, it will be treated as two separate transactions, as follows:

4a. Increase in Cash Flows from Financing Activities	100,000	
Bonds Payable		100,000
4b. Land	100,000	
Decrease in Cash Flows from Investing Activities		100,000

After these two items are inserted on the top portions of the worksheet, all the transactions in the Land and Bonds Payable accounts are analyzed. On the bottom portion of the worksheet, the increase in bonds payable is shown in the financing section, and the increase in land is shown in the investing section.

Purchase of a Building

Supplemental item no. 5 indicates that BMI also purchased a building for $100,000 cash. This is a straightforward use of cash for an investing activity. The appropriate worksheet entry is:

| 5. Building | 100,000 | |
| Decrease in Cash Flows from Investing Activities | | 100,000 |

After this entry is inserted on the worksheet, all transactions affecting the Building account have been analyzed.

Current Maturities of Notes Payable

During 1991, two transactions occurred that affected the current maturities of notes payable. The $80,000 1990 balance was paid in 1991, and $90,000 was transferred during 1991 from the long-term to the current category. On the statement of cash flows, the relevant transaction is the $80,000 payment made on the current liability. This represents a financing activity; it is recorded on the worksheet by the following entry:

| 6a. Current Maturities of Notes Payable | 80,000 | |
| Decrease in Cash Flows from Financing Activities | | 80,000 |

The following worksheet entry shows the reclassification of $90,000 of long-term debt to the current category.

| 6b. Notes Payable—Long-term | 90,000 | |
| Current Maturities of Notes Payable | | 90,000 |

This entry is inserted only on the top portion of the worksheet, since it does not involve an increase or decrease in cash.

Dividends Payable

Supplemental item no. 7 indicates that the $20,000 dividends payable at December 31, 1990 were paid, and that $35,000 of the $50,000 of dividends declared in 1991 were also paid. Thus a total of $55,000 of dividends was paid in cash during 1991. Analysis of these transactions is important because they affect the Cash, Retained Earnings, and Dividends Payable accounts. The worksheet entries involving Dividends Payable and Retained Earnings are as follows:

7a. Retained Earnings	50,000	
Dividends Payable		50,000
7b. Dividends Payable	55,000	
Decrease in Cash Flows from Financing Activities		55,000

The first entry records the declaration of dividends during 1991. This transaction does not involve cash and thus is recorded only on the top portion of the worksheet. It does, however, explain one of the major changes in Retained Earnings. After this $50,000 debit is posted to retained earnings, this T account appears as follows:

Retained Earnings		
	Bal.	170,000
(7a) 50,000	(1)	200,000
	Bal.	320,000

The second entry (no. 7b) is the entry that causes a decrease in cash. The payment of dividends is a financing activity and is reflected that way in the bottom portion of the worksheet.

Issuance of Common Stock

Supplemental item no. 8 indicates that 2,000 shares of $10 par value common stock were issued at $50 per share. The worksheet entry, keyed as no. 8, is:

8. Increase in Cash Flows from Financing Activities   100,000

       Common Stock   20,000

       Paid-in Capital in Excess of Par   80,000

After this entry is made, all items in the Common Stock and Paid-in Capital accounts are accounted for, as follows:

Common Stock			Paid-in Capital in Excess of Par		
	Bal.	80,000		Bal.	120,000
	(7)	20,000		(7)	80,000
	Bal.	100,000		Bal.	200,000
		✔			✔

■ COMPLETING THE WORKSHEET

At this point, all the changes in the noncash accounts have been accounted for. This can be verified by cross-footing the individual accounts on the top portion of the worksheet. The bottom portion of the worksheet should now be totaled. With the inclusion of the $13,000 increase in cash, the bottom portion of the worksheet should now balance. If it does not, a mistake has been made, and you should review your work.

■ PREPARING A STATEMENT OF CASH FLOWS

The bottom portion of the worksheet can be used to prepare a statement of cash flows. The statement of cash flows for BMI Computers is shown in Exhibit 16-14. The $2,475,000 is equal to the $2,500,000 sales less the $25,000 increase in accounts receivable (shown previously in entries 1 and 2a). The $2,163,000 is the combination of the $2,165,000 in entry 1 and entries 2a through 2f. Entry 2g is part of the determination of cash paid for interest. The FASB has not specified one particular format

EXHIBIT 16–14

BMI COMPUTERS Statement of Cash Flows For the Year Ended December 31, 1991		
Cash flows from operating activities		
Cash received from customers		$2,475,000
Cash disbursed for operating activities		
Cash paid to suppliers and employees	$2,163,000	
Cash paid for taxes	93,000	
Cash paid for interest	51,000	
		2,307,000
Net cash flows from operating activities		168,000
Cash flows from investing activities		
Proceeds from sale of equipment	50,000	
Acquisition of property, plant, and equipment	(170,000)	
Net cash used by investing activities		(120,000)
Cash flows from financing activities		
Issuance of common stock	100,000	
Payments to settle short-term debt	(80,000)	
Payment of dividends	(55,000)	
Net cash used by financing activities		(35,000)
Net increase in cash		$ 13,000
Schedule of noncash investing and financing activities		
Bonds issued to purchase land		$ 100,000

EXHIBIT 16–15

Sample Statement of Cash
Flows (Indirect Method)[2]

COMPANY M
Consolidated Statement of Cash Flows (Indirect Method)
For the Year Ended December 31, 19X1
Increase (Decrease) in Cash and Cash Equivalents

Cash flows from operating activities		
Net income		$ 760
Adjustments to reconcile net income to net cash		
provided by operating activities		
Depreciation and amortization	$ 445	
Provision for losses on accounts receivable	200	
Gain on sale of facility	(80)	
Undistributed earnings of affiliate	(25)	
Payment received on installment note receivable for		
sale of inventory	100	
Change in assets and liabilities net of effects from		
purchase of Company S		
Increase in accounts receivable	(215)	
Decrease in inventory	205	
Increase in prepaid expenses	(25)	
Decrease in accounts payable and accrued		
expenses	(250)	
Increase in interest and income taxes payable	50	
Increase in deferred taxes	150	
Increase in other liabilities	50	
Total adjustments		605
Net cash provided by operating activities		1,365
Cash flows from investing activities		
Proceeds from sale of facility	600	
Payment received on note for sale of plant	150	
Capital expenditures	(1,000)	
Payment for purchase of Company S, net of cash acquired	(925)	
Net cash used in investing activities		(1,175)
Cash flows from financing activities		
Net borrowings under line-of-credit agreement	300	
Principal payments under capital lease obligation	(125)	
Proceeds from issuance of long-term debt	400	
Proceeds from issuance of common stock	500	
Dividends paid	(200)	
Net cash provided by financing activities		875
Net increase in cash and cash equivalents		1,065
Cash and cash equivalents at beginning of year		600
Cash and cash equivalents at end of year		$1,665
Supplemental disclosures of cash flow information		
Cash paid during the year for		
Interest (net of amount capitalized)	$ 220	
Income taxes	325	

Supplemental schedule of noncash investing and financing activities
The Company purchased all of the capital stock of Company S for $950. In
conjunction with the acquisition, liabilities were assumed as follows:

Fair value of assets acquired	$1,580
Cash paid for the capital stock	(950)
Liabilities assumed	$ 630

A capital lease obligation of $850 was incurred when the Company entered into a
lease for new equipment.
Additional common stock was issued on conversion of $500 of long-term debt.
Disclosure of accounting policy
For purposes of this statement, the Company considers all highly liquid debt instru-
ments purchased with a maturity of three months or less to be cash equivalents.

[2]Financial Accounting Standards Board, Statement No. 95, *Statement of Cash Flows* (Stamford, Conn.:
1987), pp. 44–45. Reprinted by permission.

EXHIBIT 16–16

TOYS "R" US, INC. AND SUBSIDIARIES

Statements of Consolidated Cash Flows

(In thousands)   *Fiscal Year Ended*

	January 31 1988	February 1 1987	February 2 1986
CASH FLOWS FROM OPERATING ACTIVITIES			
Net income	$203,922	$152,217	$119,774
Adjustments to reconcile net income to net cash provided by operating activities:			
Depreciation and amortization	43,716	33,288	26,074
Deferred taxes	13,035	14,184	9,669
Change in operating assets and liabilities:			
Accounts and other receivables	(24,642)	(11,531)	(2,564)
Merchandise inventories	(243,894)	(115,446)	(15,580)
Prepaid expenses	(1,484)	(320)	(1,215)
Accounts payable, accrued expenses and taxes	144,364	102,382	(153)
Total adjustments	(68,905)	22,557	16,231
Net cash provided by operating activities	135,017	174,774	136,005
CASH FLOWS FROM INVESTING ACTIVITIES			
Capital expenditures-net	(314,827)	(259,388)	(221,794)
Other net	13,792	10,952	11,053
Net cash used in investing activities	(301,035)	(248,436)	(210,741)
CASH FLOWS FROM FINANCING ACTIVITIES			
Short-term borrowings-net	17,663	(1,136)	(19,118)
Long-term borrowings	96,611	—	2,493
Long-term debt repayments	(1,860)	(2,027)	(3,819)
Exercise of stock options	15,221	25,033	16,072
Net cash provided by financing activities	127,635	21,870	(4,372)
CASH AND SHORT-TERM INVESTMENTS			
Decrease during year	(38,383)	(51,792)	(79,108)
Beginning of year	84,379	136,171	215,279
End of year	$ 45,996	$ 84,379	$136,171

SUPPLEMENTAL DISCLOSURES OF CASH FLOW INFORMATION

The Company considers all highly liquid investments purchased as part of its daily cash management activities to be short-term investments.

During the years ended January 31, 1988, February 1, 1987 and February 2, 1986, the Company made income tax payments of $119,722,000, $79,934,000 and $70,205,000 and interest payments (net of amounts capitalized) of $9,610,000, $8,044,000 and $6,857,000 respectively.

See notes to consolidated financial statements.

that all firms must follow. Instead, it suggests a number of alternatives for presentation of cash flows from operating activities. In the BMI statement, there is a separate schedule for noncash investing and financing activities. The statement of cash flows in Exhibit 16-15 on page 607 is taken from the FASB Statement; it shows an alternative statement using the indirect method of disclosing cash flows from operations. Finally, the cash flows statement for Toys "R" Us is shown in Exhibit 16-16.

SUMMARY OF LEARNING OBJECTIVES

1. The purpose of the statement of cash flows. The statement of cash flows is one of the primary required financial statements. The purpose of the statement is to provide information about the firm's cash receipts and cash payments and information about the investing and financing activities of the firm.

2. The differences among investing, financing, and operating activities. The three major activities of a firm that cause changes in cash flows are investing, financing, and operations. Investing activities include cash flows from lending money and collecting on the loans and acquiring and selling securities that are not cash equivalents and productive assets. Financing activities include obtaining resources from owners and from creditors and repaying those borrowings. Operating activities include all transactions not considered either investing or financing.

3. Determining cash flows from operations. An important step in preparing a cash flow statement is to deter-

mine cash flows from operating activities. Either the direct or the indirect method can be used. Either method involves most of the steps for converting the income statement from the accrual to the cash basis. This requires making adjustments for those items that affected accrual-based operating income in one way but had a different effect on cash-based income. Exhibit 16-7 summarizes these items.

4. Preparing a statement of cash flows. A worksheet is often used to prepare a statement of cash flows. This involves analyzing changes in balance sheet accounts other than cash (using the balance sheet, income statement, and statement of changes in stockholders' equity) and then determining whether these transactions affected operating, investing, or financing activities. The actual statement can be prepared from the worksheet. A number of alternative formats can be used, but noncash activities must be clearly distinguished from those involving cash flows, using a separate schedule.

KEY TERMS

Cash equivalents
Direct method
Financing activities
Indirect method
Investing activities
Noncash activity
Operating activities
Statement of cash flows

PROBLEM FOR YOUR REVIEW

The following information is given to you concerning The Ikelin Corporation:

THE IKELIN CORPORATION
Comparative Balance Sheet
December 31

Assets	1991	1990	Liabilities and Stockholders' Equity	1991	1990
Current assets			Current liabilities		
Cash	$ 35,000	$ 45,000	Current maturities of notes payable	$ 100,000	$ 150,000
Accounts receivable, net	140,000	100,000	Accounts payable	240,000	190,000
Inventory	374,000	350,000	Accrued liabilities	9,000	13,000
Prepaids	8,000	10,000	Interest payable	1,000	2,000
Total current assets	$ 557,000	$ 505,000	Dividends payable	20,000	10,000
Property, plant, and equipment			Total current liabilities	370,000	365,000
Land	$ 300,000	$ 100,000	Long-term liabilities		
Building	400,000	400,000	Notes payable, long-term	350,000	450,000
Less: Accumulated depreciation	(50,000)	(40,000)	Bonds payable	100,000	0
Furniture and fixtures	140,000	120,000	Total liabilities	$ 820,000	$ 815,000
Less: Accumulated depreciation	(41,000)	(48,000)	Stockholders' equity		
Total property, plant, and equipment	$ 749,000	$ 532,000	Common stock, no par	$ 150,000	$ 100,000
Other assets			Retained earnings	380,000	170,000
Copyright, net	$ 44,000	$ 48,000	Total stockholders' equity	$ 530,000	$ 270,000
Total assets	$1,350,000	$1,085,000	Total liabilities and stockholders' equity	$1,350,000	$1,085,000

THE IKELIN CORPORATION
Income Statement
For the Year Ended December 31, 1991

Revenues		
Sales		$1,600,000
Expenses		
Cost of goods sold	$1,100,000	
Depreciation and amortization	22,000	
Loss on sale of furniture and fixtures	5,000	
Other operating expenses*	223,000	1,350,000
Net income		$ 250,000

*Includes interest expense of $40,000

ADDITIONAL INFORMATION (KEYED TO WORKSHEET ENTRIES):

1. Net income, $250,000 (see income statement).
2. Included in the depreciation and amortization expense is $4,000 of copyright amortization.
3. Furniture and fixtures with a historical cost of $40,000 were sold for $20,000 cash.
4. Land was purchased for cash.
5. Bonds and common stock were issued for cash.

REQUIRED: With the aid of a worksheet, prepare a statement of cash flows.

SOLUTION

NOTES KEYED TO WORKSHEET ENTRIES:

1. Items 1a through 1g relate to the income statement and changes in current accounts.
2. Since there is no activity in the Building account, it can be assumed that the increase in the Accumulated Depreciation account represents depreciation expense of $10,000.
3. Determination of book value of furniture and fixtures sold:

Proceeds	$20,000	
− Book value	? = 25,000	
= (Loss) or gain	($5,000)	from income statement
Historical cost	$40,000	
− Accumulated depreciation	? = 15,000	
= Book value	$25,000	from above

After these transactions are inserted in T accounts, they appear as follows:

Furniture and Fixtures

Bal.	120,000		
Purchase	60,000	40,000	Sale
Bal.	140,000		

**Accumulated Depreciation—
Furniture and Fixtures**

		Bal. 48,000	
Sale	15,000	8,000	depreciation
		Bal. 41,000	

Therefore it can be inferred:

The purchase of new furniture and fixtures of $60,000
($140,000 + $40,000 − $120,000)

Depreciation expense of $8,000
($41,000 + $15,000 − $48,000)

4. Land purchase was for cash.

5. Bonds and common stock were issued for cash.

6. Repayment of current portion of long-term notes is $150,000.

Current Maturities

		Bal.	150,000
Amount			
paid	150,000	From	
		long-	
		term	100,000
		Bal.	100,000

Notes Payable—Long-term

Reclassification		Bal.	450,000
to current			
100,000			
		Bal.	350,000

7. Dividends paid:

Dividends Payable

		Bal.	10,000
Dividends		Dividends	
paid	30,000	declared	40,000
		Bal.	20,000

THE IKELIN CORPORATION
Statement of Cash Flows—Worksheet
For the Year Ended December 31, 1991

Description	Account Balances 12/31/90	Analysis of Interim Transactions for 1991 Debit		Analysis of Interim Transactions for 1991 Credit		Account Balances 12/31/91
Debits						
Cash	$ 45,000			✔ $	10,000	$ 35,000
Accounts receivable	100,000	1b. $	40,000			140,000
Inventory	350,000	1c.	24,000			374,000
Prepaids	10,000			1d.	2,000	8,000
Land	100,000	4.	200,000			300,000
Building	400,000					400,000
Furniture and fixtures	120,000	3c.	60,000	3b.	40,000	140,000
Copyright	48,000			2b.	4,000	44,000
Total debits	$1,173,000					$1,441,000
Credits						
Current maturities—Notes payable	150,000	6b.	150,000	6a.	100,000	100,000
Accounts payable	190,000			1e.	50,000	240,000
Accrued liabilities	13,000	1f.	4,000			9,000
Interest payable	2,000	1g.	1,000			1,000
Dividends payable	10,000	7b.	30,000	7a.	40,000	20,000
Accumulated depreciation—Buildings	40,000			2a.	10,000	50,000
Accumulated depreciation—Furniture and fixtures	48,000	3b.	15,000	3a.	8,000	41,000
Notes payable—Long-term	450,000	6a.	100,000			350,000
Bonds payable	0			5a.	100,000	100,000
Common stock—No par	100,000			5b.	50,000	150,000
Retained earnings	170,000	7a.	40,000	1a.	250,000	380,000
Total credits	$1,173,000	$ 664,000		$ 664,000		$1,441,000

		Increases		Decreases	
Operating activities					
Cash received from customers		1a.	$1,600,000		
Less: Accounts receivable increase				1b. $	40,000
Cash paid to suppliers and employees				1a.	1,305,000
Add: Inventory increase				1c.	24,000
Accrued liabilities decrease				1f.	4,000
Less: Accounts payable increase		1e.	50,000		
Prepaids decrease		1d.	2,000		
Depreciation		2a.	10,000		
		3a.	8,000		
Amortization		2b.	4,000		
Cash paid for interest				1a.	40,000
Add: Interest payable decrease				1g.	1,000
Investing activities					
Loss on sale of equipment		3b.	5,000	1a.	5,000
Sale of furniture and fixtures		3b.	20,000		
Purchase of furniture and fixtures				3c.	60,000
Purchase of land				4.	200,000
Financing activities					
Issuance of bonds		5a.	100,000		
Repayment of current notes				6b.	150,000
Payment of dividends				7b.	30,000
Issue of common stock		5b.	50,000		
Decrease in cash		✔	10,000		
			$1,859,000		$1,859,000

THE IKELIN CORPORATION		
Statement of Cash Flows		
For the Year Ended December 31, 1991		
Net cash from operating activities		
Cash received from customers	$1,560,000	
Cash disbursed for operating activities	(1,259,000)	
Cash paid for interest	(41,000)	
Net cash flows from operating activities		$260,000
Cash flows from investing activities:		
Proceeds from sale of furniture and fixtures	20,000	
Acquisition of property, plant, equipment	(260,000)	
Net cash used by investing activity		(240,000)
Cash flows from financing activity		
Issuance of common stock	50,000	
Issuance of bonds	100,000	
Payments to settle short-term debt	(150,000)	
Payment of dividends	(30,000)	
Net cash used by investing activities		(30,000)
Net increase in cash		($10,000)

QUESTIONS

1. Describe the primary purposes of the statement of cash flows.

2. List the reasons that this statement is useful to present and potential investors and creditors.

3. What is meant by *cash equivalents*? Why is this definition important in preparing the statement of cash flows?

4. List and detail the three major activities of a firm that cause changes in cash flows.

5. The Ink Blot Company sold a piece of equipment used in the manufacture of its products. Would this be classified as an operating or an investing activity? Would it make any difference if the item was sold at a gain or a loss?

6. The Pumkin Company retired some long-term debt prior to its maturity. Is this an operating or a financing activity? Explain.

7. The Exchange Corporation issued 1,000 shares of its no par common stock for land with a fair market value of $500,000. How is this transaction shown, if at all, on the statement of cash flows?

8. Compare and contrast the direct and indirect methods of determining cash flows from operating activities.

9. During the year, the King Corp. earned net income of $1 million. Included in this net income figure are depreciation of $80,000 and a gain on sale of a building of $50,000. Assuming that there are no other changes in current accounts, what is the amount of cash flows from operating activities?

10. One of your fellow students said that the more depreciation a firm has, the better off it is, because depreciation is a source of cash. How would you respond to this statement?

11. During the year, a firm extinguished debt with a carrying value of $550,000 at a cost of $500,000. Explain how this transaction would be handled on a statement of cash flows.

12. At the beginning of the year, the balance in the Accounts Receivable account was $100,000, and at the end of the year, the balance was $150,000. Accrual-basis sales were $270,000. What are cash-basis sales?

13. During the year, the balance in a prepaid asset account increased. Is the related cash-basis expense more or less than the related accrual-basis expense?

14. A number of transactions that affect net income also affect cash flows from operations. List four such transactions. Also list three transactions that affect net income but do not affect cash flows from operations.

15. A statement of cash flows can be prepared by using a worksheet. Explain what items are in both the top and bottom portions of the worksheet.

16. Describe the basic format of a statement of cash flows. Does the FASB require that only one format be used?

EXERCISES

E1. **Types of Activities Affecting Cash Flows.** For each of the following transactions, state whether it would be classified as (1) an operating activity, (2) an investing activity, or (3) a financing activity.

(a) Payment of federal income taxes.

(b) Dividend payments to shareholders.

(c) Retirement of short-term obligations.

(d) Loans made to another entity.

(e) Payments made to acquire a business.

(f) Salaries paid to employees.

(g) Interest paid to lenders.

E2. **Transactions Affecting the Cash Flow Statement.** Explain whether the following transactions would have no effect, would increase, or would decrease cash flows and (if appropriate) by how much.

(a) The firm issued 100,000 shares of $5 par value stock for $20 per share.

(b) The firm obtained a $100,000 bank loan payable in five equal installments over the next five years.

(c) Sales during the year amounted to $500,000, of which $200,000 was for cash and the remainder was on credit.

(d) The firm sold one of its buildings for cash with a book value of $100,000 for $90,000.

(e) Cash collections on account amounted to $50,000.

(f) Dividends of $20,000 were declared: $18,000 was paid in the current year.

E3. **Transactions Affecting Cash Flows.** Complete the following table by placing an X in the appropriate column, depending on whether the transaction increases cash, uses cash, or has no effect on cash.

Transaction	Effect on Cash		
	Increase	**Decrease**	**No Effect**
1. Amortization of intangible asset			
2. Conversion of bonds payable to common stock			
3. Sales on account			
4. Purchase of inventory on account			
5. Declaration of a dividend			
6. Payment of current accounts payable			
7. Collection of accounts receivable			
8. Amortization of premium on bonds payable			
9. Sale of building at a loss			

E4. **Transactions Affecting Cash Flows.** Complete the table at the top of page 615 by placing an X in the appropriate column, depending on whether the transaction increases cash, uses cash, or has no effect on cash.

	Effect on Cash		
Items	**Increase**	**Decrease**	**No Effect**
1. Payment of accounts payable			
2. Sale of merchandise on account			
3. Sale of bonds			
4. Receipt of $60,000 from sale of a patent from a discontinued product			
5. Depreciation of $5,000 for the year			
6. Declaration of dividends payable in cash, $30,000			
7. Payment of dividends declared in (6)			
8. Return of merchandise to the supplier for credit of $18,000			

E5. Determining Cash Payments for Inventory Purchases. You have determined the following information relative to Accounts Payable and Inventory:

	Accounts Payable	Inventory
Beginning balance	$100,000	$500,000
Ending balance	70,000	620,000
Cost of goods sold: $1,500,000		

Determine the amount of cash paid for inventory purchases.

E6. Determining Cash Flows from Operations. Net income for the Stewart Company amounted to $200,000 for the current year-end. During that year, the following changes took place in these current accounts:

(a) Accounts Receivable increased by $25,000.

(b) Prepaid Insurance decreased by $2,000.

(c) Supplies increased by $5,000.

(d) Accounts Payable increased by $10,000.

Finally, depreciation for the year amounted to $4,000.

REQUIRED: Assuming that no other relevant changes took place, determine cash flows from operating activities.

E7. Conversion from Accrual to Cash Basis. The data below were taken from comparative trial balances on the Alka Pro Swimwear Co.

In addition, you determined that the firm keeps its books on the accrual basis. Included in operating expenses are depreciation of $2,000 and amortization expense of $1,000.

	December 31,	
	1990	1989
Accounts receivable	$190,000	$150,000
Interest receivable	500	700
Inventories	220,000	200,000
Prepaid insurance	1,800	1,000
Accounts payable	230,000	190,000
Other accrued expenses payable	8,000	10,000
Net sales	800,000	
Interest revenue	1,500	
Cost of goods sold	600,000	
Insurance expense	2,000	
Accrued operating expenses	80,000	

REQUIRED: Determine the following information:

(a) Cash-basis sales.

(b) Interest revenue collected during the year.

(c) Cash paid for insurance during the year.

(d) Cash paid for inventory purchases during the year.

(e) Cash paid for operating expenses during the year.

(f) Cash generated from operations.

E8. Account Analysis and the Statement of Cash Flows. Answer the appropriate questions for each of the following independent situations:

(a) At the beginning of the year, the balance in the Building account (shown net of accumulated depreciation) was $500,000. By the end of the year, the balance was $600,000. The income statement for the year showed that depreciation expense related to the building was $40,000 and that there was a loss of $10,000 on the sale of a building. Your investigation shows that the proceeds (cash) from the sale of the building were $80,000. Explain which events would affect the statement of cash flows and by how much.

(b) The beginning balance in the Retained Earnings account was $240,000. At the end of the year, the balance was $232,000. During the year, the company reported a loss of $5,000. Included in the net loss were a depreciation expense of $8,000 and a gain on the sale of land of $12,000. There were no other changes in current accounts. Determine cash flows from operations. What other transactions that the firm entered into may affect cash flows?

(c) At the beginning of the year, the Land account had a balance of $150,000, and at the end of the year, the balance was $190,000. During the year, the company purchased land of $80,000. The income statement reported a gain on sale of $20,000. Explain which events would affect the statement of cash flows and by how much.

E9. Preparation of a Statement of Cash Flows from Journal Entries. The condensed balance sheet of the Yam Company at the beginning of 1990 is as follows:

YAM COMPANY
Balance Sheet
January 1, 1990

Assets		Equities	
Current assets		Current liabilities	
Cash	$ 10,000	Accounts payable	$ 22,000
Accounts receivable	14,000	Current maturities	
Inventory	66,000	of long-term debt	18,000
Total current assets	$ 90,000	Total current liabilities	$ 40,000
Noncurrent assets		Long-term debt	$ 60,000
Property, plant, and		Stockholders' equity	
equipment, net	$100,000	Common stock	$ 45,000
Other assets	10,000	Retained earnings	55,000
Total noncurrent assets	$110,000		$100,000
Total assets	$200,000	Total equities	$200,000

During the year, the following transactions occurred:

1. Total sales were $250,000, of which $50,000 was for cash.

2. Cost of sales amounted to $130,000.

3. During the year, the firm purchased $100,000 of inventory on account, of which $70,000 was paid prior to year-end.

4. Cash collections on accounts receivable totaled $180,000.

5. Land of $100,000 was purchased for cash.

6. During the year, the following expenses were paid in cash:

Wages	$10,000
Advertising	5,000
Taxes	4,000
Interest	1,000

7. Depreciation expense for the year amounted to $5,000.

8. Accounts payable paid during the year amounted to $20,000.

9. Current maturities of long-term debt were paid, and $15,000 of long-term debt was re-classified as current.

REQUIRED: Prepare a statement of cash flows for the year ended December 31, 1990.

E10. Preparation of a Statement of Cash Flows. Comparative balance sheets for the Susuki Plumbing Co. as of December 31, 1990 and 1991 follow.

SUSUKI PLUMBING COMPANY
Comparative Balance Sheets

	December 31,	
Assets	**1991**	**1990**
Cash	$ 10,000	$ 5,000
Accounts receivable	12,000	15,000
Inventory	30,000	22,000
Long-term investments	23,000	25,000
Land	90,000	80,000
Building, net	100,000	103,000
Patents	50,000	0
Total assets	$315,000	$250,000
Equities		
Accounts payable	$ 35,000	$ 36,000
Interest payable	5,000	2,000
Long-term debt	120,000	100,000
Capital stock	60,000	50,000
Retained earnings	95,000	62,000
Total equities	$315,000	$250,000

In addition, you have obtained the following information:

1. Net income for the year was $38,000.

2. Land with a cost of $10,000 was sold for $12,000 cash.

3. The only change in the Building account was due to depreciation expense.

4. Patents were purchased for cash at the end of 1991. No amortization was taken in 1991.

5. Investments were sold for cash at their book value.

6. Interest expense included in net income was $5,000.

7. All other changes were due to normal transactions.

REQUIRED: Prepare a cash flows statement for the year ended December 31, 1991. Use the indirect method.

E11. Preparing a Statement of Cash Flows. At the top of page 618 are comparative balance sheets for the High Solar Coal Corporation for 1990 and 1991 and an income statement for the year ended December 31, 1991.

HIGH SOLAR COAL CORPORATION
Comparative Balance Sheets
December 31

Assets	1991	1990
Cash	$ 69,000	$ 40,000
Accounts receivable	55,000	60,000
Inventory	150,000	100,000
Land	250,000	200,000
Plant and equipment, net	390,000	400,000
Total assets	$914,000	$800,000

Equities	1991	1990
Accounts payable	$ 45,000	$ 30,000
Dividends payable	10,000	0
Interest liabilities	7,000	8,000
Long-term debt	240,000	200,000
Capital stock	300,000	300,000
Retained earnings	322,000	262,000
Treasury stock	(10,000)	0
Total equities	$914,000	$800,000

HIGH SOLAR COAL CORPORATION
Income Statement
For the Year Ended December 31, 1991

Sales		$1,000,000
Cost of goods sold		600,000
Gross margin on sales		$ 400,000
Operating expenses		
Depreciation	$ 10,000	
Other operating expenses	290,000	
Interest expense	10,000	300,000
Net income		$ 100,000

ADDITIONAL INFORMATION:

1. Dividends declared during the year were $40,000.
2. Land was purchased for $50,000 cash.
3. The only change in the Plant and Equipment account was due to depreciation.
4. All other balance sheet changes are the result of normal transactions.

REQUIRED: Prepare in good form a statement of cash flows. Include a supplemental schedule computing cash from operations. Use the direct method.

E12. Understanding the Statement of Cash Flows. You have obtained the following statement of cash flows for The Potsie Company:

THE POTSIE COMPANY
Statement of Cash Flows
For the Year Ended December 31, 1990

Cash flows from operating activities		$165,000
Cash flows from investing activities		
Proceeds from sale of plant and equipment	$ 200,000	
Investment in KCA Company	(1,000,000)	
Net cash used by investing activities		(800,000)
Cash flows from financing activities		
Proceeds from issuing common stock	$ 500,000	
Proceeds from issuing long-term debt	800,000	
Payments to extinguish bonds	(400,000)	
Dividends paid	(200,000)	
Net cash provided by financing activities		700,000
Net increase in cash		$ 65,000

REQUIRED: Based on this statement, explain in detail the net increase in cash. How would you assess the company's prospects for the future?

E13. Toys "R" Us Financial Statements. The cash flows statement from Toys "R" Us is reproduced in Exhibit 16-16. Based on that statement, answer the following questions:

(a) Was the statement prepared using the direct or the indirect method? Explain your reasoning.

(b) What was the amount of tax and interest payments the company made during the year ended January 31, 1988?

(c) The company's cash has been decreasing over the three-year period covered by the statement. Explain the primary reasons for this decrease.

PROBLEMS

P16-1 Identifying Changes in Cash. Below are a number of independent transactions. For each transaction, indicate whether it is a source (S) of cash, a use (U) of cash, or has no effect (NE) on cash. Item 1 is done for you as an example.

Item	Effect on Cash
1. Payment of accounts payable	U
2. Purchase of merchandise on account	
3. Sales on account	
4. Purchase of land for cash and long-term notes	
5. Declaration of dividends	
6. Collection of trade receivables on account	
7. Reclassification of long-term debt to current liability	
8. Conversion of preferred stock to common stock	
9. Depreciation expense	
10. Sale of long-term investments above cost	
11. Amortization of premium on bonds payable	
12. Purchase of current marketable securities	

P16-2 Types of Changes in Cash. State which of the following are (a) operating changes, (b) investing changes, (c) financing changes, or (d) neither, by placing an X in the appropriate space.

Item	Operating	Investing	Financing	Neither
1. Net income for the year, $3,000				
2. Purchase of a new building through the issuance of a mortgage for the entire amount				
3. Issuance of dividends in the form of capital stock, $20,000				
4. Collection of accounts receivable, $12,000				
5. Purchase of merchandise on credit, $9,000				
6. Declaration of cash dividends, $12,000				
7. Issuance of additional common stock, $300,000				
8. Depreciation for year, $6,000				
9. Purchase of equipment for cash, $12,000				
10. Sale of bonds, $25,000				
11. Sale of merchandise on account, $35,000				
12. Deposit of cash in a savings account, $5,000				

P16-3 Determining Cash Flows from Operations. The Alfredo Ice Cream Company reported net income of $500,000 for the year ended June 30, 1989. You have been able to gather the following additional information:

Unrealized loss on write-down of current marketable securities	$ 1,000
Depreciation expense	12,000
Bad debts expense	5,000
Loss on sale of land	20,000
Extraordinary gain on early extinguishment of debt	70,000
Purchase of long-term investment	55,000
Increase in balance of accounts receivable during year	8,000

There were no other changes in any current accounts.

REQUIRED: Prepare a schedule calculating cash flows from operations using the indirect method.

P16-4 Determining Cash Flows from Operations. The income statement for The Valentine Company follows:

THE VALENTINE COMPANY
Income Statement
For the Year Ended December 31, 1991

Revenues		
Sales	$500,000	
Interest	10,000	
Gain on sale of land	40,000	
Total revenues		$550,000
Expenses		
Cost of goods sold	$300,000	
Selling expenses	60,000	
General and administrative	40,000	
Loss on early retirement of debt	30,000	
Taxes	20,000	
Total expenses		450,000
Net income		$100,000

In addition, the following changes occurred in balance sheet accounts during the year:

	Net Increase (Decrease)
Accounts receivable	$40,000
Inventory	(25,000)
Prepaids	5,000
Accounts payable	(12,000)
Interest payable	3,000
Taxes payable	(2,000)

REQUIRED: Prepare a schedule determining cash flows from operations using the direct method.

P16-5 Determining Cash Flows from Operations. The following selected data were taken from the comparative trial balance of The Electric Horse Company:

	December 31,	
	1991	1990
Accounts receivable	$360,000	$400,000
Rent receivable	4,200	4,000
Inventories	140,000	100,000
Property, plant, and equipment	600,000	500,000
Accumulated depreciation	105,000	100,000
Supplies	1,000	700
Accounts payable	210,000	200,000
Other accrued liabilities	44,000	42,000
Retained earnings	105,200	75,000

In addition, you learned that property, plant, and equipment with a historical cost of $20,000 were sold during the year for cash. Depreciation related to the assets sold was $5,000.

THE ELECTRIC HORSE COMPANY
Income Statement
For the Year Ended December 31, 1991

Revenues		
Sales		$460,000
Rental income		7,200
Gain on sale of property, plant, and equipment		2,000
Total revenues		$469,200
Expenses		
Cost of goods sold	$345,000	
Supplies used	4,000	
Other accrued expenses	77,000	
Depreciation expense	10,000	
Total expenses		436,000
Net income		$ 33,200

REQUIRED: **(a)** Prepare a schedule determining cash generated from operations using the direct method.

(b) Determine what caused the changes in the Property, Plant, and Equipment account.

P16-6 **Preparation of a Statement of Cash Flows.** Comparative financial statements for the Cal Bear Corporation follow:

CAL BEAR CORPORATION
Comparative Balance Sheets

	December 31,	
Assets	1991	1990
Cash	$ 4,000	$ 15,000
Marketable securities	12,000	0
Accounts receivable, net	32,000	25,000
Inventories	86,500	73,000
Supplies	8,000	7,000
Property, plant, and equipment, net	97,500	0
Long-term notes receivable	0	15,000
Total assets	$240,000	$135,000

(continued)

| | December 31, | |
Equities	1991	1990
Accounts payable	$ 20,000	$ 18,000
Other accrued payables	10,000	7,000
Long-term note payable	95,000	25,000
Common stock, no par	50,000	50,000
Retained earnings	65,000	35,000
Total equities	$240,000	$135,000

In addition, you have gathered the following data:

1. Net income for the year amounted to $40,000. The other change in retained earnings was due to the declaration and payment of a cash dividend.

2. During the year, the company undertook a major expansion. Property, plant, and equipment with a cost of $100,000 were purchased. A 30% down payment was made; the rest was financed by issuing long-term notes that will mature in five years. The building has a 40-year life and no salvage value. Straight-line depreciation is used. There was no other depreciation expense recorded during the year.

3. The long-term note receivable was from a stockholder. Although it was not due until 1991, it was paid in full during 1990.

4. The company decided to invest excess cash in marketable securities.

5. Included in net income is interest expense of $5,000. There is no interest accrued at year-end.

REQUIRED: Prepare a statement of cash flows for the year ended December 31, 1991.

P16-7 Preparation of a Statement of Cash Flows. The KTLA Corporation's comparative balance sheets for December 31, 1989 and 1990 follow:

THE KTLA CORPORATION
Comparative Balance Sheets

| | December 31, | |
	1990	1989
Cash	$ 18,000	$ 20,000
Accounts receivable, net	39,600	45,000
Inventory	53,600	80,000
Supplies	5,400	6,000
Land	90,000	80,000
Plant and equipment, net	110,000	100,000
Patents	5,400	6,000
Total assets	$322,000	$337,000
Notes payable	$ 31,000	$ 32,000
Accounts payable	7,000	10,000
Current maturities of mortgages payable	6,200	6,000
Dividends payable	1,000	4,000
Long-term note payable	15,000	0
Mortgages payable, long-term portion	53,800	60,000
Common stock	100,000	100,000
Retained earnings	108,000	125,000
Total equities	$322,000	$337,000

In addition, you have been able to gather the following data:

1. During the year, the company incurred a net loss of $15,000. However, the company declared dividends of $2,000 during the year. Dividends paid in cash during the year were $5,000. Included in the net loss is interest expense of $2,000, all paid in cash.

2. During the year, land was purchased for $10,000 cash.

3. Plant and equipment with a book value of $10,000 were sold for $7,000 cash. Depreciation expense related to plant and equipment was $4,000. This was the total depreciation expense during the year.

4. No patents were sold or purchased during the year.

5. All other changes were the result of normal balance sheet transactions.

REQUIRED: Prepare a statement of cash flows for the year ended December 31, 1990.

P16-8 Preparation of a Statement of Cash Flows. The president of The Hardcastle Corporation understands that a statement of cash flows is one of the required financial statements. He asks your assistance in preparing the statement. He provides you with the following comparative balance sheets for 1990 and 1989, as well as the income statement for the year ended December 31, 1990.

THE HARDCASTLE CORPORATION
Comparative Balance Sheets

	December 31,	
Assets	**1990**	**1989**
Current assets		
Cash	$ 5,200	$ 4,200
Accounts receivable	20,000	28,000
Inventory	47,000	33,000
Prepaid expenses	1,500	1,000
Total current assets	$ 73,700	$ 66,200
Property, plant, and equipment		
Land	$ 3,800	$ 2,800
Machinery and equipment, net	8,700	8,500
Buildings, net	42,000	47,000
Total property, plant, and equipment	$ 54,500	$ 58,300
Other assets		
Patents	$ 1,500	$ 1,700
Total assets	$129,700	$126,200

Equities	**1990**	**1989**
Current liabilities		
Notes payable	$ 4,000	$ 5,800
Current maturities of long-term debt	2,000	1,900
Accounts payable	5,500	6,000
Accrued liabilities	15,000	13,000
Total current liabilities	$ 26,500	$ 26,700
Long-term debt	$ 18,000	$ 30,000
Stockholders' equity		
Common stock, no par	$ 61,000	$ 60,000
Retained earnings	24,200	9,500
Total stockholders' equity	$ 85,200	$ 69,500
Total liabilities and stockholders' equity	$129,700	$126,200

THE HARDCASTLE CORPORATION
Statement of Income and Retained Earnings
For the Year Ended December 31, 1990

Revenues		
Sales		$174,000
Expenses		
Cost of goods sold	$112,000	
General and administrative	26,000	
Depreciation and amortization	13,000	
Interest	2,000	
Loss on early retirement of long-term debt	400	
Loss on sale of machinery and equipment	200	153,600
Income before taxes		$ 20,400
Less: Taxes		4,000
Net income		$ 16,400
Retained earnings, January 1		9,500
Less: Dividends		(1,700)
Retained earnings, December 31		$ 24,200

In addition, the president has provided you with the following information:

1. Included in depreciation and amortization expense are:

Building depreciation	$12,000
Machinery and equipment depreciation	800
Patent amortization	200

2. Machinery and equipment with a book value of $300 were sold for cash.

3. Land was acquired in exchange for common stock.

4. Long-term debt with a face value of $10,000 was retired early.

5. Short-term notes payable were issued for the purchase of machinery during 1988.

6. All other changes represent normal balance sheet transactions.

7. There is no interest accrual at year-end.

REQUIRED: Prepare a statement of cash flows for the year ended December 31, 1990. Use the direct method.

P16-9 **Preparation of the Statement of Cash Flows.** The president of The King Corporation understands that a statement of cash flows is one of the required financial statements. She asks your assistance in preparing the statement. She provides you with the following comparative balance sheets for 1990 and 1991, as well as the income statement for the year ended December 31, 1991.

THE KING CORPORATION
Comparative Balance Sheets

	December 31,	
Assets	**1991**	**1990**
Current assets		
Cash	$ 9,300	$ 8,500
Marketable securities	2,000	2,000
Accounts receivable, net	20,000	24,000
Inventory	86,000	50,000
Supplies	4,500	2,000
Total current assets	$121,800	$ 86,500

(continued)

	December 31,	
Assets	**1991**	**1990**
Property, plant, and equipment		
Land	$ 40,500	$ 10,500
Equipment, net	19,500	18,500
Buildings, net	107,000	90,000
Total property, plant, and equipment	$167,000	$119,000
Other assets		
Long-term investments	$ 6,000	$ 5,000
Total assets	$294,800	$210,500
Equities		
Current liabilities		
Notes payable	$ 16,000	$ 15,000
Current maturities of long-term debt	5,000	3,000
Accounts payable	18,500	16,000
Dividends payable	8,500	6,000
Total current liabilities	$ 48,000	$ 40,000
Long-term debt	$ 65,000	$ 50,000
Stockholders' equity		
Common stock, no par	$125,000	$ 75,000
Retained earnings	56,800	45,500
Total stockholders' equity	$181,800	$120,500
Total liabilities and stockholders' equity	$294,800	$210,500

THE KING CORPORATION
Statement of Income and Retained Earnings
For the Year Ended December 31, 1991

Revenues		
Sales	$260,000	
Gain on sale of building	12,000	
Total revenues		$272,000
Expenses		
Cost of goods sold	$169,000	
General and administrative	44,000	
Depreciation	15,000	
Interest	13,000	
Loss on sale of equipment	1,200	242,200
Income before taxes		$ 29,800
Less: Taxes		6,000
Net income		$ 23,800
Retained earnings, January 1		45,500
Less dividends		(12,500)
Retained earnings, December 31		$ 56,800

In addition, the president has provided you with the following information:

1. Included in depreciation expense:

Building depreciation	$13,000
Equipment depreciation	2,000

2. Equipment was sold for cash. Other than the sale and depreciation expense, the only transaction affecting this account was the purchase of additional equipment for $6,000 cash.

3. Land was acquired in exchange for $10,000 cash and a long-term note payable for $20,000. No land was sold. The other change in the long-term note payable was due to the reclassification of the current portion.

4. Buildings with a book value of $20,000 were sold for cash. Other than depreciation expense, the only transaction affecting this account was the purchase of additional buildings in exchange for common stock.

5. There were no sales of long-term investments during the year.

6. All other changes represent normal balance sheet transactions.

7. There is no interest accrual at year-end.

REQUIRED: Prepare a statement of cash flows for the year ended December 31, 1991. Use the direct method.

■ USING THE COMPUTER

P16-10 Using the data in Problem 16-8, use an electronic spreadsheet to prepare a worksheet to facilitate the preparation of a statement of cash flows.

■ UNDERSTANDING FINANCIAL STATEMENTS

P16-11 Presented below is the cash flows statement for Westvaco Corporation. In addition to this statement, the following information is provided:

1. Net sales for the year (all on account) totaled $2,133,889,000.

2. Cost of goods sold for the year totaled $1,462,941,000. Further, assume that all inventory purchases are made on account and are recorded in the Accounts Payable and Accrued Expense account.

3. Tax expense for the year amounted to $105,000,000.

REQUIRED: **(a)** Does Westvaco Corporation use the direct or the indirect method of presenting cash flows from operating activities? Explain your answer.

(b) Determine the amount of cash paid for taxes and interest for year-end 1988.

(c) Determine the amount of cash collected on sales made on account for year-end 1988.

(d) Determine the amount paid for inventory purchases for year-end 1988.

WESTVACO CORPORATION
Consolidated Statement of Cash Flows
(in thousands)

Year Ended October 31	1988	1987	1986
Cash flows from operating activities			
Net income	$200,434	$146,191	$108,096
Adjustments to reconcile net income to net cash provided by operating activities			
Provision for depreciation and amortization	139,845	129,723	121,603
Provision for deferred income taxes	37,181	55,953	64,297
Gains on sales of plant and timberlands	(6,415)	(26,527)	(7,221)
Gain on settlement of pension obligations	—	(23,270)	—
Pension credits and other employee benefits	(16,512)	5,002	12,238
Foreign currency translation loss	10,133	10,118	4,516

(continued)

Year Ended October 31	1988	1987	1986
Changes in assets and liabilities			
(Increase) in receivables	(14,453)	(8,134)	(5,276)
(Increase) decrease in inventories	10,560	(7,688)	12,101
(Increase) decrease in prepaid expenses	(4,412)	(1,579)	4,822
Increase (decrease) in accounts payable and			
accrued expenses	11,399	(4,757)	2,195
Increase (decrease) in income taxes payable	(2,197)	15,180	(21,441)
Other, net	918	2,318	(1,778)
Net cash provided by operating activities	366,481	292,530	294,152
Cash flows from investing activities			
Additions to plant and timberlands	(366,056)	(271,341)	(236,660)
Proceeds from sales of plant and timberlands	13,154	42,906	15,831
Other, net	(1,991)	(3,982)	(2,295)
Net cash used in investing activities	(354,893)	(232,417)	(223,124)
Cash flows from financing activities			
Proceeds from issuance of common stock	18,662	749	957
Proceeds from issuance of debt	103,048	1,897	2,094
Common stock purchased	(29,105)	(6,193)	—
Dividends paid	(53,668)	(45,494)	(39,390)
Repayment of notes payable and long-term			
obligations	(18,125)	(17,812)	(3,056)
Net cash provided by (used in) financing			
activities	20,812	(66,853)	(39,395)
Effect of exchange rate changes on cash	(9,262)	(9,141)	(4,411)
Increase (decrease) in cash and marketable			
securities	23,138	(15,881)	27,222
Cash and marketable securities			
At beginning of period	163,854	179,735	152,513
At end of period	$186,992	$163,854	$179,735

■ FINANCIAL DECISION CASE

P16-12 The president of Denslowe Associates has become very concerned about the performance of his firm in the last couple of years. His controller reports that the firm has been profitable, but the president notices that the firm seems to be using cash at an alarming rate. The controller prepared the following statement of cash flows for the president.

DENSLOWE ASSOCIATES
Statement of Cash Flows
For the Year Ended December 31, 1990

Cash flows from operating activities	
Net income	$100,000
Adjustments to reconcile net income to net	
cash used by operating activities	
Provision for depreciation and amortization	40,000
Gain on sale of plant	(90,000)
Changes in assets and liabilities	
(Increase) in receivables	(20,000)
(Increase) in inventory	(30,000)
(Decrease) in payables	(20,000)
Net cash used by operating activities	(20,000)
	(continued)

Cash flows from investing activities		
Proceeds from sale of plant		120,000
Addition to plant and equipment		(45,000)
Net cash provided by investing activities		75,000
Cash flows used by financing activities		
Dividends paid		(35,000)
Repayment of notes payable		(80,000)
Net cash used by financing activities		(115,000)
Decrease in cash		$(60,000)

REQUIRED: **(a)** The president of Denslowe Associates has reviewed the above statement and has asked several questions. First, he would like you to explain in your own words what information this statement provides about the present and potential prospects of the company.

(b) He is also concerned that the company has shown a profit for the year, yet is having trouble meeting its current debts. He would like you to help explain the reason for this.

INTERPRETING FINANCIAL STATEMENT DATA

LEARNING OBJECTIVES

After studying this chapter, you should be able to:

1. State the purposes of financial statement analysis.
2. Identify the sources of financial information.
3. Discuss the techniques involved in financial statement analysis.
4. Know how to calculate common financial statement ratios.
5. State the limitations of financial statement analysis.

As previously mentioned, one of the primary objectives of financial reporting is to provide information to present and potential investors and creditors and other users in making rational investment, credit, and similar decisions. The decisions made by these people require that they look at more than the bottom line or earnings per share. They must interpret the past performance of companies and assess their future prospects. This requires detailed financial and nonfinancial information that can be compared and contrasted among firms in the same and different industries. Once this information is gathered, it must be analyzed and interpreted in a meaningful way. The purpose of this chapter is to introduce you to the tools of financial analysis and interpretation with the goal of understanding how to make meaningful decisions based upon financial data.

■ THE PURPOSES OF FINANCIAL STATEMENT ANALYSIS

Financial statement analysis is the set of techniques designed to provide relevant data to decision makers. It is generally based on the firm's published financial statements and other economic information about the firm and its industry. Major techniques involved in financial statement analysis include trend, vertical, and ratio analysis. The principal users of such analyses are a firm's present and potential investors, its creditors, and management.

■ PRESENT AND POTENTIAL INVESTORS AND CREDITORS

Relevant accounting information can help present and potential investors and creditors make predictions about the outcome of future events. Essentially, an investment or credit decision involves giving up cash today in the expectation of receiving a greater amount of cash in the future. One of the purposes of financial reporting is to help users assess the amounts, timing, and uncertainty of prospective net cash inflows to the enterprise, and ultimately to them. Thus investors and creditors analyze financial statements and other data in the hope of gaining insights into the future profitability and cash flows of companies.

In many cases, the past performance of the company and its current financial position can help predict the ability of the company to generate future cash flows. For example, if the operations of a company have caused continual decreases in net working capital in the last few years, this might indicate that the company may be facing future cash flow problems. Information concerning backlogs and back orders provides some indication about future profitability and the cash that will flow to the company. Trend analysis is often employed, using past information to make predictions about the future.

Ratio analysis is an important tool in measuring the past and current performance of a firm. By investigating key ratios such as the current ratio and debt-to-equity ratio, users are able to assess the current financial position of the firm and how it has changed over the immediate past. In addition, models using various ratios have been developed to help predict bankruptcy and financial distress. Ratio analysis will be discussed in great detail later in this chapter.

Forming expectations about the relative risk of a company is another important aspect of financial statement analysis. Investors demand a higher rate of return for riskier investments than they do for less risky investments. Furthermore, in putting together a portfolio of investments, investors often like to combine risky investments with less risky ones, in the hope that such diversification will reduce their overall risk. Thus financial statement analysis can be used by investors and creditors to assess the current and future risk of companies.

■ MANAGEMENT

A firm's management is both a major supplier and a user of financial statement analysis. Through its published financial statements, management provides much of the information used in financial statement analysis. Every day, management uses various ratios and other analytic tools in the evaluation and control of the firm and its various divisions. Control involves setting benchmarks and evaluating performance against these benchmarks. Many benchmarks are expressed as ratios, and performance is measured by determining variances from these ratios. Although this chapter will concentrate upon present and potential investors and creditors, the importance of financial statement analysis to management should not be overlooked.

■ SOURCES OF FINANCIAL INFORMATION

Most users of financial statements do not have direct access to a firm's records. They must rely on a variety of sources to gather the information necessary to analyze and interpret a firm's financial statements. For public companies, this information is readily available from the firm's annual report, business periodicals, and business and investment advisory services. For private companies, however, this information is difficult if not impossible to obtain. Therefore this section will focus on how to gather information about public companies. The two primary sources are reports published by the firm itself, such as annual reports, and external sources, such as business and investment advisory services.

■ PUBLISHED REPORTS

Public companies are required to publish annual reports to shareholders and to file certain reports with the Securities and Exchange Commission (SEC). Under certain circumstances, some of these reports required by the SEC can be combined with the firm's annual report.

SEC Reports

Under current laws, publicly held companies are required to file annual and quarterly reports, as well as documents notifying the SEC when an important event has had an impact on the company. These reports are available to shareholders, often free of charge, and to the public at large for a small fee. The annual report filed with the SEC is called **Form 10-K**. Essentially, this is an expanded version of the annual report sent to shareholders. However, nonfinancial information such as the president's letter is not included in Form 10-K. Current SEC regulations allow a company to integrate the annual report with Form 10-K, so it needs to prepare only one combined document if it so chooses. Since Form 10-K generally contains more information than can be found in the annual report alone, it is a valuable source of information for analyzing and interpreting financial statement data.

Public firms are also required to provide the SEC with quarterly reports called **Form 10-Q**. These reports give the SEC condensed quarterly information about the firm. In addition, all firms are required to file a **Form 8-K** within ten days of certain major events affecting the firm. Such an event might be the disposal of a major segment or the firing of the firm's auditor. This report is important, because it provides the SEC and other users with up-to-date information concerning the company.

The Annual Report

All public companies produce an annual report, which is mailed to shareholders and other interested parties free of charge. Most annual reports contain the following sections (not necessarily in this order):

1. The president's or chairperson's message.
2. Information about the company's activities during the year.
3. Management's discussion and analysis of operations.
4. A ten-year summary of activity.
5. The financial statements, including the auditor's report.

The president's message and the section containing information about the activities of the company are descriptive in nature and do not provide a great deal of information that is useful for financial statement analysis. Generally, these sections paint the best possible picture of the company; in some cases, they can make an unprofitable year sound like a successful one.

Management's discussion and analysis of operations is one of the newest and most informative sections of the annual report. Because of SEC requirements, it is included in both the annual report to shareholders and Form 10-K. The disclosure requirements in this section have recently been expanded; they should include discussions of the firm's liquidity, capital resources and results of operations, favorable or unfavorable trends and significant events and uncertainties, causes of material changes in the financial statements, narrative discussion of the effects of changing prices, and projections or other forward-looking information. Thus much of the data needed for financial statement analysis and interpretation can be found in this section.

The ten-year summary also provides useful information for financial analysis. The summary includes ten years of data concerning earnings, financial statistics, and other information. For example, in the ten-year summary contained in the Toys "R" Us annual report (Appendix D), such data as sales, gross profit, net income, working capital, the current ratio, number of employees, and the market price range of the common stock are reported for the ten most recent years.

From the point of view of financial analysis, the financial statements and related footnotes represent the heart of the annual report. Much of this book has centered around discussing the generally accepted accounting principles behind financial statements and how to understand the information contained in them. However, it is worth emphasizing the usefulness of the footnotes in financial statement analysis. Footnotes such as the one that summarizes the significant accounting policies used by the company and the one that reports certain financial information by segment and geographic area are valuable in comparing the activities of one company with those of another.

Finally, all public corporations issue quarterly financial reports containing condensed financial statements. These are reviewed by the firm's accountants rather than audited as the annual statements are. Quarterly reports are useful in spotting emerging trends and seasonal variations.

■ EXTERNAL SOURCES

Financial statement analysis requires that the performance and operations of one company be compared with those of another. In today's sophisticated business world, rule-of-thumb measures, such as "the current ratio should be two-to-one," are not adequate. Firms and industries have specific characteristics, and one rule of thumb cannot be applied to all firms. Thus understanding industry characteristics and the environment in which the firm operates are important ingredients of financial analysis. External reports such as business periodicals and investment advisory services are very useful in this regard.

Business Periodicals

Business periodicals represent a valuable source of information for financial analysts. General sources include *The Wall Street Journal*, *Forbes*, *Barron's*, *Business Week*, and *Fortune*. These journals may be published daily, weekly, or biweekly; they provide valuable information about the economy as a whole, specific industries, and individual firms. Trade journals are another valuable source of information. Journals such as *Retail World*, for example, give the reader detailed information about specific industries and firms within those industries.

Investment Advisory Services

A number of investment advisory services publish valuable and timely information about specific industries and companies. Included are such services as *Moody's Investors Services*, *Standard and Poor's Industrial Surveys*, and *The Value Line Investment*

Survey. These services all provide information such as the economic outlook for the industry, condensed financial information concerning specific firms, the outlook for the firm, and opinions as to the future performance of the firm.

Other Sources

Various other external sources are commonly used by financial statement analysts. They generally provide data on average industry ratios and norms. For example, Robert Morris and Associates, a banking association, publishes the *Annual Statement Studies*. This annual compendium provides industry facts and ratios for 220 companies. Other sources for industry ratios and relationships include Dun and Bradstreet's *Key Business Ratios*, and Prentice-Hall's *Almanac of Business and Industrial Financial Ratios*.

■ THE TECHNIQUES OF FINANCIAL ANALYSIS

Financial statement users and analysts have developed a number of techniques to help them analyze and interpret financial statements. The most common of these include horizontal analysis, vertical analysis, and ratio analysis. All of these techniques focus on relationships among items in the financial statements and on the financial statements themselves. However, in making decisions based on the results of your analysis, you must remember the limitations inherent in financial statement analysis; these limitations will be discussed later in the chapter.

■ HORIZONTAL AND TREND ANALYSIS

In trying to understand the current financial position of the firm and its future outlook, it is important to consider changes from year to year as well as trends over several years. One way to accomplish this is to use comparative financial statements and the ten-year summary of data found in the firm's annual report to spot important or emerging trends.

Horizontal Analysis

A technique that is commonly used in this regard is horizontal analysis. **Horizontal analysis** focuses on the dollar and percentage changes that have occurred in certain accounts from year to year. The determination of the percentage change is important because it relates the amount of the change to the actual amounts involved. Percentage changes are better for comparative purposes with other firms than are actual dollar changes. For example, a $1 million increase in General Motors' cash balance is likely to represent a much smaller percentage than a corresponding $1 million increase in Western Auto's cash balance.

In order to calculate percentage changes, the following formula should be used:

$$\text{Percentage change} = \frac{\text{Amount of dollar change}}{\text{Base-year amount}} \times 100$$

The base year is always considered to be the first year in the comparison. For example, Toys "R" Us total current assets were $2,027,059,000 in 1988 and $1,522,966,000 in 1987. This represents a dollar increase of $504,093,000 and a percentage increase of 33.1%, calculated as follows:

$$33.1\% = \frac{\$2,027,059,000 - \$1,522,966,000}{\$1,522,966,000} \times 100$$

Horizontal analysis can be used in conjunction with both the balance sheet and the income statement. As an example, Exhibit 17-1 presents comparative balance sheets for Toys "R" Us, and Exhibit 17-2 shows comparative statements of income. In both statements, dollar and percentage changes are shown. Several interesting balance sheet changes are apparent. During the year ended January 31, 1988, Toys "R" Us increased its property and equipment by more than 31%. This increase in capital expenditures is also reflected on the liability side of the balance sheet, where long-term debt increased more than 149%.

EXHIBIT 17–1

TOYS "R" US
Consolidated Balance Sheets
(in thousands)

Assets	1988	1987	Increase or (Decrease) Amount	Increase or (Decrease) Percentage
Current assets				
Cash and short-term investments	$ 45,996	$ 84,379	$(38,383)	(45.49%)
Accounts and other receivables, net	62,144	37,502	24,642	65.71
Merchandise inventories	772,833	528,939	243,894	46.11
Prepaid expenses	5,050	3,566	1,484	41.62
Total current assets	886,023	654,386	231,637	35.40
Property and equipment				
Real estate	762,082	600,747	161,335	26.86
Other	351,037	240,218	110,819	46.13
Leased property under capital leases	11,397	12,440	(1,043)	(8.38)
Total property, net	1,124,516	853,405	271,111	31.77
Other assets	16,520	15,175	1,345	8.86
Total assets	$2,027,059	$1,522,966	$504,093	33.10%
Liabilities and Stockholders' Equity				
Current liabilities				
Short-term notes payable to banks	$ 17,657	$ 0	$ 17,657	—
Accounts payable	403,105	305,705	97,400	31.86%
Accrued expenses, taxes, and other liabilities	167,280	118,260	49,020	41.45
Federal income taxes	71,003	73,059	(2,056)	(2.81)
Current portion long-term debt	876	973	(97)	(9.97)
Current obligations under capital lease	1,071	968	103	(10.64)
Total current liabilities	660,992	498,965	162,027	32.47
Deferred income taxes	53,356	40,321	13,035	32.33
Long-term debt	159,788	63,966	95,822	149.80
Obligations under capital leases	17,602	18,673	(1,071)	(5.74)
Total liabilities	891,738	621,925	269,813	43.38
Stockholders' equity				
Common stock	13,053	12,711	342	2.69
Additional paid-in capital	252,493	239,721	12,772	5.33
Retained earnings	854,421	650,499	203,922	31.35
Foreign currency translation adjustments	23,586	8,449	15,137	179.16
Treasury shares, at cost	(5,929)	(5,571)	(358)	6.43
Receivable from exercise of stock options	(2,303)	(4,768)	2,465	(51.70)
Total stockholders' equity	1,135,321	901,041	234,280	26.00
Total liabilities and stockholders' equity	$2,027,059	$1,522,966	$504,093	33.10%

Horizontal analysis of the income statement also provides some interesting information. Both sales and cost of sales increased from 1987 to 1988. However, the percentage increase in sales was less than the percentage increase in the cost of sales. The

EXHIBIT 17–2

			Increase or (Decrease)	
TOYS "R" US Consolidated Statements of Income (in thousands)				
Assets	**January 31, 1988**	**February 1, 1987**	**Amount**	**Percentage**
Net sales	$3,136,568	$2,444,903	$691,665	28.29%
Costs and expenses				
Cost of sales	2,157,017	1,668,209	488,808	29.30
Selling, advertising, gen & admin	584,120	458,528	125,592	27.39
Depreciation and amortization	43,716	33,288	10,428	31.33
Interest expense	13,849	7,890	5,959	75.53
Interest income	(8,056)	(7,229)	(827)	11.44
Total costs and expenses	2,790,646	2,160,686	629,960	29.16
Earnings before taxes on income	345,922	284,217	61,705	21.71
Taxes on income	142,000	132,000	10,000	7.58
Net earnings	$ 203,922	$ 152,217	$ 51,705	33.97%
Net earnings per share	$1.56	$1.16	$0.40	33.97%

result is a slight decrease in gross profit from 1987 to 1988. Operating and administrative expenses also increased at about the same rate. However, a fairly small increase in taxes, due to a decrease in the firm's effective corporate tax rate, resulted in almost a 40% increase in net earnings.

Trend Analysis

Horizontal analysis can easily be expanded to include more than a single change from one year to the next. This is called **trend analysis**. In many cases, it is important to look at changes over a period of time in order to evaluate emerging trends that are likely to have an impact on future years' performance. The ten-year summary of selected financial data, which is found in all annual reports, is particularly useful in this regard.

When more than two years are involved, index numbers are used instead of percentage changes. Essentially, one year is selected as the base year and is set to 100%. All other years are represented as a percentage of the base year. An index number can be calculated by the following formula:

$$\text{Index number} = \frac{\text{Index year dollar amount}}{\text{Base-year dollar amount}} \times 100$$

To illustrate, the sales of Toys "R" Us in 1984, the base year, were $1,320,000,000 (rounded to millions). Sales in 1988, the index year, were $3,137,000,000 (also rounded to millions), and the index for 1988 was 237.65, calculated as follows:

$$237.65 = \frac{\$3,137,000,000}{\$1,320,000,000} \times 100$$

This means that the sales of Toys "R" Us in 1988 were 237.65 or 2.37 times 1984 sales. Index numbers for other items are calculated in the same manner.

Index numbers are particularly useful in measuring real growth. In the Toys "R" Us example, sales increased 2.37 times from 1984 to 1988. Does this represent a real growth of sales, the same unit sales only at higher prices, or a combination of both?

One way to answer this question is to compare the index number for sales growth to the rate of inflation for the same period, measured by an index such as the Consumer Price Index for All Urban Consumers, or to a specific price index for the industry. If that index increased 1.20 times during the period, Toys "R" Us experienced some real growth in sales during the five-year period 1984 to 1988.

■ VERTICAL ANALYSIS

Vertical analysis is used to evaluate the relationships within single financial statements. Essentially, the appropriate total figure in the financial statement is set to 100%, and other items are expressed as a percentage of that figure. For the balance sheet, this figure is usually total assets or the total of liabilities plus stockholders' equity. Net sales is usually the total figure used in the income statement. The financial statements that result from using these percentages are often referred to as **common-dollar statements**. Exhibits 17-3 and 17-4 present comparative common-dollar balance sheets and income statements for Toys "R" Us.

EXHIBIT 17-3

TOYS "R" US Consolidated Common-dollar Balance Sheets				
	Thousands of Dollars		Percentage	
Assets	**1988**	**1987**	**1988**	**1987**
Current assets				
Cash and short-term investments	$ 45,996	$ 84,379	2.27%	5.54%
Accounts and other receivables, net	62,144	37,502	3.07	2.46
Merchandise inventories	772,833	528,939	38.13	34.73
Prepaid expenses	5,050	3,566	0.25	0.23
Total current assets	886,023	654,386	43.71	42.97
Property and equipment				
Real estate	762,082	600,747	37.60	39.45
Other	351,037	240,218	17.32	15.77
Leased property under capital leases	11,397	12,440	0.56	0.82
Total property, net	1,124,516	853,405	55.48	56.04
Other assets	16,520	15,175	0.81	1.00
Total assets	$2,027,059	$1,522,966	100.00%	100.00%
Liabilities and Stockholders' Equity				
Current liabilities				
Short-term notes payable to banks	$ 17,657	$ —	0.87%	0.00%
Accounts payable	403,105	305,705	19.89	20.07
Accrued expenses, taxes, and other liabilities	167,280	118,260	8.25	7.77
Federal income taxes	71,003	73,059	3.50	4.80
Current portion				
Long-term debt	876	973	0.04	0.06
Obligations under capital leases	1,071	968	0.05	0.06
Total current liabilities	660,992	498,965	32.61	32.76
Deferred income taxes	53,356	40,321	2.63	2.65
Long-term debt	159,788	63,966	7.88	4.20
Obligations under capital leases	17,602	18,673	0.87	1.23
Total liabilities	$891,738	$621,925	43.99%	40.84%

(continued)

EXHIBIT 17–3 (continued)

Liabilities and Stockholders' Equity	Thousands of Dollars		Percentage	
	1988	1987	1988	1987
Stockholders' equity				
Common stock	$ 13,053	$ 12,711	0.64%	0.83%
Additional paid-in capital	252,493	239,721	12.46	15.74
Retained earnings	854,421	650,499	42.15	42.71
Foreign currency translation adjustments	23,586	8,449	1.16	0.55
Treasury shares, at cost	(5,929)	(5,571)	(0.29)	(0.37)
Receivable from exercise of stock options	(2,303)	(4,768)	(0.11)	(0.31)
Total stockholders' equity	1,135,321	901,041	56.01	59.16
Total liabilities and stockholders' equity	$2,027,059	$1,522,966	100.00%	100.00%

EXHIBIT 17–4

TOYS "R" US Consolidated Common-dollar Statements of Income				
	Thousands of Dollars		Percentage	
	1988	1987	1988	1987
Net sales	$3,136,568	$2,444,903	100.00%	100.00%
Costs and expenses				
Cost of sales	2,157,017	1,668,209	68.77	68.23
Selling, advertising, general and administrative	584,120	458,528	18.62	18.75
Depreciation and amortization	43,716	33,288	1.39	1.36
Interest expense	13,849	7,890	0.44	0.32
Interest income	(8,056)	(7,229)	(0.26)	(0.30)
Total costs and expenses	2,790,646	2,160,686	88.97	88.38
Earnings before taxes on income	345,922	284,217	11.03	11.62
Taxes on income	142,000	132,000	4.53	5.40
Net earnings	$203,922	$152,217	6.50%	6.23%
Net earnings per share	$ 1.56	$ 1.17		

Common-dollar statements are very useful in noting important changes in the components of financial statements. For example, one would expect that current assets as a percentage of total assets would remain fairly constant over the years, or that net income as a percentage of sales would not radically change from year to year. When changes, especially radical ones, do occur, they are signals to external users as well as managers that the company has been affected by internal forces such as declining productivity or external forces such as a recession or severe competition. Exhibits 17-3 and 17-4 indicate that there were not many significant changes in these percentages for Toys "R" Us between 1987 and 1988. This is not unusual for a large, stable company. Significant financial statement changes usually do not occur rapidly, especially given the relatively stable economy that existed in 1987 and 1988. The one significant change was an increase in long-term debt. At year-end 1988, the company issued $100 million of debt, as noted in management's discussion of results of operations and financial condition:

On February 4, 1987, the Company issued $100 million of 8¼% Sinking Fund Debentures due 2017, as part of a shelf registration statement filed with the Securities and Exchange Commission for up to $200 million of debt securities.

Common-dollar statements are also useful in comparing the financial statements of different companies. For example, it is difficult to compare the dollar financial statements of Toys "R" Us with those of a smaller retail toy chain, because of the difference in the magnitude of the numbers. However, when the financial statements are expressed in percentages, the differences in magnitude disappear, and it is easier to compare the financial position and performance of two companies that are significantly different in size.

RATIO ANALYSIS

Ratio analysis is a shortcut method of expressing relationships among various items on the financial statements. However, ratios are not substitutes for looking deeper into the financial position of the company. There is a danger that inexperienced financial statement analysts might use what is called *rule-of-thumb analysis* to make important decisions. That is, one might decide that the current ratio should be two-to-one and make decisions on that basis. However, there are few rules of thumb that are adequate in today's complex financial world. Keep that caveat in mind during the following section's discussion of some of the more common ratios used by financial analysts.

COMMON FINANCIAL RATIOS

A multitude of ratios can be used in financial statement analysis. Throughout this text, important ratios have been introduced in appropriate chapters. The purpose in this chapter is to summarize and further explore these and other ratios. The most commonly used ratios will be stressed, using the data from Toys "R" Us found in Exhibits 17-1 and 17-2 where appropriate.

A useful way to discuss ratio analysis is to categorize the ratios by the type of financial statement user who is most likely to use the particular ratio. The three most common user groups in this regard are common and preferred stockholders, short-term creditors, and long-term creditors. However, these categories are not hard and fast; various users are likely to study ratios in all three groups to make their decisions. The categories do, however, serve as a useful way to organize the discussion.

COMMON AND PREFERRED STOCKHOLDERS

Common and preferred stockholders provide the permanent equity for the firm. They are interested in a variety of ratios that measure earnings per share to return on total assets. Because common shareholders have the residual equity interest in the firm and outnumber preferred shareholders, the discussion will center around ratios most useful to them. In most cases, these ratios will also be of interest to the preferred shareholder.

Earnings per Share

As discussed in Chapter 14, earnings per share (EPS) is one of the most commonly used (and possibly abused) of all the ratios. Its purpose is to provide the common shareholder with a comparative figure of the earnings of the company on a per-share basis. Chapter 14 pointed out how complex the actual EPS computation can be. When a simple capital structure exists, earnings per share is calculated as follows:

$$\text{EPS} = \frac{\text{Net income less preferred dividends, if any}}{\text{Weighted average number of common shares outstanding}}$$

Toys "R" Us has a complex capital structure, so its EPS cannot be calculated directly from the net income figure and the weighted average number of shares outstanding.

Exhibit 17-5, a footnote taken from the annual report of Toys "R" Us, explains how the EPS of $1.56 for 1988 was calculated.

EXHIBIT 17–5

Calculation of EPS
for Toys "R" Us

8. NET EARNINGS PER SHARE

Net earnings per share is computed by dividing net earnings by the weighted average number of common shares outstanding after reduction for treasury shares and assuming exercise of dilutive stock options computed by the treasury stock method using the average market price during the year.

Average weighted numbers of shares used in computing net earnings per share were as follows:

	January 31 1988	February 1 1987	February 2 1986
Common and common equivalent shares	130,792,000	130,273,000	129,242,000

Year ended

Price-Earnings Ratio

The price-earnings (P-E) ratio measures the relationship of the market price of a firm's common stock to its earnings per share. This ratio is useful to present and potential investors because it provides a comparative measure of how the stock market values the earnings of a company.

The P-E ratio is calculated as follows:

$$\text{P-E ratio} = \frac{\text{Market price per common share}}{\text{Earnings per share}}$$

A firm's P-E ratio fluctuates daily with the change in the price of the firm's stock. At the end of fiscal 1988, the P-E ratio for Toys "R" Us was 22, calculated as follows:

$$22 = \frac{\$34.25}{\$1.56}$$

This means that Toys "R" Us stock was selling at 22 times its earnings.

A P-E ratio of 22 is not meaningful by itself. It must be compared with other firms in the same industry and firms in other industries. For example, the P-E ratio for The Price Co., a comparable retail discount chain, was 28. Generally, a higher P-E ratio is an indication that investors feel that the firm's earnings are going to rise at a faster pace than for other companies. Conversely, a lower P-E ratio is often taken as a negative assessment of the future earnings of the company. However, generalizations such as these must be used carefully.

Dividend Yield

Some investors are primarily interested in dividends rather than in the appreciation of the market price of their stock. That is, they purchase the stock in the hope of receiving a steady flow of cash in the form of dividends. To these individuals, the dividend yield ratio is very important. The dividend yield ratio is determined by the following formula:

$$\text{Dividend yield ratio} = \frac{\text{Dividends per share}}{\text{Market price per share}} \times 100^{1}$$

[1] Certain ratios are customarily expressed as percentages. Therefore this ratio as well as certain others are multiplied by 100 in order to express the relationship as a percentage.

Although this ratio can be figured for both common and preferred stock, it generally refers to yield on common stock. Toys "R" Us has not issued any dividends. The company policy concerning dividends is expressed by management as follows:

> The Company has followed the policy of reinvesting earnings in the business and, consequently, has not paid any cash dividends. At the present time, no change in this policy is under consideration by the Board of Directors. The payment of cash dividends in the future will be determined by the Board of Directors in light of conditions then existing, including the Company's earnings, financial requirements and condition, opportunities for reinvesting earnings, business conditions and other factors.

Book Value per Share

Chapter 13 contained a complete discussion of the concept behind book value per share and the procedures for computing this statistic. The book value per share of Toys "R" Us common stock at the end of 1988 is calculated as follows:

$$\text{Book value per share} = \frac{\text{Total common shareholders' equity}}{\text{Number of common shares outstanding}}$$

$$\$8.70 = \frac{\$1,135,321,000}{130,530,467}$$

Return on Investment

The management of a firm obtains resources from creditors and stockholders and then is charged with maximizing the return on these resources. Two ratios are often calculated to measure management's performance in this regard: return on total assets and return on common stockholders' equity.

Return on Total Assets

The return on total assets measures how efficiently the assets of the firm are being employed. It is one of the most important ratios because it answers the basic question, "What rate of return has the firm earned on the assets under its control?" This question is not only important to stockholders as they analyze alternative investments, but is also of utmost importance to the management of the firm itself. Corporate management uses this ratio in evaluating the performance of various divisions and the managers of those divisions.

There are a number of ways to calculate this ratio, based on different levels of sophistication. For present purposes, the following standard formula will be used:

$$\text{Return on total assets} = \frac{\text{Net income + Interest expense}}{\text{Average total assets}} \times 100$$

There are two important points to note about the way this ratio is calculated. First, interest expense is added back to net income so that the numerator of the formula is net income before interest expense. Interest represents a payment or distribution to creditors for the use of funds that were used to acquire assets. The purpose of the ratio is to determine how well the assets of a business are employed, regardless of how the assets were financed. That is why interest expense is added back to net income.

Second, the denominator is average total assets, rather than assets at the end of the year. Net income accrues over the entire year, so it would not be accurate to relate that figure to assets at one point in time. For this reason, an average is used in the denominator. The more exact the average, the better. For most purposes, a two-point average, calculated as follows, is sufficient:

Asset balance at beginning of year + Asset balance at end of year

2

An average such as this should be used whenever an income statement figure is used in the numerator of a ratio and a balance sheet figure is used in the denominator.

The return on total assets for Toys "R" Us for 1988 and 1987 is calculated in Exhibit 17-6. To evaluate these ratios properly, they must be compared with those of other firms in the specialty retail industry. For example, for specialty firms of similar size, the average return on total assets is 11.5%.

EXHIBIT 17-6

TOYS "R" US Return on Total Assets (in thousands)		
	1988	1987
Net income	$ 203,922	$ 152,217
Interest expense	13,849	7,890
Income before interest expense	$ 217,771	$ 160,107
Total assets, beginning of year	$1,522,966	$1,225,916
Total assets, end of year	2,027,059	1,522,966
Average total assets	$1,775,013	$1,374,441
Return on total assets	12.26%	11.65%

Components of Return on Total Assets. Return on total assets is a summary ratio. Du Pont developed a system of financial control that broke this ratio down to its various components. As Exhibit 17-7 illustrates, the two major components are the profit margin percentage and asset turnover ratio. When these two ratios are multiplied together, the result is return on total assets.

EXHIBIT 17-7

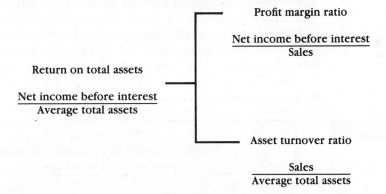

The profit margin percentage and asset turnover ratio for Toys "R" Us for 1988 are calculated in Exhibit 17-8.[2] As indicated by these ratios, Toys "R" Us generates about 6.9 cents of profit on every dollar of sales. Each dollar of assets generates about 1.8 dollars of sales. Thus the return on total assets is the combination of these two ratios, or 12.26%. For comparison purposes, the retail grocery business has a very low profit margin; gross profit percentages range between 1% and 2%. However, the asset turnover ratio tends to be higher, about 4% to 5%.

[2]For purposes of this example, the profit margin percentage has been calculated using income before interest. Traditionally, however, net income is used to calculate this percentage; this is the way in which it is calculated later in the chapter.

EXHIBIT 17-8

TOYS "R" US
Profit Margin Percentage
and Asset Turnover Ratio
(dollar amounts in thousands)

Profit margin percentage	
(based on income before interest)	
Net income before interest	$ 217,771
Sales	3,136,568
Profit margin percentage	6.94%
Asset turnover ratio	
Sales	$3,136,568
Average total assets	1,775,013
Asset turnover ratio	1.7671
Return on total assets	
12.26% = 1.7671% × 6.94	

Return on Common Stockholders' Equity

A primary concern of common shareholders is the return that is generated to them. The return on common stockholders' equity is a ratio that measures the return generated to common stockholders for each dollar they have invested. Because of interest payments to creditors and dividend payments to preferred shareholders, this ratio is likely to be different from the return on total assets. The return on common stockholders' equity is calculated as follows:

$$\frac{\text{Net income less preferred dividend requirements}}{\text{Average common stockholders' equity}} \times 100$$

Since this ratio measures the return to common stockholders, preferred dividend requirements are subtracted from net income. Since interest expense has already been subtracted from net income, the numerator of this ratio represents a figure that is net of all distributions to creditors and preferred stockholders. Thus it is the income available to common stockholders. The denominator, common stockholders' equity, is total stockholders' equity less any capital accounts related to preferred stockholders.

Since Toys "R" Us has no preferred stock, the calculation of this ratio is straightforward, as shown in Exhibit 17-9.

EXHIBIT 17-9

TOYS "R" US		
Return on Common Stockholders' Equity		
(dollar amounts in thousands)		
	1988	1987
Net income	$ 203,922	$152,217
Common stockholders' equity, beginning of year	901,041	717,394
Common stockholders' equity, end of year	1,135,321	901,041
Average common stockholders' equity	$1,018,181	$809,218
Return on common stockholders' equity	20.03%	18.81%

Leverage

Leverage (often called *trading on equity*) refers to the amount of resources raised by borrowing or by issuing preferred stock. Highly leveraged companies have a greater proportion of their assets financed through debt and preferred stock than do companies that are less leveraged. The degree of leverage affects the relationship between the return on total assets and the return on common stockholders' equity.

To illustrate the concept of leverage, let's compare the return on total assets and return on common stockholders' equity for Toys "R" Us:

	1988	1987
Return on total assets	12.26%	11.65%
Return on common stockholders' equity	20.03%	18.81%

In both cases, the return on common stockholders' equity is greater than the return on total assets. This is the result of the effective use of leverage; funds raised by borrowings or through the issuance of preferred stock earn a greater return than the required payment to creditors or preferred stockholders. That is, if a firm can borrow funds at 10% and earn a return of 12% on those funds, the common stockholder will benefit; once the creditor is paid the required interest, the differential between the interest rate and the rate of return earned on these funds accrues to the common shareholder.

However, leverage can be dangerous. If the interest rate on borrowed funds or the dividend rate on preferred stock exceeds the rate of return the company can earn on such funds, the return to common stockholders will be below the return on total assets. In the early 1980s, this happened often. Many firms had loans tied to the prime rate of interest. When this rate reached 20%, the return on common stockholders' equity began to decline; firms were unable to earn a rate of return on these funds anywhere near 20%.

The Equity Ratio

The equity ratio is a measure of the amount of leverage used by a particular firm. This ratio is calculated as follows:

$$\text{Equity ratio} = \frac{\text{Total stockholders' equity}}{\text{Total assets}} \times 100$$

This ratio relates the proportion of assets supplied by the stockholders to the proportion supplied by the creditors. The lower this ratio is, the higher the degree of leverage. Because the total assets of a particular firm must be supplied by the stockholders and creditors, 100% minus the equity ratio produces the debt ratio. This ratio measures the amount of assets supplied by the creditors. It can be calculated independently as follows:

$$\text{Debt ratio} = \frac{\text{Total liabilities}}{\text{Total assets}} \times 100$$

The equity and debt ratios for Toys "R" Us are calculated in Exhibit 17-10. Thus, in the case of Toys "R" Us, about 60% of the assets are supplied by creditors and 40% by stockholders.

EXHIBIT 17-10

TOYS "R" US Equity Ratio and Debt Ratio (dollar amounts in thousands)		
	1988	1987
Total liabilities	$ 891,738	$ 621,925
Total stockholders' equity	1,135,321	901,041
Total assets	$2,027,059	$1,522,966
Equity ratio	56.01%	59.16%
Debt ratio	43.99%	40.84%

In summary, the degree of leverage is an important financial decision of corporate management. The judicious use of leverage can lead to increased returns to common stockholders. However, too much debt, especially in a period of rising interest rates, can lead to decreased returns to common stockholders and ultimately to bankruptcy. Because of these factors, the relationship between the return on total assets and return on common stockholders' equity is closely watched by financial analysts.

Income Statement Analysis

Stockholders as well as the management of a firm are particularly interested in certain income and expense relationships. These relationships, derived through vertical analysis, were discussed previously. The most important of these from the stockholders' perspective is the profit margin percentage. This statistic measures the percentage of each sales or revenue dollar that results in net income, and it varies widely among industries. The profit margin percentage, calculated by dividing net income by total revenues, for Toys "R" Us is shown in Exhibit 17-11.

EXHIBIT 17–11

TOYS "R" US Profit Margin Percentage (dollar amounts in thousands)		
	1988	1987
Net income	$ 203,922	$ 152,217
Total sales	$3,136,568	$2,444,903
Profit margin percentage	6.5%	6.23%

Evaluation of Market Risk

Investors are interested in determining the relative risk of their current and potential investments. They demand a higher rate of return for riskier investments. In addition, information about the riskiness of stocks is useful to investors in forming portfolios. Recently, financial analysts have begun to use a measure of risk that relates the volatility of the price of a specific stock in relation to the volatility of the prices of other stocks. This measure is called **Beta** (β) and is determined through multiple regression analysis. The stockmarket as a whole is considered to have a Beta of 1. Thus the price of stocks with a Beta of higher than 1 are more volatile than the market as a whole, whereas those with a Beta of less than 1 are less volatile. Although the Beta for Toys "R" Us will not be calculated here, it is available from the investment advisory services previously discussed. At the end of 1988, the Beta for Toys "R" Us was 1.32.

In summary, the common and preferred stockholders have a long-term equity interest in the firm. As a result, they are interested in practically all aspects of the firm's operations. However, they are keenly interested in ratios that focus upon such measures as return on investment, EPS, the P-E ratio, and return on stockholders' equity. Many of these ratios are calculated by the firm and are presented in its annual report.

■ LONG-TERM CREDITORS

During their evaluation of a company, present and potential long-term creditors are particularly interested in the risk of the company, its ability to pay interest on its debt, and its ability to repay the principal of its debt. The profitability of the company interests them only to the extent that it affects the ability of the company to make timely interest and principal payments, because very few loan agreements call for the creditor to share in the profits of the firm beyond receiving interest payments.

The Debt Ratio

As noted previously, the debt ratio measures the relative proportion of assets contributed by the shareholders and the creditors. All else being equal, the higher the debt ratio, the less likely it is that a creditor would loan additional funds to the company. This is because a highly leveraged company is riskier to a potential creditor than is a less leveraged firm. Clearly, the creditor's margin of protection decreases as the total debt of a firm increases.

The Debt-to-equity Ratio

The debt-to-equity ratio is another ratio that measures the balance of funds being provided by creditors and stockholders. This ratio is calculated by dividing total liabilities by total stockholders' equity. Clearly, the higher the debt-to-equity ratio, the more debt the company has and (all else being equal) the riskier it is. The debt-to-equity ratio for Toys "R" Us is shown in Exhibit 17-12. These are low ratios, which indicate that Toys "R" Us is in a strong financial position.

EXHIBIT 17-12

TOYS "R" US Debt-to-equity Ratio (dollar amounts in thousands)		
	1988	**1987**
Total liabilities	$ 891,738	$621,925
Total stockholders' equity	$1,135,321	$901,041
Debt-to-equity ratio	.79	.69

Times Interest Earned

Creditors like to have an indication of the ability of the company to meet the required interest payments. Times interest earned is the ratio of the income that is available for interest payments to the annual interest expense. The computation of times interest earned is as follows:

$$\text{Times interest earned} = \frac{\text{Income before interest and taxes (operating profit)}}{\text{Annual interest expense}}$$

The times interest earned ratios for Toys "R" Us for 1988 and 1987 are 25.98 and 37.02, respectively. The calculation of these figures is shown in Exhibit 17-13. These figures are very high, again indicating that Toys "R" Us has a moderate amount of debt.

EXHIBIT 17-13

TOYS "R" US Times Interest Earned Ratio (dollar amounts in thousands)		
	1988	**1987**
Operating profit	$359,771	$292,107
Interest expense	$ 13,849	$ 7,890
Times interest earned	25.98	37.02

It is important to keep in mind that the times interest earned ratio does not directly measure the cash available to make the required interest payments. Operating profits are not totally equivalent to cash flows from operations. For this reason, bankers and other creditors often ask the firm to provide additional cash flow information.

In summary, long-term creditors provide substantial capital to many businesses. In evaluating credit decisions, these individuals are primarily concerned with the ability of the firm to meet its interest and principal payments. Thus long-term creditors tend to focus upon such ratios as the debt ratio and times interest earned.

■ SHORT-TERM CREDITORS

Short-term creditors, like long-term creditors, are interested in all aspects of the company. However, their interest lies primarily in measuring the ability of the company to meet its short-term commitments. Thus short-term creditors are interested in such items as liquidity and working capital. The ratios that are most often calculated are the current ratio, the quick ratio, accounts receivable turnover, and inventory turnover.

The Current Ratio

The current ratio, which is determined by dividing current assets by current liabilities, is one of the most common measures of liquidity and the ability of the company to meet its short-term debt. The current ratio of Toys "R" Us for 1988 and 1987 is shown in Exhibit 17-14. The ratio for these two years is a little lower than the industry average of about 1.5:1.

EXHIBIT 17–14

TOYS "R" US Current Ratio (dollar amounts in thousands)		
	1988	1987
Current assets	$886,023	$654,386
Current liabilities	$660,992	$498,965
Current ratio	1.34:1	1.31:1

The current ratio, like all ratios, is significantly affected by the generally accepted accounting principles a firm uses. For example, because Toys "R" Us used LIFO to cost a large portion of its inventories, its current ratio was less than if FIFO had been used.

The Quick Ratio

Inventories generally represent a large portion of a firm's current assets. Inventories are not really liquid; management cannot turn them into cash at its discretion. Thus the current ratio can overstate the liquidity of the company and its ability to meet its obligations. The quick ratio overcomes this limitation of the current ratio by comparing only cash, marketable securities, and receivables to current liabilities. Marketable securities and receivables are included because management can quickly turn them into cash if necessary.

For illustrative purposes, these ratios are calculated for Toys "R" Us in Exhibit 17-15. However, these figures are very misleading and illustrate some of the dangers of using ratios that are inappropriate for a particular firm or industry. The retail toy

EXHIBIT 17–15

TOYS "R" US Quick Ratio (dollar amounts in thousands)		
	1988	1987
Cash	$ 45,996	$ 84,379
Receivables	62,144	37,502
Total	$108,140	$121,881
Current liabilities	$660,992	$498,965
Quick ratio	.16:1	.24:1

business is a cash-and-carry business. Inventories are very liquid because of the speed in which they turn over. Thus, in this case, the current ratio is a better measure of liquidity than is the quick ratio. Obviously, there are many cases in which the quick ratio is a good measure of liquidity.

Inventory Turnover

Inventory turnover measures how quickly the inventory moves. This is an important ratio for firms such as Toys "R" Us that have significant amounts of inventory. However, the inventory turnover ratio would be meaningless when analyzing an airline. The inventory turnover ratio is calculated as follows:

$$\text{Inventory turnover} = \frac{\text{Cost of goods sold}}{\text{Average inventories}}$$

If possible, average inventories should be figured by dividing the total of inventories at the end of each month by 12, because many firms choose a year-end to be a point at which their inventories are at a yearly low. Thus a simple two-point average using the inventories at the beginning and end of the year can be misleading. However, inventory levels at the end of each month are often not available, so the simpler two-point average is often used.

The inventory turnover ratios for Toys "R" Us for 1988 and 1987 are shown in Exhibit 17-16. These ratios indicate that the inventories of Toys "R" Us turn over a little more than three times a year. Another way to express the inventory turnover is to determine the average number of days needed to turn the inventory over. This is easily calculated by dividing the inventory turnover into 365 days. In 1988, it took Toys "R" Us about 110 days to turn over its inventories ($365 \div 3.31 = 110.3$).

EXHIBIT 17-16

TOYS "R" US Inventory Turnover Ratio (dollar amounts in thousands)		
	1988	1987
Cost of goods sold	$2,157,017	$1,668,209
Inventories, beginning of year	528,939	413,493
Inventories, end of year	772,833	528,939
Average inventories	$ 650,886	$ 471,216
Inventory turnover	3.31	3.54

Accounts Receivable Turnover

For most companies, the accounts receivable turnover ratio is very important. This ratio, calculated in the same manner as the inventory turnover ratio, measures how quickly the firm is converting its accounts receivable into cash. In a cash-tight economy, a primary task of management is to turn its accounts receivable into cash quickly and thus improve its cash from operations. The accounts receivable turnover ratio is calculated as follows:

$$\text{Accounts receivable turnover} = \frac{\text{Net credit sales}}{\text{Average accounts receivable}}$$

This ratio will not be calculated for Toys "R" Us, because it would be clearly inappropriate to do so. All of the sales of Toys "R" Us are for cash, and the company's receivables result from other minor activities and from amounts due from bad checks from customers.

To illustrate how this ratio is calculated, assume the data shown in Exhibit 17-17 for the Steamer Corporation. The average age of the receivables can be determined by dividing the turnover into 365 days. For the Steamer Corporation, the average ages of the receivables are 45.63 and 38.34 days for 1988 and 1987, respectively, so the length of time needed to collect receivables has increased. This is a dangerous trend: The inflow of cash into the company has slowed. Thus it is important for the firm's management to review its credit and operating policies and to try to reverse this trend.

EXHIBIT 17–17

Accounts Receivable
Turnover

STEAMER CORPORATION		
	1988	1987
Net credit sales	$1,200,000	$1,500,000
Accounts receivable, beginning of year	140,000	175,000
Accounts receivable, end of year	160,000	140,000
Average accounts receivable	$ 150,000	$ 157,500
Accounts receivable turnover	8.0	9.52

In summary, short-term creditors provide cash or services to the firm on a short-term basis. Primarily interested in the firm's liquidity and ability to meet its short-term obligations, they focus on the current ratio, the quick ratio, and various turnover ratios.

Exhibit 17-18 describes all the ratios that have been discussed in this chapter. You should keep in mind the limitations of financial statement analysis discussed next.

■ LIMITATIONS OF FINANCIAL STATEMENT ANALYSIS

Before ending the discussion of the techniques of financial statement analysis, it is important to understand the limitations of such analysis and how these limitations can be partially overcome. Naive financial statement users, who do not fully understand the limitations of financial statement analysis, are likely to make substantive judgment errors. Two problems involved in such analysis are (1) that firms use different accounting principles and methods and (2) that it is often difficult to define what industry a firm is really part of.

EXHIBIT 17–18   Summary of Significant Ratios

Ratio	Calculation	Significance
Common and preferred stockholders		
Earnings per share	$\dfrac{\text{Net income less preferred dividend}}{\text{Average number of common shares outstanding}}$	Comparative figure of earnings on a per-share basis
Price-earnings	$\dfrac{\text{Market price per common share}}{\text{Earnings per share}}$	Comparative measure of how the market values the firm's earnings
Dividend yield	$\dfrac{\text{Dividends per share}}{\text{Market price per share}} \times 100$	Measures dividend return to investors
Book value per share	$\dfrac{\text{Common stockholders' equity}}{\text{Number of common shares outstanding}}$	Investors' share of assets at historical cost
Return on total assets	$\dfrac{\text{Net income} + \text{interest expense}}{\text{Average total assets}} \times 100$	Measures profitability of firm and how efficiently assets are employed
Return on common stockholders' equity	$\dfrac{\text{Net income} - \text{preferred dividend}}{\text{Average common stockholders' equity}} \times 100$	Measures profitability of investment to owners
Equity ratio	$\dfrac{\text{Total stockholders' equity}}{\text{Total assets}} \times 100$	Measures proportion of assets supplied by creditors and by owners
Debt ratio	$\dfrac{\text{Total liabilities}}{\text{Total assets}} \times 100$	Same as previous ratio
Profit margin	$\dfrac{\text{Net income}}{\text{Total revenues}} \times 100$	Net income per dollar of revenue
Long-term creditors		
Debt to equity	$\dfrac{\text{Total liabilities}}{\text{Total stockholders' equity}}$	Another measure of debt versus equity financing
Times interest earned	$\dfrac{\text{Income before interest and taxes}}{\text{Interest expense}}$	Ability of firm to meet interest payments

(continued)

| | EXHIBIT 17–18 | (continued) | |

Ratio	Calculation	Significance
Short-term creditors		
Current ratio	$\dfrac{\text{Current assets}}{\text{Current liabilities}}$	Measures short-term liquidity of firm
Quick ratio	$\dfrac{\text{Monetary current assets}}{\text{Current liabilities}}$	Measures ability of firm to meet immediate debt
Inventory turnover	$\dfrac{\text{Cost of goods sold}}{\text{Average inventories}}$	Measures amount of inventory carried and how quickly it moves
Receivables turnover	$\dfrac{\text{Net credit sales}}{\text{Average accounts receivable}}$	Measures amount of accounts receivable relative to sales and how quickly receivables are collected

■ DIFFERENCES IN GENERALLY ACCEPTED ACCOUNTING PRINCIPLES

A firm's management has the right to select among a set of generally accepted accounting principles and methods. Even firms in the same industry select different methods to account for the same event. For example, one firm in the steel industry may use LIFO, and another may use FIFO. Obviously, the financial statements of these two firms, as well as key ratios and relationships based on those statements, will be significantly different. This makes the direct comparison of firms within the same industry difficult.

Careful reading of management's discussion and analysis of operations and the footnotes to the financial statements can partially overcome this problem. For example, Safeway Stores, Inc. used the LIFO inventory method, but its 1985 annual report provided the following information about how the inventories would have been stated if FIFO had been used:

> Had the company valued its inventories using the FIFO method, its current ratio would have been 1.36, 1.42, and 1.35, and working capital would have been $614.5 million, $643.7 million, and $519.9 million at year-ends 1985, 1984, and 1983 respectively.

Thus financial statement analysts could use this data to compare Safeway's performance with those companies in the retail grocery industry that used FIFO (or vice versa).

The footnotes to the financial statements also provide important information concerning the use of accounting principles. Current reporting rules require that a footnote to the financial statement summarize the significant accounting policies used by the company. This is usually the first item in the footnote section (see Footnote 1 in the Toys "R" Us financial statements reproduced in Appendix D for an example). It provides such information about the firm as its basis of consolidation, translation of foreign currencies, and depreciation methods. A sophisticated financial analyst can use this data to make the necessary transformations that allow for meaningful comparisons among firms using different accounting methods.

■ THE INDUSTRY A FIRM BELONGS TO

Using industry norms as a basis for financial statement analysis presupposes being able to define what industry a firm actually is a part of. For companies such as Toys "R" Us or Apple Computer, this is an easy process, because they operate in a well-defined industry. However, many U.S. companies are truly conglomerates that operate in a variety of industries. For example, what industry is ITT in? What industry is U.S. Steel in, now that it owns a large oil subsidiary? These questions are difficult to answer, be-

EXHIBIT 17–19 (continued)

Capital expenditures by industry segments are as follows:

	(in thousands)		
	1986	**1985**	**1984**
Tobacco products	$ 85,411	$ 62,456	$ 63,543
Hardware and security	21,033	16,828	9,171
Distilled beverages	7,280	14,588	16,403
Food products	30,206	18,171	18,410
Office products	28,860	13,635	14,320
Other	80,970	43,811	42,061
Total	$253,760	$169,489	$163,908

	Business by Industry Segments (in millions)					
	1986	**1985**	**1984**	**1983**	**1982**	**1981**
Net sales						
Tobacco products	$5,169.4	$4,390.0	$4,229.0	$4,416.9	$4,196.4	$4,183.1
Hardware and security	679.1	569.3	519.3	462.4	173.5	194.1
Distilled beverages	254.5	249.8	246.4	241.2	227.3	210.7
Food products	532.7	507.0	493.8	479.3	469.9	560.8
Office products	346.9	336.7	335.5	318.5	312.8	255.5
Other	1,487.0	1,255.5	1,171.2	1,175.1	1,125.1	1,134.0
	$8,469.6	$7,308.3	$6,995.2	$7,093.4	$6,505.0	$6,538.2
Operating income						
Tobacco products	$498.6	$519.6	$496.7	$493.5	$464.0	$437.9
Hardware and security	43.0	43.4	48.4	43.8	26.7	38.2
Distilled beverages	35.0	40.2	39.3	36.7	32.6	30.6
Food products	28.1	27.4	28.6	33.2	32.1	35.0
Office products	(12.1)	17.1	33.8	31.3	25.4	38.8
Other	78.6	76.5	72.5	80.6	71.3	68.8
	671.2	724.2	719.3	719.1	652.1	649.3
Financial services	176.1	174.1	172.9	132.1	129.7	134.2
	$847.3	$898.3	$892.2	$851.2	$781.8	$783.5
Identifiable assets						
Tobacco products	$1,692.6	$1,647.5	$1,439.6	$1,620.1	$1,633.1	$1,663.6
Hardware and security	488.1	458.2	422.9	341.9	179.7	204.1
Distilled beverages	252.4	259.5	259.3	245.5	244.6	231.7
Food products	207.7	178.7	174.8	167.2	158.7	242.0
Office products	412.9	427.5	420.3	420.7	411.3	409.3
Other	995.8	760.8	591.4	612.0	566.5	611.9
	$4,049.5	$3,732.2	$3,308.3	$3,407.4	$3,193.9	$3,362.6

	Business by Geographic Areas (in millions)					
Net sales						
United States	$3,322.8	$3,150.0	$3,064.9	$3.048.1	$2,525.2	$2,562.2
Europe	4,912.9	3,930.4	3,704.8	3,826.1	3,828.1	3,844.6
Other	233.9	227.9	225.5	219.2	151.7	131.4
	$8,469.6	$7,308.3	$6,995.2	$7,093.4	$6,505.0	$6,538.2

(continued)

EXHIBIT 17–19   (continued)

	Business by Geographic Areas (in millions)					
Operating income						
United States	$470.3	$551.4	$550.5	$536.0	$486.0	$473.8
Europe	205.2	163.3	156.1	170.9	158.1	163.8
Other	(4.3)	9.5	12.7	12.2	8.0	11.7
	671.2	724.2	719.3	719.1	652.1	649.3
Financial services						
(United States)	176.1	174.1	172.9	132.1	129.7	134.2
	$847.3	$898.3	$892.2	$851.2	$781.8	$783.5
Identifiable assets						
United States	$2,049.1	$2,059.8	$1,995.1	$2,043.1	$1,821.5	$1,876.2
Europe	1,895.6	1,565.7	1,201.0	1,249.6	1,279.1	1,404.0
Other	104.8	106.7	112.2	114.7	93.3	82.4
	$4,049.5	$3,732.2	$3,308.3	$3,407.4	$3,193.9	$3,362.6

SUMMARY OF LEARNING OBJECTIVES

1. Understanding the purposes of financial statement analysis. Present and potential investors and creditors are the primary external users of financial statement information. Financial statement analysis helps these users as well as others to assess the past performance and future prospects of a firm.

2. Sources of financial information. There are a variety of sources of information about public companies. All public companies publish an annual report to shareholders and also prepare several reports to the SEC. The SEC reports include Forms 10-K, 10-Q, and 8-K. There are several external sources of information available to interested individuals. These include general business periodicals as well as specialized trade journals.

3. Techniques of financial analysis. The most common types of financial statement analysis include horizontal, trend, vertical, and ratio analysis. Horizontal and trend analyses are useful in understanding changes in the firm's financial position from year to year as well as changes over several years. Vertical analysis is used to evaluate the relationships within single financial statements. An appropriate total figure in the financial statement is set to 100%, and other items are expressed as a percentage of that figure. Fi-

nally, ratio analysis is a method of expressing relationships among various items on a set of financial statements.

4. Common financial ratios. A number of ratios can be used by financial statement analysts. Groups with particular needs have developed their own ratios. Certain ratios are used by equity holders such as common stockholders, long-term debt holders, and short-term debt holders. These ratios are summarized in Exhibit 17-18.

5. Limitations of financial statement analysis. Although financial statement analysis is very useful, it does have a number of limitations. Firms use different accounting principles, so it is often difficult to compare the financial position and operations of different firms directly. Generally, the first footnote to the financial statements lists the accounting principles used in preparing the financial statements, so this footnote is very important to financial statement users.

Industry norms are often used in financial statement analysis. However, it is often difficult to determine exactly what industry a firm is part of. Again, the segment information contained in the footnotes to the firm's financial statements is helpful in assessing the different parts of the firm's operations.

Beta
Common-dollar statements
Financial statement analysis
Form 8-K
Form 10-K
Form 10-Q

Horizontal analysis
Leverage
Ratio analysis
Trend analysis
Vertical analysis

Following are the financial statements for the Valda Valdes Corporation.

VALDA VALDES CORPORATION
Balance Sheet
December 31, 1990

Assets	1990	1989
Current assets		
Cash	$ 26,000	$ 13,500
Accounts receivable, net	75,000	53,000
Inventory	86,000	67,000
Total current assets	$187,000	$133,500
Property, plant, and equipment		
Land	$120,000	$120,000
Buildings, net	136,000	141,000
Equipment, net	15,200	14,600
Total property, plant, and equipment	$271,200	$275,600
Other assets	$ 25,800	$ 12,400
Total assets	$484,000	$421,500

Equities		
Current liabilities		
Accounts payable	$ 68,000	$ 70,000
Current maturities of long-term debt	3,000	3,000
Wages payable	1,200	1,000
Taxes payable	10,000	8,000
Interest payable	22,800	12,500
Total current liabilities	$105,000	$ 94,500
Long-term liabilities		
Mortgage payable, less current portion above	$150,000	$153,000
Stockholders' equity		
No par common stock, 10,000 shares outstanding	$100,000	$100,000
Retained earnings	129,000	74,000
Total stockholders' equity	$229,000	$174,000
Total equities	$484,000	$421,500

VALDA VALDES CORPORATION
Income Statement
For the Year Ended December 31, 1990

Sales		$1,200,000
Cost of goods sold		768,000
Gross margin on sales		432,000
Operating expenses		
Selling	$200,000	
General and administrative	100,000	300,000
Income before taxes		132,000
Income taxes		57,000
Net income		$ 75,000

ADDITIONAL DATA: **(a)** Dividends issued during the year amounted to $20,000.

(b) Market price per share of common stock at year-end was $34.25.

(c) Included in operating expenses is interest expense of $18,000.

(d) Credit sales for the year amounted to $720,000.

REQUIRED: Calculate the following ratios for 1990:

1. Earnings per share.

2. Price-earnings ratio.

3. Dividend yield ratio.

4. Book value per share.

5. Return on total assets.

6. Return on common stockholders' equity.

7. Equity ratio.

8. Debt ratio.

9. Gross margin percentage.

10. Profit margin percentage.

11. Debt-to-equity ratio.

12. Times interest earned.

13. Current ratio.

14. Quick ratio.

15. Inventory turnover.

16. Accounts receivable turnover.

SOLUTION   **1.** Earnings per share

$$\text{EPS} = \frac{\text{Net income less preferred dividends, if any}}{\text{Weighted average number of common shares outstanding}}$$

$$\$7.50 = \frac{\$75,000}{10,000}$$

2. Price-earnings ratio

$$\text{P-E ratio} = \frac{\text{Market price per common share}}{\text{Earnings per share}}$$

$$4.57 = \frac{\$34.25}{\$ 7.50}$$

3. Dividend yield ratio

$$\text{Dividend yield} = \frac{\text{Dividends per share}}{\text{Market price per share}} \times 100$$

$$5.84\% = \frac{\$ 2.00^*}{\$34.25} \times 100$$

*$20,000 dividends ÷ 10,000 shares.

4. Book value per share

$$\text{Book value per share} = \frac{\text{Total common stockholders' equity}}{\text{Number of common shares outstanding}}$$

$$\$22.90 = \frac{\$229,000}{10,000}$$

5. Return on total assets

$$\text{Return on total assets} = \frac{\text{Net income plus interest expense}}{\text{Average total assets}} \times 100$$

$$20.54\% = \frac{\$75,000 + \$18,000}{(\$484,000 + \$421,500) \div 2} \times 100$$

6. Return on common stockholders' equity

$$\text{Return on common stockholders' equity} = \frac{\text{Net income less preferred dividends}}{\text{Average common stockholders' equity}} \times 100$$

$$37.22\% = \frac{\$75,000}{(\$229,000 + \$174,000) \div 2} \times 100$$

7. Equity ratio

$$\text{Equity ratio} = \frac{\text{Total stockholders' equity}}{\text{Total assets}} \times 100$$

$$47.31\% = \frac{\$229,000}{\$484,000} \times 100$$

8. Debt ratio

$$\text{Debt ratio} = \frac{\text{Total liabilities}}{\text{Total assets}} \times 100$$

$$52.69\% = \frac{\$255,000}{\$484,000} \times 100$$

9. Gross margin percentage

$$\text{Gross margin \%} = \frac{\text{Gross margin}}{\text{Sales}} \times 100$$

$$36\% = \frac{\$432,000}{\$1,200,000} \times 100$$

10. Profit margin percentage

$$\text{Profit margin \%} = \frac{\text{Net income}}{\text{Sales}} \times 100$$

$$6.25\% = \frac{\$75,000}{\$1,200,000} \times 100$$

11. Debt-to-equity ratio

$$\text{Debt-to-equity ratio} = \frac{\text{Total liabilities}}{\text{Total stockholders' equity}}$$

$$1.11 = \frac{\$255,000}{\$229,000}$$

12. Times interest earned

$$\text{Times interest earned} = \frac{\text{Income before interest and taxes}}{\text{Annual interest expense}}$$

$$8.33 = \frac{\$75,000 + \$18,000 + \$57,000}{\$18,000}$$

13. Current ratio

$$\text{Current ratio} = \frac{\text{Current assets}}{\text{Current liabilities}}$$

$$1.78 = \frac{\$187,000}{\$105,000}$$

14. Quick ratio

$$\text{Quick ratio} = \frac{\text{Cash} + \text{marketable securities} + \text{receivables}}{\text{Current liabilities}}$$

$$.96 = \frac{\$26,000 + \$75,000}{\$105,000}$$

15. Inventory turnover

$$\text{Inventory turnover} = \frac{\text{Cost of goods sold}}{\text{Average inventory}}$$

$$10.04 = \frac{\$768,000}{(\$86,000 + \$67,000) \div 2}$$

$$\text{Average days to turn over inventory} = \frac{365 \text{ days}}{10.04} = 36.4 \text{ days}$$

16. Accounts receivable turnover

$$\text{Accounts receivable turnover} = \frac{\text{Credit sales}}{\text{Average accounts receivable}}$$

$$11.25 = \frac{\$720,000}{(\$75,000 + \$53,000) \div 2}$$

$$\text{Average age of accounts receivable} = \frac{365 \text{ days}}{11.25} = 32.4 \text{ days}$$

QUESTIONS

1. Who are the primary users of financial statements? How do they use financial statements, and to what purposes do they use financial statement analysis?

2. How can financial statement users assess the past performance of a firm as well as its future prospects?

3. List and explain the primary reports that are published by publicly held companies.

4. What are the main sections found in most annual reports? Which do you think are most useful?

5. Financial analysts use a number of external sources in evaluating a firm. List and discuss the primary ones.

6. The fact that firms use different generally accepted accounting principles and that it is often difficult to define what industry a firm is part of are often cited as causing limitations in financial statement analysis. Do you agree or not? How can these potential problems be overcome?

7. What does the term *horizontal analysis* refer to? How is it useful in financial statement analysis?

8. Sales for the Olympic Co. during 1990 were $1.5 million. During 1991, sales grew to $1.8 million. What is the percentage change in sales from 1990 to 1991?

9. What does the term *trend analysis* mean? How is it useful in financial statement analysis?

10. Gross margin on sales in 1987 for the Caladonia Corp. was $500,000. In 1989, gross margin on sales was $600,000. If 1987 is the base year with an index of 100, what is the 1989 index?

11. What is vertical analysis and how is it useful in financial statement analysis?

12. Sometimes financial statements that are expressed in percentages are referred to as *common-dollar statements*. What does the term *common dollar* mean, and why are these statements useful?

13. If you were a common shareholder, what ratios would you find most useful in evaluating the company?

14. How are earnings per share and the price-earnings ratio related?

15. Describe the relationship among return on total assets, return on common shareholders' equity, and leverage.

16. A business person whom you know has a very conservative philosophy and feels that all debt is bad. As a result, his firm is primarily financed by stockholders. How do you feel about this financing philosophy?

17. Over the last couple of years, a firm's debt-to-equity ratio has increased. At the same time, the times interest earned ratio has decreased. As a long-term creditor, how do you feel about these trends?

18. Many people consider the current ratio a good measure of a firm's liquidity. Describe this ratio and discuss its strengths and weaknesses as a measure of liquidity.

19. Ratio analysis is the best way to evaluate the strengths and weaknesses of a firm. Do you agree or disagree with this statement? Why?

20. Do you consider accounting to be an asset or a liability?

EXERCISES

E1. Horizontal Analysis. Presented below are condensed balance sheets of the Laguna Sea Corporation.

LAGUNA SEA CORPORATION
Comparative Balance Sheets
December 31

Assets	1991	1990
Current assets	$ 34,212	$ 40,250
Property, plant, and equipment, net	150,000	120,000
Total assets	$184,212	$160,250

Liabilities and Stockholders' Equity

	1991	1990
Current liabilities	$ 27,500	$ 25,000
Long-term liabilities	62,500	50,000
Stockholders' equity	94,212	85,250
Total liabilities and stockholders' equity	$184,212	$160,250

REQUIRED: Determine the dollar and percentage changes in the accounts from 1990 to 1991 and comment on the significance of these changes.

E2. Horizontal Analysis. Comparative income statements of the Sizzler Company follow.

SIZZLER COMPANY
Comparative Income Statements
For the Years Ended December 31

	1991	1990
Sales	$1,365,000	$1,300,000
Cost of goods sold	914,550	845,000
Gross margin on sales	450,450	455,000
Operating expenses	210,000	200,000
Income before taxes	240,450	255,000
Taxes	96,180	102,000
Net income	$ 144,270	$ 153,000

REQUIRED: Determine the dollar and percentage changes in the accounts from 1990 to 1991 and comment on their significance.

E3. Trend Analysis. The following data are taken from the ten-year summary of consolidated financial data of the Coca-Cola Company.

	(in millions)				
	1986	1985	1984	1983	1982
Net operating revenues	$8,669	$7,212	$6,593	$6,154	$5,437
Operating income	1,145	984	990	937	825
Net income	934	678	622	553	494

REQUIRED: **(a)** Assume that 1982 is the base (index 100). Prepare a trend analysis for the Coca-Cola Company. (Round off to two decimal points where appropriate.)

(b) Comment on the trends.

E4. Vertical Analysis. Presented below are the comparative income statements of Silk Purse Publishers, Inc.:

SILK PURSE PUBLISHERS, INC.
Consolidated Statements of Income
(in thousands of dollars except per share data)

	1991	1990	1989
Sales of products and services	$817,797	$676,949	$529,653
Operating expenses			
Costs of products and services sold	388,933	317,636	249,169
Selling, general, and administrative	313,958	270,542	216,820
Total operating expenses	702,891	588,178	465,989
Operating income	114,906	88,771	63,664
Interest (expense), net	(11,003)	(5,234)	(3,259)
Other income (expense), net	(108)	(913)	44
Total other (expense)	(11,111)	(6,147)	(3,215)
Income before income taxes	103,795	82,624	60,449
Income taxes	46,169	37,924	27,371
Income before extraordinary items	57,626	44,700	33,078
Extraordinary items, net of income taxes	1,900	700	—
Net income	$ 59,526	$ 45,400	$ 33,078

(continued)

Earnings per common share			
Income before extraordinary items	$2.51	$2.04	$1.72
Extraordinary items	.08	.03	—
Net income	$2.59	$2.07	$1.72

REQUIRED: **(a)** Prepare a vertical analysis for 1991 and 1990. (Round off to two decimal points where appropriate.)

(b) Comment on the significance of your findings.

E5. Vertical Analysis. Presented below are comparative balance sheets of the King Smith Company.

KING SMITH COMPANY
Comparative Balance Sheets
June 30

Assets	1991	1990
Current assets	$ 50,000	$ 57,000
Property, plant, and equipment, net	200,000	180,000
Total assets	$250,000	$237,000

Liabilities and Stockholders' Equity		
Current liabilities	$ 20,000	$ 25,000
Long-term debt	70,000	60,000
Stockholders' equity	160,000	152,000
Total liabilities and stockholders' equity	$250,000	$237,000

REQUIRED: **(a)** Prepare common-dollar balance sheets for both years. (Round off to two decimal points where appropriate.)

(b) Comment on the significance of these figures and the changes that occurred.

E6. Ratio Analysis—Common and Preferred Shareholders. You have obtained the following data relating to the Summerfeld Corporation for the past two years:

	1990	1989
Earnings per share	$ 2.50	$ 2.40
Market price per share—year-end	20.00	18.00
Dividend per share	1.20	1.00
Net income	37,500	
Interest expense	1,700	
Total assets	500,000	480,000
Stockholders' equity (no preferred stock issued)	300,000	296,000

REQUIRED: Compute the following ratios for 1990 or at the end of 1990:

1. Price-earnings.

2. Dividend yield.

3. Return on total assets.

4. Return on common stockholders' equity.

5. Equity ratio.

6. Debt ratio.

E7. Ratio Analysis—Long-term Creditors. You have obtained the following data from the West Corporation:

	1991	1990
Total assets	$600,000	$550,000
Total liabilities	240,000	192,500
Interest expense	10,000	6,000
Taxes	15,000	12,000
Net income	60,000	49,500

REQUIRED: **(a)** Compute the following ratios for both years:

1. Equity ratio.

2. Debt ratio.

3. Debt-to-equity ratio.

4. Times interest earned.

(b) Comment on the changes that have taken place from 1990 to 1991.

E8. Ratio Analysis—Short-term Creditors and Liquidity Analysis. Comparative balance sheets (unclassified) for the Peterson Company are as follows:

PETERSON COMPANY
Comparative Balance Sheets
December 31

Assets	1991	1990
Cash	$ 28,000	$ 25,000
Current marketable securities	10,000	8,000
Accounts receivable, net	45,000	47,000
Inventories, FIFO cost	82,000	73,000
Supplies	5,000	2,000
Property, plant, and equipment, net	95,000	93,000
Long-term investments and receivables	10,000	12,000
Total assets	$275,000	$260,000

Liabilities and Stockholders' Equity	1991	1990
Accounts payable	$ 40,000	$ 45,000
Current maturities of long-term debt	20,000	17,000
Other accrued payables	12,000	15,000
Long-term debt, less current portion	80,000	100,000
Common stock, $5 par value	100,000	80,000
Retained earnings	23,000	3,000
Total liabilities and stockholders' equity	$275,000	$260,000

ADDITIONAL DATA:

Sales for year, all on credit	$445,000
Cost of goods sold during year	$302,600

REQUIRED: **(a)** For both years, calculate the following ratios:

1. Current ratio.

2. Quick ratio.

3. Receivables turnover and number of days receivables are outstanding (1991 only).

4. Inventory turnover and number of days to turn inventory over (1991 only).

5. Book value per share of common stock.

(b) Explain how the current ratio, the quick ratio, and the inventory turnover ratio would change if the firm had used the LIFO method of inventory costing and prices were rising during both years.

E9. Determining Missing Figures and Analysis. The financial records of the Herbal Tea Company were destroyed in a fire. You were able to gather the following fragmentary data as of year-end:

Cash	$ 50,000
Land	200,000
Plant and equipment, net	300,000
Other accrued liabilities	90,000
Current maturities of long-term debt	16,000
Common stock	300,000
Current ratio	2.5:1
Debt ratio	.48

Net credit sales are $1,200,000, and the receivable turnover ratio is 10. Cost of goods sold for the year is $1,080,000, and the inventory turnover ratio is 4. Turnover ratios are based on year-end data only.

REQUIRED: Prepare a classified balance sheet in good form. You need to determine the balances in the following accounts:

1. Accounts receivable, net.

2. Inventories.

3. Accounts payable.

4. Long-term debt.

5. Retained earnings.

E10. Company Comparisons and Industry Averages. You have obtained the following condensed income statements from the Ace and Beta companies, both in the same industry. Data for the industry average is also provided:

	Ace	Beta	Industry Average
Sales	$955,850	$136,550	100%
Cost of goods sold	573,510	71,006	53
Gross margin on sales	382,340	65,544	47
Operating expenses			
Selling	91,762	9,668	6
General and administrative	61,174	6,718	4
Total operating expenses	152,936	16,386	10
Income before tax	229,404	49,158	37
Income taxes	97,094	10,315	9
Net income	$132,310	$ 38,843	28%

REQUIRED: **(a)** Prepare common-dollar financial statements for the two companies in columnar form. Add a column for the industry averages. Round to whole percentages.

(b) Compare the performance of Ace and Beta with the industry averages. Comment on any significant differences. What areas need improvement?

E11. Differences in Accounting Methods. The Ace Company and the Zeta Company are both retailers of children's toys. The two companies are the same size and similar in their operations. The Ace Company, however, is rather conservative in its accounting policies and thus uses LIFO for inventory costing purposes and sum-of-the-years-digits for depreciation. On the other hand, the Zeta Company uses FIFO and straight-line depreciation. Both companies began business last year, and prices have increased during the year.

REQUIRED: Explain which company will have the higher amount for each of the following ratios. For simplicity, ignore taxes. If you feel that you cannot make a determination, so state.

    1. Quick ratio.

    2. Working capital ratio.

    3. Inventory turnover.

    4. Accounts receivable turnover.

    5. Return on total assets.

    6. Debt to total assets.

    7. Return on stockholders' equity.

E12. Change in Accounting Method. The following note was taken from the 1983 annual report of Wang Laboratories:

> During the year ended June 30, 1983 the Company retroactively adopted a change in accounting treatment for repairable service parts used in the maintenance of customer and internally used equipment. These parts were previously classified as inventories, with usage and provisions for obsolescence recognized as incurred. The new method of accounting results in the classification of service parts as noncurrent assets, with associated costs being depreciated over a period of seven years on a straight line basis. . . . Since the depreciation resulting from the new method is substantially equal to usage and obsolescence recognized under the prior method there is no cumulative effect of the change presented in the statement of consolidated earnings, and the change is not expected to materially affect future results of operations.

REQUIRED: How would each of the following ratios be affected by this change? Explain how you reached your conclusion.

    1. Current ratio.

    2. Asset turnover ratio.

    3. Inventory turnover ratio.

    4. Return on total assets.

    5. Earnings per share.

PROBLEMS

P17-1 Trend Analysis. The information at the top of page 663 is taken from an annual report of the Colgate-Palmolive Company.

REQUIRED: **(a)** Prepare a trend analysis for Colgate-Palmolive, assuming that 1984 is the base (index 100).

    (b) Comment on the results.

	(in millions, except per-share data)				
	1988	**1987**	**1986**	**1985**	**1984**
Net sales	$4,734	$4,365	$3,768	$3,488	$3,415
Income from continuing operations	152	001	115	122	028
Per common share:					
Operating income	$2.22	$0.01	$1.63	$1.55	$0.34
Dividends	1.48	1.39	1.36	1.30	1.28

P17-2 Horizontal and Vertical Analysis. The statements below and on the next page were taken from the 1988 annual report of the Colgate-Palmolive Company.

COLGATE-PALMOLIVE COMPANY
Consolidated Balance Sheet
(in thousands of dollars)

Assets	1988	1987*
Current assets		
Cash and cash equivalents	$ 241,358	$ 51,673
Marketable securities	124,180	46,364
Receivables (less allowance for doubtful accounts of $11,743 and $13,843)	589,253	723,297
Inventories	629,683	753,376
Other current assets	198,315	141,769
Total current assets	1,782,789	1,716,479
Property, plant and equipment, net	1,021,648	1,201,762
Other assets	413,130	309,412
	$3,217,567	$3,227,653

Liabilities and Shareholders' Equity		
Current liabilities		
Notes and loans payable	$ 84,253	$ 192,126
Current portion of long-term debt	21,205	25,024
Accounts payable	489,920	496,521
Accrued income taxes	114,230	68,055
Other accruals	362,247	495,241
Total current liabilities	1,071,855	1,276,967
Long-term debt	674,291	694,130
Deferred income taxes	183,208	126,525
Other liabilities	137,586	188,888
Shareholders' equity		
Preferred stock	12,562	12,562
Common stock (69,069,002 and 68,600,329 shares outstanding)	84,102	83,691
Additional paid-in capital	139,905	126,409
Retained earnings	1,614,664	1,380,339
Cumulative translation adjustments	(225,294)	(184,610)
	1,625,939	1,418,391
Treasury stock, at cost	(475,312)	(477,248)
Total shareholders' equity	1,150,627	941,143
	$3,217,567	$3,227,653

*Not restated for discontinued operations.

COLGATE-PALMOLIVE COMPANY
Consolidated Statement of Income
(in thousands of dollars, except per share amounts)

	1988	1987	1986
Net sales	$4,734,325	$4,365,687	$3,768,698
Cost of sales	2,725,218	2,509,440	2,226,952
Gross profit	2,009,107	1,856,247	1,541,746
Operating expenses and other items			
Marketing and selling	1,242,018	1,179,252	996,267
General and administrative	403,555	390,422	322,960
Hill's service agreement renegotiation expense	59,000	—	—
Provision for restructured operations	—	205,700	—
Interest expense	106,757	75,222	63,572
Interest income	(37,544)	(25,081)	(28,544)
Earnings from equity investments	(14,898)	(9,662)	(8,030)
Total operating expenses and other items	1,758,888	1,815,853	1,346,225
Income from continuing operations before income taxes	250,219	40,394	195,521
Provision (benefit) for income taxes			
Current	68,483	67,473	50,697
Deferred	29,069	(27,965)	29,977
	97,552	39,508	80,674
Income from continuing operations	152,667	886	114,847
Discontinued operations			
Income from discontinued operations, net of income taxes	40,134	53,136	62,618
Gain on disposal of discontinued operations, net of income taxes	125,000	—	—
Net income	$ 317,801	$ 54,022	$ 177,465
Earnings per common share			
Continuing operations	$ 2.22	$ .01	$ 1.63
Discontinued operations	.59	.77	.89
Disposal of discontinued operations	1.83	—	—
Total	$ 4.64	$ .78	$ 2.52
Average number of common shares outstanding (in thousands)	68,381	68,577	70,230

REQUIRED: **(a)** Prepare a schedule showing dollar amount and percentage changes from 1987 to 1988 for the income statement and the balance sheet. (Round percentages to one decimal point.)

(b) Prepare a common-dollar income statement and balance sheet for 1987 and 1988.

(c) Comment on the above statements, including any significant changes or apparent trends.

P17-3 **Ratio Analysis.** This problem asks you to use the data from the Colgate-Palmolive financial statements shown in Problem 17-2 to calculate certain ratios.

REQUIRED: **(a)** Calculate for both years the following ratios:

1. Book value per share of common stock. (Assume that the liquidation value of the preferred stock is the amount recorded on the financial statements.)

2. Equity ratio.

3. Debt ratio.

4. Debt-to-equity ratio.

5. Times interest earned.

6. Current ratio.

7. Quick ratio.

(b) For 1988 only, calculate the following ratios:

1. Return on total assets

2. Return on common stockholders' equity.

3. Inventory turnover.

4. Receivables turnover. (Assume all sales are on credit.)

P17-4 **Ratio Analysis and Accounting Principles.** The following data were obtained from the records of Congress Supply Store at the end of 1991:

Sales (80% on credit)	$2,000,000
Cost of goods sold (LIFO cost)	1,400,000
Average inventory (LIFO cost)	450,000
Average accounts receivable	400,000
Interest expense	30,000
Income taxes (30%)	102,000
Net income	238,000
Average total assets	1,780,000
Average total stockholders' equity	950,000

REQUIRED: **(a)** Determine the following ratios or statistics:

1. Gross margin percentage.

2. Profit margin percentage.

3. Inventory turnover.

4. Debt-to-equity ratio. (Use average figures.)

5. Return on total assets.

6. Return on total stockholders' equity.

(b) Now assume that the company is considering switching to the FIFO method of inventory accounting. The president of the firm tells you that if FIFO had been used, average inventories would have been $600,000 and cost of goods sold would have been $1.2 million. Recompute the above ratios and statistics and comment on the differences.

P17-5 **The Effect of Transactions on Certain Ratios.** The working capital accounts of the Garner Western Ware Store at December 31, 1990 are shown below:

Cash	$ 50,000
Loans receivable	25,000
Accounts receivable, net	85,000
Inventory	150,000
Supplies	10,000
Notes payable	60,000
Accounts payable	50,000
Other accrued liabilities	10,000

During 1991, the company entered into the following transactions:

1. Bonds payable, due in 1996, were issued for $50,000 cash.

2. Additional inventory of $90,000 was purchased on account.

3. A 10% stock dividend previously declared was distributed.

4. Sales of $200,000 were made, of which 60% was on account and the rest was for cash.

5. The cost of the sales in Item 4 was $125,000.

6. Collections on accounts receivable amounted to $150,000.

7. Payments on account were $100,000.

8. Land with a cost of $100,000 was sold for $120,000. $20,000 was received in cash, and a long-term note receivable was received for the remainder.

9. Convertible preferred stock was converted into common.

10. Treasury stock with a cost of $10,000 was purchased.

11. The cash balances in excess of $25,000 were invested in current marketable securities.

REQUIRED: **(a)** Compute the following items at the beginning of the year:

    1. Working capital.

    2. Current ratio.

    3. Quick ratio.

(b) For each of the 1991 transactions, show the effect on working capital, the current ratio, and the quick ratio. Use a table similar to the one below and show whether the effect is an increase, decrease, or none. The first item is done for you.

Transaction	Working Capital	Current Ratio	Quick Ratio
1	Increase	Increase	Increase

P17-6 Completing a Balance Sheet from Incomplete Data. You obtained the following information from the Lost Data Company:

LOST DATA COMPANY
Balance Sheet
December 31, 1991

Assets

Cash	$ 97,500
Accounts receivable	?
Inventory	?
Property, plant, and equipment, net	?
Total assets	$1,400,000

Equities

Accounts payable	$ 300,000
Current maturities of long-term debt	?
Long-term debt	?
Common stock	300,000
Retained earnings	?

You have obtained the following additional information:

1. The current ratio is 2:1.

2. The debt ratio is 60%.

3. The inventory turnover is 6 and cost of goods sold is $1.2 million. The beginning inventory is $190,000.

4. Sales are $2 million, of which 75% is on credit and the rest is for cash. The receivables turnover is 4. Receivables remained constant throughout the year.

REQUIRED: Using the data above, complete the balance sheet.

P17-7 Comparison of Two Companies. Presented below and on pages 668–670 are the financial statements, simplified for analysis purposes, for Lucky Stores, Inc. (below and on page 668), and Safeway Stores, Inc. (pages 669–670), large retail grocery chains.

ADDITIONAL INFORMATION:

Lucky Stores
Dividends per share:

| Common | $1.16 a share (both years) |
| Preferred | Total dividends in both years $1,368,000 |

Market prices per common share at 1985 and 1984 year-end were $25.00 and $17.50, respectively. Inventory method: LIFO.

Safeway Stores
Dividends per share:

| Common | $1.625 (both years) |
| Preferred | 0 |

Market prices per common share at 1985 and 1984 year-end were $36.875 and $29.25, respectively. Inventory method: LIFO.

In addition, you have been able to gather the following selected industry average data:

Current ratio 1.4:1	Gross margin percentage 22.2%
Quick ratio 0.4:1	Profit margin percentage 1.1%
Inventory turnover 13.5	Times interest earned 2.9

REQUIRED:

(a) Using data from Lucky Stores and Safeway Stores, compute the appropriate ratios from Exhibit 17-18 for 1985 and 1984. If an average is required for 1984, use year-end figures only.

(b) Compare the performance of Lucky with that of Safeway.

(c) If you were to make an investment, which stocks, if either, would you buy?

LUCKY STORES, INC.
Consolidated Earnings
Years ended February 2, 1986,
February 3, 1985, and January 29, 1984
(in thousands except per share amounts)

	1985 (52 weeks)	1984 (53 weeks)
Sales	$9,382,282	$9,236,529
Cost of goods sold	7,146,932	7,111,514
Gross margin	2,235,350	2,125,015
Expenses		
Selling, general and administrative	1,951,969	1,836,748
Depreciation and amortization	103,084	87,223
Interest, net of interest income of $8,230, $13,871, and $18,120	32,236	27,627
	2,087,289	1,951,598
Earnings before income taxes	148,061	173,417
Income taxes	61,535	78,786
Net earnings	$ 86,526	$ 94,631
Earnings per common share		
Primary	$ 1.67	$ 1.84
Fully diluted	$ 1.64	$ 1.81

LUCKY STORES, INC.
Consolidated Retained Earnings
Years ended February 2, 1986,
February 3, 1985, and January 29, 1984
(in thousands except per share amounts)

	1985	1984
Beginning of year	$351,025	$316,708
Net earnings	86,526	94,631
Cash dividends		
Preference	(1,368)	(1,370)
Common—$1.16 a share	(59,130)	(58,944)
Amortization of the excess of redemption value over fair value of preference shares	(2,512)	0
End of year	$374,541	$351,025

LUCKY STORES, INC.
Consolidated Balance Sheet
At February 2, 1986 and February 3, 1985 (in thousands)

	1985	1984
Current assets		
Cash, including short-term investments of $45,143 in 1984	$ 12,742	$ 119,406
Receivables	70,381	60,743
Inventories	793,193	688,520
Prepaid expenses and supplies	36,799	29,692
Total current assets	913,115	898,361
Property and equipment at depreciated cost	815,447	660,451
Property under capital leases, less $86,104 and $87,097 accumulated amortization	112,186	123,904
Property under construction	50,041	76,797
Licenses, receivables and other assets	28,724	28,695
Excess of cost over net assets acquired	12,947	13,551
Total assets	$1,932,460	$1,801,759
Current liabilities		
Accounts payable	$ 443,778	$ 404,822
Current portion of long-term and capital lease obligations	14,789	14,205
Income taxes	14,536	26,203
Other taxes	51,824	54,410
Payroll and employee benefits	104,193	93,575
Other accrued liabilities	113,370	84,143
Total current liabilities	742,490	677,358
Long-term obligations	239,701	231,903
Capital lease obligations	140,066	152,466
Deferred income taxes	52,840	56,639
Other deferred liabilities	101,140	56,551
Commitments—see Long-term leases		
Redeemable preference shares,* redemption value $22,914	19,861	17,400
Common shareholders' equity		
Common shares, $1.25 par value; outstanding 51,043 and 50,851 shares	63,804	63,563
Capital in excess of par value of shares issued	198,017	194,854
Retained earnings	374,541	351,025
Total common shareholders' equity	636,362	609,442
Total liabilities and shareholders' equity	$1,932,460	$1,801,759

*By convention, redeemable preferred shares are shown separately outside of the common shareholders' equity section and are not included in the total of common shareholders' equity. They are, however, part of total stockholders' equity.

■ USING THE COMPUTER

P17-8   Using the financial statements from Safeway Stores, Inc. (below and on page 670) determine the dollar changes and the percentage changes from 1984 to 1985 through the use of an electronic spreadsheet.

SAFEWAY STORES, INCORPORATED
Consolidated Statements of Income
For the 52 weeks ended December 28, 1985, and December 29, 1984
(in thousands, except per share amounts)

	1985	1984
Sales	$19,650,542	$19,642,201
Cost of sales	14,872,247	15,004,547
Gross profit	4,778,295	4,637,654
Operating and administrative expenses	4,350,635	4,214,443
Operating profit	427,660	423,211
Interest expense	(172,906)	(151,263)
Gain on sale of foreign operations	49,046	
Other income, net	49,816	26,874
Income before provision for income taxes	353,616	298,822
Provision for income taxes	122,316	113,811
Net income	$ 231,300	$ 185,011
Net income per share	$ 3.83	$ 3.12

SAFEWAY STORES, INCORPORATED
Consolidated Balance Sheets
As of December 28, 1985, and December 29, 1984
(in thousands, except per share amounts)

Assets	1985	1984
Current assets		
Cash	$ 54,593	$ 49,179
Short-term investments	170,021	25,263
Receivables	111,870	105,166
Merchandise inventories		
FIFO cost	1,878,281	1,881,525
Less LIFO reductions	312,715	318,281
	1,565,566	1,563,244
Prepaid expenses and other current assets	124,431	118,537
Total current assets	2,026,481	1,861,389
Property		
Land	247,769	236,876
Buildings	431,410	345,001
Leasehold improvements	600,091	557,504
Fixtures and equipment	2,164,072	2,023,914
Transport equipment	186,831	186,485
Property under capital leases	1,010,277	1,144,409
	4,640,450	4,494,189
Less accumulated depreciation and amortization	2,003,752	1,894,333
Total property, net	2,636,698	2,599,856
Investments in affiliated companies	122,195	27,251
Other assets	55,237	48,733
Total assets	$4,840,611	$4,537,229

(continued)

Liabilities and Stockholders' Equity	1985	1984
Current liabilities		
Notes payable	$ 80,848	$ 44,913
Current obligations under capital leases	43,396	45,427
Current maturities of notes and debentures	52,049	48,274
Accounts payable	1,151,426	1,038,268
Accrued salaries and wages	167,798	167,739
Other accrued expenses	201,357	170,905
Income taxes payable	27,827	20,431
Total current liabilities	1,724,701	1,535,957
Long-term debt		
Obligations under capital leases	625,551	746,178
Notes and debentures	689,470	646,532
Total long-term debt	1,315,021	1,392,710
Accrued claims and other liabilities	178,275	139,539
Total liabilities	3,217,997	3,068,206
Stockholders' equity		
Common stock—$1.66⅔ par value		
Authorized 150,000, 150,000 and 75,000 shares		
Outstanding 60,846, 59,854 and 58,760 shares	101,411	99,756
Additional paid-in capital	273,776	246,964
Cumulative translation adjustments	(164,035)	(155,994)
Retained earnings	1,411,462	1,278,297
Total stockholders' equity	1,622,614	1,469,023
Total liabilities and stockholders' equity	$4,840,611	$4,537,229

■ UNDERSTANDING FINANCIAL STATEMENTS

P17-9   The following was excerpted from an article appearing in the January 17, 1984 edition of *The Wall Street Journal* (p. 10):

> The recovering economy helped push General Electric Co.'s fourth-quarter earnings up 10% despite a slight sales decline. . . .
>
> Full-year profit rose 11% to $2.02 billion or $4.45 a share, from $1.82 or $4.00 a share earned in 1982 despite only a 1% gain in sales, to $26.8 billion.

REQUIRED: **(a)** In your opinion, what factors would cause profit to rise 11% when sales rose only 1%?

(b) General Electric common stock closed at 57⅛ on January 16, 1984. Determine the price-earnings ratio at this date.

(c) As of January 16, 1984, General Electric had a dividend yield of 3.5%. What is the amount of dividends per share issued by General Electric?

(d) Determine General Electric's profit margin ratio in 1983.

(e) Determine General Electric's profit margin ratio in 1982.

■ FINANCIAL DECISION CASE

P17-10   Professor Holder has contacted several individuals about starting a company to produce and market a super floppy disk that he invented. Professor Holder estimates that it will take about $1 million to finance the new company. One of his associates, an accounting professor, has suggested three ways of raising the needed funds:

1. All $1 million will be raised through the issuance of common stock to Holder and his associates.

2. Half ($500,000) will be raised through the issuance of common stock to Holder and his associates, and the other half will be raised by issuing preferred stock with a stated dividend rate of 12% to a venture capitalist.

3. Half ($500,000) will be raised through the issuance of common stock to Holder and his associates, and the other half will be raised by issuing convertible bonds with a stated interest rate of 12%.

REQUIRED: **(a)** Assuming that the company can earn $300,000 before interest and taxes and the tax rate is 40%, determine

1. the net income accruing to common shareholders, and

2. the return on common shareholders' equity

under each of the three methods. Assume all stocks and/or bonds are outstanding all year.

(b) Repeat your analysis, now assuming that the firm will be able to earn $100,000 before interest and taxes and the tax rate remains at 40%.

(c) Make recommendations to Professor Holder.

ACCOUNTING FOR CHANGES IN PRICES AND PROBLEMS RELATED TO MULTINATIONAL CORPORATIONS

LEARNING OBJECTIVES

After studying this chapter, you should be able to:

1. Differentiate between general and specific price-level changes.
2. List the problems that occur when historical-cost financial statements are not adjusted for changing prices.
3. State the requirements of FASB Statements 33, 82, and 89.
4. State the concepts behind financial statements adjusted for changes in price levels.
5. Show how foreign currency transactions are accounted for.
6. State the basic procedures involved in translating foreign currency statements to U.S. dollars.
7. Discuss efforts to harmonize international accounting standards.

■ ACCOUNTING FOR CHANGING PRICES

During the 1970s and the early 1980s, inflation was a persistent problem for the U.S. economy. Unfortunately, double-digit inflation became common. These inflation rates distorted normal business patterns as well as personal purchasing and saving patterns. Although inflation rates have become more moderate, about 2–4% in recent years, the potential for increasing inflation rates is still in the U.S. economy.

Not only does inflation affect the aggregate U.S. economy, but it can have substantial effects on the reported profits of specific companies. For example, Exhibit 18-1 shows part of a 1985 financial statement for Safeway Stores, Inc. The exhibit makes clear that changing price levels can have a material effect on earnings that are reported on a historical-cost basis. What is meant by changing prices, and why are earnings adjusted for changes in specific prices different from historical-cost earnings? What did Safeway really earn in 1985, and which of the income figures is most useful to present and potential investors and creditors? Such questions have caused considerable debate both within and outside of the accounting profession; they are the subject of the next part of this chapter.

EXHIBIT 18–1

	(in millions)	
	As Reported in the Statement of Income	Adjusted for Changes in Specific Prices (Current Costs)
Sales	$19,650	$19,650
Cost of sales	14,872	14,903
Other expenses, net	4,425	4,461
Income (loss) before provision for income taxes	353	286
Provision for taxes	122	122
Net income	$ 231	$ 164

■ DIFFERENT TYPES OF CHANGING PRICES

Inflation has become a common word in our daily language. Yet accountants do not speak of accounting for inflation; they speak of accounting for changing prices. This is because *changing prices* is a broader term that considers the two types of price changes that affect any economy: general price-level changes and specific price-level changes. The two changes affect historical-cost statements in different ways, so it is important to understand the distinction between them.

General Price-level Changes

General price-level changes are those that affect the ability of the dollar to purchase a variety of goods and services. As the general price level increases, the purchasing power of the dollar declines. Thus, when people talk about inflation, they are talking about a rise in the general price level and a corresponding decline in the purchasing power of the dollar. Conversely, deflation occurs when the general price level declines and the purchasing power of the dollar increases. During the early part of 1986, the U.S. economy actually enjoyed a period of deflation due to low oil prices and a sluggish economy.

General price-level changes are measured by such indexes as the Consumer Price Index for All Urban Consumers (CPI-U) and the Gross National Product Deflator. These indexes take a representative basket of goods and services and compare its current year's price to its base year's price. This ratio of the current year's price to the base year's price forms the index that measures the weighted-average general price changes in the economy. Exhibit 18-2 shows the actual CPI-U from 1960 through 1987. Note the large increases in the late 1970s and early 1980s and the relatively small increases after that.

EXHIBIT 18–2

Average Consumer Price Index for All Urban Consumers

1960	88.7	1974	147.7
1961	89.6	1975	161.2
1962	90.6	1976	170.5
1963	91.7	1977	181.5
1964	92.9	1978	195.4
1965	94.5	1979	217.4
1966	97.2	1980	246.8
1967	100.0 (base year)	1981	272.4
1968	104.2	1982	289.1
1969	109.8	1983	298.4
1970	116.3	1984	311.1
1971	121.3	1985	322.2
1972	125.3	1986	328.4
1973	133.1	1987	340.4

Exhibit 18-3 shows how a general price level index is calculated. The five commodities in the illustration are assumed to be a representative basket of goods and services, and their prices at the beginning of 1990 are compared with their prices at the end of 1990. Because the beginning of 1990 is assumed to be the base year, the index at that time is 100, and the index at the end of the year is 102. Thus there has been a 2% increase in the general price level. This means that dollars at the end of 1990 will buy 2% less than the same number of dollars at the beginning of 1990.

EXHIBIT 18–3

Calculation of General Price-level Changes

Commodity	January 1, 1990	December 31, 1990	Percentage Change in Individual Items
Diesel oil—gallon	$1.10	$1.05	−4.5
Butter—pound	1.80	1.88	+4.4
Hamburger—pound	2.40	2.60	+8.3
Wheat—bushel	1.28	1.20	−6.3
Cotton fabrics—yard	1.93	1.95	+1.0
	$8.51	$8.68	

Price index at December 31, 1990
(Assuming January 1, 1990 index is 100) $\dfrac{\$8.68}{\$8.51} \times 100 = 102$

Specific Price-level Changes

Specific price-level changes reflect the change in the value of a specific good or service vis-à-vis other goods or services. Specific price changes reflect an adjustment in the price of a particular item, such as a building or a gallon of gasoline, rather than the average change in prices of all items in the economy. In addition to the effects of general inflation, specific price changes are caused by market dynamics and distortions such as decreased supply or increased demand or both.

Specific prices are measured by looking at the change in the current cost or value of the individual item under consideration. Exhibit 18-3 also calculated the specific price changes of the individual items in the general index, ranging from a 6.3% decrease to an 8.3% increase. The U.S. government's Bureau of Labor Statistics publishes a number of specific price indexes, as do other public and private agencies.

The Relationship between General and Specific Price Changes

As Exhibit 18-3 also shows, price changes for all goods and services in the economy do not move together. In this example, the prices of diesel oil and wheat fell while the prices of other commodities rose. This situation occurs all the time; for example, the prices of small calculators and personal computers have decreased while the general price level has continued to increase.

To illustrate this concept further, assume that an acre of land is purchased at the beginning of the year for $10,000. At the end of the year, the current value of the land is determined to be $15,000. Further, the general price level increased 15% during the year. Thus, of the $5,000 increase, $1,500 ($10,000 × .15) is due to an increase in the general price level, and the remaining $3,500 is due to a specific price increase above the general price-level increase. In this example, both price changes moved in the same direction, but this is not always the case.

■ PROBLEMS WITH FINANCIAL STATEMENTS NOT ADJUSTED FOR PRICE CHANGES

Traditional financial statements in the United States are based on historical costs and are not adjusted for either general or specific prices. The FASB refers to such statements as *historical cost/nominal dollar statements*. For ease of discussion, let's refer to them as *historical-cost statements*. In a period of fluctuating prices, many users question the relevance of these statements. As the Safeway data in Exhibit 18-1 showed, earnings adjusted for specific price changes can be significantly different from earnings reported on a historical-cost basis.

General Price-level Changes Ignored

When statements are not adjusted for general price-level changes, dollars of different purchasing power are aggregated, because assets such as land, buildings, and inventories were all purchased at different times and thus with dollars of different purchasing power. Many observers feel that when this occurs, the dollar value of total assets on the balance sheet loses its significance. Furthermore, it is difficult to measure a firm's performance in relation to that of other firms when price levels are changing, because general price-level changes do not affect all firms in the same way.

Even more important, historical-cost financial statements do not measure **purchasing-power gains or losses**, which result from holding monetary assets (cash and rights to receive cash) and monetary liabilities (all liabilities other than those requiring the performance of a service). In a period of inflation, a firm that holds net monetary assets suffers a purchasing-power loss. For example, if you started the year with $5,000 in cash and held those dollars all year while the general price level rose 10%, you suffered a $500 purchasing-power loss. This occurs because you would need $5,500 at the end of the year to purchase the same goods as $5,000 had purchased at the beginning of the year, but you still have only $5,000 on hand. Conversely, a firm in a net liability position will incur a gain in a period of inflation because it pays back a fixed amount of dollars whose purchasing power is declining. This gain or loss is not measured by historical-cost statements, so income can be over- or understated. These gains or losses can be significant. For example, during 1985, Safeway showed a $103 million purchasing-power gain.

If financial statements are adjusted for general price-level changes, they can overcome some of the limitations of historical-cost statements. The FASB refers to such statements as *historical cost/constant purchasing power dollar statements*. (Again, for ease of discussion, they will be referred to here as **constant-dollar statements**.) Such statements are prepared by adjusting historical dollars to dollars of the same or constant purchasing power, using a general price index such as the CPI-U. Although complete constant-dollar statements were never required by the FASB, certain supplementary constant-dollar disclosures were required. After experimenting with these disclosures, the FASB decided in late 1984 to eliminate all constant-dollar disclosures other than the reporting of purchasing-power gains and losses. In late 1986, even these disclosures become voluntary.

Specific Price-level Changes Ignored

Historical-cost statements are based on the realization principle (discussed in Chapter 3): that assets and liabilities are recorded at their historical cost and are not adjusted until an exchange has taken place. As a result, current values are not reflected in the financial statements, and revenue is generally not recognized until a sale takes place.

To illustrate, assume that one item of inventory is purchased at a cost of $100. This inventory is held until the end of the year, at which time its replacement cost increases to $125. At the beginning of the next year, the item is sold for $135. Assuming that the firm entered into no other transactions, a traditional income statement would show no income for the first year but would show income of $35 ($135 − $100) in the second year. A number of accounting theorists argue that this is misleading, because the increase in value was not reported when it occurred. These observers say that a holding gain of $25 occurred during the first year, as the inventory increased in value from $100 to $125. In the second year, an operating gain of $10 occurred, when the inventory with a current value of $125 was sold for $135. Thus the total income over the two-year period is still $35, but it is allocated as a $25 holding gain in Year 1 and a $10 operating gain in Year 2. Further, at the end of the first year, the inventory is recorded on the balance sheet at $125, its current cost.

The FASB refers to financial statements adjusted for specific price changes as *current cost/nominal dollar*. For ease of discussion, they will be referred to here as **current-cost statements**. Although the FASB does not require firms to prepare complete current-cost statements, it does suggest certain current-cost disclosures, which are discussed later.

Statements Adjusted for Both General and Specific Prices

Some say that to reflect economic reality properly, financial statements should be adjusted for both specific and general price-level changes. Such statements, referred to as *current cost/constant purchasing power dollar statements* by the FASB, combine the attributes of both current-cost and constant-dollar statements.

■ FASB STATEMENTS 33, 82, AND 89

After years of controversy and debate, the FASB decided that the effects of changing prices were significant enough to require some recognition in financial statements. In September 1979, the FASB issued Statement 33, which required large firms to disclose on a supplemental basis certain financial information adjusted for changing prices. After studying the effects of this statement for five years, the Board issued Statement 82, which reduced the supplemental disclosures required under Statement 33. Recently, the FASB issued Statement 89, which reduced these requirements further by making all disclosures voluntary. Specifically, Statement 89 encourages the voluntary disclosure of the following items:

1. Information on income from continuing operations for the current fiscal year on a current-cost basis.

2. The purchasing-power gain or loss on net monetary items for the current fiscal year.

3. The current-cost amounts of inventory and property, plant, and equipment at the end of the current fiscal year.

4. Increases or decreases for the current fiscal year in the current-cost amounts of inventory and of property, plant, and equipment, net of inflation.

5. A summary of selected data for the five most recent fiscal years.[1]

However, most firms provide only descriptive information relating to changing prices. Exhibit 18-4, part of management's discussion in the 1988 annual report of Coca-Cola Company, is typical.

EXHIBIT 18–4

IMPACT OF INFLATION AND CHANGING PRICES

Although inflation has slowed in the United States in recent years, it is still a factor in many of the Company's markets around the world and the Company continues to seek ways to cope with its impact. Foreign currency exchange rates tend to reflect over time the difference in relative inflation rates. The Company's financial statements, prepared in accordance with generally accepted accounting principles, reflect the historical cost rather than the current or replacement cost of assets required to maintain productive capability. Income from continuing operations determined under the specific price changes method (current cost) would be less than reported in the primary financial statements.

During periods of inflation, monetary assets, such as cash and accounts receivable, lose purchasing power while monetary liabilities, such as accounts payable and debt, gain purchasing power. The Company has benefited from its net monetary liability position in recent years resulting in net purchasing power gains. These gains do not represent an increase in funds available for distribution to shareholders and do not necessarily imply that incurring more debt would be beneficial to the Company.

In general, management believes that the Company is able to adjust prices to compensate for increasing costs and to generate sufficient cash flow to maintain its productive capability.

■ THE THEORY BEHIND CONSTANT-DOLLAR ACCOUNTING

The primary objective of constant-dollar accounting is to prepare financial statements that are adjusted for general price-level changes. This means that the items on the financial statements are stated in dollars of the same purchasing power. In all other respects, the historical-cost model is maintained. However, the measuring unit becomes a constant dollar rather than the nominal dollar. The traditional realization principle is not changed. That is, historical costs are adjusted to dollars of equal purchasing power, but they are not adjusted for current costs. Take the example previously given, of land purchased for $10,000. During the year the inflation rate was 15% and the current cost of the land at year-end was $15,000. On a constant-dollar statement, the land would be shown at a constant-dollar amount of $11,500, or $10,000 + ($10,000 × .15), rather than its current cost of $15,000 or its historical cost of $10,000.

The primary constant-dollar disclosure that is currently suggested by the FASB is purchasing-power gain or loss. The first step in determining such gain or loss is to distinguish between monetary and nonmonetary assets and liabilities. As previously noted, monetary assets and liabilities are subject to purchasing-power gains and losses. However, nonmonetary assets and liabilities do not represent fixed claims on dollars; as the general price level increases, nonmonetary items retain their purchasing power.

To illustrate the concepts involved, assume that the Instant Gold Company was organized on December 31, 1990. At that time, the inventory, land, and buildings were purchased. Business commenced January 2, 1991. The financial statements reflecting the first year of operations (1991) are presented in Exhibits 18-5 (balance sheet) and 18-6 (income statement). Other relevant data are presented in Exhibit 18-7.

[1]FASB Statement No. 89, *Financial Reporting and Changing Prices* (Stamford, Conn.: FASB, December 1986), par. 7, 11, and 12.

EXHIBIT 18-5

INSTANT GOLD COMPANY Historical-cost Balance Sheet December 31						
	1991	**1990**			**1991**	**1990**
Assets			Liabilities and owner's equity			
Cash	$ 6,500	$ 3,000	Accounts payable		$ 10,000	$ 0
Accounts receivable	8,000	0	Stockholders' equity		90,000	82,000
Inventory	12,000	4,000				
Land	30,000	30,000				
Buildings, net	43,500	45,000	Total liabilities and			
Total assets	$100,000	$82,000	stockholders' equity		$100,000	$82,000

EXHIBIT 18-6

INSTANT GOLD COMPANY Historical-cost Income Statement For the Year Ended December 31, 1991		
Sales		$100,000
Cost of goods sold		
Beginning inventory	$ 4,000	
Purchases	68,000	
Cost of goods available for sale	72,000	
Less: Ending inventory	12,000	
Cost of goods sold		60,000
Gross margin on sales		40,000
Operating expenses		
Selling and general and administrative, excluding depreciation	$28,500	
Depreciation	$ 1,500	30,000
Net income		$ 10,000

EXHIBIT 18-7

INSTANT GOLD COMPANY Other Data		
Relevant General Price-level Indexes		
Date	**Index**	**Event, Where Appropriate**
December 31, 1990	150	Company formed; inventory, land, and buildings purchased
Average for 1991*	165	Used for monetary asset and liability inflows and outflows
December 31, 1991	175	Date company paid dividends
Inflation rate	16.67%[†]	

*The average for the year is a monthly average and does not necessarily equal the average of the beginning and ending price indices.

[†] $\dfrac{(175 - 150)}{150} = 16.67\%$

The monetary assets on Instant Gold's balance sheet are cash and receivables. The monetary liability is the accounts payable. In order to determine the purchasing-power gain or loss, monetary assets and liabilities must be restated to dollars of current purchasing power. This is accomplished by multiplying the historical cost of these items by a conversion factor—the current year's price index divided by the index that existed when the monetary asset or liability was recorded in the accounts. Specifically, the formula is:

$$\text{Constant-dollar amount} = \text{Historical cost} \times \frac{\text{Index at end of the year}}{\text{Index when the item was acquired}}$$

Exhibit 18-8 is a schedule showing how the purchasing-power loss of $713 suffered by the Instant Gold Company during 1991 is determined. The following procedures are used in calculating the loss:

1. Restate the net monetary assets or liabilities at the beginning of the year to their value in terms of year-end purchasing power. This is done by multiplying the conversion factor of 175/150 by the net monetary asset position at the beginning of the year. The denominator is 150, because these assets were on hand at the beginning of the year, and they are assumed to be held all year.

2. Restate all transactions during the year that increased monetary items so that they reflect year-end value. These items will include sales and the proceeds from the sale of other assets, if any. In this situation, only sales increased monetary items, and they are assumed to take place evenly throughout the year, so the conversion factor is 175/165.[2] This restated figure is added to the amount calculated in Step 1.

EXHIBIT 18–8

INSTANT GOLD COMPANY Schedule of Purchasing-power Loss For the Year Ended December 31, 1991		
Net monetary assets, 1/1/91	$ 3,000[a] × 175/150 =	$ 3,500*
Add: Sales	100,000 × 175/165 =	106,061
	$103,000	$109,561
Less		
Purchases	$ 68,000 × 175/165 =	$ 72,121
Selling and general administrative expenses	28,500 × 175/165 =	$ 30,227
Dividends	2,000 × 175/175 =	2,000
	$ 98,500	$104,348
Net monetary position, 12/31/91, restated		5,213
Net monetary position, 12/31/91, actual	4,500[b]	4,500
Purchasing-power loss		(713)

*Rounded to whole dollars where appropriate.

[a]Net monetary position, 1/1/91

Cash	$3,000

[b]Net monetary position, 12/31/91

Cash	$ 6,500
Receivables	8,000
	14,500
Less: Accounts payable	10,000
	$ 4,500

[2]It is important to note that all sales, whether for cash or on account, increase net monetary assets, because both cash and receivables are monetary items.

3. Restate all transactions that decreased monetary items so that they reflect year-end values. These items are subtracted from the total in Step 2. Included are purchases, selling and administrative expenses, and taxes. They are restated using the conversion factor, 175/165, because they are assumed to take place evenly throughout the year.

In this case, dividends must also be subtracted. However, no restatement is necessary because they were paid on December 31, 1991. Depreciation expense is ignored, because it does not affect any monetary items. That is, the depreciation entry affects only two nonmonetary accounts, Depreciation Expense (Stockholders' Equity) and Accumulated Depreciation. Only the purchases component of cost of goods sold is adjusted, because this amount represents a net monetary asset outflow in the current period.

4. Subtract the excess of monetary assets or liabilities based on actual historical costs from the figure in Step 3 to arrive at a purchasing-power gain or loss.

A $713 loss occurred because, in order to maintain its purchasing power, the Instant Gold Company needed to have net monetary assets of $5,213 at the end of the year. Since there was only $4,500 of net monetary assets on December 31, 1991, the company suffered a loss of $713 ($5,213 − $4,500).

In this example, a loss occurred because the firm held net monetary assets in a period of inflation. In reality, however, a gain or a loss may occur, depending on the firm's particular monetary position and the rate and direction of general price-level changes. Exhibit 18-9 illustrates when a purchasing-power gain or loss results.

EXHIBIT 18–9

| | Actual Monetary Position | |
Restated Amount	Net Assets	Net Liability
Exceeds actual	Loss	Gain
Less than actual	Gain	Loss

■ INTERPRETING PURCHASING-POWER GAINS AND LOSSES

The Instant Gold Company suffered a $713 purchasing-power loss due to the effect of general price-level changes or inflation upon the purchasing power of its net monetary assets. This purchasing-power loss is in addition to the results of the firm's operations computed on either a historical-cost or constant-dollar basis. In effect, if a firm had no revenues or expenses but held net monetary assets during a period of inflation, it would suffer a purchasing-power loss.

On the other hand, the information provided by the management of the Coca-Cola Company in Exhibit 18-4 indicates that the company had a purchasing-power gain. As noted in that report, "the Company has benefited from its net monetary liability position in recent years resulting in net purchasing power gains." Management goes on to note that "These gains do not represent an increase in funds available for distribution to shareholders and do not necessarily imply that incurring more debt would be beneficial to the Company."

■ CURRENT-COST FINANCIAL STATEMENTS

Current-value accounting represents a departure from historical-cost accounting in that the attribute being measured is current value rather than historical cost, whether or not adjusted for general price-level changes. In this context, when accountants speak of current value they generally mean current cost.

Current cost is the current replacement cost of an asset in its current condition with a similar asset. Current replacement cost measurements can be difficult to obtain for operational assets in which the value of the service potential of the asset rather than the value of the asset itself is being measured. Nevertheless, in most circumstances, the FASB uses current cost to measure current value. The FASB suggests the use of specific price indexes, current-price lists, or appraisals in determining current costs.

■ THE THEORY BEHIND CURRENT-COST FINANCIAL STATEMENTS

To illustrate the basic theory behind current-cost financial statements, let's return to an example previously given, in which an item of inventory was purchased during Year 1 for $100. At the end of the year, the item's current cost increased to $125. An unrealized holding gain of $25 is calculated as follows:

Current cost	$125
Less: Historical cost	100
Unrealized holding gain	$ 25

Under current-cost accounting, the inventory on the balance sheet at the end of the year is shown as $125. The $25 holding gain is shown as a separate component of current-cost net income.

When the inventory is sold in January of the next year for $135, operating income of $10 is reported, calculated as follows:

Sale	$135
Less: Current cost of inventory	125
Operating income	$ 10

Under historical-cost accounting, income of $35 ($135 − $100) is reported in the second year. Note that the $35 figure is equal to the $25 unrealized holding gain plus the $10 operating profit. Proponents of current-cost accounting argue that because it takes $125 to replace the item of inventory just sold, $10 is the real operating profit. This is the amount that remains after the company has maintained its capital in terms of productive capacity, because $25 of the historical-cost profit must be reinvested in inventory if the firm is to remain a going concern.

■ PREPARING CURRENT-COST STATEMENTS

Preparing current-cost statements involves a number of complex procedures that are beyond the scope of an introductory accounting course. Exhibit 18-10 shows a current-cost balance sheet and an income statement for the Instant Gold Company. Since the FASB requires certain current-cost disclosures, the subsections that follow discuss how they are prepared.

EXHIBIT 18–10

INSTANT GOLD COMPANY
Current-cost Balance Sheet
December 31, 1991

Assets		Liabilities and Owner's Equity	
Cash	$ 6,500	Accounts payable	$ 10,000
Accounts receivable	8,000	Stockholders' equity	94,400
Inventory	13,500		
Land	30,000		
Building, net	46,400	Total liabilities and	
Total assets	$104,400	owner's equity	$104,400

The Current-cost Balance Sheet

A current-cost balance sheet lists all the accounts at their current cost. In the Instant Gold example, it is assumed that the only items whose current costs differ from their historical costs are the inventory and the building. The current cost of the inventory is $13,500, and the gross current cost of the building before depreciation is $48,000. By the end of 1991, one year's depreciation has been taken; on a current-cost basis, it equals $1,600 ($48,000 ÷ 30 years).[3] This assumes a 30-year life, no salvage value, and straight-line depreciation. Therefore the net current cost at December 31, 1991 is $46,400, or $48,000 − $1,600. The Capital account supplies the amount needed to balance the balance sheet.

The Current-cost Income Statement

A current-cost income statement for the Instant Gold Company is shown in Exhibit 18-11. Net operating income of $7,400 is equal to sales less all expenses at current cost. In the Instant Gold Company example, only cost of goods sold and depreciation expense are different on a current-cost basis. Cost of goods sold on a current-cost basis is assumed to be $62,500, and current-cost depreciation is $1,600, as just calculated. The $7,400 net operating income represents the income available to the company after maintaining its productive capacity. This is the figure that the FASB suggests be disclosed on a supplemental basis.

EXHIBIT 18–11

INSTANT GOLD COMPANY Current-cost Income Statement For the Year Ended December 31, 1991		
Sales		$100,000
Cost of goods sold		62,500
Current-cost gross margin		37,500
Operating expenses		
Selling, general, and administrative	$28,500	
Depreciation	1,600	30,100
Net operating income		$ 7,400

Consistent with FASB disclosures, the income statement in Exhibit 18-11 does not include unrealized holding gains or losses (the increase or decrease in the current value of assets and liabilities still on hand). Instead, they are indirectly included in the Stockholders' Equity account, since the number in this account is the amount needed to balance the balance sheet. Some accountants argue that these unrealized gains and losses should be included in that income.

■ INTERPRETING CURRENT-COST STATEMENTS

The current-cost model rests on a particular theory of capital maintenance. The purpose of current-cost accounting is to maintain capital in terms of the firm's productive capacity—that is, the ability of the firm to continue to produce goods and services. As a result, income is not earned until the firm's productive capacity at the end of the period is at least as great as it was at the beginning of the period.

---

[3] In reality, the calculation of current-cost depreciation is quite complex. For example, the FASB argues that the expense should be based on the asset's average current cost for the year. For simplicity, this example calculated depreciation expense on the year-end current cost.

Referring to the Safeway example (Exhibit 18-1), net income on a historical-cost basis is $231 million, whereas on a current-cost basis, the net income is only $164 million. The causes of this difference are the excess of current-cost depreciation and costs of goods sold over historical-cost depreciation and cost of goods sold. Essentially, these figures indicate that Safeway has been able to earn enough income to maintain its productive capacity, but only by $164 million. Considering that Safeway paid over $98 million in dividends during 1985, many would argue that its productive capacity actually increased by only $66 million.

■ CURRENT-COST/CONSTANT-DOLLAR STATEMENTS

Complete current-cost/constant-dollar statements can also be prepared. The advantage of such statements is that they combine the benefits of both current-cost and constant-dollar statements. To illustrate the complete preparation of these statements is beyond the scope of an introductory course, but a simple example can illustrate the concept behind current-cost/constant-dollar statements.

In a previous example, it was assumed that an item of inventory was purchased in Year 1 for $100. At the end of the year, the item's current cost increased to $125. Now assume that the general price level increased 4% during that period. In this case, the holding gain, net of inflation, is only $21, calculated as follows:

Current cost	$125
Historical cost adjusted for 4% inflation ($100 × 1.04)	104
Holding gain, net of inflation	$ 21

In effect, $4 of the original holding gain of $25 is the result of inflation and does not represent real income available to the firm to maintain its productive capacity.

The FASB suggests only limited current-cost/constant-dollar disclosures. Under the present rules, firms are encouraged to disclose the increase in the current cost of inventories and property net of the effect of inflation. Using the above data, the firm would report a $21 increase in the current cost of its inventory net of the $4 effect of inflation.

■ ACCOUNTING PROBLEMS RELATED TO MULTINATIONAL CORPORATIONS

Since World War II, there has been an unprecedented growth in the number of U.S. corporations doing business abroad. These foreign operations range from occasional import/export activities to the establishment of worldwide production and sales activities. In fact, many of the largest U.S. corporations can be classified as multinational or transnational organizations. For example, in 1988, 61% of Coca-Cola's revenues and 73% of its operating income came from non-U.S. sources.

Multinational corporations face a number of accounting problems. The two issues that have caused the most controversy are accounting for **foreign currency transactions** and translating foreign currency statements to U.S. dollar statements. These issues, as well as attempts at the harmonization of international accounting standards, are discussed in this part of the chapter.

■ EXCHANGE RATES

Accounting for foreign currency transactions and foreign currency financial statements involves the need to translate the currency of one country into that of another. In the case of U.S. firms doing business abroad, this means translating foreign currencies into U.S. dollars. Translation is accomplished by applying an **exchange rate** (the rate at which one currency can be exchanged for another) to the foreign currency that is to be translated into U.S. dollars. For example, assume that an individual has 5,000 British pounds and wishes to exchange them for U.S. dollars. If the current exchange rate is £1.00 = $1.20, the individual would receive $6,000, or £5,000 × 1.20.

Exchange rates change daily, depending upon the supply and demand for particular currencies. The supply and demand are affected by inflation rates, interest rates, and other factors in individual countries. Exhibit 18-12 expresses several foreign currencies in U.S. dollars as of April 5, 1985, October 2, 1986, and February 17, 1989. The exhibit shows the dramatic decrease in the value of the U.S. dollar that took place between 1985 and 1989. That is, as the dollar decreased, strong foreign currencies became more valuable. For example, the British pound increased in value from $1.23 in April 1985 to $1.72 in February 1989. As will become apparent, accounting for foreign currency transactions and foreign currency financial statements is complicated by the fact that currency values continuously change.

| **EXHIBIT 18–12** | **U.S. Dollar Equivalent** | | |
| Exchange Rate Fluctuations | | | |
Currency	April 5, 1985	October 2, 1986	February 17, 1989
British pound	$1.23	$1.45	$1.72
Canadian dollar	.73	.72	.84
West German mark	.32	.49	.54
Japanese yen	.0040	.0065	.008

■ ACCOUNTING FOR FOREIGN CURRENCY TRANSACTIONS

When a U.S. firm buys and sells its goods and services abroad, it can do business in either U.S. dollars or a foreign currency. If the transaction is carried out in U.S. dollars (and U.S. dollars are received in payment or made in payment), no accounting problems arise. The entire transaction is recorded in U.S. dollars at the time of sale or purchase. For example, assume that the Kwon International Co. sells 100 computers to Mishka, Ltd., a West German company. Each computer is sold for $1,000, and payment is to be made in U.S. dollars. The journal entries to record the sale and the subsequent cash collection are:

Accounts Receivable, Mishka, Ltd.	100,000	
Sales		100,000
To record sale of 100 computers at $1,000 each, payable in U.S. dollars.		
Cash	100,000	
Accounts Receivable, Mishka, Ltd.		100,000
To record collection from Mishka, Ltd.		

Foreign purchases payable in U.S. dollars are treated in a similar manner: The purchase and the payable are recorded at the agreed-upon U.S. price and dollars. When the subsequent payment is made in U.S. dollars, Accounts Payable is debited, and Cash is credited.

In many cases, however, the transaction is denominated in the foreign currency. That is, a U.S. firm makes a sale to an overseas firm and agrees to accept payment in the foreign currency. Conversely, a purchase is made from an overseas firm, and payment must be made in the foreign currency. In this situation, an exchange gain or loss will occur if the exchange rate changes between the time the sale or purchase is made and the receivable or payable is liquidated in the foreign currency. This gain or loss must be recorded in the financial statements of the U.S. company making the sale or purchase. Further, if the transaction has not been completed at a balance sheet date, the firm must record an unrealized gain or loss on any changes in currency values.

To illustrate, assume that the Imke Company purchases £200,000 of goods on April 2 from its major British supplier. Payment in British pounds is due July 10. The firm prepares quarterly financial statements on June 30. The following exchange rates apply:

	U.S. dollars per British pound	Event
April 2	$1.25	Purchase
June 30	1.22	Financial statements prepared
July 10	1.23	Payment on account

On April 2, the Imke Company records the purchase and the account payable in the U.S. dollar equivalent of $250,000, or £200,000 × $1.25. The following entry is made:

Purchases	250,000	
Accounts Payable		250,000
To record purchase of goods at current exchange rate of $1.25.		

On June 30, the firm prepares its quarterly financial statements. Because the transaction is still open, the Imke Company must account for changes in exchange rates since the transaction was first recorded. In this case, the British pound decreased in value and is now worth only $1.22. If the Imke Company had to settle the contract on June 30, it would have to pay only $244,000, or £200,000 × $1.22. Thus the firm must record an exchange gain of $6,000, or £200,000 × ($1.25 − $1.22). To record the exchange gain, the payable is adjusted downward. However, the Purchases account is not adjusted. The credit is recorded in a separate income account, Exchange Gains and Losses. The following journal entry is made at June 30:

Accounts Payable	6,000	
Exchange Gains and Losses		6,000
To adjust liability account to current exchange rate of $1.22.		

On July 10, the Imke Company settles its liability by making a payment to its British supplier in British pounds. However, in the interim since June 30, the pound has increased in value. On July 10, the pound is currently worth $1.23, an increase of $.01. In order to satisfy this liability, the firm will need $246,000, or £200,000 × $1.23. However, the liability had been reduced to $244,000 (or $250,000 less the debit of $6,000 on June 30). As a result, the firm has suffered a $2,000 exchange loss in the period June 30 to July 10. The following journal entry is made to record this loss:

July 10	Accounts Payable	244,000	
	Exchange Gains and Losses	2,000	
	Cash		246,000
	To settle liability on July 10 and record exchange loss.		

The result of all these transactions is to record a purchase of $250,000 and a net exchange gain of $4,000, or $6,000 exchange gain less the $2,000 exchange loss. Many firms believe that the unrealized gain on June 30 should not be recorded. They feel that large currency fluctuations can distort quarterly earnings, even though by the end of the year transaction gains and losses may net out to a rather immaterial figure. However, others note that recording these transactions at their current exchange rates better reflects economic reality.

Accounting for sales denominated in a foreign currency follows the same pattern. However, Accounts Receivable and Sales are involved rather than Accounts Payable and Purchases.

■ FOREIGN CURRENCY TRANSLATION

Financial statements prepared by U.S. multinationals for distribution in the United States must be prepared according to U.S. generally accepted accounting principles and must be denominated in U.S. dollars. U.S. multinational firms conduct their business in many countries, and the host country's currency is often used as a basis for the operations in that country. For example, the French subsidiary of a U.S. firm is likely to keep its books in French francs. When this subsidiary and others in different countries are combined in the preparation of consolidated financial statements, all currencies must be translated to U.S. dollars.

Foreign currency translation means that one currency is restated in terms of another currency. For example, assume that the Land account on the French subsidiary's books is recorded at 1,000,000 French francs. When these statements are consolidated, the Land account must be restated to U.S. dollars. Assuming that the appropriate exchange rate is one French franc to $.10, the land would be shown at $100,000, or F1,000,000 × $.10.

There has been considerable controversy as to what exchange rates should be used and how the resulting accounting gain or loss from changes in exchange rates should be handled. In 1981, the FASB issued Statement 52, which requires a dual approach. For foreign subsidiaries whose operations are fairly well self-contained in the host country and which conduct most of their operations in the foreign currency, the FASB requires that all balance sheet items be translated at the current exchange rate at the date of the financial statements. Income statement items are translated at the average exchange rate for the period. This is referred to as the **current-rate method**. Further, any resulting exchange gains and losses from statement translation can be accumulated in a special stockholders' equity account, thus bypassing the income statement. Note, however, that gains and losses from foreign currency transactions are still shown on the income statement.

Some foreign subsidiaries are really just an extension of the parent company's operations. Most of their operations are conducted in U.S. dollars. For these companies, the FASB requires a different translation method. Monetary assets and liabilities are translated at current rates, whereas nonmonetary assets and liabilities are translated at the rates prevailing when the particular item was acquired. Income statement items are translated at the average exchange rate for the period. This is called the **temporal method**. In contrast to the translation method previously described, translation gains and losses on translating the subsidiary's statements go directly to the income statement.

Foreign Currency Translation Example

Because the first method is the most prevalent, a brief illustration will show how foreign currency statements are translated when a subsidiary is a self-contained unit operating in the host country and does most of its business in the host country's currency. Thus the current-rate method is used.

The Michele Corporation is a 100% owned French subsidiary of Dumfies, Inc., a U.S. multinational. Exhibit 18-13 presents a worksheet translating Michele Corporation's financial statement from French francs to U.S. dollars. At year-end, one French

EXHIBIT 18–13

DUMFIES, INC. Worksheet December 31, 1991			
Accounts	**French Francs**	**Exchange Rate**	**U.S. Dollars**
Balance Sheet			
Cash	50,000	.10	5,000
Accounts receivable, net	125,000	.10	12,500
Inventory	100,000	.10	10,000
Building, net	200,000	.10	20,000
Land	50,000	.10	5,000
Total assets	525,000		52,500
Accounts payable	35,000	.10	3,500
Notes payable	65,000	.10	6,500
Common stock	100,000	.25	25,000
Retained earnings	325,000		45,000
Cumulative translation adjustment			(27,500)
Total liabilities and stockholders' equity	525,000		52,500
Income Statement			
Sales	700,000	.12	84,000
Cost of goods sold	500,000	.12	60,000
Selling expenses	80,000	.12	9,600
General and administrative expenses	50,000	.12	6,000
Total expenses	630,000		75,600
Net income	70,000		8,400

franc equaled $.10, and the average for the year was $.12. When the subsidiary was formed and the stock issued, the exchange rate was $.25.

As shown on the worksheet, all balance sheet accounts other than common stock and retained earnings are translated at the exchange rate in effect on December 31. Retained earnings cannot be translated, because it represents many items that have been translated in the past at several different rates. It is assumed that the retained earnings at January 1 in U.S. dollars are $36,600. When the income of $8,400 is added to the beginning balance of $36,600, the ending balance of $45,000 in retained earnings is obtained. This example assumes that no dividends have been declared.

The cumulative translation adjustment is a debit of $27,500; this is the amount needed to make the liabilities and stockholders' equity equal the total assets. It is a cumulative figure that represents the net translation gains and losses from all previous periods as well as the current period.

■ INTERPRETING TRANSLATION GAINS AND LOSSES

Translation gains and losses occur when exchange rates fluctuate. In 1985, the dollar began to depreciate against most major currencies, and this depreciation accelerated from 1986 through 1988. When this occurs, firms are likely to incur a translation gain. For example, the 1988 annual report of Coca-Cola Company included the information shown in Exhibit 18-14. The report indicated that translation adjustments increased stockholders' equity significantly in 1986 and 1987, and had minor effects in 1988.

EXHIBIT 18-14

INTERNATIONAL OPERATIONS

The Company distributes its products in more than 160 countries and uses approximately 40 functional currencies. The U.S. dollar is used as the functional currency in countries considered to have hyperinflationary economies, such as Brazil and Mexico. In 1986, the Company recorded a provision for $45 million related to the Company's disinvestment from South Africa.

Approximately 76 percent of total operating income in 1988 was generated outside the United States. Management estimates that the average annual exchange rates of selected key foreign hard currencies compared to the U.S. dollar increased by an average of 10 percent and 16 percent in 1988 and 1987, respectively. Percentage increases (decreases) in average exchange rates relative to the U.S. dollar for several of the selected foreign currencies are as follows:

	1988	1987	1986
Australia	12%	5%	(4%)
Germany	2%	20%	34%
Italy	(1%)	15%	28%
Japan	12%	16%	41%
United Kingdom	9%	11%	13%

Exchange effects (net gains or (losses) on foreign currency transactions and translation of balance sheet accounts for operations in countries for which the U.S. dollar serves as the functional currency) were $(13) million in 1988, $35 million in 1987 and $18 million in 1986. Such amounts are included in other income in the consolidated statements of income.

■ INTERNATIONAL ACCOUNTING STANDARDS

As previously noted, accounting concepts in a particular country are related to that country's social, political, and economic systems. As a result, there are significant differences between accounting concepts in the United States and those in other countries. Nonetheless, present and potential investors and creditors need to compare firms that are based in various countries. Sophisticated individuals often invest in securities of non-U.S. firms. However, differences in accounting practices make it difficult to compare the results of operations and the financial position of a firm that follows generally accepted accounting principles of the United States with those of a firm that follows accounting principles of another country.

To overcome these problems the international accounting community has attempted to harmonize accounting standards. Harmonization, however, does not imply standardization. Harmonization allows different accounting information to be communicated to various users, whereas standardization implies the communication of the same information in the same manner to all users. In a broad sense, harmonization makes it possible to have compatible reporting standards among countries without requiring all countries to adopt the same standards.

Over the last 50 years, several international groups have looked at the issue of harmonization of accounting standards. The charge of the **International Accounting Standards Committee (IASC)**, created in 1973, is to develop basic accounting standards and to promote the worldwide acceptance and observance of these standards. Following a procedure similar to that of the FASB, the IASC issues international accounting standards. As of mid-1989, the IASC had issued 26 standards.

The IASC has had only an indirect effect on the external reporting practices of U.S. multinationals. The American Institute of CPAs (AICPA), for example, has pledged its best efforts to gain acceptance of IASC standards. Yet the FASB, not the AICPA, sets U.S. accounting standards, and this body has done little to harmonize its standards with those of the IASC. U.S. firms are bound by FASB and not IASC standards and are not presently required to disclose whatever differences exist between the two sets of standards. However, it should be noted that there are not many significant differences between the two sets of standards.

In 1976, the **International Federation of Accountants (IFAC)** was formed. Accounting bodies in various countries are eligible for membership in the IFAC. The broad objective of the IFAC is the development and enhancement of a coordinated worldwide accounting profession with harmonized standards. The IFAC is essentially a coordinating body of professional accounting organizations and does not have the responsibility for setting international accounting standards.

The ultimate benefit of accounting harmonization to present and potential investors and multinational firms depends to a large extent on what standards eventually evolve. If these standards are broad in nature and help to improve international disclosures, they can improve the accounting practices of multinational firms. However, if international standards evolve as detailed principles that are in conflict with many national requirements, they will not meet with acceptance. The current efforts appear to be taking the former approach and thus can serve as an integrating force in world business.

SUMMARY OF LEARNING OBJECTIVES

1. **The difference between general and specific price changes.** General price-level changes affect the ability of the dollar to purchase a variety of goods and services; such changes are measured by such indexes as the CPI-U. Specific price levels reflect the change in the value of a specific good or service vis-à-vis other goods or services. Specific price-level changes are measured by looking at the change in the current or value of an individual item.

2. **Accounting for changing prices.** Traditional financial statements are based on historical costs. However, in a period of changing prices, such statements no longer present all the relevant information informed users need to make decisions concerning resource allocation. Alternative ways of accounting for changing prices are as follows:

Type of Price Change	Accounting Alternatives Available
None or slight	Historical-cost accounting
General	Historical-cost/constant-dollar accounting
Specific	Current-cost accounting
General and specific	Current-cost/constant-dollar accounting

3. **The requirements of FASB Statements 33, 82, and 89.** The FASB position regarding accounting for changing prices has evolved over a number of years. Disclosures that were once required are now only voluntary. Voluntary disclosures include purchasing-power gain or loss and income from operations on a current-cost basis.

4. **The basic procedures involved in accounting for changing prices.** The primary constant-dollar disclosure that is presently required by the FASB is purchasing-power gain or loss. In order to determine purchasing-power gain or loss, monetary assets and liabilities must be restated to dollars of current purchasing power. Monetary assets or liabilities based on historical costs are subtracted from the restated amount to arrive at the purchasing-power gain or loss.

On a current-cost balance sheet, all items other than stockholders' equity are shown at their current cost. A current-cost income statement is prepared by subtracting expenses at their current cost from revenues recognized during the period.

5. **Accounting for foreign currency transactions.** Foreign currency transactions occur when a firm makes sales or purchases that are denominated in a foreign currency. These transactions are originally recorded in U.S. dollars, based on the exchange rate at the date of the transaction. When the transaction is settled (or at a balance sheet date prior to settlement), the firm must recognize a gain or loss due to any changes in the exchange rate. These gains and losses go directly to the income statement.

6. **Accounting for foreign currency translation.** Statements of foreign subsidiaries of U.S. companies must be translated to U.S. dollars when consolidated with the U.S. parent. In most cases, the current-rate method is used; balance sheet items are translated at the rate in effect at the balance sheet date, and income statement items are translated at the average rate for the period. Resulting translation gains and losses do not affect current period's income but are a direct adjustment to stockholders' equity.

7. The harmonization of accounting standards. In recent years, there has been an attempt by the international accounting profession to harmonize accounting standards. The two most important groups in this regard are the International Accounting Standards Committee and the International Federation of Accountants.

KEY TERMS

Constant-dollar statements
Current cost
Current-cost statements
Current-rate method
Exchange rate
Foreign currency transaction
Foreign currency translation

General price-level changes
International Accounting Standards Committee
International Federation of Accountants
Purchasing-power gains and losses
Specific price-level changes
Temporal method

PROBLEMS FOR YOUR REVIEW

A. The historical-cost income statement for Nikolai's Shoe Store follows:

NIKOLAI'S SHOE STORE
Historical–cost Income Statement
For the Year Ended December 31, 1990

Sales		$400,000
Cost of goods sold		
Beginning inventory	$ 30,000	
Purchases	270,000	
Goods available for sale	300,000	
Ending inventory	40,000	260,000
Gross margin on sales		140,000
Operating expenses		
Selling and general and administrative	55,000	
Depreciation	5,000	60,000
Income before taxes		80,000
Taxes		32,000
Net income		$ 48,000

ADDITIONAL DATA: **1.** Relevant price indexes:

Date	Index	Event
January 1, 1990	130	
Average for 1990	140	
September 30, 1990	145	Date dividends paid
December 31, 1990	150	

2. The corporation declared and paid dividends of $5,000 on September 30, 1990.

3. The firm held a net monetary asset position of $5,000 on January 1, 1990. All items affecting the position are described in the information on the previous page. (*Hint:* The net monetary asset position at 12/31/90 is $43,000.)

4. Unless otherwise indicated, assume that all items of income and expense took place evenly throughout the year.

REQUIRED: Prepare a schedule computing a purchasing-power gain or loss. Round off to whole dollars where appropriate.

SOLUTION

NIKOLAI'S SHOE STORE
Schedule of Purchasing-power Gain or Loss
For the Year Ended December 31, 1990

Net monetary position 1/1/90	$ 5,000 × 150/130[a] =	$ 5,769
Increases		
Sales	400,000 × 150/140 =	428,571
	$405,000	$434,340
Decreases[b]		
Purchases	$270,000 × 150/140 =	$289,286
Selling, general, and		
administrative expense	55,000 × 150/140 =	58,929
Taxes	32,000 × 150/140 =	34,286
Dividends[c]	5,000 × 150/145 =	5,172
	$362,000	$387,673
		46,667
Net monetary position 12/31/90	$ 43,000	43,000
Purchasing-power loss		($ 3,667)

[a] Beginning of year index; items are held all year.

[b] Depreciation not included, as it does not affect monetary item.

[c] September 30, 1990 index used, as this is when dividends were issued. All other items adjusted using 1990 average index.

B. The All American Company purchased a laser from the Canada Co., for $100,000 Canadian. The purchase was made on September 21, when the exchange rate was $.75 per Canadian dollar. Payment was made on October 15, when the exchange rate was $.70 per Canadian dollar. No interim financial statements were prepared. Make the journal entries to record the purchase and payment of the laser. Record the laser in an equipment account.

SOLUTION

Sept. 21	Equipment	75,000	
	Accounts Payable		75,000
	To record purchase of equipment when exchange rate equaled $.75.		
	$100,000 Canadian × $.75 = $75,000.		
Oct.15	Accounts Payable	75,000	
	Exchange Gains and Losses		5,000
	Cash		70,000
	To record payment of $70,000 and exchange gain of $5,000.		

Accounts Payable

Cash payment required: $100,000 Canadian × $.70

Exchange Gain:	$75,000	Accounts Payable
	70,000	Cash paid
	$ 5,000	Gain

QUESTIONS

1. Distinguish between general price-level changes and specific price-level changes. Why is it important to make this distinction when accounting for changing prices?

2. What do people mean by *inflation*? Name two common indexes used to measure inflation.

3. How are specific price-level changes measured?

4. Define the following terms:
   (a) Monetary assets.
   (b) Monetary liabilities.
   (c) Constant-dollar accounting.
   (d) Purchasing-power gain or loss.

5. Financial statements that are not adjusted for changing prices are called *historical cost/nominal dollar statements*. Some individuals contend that these statements are no longer relevant for decision makers. What are the reasons for this contention?

6. What are the basic provisions of FASB Statement No. 33? What changes were made by FASB Statements No. 82 and 89? What is the current status of disclosures related to changing prices?

7. At the beginning of the year, the Lynch Co. purchased a downtown office building for $1 million. At the end of the year, the building was appraised at $1,150,000. During the year, the inflation rate was 8%. Determine the amount of price increase due to inflation and the amount due to the specific price change.

8. What are the basic theoretical differences between current-cost accounting and current-cost/constant-dollar accounting?

9. For many large U.S. companies, the difference between

historical cost and current cost or constant-dollar cost of goods sold is not as great as the difference in historical-cost depreciation and the current-cost and constant-dollar measures of depreciation. Why do you think that this is the case?

10. Name an industry, besides those mentioned in the text, in which firms are likely to have a large purchasing-power gain. Name an industry in which firms are likely to incur large purchasing-power losses.

11. What is a foreign currency transaction? How must firms account for such transactions?

12. On April 15, the Smoothe Company sold some computer chips to an English company, agreeing to take English pounds in full payment. The price was £50,000. At the time of the sale, the exchange rate was one pound for $1.20. When the Smoothe Company received payment from the English company, one pound equaled $1.23. Determine the amount of the exchange gain or loss the Smoothe Company should recognize.

13. Why must foreign currency statements of U.S. subsidiaries operating abroad be translated to U.S. dollars?

14. Briefly describe the translation method required for foreign subsidiaries whose operations are well contained in the host country and which conduct most of their business in a foreign currency.

15. What does harmonization of accounting standards mean? Do you think it is feasible?

16. Describe the functions of the International Accounting Standards Committee and the International Federation of Accountants.

17. Do you consider accounting to be an asset or liability?

EXERCISES

E1. Accounting for Changing Prices. During 1991, the Prudential Plaza Company purchased a plot of land for $100,000. At the end of 1991, the land was appraised at $160,000. During the year, the general price level rose 12%. How would the land be listed on the December 31, 1991 balance sheet under each of the following methods?
   (a) Historical-cost.
   (b) Constant-dollar.
   (c) Current-cost.

E2. Determining a Price Index. As an accountant in the cost accounting department of Shop Here Markets, you are asked by the controller to determine the effect of inflation on the market's products, based on a representative basket of groceries. You have gathered the following data:

	Prices	
Item	**January 1**	**December 31**
Butter (pound)	$1.70	$1.79
Hamburger (pound)	1.65	1.60
Lettuce (head)	.40	.60
Diapers (dozen)	2.35	2.59
Coffee (pound)	2.20	2.14
Milk (gallon)	1.05	1.05

REQUIRED: **(a)** Determine the December 31 price index for the market, assuming that the January 1 index equals 100.

(b) What does this new price index mean when some prices are rising, some are falling, and some remain stable?

E3. Purchasing-power Gain or Loss. The Hernandez Company was formed at the beginning of 1990. Cash of $100,000 and computer equipment with a fair market value of $500,000 were contributed by the owner to the company. The company spent all of 1990 in start-up preparations and did not actually begin sales until 1991. The only transaction that occurred in 1990 was a $55,000 bank loan the firm received on July 1. At the beginning of 1990, the consumer price index was 100; it was 110 on July 1; and 120 at year-end. Determine the purchasing-power gain or loss incurred by Hernandez during the year. (Round to whole dollars.)

E4. Calculating a Purchasing-power Gain or Loss. The Pao Corporation was formed several years ago. The president of the company is concerned about how the recent high rates of inflation have affected the company. She provides you with the financial data shown below and asks you to prepare a schedule calculating the firm's purchasing-power gain or loss.

THE PAO CORPORATION
Historical-cost Income and Retained Earnings Statement
For the Year Ended December 31, 1990

Sales		$320,000
Cost of goods sold		
Beginning inventory	$ 20,000	
Purchases	280,000	
Goods available for sale	300,000	
Less ending inventory	60,000	240,000
Gross margin on sales		$ 80,000
Operating expenses, except depreciation	$ 50,000	
Depreciation	10,000	60,000
Income before taxes		$ 20,000
Taxes		6,000
Net income		$ 14,000
Beginning retained earnings		80,000
		$ 94,000
Dividends		8,000
Ending retained earnings		$ 86,000

ADDITIONAL DATA: **(a)** Relevant price indexes:

January 1, 1990	125
Average for the year	130
December 31, 1990	135

(b) The dividend was declared and paid at the end of the year.

(c) All other items were earned or incurred evenly throughout the year.

(d) Net monetary asset position:

January 1, 1990	$50,000
December 31, 1990	26,000

REQUIRED: Prepare the schedule calculating purchasing-power gain or loss. (Round to whole dollars where appropriate.)

E5. Purchasing-power Gains and Losses. The following selected accounts were taken from the records of Wingit Company:

Beginning inventory	$12,000	Sales	$50,000
Salaries expense	16,000	Depreciation expense	4,000
Sales returns	2,000	Purchases	30,000
Dividends	1,000	Rent expense	1,500
Ending inventory	14,000		

In addition, the company purchased a plot of land for $50,000 cash during the year.

REQUIRED: Which of these accounts would be involved in the computation of the purchasing-power gain or loss of the Wingit Company? Why?

E6. Current-cost Income Statements. The Beta Byte Company began operations at the beginning of 1990. At that time, the firm purchased 2,000 bytes, its main inventory item, at a cost of $20 per unit. Also at that time, the firm purchased all of its equipment at a cost of $20,000. All the equipment has an estimated useful life of ten years with no salvage value, and the firm uses the straight-line method of depreciation. During the year, the firm sold 1,400 bytes at $35 per unit. In addition, you have been able to gather the following data:

(a) The current cost of goods sold is $25 per unit.

(b) The current cost of the equipment is $22,000. This is the amount on which current-cost depreciation should be calculated.

(c) Other operating expenses totaled $2,000.

REQUIRED: Prepare a current-cost income statement for the year ended December 31, 1990. Do not include the unrealized increase in the value of the equipment in net income.

E7. Current-cost Balance Sheet. The following trial balance was prepared from the records of the Falk Company at December 31, 1990:

Account	Debit	Credit
Cash	$ 150,000	
Accounts receivable	190,000	
Inventory	250,000	
Plant and equipment, net	450,000	
Other assets	40,000	
Accounts payable		$ 200,000
Bank loan payable		100,000
E. Falk, capital		780,000
Totals	$1,080,000	$1,080,000

You have been able to determine that the items at the top of the next page had the fair market values shown at December 31, 1990:

Inventory	$275,000
Plant and equipment, net	510,000
Other assets	30,000

All other items have a fair market value equal to their recorded amounts.

REQUIRED: Prepare in good form a current-cost balance sheet at December 31, 1990.

E8. Current-cost/Constant-dollar Accounting. The Alberto Realty Co. purchased a plot of land for speculation at the beginning of 1990. The purchase price was $500,000. At the end of the year, the land was appraised at $600,000. Also during that period, the general price level rose 5%.

REQUIRED: **(a)** Determine the holding gain, net of inflation, during 1990.

(b) At what amount would the land be listed on December 31, 1990 current-cost/constant-dollar balance sheet?

E9. Foreign Currency Transactions. The Lawrence Radiation Company purchased some specially made equipment from the Liexor Corporation, a Swiss firm. The purchase was made on November 12, when one Swiss franc equaled $.40. Payment of 500,000 Swiss francs was due on December 15. When payment was made, one Swiss franc equaled $.38.

REQUIRED: Make the journal entries to record the purchase on November 12 and the payment on December 15.

E10. Foreign Currency Transactions. On December 18, the Woo Import Company, a U.S. company, purchased goods for resale from its primary Japanese supplier. The total cost, payable in yen, was Y3,000,000. Payment is due January 30. The following exchange rates apply:

Date	$ per yen
December 18	$.0035
December 31	.0040
January 30	.0038

REQUIRED: **(a)** Make the required journal entries on the books of the Woo Import Company to record these transactions. The firm closes its books each December 31.

(b) How should the exchange gains and losses be reported on the books of the Woo Import Company?

E11. Translating Financial Statements. The Hamilton Company's chief financial officer provided the following data relative to certain account balances of its foreign subsidiary:

Account	Translated at Current Rates	Translated at Historical Rates
Cash	$ 100,000	$ 105,000
Inventory	700,000	750,000
Plant and equipment	900,000	890,000
Sales	3,500,000*	3,600,000
Common stock	500,000	450,000

*Represents average for the year.

REQUIRED: Assuming that the subsidiary's operations are self-contained and that it conducts most of its business in the local currency, state at what amount each of the accounts should be translated.

PROBLEMS

P18-1 **Constant-dollar Accounting.** At the beginning of 1990, Dennis Chambliss decided to open his own CPA firm after working many years with a national firm. Presented below is his firm's comparative balance sheet for January 2, 1991 and December 31, 1991, as well as a condensed income statement for the year then ended.

DENNIS CHAMBLISS, CPA, INC.
Comparative Balance Sheet

	December 31, 1991	January 2, 1991
Assets		
Cash	$ 30,000	$ 40,000
Accounts receivable	60,000	0
Supplies	5,000	5,000
Furniture and equipment, net	50,000	55,000
Total assets	$145,000	$100,000
Equities		
Bank loan payable	$ 20,000	$ 30,000
Accounts payable	25,000	0
Capital stock	70,000	70,000
Retained earnings	30,000	0
Total equities	$145,000	$100,000

DENNIS CHAMBLISS, CPA, INC.
Income Statement
For the Year Ended December 31, 1991

Revenues from accounting services		$200,000
Expenses		
Operating expenses other than depreciation	$90,000	
Depreciation	5,000	
Taxes	55,000	150,000
Net income		$ 50,000

Dennis is concerned about how inflation may be affecting his practice and asks you to prepare a schedule determining the purchasing-power gain or loss for the year. He provides you with the additional following data:

1. During 1991, the price level increased evenly from 100 to 120, with the average for the year being 110.

2. Dennis issued himself a dividend of $20,000 on December 31.

3. All revenues earned and expenses (except for depreciation) were incurred evenly throughout the year.

REQUIRED: **(a)** Prepare a schedule computing the purchasing-power gain or loss for the year.

(b) Explain to Dennis how the 20% inflation rate has affected his business.

P18-2 **Determining Purchasing-power Gains and Losses.** As the treasurer for the Muffin Company, you were asked to prepare a schedule determining the firm's purchasing-power gain or loss. You have the following historical-cost statement and the data listed below it.

MUFFIN COMPANY

Historical-cost Income Statement

For the Year Ended December 31, 1991

Sales		$300,000
Cost of goods sold		
Beginning inventory	$ 75,000	
Net purchases	250,000	
Goods available for sale	325,000	
Ending inventory	125,000	
Cost of goods sold		200,000
Gross margin on sales		$100,000
Operating expenses		
Selling, general, and administrative	$ 35,000	
Depreciation	20,000	55,000
Income before taxes		$ 45,000
Taxes		20,000
Net income		$ 25,000

You have gathered the following additional data relative to corporate events and general price indexes:

	Price Index
December 31, 1990	140
September 30, 1990—purchase of land for $50,000	155
December 31, 1991	160
Average for 1991	150

The firm's net monetary position:

December 31, 1990	$200,000
December 31, 1991	145,000

Finally, assume that sales and expenses other than the cost of goods sold and depreciation were earned or incurred evenly throughout the year.

REQUIRED: Determine the purchasing-power gain or loss for the year. (Round off to whole dollars where appropriate.)

P18-3 **Current-cost Financial Statements.** Rose Florist has just completed its first year of operations at the end of 1990. Due to the excess demand over supply, there is a tendency for the cost of flowers to increase faster than the general price index. The owner of the florist shop was concerned about the effects of specific price-level changes in the flower business. You are asked to prepare current-cost financial statements. The historical-cost financial statements are provided for you.

ROSE FLORIST
Historical-cost Balance Sheet
As of December 31, 1990

Assets		Equities	
Cash	$ 30,000	Bank loan payable	$ 20,000
Accounts receivable, net	20,000	Accounts payable	10,000
Inventory	10,000	Stockholders' equity	70,000
Furniture and fixtures, net	40,000		
Total assets	$100,000	Total equities	$100,000

ROSE FLORIST
Historical-cost Income Statement
For the Year Ended
December 31, 1990

Sales	$150,000
Cost of goods sold	80,000
Gross margin on sales	70,000
Operating expenses	30,000
Net income	$ 40,000

In addition, you obtained the following data:

(a) Depreciation expense was included in operating expenses. On a historical-cost basis, it equals $8,000; on a current-cost basis, it equals $10,000. Thus current-cost operating expenses are $32,000.

(b) Cost of goods sold on a current-cost basis equals $100,000.

(c) The current cost of the furniture and fixtures, net, is $50,000.

(d) Current cost of inventory is $18,000.

(e) For all other items, the current cost is the same as historical cost.

REQUIRED: **(a)** Prepare a current-cost income statement for the year ended December 31, 1990. Do not include the unrealized increase in the value of the furniture and fixtures and inventory in net income.

(b) Prepare a current-cost balance sheet at December 31, 1990. The balance in the Stockholders' Equity account is the amount needed to make this balance sheet balance.

P18-4 Current-cost Accounting Data. Southern California Property Management began business on December 31, 1990. The firm offers property management for property owners and speculates in real estate. The financial statements of the firm at the end of its first year of operations are shown below and on page 699.

SOUTHERN CALIFORNIA PROPERTY MANAGEMENT
Historical-cost Balance Sheet
As of December 31

Assets	1991	1990
Cash and marketable securities	$ 500,000	$ 400,000
Accounts receivable, net	80,000	0
Building and land held for resale	1,050,000	1,000,000
Other assets	120,000	100,000
Total assets	$1,750,000	$1,500,000

(continued)

Equities	1991	1990
Bank loans payable	$1,080,000	$ 980,000
Accounts payable	70,000	20,000
Stockholders' equity	600,000	500,000
Total equities	$1,750,000	$1,500,000

SOUTHERN CALIFORNIA PROPERTY MANAGEMENT
Historical-cost Income Statement
For the Year Ended December 31, 1991

Revenues		
Management fees earned	$ 400,000	
Gross revenues from sales of real estate	1,350,000	
Total revenues		$1,750,000
Expenses		
Cost of real estate sold	$1,000,000	
Operating expenses	450,000	
Total expenses		$1,450,000
Net income		$ 300,000

In addition, you have gathered the following data at the end of 1991:

Accounts	Current Cost
Cost of real estate sold	$1,200,000
Buildings and land	1,300,000
Cash and marketable securities	550,000

REQUIRED: **(a)** What is the amount of current-cost net operating income for 1991?

(b) At what amount would buildings and land be shown on a current-cost balance sheet at December 31, 1991?

(c) At what amount would cash and marketable securities be shown on a current-cost balance sheet at December 31, 1991?

(d) What is the amount of the purchasing-power gain or loss to be reported on the current-cost income statement for 1991?

(e) At what amount would the total owner's equity be shown on the December 31, 1991 current-cost balance sheet?

P18-5 **Foreign Currency Transactions.** The Great Import Company sold some pollution control devices to a German company for $50,000. The following exchange rates applied:

Date	Event	Exchange Rate (German Mark per U.S. Dollar)
May 10	Date of purchase	$.35
June 30	Balance sheet prepared	.40
July 18	Payment made	.41

REQUIRED: **(a)** Assuming that the sale is receivable in U.S. dollars, make the appropriate entries on the books of the Great Import Company.

(b) Assuming that the sale is for 143,000 German marks, make the appropriate entries on the books of the Great Import Company.

P18-6 Translating Foreign Currency Statements. The London Company operates in England and is a 100% owned subsidiary of a U.S. company. Its operations are self-contained in England and it carries out its operations in pounds. In the process of preparing consolidated financial statements, the controller in the headquarters office must translate the English subsidiary's balance sheet to U.S. dollars. He provides you with the following information and asks your help:

THE LONDON COMPANY
Balance Sheet
December 31, 1991

Account	Amount (in Pounds)
Cash	70,000
Accounts receivable, net	95,000
Inventory	300,000
Building, net	700,000
Land	500,000
Total assets	1,665,000
Accounts payable	85,000
Notes payable	165,000
Common stock	700,000
Retained earnings	715,000
Total equities	1,665,000

ADDITIONAL INFORMATION:
1. Retained earnings at the beginning of the year in U.S. dollars is $400,000.
2. Net income in U.S. dollars is $50,000.
3. Exchange rates are as follows:

Date	Exchange Rate (Pound per Dollar)
December 31, 1991	$1.25
Average for 1991	1.20
When common stock issued	1.50

REQUIRED: Translate the English subsidiary's balance sheet to U.S. dollars.

P18-7 Translating Foreign Currency Statements. The Smithe Co. Ltd. is a 100% owned Canadian subsidiary of U.S. Oils. In preparation for consolidation with the U.S. parent, the controller of the Canadian subsidiary prepared the following financial statements in Canadian dollars.

Account	Canadian Dollars
Balance Sheet	
Cash	160,000
Accounts receivable, net	180,000
Inventory	250,000
Building, net	800,000
Land	510,000
Total assets	1,900,000

(continued)

Account	Canadian Dollars
Balance Sheet	
Accounts payable	170,000
Notes payable	365,000
Common stock	700,000
Retained earnings	665,000
Total liabilities	1,900,000
Income Statement	
Sales	1,400,000
Cost of goods sold	800,000
Selling expenses	320,000
General and administrative expenses	150,000
Total expenses	1,270,000
Net income	130,000

ADDITIONAL INFORMATION:

1. Retained earnings in U.S. dollars at the beginning of the year is $600,000.

2. The exchange rates that apply are as follows:

	$U.S. per $Canadian
December 31, 1991	$.75
Average for 1991	.70
When common stock issued	.85

REQUIRED: Prepare translated statements to be included in the consolidation with the U.S. parent.

■ USING THE COMPUTER

P18-8 The Melody Company began business at the beginning of 1985. The income statement for the year ended December 31, 1990 follows, other information is on the next page.

THE MELODY COMPANY
Income Statement
For the Year Ended December 31, 1990

Sales		$840,000
Cost of goods sold		
Inventory, beginning	$210,000	
Purchases	480,000	
Goods available for sale	690,000	
Inventory, ending	250,000	
Cost of goods sold		440,000
Gross margin on sales		$400,000
Operating expenses		
Expenses other than depreciation	$240,000	
Depreciation	70,000	
Total expenses		310,000
Income before taxes		$ 90,000
Taxes		18,000
Net income		$ 72,000

OTHER INFORMATION:	**1.** Net monetary liability position—1/1/90 = $220,000.

2. Net monetary liability position—12/31/90 = $302,000.

3. No fixed assets were acquired during the year.

4. Dividends of $20,000 were paid in cash on June 30, 1990.

5. The company's sales, purchases, and expenses were earned or incurred evenly throughout the year.

6. Relevant price indexes:

January 1, 1990	120
June 30, 1990	125
December 31, 1990	130

REQUIRED:	Using an electronic spreadsheet, prepare a schedule determining the firm's purchasing-power gain or loss.

■ UNDERSTANDING FINANCIAL STATEMENTS

P18-9	The following statement was taken from a recent financial statement of United States Tobacco Company.

Inflation Related Information

The Financial Accounting Standards Board has made voluntary the disclosure requirements of SFAS No. 33, Financial Reporting and Changing Prices. The concept of disclosing inflationary effects on a business is sound. However, the use of a universal format may not accurately reflect the impact of inflation on an individual company. Accordingly, the Company has chosen not to present recalculated financial information that attempts to measure the effects of inflation on historical data. Instead, the following narrative provides useful information on the methods employed by the Company to mitigate the overall effects of inflation.

The financial statements presented in this annual report were prepared under generally accepted accounting principles and do not attempt to measure the impact of inflation on the results of operations or financial condition of the Company. Inflation has slowed in recent years, but continues to affect both the economy and the Company. There are various means available to the Company which serve to reduce the detrimental effects of inflation. The Company has adjusted selling prices over the years to maintain overall margins, has employed inventory accounting methods that reflect current costs in operating statements, and has planned asset replacements incorporating better technology to help improve efficiencies in manufacturing operations.

A significant portion of costs of products sold is determined using the LIFO method of inventory valuation which has the effect of matching current costs with current sales. The LIFO method is used for both financial reporting purposes in the primary financial statements and for income tax purposes, resulting in improved cash flow.

The Company replaces its fixed assets in the normal course of business. Decisions are evaluated for efficiencies, tax incentives, cash flow and rates of return on investment. Although assets are usually replaced at a higher cost, technological improvements often create operating efficiencies resulting in cost savings. Over the last several years the Company has invested in new assets that are more efficient than the assets being replaced.

Inflation erodes the general purchasing power of monetary assets such as cash, marketable securities and receivables, as these assets will purchase fewer goods and services over time. However, inflation benefits the Company in relation to monetary liabilities, as the payment of these obligations will be made with less expensive dollars.

Current tax legislation does not allow deductions for the effects of inflation. Accordingly, effective tax rates levied are, in real terms, higher than established statutory rates. The Tax Reform Act of 1986 includes provisions that will reduce the effective tax rate of the Company. However, the act seems to disregard the effects of inflation on the replacement of assets by providing for longer useful lives, eliminating favorable capital gains treatment on disposals, and repealing the investment tax credit. The Company supports efforts to modify these provisions.

Overall, the Company has reduced the impact of inflation through good business judgments and the effective use of accounting and tax practices, as evidenced by the significant growth in pretax margins during the last three years.

REQUIRED: **(a)** The company states that it has reduced the impact of inflation through good business judgments and the effective use of tax and accounting policies. Which accounting policies has the company used to reduce the impact of inflation? How do they reduce that impact?

(b) Why has the company chosen simply to use a narrative disclosure? Do you agree with these reasons?

■ FINANCIAL DECISION CASES

P18-10 The owner and president of Silicon Inc., Sue Weinreb, has just reviewed the financial statements prepared by the firm's accountant and is distressed by the fact that the firm suffered a $1 million loss in the current year. This has been a very tough year for high-tech firms. Demand has slowed for Silicon's product, competition has increased, and prices have fallen.

The firm was created several years ago and was funded primarily by venture capital. Prior to this year, the firm had been profitable. As the firm's financial condition deteriorated this year, it was forced to borrow heavily from a local bank at 15%. At the beginning of the year, the firm was in a small net liability position, but by the end of the year monetary liabilities exceeded monetary assets by $5 million.

As Sue was preparing for a presentation to the board of directors, she noticed that in the footnotes to the financial statements the accountant had determined that the firm had a purchasing-power gain of $1.5 million for the current year. Adding this to the $1 million net loss for the period, Sue figured the firm had positive net income of $.5 million. With this new information, she feels that she will be able to satisfy the members of the board. In fact, she feels that the firm may now be able to declare the dividends it was planning to omit.

REQUIRED: **(a)** What do you think is the likely cause of the purchasing-power gain?

(b) As a member of the board of directors, how would you respond to Sue's logic that the income for the year amounted to $.5 million?

(c) Do you think that Sue is correct in now planning to declare the dividend?

P18-11 In Exhibit 18-12, the exchange rates for the British pound, the Canadian dollar, the West German mark, and the Japanese yen were provided. Using the *Wall Street Journal* or the financial section of your local paper, determine the current exchange rates for these currencies. Prepare a table comparing the rates in the text with the current rates. As well as you can, hypothesize how a firm such as Coca-Cola would be affected by any change in the exchange rates.

APPENDIX A

ACCOUNTING SYSTEMS AND THE ROLE OF THE COMPUTER

LEARNING OBJECTIVES

After studying this appendix, you should be able to:
1. Explain the use of subsidiary ledgers for accounts receivable and accounts payable.
2. Explain the use of specialized journals.
3. Record entries into the following specialized journals:

(a) sales journal
(b) purchases journal
(c) cash receipts journal
(d) cash payments journal.
4. List the uses of computers in accounting.

T he first six chapters explained how the accounting information system classifies, processes, and summarizes economic data. A simple accounting system was used, based on a manual set of books. The main components of that system were the general journal and the general ledger. This appendix introduces you to more complex accounting systems employing specialized journals and ledgers.

ACCOUNTING SYSTEM COMPONENTS

Although an accounting system must be designed to meet the needs of a specific firm, most accounting systems have certain elements in common: a strong internal control system (discussed in Chapter 7), subsidiary ledgers, and specialized journals.

THE NEED FOR SUBSIDIARY LEDGERS

Because of the need for timely and accurate information, as well as good internal control procedures, certain detailed accounts must be maintained. To illustrate, management needs to know the total of its accounts receivable and also the amount that each individual customer owes. The same type of information is needed on payables. Management needs to know the total owed various vendors as well as how much it owes individual vendors and when each payment is due. Similar detailed information is necessary for such items as prepaid insurance and plant and equipment.

The primary account is called a **controlling account**. It is maintained in the general ledger. For example, the general ledger contains an account called Accounts Receivable. It shows summary information about the beginning balance, the total sales on account for the period, the total cash collected on account during the period, and the total balance due from the firm's customers at the end of the period.

Detailed accounts for each individual customer are also maintained. These are called **subsidiary accounts** and are placed in a subsidiary accounts receivable ledger. A subsidiary ledger is separate from the general ledger. It contains a set of related accounts whose balances in total will equal the balance in the controlling account. Each individual account in the subsidiary accounts receivable ledger should show the customer's name, address, credit rating, and credit limit and other vital payment information. An example of such a subsidiary account is shown in Exhibit A-1. The format in this example is a running balance ledger account. That is, it provides the ability to update the balance continuously after posting each transaction.

EXHIBIT A–1

Accounts Receivable Subsidiary Ledger

Name:	Thomas Hunter		Account No.	4
Address:	125 East 55th Street		Credit Limit:	$2,500
	East Rutherford, NJ 01908		Sale Terms:	2/10

Date	Post Ref.	Debit	Credit	Balance
June 1				201.48
2	SJ-1	$1,500.00		1,701.48
12	CR-5		$1,500.00	201.48

Similar subsidiary accounts are maintained for payables and, depending on the firm's needs, for other accounts such as Property, Plant, and Equipment. For example, the general ledger account, Equipment, shows the historical cost of the total equipment owned by the firm. Often, backup cards are maintained for each item of equipment. These cards show such information as the cost of each item, its estimated life, its salvage (or residual) value, and its insurance coverage. These individual cards serve as a subsidiary ledger to the controlling Equipment account. The number of and detail in the subsidiary accounts depend on the needs of the firm's management.

Posting to Subsidiary Accounts

When subsidiary accounts are maintained, it is necessary to post journal entries to both the general ledger or controlling account and to the subsidiary account. Thus, if an entry is made to record a sale on account, two postings must be made, one to the general ledger Account Receivable account and the other to the individual subsidiary accounts. To maintain control, postings to subsidiary accounts should be made daily. Postings to general ledger accounts need to be made only periodically. Similar posting procedures are followed for subsidiary Accounts Payable and any other subsidiary accounts that are maintained.

To demonstrate these procedures, record and post three representative entries to Accounts Receivable for sales on account, sales returns, and collections on account. Assume that at the beginning of the current year (in this case, 1990), The LA Company's accounts receivable totaled $6,000 and comprised five customers with the account balances shown in Exhibit A-2.

EXHIBIT A–2

THE LA COMPANY Accounts Receivable		
Customer	Account No.	Account Balance
A. Abbot	001	$1,250
B. Battle	002	750
L. Lloyd	003	2,000
O. Ort	004	400
Q. Quint	005	1,600
Total		$6,000

Sales for January 2, 1990 were $1,500 and were recorded in the general journal as follows:

Date	Explanation	Ref.	Debit	Credit
1990 Jan. 2	Accounts Receivable	200	1,500	
	Sales	600		1,500
	To record credit sales to the following customers:			
	B. Battle	002	$700	
	O. Ort	004	300	
	Q. Quint	005	500	

On January 10, O. Ort returned $100 of the merchandise that she purchased on account on January 2. This entry is recorded as follows:

Date	Explanation	Ref.	Debit	Credit
1990 Jan. 10	Sales Returns and Allowances	610	100	
	Accounts Receivable	200		100
	To record return of merchandise by O. Ort, $100.	004		

Finally, on January 12, the firm received $5,300 of cash on account from various customers. The following entry was made to record these collections:

Date	Explanation	Ref.	Debit	Credit
1990				
Jan. 12	Cash	100	5,300	
	Accounts Receivable	200		5,300
	To record collections on account from the following customers:			
	A. Abbot	001	$1,250	
	B. Battle	002	750	
	L. Lloyd	003	1,500	
	O. Ort	004	600	
	Q. Quint	005	1,200	

The general ledger account Accounts Receivable and the subsidiary accounts are shown below. T accounts, rather than the running balance form, are used for convenience. Each entry is posted to both the appropriate general ledger accounts and the individual customer accounts. Postings to the subsidiary ledger accounts are indicated by noting the customer's account number in the Ref. column. Postings to the general ledger accounts are indicated by noting the general ledger account number in the Ref. column.

General Ledger
Accounts Receivable   200

1/1/90	Bal.	6,000	1/10	100
1/2		1,500	1/12	5,300
1/12	Bal.	2,100		

Subsidiary Ledger

A. Abbot   001

1/1/90	Bal.	1,250	1/12	1,250
1/12		0		

B. Battle   002

1/1/90	Bal.	750	1/12	750
1/2		700		
1/12	Bal.	700		

L. Lloyd   003

1/1/90	Bal.	2,000	1/12	1,500
1/12	Bal.	500		

O. Ort   004

1/1/90	Bal.	400	1/10	100
1/2		300	1/12	600
1/12	Bal.	0		

Q. Quint   005

1/1/90	Bal.	1,600	1/12	1,200
1/2		500		
1/12	Bal.	900		

At the end of the accounting period, a list of all the individual subsidiary accounts and their balances is prepared. This **schedule of accounts receivable**, often called an **accounts receivable trial balance**, is totaled, and the total should equal the balance in the related general ledger account. If these totals are not equal, this indicates a posting error. The schedule of accounts receivable for the example is shown in Exhibit A-3.

EXHIBIT A–3

THE LA COMPANY Schedule of Accounts Receivable January 31, 1990		
Accounts		**Amount**
A. Abbot	001	$ 0
B. Battle	002	700
L. Lloyd	003	500
O. Ort	004	0
Q. Quint	005	900
Total		$2,100

SPECIALIZED JOURNALS

A **specialized journal** is one that is designed to handle certain types of transactions such as only cash receipts or charge sales. The use of specialized journals significantly reduces the time necessary to record transactions and post to the ledgers.

Most of the firm's transactions can be classified into four groups. These groups, as well as the journals used to record these transactions, are shown in Exhibit A-4. If a particular transaction does not fit into one of these journals, it is recorded in the general journal. This is the journal that has been used up to this point. However, for many firms, most transactions can be recorded in specialized journals.

EXHIBIT A–4

Transaction	Specialized Journal	Posting Abbreviation
Sales of merchandise on credit	Sales journal	SJ
Purchase of merchandise on credit	Purchases journal	PJ
Receipts of cash	Cash receipts journal	CR
Payments of cash	Cash payments journal	CP

For illustrative purposes, the following discussion is based on a manual accounting system. This means that one or more individuals must record the transactions by hand in the appropriate journals. These transactions must then be posted by hand to the appropriate general and subsidiary ledgers. The widespread use of microcomputers has enabled even small firms to automate their accounting systems. A later section will describe how the accounting system can be computerized.

The specialized journals illustrated here are examples of those found in many manually kept sets of books, but they are not the only journals used. Firms design their own specialized journals to meet their particular needs.

The Sales Journal

The **sales journal**, sometimes called the *credit sales journal*, is used for recording all sales made on account. The sales journal for the Fortune Retail Store is shown in Exhibit A-5. All the sales on account for the month of June are shown in this journal; cash sales are recorded in the cash receipts journal. Sales invoices are the primary inputs into this journal. In this example, assume that all sales are made on terms of 2/10, n/30 and that the gross method is used to record sales discounts, so each account receivable is shown at its full amount. Because the sales journal is used exclusively to record credit sales, the Amount column represents both a debit to Accounts Receivable and a credit to Sales.

EXHIBIT A–5

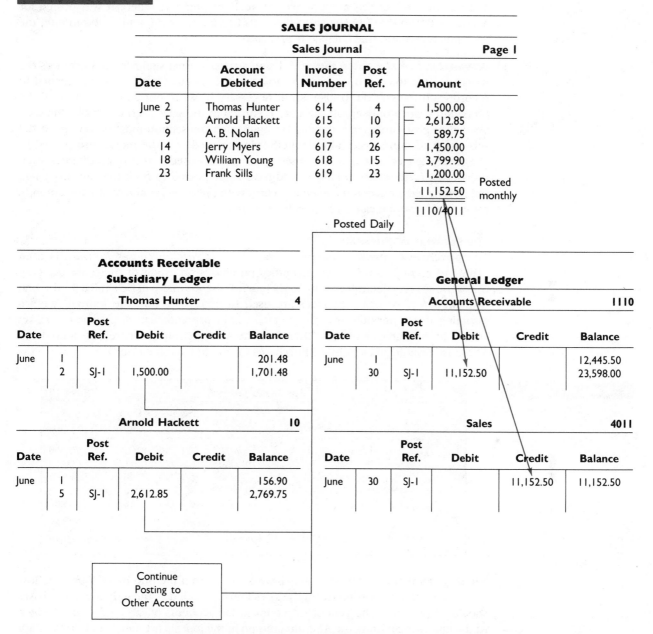

SALES JOURNAL

Sales Journal				Page 1
Date	Account Debited	Invoice Number	Post Ref.	Amount
June 2	Thomas Hunter	614	4	1,500.00
5	Arnold Hackett	615	10	2,612.85
9	A. B. Nolan	616	19	589.75
14	Jerry Myers	617	26	1,450.00
18	William Young	618	15	3,799.90
23	Frank Sills	619	23	1,200.00
				11,152.50
				1110/4011

Posted monthly

Posted Daily

Accounts Receivable Subsidiary Ledger

General Ledger

Thomas Hunter   4

Date	Post Ref.	Debit	Credit	Balance
June 1				201.48
2	SJ-1	1,500.00		1,701.48

Accounts Receivable   1110

Date	Post Ref.	Debit	Credit	Balance
June 1				12,445.50
30	SJ-1	11,152.50		23,598.00

Arnold Hackett   10

Date	Post Ref.	Debit	Credit	Balance
June 1				156.90
5	SJ-1	2,612.85		2,769.75

Sales   4011

Date	Post Ref.	Debit	Credit	Balance
June 30	SJ-1		11,152.50	11,152.50

Continue Posting to Other Accounts

Posting from the Sales Journal. Exhibit A-5 also shows how postings are made from the sales journal to both the subsidiary and the general ledger accounts. Each individual sale is posted to its appropriate subsidiary account. After the posting is made, the account number or a check is placed in the post reference (Post Ref.) column. The Post Ref. in the subsidiary ledger and controlling accounts will be labeled SJ-1 to represent page 1 of the sales journal. Postings to the subsidiary ledger should be made daily to ensure that management has up-to-date knowledge on how much each customer owes. This knowledge can be used to assure that individual customers have not exceeded their credit limits.

At the end of the month, the Amount column in the journal is totaled and posted as a debit in the Accounts Receivable control account and as a credit to the general ledger

Sales account. In the illustration shown in Exhibit A-5, this amount is $11,152.50. The numbers under this amount are the account numbers where it was posted for Accounts Receivable (1110) and Sales (4011). Finally, at the end of the month, the accounts receivable trial balance is prepared.

Advantages of the Sales Journal. Using a sales journal significantly decreases the work required to record transactions in a manual system. Only one line is needed to record each transaction. It also is not necessary to write out an explanation of the transaction, since only credit sales are recorded in the sales journal. Finally, the time needed to post entries is reduced. Although each transaction must be posted to the subsidiary accounts receivable ledger, only the totals for the month are posted to the general ledger accounts. If a general journal were used to record credit sales, each transaction (rather than totals) would have to be posted to both the subsidiary and the general ledger accounts. Even for a firm with only several hundred sales a month, using a sales journal can save considerable time.

The Purchases Journal

The **purchases journal**, sometimes called the *credit purchases journal*, is used mainly to record merchandise inventory purchases on credit. If these are the only transactions recorded in the purchases journal, the journal will be similar to the one in Exhibit A-6. Purchase invoices are used to enter data into the journal. We are assuming that a periodic inventory system is in use and that all purchases are recorded at their gross amounts. Therefore the Amount column represents a credit to Accounts Payable and a debit to Purchases for the full invoice price.

EXHIBIT A-6

Purchases Journal

| Purchases Journal | | | | | Page 12 |
Date	Account Credited	Terms	Invoice Date	Post Ref.	Amount
June 1	Super Cola	2/10, n/30	6/1 /90	5	1,700.00
6	Jones Farm	2/10, n/30	6/6 /90	11	1,000.00
18	Mrs. Smith's Bakeries	n/30	6/17/90	8	1,294.60
25	Wholesale Grocery Co.	2/10, n/30	6/25/90	15	2,800.90
30	Jim's Snacks	n/30	6/30/90	16	105.00
					6,900.50
					5011/2010

Posting from the Purchases Journal. Postings from the purchases journal follow the same pattern as postings from the sales journal. Each day, the individual purchases should be posted to the vendor's account in the accounts payable subsidiary ledger. At the end of the month, the Amount column in the journal is totaled, and this amount is posted as a debit in the general ledger Purchases account and as a credit in the general ledger Accounts Payable account. Finally, at the end of the month, a list of the individual subsidiary accounts is made. This list is often called an **accounts payable trial balance** or a **schedule of accounts payable**. The total of this list is compared with the balance in the general ledger Accounts Payable account. This procedure helps assure that all the postings have been correctly made.

Cash Receipts Journal

The **cash receipts journal** is used to record all transactions involving the receipt of cash, including cash sales, the receipt of a bank loan, the receipt of a payment on account, and the sale of assets such as marketable securities. An example of a cash receipts journal is shown in Exhibit A-7. As this exhibit shows, a typical cash receipts

EXHIBIT A–7

Cash Receipts Journal — Page 8

Date		Explanation	Cash	Sales Dis-counts	Account Title	Ref.	Amount	Account Credited	Ref.	Amount	Sales	Ref.	Amount
			Debits		**Other Accounts**				**Accounts Receivable**			**Other Accounts**	
June	1	Cash sales	506.00								506.00		
	2	Invoice of											
		May 18	184.61					Perry Alexander	17	184.61			
	10	Sale of market-						Marketable					
		able securities	2,000.00					securities				1528	1,800.00
								Other income				8021	200.00
	12	Invoice of June											
		1, less 2%	1,470.00	30.00				Thomas Hunter	4	1,500.00			
	15	Cash sales	1,200.00								1,200.00		
	20	Invoice of June											
		14, less 2%	1,421.00	29.00				Jerry Myers	26	1,450.00			
	22	Repayment—						Employee					
		employee adv.	200.00					advances				1130	200.00
	30	Invoice of											
		June 18	3,947.27					William Young	15	3,947.27			
			10,928.88	59.00						7,081.88	1,706.00		2,200.00
			(1010)	(8531)						(1110)	(4011)		(✔)

Monthly Totals Posted at End of Month

General Ledger

Cash — 1010

Date		Post Ref.	Debit	Credit	Balance
June	1				16,056.50
	30	CR-8	10,928.88		26,985.38

Accounts Receivable — 1110

Date		Post Ref.	Debit	Credit	Balance
June	1				12,445.50
	30	SJ-1	11,152.50		23,598.00
	30	CR-8		7,081.88	16,516.12

Marketable Securities — 1528

Date		Post Ref.	Debit	Credit	Balance
June	1				5,000.00
	10	CR-8		1,800.00	3,200.00

Continue posting to other general ledger accounts

Subsidiary Accounts Receivable Ledger

Perry Alexander — 17

Date		Post Ref.	Debit	Credit	Balance
June	1				184.61
	2	CR-8		184.61	0

Thomas Hunter — 4

Date		Post Ref.	Debit	Credit	Balance
June	1				201.48
	2	SJ-1	1,500.00		1,701.48
	12	CR-8		1,500.00	201.48

Continue posting to other subsidiary ledger accounts

journal has many columns. This is necessary because there are numerous transactions that result in the collection of cash. The debit columns will always include a Cash column and most likely a Sales Discount column. Other debit columns are used for routine transactions. In the journal shown in Exhibit A-7, the only additional debit column is an Other Accounts column. This column provides for the name of the account, the post reference (in this case labeled Ref.), and the amount. If desired, the name of the account can be replaced by account numbers.

The credit columns in a cash receipts journal will most often include both Accounts Receivable and Sales. Again, other columns can be used, depending on what types of routine transactions the firm has. In Exhibit A-7, the only additional credit column is Other Accounts. It is set up in the same way that the other column on the debit side is, except that the account title area is replaced by just a Ref. column.

To demonstrate the use of the cash receipts journal, assume that during June the Fortune Retail Store entered into the following transactions involving cash receipts:

- June 1: Cash sales totaled $506.

- June 2: Collected from Perry Alexander (account no. 17) $184.61 from sale made in May. No sales discount allowed.

- June 10: The firm sold marketable securities for $2,000 that it purchased for $1,800.

- June 12: Collected $1,470 on account from Thomas Hunter (account no. 4). Sales discount of $30 allowed.

- June 15: Cash sales totaled $1,200.

- June 20: Collected $1,421 on account from Jerry Myers (account no. 26). Sales discount of $29 allowed.

- June 22: Repayment of employee advances of $200.

- June 30: Collection on account from William Young (account no. 15). Total received is $3,947.27, which represents outstanding balance of $147.37 on June 1 and subsequent sale on June 18. No discount allowed.

Each of these transactions is entered chronologically in the cash receipts journal. For example, the cash sale on June 1 is recorded in the cash receipts journal by first entering June 1 in the Date column. "Cash sales" is entered in the Explanation column. The amount of $506 is then placed in both the Cash Debit column and the Sales Credit column. It is not necessary to make an entry in the Account Credited column, since the Sales column was used. Other entries are made in a similar fashion.

Posting the Cash Receipts Journal to the Ledgers. As with the other journals, the cash receipts journal is posted in two stages. Any entries in the Accounts Receivable column should be posted daily to the subsidiary accounts receivable ledger. This ensures that the individual customers' accounts are up to date and accurately reflect the balance owed at that time. As these accounts are posted, the account number is entered into the Post Reference column. In the subsidiary ledger, the post reference is CR-8, which indicates that the entries came from page 8 of the cash receipts journal.

At the end of the month, the columns in the cash receipts journal are totaled and posted to the appropriate general ledger accounts. Again, in the general ledger accounts, the post reference is CR-8 to indicate that these entries came from page 8 of the cash receipts journal.

The amounts in the Other Accounts column must be posted separately. Although these amounts are often posted at the end of the month, they could be posted more frequently. As it is posted, the account number is placed in the Post Reference column. A check is placed under the total of this column to indicate that it is not posted. The postings are shown in Exhibit A-7 for the general ledger accounts Cash, Accounts Receivable, and Marketable Securities, as well as two selected subsidiary ledger accounts receivable accounts, Perry Alexander and Thomas Hunter.

The Cash Payments Journal

The **cash payments journal** is used to record the cash disbursements made by check, including payments on account, payments for cash merchandise purchases, payments for various expenses, and other payments.

A typical cash payments journal is shown in Exhibit A-8. This journal has a Date column, a Check Number column, a Payee column, and at least two credit columns, one for cash and one for purchase discounts. In the journal in Exhibit A-8, another credit column is for Other Accounts. If necessary, other specific columns could be added if used routinely. The debit columns will include at least an Accounts Payable column, a Purchases column, and an Other Accounts column. Again, other specific columns could be added if needed. The main sources of entries for this journal are check stubs and payment requests.

EXHIBIT A-8

			Cash Payments Journal										Page 10
			Credits						**Debits**				
				Pur-chases Dis-counts	**Other Accounts**				**Accounts Payable**			**Other Accounts**	
Date	Check No.	Explanation	Cash		Account Title	Ref.	Amount	Account Debited	Ref.	Amount	Purchases	Ref.	Amount
June 1	498	Store lease	1,500.00					Lease expense				6531	1,500.00
1	499	Invoice of May 17	76.00					Ricco's Pizza	12	76.00			
2	500	Merchandise purchased	1,250.00								1,250.00		
3	501	Invoice of May 21	784.84					Super Cola	5	784.84			
9	502	Purchase of equipment	2,000.00		Loans payable	2620	8,000.00	Machinery—equipment				1520	10,000.00
10	503	Invoice of June 1, less 2%	1,660.00	40.00				Super Cola	5	1,700.00			
15	504	Paid manager's salary	2,200.00					Salaries				6011	2,200.00
16	505	Invoice of June 6, less 2%	980.00	20.00				Jones Farms	11	1,000.00			
25	506	Merchandise purchased	1,400.00								1,400.00		
30	507	Invoice of June 18	1,294.60					Mrs. Smith's Bakeries	8	1,294.60			
30	508	Loan repayment	120.00					Interest				6641	90.00
								Notes payable				2620	30.00
			13,265.44	60.00			8,000.00			4,855.44	2,650.00		13,820.00
			(1010)	(8031)			(✔)			(2010)	(5011)		(✔)

To demonstrate how entries are recorded in the cash payments journal, assume that the Fortune Retail Store made the following cash payments during the month of June:

- June 1: Payment of store lease, $1,500.

- June 1: Paid Ricco's Pizza (account no. 12) for $76 invoice dated May 17. No discount taken.

- June 2: Cash purchase of $1,250.

- June 3: Paid to Super Cola (account no. 5) $748.84 for invoice dated May 21. No purchase discount taken.

- June 9: Purchase of equipment for $10,000 with 20% down payment.
- June 10: Paid to Super Cola $1,660 for invoice dated June 1.
- June 15: Paid manager's salary, $2,200, for first half of June.
- June 16: Paid $980 to Jones Farm for invoice dated June 6. Discount taken.
- June 25: Cash purchase of $1,400.
- June 30: Paid $1,284.60 to Mrs. Smith's Bakeries for invoice dated June 18. No discount allowed.
- June 30: Loan payment of $120, of which $90 is interest.

The entries in the cash payments journal are recorded and posted in a manner similar to those in the cash receipts journal. Thus the entries are entered chronologically into the cash payments journal. The cash payments journal is also posted in two stages. Entries to the Accounts Payable account should be posted daily to the subsidiary accounts payable ledger. At the end of the month, all columns are summed, and the totals are posted to the appropriate general ledger accounts. The accounts in the other columns must be posted individually. They can be posted daily, monthly, or at other convenient intervals. Since the basic posting procedures are the same as those for the other journals, the actual postings are not shown in the exhibit.

■ THE GENERAL JOURNAL

The special-purpose journals described above can be used to record the routine transactions of the firm. However, some transactions do not involve sales, purchases, cash receipts, or cash payments or are too complex to fit conveniently into these journals. Examples are a sales or purchase return, adjusting entries, and closing entries. These entries are made in the general journal.

To illustrate, assume that the Fortune Retail Store entered into the following three transactions:

- June 5: Purchased $500 worth of wine from the Neuman Wine Company that arrived damaged. It was returned, and Fortune's account was reduced.
- June 17: A. Waller returned some merchandise because it did not meet her needs. She received a $200 credit on her account.
- June 30: Depreciation expense for the month is $1,200.

These entries are recorded in the general journal shown in Exhibit A-9. The form of this journal is the same as was used throughout the first six chapters of this book. Note that the Receivables and Payables accounts must be posted twice. That is, the entry

EXHIBIT A-9

FORTUNE RETAIL STORE
General Journal
Page 14

Date	Explanation	Post Ref.	Debit	Credit
June 5	Account Payable—Neuman Wine	2010/23	500	
	Purchase Returns and Allowances	8040		500
	To record return of damaged merchandise.			
17	Sales Returns and Allowances	8541	200	
	Accounts Receivable—A. Waller	1110/12		200
	To record refund to customer for damaged goods.			
30	Depreciation Expense	6781	1,200	
	Accumulated Depreciation	1550		1,200
	To record monthly depreciation expense.			

must be posted to both the appropriate subsidiary account and the controlling account. This posting is shown by noting both the particular controlling account number in the Post Reference column and the subsidiary ledger account number.

■ INTERNAL CONTROL AND SPECIAL JOURNALS

As previously noted, separation of duties is an important aspect of internal control. As far as possible, different individuals should record transactions in each of the special journals. Depending on the size and the complexity of the accounting department, a total separation of duties may not be possible. However, not all accounting personnel should have access to the general journal. Nonroutine transactions are recorded in this journal and should be approved by the head of the accounting department or by someone with similar authority. Routine transactions are recorded in the special journals and do not require authorization.

■ THE USE OF COMPUTERS IN ACCOUNTING

In the last 20 years, there has been a tremendous increase in the use of computers in accounting, primarily to automate accounting systems. Computerized accounting systems are now found in businesses of all sizes and complexities, due to the growth of data-processing services and the widespread use of microcomputers. Computers perform analysis for management and provide word processing and communications for the timely dissemination of financial reports. In addition, computers are beginning to play an important role in all aspects of the public accounting profession.

■ COMPUTERIZED VERSUS MANUAL ACCOUNTING SYSTEMS

A computerized accounting system differs procedurally from a manual system. For example, an accounting information system consists of three phases, as shown in Exhibit A-10. The difference between a manual and a computerized system exists in the processing and output phases. The accounting procedures performed in a manual accounting system are shown in Exhibit A-11.

A computerized accounting system makes use of the same input of raw data from source documents as does a manual accounting system, but the remaining procedures are performed automatically with total accuracy. Hours of manual processing can be

EXHIBIT A–10

Phases of an Accounting Information System

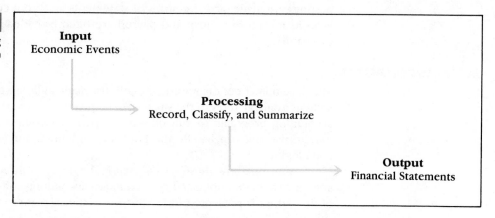

Input
Economic Events

Processing
Record, Classify, and Summarize

Output
Financial Statements

¹ This section draws heavily upon *McGee Computerized Accounting Information System*, by Earl Weiss and Donald L. Raun, PWS-KENT Publishing Co., 1988, pp. 33–34.

EXHIBIT A–11

Procedures in a Manual
Accounting System

Input
- Analyze Transactions
  (source documents)

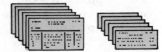

Processing
- Record Journal Entries
- Post to General Ledger
- Adjust and Close

Output
- Prepare Trial Balance
- Prepare Financial Statements
- Analyze and Interpret

accomplished in minutes. Current output is available on a continuous basis, and up-to-date financial statements can be prepared as often as needed without concern for time or cost. These benefits also extend to the very important function of analyzing and interpreting financial statements.

DATA-PROCESSING SERVICES

Data-processing services emerged when it became possible to input data from remote terminals. In effect, the data-processing service has a computer at its service center. Clients of the service lease or purchase terminals, which are located on their premises. These terminals are used to input the various transactions into the main computer. This computer processes the data; the necessary journals are generated; the postings are made; and the financial statements are produced. In addition, such services as inventory control and payroll are often provided by these data-processing companies.

MICROCOMPUTERS

The development of the microcomputer has made in-house computerized accounting systems available to even the smallest of companies. Software companies have devised accounting programs to run on various personal computers. These programs are easy to use and can handle the bookkeeping chores for firms of various sizes and complexities.

To illustrate how these systems work, the transactions used to describe a manual system have been duplicated on a common accounting software program.[2] A sample of the output is presented in Exhibit A-12 (the sales journal) and Exhibit A-13 (the

[2] The software package used in this example was developed by IBM and BPI. However, for consistency, the form of the journals has been altered.

EXHIBIT A–12

FORTUNE RETAIL STORE
Sales Journal

Date	A/R Subs. Ref.	Customer	Invoice #	Amount
06/02	4	Thomas Hunter	614	1,500.00
06/05	10	Arnold Hackett	615	2,612.85
06/09	19	A. B. Nolen	616	589.75
06/14	26	Jerry Myers	617	1,450.00
06/18	15	William Young	618	3,799.90
06/23	23	Frank Sills	619	1,200.00
Totals				11,152.50

EXHIBIT A–13

FORTUNE RETAIL STORE
Purchases Journal

Date	A/P Subs. Ref.	Supplier	Invoice #	Terms	Amount
06/01	5	Super Cola Bottling	3142	2/10, n/30	1,700.00
06/06	11	Jones Farms	217	2/10, n/30	1,000.00
06/18	8	Mrs. Smith's Bakeries	912	n/30	1,294.60
06/25	15	Wholesale Grocery Co.	128	2/10, n/30	2,800.90
06/30	16	Jim's Snacks	618	n/30	105.00
Totals					6,900.50

purchases journal). In a similar manner, cash receipts, cash purchases, and general journals are generated by the same accounting program.

These software programs are relatively inexpensive and have a number of advantages over manual systems. The programs are extremely accurate; if transactions are entered correctly, computational errors can be eliminated. Most of these software programs have subroutines that post entries after a set of transactions has been recorded. This means that both general and subsidiary ledger accounts can be updated daily. Thus management has up-to-date information on such accounts as Cash and Receivables. This information is valuable in providing data on receivable collections and cash flows.

More sophisticated software programs have the ability to generate checks on the firm's printer and make appropriate entries in the cash payments journal. Many of these same programs have payroll routines that are able to prepare the firm's periodic payroll, generate the payroll journals and ledgers, and supply the firm with the information required to prepare a variety of payroll tax forms.

Although these accounting software programs are usually versatile, they do have drawbacks. In many cases, the financial statement formats are fixed and cannot be changed easily. Programs are not designed to meet the needs of all firms; what is appropriate for a typical merchandising firm may not be best suited for a service or merchandising firm. However, in recent years, these programs have become considerably more sophisticated. Firms with complex accounting needs might still require sophisticated office computers that can handle more intricate programs.

■ FINANCIAL ANALYSIS PROGRAM

The development of spreadsheet programs that can be used on personal computers has greatly enhanced the financial analysis capability of management. A **spreadsheet** is an empty matrix of rows and columns that are individually labeled by the user. Programs such as Quattro and Lotus 1-2-3 enable individuals to perform a variety of functions, including cash flow projections, depreciation schedules, inventory management, receivables and payables management, sales projections, and product line summaries. An example of an accounts payable management worksheet that was developed using a common spreadsheet program is reproduced in Exhibit A-14. The purpose of this schedule is to show when payables should be paid so as to receive the discount and the amount of savings if the discount is taken.

EXHIBIT A–14

			MIKE'S RESTAURANT							
			Accounts Payable Schedule							
			October, 1990							
Account Name	Invoice Amount	Invoice Day	Date Month	Year	Discount Per-cent	Days for Discount	Date to Get Discount	Discount Amount	Net Payable
Kojack Corp.	$ 1,200.00	2	10	85	2%	10	12-Oct.-85	$ 24.00	$ 1,176.00
Lite Co.	675.00	2	10	85	2	10	12-Oct.-85	13.50	661.50
LaJolla Corp.	1,575.00	3	10	85	2	0	03-Oct.-85	0.00	1,575.00
Luga Inc.	700.00	5	10	85	2	10	15-Oct.-85	14.00	686.00
Olympic Co.	3,000.00	5	10	85	1	10	15-Oct.-85	30.00	2,970.00
Ripech Corp.	788.00	7	10	85	2	15	22-Oct.-85	15.76	772.24
Levins Inc.	3,277.50	9	10	85	2	10	19-Oct.-85	65.55	3,211.95
Laird Walls	908.00	10	10	85	0	0	10-Oct.-85	0.00	908.00
Hours Corp.	2,200.00	13	10	85	1	15	28-Oct.-85	22.00	2,178.00
Industrial Co.	200.00	16	10	85	1	10	26-Oct.-85	2.00	198.00
Sonics	2,567.89	20	10	85	2	10	30-Oct.-85	51.36	2,516.53
Entertainment Co.	675.00	21	10	85	2	5	26-Oct.-85	13.50	661.50
Potporri Plus	3,567.00	24	10	85	2	10	03-Nov.-85	71.34	3,495.66
Cellular Co.	2,098.25	25	10	85	2	10	04-Nov.-85	41.96	2,056.29
Devices Corp.	1,990.00	29	10	85	1	10	08-Nov.-85	19.90	1,970.10
Totals	$25,421.64							$384.87	$25,036.77

■ COMMUNICATIONS AND WORD PROCESSING

Communications and word-processing programs allow for the efficient preparation of reports as well as the communication of these reports to various users. In addition, advanced integrated software programs such as Framework, Symphony, and Excel have greatly expanded the capabilities of personal computers. Integrated programs combine spreadsheets with data base management, communications, and word processing. They allow for the creation of a data base that can be used in several applications. Specific reports can be generated and then communicated to various users, either electronically or through print.

The importance of computers in accounting and the communication of financial information is illustrated in the following *Forbes* interview with John C. (Sandy) Burton, former chief accountant of the Securities and Exchange Commission (SEC).

He began by predicting that in 10 to 15 years corporate financial statements will be supplanted by a steady flow of computer-generated information. Under the present system, investors and analysts generally must wait until the end of a quarter for earnings information, and frequently to the end of a year for crucial balance-sheet information. This existing system reflects precomputer-era difficulties in gathering data, Burton says. It took so long and cost so much back then that everyone settled for one common format. But, today, generating information is no problem, so the best method is to present the information to users—institutional analysts, mainly—via computer, as often as they wish and in as many formats as possible.

In short, he thinks, investors shouldn't have to wait until July to learn about a sales or earnings slippage that may have begun in April.[3]

In addition to the continuous data base accounting predicted by Burton, the SEC's EDGAR (Electronic Data Gathering, Analysis, and Retrieval System) project will, in the near future, allow firms to file their traditional financial statements with the SEC electronically rather than in print. Eventually, individuals will have electronic access to this data base.

■ THE USE OF COMPUTERS IN PUBLIC ACCOUNTING

The use of micro- and personal computers is beginning to have a significant impact on the public accounting profession. CPA firms of all sizes now use computers in various tax, audit, and management-consulting functions. For example, tax return preparation has been automated for many years. However, with the use of personal computers, tax and financial planning is greatly enhanced. Furthermore, the ability to access data bases containing the latest tax laws and court cases will increase the efficiency and effectiveness of tax research.

Personal computers are playing a larger role in the audit function. Audit work papers can be standardized and stored on hard disks. This greatly reduces the time currently required for their preparation. Electronic spreadsheets can be used to facilitate account analysis, and word-processing programs can be used to prepare audit programs and financial statements. Finally, communications programs assit auditors in transferring data between remote audit locations. These same programs are used to transfer data to the CPA firm's central computer, to be used in automated audit programs.

SUMMARY OF LEARNING OBJECTIVES

1. The need for subsidiary ledgers. Management needs comprehensive backup information for certain accounts such as receivables and payables. This information is contained in the subsidiary ledgers. For example, the accounts receivable subsidiary ledger contains all the individual customer accounts. The total of these accounts should equal the balance in the general ledger Accounts Receivable account. This general ledger account is called a *controlling account*.

2. Common specialized journals. Specialized journals are used to record routine transactions of the same type. These transactions and the related specialized journals are:

Transaction	Specialized Journal
Sales of merchandise on credit	Sales journal
Purchase of merchandise on credit	Purchases journal
Receipts of cash	Cash receipts journal
Payments of cash	Cash payments journal

Transactions that do not fit into any one of these journals are recorded in the general journal. Although there are standard forms for these journals, they should be designed to meet the needs of a particular firm.

[3]Geoffrey Smith, "Toward a More Perfect Market," *Forbes*, December 17, 1984, p. 73. Reprinted by permission of *Forbes* magazine. © Forbes Inc., 1984.

3. Recording transactions in specialized journals. In a manual system, transactions must be recorded by hand in specialized journals. In most cases, transactions that affect subsidiary accounts are posted daily, whereas transactions that affect general ledger accounts are posted monthly. At the end of the month, subsidiary trial balances are made, and the totals in these reports are compared with the balances in the related controlling or general ledger accounts.

4. The use of computerized systems. The recent development of microcomputers has made computerized accounting systems available to firms of all sizes. There are many software packages available to run on various makes of personal or business computers. These systems post transactions as they are recorded and supply management with up-to-date reports as needed. Spreadsheet, word processing, data base management, and integrated software programs have increased the financial analysis ability of private and public accountants. This trend will continue into the future and will enhance the efficiency of the accounting information system.

KEY TERMS

Accounts payable trial balance
Accounts receivable trial balance
Cash receipts journal
Cash payments journal
Controlling account
Purchases journal

Sales journal
Schedule of accounts payable
Schedule of accounts receivable
Specialized journal
Spreadsheet
Subsidiary account

PROBLEM FOR YOUR REVIEW

Special Journals. Business World entered into the following transactions during April:

- April 1: Cash sales amounted to $1,500.
- April 2: Sales to G. M. Smith on account amounted to $2,000. Terms are 2/10, n/30. The invoice number is 126.
- April 8: Collected $2,600 from A. L. Ford on sale made on March 2. No discount allowed.
- April 10: Sales to A.M.R. for $5,000 on account. Terms are 2/10, n/30. The invoice number is 127.
- April 11: Collected from G. M. Smith amount due from April 2 sale, less appropriate discount.
- April 18: Sold marketable securities with a cost of $2,500 for $2,200 cash.
- April 22: Collected from A.M.R. amount due from April 10 sale. Discount not taken.
- April 25: Cash sales amounted to $2,700.
- April 29: A customer returned some items, as they were defective, and received a cash refund of $500.
- April 30: Sale to N. B. Honda for $6,000. Terms are n/30. The invoice number is 128.

REQUIRED: **1.** Record these transactions in (1) the sales journal, (2) the general journal, or (3) the cash receipts journal, depending on the nature of the transaction.

2. Explain how these transactions should be posted to the subsidiary and general ledgers. It is not necessary to make the postings.

SOLUTION
(1)

Sales Journal

Date	Account Debited	Invoice Number	Post Ref.	Amount
April 2	G. M. Smith—2/10, n/30	126	✔	$ 2,000
10	A. M. R.—2/10, n/30	127	✔	5,000
30	N. B. Honda—n/30	128	✔	6,000
				$13,000

General Journal

Date	Explanation	Post Ref.	Debit	Credit
April 29	Sales Returns and Allowances	✔	500	
	Cash	✔		500
	To record cash refund to customer.			

Cash Receipts Journal

Date		Explanation	Cash	Sales Dis-counts	Other Accounts Account Title	Ref.	Amount	Account Credited	Accounts Receivable Ref.	Amount	Sales	Other Accounts Ref.	Amount
April	1	Cash sales	1,500.00								1,500.00		
	8	Invoice from March 2	2,600.00					A. L. Ford	✔	2,600.00			
	11	Invoice of April 2, less 2%	1,960.00	40.00				G. M. Smith	✔	2,000.00			
	18	Sale of marketable securities	2,200.00		Loss on sale of securities	✔	300.00	Marketable securities					2,500.00
	22	Invoice of April 10	5,000.00					A. M. R.	✔	5,000.00			
	25	Cash sales	2,700.00								2,700.00		
			15,960.00	40.00			300.00			9,600.00	4,200.00		2,500.00
			✔	✔						✔	✔		

(2) At the end of each day, postings from the sales journal and the cash receipts journal should be made to the appropriate customer accounts in the subsidiary ledger. Because account numbers were not given, these postings are shown by a check mark. At the end of the month, postings should be made to the general ledger accounts. Again, these postings are shown by a check mark.

QUESTIONS

1. What are subsidiary ledgers, and what purpose do they serve?

2. Name five general ledger accounts that are likely to be supported by subsidiary accounts. State why this is the case.

3. How are subsidiary accounts related to the controlling accounts? What purpose does the subsidiary trial balance serve in this regard?

4. What are specialized journals, and what purpose do they serve?

5. List the four most common specialized journals and the transactions that would be recorded in them.

6. Explain when and what postings are made from the sales journal to the appropriate ledgers. How might you detect an error in this posting process?

7. The purchases journal described in the text had only one amount column for purchases and accounts payable. If the journal were to be expanded to a multicolumn form, what additional columns might be included? What determines their selection?

8. One of your fellow students stated that all sales are recorded in the sales journal. Do you agree? Why or why not?

9. The Nett Company sells all its goods on a 2/10, n/30 basis. Its practice is to record all sales invoices net. Describe how this would affect the format of the cash receipts journal described in the text.

10. The Firegate Company makes its inventory purchases both by cash and on account. In what journals would these transactions be recorded? Would it be possible to record both these transactions in one journal? If so, which one?

11. Given the widespread use of specialized journals, is it still necessary to use a general journal? Why or why not?

12. A small retail store has always kept its accounting records manually. However, the company is thinking about trying to increase the efficiency and accuracy of its records. The president of the company is always complaining that the records he gets are often late and full of errors. What alternatives are available to the firm to upgrade its accounting system?

13. What is an electronic spreadsheet? Describe three accounting-related uses of such spreadsheets.

14. Mildred Jones is about to open her own CPA firm. She is considering purchasing a personal or office computer. List four functions for which such a computer could be used in her firm.

EXERCISES*

E1.   Transactions and Special Journals. The Grant Company uses a one-column sales journal, a one-column purchases journal, multicolumn cash receipts and cash payments journals, and a general journal. For each of the following transactions, state in which journal it should be recorded:

  (a) Purchase of inventory for cash.

  (b) Receipt of a $5,000 bank loan.

  (c) Sales on account.

  (d) Receipt of interest revenue for the month.

  (e) Cash withdrawal by the owner.

  (f) Purchase of inventory on account.

  (g) Payment of monthly rent.

  (h) Sale of an old delivery truck for cash. There was a loss on the sale.

  (i) Cash sales for the day from the cash register.

  (j) Return of merchandise purchased on account because it arrived damaged.

E2.   Characteristics of Special Journals. The Feel-Rite Drugstore uses the following specialized journals: a single-column sales journal, a single-column purchases journal, a multicolumn cash receipts journal, a multicolumn cash payables journal, and a general journal. Answer each of the following questions regarding these journals:

  (a) At the end of the period, the total in the sales journal should be posted to which ledger accounts?

  (b) What subsidiary ledgers would most likely be associated with the cash payments and cash receipts journals?

  (c) In which journal would the fewest transactions most likely be recorded?

*Unless otherwise noted, assume that all sales and purchases are recorded gross of any allowable sales or purchase discounts.

(d) The firm takes all available purchase discounts. In what journal would the purchase discounts be recorded?

(e) At the end of the period, the total in the purchases journal should be posted to which ledger accounts?

(f) In which journal are adjusting entries and closing entries made?

(g) In which journal would sales discounts be recorded?

E3. Characteristics of Specialized Journals and Subsidiary Ledgers. A fellow student made the following statements. State whether each statement is true or false, and explain your reasoning.

(a) All general ledger accounts must have subsidiary accounts.

(b) All entries in the cash receipts journal should be posted daily.

(c) The purchases journal can be used to record cash purchases.

(d) Daily postings in the sales journal are made to the subsidiary accounts payable ledger.

(e) Not all the column totals in the cash receipts journal are posted to specific ledger accounts.

(f) Computerized accounting systems have eliminated the need for internal controls.

E4. Making Entries in Specialized Journals. During the month of October, the Kwan Company entered into the following selected transactions:

- October 1: Purchased merchandise on account from the White Co., $10,000. Terms are 1/10, n/30.
- October 3: Purchased merchandise for cash, $1,000.
- October 5: Paid invoice of the ABC Co. from September, $8,000 less 2% discount.
- October 12: Purchased merchandise on account from the Brown Co., $6,000. Terms are n/30.
- October 15: Paid $1,000 for advertising expense.
- October 24: Returned $400 of merchandise purchased on October 12 because it was defective.
- October 30: Paid the remaining balance on the October 12 purchase.

REQUIRED: Record these transactions in the appropriate journals. Use journals similar in form to those used in this appendix.

E5. Making Entries in Specialized Journals. During November, the Spartan Company entered into the following transactions:

- November 1: Sales to The Express on account amounted to $5,000. Terms are n/30. The invoice number is 156.
- November 5: Collected $3,822 from the Raider Company from sale on October 30. The amount received represents the total invoice less the 2% discount. All sales are recorded gross.
- November 15: Cash sales for the first half of the month amounted to $10,000.
- November 18: Sales to the Invader Company on account amounted to $15,000. Terms are 2/10, n/30. The invoice number is 157.
- November 20: $300 worth of the merchandise sold to the Invader Company was defective and returned. Its account was credited.
- November 27: Collected the remaining balance due from the Invader Company, less the appropriate discount.
- November 30: Received an $8,000 bank loan from First City Bank.
- November 30: Cash sales for the remainder of the month were $13,000.

REQUIRED: Record these transactions in the appropriate journals. Use forms similar to those in this appendix. Number checks beginning with check no. 1.

E6. Posting to Ledger Accounts. The Michigan State Company uses a general journal, a one-column sales journal, a one-column purchases journal, multicolumn cash receipts and cash payments journals, and subsidiary accounts receivable and payable ledgers. As of September 30 of the current year, the following balances were in these controlling accounts:

| Accounts receivable | $180,000 |
| Accounts payable | 140,000 |

After the October transactions were recorded in the specialized journals, certain columns had the following totals:

Sales journal	$160,000
Purchases journal	190,000
Cash receipts journal —Accounts receivable column	135,000
—Sales column	40,000
Cash payments journal—Accounts payable column	200,000
—Purchases column	30,000

REQUIRED: Answer each of the following questions:

  (a) To which ledger accounts would the $160,000 column total of the sales journal be posted?

  (b) To which ledger accounts would the $190,000 column total of the purchases journal be posted?

  (c) Where would the accounts receivable total of $135,000 in the cash receipts journal be posted?

  (d) Where would the accounts payable total of $200,000 in the cash payments journal be posted?

  (e) What was the total of sales for the month of October?

  (f) What was the total of purchases for the month of October?

  (g) What are the balances in the controlling accounts receivable and the accounts payable accounts at the end of October?

E7. Posting to Subsidiary Accounts. The Raleigh Company started business on the first of January. At the end of January, the accounts receivable subsidiary trial balance appeared as follows:

Customer Name	Account Number	Balance
B. F. Good	001	$ 2,500
C. L. Cooper	002	3,000
P. M. Marwick	003	5,500
A. Y. Young	004	2,400
Total		$13,400

The sales journal for February appeared as follows:

Date	Account Debited	Invoice Number	Amount
February 2	C. D. Badd	749	$ 2,200
5	A. A. Andersen	315	6,000
14	C. L. Cooper	828	2,400
22	P. M. Marwick	170	3,000
29	P. W. Waterhouse	1,357	2,500
			$16,100

The accounts receivable column of the cash receipts journal contained the following:

B. F. Good	$2,500
C. L. Cooper	3,000
C. D. Badd	2,000
P. M. Marwick	8,000
C. L. Cooper	2,000

REQUIRED: **(a)** Post entries from the sales journal and the cash receipts journal to the appropriate accounts receivable subsidiary accounts. Where necessary, open new accounts beginning with account number 005. Use T accounts.

(b) Post the entries to the controlling Accounts Receivable and Sales accounts. Assume that the balance in the Sales account at February 1 is $70,000.

(c) Prepare an accounts receivable trial balance at February 29.

E8. Errors in Special Journals. The Budget Company records all sales on account in a one-column sales journal. During the month of July, the bookkeeper made the following errors in recording and posting in the sales journal:

(a) The amount column of the sales journal was incorrectly totaled.

(b) A sale on account to the Brinkley Company was correctly recorded in the sales journal as $100 but was posted to the subsidiary account as $1,000.

(c) A sales return of $200 was recorded in the general journal as a debit to Sales Returns and Allowances and a credit to Accounts Receivable. By mistake, the credit to Accounts Receivable was not posted to the controlling Accounts Receivable account.

(d) A mathematical error was made in determining a balance in one of the subsidiary Accounts Receivable accounts.

(e) A sale on account to the Dominici Company was posted in error to the account of the Hamm Company.

REQUIRED: Determine how each of these errors could be detected, assuming that they are independent.

PROBLEMS

A-1 Purchases Journal and Subsidiary Ledgers. Stuart's Supplies is an office supplies company in New Haven. Most of the company's purchases are made from five vendors. At the beginning of July of the current year, the controlling Accounts Payable (account no. 500) had a balance of $12,000. Analysis of the subsidiary accounts payable ledger indicated the following:

Supplier	Account No.	Balance
A. Doe	3-001	$2,800
L. Link	3-002	3,200
F. Owl	3-003	3,450
C. Roet	3-004	2,150
Z. Xu	3-005	400

During July, the following purchases were made on account from these suppliers. (No discounts are allowed on purchases.)

Supplier	Account No.	Sales
A. Doe	3-001	$2,600
L. Link	3-002	4,300
F. Owl	3-003	1,400
C. Roet	3-004	2,150

Payments on account during July were as follows:

Supplier	Account No.	Amount
A. Doe	3-001	$2,800
L. Link	3-002	5,000
F. Owl	3-003	1,500
C. Roet	3-004	4,300
Z. Xu	3-005	170

On July 22, the company returned some staplers to Xu that it previously purchased on account. The company's account was debited for $100.

REQUIRED:

(a) Set up the controlling Accounts Payable account and the appropriate accounts in the accounts payable subsidiary ledger. Use T accounts.

(b) Record the above transactions in a single-column purchases journal, as shown in the text. Record the purchase returns and the payment to suppliers in the general journal. The specific days of the month may be omitted.

(c) Post the entries to the controlling Accounts Payable account and the subsidiary accounts.

(d) Prepare a schedule of accounts payable (accounts payable trial balance) as of July 31.

A-2 Identifying Transactions in Specialized Journals. The following is an excerpt from one of the specialized journals used by Earth Resources, Inc. Describe the transaction that resulted in each entry. In addition, describe the postings that should be made daily and at the end of the month.

EARTH RESOURCES, INC.

| | | Debits | | | | | Credits | | | | | |
| | | | | Other Accounts | | | | | | | Other Accounts | |
Date	Explanation	Cash	Sales Discounts	Account Title	Ref.	Amount	Account Credited	Ref.	Accounts Receivable Amount	Sales	Ref.	Amount
September 1		3,000.00								3,000.00		
6		10,000.00					Securities					8,000.00
							Gain on sale					2,000.00
10		500.00	10.00				C. W. Poat		510.00			
14		5,500.00								5,500.00		
21		1,200.00					J. C. Ray		1,200.00			
27		100.00					Interest revenue					100.00
29		2,450.00	50.00				P. Chain		2,500.00			
30												
		6,000.00					Capital stock					6,000.00
		28,750.00	60.00						4,210.00	8,500.00		16,100.00

A-3 **Recording Transactions in the Sales and Purchases Journals.** The Fashion Coordinates Company uses a sales and purchases journal in its accounting system. The following selected transactions took place during July:

- July 1: Purchased merchandise on account from the Dimension Company for $3,000. Terms are 2/10, n/30. The invoice date is 7/1.
- July 3: Purchased inventory for $5,000 cash. Check number is 701.
- July 5: Sold on account to the Elite Company $3,500 of merchandise. Terms are 2/10, n/30. The invoice number is 927.
- July 15: Sold on account to the Large Sizes Co. $4,000 of merchandise. Terms are n/30. The invoice number is 928.
- July 22: Purchased inventory on account from the New Fashions Company, $4,500. Terms are n/30. The invoice date is 7/21.
- July 29: Sold on account to the Merton Company $7,000 of merchandise. Terms are 1/10, n/30. The invoice number is 929.

REQUIRED: **(a)** Open all the necessary general ledger accounts and accounts receivable and payable subsidiary ledger accounts. Use the following general ledger account numbers:

Accounts receivable	200	Sales	500
Accounts payable	400	Purchases	800

Assume that there are no beginning balances in any accounts.

(b) Record the above transactions in the appropriate journals.

(c) Post the transactions from the journals to the appropriate general and subsidiary ledgers. Use a check mark to indicate a posting to a subsidiary account.

(d) Prepare an accounts receivable and accounts payable trial balance as of the end of the month.

(e) Now assume that the sales and purchases are recorded net rather than gross. Describe the differences that would have to be made in the design of the sales journal, the purchases journal, the cash receipts journal, and the cash payments journal. How would this practice affect the way the entries are made in these journals?

A-4 **Recording Transactions in the Sales and Cash Receipts Journals.** The Molokai Company began business in January of the current year. The following selected transactions took place during the month of January:

- January 2: The owner, H. Molokai, invested $100,000 cash in the business.
- January 5: The firm sold short-term investments with a cost of $15,000 for $25,000 cash.
- January 7: Sales on account to the Lanai Co. amounted to $8,000. Terms are 2/10, n/30. The invoice number is 100.
- January 9: Sales on account to the New Japan Co. for $22,000. Terms are n/30. The invoice number is 101. New Japan's account balance was $4,000 prior to the sale.
- January 15: Cash sales for the first half of January are $8,000.
- January 16: The Big Island Company had an outstanding account receivable balance of $10,000. Because of financial difficulties, Big Island was having trouble paying. The Molokai Company agreed to exchange the account receivable for a $10,000, 12% note receivable due in one year.
- January 17: Received payment from Lanai Company less appropriate discount.
- January 21: Sales on account to the Kanapalli Co. amounted to $2,600. Terms are 2/10, n/30. The invoice number is 103.
- January 22: $12,000 payment on account from the New Japan Co.
- January 23: The Kanapalli Co. returned $400 of merchandise purchased on January 21 because it was defective. The company's account was credited for $400.

- January 30: Received a check for $1,000 representing rental revenue on a small building the firm owns.

- January 30: Received the amount due from the Kanapalli Co.

REQUIRED: **(a)** Enter the above transactions in either the sales journal, the cash receipts journal, or the general journal.

(b) Set up the following general ledger and subsidiary accounts:

General Ledger Accounts

Account	Account Number
Cash	100
Short-term investments (balance prior to entry, $15,000)	150
Accounts receivable (balance prior to entries, $14,000)	200
Notes receivable	250
H. Molokai, capital	500
Sales	600
Sales returns and allowances	650
Sales discounts	660
Rental revenue	900
Gain on sale of securities	950

Unless otherwise noted, assume that the account has a zero balance.

Open a subsidiary ledger for each customer. Begin with account 001 for the first customer. The second customer should be 002, and so forth.

(c) Foot and rule the specialized journals and post all entries to the appropriate ledger accounts.

A-5   **Recording Transactions in the Purchases and Cash Payments Journals.** The Rose Company's chart of accounts includes the following accounts:

Cash ($48,000)	100	Purchases	800
Office furniture ($12,000)	400	Purchase returns and allowances	920
Land	500	Purchase discounts	930
Accounts payable	600	Selling expenses	1000
Notes payable	700	General expenses	2000
Accrued expenses payable	750	Interest expense	3000

The amounts listed in parentheses represent the beginning balance on these accounts as of March 1, 1990. If no amount appears, the balance is zero.

The following transactions occurred during March:

- March 1: Purchased merchandise from the Zorn Company for $8,000 with an invoice date of March 1. Terms are 2/10, n/30.

- March 4: Made a $6,000 cash purchase from the Seaver Company.

- March 5: Purchased merchandise from the Plunkett Co. for $9,000. Terms are 2/10, n/30. The invoice is dated March 4.

- March 6: Returned $500 of merchandise to the Plunkett Co. because it arrived damaged. Received an adjustment on their account.

- March 8: Purchased a plot of land for $50,000. Made a 10% down payment and financed the rest through a 12% bank loan.

- March 10: Made required payment to the Zorn Company.

- March 15: Cash purchases totaled $1,000.

- March 18: Made appropriate payment to the Plunkett Co.

- March 19: Purchased merchandise from the Wodin Company for $8,000. Terms are 2/10, n/30. The invoice is dated March 18.

- March 22: Purchased additional office furniture for $2,000 cash.
- March 23: Purchased merchandise from the Huie Co. for $3,000. Terms are n/30. The invoice is dated March 23.
- March 27: Made appropriate payment to the Wodin Company.
- March 30: Made a $500 monthly payment on the bank loan of March 8. The interest portion is $450.
- March 30: Paid selling expenses of $3,000 and general expenses of $1,000.
- March 31: Accrued additional selling expenses of $500.

REQUIRED:
(a) Record the transactions in the appropriate journals. Use journals similar to those shown in the text, and a two-column general journal. Make all the required postings to the general ledger and subsidiary accounts. Use check marks to show the postings to the subsidiary accounts. Number the checks beginning with check no. 1.

(b) Balance the subsidiary accounts and the accounts payable general ledger account. Prepare an accounts payable trial balance. Make sure that the total in this trial balance agrees with the control account.

A-6 **Recording Transactions in Several Journals.** The Federal Company began operations on June 1 of the current year. The company's accounting system is based on a general journal, a one-column sales journal, a one-column purchases journal, a multicolumn cash receipts journal, and a multicolumn cash payments journal. The forms are similar to the ones used in the text. The following chart of accounts was set up:

Cash	10	Sales discounts	45
Accounts receivable	11	Sales returns and allowances	46
Prepaid rent	15	Purchases	50
Office furniture and equipment	18	Purchase discounts	55
Accounts payable	20	Purchase returns and allowances	56
Loan payable	21	Interest expense	59
Interest payable	25	Rent expense	60
Capital stock	30	Advertising expense	70
Sales	40	Salaries expense	80

During June, the following events occurred:

- June 1: The owner, C. Fazzi, invested $50,000 cash in the business through the purchase of capital stock.
- June 3: Borrowed $20,000 from a group of potential investors at 12%.
- June 3: Leased a store. A full year's rent of $4,800 was paid in advance.
- June 5: Purchased merchandise for cash, $6,000.
- June 6: Purchased merchandise on account from the Loutus Company, $4,000. Terms are 2/10, n/30. The invoice is dated June 5.
- June 7: Purchased merchandise on account from the Micro Co., $1,000. Terms are 2/10, n/30. The invoice is dated June 7.
- June 9: Purchased office furniture and fixtures, $5,000. Made a cash payment of $1,000; the rest on open account payable to the Furniture Company.
- June 9: Sold merchandise on account to the Chee Chee Co., $3,500. Terms are 2/10, n/30. The invoice number is 100.
- June 10: Some of the merchandise purchased from the Loutus Company arrived damaged. It was returned and the Federal Company account was reduced $200.
- June 12: The merchandise purchased from the Micro Co. was paid for.
- June 14: The appropriate payment was made to the Loutus Company for the outstanding balance of the payable.
- June 15: Cash sales for the first half of the month totaled $2,000.
- June 16: Advertising expense of $1,000 was incurred and paid for.

- June 18: Received balance owed from the Chee Chee Co.

- June 19: Purchased merchandise on account from the Rafferty Co., $1,800. Terms are n/30. The invoice is dated June 19.

- June 21: Cash purchases, $700.

- June 21: Purchased merchandise on account from the Quincy Co., $900. Terms are 2/10, n/30. The invoice is dated June 20.

- June 23: Sold merchandise on account to Carroll Co. for $4,000. Terms are 2/10, n/30. The invoice number is 102.

- June 25: Paid the Rafferty Co. $900 on account.

- June 27: Sold merchandise to the Discount Drug Store for $3,200. Terms are 2/10, n/30. The invoice number is 103.

- June 30: Salaries for the month of $2,000 were paid in cash.

- June 30: The Discount Drug Store returned some merchandise and received a credit of $200.

- June 30: Cash sales for the second half of the month, $4,500.

In addition, the following adjustments must be made:

(a) One month's prepaid rent must be written off.

(b) Interest for one month must be accrued on the loan.

REQUIRED: (a) Set up the general ledger accounts using the accounts from the chart of accounts. As necessary, set up appropriate subsidiary receivable and payable accounts.

(b) Enter the above transactions in the appropriate journals. Assume that all journals begin with page 1. Number checks beginning with check No. 1.

(c) Total the journal and make the appropriate postings to the general ledger accounts and subsidiary accounts. Use check marks to indicate a posting to the subsidiary accounts.

(d) Prepare subsidiary trial balances and check to see that they agree with the controlling accounts.

■ USING THE COMPUTER

A-7 **Electronic Spreadsheet—Cash Receipts Journal.** The Stickney Candy Company records all of its cash receipts in a cash receipts journal similar to that in the text. During August, the company entered into the following transactions:

- August 1: Cash sales amounted to $2,000.

- August 6: Sold a parcel of land for $10,000, which was purchased several years ago for $8,000.

- August 8: Received payment on account from C. W. Chang. Amount after 2% discount was $490. Receivables were recorded gross.

- August 15: Cash sales amounted to $3,500.

- August 19: Received payment on account from J. Donohoo. Amount received was $1,000. No discount was taken.

- August 24: Monthly interest revenue of $300 was received on note receivable. No monthly accruals were made.

- August 29: Received payment on account from P. Lockett. The receivable was originally recorded at a gross amount of $2,500. The 2% discount was taken.

- August 30: C. Stickney, the owner of the business, made an additional cash investment in the business of $5,000.

REQUIRED: Using an electronic spreadsheet, create a cash receipts journal similar to the one in the text. Debit columns should include cash, sales discounts, and other accounts. Credit columns should include receivables, sales, and other accounts. Enter the above transactions, and total the columns at the end of the month.

APPENDIX
B

ACCOUNTING FOR UNINCORPORATED BUSINESSES

After studying this appendix, you should be able to:
1. Account for the owners' equity section of a sole proprietorship.
2. Prepare financial statements of a sole proprietorship.

3. Explain the main concepts of a partnership.
4. Account for the operations of a partnership.

Throughout this book, the corporate form of business organization has been used to illustrate various accounting principles, because the corporation is the dominant form of business organization in the United States. However, in total numbers there are more sole proprietorships and partnerships than corporations. Furthermore, some very large service organizations such as national CPA firms and law firms are organized as partnerships. This appendix will discuss the concepts and procedures that are unique to sole proprietorships and partnerships.

■ THE SOLE PROPRIETORSHIP

A **sole proprietorship** is a business owned by a single individual. Although most sole proprietorships are relatively small, some are multimillion-dollar businesses. Legally, there is no distinction between the assets held in the business and those held personally by the owner. If the business becomes insolvent, its creditors can look to certain personal assets of the owner to meet their claims. Thus there is an unlimited liability for sole proprietorships. However, because of the entity rule, separate accounting records are maintained for the business, and there should be no commingling of business assets with the owner's assets.

■ THE OWNER'S EQUITY OF A SOLE PROPRIETORSHIP

With the exception of owner's equity transactions, all the accounting procedures and concepts you have learned apply equally well to sole proprietorships. In a sole proprietorship, since there is no legal distinction between the assets of a business and the personal assets of the owners, no attempt is made to distinguish between the original invested capital in the business and subsequent changes due to profits and losses. As a result, unlike a corporation, there is no separate invested capital account (Capital Stock) or accumulated profit account (Retained Earnings). These accounts are replaced by a permanent Capital account and a temporary Drawing account.

The Capital Account

In a sole proprietorship, the owner's **Capital account** replaces both the Capital Stock and Retained Earnings accounts. When the owner makes an original investment in the business, as well as subsequent investments, they are credited to the Capital account. At the end of the year, the profit or loss generated by the business is closed into the Capital account. Any withdrawals made by the owner are first accumulated in the Drawing account, which is closed into the Capital account at the end of the year. Thus the balance in the Capital account represents the sole proprietor's total equity in the business; it is similar to stockholders' equity in a corporation.

The Capital account is labeled with the name of the owner. For example, if Sue Lifs owned a business, her Capital account would be called Sue Lifs, Capital.

The Drawing Account

A sole proprietor often withdraws cash or other assets from the business. In order to maintain proper accounting records, withdrawals are recorded in a separate **Drawing account**. At the end of the period, the debit balance in the Drawing account, if any, is closed into the Capital account. This Drawing account (which is called, for example, Sue Lifs, Drawing) is similar to a Dividend account for a corporation.

■ ACCOUNTING FOR SOLE PROPRIETORSHIPS

To illustrate the accounting for a single proprietorship, assume that on January 2, 1990, Sue Lifs opens a retail computer store called Compton Computer Company. She invests $60,000 cash and other assets with the following fair market values:

Equipment	$25,000
Furniture and fixtures	10,000
Supplies	5,000

The following entry is made to record this investment:

Jan. 2, 1990	Cash	60,000	
	Equipment	25,000	
	Furniture and Fixtures	10,000	
	Supplies	5,000	
	Sue Lifs, Capital		100,000
	To record Sue Lifs's investment in the business.		

When assets other than cash are contributed to the sole proprietorships, they are recorded at their fair market values. Because the equipment and furniture and fixtures are now the assets of another entity (the sole proprietorship), a new basis of accounting is established. Thus the original cost of the assets to Sue Lifs is not relevant.

Proprietorship Operations

The Compton Computer Company's income statement for the year ended December 31, 1990 is shown in Exhibit B-1. As it indicates, net income for the year is $35,000. There are two important points to note when you examine this statement. First, salaries include only those of the employees, not that of the owner. Although Sue worked in the store and paid herself a salary of $1,000 per month, this amount is debited to the Drawing account and appears as a debit item on the statement of owner's equity. The monthly entry to record her salary is:

Sue Lifs, Drawing	1,000	
Cash		1,000
To record monthly salary of the owner.		

EXHIBIT B–1

| COMPTON COMPUTER COMPANY |
| Income Statement |
| For the Year Ended December 31, 1990 |

Revenue		
Sales		$280,000
Expenses		
Cost of goods sold	$182,000	
Salaries, other than owner	32,000	
Rent	15,000	
Depreciation	10,800	
Office expense	5,200	245,000
Net income		$ 35,000

Second, there is no item called "income taxes." This is because the sole proprietorship does not pay income tax. The total net income from the business is included with any other income earned by the proprietor and is taxed to the person at the individual level. The income or loss from the business is listed on a Schedule C, which is included in the personal tax return (Form 1040) of the individual owner.

Closing Entries

Based on the data from the income statement, the following closing entries are made at the end of the year:

Dec. 31, 1990	1. Sales	280,000	
	Income Summary		280,000
	To close revenue account.		

2.	Income Summary	245,000	
	Cost of Goods Sold		182,000
	Salaries		32,000
	Rent		15,000
	Depreciation		10,800
	Office Supplies		5,200
	To close expense account.		
3.	Income Summary	35,000	
	Sue Lifs, Capital		35,000
	To close income summary to capital account.		
4.	Sue Lifs, Capital	12,000	
	Sue Lifs, Drawing		12,000
	To close drawing account into capital account.		

■ FINANCIAL STATEMENTS OF A SOLE PROPRIETORSHIP

Except for owner's equity, the financial statements of a sole proprietorship are similar to those of other forms of business organizations. In a manner similar to a retained earnings statement, the statement of owner's equity is prepared for a sole proprietorship. Such a statement for the Compton Computer Company is shown in Exhibit B-2. There is no beginning balance in this statement, since this is the end of the company's first year of operations. The initial investment by Sue Lifs is shown as an investment. The net income increases the owner's equity and the monthly withdrawals decrease it. As a result, ending owner's equity is $123,000; this is the same amount shown under owner's equity on the December 31, 1990 balance sheet (Exhibit B-3).

EXHIBIT B–2

COMPTON COMPUTER COMPANY
Statement of Owner's Equity
For the Year Ended December 31, 1990

Sue Lifs, Capital—1/2/90		$ 0
Add		
Investment	$100,000	
Net income	35,000	135,000
Less: Withdrawals		12,000
Sue Lifs, Capital—12/31/90		$123,000

EXHIBIT B–3

COMPTON COMPUTER COMPANY
Balance Sheet
December 31, 1990

Assets		Liabilities and Owner's Equity	
Cash	$ 15,800	Liabilities	
Accounts receivable	17,900	Accounts payable	$ 5,400
Inventory	80,000	Notes payable	10,000
Supplies	3,000	Salaries payable	2,500
Equipment, net	17,000	Total liabilities	17,900
Furniture and fixtures, net	7,200	Owner's equity	
		Sue Lifs, Capital	123,000
		Total liabilities and	
Total assets	$140,900	owner's equity	$140,900

■ PARTNERSHIP—THE MAIN CONCEPTS

The Uniform Partnership Act defines a **partnership** as "an association of two or more persons to carry on as co-owners of a business for a profit." Traditionally, many professional firms such as law firms and CPA firms have been organized as partnerships, due to the fact that until the mid-1970s, most states prohibited professionals from incorporating. However, this prohibition has been lifted, and many professional firms are now incorporated.

■ FEATURES OF A PARTNERSHIP

Partnerships have several features or characteristics, including voluntary association, ease of formation, limited life, mutual agency, unlimited liability, co-ownership of property, and participation in partnership profits and losses.

Voluntary Association

A partnership is a voluntary association between two or more individuals. It is not a legal entity, so no federal or state income taxes are levied against the partnership. However, as in the case of the sole proprietorship, the partnership is a distinct accounting entity. Because the partnership does not represent a separate legal entity, each partner has unlimited liability for partnership debts and is bound by mutual agency by the actions of other partners.

Ease of Formation

Because a partnership is a voluntary association rather than a separate legal entity, it is relatively easy to form. In fact, any two competent individuals can verbally agree to organize a partnership. No state approval is needed.

When individuals agree to form a partnership, a partnership agreement results. This agreement constitutes a contract between the partners and states the details of the partnership. Although this document does not have to be in writing, it certainly makes good sense to have a written partnership agreement, containing the following points:

1. The name, location, and purpose of the business.
2. The names and addresses of the original partners.
3. The investment to be made by each partner.
4. The respective duties of each partner.
5. The method by which profits and losses are to be distributed.
6. The amount and timing of the withdrawals allowed by the partners.
7. Procedures for the admission or withdrawal of partners.
8. Procedures for the orderly dissolution of the partnership.

Limited Life

Because of the voluntary association aspect of a partnership, a partnership is ended every time there is a change of partners. For example, the admission of a new partner or the withdrawal or death of an old partner automatically terminates the old partnership and creates a new one. Business does not necessarily have to cease when a partnership ends; it is likely to continue if a new partnership is formed. Other events causing the termination of a partnership are the bankruptcy of a partner, incapacitation of a partner due to illness or other factors, or mutual consent of all partners.

Mutual Agency

Mutual agency means that each partner can make binding agreements for the partnership as long as the partner acts within the normal scope of partnership business. In effect, each partner is an agent of the partnership and has authority to act on behalf of the partnership. Mutual agency clearly means that individuals must be very careful in selecting partners.

Unlimited Liability

Unlimited liability means that each partner is personally liable for the debts of the partnership. Thus an individual partner's liability is not limited to the amount of the partner's investment in the partnership. For example, if a partnership is bankrupt, the creditors may seek relief from the individual partners. Furthermore, if an individual partner does not have enough personal assets to meet these debts, the creditors are able to make a claim against the personal assets of the remaining solvent partners.

In recent years, primarily for tax reasons, a form of partnership called a *limited partnership* has evolved. The primary difference between a limited partnership and a regular partnership (often referred to as a *general partnership*) involves the individual partner's liability for partnership debts. In a limited partnership, there are generally one or two general partners and several limited partners. In this type of partnership, only the general partners have unlimited liability; the liability of the limited partners is their investment in the partnership. The management control of the partnership lies with the general partners. Limited partnerships have definite advantages for tax shelter investments, but not for normal daily operations. The examples in this appendix assume a general partnership.

Co-ownership of Property and Participation in Partnership Profits and Losses

The property of the partnership is jointly owned by all partners. This means that if an individual partner contributes property to the partnership, the property becomes jointly owned by all partners. Furthermore, each partner has the right to share in partnership profits and losses. The distribution of profits and losses among partners can be in any manner agreed upon by the partners and should be clearly stated in the partnership agreement. It is possible for the partners to agree to split profits in one manner and losses in a different manner.

◾ ADVANTAGES AND DISADVANTAGES OF PARTNERSHIP

The characteristics of partnerships described above result in both advantages and disadvantages. Partnerships are advantageous because they are easy to form or dissolve. Because partnerships are not separate legal entities, they are not subject to income tax or to the same state and federal regulations as corporations. Generally, a partnership is a convenient way to pool capital and managerial skills.

However, there are three serious disadvantages to a partnership: unlimited liability, mutual agency, and limited life. The unlimited-liability and limited-life aspects of a partnership make it very difficult for partnerships to raise the capital needed to finance large businesses. This is further complicated by the fact that it is more difficult to transfer a partnership interest than to purchase and sell a share of capital stock. Finally, mutual agency means that individual partners are subject to the actions of all partners.

◾ ACCOUNTING ISSUES RELATED TO PARTNERSHIP OPERATIONS

As with sole proprietorships, the major difference in accounting for a partnership is in the owners' equity section of the balance sheet. Instead of a Capital Stock and a Retained Earnings account, the owners' equity section contains a Capital account for each partner. The Capital account is a running balance of each individual partner's investment and share of partnership profits less his or her share of partnership losses and withdrawals. In addition, a Drawing account, which is closed into the Capital account yearly, is maintained for each partner. The division of partnership profit and loss among the various partners is one of the most important aspects of partnership accounting.

■ ACCOUNTING FOR THE FORMATION OF A PARTNERSHIP

In order to illustrate the accounting procedures required when a partnership is formed, assume that Jim Levitas and Teri Brown decide to leave their positions with a large CPA firm and open their own practice on January 2, 1990. The partnership agreement states that each partner is to contribute $60,000 in cash or other assets. Levitas contributes $60,000 in cash and Brown contributes $30,000 in cash plus other assets, including office equipment and office furniture and fixtures having fair market values of $12,000 and $18,000, respectively.

The entry to record Levitas's cash investment is straightforward. Cash is debited, and J. Levitas, Capital, is credited for $60,000. The entry to record Teri Brown's capital investment is more complicated. As is the case with sole proprietorships, assets other than cash that are contributed to the partnership are recorded at their market values. Thus the original cost of the office equipment and the office furniture and fixtures to Teri Brown, or even their present net book value, is not relevant. The current fair value of these assets must be determined and becomes the basis to the partnership.

The following entries are made to record the original investments in the partnership of Levitas and Brown:

Jan. 2, 1990	Cash	60,000	
	J. Levitas, Capital		60,000
	To record $60,000 cash investment by Levitas.		
	Cash	30,000	
	Office Equipment	12,000	
	Office Furniture and Fixtures	18,000	
	T. Brown, Capital		60,000
	To record investment in cash and assets by Brown.		

■ SUBSEQUENT INVESTMENTS AND WITHDRAWALS

Subsequent investments by partners are quite common. When that occurs, cash or other assets are debited and the partners' Capital accounts are credited. Occasionally, a partner (or partners) will make loans to the partnership instead of making a capital investment. This may occur if the funds are needed only for a short period of time or when one of the partners is willing to provide additional funds to the partnership. These loans are recorded by a debit to Cash and a credit to a Partner's Loan account. However, in most states these loans are considered part of the partners' capital. In effect, liabilities to third parties always take precedence over partners' loans; in case of liquidation, these third-party liabilities must be paid in full before any partner's loans are repaid.

Partners often withdraw cash or other assets, and a Drawing account is established for each partner to record these transactions. This account is used to record cash or asset withdrawals made by the partners and other payments by the partnership for personal debts or expenses. Again, as with the sole proprietorship, partners' salaries are not considered an expense but are withdrawals in anticipation of partnership profits. As a result, all partners' withdrawals are debited to this Drawing account, even though they are referred to as salaries.

■ RECORDING PROFITS AND CLOSING ENTRIES

Continuing with the example, assume that the firm of Levitas and Brown was successful during its first year. The income statement for the year ended December 31, 1990 (shown in Exhibit B-4) is similar to that of any service business. One added feature to a partnership income statement is the bottom portion showing the distribution of profits. In this case, the net income of $80,000 is split evenly. However, profits can be split in any manner the partners desire.

EXHIBIT B—4

LEVITAS AND BROWN, CPAs Income Statement For the Year Ended December 31, 1990		
Revenues		
Fees		$210,000
Expenses		
Employee salaries	$75,000	
Rent	25,000	
Travel	12,000	
Depreciation	10,000	
Supplies used	6,500	
Delivery expense	1,500	130,000
Net income		$ 80,000
Distribution of net income		
Jim Levitas, 50%	$40,000	
Teri Brown, 50%	40,000	$80,000

Partnership Net Income and Income Taxes

As previously noted, partnerships are not required to pay income taxes on their profits. As a result, there is no income tax expense on a partnership income statement. However, partners must include their share of profits or losses in their individual tax returns. These profits and losses must be included in the partners' income in the year earned, regardless of when they are distributed to the partners. In order to ensure the proper reporting of partnership profits, the partnership must file an information tax return showing the partnership net income or loss and each partner's share of that net income or loss.

Closing Entries

The entries to close the income statement accounts into the partners' Capital accounts are:

Dec. 31, 1990	Fees	210,000	
	Income Summary		210,000
	To close revenue accounts.		
	Income Summary	130,000	
	Employee Salaries		75,000
	Rent		25,000
	Travel		12,000
	Depreciation		10,000
	Supplies Used		6,500
	Delivery Expense		1,500
	To close expense accounts.		

Income Summary	80,000	
J. Levitas, Capital		40,000
T. Brown, Capital		40,000
To close income summary into the Capital accounts.		
J. Levitas, Capital	24,000	
T. Brown, Capital	24,000	
J. Levitas, Drawing		24,000
T. Brown, Drawing		24,000
To close drawing accounts into the Capital accounts.		

These entries are based on the income statement as well as the fact that each partner withdrew $2,000 a month in salaries.

After the closing entries are made, a balance sheet (Exhibit B-5) and a statement of partners' capital (Exhibit B-6) are prepared. Again, the balance sheet is similar to that of any service business. The only feature that distinguishes it as a partnership balance sheet is the owners' equity section. The statement of partners' capital shows all changes that occurred during the period in each individual partner's Capital account.

EXHIBIT B–5

LEVITAS AND BROWN, CPAs
Balance Sheet
December 31, 1990

Assets		Liabilities and Owners' Equity	
Current assets		Liabilities	
Cash	$ 13,000	Accounts payable	$ 13,400
Accounts receivable	56,500	Salaries payable	3,600
Office supplies	9,500		
Total current assets	79,000	Total liabilities	17,000
Noncurrent assets		Owners' equity	
Store equipment, net	$20,000	Jim Levitas, Capital	76,000
Office equipment and		Teri Brown, Capital	76,000
fixtures, net	4,000	Total owners' equity	152,000
Other assets	66,000		
Total noncurrent assets	90,000	Total liabilities and	
Total assets	$169,000	owners' equity	$169,000

EXHIBIT B–6

LEVITAS AND BROWN, CPAs
Statement of Partners' Capital
For the Year Ended December 31, 1990

	Levitas	Brown	Total
Capital, 1/1/90	$ 0	$ 0	$ 0
Add: Investment during the year	60,000	60,000	120,000
Net income	40,000	40,000	80,000
	100,000	100,000	200,000
Less: Withdrawals	24,000	24,000	48,000
Capital, 12/31/90	$ 76,000	$ 76,000	$152,000

■ DISTRIBUTION OF PARTNERSHIP PROFITS

The partners can agree to share profits and losses in any manner they wish. In fact, profits can be distributed in one ratio and losses in another. The distribution of profits and losses should be clearly stated in the partnership agreement. If the agreement fails to mention how the profits are to be divided, the law generally requires an equal split. If the agreement mentions the ratio in which profits are to be split but fails to mention losses, losses will usually be split in the same ratio as profits.

Dividing Partnership Net Income or Loss

As previously noted, partners can agree to divide partnership profits and losses in any manner they desire. However, most agreements take one of three general types:

1. A fixed ratio. For example, a three-person partnership can agree to divide income and losses equally so that each partner is allocated one-third of the profits or losses. In other instances, the profits can be split 40%, 35%, and 25% and the losses, $33\frac{1}{3}$%, $33\frac{1}{3}$%, and $33\frac{1}{3}$%.

2. A set salary to partners, with the remaining net income split in any agreed-upon ratio. For example, each of three partners agrees to a salary of $12,000, and the remainder, if any, is split 35%, 35%, and 30%.

3. Salaries to partners, interest on partners' Capital accounts, and the remainder, if any, split in a fixed ratio. Thus, in addition to salaries, each partner is allocated a stated percentage rate on the capital balance. This type of agreement combines the features of each of the previous types of profit allocation.

It must be remembered that these examples are not all-inclusive; they are just representative of the types of profit-sharing arrangements that can be made.

The components found in these types of profit-sharing arrangements grew out of the nature of partnership profits. Partnership profits are assumed to be composed of three distinct elements: (1) a return on the partners' invested capital, (2) a salary or compensation for services performed for the partnership, and (3) an economic or pure profit for taking the risk of operating a business. Different profit-sharing arrangements are necessary because partners are apt to contribute in different ways. For example, one partner may make a larger investment in the business but may perform few services for the partnership. The other partner may make a smaller investment but may perform a greater portion of personal services to the partnership. A profit-sharing agreement that is based on capital investments, salaries, and a fixed ratio for the remaining profits is flexible enough to handle these situations.

To illustrate the calculations required in dividing partnership income, see Exhibit B-7, which shows data at year-end 1990 for the partnership of Maynard and Arthur, which has been in existence for several years. The partnership calls for Maynard and Arthur to receive: (1) salaries of $18,000 and $24,000, respectively, (2) 10% interest on their capital balances at the beginning of the year, and (3) any remaining income split equally. Assuming partnership net income was $100,000, Exhibit B-8 (on the next page) illustrates how this income is distributed between Maynard and Arthur.

EXHIBIT B–7

	Maynard	Arthur	Total
Capital balances, 1/1/90	$124,800	$115,200	$240,000
Additional contribution, 4/1/90	15,650		15,650
Additional contribution, 7/1/90		9,350	9,350
	$140,450	$124,550	$265,000
Income for 1990*			$100,000

*Before any partners' salaries or interest on capital balances.

EXHIBIT B–8

Distribution of Partnership
Net Income

	Maynard	Arthur	Net Income
1990 net income			$100,000
Allocation of salaries	$18,000	$24,000	(42,000)
Remaining to be allocated			58,000
Interest on beginning capital balance			
Maynard, $124,800 × .10	12,480		(12,480)
Arthur, $115,200 × .10		11,520	(11,520)
Remaining to be allocated in a fixed ratio			$ 34,000
Maynard, 50%	17,000		(17,000)
Arthur, 50%		17,000	(17,000)
Total share to each partner	$47,480	$52,520	$ 0

The closing entry to reflect this distribution is:

Income Summary	100,000	
K. Maynard, Capital		47,480
B. Arthur, Capital		52,520
To close net income for the year to partners' capital.		
K. Maynard, Capital	18,000	
B. Arthur, Capital	24,000	
K. Maynard, Drawing		18,000
B. Arthur, Drawing		24,000
To close drawing accounts into capital.		

In any particular period, the partnership's net income may not exceed the partners' salaries and the interest on their capital balances. If this occurs, the salaries or the interest on invested capital which are specified in the partnership agreement must still be allocated in the prescribed manner. Any deficit must then be allocated in the same ratio in which any positive remainder would have been allocated.

To illustrate, now assume the same facts as before, except that the partnership's net income for 1990 is only $58,000. Exhibit B-9 shows how the $58,000 is distributed between Maynard and Arthur.

EXHIBIT B–9

Distribution of Partnership
Net Income

	Maynard	Arthur	Total
1990 net income			$58,000
Allocation of salaries	$18,000	$24,000	(42,000)
Remaining to be allocated			16,000
Interest on beginning capital balances			
Maynard, $124,800 × .10	12,480		(12,480)
Arthur, $115,200 × .10		11,520	(11,520)
Deficit after salaries and interest			
allocated in a fixed ratio			(8,000)
Maynard, 50%	(4,000)		4,000
Arthur, 50%		(4,000)	4,000
Total share to each partner	$26,480	$31,520	$ 0

The closing entry to record this distribution is:

Income Summary	58,000	
K. Maynard, Capital		26,480
B. Arthur, Capital		31,520
To close net income for the year to partners' capital.		

K. Maynard, Capital	18,000	
B. Arthur, Capital	24,000	
K. Maynard, Drawing		18,000
B. Arthur, Drawing		24,000
To close drawing account to capital.		

■ OTHER ACCOUNTING ISSUES RELATED TO PARTNERSHIPS

There are various other issues related to partnership accounting. These include the admission and/or withdrawal of partners and the liquidation of the partnership. Such complex issues are beyond the scope of an introductory text.

SUMMARY OF LEARNING OBJECTIVES

1. The owner's equity section of a sole proprietorship. In a sole proprietorship, the owner's Capital account replaces both the Capital Stock and the Retained Earnings accounts. When a sole proprietor withdraws cash or other assets from the sole proprietorship, this withdrawal is recorded in a separate Drawing account.

2. Financial statements of a sole proprietorship. Except for the owner's equity section, the financial statements of a sole proprietorship are similar to those of other forms of business organizations. A statement of owner's capital (similar to a retained earnings statement) is prepared.

3. The main concepts behind partnerships. A partnership is an association of two or more persons to carry on as co-owners of a business for a profit. Partnerships have certain characteristics that make them advantageous. Included are their ease of formation and dissolution and the fact that they are not separate legal entities, which means they are not taxed. On the other hand, there are certain disadvantages to a partnership, including unlimited liability, mutual agency, and limited life. These characteristics tend to make it more difficult to raise capital than it is for a corporation.

4. Accounting issues related to partnership operations. Except for the owners' equity section of the balance sheet, accounting for a partnership is similar to the accounting for other business organizations. The partners' Capital accounts reflect the individual partners' equity in the partnership. They are used to record initial investments, subsequent investments, and the partners' share of profit or losses. Partners' withdrawals are eventually closed into their Capital accounts.

The partners can agree to share partnership profit and losses in any manner they wish. However, the profit-sharing agreement should be clearly spelled out in the partnership agreement. Generally, the distribution of profit and losses is based on one or more of the following items:

1. Partners' salaries.

2. Interest on capital balances.

3. A fixed ratio.

KEY TERMS

Capital account
Drawing account
Mutual agency
Partnership
Sole proprietorship

Accounting for Partnership Operations. The partnership of Webb, Gernon, and Rios commenced business on January 2, 1990. The financial statements at the end of 1990 are shown below and on the next page.

In addition, you have learned that the partnership agreement calls for profit and losses to be split as follows:

1. Webb is to receive a salary of $1,500 per month.

2. Gernon and Rios are to receive salaries of $2,000 per month.

3. All partners will receive interest of 10% on their opening Capital balances (in this case, the investment made on 1/2/90). The remainder of income is to be distributed as follows: Webb 40%, Gernon 30%, and Rios 30%.

WEBB, GERNON, AND RIOS, ATTORNEYS
Income Statement
For the Year Ended December 31, 1990

Revenues		
Fees earned		$330,000
Expenses		
Salaries	$140,000	
Rent	75,000	
Depreciation	15,000	
Insurance	2,500	
Office supplies	2,000	
Delivery	1,500	236,000
Net income		$ 94,000
Distribution of net income		
Webb		$ 29,200
Gernon		32,400
Rios		32,400
		$ 94,000

WEBB, GERNON, AND RIOS, ATTORNEYS
Statement of Partners' Capital
For the Year Ended December 31, 1990

	Webb	Gernon	Rios	Total
Capital, 1/1/90	$ 0	$ 0	$ 0	$ 0
Add: Investment during year	60,000	45,000	45,000	150,000
Net income	29,200	32,400	32,400	94,000
Less: Withdrawals	(18,000)	(24,000)	(24,000)	(66,000)
Capital, 12/31/90	$71,200	$53,400	$53,400	$178,000

WEBB, GERNON, AND RIOS, ATTORNEYS
Balance Sheet
December 31, 1990

Assets		Liabilities and Partners' Equity	
Cash	$ 29,000	Liabilities	
Accounts receivable	42,600	Accounts payable	$ 5,200
Office supplies	8,200	Wages payable	1,500
Prepaid insurance	9,700	Total liabilities	6,700
Office equipment, net	38,400	Partners' equity	
Office furniture, net	56,800	Webb, Capital	71,200
		Gernon, Capital	53,400
		Rios, Capital	53,400
			178,000
		Total liabilities and partners'	
Total assets	$184,700	equity	$184,700

REQUIRED:

1. Make the journal entries to record the partners' investment in the partnership on 1/2/90. Assume that all partners contributed cash.

2. Show how the profit distribution was calculated.

3. Make all the required closing entries.

4. If net income for the year was only $75,000, recalculate the profit distribution.

SOLUTION

(1) ENTRIES TO RECORD ORIGINAL INVESTMENT

1/2/90	Cash	150,000	
	Webb, Capital		60,000
	Gernon, Capital		45,000
	Rios, Capital		45,000
	To record original investment in partnership.		

(2) DISTRIBUTION OF PROFITS

WEBB, GERNON, AND RIOS, ATTORNEYS
Distribution of Income for 1990

	Webb	Gernon	Rios	Total
1990 net income				$94,000
Allocation of salaries	$18,000	$24,000	$24,000	(66,000)
Remaining to be allocated				28,000
Interest on beginning capital balance				
Webb ($60,000 × .10)	6,000			(6,000)
Gernon (45,000 × .10)		4,500		(4,500)
Rios (45,000 × .10)			4,500	(4,500)
				13,000
Remaining to be allocated in a fixed ratio				
Webb, 40%	5,200			(5,200)
Gernon, 30%		3,900		(3,900)
Rios, 30%			3,900	(3,900)
	$29,200	$32,400	$32,400	$ 0

(3) CLOSING ENTRIES

12/31/90	Fees Earned	330,000	
	Income Summary		330,000
	To close fees earned to income summary.		

Income Summary	236,000	
Salaries		140,000
Rent		75,000
Depreciation		15,000
Insurance		2,500
Office Supplies		2,000
Delivery		1,500
To close expenses to income summary.		
Income Summary	94,000	
Webb, Capital		29,200
Gernon, Capital		32,400
Rios, Capital		32,400
To close income summary to capital.		
Webb, Capital	18,000	
Gernon, Capital	24,000	
Rios, Capital	24,000	
Webb, Drawing		18,000
Gernon, Drawing		24,000
Rios, Drawing		24,000
To close drawing into partners' capital.		

(4) DISTRIBUTION OF PROFITS—NET INCOME $75,000

WEBB, GERNON, AND RIOS, ATTORNEYS
Distribution of Income for 1990

	Webb	Gernon	Rios	Total
1990 net income				$75,000
Allocation of salaries	$18,000	$24,000	$24,000	(66,000)
Remaining to be allocated				9,000
Interest on beginning capital balance:				
Webb ($60,000 × .10)	6,000			(6,000)
Gernon (45,000 × .10)		4,500		(4,500)
Rios (45,000 × .10)			4,500	(4,500)
Deficit				(6,000)
Deficit allocated in profit-sharing ratio:				
Webb ($6,000 × .40)	(2,400)			2,400
Gernon ($6,000 × .30)		(1,800)		1,800
Rios ($6,000 × .30)			(1,800)	1,800
	$21,600	$26,700	$26,700	$ 0

QUESTIONS

1. Describe the Capital accounts for a sole proprietorship.

2. How are the profits of a sole proprietorship taxed?

3. Describe the primary features of a partnership. Discuss the advantages and disadvantages of the partnership form of business organization.

4. Until recently, many personal-service businesses in the United States that had more than one owner were or-

ganized as partnerships. Why do you think that was the case?

5. What is a partnership agreement and what items should be included in the document?

6. In forming the partnership of Scully and Porter, Scully contributed only cash and Porter contributed various assets other than cash. How should these assets be re-

corded on the partnership books? What is the relevance of the book value of these assets on Porter's records?

7. Describe the nature of partnership profits and how they should be taken into consideration in developing a scheme to divide partnership profits or losses.

8. You and a potential partner are considering starting a partnership to practice law. What factors should be considered in deciding how to divide profits and losses? Is it

necessary that profits and losses be divided in the same manner?

9. The partnership of Arnold and Cherry earned $50,000 during the current year. During the year, Arnold withdrew $30,000, and Cherry withdrew $24,000. The partnership agreement calls for Arnold and Cherry to split profits and losses equally. How much income must Arnold and Cherry report on their income tax returns for the current year?

EXERCISES

E1. **Sole Proprietorship.** Jacob Smith recently decided to open a retail store selling fax machines. Prepare journal entries to record the following transactions during the company's first month of business:

- Nov. 1: Jacob invested $20,000 in cash and various pieces of equipment, valued at $12,000, in the business.
- Nov. 9: Jacob withdrew $1,000 from the business for personal use.
- Nov. 30: Closed the following revenue and expense accounts:

Sales	$16,000
Cost of Goods Sold	9,000
Rent Expense	1,500
Utility Expense	400
Depreciation Expense—Various	300

- Nov. 30: Closed Income Summary account.
- Nov. 30: Closed Drawing account.

E2. **Accounting for the Formation of a Partnership.** Emily Chang ran a small but successful CPA firm as a sole proprietorship for a number of years. During the current year, she decided to expand the firm and admit a partner, Ken Cobb. The partnership agreement calls for Cobb to contribute $100,000 and for Chang to contribute the assets of her existing practice. The partnership agreement provides the following information concerning the assets contributed by Chang:

Account	Book Value	Fair Value
Cash	$ 5,000	$ 5,000
Accounts receivable	25,000	20,000
Supplies	8,000	8,000
Office equipment	50,000	67,000

During the first year, the partnership's net income was $50,000. All profit and losses are split equally, and during the year each partner was paid a salary of $20,000.

REQUIRED: **(a)** Make the necessary summary journal entries to record these events.

(b) What is the amount of each partner's Capital account at the end of the first year of operations?

E3. **Partnership Operations.** Make the journal entries to record each of the following independent situations relating to a partnership:

(a) H. Aber contributes cash of $20,000 and assets with a book value of $40,000 and a fair market value of $25,000 to a partnership.

(b) T. O'Keefe withdraws $8,000 cash from the partnership.

(c) H. Gernon borrows $5,000 cash from the partnership.

(d) A. Zapata, one of the partners in a local CPA firm, collects a $1,000 receivable from one of the partnership clients and deposits the funds in his own bank account for his personal use.

(e) B. Crocker purchases one-half of the interest of one of the existing partners in the Express Co. for $50,000. The total Capital balance of the partner, BA America, was $80,000 before the purchase.

E4. Statement of Partners' Capital Accounts. At the beginning of the current year, 1990, the total capital of the JAR partnership was $120,000. During the year, the partnership's net income was $100,000. The following salaries were paid to each of the partners: J, $18,000; A, $24,000; R, $15,000. The partners split profit and losses as follows: J, 30%; A, 30%; R, 40%. The partners have also agreed to maintain Capital balances in that ratio, and they agree that the total capital of the partnership at the end of the year should be $130,000. Prepare a statement of the partners' Capital accounts at the end of the current year.

E5. Division of Partnership Profits. The beginning capital of the Furillo and Lombardi partnership was $200,000. Furillo's Capital balance was $120,000, and Lombardi's was $80,000. Determine how profits and losses should be split in each of the following independent situations:

(a) Partnership net income was $51,000, and the profits are split one-third to Furillo and two-thirds to Lombardi.

(b) Partnership net loss was $60,000, and profits and losses are split in the ratio of the beginning Capital balances.

(c) Partnership net income was $120,000. Each partner draws a salary of $25,000 a year. Partnership profits in excess of salaries are split 55% to Furillo and 45% to Lombardi.

(d) Partnership net income was $40,000. Each partner draws a salary of $25,000 a year. The partnership agreement is silent as to how profit and losses are to be split.

PROBLEMS

B-1 Accounting for the Formation of Partnerships. Helene Blanc and Henry Lee each operated their own CPA firms for several years before deciding to form a partnership at the beginning of the current year, 1990. The partnership agreement stipulated that Blanc and Lee were to contribute the net assets of their individual practices. In addition, because Blanc was to be the managing partner, she was to receive 55% of the profits, and Lee was to receive 45%. All losses were to be split equally.

Just prior to the merger, the individual balance sheets for Blanc and Lee were as follows:

	Blanc's Practice		Lee's Practice	
Assets	**Book Value**	**Fair Value**	**Book Value**	**Fair Value**
Cash	$ 5,000	$ 5,000	$10,000	$10,000
Accounts receivable, net	25,000	22,000	34,000	30,000
Office supplies	2,500	2,500	1,500	1,000
Office equipment, net	50,000	60,000	40,000	48,000
Total assets	$82,500	$89,500	$85,500	$89,000
Equities				
Accounts payable	$12,000	$12,500	$ 1,500	$ 1,500
Blanc, Capital	70,500	77,000		
Lee, Capital			84,000	87,500
Total equities	$82,500	$89,500	$85,500	$89,000

At the end of the firm's first year of operations, these accounts showed the following balances:

Income Summary	$80,000 credit
Blanc, Drawing	30,000 debit
Lee, Drawing	25,000 debit

No additional capital contributions were made.

REQUIRED: **(a)** Prepare the journal entries to open the partnership's books.

(b) Prepare a balance sheet on the first day of partnership operations, January 2, 1990.

(c) Prepare the closing entries at the end of 1990.

(d) Prepare a statement of partners' Capital accounts on December 31, 1990.

B-2 **Partnership Operations.** Bill Garrison, the managing partner of a partnership that owns a large department store, prepared the following income statement:

BUY-RITE DEPARTMENT STORE
Income Statement
For the Year Ended December 31, 1990

Net sales		$2,500,000
Cost of goods sold		1,625,000
Gross margin on sales		875,000
Operating expenses		
Selling	$435,000	
General and administrative	240,000	675,000
Net income		$ 200,000

In addition, the following data are also available:

1. Included in general and administrative expenses are partners' salaries of $50,000, split as follows: Garrison, $25,000; Smith, $20,000; Beaver, $5,000.

2. During the year Al Smith, one of the partners, took some merchandise home from the department store for his personal use. The bookkeeper did not record this, so the merchandise, with a cost of $5,000, was not counted in the ending inventory.

3. One of the other partners, B. Beaver, paid off a partnership bank loan of $10,000 and the related interest of $1,500. No interest accrual had been made. The bookkeeper was not notified of this transaction, so it was not recorded on the partnership books.

4. Partners' Capital balances per books at December 31, 1989 and drawings during 1990 were:

	Amount	Profit and Loss %
Garrison, Capital	$100,000	40%
Garrison, drawing during 1990	5,000	
Smith, Capital	125,000	35
Smith, drawing during 1990	0	
Beaver, Capital	90,000	25
Beaver, drawing during 1990	10,000	

REQUIRED: **(a)** Based on the information provided, make any necessary correcting entries.

(b) Prepare a revised income statement. Include a schedule showing the distribution of net income.

(c) How much income should each partner include in his income tax for 1990?

(d) Prepare a statement of partners' Capital accounts for the year ended December 31, 1990.

B-3 Distribution of Partnership Income. P. Crack and C. Pot are partners in a very successful medical practice. According to the partnership agreement, profit and losses are divided according to the ratio of the partners' year-end Capital balances. Partnership net income amounted to $200,000 during the current year. Your analysis of the partners' Capital accounts revealed the following:

Partner	Date	Transaction	Amount
P. Crack	1/2/90	Beginning balance	$200,000
	4/1/90	Capital investment	50,000
	6/1/90	Capital investment	30,000
	11/1/90	Withdrawal	40,000
C. Pot	1/2/90	Beginning balance	$220,000
	3/1/90	Withdrawal	20,000
	6/1/90	Withdrawal	20,000
	10/1/90	Capital investment	50,000

REQUIRED: **(a)** Determine how partnership profits should be divided between the two partners. (Where necessary, round to whole dollars and whole percentages.)

(b) Now assume that the partnership profits are to be split based on the ratio of the beginning Capital balances. Determine how the profits should now be split. Which arrangement do you think is more equitable? Why?

B-4 Distribution of Partnership Profits. Lotus has three partners—Padilla, Doggett, and Kari. Their beginning Capital balances, as well as certain provisions of the partnership agreement, are provided below:

Partner	Capital Balance	Annual Salary	Residual Profit and Loss %
Padilla	$100,000	$24,000	20%
Doggett	150,000	36,000	40
Kari	200,000	48,000	40

Under the partnership agreement, profits and losses are split in the following manner: Each partner receives an annual salary and then 10% interest on the beginning Capital balance. Any residual profits are split per the above percentages.

REQUIRED: Prepare schedules indicating how the partnership profits or losses should be split under each of the following independent situations:

(a) Partnership income—$600,000.

(b) Partnership income—$140,000.

(c) Partnership loss—$100,000.

■ USING THE COMPUTER

B-5 Yolo has three partners—Zachery, Silver, and Pecora. Their beginning Capital balances, as well as certain provisions of the partnership agreement, are provided below:

Partner	Capital Balance	Annual Salary	Residual Profit and Loss %
Zachery	$200,000	$48,000	40%
Silver	300,000	72,000	20
Pecora	400,000	96,000	40

Under the partnership agreement, profits and losses are split in the following manner: Each partner receives an annual salary and then 12% interest on the beginning Capital balance. Any residual profits are split per the above percentages.

REQUIRED: Using an electronic spreadsheet, prepare schedules indicating how the partnership profits or losses should be split under each of the following independent situations:

(a) Partnership income—$500,000.

(b) Partnership income—$250,000.

■ UNDERSTANDING FINANCIAL STATEMENTS

B-6   Following is a statement of partner's equity at December 31, 1983 for Transco Exploration Partners, Ltd. The general partners have unlimited liability, and the limited partners have liabilities limited to their investment.

| | Transco Exploration Partners, Ltd. | | |
	General Partners	Limited Partners	Total
Transfer of net assets of TXC	$ —	$ 914,925,579	$ 914,925,579
General partners' cash contributions	10,303,030	—	10,303,030
Sale of depositary units	—	120,000,000	120,000,000
Add (deduct)			
Syndication costs	(18,467)	(1,828,202)	(1,846,669)
Net income	104,812	10,376,424	10,481,236
Distribution	(257,576)	(28,500,000)	(28,757,576)
Reinvestment	227,273	22,500,000	22,727,273
Balance at December 31, 1983	$10,359,072	$1,037,473,801	$1,047,832,873

During the year ended December 31, 1984, the following events occurred:

Syndication costs	$ 67,568
Net income	47,107,552
Distributions	108,433,714
Reinvestments	98,168,636

REQUIRED: **(a)** Determine the distribution ratio between the general and limited partners for the syndication costs, net income, distribution, and reinvestment for the year ended December 31, 1983.

(b) Applying these ratios for 1984, prepare the statement of partners' equity at December 31, 1984, in the same format as the one above.

■ FINANCIAL DECISION CASE

B-7   For several years, Lin and Rusbarsky have operated a partnership that develops high-tech products for the Defense Department. The business is very risky in that their profit levels depend largely on the contracts received from the Defense Department. Thus some years are very profitable and others are not. Each partner's current Capital balance and other partnership data are as follows:

	Capital Balance	Annual Salary	Profit (Loss) Sharing Ratio
Lin	$300,000	$40,000	50%
Rusbarsky	400,000	50,000	50

Partnership profits during the last six years have been:

1982	$180,000
1983	(50,000)
1984	120,000
1985	(40,000)
1986	160,000
1987	90,000

Because of prior losses and uncertainty, the partners often make additional capital contributions.

One employee, C. Purvis, is being considered for admittance to the partnership. She currently receives an annual salary of $35,000. The terms of the new partnership agreement are as follows:

(a) Purvis will purchase a 15% interest in the partnership for $200,000.

(b) She will receive an annual salary of $30,000 plus her share of partnership profits. Partnership profits will now be split as follows:

Lin	42.5%
Rusbarsky	42.5
Purvis	15.0

The original two partners will receive their same yearly salaries.

Purvis is concerned about joining the partnership and asks your advice on a number of issues.

REQUIRED: **(a)** Explain to Purvis the advantages and disadvantages of the partnership form of business organization, especially as related to the current partnership under consideration.

(b) Explain to Purvis the advantages and disadvantages of the proposed partnership agreement outlined above.

APPENDIX
C

PRESENT AND FUTURE VALUE TABLES

TABLE I   Future Value of a Single Amount

(n) Periods	2%	2½%	3%	4%	5%	6%	7%	8%	9%	10%	12%	15%	(n) Periods
1	1.02000	1.02500	1.03000	1.04000	1.05000	1.06000	1.07000	1.08000	1.09000	1.10000	1.12000	1.15000	1
2	1.04040	1.05062	1.06090	1.08160	1.10250	1.12360	1.14490	1.16640	1.18810	1.21000	1.25440	1.32250	2
3	1.06121	1.07689	1.09273	1.12486	1.15763	1.19102	1.22504	1.25971	1.29503	1.33100	1.40493	1.52088	3
4	1.08243	1.10381	1.12551	1.16986	1.21551	1.26248	1.31080	1.36049	1.41158	1.46410	1.57352	1.74901	4
5	1.10408	1.13141	1.15927	1.21665	1.27628	1.33823	1.40255	1.46933	1.53862	1.61051	1.76234	2.01136	5
6	1.12616	1.15969	1.19405	1.26532	1.34010	1.41852	1.50073	1.58687	1.67710	1.77156	1.97382	2.31306	6
7	1.14869	1.18869	1.22987	1.31593	1.40710	1.50363	1.60578	1.71382	1.82804	1.94872	2.21068	2.66002	7
8	1.17166	1.21840	1.26677	1.36857	1.47746	1.59385	1.71819	1.85093	1.99256	2.14359	2.47596	3.05902	8
9	1.19509	1.24886	1.30477	1.42331	1.55133	1.68948	1.83846	1.99900	2.17189	2.35795	2.77308	3.51788	9
10	1.21899	1.28008	1.34392	1.48024	1.62889	1.79085	1.96715	2.15892	2.36736	2.59374	3.10585	4.04556	10
11	1.24337	1.31209	1.38423	1.53945	1.71034	1.89830	2.10485	2.33164	2.58043	2.85312	3.47855	4.65239	11
12	1.26824	1.34489	1.42576	1.60103	1.79586	2.01220	2.25219	2.51817	2.81267	3.13843	3.89598	5.35025	12
13	1.29361	1.37851	1.46853	1.66507	1.88565	2.13293	2.40985	2.71962	3.06581	3.45227	4.36349	6.15279	13
14	1.31948	1.41297	1.51259	1.73168	1.97993	2.26090	2.57853	2.93719	3.34173	3.79750	4.88711	7.07571	14
15	1.34587	1.44830	1.55797	1.80094	2.07893	2.39656	2.75903	3.17217	3.64248	4.17725	5.47357	8.13706	15
16	1.37279	1.48451	1.60471	1.87298	2.18287	2.54035	2.95216	3.42594	3.97031	4.59497	6.13039	9.35762	16
17	1.40024	1.52162	1.65285	1.94790	2.29202	2.69277	3.15882	3.70002	4.32763	5.05447	6.86604	10.76126	17
18	1.42825	1.55966	1.70243	2.02582	2.40662	2.85434	3.37993	3.99602	4.71712	5.55992	7.68997	12.37545	18
19	1.45681	1.59865	1.75351	2.10685	2.52695	3.02560	3.61653	4.31570	5.14166	6.11591	8.61276	14.23177	19
20	1.48595	1.63862	1.80611	2.19112	2.65330	3.20714	3.86968	4.66096	5.60441	6.72750	9.64629	16.36654	20
21	1.51567	1.67958	1.86029	2.27877	2.78596	3.39956	4.14056	5.03383	6.10881	7.40025	10.80385	18.82152	21
22	1.54598	1.72157	1.91610	2.36992	2.92526	3.60354	4.43040	5.43654	6.65860	8.14028	12.10031	21.64475	22
23	1.57690	1.76461	1.97359	2.46472	3.07152	3.81975	4.74053	5.87146	7.25787	8.95430	13.55235	24.89146	23
24	1.60844	1.80873	2.03279	2.56330	3.22510	4.04893	5.07237	6.34118	7.91108	9.84973	15.17863	28.62518	24
25	1.64061	1.85394	2.09378	2.66584	3.38635	4.29187	5.42743	6.84847	8.62308	10.83471	17.00000	32.91895	25
30	1.81136	2.09757	2.42726	3.24340	4.32194	5.74349	7.61226	10.06266	13.26768	17.44940	29.95992	66.21177	30
32	1.88454	2.20376	2.57508	3.50806	4.76494	6.45339	8.71527	11.73708	15.76333	21.11378	37.58173	87.56507	32
34	1.96068	2.31532	2.73191	3.79432	5.25335	7.25103	9.97811	13.69013	18.72841	25.54767	47.14252	115.80480	34
36	2.03989	2.43254	2.89828	4.10393	5.79182	8.14725	11.42394	15.96817	22.25123	30.91268	59.13557	153.15185	36
40	2.20804	2.68506	3.26204	4.80102	7.03999	10.23572	14.97446	21.72452	31.40942	45.25926	93.05097	267.86355	40

TABLE 2 — Present Value of a Single Amount

(n) Periods	2%	2½%	3%	4%	5%	6%	7%	8%	9%	10%	12%	15%	(n) Periods
1	.98039	.97561	.97087	.96154	.95238	.94340	.93458	.92593	.91743	.90909	.89286	.86957	1
2	.96117	.95181	.94260	.92456	.90703	.89000	.87344	.85734	.84168	.82645	.79719	.75614	2
3	.94232	.92860	.91514	.88900	.86384	.83962	.81630	.79383	.77218	.75132	.71178	.65752	3
4	.92385	.90595	.88849	.85480	.82270	.79209	.76290	.73503	.70843	.68301	.63552	.57175	4
5	.90573	.88385	.86261	.82193	.78353	.74726	.71299	.68058	.64993	.62092	.56743	.49718	5
6	.88797	.86230	.83748	.79031	.74622	.70496	.66634	.63017	.59627	.56447	.50663	.43233	6
7	.87056	.84127	.81309	.75992	.71068	.66506	.62275	.58349	.54703	.51316	.45235	.37594	7
8	.85349	.82075	.78941	.73069	.67684	.62741	.58201	.54027	.50187	.46651	.40388	.32690	8
9	.83676	.80073	.76642	.70259	.64461	.59190	.54393	.50025	.46043	.42410	.36061	.28426	9
10	.82035	.78120	.74409	.67556	.61391	.55839	.50835	.46319	.42241	.38554	.32197	.24719	10
11	.80426	.76214	.72242	.64958	.58468	.52679	.47509	.42888	.38753	.35049	.28748	.21494	11
12	.78849	.74356	.70138	.62460	.55684	.49697	.44401	.39711	.35554	.31863	.25668	.18691	12
13	.77303	.72542	.68095	.60057	.53032	.46884	.41496	.36770	.32618	.28966	.22917	.16253	13
14	.75788	.70773	.66112	.57748	.50507	.44230	.38782	.34046	.29925	.26333	.20462	.14133	14
15	.74301	.69047	.64186	.55526	.48102	.41727	.36245	.31524	.27454	.23939	.18270	.12289	15
16	.72845	.67362	.62317	.53391	.45811	.39365	.33873	.29189	.25187	.21763	.16312	.10687	16
17	.71416	.65720	.60502	.51337	.43630	.37136	.31657	.27027	.23107	.19785	.14564	.09293	17
18	.70016	.64117	.58739	.49363	.41552	.35034	.29586	.25025	.21199	.17986	.13004	.08081	18
19	.68643	.62553	.57029	.47464	.39573	.33051	.27651	.23171	.19449	.16351	.11611	.07027	19
20	.67297	.61027	.55368	.45639	.37689	.31180	.25842	.21455	.17843	.14864	.10367	.06110	20
21	.65978	.59539	.53755	.43883	.35894	.29416	.24151	.19866	.16370	.13513	.09256	.05313	21
22	.64684	.58086	.52189	.42196	.34185	.27751	.22571	.18394	.15018	.12285	.08264	.04620	22
23	.63416	.56670	.50669	.40573	.32557	.26180	.21095	.17032	.13778	.11168	.07379	.04017	23
24	.62172	.55288	.49193	.39012	.31007	.24698	.19715	.15770	.12641	.10153	.06588	.03493	24
25	.60953	.53939	.47761	.37512	.29530	.23300	.18425	.14602	.11597	.09230	.05882	.03038	25
30	.55207	.47674	.41199	.30832	.23138	.17411	.13137	.09938	.07537	.05731	.03338	.01510	30
32	.53063	.45377	.38834	.28506	.20987	.15496	.11474	.08520	.06344	.04736	.02661	.01142	32
34	.51003	.43191	.36604	.26355	.19035	.13791	.10022	.07305	.05339	.03914	.02121	.00864	34
36	.49022	.41109	.34503	.24367	.17266	.12274	.08754	.06262	.04494	.03235	.01691	.00653	36
40	.45289	.37243	.30656	.20829	.14205	.09722	.06678	.04603	.03184	.02210	.01074	.00373	40

754

(Handwritten margin notes)
.311 × 100,000 = ?
× 8000 = ?
11,468
500 × 7
3500
6√100 = 16
613.9

TABLE 3 Future Value of an Annuity

(n) Periods	2%	2½%	3%	4%	5%	6%	7%	8%	9%	10%	12%	15%	(n) Periods
1	1.00000	1.00000	1.00000	1.00000	1.00000	1.00000	1.00000	1.00000	1.00000	1.00000	1.00000	1.00000	1
2	2.02000	2.02500	2.03000	2.04000	2.05000	2.06000	2.07000	2.08000	2.09000	2.10000	2.12000	2.15000	2
3	3.06040	3.07562	3.09090	3.12160	3.15250	3.18360	3.21490	3.24640	3.27810	3.31000	3.37440	3.47250	3
4	4.12161	4.15252	4.18363	4.24646	4.31013	4.37462	4.43994	4.50611	4.57313	4.64100	4.77933	4.99338	4
5	5.20404	5.25633	5.30914	5.41632	5.52563	5.63709	5.75074	5.86660	5.98471	6.10510	6.35285	6.74238	5
6	6.30812	6.38774	6.46841	6.63298	6.80191	6.97532	7.15329	7.33592	7.52334	7.71561	8.11519	8.75374	6
7	7.43428	7.54743	7.66246	7.89829	8.14201	8.39384	8.65402	8.92280	9.20044	9.48717	10.08901	11.06680	7
8	8.58297	8.73612	8.89234	9.21423	9.54911	9.89747	10.25980	10.63663	11.02847	11.43589	12.29969	13.72682	8
9	9.75463	9.95452	10.15911	10.58280	11.02656	11.49132	11.97799	12.48756	13.02104	13.57948	14.77566	16.78584	9
10	10.94972	11.20338	11.46338	12.00611	12.57789	13.18079	13.81645	14.48656	15.19293	15.93743	17.54874	20.30372	10
11	12.16872	12.48347	12.80780	13.48635	14.20679	14.97164	15.78360	16.64549	17.56029	18.53117	20.65458	24.34928	11
12	13.41209	13.79555	14.19203	15.02581	15.91713	16.86994	17.88845	18.97713	20.14072	21.38428	24.13313	29.00167	12
13	14.68033	15.14044	15.61779	16.62684	17.71298	18.88214	20.14064	21.49530	22.95339	24.52271	28.02911	34.35192	13
14	15.97394	16.51895	17.08632	18.29191	19.59863	21.01507	22.55049	24.21492	26.01919	27.97498	32.39260	40.50471	14
15	17.29342	17.93193	18.59891	20.02359	21.57856	23.27597	25.12902	27.15211	29.36092	31.77248	37.27972	47.58041	15
16	18.63929	19.38022	20.15688	21.82453	23.65749	25.67253	27.88805	30.32428	33.00340	35.94973	42.75328	55.71747	16
17	20.01207	20.86473	21.76159	23.69751	25.84037	28.21288	30.84022	33.75023	36.97371	40.54470	48.88367	65.07509	17
18	21.41231	22.38635	23.41444	25.64541	28.13238	30.90565	33.99903	37.45024	41.30134	45.59917	55.74972	75.83636	18
19	22.84056	23.94601	25.11687	27.67123	30.53900	33.75999	37.37896	41.44626	46.01846	51.15909	63.43968	88.21181	19
20	24.29737	25.54466	26.87037	29.77808	33.06595	36.78559	40.99549	45.76196	51.16012	57.27500	72.05244	102.44358	20
21	25.78332	27.18327	28.67649	31.96920	35.71925	39.99273	44.86518	50.42292	56.76453	64.00250	81.69874	118.81012	21
22	27.29898	28.86286	30.53678	34.24797	38.50521	43.39229	49.00574	55.45676	62.87334	71.40275	92.50258	137.63164	22
23	28.84496	30.58443	32.45288	36.61789	41.43048	46.99583	53.43614	60.89330	69.53194	79.54302	104.60289	159.27638	23
24	30.42186	32.34904	34.42647	39.08260	44.50200	50.81558	58.17667	66.76476	76.78981	88.49733	118.15524	184.16784	24
25	32.03030	34.15776	36.45926	41.64591	47.72710	54.86451	63.24904	73.10594	84.70090	98.34706	133.33387	212.79302	25
30	40.56808	43.90270	47.57542	56.08494	66.43885	79.05819	94.46079	113.28321	136.30754	164.49402	241.33268	434.74515	30
32	44.22703	48.15028	52.50276	62.70147	75.29883	90.88978	110.21815	134.21354	164.03699	201.13777	304.84772	577.10046	32
34	48.03380	52.61289	57.73018	69.85791	85.06696	104.18375	128.25876	158.62667	196.98234	245.47670	384.52098	765.36535	34
36	51.99437	57.30141	63.27594	77.59831	95.83632	119.12087	148.91346	187.10215	236.12472	299.12681	484.46312	1014.34568	36
40	60.40198	67.40255	75.40126	95.02552	120.79977	154.76197	199.63511	259.05652	337.88245	442.59256	767.09142	1779.09031	40

TABLE 4   Present Value of an Annuity

(n) Periods	2%	2½%	3%	4%	5%	6%	7%	8%	9%	10%	12%	15%	(n) Periods
1	.98039	.97561	.97087	.96154	.95238	.94340	.93458	.92593	.91743	.90909	.89286	.86957	1
2	1.94156	1.92742	1.91347	1.88609	1.85941	1.83339	1.80802	1.78326	1.75911	1.73554	1.69005	1.62571	2
3	2.88388	2.85602	2.82861	2.77509	2.72325	2.67301	2.62432	2.57710	2.53130	2.48685	2.40183	2.28323	3
4	3.80773	3.76197	3.71710	3.62990	3.54595	3.46511	3.38721	3.31213	3.23972	3.16986	3.03735	2.85498	4
5	4.71346	4.64583	4.57971	4.45182	4.32948	4.21236	4.10020	3.99271	3.88965	3.79079	3.60478	3.35216	5
6	5.60143	5.50813	5.41719	5.24214	5.07569	4.91732	4.76654	4.62288	4.48592	4.35526	4.11141	3.78448	6
7	6.47199	6.34939	6.23028	6.00205	5.78637	5.58238	5.38929	5.20637	5.03295	4.86842	4.56376	4.16042	7
8	7.32548	7.17014	7.01969	6.73274	6.46321	6.20979	5.97130	5.74664	5.53482	5.33493	4.96764	4.48732	8
9	8.16224	7.97087	7.78611	7.43533	7.10782	6.80169	6.51523	6.24689	5.99525	5.75902	5.32825	4.77158	9
10	8.98259	8.75206	8.53020	8.11090	7.72173	7.36009	7.02358	6.71008	6.41766	6.14457	5.65022	5.01877	10
11	9.78685	9.51421	9.25262	8.76048	8.30641	7.88687	7.49867	7.13896	6.80519	6.49506	5.93770	5.23371	11
12	10.57534	10.25776	9.95400	9.38507	8.86325	8.38384	7.94269	7.53608	7.16073	6.81369	6.19437	5.42062	12
13	11.34837	10.98318	10.63496	9.98565	9.39357	8.85268	8.35765	7.90378	7.48690	7.10336	6.42355	5.58315	13
14	12.10625	11.69091	11.29607	10.56312	9.89864	9.29498	8.74547	8.24424	7.78615	7.36669	6.62817	5.72448	14
15	12.84926	12.38138	11.93794	11.11839	10.37966	9.71225	9.10791	8.55948	8.06069	7.60608	6.81086	5.84737	15
16	13.57771	13.05500	12.56110	11.65230	10.83777	10.10590	9.44665	8.85137	8.31256	7.82371	6.97399	5.95424	16
17	14.29187	13.71220	13.16612	12.16567	11.27407	10.47726	9.76322	9.12164	8.54363	8.02155	7.11963	6.04716	17
18	14.99203	14.35336	13.75351	12.65930	11.68959	10.82760	10.05909	9.37189	8.75563	8.20141	7.24967	6.12797	18
19	15.67846	14.97889	14.32380	13.13394	12.08532	11.15812	10.33560	9.60360	8.95012	8.36492	7.36578	6.19823	19
20	16.35143	15.58916	14.87747	13.59033	12.46221	11.46992	10.59401	9.81815	9.12855	8.51356	7.46944	6.25933	20
21	17.01121	16.18455	15.41502	14.02916	12.82115	11.76408	10.83553	10.01680	9.29224	8.64869	7.56200	6.31246	21
22	17.65805	16.76541	15.93692	14.45112	13.16300	12.04158	11.06124	10.20074	9.44243	8.77154	7.64465	6.35866	22
23	18.29220	17.33211	16.44361	14.85684	13.48857	12.30338	11.27219	10.37106	9.58021	8.88322	7.71843	6.39884	23
24	18.91393	17.88499	16.93554	15.24696	13.79864	12.55036	11.46933	10.52876	9.70661	8.98474	7.78432	6.43377	24
25	19.52346	18.42438	17.41315	15.62208	14.09394	12.78336	11.65358	10.67478	9.82258	9.07704	7.84314	6.46415	25
30	22.39646	20.93029	19.60044	17.29203	15.37245	13.76483	12.40904	11.25778	10.27365	9.42691	8.05518	6.56598	30
32	23.46833	21.84918	20.38877	17.87355	15.80268	14.08404	12.64656	11.43500	10.40624	9.52638	8.11159	6.59053	32
34	24.49859	22.72379	21.13184	18.41120	16.19290	14.36814	12.85401	11.58693	10.51784	9.60857	8.15656	6.60910	34
36	25.48884	23.55625	21.83225	18.90828	16.54685	14.62099	13.03521	11.71719	10.61176	9.67651	8.19241	6.62314	36
40	27.35548	25.10278	23.11477	19.79277	17.15909	15.04628	13.33171	11.92461	10.75736	9.77905	8.24378	6.64179	40

APPENDIX
D

ILLUSTRATIVE
FINANCIAL STATEMENTS

This appendix consists of excerpts from the 1988 annual reports of two companies (reproduced courtesy of those firms):

1. Toys "R" Us, Inc. and subsidiaries

2. Heineken N.V. (a Dutch multinational company)

■ ANNUAL REPORT OF TOYS "R" US, INC. AND SUBSIDIARIES

TOYS "R" US, INC. AND SUBSIDIARIES

■Financial Highlights

(In millions except per share information)   Fiscal Year Ended

	Jan. 31 1988	Feb. 1 1987	Feb. 2 1986	Feb. 3 1985	Jan. 29 1984	Jan. 30 1983	Jan. 31 1982	Feb. 1 1981	Feb. 3 1980	Jan. 28 1979
■OPERATIONS:										
Net Sales.............................	$3,137	$2,445	$1,976	$1,702	$1,320	$1,042	$783	$597	$480	$349
Net Earnings.........................	204	152	120	111	92	64	49	29	27	17
Net Earnings Per Share	1.56	1.17	.93	.87	.72	.52	.42	.26	.24	.16
■FINANCIAL POSITION AT YEAR-END:										
Working Capital	225	155	181	222	220	157	137	91	77	60
Real Estate-Net......................	762	601	423	279	185	121	79	28	21	19
Total Assets	2,027	1,523	1,226	1,099	820	559	442	312	232	184
Long-term Obligations	179	85	88	88	55	42	88	41	49	66
Stockholders' Equity	1,135	901	717	579	460	323	206	151	121	79
■NUMBER OF STORES AT YEAR-END:										
Toys "R" Us · United States	313	271	233	198	169	144	120	101	85	72
Toys "R" Us · International	37	24	13	5	—	—	—	—	—	—
Kids "R" Us.........................	74	43	23	10	2	—	—	—	—	—

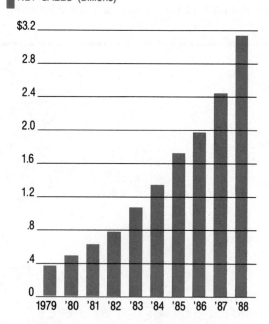

■ NET SALES (Billions)

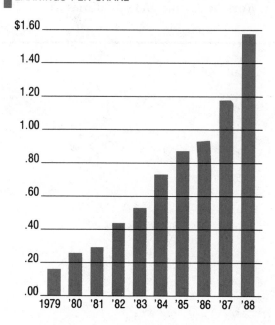

■ EARNINGS PER SHARE

Management's Discussion—Results of Operations and Financial Condition

RESULTS OF OPERATIONS

The Company has experienced strong sales growth in each of its last three years; sales were up 28.3% in fiscal 1988, 23.7% in fiscal 1987, and 16.1% in fiscal 1986. Part of the growth is attributable to the opening of 115 new U.S. toy stores, 32 international toy stores and 64 children's clothing stores during the three-year period, and a portion of the increase is due to comparable U.S. toy store sales increases as follows: fiscal 1988—10.1%, fiscal 1987—8.5%, fiscal 1986—2.4%.

Cost of sales as a percentage of sales increased in fiscal 1988 over fiscal 1987 and 1986 due primarily to more competitive pricing. In addition, the Company experienced a LIFO benefit of $4,836,000 in fiscal 1986 and none in fiscal 1987 or 1988.

Selling, advertising, general and administrative expenses as a percent of sales decreased from 20.7% in fiscal 1986 to 18.8% in fiscal 1987 and 18.6% in fiscal 1988 as a result of labor productivity gains and other cost-cutting measures.

Interest expense increased in both fiscal 1988 and fiscal 1987 from fiscal 1986, primarily due to increased seasonal borrowings as well as a $100 million bond financing in February 1987.

Interest income increased in fiscal 1988 over 1987 due to greater prepayments of vendor invoices. Interest income decreased in fiscal 1987 from fiscal 1986 due to less funds invested and lower interest rates.

As a result of the 1986 Tax Reform Act, including the elimination of the investment tax credit after fiscal 1986, the Company's effective tax rate has changed as follows:

Fiscal 1988 - 41.0%
Fiscal 1987 - 46.4%
Fiscal 1986 - 45.5%

It is expected that the rate will be further reduced to approximately 37.5% in fiscal 1989 as a result of that Act.

In December 1987, the Financial Accounting Standards Board issued a new standard on accounting for income taxes (SFAS 96) which changes the accounting for deferred income taxes. Adoption of the new standard is required no later than the fiscal year ending January 28, 1990. Upon adoption of SFAS 96, the Company will recognize some income; the amount, however, has not been determined.

Inflation has had little effect on the Company's operations in the last three years.

LIQUIDITY AND CAPITAL

The Company is in a strong financial position as evidenced by the following:

	Year ended		
	January 31 1988	February 1 1987	February 2 1986
Net working capital (in millions)	$225.0	$155.4	$181.2
Long-term debt to equity (including capital leases)	15.8%	9.4%	12.2%
Long-term debt to equity (excluding capital leases)	14.2%	7.2%	9.4%

The Company opened 43 toy stores in fiscal 1986, 49 in fiscal 1987 and 55 in fiscal 1988. Approximately 60 new toy store openings are planned for fiscal 1989 in the United States, Canada, the United Kingdom and West Germany. The Company opened 13 Kids "R" Us children's clothing stores in fiscal 1986, 20 in fiscal 1987 and 31 in fiscal 1988 and plans to open about 35 in fiscal 1989. The Company also operates 4 department stores.

Since fiscal 1982, the Company has been acquiring most of its real estate for its U.S. toy stores and plans to continue this policy in fiscal 1989. In the last three fiscal years, the Company financed most of its real estate acquisitions through internally generated funds. On February 4, 1987, the Company issued $100 million of 8¼% Sinking Fund Debentures due 2017, as part of a shelf registration statement filed with the Securities and Exchange Commission for up to $200 million of debt securities.

For fiscal 1989, capital requirements for real estate, store and warehouse fixtures and equipment, leasehold improvements, betterments, and other additions to property and equipment are estimated at $325 million (including real estate of $250 million), which the Company plans to finance primarily through operations.

Because of the seasonal nature of the business (approximately 50% of sales take place in the fourth quarter), cash typically declines from the beginning of the year through October as inventory is built up for the Christmas season and funds are used for land purchases and construction of new stores which usually open in the third quarter of the year. The Company expects that seasonal cash requirements will continue to be met primarily through operations and issuance of short-term commercial paper.

▌Market Information

The Company's Common Stock is listed on the New York Stock Exchange. The following table reflects the high and low prices based on New York Stock Exchange trading since January 1, 1986. Prices (rounded to the nearest one-eighth) have been restated to reflect the three-for-two stock split effected on June 27, 1986. Price ranges are for calendar quarters.

The Company has followed the policy of reinvesting earnings in the business and, consequently, has not paid any cash dividends. At the present time, no change in this policy is under consideration by the Board of Directors. The payment of cash dividends in the future will be determined by the Board of Directors in light of conditions then existing, including the Company's earnings, financial requirements and condition, opportunities for reinvesting earnings, business conditions and other factors.

The number of shareholders of record of common stock on March 15, 1988, was approximately 11,200.

	High	Low
1986		
1st Quarter	29⅜	21⅞
2nd Quarter	34⅜	27⅛
3rd Quarter	33⅞	26⅝
4th Quarter	32¾	26⅞
1987		
1st Quarter	39⅝	29
2nd Quarter	39½	32⅜
3rd Quarter	42⅝	34⅝
4th Quarter	40⅜	22

▌Report of Management

Responsibility for the integrity and objectivity of the financial information presented in this Annual Report rests with Toys "R" Us management. The accompanying financial statements have been prepared from accounting records which management believes fairly and accurately reflect the operations and financial position of the Company. Management has established a system of internal controls to provide reasonable assurance that assets are maintained and accounted for in accordance with its policies and that transactions are recorded accurately on the Company's books and records.

The Company's comprehensive internal audit program provides for constant evaluation of the adequacy of and adherence to management's established policies and procedures. The Company has distributed to key employees its policies for conducting business affairs in a lawful and ethical manner.

The financial statements of the Company have been examined by Touche Ross & Co., independent certified public accountants. Their accompanying report is based on an examination conducted in accordance with generally accepted auditing standards, including a review of internal accounting controls and financial reporting matters.

Charles Lazarus
Chairman of the Board

Michael Goldstein
*Executive Vice President-
Finance and Administration*

▌Auditors' Report

Board of Directors and Stockholders
Toys "R" Us, Inc.
Rochelle Park, New Jersey

We have examined the consolidated balance sheets of Toys "R" Us, Inc. and subsidiaries at January 31, 1988 and February 1, 1987 and the related consolidated statements of earnings, stockholders' equity and cash flows for each of the three years in the period ended January 31, 1988. Our examinations were made in accordance with generally accepted auditing standards and, accordingly, included such tests of the accounting records and such other auditing procedures as we considered necessary in the circumstances.

In our opinion, the consolidated statements referred to above present fairly the financial position of Toys "R" Us, Inc. and subsidiaries at January 31, 1988 and February 1, 1987, and the results of their operations and cash flows for each of the three years in the period ended January 31, 1988 in conformity with generally accepted accounting principles applied on a consistent basis.

Touche Ross & Co.

March 16, 1988
New York, New York

Certified Public Accountants

TOYS "R" US, INC. AND SUBSIDIARIES

Statements of Consolidated Earnings

(In thousands except per share information)   *Fiscal Year Ended*

	January 31 1988	February 1 1987	February 2 1986
Net sales	$3,136,568	$2,444,903	$1,976,134
Costs and expenses:			
Cost of sales	2,157,017	1,668,209	1,322,942
Selling, advertising, general and administrative	584,120	458,528	408,438
Depreciation and amortization	43,716	33,288	26,074
Interest expense	13,849	7,890	6,999
Interest income	(8,056)	(7,229)	(8,093)
	2,790,646	2,160,686	1,756,360
Earnings before taxes on income	345,922	284,217	219,774
Taxes on income (Note 6)	142,000	132,000	100,000
Net earnings	$ 203,922	$ 152,217	$ 119,774
Net earnings per share (Note 8)	$1.56	$1.17	$.93

See notes to consolidated financial statements.

Number of Stores

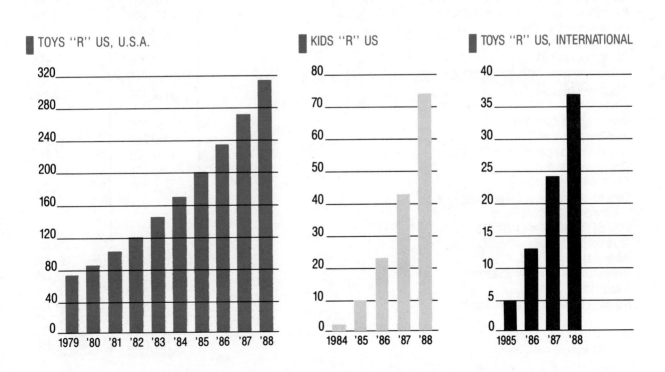

TOYS "R" US, U.S.A.

KIDS "R" US

TOYS "R" US, INTERNATIONAL

TOYS "R" US, INC. AND SUBSIDIARIES

Consolidated Balance Sheets

(In thousands)	Fiscal Year Ended January 31 1988	February 1 1987
ASSETS		
Current Assets:		
Cash and short-term investments	$ 45,996	$ 84,379
Accounts and other receivables, less allowance for doubtful accounts of $1,386 and $1,133	62,144	37,502
Merchandise inventories (Note 1)	772,833	528,939
Prepaid expenses	5,050	3,566
Total Current Assets	886,023	654,386
Property and Equipment (Notes 1, 2 and 3):		
Real estate, net of accumulated depreciation of $31,238 and $22,400	762,082	600,747
Other, net of accumulated depreciation and amortization of $116,980 and $86,207	351,037	240,218
Leased Property Under Capital Leases, net of accumulated depreciation of $16,840 and $15,797 (Note 4)	11,397	12,440
Other Assets	16,520	15,175
	$ 2,027,059	$1,522,966
LIABILITIES AND STOCKHOLDERS' EQUITY		
Current Liabilities:		
Short-term notes payable to banks	$ 17,657	$ —
Accounts payable	403,105	305,705
Accrued expenses, taxes and other liabilities	167,280	118,260
Federal income taxes (Note 6)	71,003	73,059
Current portion:		
Long-term debt (Note 3)	876	973
Obligations under capital leases (Note 4)	1,071	968
Total Current Liabilities	660,992	498,965
Deferred Income Taxes (Note 6)	53,356	40,321
Long-Term Debt (Note 3)	159,788	63,966
Obligations Under Capital Leases (Note 4)	17,602	18,673
Commitments (Note 4)		
Stockholders' Equity (Note 5):		
Common stock par value $.10 per share:		
Authorized 200,000,000 shares		
Issued 130,530,467 and 127,110,608	13,053	12,711
Additional paid-in capital	252,493	239,721
Retained earnings	854,421	650,499
Foreign currency translation adjustments	23,586	8,449
Treasury shares, at cost	(5,929)	(5,571)
Receivable from exercise of stock options	(2,303)	(4,768)
	1,135,321	901,041
	$2,027,059	$1,522,966

See notes to consolidated financial statements.

TOYS "R" US, INC. AND SUBSIDIARIES

Statements of Consolidated Cash Flows

(In thousands)			Fiscal Year Ended
	January 31 1988	February 1 1987	February 2 1986
CASH FLOWS FROM OPERATING ACTIVITIES			
Net income	$203,922	$152,217	$119,774
Adjustments to reconcile net income to net cash provided by operating activities:			
Depreciation and amortization	43,716	33,288	26,074
Deferred taxes	13,035	14,184	9,669
Change in operating assets and liabilities:			
Accounts and other receivables	(24,642)	(11,531)	(2,564)
Merchandise inventories	(243,894)	(115,446)	(15,580)
Prepaid expenses	(1,484)	(320)	(1,215)
Accounts payable, accrued expenses and taxes	144,364	102,382	(153)
Total adjustments	(68,905)	22,557	16,231
Net cash provided by operating activities	135,017	174,774	136,005
CASH FLOWS FROM INVESTING ACTIVITIES			
Capital expenditures-net	(314,827)	(259,388)	(221,794)
Other net	13,792	10,952	11,053
Net cash used in investing activities	(301,035)	(248,436)	(210,741)
CASH FLOWS FROM FINANCING ACTIVITIES			
Short-term borrowings-net	17,663	(1,136)	(19,118)
Long-term borrowings	96,611	—	2,493
Long-term debt repayments	(1,860)	(2,027)	(3,819)
Exercise of stock options	15,221	25,033	16,072
Net cash provided by financing activities	127,635	21,870	(4,372)
CASH AND SHORT-TERM INVESTMENTS			
Decrease during year	(38,383)	(51,792)	(79,108)
Beginning of year	84,379	136,171	215,279
End of year	$ 45,996	$ 84,379	$136,171

SUPPLEMENTAL DISCLOSURES OF CASH FLOW INFORMATION

The Company considers all highly liquid investments purchased as part of its daily cash management activities to be short-term investments.

During the years ended January 31, 1988, February 1, 1987 and February 2, 1986, the Company made income tax payments of $119,722,000, $79,934,000 and $70,205,000 and interest payments (net of amounts capitalized) of $9,610,000, $8,044,000 and $6,857,000 respectively.

See notes to consolidated financial statements.

TOYS "R" US, INC. AND SUBSIDIARIES

Statements of Consolidated Stockholders' Equity

		Issued	
(In thousands except shares information)		Shares	Amount
Balance, February 3, 1985		83,153,924	$ 8,315
Net earnings for the year		—	—
Exercise of stock options and other		899,992	90
Tax benefit from exercise of stock options		—	—
Foreign currency translation gain		—	—
Balance, February 2, 1986		84,053,916	8,405
Three-for-two stock split effected in the form of a 50% stock dividend payable June 27, 1986		42,338,594	4,234
Net earnings for the year		—	—
Exercise of stock options		718,098	72
Tax benefit from exercise of stock options		—	—
Repayment of stock option loans		—	—
Foreign currency translation gain		—	—
Balance, February 1, 1987		127,110,608	12,711
Net earnings for the year		—	—
Exercise of stock options		3,419,859	342
Tax benefit from exercise of stock options		—	—
Repayment of stock option loans		—	—
Foreign currency translation gain		—	—
Balance, January 31, 1988		130,530,467	$13,053

See notes to consolidated financial statements.

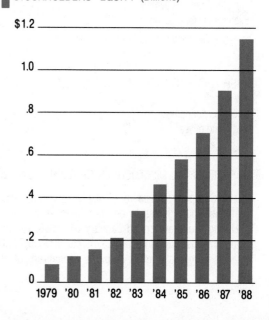

STOCKHOLDERS' EQUITY (Billions)

	Common stock In treasury		Additional paid-in	Retained	Foreign currency translation	Receivable from exercise of stock	
Shares		Amount	capital	earnings	adjustments	options	Total
(1,690,368)		$(4,352)	$200,323	$382,821	$ (383)	$(7,611)	$ 579,113
—		—	—	119,774	—	—	119,774
(1,903)		(71)	5,713	—	—	(554)	5,178
—		—	10,894	—	—	—	10,894
—		—	—	—	2,435	—	2,435
(1,692,271)		(4,423)	216,930	502,595	2,052	(8,165)	717,394
(864,629)		—	—	(4,313)	—	—	(79)
—		—	—	152,217	—	—	152,217
(33,817)		(1,148)	4,107	—	—	(92)	2,939
—		—	18,684	—	—	—	18,684
—		—	—	—	—	3,489	3,489
—		—	—	—	6,397	—	6,397
(2,590,717)		(5,571)	239,721	650,499	8,449	(4,768)	901,041
—		—	—	203,922	—	—	203,922
(9,265)		(358)	7,739	—	—	(1,313)	6,410
—		—	5,033	—	—	—	5,033
—		—	—	—	—	3,778	3,778
—		—	—	—	15,137	—	15,137
(2,599,982)		$(5,929)	$252,493	$854,421	$23,586	$(2,303)	$1,135,321

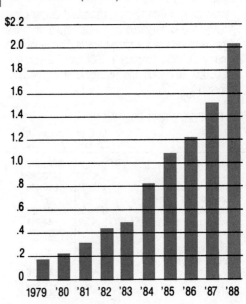

TOTAL ASSETS (Billions)

TOYS "R" US, INC. AND SUBSIDIARIES

Notes to Consolidated Financial Statements
Fiscal years ended January 31, 1988, February 1, 1987 and February 2, 1986

1. SUMMARY OF SIGNIFICANT ACCOUNTING POLICIES

A. Principles of Consolidation
The consolidated financial statements include the accounts of the Company and its subsidiaries for the 52 weeks ended January 31, 1988, February 1, 1987 and February 2, 1986. All material intercompany balances and transactions have been eliminated. In accordance with Statement of Financial Accounting Standards (SFAS) No. 52, assets and liabilities of foreign operations are translated at current rates of exchange while results of operations are translated at average rates in effect for the period. Translation gains or losses are shown as a separate component of Stockholders' Equity.

B. Merchandise Inventories
Merchandise inventories for the USA toy and children's clothing store operations, which represent over 88% of total inventories, are stated at the lower of LIFO cost (last-in, first-out) or market as determined by the retail inventory method. If inventories had been valued at the lower of FIFO cost or market, inventories would show no change at January 31, 1988 or February 1, 1987.

C. Property and Equipment
Property and equipment are recorded at cost. Depreciation and amortization are provided using the straight-line method over the estimated useful lives of the assets, or where applicable, the terms of the respective leases, whichever is shorter.

D. Preopening Costs
Preopening costs, which consist primarily of advertising, occupancy, and payroll expenses, are amortized over expected sales to the end of the fiscal year in which the store opens.

E. Capitalized Interest
Interest on borrowed funds is capitalized during construction of property and is amortized by charges to earnings over the depreciable lives of the related assets. During the years ended January 31, 1988, February 1, 1987 and February 2, 1986, $8,103,000, $6,154,000 and $4,129,000 of interest was capitalized, respectively.

2. PROPERTY AND EQUIPMENT

(In thousands)	Useful Life (In years)	January 31 1988	February 1 1987
Land		$275,012	$234,780
Buildings	20 - 50	473,397	361,732
Furniture and equipment	5 - 15	320,491	222,356
Leaseholds and lease-hold improvements	12½ - 50	147,526	104,069
Construction in progress		44,911	26,635
		1,261,337	949,572
Less accumulated depreciation and amortization		148,218	108,607
		$1,113,119	$840,965

3. LONG-TERM DEBT

(In thousands)	January 31 1988	February 1 1987
Industrial revenue bonds (a)	$ 62,319	$62,642
Mortgage notes payable at annual interest rates from 6½% to 8½% (b)	1,646	2,254
8¼% sinking fund debentures, due 2017 net of discounts of $3,314	96,686	—
Other	13	43
	160,664	64,939
Less current portion	876	973
	$159,788	$63,966

(a) At January 31, 1988, certain industrial revenue bonds are collateralized by property and equipment with an aggregate carrying value of $12,050,000. The bonds have fixed or variable interest rates with an average of 5.51% at January 31, 1988. In addition, $53,680,000 are supported by bank letters of credit expiring in 1988 and 1989. The Company expects that these letters of credit will be renewed.

(b) Mortgage notes payable are collateralized by property and equipment with an aggregate carrying value of $18,748,000 at January 31, 1988.

The annual maturities of long-term debt at January 31, 1988 are as follows:

(In thousands) Fiscal year ending in	Amount
1989	$ 876
1990	670
1991	462
1992	426
1993	435
1994 and subsequent	157,795
	$160,664

4. LEASES

The Company leases a significant portion of the real estate used in its operations. Most leases require the Company to pay real estate taxes and other expenses; some require additional amounts based on percentages of sales.

Obligations under capital leases require minimum payments as follows:

(In thousands) Fiscal year ending in	Amount
1989	$ 2,813
1990	2,813
1991	2,816
1992	2,791
1993	2,731
1994 and subsequent	19,239
Total minimum lease payments	33,203
Less amount representing interest	14,530
Obligations under capital leases (including current portion)	$18,673

Minimum rental commitments (excluding renewal options) under non-cancellable operating leases having a term of more than one year as of January 31, 1988 were as follows:

(In thousands) Fiscal year ending in	Gross minimum rentals	Sublease income	Net minimum rentals
1989	$ 52,073	$ 745	$ 51,328
1990	50,886	713	50,173
1991	50,733	598	50,135
1992	50,984	598	50,386
1993	51,589	603	50,986
1994 and subsequent	906,234	1,891	904,343
	$1,162,499	$5,148	$1,157,351

Total rental expense was as follows:

(In thousands)	Year ended		
	January 31 1988	February 1 1987	February 2 1986
Minimum rentals	$50,094	$35,633	$28,209
Additional amounts computed as percentages of sales	3,468	3,320	2,999
	53,562	38,953	31,208
Less sublease income	1,896	1,444	1,374
	$51,666	$37,509	$29,834

5. STOCK OPTIONS

All numbers of shares and prices have been restated for the three-for-two stock splits effected on June 27, 1986, January 8, 1985, July 26, 1983, July 22, 1982, July 21, 1981 and July 28, 1980

A. Key Executive Stock Options

In April 1978, pursuant to their employment agreements, four present and former key executive officers were granted options to purchase 13,668,750 shares of common stock at an exercise price of $.96 per share. For the fiscal years ended February 2, 1986, February 1, 1987, and January 31, 1988, these officers exercised options for 560,902, 222,559, and 2,633,324 shares, respectively. At January 31, 1988, all options under these agreements had been exercised. The employment agreements also provided that these executives may borrow from the Company, for the purpose of exercising these options, up to 80% of the exercise price of the options. Amounts borrowed are repayable five years after the exercise date, with interest at 6% per annum and are shown as a reduction of Stockholders' Equity.

On June 6, 1984, the Company's stockholders approved the grant of options to purchase an additional 1,687,500 shares to two of the key executive officers. These options are exercisable in five equal annual installments beginning March 6, 1985 at a price of $15.83 per share which was the market value at the date of grant. None has been exercised.

No compensation expense has been reflected with respect to the issuance of any of these options.

B. Stock Option Plan

In April 1978, the Board of Directors adopted a stock option plan (which has subsequently been amended) whereby the Company may grant options for the purchase of up to 13,668,750 shares of its common stock to key employees. On June 6, 1984, the Company's stockholders approved an amendment to the plan providing for grants of an additional 4,500,000 shares. The exercise price per share of all options heretofore granted has been the market price of the Company's common stock on the date of grant.

Outstanding options become exercisable four years and nine months from the date of grant (although this may be accelerated due to retirement or death) and must be exercised within ten years from the date of grant. At January 31, 1988, options to purchase 509,094 shares were exercisable.

Transactions are summarized as follows:

	Shares Under Option		
	Incentive	Non- Qualified	Price Range
Outstanding February 3, 1985 . .	4,778,375	1,722,187	$ .96 - 22.83
Granted	1,210,110	149,475	21.42 - 25.25
Exercised	(1,212,935)	(48,006)	2.43 - 17.59
Cancelled	(531,174)	(113,130)	2.43 - 21.92
Outstanding February 2, 1986 .	4,244,376	1,710,526	.96 - 25.25
Granted	1,318,371	194,804	28.33 - 32.50
Exercised	(496,724)	(286,168)	2.43 - 28.33
Cancelled	(621,210)	(9,340)	8.04 - 28.33
Outstanding February 1, 1987 . .	4,444,813	1,609,822	.96 - 32.50
Granted	55,120	1,036,780	26.06 - 35.75
Exercised	(663,669)	(122,866)	.96 - 28.33
Cancelled	(587,552)	(94,014)	8.04 - 28.33
Outstanding January 31, 1988 .	3,248,712	2,429,722	2.43 - 35.75

In November 1987 the Company granted non-qualified stock options at the then market price of $29.25 per share to substantially all employees in replacement of options (incentive and non-qualified) granted in May 1987 at the then market price of $35.75, subject to the employees surrendering the May options. Substantially all the May options have been surrendered and the above tabulation does not reflect the options which were granted in May and surrendered in November.

All outstanding options expire at dates ranging from May 1, 1990 to January 5, 1998. At January 31, 1988, 4,542,995 shares were available for future grant.

C. Reserved Shares

At January 31, 1988, an aggregate of 11,908,929 shares of authorized common stock was reserved for the options noted above.

D. Tax Benefit from Non-Qualified Options

The exercise of non-qualified stock options results in state and federal income tax benefits to the Company equal to the difference between the market price at the date of exercise (or six months later for officers) and the option price. During the years ended February 2, 1986, February 1, 1987, and January 31, 1988, $10,894,000, $18,684,000 and $5,033,000 respectively, was credited to additional paid-in capital.

6. TAXES ON INCOME

The provision for taxes on income consists of the following:

		Year ended	
(In thousands)	January 31 1988	February 1 1987	February 2 1986
Current			
Federal	$104,345	$100,896	$ 77,151
Foreign	3,806	2,520	280
State	20,814	14,400	12,900
	128,965	117,816	90,331
Deferred	13,035	14,184	9,669
Total	$142,000	$132,000	$100,000

Deferred income taxes result from timing differences in the recognition of certain income and expense items (primarily depreciation) for tax and financial statement purposes. In December 1987, the Financial Accounting Standards Board issued a new statement on accounting for income taxes (SFAS 96) which changes the accounting for deferred income taxes. Adoption of the new statement is required no later than the fiscal year ending January 28, 1990. Upon adoption of SFAS 96, the Company will recognize some income; the amount, however, has not been determined.

A reconciliation of the federal statutory tax rate with the effective tax rate follows:

		Year ended	
	January 31 1988	February 1 1987	February 2 1986
Statutory tax rate	38.9%	46.0%	46.0%
State income taxes, net of federal income tax benefit	3.7	2.7	3.2
Tax free interest, dividends and other	(.9)	(1.1)	(.9)
Foreign	(.3)	(.8)	(.2)
Investment tax and jobs tax credits	(.4)	(.4)	(2.6)
	41.0%	46.4%	45.5%

7. PROFIT-SHARING PLAN

The Company has a profit-sharing plan with a 401(k) salary deferral feature for eligible employees, which may be terminated at its discretion. Provisions of $9,523,000, $6,573,000, and $6,422,000 have been charged to operations in the years ended January 31, 1988, February 1, 1987 and February 2, 1986, respectively.

8. NET EARNINGS PER SHARE

Net earnings per share is computed by dividing net earnings by the weighted average number of common shares outstanding after reduction for treasury shares and assuming exercise of dilutive stock options computed by the treasury stock method using the average market price during the year.

Average weighted numbers of shares used in computing net earnings per share were as follows:

		Year ended	
	January 31 1988	February 1 1987	February 2 1986
Common and common equivalent shares	130,792,000	130,273,000	129,242,000

9. QUARTERLY FINANCIAL DATA (unaudited)

The following table sets forth certain unaudited quarterly financial information (in thousands except per share information):

Year ended January 31, 1988:

Quarter	Net sales	Cost of sales	Net earnings	Net earnings per share
1st	$ 473,985	$ 328,023	$ 14,523	$ .11
2nd	516,602	358,300	16,651	.13
3rd	600,167	415,584	18,432	.14
4th	1,545,814	1,055,110	154,316	1.19
Year	$3,136,568	$2,157,017	$203,922	$1.56

Year ended February 1, 1987:

Quarter	Net sales	Cost of sales	Net earnings	Net earnings per share
1st	$ 368,367	$ 251,539	$ 10,340	$ .08
2nd	426,031	298,336	13,062	.10
3rd	471,728	328,426	12,755	.10
4th	1,178,777	789,908	116,060	.89
Year	$2,444,903	$1,668,209	$152,217	$1.17

■ ANNUAL REPORT OF HEINEKEN N.V. (A DUTCH MULTINATIONAL COMPANY)

Annual Accounts

Consolidated Balance Sheet
(after appropriation of profit)

Assets	December 31, 1988		December 31, 1987	
(in thousands of guilders)				
Fixed assets				
Tangible fixed assets	4,167,313		3,701,848	
Financial fixed assets	314,708		317,815	
		4,482,021		4,019,663
Current assets				
Stocks	751,185		661,143	
Accounts receivable	805,689		721,216	
Securities	46,766		36,841	
Cash at bank and in hand	454,104		611,641	
		2,057,744		2,030,841
		6,539,765		6,050,504

Liabilities	December 31, 1988		December 31, 1987	
(in thousands of guilders)				
Group funds				
Shareholders' equity	2,772,089		2,464,485	
Minority interests	387,735		429,943	
		3,159,824		2,894,428
Investment facilities equalization account		199,566		182,662
Provisions		900,193		807,109
Debts				
Long-term debts	664,807		618,798	
Current liabilities	1,615,375		1,547,507	
		2,280,182		2,166,305
		6,539,765		6,050,504

Consolidated Statement of Income

	1988		1987
(in thousands of guilders)			
Net turnover	7,290,762		6,658,781
Raw materials, other materials and services	3,709,986	3,374,212	
Excise duties	1,187,041	1,028,805	
Personnel costs	1,440,555	1,358,301	
Depreciation and value adjustments	415,892	386,414	
Total operating expenditure	6,753,474		6,147,732
Trading profit	537,288		511,049
Dividend from non-consolidated participations	21,690	10,561	
Interest	− 92,292	− 47,670	
	− 70,602		− 37,109
Profit on ordinary activities before taxes	466,686		473,940
Taxes	− 160,303		− 176,838
Group profit after taxes	306,383		297,102
Minority interests	− 15,596		− 10,419
Net profit	290,787		286,683

Notes to the Consolidated Balance Sheet and Statement of Income for the financial year 1988

General

The provisions of Title 9, Book 2 of the Netherlands Civil Code, are applicable to the annual accounts and the annual report.

The financial data of Heineken N.V. are incorporated in the consolidated balance sheet and statement of income. Consequently, for the profit and loss account of Heineken N.V. use has been made of the possibility of a simplified presentation in accordance with Article 402, Title 9, Book 2 of the Netherlands Civil Code.

The amounts stated in the notes are in thousands of guilders, unless indicated otherwise.

Basis of consolidation

In the consolidated balance sheet and statement of income Heineken N.V. and its interests of more than 50% are shown as fully consolidated. The minority interests in the Group funds and in the Group profit are indicated separately. Proportionate consolidation has taken place in the case of those participations in which an interest of 50% or less is held, if the influence exerted by Heineken on management policy is equal to that of the other partners combined.

Under the heading 'Changes in the extent of the consolidation' the following statements of the movements of various assets and liabilities show those movements which relate to the increase in or reduction of our interests in consolidated participations.

Translation of foreign currencies

The items in foreign currency in the annual accounts have been translated at the rates of exchange at the balance sheet date.

Valuation differences arise as a result of the translation to guilders of the shareholders' equity at the beginning of the financial year of the foreign consolidated participations and of the financing furnished to these participations within the Group framework. These differences are regarded as a revaluation and are credited or debited to the Group funds, taking into account the possible levying of taxation.
Other differences connected with rates of exchange are incorporated in the Statement of Income.

Intangible assets

The differences between the price paid and the valuation according to these policies upon the acquisition of participations are offset against the Group funds.
Costs of other intangible assets, including patents, licences, software, research and development, are charged directly to the Statement of Income.

Accounting policies for the valuation of assets and liabilities

Fixed assets
Tangible fixed assets have been valued on the basis of replacement cost and, with the exception of sites, after deduction of cumulative depreciation. The replacement cost is based on valuations by internal and external experts, taking technical and economic developments into account. They are supported by the experience gained in the construction of new establishments all over the world. Projects under construction are stated at cost.
The valuation of non-consolidated participations is at the cost of acquisition, after deduction of provisions considered necessary.
The other financial fixed assets are shown at par value, less a provision for bad debts.

Current assets

Stocks obtained from third parties have been valued on the basis of replacement cost. The replacement cost is based on the prices of current purchase contracts and on market prices applicable on the balance sheet date.

Finished products and products in process are valued at manufacturing cost, based on replacement cost and taking into account the stage of processing. Stocks of spare parts are depreciated on a straight-line basis in view of the reduction of the possibility of use. Provisions on stocks are made up to the recoverable amount or net realizable value, respectively, if this is lower than the replacement value.

Prepayments on stocks are stated at par value.

Accounts receivable are shown at par value, after deduction of a provision for bad debts and less the amount of deposits due on account of the obligation to take back own packing materials. Securities have been valued at the cost of acquisition, unless the market price or the estimated market value of unlisted securities is lower.

Cash at bank and in hand are stated at par value.

Revaluations

Differences in valuation resulting from revaluation are credited or debited to the Group funds, if applicable, after deduction of an amount for deferred tax liabilities.

Investment facilities equalization account

The purpose of the investment facilities equalization account is to apportion the amounts received in virtue of arrangements in a number of countries with regard to investments over the estimated life of the assets concerned.

Provisions

The provision for deferred tax liabilities is calculated on the differences in valuation between the balance sheet and the statement of financial condition for fiscal purposes, in so far as these differences will be taken into account in the levying of taxation. Calculation takes place at the nominal rates of the taxes on profit in the various countries and the taxes on profit distributions which are borne by the Group.

The provision for pension liabilities is determined on the basis of present value. The provision for other personnel schemes is calculated on the basis of the present value of the benefit commitments on account of retirement, replacement, retaining pay and disability, taking into account where applicable the expected degree of participation.

Debts

Long-term debts and current liabilities are shown at par value.

Accounting policies for the determination of income

In the statement of income proceeds and expenses are in principle accounted for at the time when the relevant goods or services are supplied.

Net turnover means the proceeds of products supplied and services rendered to third parties, after deduction of turnover taxes and discounts.

The consumption of raw materials and other materials is stated at replacement cost in the statement of income.

Excise duties are stated at the actual amount incurred.

The depreciation based on replacement cost is applied on a straight-line basis, in accordance with the estimated life of each asset; the withdrawal from the investment facilities equalization account is allowed for in this calculation.

Dividend from non-consolidated participations relates to the dividends received in the financial year.

Taxes on profit are calculated on the income according to the annual accounts on the basis of nominal rates. The taxes on profit distributions which are borne by the Group and the facilities applicable are taken into account. The differences from the taxes actually payable in respect of the financial year are offset against the provision for deferred tax liabilities.

Consolidated Balance Sheet

Tangible fixed assets	Total	Plants and sites	Machinery and installations	Other fixed operating assets	Projects under construction
Position on January 1, 1988	3,701,848	1,241,191	1,496,585	708,421	255,651
Changes in the extent of the consolidation	131,142	31,875	77,103	19,817	2,347
Investments less disposals	571,367	43,671	109,207	139,035	279,454
Projects completed	–	53,977	265,969	27,013	– 346,959
Revaluation	187,747	43,943	94,706	49,098	–
Depreciation and value adjustments	– 424,791	– 52,878	– 248,336	– 123,577	–
Position on December 31, 1988	4,167,313	1,361,779	1,795,234	819,807	190,493
This book value is composed as follows:					
Replacement cost	8,538,316	2,476,663	4,253,182	1,617,978	190,493
Cumulative depreciation	– 4,371,003	– 1,114,884	– 2,457,948	– 798,171	–
	4,167,313	1,361,779	1,795,234	819,807	190,493
The cumulative amount of the revaluations included in the book value as at December 31, 1988, is:	893,000	380,000	377,000	136,000	–

Other fixed operating assets include means of transport and furniture and fittings as well as crates, kegs and returnable bottles and pallets.

Projects under construction also include prepayments related to tangible fixed assets on order.

Financial fixed assets

	Total	Non-consolidated participations		Other financial fixed assets
		Shares	Loans	
Position on January 1, 1988	317,815	221,080	1,495	95,240
Changes in the extent of the consolidation	– 10,574	– 9,500	–	– 1,074
Investments/Issues	61,448	8,479	625	52,344
Disposals/Repayments	– 50,874	– 6,580	– 791	– 43,503
Revaluation	– 482	–	– 11	– 471
Other value adjustments	– 2,625	– 237	69	– 2,457
Position on December 31, 1988	314,708	213,242	1,387	100,079

Other financial fixed assets include N.fl. 76 million for loans to customers; in 1987 the corresponding figure was N.fl. 73 million.

Stocks	1988	1987
Raw materials	152,264	127,105
Products in process	164,773	158,780
Finished products	140,807	133,330
Merchandise	59,749	41,754
Packaging materials	71,752	61,690
Sundry stocks	131,558	117,437
Prepayments on stocks	30,282	21,047
	751,185	661,143

Accounts receivable

	1988	1987
The accounts receivable becoming due and payable in at most one year relate to:		
Accounts receivable from trade debtors	854,603	755,984
Less: deposits due on own packaging materials	– 320,230	– 301,034
	534,373	454,950
Accounts receivable from non-consolidated participations	30,233	23,384
Other receivables	163,192	162,977
Prepayments and accrued income	77,891	79,905
	805,689	721,216

Securities

	1988	1987
Listed securities	15,913	29,633
Unlisted securities	30,853	7,208
	46,766	36,841

Cash at bank and in hand	1988	1987
Cash in hand, balances at banks and giro institutions	126,206	137,167
Short-term cash deposits	324,168	471,146
Bills of exchange and cheques	3,730	3,328
	454,104	611,641

Shareholders' equity

	1988
Position on January 1	2,464,485
Revaluation	161,628
Loss in value upon acquisition of participations	– 54,900
Net addition from the appropriation of profit	200,876
Position on December 31	2,772,089

For a specification of the shareholders' equity reference
may be made to the balance sheet of Heineken N.V. as at
December 31, 1988, on page 44.

Minority interests

Position on January 1	429,943
Changes in the extent of the consolidation	– 136,542
Minority interests in the Group profit	15,596
Revaluation	9,627
Share in the issue by subsidiaries	71,543
Dividend paid to outside shareholders	– 2,432
Position on December 31	387,735

Investment facilities equalization account

Position on January 1	182,662
Changes in the extent of the consolidation	3,274
Facilities granted	31,933
Withdrawn in favour of the trading profit	– 18,303
Position on December 31	199,566

Provisions

	1988	1987
These comprise:		
Provision for deferred tax liabilities	559,089	528,729
Provision for pension liabilities	125,367	98,911
Provision for other personnel schemes	201,276	172,508
Other provisions	14,461	6,961
	900,193	807,109

The provision for pension liabilities largely relates to
pensions and annuities which have not been funded by third
parties. The average rate of interest used in calculating the
present value of the provision for pension liabilities was 7%,
taking into consideration the interest rates existing in the
countries concerned.
The provisions are almost entirely to be considered as
becoming due and payable after more than one year.

Long-term debts

The debts becoming due and payable after more than one year relate to:	Total	More than 5 years	Total	More than 5 years
Euro-guilder Notes Loan, interest 6.5%, redeemable on February 1, 1991	150,000	–	150,000	–
Loan in guilders, interest 10.25%, annual repayment of N.fl. 5.3 million	26,668	5,335	32,002	10,669

Other debentures and private loans, average interest 11.3% (1987: 11.9%)	433,409	60,676	382,130	38,359
Other debts, interest-free	54,730	30,183	54,666	10,098
	664,807	96,194	618,798	59,126

The loan in guilders has been secured by the obligation not to encumber the complex at Zoeterwoude in the Netherlands. In relation to the other debentures and private loans securities in the form of mortgages have been given up to an amount of N.fl. 80 million (1987: N.fl. 111 million).

Current liabilities	1988	1987
The debts becoming due and payable in at most one year are as follows:		
Repayment obligations in 1989 on other debentures and private loans	102,108	71,218
Indebtedness to credit institutions	212,831	201,619
Suppliers	424,758	376,684
Bills of exchange and cheques payable	9,296	6,594
Taxes and social security contributions	381,551	401,220
Dividend	51,760	53,810
Deposits	98,875	78,421
Pensions	4,376	8,826
Other debts	180,349	199,626
Accruals and deferred income	149,471	149,489
	1,615,375	1,547,507

In behalf of the Collector of Excise Duties in the Netherlands the brewery at 's-Hertogenbosch is encumbered with an equitable mortgage of N.fl. 150 million as security for excise duties payable on beer, soft drinks and spirits, as well as for import duties payable.

Obligations not evident from the Balance Sheet

The obligations in question are on account of: (in millions of guilders)		
Tenancy and operating leases	111	103
Assets on order, in so far as not included under tangible fixed assets	132	178
Discounted bills of exchange and cheques	22	12
Declarations of liability	169	158

Consolidated Statement of Income	1988	1987
Net turnover		
This item comprises:		
Sales proceeds	7,182,342	6,585,099
Proceeds from services	108,420	73,682
Net turnover	7,290,762	6,658,781

The breakdown of the sales proceeds was:

	%	amount	%	amount
Europe:				
The Netherlands	24	1,701,564	26	1,715,680
Other countries	49	3,510,761	47	3,085,478
	73	5,212,325	73	4,801,158
Western Hemisphere	12	860,827	12	813,655
Africa	8	601,198	9	566,528
Asia/Australia/Oceania	7	507,992	6	403,758
	100	7,182,342	100	6,585,099

Raw materials, other materials and services

Consumption of raw materials	613,077	527,652
Consumption of packing materials	860,274	784,734
Merchandise	532,068	549,517
Selling expenses	732,208	585,848
Transport costs	218,542	190,701
Energy and water	133,275	130,539
Repair and maintenance	183,836	186,602
Other expenses	436,706	418,619
	3,709,986	3,374,212

The change in the stocks of products in process and finished products (increase of N.fl. 46.3 million, excluding revaluation and changes in the extent of the consolidation) has been offset against the production cost, i.e. raw materials, packing materials and excise duties, and, as regards the fixed costs in the stocks, against the other expenses.

Excise duties

Excise duties paid less restitutions of excise duty	1,187,041	1,028,805

Personnel costs

	1988	1987
Salaries and wages	1,003,008	943,779
Pension costs	55,077	51,480
Other social security costs	240,284	227,529
Other personnel costs	174,774	166,448
	1,473,143	1,389,236
Personnel costs capitalized in connection with production of tangible fixed assets for own purposes	− 32,588	− 30,935
	1,440,555	1,358,301

The average number of employees was:		
Production personnel	13,007	12,748
Other personnel	12,785	12,746
Heineken N.V. and subsidiaries	25,792	25,494
Heineken N.V. and Group companies	28,719	28,418

Depreciation and value adjustments

Depreciation on tangible fixed assets	424,621	370,428
Other value adjustments of tangible fixed assets	170	19,900
	424,791	390,328
Withdrawal from investment facilities equalization account	– 18,303	– 16,263
Value adjustments of other assets	9,404	12,349
	415,892	386,414

Dividend from non-consolidated participations

Dividends received in the year	21,690	10,561

Dividend from non-consolidated participations in 1988 includes a non recurring item of N.fl. 11.3 million before taxes.

Interest

Interest paid	127,406	110,239
Interest received on cash deposits, etc.	– 35,114	– 62,569
	92,292	47,670

Interest received on cash deposits, etc. in 1987 includes a profit before taxes of N.fl. 23.3 million upon the sale of marketable securities.

Taxes

Taxes on profit	160,303	176,838

Taxes amount to 36.0% (1987 38.2%) of the Group profit before taxes and before dividend from non-consolidated participations. The tax burden is influenced not only by the nominal rates of tax in the various countries of establishment, but also by factors such as losses carried forward, investment- and other facilities.

Source and application of funds

	1988	1987
(in thousands of guilders)		
Source		
Group profit after taxes	306,383	297,102
Depreciation and value adjustments	415,892	386,414
Movements in provisions	48,924	21,344
Cash flow	771,199	704,860

Application

Investments less disposals in tangible fixed assets	571,367	595,975
Investments less disposals in financial fixed assets	10,574	63,013
Increase in interests in consolidated participations	220,038	22,704
Movement in working capital, excluding cash at bank and in hand, securities and indebtedness to credit institutions	154,140	26,494
	956,119	708,186
Dividends paid	94,750	97,996
	1,050,869	806,182

Financing

Balance of source and application	− 279,670	− 101,322
Minority interests in the issue by subsidiaries	71,543	8,333
Long-term borrowings	154,656	121,256
Investment facilities received	31,933	20,544
	− 21,538	48,811
Repayments on long-term debts	− 137,286	− 193,162
Movement in cash at bank and in hand, securities and indebtedness to credit institutions	− 158,824	− 144,351

The balance of cash at bank and in hand, securities and indebtedness to credit institutions consists of:

Cash at bank and in hand	454,104	611,641
Securities	46,766	36,841
Indebtedness to credit institutions	− 212,831	− 201,619
Position on December 31	288,039	446,863

Movements as a result of revaluation and changes in the extent of the consolidation have been eliminated in the above statement, with the exception of the working capital.

GLOSSARY OF KEY TERMS

Accelerated depreciation: methods of depreciation that allocate a greater portion of the asset's cost to the early years of its useful life, and consequently less to the later years.

Account: a record that summarizes all of the transactions that affect a particular category of asset, liability, or stockholders' equity.

Account form of balance sheet: a particular form of balance sheet, with the assets shown on the left and the liabilities and stockholders' equity on the right.

Accounting: a system of providing quantitative information (primarily financial in nature) about economic entities; intended to be useful in making economic decisions.

Accounting controls: a plan of organization, plus procedures and records to assure the safeguarding of assets and the reliability of the financial records.

Accounting cycle: a set of standardized procedures performed in monthly, quarterly, or yearly sequence, depending on the needs of the business.

Accounting equation: an algebraic expression of financial position: assets = liabilities + stockholders' equity.

Accounting information system: a system designed to provide financial information about economic entities.

Accounting system: the set of methods and procedures that is used to record, classify, and summarize the financial information to be distributed to users.

Accounts payable: money owed to the enterprise's suppliers or vendors for the purchase of goods and services.

Accounts payable trial balance (schedule of accounts payable): a list of the balances in all of the subsidiary Accounts Payable accounts.

Accounts receivable trial balance (schedule of accounts receivable): a list of all the balances in all of the subsidiary Accounts Receivable accounts.

Accrual basis: the accounting system in which revenues, expenses, and other changes in assets, liabilities, and stockholders' equity are accounted for in the period in which the economic event takes place, not when the cash inflows and outflows take place.

Accruals: expenses that are incurred and revenues that are earned over time but that are recorded only periodically.

Accrued expenses: expenses that have been incurred but have not been recorded, necessitating adjusting entries. Examples include interest expense, salary expense, and tax expense.

Accrued revenues: revenues received for services completed or goods delivered that have not been recorded, necessitating adjusting entries. Examples include interest revenue and rental revenue.

Action plans: plans to achieve organizational objectives. Formulated after the organization has analyzed information about itself and the environment and then established its objectives.

Additional paid-in capital: the amount invested in a corporation by its owners, in addition to the par value of any capital stock.

Additions: enlargements, such as the addition of a new wing to an existing plant.

Adjunct account: an account, the balance of which is added to the corresponding account in the financial statements.

Adjusted trial balance: a listing of the general ledger account balances after the adjustments have been posted.

Adjusting entries: entries that record accruals and internal transactions; necessary to the application of the accrual basis of accounting.

Administrative controls: a plan of organization, procedures, and records regarding the decision processes leading to management's authorization of transactions.

Aging method: a method of estimating uncollectible accounts expense; attempts to estimate what percentage of the outstanding receivables at year-end will ultimately remain uncollected.

Allowance for uncollectible accounts: a contra Accounts Receivable account, in which appears the estimated total of those as yet unidentified accounts receivable that will remain uncollected.

Allowance method: a method of matching the uncollectible account expense for the period with the sales for the period. Requires an estimate of the uncollectible account expense in the period of the sale.

American Accounting Association (AAA): a professional association of accountants (principally academics and practicing accountants) who are concerned with accounting education and research.

American Institute of Certified Public Accountants (AICPA): the professional association of CPAs.

Amortization: periodic allocation of the cost of an intangible asset over its useful life.

Annuity: a series of equal payments or receipts at regular intervals.

Appropriation of retained earnings: a restriction of retained earnings; occurs when the board of directors transfers a portion of the Retained Earnings account into a separate Appropriated Retained Earnings account in order to indicate to stockholders and others that the balance in the Appropriated Retained Earnings account is not available for dividends.

Articulation: relationship in which the income statement, balance sheet, retained earnings statement, and statement of cash flows are all linked together. For example, the amount in one statement, such as net income on the income statement, is carried forward to another statement, in this case the retained earnings statement.

Assets: economic resources owned or controlled by the firm which are expected to have future economic benefits.

Audit: an examination of a firm's financial statements by a CPA firm.

Auditor's report: a report by an independent CPA; accompanies the financial statements and includes the ac-

countant's opinion regarding the fairness of presentation of the financial statements.

Average collection period: a ratio that measures the average number of days it takes before a receivable is collected.

Average cost: an inventory costing method by which a weighted average cost, determined by dividing the total cost of goods available for sale by the number of units available for sale, is applied to both the cost of goods sold and the ending inventory.

Balance sheet: a financial statement that shows the financial position of a firm at a particular point in time.

Bank reconciliation: the process of accounting for the differences between the balance appearing on the bank statement and the balance of cash according to the depositor's records.

Bank statement: a monthly statement that the bank prepares and mails to the depositor. The statement lists the beginning balance in the account, all deposits received, checks paid, other debits (charges) and credits (receipts), and the ending balance in the account.

Beta: a measure of risk; relates the volatility of the price of a specific stock to the volatility of the prices of the stock market as a whole.

Betterments: improvements to existing assets, such as the installation of a computer-controlled temperature-monitoring system in a department store.

Board of directors: a group of individuals elected by shareholders, charged with establishing broad corporate policies and appointing senior corporate management.

Bond: a written agreement between a borrower and lenders in which the borrower agrees to repay a stated sum on a future date and to make periodic interest payments at specified dates.

Bond indentures: written agreements (which bondholders often insist on) including restrictions as to dividends, working capital, and the issuance of additional long-term debt.

Book value: the equity that the owner of one share of common stock has in the net assets (assets less liabilities) or stockholders' equity of the corporation.

Business entity: a separate economic unit, the transactions of which are kept separate from those of its owners.

Call premium: the difference between the call price and par value of a callable preferred stock.

Callable preferred stock: preferred stock that may be called or redeemed at the option of the corporation.

Capital account: represents the owner's equity in a sole proprietorship.

Capital budgeting: the process of planning for long-term investment decisions regarding operational assets through analysis of alternative uses of funds, in order to find the greatest return on investment.

Capital expenditures: expenditures resulting in other assets that yield benefits in several accounting periods.

Capital lease: a long-term lease that is, in effect, an installment purchase of assets.

Capital stock: a component of stockholders' equity, representing the amount invested by the owners of the business. A general term for *common stock*.

Capitalized retained earnings: retained earnings transferred to permanent capital, unavailable for future cash dividends. Usually occurs when a stock dividend is issued.

Cash: any medium of exchange that a bank will accept for deposit, including coins, paper money, money orders, checks, certified and cashier's checks, and money on deposit in a bank.

Cash basis: accounting system in which revenues and expenses are not recognized until the cash is received or paid.

Cash budget: a budget that includes only items affecting cash and is made up of cash receipts and cash expenditures.

Cash equivalents: short-term liquid investments, including commercial paper, money market accounts, and U.S. Treasury notes. Can usually be converted to cash without loss of principal.

Cash payments journal: specialized journal used to record cash disbursements made by check.

Cash receipts journal: specialized journal used to record the receipt of cash.

Certified public accountant (CPA): a professional accountant licensed by an individual state to practice accounting after having met a number of requirements.

Change in accounting estimate: alteration of a previous estimate (such as service life, residual value, uncollectible receivables, or warranties), when new information is obtained. Such changes affect only current and future periods.

Change in accounting method: a change that occurs when a firm switches from one generally accepted accounting principle or method to another.

Chart of accounts: a listing of all of the accounts used by a particular firm. Each account is assigned a unique number.

Classified financial statement: financial statement subdivided into categories to allow for meaningful inter-firm and interperiod comparison.

Closing entries: journal entries made at the end of the period; used to update retained earnings to reflect the results of operations and to eliminate the balances in the revenue and expense accounts so that they may be used again in a subsequent period.

Common-dollar statements: financial statements in which the appropriate total figure is set to 100%; other items are expressed as a percentage of that figure.

Common stock equivalent: a dilutive security that, because of the terms or circumstances at the time of its issue, is essentially equivalent to common stock, allowing the holder to become a common stockholder at some future date.

Comparability: the qualitative characteristic of accounting information that presents information in such a way that users can identify similarities and differences between two sets of economic events. Can be used to evaluate the financial position and performance of one firm over time or to compare such factors with other firms.

Comparative balance sheet: a balance sheet in which data for two or more periods are shown in adjacent columns.

Compensated absences: a liability that arises as employees accrue certain fringe benefits that allow them time off with full or partial pay. Included are such benefits as vacation and sick pay.

Complex capital structure: a capital structure in which there are certain types of bonds, preferred stock, or other securities that are convertible into common shares.

Compound interest: interest computed on the principal, plus any previously accrued interest.

Conceptual framework project: a theoretical framework for accounting, used to develop objectives and concepts that the Financial Accounting Standards Board (FASB) uses to establish standards of external financial reporting.

Conservatism: prudence exercised in financial reporting, due to uncertainties surrounding business and economic activities. When faced with accounting alternatives, accountants tend to choose those that are least likely to overstate assets or income.

Consistency: an accounting convention requiring that a firm use the same accounting procedures and policies from one period to the next.

Consolidated financial statements: the combined financial statements, less certain eliminations, of a parent company and its subsidiaries.

Constant-dollar statements: financial statements that are adjusted for general price-level changes.

Contingent liability: a possible liability that may or may not occur, depending on some future event.

Contra account: an account, the balance of which is subtracted from the associated account on the financial statements.

Contributed capital: the legal capital plus any additional capital contributed by the stockholders or others.

Control environment: an expression of management's philosophy. Shaped by such factors as the entity's organizational structure, the makeup of the board of directors, and personnel policies and procedures.

Control procedures: procedures management puts in place to assure that its internal control policies are being carried out. Includes such items as segregation of duties, record-keeping procedures, and independent checks by the internal audit staff.

Controlling account: the main or primary account that is maintained in the general ledger.

Convertible bonds: bonds that can be converted at some specified future date into the firm's common stock.

Convertible preferred stock: preferred stock that the holders can convert, at a stated rate and time, to common stock.

Copyright: the exclusive right of the creator or his or her heirs to reproduce and/or sell an artistic or published work.

Corporation: a business entity legally viewed as separate and distinct from its owners—the "stockholders."

Cost of goods sold: cost allocated to the merchandise sold by a retail or merchandising firm.

Costs: resources sacrificed or given up to attain goods and services.

Coupon bonds: bonds that are not registered in the name of individual holders but are negotiable by whoever holds them.

Credit: an entry on the right side of any ledger account, representing a decrease in an asset account and an increase in an equity account.

Current assets: cash or other assets reasonably expected to be realized in cash or sold within the normal operating cycle of a business, or within one year (if the operating cycle is longer than one year).

Current cost (or **current value**): current market value of an item; often established by appraisal or examination of catalogues.

Current-cost/constant-dollar statements: financial statements that are adjusted for both specific and general price-level changes.

Current-cost statements: financial statements that are adjusted for specific price changes.

Current liabilities: liabilities that will either be paid or require the use of current assets within a year (or within the operating cycle, if longer), or that result in the creation of new current liabilities.

Current maturities of long-term debt: portions of long-term liabilities that are payable within one year of the balance sheet date and are therefore classified as current.

Current method: a method of foreign currency translation under which all balance sheet items can be translated at the current exchange rate at the date of the financial statements; income statement items are translated at the average exchange rate for the period.

Current rate maturity of long-term debt: the portion of long-term liabilities that is payable within 12 months from the balance sheet date.

Current ratio: the total of current assets divided by the total of current liabilities.

Date of record: the date the stockholders are entitled to receive the dividends as per issue.

Debenture: an unsecured bond.

Debit: an entry on the left side of any ledger account, representing an increase in an asset account and a decrease in an equity account.

Debt-to-equity ratio: total liabilities divided by total stockholders' equity.

Debt securities: long-term notes, bonds, and other liabilities.

Debt-to-total-assets ratio: total liabilities divided by total assets.

Declaration date: the date the board of directors declares the dividend.

Declining-balance method: an accelerated method of depreciation, in which an asset's book value at the beginning of each ledger is multiplied by a constant percentage.

Default: failure of the borrower or maker of a note to make the required payment at the note's maturity.

Denomination: amount on which the required interest payment is always calculated (also called *face value*, *maturity value*, or *par value*).

Depletion: process in which natural resources lose their benefits as the resources are removed. Follows the same process as units-of-production depreciation.

Deposit slip: a list of cash and checks to be deposited.

Deposits in transit: deposits made by the depositor but not yet recorded by the bank.

Depreciable base: an asset's acquisition cost, less its estimated residual value.

Depreciable cost: an asset's estimated residual value, less its acquisition cost.

Depreciation: systematic allocation of the cost of non-current, nonmonetary tangible assets (except for land) over their estimated useful life.

Direct method: procedure established by the FASB to convert an income statement from the accrual basis to the cash basis for the purpose of determining cash flows from operations. It involves adjusting net income by items not affecting cash flows, including depreciation, amortization, and changes in current assets and liabilities.

Discount: the selling or pledging of a customer's note receivable to the bank at some point prior to the note's maturity date.

Discounting: a process that determines the present value of a future cash flow in order to assess the value of a proposed investment.

Dividend payment date: date the dividend is actually paid.

Dividends: a return to stockholders of some of the assets of the corporation, which have increased as a result of the profits earned.

Dividends in arrears: accumulated unpaid dividends on cumulative preferred stock from prior years.

Double-entry accounting: system of accounting in which each transaction has equal debit and credit effects, thus ensuring that the accounting equation remains in balance.

Drawing account: in a sole proprietorship, an account used to record withdrawals by the owner.

Duration of the note: length of time that the note is outstanding, or the number of days called for by the note.

Early extinguishment of debt: retirement of debt before maturity.

Earnings per share (EPS): net income divided by the average number of common shares outstanding during the year; also called *net income per share.*

Effective-interest method: a method of determining periodic interest, in which a constant interest rate (the effective rate at the time of issue) is applied to the carrying value of the note or bond at the beginning of the period.

Effective interest rate: interest rate at which the bond is issued (*see also* Market interest rate).

Equities: liabilities and stockholders' equity.

Equity method: a method of accounting for long-term investments, in which the investment is first recorded at its acquisition cost. However, the investment account is adjusted to reflect the proportionate increase or decrease in the investee's stockholders' equity that results from the investee's net income or loss for the period and the declaration of dividends.

Equity securities: preferred and common stock, or other instruments that represent an ownership interest.

Exchange rate: rate at which one currency can be exchanged for another.

Expenditures: outflows of cash or other assets or increases in liabilities.

Expenses: dollar amount of the resources used up by the firm during a particular period of time in the process of earning revenues.

External transactions: transactions with an outside party, which are recorded in financial statements.

Extraordinary items: gains and losses that result from transactions that are both unusual in nature and infrequent in occurrence (in the environment in which the firm operates).

Extraordinary repairs: a major reconditioning or overhaul to existing assets, such as a major overhaul or the installation of a new engine.

Federal Unemployment Tax Act (FUTA): unemployment taxes that employers must pay in addition to their share of social security taxes.

FICA (Federal Insurance Contributions Act) taxes: a combination of Old Age Survivors and Disability Insurance (O.A.S.D.I.) and Medicare Insurance; also called *social security taxes.*

FIFO (first-in, first-out): an inventory costing method that assumes that the costs attached to the first goods purchased are the costs of the first goods sold.

Financial Accounting Standards Board (FASB): a private-sector body that has responsibility for developing and issuing accounting standards.

Financial statement analysis: set of techniques designed to provide relevant data to decision makers.

Financial statements: reports by which financial information about a particular enterprise is communicated to users.

Fiscal year: a year that ends on the last day of any month other than December.

FOB destination: terms of sale in which legal title of the goods does not pass until they reach the buyer's receiving point; as a result, the seller pays the freight charges.

FOB shipping point: terms of sale in which legal title to the goods transfers from the seller to the buyer when those goods leave the seller's warehouse; and as a result, the buyer pays the freight charges.

Footnotes to financial statements: footnotes accompanying financial statements; narrative explanations of important aspects of various items in the statement.

Foreign currency transactions: transactions that are denominated in foreign currency. For example, a U.S. firm makes a sale to an overseas firm and agrees to accept payment in the foreign currency, or a purchase is made from an overseas firm and payment must be made in the foreign currency.

Foreign currency translation: restatement of amounts in one currency in terms of another currency.

Form 8-K: a published report that all firms are required to file with the SEC within ten days of certain major events affecting the firm.

Form 10-K: annual report filed with the SEC.

Form 10-Q: quarterly reports filed with the SEC.

Franchise: a right to use a formula, design, or technique, or the right to conduct business in a certain territory.

Full-cost method: a method in which all exploration costs are capitalized into the cost of the natural resource asset account.

Full-disclosure principle: an accounting convention requiring that a firm's financial statements provide users with all relevant information about the various transactions in which a firm has been involved.

Fully diluted EPS: the net income available to common shareholders, as calculated by the weighted average number of common shares outstanding plus all dilutive securities, whether or not they are considered common stock equivalents.

Future value of an annuity: the amount of a series of payments or receipts taken to a future date at a specified interest rate.

Future value of a single amount: the amount of a current single amount taken to a future date at a specified interest rate.

Gains: a firm's increase in equity (net assets) during a set period from all activities (except for revenues and investments by owners).

General ledger: a general book or file containing all the company's controlling accounts, arranged in the order of the chart of accounts.

General partnership: a form of partnership in which the general partners have unlimited liability.

General price-level changes: price changes that reflect fluctuations in the ability of the dollar to purchase a variety of goods and services.

Generally accepted accounting principles (GAAP): concepts and standards underlying accounting for financial reporting purposes.

Going-concern assumption: assumption that unless there is evidence to the contrary, a firm will be in existence long enough to use its assets and derive their benefits.

Goods in transit: goods that have been purchased (and title has passed to the purchaser) but that have not yet been received by the purchaser.

Goods on consignment: goods held by a firm for resale, although title remains with the manufacturer or owner of the product.

Goodwill: future benefits that accrue to a firm as a result of its ability to earn an excess rate of return on its recorded net assets.

Governmental accounting: the practice of accounting as it relates to governmental organizations.

Governmental Accounting Standards Board (GASB): created by the Financial Accounting Foundation in 1984 with the purpose of establishing and improving financial accounting standards for state and local government.

Gross margin method: a method used to estimate the value of inventory, in which firms estimate their ending inventory without taking an actual count. Based on the firm's gross margin percentage.

Gross margin on sales: sales minus cost of goods sold.

Gross margin percentage: gross margin divided by sales.

Gross method of recording purchase discounts: a method of recording purchase discounts, in which the purchase and the payable are recorded at the gross amount, before any discount.

Gross method of recording sales discounts: a method of recording sales discounts, in which the sale and the receivable are recorded at the gross amount, before any discount.

Gross sales: total of cash sales plus sales made on credit during the period.

Historical-cost convention: the convention under which assets and liabilities are initially recorded in the accounting system at their original or historical cost and are not adjusted for subsequent increases in value.

Horizontal analysis: a technique of financial analysis, focusing on the dollar changes and percentage changes that have occurred in certain accounts from year to year.

Income from continuing operations: the excess of gross margin from sales over operating expenses.

Income statement: a financial statement that shows the amount of income earned by a firm over an accounting period.

Income summary account: a temporary account used to provide structure and to control the accuracy of the closing process.

Indirect method: procedure established by the FASB for converting an income statement from the accrual basis to the cash basis. Items not affecting cash flows (such as depreciation and amortization) are adjusted.

Intangible assets: assets that have no physical substance but have future economic benefits based on rights or benefits accruing to the assets' owner.

Interest: cost associated with the use of money over a specified period of time.

Interest rate: percentage rate of interest; usually stated in annual terms and must be prorated for periods shorter than a year.

Interim statements: financial statements issued monthly or quarterly.

Internal control: organizational plan that includes specific methods and procedures developed by management to ensure the accuracy and reliability of the accounting records and to safeguard the firm's assets.

Internal control structure: policies and procedures established by an entity to provide reasonable assurance that specific objectives will be achieved.

Internal transactions: events that affect the firm only; are usually recorded by adjusting entries.

International Accounting Standards Committee (IASC): committee whose charge is to develop basic accounting standards and to promote the worldwide acceptance and observance of those standards.

International Federation of Accountants (IFAC): international accounting body that is essentially a coordinating body of professional accounting organizations. Does not have the responsibility for setting international accounting standards; instead, the broad objective is the development and enhancement of a coordinated worldwide accounting profession with harmonized standards.

Interperiod income tax allocation: allocation of income taxes among different accounting periods.

Interpolation: a process by which it is possible to find the exact rate of interest promised by an investment.

Intraperiod income tax allocation: allocation of income taxes in such a way that the total income tax expense for the period is related to the proper component that caused the income.

Inventories: goods that are owned and held for sale in the regular course of business, including goods in transit (if shipped FOB shipping point).

Inventory profits: the amount by which the cost of replacing merchandise sold on the sale date exceeds the reported cost.

Inventory turnover: rate at which a company sells its inventory.

Investing activities: making and collecting loans and acquiring and disposing of plant and equipment.

Journal: record or book where each transaction is recorded originally. Provides a chronological record of each transaction.

Lease: a contractual agreement between the lessor (the owner of the property) and the lessee (the user of the property) that gives the lessee the right to use the lessor's property for a specific period of time in exchange for stipulated cash payments.

Leasehold improvements: improvements made by the lessee; at the end of the lease term, they revert to the ownership of the lessor.

Ledger: a book or file containing a specific account for each item in the chart of accounts.

Legal (stated) capital: the minimum amount that can be reported as contributed capital. Usually equal to the par or stated value of all capital stock.

Lessee: the user of the property in the lease contract.

Lessor: the owner of the property in the lease contract.

Leverage: use of debt financing, such as bonds and mortgages.

Liabilities: economic obligations of the enterprise; amount owed to creditors, employees, the government, or others.

LIFO (last-in, first-out): an inventory costing method that assumes that the costs attached to the latest purchases are the costs of the first items sold.

LIFO liquidation: a financial event that occurs when a firm sells more units in any year than it purchases, and LIFO layers that have been built up in the past are liquidated.

Limited liability: the owners of a corporation are not, as individuals, legally responsible for the debts incurred by the corporation, in excess of the amount that they have invested in the corporation.

Limited partnership: a form of partnership; usually made up of one or two general partners and several limited partners. Only the general partners have unlimited liability; the liability of the other partners is limited to their investment in the partnership.

Long-term investments: assets that include holdings in securities (stocks and bonds) not classified as current, and in some circumstances, investments in certain subsidiaries that have not been consolidated with the parent firm.

Long-term liabilities: debts and obligations of an entity which are due after 12 months or beyond the normal operating cycle, or are paid out of noncurrent assets.

Losses: decreases in equity (net assets) affecting the firm during a set period from all activities (except for expenses and distribution to owners).

Lower of cost or market: a method of inventory pricing, in which the inventory is priced at cost or market, whichever is lower. An application of conservatism in accounting.

Maker: individual or business that signs a note.

Management accounting: the part of accounting that provides information to managers inside the organization and helps in planning, decision making, and control. This type of accounting has a different purpose from financial accounting, which provides accounting information to users outside of the organization.

Market: current replacement cost of inventory.

Market interest rate: interest rate that the money market establishes through hundreds of individual transactions; depends on such factors as prevailing interest rates in the economy and the perceived risk of the individual company.

Matching convention: the basic rule underlying accrual accounting. Revenues are recognized as they are earned. All expenses incurred in earning those revenues are also reported in the period in which those revenues are recognized.

Materiality: the relative importance or significance of an item to an informed decision maker.

Maturity date: date a promissory note is due.

Maturity value: total proceeds of a promissory note; includes principal and interest due at the maturity date.

Merchandising firm: a firm that purchases a finished product for future sale.

Monetary liability: liabilities, such as accounts payable and taxes payable, that are liquidated by payments of cash.

Mortgage: a promissory note secured by an asset, the title of which is pledged to the lender.

Multistep income statement: a form of the income statement that has various categories and arrives at net income in steps.

Mutual agency: in a partnership, each partner can make binding agreement for the partnership as long as the individual partner acts within the normal scope of partnership business.

Natural resources: physical substances extracted from the ground and converted into inventory; when sold, they produce revenues for the firm.

Net assets: stockholders' equity—assets minus liabilities.

Net book value: the difference between the cost of a depreciable asset and the associated accumulated depreciation.

Net income: the difference between the total of revenues and gains and the total of expenses and losses.

Net method of recording purchase discounts: a method of recording purchase discounts, in which the purchase and the accounts payable are recorded net of the allowable discount.

Net method of recording sales discounts: a method of recording sales discounts, in which the receivable and the sale are recorded net of the allowable discount.

No par stock: capital stock that has no par or stated value placed on it by the board of directors.

Nominal interest rate: a stated interest rate that is specified on the note or bond at the time it is issued and that does not change over the life of the note or bond.

Nominal (temporary) accounts: the separate revenue and expense accounts used only during the period, which have a zero balance at the beginning of each period. These accounts are closed to Retained Earnings at the end of each period.

Noncash activities: exchanges of long-term assets for long-term liabilities, the settlement of debts by issuing common or preferred stock, and other transactions that involve only noncurrent accounts.

Noncurrent long-term liabilities: liabilities that will not be satisfied within one year or within the operating cycle (if longer).

Nonmonetary assets: assets (other than cash or rights to receive cash) that can generate future revenues, such as property, plant, and equipment.

Note payable: a liability that results from purchases of goods and services or loans. Usually a written instrument that includes interest.

Note receivable: an unconditional promise in writing by an individual or business to pay a definite amount at a definite date or on demand.

Objectives of financial reporting: the fundamental purposes behind financial statements.

Objectivity: a characteristic of the accounting system: that valuations of assets and liabilities must be factual and able to be verified by others.

Obsolescence: the process of becoming out-of-date, outmoded, or inadequate.

Off-balance-sheet financing: the fact that certain liabilities are not recorded on the balance—for example, leases that are in substance installment purchases, but are not recorded as liabilities.

Operating activities: all transactions and other events not defined as either investing or financing. Cash flows from operating activities generally include the cash effects of transactions that enter into the determination of net income.

Operating cycle: the average time a business takes to purchase merchandise, sell the merchandise, and receive cash.

Operating lease: a short-term lease under which regular monthly payments are made by the lessee, but the lessor retains control and ownership of the property.

Opinion: a report issued by the auditor after examination of findings regarding the financial statements of a firm. Often called the *accountant's* or *auditor's report*.

Organization costs: costs that a corporation incurs during the organization process, including filing and incorporation fees to the state, attorney's fees, promotion fees, printing and engraving fees, and similar items.

Outstanding checks: checks written by the depositor but yet to be paid by the bank.

Owners' equity: a general term used to mean the owners' residual interest for sole proprietorships, partnerships, and corporations.

Par value: an amount designated in the articles of incorporation or by the board of directors, and printed on the stock certificate.

Parent company: corporation that owns the majority of the common stock of another company.

Partnership: an unincorporated business entity owned by two or more individuals or other entities.

Patent: an exclusive right to use, manufacture, process, or sell a product. Granted by the U.S. Patent Office.

Payee: person to whom payment for a note is to be made.

Payroll register: a listing of the firm's payroll; prepared each payday.

Percentage of net sales method: a method of estimating uncollectible accounts expense, under which the amount of uncollectible accounts expense is determined by analyzing the relationship between net credit sales and the prior year's uncollectible accounts expense.

Period costs: costs associated with the accounting period rather than the units of product.

Period expenses: expenses of a business that cannot be directly related to a product or service and matched against revenues in the period when the revenues are earned.

Periodic inventory system: an inventory system that does not keep continuous track of ending inventories and cost of goods sold; instead, these items are determined periodically—at the end of each quarter, each year, or other accounting period.

Permanent differences: income items that are reported for tax purposes but not for financial statement purposes (or vice versa). These differences do not reverse.

Perpetual inventory system: an inventory system that keeps a running balance of both inventory on hand and the cost of goods sold (in dollars and units).

Petty cash fund: a small fund established by a company for miscellaneous expenditures.

Pooling-of-interests method: a method of accounting for a business combination in which the combining companies are treated as if their net assets were pooled instead of one company having purchased the other outright. Assets and liabilities are combined at their net book values.

Posting: the process of transferring information from journal entries to the ledger accounts.

Post-closing trial balance: a trial balance prepared from the ledger accounts after the closing entries have been posted. Used to help ensure that these entries have been posted correctly.

Preferred stock: a type of stock that has certain preferences over common stock.

Present value: the amount that must be invested now, at a given rate of interest, to produce a given future value.

Present value of an annuity: present value of a series of future promises to pay or receive an annuity at a specified interest rate.

Present value of a single amount: value of a future promise to pay or receive a single amount at a specified interest rate.

Price-earnings ratio: the current market price of a stock divided by the earnings per share.

Primary earnings per share: net income available to common stock, divided by the sum of the weighted-average common shares and common stock equivalents.

Principal: the original amount of a promissory note, on which interest is calculated.

Prior period adjustments: transactions that relate to an earlier accounting period but that were not determinable by management in the earlier period. Specifically limited by an FASB Statement.

Private accounting: the practice of accounting in a single firm.

Profit margin percentage: the net income divided by the sales.

Promissory note: written promise to pay a definite amount at a future time. Also called a *note*. (*See also* Note receivable.)

Proxy: a legal document signed by the shareholders, giving another individual or individuals (usually existing management) the right to vote the shares in the manner they deem best.

Public accounting: the type of accounting activity in which an accountant provides a variety of accounting services to individuals and firms, for a fee.

Publicly held corporation: a corporation whose stock is owned by outside investors, and whose stock and/or bonds are listed on national and regional exchanges.

Publicly owned: indicates that a corporation's stock is traded on an organized exchange (such as the New York or American Stock Exchange), easily enabling individuals to buy or sell shares of its stock.

Purchase discounts: allowances given for prompt payment for merchandise purchased for resale.

Purchase method: a method of preparing consolidated financial statements, in which the net assets of the purchased company are revalued to their fair market value.

Purchase order: a document prepared by the purchaser, indicating to the seller the quantity, type, and estimated price of the items the buyer wishes to purchase.

Purchase requisition: a document sent to the purchasing department, requesting that it purchase a certain quantity and type of item.

Purchase returns and allowances: refunds and other allowances given by suppliers on merchandise originally purchased for resale.

Purchases journal: specialized journal used to record merchandise purchases on account.

Purchasing-power gains or losses: gains or losses that result from holding monetary assets (cash and rights to receive cash) and monetary liabilities (all liabilities other than those requiring the performance of a service) during periods of inflation or deflation.

Quality of earnings: a judgment as to whether accounting principles and methods selected by management lead to conservative estimates of earnings or inflated earnings.

Quantifiability: a characteristic of the accounting system: acceptable inputs are only those transactions and events that can be represented in numerical (primarily monetary) terms.

Quantity discounts: reductions from list price, as a result of quantity purchases.

Ratio analysis: a shortcut method of expressing relationships among various items on the financial statements.

Real accounts: balance sheet accounts (including retained earnings), the balances of which extend beyond the accounting period.

Realization principle: the principle accountants follow to determine when revenue should be recognized.

Realized gains and losses: the difference between expenses on a current-cost basis and on a historical-cost basis, which represents the holding gains or losses the firm has realized through sales or use in the current period.

Receipts: inflows of cash or of other assets.

Receivable turnover: a ratio determined by dividing credit sales by the average accounts receivable for the period.

Redeemable preferred stock: preferred stock that can be callable and that can be returned to the issuing corporation by the owner of the stock, under certain conditions, for a stated price.

Relevance: a qualitative characteristic requiring that accounting information be relevant to a user's decision.

Reliability: a characteristic of the accounting system: accounting information must be unbiased, accurate, and verifiable.

Remittance advice: a document attached to a sales invoice that is mailed to the customer; used to identify the source of the check received.

Report form of balance sheet: a form of balance sheet in which the assets are listed first and the liabilities and stockholders' equity beneath.

Research and development costs: expenditures incurred in discovering, planning, designing, and implementing a new product or process.

Residual (salvage) value: an estimate of an asset's worth at the end of its life.

Retail method: a method of estimating inventory, in which the inventory is taken at retail prices and then converted to cost.

Retained earnings: the amount of stockholders' equity that has resulted from retaining the assets that have arisen from the profits of a corporation. Represents the accumulated earnings of the business since its inception, minus any losses, dividends, and transfers to permanent capital.

Retained earnings statement: a financial statement that details the changes in the Retained Earnings account for a certain period.

Return on stockholders' equity: ratio calculated by dividing net income by average stockholders' equity.

Return on assets: ratio determined by dividing net income by average total assets.

Revenue expenditure: expenditures, the benefits of which are used up or consumed in the current period.

Revenues: price of goods sold or services rendered by a firm to others, in exchange for cash or other assets.

Reversing entries: entries made on the first day of a new accounting period, reversing certain adjusting entries to allow the routine recording of certain entries.

Reviews and compilations: accounting services provided by CPA firms.

Sales: the essential activity of a merchandising firm. At the point of sale, the firm's earning process is completed, and objective evidence as to the sales price is available. Revenue is thus recognized under generally accepted accounting principles.

Sales allowance: a reduction in the actual sales price, occurring when the particular item does not perform to expectations or when there are other defects in the product.

Sales discount: a cash reduction offered to customers in an attempt to ensure that they make prompt payment on their trade accounts.

Sales journal: specialized journal used to record sales on account.

Sales mix: proportion in which the various products of the firm are sold.

Sales returns: a reduction in the actual sales, which occurs when a customer, for whatever reason, returns the item for a cash refund or a credit to his or her account.

Securities and Exchange Commission (SEC): a federal agency that has the legal power to set and enforce accounting standards for publicly traded firms.

Segment: a component of an entity, the activities of which represent a separate line of business or class of major customer.

Serial bonds: bonds, the principal of which is payable on various dates.

Short-term monetary assets: current assets, such as cash and items that represent a specific claim to cash.

Simple interest: interest amount for one or more periods, assuming that the amount on which interest is computed stays the same.

Single-step income statement: a form of income statement that has only major categories (revenues, expenses, income before taxes, and net income).

Sinking fund: a collection of cash or other assets such as marketable securities; set apart from the remaining assets of the firm and used only for a specified purpose.

Sole proprietorship: an unincorporated business entity in which one person is the owner.

Specialized journal: a journal that is designed to handle certain transactions, such as receipts or sales.

Specific-identification method: an inventory costing method that determines the actual acquisition cost of each item in the ending inventory.

Specific price-level changes: price changes that reflect the fluctuation in the value of specific goods or services vis-à-vis other goods or services.

Specifically identifiable intangible assets: intangible assets, the costs of which can easily be identified as part of the cost of the asset, and the benefits of which generally have a determinable life.

Spreadsheet: a computer software program containing an empty matrix of rows and columns that can be labeled individually by the user. Examples include Lotus 1-2-3 and Quattro.

Statement of cash flows: a primary financial statement that indicates the effect on cash flows of the entity's operating, investing, and financing activities.

Statement of changes in stockholders' equity: a financial statement that summarizes the transactions and events that affect a variety of stockholders' equity accounts.

Stock dividend: a distribution to current shareholders (on a proportional basis) of the corporation's own stock.

Stock registrar: an individual employed by a corporation to maintain an independent record of the number of shares outstanding.

Stock split: an increase in the number of outstanding shares, with a proportionally decreasing par or stated value.

Stock transfer agent: an individual employed by a firm (usually a large bank) to handle all stock transfer by canceling the old certificates, issuing new ones, and updating the stockholders' ledger.

Stockholders' equity: the owners' equity of a corporation, representing the residual claims of the owners.

Straight-line depreciation: a depreciation method that assumes that depreciation is a constant function of time; results in an equal allocation of the asset's cost to each accounting period of its estimated service life.

Subsidiary: a corporation that is wholly or partially owned by another company.

Subsidiary accounts: backup accounts for several particular ledger accounts.

Subsidiary ledger: a ledger containing backup or more detailed accounts than does the general ledger.

Successful-efforts method: a method by which only the exploration costs of successful finds are capitalized into the Natural Resource asset account.

Sum-of-the-years-digits: one variation of accelerated depreciation, in which the asset's depreciable base is multiplied by a declining rate.

T account: an account that has a T-shaped form. Used to analyze transactions.

Tangible assets: assets that have physical substance and capabilities, such as property, plant, equipment, and similar productive assets acquired by the company.

Temporal method: a method of foreign currency translation, in which monetary assets and liabilities are translated at current rates, while nonmonetary assets and liabilities are translated at the rates in effect when the particular item was acquired. Income statement items are translated at the average exchange rate for the period.

Temporary differences: differences between the book basis and the tax basis of an asset or a liability, which will reverse at some future date, thereby resulting in taxable income or deductions.

Term bonds: bonds for which the entire principal is due in one payment.

Time-period assumption: the division of the enterprise's life span into time periods—as short as a month or a quarter, but rarely longer than a year.

Time value of money: the concept that money on hand now is worth more than money received in the future, because money on hand now can be invested and can earn interest.

Trade accounts payable: *see* Accounts payable.

Trade discounts: discounts offered to a certain class of buyers.

Transactions: business events, measured in money and recorded in the financial records of a particular enterprise.

Treasury stock: the corporation's own stock that it has repurchased.

Trend analysis: a type of horizontal analysis that includes more than a single change from one year to the next; looks at changes over a period of time in order to evaluate emerging performance.

Trial balance: a list of the accounts in the general ledger, with their respective debit and credit balances.

Unadjusted trial balance: a listing of the balances of all ledger accounts prior to the recording of adjusting entries.

Uncollectible accounts: receivables that the firm is unable to collect the full amount due from the customer.

Underwriters: brokerage firms or groups of firms that, for a stated price, purchase an entire stock issue and assume the risks involved in marketing the stock to their clients.

Uniform Partnership Act: defines a partnership as "an association of two or more persons to carry on as co-owners of a business for a profit."

Units-of-production method: a method of depreciation that assumes that the primary depreciation factor is use rather than the passage of time; appropriate for such assets as delivery trucks and equipment, when substantial variations in use occur.

Unsecured bonds: bonds that are not secured by collateral or specified assets of the borrower. Also called *debentures*.

Verifiability: a qualitative characteristic of an accounting system: the data pertaining to the transaction or event must be available, and if two or more qualified persons examined the same data, they would reach essentially the same conclusion about the data's accounting treatment.

Vertical analysis: a technique of financial analysis, used to evaluate the relationships within single financial statements, wherein the appropriate total figure in the financial statement is set to 100%, and other items are expressed as a percentage of that figure.

Voucher: a written authorization for each expenditure.

Voucher system: an elaborate, structured system developed to provide maximum internal control over all disbursements. The primary feature of the voucher system is the high degree of separation of duties.

Weighted-average cost flow assumption: a method used in process costing systems, in which the units in beginning Work in Process are treated as if they were started and finished in the current period.

Working capital: current assets minus current liabilities. Often referred to as *net working capital*.

Worksheet: a type of working paper, used to aid in the preparation of adjusting entries and financial statements.

Yield rate: actual rate at which a bond is issued (also called *effective rate*).

INDEX